EDWARD BATES, ATT'Y GEN.
POST MASTER GENERAL
MONTGOMERY BLAIR
SECRETARY OF THE INTERIOR
JOHN P. USHER
HANNIBAL HAMLIN VICE PRESIDENT
SALMON P. CHASE, SEC. OF THE TREASURY
WILLIAM H. SEWARD, SEC. OF STATE
PRESIDENT OF THE UNITED STATES.
ABRAHAM LINCOLN.
GIDEON WELLES SEC. OF THE NAVY
EDWIN M. STANTON, SEC. OF WAR.
CALEB B. SMITH EX-SEC. OF THE INT.
SIMON CAMERON EX-SEC. OF WAR.
Entered according to act of Congress in the year 1864 by O. D. Case & Co. in the clerks office of the District Court of the United States for the District of Connecticut.
Engraved by J. C. Buttre
PRESIDENT AND CABINET

THE

AMERICAN CONFLICT:

A HISTORY

OF

THE GREAT CIVIL WAR

IN THE

UNITED STATES OF AMERICA,

1860–64:

ITS

CAUSES, INCIDENTS, AND RESULTS:

INTENDED TO EXHIBIT ESPECIALLY ITS MORAL AND POLITICAL PHASES, WITH THE DRIFT AND PROGRESS OF AMERICAN OPINION RESPECTING HUMAN SLAVERY.

FROM 1776 TO THE CLOSE OF THE WAR FOR THE UNION.

BY HORACE GREELEY.

ILLUSTRATED BY PORTRAITS ON STEEL, VIEWS, MAPS, DIAGRAMS OF BATTLE-FIELDS, ETC.

VOL. I.

HARTFORD, U.S.:
PUBLISHED BY O. D. CASE & COMPANY.
LONDON: BACON & CO., 48, PATERNOSTER ROW.
1865.

TO

JOHN BRIGHT,

BRITISH COMMONER AND CHRISTIAN STATESMAN;

THE FRIEND OF MY COUNTRY, BECAUSE THE FRIEND OF MANKIND;

This Record of a Nation's Struggle

UP

FROM DARKNESS AND BONDAGE TO LIGHT AND LIBERTY,

IS REGARDFULLY, GRATEFULLY INSCRIBED

BY

THE AUTHOR.

PRELIMINARY EGOTISM.

No one can realize more vividly than I do, that the History through whose pages our great-grand-children will contemplate the momentous struggle whereof this country has recently been and still is the arena, will not and cannot now be written; and that its author must give to the patient, careful, critical study of innumerable documents and letters, an amount of time and thought which I could not have commanded, unless I had been able to devote years, instead of months only, to the preparation of this volume. I know, at least, what History is, and how it must be made; I know how very far this work must fall short of the lofty ideal. If any of my numerous fellow-laborers in this field is deluded with the notion that he has written *the* history of our gigantic civil war, *I*, certainly, am free from like hallucination.

What I have aimed to do, is so to arrange the material facts, and so to embody the more essential documents, or parts of documents, illustrating those facts, that the attentive, intelligent reader may learn from this work not only what were the leading incidents of our civil war, but its causes, incitements, and the inevitable sequence whereby ideas proved the germ of events. I believe the thoughtful reader of this volume can hardly fail to see that the great struggle in which we are engaged was the unavoidable result of antagonisms imbedded in the very nature of our heterogeneous institutions;—that ours was indeed 'an irrepressible conflict,' which might have been precipitated or postponed, but could by no means have been prevented;—that the successive 'compromises,' whereby it was so long put off, were—however intended—deplorable mistakes, detrimental to our National character;—that we ought—so early, at least, as 1819—to have definitively and conclusively established the right of the constitutional majority to shape our National policy according to their settled convictions, subject only to the Constitution as legally expounded and applied. Had the majority then stood firm, they would have precluded the waste of thousands of millions of treasure and rivers of generous blood.

I presume this work goes further back, and devotes more attention to the remoter, more recondite causes of our civil strife, than any rival. At all events, I have aimed to give a full and fair, though necessarily condensed, view of all that impelled to our desperate struggle. I have so often heard or read this demurrer—"You Abolitionists begin with Secession, or the bombardment of Sumter, slurring over all that you had done, through a series of years, to provoke the South to hostilities," that I have endeavored to meet that objection fairly and fully. If I have failed to dig down to the foundations, the defect flows from lack of capacity or deficiency of perception in the author; for he has intently purposed and aimed to begin at the beginning.

I have made frequent and copious citations from letters, speeches, messages, and other documents, many of which have not the merit of rarity; mainly because I could only thus present the views of political antagonists in terms which they must recognize and respect as authentic. In an age of passionate controversy, few are capable even of stating an opponent's position in language that he will admit to be accurate and fair. And there are thousands who cannot to-day realize that they ever held opinions and accepted dogmas to which they unhesitatingly subscribed less than ten years ago. There is, then, but one safe and just way to deal with the tenets and positions from time to time held by contending parties—this, namely: to cite fully and fairly from the 'platforms' and other formal declarations of sentiment put forth by each; or (in the absence of these) from the speeches, messages, and other authentic utterances, of their accepted, recognized chiefs. This I have constantly and very freely done throughout this volume. Regarding the progress of Opinion toward absolute, universal justice, as the one great end which hallows effort and recompenses sacrifice, I have endeavored to set forth clearly, not only what my countrymen, at different times, have done, but what the great parties into which they are or have been divided have believed and affirmed, with regard more especially to Human Slavery, and its rights and privileges in our Union. And, however imperfectly my task may have been performed, I believe that no preëxisting work has so fully and consistently exhibited the influences of Slavery in molding the opinions of our people, as well as in shaping the destinies of our country.

To the future historian, much will be very easy that now is difficult; as much will in his day be lucid which is now obscure; and he may take for granted, and dispatch in a sentence, truths that have now to be established by pains-taking research and elaborate citation. But it is by the faithful fulfillment of the duties incumbent on us, his predecessors, that his labors will be lightened and his averments rendered concise, positive, and correct. Our work, well done, will render his task easy, while increasing the value of its fruits.

Some ancient historians favor their readers with speeches of generals and chiefs to their soldiers on the eve of battle, and on other memorable occasions; which, however characteristic and fitting, are often of questionable authenticity. Modern history draws on ampler resources, and knows that its materials are seldom apocryphal. What Franklin, Washington, Adams, Jefferson, Laurens, the Pinckneys, Marshall, Jackson, Clay, Calhoun, Webster, etc., etc., have from time to time propounded as to the nature and elements of our Federal pact, the right or wrong of Secession, the extension or restriction of Slavery under our National flag, etc., etc., is on record; and we know, beyond the possibility of mistake, its precise terms as well as its general purport. We stand, as it were, in the immediate presence of the patriot sages and heroes who made us a nation, and listen to their well-weighed utterances as if they moved in life among us to-day. Not to have cited them in exposure and condemnation of the novelties that have so fearfully disturbed our peace, would have been to slight and ignore some of the noblest lessons ever given by wisdom and virtue for the instruction and guidance of mankind.

It has been my aim to recognize more fully than has been usual the legitimate position and necessary influence of the Newspaper Press of our day in the discussion and decision of the great and grave questions from time to time arising among us. To-day, the history of our country is found recorded in the columns of her journals more fully, promptly, vividly, than elsewhere. More and more is this becoming the case with other countries throughout the civilized world. A history which takes no account of what was said by the Press in memorable emergencies befits an earlier age than ours.

As my plan does not contemplate the invention of any facts, I must, of course, in narrating the events of the war, draw largely from sources common to all writers on this theme, but especially from *The Rebellion Record* of Mr. Frank Moore, wherein the documents elucidating our great struggle are, in good part, preserved. Perhaps the events of no former war were ever so fully and promptly embodied in a single work as are those of our great contest in *The Record*, which must prove the generous fountain whence all future historians of our country may draw at will. But I am also considerably indebted to Mr. Orville J. Victor's *History of the Southern Rebellion*, wherein is embodied much valuable, important, and interesting material not contained in *The Record.* I shall doubtless appear to have made more use of Mr. Edward A. Pollard's *Southern History of the War;* which I have often cited, and shall continue to cite, for peculiar reasons. Its author is so hot-headed a devotee of Slavery and the Rebellion, that nothing which seems to favor that side is too marvelous for his deglutition; so that, if he were told that a single Confederate had constrained a Union regiment to lay down their arms and surrender, he would swallow it, without scrutiny or doubt. His work, therefore, is utterly untrustworthy as a whole; yet, in certain aspects, it has great value. He is so headlong and unquestioning a believer in the Confederacy, that he never dreams of concealing or disavowing the fundamental ideas whereon it is based; it is precisely because it stands and strikes for Slavery that he loves and glories in the Confederate cause. Then his statements of the numbers engaged or of the losses on either side are valuable in one aspect: You know that he never overstates the strength nor the losses of the Confederates; while he seems, in some instances, to have had access to official reports and other documents which have not been seen this side of the Potomac. Hence the use I have made, and shall doubtless continue to make, of his work. But I trust that it has been further serviceable to me, in putting me on my guard against those monstrous exaggerations of the numbers opposed to them with which weak, incompetent, and worsted commanders habitually excuse, or seek to cover up, their failures, defeats, and losses.

I have not found, and do not expect to find, room for biographic accounts of the generals and other commanders who figure in our great struggle, whether those who have honored and blessed or those who have betrayed and shamed their country. To have admitted these would have been to expand my work inevitably beyond the prescribed limits. By nature little inclined to man-worship, and valuing individuals only as the promoters of measures, the exponents of ideas, I have dealt with personal careers only when they clearly exhibited some phase of our National character, elucidated the state of contemporary opinion, or palpably and powerfully modified our National destinies. Thomas Jefferson, Eli Whitney, Andrew Jackson, Daniel Webster, John C. Calhoun, Benjamin Lundy, Elijah P. Lovejoy, John Brown—men differing most widely in intellectual caliber as well as in aspirations, instincts, convictions, and purposes—may fairly be regarded as, in their several spheres, representative Americans, each of whom in some sense contributed to lay the train which we have seen fired by the Secessionists of our day with so magnificent a pyrotechnic display, so majestic a resulting conflagration; and of these, accordingly, some notion may be acquired from the following pages; while, of our generals and commodores, the miniature Portraits contained in these volumes, and the record of their respective achievements, are all that I can give. So many battles, sieges, marches, campaigns, etc., remain to be narrated, that—ample as this work would seem to be, and capacious as are its pages—a naked record of the remaining events of the war, especially should it be protracted for a full year more, will test to the utmost my power of condensation to conclude the work in another volume of the generous amplitude of this.

My subject naturally divides itself into two parts: I. *How we got into the War for the Union;* and II. *How we get out of it.* I have respected this division in my cast of the present work, and submit this volume as a clear elucidation of the former of these problems, hoping to be at least equally satisfactory in my treatment of the latter.

It is the task of the historian to eliminate from the million facts that seemed important in their day and sphere respectively, the two or three thousand that have an abiding and general interest, presenting these in their due proportions, and with their proper relative emphasis. Any success in this task must, of course, be comparative and approximate; and no historical work ever was or will be written whereof a well-informed and competent critic might not forcibly say, 'Why was this fact stated and that omitted? Why give a page to this occurrence, and ignore that, which was of at least equal consequence? Why praise the achievement of A, yet pass over that of B, which was equally meritorious and important?' But, especially in dealing with events so fresh and recent as those of our great convulsion, must the historian expose himself to such strictures. Time, with its unerring perspective, reduces every incident to its true proportions; so that we are no longer liable to misconceptions and apprehensions which were once natural and all but universal. We know, beyond question, that Braddock's defeat and death before Fort Du Quesne had not the importance which they seemed to wear in the eyes of those who heard of them within the month after their occurrence; that Bunker Hill, though tactically a defeat, was practically a triumph to the arms of our Revolutionary fathers; that the return of Bonaparte from Elba exerted but little influence over the destinies of Europe, and that little of questionable beneficence; and that 'fillibusterism,' so called, since its first brilliant achievement in wresting Texas from Mexico and annexing her to this country, though attempting much, has accomplished very little, toward the diffusion either of Freedom or Slavery. And so, much that now seems of momentous consequence will doubtless have shrunk, a century hence, to very moderate dimensions, or perhaps been forgotten altogether.

The volume which is to conclude this work cannot, of course, appear till some time after the close of the contest; and I hope to be able to bestow upon it at least double the time that I was at liberty to devote to this. I shall labor constantly to guard against Mr. Pollard's chief error—that of supposing that all the heroism, devotedness, humanity, chivalry, evinced in the contest, were displayed on one side; all the cowardice, ferocity, cruelty, rapacity, and general depravity, on the other. I believe it to be the truth, and as such I shall endeavor to show, that, while this war has been signalized by some deeds disgraceful to human nature, the general behavior of the combatants on either side has been calculated to do honor even to the men who, though fearfully misguided, are still our countrymen, and to exalt the prestige of the American name.

That the issue of this terrible contest may be such as God, in His inscrutable wisdom, shall deem most directly conducive to the progress of our race in knowledge, virtue, liberty, and consequent happiness, is not more the fervent aspiration, than it is the consoling and steadfast faith, of

H. G.

NEW YORK, *April* 10, 1864.

INDEX BY CHAPTERS.

ILLUSTRATIONS.

PRESIDENT AND CABINET.

EMINENT OPPONENTS OF THE SLAVE POWER.

CONFEDERATE CHIEFTAINS.

UNION GENERALS.

CONFEDERATE GENERALS.

UNION NAVAL OFFICERS.

ILLUSTRATIONS—CONTINUED.

THE AMERICAN CONFLICT.

I.

OUR COUNTRY.

The United States of America, whose independence, won on the battle-fields of the Revolution, was tardily and reluctantly conceded by Great Britain on the 30th of November, 1782, contained at that time a population of a little less than Three Millions, of whom half a million were slaves. This population was mainly settled upon and around the bays, harbors, and inlets, which irregularly indent the western shore of the Atlantic Ocean, for a distance of about a thousand miles, from the mouth of the Penobscot to that of the Altamaha. The extent of the settlements inland from the coast may have averaged a hundred miles, although there were many points at which the primitive forest still looked off upon the broad expanse of the ocean. Nominally, and as distinguished from those of other civilized nations, the territories of the Confederation stretched westward to the Mississippi, and northward, as now, to the Great Lakes, giving a total area of a little more than eight hundred thousand square miles. At several inviting localities, the "clearings" were pushed two or three hundred miles westward, to the bases and more fertile valleys of the eastern slope of the Alleghanies; and there were three or four settlements quite beyond that formidable but not impassable barrier, mainly in that portion of Virginia which is now the State of Kentucky. But, in the absence of steam, of canals, and even of tolerable highways, and with the mouth of the Mississippi held and sealed by a jealous and not very friendly foreign power, the fertile valleys of the Illinois, the Wabash, and even of the Ohio itself, were scarcely habitable for civilized communities. No staple that their pioneer population would be likely, for many years, to produce, could be sold on the sea-board for the cost of its transportation, even from the site whereon Cincinnati has since been founded and built, much less from that of Indianapolis or Chicago. The delicate, costly fabrics of Europe, and even of Asia, could be transferred to the newest and most inland settlement for a small fraction of the price at which they would there be eagerly bought; but when the few coins which the settlers had taken with them in their journey of emigration had been exhausted, there was nothing left wherewith to pay for these costly luxuries; and debt, embarrassment, bankruptcy, were the inevitable results. A people clothed in skins, living on the products of the chase and the spontaneous abundance of nature, might maintain existence and a rude social organization amid the forests and on the prairies of the Great Valley; any other must have experienced striking alternations of factitious prosperity and universal distress; seeing its villages and commercial depots rise, flourish, and decay, after the manner of Jonah's gourd, and its rural population constantly hunted by debt and disaster to new and still newer locations. The Great West of to-day owes its unequaled growth and progress, its population, productiveness, and wealth, primarily, to the framers of the Federal Constitution, by which its development was rendered possible; but more immediately and palpably to the sagacity and statesmanship of Jefferson, the purchaser of Louisiana; to the genius of Fitch and Fulton, the projector and achiever, respectively, of steam-navigation; to De Witt Clinton, the early, unswerving, and successful champion of artificial inland navigation; and to Henry Clay, the eminent, eloquent, and effective champion of the diversification of our National Industry through the Protection of Home Manufactures.

The difficulties which surrounded the infancy and impeded the growth of the thirteen original or Atlantic States, were less formidable, but kindred, and not less real. Our fathers emerged from their arduous, protracted, desolating Revolutionary struggle, rich, indeed, in hope, but poor in worldly goods. Their country had, for seven years, been traversed and wasted by contending armies, almost from end to end. Cities and villages had been laid in ashes. Habitations had been deserted and left to decay. Farms, stripped of their fences, and deserted by their owners, had for years produced only weeds. Camp fevers, with the hardships and privations of war, had destroyed many more than the sword; and all alike had been subtracted from the most effective and valuable part of a population, always, as yet, quite inadequate. Cripples and invalids, melancholy mementoes of the yet recent struggle, abounded in every village and township. Habits of industry had been unsettled and destroyed by the anxieties and uncertainties of war. The gold and silver of ante-revolutionary days had crossed the ocean in exchange for arms and munitions. The Continental paper, which for a time more than supplied (in volume) its place, had become utterly worthless. In the absence of a tariff, which the Confederate Congress lacked power to impose, our ports, immediately after peace, were glutted with foreign luxuries—gewgaws which our people were eager enough to buy, but for which they soon found themselves utterly unable to pay. They were almost exclusively an agricultural people, and their products, save only Tobacco and Indigo, were not wanted by the Old World, and found but a very restricted and inconsiderable market even in the West Indies, whose trade was closely monopolized by the nations to which they respectively belonged.

Indian Corn and Potatoes, the two principal edibles for which the poor of the Old World are largely indebted to America, were consumed to a very limited extent, and not at all imported, by the people of the eastern hemisphere. The wheat-producing capacity of our soil, at first unsurpassed, was soon exhausted by the unskillful and thriftless cultivation of the Eighteenth Century. Though one-third of the labor of the country was probably devoted to the cutting of timber, the axe-helve was but a pudding-stick; while the plow was a rude structure of wood, clumsily pointed and shielded with iron. A thousand bushels of corn (maize) are now grown on our western prairies at a cost of fewer days' labor than were required for the production of a hundred in New York or New England eighty years ago. And, though the settlements of that day were nearly all within a hundred miles of tidewater, the cost of transporting bulky staples, for even that distance, over the execrable roads that then existed, was about equal to the present charge for transportation from Illinois to New York. Industry was paralyzed by the absence or uncertainty of markets. Idleness tempted to dissipation, of which the tumult and excitement of civil war had long been the school. Unquestionably, the moral condition of our people had sadly deteriorated through the course of the Revolution. Intemperance had extended its ravages; profanity and licentiousness had overspread the land; a coarse and scoffing infidelity had become fashionable, even in high quarters; and the letters of Washington[1] and his compatriots bear testimony to the wide-spread prevalence of venality and corruption, even while the great issue of independence or subjugation was still undecided.

The return of peace, though it arrested the calamities, the miseries, and the desolations of war, was far from ushering in that halcyon state of universal prosperity and happiness which had been fondly and sanguinely anticipated. Thousands were suddenly deprived by it of their accustomed employment and means of subsistence, and were unable at once to replace them. Those accepted though precarious avenues to fame and fortune, in which they had found at least competence, were instantly closed, and no new ones seemed to open before them. In the absence of aught that could, with justice, be termed a currency, Trade and Business were even more depressed than Industry. Commerce and Navigation, unfettered by legislative restriction, ought to have been, or ought soon to have become, most flourishing, if the dicta of the world's accepted political economists had been sound; but the facts were deplorably at variance with their inculcations. Trade, emancipated from the vexatious trammels of the custom-house marker and gauger, fell tangled and prostrate in the toils of the usurer and the sheriff. The common people, writhing under the intolerable pressure of debt, for which no means of payment existed, were continually prompting

[1] "That spirit of freedom, which, at the commencement of this contest, would have gladly sacrificed every thing to the attainment of its object, has long since subsided, and every selfish passion has taken its place. It is not the public, but private interest, which influences the generality of mankind, nor can the Americans any longer boast of an exception."—*Washington's Letter to Henry Laurens*, July 10 (1782).

"Shoddy," it seems, dates away back of 1861.

their legislators to authorize and direct those baseless issues of irredeemable paper money, by which a temporary relief is achieved, at the cost of more pervading and less curable disorders. In the year 1786, the legislature of New Hampshire, then sitting at Exeter, was surrounded, evidently by preconcert, by a gathering of angry and desperate men, intent on overawing it into an authorization of such an issue. In 1786, the famous Shays's Insurrection occurred in western Massachusetts, wherein fifteen hundred men, stung to madness by the snow-shower of writs to which they could not respond, and executions which they had no means of satisfying, undertook to relieve themselves from intolerable infestation, and save their families from being turned into the highways, by dispersing the courts and arresting the enforcement of legal process altogether. That the sea-board cities, depending entirely on foreign commerce, neither manufacturing themselves, nor having any other than foreign fabrics to dispose of, should participate in the general suffering, and earnestly scan the political and social horizon in quest of sources and conditions of comprehensive and enduring relief, was inevitable. And thus industrial paralysis, commercial embarrassment, and political disorder, combined to overbear inveterate prejudice, sectional jealousy, and the ambition of local magnates, in creating that more perfect Union, whereof the foundations were laid and the pillars erected by Washington, Hamilton, Franklin, Madison, and their compeers, in the Convention which framed the Federal Constitution.

Yet it would not be just to close this hasty and casual glance at our country, under the old federation, without noting some features which tend to relieve the darkness of the picture. The abundance and excellence of the timber, which still covered at least two-thirds of the area of the then States, enabled the common people to supply themselves with habitations, which, however rude and uncomely, were more substantial and comfortable than those possessed by the masses of any other country on earth. The luxuriant and omnipresent forests were likewise the sources of cheap and ample supplies of fuel, whereby the severity of our northern winters was mitigated, and the warm, bright fireside of even the humblest family, in the long winter evenings of our latitude, rendered centers of cheer and enjoyment. Social intercourse was more general, less formal, more hearty, more valued, than at present. Friendships were warmer and deeper. Relationship, by blood or by marriage, was more profoundly regarded. Men were not ashamed to own that they loved their cousins better than their other neighbors, and their neighbors better than the rest of mankind. To spend a month, in the dead of winter, in a visit to the dear old homestead, and in interchanges of affectionate greetings with brothers and sisters, married and settled at distances of twenty to fifty miles apart, was not deemed an absolute waste of time, nor even an experiment on fraternal civility and hospitality. And, though cultivation was far less effective than now, it must not be inferred that food was scanty or hunger predominant. The woods were alive with game, and nearly every boy and man between fifteen and sixty years of age was a hunter. The larger and smaller rivers, as yet unobstructed by the dams and wheels of the cotton-spinner and power-loom weaver, abounded in excellent fish, and at seasons fairly swarmed with them. The potato, usually planted in the vegetable mold left by recently exterminated forests, yielded its edible tubers with a bounteous profusion unknown to the husbandry of our day. Hills the most granitic and apparently sterile, from which the wood was burned one season, would, the next year, produce any grain in ample measure, and at a moderate cost of labor and care. Almost every farmer's house was a hive, wherein the 'great wheel' and the 'little wheel' —the former kept in motion by the hands and feet of all the daughters ten years old and upward, the latter plied by their not less industrious mother—hummed and whirled from morning till night. In the back room, or some convenient appendage, the loom responded day by day to the movements of the busy shuttle, whereby the fleeces of the farmer's flock and the flax of his field were slowly but steadily converted into substantial though homely cloth, sufficient for the annual wear of the family, and often with something over to exchange at the neighboring merchant's for his groceries and wares. A few bushels of corn, a few sheep, a fattened steer, with, perhaps, a few saw-logs, or loads of hoop-poles, made up the annual surplus of the husbandman's products, helping to square accounts with the blacksmith, the wheelwright, the minister, and the lawyer, if the farmer were so unfortunate as to have any dealings with the latter personage. His life, during peace, was passed in a narrower round than ours, and may well seem to us tame, limited, monotonous; but the sun which warmed him was identical with ours; the breezes which refreshed him were like those we gladly welcome; and, while his road to mill and to meeting was longer and rougher than those we daily traverse, he doubtless passed them unvexed by apprehensions of a snorting locomotive, at least as contented as we, and with small suspicion of his ill-fortune in having been born in the Eighteenth instead of the Nineteenth Century.[2]

The illusion that the times that were are better than those that are, has probably pervaded all ages. Yet a passionately earnest assertion, which many of us have heard from the lips of the old men of thirty to fifty years ago, that the days of their youth were sweeter and happier than those we have known, will doubtless justify

[2] "Vagabonds, without visible property or vocation, are placed in workhouses, where they are well clothed, fed, lodged, and made to labor. Nearly the same method of providing for the poor prevails through all the States; and, from Savannah to Portsmouth, you will seldom meet a beggar. In the larger towns, indeed, they sometimes present themselves. These are usually foreigners who have never obtained a settlement in any parish. I never saw a native American begging in the streets or highways. A subsistence is easily gained here: and if, by misfortunes, they are thrown on the charities of the world, those provided by their own country are so comfortable and so certain, that they never think of relinquishing them to become strolling beggars. Their situation, too, when sick, in the family of a good farmer, where every member is anxious to do them kind offices, where they are visited by all the neighbors, who bring them little rarities which their sickly appetites may crave, and who take by rotation the nightly watch over them, when their condition requires it, is, without comparison, better than in a general hospital, where the sick, the dying, and the dead, are crammed together in the same rooms, and often in the same beds."—*Jefferson's Notes on Virginia*, p. 196.

us in believing that they were by no means intolerable. It is not too much to assume that the men by whose valor and virtue American independence was achieved, and who lived to enjoy, for half a century thereafter, the gratitude of their country, and the honest pride of their children, saw wealth as fairly distributed, and the labor of freemen as adequately rewarded, as those of almost any other country or of any previous generation.

Eighty years had not passed since the acknowledgment of our independence, when the returns of the Eighth Decennial Census afforded us the means of measuring our country's growth and physical progress during nearly its whole national history. The retrospect and the prospect might well minister to the pride (though that were needless) of a patriotic apostle of 'manifest destiny.' During those eighty years, or within the memory of many still living, the area of our country had been expanded, by successive and, in good part, peaceful acquisitions, from Eight Hundred Thousand to about Three Millions of square miles. Its population, excluding the Aboriginal savages, had increased from Three to more than Thirty Millions. Of its two thousand millions of acres of dry land, about five hundred millions had been divided into farms; leaving three-fourths of its surface as yet unimproved, though but in part unappropriated. Its farms were officially estimated as worth six thousand six hundred and fifty millions of dollars, and were doubtless actually worth not less than Ten Thousand Millions of dollars. On these farms were over eleven hundred millions' worth of live stock, and nearly two hundred and fifty millions' worth of implements and machinery. The value of animals annually slaughtered was returned at over two hundred millions of dollars. The annual product of Wheat was more than one hundred and seventy millions of bushels, with an equal quantity of Oats, and more than eight hundred millions of bushels of Indian Corn. Of Tobacco, our annual product was more than four hundred millions of pounds; and of Rice, nearly two millions. Of Wool, our annual clip was over sixty millions of pounds, and our consumption probably double that amount. Of ginned Cotton, ready for market, our product was about one million of tuns, or more than Five Millions of bales of four hundred pounds each. Four hundred and sixty millions of pounds of Butter, and one hundred and five millions of pounds of Cheese, were likewise returned as our aggregate product for the year 1859. We made in that year three hundred and forty millions of pounds of Sugar, and more than twenty-five millions of gallons of Molasses. And, beside consuming all this, with twenty-five millions of pounds of home-made Honey, we imported from abroad to the value of over thirty-six millions of dollars. We dragged from our forests, not including fuel, Timber valued at more than Ninety-three Millions of dollars. We made Flour to the value of Two Hundred Millions. We manufactured over fifty-five millions' worth of Cotton into fabrics, worth one hundred and fifteen millions of dollars, beside importing largely from abroad. We fabricated over eighty millions of pounds of Wool, costing forty millions of dollars, into sixty-eight millions' worth of goods, though importing nearly all our finer woolen fabrics. We produced sixty-three millions' worth of Leather; eight hundred and seventy-five thousand tuns of Pig Iron, worth twenty millions of dollars; four hundred thousand tuns of Wrought Iron, worth twenty-one millions; and Agricultural Implements to the value of seventeen millions. The grand total of Manufactures, returned by this Census, amounted in value to One Thousand Nine Hundred Millions—an increase of forty-five per cent. within ten years. Our Exports, for the year ending in 1860, amounted to a little more than Four Hundred Millions of dollars, whereof all but Twenty-seven Millions were of domestic production. Our Imports were a little over Three Hundred and Sixty Millions. Of Gold and Silver, we exported, in that year, nearly fifty-seven millions of dollars, and imported about eight millions and a half; indicating that ours had become one of the great gold-producing countries on earth, if not the very greatest. The number of ocean voyages terminating in our ports during the year ending June 30, 1861, was Twenty-two Thousand, less forty; their aggregate tunnage a little more than seven millions two hundred and forty thousand—more than two-thirds of it American. About fifty thousand churches, with forty thousand clergymen; two hundred and thirty-nine Colleges, having one thousand six hundred and seventy-eight teachers and twenty-seven thousand eight hundred and twenty-one pupils; six thousand and eighty-five Academies and Private Schools, with twelve thousand two hundred and sixty teachers and two hundred and sixty-three thousand and ninety-six pupils; eighty thousand nine hundred and seventy-eight Common Schools, with three millions three hundred and fifty-four thousand and eleven pupils; three hundred and eighty-six Daily Newspapers, circulating in the aggregate one million four hundred and seventy-eight thousand four hundred and thirty-five copies; one hundred and forty-six Tri-Weekly and Semi-Weekly, and three thousand one hundred and fifty-three Weekly journals, circulating seven millions five hundred and sixty-four thousand three hundred and fourteen copies; with nineteen Quarterlies, five hundred and twenty-one Literary, and two hundred and seventy-one Religious periodicals, mainly issued weekly, sufficiently attest that our progress had not been purely physical, but intellectual and moral as well.

The temptation to increase these citations from the Census is one hard to resist. Yet any multiplication of details would tend rather to confuse than to deepen their impression on the mind of the general reader. Let it suffice, then, in conclusion, that the Real and Personal Estate of our people, which in 1850 was returned as of the aggregate value of a little over Seven Thousand Millions of dollars, was, in 1860, returned as worth over Sixteen Thousand Millions—an increase in ten years of more than one hundred and twenty-five per cent. It is quite probable that both these aggregates are largely under the truth; but, conceding their accuracy, it is perfectly safe to assume that Fifteen of the Sixteen Thousand Millions of property returned in 1860 had been created and added to the wealth of the world by the industry, enterprise, and thrift of our people during the eighty preceding years.

II.

SLAVERY BEFORE THE REVOLUTION.

Vice, whether individual or general, is ever conceived in darkness and cradled in obscurity. It challenges observation only in its hardy maturity and conscious strength. Slavery is older than Civilization—older than History. Its origin is commonly referred to war—to the captivity of the vanquished, and to the thrift and clemency of the victor, who learns by experience that the gratification of killing his prisoner is transient, while the profit of sparing him for servitude is enduring; and thus, in rude ages, not merely the vanquished warriors, but their wives and children, their dependents and subjects, were accounted legitimate "spoils of victory," along with the lands, houses, flocks and herds, the goods and chattels of the conquered people. "Woe to the conquered!" is the primary rule of savage and of barbarian warfare; and the captivity of the Jews in Babylon, the destruction by Rome of Capua, of Carthage, and of other cities and peoples which had provoked her special enmity, prove that nations which regarded themselves as far advanced in civilization, were hardly more merciful than savages, when maddened by fear and hate. War wastes and devastates. The earth, plowed however deeply with cannon-wheels, yields uncertain harvests; yet armies and their dependents must be fed. Rapacity, as well as destruction, seems almost inseparable from war. The soldier, impelled to destroy for his chief's or his country's sake, soon learns to save and appropriate for his own. The natural and necessary distinction between 'mine' and 'thine' becomes in his mind confused, if not obliterated. The right of every one to the product of his own labor is one which his vocation incites, and even compels, him to disregard. To enslave those whom, whether combatants or otherwise, he might justifiably kill, appears to him rather an act of humanity than of injustice and wrong. Hence, the warlike, conquering, dominating races of antiquity almost universally rejoiced, when at their acme of power and greatness, in the possession of innumerable slaves.

Slavery of a mild and gentle type may very well have grown up insensibly, even in the absence of war. The patriarch has shelter and food, with employment for various capacities; and his stronghold, if he be stationary, or his tents, if he be nomadic, become the refuge of the unfortunate and the destitute from the region around him. The abandoned wife, the unwedded mother, the crippled or infirm of either sex, the tender orphan, and the out-worn, seedy prodigal, betake themselves to his lodge, and humbly solicit his permission to earn bread and shelter by tending his flocks and herds, or by any other service to which their capacities are adequate. Some are accepted from motives of thrift; others under the impulse of charity; and the greater portion of either class, exulting in their escape from hunger, cold, and nakedness, gladly remain through life. Marriages are formed among them and children are born, who grow up adepts in the labor the patriarch requires of them, contented with their station, and ignorant of the world outside of his possessions. If his circumstances require a military force, he organizes it of 'servants born in his household.' His possessions steadily increase, and he becomes in time a feudal chieftain, ruling over vassals proud of his eminence and docile to his will. Thus it has been justly remarked that the condition of Slavery has ever preceded the laws by which it is ultimately regulated; and it is not without plausibility that its champions have contended for it as a natural form of society—a normal development of the necessary association of Capital with Labor in Man's progress from rude ignorance and want to abundance, refinement, and luxury.

But Slavery, primarily considered, has still another aspect—that of a natural relation of simplicity to cunning, of ignorance to knowledge, of weakness to power. Thomas Carlyle,[1] before his melancholy decline and fall into devil-worship, truly observed, that the capital mistake of Rob Roy was his failure to comprehend that it was cheaper to buy the beef he required in the grass-market at Glasgow than to obtain it without price, by harrying the lowland farms. So the first man who ever imbibed or conceived the fatal delusion that it was more advantageous to him, or to any human being, to procure whatever his necessities or his appetites required by address and scheming than by honest work—by the unrequited rather than the fairly and faithfully recompensed toil of his fellow-creatures—was, in essence and in heart, a slaveholder, and only awaited opportunity to become one in deed and practice. And this single truth, operating upon the infinite varieties of human capacity and culture, suffices to account for the universality of slaveholding in the ante-Christian ages, for its tenacity of life, and for the extreme difficulty of even its partial eradication. The ancients, while they apprehended, perhaps adequately, the bitterness of bondage, which many of them had experienced, do not seem to have perceived so vividly the corresponding evils of slaveholding. They saw that end of the chain which encircled the ankle of the bondman; they do not seem to have so clearly perceived that the other lay heavily across the throat of even his sleeping master. Homer—if we may take Pope's word for it—observed that

> "Jove fixed it certain, that whatever day
> Makes man a slave, takes half his worth away;"

but that the slaveholding relation effected an equal discount on the value of the master appears to have escaped him. It is none the less true, however, that ancient civilization, in its

[1] In a letter on Copyright.

various national developments, was habitually corrupted, debauched, and ultimately ruined, by Slavery, which rendered labor dishonorable, and divided society horizontally into a small caste of the wealthy, educated, refined, and independent, and a vast hungry, sensual, thriftless, and worthless populace; rendered impossible the preservation of republican liberty and of legalized equality, even among the nominally free. Diogenes, with his lantern, might have vainly looked, through many a long day, among the followers of Marius, or Catiline, or Cæsar, for a specimen of the poor but virtuous and self-respecting Roman citizen of the days of Cincinnatus, or even of Regulus.

The Slavery of antiquity survived the religions, the ideas, the polities, and even the empires, in which it had its origin. It should have been abolished, with gladiatorial combats and other moral abominations, on the accession of Christianity to recognized supremacy over the Roman world; but the simple and sublime doctrine of Jesus and his disciples, of Paul and the Apostles, had ere this been grievously corrupted and perverted. The subtleties of Greek speculation, the pomp and pride of imperial Rome, had already commenced drawing the Church insensibly further and further away from its divine source. A robed and mitered ecclesiasticism, treacherous to humanity and truckling to power, had usurped the place of that austere, intrepid spirit which openly rebuked the guilt of regal, voluptuous Herod, and made courtly Felix tremble. The prelates of the lately persecuted Church were the favored companions and counselors—too often, alas! the courtiers also—of Emperors and Cæsars; but they seldom improved or risked their great opportunity to demand obedience, in all cases, to the dictates of the Golden Rule. The Church had become an estate above the people; and their just complaints of the oppressions and inhumanities of the powerful were not often breathed into its reluctant ears. White Slavery gradually wore out, or faded out; but it was not grappled with and crushed as it should have been. The Dark Ages, justly so called, are still quite dark enough; but sufficient light has been shed upon them to assure us that the accord of priest and noble was complete, and that serf and peasant groaned and suffered beneath their iron sway.

The invention of Printing, the discovery of America, the Protestant Reformation, the decline and fall of Feudalism, gradually changed the condition and brightened the prospect of the masses. Ancient Slavery was dead; modern Serfdom was substantially confined to cold and barbarous Russia; but African Slavery—the slavery of heathen negroes—had been revived, or rëintroduced, on the northern coast of the Mediterranean, by Moorish traders, about the Tenth Century, and began to make its way among Spanish and Portuguese Christians somewhere near the middle of the Fifteenth.[2]

The great name of Columbus is

[2] "In the year 990, Moorish merchants from the Barbary coast first reached the cities of Nigritia, and established an uninterrupted exchange of Saracen and European luxuries for the gold and slaves of Central Africa."—*Bancroft's History of the United States*, vol. i., p. 165.

"The Portuguese are next in the market. An-

indelibly soiled and stained by his undeniable and conspicuous implication in the enslavement of the Aborigines of this continent, so improperly termed Indians. Within two years after his great discovery, before he had set foot on the continent, he was concerned in seizing some scores of natives, carrying them to Spain, and selling them there as slaves.[3] His example was extensively followed. The fierce lust for gold, which inflamed the early adventurers on his track, incited the most reckless, shameless disregard of the rights and happiness of a harmless and guileless people, whose very helplessness should have been their defense.[4] Forced to hunt incessantly for gold, and to minister in every way to the imperious appetites of their stranger tyrants, they found in speedy death their only relief from intolerable suffering. In a few years, but a miserable remnant remained. And now the western coast of Africa was thrown open to replace them by a race more indurated to hardship, toil, and suffering.[5] Religion was speciously invoked to cover this new atrocity with her broad mantle, under the plea of relieving the Indians from a servitude, which they had already escaped through the gate of death. But, though the Papacy was earnestly importuned to lend its sanction to this device, and though its compliance has been stoutly asserted, and was long widely believed, the charge rests upon no evidence, is squarely denied, and has been silently abandoned. For once, at least, avarice and cruelty have been unable to gain a sacerdotal sanction, and compelled to fall back in good order upon Canaan and Ham.[6] But, even without benefit of clergy, Negro Slavery, once introduced, rapidly, though thinly, overspread the whole vast area of Spanish and Portuguese America, with Dutch and French Guiana and the West India Islands; and the African slave-trade was, for two or three centuries, the most lucrative, though most abhorrent, traffic pursued by or known to mankind.[7] It was the subject of

tonio Gonzales, who had brought some Moorish slaves into Portugal, was commanded to release them. He did so; and the Moors gave him, as their ransom, not gold, but *black Moors with curled hair*. Thus negro slaves came into Europe."

"In 1444, Spain also took part in the traffic. The historian of her maritime discoveries even claims for her the unenviable distinction of having anticipated the Portuguese in introducing negroes into Europe."—*Ibid.*, p. 166.

[3] "Columbus himself did not escape the stain. Enslaving five hundred native Americans, he sent them to Spain, that they might be publicly sold at Seville."—*Ibid.*

[4] "In 1500, the generous Isabella commanded the liberation of the Indians held in bondage in her European possessions. Yet her native benevolence extended not to the Moors, whose valor had been punished by slavery, nor to the Africans; and even her compassion for the New World was but a transient feeling, which relieves the miserable who are in sight, not the deliberation of a just principle."—*Bancroft's Hist. U. S.*, vol. i., p. 128.

[5] "It was not Las Casas who first suggested the plan of transporting African slaves to Hispaniola; Spanish slaveholders, as they emigrated, were accompanied by their negroes."—*Ibid.*

[6] "Even the voluptuous Leo X. declared that 'not the Christian religion only, but nature herself, cries out against the state of Slavery.' And Paul III., in two separate briefs, imprecated a curse on the Europeans who would enslave Indians, or any other class of men."—*Ibid.*, p. 172.

[7] Upon the suggestion of Las Casas in favor of negroes for American slaves, in contradiction to the Indians, negroes began to be poured into the West Indies.

"It had been proposed to allow four for each emigrant. Deliberate calculation fixed the number esteemed necessary at four thousand. That very year in which Charles V. sailed with a powerful expedition against Tunis, to attack the pirates of the Barbary States, and to emancipate Christian slaves in Africa, he gave an open, legal sanction to the African slave-trade."—*Ibid.*, p. 170.

gainful and jealous monopolies, and its profits were greedily shared by philosophers, statesmen, and kings.[8]

When, in 1607, the first abiding English colony—Virginia—was founded on the Atlantic coast of what is now our country, Negro Slavery, based on the African slave-trade, was more than a century old throughout Spanish and Portuguese America, and so had already acquired the stability and respectability of an institution. It was nearly half a century old in the British West Indies. Spanish, Dutch, Portuguese, and British vessels and trading companies[9] vied with each other for the gains to be speedily acquired by purchasing, or kidnapping, young negroes on the coast of Guinea, and selling them in the American colonies of their own and other nations. The early colonists of Virginia were mainly adventurers of an unusually bad type—bankrupt prodigals, genteel spendthrifts, and incorrigible profligates, many of whom had left their native country for that country's good, in obedience to the urgent persuasion of sheriffs, judges, and juries. All were intoxicated by the common illusions of emigrants with regard to the facilities for acquiring vast wealth at the cost of little or no labor in the Eden to which they were attracted. Probably no other colony that ever succeeded or endured was so largely made up of unfit and unpromising materials. Had it not been backed by a strong and liberal London company, which enjoyed for two or three generations the special favor and patronage of the Crown, it must have perished in its infancy. But the climate of tide-water Virginia is genial, the soil remarkably fertile and facile, the timber abundant and excellent, while its numerous bays and inlets abound in the choicest shell-fish; so that a colony that would fail here could succeed nowhere. Tobacco, too, that bewitching but poisonous narcotic, wherewith Providence has seen fit to balance the inestimable gifts of Indian Corn and the Potato by the New World to the Old, grew luxuriantly on the intervals of her rivers, and was eagerly bought at high prices by the British merchants, through whom nearly every want of the colonists was supplied. Manual labor of all kinds was in great demand in the English colonies; so that, for some time, the

[8] "A Flemish favorite of Charles V. having obtained of this king a patent containing an exclusive right of importing four thousand negroes annually to the West Indies, sold it for twenty-five thousand ducats, to some Genoese merchants, who first brought into a regular form the commerce for slaves between Africa and America."—*Holmes's Annals of America*, vol. i., p. 35.

"In 1563, the English began to import negroes into the West Indies. Their first slave-trade was opened the preceding year on the coast of Guinea. John Hawkins, in the prospect of a great gain, resolved to make trial of this nefarious and inhuman traffic. Communicating the design to several gentlemen in London, who became liberal contributors and adventurers, three good ships were immediately provided; and, with these and one hundred men, Hawkins sailed to the coast of Guinea, where, by money, treachery, and force, he procured at least three hundred negroes, and now sold them at Hispaniola."—*Ibid.*, p. 83.

"Ferdinand" (in 1513) "issued a decree declaring that the servitude of the Indians is warranted by the laws of God and man."—*Ibid.*, p. 32.

"Every freeman of Carolina shall have absolute power and authority over his negro slaves, of what nation or religion whatsoever."—*Locke's Fundamental Constitution for South Carolina.*

[9] According to Bancroft, upon the establishment of the Assiento Treaty in 1713, creating a Company for the prosecution of the African Slave Trade, one-quarter of the stock was taken by Philip of Spain; Queen Anne reserved to herself another quarter, and the remaining moiety was to be divided among her subjects. "Thus did the sovereigns of England and Spain become the largest slave-merchants in the world."

banishment thither of felons from the mother country seems to have provoked no serious objection. That such a colony, in such an age, should have existed thirteen years prior to the introduction of Negro Slavery, indicates rather its weakness and poverty than its virtue. The probability is that its planters bought the first slaves that were offered them; at any rate, the first that they were able to pay for. When the Pilgrim Fathers landed on the rock of Plymouth,[10] Virginia had already received and distributed her first cargo of slaves.[11]

There is no record of any serious opposition, whether on moral or economic grounds, to the introduction of slaves and establishment of Slavery in the various British, Dutch, and Swedish Colonies, planted along the coast between the Penobscot and the Savannah rivers during the succeeding century. At the outset, it is certain that the importation of negro chattels into the various seaports, by merchants trading thither, was regarded only with vague curiosity and marvel, like that which would now be excited by the experimental introduction of elephants or hippopotami as beasts of burden. Human rights, in the abstract, had not yet been made a theme of popular discussion, hardly of philosophic speculation: for English liberty, John Hampden had not yet poured out his blood on the battle-field, nor Algernon Sidney laid his head on the block. The negroes, uncouth and repulsive, could speak no word intelligible to British or Colonial ears, when first imported, and probably had a scarcely clearer conception of their own rights and wrongs than had those by whom they were surrounded. Some time ere the middle of the Seventeenth Century, a British Attorney-General, having the question formally submitted to him, gave his official opinion, that negroes, *being pagans*, might justly be held in Slavery, even in England itself. The amount of the fee paid by the wealthy and prosperous slave-traders

[10] December 22, 1620. The first slaves brought to Virginia were sold from a Dutch vessel, which landed twenty at Jamestown, in 1620.

[11] "In the first recorded case (Butts *v.* Penny, 2 Lev., 201; 3 Kib., 785), in 1677, in which the question of property in negroes appears to have come before the English courts, it was held, 'that, being usually bought and sold among merchants as merchandise, and *also being infidels*, there might be a property in them sufficient to maintain trover.'"—*Hildreth's Hist. U. S.*, vol. ii., p. 214.

"What precisely the English law might be on the subject of Slavery, still remained a matter of doubt. Lord Holt had expressed the opinion, as quoted in a previous chapter, that Slavery was a condition unknown to English law, and that every person setting foot in England thereby became free. American planters, on their visits to England, seem to have been annoyed by claims of freedom set up on this ground, and that, also, of baptism. To relieve their embarrassments, the merchants concerned in the American trade" (in 1729) "had obtained a written opinion from Yorke and Talbot, the attorney and solicitor general of that day. According to this opinion, which passed for more than forty years as good law, not only was baptism no bar to Slavery, but negro slaves might be held in England just as well as in the Colonies. The two lawyers by whom this opinion was given rose afterward, one of them to be chief justice of England, and both to be chancellors. Yorke, sitting in the latter capacity, with the title of Lord Hardwicke" (in 1749), "had recently recognized the doctrine of that opinion as sound law. (Pearce *v.* Lisle, Ambler, 76.) He objects to Lord Holt's doctrine of freedom, secured by setting foot on English soil, that no reason could be found why slaves should not be equally free when they set foot in Jamaica, or any other English plantation. All our colonies are subject to the laws of England, although as to some purposes they have laws of their own! His argument is that, if Slavery be contrary to English law, no local enactments in the Colonies could give it any validity. To avoid overturning Slavery in the Colonies, it was absolutely necessary to uphold it in England."—*Ibid.*, p. 426.

for this remarkable display of legal erudition and acumen, is not recorded, but it probably included a liberal consideration for wear-and-tear of conscience. Two or three decisions from British courts were, at different times thereafter, obtained, substantially echoing this opinion. It was not till 1772 that Lord Mansfield pronounced, in the ever-memorable Somerset case, his judgment that, by the laws of England, no man could be held in Slavery. That judgment has never since been disturbed, nor seriously questioned.

The austere morality and democratic spirit of the Puritans ought to have kept their skirts clear from the stain of human bondage. But, beneath all their fierce antagonism, there was a certain kinship between the disciples of Calvin and those of Loyola. Each were ready to suffer and die for God's truth as they understood it, and neither cherished any appreciable sympathy or consideration for those they esteemed God's enemies, in which category the savages of America and the heathen negroes of Africa were so unlucky as to be found. The Puritan pioneers of New England were early involved in desperate, life-or-death struggles with their Aboriginal neighbors, in whom they failed to discover those poetic and fascinating traits which irradiate them in the novels of Cooper and the poems of Longfellow. Their experience of Indian ferocity and treachery, acting upon their theologic convictions, led them early and readily to the belief that these savages, and by logical inference *all* savages, were the children of the devil, to be subjugated, if not extirpated, as the Philistine inhabitants of Canaan had been by the Israelites under Joshua. Indian slavery, sometimes forbidden by law, but usually tolerated, if not entirely approved, by public opinion, was among the early usages of New England; and from this to negro slavery—the slavery of any variety of pagan barbarians—was an easy transition. That the slaves in the Eastern colonies were few, and mainly confined to the seaports, does not disprove this statement. The harsh climate, the rocky soil, the rugged topography of New England, presented formidable, though not impassable, barriers to slaveholding. Her narrow patches of arable soil, hemmed in between bogs and naked blocks of granite, were poorly adapted to cultivation by slaves. The labor of the hands without the brain, of muscle divorced from intelligence, would procure but a scanty livelihood on those bleak hills. He who was compelled, for a subsistence, to be, by turns, farmer, mechanic, lumberman, navigator, and fisherman, might possibly support one slave, but would be utterly ruined by half a dozen. Slaveholding in the Northern States was rather coveted as a social distinction, a badge of aristocracy and wealth, than resorted to with any idea of profit or pecuniary advantage.

It was different southward of the Susquehanna, but especially in South Carolina, where the cultivation of Rice and Indigo on the seaboard had early furnished lucrative employment for a number of slaves far exceeding that of the white population, and whose Sea Islands afforded peculiar facilities for limiting the intercourse of the slaves with each other, and their means of escape to the wilderness and to the savages. South Carolina, a century ago, was as intensely, conspicuously aristocratic and slaveholding as in our own day. But when Slavery had obtained everywhere a foothold, and, in most colonies, a distinct legal recognition, without encountering aught deserving the name of serious resistance, it were absurd to claim for any colony or section a moral superiority in this regard over any other.

The single and most honorable exception to the general facility with which this giant wrong was adopted and acquiesced in, is presented by the history of Georgia. That colony may owe something of her preëminence to her comparatively recent foundation; but she is far more indebted to the character and efforts of her illustrious founder. James Oglethorpe was born in 1688, or 1689, at Godalming, Surry County, England; entered the British army in 1710; and, having resigned on the restoration of peace, was, in 1714, commended by the great Marlborough to his former associate in command, the famous Prince Eugene of Savoy, by whom he was appointed one of his aids. He fought under Eugene in his brilliant and successful campaign against the Turks in 1716 and 1717, closing with the siege and capture of Belgrade, which ended the war. Declining to remain in the Austrian service, he returned, in 1722, to England, where, on the death of his elder brother about this time, he inherited the family estate; was elected to Parliament for the borough of Hazelmere, which he represented for the ensuing thirty-two years, and, becoming acquainted with the frightful abuses and inhumanities which then characterized the British system of Imprisonment for Debt, he devoted himself to their reform, and carried through the House an act to this end. His interest in the fortunes of bankrupt and needy debtors led him to plan the establishment of a colony to which they should be invited, and in which they might hope, by industry and prudence, to attain independence. This colony was also intended to afford an asylum for the oppressed Protestants of Germany and other portions of the continent. He interested many eminent and influential personages in his project, obtained for it a grant of nearly ten thousand pounds sterling from Parliament, with subscriptions to the amount of sixteen thousand more, and organized a company for its realization, whereof the directors were nearly all noblemen and members of Parliament. Its constitution forbade any director to receive any pecuniary advantage therefrom. Being himself the animating soul of the enterprise, he was persuaded to accept the arduous trust of governor of the colony, for which a royal grant had been obtained of the western coast of the Atlantic from the mouth of the Savannah to that of the Altamaha, and to which the name of Georgia was given in honor of the reigning sovereign. The trustees were incorporated in June, 1732. The pioneer colonists left England in November of that year, and landed at Charleston in January, 1733. Proceeding directly to their territory, they founded the city of Savannah in the course of the ensuing month. Oglethorpe, as director and vice-president of the African Company, had previously become acquainted with an African prince, captured and sold into slavery by some neighboring chief, and had returned him to his native country, after imbibing from his acquaintance with the facts a profound detestation of the Slave-Trade and of Slavery. One of the fundamental laws devised by Oglethorpe for the government of his colony was a prohibition of slaveholding; another was an interdiction of the sale or use of Rum—neither of them calculated to be popular with the jail-birds, idlers, and profligates, who eagerly sought escape from their debts and their miseries by becoming members of the new colony. The spectacle of men, no wiser nor better than themselves, living idly and luxuriously, just across the Savannah river, on the fruits of constrained and unpaid negro labor, doubtless inflamed their discontent and their hostility. As if to add to the governor's troubles, war between Spain and England broke out in 1739, and Georgia, as the frontier colony, contiguous to the far older and stronger Spanish settlement of East Florida, was peculiarly exposed to its ravages. Oglethorpe, at the head of the South Carolina and Georgia militia, made an attempt on Saint Augustine, which miscarried; and this, in 1742, was retaliated by a much stronger Spanish expedition, which took Fort St. Simon, on the Altamaha, and might easily have subdued the whole colony, but it was alarmed and repelled by a stratagem of his conception. Oglethorpe soon after returned to England; the trustees finally surrendered their charter to the Crown; and in 1752 Georgia became a royal colony, whereby its inhabitants were enabled to gratify, without restraint, their longing for Slavery and Rum. The struggle of Oglethorpe[12] in Georgia was aided by the presence, counsels, and active sympathy, of the famous John Wesley, the founder of Methodism, whose pungent description of Slavery as "the sum of all villainies," was based on personal observation and experience during his sojourn in these colonies. But "another king arose, who knew not Joseph;" the magisterial hostility to bondage was relaxed, if not wholly withdrawn; the temptation remained and increased, while the resistance faded and disappeared; and soon Georgia yielded silently, passively, to the contagion of evil example, and soon became not only slaveholding, but, next to South Carolina, the most infatuated of all the thirteen colonies in its devotion to the mighty evil.

[12] Oglethorpe lived to be nearly a hundred years old—dying at Cranham Hall, Essex, England, June 30, 1787. It is not recorded nor probable that he ever revisited America after his relinquishment of the governorship of Georgia; but he remained a warm, active, well-informed friend of our country after, as well as before and during, her struggle for independence. In 1784, Hannah More thus wrote of him:

"I have got a new admirer; it is Gen. Oglethorpe, perhaps the most remarkable man of his time. He was foster-brother to the Pretender, and is much above ninety years old; the finest figure you ever saw. He perfectly realizes all my ideas of Nestor. His literature is great, his knowledge of the world extensive, and his faculties as bright as ever. * * He is quite a *preux chevalier;* heroic, romantic, and full of the old gallantry."

Pope—who praised so sparingly—had spoken of him, not quite half a century earlier, in terms evincing like admiration; and many other contemporaries of literary eminence bore testimony to his signal merits.—See *Sparks's American Biography.*

III.

SLAVERY IN THE REVOLUTION.

The American Revolution was no sudden outbreak. It was preceded by eleven years of peaceful remonstrance and animated discussion. The vital question concerned the right of the British Parliament to impose taxes, at its discretion, on British subjects in any and every part of the empire. This question presented many phases, and prompted various acts and propositions. But its essence was always the same; and it was impossible that such men as James Otis, John Adams, Thomas Jefferson, and Patrick Henry, should discuss it without laying broad foundations for their argument in premises affecting the natural and general Rights of Man to self-government, with the control of his own products or earnings. The enthusiast who imagines that our patriots were *all* convinced of the danger and essential iniquity of Slavery, and the conservative who argues that few or none perceived and admitted the direct application of their logic to the case of men held in perpetual and limitless bondage, are alike mistaken. There were doubtless some who did not perceive, or did not admit, the inseparable connection between the rights they claimed as British freemen and the rights of all men everywhere; but the more discerning and logical of the patriots comprehended and confessed that their assertion of the rightful inseparability of Representation from Taxation necessarily affirmed the grander and more essential right of each innocent, rational being to the control and use of his own capacities and faculties, and to the enjoyment of his own earnings.[1]

[1] Witness the Darien (Ga.) resolutions. In the Darien committee, Thursday, June 12, 1775:

"When the most valuable privileges of a people are invaded, not only by open violence, but by every kind of fraud, sophistry, and cunning, it behooves every individual to be upon his guard, and every member of society, like beacons in a country surrounded by enemies, to give the alarm, not only when their liberties in general are invaded, but separately, lest the precedent in one may affect the whole; and to enable the collective wisdom of such a people to judge of its consequences, and how far their respective grievances concern all, or should be opposed to preserve their necessary union. Every laudable attempt of this kind by the good people of this Colony, in a constitutional manner, has been hitherto frustrated by the influence and authority of men in office and their numerous dependents, and in every other natural and just way by the various arts they have put in practice. We, therefore, the representatives of the extensive district of Darien, in the colony of Georgia, being now assembled in congress by the authority and free choice of the inhabitants of the said district, now free from their fetters, do Resolve—"

There are six resolutions in all. The first eulogizes "the firm and manly conduct of the people of Boston and Massachusetts," acquiescing in all the resolutions of the "grand American Congress in Philadelphia last October." The second resolution is denunciatory of England, in shutting up the land office, and in other oppressive acts. The third is opposed to ministerial mandates under the name of constitutions. The fourth is denunciatory of the number of officers appointed over the colonies by the British crown, and their exorbitant salaries. The fifth is as follows:

"5th. To show the world that we are not influenced by any contracted or interested motive, but a general philanthropy for all mankind, of whatever climate, language, or complexion, we hereby declare our disapprobation and abhorrence of the unnatural practice of Slavery in America (however the uncultivated state of our country, and other specious arguments, may plead for it), a practice founded in injustice and cruelty, and highly dangerous to our liberties (as well as lives), debasing part of our fellow-creatures below men, and corrupting the virtue and morals of the rest, and as laying the basis of that liberty we contend for (and which we pray the Almighty to continue to the latest posterity) upon a very wrong foundation. We therefore resolve at all times to use our utmost efforts for the manumis-

The principles of civil and political liberty, so patiently evolved and so thoroughly commended during the long controversy which preceded the appeal to arms, were reduced to axioms, and became portions of the popular faith. When Jefferson, in drafting our immortal Declaration of Independence, embodied in its preamble a formal and emphatic assertion of the inalienable Rights of Man, he set forth propositions novel and startling to European ears, but which eloquence and patriotic fervor had already engraven deeply on the American heart. That Declaration was not merely, as Mr. Choate has termed it, "the passionate manifesto of a revolutionary war;" it was the embodiment of our forefathers' deepest and most rooted convictions; and when, in penning that Declaration, he charged the British government with upholding and promoting the African slave-trade against the protests of the colonists,[2] and in violation of the dictates of humanity, he asserted truths which the jealous devotion of South Carolina and Georgia to slaveholding rendered it impolitic to send forth as an integral portion of our arraignment of British tyranny; but which were, nevertheless, widely and deeply felt to be an important and integral portion of our case.[3] Even divested of this, the Declaration stands to-day an evidence that our fathers regarded the rule of Great Britain as no more destructive to their own rights than to the rights of mankind.

No other document was ever issued which so completely reflected and developed the popular convictions which underlaid and impelled it as that Declaration of Independence. The cavil that its ideas were *not original* with Jefferson is a striking testimonial to its worth. Originality of conception was the very last merit to which he would have chosen to lay claim, his purpose being to embody the general convictions of his countrymen — their conceptions of human, as well as colonial, rights and British wrongs, in the fewest, strongest, and clearest words. The fact that some of these words had already been employed—some of them a hundred times—to set forth the same general truths, in no manner unfitted them for his use.

The claim that his draft was a pla-

sion of our slaves in this colony upon the most safe and equitable footing for the masters and themselves."—*American Archives, 4th Series,* vol. i., 1774 and 1775.

[2] The following is the indictment of George III., as a patron and upholder of the African slave-trade, embodied by Mr. Jefferson in his original draft of the Declaration:

"*Determined to keep open a market where* MEN *should be bought and sold, he has prostituted his negative for suppressing every legislative attempt to prohibit or to restrain this execrable commerce. And that this assemblage of horrors might want no fact of distinguished dye, he is now exciting those very people to rise in arms among us, and purchase that liberty of which he has deprived them, by murdering the people on whom he also obtruded them: thus paying off former crimes committed against the* LIBERTIES *of one people, with crimes which he urges them to commit against the* LIVES *of another.*"

[3] Mr. Jefferson, in his Autobiography, gives the following reason for the omission of this remarkable passage from the Declaration as adopted, issued, and published:

"The clause, too, reprobating the enslaving the inhabitants of Africa, was struck out in complaisance to *South Carolina* and *Georgia*, who had never attempted to restrain the importation of slaves, and who, on the contrary, still wished to continue it. Our Northern brethren also, I believe, felt a little tender under those censures; for, though their people had very few slaves themselves, yet they had been pretty considerable carriers of them to others." — *Jefferson's Works,* vol. i., p. 170.

giarism from the Mecklenburg (N. C.) Declaration of April 20th, preceding, he indignantly repelled; but he always observed that he employed whatever terms best expressed his thought, and would not say how far he was indebted for them to his reading, how far to his original reflections. Even the great fundamental assertion of Human Rights, which he has so memorably set forth as follows: "We hold these truths to be self-evident, that all men are created equal; that they are endowed by their Creator with certain inalienable rights; that among these, are life, liberty, and the pursuit of happiness; that to secure these rights governments are instituted among men, deriving their just powers from the consent of the governed; that, whenever any form of government becomes destructive of these ends, it is the right of the people to alter or to abolish it, and to institute a new government, laying its foundations on such principles, and organizing its powers in such form, as to them shall seem most likely to effect their safety and happiness," was no novelty to those who hailed and responded to it. Three weeks before, the Virginia Convention had unanimously adopted a Declaration of Rights, reported on the 27th of May by George Mason,[4] which proclaims that "All men are by nature equally free, and have inherent rights, of which, when they enter into a state of society, they cannot, by any compact, deprive or divest their posterity; namely, the enjoyment of life and liberty, with the means of acquiring and possessing property, and pursuing and obtaining happiness and safety." See also the Mecklenburg Declaration.

The original draft of the Declaration of American Independence was first communicated by Mr. Jefferson separately to two of his colleagues, John Adams and Benjamin Franklin, on the committee chosen by Congress to prepare it; then to the whole committee, consisting, in addition, of Roger Sherman and Robert R. Livingston; reported, after *twenty days'* gestation, on the 28th of June; read in Committee of the Whole on the 1st of July; earnestly debated and scanned throughout the three following days, until finally adopted on the evening of the 4th. It may safely be said that not an affirmation, not a sentiment, was put forth therein to the world, which had not received the deliberate approbation of such cautious, conservative minds as those of Franklin, John Adams, and Roger Sherman, and of the American People, as well as their representatives in Congress, those of South Carolina and Georgia included.

The progress of the Revolution justified and deepened these convictions. Slavery was soon proved our chief source of weakness and of peril. Of our three millions of people, half a million were the chattels of others; and though all the colonies tolerated, and most of them expressly legalized slaveholding, the slaves, nearly concentrated in the Southern States, paralyzed the energies and enfeebled the efforts of their patriots. Incited by proclamations of royal governors and military commanders, thousands of the negroes escaped to British camps and garrisons, and were there

[4] The grandfather of James M. Mason, late U.S. Senator from Virginia, since Confederate Emissary to England. *George* Mason was one of Virginia's most illustrious sons.

manumitted and protected; while the master race, alarmed for the safety of their families, were unable or unwilling to enlist in the Continental armies, or even to be called into service as militia.[5]

The number of slaves in the States respectively, at the time of the Revolution, is not known. But it may be closely approximated by the aid of the census of 1790, wherein the slave population is returned as follows:

NORTH.		SOUTH.	
New Hampshire	158	Delaware	8,887
Vermont	17	Maryland	103,036
Rhode Island	952	Virginia	293,427
Connecticut	2,759	North Carolina	100,572
Massachusetts [6]	none	South Carolina	107,094
New York	21,324	Georgia	29,264
New Jersey	11,423	Kentucky	11,830
Pennsylvania [7]	3,737	Tennessee	3,417
Total	40,370	Total	657,527

The documents and correspondence of the Revolution are full of complaints by Southern slaveholders of their helplessness and peril, because of Slavery, and of the necessity thereby created of their more efficient defense and protection.[8] The New England States, with a population less numerous than that of Virginia, the Carolinas, and Georgia, furnished more than double the number of soldiers to battle for the common cause. The South was repeatedly overrun, and regarded as substantially subdued, by armies that would not have ventured to invade New England, and could not have maintained themselves a month on her soil. Indeed, after Gage's expulsion

[5] The number of troops employed by the Colonies during the entire Revolutionary war, as well as the number furnished by each, is shown by the following, which is compiled from statistics contained in a work published by Jacob Moore, Concord, entitled, "Collections of the New Hampshire Historical Society for the year 1824," vol. i., p. 236.

	CONTINENTAL.	MILITIA.
New Hampshire	12,496	2,093
Massachusetts	68,007	15,155
Rhode Island	5,878	4,284
Connecticut	32,039	7,792
New York	18,331	3,304
New Jersey	10,726	6,055
Pennsylvania	25,608	7,357
Delaware	2,317	376
Maryland	13,912	4,127
Virginia	26,668	5,620
North Carolina	7,263	
South Carolina	6,417	
Georgia	2,679	
Total	232,341	56,163

[6] Massachusetts adopted a new State Constitution in 1780, to which a bill of rights was prefixed, which her Supreme Court soon after decided was inconsistent with the maintenance of Slavery, which had been thus abolished.

[7] Pennsylvania had passed an act of Gradual Emancipation in 1780.

[8] Henry Laurens of South Carolina, two years President of the Continental Congress, appointed Minister to Holland, and captured on his way thither by a British cruiser, finally Commissioner with Franklin and Jay for negotiating peace with Great Britain, on the 14th of August, 1776, wrote from Charleston, S. C., to his son, then in England, a letter explaining and justifying his resolution to stand or fall with the cause of American Independence, in which he said:

"You know, my dear son, I abhor Slavery. I was born in a country where Slavery had been established by British kings and parliaments, as by the laws of that country, ages before my existence. I found the Christian religion and Slavery growing under the same authority and cultivation. I nevertheless disliked it. In former days, there was no combating the prejudices of men supported by interest: the day, I hope, is approaching, when from principles of gratitude, as well as justice, every man shall strive to be foremost in showing his readiness to comply with the golden rule. Not less than twenty thousand pounds sterling would all my negroes produce, if sold at public auction tomorrow. I am not the man who enslaved them; they are indebted to Englishmen for that favor: nevertheless, I am devising means for manumitting many of them, and for cutting off the entail of slavery. Great powers oppose me,—the laws and customs of my country, my own and the avarice of my countrymen. What will my children say if I deprive them of so much estate? These are difficulties, but not insuperable. I will do as much as I can in my time, and leave the rest to a better hand.

"I am not one of those who arrogate the peculiar care of Providence in each fortunate event; nor one of those who dare trust in Providence for defense and security of their own liberty, while they enslave, and wish to continue in slavery, thousands who are as well entitled to

from Boston, and Burgoyne's surrender at Saratoga, New England, save the islands on her coast, was pretty carefully avoided by the Royalist generals, and only assailed by raids, which were finished almost as soon as begun. These facts, vividly impressed on the general mind by the necessities and sacrifices of the times,[9] in connection with the discovery and elucidation, already noticed, of elemental principles, had pretty thoroughly cured the North of all attachment to, or disposition to justify Slavery before the close of the Revolutionary war.

IV.

SLAVERY UNDER THE CONFEDERATION.

As the public burdens were constantly swelled, and the debts of the several States increased, by the magnitude and duration of our Revolutionary struggle, the sale of yet unsettled lands, especially in the vast and fertile West, began to be regarded as a principal resource for the ultimate discharge of these constantly augmenting liabilities: and it became a matter of just complaint and uneasiness on the part of those States—Rhode Island, New Jersey, Delaware, and South Carolina—which had no chartered claim to such lands much beyond the limits of their then actual settlements, that their partners in the efforts, responsibilities, and sacrifices of the common struggle were likely to reap a peculiar and disproportionate advantage from its success. Massachusetts, Connecticut, New York, Virginia, North Carolina, and Georgia, each claimed, under their several charters, a right of almost infinite extension westward, and, in the event of the establishment of American independence, would naturally

---

freedom as themselves. I perceive the work before me is great. I shall appear to many as a promoter not only of strange, but of dangerous doctrines: it will therefore be necessary to proceed with caution. You are apparently deeply interested in this affair; but, as I have no doubts concerning your concurrence and approbation, I most sincerely wish for your advice and assistance, and hope to receive both in good time."—*Collection of the Zenger Club*, pp. 20, 21.

[9] The famous Rev. Samuel Hopkins, D.D., an eminent Calvinist divine, published, soon after the commencement of the war, a dialogue concerning the slavery of the Africans, which he dedicated to "The Honorable Continental Congress," and of which the following passage exhibits the drift and purpose:

"God is so ordering it in his providence, that it seems absolutely necessary something should be speedily done with respect to the slaves among us, in order to our safety, and to prevent their turning against us in our present struggle, in order to get their liberty. Our oppressors have planned to gain the blacks, and induce them to take up arms against us, by promising them liberty on this condition; and this plan they are prosecuting to the utmost of their power, by which means they have persuaded numbers to join them. And, should we attempt to restrain them by force and severity, keeping a strict guard over them, and punishing them severely who shall be detected in attempting to join our opposers, this will only be making bad worse, and serve to render our inconsistence, oppression, and cruelty more criminal, perspicuous, and shocking, and bring down the righteous vengeance of Heaven on our heads. The only way pointed out to prevent this threatening evil is to set the blacks at liberty ourselves, by some public acts and laws, and then give them proper encouragement to labor, or take arms in the defense of the American cause, as they shall choose. This would at once be doing them some degree of justice, and defeating our enemies in the scheme that they are prosecuting."—*Hopkins's Works*, vol. ii., p. 584.

each possess a vast area of unpeopled, ungranted, and ultimately valuable lands. The landless States, with obvious reason and justice, insisted that these lands, won by the common valor and sacrifices of the whole American people, should be regarded as their common property, and to this end should be surrendered or ceded by the States claiming them respectively to the Confederation. The colonial charters, moreover, were glaringly inconsistent with each other; vast tracts being ceded by them to two or more colonies respectively; and it was a puzzling question, even for lawyers, to determine whether the earliest or the latest royal concession, if either, should have the precedence. There was but one beneficent and just solution for all disputes and difficulties in the premises; and this was a quit-claim by the respective States of their several rights and pretensions to lands exterior to their own proper boundaries, in favor of the common Confederacy. This consummation was, for the most part, seasonably and cheerfully agreed to. Connecticut made a moderate reservation of wild lands assured to her by her charter in what is now Northern Ohio. Virginia, beside retaining her partially settled country south of the Ohio, now forming the State of Kentucky, reserved a sufficiency north of the Ohio to provide liberal bounties for her officers and soldiers who fought in the war of the Revolution, conceding all other territory north of the river, and all jurisdiction over this. And it was presumed, at the close of the war, that North Carolina and Georgia would promptly make similar concessions of the then savage regions covered by their respective charters, now known as Tennessee, Alabama, and Mississippi.

Though the war was practically concluded by the surrender of Cornwallis at Yorktown, October 19, 1781, and though the treaty of peace was signed at Paris, November 30, 1782, the British did not evacuate New York till November 25, 1783; and the Ninth Continental Congress, which convened at Philadelphia on the 3d of that month, adjourned next day to Annapolis. A bare quorum of members responded to their names, but one and another soon dropped off; so that the journal of most days records no quorum present, and no business done, until about the 1st day of March, 1784. On that day, Mr. Jefferson, on behalf of the delegates from his State, presented the deed of cession to the Confederation, by Virginia, of all her claims to jurisdiction over territory northwest of the Ohio, and to the soil also of that territory, subject to the reservation in behalf of her soldiers already noted. This deed being formally accepted, Mr. Jefferson moved the appointment of a select committee to report a plan of government for the western territory; and Messrs. Jefferson, Chase of Maryland, and Howell of Rhode Island, were appointed such committee. From this committee, Mr. Jefferson, in due time, reported an Ordinance for the government of "the territory, ceded already, or *to be* ceded, by individual States to the United States," specifying that such territory extends from the 31st to the 47th degree of north latitude, so as to include what now constitutes the States of Tennessee, Alabama, and Mississippi, but which was then, and remained for some years thereafter, unceded to the Union by North Carolina and Georgia. This entire territory, ceded and to be ceded, was divided prospectively by the Ordinance into embryo States, to which names were given; each of them to receive, in due time, a temporary or territorial government, and ultimately to be admitted into the Confederation of States upon the express assent of two-thirds of the preceding States; but both their temporary and their permanent governments were to be established on these fundamental conditions:

"1. That they shall *forever* remain a part of the United States of America.

"2. That, in their persons, property, and territory, they shall be subject to the government of the United States, in Congress assembled, and to the Articles of Confederation, in all those cases in which the original States shall be so subject.

"3. That they shall be subject to pay a part of the Federal debts, contracted or to be contracted; to be apportioned on them by Congress, according to the same common rule and measure by which apportionments thereof shall be made on the other States.

"4. That their respective governments shall be in republican forms, and shall admit no person to be a citizen who holds an hereditary title.

"5. *That after the year* 1800 *of the Christian era, there shall be neither Slavery nor involuntary servitude in any of the said States*, otherwise than in punishment of crimes, whereof the party shall have been duly convicted to have been personally guilty."

The Ordinance concluded as follows:

"*That all the preceding articles shall be formed into a charter of compact;* shall be duly executed by the President of the United States, in Congress assembled, under his hand and the seal of the United States; shall be promulgated, and *shall stand as fundamental conditions* between the thirteen original States and those newly described, *unalterable* but by the joint consent of the United States, in Congress assembled, and of the particular State within which such alteration is proposed to be made."

On the 19th of April, Congress took up this plan for consideration and action, and Mr. Spaight of N. C. moved that the fifth proposition above quoted, prohibiting Slavery after the year 1800, be stricken out of the Ordinance; and Mr. Read of S. C. seconded the motion. The question was put in this form: "Shall the words moved to be stricken out stand?" and on this question the Ays and Noes were required and taken, with the following result:

State	Member	Vote	Result
N. HAMP.	Mr. Foster	ay,	*Ay.*
	Mr. Blanchard	ay,	
MASSACHU.	Mr. Gerry	ay,	*Ay.*
	Mr. Partridge	ay,	
R. ISLAND.	Mr. Ellery	ay,	*Ay.*
	Mr. Howell	ay,	
CONNECT.	Mr. Sherman	ay,	*Ay.*
	Mr. Wadsworth	ay,	
NEW YORK.	Mr. De Witt	ay,	*Ay.*
	Mr. Paine	ay,	
N. JERSEY.	Mr. Dick	ay,	*No vote.*[1]
PENNSYL.	Mr. Mifflin	ay,	*Ay.*
	Mr. Montgomery	ay,	
	Mr. Hand	ay,	
MARYLAND.	Mr. Henry	no,	*No.*
	Mr. Stone	no,	
VIRGINIA.	Mr. Jefferson	ay,	*No.*
	Mr. Hardy	no,	
	Mr. Mercer	no,	
N. CAROLI.	Mr. Williamson	ay,	*Divided.*
	Mr. Spaight	no,	
S. CAROLI.	Mr. Read	no,	*No.*
	Mr. Beresford	no,	

The votes of members were *sixteen* for Mr. Jefferson's interdiction of Slavery to *seven* against it, and the States stood recorded *six* for it to *three* against it. But the Articles of Confederation required an affirmative vote of a majority of all the States to sustain a proposition; and thus the restriction failed through the absence of a member from New Jersey, rendering the vote of that State null for

[1] By the Articles of Confederation, two or more delegates were required to be present to cast the vote of a State. New Jersey, therefore, failed to vote.

want of a quorum. Had Delaware been then represented, she might, and might not, have voted in the affirmative; but it is not probable that Georgia, had she been present, would have cast an affirmative vote. Humanly speaking, we may say that the accident—a most deplorable and fatal accident—of the absence of a member from New Jersey, prevented the adoption, at that time, of a proposition which would have confined Slavery in our country within the limits of the then existing States, and precluded all reasonable probability of subsequent contentions, collisions, and bloody strife touching its extension.

The Jeffersonian Ordinance, thus shorn of its strength—the play of Hamlet with the part of Hamlet omitted—after undergoing some further amendments, was finally adopted, four days later: all the delegates but those from South Carolina voting in its favor.

In 1787, the last Continental Congress, sitting in New York, simultaneously with the Convention at Philadelphia which framed our present Constitution, took further action on the subject of the government of the western territory, raising a Select Committee thereon, of which Nathan Dane, of Massachusetts, was Chairman. That committtee reported, July 11, "An Ordinance for the government of the Territories of the United States northwest of the Ohio," excluding, by its silence, the territories south of that river, which were expressly brought within the purview and operation of Mr. Jefferson's Ordinance—those territories not having, as yet, been ceded by the States claiming them respectively as their peculiar possessions. Mr. Dane's ordinance embodies many provisions originally drafted and reported by Mr. Jefferson in 1784, but with some modifications. The act concludes with six unalterable Articles of *Perpetual* Compact between the embryo States respectively and the Union: the last of them in these words:

> "*There shall be neither Slavery nor involuntary servitude in the said Territory, otherwise than in punishment of crimes, whereof the parties shall be duly convicted.*"

To this was added, prior to its passage, the stipulation for the rendition of fugitives from labor or service, which either had just been, or was just about to be, embodied in the Federal Constitution, then being framed; and in this shape the entire Ordinance was adopted, July 13, by the unanimous vote of the States then represented in Congress, including Georgia and the Carolinas; no effort having been made to strike out the inhibition of Slavery. Mr. Robert Yates, of New York, voted alone in the negative on the passage of the Ordinance, but was overborne by the vote of his two colleagues, then present.[2]

[2] As the American people of our day evidently presume themselves much wiser than their grandfathers, especially in the science of government, the more essential portion of this celebrated Ordinance of 1787 is hereto appended, as affording a standard of comparison with the latest improvements in the art of Constitution-making. It reads:

"And for extending the fundamental principles of civil and religious liberty, which form the basis whereon these Republics, their laws and constitutions, are erected; to fix and establish these principles as the basis of all laws, constitutions, and governments, which forever hereafter shall be formed in the said Territory; to provide, also, for the establishment of States and permanent government therein, and for their admission to a share in the Federal councils on an equal footing with the original States at as early periods as may be consistent with the general interest:

V.

THE CONVENTION AND THE CONSTITUTION.

THE experiment of a Confederation, as contra-distinguished from a more intimate and positive Union, was fairly tried by our fathers. Its only beneficent result was the demonstration thereby afforded of its

---

"It is hereby ordained and declared, by the authority aforesaid, that the following articles shall be considered as articles of compact between the original States and the people and States in the said Territory, and *forever* remain unalterable, unless by common consent, to wit:

"ARTICLE 1. No person demeaning himself in a peaceable, orderly manner, shall ever be molested on account of his mode of worship, or religious sentiments, in the Territory.

"ART. 2. The inhabitants of the said Territory shall always be entitled to the benefits of the right of *habeas corpus*, and to the trial by jury; of a proportionate representation of the people in the Legislature, and of judicial proceedings according to the course of the common law. All persons shall be bailable, unless for capital offenses, where the proof shall be evident or the presumption great. All fines shall be moderate, and no cruel or unusual punishment shall be inflicted. No man shall be deprived of his liberty, or property, but by the judgment of his peers, or the law of the land; and, should the public exigencies make it necessary for the common preservation to take any person's property, or to demand his particular services, full compensation shall be made for the same. And in the just preservation of rights and property, it is understood and declared, that no law ought ever to be made, or have force, in the said Territory, that shall, in any manner whatever, interfere with, or affect, private contracts or engagements, *bonâ fide*, and without fraud, previously formed.

"ART. 3. General morality and knowledge being necessary to good government and the happiness of mankind, schools and the means of education shall be forever encouraged. The utmost good faith shall always be observed toward the Indians; their lands and property shall never be taken from them, without their consent; and in their property, rights, and liberty, they shall never be invaded or disturbed, unless in just and lawful wars, authorized by Congress; and laws, founded in justice and humanity, shall from time to time be made for preventing wrongs being done to them, and for preserving peace and friendship with them.

"ART. 4. The said Territory, and the States which may be formed therein, shall *forever* remain a part of this confederacy of the United States of America, subject to the Articles of Confederation, and to such alterations therein as shall be constitutionally made, and to all acts and ordinances of the United States, in Congress assembled, conformable thereto. The inhabitants and settlers in the said Territory shall be subject to pay a part of the Federal debts, apportioned on them by Congress, according to the same common rule and measure by which apportionments shall be made on the other States; and the taxes for paying their proportion shall be laid and levied by the authority and direction of the legislatures of the district, or districts, or new States, as in the original States, within the time agreed upon by the United States, in Congress assembled. The Legislatures of those districts, or States, shall *never* interfere with the primary disposal of the soil by the United States in Congress assembled, nor with any regulations Congress may find necessary for securing the title in such soil to the *bonâ fide* purchasers. No taxes shall be imposed on the lands and property of the United States; and in no case shall non-resident proprietors be taxed higher than residents. The navigable waters leading into the Mississippi and Saint Lawrence, and the conveying-places between the same, shall be common highways, and forever free, as well to the inhabitants of the said Territory as to the citizens of the United States, and those of any other State that may be admitted into the Confederacy, without any tax, impost, or duty, therefor.

"ART. 5. There shall be formed in the said Territory no less than three, nor more than five States; and the boundaries of the States, as soon as Virginia shall alter her act of cession and consent to the same, shall be fixed and established as follows, to wit: The western State in the said Territory shall be bounded by the Mississippi, the Ohio, and Wabash rivers; a direct line drawn from the Wabash and Post Vincent's due north to the territorial line between the United States and Canada; and by the said territorial line to the Lake of the Woods and Mississippi. The middle State shall be bounded by the said direct line, the Wabash, from Post Vincent's to the Ohio; by the Ohio; by a direct line, drawn due north, from the mouth of the Great Miami to the said territorial line; and by the said national line. The eastern State shall be bounded by the last mentioned direct line, the Ohio, Pennsylvania, and the said territorial line. Provided, however, and it is further understood and declared, that the boundaries of these three States shall be subject so far to be altered, that, if Congress shall hereafter find it expedient, they shall have authority to form one or two States in that part of the said Territory which lies north of an east and west line drawn through the southerly bend or extremity of Lake Michigan. And

vital and incurable defects.[1] Our country attained under it neither dignity, consideration, security, nor even solvency. The central or national authority, left dependent on the concurrent action of the several States for the very means of existence, was exhibited often in the attitude of a genteel beggar, rather than of a sovereign. Congress attempted to impose a very moderate tariff for the payment of interest on the general or foreign debt, contracted in support of the Revolutionary armies, but was baffled by the Legislature of Rhode Island—then a State of relatively extensive foreign commerce—which interposed its paralyzing veto. Political impotence, commercial embarrassment, and general distress, finally overbore or temporarily silenced sectional jealousies and State pride, to such an extent that a Convention of delegates from a quorum of the States, called together rather to amend than to supersede the Articles of Confederation, was legally assembled at Philadelphia in 1787, George Washington, Benjamin Franklin, Alexander Hamilton, James Madison, Edmund Randolph, and Charles C. Pinckney, being among its most eminent members. John Adams and Thomas Jefferson were absent as Embassadors in Europe. Samuel Adams, George Clinton, and Patrick Henry stood aloof, watching the movement with jealous appre-

whenever any of the said States shall have 60,000 free inhabitants therein, such State shall be admitted, by its delegates, into the Congress of the United States, on an equal footing with the original States in all respects whatever, and shall be at liberty to form a permanent constitution and State government; provided the constitution and government so to be formed shall be republican, and in conformity to the principles contained in these articles. And so far as it can be consistent with the general interest of the confederacy, such admission shall be allowed at an earlier period, and when there may be a less number of free inhabitants in the State than 60,000.

"Art. 6. There shall be neither Slavery nor involuntary servitude in the said Territory, otherwise than in punishment of crimes, whereof the party shall have been duly convicted; provided always, that any person escaping into the same from whom labor or service is lawfully claimed in any one of the original States, such fugitive may be lawfully reclaimed, and conveyed to the person claiming his or her labor, or service, as aforesaid."

On passing the above Ordinance, the Yeas and Nays being required by Mr. Yates, they were taken, with the following result:

State	Member	Vote	State vote
Massachusetts	Mr. Holton	ay,	*Ay.*
	Mr. Dane	ay,	
New York	Mr. Smith	ay,	*Ay.*
	Mr. Haring	ay,	
	Mr. Yates	no,	
New Jersey	Mr. Clarke	ay,	*Ay.*
	Mr. Sherman	ay,	
Delaware	Mr. Kearney	ay,	*Ay.*
	Mr. Mitchell	ay,	
Virginia	Mr. Grayson	ay,	*Ay.*
	Mr. R. H. Lee	ay,	
	Mr. Carrington	ay,	
North Carolina	Mr. Blount	ay,	*Ay.*
	Mr. Hawkins	ay,	
South Carolina	Mr. Kean	ay,	*Ay.*
	Mr. Huger	ay,	
Georgia	Mr. Few	ay,	*Ay.*
	Mr. Pierce	ay,	

Journal of Congress, vol. iv., 1787.

[1] "It may perhaps be thought superfluous to offer arguments to prove the utility of the Union—a point, no doubt deeply engraven on the hearts of the great body of the people in every State, and one which, it may be imagined, has no adversaries. * * * But the fact is that we already hear it whispered in the private circles of those who oppose the new Constitution, that the thirteen States are of too great extent for any general system, and that we must of necessity resort to separate confederacies of distinct portions of the whole. This doctrine will, in all probability, be gradually propagated, till it has votaries enough to countenance its open avowal. For nothing can be more evident to those who are able to take an enlarged view of the subject, than the alternative of an adoption of the Constitution or a dismemberment of the Union."—*The Federalist*, N. Y. edition of 1802, vol. i., p. 5.

"The melancholy story of the Federation showed the stern necessity of a compulsory power in the General Government to execute the duties confided to it; and the history of the present government itself has, on more than one occasion, manifested that the power of the Union is barely adequate to compel the execution of its laws, when resisted even by a single State."—*Oliver Wolcott*, vol. ii., p. 323.

hension. Franklin, then over eighty-one years of age, declined the chair on account of his increasing infirmities; and, on his motion, George Washington was unanimously elected President.

The Convention sat with closed doors; and no circumstantial nor adequate report of its deliberations was made. The only accounts of them which have reached us are those of delegates who took notes at the time, or taxed their recollection in after years, when the matter had attained an importance not anticipated at the time of its occurrence; and these reminiscences are not free from the suspicion of having been colored, if not recast, in accordance with the ambitions and ultimate political relations of the recorders. The general outline, however, of the deliberations and decisions of the Convention are sufficiently exhibited in the Constitution, and in what we know of the various propositions rejected in the course of its formation. The purpose of this work will require only a rapid summary of what was done, and what left undone, in relation to Human Slavery.

A majority of the framers of the Constitution, like nearly all their compatriots of our Revolutionary era, were adverse to Slavery.[2] Their judgments condemned, and their con-

[2] In the debate of Wednesday, August 8, on the adoption of the report of the Committee,

"Mr. RUFUS KING [then of Massachusetts, afterward an eminent Senator from New York] wished to know what influence the vote just passed was meant to have on the succeeding part of the report concerning the admission of slaves into the rule of representation. He could not reconcile his mind to the Article (Art. VII., Sect. 3), if it was to prevent objections to the latter part. The admission of slaves was a most grating circumstance to his mind, because he had hoped that this concession would have produced a readiness, which had not been manifested, to strengthen the General Government, and to make a full confidence in it. The report under consideration had, by the tenor of it, put an end to all his hopes. In two great points, the hands of the Legislature were absolutely tied. The importation of slaves could not be prohibited. Exports could not be taxed. Is this reasonable? What are the great objects of the general system? First, defense against foreign invasion; second, against internal sedition. Shall all the States, then, be bound to defend each, and shall each be at liberty to introduce a weakness which will render defense more difficult? Shall one part of the United States be bound to defend another part, and that other part be at liberty, not only to increase its own danger, but to withhold a compensation for the burden? If slaves are to be imported, shall not the exports produced by their labor supply a revenue, the better to enable the General Government to defend their masters? * * * He never could agree to let them be imported without limitation, and then be represented in the National Legislature. Indeed, he could so little persuade himself of the rectitude of such a practice, that he was not sure that he could assent to it under any circumstances.

"Mr. SHERMAN [Roger, of Connecticut] regarded the Slave-Trade as iniquitous; but, the point of representation having been settled after much difficulty and deliberation, he did not think himself bound to make opposition; especially as the present article, as amended, did not preclude any arrangement whatever on that point in another place reported.

"Mr. MADISON objected to one for every forty thousand inhabitants as a perpetual rule. The future increase of population, if the Union should be permanent, will render the number of representatives excessive.

"Mr. SHERMAN and Mr. MADISON moved to insert the words 'not exceeding' before the words 'one for every forty thousand inhabitants,' which was agreed to *nem. con.*

"Mr. GOUVERNEUR MORRIS moved to insert 'free' before the word 'inhabitants.' Much, he said, would depend on this point. He never could concur in upholding Domestic Slavery. It was a nefarious institution. It was the curse of heaven on the States where it prevailed. Compare the free regions of the Middle States, where a rich and noble cultivation marks the prosperity and happiness of the people, with the misery and poverty which overspreads the barren wastes of Virginia, Maryland, and the other States having slaves. Travel through the whole continent, and you behold the prospect continually varying with the appearance and disappearance of Slavery. * * * Upon what principle is it that the slaves shall be computed in the representation? Are they men? Then make them citizens, and let them vote. Are they property? Why, then, is no other property included? The houses in this city [Philadelphia] are worth more than all the wretched slaves that cover the rice-swamps of South Carolina. The admission of slaves into the representation, when fairly explained, comes to this: that the inhabit-

sciences reprobated it. They would evidently have preferred to pass over the subject in silence, and frame a Constitution wherein the existence of human bondage was not impliedly or constructively recognized. Hence it may be noted, that those provisions favoring or upholding Slavery, which deform our great charter, are not original and integral parts of the fabric, and, as such, contained in the original draft thereof; but are unsightly and abnormal additions, rather fastened upon than interwoven with the body of the structure. Could the majority have made such

ant of Georgia or South Carolina, who goes to the coast of Africa, and, in defiance of the most sacred laws of humanity, tears away his fellow-creatures from their dearest connections, and dooms them to the most cruel bondage, shall have more votes in a government instituted for the protection of the rights of mankind than the citizen of Pennsylvania or New Jersey, who views with a laudable horror so nefarious a practice. He would add, that Domestic Slavery is the most prominent feature in the aristocratic countenance of the proposed Constitution. * * * Let it not be said that Direct Taxation is to be proportioned to Representation. It is idle to suppose that the General Government can stretch its hand directly into the pockets of the people, scattered over so vast a country. They can only do it through the medium of exports, imports, and excises. For what, then, are all the sacrifices to be made? He would sooner submit himself to a tax, paying for all the negroes in the United States, than *saddle posterity with such a Constitution.*

"Mr. DAYTON [of New Jersey] seconded the motion. He did it, he said, that his sentiments on the subject might appear, whatever might be the fate of the amendment.

"Mr. SHERMAN did not regard the admission of negroes into the ratio of representation as liable to such insuperable objections," etc., etc.

"Mr. PINCKNEY [C. C., of South Carolina] considered the Fisheries and the Western Frontier as more burdensome to the United States than the slaves. He thought this could be demonstrated, if the occasion were a proper one."

On the question on the motion to insert "free" before "inhabitants," it was disagreed to; New Jersey alone voting in the affirmative. —*Madison's Papers*, vol. iii., p. 1261.

Tuesday, August 21st:

"Mr. LUTHER MARTIN [of Maryland] proposed to vary Article VII., Section 4, so as to allow a prohibition or tax on the importation of slaves. In the first place, as five slaves are to be counted as three freemen in the apportionment of representatives, such a clause would leave an encouragement to this traffic. In the second place, slaves weakened one part of the Union, which the other parts were bound to protect. The privilege of importing was therefore unreasonable. And in the third place, *it was inconsistent with the principles of the Revolution, and dishonorable to the American character, to have such a feature in the Constitution.*

"Mr. RUTLEDGE [of South Carolina] did not see how the importation of slaves could be encouraged by this section. He was not apprehensive of insurrections, and would readily exempt the other States from the obligation to protect the Southern against them. *Religion and humanity had nothing to do with this question. Interest* alone is the governing principle with nations," etc.

"Mr. ELLSWORTH [of Connecticut] was for leaving the clause as it stands," etc.

"Mr. PINCKNEY.—South Carolina *can never receive the plan if it prohibits the Slave-Trade.* In every proposed extension of the powers of Congress, that State expressly and watchfully excepted that of meddling with the importation of negroes. If the States should be all left at liberty on this subject, South Carolina may, perhaps, by degrees, do of herself what is wished, as Virginia and Maryland have already done."

"Adjourned."—*Ibid.*, p. 1388.

Again: in the debate of the following day—the consideration of Article VII., Section 4, being resumed—Colonel MASON [George, grandfather of James M., late United States Senator, and late Confederate emissary to England] gave utterance to the following sentiments:

"This *infernal traffic* originated in the avarice of British merchants. The British government has constantly checked the attempts of Virginia to put a stop to it. The present question concerned not the importing of slaves alone, but the whole Union. *The evil of having slaves was experienced during the late war. Had slaves been treated as they might have been by the enemy, they would have proved dangerous instruments in their hands.* But their folly dealt by the slaves as it did by the Tories. * * * Maryland and Virginia, he said, had already prohibited the importation of slaves. North Carolina had done the same in substance. All this would be vain, if South Carolina and Georgia be at liberty to import. The Western people are already calling for slaves for their new lands; and will fill that country with slaves, if they can be got through South Carolina and Georgia. Slavery discourages the arts and manufactures. The poor despise labor when performed by slaves. They prevent the emigration of whites, who really enrich and strengthen a country. They produce the most pernicious effect on manners. Every master of slaves is born a petty tyrant. They bring the judgment of heaven on a country. *As nations can not be punished in the next world, they must be in this. By an inevitable chain of causes and effects, Providence punishes national sins by national calamities.* * * * He held it essential, in every point of view, that the General Government should have power to prevent the increase of Slavery."—*Ibid.*, p. 1390.

a Constitution as they would have preferred, Slavery would have found no lodgment in it; but already the whip of Disunion was brandished, and the fatal necessity of Compromise made manifest. The Convention would have at once and forever prohibited, so far as our country and her people were concerned, the African Slave-Trade; but South Carolina and Georgia were present, by their delegates, to admonish, and, if admonition did not answer, to menace, that this must not be.[3] "No Slave-Trade, no Union!" Such was the short and sharp alternative presented by the delegates from those States. North Carolina was passive; Virginia and her more northern sisters more than willing to prohibit at once the further importation of Slaves; in fact, several, if not all, of these States, including Virginia and Maryland, had already expressly forbidden it. But the ultimatum presented by the still slave-hungry States of the extreme South was imperative, and the necessity of submitting to it was quite too easily conceded. Roger Sherman, of Connecticut, was among the first to admit it. The conscience of the North was quieted[4] by em-

[3] In the debate of the same day, "General Pinckney declared it to be his firm conviction, that, if himself and all his colleagues were to sign the Constitution, and use their personal influence, it would be of no avail toward obtaining the consent of their constituents. South Carolina and Georgia can not do without slaves. * * He contended that the importation of slaves would be for the interest of the whole Union. The more slaves, the more products to employ the carrying trade; the more consumption also; and the more of this, the more revenue for the common treasury. He admitted it to be reasonable, that slaves should be dutied, like other imports, *but should consider a rejection of the clause as an exclusion of South Carolina from the Union.*

"Mr. BALDWIN has similar conceptions in the case of Georgia.

"Mr. WILSON (of Pennsylvania) observed, that, if South Carolina and Georgia were thus disposed to get rid of the importation of slaves in a short time, as had been suggested, they would never refuse to unite, because the importation might be prohibited. As the section now stands, all articles imported are to be taxed. Slaves alone are exempt. This is, in fact, a *bounty* on that article.

"Mr. DICKINSON [of Delaware] expressed his sentiments as of a similar character. And Messrs. KING and LANGDON [of New Hampshire] were also in favor of giving the power to the General Government.

"General PINCKNEY thought himself bound to declare candidly, *that he did not think South Carolina would stop her importations of slaves in any short time;* but only stop them occasionally, as she now does. He moved to commit the clause, that slaves might be made liable to an equal tax with other imports; which he thought right, and which would remove one difficulty that had been started.

"Mr. RUTLEDGE seconded the motion of General Pinckney.

"Mr. GOUVERNEUR MORRIS wished the whole subject to be committed, including the clause relating to taxes on exports, and the navigation act. These things may form a *bargain* among the Northern and Southern States.

"Mr. BUTLER [of South Carolina] declared that he would never agree to the power of taxing exports.

"Mr. SHERMAN said it was better to let the Southern States import slaves than to part with them, if they made that a *sine quâ non.*"

On the question for committing the remaining part of Sections 4 and 5, of Article VII., the vote was 7 in the affirmative; 3 in the negative; Massachusetts absent.—*Ibid.*, p. 1392.

[4] An instance of this *quieting* influence, as exerted by *The Federalist*, a series of letters, urging upon the Northern people the adoption of the new Constitution, as framed and presented to their several legislatures for ratification by the Federal Convention, may be shown in the following:

"It were, doubtless, to be wished that the power of prohibiting the importation of slaves had not been postponed until the year 1808; or rather, that it had been suffered to have immediate operation. But it is not difficult to account either for this restriction on the General Government, or for the manner in which the whole clause is expressed. It ought to be considered as a great point gained in favor of humanity, that a period of twenty years may terminate forever, within these States, a traffic which has so long and so loudly upbraided the barbarism of modern policy; that within that period it will receive a considerable discouragement from the Federal Government, and may be totally abolished by the concurrence of the few States which continue the unnatural traffic, in the prohibitory example which is given by so *large a majority of the Union.* Happy would it be for the unfortunate Africans if an equal prospect lay before them of being redeemed from the

bodying in the Constitution a proviso that Congress might interdict the foreign Slave-Trade after the expiration of twenty years—a term which, it was generally agreed, ought fully to satisfy the craving of Carolina and Georgia.[5] The modified proposition to prohibit the Slave-Trade now encountering no opposition, the recognition of slaves, as a basis of political power, presented a grave and intricate problem. It was one calculated, at least, to place the antagonistic parties respectively in false positions. If slaves are human beings, why should they not be represented like other human beings—that is, like women and children, and other persons, ignorant, humble, and powerless, like themselves? If, on the other hand, you consider them property—mere chattels personal, why should they be represented any more than ships, or houses, or cattle? Here is a nabob, who values his favorite high-bred horse at five thousand dollars, and five of his able-bodied negroes at the same amount. Why should his five negroes count as three men in apportioning the representatives in Congress among the several States, while the blooded horse counts just nothing at all? We can only answer that Slavery and Reason travel different roads, and that he strives in vain who labors to make those roads even *seem* parallel. The Convention, without much debate or demur, split the difference, by deciding that the basis alike of Representation in Congress, and of Direct Taxation, should be the entire free population of each State, with "three-fifths of all other persons."[6]

---

oppression of their European brethren."—*The Federalist*, vol. i., p. 276.

[5] *The Encyclopædia Britannica* (latest edition —Art., *Slavery*) states that the African Slave-Trade was abolished by Great Britain, after years of ineffectual struggle under the lead of Granville Sharp, Thomas Clarkson, Wilberforce, etc., on the 25th of March, 1807; and most inaccurately and unjustly adds:

"The great measure of the British legislature was *imitated*, in the first instance, by the United States."

To say nothing of acts prohibiting the importation of slaves by several of our States, Virginia and Maryland inclusive, prior to the framing of our Federal Constitution, and the provisions incorporated in that instrument looking to a complete suppression of the Slave-Trade after twenty years, our Congress, on the 22d day of March, 1794, passed an act forbidding and punishing any participation by our citizens in the Slave-Trade to foreign countries, which had long been very zealously pursued and protected by Great Britain as a large and lucrative branch of her foreign commerce and navigation. In 1800, our Congress passed a further act, to the same effect, but more sweeping in its provisions and severe in its penalties. On the 2d of March, 1807—twenty-three days *before* the passage of the British act—Congress passed one which prohibits the African Slave-Trade utterly—to our own country as well as to foreign lands. True, this act did not take effect till the 1st of January ensuing, because of the constitutional inhibition aforesaid; but we submit that this does not invalidate our claim for our country and her Revolutionary Statesmen of the honor of having pioneered thus far the advance of Justice and Humanity, to the overthrow of a giant iniquity.

The Encyclopædia aforesaid, in noting the fact that the African Slave-Trade was abolished by Great Britain under the brief Whig ministry of Fox and Grenville, after such abolition had been boldly urged for twenty years under the all but dictatorial Tory rule of Pitt, who was professedly its friend, forcibly and truly adds:

"The proud son of Chatham *loved truth and justice not a little, but he loved power and place greatly more;* and he was resolved that Negro Emancipation should not lose him either a shred of political influence or a beam of [royal] favor."

The particular individual of whom this is said is now some sixty years dead; but the breed was not extinct, in either hemisphere, at the date of our latest advices.

[6] "We subscribe to the doctrine, *might one of our Southern brethren observe,* that Representation relates more immediately to persons, and Taxation more immediately to property; and we join in the application of this distinction to the case of our slaves. But we deny the fact, that

At length, when the Constitution was nearly completed, Slavery, through its attorney, Mr. Butler, of South Carolina, presented its little Bill for extras. Like Oliver Twist, it wanted 'some more.' Its new demand was that slaves escaping from one State into another, might be followed and legally reclaimed. This requirement, be it observed, was entirely outside of any general and obvious necessity. No one could pretend that there was any thing mutual in the obligation it sought to impose—that Massachusetts or New Hampshire was either anxious to secure the privilege of reclaiming her fugitive slaves who might escape into Carolina or Georgia, or had any desire to enter into reciprocal engagements to this end. Nor could any one gravely insist that the provision for the mutual rendition of slaves was essential to the completeness of the Federal pact. The old Confederation had known nothing like it; yet no one asserted that the want of an inter-State Fugitive Slave law was among the necessities or grievances which had impelled the assembling of this Convention. But the insertion of a slave-catching clause in the Constitution would undoubtedly be regarded with favor by the slaveholding interest, and would strongly tend to render the new frame-work of government more acceptable to the extreme South. So, after one or two unsuccessful attempts, Mr. Butler finally gave to his proposition a shape in which it proved acceptable to a majority; and it was adopted, with slight apparent resistance or consideration.[7]

In these latter days, since the radical injustice and iniquity of slaveholding have been more profoundly realized and generally appreciated, many subtle and some able attempts have been made to explain away this most unfortunate provision, for the reason that the Convention wisely and decorously excluded the terms *Slave* and *Slavery* from the Constitution; "because," as Mr. Madison says, "they did not choose to admit

slaves are considered *merely* as property, and in no respect whatever as persons. The true state of the case is, that they partake of both these qualities, being considered by our laws in some respects as persons, and in other respects as property. In being compelled to labor, not merely for himself, but for a master—in being vendible by one master to another master, and being subject, at all times, to being restrained in his liberty and chastised in his body by the capricious will of his owner, the slave may appear to be degraded from the human rank, and classed with that of the irrational animals, which fall under the legal denomination of property. In being protected, on the other hand, in his life and in his limbs, against the violence of all others, even the master of his labor and his liberty, and in being punished himself for all violence committed against others, the slave is no less regarded by the law as a member of society, not as a part of the irrational creation—as a moral person, not a mere object of property. The Federal Constitution, therefore, decides, *with great propriety*, on the case of our slaves, when it views them in the mixed character of persons and property. This is, in fact, their true character. It is the character bestowed on them by the laws under which they live; and it will not be disputed that these are the proper criterion, because it is only under the pretext that the laws have transformed negroes into subjects of property, that a place is denied to them in the computation of numbers; *and it is admitted that, if the laws were to restore the rights which have been taken away, the negroes would no longer be refused an equal share of representation with the other inhabitants.*"—*The Federalist*, vol. ii., p. 46.

[7] In Convention, Wednesday, August 29, 1787.

"Mr. Butler moved to insert, after Article XV., 'if any person bound to service or labor in any of the United States shall escape into another State, he or she shall not be discharged from such service or labor in consequence of any regulations existing in the State to which they escape, but shall be delivered up to the person justly claiming their service or labor'—which, after some verbal modification, was agreed to, *nem. con.*"—*Madison's Papers*, vol. iii., p. 145, 6.

the right of property in man."[8] It has been argued that this provision does not contemplate the rendition of fugitives from Slavery, but rather of runaway apprentices, persons who, having entered into contracts for their own labor, have repudiated their engagements, and other such Jonahs. The records and reminiscences of the Convention, however, utterly refute and dissipate these vain and idle pretenses. It is sheer absurdity to contend that South Carolina in the Convention was absorbingly intent on engrafting upon the Federal Constitution a provision for the recapture of runaway apprentices, or any thing of the sort. What she meant was, to extort from the apprehensions of a majority, anxious for a more perfect Union, a concession of authority to hunt fugitive slaves in any part of our broad national area, and legally to drag them thence back into perpetual bondage. If the Convention did not mean to grant exactly that, it trifled with a very grave subject, and stooped to an unworthy deception. How much better to meet the issue broadly and manfully, saying frankly to the slaveholders: "This provision is contrary to equity and good conscience; hence we can not obey it. To seize our fellow-man and thrust him into an abhorred bondage may in your eyes be innocent, in ours it would be crime. If, then, you are aggrieved in any case, by our refusal or neglect to return your fugitives, make out your bill for their fair market value and call upon us for its payment. If we refuse it, you will then have a real grievance to allege —this, namely: that we have deprived you of what the Constitution recognizes as your property, and have failed to make recompense therefor. But you surely can not blame us, that, having been enlightened as to the immoral nature of acts consented to, or stipulated for, by our fathers, we are unable longer to commit them. Take our property, if you think yourselves entitled to it; but allow us to be faithful to our convictions of duty and the promptings of humanity."[9]

General Charles C. Pinckney, in laying the Federal Constitution before the Convention of South Carolina, which assembled January 15, 1788, to pass upon it, made a speech,

[8] In the debate of Tuesday, July 29, 1788, in the North Carolina ratification convention, which was organized at Hillsborough, July 21, 1788:

"Mr. Iredell begged leave to explain the reason of this clause (last clause, Section 2, Article IV.). In some of the Northern States, they have emancipated all their *slaves*. If any of our *slaves*, said he, go there and remain there a certain time, they would, by the present laws, be entitled to their freedom, so that their masters could not get them again. This would be extremely prejudicial to the inhabitants of the Southern States; and to prevent it, this clause is inserted in the Constitution. Though the word *slave* is not mentioned, this is the meaning of it. The Northern delegates, owing to their peculiar scruples on the subject of Slavery, did not choose the word *slave* to be mentioned."—*Elliot's Debates*, vol. iv., p. 176.

[9] Governor Seward, in his speech of March 11, 1850, on Freedom in the Territories, forcibly set forth the true and manly Northern ground on this subject, as follows:

"The law of nations disavows such compacts; the law of nature, written on the hearts and consciences of freemen, repudiates them. I know that there are laws, of various sorts, which regulate the conduct of men. There are constitutions and statutes, codes mercantile and codes civil; but when we are legislating for States, especially when we are founding States, all these laws must be brought to the standard of the law of God, must be tried by that standard, and must stand or fall by it. To conclude on this point: We are not slaveholders. We can not, in our judgment, be either true Christians or real freemen, if we impose on another a chain that we defy all human power to fasten on ourselves."—*Seward's Works*, vol. i., p. 66.

in which he dwelt with reasonable and justifiable complacency on the advantages secured to Slavery by the Constitution;[10] and these, doubtless, were among the considerations which secured its ratification, by that body, by a vote of 149 to 73. Other Southern States may have been thus affected.

VI.

SLAVERY UNDER THE CONSTITUTION.

It has been plausibly argued that the constitutional provision for the surrender of fugitive slaves, and the inhibition of Slavery in the Territories simultaneously embodied in the Ordinance of 1787, were parts of an implied, rather than clearly expressed, compact, whereby Slavery in the old States was to be protected, upheld, and guaranteed, on condition that it should rest content within its existing boundaries. In seeming accordance with this hypothesis, the first Federal Congress, which met at New York on the first Wednesday in March, 1789, proceeded forthwith to adopt and reënact the prohibition of Slavery in the Territories, already contained in the Ordinance of '87 aforesaid, and to adapt that Ordinance in all respects to the new state of things created by the Federal Constitution. No voice was raised in dissent from this action. On the other hand, the next Congress proceeded to enact, with very little opposition, a stringent and comprehensive fugitive slave law.[1]

North Carolina, on the 22d of December, 1789—one month after ratifying the Federal Constitution—passed an act ceding, on certain conditions, her western territory—now constituting the State of Tennessee—to the Federal Union. She exacted and required Congress to assent to this, among other conditions:

> "*Provided always*, that no regulation made, or to be made, by Congress, shall tend to emancipate slaves."

Georgia, likewise, in ceding to the Union (April 2, 1802) her outlying territories, now forming the States of Alabama and Mississippi, imposed upon the Union, and required Con-

[10] The following is an extract from General Chas. C. Pinckney's speech, delivered in the South Carolina ratification convention, January 17, 1788:

"I am of the same opinion now as I was two years ago—that, while there remained one acre of swamp land uncleared in South Carolina, I would raise my voice against restricting the importation of negroes. * * * * The Middle States and Virginia were for an immediate and total prohibition. We endeavored to obviate the objections which were urged in the best manner we could, and assigned reasons for our insisting on the importation, which there is no occasion to repeat, as they must occur to every gentleman in the House: a committee of the States was appointed in order to accommodate this matter; and, after a great deal of difficulty, it was settled, on the footing of the Constitution. By this settlement, we have secured an unlimited importation of negroes for twenty years. Nor is it declared when that importation shall be stopped; it may be continued. We have a right to recover our slaves in whatever part of America they may take refuge. In short, considering all circumstances, we have made the best terms for the security of this species of property it was in our power to make. *We would have made better if we could; but, on the whole, I do not think them bad.*"—*Elliot's Debates*, vol. iv., p. 285.

[1] For this act, see *Brightley's Digest*, p. 294.

gress to accede to, the following condition:

"Fifthly. That the territory thus ceded shall become a State, and be admitted into the Union as soon as it shall contain sixty thousand inhabitants, or at an earlier period, if Congress shall think it expedient, on the same conditions and restrictions, with the same privileges, and in the same manner, as is provided in the ordinance of Congress of the 13th day of July, 1787, for the government of the western territory of the United States; which ordinance shall, in all its parts, extend to the territory contained in the present act of cession, *the article only excepted which forbids Slavery.*"

Congress was thus precluded, by the unprecedented and peremptory conditions affixed to their respective cessions of their western territory by North Carolina and Georgia, from continuing and perfecting the Jeffersonian policy of fundamental and imperative Slavery inhibition in the Federal Territories. Had Mr. Jefferson's Ordinance of 1784 been passed as he reported it, this beneficent end would have been secured. Accident, and the peculiar requirements of the Articles of Confederation, prevented this. Mr. Dane's Ordinance of 1787 contemplated only the territories already ceded to the Confederation, leaving those still *to be* ceded to be governed by some future act. The assumption, however, that there was between the North and the South an original and subsisting compact, arrangement, understanding, or whatever it may be called, whereby so much of the common territories of the Republic as lay south of the Ohio, or of any particular latitude, were to be surrendered to Slavery, on the condition that the residue should be quitclaimed to free labor, is utterly unfounded and mistaken. The author of the original restriction was himself a slaveholder; yet he contemplated and provided for (as we have seen) the consignment of every acre of those territories, north as well as south of the Ohio, and down to the southernmost limit of our domain, to Free Labor evermore. A majority of the States which sustained that proposition were then slaveholding, and had taken no decided steps toward Emancipation. Yet they none the less regarded Slavery as an evil and a blunder,[2] to be endured,

---

[2] The Rev. Jonathan Edwards (son of the famous Jonathan Edwards, who was the greatest theologian, and one of the greatest men whom New England has ever produced), preached a sermon against the African Slave-Trade, September 15, 1791, at New Haven, Connecticut, then a Slave State. Text: The Golden Rule; Matthew vii., 12.

It is so commonly urged that the Abolitionists condemn a relation whereof they are *grossly ignorant*, that the following extract from that sermon is of interest, as the testimony of one living amid Slavery, and as proving how essentially identical are the objections urged to human chattelhood at all times, and under whatever circumstances. Mr. Edwards said:

"African Slavery is exceedingly impolitic, as it discourages industry. Nothing is more essential to the political prospect of any State than industry in the citizens. But, in proportion as Slaves are multiplied, every kind of labor becomes ignominious; and, in fact, in those of the United States in which slaves are the most numerous, gentlemen and ladies of any fashion disdain to employ themselves in business, which in other States is consistent with the dignity of the first families and the first offices. In a country filled with negro slaves, labor belongs to them only, and a white man is despised in proportion as he applies to it. Now, how destructive of industry in all of the lowest and middle class of citizens such a situation, and the prevalence of such ideas will be, you can easily conceive. The consequence is that some will nearly starve, others will betake themselves to the most dishonest practices to obtain a means of living. As Slavery produces an indolence in the white people, so it produces all those vices which are naturally connected with it, such as intemperance, lewdness, and prodigality. These vices enfeeble both the body and the mind, and unfit men for any vigorous exertions and employments, either external or mental. And those who are unfit for such exertions are already very degenerate; degenerate, not only in

perhaps, for a season where already established, rather than to invoke greater mischiefs and perils by its too sudden and violent extirpation than were likely to flow from its more patient and gradual extinction. But to plant Slavery on virgin soil—to consecrate vast and yet vacant territories to its extension and perpetuation—to conquer and annex still further domains expressly to increase its security and enlarge its power—are guilty dreams which never troubled the repose of the great body of our Revolutionary sages and patriots. Enlightened by their own experience as to the evils and dangers of arbitrary, despotic, irresponsible power, they were too upright and too logical to seek to fasten for all time on a helpless and inoffensive race chains far heavier and more galling than those they had just shaken off. Most of them held slaves, but held them under protest against the anomaly presented to the world by republican bondage, and in the confident hope that the day would soon dawn that would rid themselves of the burden and their country of the curse and shame of human chattelhood.[3] Had they been asked to unite in any of

---

a moral, but a natural sense. They are contemptible too, and will soon be despised, even by their negroes themselves.

"Slavery tends to lewdness, not only as it produces indolence, but as it affords abundant opportunity for that wickedness, without either the danger or difficulty of an attack on the virtue of a woman of chastity, or the danger of a connection with one of ill fame. A planter, with his hundred wenches about him, is, in some respects at least, like the Sultan in his seraglio; and we learn too frequently the influence and effect of such a situation, not only from common fame, but from the multitude of mulattoes in countries where slaves are very numerous.

"Slavery has a most direct tendency to haughtiness also, and a domineering spirit and conduct in the proprietors of slaves, and in their children, and in all who have control of them. A man who has been brought up in domineering over negroes can scarcely avoid contracting such a habit of haughtiness and domination as will express itself in his general treatment of mankind, whether in his private capacity, or any office, civil or military, with which he may be vested. Despotism in economics naturally leads to despotism in politics, and domestic Slavery in a free government is a perfect solecism in human affairs.

"How baneful all these tendencies and effects of Slavery must be to the public good, and especially to the public good of such a free country as ours, I need not inform you."—*Sermons*, 1775-99, p. 10.

[3] The opinion of the Father of his Country respecting the "peculiar institution" of the South may be perceived from the following extracts. In a letter to Lafayette, bearing date April 5, 1783, he says:

"The scheme, my dear Marquis, which you propose as a precedent to encourage the emancipation of the black people in this country from that state of bondage in which they are held, is a striking evidence of the benevolence of your heart. I shall be happy to join you in so laudable a work; but will defer going into a detail of the business until I have the pleasure of seeing you."—*Sparks's Washington*, vol. viii., p 414.

Again, in a letter to the same, of May 10, 1786:

"The benevolence of your heart, my dear Marquis, is so conspicuous upon all occasions, that I never wonder at any fresh proofs of it; but your late purchase of an estate in the colony of Cayenne, with a view to emancipate the slaves on it, is a generous and noble proof of your humanity. *Would to God a like spirit might diffuse itself in the minds of the people of this country!* But I despair of seeing it. Some petitions were presented to the Assembly at its last session, for the Abolition of Slavery, but they could scarcely obtain a reading."—*Ibid.*, vol. ix., p. 163.

In a remarkable and very interesting letter written by Lafayette in the prison of Magdeburg, he said:

"I know not what disposition has been made of my plantation at Cayenne; but I hope Madam De Lafayette will take care that the negroes who cultivate it shall preserve their liberty."

The following language is also Lafayette's, in a letter to Hamilton, from Paris, April 13, 1785:

"In one of your New York Gazettes, I find an association against the Slavery of the negroes, which seems to me worded in such a way as to give no offense to the moderate men in the Southern States. *As I have ever been partial to my brethren of that color*, I wish, if you are one in the society, you would move, in your own name, for my being admitted on the list."—*Works of Alex. Hamilton, N. Y.*, 1851, vol. i., p. 423.

John Adams, in a letter to Robert J. Evans, June 8, 1819, expresses himself as follows:

"I respect the sentiments and motives which

the projects of the Sam Houstons, William Walkers, Quitmans, and Slidells of our day, they would have retorted as indignantly as the astonished Syrian to the Hebrew prophet —"Is thy servant a dog, that he should do this thing?" Oh that they had but known and realized that the wrong which to-day is barely tolerated for the moment, is to-morrow cherished, and the next day sustained, eulogized, and propagated!

When Ohio was made a State, in 1803, the residue of the North-West Territory became Indiana Territory, with William Henry Harrison—since President of the United States —as Governor. Its earlier settlements were mainly on the banks of the Ohio and of its northern tributaries, and were principally by emigrants from Virginia, Kentucky, and other Slave States. These emigrants, realizing an urgent need of labor, and being accustomed to supply that need by the employment of slaves, almost unanimously memorialized Congress, through a Convention assembled in 1802, and presided over by their Governor, for a *temporary* suspension of the sixth article of the Ordinance of '87, whereby Slavery was expressly prohibited. Their memorial was referred by the House of Representatives to a Select Committee of three, two of them from the Slave States, with the since famous John Randolph of Roanoke, then a young member, as its chairman. On the 2d of March, 1803, Mr. Randolph made a unanimous report from this Committee, recommending a denial of the prayer of the petitioners, for these reasons:

"The rapid population of the State of Ohio sufficiently evinces, in the opinion of your Committee, that the labor of slaves is not necessary to promote the growth and settlement of colonies in that region; that this labor—demonstrably the dearest of any —can only be employed in the cultivation of products more valuable than any known to that quarter of the United States; that the Committee deem it highly dangerous and inexpedient to impair a provision wisely calculated to promote the happiness and prosperity of the North-Western Country, and to give strength and security to that extensive frontier. In the salutary operation of this sagacious and benevolent restraint, it is believed that the inhabitants of Indiana will, at no very distant day, find ample remuneration for a temporary privation of labor, and of emigration."

The session terminated the next day; and the subject was, the next winter, referred to a new committee, whereof Cæsar Rodney, of Delaware, was chairman. This committee reported in favor "of a qualified suspension, for a limited time," of the inhibition aforesaid. But Congress took no action on the report.

The people of Indiana Territory persisted in their seemingly unanimous supplication to be allowed, for a limited period, the use of Slave Labor; and Mr. Garnett, of Virginia, on the 14th of February, 1806, made

have prompted you to engage in your present occupation so much, that I feel an esteem and affection for your person, as I do a veneration for your assumed signature of Benjamin Rush. The turpitude, the inhumanity, the cruelty, and the infamy of the African commerce, have been so impressively represented to the public by the highest powers of eloquence, that nothing that I could say would increase the just odium in which it is, and ought to be, held. *Every measure of prudence, therefore, ought to be assumed for the eventual total extirpation of Slavery from the United States.* * * * I have, through my whole life, held the practice of Slavery in such abhorrence, that I have never owned a negro or any other slave, though I have lived for many years in times when the practice was not disgraceful—when the best men in my vicinity thought it not inconsistent with their character; and when it has cost me thousands of dollars for the labor and subsistence of free men, which I might have saved by the purchase of negroes, at times when they were very cheap."—*Works of John Adams*, Boston, 1856, vol. x., p. 386.

another report from a Select Committee in favor of granting their request. But Congress never took this report into consideration. At the next session, a fresh letter from Governor Harrison, inclosing resolves of the Legislative Council and House of Representatives in favor of suspending temporarily the inhibition of Slavery, was received, and referred (January 21, 1807) to a Select Committee, whereof Mr. B. Parke, Delegate from said Territory, was made chairman. This Committee, composed mainly of members from Slave States, made (February 12th) a *third* report in favor of the petitioners; but Congress never acted upon the subject.

At the next session, the matter was brought before the Senate, on the apparently unanimous prayer of Governor Harrison and his Legislature for permission temporarily to employ slaves; but there was now, for the first time, a remonstrance of citizens of the Territory against the measure. The Senate referred the subject to a Select Committee of three, whereof Mr. Jesse Franklin, of N. C., was chairman; and Mr. Franklin, on the 13th of November, 1807, reported briefly against the petition, closing as follows:

"Your Committee, after duly considering the matter, respectfully submit the following resolution:

"*Resolved*, That it is *not* expedient at this time to suspend the sixth article of compact for the government of the Territory of the United States North-West of the river Ohio."

And here the long and fruitless struggle to fasten Slavery upon the vast Territory now forming the States of Indiana, Illinois, Michigan, and Wisconsin, appears to have ended. By this time, emigration from the Free States into that Territory had begun. But it is probable that, at any time prior to 1818–20, a majority of the white settlers actually resident in that Territory would have voted in favor of the introduction of slaves.

For a counter-revolution had been silently proceeding for some years previous, and had almost eradicated the lessons and the principles of the Revolution from the hearts of the South, saving, of course, those portions wherein they seem to have never been learned. The bases of this revolution are the acquisition of Louisiana and the invention of the Cotton Gin;[4] events for which Thomas Jefferson and Eli Whitney—neither of them pro-slavery—are primarily responsible. The acquisition of Louisiana, though second in occurrence and in importance, first attracted and fixed the attention of mankind, and shall, therefore, be first considered.

The river Mississippi was first discovered in 1541, by the Spanish adventurer De Soto, in the course of his three or four years' fantastic wanderings and fightings throughout the region which now constitutes the Gulf States of our Union, in quest of the fabled Eldorado, or Land of Gold. He left Spain in 1538, at the head of six hundred ambitious and enthusiastic followers, all eager and sanguine as himself in their quest of the fountain of perpetual youth and life. He died of a malignant fever on the bank of the Mississippi, in the spring or early summer of 1542; and his body,

[4] This word is merely a corruption of *engine*.

to conceal his death from the surrounding hostile savages, was sunk by his surviving followers in the deep current of that mighty stream. Of the entire expedition, less than half, an enfeebled and wretched remnant, finally reached the coast of Mexico, in the summer of 1543, glad to have escaped with their bare lives from the inhospitable swamps and savages they had so recklessly encountered. It does not appear that any of them, nor even De Soto himself, had formed any adequate conception of the importance of their discovery, of the magnitude of the river, or of the extent and fertility of the regions drained by its tributaries; since more than a century was allowed to transpire before the Mississippi was revisited by civilized men. And its next discoverers were not Spaniards, but Frenchmen; although Spain had long possessed and colonized Florida and Mexico on either side of its mouth. But the French—now firmly established in Canada, and penetrating by their traders and *voyageurs* the wild region stretching westward and south-westward from that Colony—obtained from the savages some account of this river about the year 1660; and in 1673, Marquette and Joliet, proceeding westward from Montreal, through the Great Lakes, reached the Mississippi above its junction with the Missouri, and descended it to within three days' journey of its mouth. In 1682, La Salle descended it to the Gulf of Mexico, and took formal possession of the region in the name of his king and country. A fort was erected on its banks by Iberville, about the year 1699; and in 1703, a settlement was made at St. Peters, on the Yazoo. New Orleans was first chosen as the site of a city in 1717, laid out in 1718, when the levees which protect it from the annual inundations of the river were immediately commenced, and steadily prosecuted to completion, ten years afterward. The colony of Louisiana (so named after Louis XIV.) remained a French possession until 1762, when it was ceded to Spain. New Orleans gradually increased in trade and population, but the colony outside of that city was of slight importance under its Spanish rulers, who did little to develop its resources, and were not popular with its mainly French inhabitants. In 1802, Napoleon Bonaparte, then First Consul, induced the feeble and decaying Bourbons of Spain, then in close alliance with revolutionary France, to retrocede to her Louisiana, almost without consideration; and the French flag once more waved over delighted New Orleans.

In the United States, however, the transfer was regarded with regret and apprehension. Our settlers beyond the Alleghanies, who must export their surplus products through the lower Mississippi, or see them perish useless and valueless on their hands, had been for fifteen years in a state of chronic and by no means voiceless dissatisfaction with the alleged jealous hostility and obstructive regulations of the Spanish rulers of that essential outlet. Threats were freely uttered that they would soon descend the river and clear its lower banks of the Dons and drones who seemed to burrow there only as an impediment and a nuisance. The Spaniards were charged with fomenting intrigues in Kentucky and Tennessee, which had for their object the alienation of the entire valley of the Ohio from the Union; and certain discontented or desperate spirits were pointed at and named by their neighbors as having sold themselves for money to the Spanish governor at New Orleans, agreeing to lend all their energies to the promotion of his absurd scheme. So long as Spain held the gateway of the Mississippi, it seemed that no other sway there could be more unpopular or odious with our Western pioneers.

But a 'sober second thought' was evinced from the moment that her flag had been supplanted by that of republican France. It was instinctively and universally felt that even the growls and threats, in which our people so freely indulged so long as the effete and despised Spaniard was their object, would no longer be politic nor safe. Directly after the general pacification of Europe, in 1802, by the treaty of Amiens, a powerful French expedition had sailed for the West Indies; and, though its ostensible and real destination was Hayti, the apprehension was here general and reasonable that it would ultimately, if not immediately, be debarked on the banks of the Mississippi. The privileges of navigation and of deposit, which had seemed so niggardly when conceded by the weakness of Spain, were now rather contracted than enlarged, and were likely to be withdrawn altogether. We had freely contemned and denounced the stupidity and blindness of King Log, but became suddenly grave and silent on the unexpected advent of King Stork.

Mr. Jefferson, who had recently been called to the Presidency, and who mainly did the deeper thinking of the young and vigorous party which now ruled the country, regarded the change with alarm from still another aspect. Popular sympathy with and admiration for republican France, with a corresponding aversion to and hatred of aristocratic England, were among the most potent influences which had combined to overthrow the Federalists here and bring the Republicans into power. But all this was now morally certain to be reversed. France, planting herself, as it were, at our back door, there erecting fortifications, and jealously scrutinizing, if not positively arresting, every one who should undertake to pass in or out, became inevitably and predominantly the object of American distrust and hostility.[5] And now the great advantage

[5] Upon learning of this important transfer, Mr. Jefferson (April 18, 1802) wrote to Mr. Livingston, our Minister at Paris, as follows:

"The cession of Louisiana and the Floridas by Spain to France, works most sorely on the United States. On this subject, the Secretary of State has written to you fully, yet I cannot forbear recurring to it personally, so deep is the impression it makes on my mind. It completely reverses all the political relations of the United States, and will form a new epoch in our political course. Of all nations of any consideration, France is the one which hitherto has offered the fewest points on which we could have any conflict of rights, and the most points of a communion of interests. From these causes, we have ever looked to her as our *natural friend*, as one with which we could never have an occasion of difference. Her growth, therefore, we viewed as our own—her misfortunes ours. There is on the globe one single spot, the possessor of which is our natural and habitual enemy. It is New Orleans, through which the produce of three-eighths of our territory must pass to market; and, from its fertility, it will ere long yield more than half of our whole produce, and contain more than half of our inhabitants. France, placing herself in that door, assumes to us the attitude of defiance. Spain might have retained it quietly for years. Her pacific dispositions, her feeble state, would induce her to increase our facilities there, so that her possession of the place would be hardly felt by us, and it would not, perhaps, be very long before some circumstances might arise, which might make the cession

hitherto accruing to the Republican or Democratic party from our relations with Europe, and our sympathies with one or the other of the parties which divided her, would be transferred at once to the Federalists, and probably doubled or quadrupled in intensity and efficiency. The vigilant and far-seeing Jefferson, always a patriot, and always intensely a partisan, perceived the peril at once to his country and his party, and resolved by a bold stroke to avert it. He determined that Louisiana should be ours, and perceived, in the gathering storm of war, destined so soon to sweep away the fragile frost-work of the recent and unreal peace, a means of bending the astute and selfish Napoleon to his will. Louisiana, so recently and easily rëacquired by France, must become a peril and a burden to her upon the outbreak of fresh hostilities with a power so superior in maritime strength as Great Britain. Tamely to surrender it, would be damaging, if not disgraceful; to hold it, would cost a fleet and an army, and the transfer of this fleet and army to a point so distant as the Mexican Gulf was at best a hazardous enterprise. France badly needed money; we needed, or at least coveted, Louisiana: and, where the rulers on either side are men so capable and clear-sighted as Bonaparte and Jefferson, an arrangement mutually advantageous is not likely to fail. After some skillful diplomatic fencing—Mr. Jefferson talking as if the island of Orleans and the Floridas were all that we greatly cared for, when he meant from the first to have the whole—and after some natural higgling about the price, the bargain was struck on the 30th of April, 1803. The hungry treasury of France was richer by twelve millions of dollars; four millions more were paid by our government to our own citizens, in satisfaction of their righteous claims against France for spoliations and other damages; and the United States became the unquestioned owner and possessor of the entire Valley of the Mississippi; acquiring by this bloodless purchase an area of virgin soil, subject to the Indians' rights of inheritance and occupancy, worth many times its entire cost.

There is no evidence that this purchase was made in the interest of Slavery, or with any reference to the perpetuation of its existence or the increase of its power. But this does not at all impinge on the fact that

of it to us the price of something of more worth to her. Not so can it ever be in the hands of France. The impetuosity of her temper, the energy and restlessness of her character, placed in a point of eternal friction with us, and our character, which, though quiet and loving peace and the pursuit of wealth, is high-minded, despising wealth in competition with insult or injury, enterprising and energetic as any nation on earth; these circumstances render it impossible that France and the United States can continue long friends, when they meet in so irritable a position. They, as well as we, must be blind if they do not see this; and we must be very improvident if we do not begin to make arrangements on that hypothesis. The day that France takes possession of New Orleans fixes the sentence which is to restrain her forever within her low-water mark. It seals the union of two nations, who, in conjunction, can maintain exclusive possession of the ocean. From that moment, we must marry ourselves to the British fleet and nation. We must turn all our attention to a maritime force, for which our resources place us on very high ground: and, having formed and connected together a power which may render re-enforcement of her settlements here impossible to France, make the first cannon which shall be fired in Europe the signal for tearing up any settlement she may have made, and for holding the two continents of America in sequestration for the common purpose of the united British and American nations. This is not a state of things we seek or desire. It is one which this measure, if adopted by France, forces on us, as necessarily as any other cause, by the laws of nature, brings on its necessary effect."—*Jefferson's Works*, vol. iv., p. 431.

Slavery in our Union *did* secure by this acquisition a vast extension of its power and influence. Louisiana came to us a slaveholding territory; had been such, whether under French or Spanish rule, for generations. Though its population was sparse, it was nevertheless widely dispersed along the Mississippi and its lower tributaries, there being quite considerable settlements at and in the vicinity of St. Louis. Slavery had thus already achieved a lodgment and a firm foothold in this vast, inviting domain. Possession is notoriously nine points of the law; but in this case the tenth was not wanting. The white inhabitants were habituated to slaveholding, liked it, and indolently believed it to be conducive to their importance, their wealth, and their comfort. Of the swarm of emigrants and adventurers certain to pour in upon them as a consequence of our acquisition, a large majority would naturally come from the States nearest them, that is, from the preponderantly and inveterately Slave States; while the Northern adventurers, hying with alacrity to such a tempting field for speculation and experiment, were pretty sure to interpose no *fanatical* objection to a social condition unanimously pronounced so pleasant and profitable by all who were permitted to speak at all on the subject. Moreover, the treaty of cession had expressly stipulated that the inhabitants of Louisiana "should be incorporated into the Union of the United States, and admitted, as soon as possible, according to the principles of the Federal Constitution, to the enjoyment of all the rights, advantages, and immunities of citizens of the United States. And, in the mean time, they should be maintained and protected in the free enjoyment of their liberty, *property*, and the religion which they professed." A just—no, even a literal construction of this provision, giving to the word "inhabitants" its natural and full signification—might have secured liberty, with the enjoyment of all the "rights, advantages, and immunities of citizens of the United States," to the colored as well as the white Louisianians of that day. But it is hardly supposable that this was really intended by the treacherous murderer of Toussaint, just signally baffled in his formidable attempt to reënslave the freedmen of Hayti. It is very certain that this construction was never put in practice, but that those who had been slaves under Spanish and French rule in Louisiana remained so under the flag of our country, dying in bondage unless specially emancipated, and leaving their children the sole inheritance of their sad condition; and that slaveholders, whether in fact or in purpose only, eagerly hastened to our new purchase and rapidly covered its most inviting localities with cotton-fields and slave-huts. The day that saw Louisiana transferred to our Union is one of woeful memory to the enslaved children of unhappy Africa.

The plant known as *Cotton*, whence the fiber of that name is mainly obtained, appears to be indigenous in most tropical and semi-tropical countries, having been found growing wild by Columbus in St. Domingo, and by later explorers throughout the region of the lower Mississippi and its tributaries.

Cortes found it in use by the half-civilized Mexicans; and it has been rudely fabricated in Africa from time immemorial. India, however, is the earliest known seat of the cotton manufacture, and here it long ago attained the highest perfection possible prior to the application of steam, with complicated machinery, to its various processes; and hence it appears to have gradually extended westward through Persia and Arabia, until it attracted the attention of the Greeks, and was noticed by Herodotus about 450 B. C., as the product of an Indian tree, and the staple of an extensive manufacture. Later Greek accounts confirm the impression that the tree or shrub variety was cultivated in India previously to the plant or annual now by far the more commonly grown. The Romans began to use cotton fabrics before the time of Julius Cæsar, and the cotton-plant was grown in Sicily and along the northern coast of the Mediterranean so early as the tenth century. The culture, however, does not appear to have ever attained a great importance in any portion of the world regarded by the Greeks and Romans as civilized, prior to its recent establishment in Egypt, in obedience to the despotic will of Ibrahim Pacha.

In the British colonies now composing this country, the experiment of cotton-planting was tried so early as 1621; and in 1666 the growth of the cotton-plant is on record. The cultivation slowly and fitfully expanded throughout the following century, extending northward to the eastern shore of Maryland and the southernmost point of New Jersey—where, however, the plant was grown more for ornament than use. It is stated that "seven bags of cotton-wool" were among the exports of Charleston, S. C., in 1748, and that trifling shipments from that port were likewise made in 1754 and 1757. In 1784, it is recorded that eight bags, shipped to England, were seized at the custom-house as fraudulently entered: "cotton not being a production of the United States." The export of 1790, as returned, was eighty-one bags; and the entire cotton crop of the United States at that time was probably less than the product of some single plantation in our day.

For, though the plant grew luxuriantly and produced abundantly throughout tide-water Virginia and all that portion of our country lying southward and south-westward of Richmond, yet the enormous labor required to separate the seed from the tiny handful of fibres wherein it was imbedded, precluded its extensive and profitable cultivation. It was calcuted that the perfect separation of one pound of fibre from the seed was an average day's work; and this fact presented a formidable barrier to the production of the staple in any but a region like India, where labor can be hired for a price below the cost of subsisting slaves, however wretchedly, in this country. It seemed that the limit of American cotton cultivation had been fully reached, when an event occurred which speedily revolutionized the industry of our slave-holding States and the commerce and manufactures of the world.

Eli Whitney, a native of Westborough, Worcester County, Massachusetts, born December 8, 1765, was descended on both sides from ancestors of English stock, who dated their migration from the old country nearly back to the memorable voyage of the Mayflower. They were generally farmers, and, like most farmers of those days, in very moderate circumstances. Eli's father, poor, industrious, and ingenious, had a workshop wherein he devoted the inclement season to the making of wheels and of chairs. Here the son early developed a remarkable ingenuity and mechanical skill; establishing, when only fifteen years of age, the manufacture by hand of wrought nails, for which there was, in those later years of our Revolutionary struggle, a demand at high prices. Though he had had no instruction in nail-making, and his few implements were of the rudest description, he pursued the business through two winters with profit to his father, devoting the summers, as before and afterward, to the labors of the farm. After the close of the war, his nails being no longer in demand, he engaged in the manufacture of the pins then in fashion for fastening ladies' bonnets, and nearly monopolized the market through the excellence of his product. Walking-canes also were among his winter manufactures, and were esteemed peculiarly well made and handsome. Meantime, he continued the devotion of his summers to the labors of the farm, attending the common school of his district through its winter session, and being therein noted for devotion to, and eminent skill in, arithmetic. At fourteen, he was looked upon by his neighbors as a very remarkable, energetic, and intelligent youth. At nineteen, he resolved to obtain a liberal education; but it was not until he had reached the mature age of twenty-three that he was enabled to enter college. By turns laboring with his hands and teaching school, he obtained the means of prosecuting his studies in Yale, which he entered in May, 1789. He borrowed some money to aid him in his progress, giving his note therefor, and paying it so soon as he could. On the decease of his father some years afterward, he took an active part in settling the estate, but relinquished his portion to his co-heirs. It is scarcely probable that the amount he thus sacrificed was large, but the generous spirit he evinced is not thereby obscured.

While in college, his natural superiority in mechanism and proclivity to invention were frequently manifested. On one occasion, a tutor regretted to his pupils that he could not exhibit a desired philosophical experiment, because the apparatus was out of order, and could only be repaired in Europe. Young Whitney thereupon proposed to undertake the repair, and made it to perfect satisfaction. At another time, he asked permission to use at intervals the tools of a carpenter who worked near his boarding-place; but the careful mechanic declined to trust them in the hands of a student, unless the gentleman with whom Mr. W. boarded would become responsible for their safe return. The guarantee was given, and Mr. Whitney took the tools in hand; when the carpenter, surprised at his dexterity, exclaimed: "There was one good mechanic spoiled when *you* went to college."

Mr. Whitney graduated in the fall of 1792, and directly engaged with a Mr. B., from Georgia, to proceed to that State and reside in his employer's family as a private teacher. On his way thither, he had as a traveling companion Mrs. Greene, widow of the eminent Revolutionary general, Nathaniel Greene, who was returning with her children to Savannah, after spending the summer at the North. His health being infirm on his arrival at Savannah, Mrs. Greene kindly invited him to the hospitalities of her residence until he should become fully restored. Short of money and in a land of strangers, he was now coolly informed by his employer that his services were not required, he (B.) having employed another teacher in his stead! Mrs. Greene hereupon urged him to make her house his home so long as that should be desirable, and pursue under her roof the study of the law, which he then contemplated. He gratefully accepted the offer, and commenced the study accordingly.

Mrs. Greene happened to be engaged in embroidering on a peculiar frame known as a tambour. It was badly constructed, so that it injured the fabric while it impeded its production. Mr. Whitney eagerly volunteered to make her a better, and did so on a plan wholly new, to her great delight and that of her children.

A large party of Georgians, from Augusta and the plantations above, soon after paid Mrs. G. a visit, several of them being officers who had served under her husband in the Revolutionary war. Among the topics discussed by them around her fireside was the depressed state of Agriculture, and the impossibility of profitably extending the culture of the green-seed Cotton, because of the trouble and expense incurred in separating the seed from the fiber. These representations impelled Mrs. Greene to say: "Gentlemen, apply to my young friend, Mr. Whitney—*he* can make any thing." She thereupon took them into an adjacent room, where she showed them her tambour-frame and several ingenious toys which Mr. W. had made for the gratification of her children. She then introduced them to Whitney himself, extolling his genius and commending him to their confidence and friendship. In the conversation which ensued, he observed that he had never seen cotton nor cotton-seed in his life.

Mr. Whitney promised nothing and gave little encouragement, but went to work. No cotton in the seed being at hand, he went to Savannah and searched there among warehouses and boats until he found a small parcel. This he carried home and secluded with himself in a basement room, where he set himself at work to devise and construct the implement required. Tools being few and rude, he was constrained to make better—drawing his own wire, because none could, at that time, be bought in the city of Savannah. Mrs. Greene and her next friend, Mr. Miller, whom she soon after married, were the only persons beside himself who were allowed the entrée of his workshop—in fact, the only ones who clearly knew what he was about. His mysterious hammering and tinkering in that solitary cell were subjects of infinite curiosity, marvel, and ridicule among the younger members of the family. But he did not interfere with their merriment, nor allow them to interfere with his enterprise; and, before the close of the winter, his machine was so nearly perfected that its success was no longer doubtful.

Mrs. Greene, too eager to realize and enjoy her friend's triumph, in view of the existing stagnation of Georgian industry, invited an assemblage at her house of leading gentlemen from various parts of the State, and, on the first day after their meeting, conducted them to a temporary building, erected for the machine, in which they saw, with astonishment and delight, that one man with Whitney's invention could separate more cotton from the seed in a single day than he could without it by the labor of months.

Mr. Phineas Miller, a native of Connecticut and a graduate of Yale, who had come to Georgia as the teacher of General Greene's children, and who, about this time, became the husband of his widow, now proposed a partnership with Mr. Whitney, by which he engaged to furnish funds to perfect the invention, secure the requisite patents, and manufacture the needed machines; the partners to share equally all profits and emoluments thence resulting. Their contract bears date May 27, 1793; and the firm of Miller & Whitney immediately commenced what they had good reason to expect would prove a most extensive and highly lucrative business. Mr. Whitney thereupon repaired to Connecticut, there to perfect his invention, secure his patent, and manufacture machines for the Southern market.

But his just and sanguine hopes were destined to signal and bitter disappointment. His invention was too valuable to be peacefully enjoyed; or, rather, it was the seeming and urgent interest of too many to rob him of the just reward of his achievement. He ought not to have expected that those who lived idly and luxuriously by stealing the wife from her husband, and the child from its mother, would hesitate to steal, also, the fruit of *his* brain-work, in order to render thereby the original theft ten-fold more advantageous than it otherwise could be. Reports of the nature and value of his invention were widely and rapidly circulated, creating intense excitement. Multitudes hastened from all quarters to see his original machine; but, no patent having yet been secured, it was deemed unsafe to gratify their curiosity; so they broke open the building by night, and carried off the wonderful prize. Before he could complete his model and secure his patent, a number of imitations had been made and set to work, deviating in some respects from the original, in the hope of thus evading all penalty. Before Whitney had been three days on his northward trip, a letter from his partner followed on his track, which said:

> "It will be necessary to have a considerable number of gins made, to be in readiness to send out as soon as the patent is obtained, in order to satisfy the absolute demands, and make people's heads easy on the subject; *for I am informed of two other claimants for the honor of the invention of the cotton gins, in addition to those we knew before.*"

Messrs. Miller and Whitney's plan of operations was essentially vicious. They proposed to construct and retain the ownership of all the machines that might be needed, setting one up in each cotton-growing neighborhood, and ginning all the staple for every third pound of the product. Even at this rate, the invention would have been one of enormous benefit to the planters—cotton being then worth from twenty-five to thirty-three cents per pound. But no single manufactory could turn out the gins so fast as wanted, and planters who might readily have consented to the terms of the patentees, had the machines been furnished so fast as required, could hardly be expected to acquiesce so readily in the necessity of doing without machines altogether because the patentees could not, though others could, supply them. And then the manufacture of machines, to be constructed and worked by the patentees alone, involved a very large outlay of money, which must mainly be obtained by borrowing. Miller's means being soon exhausted, their first loan of two thousand dollars was made on the comparatively favorable condition of five per cent. premium, in addition to lawful interest. But they were soon borrowing at twenty per cent. *per month.* Then there was sickness; Mr. Whitney having a severe and tedious attack in 1794; after which the scarlet fever raged in New Haven, disabling many of his workmen; and soon the lawsuits, into which they were driven in defense of their patent, began to devour all the money they could make or borrow. In 1795, Whitney had another attack of sickness; and, on his return to New Haven, from three weeks of suffering in New York, learned that his manufactory, with all his machines and papers, had just been consumed by fire, whereby he found himself suddenly reduced to utter bankruptcy. Next came a report from England that the British manufacturers condemned and rejected the cotton cleaned by his machines, on the ground that *the staple was greatly injured by the ginning process!* And now no one would touch the ginned cotton; and blockheads were found to insist that the roller-gin—a preposterous rival to Whitney's, whereby the seed was crushed in the fibre, instead of being separated from it—was actually a better machine than Whitney's! In the depths of their distress and insolvency, Miller wrote (April 27, 1796) from Georgia to Whitney, urging him to hasten to London, there to counteract the stupid prejudice which had been excited against ginned cotton; adding:

> "Our fortune, our fate, depends on it. The process of patent ginning is now quite at a stand. I hear nothing of it except the condolence of a few real friends, who express their regret that so promising an invention has entirely failed."

Whitney endeavored to obey this injunction, but could nowhere obtain the necessary funds; though he had several times fixed the day of his departure, and on one occasion had actually engaged his passage, and taken leave of some of his friends. October 7, 1797, Mr. Whitney wrote to an intimate friend a letter, wherefrom the following is an extract:

> "The extreme embarrassments which have been for a long time accumulating upon me are now become so great that it will be impossible for me to struggle against them many days longer. It has required my utmost exertions *to exist*, without making the least progress in our business. I have labored hard against the strong current of disappointment, which has been threatening to carry us down the cataract; but I have labored with a shattered oar, and struggled in vain, unless some speedy relief is obtained. I am now quite far enough advanced in life to think seriously of marrying. I have ever looked forward with pleasure to an alliance with an amiable and virtuous companion, as a source from whence I have expected one day to derive the greatest happiness. But the accomplishment of my tour to Europe, and the acquisition of

something which I can call my own, appear to be absolutely necessary, before it will be admissible for me even *to think* of family engagements. Probably a year and a half, at least, will be required to perform that tour, after it is entered upon. Life is but short, at best, and six or seven years out of the midst of it is, to him who makes it, an immense sacrifice. My most unremitted attention has been devoted to our business. I have sacrificed to it other objects, from which, before this time, I might certainly have gained twenty or thirty thousand dollars. My whole prospects have been embarked in it, with the expectation that I should, before this time, have realized something from it."

At length the ridiculous prejudice against cotton cleaned by Whitney's gin gradually and slowly gave way, and the value of the invention began to be perceived and acknowledged. But Miller & Whitney's first suit against infringers now came to trial, before a Georgia jury; and, in spite of the judge's charge directly in the plaintiffs' favor, a verdict was given for the defendant—a verdict from which there was no appeal. When the second suit was ready for trial at Savannah, no judge appeared, and, of course, no court was held. Meantime, the South fairly swarmed with pirates on the invention, of all kinds and degrees. In April, 1799, Miller writes to Whitney as follows:

"The prospect of making anything by ginning in this State is at an end. Surreptitious gins are erected in every part of the country; and the jurymen at Augusta have come to an understanding among themselves that they will never give a cause in our favor, let the merits of the case be as they may."

It would not be surprising if the firm would now have gladly relinquished the working of their machines, and confined themselves to the sale of patent rights. But few would buy what they could safely steal, and those few gave notes which they generally took care not to pay. If sued, juries would often return a verdict of no consideration, or a trial would be staved off until collection was barred by the statute of limitation, which outlawed a debt that had existed through a period of four years. On one occasion, the agent of the patentees, who was dispatched on a collecting tour through the State of Georgia, was unable to obtain money enough to pay his expenses, and was compelled to draw on his employers for nearly the full amount.

Finally, in 1801, this agent wrote to his principals that, though the planters of South Carolina would not pay their notes, many of them suggested a purchase of the right of the patentees for that State by its Legislature; and he urged Mr. Whitney to come to Columbia, and try to make an arrangement on this basis. Whitney did so, taking some letters and testimonials from the new President, Jefferson, and his Secretary of State, Madison, which were doubtless of service to him in his negotiations. His memorial having been duly submitted to the Legislature, proposing to sell the patent right for South Carolina for one hundred thousand dollars, the Legislature debated it, and finally offered for it fifty thousand — twenty thousand down, and ten thousand per annum for three years. Whitney, in a letter written the day after the passage of the act, says:

"The use of the machine here is amazingly extensive, and the value of it beyond all calculation. It may, without exaggeration, be said to have raised the value of seven-eighths of all the three Southern States from fifty to one hundred per cent. We get but a song for it in comparison with the worth of the thing; but it is *securing* something. It will enable Miller & Whitney to pay all their debts, and divide something between them. It establishes a precedent which will be valuable as it respects our collections in other States, and I think there is now a fair prospect that I shall in the event realize property enough to render me comfortable, and, in some measure, independent."

He was mistaken. The next Legislature of South Carolina nullified the contract, suspended payment on the thirty thousand still due, and instituted a suit for the recovery of the twenty thousand that had been already paid! The pretenses on which this remarkable course was taken are more fully set forth in the action of the Legislature of Georgia in 1803, based on a Message from the governor, urging the inexpediency of granting any thing to Miller & Whitney. The Committee to whom this matter was referred, made a report, in which they—

"cordially agreed with the governor in his observations, that monopolies are at all times odious, particularly in free governments, and that some remedy ought to be applied to the wound which the Cotton-Gin monopoly has given, and will otherwise continue to give, to the culture and cleaning of that precious and increasing staple. They have examined the Rev. James Hutchinson, who declares that Edward Lyon, at least twelve months before Miller & Whitney's machine was brought into view, had in possession a saw or cotton-gin, in miniature, of the same construction; and it further appears to them, from the information of Doctor Cortes Pedro Dampiere, an old and respectable citizen of Columbia county, that a machine of a construction similar to that of Miller & Whitney, was used in Switzerland at least forty years ago, *for the purpose of picking rags to make lint and paper.*"

This astonishing Committee closed their report with the following resolution:

"*Resolved*, That the Senators and Representatives of this State in Congress be, and they hereby are, instructed to use their utmost endeavors to obtain a modification of the act, entitled, 'An act to extend the privileges of obtaining Patents for useful discoveries and inventions, to certain persons therein mentioned, and to enlarge and define the penalties for violating the rights of patentees,' so as to prevent the operation of it to the injury of that most valuable staple, cotton, and the cramping of genius in improvements on Miller & Whitney's patent Gin, as well as to limit the price of obtaining a right of using it, the price at present being unbounded, and the planter and poor artificer altogether at the mercy of the patentees, who may raise the price to any sum they please.

"And, in case the said Senators and Representatives of this State shall find such modification impracticable, that they do then use their best endeavors to induce Congress, from the example of other nations, to make compensation to Miller & Whitney for their discovery, take up the patent right, and release the Southern States from so burthensome a grievance."

North Carolina, to her honor be it recorded, in December, 1802, negotiated an arrangement with Mr. Whitney, whereby the legislature laid a tax of two shillings and sixpence upon *every saw* employed in ginning cotton, to be continued for five years, which sum was to be collected by the sheriffs in the same manner as the public taxes; and, after deducting the expenses of collection, the avails were faithfully paid over to the patentee. The old North State was not extensively engaged in cotton-growing, and the pecuniary avails of this action were probably not large; but the arrangement seems to have been a fair one, and it was never repudiated. South Carolina, it should in justice be said, through her legislature of 1804, receded from her repudiation, and fulfilled her original contract.

Mr. Miller, the partner of Whitney, died, poor and embarrassed, on the 7th of December, 1803. At the term of the United States District Court for Georgia, held at Savannah in December, 1807, Mr. Whitney obtained a verdict against the pirates on his invention; his patent being now in the last year of its existence. Judge Johnson, in entering judgment for the plaintiff, said:

"With regard to the utility of this discovery, the court would deem it a waste of time to dwell long upon this topic. Is there a man who hears us, who has not experienced its utility? The whole interior of the Southern States was languishing, and its inhabitants emigrating for want of some object to engage their attention, and employ their industry, when the invention of this machine at once opened views to them which set the whole country in active motion. From childhood to age, it has presented to us a lucrative employment. Individuals who were depressed with poverty, and sunk in idleness, have suddenly risen to wealth and respectability. Our debts have been paid off. Our capitals have increased, and our lands trebled themselves in value. We cannot express the weight of the obligation which the country owes to this invention. The extent of it cannot now be seen. Some faint presentiment may be formed from the reflection that Cotton is rapidly supplanting Wool, Flax, Silk, and even Furs, in manufactures, and may one day profitably supply the use of specie in our East India trade. Our sister States also participate in the benefits of this invention; for, beside affording the raw material for their manufacturers, the bulkiness and quantity of the article afford a valuable employment for their shipping."

Mr. Whitney's patent expired in 1808, leaving him a poorer man, doubtless, than though he had never listened to the suggestions of his friend Mrs. Greene, and undertaken the invention of a machine, by means of which the annual production of cotton in the Southern States has been augmented from some five or ten thousand bales in 1793 to over *five millions of bales*, or one million tons, in 1859; this amount being at least three-fourths in weight, and seven-eighths in value, of all the cotton produced on the globe. To say that this invention was worth one thousand millions of dollars to the Slave States of this country, is to place a very moderate estimate on its value. Mr. Whitney petitioned Congress, in 1812, for a renewal of his patent, setting forth the costly and embarrassing struggles he had been forced to make in defense of his right, and observing that he had been unable to obtain any decision on the merits of his claim until he had been eleven years in the law, and until thirteen of the fourteen years' lifetime of his patent had expired. But the immense value of his invention stood directly in the way of any such acknowledgment of its merits and his righteous claims as the renewal he sought would have involved. Some liberal members from the cotton-growing region favored his petition, but a majority of the Southrons fiercely opposed it, and it was lost.

Mr. Whitney, in the course of a correspondence with Robert Fulton, inventor of the first successful steamboat, remarks:

"The difficulties with which I have had to contend have originated, principally, in the want of a disposition in mankind to do justice. My invention was new and distinct from every other: it stood alone. It was not interwoven with anything before known; and it can seldom happen that an invention or improvement is so strongly marked, and can be so clearly and specifically identified; and I have always believed that I should have had no difficulty in causing my rights to be respected, if it had been less valuable, and been used only by a small portion of the community. But the use of this machine being immensely profitable to almost every planter in the cotton districts, all were interested in trespassing upon the patent right, and each kept the other in countenance. Demagogues made themselves popular by misrepresentation and unfounded clamors, both against the right and the law made for its protection. Hence there arose associations and combinations to oppose both. At one time, but few men in Georgia dared to come into court and testify to the most simple facts within their knowledge, relative to the use of the machine. In one instance, I had great difficulty in proving that the machine *had been used in Georgia*, although, at the same moment, there were three separate sets of this machinery in motion within fifty yards of the building in which the court sat, and all so near that the rattling of the wheels was distinctly heard on the steps of the courthouse."

In 1798, Mr. Whitney, despairing of ever achieving a competence from the proceeds of his cotton-gin, engaged in the manufacture of arms, near New Haven; and his rare capacity for this or any similar undertaking, joined with his invincible perseverance and energy, was finally rewarded with success. He was a most indefatigable worker; one of the first in his manufactory in the morning, and the last to leave it at night; able to make any implement or machine he required, or to invent a new one when that might be needed; and he ultimately achieved a competency. He made great improvements in the manufacture of fire-arms—improvements that have since been continued and perfected, until the American rifled musket of our day, made at the National Armory in Springfield, Massachusetts, is doubtless the most effective and perfect weapon known to mankind. In 1817, Mr. Whitney, now fifty-two years old, found himself fully relieved from pecuniary embarrassments and the harassing anxieties resulting therefrom. He was now married to Miss Henrietta F. Edwards, daughter of the Hon. Pierpont Edwards, United States District Judge for Connecticut; and four children, a son and three daughters, were born to him in the next five years. In September, 1822, he was attacked by a dangerous and painful disease, which, with alternations of terrible suffering and comparative ease, preyed upon him until January 8, 1826, when he died, not quite sixty years of age.[6]

The African Slave-Trade, so far as it had any legal or tolerated existence, was peremptorily closed, as we have seen, on the 1st day of January, 1808. This was the period from which, according to the fond anticipations of optimists and quietists, Slavery in our country should have commenced its decadence, and thence gone steadily and surely forward to its ultimate and early extinction. And these sanguine hopes were measurably justified by the teachings of history. In all former ages, in all other countries, Slavery, so long as it existed and flourished, was kept alive by a constant or frequent enslavement of captives, or by importations of bondmen. Whenever that enslavement, that importation, ceased, Slavery began to decline. The gratitude of masters to faithful, devoted servants, who had nursed them in ill-

[6] The inventor of the cotton-gin is not deemed worthy of even the slightest distinct biographical notice in the *Encyclopædia Britannica.* The only, and not very accurate, allusion to him that I have been able to find in that immense work, is as follows:

"The Upland Cotton is a different species from the Sea Island, and is separated with such difficulty from the seed, that the expense of cleaning the wool must have put a stop to its further cultivation, had not a machine, by which the operation of cleaning is easily and successfully accomplished, been invented. This machine was invented in 1795, by Mr. Eli Whitney, of Massachusetts. There are two qualities of this cotton, the one termed Upland Georgia, grown in the States of Georgia and South Carolina, and the other of superior quality, raised upon the banks of the Mississippi, and distinguished in the market by the name of New Orleans cotton," &c., &c.—*Encyclopædia Britannica, Eighth* (*last*) *Edition*, vol. vii., p. 447.

Truly, the world knows little of its greatest men.

ness, or adhered to them in times of peril or calamity, or who had simply given the best years of their lives to the enlargement of their wealth, had been effectual in reducing, by manumission, the aggregate number of slaves much faster than it was increased by the preponderance of births over deaths. The chances of war, of invasion, and still more of insurrection and civil convulsion, had operated from time to time still further to reduce the number of slaves. Even the licentious and immoral connections between masters and their bondwomen, so inseparable from the existence of Slavery, tended strongly toward a like result; since it was seldom or never reputable, save in slaveholding America—if even there—for a master to send his own children to the auction-block and consign them to eternal bondage among strangers.[7] Quite often, the slave-mother, as well as her child or children, owed her emancipation to the affection, the remorse, or the shame, of her master and paramour. So long as slaves were mainly foreigners and barbarians, often public enemies, of fierce, strange aspect and unintelligible speech, there would naturally be little sympathy betwixt them and their masters; but when children who had grown up together—sprung, indeed, from different castes, but still members of the same household—familiar from infancy, and to some extent playmates, came to hold the relation, respectively, of master and slave, it was inevitable that kindly feelings should frequently be reciprocated between them, leading often to devotion on the one hand and emancipation on the other. It was not without reason, therefore, that the founders of our Republic and the framers of our Constitution supposed they had provided for the gradual but certain disappearance of Slavery, by limiting its area on the one hand, and providing for an early inhibition of the Slave-Trade on the other.

But the unexpected results of the purchase of Louisiana and the invention of the Cotton-Gin were such as to set at naught all these calculations. The former opened to slaveholding settlement and culture a vast domain of the richest soil on earth, in a region peculiarly adapted to the now rapidly and profitably expanding production of Cotton; for Whitney's invention had rendered this staple far more remunerative to its producer than any rival which the South

[7] "That the practice of buying and selling servants, thus early begun amongst the patriarchs, descended to their posterity, is known to every attentive reader of the Bible. It was expressly authorized by the Jewish law, in which were many directions how such servants were to be treated. They were to be bought only of the heathen; for, if an Israelite grew poor and sold himself, either to discharge a debt or to procure the means of subsistence, he was to be treated, not as a slave, but as a hired servant, and restored to freedom at the year of Jubilee. Unlimited as the power thus given to the Hebrews over their bondservants of heathen extraction appears to have been, they were strictly prohibited from acquiring such property by any other means than fair purchase. 'He that stealeth a man and selleth him,' said their great Lawgiver, 'shall surely be put to death.'"—*Encyclopædia Britannica*, vol. xx., p. 319.

The above passage seems scarcely just to the Law given by Moses. The true object and purpose of that Law, so far as bondage is concerned, was rather a mitigation of the harsher features of an existing institution than the creation of a new one. Moses, 'for the hardness of your hearts,' says Jesus, allowed or tolerated some things which 'from the beginning were not so.' How any one can quote the Law of Moses as a warrant for Slavery, yet not admit it as a justification of free-and-easy Divorce, is not apparent.

had ever, or has ever yet, attempted to grow; while the nearly simultaneous inventions of Hargreaves, Arkwright, and others,[8] whereby steam was applied to the propulsion of machinery admirably adapted to the fabrication of Cotton, secured the cultivators against all reasonable apprehension of a permanently glutted market. As the production was doubled, and even quadrupled, every few years, it would sometimes seem that the demand had been exceeded; and two or three great commercial convulsions gave warning that even the capacity of the world's steadily expanding markets could be over-estimated and surpassed by the producers of Cotton and its various fabrics. But two years at most sufficed to clear off the surplus and enlarge this steadily growing demand up to the full measure of the momentarily checked production. The five millions of bales, produced by the United States in 1859–60, were sold as readily and quickly as the one million bales produced in 1830–31, and at considerably higher prices per pound.

But the relatively frigid climate and superficially exhausted soil of Maryland, Virginia, and North Carolina—wherein the greater number of slaves were originally held—were poorly, or not at all, adapted to the production of cotton, whereof slave-labor early claimed, and succeeded in substantially maintaining, a monopoly. No other out-door work afforded such constant and nearly uniform employment for this description of labor. Throughout the greater part of the South-West, plowing for the cotton-crop may be commenced in January; to be followed directly by planting; this by weeding; and hardly has the cultivation of the crop been completed when the picking of the more advanced bolls may be commenced; and this, with ginning, often employs the whole force of the plantation nearly or quite up to the commencement of the Christmas holidays. These being over, the preparation of the fields for plowing is again commenced; so that there is no season when the hands need stand idle; and, though long spring and summer rains, impeding tillage while impelling the growth of weeds and of grass, sometimes induce weeks of necessary hurry and unusual effort, there is absolutely no day of the year wherein the experienced planter or competent overseer cannot find full employment for his hands in some detail of the cultivation of Cotton.

The forest-covered and unhealthy, but facile and marvelously fertile, South-West hungered for slaves, as we have seen evinced in the case of Indiana Territory. Impoverished, but salubrious and corn-growing Maryland, Virginia, etc., were ready to supply them. Enterprising, adventurous whites, avaricious men from the North and from Europe, but still more from the older Slave States, hied to the South-West, in hot pur-

[8] James Hargreaves had invented the Spinning-Jenny in 1764; this was supplanted by the invention by Sir Richard Arkwright, in 1768, of a superior machine for spinning cotton thread. James Watt patented his Steam Engine in 1769, and his improvement, whereby a rotary motion was produced, in 1782; and its first application to cotton-spinning occurred in 1787, but it was many years in winning its way into general use. John Fitch's first success in steam navigation was achieved in 1786. Fulton's patents were granted in 1809–11, and claimed the simple means of adapting paddle-wheels to the axle of the crank of Watt's engine.

suit of wealth by means of cotton-planting and subsidiary callings; and each became a purchaser of slaves to the full extent of his means. To clear more land and grow more cotton, wherewith to buy more negroes, was the general and absorbing aspiration —the more negroes to be employed in clearing still more land and growing still more cotton. Under this dispensation, the price of slaves necessarily and rapidly advanced, until it was roughly computed that each average field-hand was worth so many hundred dollars as cotton commanded cents per pound: That is, when cotton was worth ten cents per pound, field-hands were worth a thousand dollars each; with cotton at twelve cents, they were worth twelve hundred; and when it rose, as it sometimes did even in later days, to fifteen cents per pound for a fair article of middling Orleans, a stout negro, from seventeen to thirty years old, with no particular skill but that necessarily acquired in the rude experience of farm labor anywhere, would often bring fifteen hundred dollars on a New Orleans auction-block. Hence the business of negro-trading, or the systematic buying of slaves to sell again, though never quite reputable, and, down to the last thirty or forty years, very generally regarded with abhorrence—became a highly important and influential, as well as gainful, occupation. The negro-trader, often picking up bargains at executors' or assignees' sales in the older States, or when a sudden shift must be made to save a merchant from bankruptcy or a farm from the sheriff, controlled large sums of money, often in good part his own. He was the Providence to whom indolent, dissipated, easy-going Virginians looked for extrication, at the last gasp, from their constantly recurring pecuniary embarrassments; while, on the other hand, a majority of the South-Western planters were eager to buy of him at large prices, provided he would sell on one or two years' credit. He patronized hotels and railroads; he often chartered vessels for the transportation of his human merchandise; he was necessarily shrewd, keen, and intelligent, and frequently acquired, or at least wielded, so much wealth and influence as to become almost respectable. Quite usually, he was an active politician, almost uniformly of the most ultra Pro-Slavery type, and naturally attached to the Democratic party. Traveling extensively and almost constantly, his information and volubility rendered him mail and telegraph, newspaper and stump orator, to those comparatively ignorant and secluded planters whom he visited twice or more per year, as buyer or seller, or collector of his dues for slaves already sold; while his power as profitable customer on the one hand, or lenient creditor on the other, was by no means inconsiderable. It was this power, in connection with that of the strongly sympathizing and closely affiliated class of gamblers and blacklegs, by which Van Buren's renomination for the Presidency was defeated in the Baltimore Convention of 1844, and the Democratic party committed, through the nomination of Polk and its accessories, to the policy of annexing Texas, thus securing a fresh and boundless expansion to Slavery. When that Annexation was suddenly, and to most unexpectedly, achieved, at the close of John Tyler's administration, relays of horses, prëarranged in the absence of telegraphs, conveyed from the deeply interested negro-traders, who were watching the doings of Congress at the national metropolis, to their confederates and agents in the slave-selling districts of the neighboring States, the joyful tidings which insured an advance of twelve to fifteen per cent. in the market value of human flesh, and enabled the exclusive possessors of the intelligence to make it the basis of extensive and lucrative speculations.

Slave-breeding for gain, deliberately purposed and systematically pursued, appears to be among the latest devices and illustrations of human depravity. Neither Cowper, nor Wesley, nor Jonathan Edwards, nor Granville Sharp, nor Clarkson, nor any of the philanthropists or divines who, in the last century, bore fearless and emphatic testimony to the flagrant iniquity of slave-making, slave-holding, and slave-selling, seem to have had any clear conception of it. For the infant slave of past ages was rather an incumbrance and a burden than a valued addition to his master's stock. To raise him, however roughly, must cost all he would ultimately be worth. That it was cheaper to buy slaves than to rear them, was quite generally regarded as self-evident. But the suppression of the African Slave-Trade, coinciding with the rapid settlement of the Louisiana purchase and the triumph of the Cotton-Gin, wrought here an entire transformation. When field-hands brought from ten to fifteen hundred dollars, and young negroes were held at about ten dollars per pound, the newly born infant, if well-formed, healthy, and likely to live, was deemed an addition to his master's wealth of not less than one hundred dollars, even in Virginia or Maryland. It had now become the interest of the master to increase the number of births in his slave-cabins; and few evinced scruples as to the means whereby this result was attained. The chastity of female slaves was never esteemed of much account, even where they were white; and, now that it had become an impediment to the increase of their masters' wealth, it was wholly disregarded. No slave-girl, however young, was valued lower for having become a mother, without waiting to be first made a wife; nor were many masters likely to rebuke this as a fault, or brand it as a shame. Women were publicly advertised by sellers as extraordinary breeders, and commanded a higher price on that account.[9] Wives, sold into separation from their husbands, were imperatively required to accept new partners, in order that the fruitfulness of the

[9] Mr. Edward Yates, a zealous and active friend of the Union cause, in "A letter to the Women of England, on Slavery in the Southern States of America," founded on personal observation in 1855, gives revolting instances of the brutal handling of delicate and beautiful women, apparently white, by slave-dealers and their customers, in Southern sale-rooms. He adds:

"At Richmond and New Orleans, I was present at slave-auctions, *and did not see one instance of a married pair being sold together*, but, without exception, so far as I was able to learn from the negroes sold by the auctioneers, *every grown-up man left a wife and every grown-up woman a husband.* * * * I saw Mr. Pulliam (of Richmond) sell, to different buyers, two daughters away from their mother, who was also to be sold. This unfortunate woman was a quadroon; and I shall not soon forget the large tears that started to her eyes as she saw her two children sold away from her."

Testimony like this is abundant.

plantation might not suffer. We need not dwell on this new phase of Slavery, its revolting features, and still more revolting consequences. The simple and notorious fact that clergymen, marrying slaves, were accustomed to require of them fidelity in their marital relation, until separated by death, or by *inexorable necessity*, suffices of itself to stamp the social condition thus photographed with the indignant reprobation of mankind. And when we add that slave-girls were not only daily sold on the auction-blocks of New Orleans, and constantly advertised in her journals, as very nearly white, well-educated, and possessed of the rarest personal attractions, and that they commanded double and treble prices on this account, we leave nothing to be added to complete the outlines of a system of legalized and priest-sanctioned iniquity, more gigantic and infernal than heathenism and barbarism ever devised. For the Circassian beauty, whose charms seek and find a market at Constantinople, is sent thither by her parents, and is herself a willing party to the speculation. She hopefully bids a last adieu to the home of her infancy, to find another in the harem of some wealthy and powerful Turk, where she will achieve the life of luxury and idleness she covets. But the American-born woman, consigned by the laws of her country and the fiat of her owner to the absolute possession of whomsoever bids most for her, neither consents to the transfer, nor is at all consulted as to the person to whom she is helplessly consigned. The Circassian knows that her children will be free and honored. The American is keenly aware that hers must share her own bitter and hopeless degradation. It was long ago observed that American Slavery, with its habitual and life-long separations of husband from wife, of parent from child, its exile of perhaps the larger portion of its victims from the humble but cherished homes of their childhood to the strange and repulsive swamps and forests of the far South-West, is harsher and viler than any other system of bondage on which the sun ever shone. And when we add that it has been carefully computed that the State of Virginia, since the date of the purchase of Louisiana, had received more money for her own flesh and blood, regularly sold and exported, than her soil and all that was upon it would have sold for on the day when she seceded from the Union, we need adduce no more of the million facts which unite to prove every wrong a blunder as well as a crime—that God has implanted in every evil the seeds of its overthrow and ultimate destruction.

The conflicting currents of American thought and action with regard to Slavery—that which was cherished by the Revolutionary patriots, and gradually died with them, and that by which the former was imperceptibly supplanted—are strikingly exhibited in the history and progress of the movement for African Colonization. Its originator was the Rev. Samuel Hopkins, D. D., who was settled as a clergyman at Newport, R. I., in 1770, and found that thriving sea-port a focus of Slavery and the Slave-Trade, upon both of which he soon commenced an active and determined war. The idea of counteracting, and ultimately suppressing, the Slave-Trade, through a systematic colonization of the western coast of Africa with emancipated blacks from America, was matured and suggested by him to others, even before the outbreak of the Revolutionary war; and its realization, interrupted by that struggle, was resumed by him directly after it had been closed. This was anterior to the British settlement of Sierra Leone, and preceded the appearance of Clarkson's prize essay, commanding public attention to the horrors of the Slave-Trade. Among Dr. Hopkins's European correspondents were Granville Sharp and Zachary Macaulay, who were among the earliest and least compromising of British abolitionists. Through his influence and efforts, three colored youth were educated in New England, toward the close of the last century, with express reference to missionary labor in Africa in connection with the Colonization movement. Two of these ultimately, though at a mature age, migrated to Liberia, where they died soon after. Thirty-eight American blacks emigrated to Sierra Leone in 1815, under the auspices and in the vessel of one of their own number. The initial organization of the American Colonization Society took place at Princeton, N. J., in the autumn of 1816; and that Society was formally organized at Washington, by the choice of officers, on the 1st of January, 1817. Its first attempt at practical colonization was made in 1820 on Sherbro Island, which proved an unfortunate location; its present position on the main land, at Cape Mesurado, was purchased December 15, 1821, and some colonists landed on it early in the following year. About one thousand emigrants were dispatched thither in the course of the following seven years, including a small church of colored persons which migrated from Boston in 1826. The additional number dispatched during the succeeding thirty years was not far from eight thousand. The city founded by the original emigrants received the name of Monrovia, and in 1847 the colony declared itself an independent republic under the name of Liberia. That republic still exists, enjoying a moderate and equable prosperity, in spite of its unhealthiness for whites, and for all but duly acclimated blacks, on account of its tropical and humid location.

But the Colonization movement, though bountifully lauded and glorified by the eminent in Church and State, and though the Society numbered among its Presidents Bushrod Washington, Charles Carroll, James Madison, and Henry Clay, has not achieved a decided success, and for the last twenty years has steadily and stubbornly declined in importance and consideration. It has ceased to command or deserve the sympathy of abolitionists, without achieving the hearty confidence, though it has been blessed or cursed with the abundant verbal commendations, of their antagonists. It was soon discovered that, while it was presented to the former class as a safe and unobjectionable device for mitigating the evils, while gradually undermining the existence, of human bondage in our country, it was, at the same time, commended to the favor and patronage of slaveholders as a means of relieving the South of its dangerous free-negro element, and thus augmenting the security and insuring the perpetuity of their beloved institution. Moreover, as the enhanced and constantly increasing market value of slaves obstructed and diminished manumissions with a view to colonization, the class of subjects for deportation to Africa steadily fell off in numbers, and in the quality of those composing it. When, at last, the South, under the lead of Mr. Calhoun, quite generally adopted the novel and extraordinary doctrine of the essential righteousness and signal beneficence of Slavery—when the relation of life-long servitude and utter subjugation to the will of a master was declared the true, natural, and most enviable condition of the laboring class anywhere—the condition most conducive to their happiness,[10] moral culture, and social well-being—the idea of liberating individuals or families from this subjugation, and sending them from peaceful, plentiful, and prosperous America to benighted, barbarous, and inhospitable Africa, became, in this view, a transparent absurdity. No disciple of Calhoun could be a logical, consistent colonizationist, any more than a follower of Garrison and Wendell Phillips. The constantly and widely diverging currents of American opinion soon left the Colonization movement hopelessly stranded. The teachings of the new Southern school tended palpably toward the extirpation from the South of the free-negro anomaly, through reënslavement rather than exile. Legislative efforts to decree a general sale of free negroes into absolute slavery were made in several States, barely defeated in two or three, and fully successful in one. Arkansas, in 1858–9, enacted the enslavement of all free colored persons within her limits, who should not remove beyond them before the ensuing 4th of July, and this atrocious edict was actually enforced by her authorities. The negroes generally escaped; but, if any remained, they did so in view of the fact that the first sheriff who could lay hands on them would hurry them to the auction-block, and sell them to the highest bidder. And this was but a foretaste of the fate to which the new Southern dogma was morally certain, in a few years, to consign the whole free colored population of the

[10] "What disposition God, in His providence, will eventually make of these blacks, cannot be foretold; but it is our duty to provide for our own happiness and theirs as long as we can. In dealing with this question, it will not do to be guided by abstract notions of liberty and slavery. We can only judge the future by the past; and, as experience proves that the negro is better off in slavery at the South than in freedom elsewhere, it is the part of philanthropy to keep him here, as we keep our children in subjection for their own good."—*De Bow's Review*, vol. ii., p. 310.

Mr. Chestnut of S. C., in a long pro-slavery speech in the U. S. Senate, April 9, 1860, presented his views of the inherent excellence of human bondage, as regards the slaves themselves, as follows:

"But you say, 'I leave out of the consideration the happiness of the race enslaved.' By no means. It is an important element of the moral argument. * * * In the general march of human progress, there is no one interest of humanity which has advanced more rapidly than the institution of African Slavery as it is in the Southern States. It has stood the test of every trial. Its mission is to subdue the unbroken regions of the warm and fertile South, and its end is the happiness and civilization of the human race, *including the race of the slave*, in all respects."

Said Mr. Jas. M. Mason, of Va., in the debate of the following day:

"As to the slave population, I agree with the Senator from South Carolina. if a problem, it has worked itself out; the thing is settled here, so far as the South is concerned, or the opinions and purposes of the South, or their ability to make their opinions and purposes good. It will become, as it has already begun to be, the established policy of the South to have no more emancipation. Let them continue in bondage as they now exist, as the best condition of both races."

Slave States, had not those States been precipitated into their great Rebellion. Individuals would have resisted and protested, but only to be overborne by inexorable logic, and even more inexorable majorities.

VII.

THE MISSOURI STRUGGLE.

When the State of Louisiana, previously known as the Territory of Orleans, was admitted into the Union,[1] the remainder of the Louisiana purchase, which had formerly borne the designation of Louisiana Territory, was renamed the Territory of Missouri. The people of a portion of this Territory, stretching westward from the Mississippi on both sides of the river Missouri, petitioned Congress for admission into the Union as the State of Missouri; and their memorials[2] were referred by the House to a Select Committee, whereof Mr. Scott, their delegate, was chairman. This Committee reported[3] a bill in accordance with their prayer, which was read twice and committed; but no further action was taken thereon during that session.

The same Congress reconvened for its second session on the 16th of the following November, and the House resolved itself into a Committee of the whole,[4] and in due time took up the Missouri bill aforesaid, which was considered throughout that sitting and that of the next day but one, during which several amendments were adopted, the most important of which, moved by General James Tallmadge, of Dutchess County, New York, was as follows:

"*And provided*, That the introduction of Slavery, or involuntary servitude, be prohibited, except for the punishment of crimes, whereof the party has been duly convicted; and that all children born within the said State, after the admission thereof into the Union, shall be declared free at the age of twenty-five years."

On the rising of the Committee, the Yeas and Nays were demanded in the House on the question of agreeing to this amendment; when a division was called, and so much of it as precedes and includes the word "convicted" was adopted by 87 Yeas—all from the substantially Free States[5] except one of the two members from Delaware—to 76 Nays, whereof ten were from Free States—Massachusetts (then including Maine) supplying three of them, New York three, with one each from New Jersey, New Hampshire, Ohio, and Illinois. The residue of the amendment was likewise sustained, by the close vote of 82 Yeas to 78 Nays. The bill thus amended was ordered to a third reading by 98 Yeas to 56 Nays, and the next day was passed and sent to the Senate, where the restriction aforesaid was stricken out by a vote of 22 to 16, and the bill thus amended passed without a division, on the last day but one of the session. Being now returned to the House, General Tall-

[1] April 8, 1812.

[2] On the 16th of March, 1818.

[3] April 3d.

[4] February 13, 1819.

[5] New York and New Jersey still held a few slaves, but the former had decreed their manumission.

madge moved its indefinite postponement, which was defeated—Yeas 69, Nays 74. But the question next presented, of concurrence in the Senate's amendment aforesaid, was decided in the negative—Yeas 76, Nays 78; and the bill returned to the Senate accordingly. The Senate insisted on its amendment without a division; and, on the return of the bill to the House, Mr. John W. Taylor,[6] of New York, moved that the House adhere to its disagreement; which prevailed—Yeas 78, Nays 66. And so the bill failed for that session.

A bill, organizing so much of the Territory of Missouri as was not included within the borders of the proposed State of that name, to be known as the Territory of Arkansas, was considered at this session, and Mr. Taylor, of New York, moved the application thereto of the restriction aforesaid. So much of it as required that all slaves born within the Territory after the passage of this act should be free at twenty-five years of age, was carried,[7] by 75 Yeas to 72 Nays, and the residue defeated by 70 Yeas to 71 Nays. Next day, however, the adopted clause was reconsidered and stricken out, and the bill ultimately passed without any reference to Slavery. Arkansas became in consequence a Slave Territory, and ultimately a Slave State.

A new Congress convened December 6, 1819; and Mr. Scott[8] moved a reference to a Select Committee of the memorials from Missouri, including that of her Territorial Legislature, asking admission into the Union. This motion prevailed, and Mr. Speaker Clay appointed as such Committee three members from Slave States, beside Mr. Scott, who was chairman, with but one from a Free State. In the Senate, the legislative memorial aforesaid was referred to the Judiciary Committee, consisting of three members from Slave States with but two from Free States.

Upon the conflict which ensued, the Slave Power entered with very great incidental advantages. The President, Mr. Monroe, though he took no conspicuous part in the strife, was well known to favor that side, as did a majority of his Cabinet, so that the patronage of the Government and the hopes of aspirants to its favor were powerful makeweights against the policy of Restriction. The two ex-Presidents of the dominant party, Messrs. Jefferson and Madison, still survived, and gave their powerful influence openly in accordance with their Southern sympathies rather than their Anti-Slavery convictions. Mr. Clay, the popular and potent Speaker of the House, though likewise Anti-Slavery in principle, was a zealous and most efficient adversary of Restriction. The natural fears of a destruction, or at least a temporary prostration, of the Republican ascendency, through the rëformation of parties on what were called geographical lines, also tended strongly to defeat the proposed inhibition of Slavery. The North, it had by this time come to be understood, if beaten in such a struggle, would quietly submit; while the South, it was very clearly intimated and generally believed, would shiver all party bands, and perhaps even the Union itself, rather than submit to a defeat on this issue.

[6] Some years afterward, Speaker of the House.

[7] February 17th.

[8] December 8th.

Moreover, the shape and manner in which the question was presented were exceedingly favorable to the Southern side. Its advocates, in accordance with their general policy of defending and promoting Slavery in the abused name of Liberty, fought their battle under the flag of State Sovereignty, State Equality, etc. The Right of the People to form and modify their institutions in accordance with their own judgment, interest, feelings, or convictions, was the burden of their strain. Said Mr. William Pinkney,[9] of Maryland, their most pretentious and ornate, if not their ablest champion:

"Slavery, we are told in many a pamphlet, memorial, and speech, with which the press has lately groaned, is a foul blot on our otherwise immaculate reputation. Let this be conceded—yet you are no nearer than before to the conclusion that you possess power which may deal with other objects as effectually as with this. Slavery, we are further told, with some pomp of metaphor, is a canker at the root of all that is excellent in this republican empire, a pestilent disease that is snatching the youthful bloom from its cheek, prostrating its honor and withering its strength. Be it so—yet, if you have power to medicine to it in the way proposed, and in virtue of the diploma which you claim, you also have the power, in the distribution of your political alexipharmics, to present the deadliest drugs to every Territory that would become a State, and bid it drink or remain a colony forever. Slavery, we are also told, is now 'rolling onward with a rapid tide toward the boundless regions of the West,' threatening to doom them to sterility and sorrow, unless some potent voice can say to it, Thus far shalt thou go and no farther. Slavery engenders pride and indolence in him who commands, and inflicts intellectual and moral degradation on him who serves. Slavery, in fine, is unchristian and abominable. Sir, I shall not stop to deny that Slavery is all this and more; but I shall not think myself the less authorized to deny that it is for *you* to stay the course of this dark torrent, by opposing to it a mound raised up by the labors of this portentous discretion on the domain of others; a mound which you cannot erect but through the instrumentality of a trespass of no ordinary kind—not the comparatively innocent trespass that beats down a few blades of grass, which the first kind sun or the next refreshing shower may cause to spring again—but that which levels with the ground the lordliest trees of the forest, and claims immortality for the destruction which it inflicts."

Throughout the discussion, the argument that Missouri, by the adoption of this amendment, would be subject to unprecedented, invidious, and degrading exactions—that she would be brought into the Union not as the equal, but as the subject of her elder sisters—that the power thus exercised involved the assertion of unlimited and utterly irresponsible authority to shape and mold the institutions of every new State—was pressed with eminent subtlety, pertinacity, and vigor. The right to prohibit Slavery in any or all of the Territories, denied by none, was expressly admitted by Mr. Philip P. Barbour,[10] of Virginia. But this admission, however generally made,

[9] Speech in the U. S. Senate, February 15, 1820.

[10] In the debate of Monday, Feb. 15, 1819, Mr. P. P. Barbour, of Va., said:

"The effect of the proposed amendment is to prohibit the further introduction of slaves into the new State of Missouri, and to emancipate, at the age of twenty-five years, the children of all those slaves who are now within its limits. The first objection, said he, which meets us at the very threshold of the discussion, is this: that we have no constitutional right to enact the proposed provision. Our power, in relation to this subject, is derived from the first clause of the third section of the fourth article of the Constitution, which is in these words: 'New States may be admitted by the Congress into this Union.' Now, Sir, although by the next succeeding clause of the same section, 'Congress has the power to make all needful rules and regulations respecting the Territory of the United States;' and although, therefore, whilst the proposed State continued a part of our *Territory*, upon the footing of a Territorial government, *it would have been competent for us*, under the power expressly given to make needful rules and regulations—*to have established the principle now proposed;* yet the question assumes a totally different aspect when that principle is intended to apply to a STATE."—*Benton's Abridgment.* N. Y., 1858., vol. vi., p. 341.

did not gain a single Southern vote for the policy of Restriction when the bill to organize Arkansas Territory was under consideration; whereon Mr. Walker, of North Carolina, in opposing that policy, gravely, and without the least suspicion of irony, observed: "Let it not be forgotten that we are legislating in a *free* country, and for a *free* people." But the champions of Restriction, though less agile and skillful of fence than their opponents, were by no means worsted in the argument. Here is a specimen of their logic, from the speech of John W. Taylor:[11]

"Gentlemen have said the amendment is in violation of the treaty, because it impairs the property of a master in his slave. Is it then pretended that, notwithstanding the declaration in our bill of rights 'that all men are created equal,' one individual can have a vested property, not only in the flesh and blood of his fellow-man, but also in generations not yet called into existence? Can it be believed that the supreme legislature has no power to provide rules and regulations for meliorating the condition of future ages? And this, too, when the Constitution itself has vested in Congress full sovereignty, by authorizing the enactment of whatever law it may deem conducive to the welfare of the country? The sovereignty of Congress in relation to the States is limited by specific grants, but in regard to the Territories it is unlimited. Missouri was purchased with our money; and, until incorporated into the family of States, it may be sold for money. Can it, then, be maintained that, though we have the power to dispose of the whole Territory, we have no right to provide against the further increase of Slavery within its limits? That, although we may change the political relations of its free citizens by transferring their country to a foreign power, we cannot provide for the gradual abolition of Slavery within its limits, nor establish those civil regulations which naturally flow from self-evident truth? No, Sir; it cannot: the practice of nations, and the common sense of mankind have long since decided these questions.

"Having proved, as I apprehend, our right to legislate in the manner proposed, I proceed to illustrate the propriety of exercising it. And here I might rest satisfied with reminding my opponents of their own declarations on the subject of Slavery. How often and how eloquently have they deplored its existence among them! What willingness, nay, what solicitude, have they not manifested to be relieved from this burden! How have they wept over the unfortunate policy which first introduced slaves into this country! How have they disclaimed the guilt and shame of that original sin, and thrown it back upon their ancestors! I have with pleasure heard these avowals of regret, and confided in their sincerity; I have hoped to see its effects in the advancement of the cause of Humanity. Gentlemen have now an opportunity of putting their principles into practice. If they have tried Slavery and found it a curse—if they desire to dissipate the gloom with which it covers their land—I call upon them to exclude it from the Territory in question; plant not its seeds in this uncorrupt soil; let not our children, looking back to the proceedings of this day, say of them, as they have been constrained to speak of *their* fathers, 'We wish their decision had been different; we regret the existence of this unfortunate population among us; but we found them here; we know not what to do with them; it is our misfortune; we must bear it with patience.'

"History will record the decision of this day as exerting its influence for centuries to come over the population of half our continent. If we reject the amendment, and suffer this evil, now easily eradicated, to strike its roots so deep into the soil that it can never be removed, shall we not furnish some apology for doubting our sincerity when we deplore its existence? Shall we not expose ourselves to the same kind of censure which was pronounced by the Saviour of mankind on the Scribes and Pharisees, who builded the tombs of the prophets, and garnished the sepulchres of the righteous, and said, if they had lived in the days of their fathers, they would not have been partakers with them in the blood of the prophets, while they manifested a spirit which clearly proved them the legitimate descendants of those who killed the prophets, and thus filled up the measure of their fathers' iniquities?"

The Legislatures of New York, New Jersey, and Pennsylvania unanimously adopted and transmitted resolves in favor of the proposed Restriction; and like resolves were

[11] February 15, 1819.

adopted by the Legislature of the Slave State of Delaware. A frank and forcible memorial from inhabitants of Boston and its vicinity, drafted by Daniel Webster,[12] and signed by the principal citizens of all parties, asserted the complete authority of Congress over the subject, and demanded Restriction on those grounds of expediency, morality, and justice, with which thoughtful readers are by this time abundantly familiar. The following extract from this memorial is eminently worthy of its author:

"Your memorialists were not without the hope that the time had at length arrived when the inconvenience and danger of this description of population had become apparent in all parts of this country and in all parts of the civilized world. It might have been hoped that the new States themselves would have had such a view of their own permanent interests and prosperity as would have led them to prohibit its extension and increase. The wonderful growth and prosperity of the States north of the Ohio are unquestionably to be ascribed, in a great measure, to the consequences of the Ordinance of 1787; and few, indeed, are the occasions in the history of nations, in which so much can be done, by a single act, for the benefit of future generations, as was done by that Ordinance, and as may now be done by the Congress of the United States. We appeal to the justice and to the wisdom of the National Councils to prevent the further progress of a great and serious evil. We appeal to those who look forward to the remote consequences of their measures, and who cannot balance a temporary or trifling inconvenience, if there were such, against a permanent, growing, and desolating evil. We cannot forbear to remind the two Houses of Congress that the early and decisive measures adopted by the American Government for the abolition of the Slave-Trade, are among the proudest memorials of our nation's glory. That Slavery was ever tolerated in the Republic is, as yet, to be attributed to the policy of another Government. No imputation, thus far, rests on any portion of the American Confederacy. The Missouri Territory is a new country. If its extensive and fertile fields shall be opened as a market for slaves, the Government will seem to become a party to a traffic which, in so many acts, through so many years, it has denounced as impolitic, unchristian, inhuman. To enact laws to punish the traffic, and at the same time to tempt cupidity and avarice by the allurements of an insatiable market, is inconsistent and irreconcilable. Government, by such a course, would only defeat its own purposes, and render nugatory its own measures. Nor can the laws derive support from the manners of the people, if the power of moral sentiment be weakened by enjoying, under the permission of Government, great facilities to commit offenses. The laws of the United States have denounced heavy penalties against the traffic in slaves, because such traffic is deemed unjust and inhuman. We appeal to the spirit of these laws. We appeal to this justice and humanity. We ask whether they ought not to operate, on the present occasion, with all their force? We have a strong feeling of the injustice of any toleration of Slavery. Circumstances have entailed it on a portion of our community, which cannot be immediately relieved of it without consequences more injurious than the suffering of the evil. But to permit it in a new country, where, as yet, no habits are formed which render it indispensable, what is it, but to encourage that rapacity, and fraud, and violence, against which we have so long pointed the denunciations of our penal code? What is it, but to tarnish the proud fame of the country? What is it, but to throw suspicion on its good faith, and to render questionable all its professions of regard for the rights of Humanity and the liberties of mankind?

"As inhabitants of a free country—as citizens of a great and rising Republic—as members of a Christian community—as living in a liberal and enlightened age, and as feeling ourselves called upon, by the dictates of religion and humanity, we have presumed to offer our sentiments to Congress on this question, with a solicitude for the event far beyond what a common occasion could inspire."

The House Committee, of course, reported the bill without restriction, and it came up as a special order.[13] Mr. Taylor moved its postponement for a week, which was voted down—Yeas 87; Nays 88. It was considered in Committee the next day,[14] as also on the 28th, and 30th, and thence

[12] Then a recent emigrant to Massachusetts from the neighboring State of New Hampshire.

[13] January 24, 1820.

[14] Missouri impatiently awaited admission.

debated daily, until the 19th of February, when a bill came down from the Senate "to admit the State of *Maine* into the Union," with a rider, authorizing the people of Missouri to form a State Constitution, etc.—the connection being intended to force the Missouri measure through the House upon the strength of the other proposition.

The Maine bill had passed the House weeks before, without serious opposition. Reaching the Senate, it was sent to its Judiciary Committee, which appended to it the provision for organizing Missouri. An attempt to shake this off was defeated by 25 Nays to 18 Yeas, and the bill returned to the House accordingly. The House refused to concur by the decisive vote of 93 to 72—only four members from the Free States voting in the minority. The House further disagreed, by the strong vote of 102 to 68, to the Senate's amendment striking the Restriction out of the Missouri bill. Hereupon, what is known in history as the Missouri *Compromise* was concocted. It was the work, not of the advocates, but of the opponents, of Slavery *Restriction*, intended solely to win votes enough from the majority in the House to secure the admission of Missouri as a Slave State. It was first proposed in the Senate by Mr. Thomas, of Illinois—a uniform opponent of Restriction on Missouri—and introduced by him[14] in this shape:

"*And be it further enacted*, That in all that Territory ceded by France to the United States, under the name of Louisiana, which lies north of thirty-six degrees thirty minutes north latitude, excepting only such part thereof as is included within the limits of the State contemplated by this act, Slavery and involuntary servitude, otherwise than in the punishment of crime, whereof the party shall have been duly convicted, shall be and is hereby forever prohibited. *Provided always*, That any person escaping into the same, from whom labor or service is lawfully claimed in any State or Territory of the United States, such fugitive may be lawfully reclaimed and conveyed to the person claiming his or her labor or service as aforesaid."

The Senate adopted this proposition by 34 Yeas to 10 Nays, and passed the Missouri bill, thus amended, by 24 Yeas to 20 Nays—the minority embracing both advocates and opponents of Restriction. The House at first rejected Mr. Thomas's amendment by the overwhelming vote of 159 Yeas to 18 Nays. The Senate refused to recede from its amendments, and the House decisively insisted on its disagreement to them; whereupon the Senate asked a conference, and the House granted it without a division. The Committee of Conference was framed so as to give the anti-Restrictionists a decided preponderance; and John Holmes, of Massachusetts, reported[15] from said Committee, that the Senate should give up its combination of Missouri with Maine; that the House should abandon its attempt to restrict Slavery in Missouri; and that both Houses should concur in passing the bill to admit Missouri as a State, with Mr. Thomas's restriction or proviso, excluding Slavery from all Territory North and West of the new State. Fourteen members, in all, from the Free States[16] voted to adopt this Compromise, with 76 from the Slave States, making 90 in all; while 87 members from the Free States, and *none* from the Slave States, voted

[14] February 17, 1820. [15] March 2, 1820.

[16] The names of the fourteen members from the Free States, thus voting with the Anti-Restrictionists, are as follows:

against the Compromise. So the bill passed both Houses, as did that for the admission of Maine on the same day.

This virtually ended the Missouri struggle;[17] though, at the next Session, when Missouri presented herself for admission as a State, with a Constitution denying to her Legislature any power to emancipate slaves or to prevent their immigration, and requiring said Legislature to pass laws to prevent the immigration of free negroes or mulattoes at any time or under any circumstances, the Northern members for the moment revolted. They keenly felt that this was not the "liberty" and "equality" which had been so stoutly demanded and eulogized by the opponents of Slavery Restriction; and they further objected that this arbitrary and irrevocable prohibition of free colored immigration was in palpable violation of that clause of the Federal Constitution which guarantees to the citizens of each State the rights of citizens in every State. Her admission was at first voted down in the House by 93 Nays to 79 Yeas; but, finally, a fresh Compromise, concocted by a select Joint Committee, whereof Mr. Clay[18] was chairman, was adopted. By this Compromise, Missouri was required to pledge herself that no act should be passed by her Legislature, "by which any of the citizens of either of the States should be excluded from the enjoyment of the privileges and immunities to which they are entitled under the Constitution of the United States." With this added as a proviso, the joint resolve admitting Missouri finally passed the House by 86 Yeas to 82 Nays; and the Senate concurred[19] by 26 Yeas to 15 Nays. Missouri, through her legislature, complied with the condition, and thereby became an admitted State. And thus closed the memorable Missouri controversy, which had for two years disturbed the harmony, and threatened the peace of the Union.[20]

MASSACHUSETTS.—Mark Langdon Hill, John Holmes, Jonathan Mason, Henry Shaw—4.

RHODE ISLAND.—Samuel Eddy—1.

CONNECTICUT.—Samuel A. Foot, James Stephens—2.

NEW YORK.—Henry Meigs, Henry R. Storrs 2.

NEW JERSEY.—Joseph Bloomfield, Charles Kinsey, Bernard Smith—3.

PENNSYLVANIA.—Henry Baldwin, David Fullerton—2.

[17] Some idea of the state of feeling in Missouri, as well as of that in some of the original States, at this period of the Missouri struggle, may be gathered from the following extract:

"IMPRUDENCE—OR WORSE.—The *St. Louis Enquirer*, intimating that the Restrictionists intend to renew their designs at the next session of Congress, says—Missouri will then appear 'as a *sovereign State*, according to the law of Congress, and not as a Territorial orphan;' that her people will, in that case, 'give fresh proof to the world that they know their rights, and are able to defend them.' What signifies such language as this? All things considered, we wish that the Missouri question may be suffered to rest where it is, as the lesser evil; but, if Congress pleases to take it up again, and refuses to admit the Territory under the Constitution which its Convention has formed, and is without power to enforce its determination, it is high time, indeed, that a new organization of affairs should take place."—*Niles' Register*, August 26, 1820, vol. xviii., p. 451.

[18] Colonel William H. Russell, of Missouri, a distant relative and life-long friend of Mr. Clay, in a letter (1862) to Hon. James S. Rollins, M. C., from his State, says that Mr. Scott, the Delegate from Missouri at the time of her admission, told him that Mr. Clay, at the close of the struggle, said to him: "Now, go home, and prepare your State for gradual Emancipation."

[19] February 27, 1821.

[20] Even John Adams's faith in the Union was somewhat shaken in this stormy passage of its

VIII.

STATE RIGHTS—NULLIFICATION.

So long as the people of any State withheld their assent from the Federal Constitution, it was represented and reprobated by its adversaries as a scheme of absolute and undisguised consolidation. They pointed to its sweeping provisions, whereby all power with regard to war, to treaties, and to diplomatic or commercial intercourse with foreign nations, to the currency, to naturalization, to the support of armies, etc., etc., was expressly withdrawn from the States and concentrated in the Federal Government,[1] as proof irresistible of the correctness of their position. The express inhibition of any alliance, compact, or treaty between two or more of the States, was even more conclusive on this head. They pointed to the fact, that the very preamble to this instrument proclaimed it the work of "the people of the United States," and not a mere alliance or pact between the States themselves in their capacity of separate and sovereign political communities. Patrick Henry urged this latter objection with much force in the Virginia ratifying Convention.[2] These cavilers were answered, frankly and firmly: "It *is* the work of 'the people of the United States,' as distinguished from the States in their primary and sovereign capacity; and why should not the fact be truly stated?" General Washington did not hesitate to assert, in his plain, earnest, practical way, that the end sought by the new framework was the "*consolidation* of

history. In a letter to Thomas Jefferson, December 18, 1819, he said:

"The Missouri question, I hope, will follow the other waves under the ship, and do no harm. I know it is high treason to express a doubt of the perpetual duration of our vast American empire, and our free institutions; and I say as devoutly as father Paul, *esto perpetua:* and I am sometimes Cassandra enough to dream that another Hamilton, another Burr, may rend this mighty fabric in twain, or perhaps into a leash, and a few more choice spirits of the same stamp might produce as many nations in North America as there are in Europe."—*Adams's Works*, vol. x., p. 386.

[1] "1. No State shall enter into any treaty, or confederation; grant letters of marque or reprisal; coin money; emit bills of credit; make any thing but gold and silver coin a tender in payment of debts; pass any bill of attainder, *ex-post-facto* law, or law impairing the obligation of contracts; or grant any title of nobility.

"2. No State shall, without the consent of the Congress, lay any imposts or duties on imports or exports, except what may be absolutely necessary for executing its inspection laws; and the net produce of all duties and imposts laid by any State on imports or exports, shall be for the use of the treasury of the United States; and all such laws shall be subject to the revision and control of the Congress. No State shall, without the consent of Congress, lay any duty on tonnage, keep troops or ships of war in time of peace, enter into any agreement or compact with another State or with a foreign power, or engage in war unless actually invaded, or in such imminent danger as will not admit of delay."—*The Constitution*, Art. I., sec. 10.

[2] In the Virginia Convention (Wednesday, June 4, 1788, and the day following) Mr. Henry spoke as follows:

"That this is a consolidated government is demonstrably clear; and the danger of such a government is, to my mind, very striking. I have the highest veneration for those gentlemen [who formed the Constitution]; but, Sir, give me leave to demand, What right had they to say, *We, the people?* My political curiosity, exclusive of my anxious solicitude for the public welfare, leads me to ask, Who authorized them to say, *We, the people*, instead of *We, the States?* States are the characteristics and the soul of a confederation. If the States be not the agents of this compact, it must be one great, consolidated, national government, of the people of all the States. * * * I need not take much pains to show that the principles of this system are extremely pernicious, impolitic, and dangerous." —*Elliot's Debates*, vol. iii., pp. 22, 44.

our Union,"[3] which he never ceased to regard as of the highest importance and the greatest beneficence. History teaches scarcely anything more clearly than that it was the purpose of the framers of the Constitution to render the inhabitants of all the States substantially and perpetually one people, living under a common Government, and known to the rest of mankind by a common national designation.[4] The advantages secured to the people of all the States by the "more perfect Union" attained through the Constitution, were so striking and manifest that, after they had been for a few years experienced and enjoyed, they silenced all direct and straightforward opposition. Those who had originally opposed and denounced the Constitution became—at least in profession—its most ardent admirers and vigilant guardians. They volunteered their services as its champions and protectors against those who had framed it and with difficulty achieved its ratification. These were plainly and persistently accused of seeking its subversion through the continual enlargement of Federal power by latitudinous and unwarranted construction.[5] They vehemently disclaimed any desire to return to the chronic feebleness and anarchy of the supplanted Confederation, and consecrated their energies to battling against the measureless ills of an unbalanced and centralized despotism. They generally rejected the appellation of Anti-Federalists, and chose to be distinctively known as *Republicans*. Thomas Jefferson, who had been absent as embassador to France throughout the five or six preceding years, and who had therefore taken no conspicuous or decided part either for or against the Constitution in its incipiency, became the leader, and was for many years thereafter the oracle, of their party.

The Federalists, strong in the possession of power, and in the popularity and influence of their great chief, Washington, were early misled into some capital blunders. Among these was the passage of the acts of Congress, famous as the Alien and Sedition laws. The aliens, whom the political tempests then convulsing Europe had drifted in large numbers to our shores, were in good part turbulent, restless adventurers, of desperate fortunes, who sought to embroil

[3] In the address of the Federal Convention to the people, signed by Washington as its President, September 17, 1787.

[4] "Citizens by birth or choice of a common country, that country has a right to concentrate your affections. The name of AMERICAN, which belongs to you in your National capacity, must always exalt the just pride of Patriotism, more than any appellation derived from local discriminations."—*Washington's Farewell Address.*

[5] In the Federal Convention of 1787 (Debate of Monday, June 18th):

Mr. HAMILTON, of New York, said: "The General power, whatever be its form, if it preserves itself, must swallow up the State Governments. Otherwise, it would be swallowed up by them. It is against all the principles of good government to vest the requisite powers in such a body as Congress. Two sovereignties cannot exist within the same limits."

Mr. WILSON, of Pennsylvania (June 20th), "was tenacious of the idea of preserving the State Governments." But in the next day's debate: "Taking the matter in the more general view, he saw no danger to the States from the General Government. On the contrary, he conceived that, in spite of every precaution, the General Government would be in perpetual danger of encroachments from the State Governments." And

Mr. MADISON, of Virginia, "was of the opinion, in the first place, that there was less danger of encroachment from the General Government than from the State Governments; and, in the second place, that the mischiefs from the encroachments would be less fatal, if made by the former, than if made by the latter."—*Madison's Papers*, vol. ii., pp. 884, 903, 921.

us in the contest then devastating the Old World. Washington, and the Federal magnates who surrounded him, were inflexibly averse to this, and baffled all attempts to involve us in a foreign war. This very naturally offended the European refugees among us, who looked anxiously to this country for interference to reëstablish them in power and prosperity in their own. Hence, they generally took the lead in reprobating and stigmatizing the negotiation and approval of Jay's treaty[6] with Great Britain, whereby our past differences and misunderstandings with that power were adjusted. They were in good part politicians and agitators by trade, instinctively hostile to a government so cold-blooded and unimpulsive as ours, and ardently desired a change. Regarding them as dangerous and implacable enemies to the established policy of non-intervention, and to those who upheld it, the Alien law assumed to empower the President to send out of the country any foreigner whose further stay among us should be deemed by him incompatible with the public safety or tranquillity. The Sedition law provided for the prosecution and punishment of the authors of false, malicious, and wicked libels on the President, and others high in authority. The facts that no one ever *was* sent away under the Alien act, and that the Sedition law was hardly more than the common law of libel applied specially to those who should venture to speak evil of dignities, proved rather the folly of such legislation than its necessity or its accordance with the Constitution. Party spirit and party feeling ran high. It was far easier to libel a hated opponent than to refute his arguments. The best newspapers of that day would hardly maintain a comparison, either for ability or decorum, with the third class of our time; and personalities largely supplied the place of learning and logic. Hence, many prosecutions under the Sedition law; some of them, doubtless, richly deserved; but all tending to excite hostility to the act and its authors. No other contributed half so palpably to the ultimate overthrow of the Federal ascendency.

When John Adams became President, in 1797, the South had become the stronghold of the Opposition. Mr. Madison had dissolved his earlier association with the great body of the framers of the Constitution, and become the lieutenant of Mr. Jefferson. Kentucky—a Virginia colony and offset—was ardently and almost unanimously devoted to the ideas and the fortunes of Jefferson; and he was privately solicited to draft the manifesto, through which the new State beyond the Alleghanies proclaimed, in 1798, her intense hostility to Federal rule. The famous "Resolutions of '98" were thus originated; Mr. Jefferson's authorship, though suspected, was never established until he avowed it in a letter more than twenty years afterward. These resolutions are too long to be here quoted in full, but the first is as follows:

"*Resolved*, That the several States composing the United States of America are not united on the principle of unlimited submission to their General Government; but that, by a compact under the style and title of a Constitution for the United States, and of amendments thereto, they constituted a General Government for special purposes—

[6] Signed November 19, 1794; ratified by Washington, August 14, 1795.

delegated to that Government certain definite powers, reserving, each State to itself, the residuary mass of right to their own self-government; and that whensoever the General Government assumes undelegated powers, its acts are unauthoritative, void, and of no force; that to this compact each State acceded as a State, and as an integral party, its co-States forming, as to itself, the other party; that the Government created by this compact was not made the exclusive or final judge of the extent of the powers delegated to itself; since that would have made its discretion, and not the Constitution, the measure of its powers; but that, as in all other cases of compact among powers having no common judge, each party has an equal right to judge for itself, as well of infractions as of the mode and measure of redress."

The resolves proceed, at great length, to condemn not only the Alien and Sedition laws, as utterly unconstitutional and void, but even the act, recently passed, to punish frauds committed on the Bank of the United States, as well as other acts and parts of acts; and conclude with a call on the other States to unite with Kentucky in condemning and opposing all such usurpations of power by the Federal Government, and by expressing her undoubting confidence

"That they will concur with this commonwealth in considering the said acts as so palpably against the Constitution as to amount to an undisguised declaration that that compact is not meant to be the measure of the powers of the General Government, but that it will proceed in the exercise, over these States, of all powers whatsoever: that they will view this as seizing the rights of the States, and consolidating them in the hands of the General Government, with the power assumed to bind the States (not merely as to the cases made federal (*casus fœderis*), but) in all cases whatsoever, by laws made, not with their consent, but by others against their consent: that this would be to surrender the form of government we have chosen, and live under one deriving its powers from its own will, and not from our authority; and that the co-States, returning to their natural right in cases not made federal, will concur in declaring these acts void and of no force, and will each take measures of its own in providing that neither these acts, nor any others of the General Government, not plainly and intentionally authorized by the Constitution, shall be exercised within their respective territories.

"9th. *Resolved*, That the said Committee be authorized to communicate, by writing or personal conferences, at any times or places whatever, with any person or persons who may be appointed by any one or more co-States to correspond or confer with them, and that they lay their proceedings before the next session of Assembly."

The Virginia resolves on the same subject, passed by her Legislature in 1799, were drafted by Mr. Madison—doubtless after consultation with his chief, Mr. Jefferson—and did not differ materially in spirit or expression from those of Kentucky.

Mr. Jefferson became President on the 4th of March, 1801. Up to this hour, he had been an extreme and relentless stickler for the most rigid and literal construction of the Federal pact, and for denying to the Government all authority for which express warrant could not be found in the provisions of that instrument. Said he[7]: "In questions of power, then, let no more be heard of confidence in man, but bind him down from mischief by the chains of the Constitution."

His fidelity to his declared principle was soon subjected to a searching ordeal. Louisiana fell into the hands of Bonaparte, who, it was not improbable, might be induced to sell it. It was for us a desirable acquisition; but where was the authority for buying it? In the Constitution, there clearly was none, unless under that very power to provide for the general welfare, which, as he had expressly declared, was meant by the instrument "to be subsidiary only to the execution of limited powers."[8] He

[7] Eighth Kentucky Resolve.

[8] Seventh Kentucky Resolve.

was quite too large and frank a man to pretend that his action in this case was justified by the Constitution, as he understood and had always interpreted it. He said:[9]

"This treaty must of course be laid before both Houses, because both have important functions to exercise respecting it. They, I presume, will see their duty to their country in ratifying and paying for it, so as to secure a good which would otherwise be probably never again in their power. But I suppose they must then appeal to the nation for an additional article to the Constitution, approving and confirming an act which the nation had not previously authorized. The Constitution has made no provision for our holding foreign territory, still less for incorporating foreign nations into our Union. The Executive, in seizing the fugitive occurrence which so much advances the good of their country, have done an act beyond the Constitution. The Legislature, in casting behind them metaphysical subtleties, and risking themselves like faithful servants, must ratify and pay for it, and throw themselves on their country for doing for them unauthorized what we know they would have done for themselves had they been in a situation to do it. It is the case of a guardian, investing the money of his ward in purchasing an important adjacent territory; and saying to him, when of age, 'I did this for your good; I pretend to no right to bind you: you may disavow me, and I must get out of the scrape as I can. I thought it my duty to risk myself for you.' But we shall not be disavowed by the nation, and their act of indemnity will confirm, and not weaken, the Constitution, by more strongly marking out its lines."

In a letter to Wilson C. Nicholas,[10] he examines and thoroughly refutes the assumption, suggested by Mr. N., that the power to purchase Louisiana "might possibly be distilled from the authority given to Congress to admit new States into the Union." He says: "But when I consider that the limits of the United States are precisely fixed by the treaty of 1783, and that the Constitution expressly declares itself to be made for the United States, I cannot help believing the intention was not to permit Congress to admit into the Union new States, which should be formed outside of the territory for which, and under whose authority alone, they were then acting. I do not believe it was meant that they might receive England, Ireland, Holland, etc., into it, which would be the case on your construction." After disposing in like manner of "the opinion of those who consider the grant of the treaty-making power as boundless," and completing his demonstration that there was no power whatever in the Constitution, as he construed it, to make this purchase, he, with more good sense than consistency, concludes: "I confess, then, I think it important, in the present case, to set an example against broad construction, by appealing for new power to the people. If, however, our friends shall think differently, certainly I shall acquiesce with satisfaction; confiding, that the good sense of our country will correct the evil of construction when it shall produce ill effects."

When, in 1811, the Territory of Orleans was moulded into the State of Louisiana, Mr. Josiah Quincy, a young and very ardent Federalist who then represented the city of Boston in the House, indulged in what resembled very closely a menace of contingent secession; and similar fulminations were uttered by sundry New England Federalists under the pressure of Mr. Jefferson's Embargo and of the War of 1812. The famous but unsavory Hartford Convention,[11] held near the close of that war, and

[9] Letter to Senator Breckinridge, August 12, 1803.

[10] September 7, 1803.

[11] For proceedings of this Convention, see *Niles's Register*, January 14, 1815.

by which the ruin of the Federal party was completed, evinced its discontent with matters in general, but especially with Democracy and the War, by a resort to rhetoric which was denounced as tending to disunion, but which does not seem to warrant the imputation. And whenever the right of secession or of nullification has been asserted, whether directly or by clear implication, in any part of the country, or by any party out of power, such assertion has called forth expressions of emphatic rebuke and dissent from other sections[12] and antagonistic parties. Mr. Webster,[13] in replying to Mr. Hayne of South Carolina on this subject, forcibly said:

"I understood the gentleman to maintain, that, without revolution, without civil commotion, without rebellion, a remedy for supposed abuse and transgression of the powers of the General Government lies in a direct appeal to the interference of the State Governments."

Mr. Hayne here rose and said: "He did not contend for the mere right of revolution, but for the right of constitutional resistance. What he maintained was that, in case of a plain, palpable violation of the Constitution by the General Government, a State may interpose; and that this interposition is constitutional."

Mr. Webster resumed:—"So, Sir, I understood the gentleman, and am happy to find that I did not misunderstand him. What he contends for is, that it is constitutional to interrupt the administration of the Constitution itself, in the hands of those who are chosen and sworn to administer it, by the direct interference, in form of law, of the States, in virtue of their sovereign capacity. The inherent right of the people to reform their government, I do not deny; and they have another right, and that is, to resist unconstitutional laws, without overturning the government. It is no doctrine of mine that unconstitutional laws bind the people. The great question is, 'Whose prerogative is it to decide on the constitutionality or unconstitutionality of the laws?' On that, the main debate hinges. The proposition that, in case of a supposed violation of the Constitution by Congress, the States have a constitutional right to interfere and annul the law of Congress, is the proposition of the gentleman. I do not admit it. If the gentleman had intended no more than to assert the right of revolution for justifiable cause, he would have said only what all agree to. But I cannot conceive that there can be a middle course between submission to the laws, when regularly pronounced constitutional, on the one hand, and open resistance, which is revolution or rebellion, on the other. I say, the right of a State to annul a law of Congress cannot be maintained, but on the ground of the inalienable right of man to resist oppression; that is to say, upon the ground of revolution. I admit that there is an ultimate violent remedy, above the Constitution and in defiance of the Constitution, which may be resorted to when a revolution is to be justified. But I *do not* admit that, under the Constitution, and in conformity with it, there is any mode in which a State Government, as a member of the Union, can interfere and stop the progress of the general movement, by force of her own laws, under any circumstances whatever. * * * Sir, the human mind is so constituted that the merits of both sides of a controversy appear very clear, and very palpable, to those who respectively espouse them; and both sides usually grow clearer as the controversy advances. South Carolina sees unconstitutionality in the tariff; she sees oppression there also; and she sees danger. Pennsylvania, with a vision not less sharp, looks at the same tariff, and sees no such thing in it; she sees it all constitutional, all useful, all safe. The faith of South Carolina is strengthened by opposition, and she now not only sees, but *resolves*, that the tariff is palpably unconstitutional, oppressive, and dangerous; but Pennsylvania, not to be behind her neighbors, and equally willing to strengthen her own faith by a confident asseveration, *resolves* also, and gives to every

[12] The following extract is a fair specimen of the prevailing sentiment, at the time of the assembling of the "Hartford Convention," of the South—including South Carolina—on the subject of Secession:

"No man, no association of men, *no State or set of States*, has a right to withdraw itself from this Union, of its own account. The same power that knit us together can unknit. The same formality which formed the links of the Union is necessary to dissolve it. The majority of the States which formed the Union must consent to the withdrawal of any branch of it. *Until that consent has been obtained, any attempt to dissolve the Union, or distract the efficacy of its laws, is* TREASON—*treason to all intents and purposes.*"—*Richmond Enquirer*, November 1, 1814.

[13] Debate on Foot's resolutions, January 26, 1830.

warm affirmative of South Carolina a plain, downright, Pennsylvania negative. South Carolina, to show the strength and unity of her opinion, brings her assembly to a unanimity, within seven voices; Pennsylvania, not to be outdone in this respect any more than in others, reduces her dissentient fraction to a single vote. Now, Sir, again I ask the gentleman, What is to be done? Are these States both right? If not, which is in the wrong? or, rather, which has the best right to decide? And if he, and if I, are not to know what the Constitution means, and what it is, till those two State Legislatures, and the twenty-two others, shall agree in its construction, what have we sworn to when we have sworn to maintain it? I was forcibly struck, Sir, with one reflection, as the gentleman went on in his speech. He quoted Mr. Madison's resolutions[14] to prove that a State may interfere, in a case of deliberate, palpable, and dangerous exercise of a power not granted. The honorable member supposes the tariff law to be such an exercise of power; and that, consequently, a case has arisen in which the State may, if it see fit, interfere by its own law. Now it so happens, nevertheless, that Mr. Madison deems this same tariff law quite constitutional! Instead of a clear and palpable violation, it is, in his judgment, no violation at all. So that, while they use his authority for a hypothetical case, they reject it in the very case before them. All this, Sir, shows the inherent futility—I had almost used a stronger word—of conceding this power of interference to the States, and then attempting to secure it from abuse by imposing qualifications of which the States themselves are to judge. One of two things is true: either the laws of the Union are beyond the discretion and beyond the control of the States; or else we have no constitution of General Government, and are thrust back again to the days of the Confederation."

In his brief speech, which closed that debate, and finished the doctrine of Nullification, Mr. Webster said:

"Sir, if I were to concede to the gentleman his principal proposition, namely, that the Constitution is a compact between States, the question would still be, What provision is made in this compact to settle points of disputed construction, or contested power, that shall come into controversy? And this question would still be answered, and conclusively answered, by the Constitution itself. While the gentleman is contending against construction, he himself is setting up the most dangerous and loose construction. The Constitution declares that, *the laws of Congress passed in pursuance of the Constitution shall be the supreme law of the land.* No construction is necessary here. It declares also, with equal plainness and precision, *that the judicial power of the United States shall extend to every case arising under the laws of Congress.* This needs no construction. Here is a law, then, which is declared to be supreme; and here is a power established, which is to interpret that law. Now, Sir, how has the gentleman met this? Suppose the Constitution to be a compact, yet here are its terms; and how does the gentleman get rid of them? He cannot argue the *seal off the bond*, nor the words out of the instrument. Here they are; what answer does he give to them? None in the world, Sir, except, that the effect of this would be to place the States in a condition of inferiority; and that it results from the very nature of things, there being no superior, that the parties must be their own judges! Thus closely and cogently does the honorable gentleman reason on the words of the Constitution! The gentleman says, if there be such a power of final decision in the General Government, he asks for the grant of that power. Well, Sir, I show him the grant. I turn him to the very words. I show him that the laws of Congress are made supreme; and that the judicial power extends, by express words, to the interpretation of these laws. Instead of answering this, he retreats into the general reflection, that it must result *from the nature of things*, that the States, being parties, must judge for themselves.

"I have admitted, that, if the Constitution were to be considered as the creature of the State governments, it might be modified, interpreted, or construed according to their pleasure. But, even in that case, it would be necessary that they should *agree.* One alone could not interpret it conclusively; one alone could not construe it; one alone could not modify it. Yet the gentleman's doctrine is, that Carolina alone may construe and interpret that compact, which equally binds all, and gives equal rights to all.

"So, then, Sir, even supposing the Constitution to be a compact between the States, the gentleman's doctrine, nevertheless, is not maintainable; because first, the General Government is not a party to the compact, but a *government* established by it, and vested by it with the powers of trying and deciding doubtful questions; and, secondly, because, if the Constitution be regarded as a compact, not one State only, but *all* the States, are parties to that compact, and one

[14] The Virginia Resolves of 1799.

can have no right to fix upon it her own peculiar construction."

Andrew Jackson and John C. Calhoun—two of the most remarkable men ever produced in this or any other country—were destined to lead the rival forces by which the Nullification issue was finally brought to a practical conclusion. Though they became and died fierce antagonists, and even bitter personal enemies, their respective characters and careers exhibited many points of resemblance. Each was of that "Scotch-Irish" Presbyterian stock with which Cromwell repeopled the north of Ireland from Scotland, after having all but exterminated its original Celtic and Catholic inhabitants, who resisted and defied his authority. That Scotch-Irish blood to this day evinces something of the Cromwellian energy, courage, and sturdiness. Each was of Revolutionary Whig antecedents—Jackson, though but thirteen years of age, having been in arms for the patriotic cause in 1780; his brother Hugh having died in the service the preceding year. Andrew (then but fourteen), with his brother Robert, was taken prisoner by the British in 1781, and wounded in the head and arm while a captive, for refusing to clean his captor's boots. His brother was, for a like offense, knocked down and disabled. John C. Calhoun was only born in the last year of the Revolutionary War; but his father, Patrick Calhoun, was an ardent and active Whig throughout the struggle. Each was early left fatherless—Andrew Jackson's father having died before his illustrious son was born; while the father of John C. Calhoun died when his son was still in his early teens. Each was by birth a South Carolinian; for, though General Jackson's birth-place is claimed by his biographers for North Carolina, he expressly asserted South Carolina[15] to be his native State, in the most important and memorable document to which his name is appended, and which flowed not merely from his pen, but from his heart. Each was of the original Anti-Federal, strict-construction school in our politics—Calhoun's father having vehemently opposed the adoption of the Federal Constitution; while Jackson, entering Congress as the sole representative of the newly admitted State of Tennessee (December 5, 1796), voted in a minority of twelve against the address tendering to General Washington, on his retirement from the Presidency, a respectful expression of the profound admiration and gratitude wherewith his whole public career was regarded by Congress and the country. General Jackson was not merely an extreme Republican of the Jeffersonian State-Rights School; he was understood to side with Colonel Hayne at the time of his great debate on Nullification with Mr. Webster. Each entered Congress before attaining his thirtieth year, having already taken a conspicuous part in public affairs. Each was first chosen to the House, but served later and longer in the Senate. Each was a slaveholder through most of his career, always found on the side of Slavery in any controversy affecting its claims or interests during his public life; and neither emanci-

[15] "Fellow-citizens of *my native State!*"—appealing to South Carolinians in his Proclamation against the Nullifiers, Dec. 11, 1832. He can hardly have been mistaken on this head.

pated his slaves by his will. Each became, for the first time, a candidate for the Presidency in 1824, when each counted with confidence on the powerful support of Pennsylvania. When that State, through her leading politicians, decided to support Jackson, Calhoun fell out of the race, but was made Vice-President without serious opposition; General Jackson receiving a plurality of the electoral votes for President, but failing of success in the House. In 1828, their names were placed on the same ticket, and they were triumphantly elected President and Vice-President respectively, receiving more than two-thirds of the electoral votes, including those of every State south of the Potomac. This is the only instance wherein the President and Vice-President were both chosen from those distinctively known as Slave States; though New York was nominally and legally a Slave State when her Aaron Burr, George Clinton, and Daniel D. Tompkins were each chosen Vice-President with the last three Virginian Presidents respectively. Alike tall in stature, spare in frame, erect in carriage, austere in morals, imperious in temper, of dauntless courage, and inflexible will, Jackson and Calhoun were each fitted by nature to direct, to govern, and to mould feebler men to his ends; but they were not fitted to coalesce and work harmoniously together. They had hardly become the accepted chiefs of the same great, predominant party, before they quarreled; and their feud, never healed, exerted a signal and baneful influence on the future of their country.

The Protective Policy, though its earliest conspicuous champion in our national councils was Alexander Hamilton, General Washington's Secretary of the Treasury, came, at a later day, to be mainly championed by Republicans. The great merchants were leading Federalists; the great sea-ports were mainly Federal strongholds; the seaboard was in good part Federal: it yearned for extensive and ever-expanding commerce, and mistakenly, but naturally, regarded the fostering of Home Manufactures as hostile to the consummation it desired. Mr. Jefferson's Embargo had borne with great severity upon the mercantile class, inciting a dislike to all manner of commercial restrictions. The interior, on the other hand, was preponderantly Republican, and early comprehended the advantage of a more symmetrical development, a wider diversification, of our National Industry, through the legislative encouragement of Home Manufactures. The Messages of all the Republican Presidents, down to and including General Jackson, recognize and affirm the wisdom, beneficence, and constitutionality of Protective legislation. The prëamble to the first tariff act passed by Congress under the Federal Constitution explicitly affirms the propriety of levying imposts, among other ends, "for the protection of Domestic Manufactures." Mr. Jefferson, in his Annual Message of December 14, 1806, after announcing that there is a prospect of an early surplus of Federal revenue over expenditure, proceeds:

"The question, therefore, now comes forward—to what other objects shall these surpluses be appropriated, and the whole surplus of impost, after the entire discharge of the public debt, and during those intervals when the purposes of war shall not call for them? *Shall we suppress the impost and give that advantage to foreign over domestic manufactures?* On a few articles of more general and necessary use, the suppression, in due season, will doubtless be right; but the great mass of the articles on which impost is paid is foreign luxuries, purchased by those only who are rich enough to afford themselves the use of them. Their patriotism would certainly prefer its continuance and application to the great purposes of the public education, roads, rivers, canals, and such other objects of public improvement as it may be thought proper to add to the constitutional enumeration of federal powers. By these operations, new channels of communication will be opened between the States; the lines of separation will disappear; their interests will be identified, and their Union cemented by new and indissoluble ties."

"Education is here placed among the articles of public care, not that it would be proposed to take its ordinary branches out of the hands of private enterprise, which manages so much better all the concerns to which it is equal; but a public institution can alone supply those sciences which, though rarely called for, are yet necessary to complete the circle, all the parts of which contribute to the improvement of the country, and some of them to its preservation. The subject is now proposed for the consideration of Congress, because, if approved, by the time the State Legislatures shall have deliberated on this extension of the federal trusts, and the laws shall be passed, and other arrangements made for their execution, the necessary funds will be on hand and without employment. I suppose an amendment to the Constitution, by consent of the States, necessary, because the objects now recommended are not among those enumerated in the Constitution, and to which it permits the public moneys to be applied."

Mr. Jefferson, it will be seen, suggests an amendment to the Constitution, to give Congress power to raise and appropriate money to the "great purposes of education, roads, rivers, canals," etc.; but he betrays no suspicion that the incidental Protection then confessedly enjoyed by our Home Manufactures was given in defiance of "the Constitution as it is." On the contrary, an enlargement of federal power was suggested by him with reference to *new* objects, not to those already provided for. Had *these* required such enlargement, the duties should have been repealed or reduced at once, to be reimposed whenever Congress should be clothed with the requisite constitutional power.

Henry Clay entered Congress under Jefferson, in 1806, and was an earnest, thorough, enlightened Protectionist from the start. Mr. Calhoun first took his seat in 1811, when the question of war with Great Britain dwarfed all others; and his zealous efforts, together with those of Clay, Felix Grundy, and other ardent young Republicans, finally overbore the reluctance of Madison and his more sedate councilors, and secured a Declaration of War on the 18th of June, 1812. At the close of that war, a revision of the existing Tariff was imperatively required; and no man did more than John C. Calhoun—then, for his last term, a leading member of the House—to secure the efficient Protection of Home Manufactures, but especially of the Cotton Manufacture, by the Tariff of 1816; which Massachusetts, and most of New England, opposed, precisely because it *was* Protective, and therefore, in the short-sighted view, hostile to the interests of Commerce and Navigation. Internal Improvements, and all other features of what was termed the National in contradistinction to the Radical or strict-construction theory of the nature and functions of our Federal Government, found in Mr. Calhoun and his personal adherents their most thorough-going champions: and South Carolina was, about 1820, the arena of a stirring conflict between her "National" school of politicians, headed by Calhoun and McDuffie, and the "Radicals," whose chief was William H. Crawford, of Georgia. Repeated duels between Mr. McDuffie and Colonel William Cuming, of Georgia, in one of which McDuffie was severely wounded, were among the incidents of this controversy. Yet but few years elapsed before Mr. Calhoun and his trusty henchman, McDuffie, appeared in the novel character of champions of "State Rights," and relentless antagonists of Protection, and all the "National" projects they had hitherto supported! Mr. Calhoun attempted, some years afterward, to reconcile this flagrant inconsistency; but it was like "arguing the seal off the bond"—a feat to which the subtlest powers of casuistry are utterly inadequate. He *did* prove, however, that his change did not follow, but preceded, his quarrel with General Jackson—his original, though then unacknowledged, demonstration against Protection as unconstitutional, and in favor of Nullification as a reserved right of each State, having been embodied in an elaborate document known as "The South Carolina Exposition," adopted and put forth by the Legislature of his State near the close of 1828. The doctrines therein affirmed were those propounded by Hayne and refuted by Webster in the great debate already noticed.

The Tariff of 1828—the highest and most protective ever adopted in this country—was passed by a Jackson Congress, of which Van Buren, Silas Wright, and the Jacksonian leaders in Pennsylvania and Ohio, were master-spirits. It was opposed by most of the members from the Cotton States, and by a majority of those from New England—some provisions having been engrafted upon it with the alleged purpose and the certain effect of making it obnoxious to Massachusetts and the States which, on either side, adjoined her. On the other hand, the members from the Middle and Western Free States, without distinction of party, supported it almost unanimously. This Tariff imposed high duties on Iron, Lead, Hemp, Wool, and other bulky staples, and was very generally popular. Under it, the industry of the Free States, regarded as a whole, was more productive, more prosperous, better rewarded, than ever before, and the country exhibited a rapid growth in wealth, intelligence, and general comfort.

The South—that is, the cotton-growing region—for Louisiana, through her sugar-planting interest, sustained the Protective policy, and shared in the prosperity thence resulting—now vehemently opposed the Tariff, declaring herself thereby plundered and impoverished. There is no evidence that her condition was less favorable, her people less comfortable, than they had been; but the contrast between the thrift, progress, and activity of the Free States, and the stagnation, the inertia, the poverty, of the cotton region, was very striking. And, as the South was gradually unlearning her Revolutionary principles, and adopting instead the dogma that Slavery is essentially right and beneficent, she could not now be induced to apprehend, nor even to consider, the real cause of her comparative wretchedness; though she was more than once kindly and delicately reminded of it. Mr. George M. Dallas,[16] of Pennsylvania—a life-long Democrat and anti-Abolitionist, cautious, conservative, conciliatory—replying to one of Mr. Hayne's eloquent and high-wrought portrayals of the miserable state to which the South and her industry had been reduced by the Protective policy, forcibly and truthfully said:

"What, Sir, is the cause of Southern distress? Has any gentleman yet ventured to designate it? I am neither willing nor competent to flatter. To praise the honorable Senator from South Carolina would be

'To add perfume to the violet—
Wasteful and ridiculous excess.'

But, if *he* has failed to discover the source of the evils he deplores, who can unfold it? Amid the warm and indiscriminating denunciations with which he has assailed the policy of protecting domestic manufactures and native produce, he frankly avows that he would not 'deny that there are other causes, besides the Tariff, which have contributed to produce the evils which he has depicted.' What are those 'other causes?' In what proportion have they acted? How much of this dark shadowing is ascribable to each singly, and to all in combination? Would the Tariff be at all felt or denounced, if those other causes were not in operation? Would not, in fact, its influence, its discriminations, its inequalities, its oppressions, but for those 'other causes,' be shaken, by the elasticity, energy, and exhaustless spirit of the South, as 'dew-drops from the lion's mane?' These inquiries must be satisfactorily answered before we can be justly required to legislate away an entire system. If it be the root of all evil, let it be exposed and demolished. If its poisonous exhalations be but partial, let us preserve such portions as are innoxious. If, as the luminary of day, it be pure and salutary in itself, let us not wish it extinguished, because of the shadows, clouds, and darkness, which obscure its brightness, or impede its vivifying power.

"That 'other causes' still, Mr. President, for Southern distress, do exist, cannot be doubted. They combine with the one I have indicated, and are equally unconnected with the manufacturing policy. One of these it is peculiarly painful to advert to; and when I mention it, I beg honorable Senators not to suppose that I do it in the spirit of taunt, of reproach, or of idle declamation. Regarding it as a misfortune merely, not as a fault—as a disease inherited, not incurred—perhaps to be alleviated, but not eradicated—I should feel self-condemned were I to treat it other than as an existing fact, whose merit or demerit, apart from the question under debate, is shielded from commentary by the highest and most just considerations. I refer, Sir, to the character of Southern labor, in itself, and in its influence on others. Incapable of adaptation to the ever-varying changes of human society and existence, it retains the communities in which it is established, in a condition of apparent and comparative inertness. The lights of Science and the improvements of Art, which vivify and accelerate elsewhere, cannot penetrate, or if they do, penetrate with dilatory inefficiency, among its operatives. They are not merely instinctive and passive. While the intellectual industry of other parts of this country springs elastically forward at every fresh impulse, and manual labor is propelled and redoubled by countless inventions, machines, and contrivances, instantly understood and at once exercised, the South remains stationary, inaccessible to such encouraging and invigorating aids. Nor is it possible to be wholly blind to the moral effect of this species of labor upon those freemen among whom it exists. A disrelish for humble and hardy occupation; a pride adverse to drudgery and toil; a dread that to partake in the employments allotted to color may be accompanied also by its degradation, are natural and inevitable. The high and lofty qualities which, in other scenes and for other purposes, characterize and adorn our Southern brethren, are fatal to the enduring patience, the corporal exertion, and the painstaking simplicity, by which only a successful yeomanry can be formed. When, in fact, Sir, the Senator from South Carolina asserts that 'Slaves are too improvident, too incapable of that minute, constant, delicate attention, and that persevering industry which are essential to manufacturing establishments,' he himself admits the defect in Southern labor, by which the progress of his favorite section must be retarded. He admits an inability to keep pace with the rest of the world. He admits an inherent weakness; a weakness neither engendered nor aggravated by the Tariff—which, as societies are now constituted and directed, must drag in the rear, and be distanced in the common race."

South Carolina did not heed these

[16] Speech in the Senate, February 27, 1832.

gentle admonitions. The convictions of her leading men were, doubtless, Pro-Slavery and Anti-Tariff; but their aspirations and exasperations likewise tended to confirm them in the course on which they had resolved and entered. General Jackson and Mr. Calhoun had become estranged and hostile not long after their joint election as President and Vice-President, in 1828. Mr. Calhoun's sanguine hopes of succeeding to the Presidency had been blasted. Mr. Van Buren supplanted him as Vice-President in 1832, sharing in Jackson's second and most decided triumph. And, though the Tariff of 1828 had been essentially modified during the preceding session of Congress, South Carolina proceeded, directly after throwing away her vote in the election of 1832, to call a Convention of her people, which met at her Capitol on the 19th of November. That Convention was composed of her leading politicians of the Calhoun school, with the heads of her great families, forming a respectable and dignified assemblage. The net result of its labors was an Ordinance of Nullification, drafted by a grand Committee of twenty-one, and adopted with entire unanimity. By its terms, the existing Tariff was formally pronounced "null, void, and no law, nor binding on this State, its officers, or citizens," and the duties on imports imposed by that law were forbidden to be paid within the State of South Carolina after the 1st day of February ensuing. The Ordinance contemplated an act of the Legislature nullifying the Tariff as aforesaid; and prescribed that no appeal to the Supreme Court of the United States against the validity of said act should be permitted; no copy of the proceedings should be taken for the purpose of making such appeal; and any attempt to appeal to the Judiciary of the United States from any decision of a State court affirming and upholding this Ordinance, should be "dealt with as for a contempt of the court" thus upholding and affirming. Every office-holder of the State, and "every juror" was required expressly to swear to obey this Ordinance, and all legislative acts based thereon. Should the Federal Government undertake to enforce the law thus nullified, or in any manner to harass or obstruct the foreign commerce of the State, South Carolina should thereupon consider herself no longer a member of the Federal Union:

> "The people of this State will thenceforth hold themselves absolved from all further obligation to maintain or preserve their political connection with the people of the other States, and will forthwith proceed to organize a separate government, and do all other acts and things which sovereign and independent States may of right do."

Thus was Nullification[17] embodied in an Ordinance preparatory to its reduction to practice. The Legislature, in which the Nullifiers were an overwhelming majority, elected Mr. Webster's luckless antagonist, Robert Y. Hayne, Governor of the State; and the Governor, in his Message, thoroughly indorsed the action of the nullifying Convention, whereof he had been a member.

> "I recognize," said he, "no allegiance as paramount to that which the citizens of South Carolina owe to the State of their birth or their adoption. I here publicly declare, and wish it to be distinctly understood, that I shall hold myself bound, by the highest of all obligations, to carry into effect, not only the Ordinance of the Con-

[17] November 24, 1832.

vention, but every act of the Legislature, and every judgment of our own courts, the enforcement of which may devolve upon the executive. I claim no right to revise their acts. It will be my duty to execute them; and that duty I mean, to the utmost of my power, faithfully to perform."

He proceeded:

"If the sacred soil of Carolina should be polluted by the footsteps of an invader, or be stained with the blood of her citizens, shed in her defense, I trust in Almighty God that no son of hers, native or adopted, who has been nourished at her bosom, or been cherished by her bounty, will be found raising a parricidal arm against our common mother. And even should she stand ALONE in this great struggle for constitutional liberty, encompassed by her enemies, that there will not be found, in the wide limits of the State, one recreant son who will not fly to the rescue, and be ready to lay down his life in her defense. South Carolina cannot be drawn down from the proud eminence on which she has now placed herself, except by the hands of her own children. Give her but a fair field, and she asks no more. Should she succeed, hers will be glory enough to have led the way in the noble work of REFORM. And if, after making these efforts due to her own honor, and the greatness of the cause, she is destined utterly to fail, the bitter fruits of that failure, not to herself alone, but to the entire South, nay, to the whole Union, will attest her virtue."

The Legislature proceeded to pass the acts requisite to give practical effect to the Ordinance, and the Governor to accept the services of volunteers, who were not mustered into service, but directed to hold themselves in readiness for action at a moment's notice. Mr. Calhoun resigned the Vice-Presidency when he had three months still to serve, and was chosen to the Senate to fill the seat vacated by Mr. Hayne's acceptance of the governorship. Leaving his State foaming and surging with preparations for war, Mr. Calhoun, in December, calmly proceeded to Washington, where he took his seat in the Senate, and swore afresh to maintain the Constitution, as if unconscious of the tempest he had excited, and which was now preparing to burst upon his head.

General Jackson had already[18] made provision for the threatened emergency. Ordering General Scott to proceed to Charleston for the purpose of "superintending the safety of the ports of the United States in that vicinity," and making the requisite disposition of the slender military and naval forces at his command, the President sent confidential orders to the Collector for the port of Charleston, whereof the following extract sufficiently indicates the character and purpose:

"Upon the supposition that the measures of the Convention, or the acts of the Legislature may consist, in part, at least, in declaring the laws of the United States imposing duties unconstitutional, and null and void, and in forbidding their execution, and the collection of the duties within the State of South Carolina, you will, immediately after it shall be formally announced, resort to all the means provided by the laws, and particularly by the act of the 2d of March, 1799, to counteract the measures which may be adopted to give effect to that declaration.

"For this purpose, you will consider yourself authorized to employ the revenue cutters which may be within your district, and provide as many boats and employ as many inspectors as may be necessary for the execution of the law, and for the purposes of the act already referred to. You will, moreover, cause a sufficient number of officers of cutters and inspectors to be placed on board, and in charge of every vessel arriving from a foreign port or place, with goods, wares, or merchandise, as soon as practicable after her first coming within your district, and direct them to anchor her in some safe place within the harbor, where she may be secure from any act of violence, and from any unauthorized attempt to discharge her cargo before a compliance with the laws; and they will remain on board of her at such place until the reports and entries required by law shall be made, both of vessel and cargo, and the duties paid, or secured to be paid, to your satisfaction, and until the regular permit shall be granted for

[18] November 6th.

landing the cargo; and it will be your duty, against any forcible attempt, to retain and defend the custody of the said vessel, by the aid of the officers of the customs, inspectors, and officers of the cutters, until the requisitions of the law shall be fully complied with; and, in case of any attempt to remove her or her cargo from the custody of the officers of the customs, by the form of legal process from State tribunals, you will not yield the custody to such attempt, but will consult the law officer of the district, and employ such means as, under the particular circumstances, you may legally do, to resist such process, and prevent the removal of the vessel and cargo.

"Should the entry of such vessel and cargo not be completed, and the duties paid, or secured to be paid, by bond or bonds, with sureties to your satisfaction, within the time limited by law, you will, at the expiration of that time, take possession of the cargo, and land and store the same at Castle Pinckney, or some other safe place, and, in due time, if the duties are not paid, sell the same, according to the direction of the 56th section of the act of the 2d of March, 1799; and you are authorized to provide such stores as may be necessary for that purpose."

The contrast between the spirit evinced in these instructions, and that exhibited by General Jackson's successor, on the occurrence of a similar outbreak at Charleston twenty-eight years later, is very striking.

Congress reconvened on the 3d of December; but the President's Message, delivered on the following day, made no allusion to the impending peril of civil convulsion and war. One week later, however, the country was electrified by the appearance of the famous Proclamation, wherein the President's stern resolve to crush Nullification as Treason was fully manifested. And, though this document received its final fashion and polish from the pen of the able and eminent Edward Livingston, who then worthily filled the post of Secretary of State, it is abundantly established[19] that the original draft was the President's own, and that he insisted throughout on expressing and enforcing his own sentiments and convictions. The language may in part be Livingston's; the positions and the principles are wholly Jackson's; and their condemnation of the Calhoun or South Carolina theory of the nature, genius, and limitations of our Federal pact, are as decided and sweeping as any ever propounded by Hamilton, by Marshall, or by Webster himself.

After reciting the purport and effect of the South Carolina Ordinance, General Jackson proceeds:

"The Ordinance is founded, not on the indefeasible right of resisting acts which are plainly unconstitutional and too oppressive to be endured; but on the strange position that any one State may not only declare an act of Congress void, but prohibit its execution; that they may do this consistently with the Constitution; that the true construction of that instrument permits a State to retain its place in the Union, and yet be bound by no other of its laws than those it may choose to consider as constitutional! It is true, they add that, to justify this abrogation of a law, it must be palpably contrary to the Constitution; but it is evident that, to give the right of resisting laws of that description, coupled with the uncontrolled right to decide what laws deserve that character, is to give the power of resisting *all* laws. For, as, by this theory, there is no appeal, the reasons alleged by the State, good or bad, must prevail. If it should be said that public opinion is a sufficient check against the abuse of this power, it may be asked why it is not deemed a sufficient guard against the passage of an unconstitutional act by Congress. There is, however, a restraint in this last case, which makes the assumed power of a State more indefensible, and which does not exist in the other. There are two appeals from an unconstitutional act passed by Congress—one to the Judiciary, the other to the people and the States. There is no appeal from the State decision in theory, and the practical illustration shows that the courts are closed against an application to review it, both judges and jurors being sworn to decide in its favor. But reasoning on this subject is

[19] See Parton's Life of Jackson, pp. 455-6.

superfluous when our social compact in express terms declares that the laws of the United States, its Constitution, and the treaties made under it, are the supreme law of the land; and, for greater caution, adds, 'that the judges in every State shall be bound thereby, anything in the constitution or laws of any State to the contrary notwithstanding.' And it may be asserted, without fear of refutation, that no federative government could exist without a similar provision. Look, for a moment, to the consequences. If South Carolina considers the revenue laws unconstitutional, and has a right to prevent their execution in the port of Charleston, there would be a clear constitutional objection to their collection in every other port, and no revenue could be collected anywhere; for all imposts must be equal. It is no answer to repeat, that an unconstitutional law is no law, so long as the question of legality is to be decided by the State itself; for every law, operating injuriously upon any local interest, will be perhaps thought, and certainly represented as, unconstitutional; and, as has been shown, there is no appeal.

"If this doctrine had been established at an earlier day, the Union would have been dissolved in its infancy. The Excise law in Pennsylvania, the Embargo and Non-Intercourse law in the Eastern States, the carriage-tax in Virginia, were all deemed unconstitutional, and were more unequal in their operation than any of the laws now complained of; but, fortunately, none of those States discovered that they had the right now claimed by South Carolina. The war into which we were forced, to support the dignity of the nation and the rights of our citizens, might have ended in defeat and disgrace, instead of victory and honor, if the States who supposed it a ruinous and unconstitutional measure had thought they possessed the right of nullifying the act by which it was declared, and denying supplies for its prosecution. Hardly and unequally as those measures bore upon several members of the Union, to the Legislatures of none did this efficient and peaceable remedy, as it is called, suggest itself. The discovery of this important feature in our Constitution was reserved for the present day. To the statesmen of South Carolina belongs the invention, and upon the citizens of that State will unfortunately fall the evils of reducing it to practice."

General Jackson summed up his objections to Nullification in these unambiguous terms:

"I consider, then, the power to annul a law of the United States, assumed by one State, *incompatible with the existence of the Union, contradicted expressly by the letter of the Constitution, unauthorized by its spirit, inconsistent with every principle on which it was founded, and destructive of the great object for which it was formed.*"

A little farther on, he proclaimed his concurrence in the "National," as contradistinguished from the "State Rights," theory of our Federation, in these words:

"The Constitution of the United States, then, forms a Government, not a league; and, whether it be formed by compact between the States, or in any other manner, its character is the same. It is a government in which all the people are represented, which acts directly on the people individually, not upon the States—they retained all the power they did not grant. But each State, having expressly parted with so many powers, as to constitute, jointly with the other States, a single nation, cannot, from that period, possess any right to secede; because such secession does not break a league, but destroys the unity of a nation, and any injury to that unity is not only a breach which would result from the contravention of a compact, but it is an offense against the whole Union. *To say that any State may at pleasure secede from the Union, is to say that the United States are not a nation, because it would be a solecism to contend that any part of a nation might dissolve its connection with the other parts, to their injury or ruin, without committing any offense.* Secession, like any other revolutionary act, may be morally justified by the extremity of oppression; but to call it a constitutional right, is confounding the meaning of terms, and can only be done through gross error, or to deceive those who are willing to assert a right, but would pause before they make a revolution, or incur the penalties consequent on a failure."

The dogma of State Sovereignty, as contravening or limiting the proper Nationality of the Republic, is thus squarely confronted:

"The States severally have *not* retained their entire sovereignty. It has been shown that, in becoming parts of a nation, not members of a league, they surrendered many of their essential parts of sovereignty. The right to make treaties, declare war, levy taxes, exercise exclusive judicial and legislative powers, were all of them functions of sovereign power. The States, then, for all these important purposes, were no longer sovereign. The allegiance of their citizens was transferred, in the first instance, to the Government of the United States; they became American citizens, and owed obedience to the Constitution of the United States, and to laws made in conformity with the powers it vested in Congress. This last position has not been, and cannot be, denied. How, then, can that State be said to be sovereign and independent, whose citizens owe obedience to laws not made by it, and whose magistrates are sworn to disregard those laws, when they come in conflict with those passed by another? What shows, conclusively, that the States cannot be said to have reserved an undivided sovereignty, is, that they expressly ceded the right to punish treason—not treason against their separate power, but treason against the United States. Treason is an offense against *sovereignty*, and sovereignty must reside with the power to punish it."

Mr. Jefferson Davis, in one of his earlier manifestoes from Richmond, saw fit to speak of the severance of our Union as "the dissolution of a league." General Jackson anticipated and refuted this assumption as follows:

"How is it that the most perfect of those several modes of Union should now be considered as a mere league, that may be dissolved at pleasure? It is from an abuse of terms. Compact is used as synonymous with league, although the true term is not employed, because it would at once show the fallacy of the reasoning. It would not do to say that our Constitution was only a league, but it is labored to prove it a compact (which, in one sense, it is), and then to argue that, as a league is a compact, every compact between nations must, of course, be a league, and that, from such an engagement, every sovereign power has a right to recede. But it has been shown that, in this sense, the States are *not* sovereign, and that, even if they were, and the national constitution had been formed by compact, there would be no right in any one State to exonerate itself from its obligations.

"So obvious are the reasons which forbid this secession, that it is necessary only to allude to them. The Union was formed for the benefit of all. It was produced by mutual sacrifices of interests and opinions. Can those sacrifices be recalled? Can the States who magnanimously surrendered their title to the territories of the West, recall the grant? Will the inhabitants of the inland States agree to pay the duties that may be imposed without their assent by those on the Atlantic or the Gulf, for their own benefit? Shall there be a free port in one State and onerous duties in another? No one believes that any right exists in a single State to involve all the others in these and countless other evils, contrary to engagements solemnly made. Every one must see that the other States, in self-defense, must oppose it at all hazards."

Having thus frankly and vigorously set forth the fundamental principles of our political system, though at much greater length, and with a variety and fullness of illustration, General Jackson proceeds to proclaim

"That the duty imposed on me by the Constitution 'to take care that the laws be faithfully executed' shall be performed to the extent of the powers already vested in me by law, or of such others as the wisdom of Congress shall devise and intrust to me for that purpose; and to warn the citizens of South Carolina, who have been deluded into an opposition to the laws, of the danger they will incur by obedience to the illegal and disorganizing Ordinance of the Convention."

And he closes a most pathetic and eloquent appeal to the people of South Carolina in these memorable and stirring words:

"Contemplate the condition of that country of which you still form an important part!—consider its Government, uniting in one bond of common interest and general protection so many different States—giving to all their inhabitants the proud title of American citizens—protecting their commerce—securing their literature and their arts—facilitating their intercommunication—defending their frontiers—and making their names respected in the remotest parts of the earth! Consider the extent of its territory, its increasing and happy population, its advance in the arts, which render life agreeable, and the sciences which elevate the mind! See education spreading the lights of religion, humanity, and general information, into every cottage in this wide extent of our territories and States! Behold it as the asylum where the wretched and the oppressed find a refuge and support! Look on this picture of happiness and honor, and say, WE, TOO, ARE CITIZENS OF AMERICA. Carolina is one of these proud States; her arms have defended, her best blood has cemented, this happy Union! And then add, if you can, without horror and remorse, 'This happy Union we will dissolve —this picture of peace and prosperity we will deface—this free intercourse we will interrupt—these fertile fields we will deluge with blood—the protection of that glorious flag we renounce—the very name of Americans we discard.' And for what, mistaken men! for what do you throw away these inestimable blessings—for what would you exchange your share in the advantages and honor of the Union? For the dream of a separate independence—a dream interrupted by bloody conflicts with your neighbors, and a vile dependence on foreign power! If your leaders could succeed in establishing a separation, what would be your situation? Are you united at home? Are you free from the apprehension of civil discord, with all its fearful consequences? Do our neighboring republics, every day suffering some new revolution or contending with some new insurrection, do they excite your envy?

"But the dictates of a high duty oblige me solemnly to announce that you cannot succeed. The laws of the United States must be executed. I have no discretionary power on the subject—my duty is emphatically pronounced in the Constitution. Those who told you that you might peaceably prevent their execution, deceived you—they could not have been deceived themselves. They know that a forcible opposition could alone prevent the execution of the laws, and they know that such opposition must be repelled. Their object is disunion: be not deceived by names. Disunion, by armed force, is *treason*. Are you really ready to incur its guilt? If you are, on the heads of the instigators of the act be the dreadful consequences—on their heads be the dishonor; but on yours may fall the punishment—on your unhappy State will inevitably fall all the evils of the conflict you force upon the Government of your country. It cannot accede to the mad project of disunion, of which you would be the first victims—its first magistrate cannot, if he would, avoid the performance of his duty—the consequence must be fearful for you, distressing to your fellow-citizens here, and the friends of good government throughout the world. Its enemies have beheld our prosperity with a vexation they could not conceal—it was a standing refutation of their slavish doctrines, and they would point to our discords with the triumph of malignant joy. It is yet in your power to disappoint them. There is yet time to show that the descendants of the Pinckneys, the Sumpters, the Rutledges, and of the thousand other names which adorn the pages of your Revolutionary history, will not abandon that Union, to support which so many of them fought, and bled, and died. I adjure you, as you honor their memory, as you love the cause of freedom to which they dedicated their lives—as you prize the peace of your country, the lives of its best citizens, and your own fair fame, to retrace your steps. Snatch from the archives of your State the disorganizing edict of its Convention—bid its members to reassemble and promulgate the decided expression of your will to remain in the path which alone can conduct you to safety, prosperity, and honor—tell them that, compared to disunion, all other evils are light, because that brings with it an accumulation of all—declare that you will never take the field unless the star-spangled banner of your country shall float over you—that you will not be stigmatized when dead, and dishonored and scorned while you live, as the authors of the first attack on the Constitution of your country! Its destroyers you cannot be. You may disturb its peace—you may interrupt the course of its prosperity—you may cloud its reputation for stability—but its tranquillity will be restored, its prosperity will return, and the stain upon its national character will be transferred, and remain an eternal blot on the memory of those who caused the disorder."

Turning from the deluded minority to the loyal and Union-loving majority of the American people, the President concludes his Proclamation as follows:

"Fellow-citizens of the United States! The threat of unhallowed disunion, the names of those (once respected) by whom it was uttered, the array of military force to support it, denote the approach of a crisis in our affairs, on which the continuance of our unexampled prosperity, our political existence, and perhaps that of all free governments, may depend. The conjuncture demanded a full, a free, and explicit annunciation, not only of my intentions, but of my principles of action; and, as the claim was asserted of a right by a State to annul the laws of the Union, and even to secede from it, at pleasure, a frank exposition of my opinions in relation to the origin and form of our Government, and the construction I give to the instrument by which it was created, seemed to be proper. Having the fullest confidence in the justness of the legal and constitutional opinion of my duties, which has been expressed, I rely with equal confidence on your undivided support in my determination to execute the laws—to preserve the Union by all constitutional means—to arrest, if possible, by moderate, but firm measures, the necessity of a recourse to force. And if it be the will of Heaven that the recurrence of its primeval curse on man for the shedding of a brother's blood should fall upon our land, that it be not called down by any offensive act of the United States.

"Fellow-citizens! the momentous case is before you. On your undivided support of your Government depends the decision of the great question it involves, whether your sacred Union will be preserved, and the blessing it secures to us as one people shall be perpetuated. No one can doubt that the unanimity with which that decision will be expressed will be such as to inspire new confidence in republican institutions, and that the prudence, the wisdom, and the courage which it will bring to their defense, will transmit them unimpaired and invigorated to our children.

"May the great Ruler of nations grant, that the signal blessings with which He has favored ours may not, by the madness of party, or personal ambition, be disregarded and lost: and may His wise providence bring those who have produced this crisis to see the folly, before they feel the misery, of civil strife; and inspire a returning veneration for that Union, which, if we may dare to penetrate His designs, He has chosen as the only means of attaining the high destinies to which we may reasonably aspire."

General Jackson's Special Message against Nullification[20] is equally decided and thorough in its hostility to the Calhoun heresy, under all its aspects, and dissects the Ordinance of Nullification, and the legislative acts based thereon, with signal ability and cogency. A single extract, bearing directly upon the alleged right of Secession, will here be given:

"The right of the people of a single State to absolve themselves at will, and without the consent of the other States, from their most solemn obligations, and hazard the liberties and happiness of the millions composing this Union, cannot be acknowledged. Such authority is believed to be utterly repugnant both to the principles upon which the General Government is constituted, and to the objects which it was expressly formed to attain.

"Against all acts which may be alleged to transcend the constitutional power of Government, or which may be inconvenient or oppressive in their operation, the Constitution itself has prescribed the modes of redress. It is the attribute of free institutions that, under them, the empire of reason and law is substituted for the power of the sword. To no other source can appeals for supposed wrongs be made, consistently with the obligations of South Carolina; to no other can such appeals be made with safety at any time; and to their decisions, when constitutionally pronounced, it becomes the duty, no less of the public authorities than of the people, in every case to yield a patriotic submission.

"That a State, or any other great portion of the people, suffering under long and intolerable oppressions, and having tried all constitutional remedies without the hope of redress, may have a natural right, when their happiness can be no otherwise secured, and when they can do so without greater injury to others, to absolve themselves from their obligations to the Government, and appeal to the last resort, need not, on the present occasion, be denied.

"The existence of this right, however, must depend on the causes which justify its exercise. It is the *ultima ratio*, which presupposes that the proper appeals to all other means of redress have been made in good faith, and which can never be rightfully resorted to unless it be unavoidable. It is not the right of the State, but of the individual, and of all the individuals in the State. It is the right of mankind generally to secure, by all means in their power, the blessings of liberty and happiness; but when for these purposes any body of men have voluntarily associated themselves under any particular form of government, no portion of them can dissolve the association without acknowledging the correlative right in the remainder to decide whether that dissolution can be permitted consistently with the general happiness. In this view, it is a right dependent upon the power to enforce it. Such a right, though it may be admitted to preëxist, and cannot be wholly surrendered, is necessarily subjected to limitations in all free governments, and in compacts of all kinds, freely and voluntarily entered into, and in which the interest and welfare of the individual become identified with those of the community of which he is a member. In compacts between individuals, however deeply they may affect their relations, these principles are acknowledged to create a

[20] January 16, 1833.

sacred obligation; and in compacts of civil government, involving the liberty and happiness of millions of mankind, the obligation cannot be less."

The unanimity and enthusiasm, with which the people of the Free States responded to these downright manifestations of a purpose to preserve at all hazards the integrity of the Union, are still freshly remembered. Those States had just been convulsed by a Presidential contest, wherein their people were about equally divided into zealous advocates and equally zealous opponents of General Jackson's re-election. Though his triumph had been overwhelming, so far as the choice of Electors was concerned, the popular majorities, whereby those electors were chosen, were very meager in several of the States, including New York, Ohio, and New Jersey; while the majorities against him in Massachusetts, Connecticut, Rhode Island, Vermont, and Kentucky, were heavy. But the States which had opposed his re-election, the citizens who had deprecated it as confirming and renewing a lease of virtually absolute power in hands too prone to stretch Authority and Prerogative to the utmost, now vied with their late antagonists in pledging devotion and support to the elected chief of the Republic in his efforts to preserve its unity and vitality. Great public meetings were held in the principal cities to give formal and influential expression to the sentiment; the Press, all but unanimously, echoed and stimulated the popular plaudits; and General Jackson was never before nor afterward so strong throughout the Free States, as during the few months which followed a most vigorous and determined struggle to defeat his re-election.

At the South, the case was somewhat different, though in every State—South Carolina, of course, excepted—the President's course was approved by a decided majority. The great mass of the voting population of nearly all these States had just given General Jackson their suffrages for the second or third time—they had long enough been told that he was a despot, an usurper, a tyrant, etc., without believing it; and they were little inclined to repudiate in a moment the convictions and the associations of a lifetime. In Virginia alone was there any official exhibition of sympathy with South Carolina in her self-invoked peril; and she sent a commissioner[21] to that State rather to indicate her fraternal regard than to proffer any substantial assistance.

There was some windy talk of opposing by force the passage of a Federal army southward through the Old Dominion on an errand of "subjugation;" and her Governor,[22] in his annual Message, said something implying such a purpose. Ex-Governor Troup, of Georgia, and a few other *doctrinaires* of the extreme State Rights school, muttered some words of sympathy with the Nullifiers, about to be crushed under the iron heel of Federal power—some vague protest against Consolidation; but that was all. Had it become necessary to call for volunteers to assert and maintain the National authority on the soil of the perverse State, they would doubtless have offered themselves by thousands from nearly or quite

[21] Benjamin Watkins Leigh.

[22] John Floyd, father of the late John B. Floyd, Mr. Buchanan's Secretary of War.

every Southern as well as Northern State.

But it did not become necessary. Congress in due time took up the Tariff, with a view to its revision and reduction. The Jacksonian ascendency was decided in every department of the Government. Andrew Stevenson (anti-Tariff), of Virginia, was Speaker of the House, Gulian C. Verplanck (anti-Tariff) was Chairman of its Committee of Ways and Means, whence a bill containing sweeping reductions and equalizations of duties was, at an early period of the session, reported; and, though no conclusive action was had on this measure, the mere fact of its introduction was seized upon by the Nullifiers as an excuse for recoiling from the perilous position they had so recklessly assumed. A few days before the 1st of February, the Nullifying chiefs met at Charleston, and gravely resolved that, inasmuch as measures were then pending in Congress which contemplated such reductions of duties on imports as South Carolina demanded, the execution of the Nullifying Ordinance, and of course of all legislative acts subsidiary thereto, should be postponed till after the adjournment of that body!

But Mr. Verplanck's bill[23] made such slow progress that its passage, even at the last moment, seemed exceedingly doubtful. Mr. Webster forcibly urged that no concession should be made to South Carolina until she should have abandoned her treasonable attitude. The manufacturers beset the Capitol in crowds, remonstrating against legislation under duress, in defiance of the public interest and the convictions of a majority of the members, which would whelm them in one common ruin. Finally[24], Mr. Clay was induced to submit his Compromise Tariff, whereby one-tenth of the excess over twenty per cent. of each and every existing impost was to be taken off at the close of that year; another tenth two years thereafter; so proceeding until the 31st of June, 1842, when all duties should be reduced to a maximum of twenty per cent. This Compromise Tariff, being accepted and supported by Mr. Calhoun and the Nullifiers, was offered in the House, as a substitute for Mr. Verplanck's bill, by Mr. Letcher, of Kentucky (Mr. Clay's immediate representative and devoted friend), on the 25th of February; adopted and passed at once by a vote of 119 to 85; agreed to by the Senate; and became a law in the last hours of the session: General Jackson, though he openly condemned it as an unwise and untimely concession to rampant treason, not choosing to take the responsibility of vetoing, nor even of pocketing it, as he clearly might have done. South Carolina thereupon abandoned her Ordinance and attitude of Nullification; and the storm that lowered so black and imminent suddenly gave place to a sunny and smiling calm.

But General Jackson was deeply dissatisfied, and with reason. He saw in this easy accommodation the seeds of future perils and calamities. He insisted that Calhoun was a traitor; and to the end of his days regretted that he had not promptly arrested and tried him as such. He denied that dissatisfaction with the Protective policy was the real incite-

[23] Reported December 28th.

[24] February 12, 1833.

ment to the ambitious and restless Carolinian's attempt at practical Nullification. "The Tariff," he wrote in 1834, to an intimate friend in Georgia, "was but a pretext. *The next will be the Slavery or Negro question.*"

But while Nullification was thus sternly crushed out in South Carolina, it was simultaneously allowed a complete triumph in the adjoining State of Georgia. The circumstances were briefly as follows:

The once powerful and warlike Aboriginal tribes known to us as "Cherokees" and "Creeks," originally possessed respectively large territories, which are now included within the States of North Carolina, Georgia, Tennessee, and Alabama. With those tribes, treaties were from time to time made by our Government, whereof each had for its main object the transfer, for a specified consideration, of lands by the Indians to the United States. One of the conditions on which we sought and obtained those lands was thus succinctly expressed in the treaty with the Cherokees negotiated on the bank of the Holston, in 1791, under the Presidency of Washington:

> "ARTICLE 7. The United States solemnly GUARANTY to the Cherokee Nation *all their lands not hereby ceded.*"

The stipulations of this treaty were recognized, and their validity confirmed by the treaty of 1794, negotiated by Henry Knox, Secretary of War, "being authorized thereto by the President of the United States." A further treaty, negotiated in 1798, under John Adams, recognized and ratified afresh all the obligations incurred, the guaranties given, by former treaties. Such stipulations continued to be made, at least down to 1817, when one was negotiated on our part by Andrew Jackson and others, again renewing and confirming to the Cherokees all former stipulations and guaranties.

Still more: when, in 1814, the Treaty of Ghent was negotiated, whereby the war of 1812 with Great Britain was terminated, the British commissioners long and fairly insisted on including her Aboriginal allies in that war in the provisions and stipulations of the treaty, especially that which exacted a mutual restoration of all territories or places taken by one party from the other during the preceding contest. Our commissioners naturally demurred to this, preferring to insert an article which set forth the humane and benevolent principles whereby (as it alleged) our Government regulates its conduct toward the Indian tribes within our borders.[25] And Mr. Clay, one of the negotiators of that treaty, declared, in his speech on the Cherokee Grievances in 1835, that the British commissioners would never have been satisfied with this, if they had understood that those tribes

---

[25] The following is that portion of the Treaty of Ghent relating to the Indians:

"*Article the Ninth.* The United States of America engage to put an end, immediately after the ratification of the present treaty, to hostilities with all the tribes or nations of Indians with whom they may be at war at the time of such ratification; and forthwith to restore to such tribes or nations, respectively, all the possessions, rights, and privileges, which they may have enjoyed or been entitled to in one thousand eight hundred and eleven, previous to such hostilities. *Provided always,* That such tribes or nations shall agree to desist from all hostilities against the United States of America, their citizens and subjects, upon the ratification of the present treaty being notified to such tribes or nations, and shall so desist accordingly."

held their rights and possessions guaranteed to them by Federal treaties subject to the good-will and pleasure of the several States, or any of them.

In 1802, Georgia ceded, on certain conditions, her western territory, now composing the States of Alabama and Mississippi, to the Union. Among these conditions, our Government undertook to extinguish the Indian title to all lands within the boundaries of the State as thereby constituted, so soon as this could be effected "peaceably and on reasonable terms."[26] And this object was urgently, perseveringly, and not always honorably, pursued. In February, 1825, just as Mr. Monroe's Administration was passing away, certain commissioners, selected by Mr. Calhoun, then Secretary of War, attempted to obtain from the Creeks, at a council held at Indian Springs, a cession of their lands; but were baffled by the stern resolve of chiefs and people—the tribe having previously prescribed the penalty of death for any one who should make such sale. Thus defeated, the commissioners resorted to a too common practice: they bribed an inconsiderable minority of the Creeks, including one or two alleged chiefs, to give their formal assent to such an instrument as they desired. This sham treaty was hurried to Washington, and forced through the expiring Senate on the last day of the session, before its true character could be generally known. The Creeks, upon learning that such a pretended treaty had been made, held a general council, wherein it was formally disavowed and denounced, and a party was at once dispatched to the home of McIntosh, a chief who had signed the fraud, to execute the sentence of the law upon him. McIntosh and another principal signer were shot dead on sight, and due notice given that the pretended treaty was utterly repudiated.

Governor Troup, of Georgia, of course assumed the validity of the instrument, and prepared to take forcible possession of the Creek lands. The Creeks appealed to the Government, demanding the enforcement of the treaties whereby they were guaranteed protection in the peaceable enjoyment of their clearly defined territorial possessions. Mr. Adams, who had now succeeded to the Presidency, looked fully into the matter, saw that their claim was just, and assured them that they should be defended. Governor Troup threatened to employ force; Mr. Adams *did* employ it. He ordered General Gaines, with a body of regulars, to the scene of apprehended conflict, and gave Georgia fair notice that she must behave herself. The Governor talked loudly, but did not see fit to proceed from words to blows. The Indian Springs fraud proved abortive; but Georgia and her backers scored up a heavy account against

[26] The following is the entire article:

"*Fourthly*, That the United States shall, at their own expense, extinguish, for the use of Georgia, as early as the same can be peaceably obtained, on reasonable terms, the Indian title to the country of Talassee, to the lands left out by the line drawn with the Creeks, in the year one thousand seven hundred and ninety-eight, which had been previously granted by the State of Georgia, both which tracts had formally been yielded by the Indians; and to the lands within the forks of the Oconee and Ocmulgee rivers; for which several objects, the President of the United States has directed that a treaty should be immediately held with the Creeks; and that the United States shall, in the same manner, also extinguish the Indian title to all other lands within the State of Georgia."—*American State Papers*, vol. xvi., p. 114.

Mr. Adams, to be held good against him not only, but all future 'Yankee' and 'Puritan' aspirants to the Presidency.

General Jackson was chosen President in 1828, receiving more than two-thirds of the Electoral votes, including those of all the Slave States but Delaware and a part of Maryland. In Georgia, there were two Jackson Electoral tickets run, but none for Adams. And the first Annual Message of the new President gave the Indians due notice that Georgia had not so voted from blind impulse—that their dearest rights, their most cherished possessions, were among her "spoils of victory." In this Message, the solemn obligations which our Government had volunteered to assume, in treaty after treaty with the Creeks and Cherokees, were utterly ignored, and the rights and possessions of the Indians dealt with precisely as if no such treaties had ever existed! Georgia had herself, through her citizens, participated in negotiating, and, through her Senators, united in ratifying those treaties; yet not only was she held at liberty to disobey and trample on them, but the United States was regarded as equally absolved, by the convenient fiction of State Sovereignty, from all liability to maintain and enforce them! No one could deny that we had solemnly engaged, by repeated treaties, to protect the Indians in the undisturbed use and enjoyment forever of the lands which we had admitted to be, and marked out as, theirs. No one could deny that we had obtained large cessions of valuable lands by these treaties. No one doubted that Georgia had urged us to make these treaties, and had eagerly appropriated the lands thus obtained by the Union, and passed directly over to her: but then, Georgia was a sovereign State, and entitled to do as she liked with all the lands within her borders, and all the people living thereon, no matter if in flagrant violation of the laws and treaties of the United States! And the new President did not scruple to assert and reiterate the untruth that the Creeks and Cherokees respectively were attempting to "*erect* an independent government within the limits of Georgia and Alabama," ringing all possible changes on the falsehood, and gravely quoting from the Constitution that "No new State shall be *formed or erected* within the limits of any other State," as precluding the maintenance by the Creeks and Cherokees of their governments in territories which they had possessed and governed long before Georgia had been colonized, or the name Alabama invented.

This deliberate and flagrant perversion of the question to be decided was persisted in through several pages of the Message. Says the President:

> "Actuated by this view of the subject, I informed the Indians inhabiting parts of Georgia and Alabama that their attempt *to* ESTABLISH *an independent government* would not be countenanced by the Executive of the United States, and advised them to emigrate beyond the Mississippi, or submit to the laws of those States."

What the Indians demanded was simply that the portion of their immemorial possessions which they had reserved for their own use and enjoyment in making liberal cessions to our Government, should still be left to them—that they should be protected in such enjoyment, by the United States, as we had solemnly stipulated by treaty that they should be, taking our pay for it in advance. But General Jackson, in urging them to migrate beyond the Mississippi, did not hesitate to speak of their rights and their immunities as follows:

"This emigration should be voluntary; for it would be as cruel as unjust to compel the Aborigines to abandon the graves of their fathers, and seek a home in a distant land. But they should be distinctly informed that, if they remain within the limits of the States, they must be subject to their laws. In return for their obedience, as individuals, they will, without a doubt, be protected in the enjoyment of those possessions which they have improved by their industry. But it seems to me visionary to suppose that, in this state of things, *claims can be allowed on tracts of country on which they have neither dwelt nor made improvements, merely because they have seen them from the mountain, or passed them in the chase.* Submitting to the laws of the States, and receiving, like other citizens, protection in their persons and property, they will ere long become merged in the mass of our population."

How "voluntary" their emigration was to be, and what sort of "protection in their persons and property" they were likely to receive in case they refused to "abandon the graves of their fathers, and seek a home in a distant land," let the laws which Georgia proceeded to enact bear witness. Grown weary of awaiting the operation of the methods whereby she had already secured, at no cost to herself, the gradual acquisition of the greater part of the Indian lands within her borders when she acceded to the Union, that State passed acts abolishing the government of the Cherokees, and reducing them at a word to the condition of unprotected vassals. Their lands were thereupon divided into counties, surveyed, and ordered to be distributed by lottery among the white citizens of the State, of whom each was to have a ticket. A reservation of one hundred and sixty acres to each head of a Cherokee family was made; but this reservation conferred or recognized only a right of possession during the good pleasure of the State Legislature. The Indians, whose government was thus abolished, were allowed no voice in that to which they were arbitrarily subjected; they could not even give testimony in a Georgia court, though denied a resort to any other. The fortunate drawer of Cherokee lands in the Georgia State lottery was entitled to call upon the Governor to put him in summary possession, expelling any adverse [Indian] claimant. If there were two or more antagonist *white* claimants, their respective claims were to be deliberately adjudicated by the courts, according to the dictates of ordinary jurisprudence. If any one sought to legally hold or recover lands against a claimant under this rule, he must make express affidavit that he

"was not liable to be dispossessed of said land by or under any one of the provisions of the said act of the General Assembly of Georgia, passed December 20, 1833: * * * in which issue the person to whom possession of said land was delivered shall join: *and which issue shall constitute the entire pleadings between the parties; nor shall the court allow any matter other than is contained in said issue to be placed upon the regular files of said court;* * * * nor shall said court, at the instance of either party, pass any order, or grant any injunction, to stay said cause, *nor permit to be ingrafted on said cause any other proceedings whatever.*"

It can hardly be necessary to say that the sole, unconcealed object of this legislation was to deprive the Cherokees of the protection of the courts of the United States, or any adjudication therein touching their rights, by precluding any appeal to said courts for the sake of testing the validity of these acts of the Legislature of Georgia.

That State had already decisively indicated that, if unable to make or control such adjudication, she was abundantly ready to defy it.

A Cherokee named Tassells was arrested on a Georgia warrant for killing another Indian within the Cherokee territory. His counsel obtained a writ of error from a United States court, requiring Georgia to show cause why he should not be discharged and his case remitted to the Cherokee authorities, according to existing treaties. Georgia defied the writ and hung the Indian. And this finished the case.

Some time thereafter, two missionaries of the American Board among the Cherokees were arrested on a Georgia process, tried for, and convicted of, inciting the Indians to resist the policy of the State of Georgia designed to effect the expulsion of the Indians from her soil. They were of course sentenced to the State Prison. They appealed by writ of error to the courts of the United States, and the final adjudication thereon was had before the Supreme Court at Washington, the decision being pronounced by Chief Justice Marshall. It was entirely in favor of the missionaries and against the pretensions of Georgia, holding that the treaties between the United States and the Cherokees were valid and binding on all the States, and paramount to all State laws, according to that provision of the Federal Constitution which prescribes:

"Article VI., § 2. This Constitution, and the laws of the United States which shall be made in pursuance thereof; and all *treaties* made, or which shall be made, under the authority of the United States, shall be the *supreme law of the land;* and the judges in every State shall be bound thereby, anything in the constitution or laws of any State to the contrary notwithstanding."

The attorneys for the missionaries sought to have this judgment enforced, but could not. General Jackson was President, and would do nothing of the sort. "Well: John Marshall has made his decision: *now let him enforce it!*"[27] was his commentary on the matter. So the missionaries languished years in prison, and the Cherokees were finally (1838) driven into exile, in defiance of the mandate of our highest judicial tribunal.[28] Georgia was permitted to violate the faith of solemn treaties and defy the adjudications of our highest court. South Carolina was put down in a similar attempt: for the will of Andrew Jackson, not the Constitution, was in those years "the supreme law of the land."[29]

---

[27] I am indebted for this fact to the late Governor George N. Briggs, of Massachusetts, who was in Washington as a member of Congress when the decision was rendered.

[28] President Jackson, in his first Annual Message, already referred to, had said:

"A portion of the Southern tribes, having mingled much with the whites, and made some progress in the arts of civilized life, have lately attempted to *erect* an independent government within the limits of the States of Georgia and Alabama."

And Colonel Benton, in his "Thirty Years' View," says (vol. i., p. 164), General Jackson "refused to sustain those Southern tribes in their attempt to *set up* an independent government within the States of Alabama and Georgia."

Both these gentlemen well knew—Colonel Benton could not *but* know—that the Cherokees only claimed or sought the rights which they had possessed and enjoyed from time immemorial, which were solemnly guaranteed to them by treaty after treaty, whereof the subsisting validity and pertinence were clearly affirmed by the tribunal of ultimate resort.

[29] The late Jeremiah Evarts, long the efficient and honored Secretary of the American Board

IX.

THE RISE AND PROGRESS OF ABOLITION.

The General Congress which convened at Philadelphia in 1774, framed articles of Association between the colonies, one of which was a solemn agreement "that we will neither import nor purchase any slave imported after the 1st of December next;" being moved thereto by State action of like character, wherein Virginia and North Carolina were honorably conspicuous. Most of the States, accordingly, prohibited the Slave-Trade during or soon after the Revolution. Throughout the war for independence, the Rights of Man were proclaimed as the great objects of our struggle. General Gates, the hero of Saratoga, emancipated his slaves in 1780. The first recorded Abolition Society—that of Pennsylvania—was formed in 1774. The New York Manumission Society was founded in 1785: John Jay was its first President; Alexander Hamilton its second. Rhode Island followed in 1786; Maryland in 1789; Connecticut in 1790; Virginia in 1791; New Jersey in 1792. The discovery that such societies were at war with the Federal Constitution, or with the reciprocal duties of citizens of the several States, was not made till nearly forty years afterward. These Abolition Societies were largely composed of the most eminent as well as the worthiest citizens. Among them were, in Maryland, Samuel Chase, a signer of the Declaration, and Luther Martin, one of the framers of the Constitution; in Delaware, James A. Bayard,[1] afterward in Congress, and Cæsar A. Rodney, who became Attorney-General. The Pennsylvania Society had Benjamin Franklin for its President, and Benjamin Rush for Secretary—both signers of the Declaration. This,[2] among other such societies, memorialized the first Federal Congress, then sitting at Philadelphia, against Slavery, asking

> "that you will be pleased to countenance the restoration to liberty of those unhappy men who, alone in this land of freedom, are degraded into perpetual bondage, and who, amid the general joy of surrounding freemen, are groaning in servile subjection; that you will devise means for removing this inconsistency of character from the American people; that you will promote mercy and justice toward this distressed race; and that you will step to the very verge of the power vested in you for discouraging every species of traffic in the persons of our fellow-men."

Congress courteously received this and similar memorials, calmly considered them, and decided that it had no power to abolish Slavery in the

of Commissioners for Foreign Missions, who devoted the best of his life to the cause of the Cherokees, has summed up, in a letter to a sympathizing friend, his convictions as to the ultimate cause of the perfidy and oppression of which they were the victims:

"Without that disregard of human rights which is to be found among slaveholders only, nothing could have been done against the Indians; and without the base surrender of all personal dignity and independence to the capricious mandate of party discipline, the slaveholders would not have received aid enough to carry their point."—*Life of Jeremiah Evarts*, Boston, 1845, p. 367.

[1] Father of one of her present U. S. Senators.

[2] Franklin, then 84 years of age, signed this memorial on the 3d of February, 1790, and died on the 17th of April following.

States which saw fit to authorize and cherish it. There was no excitement, no menace, no fury. South Carolina and Georgia, of course, opposed the prayer, but in parliamentary language. It is noteworthy, that among those who leaned furthest toward the petitioners were Messrs. Parker and Page, of Virginia—the latter in due time her Governor. They urged, not that the prayer should be granted, but that the memorial be referred, and respectfully considered.

Vermont framed a State Constitution in 1777, and embodied in it a Bill of Rights, whereof the first article precluded Slavery.

Massachusetts framed a constitution in 1780, wherein was embodied a Declaration of Rights, affirming that

> "All men are born free and equal, and have certain natural, essential, and inalienable rights, among which are the right of enjoying and defending their lives and liberties, and that of acquiring, possessing, and protecting property."

The Supreme Court of that State, upon the first case arising which involved the question, decided that this provision had abolished Slavery.

New Hampshire was, in like manner, held to have abolished Slavery by her Constitution, framed in 1783.

Pennsylvania passed a Gradual Emancipation Act, March 1, 1780. All persons born in that State after that day, were to be free at the age of twenty-eight.

Rhode Island provided by law that all persons born in that State after March, 1784, should be free.

Connecticut, in 1784, passed an act providing for gradual Abolition. She had still two thousand seven hundred and fifty-nine slaves in 1790.

New York provided for Gradual Emancipation in 1799. In 1817, a further act was passed, decreeing that there should be no Slavery in the State after the 4th of July, 1827. Ten thousand slaves were set free at once by this act.

New Jersey passed an act, in 1804, designed to put an end to Slavery. It was so very gradual in its operation, that the census of 1840 reported six hundred and seventy-four slaves as still held in that State.

The frequently reiterated Southern assertion that the Northern States "sold their slaves to the South, and *then* abolished Slavery," is abundantly refuted. Pennsylvania, New York, and doubtless most other States, by their acts of emancipation, imposed severe penalties on the exportation of slaves. Delaware, though a Slave State, long since did. and still does, the same.

The North emerged from the Missouri struggle chafed and mortified. It felt that, with Right and Power both on its side, it had been badly beaten, through the treachery of certain of its own representatives, whom it proceeded to deal with accordingly. Few, indeed—hardly one—of those Northern members who had sided with the South in that struggle were reëlected. That lesson given, what more could be done? Missouri was in the Union, and could not be turned out. Arkansas was organized as a Slave Territory, and would in due time become a Slave State. What use in protracting an agitation which had no longer a definite object? Mr. Monroe had just been reëlected President, and the harmony of the party would be disturbed by permitting the feud to become chronic. Those who perpetuated it would be most unlikely to share bounteously in the distribution of Federal offices and honors. Then a new Presidential contest began to loom up in the distance, and all manner of speculations were current, and hopes were buoyant, with regard to it. Yet more: the Cotton culture was rapidly expanding, and with it Southern trade, bringing the Northern seaports more and more under their sway.

There had been an effort, in 1817, to secure the passage through Congress of a more effective Fugitive Slave Law, which was defeated, after a most spirited discussion. In 1826 (March 9th), the subject of Slavery was brought before the House by Mr. Edward Everett—then a new and very young member from Massachusetts—who incidentally expressed his hostility to all projects of violent Abolition, his readiness to shoulder a musket to put down a slave insurrection, and his conviction, with regard to Slavery, that, "*while* it subsists, *where* it subsists, its duties are presupposed and sanctioned by religion," etc., etc. But this strange outburst, instead of being gratefully hailed and welcomed, was repelled and reprobated by the South. Mr. Mitchell, of Tennessee, though himself a slaveholder, pointedly dissented from it. Mr. C. C. Cambreleng, of New York, (a North Carolinian by birth and training), said:

"The gentleman from Massachusetts has gone too far. He has expressed opinions which ought not to escape animadversion. I heard them with great surprise and regret. I was astonished to hear him declare that Slavery—domestic Slavery—say what you will, is a condition of life, as well as any other, to be justified by morality, religion, and international law," etc., etc.

And John Randolph, of Virginia —himself a life-long slaveholder and opponent of the North—saw fit to say:

"Sir, I envy neither the head nor the heart of that man from the North, who rises here to defend Slavery upon principle."

So that, so late as 1826, the doctrine of the essential righteousness and beneficence of Slavery had not yet been accepted in any quarter.[3]

Virginia, in 1829, assembled[4] a Convention of her people to revise their Constitution. Ex-President James Monroe[5] was chosen to preside, and was conducted to the chair by ex-President James Madison and Chief Justice Marshall. The first

[3] Roger Brooke Taney—now Chief Justice of the United States—in defending as a lawyer, in 1818, before a Maryland court, Rev. Jacob Gruber, charged with anti-Slavery inculcations and acts, thus happily set forth the old Revolutionary idea of Slavery, and the obligations it imposes:

"A hard necessity, indeed, compels us to endure the evils of Slavery for a time. It was imposed upon us by another nation, while yet we were in a state of colonial vassalage. It cannot be easily or suddenly removed. Yet, while it continues, it is a blot on our national character, and every real lover of freedom confidently hopes that it will be effectually, though it must be gradually, wiped away, and earnestly looks for the means by which this necessary object may be attained. And, until it shall be accomplished, until the time come when we can point without a blush to the language held in the Declaration of Independence, every friend of humanity will seek to lighten the galling chain of Slavery, and better, to the utmost of his power, the wretched condition of the slave."

[4] At Richmond, October 5th.

[5] Mr. Monroe, in a speech (November 2d), on the Basis of Representation, said, incidentally of Slavery:

"No imputation can be cast on Virginia in this matter. She did all that it was in her power to do to *prevent the extension of Slavery*, and to mitigate its evils so far as she could."

earnest collision was on the *White Basis*, so called—that is, on the proposition that representation and political power should be apportioned to the several counties on the basis of their White population alone. The Committee on the Legislative department decided in favor of the White Basis by 13 to 11—James Madison's vote giving that side the majority; but he voted also *against* the White Basis for the Senate, making a tie on that point. A strong excitement having arisen on this question, General Robert B. Taylor, of Norfolk, an advocate of the White Basis, resigned, and his seat was filled by Hugh B. Grigsby, of opposite views. At length,[6] the Convention came to a vote, on the proposition of a Mr. Green, of Culpepper, that the White Basis be stricken out, and the Federal Basis (the white inhabitants with "three-fifths of all other persons") be substituted. This was defeated—Yeas 47 (including Grigsby aforesaid); Nays 49—every delegate voting. Among the Yeas were ex-President Madison, Chief Justice Marshall, Benjamin Watkins Leigh, Philip P. Barbour, John Randolph of Roanoke, William B. Giles, John Tyler, etc. Among the Nays (*for* the White Basis) were ex-President Monroe, Philip Doddridge, Charles F. Mercer, Chapman Johnson, Lewis Summers, etc. As a rule, Western (comparatively Free) Virginia voted for the White Basis, with some help from the East; and it was computed that the majority represented 402,631 of Free Population, and the minority but 280,000. But the minority was strong in intellect, in numbers, and in resolution, and it fought desperately through weeks of earnest debate and skillful maneuvering. President Monroe, in December, resigned the chair, and his seat, and his constituents offered the latter to General R. B. Taylor aforesaid, who declined, when it was given to a Mr. Osborne. Finally, a proposition by Mr. Upshur (afterward Secretary of State) was so amended, on motion of Mr. Gordon, as to prescribe, arbitrarily, that thirteen Senators should be apportioned to counties west of the Blue Ridge, and nineteen to those east of it, with a corresponding allotment of Delegates in four parcels to the various natural divisions of the State, and was carried by 55 Yeas to 41 Nays—a motion that the Senate apportionment be based on Federal numbers, and that for the House on the White population, having first been voted down—48 to 48. So the effort of the West, and of the relatively non-slaveholding sections of Virginia, to wrest political power from the slave-holding oligarchy of the tide-water counties, was defeated, despite the sanguine promise at the outset; and the Old Dominion sunk again into the arms of the negro-breeders.[7]

[6] November 16th.

[7] Hezekiah Niles, in his *Weekly Register* of October 31, 1829, thus forcibly depicted the momentous issues for Virginia and the country, then hinging on the struggle in Richmond:

"VIRGINIA CONVENTION.—The committees having chiefly reported, 'the tug of war' between the 'old lights' and the new has commenced; and the question is to be settled whether trees and stones, and arbitrary divisions of land, with almost as senseless herds of black slaves, or the free, tax-paying inhabitants of the State, shall have political power. Very important events will grow out of this convention, and their effect will not be confined to Virginia. We hope and believe, that the free white population of the State will be adopted as the basis of representation in the popular branch of the Legislature—indeed, it cannot be *popular* without it; but perhaps the Senate may be apportioned according to 'federal numbers,' in which three-fifths of the

Some years later (in 1831–2), on the occurrence of the slave insurrection in Southampton county, known as Nat. Turner's, her people were aroused to a fresh and vivid conception of the perils and evils of Slavery, and her Legislature, for a time, seemed on the point of inaugurating a system of Gradual Emancipation; but the impulse was finally, though with difficulty, overborne. Several who have since cast in their lot with the Slaveholders' Rebellion—among them Jas. C. Faulkner, late Minister to England—at that time spoke earnestly and forcibly for Emancipation, as an imperative necessity. And this is noteworthy as the last serious effort by the politicians of any Slave State[8] to rid her of the giant curse, prior to the outbreak of the Slaveholders' Rebellion.

Benjamin Lundy deserves the high honor of ranking as the pioneer of direct and distinctive Anti-Slavery in America. Many who lived before and cotemporary with him were Abolitionists: but he was the first of our countrymen who devoted his life and all his powers exclusively to the cause of the slave. Born in Sussex county, New Jersey, January 4, 1789, of Quaker parents, whose ancestors for several generations had lived and died in this country, he injured himself, while still a mere boy, by excessive labor on his father's farm, incurring thereby a partial loss of hearing, from which he never recovered. Slight in frame and below the common hight, unassuming in manner and gentle in spirit, he gave to the cause of Emancipation neither wealth, nor eloquence, nor lofty abilities, for he had them not; but his courage, perseverance, and devotion were unsurpassed; and these combined to render him a formidable, though disregarded if not despised, antagonist to our national crime. Leaving his father's farm at nineteen years of age, he wandered

slaves are counted. If the latter may stand as a peace-offering to the departing power of the old lights, we would let them have it—in a few years, under a liberal Constitution, the free population of middle and western Virginia will be so increased, that the power in the Senate, derived from slaves, will not be injuriously felt. And then will the *tacticians*, who have kept Virginia back half a century, compared with New York and Pennsylvania, disappear, and give place to *practical* men—then will roads and canals be made, domestic manufactures encouraged, and a free and virtuous and laborious people give wealth and power and security to the commonwealtn—the 'old families,' as they are called—persons much partaking of the character of the old nobility of France, imbecile and incorrigible—pass away, and a healthful and happy, bold and intelligent middle class rise up to sweeten and invigorate society, by rendering labor honorable; and Richmond will not any longer be ALL Virginia, as a distinguished gentleman used to proclaim, in matters of politics or policy. The moral effects of these things over the slave population of Virginia, and in the adjacent States, are hardly to be calculated. The presence of numerous slaves is incompatible with that of a numerous free population; and it is shown that the labor of the latter, in all the important operations of agriculture or the arts, except the cultivation of cotton, sugar, tobacco, and rice (as at present carried on), is the cheapest and the best. And in truth, it would not perhaps be straining the facts too far, to express an opinion, that the greatest question before the Virginia convention is, the perpetual duration of negro slavery, or the increase of a generous and free white population."

[8] In 1849, when Kentucky revised her State Constitution, Henry Clay formally renewed the appeal in favor of Gradual Emancipation, which he had made, when a very young man, on the occasion of her organization as a State; but the response from the people was feeble and ineffective. Delaware has repeatedly endeavored to rid herself of Slavery by legislation; but partisan Democracy has uniformly opposed and defeated every movement looking to this end. She, though slaveholding, has for sixty years or more been truly, emphatically, a Border State. Slavery has only been kept so long alive within her limits for the benefit, and by the strenuous efforts, of the Democratic party. It is now evidently near its end.

westward to Wheeling, Virginia, where, during the next four years, he learned the trade of a saddler, and gained an insight into the cruelties and villainies of slaveholding—Wheeling being at that time a great thoroughfare for negro-traders and their prey on their route from Maryland and Virginia to the lower Mississippi. Before he made Wheeling his home, he had spent some time at Mount Pleasant, Ohio, whither he returned after learning his trade, and remained there two years, during which he married a young woman of like spirit to his own. He then, after a long visit to his father in New Jersey, settled at St. Clairsville, Ohio, near Wheeling, and opened a shop, by which in four years he made about three thousand dollars above his expenses, and, with a loving wife and two children, was as happy and contented with his lot as any man need be.

But the impression made on his mind by his experiences of Slavery in Wheeling could not be shaken off nor resisted. In the year 1815, when twenty-six years of age, he organized an anti-Slavery association known as the "Union Humane Society," whereof the first meeting was held at his own house, and consisted of but five or six persons. Within a few months, its numbers were swelled to four or five hundred, and included the best and most prominent citizens of Belmont and the adjacent counties. Lundy wrote an appeal to philanthropists on the subject of Slavery, which was first printed on the 4th of January, 1816, being his twenty-seventh birthday. Short and simple as it was, it contained the germ of the entire anti-Slavery movement. A weekly journal entitled *The Philanthropist* was soon after started at Mount Pleasant by Charles Osborne; and Lundy, at the editor's invitation, contributed to its columns, mainly by selections. In a few months, he was urged by Osborne to join him in the newspaper enterprise, and finally consented to do so, removing to Mount Pleasant. Meantime, he made a voyage to St. Louis in a flat-boat to dispose of his stock of saddlery. Arriving at that city in the fall of 1819, when the whole region was convulsed by the Missouri Question, he was impelled to write on the side there unpopular in the journals of the day. His speculation proved unfortunate—the whole West, and, indeed, the whole country, being then involved in a commercial convulsion, with trade stagnant and almost every one bankrupt. He returned to his home on foot during the ensuing winter, having been absent nearly two years, and lost all he was worth.

Meantime, Osborne, tired of his thankless and profitless vocation, had sold out his establishment, and it had been removed to Jonesborough, Tennessee, where his newspaper took the title of *The Emancipator*. Lundy removed, as he had purposed, to Mount Pleasant, and there started, in January, 1821, a monthly entitled *The Genius of Universal Emancipation*. He commenced it with six subscribers; himself ignorant of printing and without materials; having his work done at Steubenville, twenty miles distant; traveling thither frequently on foot, and returning with his edition on his back. Four months later, he had a very considerable subscription list. About this time, Elihu Embree, who had started *The Eman-*

JOHN QUINCY ADAMS
HENRY WARD BEECHER
WILLIAM LLOYD GARRISON
JOHN GREENLEAF WHITTIER
WILLIAM CULLEN BRYANT
JOSHUA R. GIDDINGS
WENDELL PHILLIPS
CHARLES SUMNER
GERRIT SMITH
CASSIUS M. CLAY
OWEN LOVEJOY
BENJAMIN LUNDY
Engraved by J. C. Buttre, New York.
EMINENT OPPONENTS OF THE SLAVE POWER

cipator in Tennessee, died, and Lundy was urged to go thither, unite the two journals, and print them himself from the materials of *The Emancipator*. He consented, and made the journey of eight hundred miles, one-half on foot and the rest by water. At Jonesborough, he learned the art of printing, and was soon issuing a weekly newspaper beside *The Genius*, and a monthly agricultural work. He removed his family a few months later, and East Tennessee was thenceforward his home for nearly three years, during which *The Genius of Universal Emancipation* was the only distinctively and exclusively anti-Slavery periodical issued in the United States, constantly increasing in circulation and influence. And, though often threatened with personal assault, and once shut up in a private room with two ruffians, who undertook to bully him into some concession by a flourish of deadly weapons, he was at no time subjected to mob violence or legal prosecution.

In the winter of 1823-4, the first American Convention for the Abolition of Slavery was held in Philadelphia; and Lundy made the journey of six hundred miles and back on purpose to attend it. During his tour, he decided on transferring his establishment to Baltimore; and, in the summer of 1824, knapsack on shoulder, he set out on foot for that city. On the way, he delivered, at Deep Creek, North Carolina, his first public address against Slavery. He spoke in a beautiful grove, near the Friends' meeting-house at that place, directly after divine worship; and the audience were so well satisfied that they invited him to speak again, in their place of worship. Before this second meeting adjourned, an anti-Slavery society was formed; and he proceeded to hold fifteen or twenty similar meetings at other places within that State. In one instance, he spoke at a house-raising; in another, at a militia muster. Here an anti-Slavery society of fourteen members was thereupon formed, with the captain of the militia company for its President. One of his meetings was held at Raleigh, the capital. Before he had left the State, he had organized twelve or fourteen Abolition Societies. He continued his journey through Virginia, holding several meetings, and organizing societies—of course, not very numerous, nor composed of the most influential persons. It is probable that his Quaker brethren supplied him with introductions from place to place, and that his meetings were held at the points where violent opposition was least likely to be offered.

He reached Baltimore about the 1st of October, and issued on the 10th No. 1 of Volume IV. of the "Genius," which continued to be well supported, though receiving little encouragement from Baltimore itself. A year afterward, it began to be issued weekly.

Lundy visited Hayti in the latter part of 1825, in order to make arrangements there for the reception of a number of slaves, whose masters were willing to emancipate them on condition of their removal from the country—in fact, were not allowed, by the laws of their respective States, to free them otherwise. Being detained longer than he had expected, he was met, on his return to Baltimore, with tidings of the death of his wife, after giving birth to twins, and hastened to his dwelling to find it entirely deserted, his five children having been distributed among his friends. In that hour of intense affliction, he renewed his solemn vow to devote his entire energies to the cause of the slave, and to efforts designed to awaken his countrymen to a sense of their responsibility and their danger. In 1828, he traveled eastward, lecturing and soliciting subscribers to his "Genius," and calling, in New York, on Arthur Tappan, William Goodell, and other anti-Slavery men. At Boston, he could hear of no Abolitionists, but made the acquaintance, at his boarding-house, of William Lloyd Garrison, a fellow-boarder, whose attention had not previously been drawn to the Slavery question, but who readily embraced his views. He visited successively most of the clergymen of Boston, and induced eight of them, belonging to various sects, to meet him. All of them, on explanation, approved his labors, and subscribed for his periodical; and, in the course of a few days, they aided him to hold an anti-Slavery meeting, which was largely attended. At the close of his remarks, several clergymen expressed a general concurrence in his views. He extended his journey to New Hampshire and Maine, lecturing where he could, and obtaining some encouragement. He spoke also in the principal towns of Massachusetts, Rhode Island, and Connecticut; and, on his homeward route, traversed the State of New York, speaking at Poughkeepsie, Albany,[9] Lockport, Utica, and Buffalo, reaching Baltimore late in October.

Lundy made at least one other visit to Hayti, to colonize emancipated slaves; was beaten nearly to death in Baltimore by a slave-trader, on whose conduct he had commented in terms which seemed disrespectful to the profession; was flattered by the judge's assurance, when the trader came to be tried for the assault, that "he [L.] had got nothing more than he deserved;" and he made two long journeys through Texas, to the Mexican departments across the Rio Grande, in quest of a suitable location on which to plant a colony of freed blacks from the United States, but without success. He traveled in good part on foot, observing the strictest economy, and supporting himself by working at saddlery and harness-mending, from place to place, as circumstances required. Meantime, he had been compelled to remove his paper from Baltimore to Washington; and finally (in 1836), to Philadelphia, where it was entitled *The National Inquirer*, and at last merged into *The Pennsylvania Freeman*. His colonizing enterprise took him to Monclova, Comargo, Monterey, Matamoras, and Victoria, in Mexico, and consumed the better part of several years, closing in 1835. He also made a visit to the settlements in Canada, of fugitives from American Slavery, to inquire into the welfare of their inhabitants. On the 17th of May,

[9] Lundy's brief journal of this tour has been preserved; and, next to an entry running—"On the 25th I arrived at Northampton, Mass., after 9 o'clock in the evening, and called at three taverns before I could get lodgings or polite treatment"—we find the following:

"*September 6th*—At Albany, I made some acquaintances. *Philanthropists are the slowest creatures breathing. They think forty times before they act.*"

There is reason to fear that the little Quaker was a 'fanatic.'

1838, at the burning by a mob of Pennsylvania Hall—built by Abolitionists, because they could be heard in no other—his little property, consisting mainly of papers, books, clothes, etc., which had been collected in one of the rooms of that Hall, with a view to his migration westward, was totally destroyed. In July, he started for Illinois, where his children then resided, and reached them in the September following. He planted himself at Lowell, La Salle county, gathered his offspring about him, purchased a printing-office, and renewed the issues of his "Genius." But in August, 1839, he was attacked by a prevailing fever, of which he died on the 22d of that month, in the 51st year of his age. Thus closed the record of one of the most heroic, devoted, unselfish, courageous lives, that has ever been lived on this continent.[10]

William Lloyd Garrison, born in obscurity and indigence, at Newburyport, Massachusetts, in 1805, and educated a printer, after having tried his boyish hand at shoe-making, wood-sawing, and cabinet-making, started *The Free Press*, in his native place, directly upon attaining his majority; but Newburyport was even then a slow old town, and his enterprise soon proved unsuccessful. He migrated to Boston, worked a few months as a journeyman printer, and then became editor of *The National Philanthropist*, an organ of the Temperance movement. He left this early in 1828, to become editor, at Bennington, Vermont, of *The Journal of the Times*, a "National Republican" gazette, and about the ablest and most interesting newspaper ever issued in that State. Though earnestly devoted to the reëlection of John Quincy Adams, as President, it gave a hearty support to the Temperance, Anti-Slavery, and other Reform projects, and promoted the extensive circulation and signature of memorials to Congress, urging the banishment of Slavery from the District of Columbia. But its patronage was unequal to its merits; and, Mr. Adams having been defeated, its publication was soon afterward discontinued.

Mr. Garrison was, about this time, visited by Lundy, and induced to join him in the editorship of *The Genius* at Baltimore, whither he accordingly proceeded in the Autumn of 1829. Lundy had been a zealous supporter of Adams; and, under his auspices, a single Emancipation candidate for the Legislature had been repeatedly presented in Baltimore, receiving, at one election, more than nine hundred votes. Garrison, in his first issue, insisted on immediate and unconditional Emancipation as the right of the slave and the duty of the master, and disclaimed all temporizing, all make-shifts, all compromises, condemning Colonization, and everything else that involved or implied affiliation or sympathy with slaveholders. Having, at length, denounced the coastwise slave-trade between Baltimore and New Orleans as "domestic piracy," and stigmatized by name certain Baltimoreans concerned therein, he was indicted for "a gross and malicious libel" on those worthies, convicted, sentenced to pay fifty dollars' fine and costs, and, in default thereof, committed to jail. A judgment

[10] Condensed from the "Life of Benjamin Lundy," by Thomas Earle.

in behalf of one of these aggrieved persons of $1,000 and costs was likewise obtained against him on a civil suit, but never enforced. He remained forty-nine days in prison, during which his case excited much sympathy, a protest against his incarceration having been issued by the Manumission Society of North Carolina. At length, the fine and costs were paid by Arthur Tappan, then a wealthy and generous New York merchant, who anticipated, by a few days, a similar act meditated by Henry Clay. Separating himself from Lundy and *The Genius*, Mr. Garrison now proposed the publication of an anti-Slavery organ in Washington City; but, after traveling and lecturing through the great cities, and being prevented by violence from speaking in Baltimore, he concluded to issue his journal from Boston instead of Washington; and the first number of *The Liberator* appeared accordingly on the 1st of January, 1830. It was, from the outset, as thorough-going as its editor; and its motto—"Our Country is the World—Our Countrymen are all Mankind"—truly denoted its character and spirit. "No Union with slaveholders" was adopted as a principle some years later; as was the doctrine that "The [Federal] Constitution is a covenant with death, and an agreement with hell." To wage against Slavery an uncompromising, unrelenting war, asking no quarter and giving none—to regard and proclaim the equal and inalienable rights of every innocent human being as inferior or subordinate to those of no other, and to repudiate all creeds, all alleged revelations, rituals, constitutions, governments, parties, politics, that reject, defy, or ignore this fundamental truth—such is and has been the distinctive idea of the numerically small, but able and thoroughly earnest class, known as "Garrisonians."[11] They for many years generally declined, and some of them still decline, to vote, deeming the Government and all parties so profoundly corrupted by Slavery, that no one could do so without dereliction from principle and moral defilement. And, though the formal and definitive separation did not take place till 1839, the alienation between the Garrisonians and the larger number of Anti-Slavery men had long been decided and irremediable. A very few years,

[11] "The broadest and most far-sighted intellect is utterly unable to see the ultimate consequences of any great social change. Ask yourself, on all such occasions, if there be any element of right or wrong in the question, any principle of clear, natural justice, that turns the scale. If so, take your part with the perfect and abstract right, and trust God to see that it shall prove the expedient."—*Wendell Phillips's Speeches and Lectures*, p. 18.

"The time has been when it was the duty of the reformer to show cause why he offered to disturb the quiet of the world. But, during the discussion of the many reforms which have been advocated, and which have more or less succeeded, one after another—freedom of the lower classes, freedom of food, freedom of the press, freedom of thought, reform in penal legislation, and a thousand other matters—it seems to me to have been proved conclusively, that government commenced in usurpation and oppression; that liberty and civilization, at present, are nothing else than the fragments of rights which the scaffold and the stake have wrung from the strong hands of the usurpers. Every step of progress the world has made has been from scaffold to scaffold, and from stake to stake. It would hardly be exaggeration to say, that all the great truths relating to society and government have been first heard in the solemn protests of martyred patriotism, or the loud cries of crushed and starving labor. The law has been always wrong."—*Ibid.*, p. 14.

"An intelligent democracy says of Slavery as of a church, 'This is justice and that iniquity.' The track of God's thunderbolt is a straight line from one to the other, and the Church or State that cannot stand it, must get out of the way."—*Ibid.*, p. 267.

dating from 1832-3, when the New England and the American Anti-Slavery Societies were formed respectively, sufficed to segregate the American opponents of Slavery into four general divisions, as follows:

1. The "Garrisonians" aforesaid.

2. The members of the "Liberty party,"[12] who, regarding the Federal Constitution as essentially anti-Slavery, swore with good conscience to uphold it, and supported only candidates who were distinctively, determinedly, pre-eminently, champions of "Liberty for all."

3. Various small sects and parties, which occupied a middle ground between the above positions; some of the sects agreeing with the latter in interpreting and revering the Bible as consistently anti-Slavery, while refusing, with the former, to vote.

4. A large and steadily increasing class who, though decidedly anti-Slavery, refused either to withhold their votes, or to throw them away on candidates whose election was impossible, but persisted in voting, at nearly every election, so as to effect good and prevent evil to the extent of their power.

An artful and persistent ignoring of all distinction between these classes, and thus covering Abolitionists indiscriminately with odium, as hostile to Christianity and to the Constitution, was long the most effective weapon in the armory of their common foes. Thousands, whose consciences and hearts would naturally have drawn them to the side of humanity and justice, were repelled by vociferous representations that to do so would identify them with the "disunion" of Wendell Phillips, the "radicalism" of Henry C. Wright, and the "infidelity" of Pillsbury, Theodore Parker, and Garrison.

X.

THE CHURCHES AND SLAVERY.

We have seen that the Revolutionary era and the Revolutionary spirit of our country were profoundly hostile to Slavery, and that they were not content with mere protests against an evil which positive efforts, determined acts, were required to remove. Before the Revolution, indeed, a religious opposition to Slavery, whereof the society of Christian Friends or Quakers were the pioneers, had been developed both in the mother country and in her colonies. George Fox, the first Quaker, bore earnest testimony, so early as 1671, on the occasion of his visit to

[12] Sundry differences respecting "Woman's Rights"—whereof the Garrisonians were stanch asserters—and other incidental questions, were the immediate causes of the rupture between the Garrisonians and the political Abolitionists, whereby the American Anti-Slavery Society was convulsed by the secession of the latter in 1840; but the ultimate causes of the rupture were deeper than these. As a body, the Garrisonians were regarded as radical in politics and heterodox in theology; and the more Orthodox, conservative, and especially the clerical Abolitionists, increasingly disliked the odium incited by the sweeping utterances of the Garrisonian leaders.

Barbadoes, against the prevalent cruelty and inhumanity with which negro slaves were then treated in that island, and urged their gradual emancipation. His letter implies that some of his disciples were slaveholders. Yet it was not till 1727 that the yearly meeting of the whole society in London declared "the importing of negroes from their native country and relations, by Friends, not a *commendable* or allowable practice." Nearly thirty years before, the yearly meeting in Philadelphia (1696) took a step in advance of this, admonishing their members to be careful not to encourage the *bringing in* of *any more negroes*, and that those who *have* negroes be careful of them, bring them to meeting, etc., etc. It thus appears that Quakers, like other Christians, were then not only slaveholders, but engaged in the Slave-Trade. In 1754, the American Quakers had advanced to the point of publicly recommending their societies to "advise and deal with such as engage in" the Slave-Trade. Again: slaveholding Quakers were urged—not to emancipate their slaves—but to care for their morals, and treat them humanely. The British Quakers came up to this mark in 1758—four years later; and more decidedly in 1761 and 1763. In 1774, the Philadelphia meeting directed that all persons engaged in any form of slave-trading be "disowned;" and in 1776 took the decisive and final step by directing "that the *owners* of slaves, who refused to execute the proper instruments for giving them their freedom, be disowned likewise." This blow hit the nail on the head. In 1781, but "one case" requiring discipline under this head was reported; and in 1783, it duly appeared that there were *no* slaves owned by its members.[1] The cöincidence of these later dates with the origin, progress, and close of our Revolutionary struggle, is noteworthy. The New York and Rhode Island yearly meetings passed almost simultaneously through the same stages to like results; that of Virginia pursued a like course; but, meeting greater obstacles, was longer in overcoming them. It discouraged the *purchasing* of slaves in 1766; urgently recommended manumission in 1773; yet, so late as 1787, its annual reports stated that some members still held slaves. But it is understood that Slavery and Quakerism, throughout the South, had very little communion or sympathy after the Revolution, and were gradually and finally divorced so early as 1800. Hence, as Slavery grew stronger and more intolerant there, Quakerism gradually faded out; so that its adherents were probably fewer in that section in 1860 than they had been eighty years before.

Of other religious denominations, none of the more important and popular, which date back to the earlier periods of our colonial history, can show even so fair a record as the above. By the Roman Catholics and Protestant Episcopalians, generally, Slaveholding has never been, and is not yet, considered inconsistent with piety, and a blameless, exemplary, Christian life. Individuals in these, as in other communions, have conspicuously condemned and earnestly opposed Human Slavery; but the general influence of these churches in our country, and especially of their

[1] Clarkson's History.

hierarchies, has been adverse to the practical recognition of every innocent man's right to his own limbs and sinews, and to sell or employ his own labor as to himself shall seem best.

The Presbyterian, Congregational, Baptist, and kindred "Orthodox" denominations, have no very consistent or luminous record on this subject. Thus, the Presbyterian General Assembly did, at its session in 1794—long before its division into "Old School" and "New School"—adopt a note to one of the questions in its longer Catechism, wherein, expounding and applying the Eighth Commandment, it affirmed that the Biblical condemnation of "*man-stealers*"

> "comprehends all who are concerned in bringing any of the human race into Slavery, *or retaining them therein.* Stealers of men are those who bring off slaves or freemen, and *keep*, *sell*, *or buy them.* To steal a freeman, says Grotius, is the highest kind of theft," etc., etc.

But this note was directed to be *erased* by the General Assembly of 1816, in a resolve which characterizes Slavery as a "mournful evil," but does not direct that the churches be purged of it. In 1818, a fresh Assembly adopted an "Expression of Views," wherein Slavery is reprobated as a

> "gross violation of the most precious and sacred rights of human nature, utterly inconsistent with the law of God, which requires us to love our neighbor as ourselves, and totally irreconcilable with the spirit and principles of the gospel of Christ, which enjoin that 'all things whatsoever ye would that men should do to you, do ye also to them.'"

But, instead of requiring its members to clear themselves, and *keep* clear, of slaveholding, the Assembly exhorted them to "continue and increase their exertions to effect a total abolition of Slavery, *with no greater delay than a regard for the public welfare demands!*" and recommended that, if "a Christian professor shall *sell* a slave, *who is also in communion with our Church*"—said slave not being a consenting party to the sale—the seller be "suspended till he shall repent and make reparation!" It need hardly be added that, with few and spasmodic exceptions, the Presbyterian Church thenceforth was found apologizing for Slavery, and censuring its determined assailants far oftener than doing or devising anything to hasten that "total abolition," which it had solemnly pronounced a requirement of Christianity. And, though the Synod of Kentucky, in 1835, adopted a report on Slavery, which condemned slaveholding broadly and thoroughly, and reprobated the domestic slave-trade as revolting, even horrible, in its cruelty, the same report admits that "those who hold to our communion, are involved in it;" and no action was taken whereby they should be required to choose between their connection with the Church and persistence in buying, holding, and selling men, women, and children, as slaves.

Nor did the division of this Church, which occurred not long afterward, work any improvement in this respect. A majority of the slaveholding members, doubtless, adhered to the "Old School;" but the "New School" did not see fit to make slaveholding a bar to its communion. On the contrary, certain Presbyteries having done so, the General Assembly of 1843 censured their action, and required that it be rescinded. And though, in 1846, the next General Assembly reiterated, in substance, the broad condemnation of Slavery contained in the Expression of Views in 1818, and in 1849 proclaimed that

"there has been no information before this Assembly to prove that the members of our Church, in the Slave States, are not doing all they can (situated as they are, in the providence of God) to bring about the possession and enjoyment of liberty by the enslaved,"

it is as certain as that "fine words butter no parsnips," that slaves continued to be bought, held, and sold by members of the "New," as well as of the "Old School" Presbyterian Church, and that, while Abolitionists were subject to continued and unsparing denunciation in the common as well as the special organs and utterances of these rival sects, slaveholders often filled the highest seats in their respective synagogues, and Slavery regarded their aimless denunciations and practical tolerance with serene complacency.

With the Baptists and Methodists—two very numerous and important denominations—the case was somewhat different. Each of these churches was originally anti-Slavery. The Methodists, in the infancy of their communion, were gathered mainly from among the poor and despised classes, and had much more affiliation with slaves than with their masters. Their discipline could with great difficulty be reconciled with slaveholding by their laity, while it decidedly could *not* be made to permit slaveholding on the part of their Bishops; and this impelled the secession, some twenty years since, of the "Methodist Church South," carrying off most, but not all, of the churches located in the Slave States. The General Conference held at Cincinnati in 1836 solemnly disclaimed "any right, wish, or intention, to interfere with the civil and political relation between master and slave, as it exists in the slaveholding States of this Union," condemned two ministers who had delivered Abolition lectures, and declared the opponents of Abolition "true friends to the Church, to the slaves of the South, and to the Constitution of our Country."

The Baptists of Virginia, in General Assembly, 1789, upon a reference from the session of the preceding year, on motion of Elder John Leland,

"*Resolved*, That Slavery is a violent deprivation of the rights of nature, and inconsistent with republican government; and therefore we recommend it to our brethren to make use of every measure to extirpate this horrid evil from the land; and pray Almighty God that our honorable Legislature may have it in their power to proclaim the great jubilee, consistent with the principles of good policy."

But no similar declaration has been made by any Southern Baptist State Convention since field-hands rose to $1,000 each, and black infants, at birth, were accounted worth $100. On the contrary, the Southern Baptists have for thirty years been among the foremost champions of slaveholding as righteous and Christian, and the Savannah River Baptist Association in 1835 gravely decided that slave husbands and wives, separated by sale, should be at liberty to take new partners; because

"such separation, among persons situated as our slaves are, is civilly a separation by death, and they believe that, in the sight of God, it would be so viewed. To forbid second marriages, in such cases, would be to expose the parties not only to greater hardships and stronger temptations, but to *church censure* for acting *in obedience to their masters*," etc., etc.

Thus adapting Christianity to Slavery, instead of requiring that Slavery be made to square with the requirements of Christianity. And this is a fair specimen of what has passed for religion at the South for the last thirty or forty years.

In full view of these facts, the Northern and Southern Baptists met for thirty years in Triennial Convention, over which slaveholders usually presided, and wherein the righteousness of slaveholding could not, therefore, without seeming rudeness, be questioned. Abolition might be freely stigmatized; slaveholding was tacitly admitted to be just and proper by the very constitution of the body. And by no sect or class have anti-Slavery inculcations been more virulently reprobated than by the Baptists of the South.

The Free-Will Baptists, several bodies of Scottish Covenanters, and other offsets from the original Presbyterian stock, with certain of the Methodist dissenters or seceders from the great Methodist Episcopal organization, have generally maintained an attitude of hostility to Slavery. So, of late years, have the greater number of Unitarian and Universalist conventions. But all these together are a decided minority of the American People, or even of the professing Christians among them; and they do not at all shake the general truth that the anti-Slavery cause, throughout the years of its arduous and perilous struggle up from contempt and odium to respect and power, received far more of hindrance than of help from our ecclesiastical organizations. And this fact explains, if it does not excuse, the un-Orthodox, irreverent, and "infidel" tendencies which have been so freely, and not always unreasonably, ascribed to the apostles of Abolition. These have justly felt that the organized and recognized religion of the country has not treated their cause as it deserved and as they had a right to expect. The pioneers of "modern Abolition" were almost uniformly devout, pious, church-nurtured men, who, at the outset of their enterprise, took the cause of the slave[2] to the Clergy and the Church, with undoubting faith that it would there be recognized and by them adopted as the cause of vital Christianity. Speaking generally, they were repulsed and resisted, quite as much to their astonishment as their mortification; and the resulting estrangement and hostility were proportioned to the fullness of their trust, the bitterness of their disappointment.[3] It would have been wiser, doubtless, to have forborne, and trusted, and reasoned, and remonstrated, and supplicated; but patience and policy are not the virtues for which reformers are apt to be distinguished; since, were they prudent and politic, they would choose some safer and sunnier path. No insurance company that had taken a large risk on the life of John the Baptist would have counseled or approved his freedom of speech with regard to the domestic relations of Herod.

[2] Witness Lundy and Garrison at Boston, 1828.

[3] "Alas! they had been friends in youth;
But whispering tongues can poison truth,
And constancy lives in realms above;
And life is thorny and youth is vain;
And to be wroth with one we love,
Doth work like madness on the brain."
—*Coleridge's Christabel.*

XI.

THE PRO-SLAVERY REACTION.

The Liberator, by its uncompromising spirit and unsparing denunciations, soon challenged and secured, to an extent quite unprecedented, the attention of adversaries. Treating Slavery uniformly as a crime to be repented, a wrong to be righted at the earliest moment, if it did not convince the understanding of slaveholders, it at least excited their wrath. Before it had been issued a year, while it had probably less than a thousand subscribers, and while its editor and his partner were still working all day as journeymen printers, sleeping, after some hours' editorial labor, at night on the floor of their little sky-parlor office, and dreaming rather of how or where to get money or credit for the paper required for next week's issue than of troubling the repose of States, they were flattered by an act of the Legislature of Georgia, unanimously passed, and duly approved by Governor Lumpkin, offering the liberal reward of $5,000 to whomsoever should arrest, bring to trial, and prosecute to conviction, either of them under the laws of that State—the arrest being the only difficult matter.[1] There was no reason to doubt that the proffer was made in good faith, and that the stipulated reward would have been more promptly and cheerfully paid than Southern debts are apt to be. Other such rewards of $10,000, $50,000, and even $100,000, for the bodies or the heads of prominent Abolitionists, were from time to time advertised; but these plagiarisms were seldom responsibly backed, and proved only the anxiety of the offerers to distinguish themselves and cheaply win a local popularity. Their aspect was not business-like. In several instances, Southern grand juries gravely indicted Northern "agitators" for offenses against the peace and dignity of their respective States; and in at least one case a formal requisition was made upon the Governor of New York for the surrender of an Abolitionist who had never trod the soil of the offended State; but the Governor (Marcy), though ready to do what he lawfully could to propitiate Southern favor, was constrained respectfully to decline.

That "error of opinion may be safely tolerated where reason is left free to combat it,"[2] is a truth that does not seem to have occurred either to the Southern or Northern contemners of the Garrisonian ultras. In fact, it does not seem to have irradiated the minds of the chief priests, scribes and Pharisees of Christ's day, nor those of the hereditary champions of established institutions and gainful traditions at almost any time. The South-

[1] Harrison Gray Otis, the wealthy and aristocratic Mayor of Boston, being required by a Southern magistrate to suppress *The Liberator*—which was probably the first he had heard of it—in due season reported that his officers had "ferreted out the paper and its editor, whose office was an obscure hole, his only visible auxiliary a negro boy, his supporters a few *insignificant* persons of all colors"—whence the said Otis concluded that his paper ought not to disturb the slumbers of the quite significant and potent Southrons. The superficial, purblind Mayor!

[2] Jefferson's Inaugural Address.

ern journals and other oracles imperiously, wrathfully, demanded the instant suppression and extinction of the "incendiaries" and "fanatics," under the usual penalty of a dissolution of the Union;[3] to which was now added the annihilation of Northern prosperity and consequence through a retributive withdrawal of Southern trade.[4] The commercial and political interests at the North, which regarded Southern favor as the sheet-anchor of their hopes, eagerly responded to these overtures, clamoring for penal enactments and popular proofs of Northern fidelity to Constitutional obligations. The former were not forthcoming; in fact, the most adroit and skillful draftsman would have found it difficult to frame any such law as was required—any one that would have subserved the end in view—that would not have directly and glaringly contravened the constitution or bill of rights of even the most "conservative" State. Yet President Jackson did not hesitate, in his Annual Message of December 2, 1835, to say:

"I must also invite your attention to the painful excitement produced in the South by attempts to circulate, through the mails, inflammatory appeals addressed to the passions of the slaves, in prints, and in various sorts of publications, calculated to stimulate them to insurrection, and to produce all the horrors of a servile war.

"There is, doubtless, no respectable portion of our fellow-countrymen who can be so far misled as to feel any other sentiment than that of indignant regret at conduct so destructive of the harmony and peace of the country, and so repugnant to the principles of our national compact, and to the dictates of humanity and religion. Our happiness and prosperity essentially depend upon peace within our borders—and peace depends upon the maintenance, in good faith, of those compromises of the Constitution upon which the Union is founded. It is fortunate for the country that the good sense, the generous feeling, and the deep-rooted attachment of the people of the non-slaveholding States to the Union, and to their fellow-citizens of the same blood in the South, have given so strong and impressive a tone to the sentiments entertained against the proceedings of the misguided persons who have engaged in these unconstitutional and wicked attempts, and especially against the emissaries from foreign parts who have dared to interfere in this matter, as to authorize the hope that those attempts will no longer be persisted in. But, if these expressions of the public will shall not be sufficient to effect so desirable a result, not a doubt can be entertained that the non-slaveholding States, so far from countenancing the slightest interference with the constitutional rights of the South, will be prompt to exercise their authority in suppressing, so far as in them lies, whatever is calculated to produce the evil.

"In leaving the care of other branches of this interesting subject to the State authorities, to whom they properly belong, it is nevertheless proper for Congress to take such measures as will prevent the Post-Office Department, which was designed to

[3] The following is an extract from the *Augusta* (Ga.) *Chronicle* of October, 1833.

"We firmly believe that, if the Southern States do not quickly unite, and declare to the North, if the question of Slavery be longer *discussed* in any shape, they will instantly secede from the Union, that the question must be settled, and very soon, by the SWORD, as the only possible means of self-preservation."

February 16, 1836, both houses of the Virginia Legislature agreed to the following:

"*Resolved*, That the non-slaveholding States of the Union are respectfully but *earnestly* requested promptly to adopt *penal enactments*, or such other measures as will *effectually suppress all associations* within their respective limits purporting to be, or having the character of, Abolition societies."

Resolutions, similar in spirit and demand, were adopted by the Legislatures of South Carolina, North Carolina, Alabama, and doubtless other Slave States.

[4] *The Richmond Whig*, in the course of a fulmination against the Abolitionists, said:

"The people of the North must go to hanging these fanatics *if they would not lose the benefit of the Southern trade*, and they *will* do it. * * * Depend upon it, the Northern people *will never sacrifice their present lucrative trade with the South, so long as the hanging of a few thousands will prevent it.*"

Not a bad calculation, *provided* "the Northern people" and the enjoyers of "the lucrative trade" aforesaid had been identical; but they were not.

foster an amicable intercourse and correspondence between all the members of the confederacy, from being used as an instrument of an opposite character. The General Government, to which the great trust is confided of preserving inviolate the relations created among the States by the Constitution, is especially bound to avoid, in its own action, any thing that may disturb them. I would therefore call the special attention of Congress to the subject, and respectfully suggest the propriety of passing such a law as will prohibit, under severe penalties, the circulation in the Southern States, through the mail, of incendiary publications intended to instigate the slaves to insurrection."

Had the President been asked to justify his charges against his fellow-citizens of having "attempted to circulate, through the mails, inflammatory appeals, addressed to the passions of *slaves*, in *prints*," etc., etc., he must have answered that he had heard or read charges to this effect, and had believed them. But it was in vain that the Abolitionists remonstrated, and protested, and called for proofs. The slaveholding interest detested and feared them; the mob was in full cry at their heels; and it was the seeming interest of the great majority of speakers and writers to join in the hunt.[5]

Governor Marcy followed in the footsteps of his party chief. In his Annual Message of January 5, 1836—five weeks later than the foregoing—he said:

"Relying on the influence of a sound and enlightened public opinion to restrain and control the misconduct of the citizens of a free government, especially when directed, as it has been in this case, with unexampled energy and unanimity, to the particular evils under consideration, and perceiving that its operations have been thus far salutary, I entertain the best hopes that this remedy, of itself, will entirely remove these evils, or render them comparatively harmless. But, if these reasonable expectations should, unhappily, be disappointed; if, in the face of numerous and striking exhibitions of public reprobation, elicited from our constituents by a just fear of the fatal issues in which the uncurbed efforts of the Abolitionists may ultimately end, any considerable portion of these misguided men shall persist in pushing them forward to disastrous consequences, then a question, new to our confederacy, will necessarily arise, and must be met. It must then be determined how far the several States can provide, within the proper exercise of their constitutional powers, and how far, in fulfillment of the obligations resulting from their federal relations, they ought to provide, by their own laws, for the trial and punishment by their own judicatories, of residents within their limits, guilty of acts therein, which are calculated and intended to excite insurrection and rebellion in a sister State. * * * I cannot doubt that the Legislature possesses the power to pass such penal laws as will have the effect of preventing the citizens of this State and residents within it from availing themselves, with impunity, of the protection of its sovereignty and laws, while they are actually employed in exciting insurrection and sedition in a sister State, or engaged in treasonable enterprises, intended to be executed therein."

A legislative Report responsive to these recommendations was made in *May* following, just at the close of the session, which assumed to pledge the faith of the State to pass such laws as were suggested by the Governor, *whenever they shall be requisite!* This report was duly forwarded to the Southern Governors, but not circulated at large, nor was any such action as it proposed ever taken—or meant to be. Governor Edward Everett (Whig), of Massachusetts, sent[6] a Message to the Legislature of his State, communicating the demands of certain Southern States that anti-Slavery inculcations in the Free States should be legally suppressed, and saying:

"Whatever by direct and necessary ope-

[5] "Now we tell them [the Abolitionists] that when they openly and publicly promulgate doctrines which outrage public feeling, they have no right to demand protection of the people they insult. Ought not, we ask, our city authorities to make them understand this—to tell them that they prosecute their TREASONABLE and BEASTLY plans at their own peril?"—*New York Courier and Enquirer*, 11th July, 1834.

[6] January 6, 1836.

ration is *calculated* to excite an insurrection among the slaves, has been held, by highly respectable legal authority, an offense against the peace of this commonwealth, which may be prosecuted as a *misdemeanor at common law.*"

The Legislature referred the subject to a joint Committee, whereof a conspicuous champion of Slavery was Chairman. The Abolitionists perceived and eagerly embraced their opportunity. They demanded a hearing before this Committee—they being accused of grave misdemeanors in the documents whereon it was to act—and their request was tardily acceded to. On the 3d of March, 1836, they were apprised that they would be heard *next day*. They were duly present accordingly—the Committee sitting in the spacious Representatives' Hall, neither House being in session. Brief addresses in their behalf were heard from Rev. Samuel J. May and Ellis Gray Loring, who were followed by Professor Charles Follen, who, in the course of his remarks, alluded to the mob outrages to which the Abolitionists had recently been subjected, remarking that any legislative enactment to their prejudice would tend to encourage their adversaries to repeat those outrages. The Chairman treated this remark as disrespectful to the Committee, and abruptly terminated the hearing. The Abolitionists thereupon completed promptly their defense, and issued it in a pamphlet, which naturally attracted public attention, and a popular conviction that fair play had not been accorded them was manifested. The Legislature shared it, and directed its Committee to allow them a full hearing. Monday, the 8th, was accordingly appointed for the purpose. By this time, the public interest had become diffused and intensified, and the Hall was crowded with earnest auditors. The Rev. William E. Channing, then the most eminent clergyman in New England, appeared among the champions of Free Speech. Professor Follen concluded, and was followed by Samuel E. Sewall, William Lloyd Garrison, and William Goodell—the last-named stigmatizing the demand of the South and its backers as an assault on the liberties of the North. Mr. Bond, a Boston merchant, and Dr. Bradley, from Plymouth, were prompted by the impulse of the hour to add their unpremeditated remonstrances against the contemplated invasion of time-honored rights. Darkness had set in when the Committee rose, and a low murmur of approving multitudes gave token that the cause of liberty had triumphed. The Committee reported adversely to the "agitators" and "fanatics" at the heel of the session, but in evident despair of any accordant action; and none was ever had. Massachusetts refused to manacle her own people in order to rivet more securely the shackles of others.

Rhode Island was the theatre of a similar attempt, ending in a similar failure. And if, in any other State, like efforts were made, they were likewise defeated. No nominally Free State, however hostile to Abolition, consented to make it a crime on the part of her people to "preach deliverance to the captive."

But the systematic suppression of anti-Slavery teaching by riot and mob-violence was, for a time, well-nigh universal. In New York, a meeting at Clinton Hall, to organize a City Anti-Slavery Society, having been called for the evening of October 2, 1833, there appeared a counter-call from "Many Southrons" for a meeting at the same time and place. In apprehension of a riot, Clinton Hall was not opened; but such of the Abolitionists as could be notified on the instant repaired to the Chatham-street Chapel. Their opponents met in Tammany Hall, and, after making their speeches and passing their resolves unquestioned, were about to adjourn, when they were apprised of the meeting in the Chapel. "Let us rout them!" was the general cry; and they rushed noisily to the Chapel only to find that the Abolitionists had departed. "Ten thousand dollars for Arthur Tappan!" was shouted; but no one was molested, and the crowd dissolved in the comforting assurance that the Union was safe.

But on the 4th of July, 1834, an attempt to hold an anti-Slavery celebration in Chatham-street Chapel was the signal for a furious and alarming riot. The prayer, the singing, and the reading of the Declaration, were endured with tolerable patience; but a Declaration of the Sentiments of the Anti-Slavery Society by Lewis Tappan was interrupted by hisses; and when David Paul Brown, of Philadelphia, commenced his oration, it was soon manifest that a large portion of the audience had come expressly *not* to hear him, nor let any one else. Rev. Samuel H. Cox interposed in behalf of Free Speech; but both were clamored down with cries of "Treason! Treason! Hurrah for the Union!" and the meeting quietly dispersed, without awaiting or provoking further violence.

The leading commercial journals having commended this experiment in Union-saving, the actors were naturally impelled to extend it. At midnight on the 9th, the dwelling of Lewis Tappan was broken open by a mob, his furniture carried into the street, and consigned to the flames. The burning of the house was then proposed; but the Mayor remonstrated, and it was forborne. The riots were continued through the next day; the doors and windows of Dr. Cox's (Presbyterian) church being broken, with those of Dr. Ludlow's church; while a Baptist, a Methodist, and a Protestant Episcopal church, belonging to colored congregations, were badly shattered, and one of them nearly destroyed, as was a school-house for colored children, and many dwellings inhabited by negroes, while others were seriously injured. Many rioters were arrested during these days by the police, but none of them was ever punished.

Newark, New Jersey, imitated this riot on the 11th, but with indifferent success. A church was somewhat injured.

Philadelphia followed on the 13th of August. Her riots lasted three nights, and the harmless and powerless blacks were mainly their victims. Forty-four houses (mostly small) were destroyed or seriously injured. Among them was a colored Presbyterian church. Several of the blacks were chased and assaulted, one of them being beaten to death, and another losing his life in attempting to swim the Schuylkill to escape his pursuers.

At Worcester, Massachusetts, August 10, 1835, the Rev. Orange Scott, who was lecturing against Slavery, was assaulted, his notes torn up, and personal violence attempted.

At Concord, New Hampshire, on the same day, a mob demolished an academy, because colored boys were admitted as pupils.

At Canterbury, Connecticut, Miss Prudence Crandall having attempted, in 1833, to open a school for colored children, an act was passed by the Legislature forbidding any teaching within that State of colored youth from other States. She persisted, and was imprisoned for it as a malefactor. Having been liberated, she resumed her school; when it was broken up by mob-violence.

The riots whereof the foregoing are specimens were too numerous and wide-spread to be even glanced at severally. They were, doubtless, multiplied and intensified by the presence in our country of GEORGE THOMPSON, an eminent and ardent English Abolitionist, who—now that the triumph of Emancipation in the British West Indies was secured—came over to aid the kindred struggle in this country. That a Briton should presume to plead for Liberty in this free and enlightened country was not to be endured; and Mr. Thompson's eloquence, fervor, and thoroughness, increased the hostility excited by his presence, which, of itself, was held an ample excuse for mobs. He was finally induced to desist and return to England, from a conviction that the prejudice aroused by his interference in what was esteemed a domestic difference overbalanced the good effect of his lectures. The close of this year (1835) was signalized by the conversion of GERRIT SMITH—hitherto a leading and zealous Colonizationist—to the principles of the Abolitionists.

In Northfield, New Hampshire, December 14, 1835, Rev. George Storrs attempted to deliver an anti-Slavery lecture, but was dragged from his knees while at prayer, preliminary to his address, by a deputy sheriff, on the strength of a warrant issued by a justice, on a complaint charging him with being "a common rioter and brawler," "an idle and disorderly person, going about the town and county disturbing the public peace." On trial, he was acquitted; but, on the 31st of March following, after having lectured at Pittsfield, New Hampshire, he was again arrested while at prayer, on a writ issued by one who afterward became a Member of Congress, tried the same day, convicted, and sentenced to three months' imprisonment in the House of Correction. He appealed, and that was probably the end of the matter.

At Boston, October 21, 1835, a large and most respectable mob, composed in good part of merchants, assailed a meeting of the Female Anti-Slavery Society, while its President was at prayer, and dispersed it. William Lloyd Garrison, having escaped, was found concealed in a cabinet-maker's shop, seized and dragged through the streets with a rope around his body, threatened with tar and feathers, but finally conducted to the Mayor, who lodged him in jail till the next day, to protect him from further violence. At the earnest request of the authorities, he left town for a time.

At Utica, New York, the same day, a meeting, convened to form a State Anti-Slavery Society, was broken up by a most respectable Committee, appointed by a large meeting of citizens. The office of a Democratic journal that had spoken kindly of the Abolitionists was assailed and its press thrown down. The discipline proved effective. No Democratic journal issued in that city has since ventured to speak a word for Freedom or Humanity. The Abolitionists, at Gerrit Smith's invitation, adjourned to his home at Peterborough, Madison County, and there completed their organization.

At the South, there was but one mode of dealing with Abolitionists—that described by Henry A. Wise as made up of "Dupont's best [gunpowder], and cold steel." "Let your emissaries cross the Potomac," writes the Rev. T. S. Witherspoon from Alabama to *The Emancipator*, "and I can promise you that your fate will be no less than Haman's."[7] Says the Rev. William Plummer, D. D., of Richmond, Virginia, in response (July, 1835) to a call for a meeting of the clergy to take action on the exciting topic, "Let the Abolitionists understand that they *will be caught* if they come among us, and they will take good care to stay away."[8] The calculation was a tolerably sound one; yet it did not save quite a number of persons—mainly of Northern birth—who were seized at various points throughout the South on suspicion of being anti-Slavery, and very summarily put to death—some with, and some without, a mob trial. Had there been any proof[9] against them, they would doubtless have been left to the operation of the laws for such cases made and provided; for these were certainly harsh enough to satisfy even Wise himself.

At Charleston, S. C., July 29, 1835, it was noised about that the mails just arrived from the North contained a quantity of Abolition periodicals and documents. A public meeting was thereupon called, which the Reverend Clergy of the

[7] At a public meeting convened in the *church* in the town of Clinton, Mississippi, September 5, 1835, it was

"*Resolved*, That it is our decided opinion, that any individual who dares to circulate, with a view to effectuate the designs of the Abolitionists, any of the incendiary tracts or newspapers now in the course of transmission to this country, is justly worthy, in the sight of God and man, of immediate death: and we doubt not that such would be the punishment of any such offender, in any part of the State of Mississippi where he may be found."

[8] "The cry of the whole South should be death—instant death—to the abolitionist, wherever he is caught."—*Augusta* (Ga.) *Chronicle.*

"We can assure the Bostonians, one and all, who have embarked in the nefarious scheme of abolishing Slavery at the South, that lashes will hereafter be spared the backs of their emissaries. Let them send out their men to Louisiana; they will never return to tell their sufferings, but they shall expiate the crime of interfering with our domestic institutions, by being BURNED AT THE STAKE."—*New Orleans True American.*

"Abolition editors in Slave States will not dare to avow their opinions. It would be instant DEATH to them."—*Missouri Argus.*

And Mr. Preston, of South Carolina, who once delivered a speech at Columbia in reference to a proposed railroad, in which he despondingly drew a forcible contrast between the energy, enterprise, knowledge, and happiness of the North, and the inertia, indigence, and decay of the South, in the U. S. Senate afterward declared:

"Let an abolitionist come within the borders of South Carolina, if we can catch we will try him, and, notwithstanding all the interference of all the governments of the earth, including the Federal Government, we will HANG him."—*See "N. Y. Journal of Commerce,"* June 6, 1838.

[9] In 1835, a suspicion was aroused in Madison County, Mississippi, that a conspiracy for a slave insurrection existed. Five negroes were first hung; then five white men. The pamphlet put forth by their mob-murderers shows that there was no real evidence against any of them—that their lives were sacrificed to a cowardly panic, which would not be appeased without bloodshed. The whites were hung at an hour's notice, protesting their innocence to the last. And this is but one case out of many such. In a panic of this kind, every non-slaveholder who ever said a kind word or did a humane act for a negro is a doomed man.

city attended in a body, "lending," says *The Courier* of next morning, "their sanction to the proceedings, and adding, by their presence, to the impressive character of the scene." This meeting unanimously resolved that all the mail matter in question should be burnt, and it *was* burnt accordingly—the mails being searched and rifled for the purpose; "although," (says *The Courier*), "arrangements had previously been made at the Post-office to arrest the circulation of incendiary matter, until instructions could be received from the Department at Washington;" and "it might have been better, perhaps, to have awaited the answer before proceeding to extremities." But Mr. Amos Kendall, then Postmaster-General, was not the man to "hint a fault, or hesitate dislike," with regard to such mail robbery, though obliged to confess that it was not strictly according to act of Congress.

"I am satisfied," he replied to the Postmaster's application, "that the Postmaster-General has no legal authority to exclude newspapers from the mail, nor to prohibit their carriage or delivery on account of their character or tendency, real or supposed." "But I am not prepared to direct you to forward or deliver the papers of which you speak." "By no act or direction of mine, official or private, could I be induced to aid, knowingly, in giving circulation to papers of this description, directly or indirectly. We owe an obligation to the *laws*, but a *higher* one to the communities in which we live; and, if the *former* be permitted to destroy the *latter*, it is patriotism to disregard them. Entertaining these views, I *cannot sanction*, and will *not condemn*, the step you have taken. Your justification must be looked for in the character of the papers detained, and the circumstances by which you are surrounded."

Governor Seward has been widely charged and credited with the authorship of the "higher law" doctrine; but here we find it clearly set forth in a grave Democratic State paper, fifteen years before he uttered it. And it is yet far older than this.

General Jackson's recommendation of repression by law of the circulation of "incendiary" matter through the mails, was referred by the Senate to a Select Committee, whereof John C. Calhoun was Chairman. The perilous *scope* of any such legislation was at once clear to the keen intellect of that statesman, who had by this time learned to dread "Consolidation" as intensely as he detested "Abolition." He reported (February 4, 1836), that the measure proposed by the President would violate the Constitution, and imperil public liberty.

"Nothing is more clear," says the Report, "than that the admission of the right of Congress to determine what papers are incendiary, and, as such, to prohibit their circulation through the mail, necessarily involves the RIGHT to determine what are NOT incendiary, and ENFORCE their circulation. * * * If Congress may this year decide what incendiary publications ARE, they may, next year, decide what they are NOT, and thus laden their mails with real or covert abolitionism. * * * It belongs to the STATES, and not to Congress, to determine what is or is not calculated to disturb their security."

He proposed, therefore, that each *State* should determine for itself what kind of reading it would deem "incendiary," and that Congress should thereupon prohibit the transmission by mail of such matter to *that State*. He concluded with a bill, which contained this provision:

"*Be it enacted, etc.*, That it shall not be lawful for any deputy postmaster, in any State, Territory, or District, of the United States, knowingly, to deliver to any person whatsoever, any pamphlet, newspaper, handbill, or other printed paper or pictorial representation, touching the subject of Slavery, where, by the laws of the said State, Territory, or District, their circulation is prohibited; and any deputy postmaster who shall be guilty thereof, shall be forthwith removed from office."

This bill was ordered to a third reading by 18 Yeas to 18 Nays—Mr. Van Buren, then Vice-President, giving the casting vote in the affirmative. It failed, however, to pass; and that ended the matter.

ELIJAH P. LOVEJOY, son of Rev. Daniel Lovejoy, and the eldest of seven children, was born at Albion, Maine, November 9, 1802. His ancestors, partly English and partly Scotch, all of the industrious middle class, had been citizens of New Hampshire and of Maine for several generations. He was distinguished, from early youth, alike for diligence in labor and for zeal and success in the acquisition of knowledge. He graduated with high honors at Waterville College, Maine, in September, 1826. In May following, he turned his face westward, and in the autumn of that year found employment as a teacher in St. Louis. In 1828, he became editor of a political journal, of the "National Republican" faith, and was thence actively engaged in politics of the Clay and Webster school, until January, 1832, when he was brought under deep religious impressions, and the next month united with the Presbyterian Church. Relinquishing his political pursuits and prospects, he engaged in a course of study preparatory for the ministry, entering the Theological Seminary at Princeton, New Jersey, on the 24th of March. He received, next Spring, a license to preach from the second Presbytery of Philadelphia, and spent the Summer as an evangelist in Newport, R. I., and in New York. He left the last-named city in the autumn of that year, and returned to St. Louis, at the urgent invitation of a circle of fellow-Christians, who desired him to establish and edit a religious newspaper in that city—furnishing a capital of twelve hundred dollars for the purpose, and guaranteeing him, in writing, the entire control of the concern. *The St. Louis Observer*, weekly, was accordingly first issued on the 22d of November. It was of the "Evangelical" or Orthodox Protestant school, but had no controversy, save with wickedness, and no purpose, but to quicken the zeal and enlarge the usefulness of professing Christians, while adding, if possible, to their number. There is no evidence that it was commenced with any intent to war on Slavery, or with any expectation of exciting the special hostility of any interest but that of Satan. Its first exhibition of a combative or belligerent tendency had for its object the Roman Catholics and their dogmas; but this, though it naturally provoked some resentment in a city so largely Catholic as St. Louis, excited no tumult or violence. Its first articles concerning Slavery were exceedingly moderate in their tone, and favorable rather to Colonization than to immediate Abolition. Even when the editor first took decided ground against Slavery,[10] he still affirmed his hostility to immediate, unconditional emancipation. This article was, in part, based on an editorial in *The St. Louis Republican*, of the preceding week, which—discussing a proposed Convention to revise the Constitution of that State—said:

---

[10] April 16, 1835.

"We look to the Convention as a happy means of relieving the State, at some future day, of an evil which is destroying all our wholesome energies, and leaving us, in morals, in enterprise, and in wealth, behind the neighboring States. We mean, of course, the curse of *Slavery*. We are not about to make any attack upon the rights of those who at present hold this description of property. They ought to be respected to the letter. We only propose that measures shall now be taken for the Abolition of Slavery, at such distant period of time as may be thought expedient, and eventually for ridding the country altogether of a colored population."

Mr. Lovejoy, commenting on the foregoing, wished that some Southern-born man, of high character, decided ability, and fervent piety, would take up the subject of Slavery in a proper spirit, and, being familiar, experimentally, with all its evils and its difficulties, would show the people, practically, what they ought to do with regard to it. He continued:

"To such a man, a golden opportunity of doing good is offered. We believe the minds of the good people of this State are fully prepared to listen to him—to give a dispassionate consideration to the facts and reasonings he might present connected with the subject of Slavery. Public sentiment, amongst us, is already moving in this great matter—it now wants to be directed in some defined channel, to some definite end.

"Taken all in all, there is not a State in this Union possessing superior natural advantages to our own. At present, Slavery, like an incubus, is paralyzing our energies, and, like a cloud of evil portent, darkening all our prospects. Let this be removed, and Missouri would at once start forward in the race of improvement, with an energy and rapidity of movement that would soon place her in the front rank along with the most favored of her sister States."

He continued to speak of Slavery at intervals, through that summer, leaving his post in October to attend a regular meeting of the Presbyterian Synod.

Directly after his departure, an excitement commenced with regard to his strictures on Slavery; and the proprietors of *The Observer*, alarmed by threats of mob-violence, issued a card, promising that nothing should be said on the exciting subject until the editor's return; and, this not proving satisfactory, they issued a further card on the 21st, declaring themselves, "one and all," opposed to the mad schemes of the Abolitionists. Before this, a letter[11] had been written

[11] ST. LOUIS, October 5, 1835.

To the Rev. E. P. Lovejoy, Editor of The Observer:

Sir:—The undersigned, friends and supporters of the "Observer," beg leave to suggest, that the present temper of the times requires a change in the manner of conducting that print in relation to the subject of domestic Slavery.

The public mind is greatly excited, and, owing to the unjustifiable interference of our Northern brethren with our social relations, the community are, perhaps, not in a situation to endure sound doctrine in relation to this subject. Indeed, we have reason to believe, that violence is even now meditated against the "Observer Office;" and we do believe that true policy and the interests of religion require that the discussion of this exciting question should be at least postponed in this State.

Although we do not claim the right to prescribe your course as an Editor, we hope that the concurring opinions of so many persons, having the interest of your paper and of religion both at heart, may induce you to distrust your own judgment, and so far change the character of the "Observer," as to pass over in silence everything connected with the subject of Slavery. We would like that you announce in your paper, your intention so to do.

We shall be glad to be informed of your determination in relation to this matter.

Respectfully, your obedient servants,

ARCHIBALD GAMBLE, G. W. CALL,
NATHAN RANNEY, H. R. GAMBLE,
WILLIAM S. POTTS, HEZEKIAH KING,
JNO. KERR.

I concur in the object intended by this communication.

BEVERLY ALLEN.

I concur in the foregoing.

J. B. BRYANT.

This document is indorsed as follows:

"I did not yield to the wishes here expressed, and in consequence have been persecuted ever since. But I have kept a good conscience in the matter, and that more than repays me for all I have suffered, or can suffer. I have sworn eternal opposition to Slavery, and, by the blessing of God, I will never go back. Amen.

"E. P. L.

"*October* 24, 1837."

to the editor by nine eminent citizens of St. Louis (including H. R. Gamble, her present provisional Governor), urging him "to pass over in silence everything connected with the subject of Slavery;" which, in due time, he respectfully declined.

The immediate cause of the excitement here alleged was the illegal and violent seizure, in Illinois, of two white men suspected of having decoyed slaves away from Saint Louis. The suspected persons, having been forcibly brought to St. Louis, and there tried and convicted by a mob, which voted, 40 to 20, to whip, rather than hang them, were accordingly taken two miles back of the city, and there whipped between one and two hundred lashes—the sixty wealthy and respectable citizens taking turns in applying the lash. A public meeting was thereupon held, wherein it was gravely

"2. *Resolved*, That the right of free discussion and freedom of speech exists under the Constitution; but that, being a conventional reservation made by the people in their sovereign capacity, does not imply a moral right, on the part of the Abolitionists, to freely discuss the subject of Slavery, either orally or through the medium of the press. It is the agitation of a question too nearly allied to the vital interests of the slaveholding States to admit of public disputation; and so far from the fact, that the movements of the Abolitionists are constitutional, they are in the greatest degree seditious, and calculated to excite insurrection and anarchy, and, ultimately, a disseverment of our prosperous Union.

"3. *Resolved*, That we consider the course pursued by the Abolitionists, as one calculated to paralyze every social tie by which we are now united to our fellow-man, and that, if persisted in, it must eventually be the cause of the disseverment of these United States; and that the doctrine of *amalgamation* is peculiarly baneful to the interests and happiness of society. The union of black and white, in a moral point of view, we consider as the most preposterous and impudent doctrine advanced by the infatuated Abolitionists—as repugnant to judgment and science, as it is degrading to the feelings of all sensitive minds—as destructive to the intellect of after generations, as the advance of science and literature has contributed to the improvement of our own. In short, its practice would reduce the high intellectual standard of the American mind to a level with the Hottentot; and the United States, now second to no nation on earth, would, in a few years, be what Europe was in the darkest ages.

"4. *Resolved*, That the Sacred Writings furnish abundant evidence of the existence of Slavery from the earliest periods. The patriarchs and prophets possessed slaves—our Saviour recognized the relation between master and slave, and deprecated it not: hence, we know that He did not condemn that relation; on the contrary, His disciples, in all countries, designated their respective duties to each other.

"Therefore, *Resolved*, That we consider Slavery, as it now exists in the United States, as sanctioned by the sacred Scriptures."

Mr. Lovejoy, on his return to the city, put forth an address to "My Fellow-Citizens," wherein he said:

"Of the first resolution passed at the meeting of the 24th October, I have nothing to say, except that I perfectly agree with the sentiment, that the citizens of the non-slaveholding States have no right to interfere with the domestic relations between master and slave.

"The second resolution, strictly speaking, neither affirms nor denies anything in reference to the matter in hand. No man has a *moral* right to do anything improper. Whether, therefore, he has the moral right to discuss the question of Slavery, is a point with which human legislation or resolutions have nothing to do. The true issue to be decided is, whether he has the *civil*, the *political* right, to discuss it, or not. And this is a mere question of fact. In Russia, in Turkey, in Austria, nay, even in France, this right most certainly does not exist. But does it exist in Missouri? We decide this question by turning to the Constitution of the State. The sixteenth section, article thirteenth, of the Constitution of Missouri, reads as follows:

"'That the free communication of thoughts 'and opinions is one of the invaluable rights 'of man, and that every person may freely 'speak, write, and print ON ANY SUBJECT, 'being responsible for the abuse of that liber-'ty.'

"Here, then, I find my warrant for using, as Paul did, all freedom of speech. If I abuse that right, I freely acknowledge myself amenable to the laws. But it is said that the right to hold slaves is a constitutional one, and therefore not to be called in question. I admit the premise, but deny the conclusion.

Mr. Lovejoy proceeded to set forth that Robert Dale Owen and Frances Wright had recently landed on our shores from Great Britain, and had traversed our country, publicly propagating doctrines respecting Divorce which were generally regarded as utterly destructive to the institution of Marriage, yet they were nowhere mobbed nor assaulted for so doing. "And yet, most surely, the institutions "of Slavery are not more interwoven "with the structure of our society "than those of Marriage." He continued:

"See the danger, and the natural and inevitable result, to which the first step here will lead. To-day, a public meeting declares that you shall not discuss the subject of Slavery in any of its bearings, civil or religious. Right or wrong, the press must be silent. To-morrow, another meeting decides that it is against the peace of society that the principles of Popery shall be discussed, and the edict goes forth to muzzle the press. The next day it is, in a similar manner, declared that not a word must be said against distilleries, dram-shops, or drunkenness: and so on to the end of the chapter. The truth is, my fellow-citizens, if you give ground a single inch, there is no stopping-place. I deem it, therefore, my duty to take my stand upon the Constitution. Here is firm ground—I feel it to be such. And I do, most respectfully, yet decidedly, declare to you my fixed determination to maintain this ground. We have slaves, it is true; but *I* am not one. I am a citizen of these United States, a citizen of Missouri, free-born; and, having never forfeited the inestimable privileges attached to such a condition, I cannot consent to surrender them. But, while I maintain them, I hope to do it with all that meekness and humility that become a Christian, and especially a Christian minister. I am ready, not to fight, but to suffer, and, if need be, to die for them. Kindred blood to that which flows in my veins flowed freely to water the tree of Christian liberty, planted by the Puritans on the rugged soil of New England. It flowed as freely on the plains of Lexington, the hights of Bunker Hill, and the fields of Saratoga. And freely, too, shall mine flow—yea, as freely as if it were so much water—ere I surrender my right to plead the cause of truth and righteousness, before my fellow-citizens, and in the face of all their opposers."

He continued in this strain to review and refute all the positions and doctrines of these resolutions, and, toward the close of his appeal, said:

"If in anything I have offended against the laws of my country, or its Constitution, I stand ready to answer. If I have not, then I call upon those laws and that Constitution, and those who revere them, to protect me.

"I *do*, therefore, as an American citizen, and Christian patriot, and in the name of Liberty, and Law, and RELIGION, solemnly PROTEST against all these attempts, howsoever or by whomsoever made, to frown down the liberty of the press, and forbid the free expression of opinion. Under a deep sense of my obligations to my country, the Church, and my God, I declare it to be my fixed purpose to submit to no such dictation. *And I am prepared to abide the consequences.* I have appealed to the Constitution and laws of my country; if they fail to protect me, I APPEAL TO GOD, and with Him I cheerfully rest my cause."

The Observer failed for one week to appear, but was issued regularly thereafter. On the request of its proprietors, Mr. Lovejoy gave up the establishment to them, intending to leave St. Louis; but they handed it over in payment of a debt of five hundred dollars, and the new owner immediately presented it to Mr. Lovejoy, telling him to go on with the paper as before. He had gone to Alton, Illinois, expecting to remove it to that city; but, while there, a letter reached him from St. Louis, urging him to return and remain, which he did.

On the 28th of April, 1836, a quarrel occurred between two sailors, or boatmen, at the steamboat landing in St. Louis. When the civil officers attempted to arrest them for a breach of the peace, a mulatto named Francis J. McIntosh interfered, and enabled the boatmen to escape, for which he was very properly arrested, carried before a justice of the peace, and committed to jail. On his way thither, being informed that his punishment would be not less than five years in the State Prison, he immediately broke loose from the officers, drew a knife, and stabbed one of them fatally, severely wounding the other. He was instantly secured and lodged in jail. A mob thereupon collected, broke open the jail, tore him from his cell, carried him out of town, and chained him to a tree, around which they piled rails, plank, shavings, etc., to the hight of his knees, and then applied fire. He was burning in fearful agony about twenty minutes before life became extinct. When the fire had nearly died out, a rabble of boys amused themselves by throwing stones at the black and disfigured corpse, each endeavoring to be first in breaking the skull.

This horrible affair came in due course before the grand jury of St. Louis for investigation, and a Judge, who bore the apposite name of Lawless, was required to charge said jury with regard to it. Here is a specimen of his charge:

> "If, on the other hand, the destruction of the murderer of Hammond was the act, as I have said, of the many—of the multitude, in the ordinary sense of these words—not the act of numerable and ascertainable malefactors, but of congregated thousands, seized upon and impelled by that mysterious, metaphysical, and almost electric frenzy, which, in all ages and nations, has hurried on the infuriated multitude to deeds of death and destruction—then, I say, act not at all in the matter; the case then transcends[12] your jurisdiction—it is beyond the reach of human law"!!!

On this charge, Mr. Lovejoy commented with entire unreserve; whereupon a mob surrounded and tore down his office—although, in the issue which contained his strictures, he had announced his decision to remove the paper to Alton, believing that it would be there more useful and better supported than at St. Louis. His first issue at Alton is dated September 8th.

Meantime, his press was taken from St. Louis, by steamboat, to Alton, and landed on the bank about daylight on Sunday morning. It lay there in safety through the Sabbath; but, before the next morning, it had been destroyed by some five or six individuals. On Monday, a meeting of citizens was held, and a pledge voluntarily given to make good to Mr. Lovejoy his loss. The meeting passed some resolutions condemnatory of Abolitionism, and Mr. Lovejoy assured them that he had not come to Alton to establish an abolition, but a religious, journal; that he was not an Abolitionist, as they understood the term, but was an uncompromising enemy of Slavery, and so expected to live and die.

He started for Cincinnati to procure new printing materials, was taken sick on the way, and, upon reaching Louisville, on his return, was impelled by increasing illness to stop. He remained there sick, in the house of a friend, for a week, and was still quite ill after his return.

The Observer was issued regularly

[12] "Higher law" again—fourteen years ahead of Gov. Seward.

at Alton until the 17th of August, 1837 — discussing Slavery among other topics, but occasionally, and in a spirit of decided moderation. But no moderation could satisfy those who had determined that the subject should not be discussed at all. On the 11th of July, an anonymous hand-bill appeared, calling a meeting at the market-place for the next Thursday, at which time a large concourse assembled. Dr. J. A. Halderman[13] presided, and Mr. J. P. Jordon was Secretary. This meeting passed the following resolves:

"1. *Resolved*, That the Rev. E. P. Lovejoy has again taken up and advocated the principles of Abolitionism through his paper, the 'Observer,' contrary to the disposition and will of a majority of the citizens of Alton, and in direct violation of a sacred pledge and assurance that this paper, when established in Alton, should not be devoted to Abolitionism.

"2. *Resolved*, That we disapprove of the course of the 'Observer,' in publishing any articles favorable to Abolitionism, and that we *censure* Mr. Lovejoy for permitting such publications to appear in his paper, when a pledge or assurance has been given to this community, by him, that such doctrines should not be advocated.

"3. *Resolved*, That a committee of five citizens be appointed by this meeting to wait upon and confer with Mr. Lovejoy, and ascertain from him whether he intends, in future, to disseminate, through the columns of the 'Observer,' the doctrines of Abolitionism, and report the result of their conference to the public."

The only point requiring comment in these resolves is the allegation that Mr. Lovejoy had pledged himself not to discuss the subject of Slavery or its Abolition. This point was answered by ten respectable citizens of Alton, who united in the following statement:

"Whereas it has been frequently represented that the Rev. Elijah P. Lovejoy, late Editor of the 'Alton Observer,' solemnly pledged himself at a public meeting, called for the purpose of taking measures to bring to justice the persons engaged in the destruction of the first press brought to Alton by said Lovejoy, not to discuss the subject of Slavery; we, the undersigned, declare the following to be his language, in substance: 'My principal object in coming to this place is to establish a religious paper. When I was in St. Louis, I felt myself called upon to treat at large upon the subject of Slavery, as I was in a State where the evil existed, and as a citizen of that State I felt it my duty to devote a part of my columns to that subject; but, gentlemen, I am not, and never was, in full fellowship with the Abolitionists; but, on the contrary, have had some spirited discussions with some of the leading Abolitionists of the East, and am not now considered by them as one of them. And now, having come into a Free State, where the evil does not exist, I feel myself less called upon to discuss the subject than when I was in St. Louis.' The above, as we have stated, was his language in substance. The following, we are willing to testify, to be his words in conclusion:

"'But, gentlemen, so long as I am an American citizen, so long as American blood runs in these veins, I shall hold myself at liberty to speak, to write, and to publish, whatever I please on any subject, being amenable to the laws of my country for the same.'"

On the 24th, a Committee from the meeting aforesaid presented its resolves to Mr. Lovejoy, asking a response thereto. That response was given on the 26th, and its material portion is as follows:

"You will, therefore, permit me to say that, with the most respectful feelings toward you individually, I cannot consent, in this answer, to recognize you as the official organ of a public meeting, convened to discuss the question, whether certain sentiments should, or should not, be discussed in the public newspaper, of which I am the Editor. By doing so, I should virtually admit that the liberty of the press, and the freedom of speech, were rightfully subject to other supervision and control than those of the law. But this I cannot admit. On the contrary, in the language of one of the speakers at the meeting, I believe that 'the valor of our forefathers has won for us the liberty of speech,' and that it is 'our duty

[13] This name reäppears in the "Border Ruffian" trials of Kansas. 1856–8.

and our high privilege to act and speak on *all questions* touching this great commonwealth.' I am happy, gentlemen, in being able to concur in the above sentiments, which, I perceive, were uttered by one of your own members, and in which, I cannot doubt, you all agree. I would only add, that I consider this 'liberty' was ascertained, but never originated, by our forefathers. It comes to us, as I conceive, from our Maker, and is, in its nature, inalienable, belonging to man as man.

"Believing, therefore, that everything having a tendency to bring this right into jeopardy is eminently dangerous as a precedent, I cannot admit that it can be called into question by any man, or body of men, or that they can, with any propriety, question me as to my exercise of it."

These proceedings attracted attention from abroad, especially in St. Louis, to whose pro-Slavery politicians the publication of *The Observer*, though not in their city or State, was still an eyesore. On the 17th of August, *The Missouri Republican*, in an article entitled "Abolition," said:

"We perceive that an Anti-Slavery Society has been formed at Upper Alton, and many others, doubtless, will shortly spring up in different parts of the State. We had hoped that our neighbors would have ejected from amongst them that minister of mischief, the 'Observer,' or at least corrected its course. Something must be done in this matter, and that speedily! The good people of Illinois must either put a stop to the efforts of these fanatics, or expel them from their community. *If this is not done, the travel of emigrants through their State, and the trade of the slaveholding States, and particularly Missouri, must stop.* Every one who desires the harmony of the country, and the peace and prosperity of all, should unite to put them down. They can do no positive good, and may do much irreparable harm. We would not desire to see this done at the expense of public order or legal restraint; but there is a moral indignation which the virtuous portion of a community may exert, which is sufficient to crush this faction and forever disgrace its fanatic instigators. It is to this we appeal, and hope that the appeal will not be unheeded."

These recommendations and incitements were not unfruitful. Four days thereafter—two unsuccessful attempts having already been made—the office of *The Observer* was entered between the hours of ten and eleven, P. M., by a band of fifteen or twenty persons, and the press, type, etc., utterly destroyed. The mob commenced, as usual, by throwing stones at the building, whereby one man was hit on the head and severely wounded; whereupon the office was deserted, and the destroyers finished their work without opposition, while a large concourse were "looking on and consenting." The authorities did nothing most rigorously. Mr. Lovejoy was absent at the time, but was met in the street by the mob, who stopped him, threatened him, and assailed him with vile language, but did him no serious harm. In *The Observer* of the preceding day, he had made an explicit and effective response to the question—"What are the doctrines of Anti-Slavery men?" wherein he had succeeded in being at once moderate and forcible—affirming most explicitly the flagrant wrong of slaveholding, with the right and policy of immediate emancipation, but explaining that such an emancipation was to be effected "by the masters themselves, and no others," who were to be persuaded to it, exactly as a distiller is to be dissuaded from making intoxicating liquors, or a tippler from drinking them. But, though his doctrines were peaceful and his language mild and deprecatory, he doubtless irritated and annoyed his adversaries by pointing to the fact—in refuting their slang about amalgamation—that the then [14]Vice-

[14] Col. Richard M. Johnson.

President of the United States "has been, if he is not now, the father of slaves. And thousands have voted to elevate him to his present condition, who would crucify an Abolitionist on the bare suspicion of favoring, though only in theory, such an amalgamation. How shall we account for such inconsistency?" On the 24th of August, he issued an appeal to the friends of law and order for aid in reëstablishing *The Observer;* and this appeal was promptly and generously responded to. Having obtained a sufficient amount in Alton and Quincy alone, he sent to Cincinnati to purchase new printing materials. Meantime, he issued an address, submitting "To the Friends of the Redeemer in Alton" his resignation of the editorship of the paper, offering to hand over to them the subscription-list, now exceeding two thousand names, on condition that they pay the debts of the concern, receive all dues and assets, and furnish him sufficient means to remove himself and family to another field of labor. A meeting was accordingly held, which resolved that *The Observer* ought to be continued, while the question of retaining Mr. Lovejoy as its editor was discussed through two or three evenings, but left undecided. Meantime, while he was absent, attending a meeting of the Presbytery, his new press—the third which he had brought to Alton within a little more than a year—arrived on the 21st of September, was landed about sunset, and immediately conveyed by his friends to the warehouse of Geary & Weller. As it passed along the streets—"There goes the Abolition press! stop it! stop it!" was cried, but no violence was attempted. The Mayor, apprised of its arrival and also of its peril, gave assurance that it should be protected, and asked its friends to leave the matter entirely in his hands, which they did. A constable was posted by the Mayor at the door of the warehouse, with orders to remain until a certain hour. He left at that hour; and immediately ten or twenty ruffians, with handkerchiefs tied over their faces, broke open the store, rolled the press across the street to the river-bank, broke it into pieces, and threw it in. Before they had finished the job, the Mayor was on hand, and ordered them to disperse. They replied, that they would, so soon as they got through, and were as good as their word. The Mayor declared that he had never witnessed a more quiet and gentlemanly mob!

Mr. Lovejoy preached at St. Charles, Missouri, the home of his wife's relatives, a few days after—October 1st—and was mobbed at the house of his mother-in-law, directly after his return from evening church. The mob attempted, with oaths and blows, to drag him from the house, but were defeated, mainly through the courageous efforts of his wife and one or two friends. Three times the house was broken into and a rush made up stairs; and, finally, Mr. L. was induced, through the entreaties of his wife, to leave it clandestinely and take refuge with a friend, a mile distant, whence he and his wife made their way back to Alton next day. Nearly the first person they met there was one of those who had first broken into the house at St. Charles; and the hunted clergyman had the cold comfort of hearing, from many of his religious brethren, that he had no one to thank but himself for his persecutions, and that, if *The Observer* were reëstablished, they would do nothing to protect it. During the following month, Mr. Lovejoy attended the meeting of the Presbyterian Synod of Illinois, at Springfield, as also meetings of an anti-Slavery Convention in Upper Alton, and one or two meetings held at the Court House in Alton, to discuss and determine the propriety of allowing him to continue the publication of *The Observer*. At the last of these meetings (November 3d), having obtained the floor, he said:

"Mr. Chairman: It is not true, as has been charged upon me, that I hold in contempt the feelings and sentiments of this community, in reference to the question which is now agitating it. I respect and appreciate the feelings of my fellow-citizens; and it is one of the most painful and unpleasant duties of my life, that I am called upon to act in opposition to them. If you suppose, Sir, that I have published sentiments contrary to those generally held in this community, because I delighted in differing from them, you have entirely misapprehended me. But, Sir, while I value the good opinion of my fellow-citizens as highly as any one, I may be permitted to say that I am governed by higher considerations than either the favor or the fear of man. I am impelled to the course I have taken, because I fear God. As I shall answer it to my God in the great day, I dare not abandon my sentiments, nor cease in all proper ways to propagate them.

"I, Mr. Chairman, have not desired nor asked any *compromise*. I have asked for nothing but to be protected in my rights as a citizen—rights which God has given me, and which are guaranteed to me by the Constitution of my country. Have I, Sir, been guilty of any infraction of the laws? Whose good name have I injured? When and where have I published anything injurious to the reputation of Alton? Have I not, on the other hand, labored, in common with the rest of my fellow-citizens, to promote the reputation and interests of this city? What, Sir, I ask, has been my offense? Put your finger upon it—define it—and I stand ready to answer for it. If I have committed any crime, you can easily convict me. You have public sentiment in your favor. You have your juries, and you have your attorney (looking at the Attorney-General), and I have *no doubt* you can *convict* me. But if I have been guilty of no violation of law, why am I hunted up and down continually like a partridge upon the mountains? Why am I threatened with the *tar-barrel?* Why am I waylaid every day, and from night to night? and why is my life in jeopardy every hour?

"You have, Sir, made up, as the lawyers say, a false issue; there are not two parties between whom there can be a *compromise.* I plant myself, Sir, down on my unquestionable *rights;* and the question to be decided is, whether I shall be protected in the exercise and enjoyment of those rights—*that is the question, Sir;*—whether my property shall be protected—whether I shall be suffered to go home to my family at night without being assailed, and threatened with tar and feathers, and assassination; whether my afflicted wife, whose life has been in jeopardy from continued alarm and excitement, shall night after night be driven from a sick-bed into the garret to save her life from the brickbats and violence of the mob; that, Sir, is the question." Here, much affected and overcome by his feelings, he burst into tears. Many, not excepting even his enemies, wept—several sobbed aloud, and the sympathies of the whole meeting were deeply excited. He continued: "Forgive me, Sir, that I have thus betrayed my weakness. It was the allusion to my family that overcame my feelings. Not, Sir, I assure you, from any fears on my part. I have no personal fears. Not that I feel able to contest the matter with the whole community; I know perfectly well that I am not. I know, Sir, that you can tar and feather me, hang me up, or put me into the Mississippi, without the least difficulty. But what then? Where shall I go? I have been made to feel that, if I am not safe at Alton, I shall not be safe anywhere. I recently visited St. Charles to bring home my family, and was torn from their frantic embrace by a mob. I have been beset night and day at Alton. And now, if I leave here and go elsewhere, violence may overtake me in my retreat, and I have no more claim upon the protection of another community than I have upon this; and I have concluded, after consultation with my friends, and earnestly seeking counsel of God, *to remain at Alton*, and here to insist on protection in the exercise of my rights. If the civil authorities refuse to protect me, I must look to God; and, if I die, I have determined to make my grave in Alton."

It was known in Alton that a new press was now on the way to Mr. Lovejoy, and might arrive at any time. Great excitement pervaded the community. Friends were on the alert to protect it on its arrival, and enemies to insure its destruction. It finally reached St. Louis on the night of the 5th, and an arrangement was made to have it landed at Alton at three o'clock on the morning of the 7th. Meantime, Mr. Lovejoy and a friend went to the Mayor and notified him of its expected arrival, and of the threats that it should be destroyed, requesting the appointment of special constables to protect it. A meeting of the City Council was held, and some discussion had; but the subject was laid on the table and nothing done.

On that evening (November 6), between forty and fifty citizens met in the warehouse of Godfrey, Gilman & Co., where the press was to be stored, to organize a volunteer company to aid in the defense of law and order. At ten o'clock, several left; but about thirty remained in the building, with one city constable to command them. They were armed. Mr. Lovejoy was not among them. His dwelling had been attacked but a few nights before, when he and a sister narrowly escaped a brick-bat, thrown with sufficient force to have done mortal injury. Expecting an assault, his wife in very delicate health, and in a state of nervous alarm from her recent experience at St. Charles, Mr. Lovejoy had arranged with a brother that they should watch alternate nights at home and at the store. At three in the morning, a steamboat brought the expected press. A sentinel of the mob was watching for it, and immediately gave the alarm, when horns were blown throughout the city. The Mayor had already been called, and was in the building. He requested those who guarded there, to remain and keep quiet till he called for them, saying that he would attend to the storing of the press, which he did. A few stones were thrown, but no serious damage effected, and the press was safely deposited in the garret of a strong stone warehouse, where it was thought to be safe.

Throughout the following day, general quiet prevailed, though it was well known that "the Abolition press" had been received, and was stored in Godfrey & Gilman's warehouse. The Mayor made inquiries at several points, and was satisfied that no further violence was intended. At evening, the volunteer defenders of Mr. Lovejoy's rights dropped in at the warehouse, and remained until nine o'clock; when, there being no signs of trouble, all but twelve went away. Mr. Lovejoy remained, with one or two others who were called Abolitionists. The residue were simply citizens, opposed to burglary and robbery, and willing to risk their lives in defense of the rights of property and the freedom of the press.

About ten o'clock, some thirty persons, as if by preconcert, suddenly emerged from a neighboring grog-shop—a few of them with arms, but the majority with only stones in their hands—formed a line at the south end of the store, next the river, knocked and hailed. Mr. Gilman, from the garret door, asked what they wanted. Their leader replied: "The press." Mr. Gilman assured them that it would not be given up; adding, "We have no ill feelings toward any of you, and should much regret to do you any injury; but we are authorized by the Mayor to defend our property, and shall do so with our lives." The leader replied that they were resolved to have the press at any sacrifice, and presented a pistol, whereupon Mr. G. retired into the building. The mob then passed around to the opposite end of the warehouse, and commenced throwing stones, which soon demolished several of the windows. No resistance was offered; the inmates having agreed not to fire unless their lives were in danger. The warehouse being of stone, and solidly built, no further impression was made on it by this assault. Finding their missiles ineffectual, the mob fired two or three guns into the building, by which no one was hit. The fire was then returned, and several of the rioters wounded, one of them mortally. Hereupon, the mob recoiled, carrying off their wounded. But they soon returned with ladders, and other preparations for firing the roof of the warehouse, cursing and shouting, "Burn them out! burn them out!" They kept carefully on the side of the building where there were no windows, so that they could not be injured or repelled by its defenders. The Mayor and a justice were now deputed by the mob to bear a message to the inmates of the building, proposing that, on condition the press were given up, no one should be further molested, and no more property destroyed. The proposition was quietly declined. Mr. Gilman, in turn, requested the Mayor to call on certain citizens to save his store from the threatened destruction by fire. The Mayor replied that the mob was so strong and so determined that he could do nothing—that he had already tried to command and persuade them to desist, but without success. He was asked if those in the building should defend their property with arms; to which he replied, as he had repeatedly done before, that they had a perfect right to do so, and that the law justified them in that course. He then left the building, and reported the result of his mission, which was received with yells of "Fire the building!" "Fire the building!" "Burn 'em out!" "Burn 'em out!" "Shoot every d——d Abolitionist as he leaves!" It was now near midnight, and the bells had been rung, collecting a large concourse, who stood passive spectators of what followed.

The mob now raised their ladders against the building, mounted to the roof, and kindled a fire there, which burned rather slowly. Five of the defenders hereupon volunteered to sally out and drive them away. They left by the south door, passed around the corner to the east side of the building, and fired upon the man who guarded the foot of the ladder, drove him off, and dispersed his immediate comrades, returning to the store to reload. Mr. Lovejoy and two others stepped again to the door, and stood looking around just without the building—Mr. L. in advance of the others. Several of the rioters were concealed from their view behind a pile of lumber a few rods in their front. One of these had a two-barreled gun, which he fired. Mr. Lovejoy received five balls, three of them in his breast, probably each mortal. He turned quickly, ran into the store, and up a flight of stairs into the counting-room, where he fell, exclaiming, "Oh God, I am shot! I am shot!" and almost instantly expired. One of his friends received at the same time a ball in his leg, of which he recovered. Those remaining alive in the building now held a consultation, and concluded to surrender. One of their number went up to the scuttle and apprised the mob that Mr. Lovejoy was dead, and that the press would now be given up. A yell of exultation was sent up by the rioters, and the proposed surrender declined. Another of the inmates now resolved to go out and make some terms, if possible; but he had hardly opened the door when he was fired upon and severely wounded. A citizen now came to the door at the opposite end, and begged those within to leave the building, as it was on fire, and their remaining would be utterly useless. All but two or three hereupon laid down their arms, left the building, and fled, being fired upon by the mob as they escaped. The rioters then rushed into the building, threw the press out of the window, broke it up, and pitched the pieces into the river. They destroyed no other property, save a few guns. One of them—a doctor—offered to extract the ball from the wounded man's leg; but he declined their assistance. At two o'clock, they had dispersed, and all was again quiet.

Mr. Lovejoy's remains were borne away next morning to his dwelling, amid the jeers and scoffs of his murderers. He was buried the day following — Thursday, November 9—the day which, had he been living, would have completed his thirty-fifth year. His wife, who, on account of the critical state of her health, had been sent away from Alton, was unable to attend his funeral. Of their two children, one was born after his death.

The defenders of the warehouse, as well as the recognized leaders of their assailants, were respectively indicted for riot, and tried, or rather, Mr. Gilman alone of the defenders was tried; and upon his acquittal the City Attorney entered a *nolle prosequi* as to the other defendants. The leading rioters were next placed on trial, and were likewise acquitted. The testimony of the Mayor, John M. Krum, was much relied on by the defenders of the press, who expected to prove by it that they acted throughout under his authority, as ministers of the law and official guardians of the rights of property. His testimony, however, did not sustain this assumption. The Mayor fully admitted that he had repeatedly and freely consulted with them as to their course in the premises, and had advised them that they would be entirely justified in defending their rights by arms, if necessary. But, he said, he had given this advice as a lawyer, a neighbor, and citizen; not as Mayor.

The details of this tragedy are important, as they serve to silence two cavils, which have been most familiar in the mouths of the champions of Slavery. "If you want to oppose Slavery, why do n't you go where it is?" has been triumphantly asked many thousands of times. Mr. Lovejoy did exactly this—as Lundy, and Garrison, and many others had done before him—and only left a Slave for a Free State when such removal was imperatively demanded. "Why do n't you keep clear of the fanatical Abolitionists, and discuss the question in moderation and good temper?" Mr. Lovejoy did exactly this, also. He was not the advocate of Garrisonism; on the contrary, he condemned it. He was not the champion of any political party, nor of any peculiar line of anti-Slavery action. He did not publish an Abolition journal. His was simply and purely a religious newspaper, in which Slavery was from time to time discussed, and its evils exposed, like those of intemperance, or any other immorality. But this he was not permitted to do, whether in a Slave or in a Free State. He was proscribed, hunted, persecuted, assaulted, plundered, and finally killed—not because he persisted in opposing Slavery in the wrong place, or in a peculiarly objectionable manner, but because he would not desist from opposing it at all.[15]

The District of Columbia was originally composed of a hundred square miles of territory, lying on both sides of the river Potomac, at the head of navigation on that stream. The forty square miles south of that river, forming the county and including the city of Alexandria, were ceded to the Union in 1789 by Virginia, and retroceded to that State in 1846—the movement for retrocession having, doubtless, some covert reference to the probability or prospect of disunion. The sixty square miles lying north of the Potomac—forming the county of Washington, and including the cities of Washington and Georgetown—were ceded by Maryland in 1788, and now compose the entire District; so that Washington is commanded, within easy shelling distance, by hights which, in case the separation of Virginia from the Union were conceded, would be part and parcel of a foreign country.

The Federal Constitution (Art. I., Section 8) provides that, "The Congress shall have power to exercise exclusive legislation in all cases whatsoever, over such District (not exceeding ten miles square) as may, by cession of particular States, and the acceptance of Congress, become the seat of the Government of the United States." The cession by Maryland was without qualification. But Congress proceeded, soon after, to pass an act, apparently without much consideration or forecast, whereby the then existing laws of Maryland and Virginia were to continue in full force and effect over those portions of the Federal District ceded by them respectively, until Congress should otherwise enact; and, as those States were undoubtedly Slave States, their slave laws continued operative herein, with little or no modification or improvement, down to the passage of the Compromise measures of 1850.

Very naturally, the creation out of nothing of such a city as Washington, with its adoption as the capital of the Republic, combined with its favorable location, served to render it an extensive mart for the prosecution of the domestic Slave-Trade.

---

[15] WENDELL PHILLIPS, then a young Whig lawyer, first conspicuously identified himself with the anti-Slavery movement, at a meeting held in Boston (December 8, 1837), at the old Court House—Faneuil Hall having been asked for, and refused, to a petition headed by Rev. William E. Channing—to consider the circumstances attending the death of Mr. Lovejoy.

Some of the largest purchasers in Maryland and Virginia for the cotton and sugar region located themselves at this point, fitted up their slave-pens, and advertised in the leading journals of the Capital their readiness to buy and sell young and likely negroes. Vessels were regularly dispatched from Alexandria to New Orleans, laden with their human merchandise. So that, in the absence of manufactures, and of any but a petty retail trade, slaves were long a chief staple of the commerce, and certainly the leading export, of the American metropolis.

Under the slave laws, so hastily bolted by Congress, every negro or mulatto was presumptively a slave; and, if unable to indicate his master, or to establish specially his right to freedom, was liable to be arrested and imprisoned, advertised, and sold, in default of a claimant, to pay the costs of this worse than Algerine procedure; and, as Washington steadily increased in population and importance, the number of colored persons drifting thither from all quarters increased with it, until the business of arresting, detaining, advertising, and selling unowned negroes became a most lucrative perquisite of the Federal Marshal for the District, yielding him a net profit of many thousands of dollars per annum. The advertisements in *The National Intelligencer*, *United States Telegraph*, *Globe*, *Union*, etc., of negroes whom he had caught and caged, and, in default of an owner, was about to sell, were widely copied in both hemispheres, provoking comments by no means flattering to our country nor its institutions. The plumage of the American eagle was often ruffled by criticisms and comparisons between these legal proceedings, under the shadow of our Capitol, and the harsher dealings of savages and heathen with strangers so luckless as to fall into their hands; and the point of these invidious comparisons was barbed by their undeniable justice.

Petitions for the Abolition of Slavery in the Federal District, or, at least, of the Slave-Trade so flourishing therein, had been from time immemorial presented to Congress, and treated with no more disrespect or disregard than petitions to legislative bodies usually encounter. One of these, presented in 1828, was signed by United States District Judge Cranch, and about one thousand more of the most respectable citizens of the District; but, while it was treated decorously, no decisive step was taken toward compliance with its prayer. As the distinctive Abolition movement gained strength in the North, and the excitement caused thereby rose higher in the South—especially after the Message of Gen. Jackson, already quoted, urging that anti-Slavery agitation be made a penal offense—a more decisive hostility was resolved on by the champions of Slavery, under the lead of Mr. Calhoun.

On the presentation, by Mr. Fairfield, of Maine (December 16, 1835), of the petition of one hundred and seventy-two women, praying the Abolition of the Slave-Trade in the District, it was decisively laid on the table of the House; Yeas 180, Nays 31—the Nays all from the North, and mainly Whigs.

On the 18th, Mr Jackson, of Massachusetts, offered a similar petition from the citizens of the town of

Wrentham; and Mr. Hammond of South Carolina, moved that it be not received; which was met by a motion to lay on the table. This was rejected—Yeas 95, Nays 121. But, finally, a proposition that the petition and all motions regarding it be laid on the table was carried—Yeas 140; Nays 76.

Mr. Buchanan[16] presented a memorial of the Caln (Pennsylvania) quarterly meeting of Friends, asking for the same in substance as the above. Though opposed to granting the prayer of the petition, he preferred its reference to a Select Committee or that on the District. But, finding that there were insurmountable obstacles to such a reference, he would move that the memorial be read, and that the prayer of the memorialists be rejected. The question being demanded on Mr. Buchanan's motion, it was carried by the decisive vote of 34 to 6.

Mr. Morris, of Ohio, soon after presented similar memorials from his State; whereupon Mr. Calhoun raised the question of reception, declaring "that the petitions just read contained a gross, false, and malicious slander on eleven States represented on this floor." "That Congress had no jurisdiction over the subject, no more in this District than in the State of South Carolina." After a long and spirited debate, mainly by Southern senators, Mr. Calhoun's motion to reject was defeated by a vote to receive the petition—Yeas 35, Nays 10, as follows:

"Yeas: Messrs. Benton, Brown, Buchanan, Clay, Clayton, Crittenden, Davis, Ewing of Illinois, Ewing of Ohio, Goldsborough, Grundy, Hendricks, Hill, Hubbard, Kent, King of Alabama, King of Georgia, Knight, Linn, McKean, Morris, Naudain, Niles, Prentiss, Robbins, Robinson, Ruggles, Shepley, Southard, Swift, Tallmadge, Tipton, Tomlinson, Wall, Webster, Wright. Nays: Messrs. Black, Calhoun, Cuthbert, Leigh, Moore, Nicholas, Porter, Preston, Walker, White."

In the House,[17] Mr. Henry L. Pinckney, of South Carolina, submitted the following resolve:

"*Resolved*, That all the memorials which have been offered, or may hereafter be presented to this House, praying for the abolition of Slavery in the District of Columbia, and also the resolutions offered by an honorable member from Maine (Mr. Jarvis), with the amendment thereto, proposed by an honorable member from Virginia (Mr. Wise), and every other paper or proposition that may be submitted in relation to that subject, be referred to a Select Committee, with instructions to report that Congress has no constitutional authority to interfere in any way with the institution of Slavery in any of the States of this confederacy; and that, in the opinion of this House, Congress ought not to interfere in any way with Slavery in the District of Columbia, because it would be a violation of the public faith, unwise, impolitic, and dangerous to the Union; assigning such reasons for these conclusions as, in the judgment of the Committee, may be best calculated to enlighten the public mind, to repress agitation, to allay excitement, to sustain and preserve the just rights of the slave-holding States, and of the people of this District, and to reëstablish harmony and tranquillity amongst the various sections of the Union."

After some demur by Mr. Hammond, of South Carolina, and Mr. Wise, of Virginia, the Previous Question was ordered on this resolve —Yeas 118, Nays 47. Mr. Vinton, of Ohio, now demanded a division of the resolve into three parts, which demand was sustained by the Chair; and the first proposition, requiring a reference of all memorials on this subject to a Select Committee, was carried—Yeas 174, Nays 48: the Nays all from the South. The second proposition, regarding Slavery

[16] January 11, 1836.

[17] February 5, 1836.

in the States, was affirmed—Yeas 201, Nays 7. The third proposition, affirming that "Congress ought not to interfere in any way with Slavery in the District of Columbia," prevailed—Yeas 163, Nays 47—the Nays, of course, from the North. And the third clause, being now divided, the question was taken on the remaining part—"because it would be a violation of the public faith, unwise, impolitic, and dangerous to the Union"—and that was also affirmed—Yeas 129; Nays 74: the Nays being all from the North, and nearly all Whigs. The remainder of the proposition was then affirmed—Yeas 169; Nays 6.

The Committee appointed under the above resolution consisted of Messrs. Pinckney of South Carolina; Hamer of Ohio; Pierce of New Hampshire; Hardin of Kentucky; Jarvis of Maine; Owens of Georgia; Muhlenberg of Pennsylvania; Dromgoole of Virginia; and Turrill of New York—all Democrats, but Hardin, a Southern Whig. This Committee, in due season, reported, *First*, That Congress possesses no constitutional authority to interfere, in any way, with the institution of Slavery in any State of this confederacy. *Secondly*, That Congress ought not to interfere in any way with Slavery in the District of Columbia. And, "for the purpose of arresting agitation, and restoring tranquillity to the public mind," they recommended the adoption of this resolve:

"That all petitions, memorials, resolutions, propositions, or papers relating in any way to the subject of Slavery, or the abolition of Slavery, shall, without either being printed or referred, be laid upon the table."

This resolve was adopted—Yeas 117, Nays 68; the Nays being substantially, but not entirely, composed of the Whig members from the Free States.

Amazing as it may seem, this heroic treatment was not successful in "arresting agitation, and restoring tranquillity to the public mind;" so that, when this Congress met for the second session, it was found necessary to do the work all over again. Accordingly, Mr. Albert G. Hawes, (Democrat) of Kentucky,[18] offered a resolution, providing:

"That all memorials, etc., on the subject of the abolition of Slavery, should be laid on the table, without being referred or printed, and that no further action should be had thereon."

Which was adopted—Yeas 129; Nays 69—the Nays mainly Northern Whigs, as before. All debate was precluded by the Previous Question.

And still the agitation refused to be controlled or allayed; so that, on the meeting of the next Congress, Mr. Patton, of Virginia,[19] offered the following "as a timely sacrifice to the peace and harmony of the country:"

"*Resolved*, That all petitions, memorials, and papers touching the abolition of Slavery, or the buying, selling, or transferring of slaves in any State, District, or Territory of the United States, be laid upon the table without being debated, printed, read, or referred; and no further action whatever shall be had thereon."

The Previous Question having again been ordered, this resolve was adopted—Yeas 122; Nays 74—the Nays, as before, mainly, if not entirely, the Whig members from the Free States.

[18] January 18, 1837.

[19] December 21, 1837.

At the next session,[20] Mr. Charles G. Atherton, of New Hampshire, moved the following resolutions:

"*Resolved*, That this government is a government of limited powers; and that, by the Constitution of the United States, Congress has no jurisdiction whatever over the institution of Slavery in the several States of the confederacy.

"*Resolved*, That the petitions for the abolition of Slavery in the District of Columbia and the Territories of the United States, and against the removal of slaves from one State to another, are a part of the plan of operations set on foot to affect the institution of Slavery in the several States, and thus indirectly to destroy that institution within their limits.

"*Resolved*, That Congress has no right to do that indirectly which it cannot do directly; and that the agitation of the subject of Slavery in the District of Columbia, or the Territories, as a means or with a view of disturbing or overthrowing that institution in the several States, is against the true spirit and meaning of the Constitution, an infringement of the rights of the States affected, and a breach of the public faith on which they entered into the confederacy.

"*Resolved*, That the Constitution rests on the broad principle of equality among the members of this confederacy; and that Congress, in the exercise of its acknowledged powers, has no right to discriminate between the institutions of one portion of the States and another, with a view of abolishing the one and promoting the other.

"*Resolved, therefore*, That all attempts on the part of Congress to abolish Slavery in the District of Columbia or the Territories, or to prohibit the removal of slaves from State to State, or to discriminate between the institutions of one portion of the country and another with the views aforesaid, are in violation of the Constitution, destructive of the fundamental principles on which the Union of these States rests, and beyond the jurisdiction of Congress; and that every petition, memorial, resolution, proposition, or paper, touching or relating in any way, or to any extent whatever, to Slavery as aforesaid, or the abolition thereof, shall, on the presentation thereof, without any further action thereon, be laid on the table, without being debated, printed, or referred."

Mr. Cushing, of Massachusetts, objecting, on motion of Mr. Atherton, the rules were suspended; and Mr. A.'s resolves duly passed, as follows: No. 1—Yeas 198; Nays 6. No. 2—Yeas 134; Nays 67—mainly, if not wholly, Northern Whigs. The third resolution having been divided, the House first resolved "That Congress has no right to do that indirectly which it cannot do directly," etc.—Yeas 170, Nays 30. The residue of the third resolve passed—Yeas 164, Nays 39. The fourth resolve was in like manner divided, and passed in two parts, by 182 and 175 Yeas to 26 Nays. The last of Mr. Atherton's resolves was in like manner divided, and the former part adopted by Yeas 147 to Nays 51; and the latter or *gag* portion by Yeas 127, Nays 78—Henry A. Wise refusing to vote.

This would seem quite stringent enough; but, two years later,[21] the House, on motion of William Cost Johnson (Whig), of Maryland, further

"*Resolved*, That upon the presentation of any memorial or petition, praying for the abolition of Slavery or the Slave-Trade in any District, Territory, or State of the Union, and upon the presentation of any resolution or other paper touching that subject, the reception of such memorial, petition, resolution, or paper, shall be considered as objected to, and the question of its reception laid on the table, without debate or further action thereon.

"*Resolved*, That no petition, memorial, resolution, or other paper, praying for the abolition of Slavery in the District of Columbia, or any State or Territory, or the Slave-Trade between the States or Territories of the United States, in which it now exists, shall be received by this House, or entertained in any way whatever."

On this proposition, the votes were—Yeas 114; Nays 108—several Northern Democrats and some Southern Whigs voting with all the Northern Whigs in the minority.[22]

In a little more than ten years

[20] December 11, 1838. [21] January 18, 1840.

[22] The members from the Free States, twenty-eight in all (all Democrats but Proffit, a Tylerized Whig), who voted for this resolve, were as follows:

Maine.—Virgil D. Parris, Albert Smith.—

after this, Congress prohibited the Slave-Trade in the District; and, within twenty-two years, Slavery itself, in that District, was likewise abolished by a decided vote. Thus Congress at last discovered and applied the true, enduring remedy for 'agitation,' in hearing and heeding the demands of Justice, Humanity, and Freedom.

XII.

TEXAS AND HER ANNEXATION.

The name *Texas* originally designated an ill-defined and mainly uninhabited region lying between the French possessions on the Mississippi, and the Spanish on the Rio Grande, but including no portion of the valley of either of those great rivers. Though the first European settlement on its soil appears to have been made by La Salle, a Frenchman, who landed in Matagorda Bay, and erected fort St. Louis on the Lavacca, prior to 1687, he is known to have intended to settle on the Mississippi, and to have drifted so far westward by mistake. The region since known as Texas was, even then, claimed by Spain as a part of Mexico; and a Spanish expedition under De Leon was dispatched to the Lavacca in 1689 to expel La Salle; but, on entering that river, learned that he had been assassinated by one of his followers, and his entire company dispersed. De Leon returned next year, and founded the mission of San Francisco on the site of the dismantled fort St. Louis. From that time, the Spanish claim to the country was never seriously disputed, though another French attempt to colonize it was made in 1714, and proved as futile as La Salle's. The cession of Louisiana by France to Spain in 1763, of course foreclosed all possibility of collision; and when Louisiana, having been retroceded by Spain to France, was sold to the United States, we took our grand purchase without specification of boundaries or guaranty of title. For a time, there was apparent danger of collision respecting our western boundary, between our young, self-confident, and grasping republic, and the feeble, decaying monarchy of Spain; but the wise moderation of Mr. Jefferson was manifested through the action of his subordinates, so that Gen. Wilkinson, our military commander in Louisiana, and Gen. Herrera, who directed the small Spanish force on our frontier, after some threatening demonstrations, came to an understanding in October, 1806, whereby the Sabine was practically recognized as our western boundary, and all peril of collision obviated by

New Hampshire.—Charles G. Atherton, Edmund Burke, Ira A. Eastman, Tristram Shaw.—*New York.*—Nehemiah H. Earle, John Fine, Nathaniel Jones, Gouverneur Kemble, James de la Montanya, John H. Prentiss, Theron R. Strong. *Pennsylvania.*—John Davis, Joseph Fornance, James Gerry, George M'Cullough, David Petriken, William S. Ramsay. *Ohio.*—D. P. Leadbetter, William Medill, Isaac Parrish, George Sweeney, Jonathan Taylor, John B. Weller. *Indiana.*—John Davis, George H. Proffit.—*Illinois.*—John Reynolds.

a withdrawal of the Spanish troops behind the Arroyo Honda, some miles further west. The weakness of Spain, the absorption of her energies and means in the desolating wars for her independence into which she was soon after forced by the rapacity of Napoleon, and the consequent revolutions in her continental American colonies, whereby they were each and all lost to her forever, afforded tempting opportunities to adventurer after adventurer, from Burr to Lafitte and Long, to attempt the conquest of Texas, with a view to planting an independent power on her inviting prairies, or of annexing her to the United States. Two or three of these expeditions seemed for a time on the verge of success; but each in turn closed in defeat and disaster; so that, when Spanish power was expelled from Mexico, Texas became an undisputed Mexican possession without costing the new nation a drop of blood. About this time (1819), our long-standing differences with Spain were settled by treaty, whereby Florida was ceded by her to this country, and the Sabine was mutually acknowledged and established as our western boundary. In other words, it was agreed that the region known as Texas appertained not to Louisiana, but to Mexico. Mr. Clay—then in *quasi* opposition to Mr. Monroe's Administration—demurred to this, and there were a few others who indicated dissatisfaction with it; but this stipulation of the treaty was so clearly right, and the course of the Administration in negotiating it so wise and proper, that all dissent was speedily drowned in avowals of general and hearty satisfaction.

Mexico having practically vindicated her independence, and all attempts to grasp Texas by force having proved abortive, Mr. Moses Austin—a native of Connecticut settled in Missouri—tried a new tack. Representing himself as a leader and mouth-piece of a band of Roman Catholics suffering from Protestant intolerance and persecution in this country, he petitioned the Mexican government for a grant of land, and permission to settle in the then almost unpeopled wilderness, vaguely known as Texas. His prayer was granted, though he did not live to profit by it. Returning, in the early months of 1821, from western Texas to Louisiana, he was robbed and left exposed to every hardship in that uninhabited region, thus contracting a severe cold, whereof he died the following June. His son, Stephen F. Austin, received the grant for which his father had sued, and under it made a settlement on a site which now includes the city of Austin.

Swarms of like adventurers, invited by the climate, soil, and varied natural resources of Texas, from this time poured into it; some of them on the strength of real or pretended concessions of territory—others without leave or license. They found very few Mexicans to dispute or share with them the advantages it presented; of government there was very little, and that not good; Texas being a portion, or rather appendage, of Coahuila, a Mexican State situated on the lower Rio Grande, with the bulk of its population west of that river. Revolutions succeeded each other at short intervals in Mexico, as in most Spanish American countries; and it was fairly a question whether the allegiance sworn to the government of last year, was binding in favor of that whereby it had since been arbitrarily supplanted.

In the year 1827—Mr. John Q. Adams being President—Mr. Clay, his Secretary of State, instructed Joel R. Poinsett, our Minister to Mexico, to offer one million of dollars for the cession to us by the republic of Mexico of her territory this side of the Rio Grande. Mr. Poinsett did not make the offer, perceiving that it would only irritate and alienate the Mexicans to no good purpose.

In 1829, Mr. Van Buren, as Gen. Jackson's Secretary of State, instructed our Minister at Mexico to make a similar offer of four or five millions for Texas, including no part of the valley of the Rio Grande, nor of that of the Nueces, this side of it, and, of course, no part of New Mexico. Still, Mexico would not sell.

Sam Houston, born in Rockbridge County, Virginia, in 1793, had early migrated to Tennessee, settling very near the reserved lands of the Cherokee Indians, to whom he speedily absconded, living three years among them. More than twenty years later—having, meantime, been a gallant soldier in the War of 1812, an Indian agent, a lawyer, district attorney, major-general of militia, member of Congress, and Governor of Tennessee—he abruptly separated from his newly-married wife, and repaired again to the Cherokees, now settled west of the Mississippi, by whom he was welcomed and made a chief. After living with them three years longer as a savage, he suddenly left them again, returned to civilization—of the Arkansas pattern—set out from Little Rock, with a few companions of like spirit, for the new country to which adventurers and lawless characters throughout the Southwest were silently tending. A Little Rock journal, noticing his departure for Texas, significantly said: "We shall doubtless hear of his *raising his flag* there shortly." The guess was a perfectly safe one.

For the Slave Power had already perceived its opportunity, and resolved to profit by it. Houston and other restless spirits of his sort were pushed into Texas expressly to seize upon the first opportunity to foment a revolution,[1] expel the Mexican au-

[1] In the Winter of 1830, the first year of Jackson rule at Washington, Houston came to that city from the wilds of the far West, in company with a band of Indians, who professed to have business there. He remained some weeks or months, ostensibly attending to this business, and made or renewed the acquaintance of one Dr. Robert Mayo, with whom he became intimate, and to whom he imparted his Texas project; and by him it was betrayed to President Jackson, who, very probably, had already heard it from Houston himself.

"I learned from him," wrote Mayo, "that he was organizing an expedition against Texas; to afford a cloak to which, he had assumed the Indian costume, habits, and associations, by settling among them in the neighborhood of Texas. That nothing was more easy to accomplish than the conquest and possession of that extensive and fertile country, by the coöperation of the Indians in the Arkansas Territory, and recruits among the citizens of the United States. That, in his view, it would hardly be necessary to strike a blow to wrest Texas from Mexico. That it was ample for the establishment and maintenance of a separate and independent government from the United States. That the expedition would be got ready with all possible dispatch. That the demonstration would and *must* be made in about twelve months from that time. That the event of success opened the most unbounded prospects of wealth to those who would embark in it," etc., etc.

Dr. Mayo further learned from one Hunter, a confederate of Houston, that there were then secret agencies in all the principal cities of the Union, enlisting men for the Texas enterprise.

thorities, and prepare the region for speedy Annexation to this country, as a new make-weight in Mr. Calhoun's scheme of a perpetual balance of power betwen the Free and the Slave States. Houston had scarcely reached Nacogdoches, near the eastern boundary of Texas, when he was elected therefrom a delegate to a Convention called to frame a Constitution for that country as a distinct State, which met April 1, 1833, and did its predestined work. Texas proclaimed her entire independence of Mexico, March 2, 1836. War, of course, ensued—in fact, was already beginning—and Houston soon succeeded Austin in the command of the insurgent forces. On the 10th, Houston repaired to the camp at Gonzales, where 374 poorly-armed, ill-supplied men, were mustered to dispute the force, 5,000 strong, with which Santa Anna had already crossed the Rio Grande and advanced to the frontier fort, known as the Alamo, held by Col. Travis, with 185 men, who were captured and all put to death. Houston, of course, retreated, hoping to be joined by Col. Fannin, who held Goliad with 500 men, and several pieces of artillery, whereas Houston had not one. But Fannin, while on his way to join Houston, was intercepted and surrounded by a strong Mexican detachment under Urrea, by whom, after two days' fighting, he was captured (March 20), and all his survivors, 357 men, treacherously shot in cold blood. Houston, of course, continued his retreat, pursued by Santa Anna, but having too little to carry to be easily overtaken. He received some slight reënforcements on his march, and at the San Jacinto, April 10, met two guns (six-pounders), sent him from Cincinnati—his first. Santa Anna, still eagerly pressing on, had burned Harrisburg, the Texan capital, and crossed the San Jacinto with the advance of his army, the main body being detained on the other side by a freshet. Houston perceived his opportunity, and embraced it. Facing suddenly about, he attacked the Mexican vanguard with great fury, firing several rounds of grape and canister at short range, then rushing to the attack with clubbed muskets (having no bayonets), and yells of "Remember the Alamo!" "Remember Goliad!" The Mexicans were utterly routed and dispersed—the return of 630 *killed* to 208 *wounded*, proving that very little mercy was shown by the Texans, who nevertheless took 730 prisoners (about their own number), who were probably picked up after the battle, as their General was, in the trees and bushes among which they had sought safety in concealment. Santa Anna's life was barely saved by Houston, who was among the twenty-five wounded, who, with eight killed, formed the sum total of Texan loss in the fight. Houston made a treaty with his prisoner, in obedience to which the main body of the Mexicans retreated and abandoned the country, as they doubtless would, at any rate, have done. This treaty further stipulated for the independence of Texas; but no one could have seriously supposed that such a stipulation, wrested from a prisoner of war in imminent and well-grounded fear of massacre, would bind his country, even had he, when free, had power to make such a treaty. The victory, not the treaty, was the true basis and assurance of Texan independence.

Gen. Houston—who had meantime returned to the United States to obtain proper treatment for his wounded ankle, and to confer with Gen. Jackson and other friends of Texas — was immediately chosen President of the new republic, and inaugurated, October 22, 1836. In March following, the United States took the lead in acknowledging the independence of Texas, and other nations in due time followed. Expeditions, fitted out in western Texas, were sent to Santa Fé on the north, and to Mier on the Rio Grande, and each badly handled by the Mexicans, who captured the Santa Fé party entire, and sent them prisoners to their capital; but, within her original boundaries, no serious demonstration was made against the new republic by Mexico, subsequently to Santa Anna's disastrous failure in 1836. Meantime, her population steadily increased by migration from the United States, and, to some extent, from Europe; so that, though her finances were in woeful disorder, and her northern frontier constantly harassed by savage raids, there was very little probability that Texas would ever have been reconquered by Mexico.

In August, 1837, Gen. Memucan Hunt, envoy of Texas at Washington, proposed to our Government the Annexation of his country to the United States. Mr. Van Buren was then President, with John C. Forsyth, of Georgia—an extreme Southron—for his Secretary of State. The subject was fully considered, and a decisive negative returned. Mr. Forsyth, in his official reply to Gen. Hunt's proffer, said:

"So long as Texas shall remain at war, while the United States are at peace with her adversary, the proposition of the Texan Minister Plenipotentiary necessarily involves the question of war with that adversary. The United States are bound to Mexico by a treaty of amity and commerce, which will be scrupulously observed on their part so long as it can be reasonably hoped that Mexico will perform her duties and respect our rights under it. The United States might justly be suspected of a disregard of the friendly purposes of the compact, if the overture of Gen. Hunt were to be even reserved for future consideration; as this would imply a disposition on our part to espouse the quarrel of Texas with Mexico—a disposition wholly at variance with the spirit of the treaty, and with the uniform policy and the obvious welfare of the United States.

"The inducements mentioned by Gen. Hunt for the United States to annex Texas to their Territory are duly appreciated; but, powerful and weighty as certainly they are, they are light when opposed in the scale of reason to treaty obligations, and respect for that integrity of character by which the United States have sought to distinguish themselves since the establishment of their right to claim a place in the great family of Nations."

Gen. Hunt's letter having intimated that Texas might be impelled, by a discouraging response to her advances, to grant special commercial favors to other nations to the prejudice of this, Mr. Forsyth—writing in the name and under the immediate inspiration of the President—responded as follows:

"It is presumed, however, that the motives by which Texas has been governed in making this overture, will have equal force in impelling her to preserve, as an independent power, the most liberal commercial relations with the United States. Such a disposition will be cheerfully met, in a corresponding spirit, by this Government. If the answer which the undersigned has been directed to give to the proposition of Gen. Hunt should, unfortunately, evoke such a change in the sentiments of that Government as to induce an attempt to extend commercial relations elsewhere, upon terms prejudicial to the United States, this Government will be consoled by the rectitude of its intentions, and a certainty that, although the hazard of transient losses may be incurred by a rigid adherence to just principles, no lasting prosperity can be secured when they are disregarded."

This ended the negotiations, and foreclosed all discussion of the subject by our Government during Mr. Van Buren's term. Yet, so early as 1837, it had become evident to careful observers among us, that intrigues were then on foot for the Annexation of Texas to the United States, and that the chief impulse to this was the prospect of thereby increasing the influence and power of Slavery in our Government. It had, indeed, been notorious from the first, that this purpose was cherished by a large portion of those who had actively contributed to colonize Texas from this country and to fight the battles of her Independence. Benjamin Lundy saw and reported this during his repeated journeys through the whole extent of Texas, in quest of a region whereon to found a colony of free blacks. On this ground, he was a determined foe to the whole scheme of Texan colonization and independence, regarding it but as a new device of American Slavery for extending and perpetuating its power. Earnest Abolitionists generally contemplated the events transpiring in Texas with growing apprehension; while, on the other hand, the slaveholding region was unanimous and enthusiastic in favor of the new republic. Men were openly recruited throughout the valley of the lower Mississippi for her slender armies; while arms and munitions were supplied from our South-western cities with little disguise or pretense of payment. The Slave Power had made sacrifices to wrest Texas from Mexico—with what intent? Mr. Webster, in his speech at Niblo's Garden, March 15, 1837, thus cautiously, but with majestic and impressive oratory, gave utterance to the more considerate Northern view of the subject:

"Gentlemen, proposing to express opinions on the principal subjects of interest at the present moment, it is impossible to overlook the delicate question which has arisen from events which have happened in the late Mexican province of Texas. The independence of that province has now been recognized by the government of the United States. Congress gave the President the means, to be used when he saw fit, of opening a diplomatic intercourse with its government, and the late President immediately made use of those means.

"I saw no objection, under the circumstances, to voting an appropriation to be used when the President should think the proper time had come; and he deemed—very promptly, it is true,—that the time had already arrived. Certainly, gentlemen, the history of Texas is not a little wonderful. A very few people, in a very short time, have established a government for themselves, against the authority of the parent state; and this government, it is generally supposed, there is little probability, at the present moment, of the parent state being able to overturn.

"This government is, in form, a copy of our own. It is an American constitution, substantially after the great American model. We all, therefore, must wish it success; and there is no one who will more heartily rejoice than I shall, to see an independent community, intelligent, industrious, and friendly toward us, springing up and rising into happiness, distinction, and power, upon our own principles of liberty and government.

"But it cannot be disguised, gentlemen, that a desire, or an intention, is already manifested to annex Texas to the United States. On a subject of such mighty magnitude as this, and at a moment when the public attention is drawn to it, I should feel myself wanting in candor, if I did not express my opinion; since all must suppose that, on such a question, it is impossible that I should be without some opinion.

"I say, then, gentlemen, in all frankness, that I see objections—I think insurmountable objections—to the annexation of Texas to the United States. When the Constitution was formed, it is not probable that either its framers or the people ever looked to the admission of any States into the Union, except such as then already existed, and such as should be formed out of territories then already belonging to the United States. Fifteen years after the adoption of the Constitution, however, the case of Louisiana arose. Louisiana was obtained by treaty with France, who had already obtained it from Spain; but the object of this acquisition, certainly, was not mere extension of territory. Other great political interests were connected with it. Spain, while she possessed Louisiana, had held the mouths of the great rivers which rise in the Western States, and flow into the Gulf of Mexico. She had disputed our use of these rivers already; and, with a powerful nation in possession of these outlets to the sea, it is obvious that the commerce of all the West was in danger of perpetual vexation. The command of these rivers to the sea was, therefore, the great object aimed at in the acquisition of Louisiana. But that acquisition necessarily brought territory along with it; and three States now exist, formed out of that ancient province.

"A similar policy, and a similar necessity, though perhaps not entirely so urgent, led to the acquisition of Florida.

"Now, no such necessity, no such policy, requires the annexation of Texas. The accession of Texas to our territory is not necessary to the full and complete enjoyment of all which we already possess. Her case, therefore, stands upon a footing entirely different from that of Louisiana and Florida. There being no necessity for extending the limits of the Union in that direction, we ought, I think, for numerous and powerful reasons, to be content with our present boundaries.

"Gentlemen, we all see that, by whomsoever possessed, Texas is likely to be a slave-holding country; and I frankly avow my unwillingness to do anything that shall extend the slavery of the African race on this continent, or add other slave-holding States to the Union. When I say that I regard Slavery in itself as a great moral, social, and political evil, I only use language which has been adopted by distinguished men, themselves citizens of slaveholding States. I shall do nothing, therefore, to favor or encourage its further extension. We have Slavery already amongst us. The Constitution found it in the Union; it recognized it, and gave it solemn guaranties. To the full extent of those guaranties, we all are bound, in honor, in justice, and by the Constitution. All the stipulations contained in the Constitution in favor of the slaveholding States which are already in the Union, ought to be fulfilled, in the fullness of their spirit and to the exactness of their letter. Slavery, as it exists in the States, is beyond the reach of Congress. It is a concern of the States themselves; they have never submitted it to Congress, and Congress has no rightful power over it. I shall concur, therefore, in no act, no measure, no menace, no indication of purpose, which shall interfere, or threaten to interfere, with the exclusive authority of the several States over the subject of Slavery as it exists within their respective limits. All this appears to me to be a matter of plain, imperative duty.

"But, when we come to speak of admitting new States, the subject assumes an entirely different aspect. Our rights and our duties are then both different.

"The free States, and all the States, are then at liberty to accept or to reject. When it is proposed to bring new members into this political partnership, the old members have a right to say on what terms such new partners are to come in, and what they are to bring along with them. In my opinion, the people of the United States will not consent to bring into the Union a new, vastly extensive, and slaveholding country, large enough for half a dozen or a dozen States. In my opinion, they ought not to consent to it. Indeed, I am altogether at a loss how to conceive what possible benefit any part of this country can expect to derive from such annexation. Any benefit to any part is at least doubtful and uncertain; the objections are obvious, plain, and strong. On the general question of Slavery, a great portion of the community is already strongly excited. The subject has not only attracted attention as a question of politics, but it has struck a far deeper-toned chord. It has arrested the religious feeling of the country; it has taken strong hold on the consciences of men. He is a rash man, indeed, and little conversant with human nature, and especially has he a very erroneous estimate of the character of the people of this country, who supposes that a feeling of this kind is to be trifled with or despised. It will assuredly cause itself to be respected. It may be reasoned with; it may be made willing—I believe it is entirely willing—to fulfill all existing engagements and all existing duties—to uphold and defend the Constitution as it is established, with whatever regrets about some provisions which it does actually contain. But to coerce it into silence, to endeavor to restrain its free expression, to seek to compress and confine it, warm as it is, and more heated as such endeavors would inevitably render it,—should this be attempted, I know nothing, even in the Constitution or in the Union itself, which would not be endangered by the explosion which might follow.

"I see, therefore, no political necessity for the annexation of Texas to the Union, no advantages to be derived from it, and objections to it of a strong, and, in my judgment, decisive character.

"I believe it to be for the interest and happiness of the whole Union to remain as it is, without diminution, and without addition."

William Henry Harrison was, in 1840, elected ninth President of the United States, after a most animated and vigorous canvass, receiving 234 electoral votes to 60 cast for his predecessor and rival, Martin Van Buren. Gen. Harrison was the son of Benjamin Harrison, a signer of the Declaration of Independence, and was, like his father, a native of Virginia; but he migrated, while still young, to a point just below the site of Cincinnati, and thereafter resided in some Free Territory or State, mainly in Ohio. While Governor of Indiana Territory, he had favored the temporary allowance of Slavery therein; and in 1819, being then an applicant for office at the hands of President Monroe, he had opposed the Missouri Restriction. Gen. Harrison was, therefore, on the whole, quite as acceptable, personally, to the Slave Power as Mr. Van Buren; and he received the votes of Delaware, Maryland, North Carolina, Kentucky, Tennessee, Mississippi, and Louisiana. He failed, however, to win the favor of Mr. Calhoun, and so had no considerable support in South Carolina; which State gave its vote, without opposition, to Mr. Van Buren, though it had opposed his election as Vice-President in '32, and as President in '36. Virginia, Alabama, and Missouri also supported Mr. Van Buren. Gen. Harrison was inaugurated on the 4th of March, 1841, and died barely one month thereafter.

John Tyler—son of a revolutionary patriot of like name, who rose to the Governorship of his State—was elected Vice-President with General Harrison. He was originally a Republican of the Virginia school, and as such had supported Madison, Monroe, and, in 1824, William H. Crawford. Elected to the Legislature of his State in 1811, when but twenty-one years of age, he had served repeatedly in that body, and in Congress, before he was, in 1825, elected to the Governorship of Virginia by her Legislature. In March, 1827, he was chosen to the United States Senate by the combined votes of the "National Republican," or Adams and Clay members, with those of a portion of the Jacksonians, who were dissatisfied with the erratic conduct and bitter personalities of John Randolph of Roanoke, Mr. Tyler's competitor and predecessor. Mr. Tyler had (in 1825) written to Mr. Clay, commending his preference of Mr Adams to Gen. Jackson, but had afterward gone with the current in Virginia for Jackson—basing this preference on his adhesion to the 'State Rights,' or Strict Construction theory of our Government, which was deemed by him at variance with some of the recommendations in Mr. Adams's first Message. In the Senate, Mr. Tyler was anti-Tariff, anti-Improvement, anti-Bank, and anti-Coërcion; having voted alone (in February, 1833) in opposition to the passage of Gen. Jackson's "Force Bill," against South Carolina's Nullification. He supported Mr Clay's Compromise Tariff. Being reëlected for a second full term, commencing December, 1833, he opposed the removal of the public deposits from the United States Bank by Gen. Jackson, and supported Mr. Clay's resolution censuring that removal. He was fully sustained in so doing, at the time, by the public opinion and the Legislature of Virginia; but, two or three years thereafter, the thorough-going supporters of Gen. Jackson, having elected a decided majority to the Legislature, proceeded to "instruct" him to vote for expunging from the journal of the Senate that resolution; whereupon, refusing to comply, he resigned his seat, and returned to private life. In the desultory and tumultuous Presidential canvass that soon followed, he was supported by the Whigs, or anti-Jackson men, of the Slave States for Vice-President, and received the electoral votes of Maryland, Georgia, South Carolina, and Tennessee. In 1838, he was elected as a Whig to the Legislature of Virginia, and as such made a delegate to the Whig National Convention, which met at Harrisburg, Pa., in December, 1839. He there, along with his Virginia colleagues, zealously supported Mr. Clay for President, and was affected to tears when the choice of a majority of the Convention finally designated Gen. Harrison as the Whig candidate. The next day, he was, with little opposition, nominated for Vice-President—the friends of Gen. Harrison urging this nomination as a peace-offering to the friends of Mr. Clay. Every elector who voted for Gen. Harrison voted for him also.

If Mr. Tyler's past political course might, by a severe critic, have been judged unstable, and indicative rather of pervading personal aspirations than of profound political convictions, there was one grave topic—that of Slavery—on which not even the harshest judgment could pronounce him a waverer, or infirm of purpose. Born, reared, and living, in one of the most aristocratic counties of tidewater Virginia—that of Charles City, removing subsequently to that of Williamsburg—by no act, no vote, no speech, had he forfeited the confidence or incurred the distrust of the Slave Power; and his fidelity to its behests and presumed interests, was about to be conspicuously manifested.

He soon contrived to quarrel immedicably with Mr. Clay, and with the great majority of those whose votes had elected him, by vetoing, first, a National Bank bill, passed by both Houses, while all the leading provisions were suggested by his Secretary of the Treasury; and then, Congress having passed another Bank bill, based entirely on his own suggestions, and conforming in all points to his requirements, he vetoed that also. Hereupon, all the members of his Cabinet—which was that originally selected by Gen. Harrison—peremptorily resigned their places, Mr. Webster alone excepted, who retained the position of Secretary of State until May, 1843, when he also resigned, and was succeeded by Abel P. Upshur, of Virginia, a gentleman of considerable ability and spotless private character, but a *doctrinaire* of the extreme State Rights, Pro-Slavery school, under whom the project of annexing Texas to this country was more openly and actively pushed than it had hitherto been. Mr. Upshur was killed by the bursting of a gun, on the 28th of February, 1844, and was succeeded by John C. Calhoun, who prosecuted the scheme still more openly and vigorously, and under whose auspices a Treaty of Annexation was concluded April 12, 1844, but which was resolutely opposed in the Senate, and rejected, receiving but fifteen votes.

It is not probable that the master-spirits of the Annexation intrigue were either disappointed or displeased by this signal defeat of their first public movement. It is very certain that they were not disconcerted. For the Presidential Election of 1844 was now in immediate prospect; and they had two darling objects to achieve by the Annexation project: first, the defeat of Mr. Van Buren in the Democratic National Convention; next, the defeat of Mr. Clay before the people.

The defeat of Mr. Van Buren's nomination was first in order, and a matter of very considerable difficulty. He had been the candidate of the party at the preceding election, and beaten, as his supporters contended, "without a why or wherefore," by a popular frenzy incited by disgusting, though artful, appeals to ignorance, sensuality, and every vulgar prejudice and misconception. The disorganization of the Whigs, following Gen. Harrison's death and Tyler's defection, had brought their antagonists into power in at least two-thirds of the States, and they were quite as confident as the Whigs of their ability to triumph in the approaching Presidential election.

"The sober second thought" of the people had been specially appealed to by Mr. Van Buren for the vindication of his conduct of public affairs, and that appeal had been favorably responded to by his party. There was no room for reasonable doubt that a great majority of his fellow-Democrats earnestly desired and expected his nomination and election. To prevent the former was the more immediate object of the preternatural activity suddenly given to the Texas intrigue, which, never abandoned, had for several years apparently remained in a state of suspended animation. Mr. Thomas W. Gilmer, of Va., formerly a State Rights Whig member of Congress, now an ardent disciple of Calhoun and a partisan of John Tyler, by whom he was made Secretary of the Navy a few days before he was killed (February 28, 1844, on board the U. S. war steamer Princeton, by the bursting of the big gun already noticed), was the man selected to bring the subject freshly before the public. In a letter dated Washington, January 10, 1843, and published soon after in *The Madisonian*, Mr. Tyler's organ, he says:

"Dear Sir:—You ask if I have expressed the opinion that Texas would be annexed to the United States. I answer, yes: and this opinion has not been adopted without reflection, nor without a careful observation of causes, which I believe are rapidly bringing about this result. I do not know how far these causes have made the same impression on others; but I am persuaded that the time is not distant when they will be felt in all their force. The *excitement*, which you apprehend, may arise; but it will be *temporary*, and, in the end, *salutary*. * * * I am, as you know, a strict constructionist of the powers of our Federal Government; and I do not admit the force of mere precedent to establish authority under written constitutions. The power conferred by the Constitution over our foreign relations, and the repeated acquisitions of territory under it, seem to me to leave this question open as one of expediency.

"But you anticipate objections with regard to the subject of Slavery. This is, indeed, a subject of *extreme delicacy*, but *it is one on which the annexation of Texas will have the most salutary influence.* Some have thought that the proposition would endanger our Union. I am of a different opinion. I believe it will bring about a better understanding of our relative rights and obligations. * * * Having acquired Louisiana and Florida, we have an interest and a frontier on the Gulf of Mexico, and along our interior to the Pacific, which will not permit us to close our eyes or fold our arms with indifference to the events which a few years may disclose in that quarter. We have already had one question of boundary with Texas; other questions must soon arise, under our revenue laws, and on other points of necessary intercourse, which it will be difficult to adjust. *The institutions of Texas, and her relations with other governments, are yet in that condition which inclines her people (who are our countrymen) to unite their destiny with ours. This must be done soon, or not at all.* There are numerous tribes of Indians along both frontiers, which can easily become the cause or the instrument of border wars. Our own population is pressing onward to the Pacific. No power can restrain it. The pioneer from our Atlantic seaboard will soon kindle his fires, and erect his cabin, beyond the Rocky Mountains, and on the Gulf of California. If Mahomed comes not to the mountain, the mountain will go to Mahomed. Every year adds new difficulties to our progress, as natural and as inevitable as the current of the Mississippi. These difficulties will soon, like mountains interposed—

'Make enemies of nations,
Which now, like kindred drops,
Might mingle into one.' "

Following immediately on the publication of this letter, the Legislatures of Alabama, of Mississippi, and probably of other Southwestern States, were induced to take ground in favor of Annexation; with what views, and for what purpose, the following extract from the report adopted by that of Mississippi will sufficiently indicate:

"But we hasten to suggest the importance of the Annexation of Texas to this Republic upon grounds somewhat local in their complexion, but of an import infinitely grave and interesting to the people who inhabit the Southern portion of this confederacy, where it is known that a species of Domestic Slavery is tolerated and protected by law, whose existence is prohibited by the legal regulations of other States of this confederacy; which system of Slavery is held by all, who are familiarly acquainted with its practical effects, to be of highly beneficial influence to the country within whose limits it is permitted to exist.

"The Committee feel authorized to say that this system is cherished by our constituents as *the very palladium of their prosperity and happiness;* and, whatever ignorant fanatics may elsewhere conjecture, the Committee are fully assured, upon the most diligent observation and reflection on the subject, that *the South does not possess within her limits a blessing with which the affections of her people are so closely entwined and so completely enfibered*, and whose value is more highly appreciated, than that which we are now considering. * * *

"It may not be improper here to remark that, during the last session of Congress, when a Senator from Mississippi proposed the acknowledgment of Texan independence, it was found, with a few exceptions, the members of that body were ready to take ground upon it as upon the subject of Slavery itself.

"With all these facts before us, we do not hesitate in believing that these feelings influenced the New England Senators; but one voting in favor of the measure; and, indeed, Mr. Webster has been bold enough, in a public speech recently delivered in New York to many thousands of citizens, to declare that the reasons which influenced his opposition was his abhorrence of Slavery in the South, and that it might, in the event of its recognition, become a slaveholding State. He also spoke of the effort making in favor of Abolition; and that, being predicated upon and aided by the powerful influence of religious feeling, it would become irresistible and overwhelming.

"This language, coming from so distinguished an individual as Mr. Webster, so familiar with the feelings of the North, and entertaining so high a respect for public sentiment in New England, speaks so plainly the voice of the North as not to be misunderstood.

"We sincerely hope there is enough good sense and genuine love of country among our fellow-countrymen of the Northern States to secure us final justice on this subject; yet we cannot consider it safe or expedient for the people of the South to entirely disregard the efforts of the fanatics, and the efforts of such men as Webster, and others who countenance such dangerous doctrines.

"The Northern States have no interests of their own which require any *special* safeguards for their defense, save only their domestic manufactures; and God knows they have already received protection from Government on a most liberal scale; under which encouragement they have improved and flourished beyond example. *The South has very peculiar interests to preserve*, interests already violently assailed and boldly threatened.

"*Your Committee are fully persuaded that this protection to her best interests will be afforded by the Annexation of Texas; an equipoise of influence in the halls of Congress will be secured, which will furnish us a permanent guarantee of protection.*"

Mr. Henry A. Wise, of Virginia, of the same political school with Gilmer, in a speech in the House, January 26, 1842, said:

"True, if Iowa be added on the one side, Florida will be added on the other. But there the equation must stop. Let one more Northern State be admitted, and the equilibrium is gone — gone forever. The *balance of interests* is gone—the *safeguard* of American property — of the American Constitution—of the American Union, vanished into thin air. This must be the inevitable result, unless, by a treaty with Mexico, the South can add *more weight to her end of the lever*. Let the South stop at the Sabine, while the North may spread unchecked beyond the Rocky Mountains, and the Southern scale must kick the beam."

The letter of Mr. Gilmer, when printed, was, by Mr. Aaron V. Brown, a Democratic member of Congress from Tennessee, inclosed in a letter to Gen. Jackson, asking the General's opinion thereon. That request promptly elicited the following response:

"HERMITAGE, *February* 13, 1843.

"MY DEAR SIR:—Yours of the 23d ultimo has been received, and with it *The Madisonian*, containing Gov. Gilmer's letter on the subject of the annexation of Texas to the United States.

"You are not mistaken in supposing that I have formed an opinion on this interesting subject. *It occupied much of my time during my Presidency*, and, I am sure, has lost none of its importance by what has since transpired.

"Soon after my election in 1829, it was made known to me by Mr. Erwin, formerly our minister to the Court of Madrid, that, whilst at that Court, he had laid the foundation of a treaty with Spain for the cession of the Floridas and the settlement of the boundary of Louisiana, fixing the western limit of the latter at the Rio Grande, agreeably to the understanding of France; that he had written home to our Government for powers to complete and sign this negotiation; but that, instead of receiving such authority, the negotiation was taken out of his hands and transferred to Washington, and a new treaty was there concluded by which the Sabine, and not the Rio Grande, was recognized and established as the boundary of Louisiana.

"Finding that these statements were true, and that our Government *did* really give up that important territory, when it was at its option to retain it, I was filled with astonishment. The right of the territory was obtained from France; Spain stood ready to acknowledge it to the Rio Grande; and yet the authority asked by our Minister to insert the true boundary was not only withheld, but, in lieu of it, a limit was adopted which stripped us of the whole of the vast country lying between the two rivers.

"On such a subject, I thought, with the ancient Romans, that it was right never to cede any land or boundary of the republic, but always to add to it by honorable treaty, thus extending the area of freedom; and it was in accordance with this feeling that I gave our Minister to Mexico instructions to enter upon a negotiation for the retrocession of Texas to the United States.

"This negotiation failed; and I shall ever regret it as a misfortune both to Mexico and the United States. Mr. Gilmer's letter presents many of the considerations which, in my judgment, rendered the step necessary to the peace and harmony of the two countries; but the point in it, at that time, which most strongly impelled me to the course I pursued, was the injustice done to us by the surrender of the territory, when it was obvious that it could have been retained, without increasing the consideration afterward given for the Floridas. I could not but feel that the surrender of so vast and important a territory was attributable to an erroneous estimate of the tendency of our institutions, in which there was mingled somewhat of jealousy as to the rising greatness of the South and West.

"But I forbear to dwell on this part of the history of this question. It is past, and cannot now be undone. We can now only look at it as one of annexation, if Texas presents it to us; and, if she does, I do not hesitate to say that the welfare and happiness of our Union require that it should be accepted.

"If, in a military point of view alone, the question be examined, it will be found to be most important to the United States to be in possession of the territory.

"Great Britain has already made treaties with Texas; and we know that far-seeing nation never omits a circumstance, in her extensive intercourse with the world, which can be turned to account in increasing her military resources. May she not enter into an alliance with Texas? and, reserving, as she doubtless will, the North-Western Boundary question as the cause of war with us whenever she chooses to declare it, let us suppose that, as an ally with Texas, we are to fight her! Preparatory to such a movement, she sends her 20,000 or 30,000 men to Texas; organizes them on the Sabine, where supplies and arms can be concentrated before we have even notice of her intentions; makes a lodgment on the Mississippi; *excites the negroes to insurrection;* the lower country falls, and with it New Orleans; and a servile war rages through the whole South and West.

"In the mean time, she is also moving an army along the western frontier from Canada, which, in coöperation with the army from Texas, spreads ruin and havoc from the Lakes to the Gulf of Mexico.

"Who can estimate the national loss we may sustain, before such a movement could be repelled with such forces as we could organize on short notice?

"Remember that Texas borders upon us, on our west *to 42° of north latitude*, and is our southern boundary *to the Pacific*. Remember also, that, if annexed to the United States, our Western boundary would be the Rio Grande, which is of itself a fortification, on account of its extensive, barren, and uninhabitable plains. With such a barrier on our west, we are invincible. The whole European world could not, in combination against us, make an impression on our Union. Our population on the Pacific would rapidly increase, and soon be strong enough for the protection of our eastern whalers, and, in the worst event, could always be sustained by timely aids from the intermediate country.

"From the Rio Grande, overland, a large army could not march, or be supplied, unless from the Gulf by water, which, by vigilance, could always be intercepted; and to march an army near the Gulf, they could be harassed by militia, and detained until an organized force could be raised to meet them.

"But I am in danger of running into unnecessary details, which my debility will not enable me to close. The question is full of interest also as it affects our domestic relations, and as it may bear upon those of Mexico to us. I will not undertake to follow it out to its consequences in those respects; though I must say that, in all aspects, the annexation of Texas to the United States promises to enlarge the circle of free institutions, and is essential to the United States, particularly as lessening the probabilities of future collision with foreign powers, and giving them greater efficiency in spreading the blessings of peace.

"I return you my thanks for your kind letter on this subject, and subscribe myself, with great sincerity, your friend and obedient servant, ANDREW JACKSON.

"HON. A. V. BROWN."

This letter was secretly circulated, but carefully withheld from the press for a full year, and finally appeared in *The Richmond Enquirer*, with its date altered from 1843 to 1844, as if it had been written in immediate support of the Tyler-Calhoun negotiation.

Col. Benton, in his "Thirty Years' View," directly charges that the letter was drawn from Gen. Jackson expressly to be used to defeat Mr. Van Buren's nomination, and secure, if possible, that of Mr. Calhoun instead; and it doubtless exerted a strong influence adverse to the former, although Gen. Jackson was among his most unflinching supporters to the last.

Mr. John Quincy Adams had united with Mr. William Slade, Joshua R. Giddings, and ten other anti-Slavery Whig members of the XXVIIth Congress (March 3, 1843), in a stirring address to the people of the Free States, warning them against the Annexation intrigue, as by no means abandoned, but still energetically, though secretly, prosecuted. In that address, they recited such of the foregoing facts as were then known to them, saying:

"We, the undersigned, in closing our duties to our constituents and our country as members of the Twenty-Seventh Congress, feel bound to call your attention, very briefly, to the project, long entertained by a portion of the people of these United States, still pertinaciously adhered to, and intended soon to be consummated: *The Annexation of Texas to this Union.* In the press of business incident to the last days of a session of Congress, we have not time, did we deem it necessary, to enter upon a detailed statement of the reasons which force upon our minds the conviction that this project is by no means abandoned; that a large portion of the country, interested in the continuance of Domestic Slavery and the Slave-Trade in these United States, have solemnly and unalterably determined that it shall be speedily carried into execution; and that, by this admission of new Slave territory and Slave States, the undue ascendency of the Slaveholding Power in the Government shall be secured and riveted beyond all redemption.

"That it was with these views and intentions that settlements were effected in the province, by citizens of the United States, difficulties fomented with the Mexican Government, a revolt brought about, and an independent government declared, cannot now admit of a doubt; and that, hitherto, all attempts of Mexico to reduce her revolted province to obedience have proved unsuccessful, is to be attributed to the unlawful aid and assistance of designing and interested individuals in the United States; and the direct and indirect coöperation of our own Government, *with similar views*, is not the less certain and demonstrable.

"The open and repeated enlistment of troops in several States of this Union, in aid of the Texan Revolution; the intrusion of an American army, by order of the President, far into the territory of the Mexican Government, at a moment critical for the fate of the insurgents, under pretense of preventing Mexican soldiers from fomenting Indian disturbances, but in reality in aid of, and acting in singular concert and cöincidence with, the army of the Revolutionists; the entire neglect of our Government to adopt any efficient measures to prevent the most unwarrantable aggressions of bodies of our own citizens, enlisted, organized, and officered within our own borders, and marched in arms and battle array upon the territory and against the inhabitants of a friendly government, in aid of freebooters and insurgents; and the premature recognition of the Independence of Texas, by a snap vote, at the heel of a session of Congress, and that, too, at the very session when President Jackson had, by special Message, insisted that 'the measure would be contrary to the policy invariably observed by the United States in all similar cases,' would be marked with great injustice to Mexico, and peculiarly liable to the darkest suspicions, inasmuch as the Texans were almost all emigrants from the United States, and sought the recognition of their independence with the avowed purpose of obtaining their annexation to the United States. * * *

"The open avowal of the Texans themselves — the frequent and anxious negotiations of our own Government—the resolutions of various States of the Union — the numerous declarations of members of Congress—the tone of the Southern press—as well as the direct application of the Texan Government — make it impossible for any man to doubt that Annexation, and the formation of several new Slaveholding States, were originally the policy and design of the Slaveholding States and the Executive of the Nation.

"The same references will show very conclusively that the particular objects of this new acquisition of Slave territory were the perpetuation of Slavery and the continued ascendency of the Slave Power. * * *

"We hold that there is not only 'no political necessity' for it, 'no advantages to be derived from it,' but that there is no constitutional power delegated to any department of the National Government to authorize it; that no act of Congress, or treaty for annexation, can impose the least obligation upon the several States of this Union to submit to such an unwarrantable act, or to receive into their family and fraternity such misbegotten and illegitimate progeny.

"We hesitate not to say that Annexation, effected by any act or proceeding of the Federal Government, or any of its departments, *would be identical with dissolution.* It would be a violation of our National compact, its objects, designs, and the great elementary principles which entered into its formation, of a character so deep and fundamental, and would be an attempt to eternize an institution and a power of a nature so unjust in themselves, so injurious to the interests and abhorrent to the feelings of the people of the Free States, as, in our opinion, not only inevitably to result in a dissolution of the Union, but *fully to justify it;* and we not only assert that the people of the Free States 'ought not to submit to it,' but, we say with confidence, they *would not* submit to it. We know their present temper and spirit on this subject too well to believe for a moment that they would become *particeps criminis* in any subtle contrivance for the irremediable perpetuation of an institution, which the wisest and best men who formed our Federal Constitution, as well from the Slave as the Free States, regarded as an evil and a curse, soon to become extinct under the operation of laws to be passed prohibiting the Slave-Trade, and the progressive influence of the principles of the Revolution.

"To prevent the success of this nefarious project—to preserve from such gross viola-

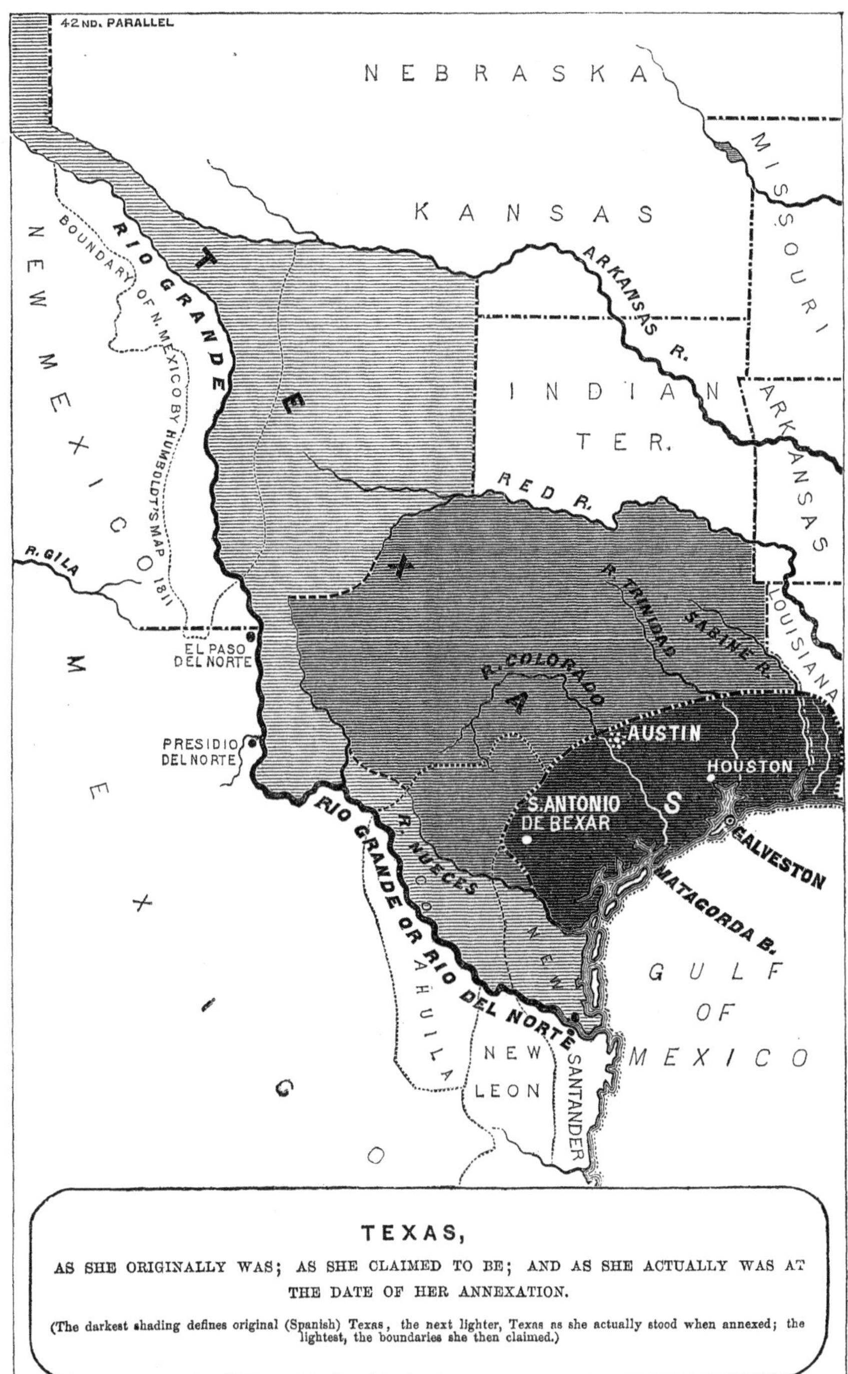

TEXAS,

AS SHE ORIGINALLY WAS; AS SHE CLAIMED TO BE; AND AS SHE ACTUALLY WAS AT THE DATE OF HER ANNEXATION.

(The darkest shading defines original (Spanish) Texas, the next lighter, Texas as she actually stood when annexed; the lightest, the boundaries she then claimed.)

tion the Constitution of our country, adopted expressly 'to secure the blessings of liberty,' and not the perpetuation of Slavery—and to prevent the speedy and violent dissolution of the Union—we invite you to unite, without distinction of party, in an immediate exposition of your views on this subject, in such manner as you may deem best calculated to answer the end proposed."

On the 27th of March, 1844, Mr. Wm. H. Hammet, Representative in Congress from Mississippi, and an unpledged delegate elect to the approaching Democratic National Convention, addressed, from his seat in the House, a letter of inquiry to Mr. Van Buren, asking an expression of his "opinions as to the constitutionality and expediency of immediately annexing Texas to the United States, so soon as the consent *of Texas* may be had to such Annexation." The writer commended himself to Mr. Van Buren as "one of your warmest supporters in 1836 and 1840, and an unpledged delegate to the Baltimore Convention;" and, though courteous in its terms, the letter gave him very clearly to understand that his answer would govern the course of the querist in the Convention aforesaid, and be very likely to influence the result of its deliberations.

Mr. Van Buren replied in a very long and elaborate letter, dated Lindenwald, April 20th, whereof the drift and purport were very clearly hostile to the contemplated Annexation. He fully admitted that Annexation was *per se* desirable; encouraging hopes that he might consent to it, as a measure of imperative self-defense, rather than permit Texas to become a British dependency, or the colony of any European power; and intimating that Mexico might too long persist "in refusing to acknowledge the independence of Texas, and in destructive but fruitless efforts to reconquer that State," so as to produce a general conviction of the necessity of Annexation to the permanent welfare, if not absolute safety, of all concerned. He, nevertheless, decidedly negatived any presumption that he could, under existing circumstances, or under any in immediate prospect, give his support to the scheme, even though assured that his re-election to the Presidency depended thereon. His view of the main question directly presented, is fairly and forcibly set forth in the following passage of his letter:

"The question, then, recurs, if, as sensible men, we cannot avoid the conclusion that the immediate Annexation of Texas would, in all human probability, draw after it a war with Mexico, can it be expedient to attempt it? Of the consequences of such a war, the character it might be made to assume, the entanglements with other nations which the position of a belligerent almost unavoidably draws after it, and the undoubted injuries which might be inflicted on each, notwithstanding the great disparity of their respective forces, I will not say a word. God forbid that an American citizen should ever count the cost of any appeal to what is appropriately denominated the last resort of nations, whenever that resort becomes necessary, either for the safety, or to vindicate the honor, of his country. There is, I trust, not one so base as not to regard himself, and all he has, to be forever, and at all times, subject to such a requisition. But would a war with Mexico, brought on under such circumstances, be a contest of that character? Could we hope to stand perfectly justified in the eyes of mankind for entering into it; more especially if its commencement is to be preceded by the appropriation to our own uses of the territory, the sovereignty of which is in dispute between two nations, one of which we are to join in the struggle? This, Sir, is a matter of the very gravest import—one in respect to which no American statesman or citizen can possibly be indifferent. We have a character among the nations of the earth to maintain. All our public functionaries, as well those who advocate this measure as those who oppose it, however much they may differ as to its effects, will, I am sure, be equally solicitous for the performance of this first of duties.

"It has hitherto been our pride and our

boast that, whilst the lust of power, with fraud and violence in its train, has led other and differently constituted Governments to aggression and conquest, *our* movements in these respects have always been regulated by reason and justice. A disposition to detract from our pretensions in this respect will, in the nature of things, be always prevalent elsewhere, and has, at this very moment, and from special causes, assumed, in some quarters, the most rabid character. Should not every one, then, who sincerely loves his country—who venerates its time-honored and glorious institutions—who dwells with pride and delight on associations connected with our rise, progress, and present condition—on the steady step with which we have advanced to our present eminence, in despite of the hostility, and in contempt of the bitter revilings, of the enemies of freedom in all parts of the globe—consider, and that deeply, whether we would not, by the immediate Annexation of Texas, place a weapon in the hands of those who now look upon us and our institutions with distrustful and envious eyes, that would do us more real, lasting injury as a nation, than the acquisition of such a territory, valuable as it undoubtedly is, could possibly repair?

"It is said, and truly said, that this war between Texas and Mexico has already been of too long duration. We are, and must continue to be, annoyed by its prosecution, and have undoubtedly, as has been remarked, an interest in seeing it terminated. But can we appeal to any principle in the law of Nations, to which we practice a scrupulous adherence, that would, under present circumstances, justify us in interfering for its suppression in a manner that would unavoidably make us a party to its further prosecution? Can this position be made sufficiently clear to justify us in committing the peace and honor of the country to its support?

"In regard to the performance by us of that duty, so difficult for any Government to perform—the observance of an honest neutrality between nations at war—we can now look through our whole career, since our first admission into the family of nations, not only without a blush, but with feelings of honest pride and satisfaction. The way was opened by President Washington himself, under circumstances of the most difficult character, and at no less a hazard than that of exposing ourselves to plausible, yet unjust, imputations of infidelity to treaty stipulations. The path he trod with such unfaltering steps, and which led to such beneficial results, has hitherto been pursued with unvarying fidelity by every one of his successors, of whom it becomes me to speak."

The Whigs were unanimous and enthusiastic in their determination that no other than Mr. Clay should be their candidate, and that no other than he should be elected. He had spent the Winter of 1843–4, mainly in New Orleans—then a hot-bed of the Texas intrigue—but had left it unshaken in his opposition to the plot—not to Annexation itself, at a suitable time, and under satisfactory conditions; but to its accomplishment while the boundaries of Texas remained undetermined and disputed, her independence unacknowledged by Mexico, and her war with that country unconcluded.

Mr. Clay set forth his view of the matter in a letter to *The National Intelligencer*, dated "Raleigh, N. C., April 17, 1844"—three days earlier than the date of Mr. Van Buren's letter. Premising that he had believed and maintained that Texas was included in the Louisiana purchase, and had, therefore, opposed the treaty of 1819, with Spain, by which Florida was acquired, and the Sabine recognized as our western boundary, he says:

"My opinions of the inexpediency of the treaty of 1819 did not prevail. The country and Congress were satisfied with it; appropriations were made to carry it into effect; the line of the Sabine was recognized by us as our boundary, in negotiations both with Spain and Mexico, after Mexico became independent; and measures have been in actual progress to mark the line, from the Sabine to the Red river, and thence to the Pacific ocean. We have thus fairly alienated our title to Texas, by solemn National compacts, to the fulfillment of which we stand bound by good faith and National honor. It is, therefore, perfectly idle and ridiculous, if not dishonorable, to talk of resuming our title to Texas, as if we had never parted with it. We can no more do that than Spain can resume Florida, France Louisiana, or Great Britain the thirteen colonies now comprising a part of the United States."

After glancing at the recent history of Texas, Mr. Clay continues:

"Mexico has not abandoned, but perseveres in, the assertion of her rights by actual force of arms, which, if suspended, are intended to be renewed. Under these circumstances, if the Government of the United States were to acquire Texas, it would acquire along with it all the encumbrances which Texas is under, and, among them, the actual or suspended war between Mexico and Texas. Of that consequence, there cannot be a doubt. Annexation and war with Mexico are identical. Now, for one, I certainly am not willing to involve this country in a foreign war for the object of acquiring Texas. I know there are those who regard such a war with indifference, and as a trifling affair, on account of the weakness of Mexico, and her inability to inflict serious injury on this country. But I do not look upon it thus lightly. I regard all wars as great calamities, to be avoided, if possible, and honorable peace as the wisest and truest policy of this country. What the United States most need are union, peace, and patience. Nor do I think that the weakness of a power should form a motive, in any case, for inducing us to engage in, or to depreciate, the evils of war. Honor, and good faith, and justice, are equally due from this country toward the weak as toward the strong. And, if an act of injustice were to be perpetrated toward any power, it would be more compatible with the dignity of the nation, and, in my judgment, less dishonorable, to inflict it upon a powerful, instead of a weak, foreign nation."

Mr. Van Buren, in his very long letter, had studiously avoided all allusion to what, in the cant of a later day, would have been termed the "sectional" aspect of the question; that is, the earnest and invincible repugnance of a large portion of our people to the annexation proposed, because of its necessary tendency to extend and strengthen Slavery. Mr. Clay confronted this view of the case cautiously, yet manfully, saying:

"I have hitherto considered the question upon the supposition that the annexation is attempted without the assent of Mexico. If she yields her consent, that would materially affect the foreign aspect of the question, if it did not remove all foreign difficulties. On the assumption of that assent, the question would be confined to the domestic considerations which belong to it, embracing the terms and conditions upon which annexation is proposed. I do not think Texas ought to be received into the Union, as an integral part of it, in decided opposition to the wishes of a considerable and respectable portion of the confederacy. I think it far more wise and important to compose and harmonize the present confederacy, as it now exists, than to introduce a new element of discord and distraction into it. In my humble opinion, it should be the constant and earnest endeavor of American statesmen to eradicate prejudices, to cultivate and foster concord, and to produce general contentment among all parts of our confederacy. And true wisdom, it seems to me, points to the duty of rendering its present members happy, prosperous, and satisfied with each other, rather than to attempt to introduce alien members, against the common consent, and with the certainty of deep dissatisfaction. Mr. Jefferson expressed the opinion, and others believed, that it never was in the contemplation of the framers of the Constitution to add foreign territory to the confederacy, out of which new States were to be formed. The acquisitions of Louisiana and Florida may be defended upon the peculiar ground of the relation in which they stood to the States of the Union. After they were admitted, we might well pause a while, people our vast wastes, develop our resources, prepare the means of defending what we possess, and augment our strength, power, and greatness. If, hereafter, further territory should be wanted for an increased population, we need entertain no apprehension but that it will be acquired, by means, it is to be hoped, fair, honorable, and constitutional. It is useless to disguise that there are those who espouse, and those who oppose, the annexation of Texas upon the ground of the influence which it would exert on the balance of political power between two great sections of the Union. I conceive that no motive for the acquisition of foreign territory could be more unfortunate, or pregnant with more fatal consequences, than that of obtaining it for the purpose of strengthening one part against another part of the common confederacy. Such a principle, put into practical operation, would menace the existence, if it did not certainly sow the seeds of a dissolution of the Union."

He closed his letter—which is not quite a third so long as Mr. Van

Buren's—with the following summing up of his convictions:

"I consider the Annexation of Texas, at this time, without the consent of Mexico, as a measure compromising the National character, involving us certainly in war with Mexico, probably with other foreign Powers, dangerous to the integrity of the Union, inexpedient in the present financial condition of the country, and not called for by any general expression of public opinion."

The Whig National Convention met at Baltimore, May 1—every district in the United States fully represented. HENRY CLAY was at once nominated for President by acclamation, and Theodore Frelinghuysen for Vice-President on the third ballot. The number in attendance was estimated by tens of thousands, and the enthusiasm was immense. The multitude separated in undoubting confidence that Mr. Clay would be our next President.

The Democratic National Convention met in the same city on the 27th of that month. A majority of its delegates had been elected expressly to nominate Mr. Van Buren, and were under explicit instructions to support him. But it was already settled among the master-spirits of the party that his nomination should be defeated. To this end, before the Convention had been fully organized, Gen. R. M. Saunders, of North Carolina, moved the adoption of the rules and regulations of the Democratic National Conventions of May, 1832, and May, 1835, for the government of this body; his object being the enactment of that rule which required a vote of two-thirds of the delegates to nominate a candidate. After a heated discussion, the two-thirds rule was adopted, on the second day, by 148 Yeas to 118 Nays, and the fate of Van Buren sealed. On the first ballot, he received 146 votes to 116 for all others; but he fell, on the second, to 127, and settled gradually to 104 on the eighth, when he was withdrawn—Gen. Cass, who began with 83, having run up to 114. On the next ballot, JAMES K. POLK, of Tennessee, who had received no vote at all till the eighth ballot, and then but 44, was nominated, receiving 233 out of 266 votes. This was on the third day of the Convention, when Silas Wright, of New York, was immediately nominated for Vice-President. He peremptorily declined, and George M. Dallas, of Pennsylvania, was selected in his stead. Mr. Polk had been an early, and was a zealous, champion of Annexation, as always of every proposition or project calculated to aggrandize the Slave Power. The Convention, in its platform,

"*Resolved*, That our title to the whole[2] territory of Oregon is clear and unquestionable; that no portion of the same ought to be ceded to England or any other power; and that the rëoccupation of Oregon, and the rëannexation of Texas, at the earliest practicable period, are great American measures, which the Convention recommends to the cordial support of the Democracy of the Union."

Col. Thomas H. Benton, in a speech in the Senate, May 6, had set forth the objections to Messrs. Tyler and Calhoun's Treaty of Annexation, on the ground of its assuming, on the one hand, to cede, and on the other, to accept and maintain, the entire territory claimed by Texas, including all that portion of New Mexico lying east of the Rio Grande, in these forcible terms:

"These former provinces of the Mexican

[2] That is, up to 54° 40′; including what is now British Columbia.

Vice-royalty, now departments of the Mexican Republic, lying on both sides of the Rio Grande from its head to its mouth, we now propose to incorporate, so far as they lie on the left bank of the river, into our Union, by virtue of a treaty of *rë*annexation with Texas. Let us pause and look at our new and important proposed acquisitions in this quarter. First: There is the department, formerly the province, of New Mexico, lying on both sides of the river from its head-spring to near the Pass del Norte—that is to say, half way down the river. This department is studded with towns and villages—is populated, well cultivated, and covered with flocks and herds. On its left bank (for I only speak of the part which we propose to *rë*annex) is, first, the frontier village Taos, 3,000 souls, and where the custom-house is kept at which the Missouri caravans enter their goods. Then comes Santa Fé, the capital, 4,000 souls; then Albuquerque, 6,000 souls; then some scores of other towns and villages—all more or less populated and surrounded by flocks and fields. Then come the departments of Chihuahua, Cöahuila, and Tamaulipas, without settlements on the left bank of the river, but occupying the right bank, and commanding the left. All this—being parts of four Mexican departments, now under Mexican Governors and Governments—is permanently *rë*annexed to this Union, if this treaty is ratified, and is actually *rë*annexed from the moment of the signature of the treaty, according to the President's last Message, to remain so until the acquisition is rejected by rejecting the treaty! The one-half of the department of New Mexico, with its capital, becomes a territory of the United States; an angle of Chihuahua, at the Pass del Norte, famous for its wine, also becomes ours; a part of the department of Cöahuila, not populated on the left bank, which we take, but commanded from the right bank by Mexican authorities; the same of Tamaulipas, the ancient Nuevo Santander (New St. Andrew), and which covers both sides of the river from its mouth for some hundred miles up, and all the left bank of which is in the power and possession of Mexico. These, in addition to old Texas; these parts of four States—these towns and villages—these people and territory—these flocks and herds—this slice of the Republic of Mexico, two thousand miles long and some hundred broad—all this our President has cut off from its mother empire, and presents to us, and declares it ours till the Senate rejects it! He calls it Texas! and the cutting off he calls *rë*annexation! Humboldt calls it New Mexico, Chihuahua, Cöahuila, and Nuevo Santander—now Tamaulipas; and the civilized world may qualify this *rë*annexation by the application of some odious and terrible epithet. Demosthenes advised the people of Athens not to take, but to *re*take, a certain city; and in that *re* lay the virtue which saved the act from the character of spoliation and robbery. Will it be equally potent with us? and will the *re* prefixed to the annexation legitimate the seizure of two thousand miles of a neighbor's dominion, with whom we have treaties of peace, and friendship, and commerce? Will it legitimate this seizure, made by virtue of a treaty with Texas, when no Texan force—witness the disastrous expeditions to Mier and to Santa Fé—have been seen near it without being killed or taken, to the last man?

"I wash my hands of all attempts to dismember the Mexican Republic by seizing her dominions in New Mexico, Chihuahua, Coahuila, and Tamaulipas. The treaty, in all that relates to the boundary of the Rio Grande, is an act of unparalleled outrage on Mexico. It is the seizure of two thousand miles of her territory, without a word of explanation with her, and by virtue of a treaty with Texas, to which she is no party. Our Secretary of State, in his letter to the United States Chargé in Mexico several days after the treaty was signed, and after the Mexican Minister had withdrawn from our seat of Government, shows full well that he was conscious of the enormity of this outrage; knew it was war; and proffered volunteer apologies to avert the consequences which he knew he had provoked.

"I therefore propose, as an additional resolution, applicable to the Rio del Norte boundary alone—the one which I will read and send to the Secretary's table, and on which, at the proper time, I shall ask the vote of the Senate. This is the resolution:

"*Resolved*, That the incorporation of the left bank of the Rio Del Norte into the American Union, by virtue of a treaty with Texas, comprehending, as the said incorporation would do, a part of the Mexican departments of New Mexico, Chihuahua, Cöahuila, and Tamaulipas, would be an act of direct aggression on Mexico; for all the consequences of which the United States would stand responsible."

The opposition of the Northern Democrats to the Annexation project, though crippled by the action of their National Convention, was not entirely suppressed. Especially in New York, where attachment to the person and the fortunes of Mr. Van Buren had been peculiarly strong,

Democratic repugnance to this measure was still manifested. Messrs. George P. Barker, William C. Bryant, John W. Edmonds, David Dudley Field, Theodore Sedgwick, and others, united in a letter—stigmatized by annexationists as a "secret circular"—urging their fellow-Democrats, while supporting Polk and Dallas, to repudiate the Texas resolution, and to unite in supporting, for Congress, Democratic candidates hostile to Annexation. Silas Wright, who had prominently opposed the Tyler treaty in the United States Senate, and had refused to run for Vice-President with Polk, was made the Democratic candidate for Governor of New York, which State could not otherwise have been carried for Polk. In a canvassing speech at Skaneateles, Mr. Wright referred to his opposition as unabated, and declared that he could never consent to Annexation on any terms which would give Slavery an advantage over Freedom. This sentiment was reiterated, and emphasized in a great Democratic convention held at Herkimer in the autumn of that year.

The canvass of 1844 was opened with signal animation, earnestness, and confidence on the part of the Whigs, who felt that they should not, and believed that they could not, be beaten on the issue made up for them by their adversaries. So late as the 4th of July, their prospect of carrying New York and Pennsylvania, and thus overwhelmingly electing their candidates, was very flattering. On the 16th of August, however, *The North Alabamian* published a letter from Mr. Clay to two Alabama friends, who had urged him to make a further statement of his views on the Annexation question. The material portion of that letter concluded as follows:

"I do not think it right to announce in advance what will be the course of a future Administration in respect to a question with a foreign power. I have, however, no hesitation in saying, that, far from having any *personal* objection to the Annexation of Texas, *I should be glad to see it*—without dishonor, without war, with the common consent of the Union, and upon just and fair terms.

"I do not think that the subject of Slavery ought to affect the question, one way or the other. Whether Texas be independent, or incorporated in the United States, I do not believe it will prolong or shorten the duration of that institution. It is destined to become extinct, at some distant day, in my opinion, by the operation of the inevitable laws of population. It would be unwise to refuse a permanent acquisition, which will exist as long as the globe remains, on account of a temporary institution.

"In the contingency of my election, to which you have adverted, if the affair of acquiring Texas should become a subject of consideration, I should be governed by the state of facts, and the state of public opinion existing at the time I might be called upon to act. Above all, I should be governed by the paramount duty of preserving the Union entire, and in harmony, regarding it, as I do, as the great guaranty of every political and public blessing, under Providence, which, as a free people, we are permitted to enjoy."

This letter was at once seized upon by Mr. Clay's adversaries, whether Democrats or Abolitionists, as evincing a complete change of base on his part. It placed the Northern advocates of his election on the defensive for the remainder of the canvass, and weakened their previous hold on the moral convictions of the more considerate and conscientious voters of the Free States. These were generally hostile to Annexation precisely or mainly because of its bearings upon Slavery; and the declaration of their candidate that such considerations "ought not to affect the question, one way or the other," was most embarrassing. The "Liberty party," so called, pushed this view of the matter beyond all justice and reason, insisting that Mr. Clay's antagonism to Annexation, not being founded in anti-Slavery conviction, was of no account whatever, and that his election should, on that ground, be opposed. Mr. James G. Birney, their candidate for President, went still further, and, in a letter published on the eve of the election, proclaimed that Mr. Clay's election would be *more* likely to promote Annexation than Mr. Polk's, because of Mr. C.'s superior ability and influence! It was in vain that Mr. Clay attempted to retrieve his error—if error it was—by a final letter to *The National Intelligencer*, reässerting his unchanged and invincible objections to any such Annexation as was then proposed or practicable.[3] The State of New York was carried against him by the lean plurality of 5,106 in nearly 500,000 votes—the totals being, Clay, 232,482, Polk, 237,588, Birney, 15,812;—one-third of the intensely anti-Slavery votes thrown away on Birney would have given the State to Mr. Clay, and elected him. The vote of Michigan was, in like manner, given to Polk by the diversion of anti-Slavery suffrages to Birney; but New York alone would have secured Mr. Clay's election, giving him 141 electoral votes to 134 for his opponent. As it was, Mr. Clay received the electoral votes of Massachusetts, Rhode Island, Connecticut, Vermont, New Jersey, Delaware, Maryland, North Carolina, Ohio, Kentucky, and Tennessee—105 in all, being those of eleven States; while Mr. Polk was supported by Maine, New Hampshire, New York, Pennsylvania, Virginia, South Carolina, Georgia, Alabama, Mississippi, Louisiana, Indiana, Illinois, Michigan, Missouri, and Arkansas—fifteen States, casting 170 electoral votes. The popular votes throughout the country, as returned, were, for Clay, 1,288,533; for Polk, 1,327,325; for Birney, 62,263. So the triumph of Annexation had been secured by the indirect aid of the more intense partisans of Abolition.

[3] This letter bears date "Ashland, September 23, 1844," and says:

"In announcing my determination to permit no other letters to be drawn from me on public affairs, I think it right to avail myself of the present occasion to correct the erroneous interpretation of one or two of those which I had previously written. In April last, I addressed to you from Raleigh a letter in respect to the proposed treaty annexing Texas to the United States, and I have since addressed two letters to Alabama upon the same subject. Most unwarranted allegations have been made that those letters are inconsistent with each other, and, to make it out, particular phrases or expressions have been torn from their context, and a meaning attributed to me which I never entertained.

"I wish now distinctly to say, that there is not a feeling, a sentiment, or an opinion, expressed in my Raleigh letter to which I do not adhere. I am decidedly opposed to the immediate Annexation of Texas to the United States. I think it would be dishonorable, might involve us in war, would be dangerous to the integrity and harmony of the Union; and, if all these objections were removed, could not be effected upon just and admissible conditions.

"It was not my intention, in either of the two letters which I addressed to Alabama, to express any contrary opinion. Representations had been made to me that I was considered as inflexibly opposed to the Annexation of Texas under any circumstances; and that my position was so extreme that I would not waive it, even if there was a general consent to the measure by all the States of the Union. I replied, in my first letter to Alabama, that, personally, I had no objection to Annexation. I thought that my meaning was sufficiently obvious, that I had no personal, individual, or private motives for opposing, as I have none for espousing, the measure—my judgment being altogether influenced by general and political considerations, which have ever been the guide of my public conduct."

The Presidential canvass of 1844 had been not only the most arduous but the most equal of any that the country had ever known, with the possible exception of that of 1800. The election of Madison in 1812, of Jackson in 1828, and of Harrison in 1840, had probably been contested with equal spirit and energy; but the disparity of forces in either case was, to the intelligent, impartial observer, quite obvious. In the contest of 1844, on the contrary, the battle raged with uniform fury from extreme North to furthest South—Maine and New Hampshire voting strongly for Polk, while Tennessee (his own State) went against him by a small majority, and Louisiana was carried against Clay only by fraud, and by a majority of less than seven hundred in nearly twenty-seven thousand votes. Up to the appearance of Mr. Clay's luckless Alabama letter, he seemed quite likely to carry every great Free State, including New York, Pennsylvania, and Indiana. Not till the election (October 8) of Shunk, the Democratic candidate for Governor of Pennsylvania, by 160,759 votes to 156,562 for his Clay competitor, Markle, did the chances for Polk seem decidedly promising; had Markle received the full vote (161,203) polled, some three weeks later, for Clay himself, the electoral votes of Pennsylvania, New York, Indiana, and Louisiana, would probably have been cast for the latter, giving him 185, and leaving his antagonist but 90. As it was, with Pennsylvania carried for Polk at the State election, the vote of no less than fourteen of the twenty-eight States, choosing 166 of the 275 Electors, was doubtful up to the evening after the election. So close a Presidential race was and remains without parallel. Mr. Clay had the ardent support of a decided majority of the native-born voters, as well as of those who could read the ballots they cast—of all who had either property or social consideration, and probably of all who had a legal right to vote. But the baleful "Nativism" which had just broken out in the great cities, and had been made the occasion of riot, devastation, and bloodshed in Philadelphia, had alarmed the foreign-born population, and thrown them almost unanimously into the ranks of his adversaries; so that, estimating the vote cast by Adopted or to-be Adopted Citizens at Half a Million, it is nearly certain that four hundred and seventy-five thousand of it was cast for Polk—not with special intent to annex Texas, but in order to defeat and prostrate Nativism. Under other auspices, Mr. Clay's portion of this vote could hardly have been less than a fifth.

The election of Polk secured the immediate Annexation of Texas. That event would probably have taken place at some future day, had Mr. Van Buren or Mr. Clay been chosen, as their avowals fully indicated. But Mr. Polk was the outspoken, unequivocal champion of Annexation forthwith—Annexation in defiance of Mexico—Annexation regardless of her protest and the existing War—Annexation with our unjustifiable claim to the boundary of the Rio Grande ready to convert the danger of war with Mexico into a certainty—Annexation in defiance of the susceptibilities and convictions of the more conscientious and considerate half of the population of the Free States as to the evil and peril, the guilt and shame of extending and fortifying Slavery by the power and under the flag of our Union. No matter what the People *meant* by electing him President—they had voted with their eyes open; and he, while equivocating[4] and dissembling on the Tariff question, had been frank and open on this. Nor had the ruling purpose with which the acquisition of Texas was pursued been disguised by its champions. "It will give a Gibraltar *to the South*," said Gen. James Hamilton, jr., of S. C., an eminent disciple of Calhoun, who had migrated from South Carolina to Texas, and taken a leading part in her affairs, in furtherance of the project. Such was the drift of Southern inculcation on this subject; and the colonizing, the revolutionizing, and the annexing of the coveted region, were but three acts in the same drama, and all the work of 'the South.' When a Tennessee slaveholder and unflinching devotee of the Slave Power, well known as an earnest and self-proclaimed Annexationist, had been chosen President, and thus invested with the Executive power and patronage of the Republic for the four years ensuing, the speedy and complete triumph of the measure was rendered inevitable.

Mr. Tyler was still President, with John C. Calhoun as Secretary of State, and would so remain until the 4th of March. On the first Monday in December, the Twenty-Eighth Congress reässembled, and the President laid before it, among others, a dispatch from Mr. Calhoun, dated August 12, 1844, to Hon. William R. King, our Minister at Paris, instructing him to represent to the French Government the advantages and the necessity of Annexation on many grounds, but especially on that of its tendency to uphold Slavery, primarily in Texas itself, but "ultimately in the United States, and throughout the whole of this continent." Mr. Calhoun assumed that Great Britain was intent on Abolition generally; that she had destroyed her own West India Colonies in a futile attempt "to combine philanthropy with profit and power, as is not unusual with fanaticism;" and that she was now employing all her diplomacy and influence to drag down, first Texas, then the residue of this continent, to her own degraded level. Says Mr. Calhoun:

"In order to regain her superiority, she not only seeks to revive and increase her

---

[4] Witness the following letter:

"COLUMBIA, TENN., *June* 19, 1844.

"DEAR SIR:—I have recently received several letters in reference to my opinions on the subject of the Tariff, and among others yours of the 10th ultimo. My opinions on this subject have been often given to the public. They are to be found in my public acts, and in the public discussions in which I have participated.

"I am in favor of a Tariff for revenue, such a one as will yield a sufficient amount to the Treasury to defray the expenses of Government economically administered. In adjusting the details of a revenue Tariff, I have heretofore sanctioned such moderate discriminating duties, as would produce the amount of revenue needed, and at the same time afford reasonable incidental protection to our home industry. I am opposed to a Tariff for protection *merely*, and not for revenue. * * * * * *

"In my judgment, it is the duty of the Government to extend, as far as it may be practicable to do so, by its revenue laws and all other means within its power, fair and just protection to all the great interests of the whole Union, embracing agriculture, manufactures, and the mechanic arts, commerce, and navigation. I heartily approve the resolutions upon this subject as passed by the Democratic National Convention, lately assembled at Baltimore.

"I am with great respect,
"Dear Sir, your ob't serv't,
"JAMES K. POLK.

"JOHN K. KANE, Esq., *Philadelphia*."

own capacity to produce tropical productions, but to diminish and destroy the capacity of those who have so far outstripped her in consequence of her error. In pursuit of the former, she has cast her eyes to her East India possessions — to central and eastern Africa—with the view of establishing colonies there, and even to restore, substantially, the Slave-Trade itself, under the specious name of transporting free laborers from Africa to her West India possessions, in order, if possible, to compete successfully with those who have refused to follow her suicidal policy. But these all afford but uncertain and distant hopes of recovering her lost superiority. Her main reliance is on the other alternative—to cripple or destroy the productions of her successful rivals. There is but one way by which it can be done, and that is, by abolishing African Slavery throughout this continent: and that she openly avows to be the constant object of her policy and exertions. It matters not how, or from what motive, it may be done—whether it be done by diplomacy, influence, or force; by secret or open means; and whether the motive be humane or selfish, without regard to manner, means, or motive. The thing itself, should it be accomplished, would put down all rivalry, and give her the undisputed supremacy in supplying her own wants and those of the rest of the world; and thereby more than fully retrieve what she lost by her errors. It would give her the monopoly of tropical productions, which I shall next proceed to show.

"What would be the consequence, if this object of her unceasing solicitude and exertions should be effected by the abolition of Negro Slavery throughout this continent? Some idea may be formed from the immense diminution of productions, as has been shown, which has followed abolition in her West India possessions. But, as great as that has been, it is nothing compared with what would be the effect, if she should succeed in abolishing Slavery in the United States, Cuba, Brazil, and throughout this continent. The experiment in her own colonies was made under the most favorable circumstances. It was brought about gradually and peaceably by the steady and firm operation of the parent country, armed with complete power to prevent or crush at once all insurrectionary movements on the part of the negroes, and able and disposed to maintain, to the full, the political and social ascendency of the former masters over their former slaves. It is not at all wonderful that the change of the relations of master and slave took place, under such circumstances, without violence and bloodshed, and that order and peace should have been since preserved. Very different would be the result of Abolition should it be effected by her influence and exertions in the possessions of other countries on this continent —and specially in the United States, Cuba, and Brazil, the great cultivators of the principal tropical products of America. To form a correct conception of what would be the result with them, we must look, not to Jamaica, but to St. Domingo, for example. The change would be followed by unforgiving hate between the two races, and end in a bloody and deadly struggle between them for the superiority. One or the other would have to be subjugated, extirpated, or expelled; and desolation would overspread their territories, as in St. Domingo, from which it would take centuries to recover. The end would be, that the superiority in cultivating the great tropical staples would be transferred from them to the British tropical possessions.

"These are of vast extent, and those beyond the Cape of Good Hope, possessed of an unlimited amount of labor, standing ready, by the aid of British capital, to supply the deficit which would be occasioned by destroying the tropical productions of the United States, Cuba, Brazil, and other countries cultivated by Slave labor on this continent, as soon as the increased prices, in consequence, would yield a profit. It is the successful competition of that labor which keeps the prices of the great tropical staples so low as to prevent their cultivation with profit in the possessions of Great Britain, by what she is pleased to call free labor.

"If she can destroy its competition, she would have a monopoly of these productions. She has all the means of furnishing an unlimited supply—vast and fertile possessions in both Indies, boundless command of capital and labor, and ample power to suppress disturbances and preserve order throughout her wide domain.

"It is unquestionable that she regards abolition in Texas as a most important step toward this great object of policy, so much the aim of her solicitude and exertions; and the defeat of the Annexation of Texas to our Union as indispensable to the abolition of Slavery there. She is too sagacious not to see what a fatal blow it would give to Slavery in the United States, and how certainly its abolition with us will abolish it over the whole continent, and thereby give her a monopoly in the production of the great tropical staples, and the command of the commerce, navigation, and manufactures of the world, with an established naval ascendency and political preponderance. To this continent, the blow would be calamitous beyond description. It would destroy, in a great measure, the cultivation and production of the great tropical staples, amounting annually in value to nearly $300,000,000, the fund which stimulates and upholds almost every other branch of its industry, commerce, navigation, and manufactures. The whole, by their joint influence, are rapidly spreading population, wealth, improvement, and civilization, over the whole continent, and vivifying, by their overflow, the industry of Europe, thereby increasing its population, wealth, and advancement in the arts, in power, and in civilization.

"Such must be the result, should Great Britain succeed in accomplishing the constant object of her desire and exertions—the Abolition of Negro Slavery over this continent—and toward the effecting of which she regards the defeat of the Annexation of Texas to our Union as so important."

Such were the grounds on which France was asked to give her sympathy and moral support to the Annexation of Texas to this country.

On the 19th of December, Mr. John B. Weller, of Ohio, by leave, introduced to the House a joint resolve, providing for the Annexation of Texas to the United States; which was sent to the Committee of the whole. Mr. John P. Hale, of New Hampshire, then also a Democrat, proposed (January 10, 1845), an amendment, as follows:

"*Provided*, That, immediately after the question of boundary between the United States of America and Mexico shall have been definitively settled by the two governments, and before any State formed out of the territory of Texas shall be admitted into the Union, the said territory of Texas shall be divided as follows, to wit: beginning at a point on the Gulf of Mexico midway between the Northern and Southern boundaries thereof on the coast; and thence by a line running in a northwesterly direction to the extreme boundary thereof, so as to divide the same as nearly as possible into two equal parts, and in that portion of the said territory lying south and west of the line to be run as aforesaid, there shall be neither Slavery nor involuntary servitude, otherwise than in the punishment of crimes, whereof the party shall have been duly convicted.

"*And provided further*, That this provision shall be considered as a compact between the people of the United States and the people of the said territory, and forever remain unalterable, unless by the consent of three-fourths of the States of the Union."

Mr. Hale's motion that the rules be suspended, to enable him to offer this proposition, was defeated—Yeas 92 (not two-thirds) to Nays 81. Mr. Charles J. Ingersoll, of Pa., reported (Jan. 12), from the Committee on Foreign Affairs a joint resolve in favor of Annexation, which was sent to the Committee of the Whole January 25th, the debate was brought to a close, and the following joint resolution adopted—that portion relating to Slavery having been added in Committee, on motion of Mr. Milton Brown (Whig), of Tennessee:

"*Resolved, by the Senate and House of Representatives in Congress assembled*, That Congress doth consent that the territory properly included in, and rightfully belonging to, the Republic of Texas, may be erected into a new State, to be called the State of Texas, with a republican form of government, to be adopted by the people of said Republic, by deputies in Convention assembled, with the consent of the existing government, in order that the same may be admitted as one of the States of this Union.

"2. *And be it further resolved*, That the foregoing consent of Congress is given on the following conditions, and with the following guarantees, to wit:

"First. Said State to be formed, subject to the adjustment by this Government of all questions of boundary that may arise with other governments; and the Constitution thereof, with the proper evidence of its adoption by the people of said Republic of Texas, shall be transmitted to the President of the United States, to be laid before Congress for its final action, on or before the 1st day of January, 1846.

"Second. Said State, when admitted into the Union, after ceding to the United States all public edifices, fortifications, barracks, ports and harbors, navy and navy yards, docks, magazines, arms, armaments, and all other property and means pertaining to the public defense, belonging to the said Republic of Texas, shall retain all the public funds, debts, taxes, and dues of every kind, which may belong to, or be due or owing said Republic; and shall also retain all the vacant and unappropriated lands, lying within its limits, to be applied to the payment of the debts and liabilities of said Republic of Texas; and the residue of said lands, after discharging said debts and liabilities, to be disposed of as said State may direct; but in no event are said debts and liabilities to become a charge upon the United States.

"Third. New States, of convenient size, not exceeding four in number, in addition to said State of Texas, and having sufficient population, may hereafter, by the consent of said State, be formed out of the territory thereof, which shall be entitled to admission, under the provisions of the Federal Constitution. And such States as may be formed out of that portion of said territory lying south of thirty-six degrees thirty minutes of North latitude, commonly known as the Missouri Compromise line, shall be admitted into the Union with or without Slavery, as the people of each State asking admission may desire; and in such State or States as may be formed out of said territory north of said Missouri Compromise line, Slavery or involuntary servitude (except for crime) shall be prohibited."

The amendment of Mr. Brown was adopted by Yeas 118 to Nays 101—the Yeas consisting of 114 Democrats and 4 Southern Whigs (as yet)—Milton Brown, of Tennessee; James Dellet, of Alabama; Duncan L. Clinch and Alexander Stephens, of Georgia. The Nays were 78 Whigs and 23 Democrats (from Free States), among them, Hannibal Hamlin, John P. Hale, Preston King, George Rathbun, and Jacob Brinckerhoff—since known as Republicans. The joint resolve, as thus amended, passed the House by Yeas 120 to Nays 98—the division being substantially as before.

In the Senate, this resolve was taken up for action, February 24th; and, on the 27th, Mr. Foster (Whig), of Tennessee, proposed the following:

"*And provided further*, That, in fixing the terms and conditions of such admission, it shall be expressly stipulated and declared, that the State of Texas, and such other States as may be formed out of that portion of the present territory lying south of thirty-six degrees thirty minutes north latitude, commonly known as the Missouri Compromise line, shall be admitted into the Union with or without Slavery, as the people of each State, so hereafter asking admission, may desire: *And provided furthermore*, That it shall be also stipulated and declared that the public debt of Texas shall in no event become a charge upon the Government of the United States."

This was voted down, as were one or two kindred propositions. Mr. Miller (Whig), of New Jersey, moved to strike out all after the enacting clause, and insert as follows:

"That the President of the United States be, and he hereby is, authorized and advised to open negotiations with Mexico and Texas, for the adjustment of their boundaries, and the annexation of the latter to the United States, on the following basis, to wit:

"I. The boundary of the annexed territory to be in the desert prairie west of the Nueces, and along the highlands and mountain hights which divide the waters of the Mississippi from the waters of the Rio del Norte, and to latitude forty-two degrees north.

"II. The people of Texas, by a legislative act, or by any authentic act which shows the will of the majority, to express their assent to said annexation.

"III. A State, to be called 'the State of Texas,' with boundaries fixed by herself, and extent not exceeding the largest State of the Union, to be admitted into the Union, by virtue of this act, on an equal footing with the original States.

"IV. The remainder of the annexed territory, to be held and disposed of by the United States, as one of their Territories, to be called 'the South-west Territory.'

"V. The existence of Slavery to be forever prohibited in the northern and northwestern part of said Territory, west of the 100th degree of longitude west from Greenwich, so as to divide, as equally as may be, the whole of the annexed country between slaveholding and non-slaveholding States.

"VI. The assent of Mexico to be obtained by treaty to such annexation and boundary, or to be dispensed with when the Congress of the United States may deem such assent to be unnecessary.

"VII. Other details of the annexation to be adjusted by treaty, so far as the same may come within the scope of the treaty-making power."

This was rejected by 11 Yeas—all Whigs from Free States—to 33 Nays.

Mr. Walker, of Wisconsin, moved to add to the House proposition an alternative contemplating negotiation as a means of effecting the end proposed: and this was carried by 27 Yeas, to 25 Nays—the Nays all Whigs. The measure, as thus amended, passed the Senate by Yeas 27—all the Democrats present and three Whigs, of whom two thereupon turned Democrats—to 25 Nays—all Whigs;[5] and the proposition being returned to the House, the amendment of the Senate was concurred in by 134 Yeas to 77 Nays—a party vote: so the Annexation of Texas was decreed, in the following terms:

"*Resolved, by the Senate and House of Representatives of the United States in Congress assembled*, That Congress doth consent that the territory properly included within, and rightfully belonging to, the Republic of Texas, may be erected into a new State, to be called *the State of Texas*, with a republican form of government, to be adopted by the people of said republic, by deputies in Convention assembled, with the consent of the existing government, in order that the same may be admitted as one of the States of the Union.

"*Sec.* 2. *And be it further resolved*, That the foregoing consent of Congress is given upon the following conditions, and with the following guarantees, to wit:

"*First:* Said State to be formed, subject to the adjustment by this Government of all questions of boundary that may arise with other governments; and the Constitution thereof, with the proper evidence of its adoption by the people of said Republic of Texas, shall be transmitted to the President of the United States, to be laid before Congress for its final action, on or before the first day of January, one thousand eight hundred and forty six.

"*Second:* Said State, when admitted into the Union, after ceding to the United States all public edifices, fortifications, barracks, forts and harbors, navy and navy-yards, docks, magazines, arms, armaments, and all other property and means pertaining to the public defense, belonging to the said Republic of Texas, shall retain all public funds, debts, taxes, and dues of every kind, which may belong to, or be due or owing said Republic; and shall also retain all the vacant or unappropriated lands lying within its limits, to be applied to the payment of the debts and liabilities of said Republic of Texas; and the residue of said lands, after discharging said debts and liabilities, to be disposed of as said State may direct; but in no event are said debts and liabilities to become a charge upon the United States.

"*Third.* New States of convenient size, not exceeding four in number, in addition to the said State of Texas, and having sufficient population, may hereafter, by the consent of said State, be formed out of the territory thereof, which shall be entitled to admission under the provisions of the Federal Constitution; and such States as may be formed out of that portion of said territory lying south of thirty-six degrees thirty minutes north latitude, commonly known as the Missouri Compromise line, shall be admitted into the Union with or without Slavery, as the people of each State asking admission may desire. And in such State or States as shall be formed out of said territory north of said Missouri Compromise line, Slavery or involuntary servitude (except for crime) shall be prohibited.

[WALKER'S AMENDMENT—ADDED.]

"*And be it further resolved*, That if the President of the United States shall, in his judgment and discretion, deem it most advisable, instead of proceeding to submit the foregoing resolutions to the Republic of Texas, as an overture on the part of the United States for admission, to negotiate with that Republic; then,

"*Be it resolved*, That a State to be formed out of the present Republic of Texas, with suitable extent and boundaries, and with two representatives in Congress, until the next apportionment of representation, shall be admitted into the Union by virtue of this act, on an equal footing with the existing States, as soon as the terms and conditions of such admission, and the

[5] On the final vote in the Senate, the YEAS—*for* the Proposition as amended—were as follows—the names in *italics* being those of Whigs:

Messrs. Allen, Ashley, Atchison, Atherton, Bagby, Benton, Breese, Buchanan, Colquitt, Dickinson, Dix, Fairfield, Hannegan, Haywood, *Henderson*, Huger, *Johnson*, Lewis, McDuffie, *Merrick*, Niles, Semple, Sevier, Sturgeon, Tappan, Walker, Woodbury—27.

The NAYS—*against* the proposed Annexation—were:

Messrs. Archer, Barrow, Bates, Bayard, Berrien, Choate, Clayton, Crittenden, Dayton, Evans, Foster, Francis, Huntington, Jarnagin, Mangum, Miller, Morehead, Pearce, Phelps, Porter, Rives, Simmons, Upham, White, Woodbridge—25.

YEAS: From Free States, 13; Slave States, 14.
NAYS: " " " 12; " " 13.

cession of the remaining Texan territory to the United States, shall be agreed upon by the Governments of Texas and the United States.

"*And be it further enacted*, That the sum of one hundred thousand dollars be, and the same is hereby, appropriated to defray the expenses of missions and negotiations, to agree upon the terms of said admission and cession, either by treaty to be submitted to the Senate, or by articles to be submitted to the two Houses of Congress, as the President may direct.

"Approved, March 2, 1845."

President Tyler immediately, on the last day of his term, rendered the Walker amendment nugatory by dispatching a messenger to Texas to secure her assent to Annexation, pure and simple; and thus the triumph of the measure was secured.

The pretext or show of compromise with respect to Slavery, by a partition of territory, was one of the worst features of this most objectionable measure. So much of Texas as lay north of the parallel of 36° 30′ north latitude was thereby allotted to Free labor, when Texas had never controlled, and did not at that moment possess, a single acre north of that parallel, nor for two hundred miles south of it. All the territory claimed by her north of that line was New Mexico, which had never been for a week under the flag of Texas. While seeming to curtail and circumscribe Slavery north of the above parallel, this measure really extended it northward *to* that parallel, which it had not yet approached, under the flag of Texas, within hundreds of miles. But the chief end of this sham compromise was the involving of Congress and the country in an indirect indorsement of the claim of Texas to the entire left bank of the Rio Grande, from its mouth to its source; and this was effected.

This complete triumph of Annexation, even before the inauguration of Mr. Polk, was hailed with exultation throughout the South, and received with profound sensation and concern at the North. It excited, moreover, some surprise; as, three days before it occurred, its defeat for that session appeared almost certain. Mr. Bagby, a Democratic Senator from Alabama, positively declared from his seat that he would not support it; while the opposition of Messrs. Niles, of Connecticut, Dix, of New York, and Benton, of Missouri, was deemed invincible; but the Alabamian was tamed by private, but unquestionable, intimations, that it would not be safe for him to return to his own State, nor even to remain in Washington, if his vote should defeat the darling project; and the repugnance of Messrs. Niles, Dix, and Benton, was somehow overcome—the Walker amendment serving as a pretext for submission to the party behest, when no plausible excuse could be given. Mr. Polk was already in Washington, engaged in making up his jewels; and he had very freely intimated that no man who opposed Annexation should receive office or consideration at his hands. The three Tylerized Whigs from the South, who voted in the affirmative, had not been counted on as opponents of the scheme.

The Democrats of the North, having elected Mr. Polk after a desperate struggle, and being intent on the imminent distribution of the spoils, might regret this early fruit of their triumph, but could hardly be expected openly to denounce it. Mr. John P. Hale, of New Hampshire, who had evinced (as we have seen) insubordination in the House, and who was then the regular Democratic nominee for the next House in the election just at hand, was thrown off the ticket unceremoniously, and another nominated in his stead—who, however, failed of success; the election resulting in no choice, so far as this seat was concerned. Three regular Democrats were elected to the others. In no other State was there any open and formidable opposition manifested by Democrats to this sudden consummation of the Texan intrigue.

The Whigs and Abolitionists of the Free States, of course, murmured; but to what end? What could they do? The new Democratic Administration must hold the reins for the ensuing four years, and its decided ascendency in both Houses of the next Congress was already amply secured. There were the usual editorial thunderings; perhaps a few sermons, and less than half-a-dozen rather thinly-attended public meetings, mainly in Massachusetts, whereat ominous whispers may have been heard, that, if things were to go on in this way much longer, the Union would, or should, be dissolved. This covert menace was emphatically rebuked by Mr. Robert C. Winthrop, of Boston, speaking the sentiment of the great majority of leading Whigs. "Our country, however bounded," was declared by him entitled to his allegiance, and the object of his affections. The great majority, even of the murmurers, went on with their industry and their trade, their pursuits and their aspirations, as though nothing of special moment had happened.

Yet it did not escape the regard of keen observers that our country had placed herself, by annexing Texas under the circumstances, not merely in the light of a powerful aggressor on the rights of neighboring helplessness, but of a champion and propagandist of Slavery, as the fit, beneficent condition of the producers of tropical and semi-tropical staples throughout the world. The dispatch of Mr. Calhoun to France, with one or two others of like purport, aimed more directly at England, justified and commended our designs on Texas expressly and emphatically on this ground. England, he argued, was plotting the extinction of Slavery throughout the Western Hemisphere. The United States must clutch Texas, or she would soon fall a prey to British intrigue and British influence—being induced thereby to emancipate her slaves; thus dealing a damaging, if not mortal, blow to Slavery throughout the New World. To avert this blow, and to shield the social and industrial system which it menaced, were the chief ends of Annexation.

Now, it was not literally true that our country was thus presented, for the first time, in the questionable attitude of a champion of Slavery. In our last treaty of peace with Great Britain, our commissioners at Ghent, acting under special instructions from the State Department,[6] had adroitly bound Great Britain to return to

[6] "The negroes taken from the Southern States should be returned to their owners, or paid for at their full value. If these slaves were considered as non-combatants, they ought to be restored; if as property, they ought to be paid for." This stipulation is, moreover, expressly included "in the conditions on which you are to *insist* in the proposed negotiations."—*Letter of Instructions from Mr. Monroe, Secretary of State, 28th January*, 1814.

us such slaves as had escaped from our coast to her cruisers, during the progress of the war.[7] And, under this treaty, after a tedious controversy, Great Britain—refusing, of course, to surrender persons who had fled from her enemies to her protection—was compelled, in 1818, on the award of Alexander I. of Russia to pay over to us no less than twelve hundred thousand dollars, to be divided among our bereft slaveholders. Before this sum was received (1826–7), our Government had made application to the British for a mutual stipulation, by treaty, to return fugitives from labor. But, though Great Britain, through her colonies, was then a slave-holding nation, she peremptorily declined the proposed reciprocity. The first application for such a nice arrangement was made by Mr. Gallatin, our Minister at London, under instructions from Mr. Clay, as Secretary of State, dated June 19, 1826. On the 5th of July, 1827, Mr. Gallatin communicated to his Government the final answer of the British Minister, that "it was utterly impossible for them to agree to the stipulation for the surrender of fugitive slaves;" and, when the application was renewed through our next Minister, Mr. James Barbour, the British Minister conclusively replied that "the law of Parliament gives freedom to every slave who effects his landing on British ground." Yet a Democratic House of Representatives, in 1828, (May 10), requested the President

"To open a negotiation with the British Government, in the view to obtain an arrangement, whereby fugitive slaves, who have taken refuge in the Canadian provinces of that Government, may be surrendered by the functionaries thereof to their masters, upon making satisfactory proof of their ownership of said slaves."

A Presidential Election was then imminent, and neither party willing to provoke the jealousy of the Slave Power: so this disgraceful resolve passed the House without a division.

In 1826, Joel R. Poinsett, our Minister to Mexico, acting under instructions from Mr. Clay, negotiated with the Mexican Government a treaty for the mutual restoration of runaway slaves, but the Mexican Senate refused to ratify it. In 1831 (January 3), the brig Comet, a regular slaver from the District of Columbia, on her voyage to New Orleans, with a cargo of 164 slaves, was lost off the island of Abaco. The slaves were saved, and carried into New Providence, a British port, whose authorities immediately set them at liberty. And in 1833 (February 4), the brig Encomium, from Charleston to New Orleans with 45 slaves, was also wrecked near Abaco, and the slaves, in like manner, carried into New Providence, and there declared free. In February, 1835, the Enterprise, another slaver from the Federal District, proceeding to Charleston with 78 slaves, was driven in distress into Bermuda, where the slaves were immediately set at liberty. After long and earnest efforts on the part of our Government, the British Cabinet reluctantly consented to pay for the cargoes of the Comet and Encomium, expressly on the grounds that Slavery

[7] "ART. I. All territory, places, and possessions whatever, taken from either party by the other, during the war, or which may be taken after the signing of this treaty, shall be restored without delay; and without causing any destruction or the carrying away of the artillery, or other public property *originally captured* in said forts or places, and which shall *remain* upon the exchange of the ratifications of this treaty, or any *slaves*, or other private property."

still existed in the British West Indies at the time their slaves were liberated; but refused to pay for those of the Enterprise, or any other slaver that might be brought on British soil subsequently to the passage of her Emancipation act. Importunity and menace were alike exhausted by our diplomatists down to a recent period, but to no purpose. Great Britain stubbornly refused either to unite with us in a reciprocal surrender of fugitive slaves to their masters, or in paying for such as, by their own efforts, or through the interposition of Providence, might emerge from American bondage into British liberty.

Our repeated invasions of Florida, while a Spanish colony, our purchase of that colony from Spain, and our unjust, costly, and discreditable wars upon her Aboriginal tribes, were all prompted by a concern for the interests and security of the slaveholders of southern Georgia and Alabama, whose chattels would persist in following each other out of Christian bondage into savage freedom. Gen. Jackson, in 1816, wrote to Gen. Gaines with respect to a fort in Florida, then a Spanish possession:

"If the fort harbors the negroes of our citizens, or of friendly Indians living within our territory, or holds out inducements to the slaves of our citizens to desert from their owners' service, it must be destroyed. Notify the Governor of Pensacola of your advance into his territory, and for the express purpose of destroying these lawless banditti."

Gen. Gaines, for some reason, did not execute this order; but a gunboat, sent up the Apalachicola river by our Commodore Patterson, on the 27th of July, attacked and destroyed the fort by firing red-hot shot, exploding its magazine. The result is thus summed up in the official report:

"Three hundred negroes, *men*, *women*, *and children*, and about twenty Indians, were in the fort; of these two hundred and seventy were killed, and the greater part of the rest *mortally* wounded."

Commodore Patterson, in his official letter to the Secretary of the Navy, expressly justifies the destruction of this fort on the ground of its affording a harbor "for runaway slaves and disaffected Indians:" adding, "they have no longer a place to fly to, and will not be so liable to abscond."

The resistance interposed by Gen. Cass, our Minister at Paris in 1840–41, to the treaty negotiated between the Great Powers, conceding a mutual right to search on the slave-coast of Africa, with a view to the more effectual suppression of the Slave-Trade, though cloaked by a jealousy of British maritime preponderance, was really a bid for the favor of the Slave Power. The concession, by our Government, of the right to search, since that Government has passed out of the hands of the devotees of Slavery, is suggestive. It was American Slavery, not American commerce, that dreaded the visitation of our vessels on the western coast of central Africa by National cruisers, intent on the punishment of a crime which had already been pronounced piracy by the awakened conscience of Christendom.

In fact, so long as more than one hundred members of Congress were chosen to represent, to advance, and to guard, before all else, the interests of Slavery, and one hundred electoral votes were controlled, primarily, by that interest, it was morally impossible that our Government should not be warped into subserviency to our National cancer. A 'peculiar institution,' creating and upholding the title to a species of property valued at Four Thousand Millions of dollars, could hardly fail to make itself respected and influential in every department of the public service, and through every act of the Federal authorities calculated to affect its stability, its prosperity, or its power.

But, up to this time, Slavery had sought and obtained the protection and championship of the Federal Government expressly as a domestic institution—as an important interest of a certain portion of the American people. In the Annexation of Texas, and in the reasons officially adduced therefor, it challenged the regard of mankind and defied the consciences of our own citizens as a great National interest, to the protection of which, at all hazards and under all circumstances, our Government was inflexibly committed, and with whose fortunes those of our country were inextricably blended. For the first time, our Union stood before the nations, not merely as an upholder, but as a zealous, unscrupulous propagandist of Human Slavery.

XIII.

THE MISSION OF SAMUEL HOAR.

The Federal Constitution (Art. iv. § 2) provides that "The citizens "of each State shall be entitled to all "the privileges and immunities of "citizens in the several States."

This is plainly condensed from the corresponding provision of the Articles of Confederation, adopted in 1778, and thenceforth our bond of Union, until superseded in 1787–8 by the Federal Constitution aforesaid. That provision is as follows:

"Art. 4. The better to secure and perpetuate mutual friendship and intercourse among the people of the different States in the Union, the free inhabitants of each State — paupers, vagabonds, and fugitives from justice excepted — shall be entitled to all the privileges and immunities of free citizens in the several States; and the people of each State shall have free ingress and egress to and from any other State, and shall enjoy therein all the privileges of trade and commerce, subject to the same duties, impositions, and restrictions, as the inhabitants thereof respectively."

When this Article was under consideration, the delegates from South Carolina moved to amend by inserting the word "*white*" between "free" and "inhabitants;" which was emphatically negatived — only *two* States voting for it: so it was determined that States had, or might have, citizens who were not "white," and that these should be entitled to all the privileges of citizens in every other State.

We have seen[1] that Congress, in 1821, resisted the attempt of Missouri to prohibit the immigration of free colored persons, deeming it a palpable violation of that requirement of the Federal Constitution above quoted; and would not admit that State into the Union until, by a second compromise, she was required to pledge herself that her

---

[1] Page 80.

Legislature should pass no act "by "which any of the citizens of either "of the States should be excluded "from the enjoyment of the privi- "leges and immunities to which they "are entitled under the Constitution "of the United States." There was no question pending, no proscription or exclusion meditated, but that affecting colored persons only; and Congress, by the above action, clearly affirmed their right, when citizens of any State, to the privileges and immunities of citizens in all other States.

The assumption that negroes are not, and cannot be, citizens, is abundantly refuted by the action of several of the Slave States themselves. Till within a recent period, free negroes were not merely citizens, but electors, of those States—which all citizens are not, or need not be. John Bell, when first elected to Congress, in 1827, running out Felix Grundy, received the votes of several colored electors, and used, long after, to confess his obligation to them.

North Carolina allowed *her* free negroes, who possessed the requisite qualifications in other respects, to vote, regardless of their color, down to about 1830. Their habit of voting for the Federal or Whig candidates, and against the Democratic, was a subject of frequent and jocular remark—the Whigs insisting that the instincts of the negro impelled him uniformly to associate, so far as practicable, with the more gentlemanly portion of the white race.

In the year 1835,[2] the Legislature of South Carolina saw fit to pass an act, whereby any and every colored person found on board of any vessel entering one of her ports was to be forthwith seized by her municipal officers, and lodged in jail; there to remain until the vessel should be cleared for departure, when said colored person or persons should be restored to said vessel, on payment of the cost and charges of arrest, detention, and subsistence.[3]

This act necessarily bore with great hardship on the colored sea-

[2] December 19th.

[3] The following is a portion of the act in question:

"II. *And be it further enacted by the authority aforesaid*, That it shall not be lawful for any free negro, or person of color, to come into this State, on board any vessel, as a cook, steward, or mariner, or in any other employment on board such vessel; and, in case any vessel shall arrive in any port or harbor of this State, from any other State or foreign port, having on board any free negro or person of color, employed on board such vessel as a cook, steward, or mariner, or in any other employment, it shall be the duty of the sheriff of the district in which such port or harbor is situated, immediately on the arrival of such vessel, to apprehend such free negro or person of color, so arriving contrary to this Act, and to confine him or her closely in jail, until such vessel shall be hauled off from the wharf, and ready to proceed to sea. And that, when said vessel is ready to sail, the captain of the said vessel shall be bound to carry away such free negro or person of color, and to pay the expenses of his or her detention. And in every such case it shall be the duty of the sheriff aforesaid, immediately on the apprehension of any free negro or person of color, to cause said captain to enter into a recognizance, with good and sufficient security, in the sum of one thousand dollars, for such free negro or slave so brought into this State, that he will comply with the requisitions of this act; and that, on his neglect, or refusal, or disability to do the same, he shall be compelled by the sheriff aforesaid to haul said vessel into the stream, one hundred yards distant from the shore, and remain until said vessel shall proceed to sea. And if said vessel shall not be hauled off from the shore as aforesaid on the order of the sheriff aforesaid, the captain or commanding officer of said vessel shall be indicted therefor, and, on conviction, forfeit and pay one thousand dollars, and suffer imprisonment not exceeding six months.

"III. *And be it further enacted by the authority aforesaid*, That whenever any free negro or person of color shall be apprehended or committed to jail, as having arrived in any vessel in the capacity of cook, steward, mariner, or otherwise, contrary to this Act, it shall be the duty of the

men, cooks, etc., of Northern vessels trading to Charleston. Massachusetts, therefore, at length resolved, through the action of her Legislature,[4] to test its constitutionality by instituting legal proceedings, which should bring it ultimately to an adjudication by the Supreme Court of the United States. To this end, Gov. Briggs appointed Hon. Samuel Hoar—one of her most eminent and venerable citizens, who had served her with honor in many important trusts, including a seat in Congress—to proceed to Charleston, and there institute the necessary proceedings, in order to bring the matter to judgment. Mr. Hoar accepted this new duty, and left home accordingly in November, 1844, for Charleston; reaching that city on the 28th of that month. So utterly unsuspecting was he of giving offense, or provoking violence, that his young daughter accompanied him.

On the day of his arrival, Mr. Hoar addressed a letter to the Governor of South Carolina,[5] announcing the fact, and stating the purpose of his mission to be, "the collecting and transmission of accurate information respecting the number and the names of citizens of Massachusetts, who have heretofore been, or may be, during the period of the engagement of the agent, imprisoned without the allegation of any crime." He further stated that he was authorized to bring and prosecute one or more suits in behalf of any citizen so imprisoned, for the purpose of having the legality of such imprisonment tried and determined in the Supreme Court of the United States.

The next morning, Mr. Hoar called on Mr. Eggleston, who had been appointed to the same agency before him, and requested of him an introduction to the Mayor of Charleston, his object being to procure access to the records of orders or sentences, under which citizens of Massachusetts, it was understood, had been imprisoned. Mr. Eggleston acceded to his request, but said it would be best that *he* should first see the

sheriff, during the confinement in jail of such free negro or person of color, to call upon some justice of the peace or quorum, to warn such free negro or person of color never to enter the said State after he shall have departed therefrom, and such justice of the peace, or quorum, shall, at the time of warning such free negro, or person of color, insert his or her name in a book, to be provided for that purpose by the sheriff, and shall therein specify his or her age, occupation, hight, and distinguishing marks; which book shall be good and sufficient evidence to such warning; and said book shall be a public record, and be subject and open to the examination of all persons who may make application to the clerk of the court of general sessions, in whose office it shall be deposited. And such justice shall receive the sum of two dollars, payable by the captain of the vessel in which said free negro or person of color shall be introduced into this State, for the services rendered in making said entry. And every free negro, or person of color, who shall not depart the State, in case of the captain refusing or neglecting to carry him or her away, or, having departed, shall again enter into the limits of this State, by land or by water, after having been warned as aforesaid, shall be dealt with as the first section of this Act directs in regard to persons of color, who shall migrate, or be brought, into this State."

It may be as well to add that the penalty of the first section referred to, is corporal punishment for the first offense: "and if, after said sentence or punishment, such free negro or person of color shall still remain in the State longer than the time allowed, or, having left the State, shall thereafter return to the same, upon proof and conviction thereof before a court, to be constituted as hereinbefore directed, *he or she shall be appropriated and applied, one half thereof to the use of the State, and the other half to the use of the informer.*"

[4] Resolves of March 24, 1843, and March 16, 1844.

[5] Hon. James H. Hammond, since distinguished as a U. S. Senator.

Mayor, and explain the matter in advance of the proposed introduction. Mr. Hoar assented, and Eggleston left Mr. H. waiting in his office, while he proceeded to confer with the Mayor. After a considerable absence, he returned, and stated that the Mayor was at Columbia, attending the session of the Legislature, and that the gentleman who temporarily discharged the duties of the officer judged it best that all further proceedings should await his return. This was assented to, and Mr. Hoar waited through the next three days accordingly.

Meantime, Gov. Hammond had received Mr. Hoar's letter, and communicated it to the Legislature, by which it was received in high dudgeon. That Legislature proceeded to pass, by a substantially unanimous vote, the following resolutions:

"*Resolved*, 1st, That the right to exclude from their territories *seditious persons*, or others whose presence may be dangerous to their peace, is essential to every independent State.

"*Resolved*, 2d, That free and other persons of color are *not* citizens of the United States, within the meaning of the Constitution, which confers upon the citizens of one State the privileges and immunities of citizens of the several States.

"*Resolved*, 3d, That the *emissary* sent by the State of Massachusetts to the State of South Carolina, with *the avowed purpose* of interfering with her institutions, and *disturbing her peace*, is to be regarded in the character he has assumed, and to be treated accordingly.

"*Resolved*, 4th, That his Excellency the Governor be requested to expel from our territory the said agent, after due notice to depart; and that the Legislature will sustain the Executive authority in any measure it may adopt for the purpose aforesaid."

The Legislature proceeded directly thereafter to pass an act forbidding and punishing such missions as that of Mr. Hoar, whereof the more material provisions are as follows:

"I. *Be it enacted by the Senate and House of Representatives, now met and sitting in General Assembly and by authority of the same*, That any person or persons who shall on his, her, or their own behalf, or under any color, or in virtue of any commission or authority from any State in this Union, or of any foreign power, come within the limits of this State for the purpose or with the intent to disturb, counteract, or hinder the operation of such laws as have been or shall be made by the public authorities of this State, in relation to slaves or free persons of color, such person or persons shall be deemed guilty of a high misdemeanor, and shall be committed for trial to the common jail of the district, by any one of the judges of the courts of law or equity, or the recorder of the city of Charleston, unless admitted to bail by the said judge or recorder; and, upon due conviction thereof by any court of competent jurisdiction, shall be sentenced to banishment from the State, and to such fine and imprisonment as may be deemed fitting by the court which shall have tried such offense.

"II. That any person within this State who shall at any time accept any commission or authority from any State, or public authority of any State in this Union, or from any foreign power, in relation to slaves or free persons of color, and who shall commit any overt act with intent to disturb the peace or security of this State, or with intent to disturb, counteract, or hinder the operation of the laws or regulations of the public authorities of this State, made or to be made, in relation to slaves or free persons of color, such person shall be deemed guilty of a misdemeanor, and, on conviction thereof, before any competent court, shall be sentenced to pay, for the first offense, a fine not exceeding one thousand dollars, and to be imprisoned not exceeding one year; for the second offense, he shall be imprisoned for seven years, and pay a fine not less than one thousand dollars, or be banished from the State, as the court may see fit."

[The act furthermore requires that the Governor for the time being shall require the aforesaid emissary or emissaries from another State, or from a foreign power, to depart from the limits of the State in forty-eight hours—such person or persons, neglecting to depart within the specified time, to be committed (unless admitted to bail), and to be tried and punished as before stated; and provides that the Sheriff shall see that the sentence of banishment be executed, and imprison such offender if he returns, unless by unavoidable accident.]

On Monday, December 2d, Mr. Hoar was, for the first time, apprised of the reception accorded at Columbia to his mission, and of the commotion it had raised. After discussing the matter freely with those around him, he walked out for some distance, and, returning at dark to his hotel, he encountered three persons standing on the piazza. One of them stepped forward and asked, "Is your name Hoar, Sir?" and, being answered in the affirmative, announced himself as follows: "I am the Sheriff of Charleston District, and I have some business with you, Sir." He then introduced his associates as the acting mayor and another alderman of the city. Mr. Hoar invited them to walk up into the parlor of the house. When seated, the sheriff inquired his business in Charleston; and was answered that he had already communicated it to the Governor; but he stated it afresh to the sheriff, who said: "It is suspected that you are an Abolitionist, and have come here to accomplish some of their measures." After some hesitation, Mr. Hoar assured him that he was no Abolitionist, but had been, for many years, a member of the Colonization Society. The sheriff intimating some suspicion that Mr. Hoar was not duly accredited, the latter exhibited his commission from the Governor of Massachusetts, and gave permission to copy it, as also the resolves of the Legislature on which it was founded.

The Sheriff continued: "It is considered a great insult on South Carolina by Massachusetts to send an agent here on such business. The city is highly incensed. You are in great danger, and you had better leave the city as soon as possible." Mr. H. replied that he had been sent there by the Governor of Massachusetts on lawful business, and could not leave until he had at least attempted to perform the duty imposed on him. The sheriff then produced a letter purporting to be from the Attorney-General of South Carolina, urging the avoidance of a resort to *lynching*, as that would disgrace the city, and adding that the person to prevent such a procedure was the sheriff. That functionary declared that he should endeavor to defend Mr. H., even at the hazard of his own life, but doubted his ability to do it in view of the prevailing excitement, and urged him, as a friend, to leave at the earliest moment. Mr. H. repeated his answer already given, and thereupon his visitors left him.

The next morning, the sheriff returned and repeated his representations and entreaties of the evening. "What do you expect?" he asked; "you can never get a verdict; and, if you should, the marshal would need all the troops of the United States to enforce the judgment." Mr. Hoar remarked that enforcing the judgment was no part of his business, and they thereupon separated.

During the day, several gentlemen called, making representations substantially like the sheriff's, and setting forth the various plans suggested for ridding the city of his presence. He could only reply that he should not voluntarily leave until he had fulfilled the duty he had undertaken.

In the evening, a gentleman to whom Mr. Hoar had a letter of introduction called, and said the sheriff had offered, in case he would leave, to agree on a case to be submitted to the U. S. Circuit Court, and thence carried to the Supreme Court for final decision. To this, Mr. Hoar readily assented, observing that such an agreement would very much expedite his departure. He had prepared himself, in Boston, with the names of a number of colored seamen who had been taken out of Massachusetts vessels in Charleston, and there imprisoned under the law in question, and he felt authorized by his commission to commence a suit in the name of either of two of them. It was agreed that a meeting should be held at the sheriff's office next morning at nine o'clock, for the purpose of perfecting this arrangement. At that hour, Mr. H. duly appeared at the sheriff's office, but found there neither the sheriff nor any other of the gentlemen who were to meet him. Being informed by one of the clerks that the sheriff had just stepped out on business, and would probably soon return, he waited half or three-quarters of an hour to no purpose, and was about to leave, when the clerk said that, if he would name a future hour when he would be there, he would inform the sheriff, so that he might meet him. He named twelve o'clock, and, returning at that time, found the sheriff. That personage now admitted that the gentleman who had conferred with Mr. H. the evening previous had correctly represented his proposal; but said, that, on further reflection and consultation, he must retract the offer; as what he had proposed might thwart the purposes of the State; that he had not been long in office, and did not know that there was any case which would properly present the question in controversy. At all events, he could not abide by his agreement. He added that he had information from Gov. Hammond which removed all personal objection, but rëiterated his former remarks about the insult by Massachusetts to South Carolina, and her determination to be rid of Mr. Hoar by some means.

On leaving the sheriff's office, Mr. Hoar was proceeding to make a call, when he was stopped by a middle-aged, decently-dressed man, who presented a cane or club, asking, "Is your name Hoar?" "Yes," was the answer. He then said, "You had better be traveling, and the sooner, the better for you, I can tell you; if you stay here until to-morrow morning, you will feel something you will not like, I am thinking." Mr. Hoar walked on, passing a number of young men assembled on the street-corner, who offered him no molestation. In the evening, a Dr. Whitredge, to whom Mr. Hoar had brought a letter from Boston, called upon him and urged him to leave the city at the earliest moment. Dr. W. had been around the city, had just come from the Council, and regarded the danger to Mr. H. as not only great, but imminent. But a word was needed to bring on the meditated attack. Yet he thought Mr. Hoar, should he start at once, might get safely out of the city. He urged him to procure a carriage, and go to his (W.'s) plantation, about twenty miles distant, where he would be hospitably treated. Mr. Hoar thanked him, but concluded that he could not accept his offer, but must remain, and abide the consequences.

The following night passed without any disturbance. The next day at noon, three leading citizens of Charleston, two of them eminent lawyers, and the third a president of one of the city banks, called on Mr. H. for the first time, and gave their names, saying they had come to see if they could not induce him to leave the city. After the usual appeals on the one side and replies on the other had consumed half an hour, the bank president gave Mr. H. notice that a number of gentlemen would call on him at two o'clock and conduct him to the boat. Mr. H. responded that he would be found there; that he did not propose to fight a whole city, and was too old to run, so that they could do with him as they thought proper. He added that he had a daughter with him; on which the bank president observed, "It is that which creates [or created] our embarrassment." They left him about one o'clock.

Mr. H. and his daughter now prepared for their departure, and waited from two till three o'clock, but no one came. He afterward learned that an accident had prevented the arrival of the boat at the usual hour. The next day at noon, Dr. Whitredge called and informed Mr. H. that the keeper of the hotel had requested the city government to take measures to remove Mr. H. from his house, in order to preserve it from the impending danger. He had never intimated such a request to Mr. Hoar, nor anything approaching it. But the fact that his host wished to get rid of him, and that he could find no other lodging without exposing whoever sheltered him to annoyance, if not peril, created a fresh embarrassment. At this moment, a waiter informed Mr. Hoar that some gentlemen wished to see him in the hall. He descended, and found there the bank-president and his associates surrounded by a considerable bevy, with an assemblage about the door, on the piazza, and in the street, where a number of carriages were in waiting. The president announced that they were there to conduct him to the boat. Mr. Hoar now stated that there was a report in circulation that he had consented to leave the city, which was not true. If he left, it would be not because he *would*, but because he *must*. The bank-president remarked that there was a misunderstanding; that he had understood that Mr. Hoar had consented to leave for the sake of preserving [or restoring] the peace of the city; but that, if he refused, they had no power to order him away; all they could do was to warn him of the consequences of remaining. Mr. H. repeated his language at the preceding interview, which the president did not deny to be accurate, but said that he had understood Mr. H. as consenting to leave.

Hereupon, several of the party united in urging his departure at once, saying it was impossible that he should remain, and that the purpose of his mission could not be effected. Among these, were two to whom he had been specially commended. Finding that he had but the choice between walking to the carriage and being dragged to it, Mr. Hoar paid his bill at the hotel, called down his daughter from her room, and entered with her the carriage pointed out to him, and one of the crowd ordered the coachman to drive on. He was thus taken to the boat, which was very soon bearing him on his homeward way. Mr. Hoar, in closing the official report of his visit to and expulsion from South Carolina, asked the following portentous questions:

"Has the Constitution of the United States the least practical validity or binding force in South Carolina, except where she thinks its operation favorable to her? She prohibits the trial of an action in the tribunals established under the Constitution for determining such cases, in which a citizen of Massachusetts complains that a citizen of South Carolina had done him an injury; saying that she has herself already tried that cause, and decided against the plaintiff. She prohibits, not only by her mobs, but by her Legislature, the residence of a free white citizen of Massachusetts within the limits of South Carolina, whenever she thinks his presence there inconsistent with her policy. Are the other States of the Union to be regarded as the conquered provinces of South Carolina?"

Such was the manner in which South Carolina, with the hearty approval of her slaveholding sisters, received and repelled the attempt of Massachusetts to determine and enforce the rights, while protecting the liberties, of her free citizens, as guaranteed by the Constitution of the United States. Massachusetts proposed no appeal to her own courts, no reliance on her own views of constitutional right and duty, but an arbitration before, and a judgment by, the tribunals of the Union, specially clothed by our Federal pact with jurisdiction over "all cases in law and equity arising under this Constitution." Here was the precise case meditated—a complaint by one State that the rights and liberties of her citizens were subverted by the legislation of a sister State; here was the tribunal created by the Constitution for the trial of such issues. South Carolina repudiated its jurisdiction, as she had previously, with regard to the Tariff, repudiated the authority of Congress, or any other that should contravene her own sovereign will. When we are told that the North failed, some years later, to evince sufficient alacrity in slave-catching, let these facts be freshly remembered.

XIV.

THE WILMOT PROVISO.

Mr. Polk succeeded Mr. Tyler as President of the United States, March 4, 1845. No change in the policy of the former with regard to Annexation was made, or, with reason, expected. The agent so hastily dispatched to Texas by Mr. Tyler to speed the consummation of the decreed union, was not, of course, recalled. The new President was doubtless gratified to find his predestined work, in which he had expected to encounter some impediments at the hands of Northern members of his own party, so nearly completed to his hand. On the 18th of June, joint resolutions, giving their final consent to Annexation, passed both Houses of the Congress of Texas by a unanimous vote; and this action was ratified by a Convention of the People of Texas on the ensuing 4th of July.

The XXIXth Congress met at Washington December 1, 1845, with a strong Democratic majority in either branch. John W. Davis, of Indiana, was chosen Speaker of the House by 120 votes to 72 for Samuel F. Vinton (Whig), of Ohio, and 18 scattering. On the 16th, a joint resolve, reported on the 10th from the Committee on Territories by Mr. Douglas, of Illinois, formally admitting Texas as a State into our Union, was carried by the decisive vote of 141 to 56. The Senate concurred, on the 22d, by 31 Yeas to 13 Nays.

Thus far, the confident predictions of War with Mexico, as a necessary consequence of our annexing Texas, had not been realized. Technically and legally, we might, perhaps, be said to have been at war ever since we had determined on Annexation; practically and in fact, we were not. No belligerent action on the part of Mexico directly followed the decisive step, or its official promulgation. Our commerce and our flag were still welcomed in the Mexican ports. The disposable portion of our little army, some 1,500 strong, under Gen. Zachary Taylor, commander of the Southwestern department, in obedience to orders from Washington, embarked (July, 1845) at New Orleans, and landed, early in August, at Corpus Christi, on Aransas Bay, near the mouth of the Nueces, which was the extreme western limit of Texan occupation.[1] The correspondence between the Secretary of War (Gov. Marcy) and Gen. Taylor, which preceded and inspired this movement, clearly indicates that Mr. Polk and his Cabinet desired Gen. Taylor to debark at, occupy, and hold, the east bank of the Rio Grande, though they shrank from the responsibility of giving an order to that effect, hoping that Gen. Taylor would take a hint, as Gen. Jackson was accustomed to do in his Florida operations, and do what was desired in such manner as would enable the Government to disavow him, and evade the responsibility of his course. Gen. Taylor, however, demanded explicit instructions, and, being thereupon directed to take position so as to be prepared to defend the soil of our new acquisition "to the extent that it had been occupied by the people of Texas," he stopped at the Nueces, as aforesaid. Here, though no hostilities were offered or threatened, 2,500 more troops were sent him in November. Official hints and innuendoes that he was expected to advance to the Rio Grande continued to reach him, but he disregarded them; and at length, about the 1st of March, he received positive orders from the President to ad-

[1] Hon. Charles J. Ingersoll, a leading Democratic representative in Congress from Pennsylvania, and a zealous Annexationist, in a speech in the House, January 3, 1845, said:

"The territorial limits are marked in the configuration of this continent by an Almighty hand. The Platte, the Arkansas, the Red, and the Mississippi Rivers * * * these are naturally our waters, with their estuaries in the Bay of Mexico. The stupendous deserts between the Nueces and the Bravo rivers, are the natural boundaries between the Anglo-Saxon and the Mauritanian races. There ends the valley of the West. There Mexico begins. * * * We ought to stop there, because interminable conflicts must ensue, either on our going South or their coming North of that gigantic boundary. While peace is cherished, that boundary will be kept sacred. Not till the spirit of conquest rages, will the people on either side molest or mix with each other."

vance. He accordingly put his column in motion on the 8th of that month, crossing the arid waste, over one hundred miles wide, that stretches south-westward nearly to the Rio Grande, and reached the bank of that river, opposite Matamoras, on the 28th. Here[2] he erected Fort Brown, commanding Matamoras—the Mexicans, under Ampudia, being at the same time engaged in throwing up batteries on their side. These being completed, Ampudia (April 12th) addressed Gen. Taylor, requiring him to return to the Nueces forthwith, there to remain "while our Governments are regulating the pending question relative to Texas;" with a warning that his refusal would be regarded by Mexico as a declaration of war. Gen. Taylor courteously replied that he was acting under instructions that were incompatible with the Mexican's requirement. Ampudia was soon after superseded by Arista, who, early in May, crossed the Rio Grande at the head of 6,000 men, and, on the 8th, attacked Gen. Taylor's 2,300 at Palo Alto, and was badly defeated. Retreating to a strong position at Resaca de la Palma, a few miles distant, he was there attacked next day by Gen. Taylor, who routed his forces, after a sharp conflict, and drove them in disorder across the river. The Mexican loss in these two affairs was 1,000 men, with eight guns, and a large amount of baggage. The undisturbed possession of the entire left bank of the Rio Grande was among the "spoils of victory."

President Polk (May 11th) communicated some of these facts to Congress in a Special Message, wherein he averred that the Mexicans had "*at last invaded our territory, and shed the blood of our fellow-citizens on our own soil.*" Congress, two days afterward, responded, by the passage of an act, calling out 50,000 volunteers, and appropriating $10,000,000 for the prosecution of the struggle thus begun, with a prëamble, running,

> "Whereas, *by the act of the Republic of Mexico*, a state of war exists between that Government and the United States, *Be it enacted*," etc.

Only 14 votes in the House, and 2 in the Senate were cast against this bill, though several members (among them Mr. Calhoun) refused to vote on it at all; and a motion in the House to strike out the prëamble was sustained by nearly every member elected as a Whig.

Congress remained in session till the 10th of August; before which time, it had become evident that Mexico, distracted and enfeebled by so many revolutions, could make no effective resistance to the progress of our arms. President Polk, not without reason, believed that a treaty of peace might be negotiated with her rickety government, whereby, on the payment of a sum of money on our part, not only the boundary of the Rio Grande, but a very consider-

[2] The following is extracted from a letter written by one of our officers, soon after Gen. Taylor's arrival on the Rio Grande, and before the outbreak of actual hostilities:

"CAMP OPPOSITE MATAMORAS, *April* 19, 1846.

"Our situation here is an extraordinary one. Right in the enemy's country, actually occupying their corn and cotton fields, the people of the soil leaving their homes, and we, with a small handful of men, marching with colors flying, and drums beating, right under the very guns of one of their principal cities, displaying the star-spangled banner, as if in defiance, under their very nose, and they, with an army twice our size, at least, sit quietly down, and make not the least resistance, not the first effort to drive the invaders off. There is no parallel to it."

able acquisition of hitherto Mexican territory beyond that river, might be secured. He accordingly (August 8) sent a Special Message to Congress, asking that a considerable sum be placed at his disposal for these purposes. A bill was immediately reported and considered in Committee of the Whole, making appropriations of $30,000 for expenses of negotiations, and $2,000,000, to be used at the discretion of the President, in making such a treaty. This bill seemed on the point of passing through all its stages without serious opposition.

But what should be the Social or Labor system of the territories about to be acquired? This question could be no longer postponed nor evaded. Hitherto, Slavery had entered upon each succeeding struggle for a new territory with the great advantage of prior possession. Virginia, which claimed the ownership of most of the territory North-west of the Ohio, and between that river and the Mississippi, was a Slave State, and her outlying territories, it might fairly be argued, inherited her domestic institutions; Alabama and Mississippi were, in like manner, constructively slaveholding at the outset, by virtue of the laws of North Carolina and Georgia, from which States they were cut off. Louisiana (including Missouri) had come to us slaveholding from France; so had Florida from Spain; while Texas had been colonized and revolutionized mainly by Southerners, who imprinted on her their darling "institution" before we had any voice in the matter. In the case of each, it had been plausibly and successfully contended that their Slavery was no concern of ours—that it was established and legalized before we were empowered to speak in the matter, and must be upheld until those more immediately interested should see fit to abolish it. This consideration had prevailed even in the recent instance of Texas, where all partition had been refused, all real compromise scouted, on the assumption that Slavery was already in possession, and did not care to divide what was wholly its own.

The case was now decidedly altered. Mexico had utterly abolished Slavery some twenty years before; and every acre that she should cede to us beyond the Rio Grande would come to us free soil. Should it so remain, or be surrendered to the domination and uses of Slavery? It was well known that Mr. Calhoun had elaborated a new dogma adapted to the exigency, whereby the Federal Constitution was held to carry Slavery into every rood of Federal territory whence it was not excluded by positive law. In other words, every citizen of any State had a constitutional right to migrate into any territory of the Union, carrying with him whatever the law of his own State recognized as property; and this must, therefore, be guarded and defended as his property by the Federal authorities of and within said territory. Should this view not be precluded by some decided protest, some positive action, it was morally certain that President Polk, with every successor of like faith, would adopt it, and that the vast and, as yet, nearly unpeopled regions about to be acquired from Mexico would thus be added to the already spacious dominions of the Slave Power.

There was a hasty consultation, in

default of time or opportunity for one more deliberate, among those Democratic members from Free States who felt that the extreme limit of justifiable or tolerable concession to Slavery had already been reached; wherein Messrs. Hamlin, of Maine, George Rathbun, Martin Grover and Preston King, of New York, David Wilmot, of Pennsylvania, Jacob Brinckerhoff and James J. Faran, of Ohio, McClelland, of Michigan, and others, took part; as the result of which, Mr. Wilmot moved to add to the first section of the bill the following:

"*Provided*, That, as an express and fundamental condition to the acquisition of any territory from the Republic of Mexico by the United States, by virtue of any treaty that may be negotiated between them, and to the use by the Executive of the moneys herein appropriated, neither Slavery nor involuntary servitude shall ever exist in any part of said territory, except for crime, whereof the party shall first be duly convicted."

This Proviso was adopted in Committee by 80 Ays to 64 Noes — only three members (Democrats), it was said, from the Free States, passing through the tellers in response to the call for the Noes. The bill was thereupon reported to the House; and Mr. Rathbun, of New York, moved the Previous Question on its engrossment (so as to preclude a motion to strike out this Proviso). This was met by Mr. Tibbatts, of Kentucky, with a motion that the bill *do lie on the table*—in other words, that the original measure, but a moment since deemed so vital, be voted down, in order to kill the Proviso. This was defeated on a call of the Yeas and Nays—all the members from Slave States but Messrs. William P. Thomasson and Henry Grider (Whigs), of Kentucky, voting to lay on the table, with Messrs. John Pettit, of Indiana, and Stephen A. Douglas, John A. McClernand (Democrats), of Illinois, and Robert C. Schenck (Whig), of Ohio, making 79; while the Yeas (comprising all the Whigs but one, and nearly all the Democrats from Free States, with the two Kentucky Whigs aforesaid), were 93. The bill was thereupon ordered to be engrossed for a third reading by 85 Yeas to 80 Nays, passed, and sent to the Senate, then in the last hours of the session. On its being taken up, Mr. Dixon H. Lewis, of Alabama (a close adherent of Mr. Calhoun), moved that the Proviso aforesaid be stricken out; whereupon Mr. John Davis (Whig), of Massachusetts, rose to debate, and persisted in speaking, as though against time, until noon, which had been concurrently fixed as the hour of adjournment; so the session terminated, and the bill and proviso failed together. It is probable that President Polk would have vetoed the bill, because of the Proviso, had they then passed.

Mr. Davis died[3] not many years afterward, and no explanation of his course in this instance was ever given to the public. He may have desired only to defeat some obnoxious measure which would have come up and which would probably have passed if this bill had been promptly disposed of. It is certain that Gen. Cass, then a Senator, complained, on his homeward journey, of Mr. Davis having defeated a measure which should have been passed, so as to preclude all further controversy with regard to the Extension of Slavery.

[3] At Worcester, Mass., April 19th, 1854.

More than a year thereafter, with a Baltimore Convention and a Presidential election in immediate prospect, Gen. Cass was interrogated by Mr. A. O. P. Nicholson, of Tennessee, with regard to his opinion of the Wilmot Proviso. In his reply,[4] Gen. C. says:

"The Wilmot Proviso has been before the country for some time. It has been repeatedly discussed in Congress and by the public press. I am strongly impressed with the opinion that *a great change* has been going on in the public mind upon this subject, in *my own* as well as others, and that doubts are resolving themselves into convictions, that the principle it involves should be kept out of the National Legislature, and left to the people of the confederacy in their respective local governments."

This letter is notable as the first clear enunciation of the doctrine termed *Popular* (otherwise squatter) *Sovereignty*—that is, of the lack of legitimate power in the Federal Government to exclude Slavery from its territories. Gen. Cass's position was thoroughly canvassed, six months after it was taken, in a letter[5] from Martin Van Buren to N. J. Waterbury and other Free Soil Democrats of his State, wherein he said:

"The power, the existence of which is at this late day denied, is, in my opinion, fully granted to Congress by the Constitution. Its language, the circumstances under which it was adopted, the recorded explanations which accompanied its formation—the construction it has received from our highest judicial tribunals, and the very solemn and repeated confirmations it has derived from the measures of the Government—leave not the shadow of a doubt in my mind in regard to the authority of Congress to exercise the power in question. This is not a new opinion on my part, nor the first occasion on which it has been avowed. While the candidate of my friends for the Presidency, I distinctly announced my opinion in favor of the power of Congress to abolish Slavery in the District of Columbia, although I was, for reasons which were then, and are still, satisfactory to my mind, very decidedly opposed to its exercise there. The question of power is certainly as clear in respect to the Territories as it is in regard to the District; and, as to the Territories, my opinion was also made known in a still more solemn form, by giving the Executive approval required by the Constitution to the bill for the organization of the Territorial Government of Iowa, which prohibited the introduction of Slavery into that Territory."

The XXXth Congress assembled December 6th, 1847, when Robert C. Winthrop (Whig), of Massachusetts, was chosen Speaker of the House by a majority of *one;* and, on the 28th of February ensuing, Mr. Harvey Putnam, of New York, having moved an independent resolve embodying the substance of the Wilmot Proviso, Mr. Richard Brodhead, of Pennsylvania, moved that the same do lie on the table, which prevailed—Yeas 105, Nays 93—twenty-five Democrats and one 'Native' (L. C. Levin) from the Free States voting with the entire South to lay on the table; all the Whigs and a large majority of the Democrats from Free States against it.

Peace with Mexico having been made,[6] a bill providing a Territorial Government for Oregon being before Congress at this session, and referred in the Senate to a Select Committee, Mr. John M. Clayton, of Delaware, from that Committee, reported it with amendments establishing Territorial Governments also for New Mexico and California. An original feature of this bill was a proposition embodied therein that all questions concerning Slavery in those Territories be referred directly to the arbitration of the Supreme Court of the United States. This measure

[4] Dated Washington, December 24, 1847.

[5] Dated Lindenwald, June 20, 1848.

[6] By the treaty of Guadalupe Hidalgo, February, 1848.

passed the Senate by the strong vote of 33 Yeas to 22 Nays—all from Free States—but, on its reaching the House, Mr. Alex. H. Stephens, of Georgia, moved that it *do lie on the table*, which prevailed; Yeas 112 (30 of them Democrats from Free States; 8 Whigs from Slave States; and 74 Whigs from Free States); Nays 97; (21 Democrats from Free States, with all the Democrats, and all but 8, as aforesaid, of the Whigs, from Slave States). As the Court was then constituted, there was little room for doubt that its award would have been favorable to Slavery Extension; hence this vote. Mr. Clayton's Compromise, thus defeated, was never revived.

The Democratic National Convention for 1848 assembled at Baltimore on the 22d of May. Gen. LEWIS CASS, of Michigan, received 125 votes for President on the first ballot, to 55 for James Buchanan, 53 for Levi Woodbury, 9 for John C. Calhoun, 6 for Gen. Worth, and 3 for Geo. M. Dallas. On the fourth ballot, Gen. Cass had 179 to 75 for all others, and was declared nominated. Gen. WILLIAM O. BUTLER, of Kentucky, received 114 votes for Vice-President on the first ballot, and was unanimously nominated on the third. Two delegations from New York presenting themselves to this Convention—that of the Free Soilers, Radicals, or "Barnburners," whose leader was Samuel Young, and that of the Conservatives or "Hunkers," whose chief was Daniel S. Dickinson—the Convention attempted to split the difference by admitting both, and giving each half the vote to which the State was entitled. This the "Barnburners" rejected, leaving the Convention and refusing to be bound by its conclusions. The great body of them heartily united in the Free Soil movement, which culminated in a National Convention at Buffalo,[7] whereby MARTIN VAN BUREN was nominated for President, with CHARLES FRANCIS ADAMS, of Massachusetts, for Vice-President.

The regular Democratic or Cass and Butler Convention rëiterated most of the resolves of its two predecessors, adding two or three in commendation of the War with Mexico; warmly congratulated France on her recent return to a republican form of government, and ambiguously indorsed the new Popular Sovereignty discovery as follows:

"*Resolved*, That in the recent development of this grand political truth, of the sovereignty of the people and their capacity for self-government, which is prostrating thrones and erecting republics on the ruins of despotism in the Old World, we feel that a high and sacred duty is devolved, with increased responsibility, upon the Democratic party of this country, as the party of the People, to sustain and advance among us Constitutional Liberty, Equality and Fraternity, by continuing to resist all monopolies and exclusive legislation for the benefit of the few at the expense of the many, and by a vigilant and consistent adherence to those principles and compromises of the Constitution which are broad enough and strong enough to embrace and uphold the Union as it was, as it is, and the Union as it shall be, in the full expansion of the energies and capacity of this great and progressive people."

At this Convention, the Calhoun or extreme Southern dogma of the constitutional right of each slaveholder to remove with his slaves into any Federal Territory, and hold them there in defiance of Congress

[7] August 9, 1848.

or any local authority, was submitted by Mr. William L. Yancey, of Alabama, in the following guise:

"*Resolved*, That the doctrine of non-interference with the rights of property of any portion of the people of this confederacy, be it in the States or Territories thereof, by any other than the parties interested in them, is the true Republican doctrine recognized by this body."

The party was not yet ready for such strong meat, and this resolve was rejected: Nays 216; Yeas 36—South Carolina 9; Alabama 9; Georgia 9; Arkansas 3; Florida 3; Maryland 1; Kentucky 1; Tennessee 1.

The Whig National Convention assembled in Philadelphia, June 7th. Gen. Zachary Taylor, of Louisiana, had on the first ballot 111 votes for President to 97 for Henry Clay, 43 for General Scott, 22 for Mr. Webster, and 6 scattering. On the fourth ballot (next day), Gen. Taylor had 171 to 107 for all others, and was declared nominated. Millard Fillmore, of New York, had 115 votes for Vice-President, on the first ballot, to 109 for Abbott Lawrence, of Massachusetts, and 50 scattering. On the second ballot, Mr. Fillmore had 173, and was nominated. No resolves affirming distinctive principles were passed; repeated efforts to interpose one affirming the principle of the Wilmot Proviso being met by successful motions to lay on the table.

The Buffalo or Free Soil Convention was as frank and explicit in its declaration of principles as its more powerful rivals had been ambiguous or reticent. The following are its most material averments:

"*Resolved*, That the Proviso of Jefferson, to prohibit the existence of Slavery after 1800, in all the Territories of the United States, Southern and Northern; the votes of six States and sixteen delegates, in the Congress of 1784, for the Proviso, to three States and seven delegates against it; the actual exclusion of Slavery from the North-western Territory, by the Ordinance of 1787, unanimously adopted by the States in Congress; and the entire history of that period, clearly show that it was the policy of the Nation not to extend, nationalize, or encourage, but to limit, localize, and *dis*courage Slavery; and to this policy, which should never have been departed from, the Government ought to return.

"*Resolved*, That our fathers ordained the Constitution of the United States, in order, among other great National objects, to 'establish justice, promote the general welfare, and secure the blessings of liberty;' but expressly denied to the Federal Government, which they created, all constitutional power to deprive any person of life, liberty, or property, without due legal process.

"*Resolved*, That, in the judgment of this Convention, Congress has no more power to make a slave than to make a king; no more power to institute or establish Slavery, than to institute or establish monarchy: no such power can be found among those specifically conferred by the Constitution, or derived by just implication from them.

"*Resolved*, That it is the duty of the Federal Government to relieve itself from all responsibility for the existence or continuance of Slavery, wherever the Government possesses constitutional authority to legislate on that subject, and it is thus responsible for its existence.

"*Resolved*, That the true, and, in the judgment of this Convention, the only safe means of preventing the extension of Slavery into territory now Free, is to prohibit its extension in *all* such territory by an act of Congress."

In the event, Gen. Taylor was chosen President, receiving the votes of New York, Pennsylvania, and thirteen other States, choosing 163 Electors. The strong Free Soil vote for Van Buren ensured to Gen. Cass the votes of Ohio, and of every other State North-west of the Ohio, most of them by a plurality only over Taylor. Gen. Cass carried fifteen States, choosing 137 Electors. Mr. Van Buren carried no Electors, but received a respectable support in every Free State, Rhode Island and New Jersey excepted. New York, Massachusetts, and Vermont, each gave a larger popular vote to him than to Gen. Cass; Wisconsin gave him nearly as many as Gen. Taylor. The entire popular vote (South Carolina not casting any) stood—Taylor and Fillmore, 1,360,752; Cass and Butler, 1,219,962; Van Buren and Adams, 291,342. Gen. Taylor had a majority of the Electoral and a plurality of the Popular vote, both in the Free and in the Slave States respectively.

The struggle for the organization of the territories was resumed in Congress the ensuing Winter; and, though there had been very few changes of members, there had been a very considerable change of feeling on the part of a great many Democrats from Free States. They indignantly felt that, by the vote cast for Gen. Taylor in the South, the services and sacrifices of their party had been ungratefully requited. That eight of the fifteen Slave States should cast their votes for the Whig candidate for President, leaving Virginia, Alabama, and Mississippi to be carried against him by the very leanest majorities, was not the entertainment to which they had been invited when they risked their ascendency at home, and their seats, by voting for Gag-Rules, and against the establishment by law of Freedom in the Territories. Some of them were permanently alienated, though the far greater number were but temporarily estranged, from the councils of their Southern chiefs. But the change was made evident, soon after the assembling of the XXXth Congress for its second session, when, (December 13, 1848), on motion of Hon. Joseph M. Root, of Ohio, the House

"*Resolved*, That the Committee on Territories be instructed to report to this House, with as little delay as practicable, a bill or bills providing a territorial government for each of the Territories of New Mexico and California, and excluding Slavery therefrom."

This passed by Yeas 108, including every Whig, and all but eight of the Democrats[8] from Free States; Nays 80—all from the Slave States but the eight aforesaid.

A further evidence of the altered feeling of the House was afforded, when, a few days thereafter, the following was, during the morning hour, moved by Mr. Daniel Gott, of New York:

"*Whereas*, the traffic now prosecuted in this metropolis of the Republic in human beings, as chattels, is contrary to natural justice, and the fundamental principles of our political system, is notoriously a reproach to our country throughout Christendom, and a serious hindrance to the progress of republican liberty among the nations of the earth: Therefore,

"*Resolved*, That the Committee on the District of Columbia be instructed to report

---

[8] The members from Free States (all Democrats), who had voted at the last session to lay the Wilmot Proviso on the table, and who now voted *for* the principle as above, were as follow: MAINE.—Asa W. H. Clapp, James S. Wiley —2. NEW YORK.—Frederick W. Lord—1. OHIO.—Thomas Richey—1. INDIANA.—Charles W. Cathcart, Thomas J. Henley, John L. Robinson, William W. Wick—4. ILLINOIS.—Robert Smith—1. Messrs. Clark and H. Williams, of Maine, Birdsall and Maclay, of New York, Brodhead and Mann, of Pennsylvania; Pettit, of Indiana; Ficklin and McClernand, of Illinois, who voted with the South at the former session —now failed to vote. Mr. D. S. Jackson, of New York, who then voted with the South, had been succeeded by Mr. H. Greeley, who voted with the North.

a bill, as soon as practicable, prohibiting the Slave-Trade in said District."

The Previous Question having been required and ordered, this resolution was adopted by Yeas 98 to Nays 88. Hereupon there was a call for the Southern members to leave the Hall, and various demonstrations of the sort, which resulted in a meeting of members from the Slave States; which resulted in an address to their constituents, drafted and reported by Mr. Calhoun; which resulted in nothing. The House Committee on the District, being Pro-Slavery, of course took good care *not* to report as instructed above.

The Territorial bill for California, foreshadowed and commended by Mr. Root's resolve, was reported by Caleb B. Smith, of Indiana, on the 20th, and that for New Mexico followed on the 3d of January, 1849. An effort (January 15), by Mr. Julius Rockwell, of Massachusetts, to make the former a special order, failed, lacking a two-thirds vote, but received the vote of nearly every member from the Free States—114 to 71. The bill was finally taken out of Committee of the Whole on the 26th of February, and engrossed for a third reading next day; when Mr. R. K. Meade, of Virginia, moved that it do lie on the table, which was decisively negatived; and then the bill passed the House by 126 Yeas to 87 Nays. Mr. Aylett Buckner (Whig of Kentucky), who had made a forcible and thorough-going speech in favor of excluding Slavery from the Territories, voted with his Whig colleague, Green Adams, and all the Whigs and all but four[9] of the Democrats from the Free States, in the affirmative; while all the members present from the Slave States but Messrs. Adams and Buckner voted in the negative: so that the House divided very nearly on Mason and Dixon's line. But Mr. Buckner paid for his speech and vote on this occasion with his seat. He had succeeded in 1847, over his Democratic opponent, by 386 majority; he was thrown out in 1849 by 1140 majority. Mr. Adams did not stand for re-election. And the bill thus passed was not even considered in the Senate—a motion by Mr. Douglas (February 28), that it be taken up for reference, having been promptly voted down by 28 Nays to 25 Yeas.

For the Pro-Slavery majority in that Senate had already resolved on their course, and it did not lie at all in this direction. They believed that their opportunity was at hand; that the more especial friends of the incoming Administration were anxious to have the Slavery question settled—that is, the opposition to Slavery Extension defeated or withdrawn, that being the way such questions were usually settled—in order to make matters smooth and pleasant for the powers soon to be; and they knew that the irritation of the Northern Democrats against the South for giving a majority of its votes for Gen. Taylor as against Gen. Cass had been gradually dying out under the pressure of social influences and of party necessities. They believed that, if a proper issue were made, the Northern repugnance to the organization of the Territories in profound silence as to Slavery, might be overcome. They had, therefore, determined to

[9] Messrs. Samuel A. Bridges of Pennsylvania, and William Kennon, jr., John K. Miller, and William Sawyer, of Ohio. Messrs. Chas. Brown, Chas. J. Ingersoll, and other such, did not vote.

fasten to the Civil and Diplomatic Appropriation bill, a "rider," organizing the new Territories with no restriction on or impediment to the introduction of Slavery, calculating that a sufficient number of the Northern friends of the Administration would permit this to pass rather than see the Government crippled and the President constrained to call an extra session of Congress—always a portent of evil to the party in power. Accordingly, the great Appropriation bill having passed the House, and been reported to and several days debated in the Senate, Mr. Walker, of Wisconsin, moved to add a section extending the laws of the United States over "the territory west of the Rio del Norte, acquired from Mexico by the treaty of February 22, 1848," and authorizing the President to "prescribe and establish all proper and needful regulations for the enforcement" of the Constitution and laws in said Territory; as also "to appoint and commission such officers as may be necessary to administer such laws," etc., etc. This passed the Senate by 29 Yeas[10] to 27 Nays; but the bill being thus returned to the House, the Senate's amendment was there (March 2) rejected: Yeas 100 (thirteen of them from Free States) to Nays 114 (all from Free States). The bill was then returned in its original shape to the Senate. The Senate insisted on its amendment, and asked a conference, which was granted, but nothing came of it. The Committee reported to either House its inability to agree, and was discharged.

Mr. McClernand (Democrat), of Illinois, now moved that the House recede from its non-concurrence in the Senate's amendment, which prevailed—Yeas 111; Nays 106; whereupon Mr. Richard W. Thompson (Whig), of Indiana, moved that the House *do concur with the Senate with an amendment*, which was, in fact, a substitute for the Senate's project, and of which the gist was a provision that "until the 4th of July, 1850, unless Congress shall sooner provide for the government of said Territories, *the existing laws thereof shall be retained and observed*"—in other words, that the laws of Mexico, whereby Slavery was abolished throughout her entire area, should continue in force in said Territories of New Mexico and California. The Senate's amendment, *as amended*, was then agreed to: Yeas 110; Nays 103. And thus the bill, late at night of what was necessarily the last day of the session, was returned to the Senate.

The majority of that body were fairly caught in their own snare. They had vociferously protested that Congress should not adjourn without providing for the government and quiet of the new territories; and had threatened to defeat the General Appropriation bill and leave the Government penniless if this were not acceded to by the House. And here was the bill proposing to do just what they had insisted *must* be done, and could not with safety be postponed. It was only objectionable in that it provided (as was done in the case of Louisiana and Florida) that the social conditions which had existed prior to our acquisition should remain unchanged until Congress, or the People more

[10] Including only Messrs. Dickinson of New York, A. C. Dodge of Iowa, Douglas of Illinois, Fitzgerald of Michigan, and Hannegan of Indiana (all Democrats), from Free States.

immediately interested, should see fit to change them. But this was exactly what the majority determined should not be, and were working to prevent. Yet they did not care to make up an issue with the House majority on this point, and go to the country on the defeat of the chief Appropriation bill, and consequent embarrassment of the Government, for no other reason than that the House had refused to unite in opening the Territories to Slavery. And so, after spending most of the night in heated discussion—much of it mere talking against time—the Senate, toward morning, struck out of the Appropriation bill its materially amended amendment, and passed the bill as it originally came from the House—at all events, with no provision for the organization or government of New Mexico and California. And thus ended the Administration of Mr. Polk, along with the XXXth Congress.

The action of the XXIXth and XXXth Congresses respectively with regard to the Territory of *Oregon*, though proceeding simultaneously with the incidents already recorded in this chapter, and involving essentially identical principles, requires distinct presentation, that the two diverse and somewhat conflicting threads of narrative may not be blended in hopeless entanglement. That action, briefly summed up, was as follows:

At the first session of the XXIXth Congress, Mr. Stephen A. Douglas reported to the House (August 6, 1846) a bill organizing the Territory of Oregon, whereof the northern boundary had just been fixed at latitude 49° by treaty with Great Britain. The bill, as reported, was silent respecting Slavery; but, while under discussion in Committee of the Whole, the following amendment was added:

> "And neither Slavery nor involuntary servitude shall ever exist in said Territory, except for crime, whereof the party shall have been duly convicted."

In the House, on coming out of Committee, the Yeas and Nays were demanded on this amendment, which was sustained: Yeas 108; Nays 44—only three or four Northern Democrats and five or six Southern Whigs being found among the Nays, whereof the residue were Southern Democrats. The bill, as thus amended, passed the House, but went to the Senate so near the close of the session that, though referred to and reported by the Committee on Territories, no further action was had thereon.

On the assembling of this Congress for its second session, Mr. Douglas again reported to the House a bill to provide a Territorial Government for Oregon, which was read twice, and sent to the Committee of the Whole; where it was debated through the 11th, 12th, and 14th of January, and ordered to be taken out of Committee on the 15th. On that day, Gen. Armistead Burt, of South Carolina, moved (having already done so in Committee of the Whole) this addition to the clause inhibiting Slavery, as above given:

> "Inasmuch as the whole of the said Territory lies north of thirty-six degrees thirty minutes north latitude, known as the line of the Missouri Compromise."

The object of this amendment was to obtain from the House a recognition of the parallel 36° 30′ as a dividing line between Slave and Free territory across the entire continent, or so far as our possessions might extend. The House voted down Gen. Burt's proposition: Yeas 82; Nays 114—every member from the Slave States, with four[11] Democrats from Free States, voting in the affirmative; while every Whig from the Free States, with every Democrat from those States but the four aforesaid, voted in the negative. The bill thereupon passed the House by 134 Yeas to 35 Nays—all from Slave States; but, on reaching the Senate, it was referred, reported, sent back again, and finally, on the last day of the session, laid on the table—Yeas 26; Nays 18—there to sleep the sleep of death.

In the next (XXXth) Congress, Mr. Caleb B. Smith (Whig), of Indiana (since Secretary of the Interior, under President Lincoln), was chairman of the Committee on Territories; and a bill creating a Territorial Government for Oregon, and prohibiting Slavery therein, was reported by him on the 9th of February, 1848. This bill was made a special order five weeks thereafter, but was so pertinaciously resisted by the Slavery Extensionists that it could not be got out of Committee till August 1; when an amendment made in Committee, striking out that clause of the original bill whereby the provisions of the Ordinance of '87 were extended to this Territory—in other words, Slavery was prohibited therein—was negatived; Yeas 88; Nays 114. On this division, Mr. John W. Houston (Whig), of Delaware, voted with the majority, which was otherwise entirely composed of members from Free States; eight[12] Democrats from Free States voted in the minority, otherwise composed of all the members from Slave States present, Mr. Houston, of Delaware, excepted. The bill then passed the House by a "sectional" vote—Yeas 128; Nays 71.

In the Senate, Mr. Douglas[13] promptly (August 5th) reported this bill with amendments, and a proposition from Mr. Foote, of Mississippi, that it "do lie on the table," was defeated by 15 (ultra Southern) Yeas to 36 Nays. Among the amendments reported by Mr. Douglas was a reproduction in substance of Gen. Burt's, defeated the year before in the House, which now received but two votes—those of Messrs. Bright and Douglas. Mr. Douglas thereupon moved to amend the bill, by inserting as follows:

> "That the line of thirty-six degrees and thirty minutes of north latitude, known as the Missouri Compromise line, as defined in the eighth section of an act entitled, 'An Act to authorize the people of the Missouri Territory to form a Constitution and State Government, and for the admission of such State into the Union, on an equal footing with the original States, and to prohibit Slavery in certain Territories, approved March 6, 1820,' be, and the same is hereby, declared to extend to the Pacific Ocean; and the said eighth section, together with the compromise therein effected, is hereby revived, and declared to be in full force, and binding, for the future organization of the Territories of the United States, in the same sense, and with the same understanding, with which it was generally adopted."

This was carried by 33 Yeas—in-

---

[11] PENNSYLVANIA.—Charles J. Ingersoll—1. ILLINOIS.—Stephen A. Douglas, Robert Smith—2. IOWA.—S. C. Hastings—1. In all, 4.

[12] NEW YORK.—Ausburn Birdsall—1. OHIO.—William Kennon, jr., John K. Miller—2. ILLINOIS.—Orlando B. Ficklin, John A. McClernand, William A. Richardson—3. INDIANA.—John L. Robinson, William W. Wick—2.

[13] Recently transferred from the House; now chairman of the Senate's Committee on Territories.

cluding Messrs. Calhoun, Jefferson Davis, John Bell, Benton, and every member present from the Slave States, with Messrs. Cameron, of Pennsylvania; Douglas, of Illinois; Bright, of Indiana; Dickinson, of New York; and Fitzgerald, of Michigan, from Free States—to 21 Nays, including Messrs. Webster, of Massachusetts, Hamlin, of Maine, Dix, of New York, and Breese, of Illinois. The bill, thus amended, passed the Senate by 33 Yeas to 22 Nays.

But the House, on its return, thus amended, utterly refused (August 11th) to concur in any such partition of the territories of the Union, on the line of 36° 30′, between Free and Slave Labor. The proposition of Mr. Douglas, above cited, was rejected by the decisive majority of 39: Yeas 82; Nays 121—only three[14] members from Free States voting in the minority. So the bill was returned to the Senate with its amendment struck out; and that body thereupon *receded*—Yeas 29; Nays 25—from its amendment, and allowed the bill to become a law in the shape given it by the House. On this memorable division, Messrs. Benton, Bright, Cameron, Dickinson, Douglas, Fitzgerald, Hannegan, Spruance, of Delaware, and Houston, of Texas, voted to yield to the House, leaving none but Senators from Slave States, and not all of them, insisting on the partition demanded. So Oregon became a Territory, consecrated to Free Labor, without compromise or counterbalance; and the Free States gave fair notice that they would *not* divide with Slavery the vast and hitherto free territories then just acquired from Mexico.

XV.

THE COMPROMISE OF 1850.

Gen. Zachary Taylor was inaugurated as President on the 4th of March, 1849. He had received, as we have seen, both an electoral majority and a popular plurality, alike in the Free and in the Slave States, mainly by reason of his persistent and obstinate silence and reserve on the vexed question of Slavery in the Territories. He had written letters—not always wise nor judicious—during the canvass, mainly in its early stages; but they were not calculated, decisively, to alienate either the champions or the opponents of Slavery Restriction. It is among the traditions of the canvass that he, some time in 1848, received a letter from a planter running thus: "Sir: I have worked hard and been frugal all my life, and the results of my industry have mainly taken the form of slaves, of whom I own about a hundred. Before I vote for President, I want to be sure that the candidate I support will not so act as to divest me of my property." To which the General, with a dexterity that would have done credit to a diplomatist, and would have proved

[14] New York.—Ausburn Birdsall—1. Pennsylvania.—Charles Brown, Charles J. Ingersoll—2.

exceedingly useful to Mr. Clay, responded: "Sir: I have the honor to inform you that *I*, too, have been all my life industrious and frugal, and that the fruits thereof are mainly invested in slaves, of whom I own *three* hundred. Yours," etc. South Carolina did not see fit to repose her faith in him; no more did Texas: his own son-in-law, Jefferson Davis, went against him: so did the great body of Slavery Propagandists; yet it is, nevertheless, true that he received many more votes at the South than would have been given for Mr. Webster, or even Mr. Clay.

In the Free States, very many Northern Whigs[1] had refused to support him, and given their votes to Van Buren as an open, unequivocal champion of Slavery Restriction; and it was by the votes thus diverted from Gen. Taylor that Ohio, with perhaps Indiana and Wisconsin also, were given to Gen. Cass. The great body of the Northern Whigs, however, had supported the nominees of their party, not fully satisfied with Gen. Taylor's position on the Slavery question, but trusting that the influence necessarily exerted over his Administration by the desires and convictions of the far greater number of its supporters, whether in or out of Congress, led by such determined Slavery Restrictionists as Mr. Webster and Gov. Seward, would insure his political adhesion to the right side. Many acted or voted in accordance with this view who were not exactly satisfied with it; and the Whig canvassers were doubtless more decided and thorough in their "Free Soil" inculcations than they would have been had their Presidential candidate been one of themselves. Mr. Webster[2] claimed "Free Soil" as a distinctive Whig doctrine, and declared that, were the Whigs to join the peculiar "Free Soil" organization, they would only make that the Whig party *with Martin Van Buren at its head.* Gov. Seward[3] declared the Slavery question the great, living, and pre-

[1] Among those Whigs who took this course in New York City, the names of Willis Hall, Joseph L. White, Philip W. Engs, and Wilson G. Hunt, are conspicuous.

[2] The following are extracts from Mr. Webster's speech at Abingdon, Mass., Oct. 9, 1848:

"The gentlemen who have joined this new party, from among the Whigs, pretend that they are greater lovers of Liberty and greater haters of Slavery than those they leave behind them. I do not admit it. I do not admit any such thing. [Applause.] I think we are as good Free Soil men as they are, though we do not set up any such great prëeminence over our neighbors. * * * There was an actual outbreak, years ago, between these two parties of the Democracy of New York, and this 'Barnburning' party existed long before there was any question of Free Soil among them—long before there was any question of the Wilmot Proviso, or any opposition by that party to the extension of Slavery. And, up to the Annexation of Texas, every man of the party went straightforward for that Annexation, Slavery Extension and all.

"But the Whigs, and they alone, raised a strong opposition to the measure. I say the Whigs alone—for nobody else, either in the East, West, South, or North, stirred a finger in the cause—or, at least, made so small an effort that it could not be discerned until the Whigs roused the people to a sentiment of opposition to the further spread of the Slave Power. Then this portion of the New York Loco-Focos, these Barnburners, seized upon this Whig doctrine, and attached to it their policy, merely to give them the predominance over their rivals. * * *

"In this Buffalo platform, this Collect of the new school, there is nothing new. * * * Suppose all the Whigs should go over to the Free Soil party: It would only be a change of name; the principles would still be the same. But there would be one change which, I admit, would be monstrous—*it would make Mr. Van Buren the head of the Whig party.* [Laughter.]"

[3] In his speech at Cleveland, Ohio, October 26, 1848, Gov. Seward said:

"A sixth principle is, that Slavery must be abolished. I think these are the principles of the Whigs of the Western Reserve of Ohio. I

dominant issue between the two National parties, and urged the duty of abolishing Slavery as a reason for supporting Gen. Taylor. Mr. Washington Hunt[4] wrote an elaborate letter to Ohio, urging the duty of standing by Whig principles by electing Gen. Taylor, and by choosing at the same time members of Congress who would inflexibly resist, and legislate to prohibit, the Extension of Slavery. At no time previously,[5] had Whig inculcations throughout the Free States been so decidedly and strongly hostile to the Extension of Slavery, and so determined in requiring its inhibition by Congress, as during the canvass of 1848.

Among the results of that canvass was—as we have seen—a temporary alienation of many Northern Democrats from their former devotion to Southern ideas and docility to Southern leadership. This alienation was further evinced in the coälitions formed the next summer between the Democratic and Free Soil parties of Vermont and Massachusetts, which in Vermont proved too weak to overcome the Whig ascendency, but in Massachusetts ultimately triumphed in the election of George S. Boutwell (Democrat), as Governor, and Charles Sumner (Free Soil), as Senator. In New York, a fusion was with difficulty effected (in 1849) of the parties which had in 1848 supported Van Buren and Cass respectively—the nominal basis of agreement being a resolve[6] of mutual hostility to the

am not now to say for the first time that they are mine. * * *

"There are two antagonistic elements of society in America, Freedom and Slavery. Freedom is in harmony with our system of government, and with the spirit of the age, and is therefore passive and quiescent. Slavery is in conflict with that system, with justice, and with humanity, and is therefore organized, defensive, active, and perpetually aggressive.

"Freedom insists on the emancipation and development of labor; Slavery demands a soil moistened with tears and blood—Freedom a soil that exults under the elastic tread of man in his native majesty.

"These elements divide and classify the American people into two parties. Each of these parties has its court and its scepter. The throne of one is amid the rocks of the Alleghany Mountains; the throne of the other is reared on the sands of South Carolina. One of these parties, the party of Slavery, regards disunion as among the means of defense, and not always the last to be employed. The other maintains the Union of the States, one and inseparable, now and forever, as the highest duty of the American people to themselves, to posterity, to mankind," etc., etc.

"The party of Freedom seeks complete and universal emancipation."

[4] Then a Whig member of Congress; since, Governor of New York.

[5] Mr. James Brooks, Editor of *The New York Express*, reported to the New York Whig State Convention of 1847 (October 6th), an Address condemning the objects of the Mexican War then raging, which was unanimously adopted. In the course of it, he said:

"Fellow Citizens: Disguise the Mexican War as sophistry may, the great truth cannot be put down, nor lied down, that it exists because of the Annexation of Texas; that from such a cause we predicted such a consequence would follow; and that, but for that cause, no war would have existed at all. Disguise its intents, purposes and consequences, as sophistry may struggle to do, the further great truth cannot be hidden, that its main object is the conquest of a market for slaves, and that the flag our victorious legions rally around, fight under, and fall for, is to be desecrated from its holy character of Liberty and Emancipation into an errand of Bondage and Slavery. * * * We protest, too, in the name of the rights of Man and of Liberty, against the further extension of Slavery in North America. The curse which our mother country inflicted upon us, in spite of our fathers' remonstrances, we demand shall never blight the virgin soil of the North Pacific. * * * * We will not pour out the blood of our countrymen, if we can help it, to turn a *Free* into a *Slave* soil; we will not spend from fifty to a hundred millions of dollars per year to make a Slave market for any portion of our countrymen. * * * The Union as it is, the *whole* Union, and *nothing but* the Union, we will stand by to the last—but *No More Territory* is our watchword—unless it be *Free.*"

[6] The last Convention of the Cass Democrats, or "Hunkers," which was held at Syracuse in September, 1849, proposing a conciliatory course toward the "Barnburners," as an overture to-

Extension of Slavery. There were local exceptions; but in the main the Democratic party was materially strengthened by the rapid and general disintegration of the Free Soil party, and by the apparent falling away of the Whigs of the Free States from a decided, open, inflexible maintenance of the principle of Slavery Restriction. Gen. Taylor's election had exhausted the personal popularity based on his achievements as a soldier; his attitude as a slaveholder, and his tacit negation of the principle aforesaid, were awkward facts; and, though the President himself could not be justly accused of doing or saying any thing clearly objectionable, yet each successive State election of 1849 indicated a diminished and declining popularity on the part of the new Administration.

Neither Mr. Webster nor Gov. Seward had a seat in Gen. Taylor's Cabinet, though either, doubtless, might have had, had he desired it. Mr. Webster remained in the Senate, where Messrs. Clay and Calhoun still lingered, and Gov. Seward first took his seat in that body on the day of Gen. Taylor's inauguration.

The proper organization of the spacious territories recently acquired from Mexico necessarily attracted the early and earnest attention of the new President and his official counselors. It could not be justifiably postponed; for the military rule that had thus far been endured by those territories, exceptional at best, had been rendered anomalous and indefensible by the lapse of a year since the complete restoration of peace. Meantime, the discovery of gold in California was already attracting swarms of adventurers to that country and rendering its speedy and extensive colonization inevitable. That it should soon receive a suitable and legitimate civil government was imperative. New Mexico, likewise, having a population of sixty thousand, mainly native-born, and divested by our conquest of a civil government substantially of her own choice, had a right to expect an early and complete deliverance from military rule.

The new Administration appears to have promptly resolved on its course. It decided to invite and favor an early organization of both California and New Mexico (including all the vast area recently ceded by Mexico, apart from Texas proper) as incipient States, and to urge their admission, as such, into the Union at the earliest practicable day. Of course, it was understood that, being thus organized, in the absence of both slaveholders and slaves, they would almost necessarily become Free States.

According to this programme, Mr. Thomas Butler King[7] was dispatched to California on the 3d of April, 1849, as a special agent from the Executive, with instructions to favor the early formation of a State Constitution and Government. The President, in a Special Message to Congress on the 21st of January, 1850, replying to a resolution of inquiry from the

wards a neutral basis of rëunion with them, adopted the following:

"*Resolved*, That we are opposed to the extension of Slavery to the free territories of the United States; but we do not regard the Slavery question, in any form of its agitation, or any opinion in relation thereto, as a test of political faith, or as a rule of party action."

[7] For most of the ten years preceding, a Whig member of Congress from Georgia.

House, stated that he had sent Mr. King "as bearer of dispatches," and added:

"I did not hesitate to express to the people of those territories my desire that each territory should, if prepared to comply with the requisitions of the Constitution of the United States, form a plan of a State constitution, and submit the same to Congress, with a prayer for admission into the Union as a State; but I did not anticipate, suggest, nor authorize, the establishment of any such government without the assent of Congress; nor did I authorize any government agent or officer to interfere with, or exercise any influence or control over, the election of delegates, or over any convention, in making or modifying their domestic institutions, or any of the provisions of their proposed constitution. On the contrary, the instructions given by my orders were, that all measures of domestic policy adopted by the people of California must originate solely with themselves; and, while the Executive of the United States was desirous to protect them in the formation of any government, republican in its character, to be, at the proper time, submitted to Congress, yet it was to be distinctly understood that the plan of such government must, at the same time, be the result of their own deliberate choice, and originate with themselves, without the interference of the Executive."

In his Annual Message, transmitted some weeks previously, the President had said:

"No civil government having been provided by Congress for California, the people of that territory, impelled by the necessities of their political condition, recently met in convention, for the purpose of forming a constitution and State government, which, the latest advices give me reason to suppose, has been accomplished; and it is believed that they will shortly apply for the admission of California into the Union as a sovereign State. Should such be the case, and should their constitution be conformable to the requisitions of the Constitution of the United States, I recommend their application to the favorable consideration of Congress.

"The people of New Mexico will also, it is believed, at no very distant period, present themselves for admission into the Union. Preparatory to the admission of California and New Mexico, the people of each will have instituted for themselves a republican form of government, 'laying its foundations in such principles, and organizing its powers in such form, as to them shall seem most likely to effect their safety and happiness.'

"By awaiting their action, all causes of uneasiness may be avoided, and confidence and kind feeling preserved. With a view of maintaining the harmony and tranquillity so dear to all, we should abstain from the introduction of those exciting topics of a sectional character which have hitherto produced painful apprehensions in the public mind; and I repeat the solemn warning of the first and most illustrious of my predecessors against furnishing 'any ground for characterizing parties by geographical discriminations.'"

It would seem that this programme might have secured the support of a majority in Congress and commanded the assent of the country. It insured, almost inevitably, to the champions of Free Labor a practical triumph in the organization and future character of the vast territories recently acquired, while according full scope to that "Popular Sovereignty" whereof Gen. Cass, Mr. Douglas, and other Democratic chiefs, were such resolute champions.

But Congress was not disposed to regard with favor any policy recommended by the Administration; while the Slave Power was fully determined, maugre any theory or profession, to exact a partition of the newly acquired territories, or a consideration for surrendering the alleged right to plant Slavery therein. There was an Opposition majority in the Senate; and the House, after a tedious contest, wherein the especial "Free Soil" or Buffalo Platform members refused to support either Mr. Winthrop (Whig), or Mr. Cobb (Democrat), for the speakership, was finally organized under the Plurality rule, whereby, after taking three more ballots, the highest number of votes was to elect. This rule was adopted,[8] by 113 Yeas to 106 Nays.

[8] December 22, 1849.

after nearly three weeks' fruitless balloting, and under it Howell Cobb, of Georgia, was chosen Speaker on the 63d ballot, receiving 102 votes to 99 for Winthrop, and 20 scattering (mainly on the Buffalo platform). Mr. Cobb[9] was one of the most determined Democratic advocates of Slavery Extension, and constituted the Committees of the House accordingly.

Gen. B. Riley, the Military Governor of California, had issued[10] a Proclamation calling a Convention of the People of California to frame a State Constitution. Such Convention was accordingly held, and formed a State Constitution whereby Slavery was expressly prohibited. State officers and members of Congress (all Democrats) were in due course elected under it; and Gen. Taylor communicated[11] the Constitution to Congress, at whose doors the members elect from the new State stood for many ensuing months patiently awaiting their admission to seats. For, among the various propositions introduced at this session, looking to the same end, Mr. Clay had already submitted[12] the following basis of a proposed Compromise of all differences relating to the territories and to Slavery:

"1. *Resolved*, That California, with suitable boundaries, ought, upon her application, to be admitted as one of the States of this Union, without the imposition by Congress of any restriction in respect to the exclusion or introduction of Slavery within those boundaries.

"2. *Resolved*, That, as Slavery does not exist by law, and is not likely to be introduced into any of the territory acquired by the United States from the Republic of Mexico, it is inexpedient for Congress to provide by law, either for its introduction into, or exclusion from, any part of the said territory; and that appropriate territorial governments ought to be established by Congress in all the said territory not assigned as within the boundaries of the proposed State of California, without the adoption of any restriction or condition on the subject of Slavery.[13]

"5. *Resolved*, That it is inexpedient to abolish Slavery in the District of Columbia, whilst the institution continues to exist in the State of Maryland, without the consent of that State, without the consent of the people of the District, and without just compensation to the owners of Slaves within the District.

"6. *But Resolved*, That it *is* expedient to prohibit, within the District, the Slave-Trade in slaves brought into it from States or places beyond the limits of the District, either to be sold therein as merchandise, or to be transported to other markets without the District of Columbia.

"7. *Resolved*, That more effectual provision ought to be made by law, according to the requirement of the Constitution, for the restitution or delivery of persons bound to service or labor in any State, who may escape into any other State or Territory in the Union. And,

"8. *Resolved*, That Congress has no power to prohibit or obstruct the trade in slaves between the slaveholding States, but that the admission or exclusion of slaves brought from one into another of them, depends exclusively upon their own particular laws."

The debate on this proposition of compromise was opened by Southern Democrats, all speaking in disparagement of its leading suggestions, or in scarcely qualified opposition to the whole scheme. Mr. H. S. Foote, of Mississippi, condemned especially the proposition "that it is *inexpedient* to abolish Slavery in the District of Columbia," as implying a *right* in Congress to legislate on that subject, which he utterly denied. He condemned still more emphatically the assertion that "Slavery does not now exist by law in the territories recently acquired from Mexico;" insisting that the mere fact of Annexation carried the Constitution, with all its guaranties, to all the territories ob-

[9] Since, a Confederate Major-General.

[10] June 3, 1849.

[11] February 13, 1850.

[12] January 29, 1850.

[13] 3, 4, relate to Texas and her boundary.

tained by treaty, and secured the privilege to any "Southern slaveholder to enter any part of it, attended by his slave property, and to enjoy the same therein, free from all molestation or hindrance whatsoever." He also condemned the resolve relating to the boundaries of Texas, contending that "her right to that part of New Mexico, lying east of the Rio Grande, was full, complete, and undeniable." But he did not object to abolishing the Slave-Trade in the District, "provided it is done in a delicate and judicious manner;" and he would consent to the admission of California, "*above the line of* 36° 30′," "provided another new Slave State can be laid off within the present limits of Texas, so as to keep up the present equiponderance between the Slave and Free States of the Union, and provided further, all this is done by way of compromise, and *in order to save the Union*—as dear to me as any man living." Mr. J. M. Mason, of Virginia, though anxious to do his utmost for "adjusting these unhappy differences," still more pointedly dissented from Mr. Clay's scheme. He said:

"Sir, so far as I have read these resolutions, there is but one proposition to which I can give a hearty assent, and that is the resolution which proposes to organize territorial governments at once in these territories, without a declaration, one way or the other, as to their domestic institutions. But there is another which I deeply regret to see introduced into this Senate, by a Senator from a Slaveholding State; it is that which assumes that Slavery does not now exist by law in those countries. I understand one of these propositions to declare that, by law, Slavery is now abolished in New Mexico and California. That was the very proposition advanced by the non-slaveholding States at the last Session; combated and disproved, as I thought, by gentlemen from the Slaveholding States, and which the Compromise bill[14] was framed to test. So far, I regarded the question of law as disposed of; and it was very clearly and satisfactorily shown to be against the spirit of the resolution of the Senator of Kentucky. If the contrary is true, I presume the Senator from Kentucky would declare that, if a law is now valid in the territories abolishing Slavery, it could not be introduced there, even if a law was passed creating the institution, or repealing the statutes already existing—a doctrine never assented to, so far as I know, until now, by any Senator representing one of the slaveholding States. Sir, I hold the very opposite, and with such confidence, that, in the last Congress, I was willing, and did vote for a bill to test this question in the Supreme Court. Yet this resolution assumes the other doctrine to be true, and our assent is challenged to it as a proposition of law."

Mr. Jefferson Davis, of Mississippi, with equal energy, objected to so much of Mr. Clay's propositions as relate to the boundary of Texas, to the Slave-Trade in the Federal District, and to the concession that Slavery does not exist by law in the newly acquired territories. He added:

"But, Sir, we are called upon to receive this as a measure of compromise! As a measure in which we of the minority are to receive something. A measure of compromise! I look upon it as but a modest mode of taking that, the claim to which has been more boldly asserted by others; and, that I may be understood upon this question, and that my position may go forth to the country in the same columns that convey the sentiments of the Senator from Kentucky, I here assert, that never will I take less than the Missouri Compromise line extending to the Pacific Ocean, with the specific recognition of the right to hold Slaves in the territory below that line; and that, before such territories are admitted into the Union as States, slaves may be taken there from any of the United States, at the option of the owners. I can never consent to give additional power to a majority to commit further aggressions upon the minority in this Union; and I will never consent to any proposition which will have such a tendency, without a full guar-

[14] That of Mr. Clayton—laid on the table of the House, on motion of Mr. Stephens, of Georgia.

antee or counteracting measure is connected with it."

Mr. Clay, in reply to Mr. Davis, spoke as follows:

"I am extremely sorry to hear the Senator from Mississippi say that he requires, first, the extension of the Missouri Compromise line to the Pacific; and, also, that he is not satisfied with that, but requires, if I understand him correctly, a positive provision for the admission of Slavery south of that line. And now, Sir, coming from a Slave State, as I do, I owe it to myself, I owe it to truth, I owe it to the subject, to state that no earthly power could induce me to vote for a specific measure for the introduction of Slavery where it had not before existed, either south or north of that line. Coming, as I do, from a Slave State, it is my solemn, deliberate, and well-matured determination that no power—no earthly power—shall compel me to vote for the positive introduction of Slavery, either south or north of that line. Sir, while you reproach, and justly, too, our British ancestors, for the introduction of this institution upon the continent of America, I am, for one, unwilling that the posterity of the present inhabitants of California and New Mexico shall reproach *us* for doing just what we reproach Great Britain for doing *to* us. If the citizens of those territories choose to establish Slavery, I am for admitting them with such provisions in their Constitutions; but then it will be their own work, and not ours; and their posterity will have to reproach them, and not us, for forming Constitutions allowing the institution of Slavery to exist among them. These are my views, Sir; and I choose to express them; and I care not how extensively and universally they are known. The honorable Senator from Virginia (Mr. Mason) has expressed his opinion that Slavery exists in these territories; and I have no doubt that opinion is sincerely and honestly entertained by him; and I would say, with equal sincerity and honesty, that *I* believe that Slavery nowhere exists within any portion of the territory acquired by us from Mexico. He holds a directly contrary opinion to mine, as he has a perfect right to do; and we will not quarrel about that difference of opinion."

Messrs. William R. King, of Alabama, Downs, of Louisiana, and Butler, of South Carolina, swelled the chorus of denunciation. They could see nothing in Mr. Clay's proposition that looked like compromise; nothing but concession and surrender of all the rights of the South in the territories. In their view, it was only a skillful and plausible device for reconciling the South to the sacrifice of its rights, and to a concession of all the new territories to Free Labor. They were, therefore, utterly averse to it.

The most remarkable speech elicited by these resolves was that of Mr. Webster,[15] wherein he took ground against the Abolitionists; against the assumed Right of Instruction; against further legislation prohibitory of Slavery in the Territories; against Secession or Disunion; against whatever seemed calculated to produce irritation or alienation between the North and the South; and in favor of liberal grants by Congress in aid of the colonization by Slave States of their free colored population. His reasons for opposing any prohibitive legislation with regard to Slavery in the new territories were set forth as follows:

"Now, as to California and New Mexico, I hold Slavery to be excluded from those territories by a law even superior to that which admits and sanctions it in Texas. I mean the law of nature, of physical geography, the law of the formation of the earth. That law settles forever, with a strength beyond all terms of human enactment, that Slavery cannot exist in California or New Mexico. Understand me, Sir; I mean Slavery as we regard it; the Slavery of the colored race as it exists in the Southern States. I shall not discuss the point, but leave it to the learned gentlemen who have undertaken to discuss it; but I suppose there is no Slavery of that description in California now. I understand that *peonism*, a sort of penal servitude, exists there, or rather a sort of voluntary sale of a man and his offspring for debt—an arrangement of a peculiar nature known to the law of Mexico.

[15] March 7, 1850.

But what I mean to say is, that it is as impossible that African Slavery, as we see it among us, should find its way, or be introduced, into California and New Mexico, as any other natural impossibility. California and New Mexico are Asiatic in their formation and scenery. They are composed of vast ridges of mountains, of great hight, with broken ridges and deep valleys. The sides of these mountains are entirely barren; their tops capped by perennial snow. There may be in California, now made free by its constitution, and no doubt there are, some tracts of valuable land. But it is not so in New Mexico. Pray, what is the evidence which every gentleman must have obtained on this subject, from information sought by himself or communicated by others? I have inquired and read all I could find, in order to acquire information on this important subject. What is there in New Mexico that could, by any possibility, induce any body to go there with slaves? There are some narrow strips of tillable land on the borders of the rivers; but the rivers themselves dry up before midsummer is gone. All that the people can do in that region is to raise some little articles, some little wheat for their *tortillas*, and that by irrigation. And who expects to see a hundred black men cultivating tobacco, corn, cotton, rice, or anything else, on lands in New Mexico made fertile only by irrigation?

"I look upon it, therefore, as a fixed fact, to use the current expression of the day, that both California and New Mexico are destined to be free, so far as they are settled at all; which I believe, in regard to New Mexico, will be but partially for a great length of time; free by the arrangement of things ordained by the Power above us. I have, therefore, to say, in this respect also, that this country is fixed for freedom, to as many persons as shall ever live in it, by a less repealable law than that which attaches to the holding of slaves in Texas; and I will say further, that, if a resolution or a bill were now before us to provide a Territorial government for New Mexico, I would not vote to put any prohibition into it whatever. Such a prohibition would be idle, as it respects any effect it would have upon the Territory; and I would not take pains uselessly to reäffirm an ordinance of nature, nor to reënact the will of God. I would put in no Wilmot Proviso for the mere purpose of a taunt or a reproach. I would put into it no evidence of the votes of superior power, exercised for no purpose but to wound the pride, whether a just and rational pride, or an irrational pride, of the citizens of the Southern States. I have no such object, no such purpose, They would think it a taunt, an indignity; they would think it to be an act taking away from them what they regard as a proper equality of privilege. Whether they expect to realize any benefit from it or not, they would think it at least a plain theoretic wrong; that something more or less derogatory to their character and their rights had taken place. I propose to inflict no such wound upon any body, unless something essentially important to the country, and efficient to the preservation of liberty and freedom, is to be effected. I repeat, therefore, Sir, and, as I do not propose to address the Senate often upon this subject, I repeat it because I wish it to be distinctly understood, that, for the reasons stated, if a proposition were now here to establish a government for New Mexico, and if it was moved to insert a provision for the prohibition of Slavery, I would not vote for it.

"Sir, if we were now making a government for New Mexico, and any body should propose a Wilmot Proviso, I should treat it exactly as Mr. Polk treated that provision for excluding Slavery from Oregon. Mr. Polk was known to be, in opinion, decidedly averse to the Wilmot Proviso; but he felt the necessity of establishing a government for the territory of Oregon. The Proviso was in the bill; but he knew it would be entirely nugatory, since it took away no right, no describable, no tangible, no appreciable right of the South; he said he would sign the bill for the sake of enacting a law to form a government in that Territory, and let that entirely useless, and, in that connection, entirely senseless, proviso remain. Sir, we hear occasionally of the Annexation of Canada; and, if there be any man, any of the Northern Democracy, or any one of the Free Soil party, who supposes it necessary to insert a Wilmot Proviso in a territorial government for New Mexico, that man would, of course, be of opinion that it is necessary to protect the everlasting snows of Canada from the foot of Slavery by the same overspreading wing of an act of Congress. Sir, wherever there is a substantial good to be done, wherever there is a foot of land to be prevented from becoming slave territory, I am ready to assert the principle of the exclusion of Slavery. I am pledged to it from the year 1837; I have been pledged to it again and again; and I will perform those pledges; but I will not do a thing unnecessarily that wounds the feelings of others, or that does discredit to my own understanding."

It seems not a little remarkable that a man of Mr. Webster's strength should have traversed the whole ground of controversy so thoroughly in a speech inevitably calculated to excite deep dissatisfaction among the great mass of his constituents, without once considering or even touching this question: "What need exists for any compromise whatever?" Admitting the correctness of his views and general positions with regard to California, New Mexico, Texas, etc., why not permit each subject demanding legislation to be presented in its order, and all questions respecting it to be decided on their intrinsic merits? He, of course, contended throughout that his position was unchanged, that his views were substantially those he had always held; yet the eagerness and satisfaction wherewith his speech was received and reprinted at Richmond, Charleston, New Orleans, and throughout the South, should, it seems, have convinced him, if the disappointment and displeasure of his constituents did not, that either he had undergone a great transformation, or nearly every one else had. His speech, though it contained little or nothing referring directly to the compromise proposed by Mr. Clay, exerted a powerful influence in favor of its ultimate triumph.

Mr. Douglas having reported[16] a bill for the admission of California into the Union, as also one to establish territorial governments for Utah and New Mexico, Col. Benton moved[17] that the previous orders be postponed, and the California bill taken up. Mr. Clay proposed the laying of this motion on the table, which was carried by 27 Yeas to 24 Nays. The Senate now proceeded, on motion of Mr. Foote, of Mississippi, to constitute a Select Committee of thirteen, to consider the questions raised by Mr. Clay's proposition, and also by resolves submitted a month later by Mr. Bell, of Tennessee; and on the 19th this Committee was elected by ballot and composed as follows:

Mr. Henry Clay, of Kentucky, *Chairman.*

Messrs.	Dickinson, of N. Y.,	Cooper, of Pa.,
	Phelps, of Vt.,	Downs, of La.,
	Bell, of Tenn.,	King, of Ala.,
	Cass, of Mich.,	Mangum, of N. C.,
	Webster, of Mass.,	Mason, of Va.,
	Berrien, of Ga.,	Bright, of Ind.

Mr. Clay reported[18] from said Committee a recommendation, substantially, of his original proposition of compromise, save that he now provided for organizing Utah as a distinct Territory. His report recommended the following bases of a general Compromise:

"1. The admission of any new State or States formed out of Texas to be postponed until they shall hereafter present themselves to be received into the Union, when it will be the duty of Congress fairly and faithfully to execute the compact with Texas, by admitting such new State or States.

"2. The admission forthwith of California into the Union, with the boundaries which she has proposed.

"3. The establishment of Territorial Governments, without the Wilmot Proviso, for New Mexico and Utah, embracing all the territory recently acquired from Mexico, not contained in the boundaries of California.

"4. The combination of these two last measures in the same bill.

"5. The establishment of the western and northern boundaries of Texas, and the exclusion from her jurisdiction of all New Mexico, with the grant to Texas of a pecuniary equivalent; and the section for that purpose to be incorporated in the bill admitting California, and establishing Territorial Governments for Utah and New Mexico.

"6. More effectual enactments of law to secure the prompt delivery of persons bound to service or labor in one State, under the laws thereof, who escape into another State; and

"7. Abstaining from abolishing Slavery, but, under a heavy penalty, prohibiting the Slave-Trade, in the District of Columbia."

[16] March 25, 1850. [17] April 5th. [18] May 8th.

And still the debate went on, hardly interrupted by the death (July 10th) of Gen. Taylor, and the accession of Vice-President Fillmore to the Presidency. Repeated efforts to cut off from California all her territory south of 36° 30′; to send back her constitution to a new convention of her people, etc., etc., were made by Southern ultras, but defeated; and finally[19] the bill to admit California passed the Senate by 34 Yeas to 18 Nays—all Southern—and the bill organizing the Territories of New Mexico and Utah, as proposed, likewise passed two days thereafter: Yeas 27; Nays 10. The other measures embraced in the proposition of compromise were in like manner successively carried with little serious opposition.

When these measures reached the House, they encountered a spirited opposition; but the bill organizing the Territory of New Mexico was added as an amendment or "rider" to the bill defining the Northern boundary of Texas, and paying her ten millions for assenting to such demarkation. This was moved by Mr. Linn Boyd (Democrat), of Kentucky, and prevailed by Yeas 107, Nays 99. The bill, as thus amended, was first defeated—Yeas 99; Nays 107; but Mr. Howard, of Texas, who had voted in the negative, now moved a reconsideration, which was carried—Yeas 122; Nays 84; whereupon the Previous Question was seconded—Yeas 115; Nays 97; and the bill passed[20] as amended—Yeas 108; Nays 97. The California bill was next[21] taken up and passed—Yeas 150; Nays 56—(all Southern); and then the Utah bill was in like manner passed—Yeas 97; Nays 85—(mainly Northern Free Soil). The bills providing more effectually for the recovery of fugitive Slaves, and abolishing the Slave-trade in the District, were likewise passed by decided majorities; and the Senate[22] concurred in the House amendment, whereby two of its measures had been welded together—Yeas 31; Nays 10 (Northern Free Soil). So all the measures originally included in Mr. Clay's proposition of compromise became laws of the land.

The propelling force, whereby these acts were pushed through Congress, in defiance of the original convictions of a majority of its members, or at least the lubricating oil wherewith the ways were rendered passable, was contained in that article of the bill proposing to the State of Texas the establishment of her Northern boundary, which reads:

"*Fourth.* The United States, in consideration of said establishment of boundaries, cession of claims to territory, and relinquishment of claims, will pay to the State of Texas the sum of ten millions of dollars, in a stock bearing five per cent. interest, and redeemable at the end of fourteen years; the interest payable half-yearly, at the Treasury of the United States."

By this article, the public debt of Texas, previously worth in market but some twenty to thirty per cent. of its face, was suddenly raised nearly or quite to par, to the entire satisfaction of its holders—many of them members of Congress, or their very intimate friends. Corruption, thinly

19 August 13th. 20 September 4th. 21 September 7th. 22 September 9th.

disguised, haunted the purlieus and stalked through the halls of the Capitol; and numbers, hitherto in needy circumstances, suddenly found themselves rich. The great majority, of course, were impervious to such influences; but the controlling and controllable minority were not. This was probably the first instance in which measures of vital consequence to the country were carried or defeated in Congress under the direct spur of pecuniary interest.

Political compromises, though they have been rendered unsavory by abuse, are a necessary incident of mixed or balanced governments—that is, of all but simple, unchecked despotisms. Wherever liberty exists, there diversities of judgment will be developed; and, unless one will dominates over all others, a practical mean between widely differing convictions must sometimes be sought. If, for example, a legislature is composed of two distinct bodies or houses, and they differ, as they occasionally will, with regard to the propriety or the amount of an appropriation required for a certain purpose, and neither is disposed to give way, a partial concession on either hand is often the most feasible mode of practical adjustment. Where the object contemplated is novel, or non-essential to the general efficiency of the public service—such as the construction of a new railroad, canal, or other public work—the repugnance of either house should suffice entirely to defeat, or, at least, to postpone it; for neither branch has a right to exact from the other conformity with its views on a disputed point as the price of its own concurrence in measures essential to the existence of the Government. The attempt, therefore, of the Senate of February–March, 1849, to dictate to the House, "You shall consent to such an organization of the territories as we prescribe, or we will defeat the Civil Appropriation bill, and thus derange, if not arrest, the most vital machinery of the Government," was utterly unjustifiable. Yet this should not blind us to the fact that differences of opinion are at times developed on questions of decided moment, where the rights of each party are equal, and where an ultimate concurrence in one common line of action is essential. Without some deference to adverse convictions, no confederation of the insurgent colonies was attainable—no Union of the States could have been effected. And where the Executive is, by according him the veto, clothed with a limited power over the making of laws, it is inevitable that some deference to his views, his convictions, should be evinced by those who fashion and mature those laws. Under this aspect, compromise in government is sometimes indispensable and laudable.

But what is known in State legislation as *log-rolling* is quite another matter. A. has a bill, which he is intent on passing, but which has no intrinsic worth that commends it to his fellow-members. But B., C., D., and the residue of the alphabet, have each his "little bill;" not, perhaps, specially obnoxious or objectionable, but such as could not be passed on its naked merits. All alike must fail, unless carried by that reciprocity of support suggested by their common need and peril. An understanding is effected between their several backers, so that A. votes for the bills of B., C., D., etc., as the indispensable means of securing the passage of his own darling ; and thus a whole litter of bills become laws, whereof no single one was demanded by the public interest, or could have passed without the aid of others as unworthy as itself. Such is substantially the process whereby our statute-books are loaded with acts which subserve no end but to fill the pockets of the few, at the expense of the rights or the interests of the many.

It was entirely proper that Congress should provide at once for the temporary government of all the territories newly acquired from Mexico; and there was no radical objection to doing this in one bill, if that should seem advisable. As the establishment of a definite boundary between New Mexico and Texas was essential to the tranquillity and security of the Territory, that object might fairly be contemplated in the act providing a civil government therefor. But why Texas should be paid Ten Millions of dollars for relinquishing her pretensions to territory never possessed by, nor belonging to, her — territory which had been first acquired from Mexico by the forces and then bought of her by the money of the Union — is not obvious; and why this payment, if made at all, should be a make-weight in a bargain covering a variety of arrangements with which it had no proper connection, is still less explicable. And when, on the back of this, was piled an act to provide new facilities for slave-catching in the Free States, ostensibly balanced by another which required the slave-traders of Washington to remove their jails and auction-rooms across the Potomac to that dull old dwarf of a city which had recently been retroceded to Virginia, as if on purpose to facilitate this arrangement, the net product was a corrupt monstrosity in legislation and morals which even the great name of Henry Clay should not shield from lasting opprobrium.

XVI.

THE ERA OF SLAVE-HUNTING.

But, whatever theoretic or practical objections may be justly made to the Compromise of 1850, there can be no doubt that it was accepted and ratified by a great majority of the American People, whether in the North or in the South. They were intent on business — then remarkably prosperous —on planting, building, trading, and getting gain—and they hailed with general joy the announcement that all the differences between the diverse 'sections' had been adjusted and settled. The terms of settlement were, to that majority, of quite subordinate consequence; they wanted peace and prosperity, and were nowise inclined to cut each other's throats and burn each other's houses in a quarrel concerning (as they regarded it) only the *status* of negroes. The Compromise had taken no money from their pockets; it had imposed upon them no pecuniary burdens; it had exposed them to no personal and palpable dangers: it had rather repelled the gaunt specter of Civil War and Disunion (habitually conjured up when Slavery had a point to carry), and increased the facilities for making money, while opening a boundless vista of National greatness, security, and internal harmony. Especially by the trading class, and the great majority of the dwellers in seaboard cities, was this view cherished with intense, intolerant vehemence.

The Compromise had been violently opposed alike from the South and from the North—of course, on opposite grounds. The "Fire-Eaters," or disciples of Mr. Calhoun, regarded it as surrendering the substance of all that was in dispute—the newly acquired territories—to the North, while amusing the South with a mere shadow of triumph in the waiver of any positive, peremptory exclusion of Slavery therefrom. They resolved not to submit to it, but to rouse their section at first to theoretical, ultimately to forcible, resistance. To this end, a direct issue was made against the Compromise in Mississippi—next to South Carolina, the most intensely Pro-Slavery State in the Union—by nominating a "State Rights" ticket, headed by Jefferson Davis for Governor—Mr. Davis having opposed the Compromise in the Senate with determined pertinacity. His adversaries accepted the challenge, and nominated a "Union" ticket in opposition, headed by Henry S. Foote for Governor—Mr. Foote, as Mr. Davis's colleague, though he demurred to Mr. Clay's programme at the outset, having supported the Compromise to the extent of his ability. The election occurred early in November, 1851; when the "Union" party won a complete triumph—the vote being the largest ever yet polled, and Mr. Foote elected by over 1,000[1] majority. The rest of the "Union" State ticket, with a strongly "Union" Legislature, succeeded by still larger majorities. Alabama, likewise, chose a "Union" Legislature, and a "Union" majority of Congressmen. Louisiana, this year, elected a "Whig" Auditor and Legislature—meaning much the same thing. And even South Carolina—having been summoned by her chieftains (Mr. Calhoun being now dead) to elect a Convention, whereby her course in the exigency should be determined—gave a "Coöperation" majority of over 7,000 on the popular[2] vote, electing 114 "Coöperationists" to 54 unqualified "Secessionists." In other words, she voted not to attempt Secession without the concurrence and support of her Southern sisters—this being the shape wherein she could, with least sacrifice of pride or consistency, indicate her disposition not to rush madly upon the perils of Disunion and Civil War. Thus the triumph of the Compromise in the Slave States was complete; for it was felt to be preposterous to make the issue in any other States if it could not be upheld in these.

In the North, likewise, the acquiescence in the Compromise was general and decisive; though here, too,

[1] Foote, 28,738; Davis, 27,729.

[2] For Coöperation, 25,098; for Secession, 17,796. These totals are obtained by adding up the votes for delegates in the several "parishes."

some of its cardinal provisions provoked strenuous opposition. The new Fugitive Slave Law proved especially obnoxious, both in principle and practice, to a large and earnest minority. It had been originally drafted by Senator Mason, of Virginia—a man conspicuously charged with that pro-Slavery venom which has since made him a leading Rebel—and who had already signalized himself by his efforts to render the maintenance of the Union impossible on any other terms than those of the most utter and abject devotion, on the part of the North, to the most extreme Pro-Slavery aspirations and policy of the South. He opposed, as we have seen, Mr. Clay's programme of compromise, as entirely too favorable to the North; he had been among the foremost of the Southern ultras in defeating that programme in its primitive shape; and he had stubbornly resisted the admission of California as a Free State, unless and until paid for by concessions on the part of the North. Yet his draft of a Fugitive Slave Law was adopted by the great Compromise Committee, and ultimately rushed through the two Houses with little consideration and less scrutiny. When it was reached in its order in the lower, Judge James Thompson[3] obtained the floor[4]—doubtless by prearrangement with Speaker Cobb—and spoke in favor of the measure as just and necessary, closing his remarks by a demand of the Previous Question. This was sustained by a majority; and the bill—with all its imperfections on its head, and without affording any opportunity for amendment—was ordered to a third reading by 109 Yeas to 75 Nays—every member from a Slave State who voted at all, voting Yea, with 28 Democrats and 3[5] Whigs from Free States. From the Free States 33, from the Slave States 15 members were absent, or withheld their votes; and, as the vote in the Senate stood 27 for to 12 against it, with 21 absent, it is noteworthy that it passed either House by the votes of a decided minority of the members thereof. Still, it is hardly probable that, had every member been present and voted, it would have been defeated.

This measure, so inconsiderately adopted, was specially objectionable to the humaner instincts of the Free States in these particulars:

1. It directed and provided for the surrender to the claimant of each alleged fugitive from Slavery without allowing such alleged fugitive a trial by jury; though the Federal Constitution[6] expressly provides that

> "In suits at common law, where the value in controversy shall exceed twenty dollars, the right of trial by jury shall be preserved:"

So that, while any person, of whom damages are claimed to the amount of twenty dollars, is entitled to a trial of the issue by jury, he whose liberty, or whose wife and children, are in jeopardy, is especially denied that right by this act. He may be entirely and unimpeachably white—for this act knows nothing of color; he may be the Governor of a State, the Bishop of a great Church; he may be General-in-Chief of the armies of the Union, engaged in a momentous war; but, if any one chooses

[3] Democrat, of Erie, Pa. [4] September, 12th.

[5] Samuel A. Eliot, Massachusetts, John L. Taylor, Ohio, Edward W. McGaughey, Indiana.

[6] Amendments—Article VII.

to swear that he is a slave who has escaped from his owner's service, he cannot require a trial by jury of the issue so raised, although the judge or commissioner before whom the claimant sees fit to bring him may be in league with that claimant to get him out of the protection of the law and into the power of his deadly enemies. And it is specially provided by this act[7] that

> "In no trial or hearing under this act shall the testimony of such alleged fugitive be admitted in evidence."

2. It did not even allow him a hearing before a judge; but authorized the captor to take him at once before any commissioner appointed to take depositions, etc., by a Judge of the Federal Courts, who was clothed by this act with plenary power in the premises; on whose rendition and certificate he might be hurried off at once into Slavery, without stay or appeal.

3. Said commissioner was to receive $10 for his services in case he directed the surrender of the alleged fugitive, but only $5 in case he, for any cause, decided against the claimant. The act thus, in effect, offered him a bribe to decide against the person charged with owing "service or labor."[8]

4. The persons charged with the duty of arresting the alleged fugitives were, in every instance, authorized and empowered by the act to "summon and call to their aid the bystanders, or *posse comitatus* of the proper county," to aid them in their work; "and all good citizens are hereby *commanded* to aid and assist in the prompt and efficient execution of this law."

Mr. John Van Buren, in a letter[9] to a Massachusetts Convention of opponents of this law, while admitting the right to reclaim and the duty of surrendering fugitives from Slavery, condemned the enactment in all its more important features: first, as an assumption by Congress of a duty properly devolving on the States,[10] and to be rightfully executed by State laws, tribunals, and functionaries. The demurrer that the Supreme Court had decided[11] adversely to this position was met by Mr. Van Buren as follows:

> "By this decision, judges in determining the question of authority would probably be concluded. But, in a popular discussion of the propriety of a law, with a view to its repeal or modification, I suppose we are at liberty to believe in opposition to a decision of the Supreme Court. Even the executive and legislative departments deny its authority to bind them. The Supreme Court decided that the Alien and Sedition Law was constitutional, and Matthew Lyon was imprisoned under it. The President, Mr. Jefferson, decided that it was not, and pardoned Mr. Lyon. The Supreme Court decided that Congress could constitutionally charter a Bank of the United States, and that the propriety and necessity of doing so were to be judged by Congress. The President, Gen. Jackson, decided that such an act was unconstitutional, and vetoed it. With these examples before me, I feel authorized to express the opinion which I entertain, that the Fugitive Slave Act is unconstitutional, because Congress has no power to legislate upon the subject."

With regard to the denial by this act of all semblance of a jury trial to persons claimed under it as fugitive slaves, Mr. Van Buren was equally

[7] Sec. 6.

[8] The reason, or, at least, the excuse, offered for this, imported that the labor of making out the necessary papers was greater in case of a rendition than in the alternative.

[9] Dated New York, April 4, 1851.

[10] This view was also taken by many Southrons of the "State Rights" school, especially by several eminent South Carolinians.

[11] In the case of Prigg against Pennsylvania.

decided and forcible, as is evinced by these further extracts from his letter:

"But, to those who regard the decision of the Supreme Court as conclusive, it is important to consider other objections to the act. Conceding the power of Congress to legislate upon this subject, I think the act in question is unconstitutional, because it does not give the person seized a trial by jury at the place where he is so seized, and before he is put in the custody of the claimant, with a warrant to transport him. * * *

"In my judgment, the claim of service secured by the Constitution, if it requires a law to enforce it, and if Congress can pass such a law, can only be provided for by an act which secures the trial of a question in a regular suit before a jury. The seventh amendment to the Constitution provides that, 'in suits at common law, where the value in controversy shall exceed twenty dollars, the right of trial by jury shall be preserved,' etc. This amendment, as well as the fifth, which declares that 'no person shall be deprived of life, liberty, or property, without due process of law,' grew out of the opposition manifested to the adoption of the Constitution, because it did not, in terms, provide for the trial by jury in civil cases. It is needless to remind an American of the anxiety with which this institution has been watched. It is well described by Mr. Justice Story, in the case of Parsons *vs.* Bedford, 3 Peters, 446. Justice Story also explains what is meant by 'a suit at common law,' in the section quoted. It covers *all* suits except those of equity, admiralty, or maritime jurisdiction; and the Judiciary Act of 1789 (chapter 20, sections 9, 12, and 13), carries this construction into practical operation. It will hardly be claimed that Congress can take *a case* which entitles a party to a jury, and deprive him of a jury by converting it into a summary proceeding, or that they can, in the same way, deprive him of his liberty or property without due process of law. If they could do this, the trial by jury and the due process of law secured by the Constitution become a mockery. Treating this as a mere question of property exceeding twenty dollars in value, I entertain no doubt that it is a case where a jury trial is secured by the Constitution.

"It may be said that a person seized can try the question of his right to freedom by a jury at the place whence he fled. This is a consolation, to be sure, to a man whose freedom has been destroyed by seizure and transportation from his home; and, if he could get his witnesses to the place where the claimant concludes to take him, he could have a trial. But the act in question provides no jury trial anywhere; there is no obligation on the claimant to take the person he seizes to any particular place; and if I have a right to try the question of title to property I hold at the place where the property is, and where the demand is made, how can it be argued that I have no such right when the demand made is for my thews and sinews?

"It is urged that juries would not render verdicts in favor of claimants, where the right was established. This does not correspond with my observation of jury trials. On the contrary, whatever prejudice jurors may feel against the law, I have hardly ever known them to fail in obeying the directions of the Court upon a point of law.

"It is also suggested, that the expense of recovering a fugitive by this mode would amount to a destruction of the right. If such an evil exists, it is incident to this unfortunate relation. It certainly furnishes no reason why the Constitution should be violated, and a safeguard broken down in reference to the liberty of a human being, which is secured to him in defending a horse or a bale of cotton."

That the provisions of this act were harsh and cruel is certain; but that any act providing for the recovery of fugitives from Slavery could have been at once humane and efficient, is not obvious. And, as the capture and rendition of alleged slaves under this act claimed a large share of public attention during the three or four years immediately following its passage, while the residue of the Compromise measures evoked no special excitement, and had none other than a noiseless, passive operation, it is not remarkable that greater success in slave-hunting, with greater alacrity on the part of the Free States in ministering to such success, seemed to the general Northern mind the sum and substance, the "being's end and aim," of the Compromises of 1850. And, as the Federal Administration, whereof Mr. Fillmore remained the official head, and Mr. Webster became the animating soul, gave prominence and emphasis to the exertions of its subordinates in aid of slave-catching, the alienation from it of anti-Slavery Whigs became more and more decided and formidable.

Numerous arrests of alleged fugitives were made in various parts of the country, but not with uniform success. In New York City, Philadelphia, and other marts largely engaged in Southern trade, no serious resistance was offered; though in one case a black man remanded to Maryland as a fugitive was honorably rejected and set at liberty by the claimant, as not the slave for whom he had been mistaken. In Boston, serious popular repugnance to rendition was repeatedly manifested; and in one case a negro known as Shadrach, who had been arrested as a fugitive, was rescued and escaped. In other cases, however, and conspicuously in those of Thomas Sims[12] and Anthony Burns,[13] the State and City authorities, the Judiciary, the Military, the merchants, and probably a decided majority of the citizens, approved and aided the surrender. There were cases, however, wherein the popular sentiment of the country was on the side of the hunted blacks—as was evinced at Syracuse,[14] N. Y., in the rescue of Jerry Loguen, an alleged fugitive, from the hands of the authorities, and his protection by alternately hiding and forwarding him until he made his escape into Canada. At Christiana, Lancaster Co., Pa.,[15] where a considerable number of negroes were compactly settled, Edward Gorsuch, a Maryland slaveholder, who attempted, with two or three accomplices, to seize his alleged slaves, four in number, was resisted by the alarmed, indignant blacks, and received a ball from a musket fired by one of them which proved fatal; and his son, who had accompanied him, was wounded. And in Milwaukee, Wis., Sherman M. Booth having been convicted in the U. S. District Court of aiding in the rescue of Joshua Glover, a fugitive from St. Louis, the Supreme Court of that State, on a *habeas corpus* sued out in his behalf, decided the Fugitive Slave Law unconstitutional and void, and set him at liberty. This decision was overruled, however, by the Supreme Court of the United States in a unanimous decision affirming the validity of the Fugitive Slave Law, and directing that, though a State Court might properly grant a *habeas corpus* in behalf of a person imprisoned under Federal authority, yet that the custodian in such case had only to make return that he *was* so held, and that this return, being proved truthful, must be accepted by the State Court as sufficient and conclusive—the Federal and State jurisdictions being each sovereign within its proper sphere, and each entitled to entire respect from the other, though operative over the same territory. And this remains to this day the adjudicated law of the land.

The activity and universality of slave-hunting, under the act of 1850, were most remarkable. That act became a law on the 18th of September; and, within ten days thereafter, a negro named James Hamlet had been seized in the city of New York, and very summarily dispatched to a woman in Baltimore, who claimed

[12] April 12, 1851. [13] May 27, 1854. [14] October 1, 1851. [15] September 11, 1851.

him as her slave. Before the act was a month old, there had been several arrests under it, at Harrisburg and near Bedford, Pa., in Philadelphia, at Detroit, and in other places. Within the first year of its existence, more persons, probably, were seized as fugitive slaves than during the preceding sixty years. Many of these seizures were made under circumstances of great aggravation. Thus, in Philadelphia, Euphemia Williams, who had lived in Pennsylvania in freedom all her life, as she affirmed, and had there become the mother of six living children, of whom the oldest was seventeen, was arrested in 1851 as the slave of a Marylander named Purnell, from whom she was charged with escaping twenty-two years before. Her six children were claimed, of course, as also the property of her alleged master. Upon a full hearing, Judge Kane decided that she was not the person claimed by Burnell as his slave Mahala. But there were several instances in which persons who had lived in unchallenged freedom from fifteen to twenty-five years were seized, surrendered, and carried away into life-long Slavery.

The needless brutality with which these seizures were often made, tended to intensify the popular repugnance which they occasioned. In repeated instances, the first notice the alleged fugitive had of his peril was given him by a blow on the head, sometimes with a heavy club or stick of wood; and, being thus knocked down, he was carried, bleeding and insensible, before the facile commissioner, who made short work of identifying him, and earning his ten dollars, by remanding him into Slavery. In Columbia, Pa., March, 1852, a negro, named William Smith, was seized as a fugitive by a Baltimore police officer, while working in a lumber-yard, and, attempting to escape, the officer drew a pistol and shot him dead. In Wilkesbarre, Pa., a deputy marshal and three or four Virginians suddenly came upon a nearly white mulatto waiter at a hotel, and, falling upon him from behind with a club, partially shackled him. He fought them off with the hand-cuff which they had secured to his right wrist, and, covered with blood, rushed from the house and plunged into the Susquehanna, exclaiming: "I will be drowned rather than taken alive!" He was pursued to the river-bank, and thence fired upon repeatedly, at a very short distance, as he stood in the water, up to his neck, until a ball entered his head, instantly covering his face with blood. The by-standers, who had by this time collected, were disgusted and indignant, and the hunters, fearing their interposition, retired for consultation. He thereupon came out of the water, apparently dying, and lay down on the shore. One of his pursuers remarked that "dead niggers were not worth taking South." His clothes having been torn off in the scuffle, some one brought a pair of pantaloons, and put them on him, and he was helped to his feet by a negro named Rex; on seeing which, the hunters returned and presented their revolvers, driving him again into the river, where he remained more than an hour, with only his head above the water. His claimants dared not come within his powerful grasp, as he afterward said, "he would have died contented, could he have carried two or three of them down with him." And the hunters were deterred or shamed by the spectators from further firing. Preparations being made to arrest them as rioters, they absconded; whereupon, their victim waded some distance up the stream, and was soon after found by some women, lying flat on his face in a corn-field, insensible. He was then duly cared for, and his wounds dressed, which was the last that was seen of him. His assailants were afterward arrested in Philadelphia, on a charge of riot, on a warrant issued on due complaint by a State magistrate; but Justice Grier, of the United States Supreme Court, arrested the proceedings as an unauthorized interference with Federal officers in the discharge of their duty. In his opinion, discharging the prisoners, he said:

> "We are unable to perceive in this transaction anything worthy of blame in the conduct of these officers, in their unsuccessful endeavors to fulfill a most dangerous and disgusting duty; except, perhaps, a want of sufficient courage and perseverance in the attempt to execute the writ!"

Of course, a law affording such facilities and temptations to kidnapping was not allowed to pass unimproved by the numerous villains who regarded negroes as the natural and lawful prey of whites under all circumstances. *The Kentucky Yeoman*, a Democratic pro-Slavery organ, once remarked that the work of arresting fugitives had become a regular business along the border line between the Slave and Free States, and that some of those engaged in it were not at all particular as to the previous slavery or freedom of those they arrested. How could it be expected that they should be? In many instances, free colored girls were hired for household service at some point distant from that where they had previously resided, and were known; and, being thus unsuspectingly spirited away from all who could identify them, were hurried off into Slavery. Sometimes, though not often, negroes were tempted by heavy bribes to betray their brethren into the hands of the slave-hunters. In one instance, a clerk in a dry-goods store in western New York, who was of full age, a member of a church, and had hitherto borne a respectable character, hired two colored boys to work for him in a hotel in Ohio, and on his way thither sold them as fugitive slaves to three Kentuckians, who appear to have believed his representations. One of the intended victims, detecting the plot, escaped from the cars, knocking down the Kentuckian who undertook to prevent him. The other was sold for $750 to an honorable slaveholder in Warsaw, Ky., who, upon proof of the outrage, promptly and cheerfully returned him to freedom. One girl, who was hired from New York, to live as a servant in Newark, N. J., was taken directly through Newark to Washington, and there offered to a slave-trader for $600, but not accepted; when she, having become alarmed, appealed to the hotel-keeper for protection; whereupon the kidnappers abandoned her, but were ultimately arrested at Ellicott's Mills, Md., and returned to New-York, where the husband was convicted, and sent to the penitentiary. In one instance, a negro, near Edwardsville, Ills., who had been employed in the work of capturing several alleged fugitives, finally met a white man on the highway, presented a pistol, and arrested him as a runaway slave, for whom a reward of $200 had been offered. The white man happened, however, to be acquainted in Edwardsville, and was thus enabled to establish his right to himself.

The business of slave-hunting became so profitable that the sheriff of Montreal, Canada, received, in January, 1855, a letter from a police officer and constable, in Frederick, Md., making him this tempting proposition:

"Vast numbers of slaves," says the Frederick official, "escaping from their masters or owners, succeed in reaching your Provinces, and are, therefore, without the pale of the 'Fugitive Slave Law,' and can only be restored by cunning, together with skill. Large rewards are offered, and will be paid, for their return; and, could I find an efficient person to act with me, a great deal of money could be made, as I would equally divide. * * * The only apprehension we have of approaching too far into Canada is the fear of being arrested; and, had I a good assistant in your city, who would induce the negroes to the frontier, I would be there to pay the cash. On your answer, I can furnish names and descriptions of negroes."

Some of the judicial decisions evoked by this carnival of man-hunting were most remarkable. In Sandusky, Ohio, four men and women, with several children, were seized from a boat about to leave for Detroit, by one who claimed to be their owner. Mr. Rush R. Sloane, a lawyer, was employed to act as their counsel. As no one claimed custody of these persons, or produced any right or warrant justifying their detention, Mr. Sloane declared to the bystanders that their seizure seemed to be unjustifiable; whereupon, a rush was made for the door. A man who had hitherto been silent, now said: "Here are the papers; I own the slaves; I will hold you individually responsible for their escape." They *did* escape, and Mr. Sloane was thereupon prosecuted for their value, and compelled by the judgment of a Federal Court to pay the sum of $3,950 and costs. In California, then completely under the domination of the Slave Power, which was especially strong in the selection of judges, matters were carried with a very high hand. In several instances, masters who had migrated or sent their sons to that region attended by slaves, undertook to reclaim them as fugitives and return them by force to the banks of the lower Mississippi; and the Supreme Court of that State became their accomplices for this purpose. The violation of law to this end was so palpable and shameless as to excite general remark, if not general indignation. In one leading case, the Court ruled, in effect, that the petitioner being young, in bad health, and probably unadvised of the constitutional provision of that State making all its inhabitants free, "is permitted to take Archy back to Mississippi." An old lawyer dryly remarked, while all around were stigmatizing this decision as atrocious, that "he thought it a very fair compromise, since it gave the law to the North and the negro to the South."

On Sunday, January 27, 1856, two slaves, with their wives and four children, escaped from Boone County, Ky., drove sixteen miles to Covington, and crossed to Cincinnati on the ice. They were missed before nightfall, and the master of five of them followed rapidly on horseback. After a few hours' inquiry, he traced them to the house of a negro named Kite, and, procuring the necessary warrants, with a marshal and assistants, proceeded thither on Monday. He summoned them to surrender. They refused. Whereupon the officers broke in the door, and were assailed with clubs and pistols by the desperate fugitives. Only one of the marshal's deputies was struck, and he not seriously injured; the negroes being disarmed before they could reload.

On a first survey of the premises they had captured, a horrible sight met the officers' eyes. In one corner of the room, a child nearly white lay bleeding to death, her throat cut from ear to ear. A scream from an adjoining room drew their attention thither, when a glance revealed a negro woman holding a knife dripping with gore over the heads of two children, who were crouched upon the floor, uttering cries of pain and terror. Wresting the knife from her hand, they discovered that the children were cut across the head and shoulders, but, though bleeding freely, not dangerously wounded. The woman proclaimed herself the mother of the dead child, as also of these, whom she desired also to kill rather than see them returned to Slavery. All were secured and taken to the marshal's office, where they sat quiet and dejected, answering all questions in monosyllables, or not answering at all. An excellent character was given to the adults by their owners. The mother of the dead child, Margaret Garner, a dark mulatto, twenty-three years of age, seemed simply stupefied and dumb from excess of agony; but, on being complimented on the looks of her little boy beside her, quickly replied, "You should have seen my little girl that—that—that died. *That* was the bird!" That girl was almost white, and of rare beauty. The mother alleged cruel treatment on the part of her master, and said she had resolved to kill all her children and then herself, in order to escape the horrors of Slavery. A coroner's jury having rendered a verdict, in the case of the dead child, that it was killed by its mother, Margaret Garner, with a knife, great efforts were made by the State authorities to hold her for trial on a charge of murder. All the adult slaves declared that they would go dancing to the gallows rather than be sent back to Slavery. But Judges McLean and Leavitt, of the Federal Court, decided that they were in the custody of the U. S. Marshal, and could not be taken out of it by the *habeas corpus* of a State Court, whether under a civil or criminal process; so they were all returned to Slavery. The owner of Margaret pledged himself to hold her subject to a requisition from the Governor of Ohio to answer the charge of crime; but he failed to keep his promise, and sent her, with the rest of the fugitives, down the river for sale, where all trace of her was lost. The cost to the Federal Treasury of this single rendition was about $22,000, whereof at least $20,000 was shamefully squandered or embezzled, as $2,000 would have amply sufficed.

The surrender of Anthony Burns probably excited more feeling than that of any other alleged fugitive, in that it attained unusual publicity, and took place in New England after the North had begun to feel the first throbs of the profound agitation excited by the repudiation of the Missouri Compromise in the passage of the Kansas-Nebraska bill.[16]

In this protracted and angry controversy respecting the surrender of Fugitive Slaves, the advocates of such surrender uniformly treated it as a high moral and political duty. Mr. Webster,[17] in announcing his determination to vote for Mr. Mason's Fugitive Slave bill, used this strong language:

"I desire to call the attention of all sober-minded men at the North, of all conscientious men, of all men who are not carried away by some fanatical idea, or some false impression, to their constitutional obligations. I put it to all the sober and sound minds at the North as a question of morals and a question of conscience," etc., etc.

And on this theme he discoursed every variation, in speeches, in letters, and in personal intercourse, during the brief remainder of his life. And every "conservative" pulpit and rostrum resounded with feebler and duller imitations, in drift and substance, of this language—the purport of all being that whoever failed to do "with alacrity,"[18] whatever he could toward securing the return of fugitive slaves to their masters, was guilty of a flagrant breach, not only of constitutional, but of moral obligation.

---

[16] On the 2d of June, 1854—the repudiation of the Missouri compact having recently been consummated in the passage and Presidential approval of the Kansas-Nebraska bill—Anthony Burns having been adjudged a fugitive at Boston, President Pierce ordered the U. S. cutter Morris to take him from that city to life-long bondage in Virginia. The following spirited stanzas thereupon appeared (June 13th) in *The New York Tribune:*

HAIL TO THE STARS AND STRIPES.

HAIL to the Stars and Stripes!
  The boastful flag all hail!
The tyrant trembles now,
  And at the sight grows pale;
The Old World groans in pain,
  And turns her eye to see,
Beyond the Western Main,
  The emblem of the Free.

Hail to the Stars and Stripes!
  Hope beams in every ray!
And, shining through the bars
  Of gloom, points out the way:
The Old World sees the light
  That shall her cells illume;
And, shrinking back to night,
  Oppression reads her doom.

Hail to the Stars and Stripes!
  They float in every sea;
The crystal waves speed on
  The emblem of the Free!
Beneath the azure sky
  Of soft Italia's clime,
Or where Auroras die
  In solitude sublime.

All hail the flaunting Lie!
  The Stars grow pale and dim—
The Stripes are bloody scars,
  A lie the flaunting hymn!
It shields the pirate's deck,
  It binds a man in chains;
It yokes the captive's neck,
  And wipes the bloody stains.

Tear down the flaunting Lie!
  Half-mast the starry flag!
Insult no sunny sky
  With Hate's polluted rag!
Destroy it, ye who can!
  Deep sink it in the waves!
It bears a fellow-man
  To groan with fellow-slaves.

Awake the burning scorn!
  The vengeance long and deep,
That, till a better morn,
  Shall neither tire nor sleep!
Swear once again the vow,
  O, freeman! dare to do!
God's will is ever NOW!
  May His *thy* will renew!

Enfurl the boasted Lie!
  Till Freedom lives again,
To reign once more in truth
  Among untrammeled men!
Roll up the starry sheen—
  Conceal its bloody stains;
For in its folds are seen
  The stamp of rusting chains.

Be bold, ye heroes all!
  Spurn, spurn the flaunting Lie,
Till Peace, and Truth, and Love
  Shall fill the bending sky;
Then, floating in the air,
  O'er hill, and dale, and sea,
'T will stand forever fair,
  The emblem of the Free!

[17] In his 7th of March speech. [18] Ibid.

In the South, where every adult white male was accustomed to join instinctively and eagerly in the hunt for a fugitive slave, precisely as though he were some domestic animal that had escaped from his owner's inclosure, and taken to the highway or the woods, such language might have been used with consistency: In the North, it was otherwise; and for this reason: The essence of obedience to law is the acceptance of the obligation, not in its letter merely, but in its spirit. In other words, he only can render full, effective obedience to a law who recognizes in such obedience the fulfillment of an *intrinsic* obligation—of a Divine requirement. Let us suppose, now, that Mr. Webster, while riding on one of the highways near Boston, or near Washington, had encountered a black mother with a child in her arms, fleeing on foot, with all possible speed, and had seen in the distance three or four white men, mounted and armed, fiercely pursuing. He would, of course, have comprehended at once that the woman and child were presumptively fugitive slaves, and that the pursuers were her master, or his agent, with assistants, in quest of her. But would he have thereupon attempted, "with alacrity," to stop the fleeing woman, and forcibly detain her, until they should overtake and seize her? Nay, if he had seen her, while in a hollow out of their sight, make a dexterous plunge into a wood, so as to throw them completely off her track, would he have ridden to tell them where she had left the road, and how they must vary their course to catch her? It would be a libel on his memory to suppose him capable of any such baseness.[19] He might have refrained from giving the woman a hint, by nodding or finger-pointing, as to the proper place at which to leave the road; he probably would have refrained from misleading her pursuers, by wink or sign, as to the course she had actually taken; but he would have rendered them no positive aid. His soul would have instinctively revolted from becoming a volunteer personal accomplice of the woman-hunters. Yet to refuse this was to withhold a genuine and hearty obedience to the vaunted constitutional obligation, that fugitives from Slavery "shall be delivered up on claim" of their masters. It was to repudiate in acts what he so stoutly affirmed in words. It was to "keep the word of promise to the ear, but break it to the hope." And hence—for this discrepancy was general and obvious—the yard-stick clamor throughout the North for a vigorous and thorough execution of the Fugitive Slave law was calculated rather to disgust than conciliate the Slave Power, every day quietly inclining more and more to the desperate expedient of Disunion. It widened and deepened the Southern impression that the North was, at heart, thoroughly anti-Slavery, but would profess or do anything base in its own eyes for the sake of securing the immense pecuniary advantages derived by it from the Union.

The National Conventions of the

[19] It is within the personal knowledge of the writer that politicians who declaimed loudly in public of our constitutional obligations to surrender fugitives, and reproached their neighbors for infidelity thereto, privately gave money to aid the escape of fugitive slaves to Canada.

rival Whig and Democratic parties for 1852 were not held till very late —convening in Baltimore, the Democratic on the 1st, and the Whig on the 16th of June. But it had already been made manifest that a new article—acquiescence in the Compromise of 1850—was to be interpolated into the creed of one or both of these parties, if the strength of its champions should be found sufficient. Indeed, a public pledge had, several months before, been signed by Henry Clay, Howell Cobb, and some fifty other members of Congress, of either party, that they would support no candidate thereafter who did not approve and agree to abide by that Adjustment. And this Compromise, according to the interpretation now put upon it by its leading supporters, was in essence a compact to refrain from and oppose all future "agitation" or discussion adverse to the security, or the presumed interests, of Human Slavery.

In the Democratic National Convention, on the first ballot for a Presidential candidate, Gen. Cass received 117 votes, Mr. Buchanan 93, and there were 78 scattered among eight others, of whom Gov. Marcy and Mr. Douglas were foremost. On the third ballot, Gen. Cass received 119; but he then began to decline; and on the thirteenth his vote had sunk to 99, while Mr. Douglas's had risen to 50, and his friends had high hopes. On the fourteenth ballot, Mr. Douglas's vote, which had risen gradually, was 92; while Gen. Cass's had settled to 33. On the next ballot, Mr. Douglas for the first time fell off; the result announced being—Douglas 92; Buchanan 83; Cass 64; all others 53. On the thirty-third, Gen. Cass ran up again to 123; and on the thirty-fifth to 131, which was *his* highest—Mr. Douglas dropping to 60 on the thirty-third, and to 53 on this. FRANKLIN PIERCE, of New Hampshire, was first named on this ballot, receiving 15 votes. He ran up to 30 on the next; fell back to 29 on the following; and there stood till the forty-sixth, when he received 44; while Gov. Marcy received 97; Gen. Cass 78; Mr. Buchanan 28; and Mr. Douglas 32, with 8 scattering. On the forty-eighth, Gen. Pierce received 55, and on the next 232 votes—being all that were cast but six—and was declared the candidate. For Vice-President, WILLIAM R. KING, of Alabama, received 126 on the first ballot, to 174 scattered among nine rivals; and on the second ballot he had 277 to 11 for Jefferson Davis, and was nominated.

This Convention, beside reäffirming the more essential propositions of its three predecessors, and one or two others condemning Nativism, indorsing the famous Kentucky and Virginia Resolutions of 1798 and 1799, etc., etc.; with reference to Slavery,

"*Resolved*, That Congress has no power under the Constitution to interfere with or control the domestic institutions of the several States, and that such States are the sole and proper judges of everything appertaining to their own affairs, and not prohibited by the Constitution; that all efforts of Abolitionists or others, made to induce Congress to interfere with questions of Slavery, or to take incipient steps in relation thereto, are calculated to lead to the most alarming and dangerous consequences; and that all such efforts have an inevitable tendency to diminish the happiness of the people, and to endanger the stability and permanency of the Union, and ought not to be countenanced by any friend of our political institutions.

"*Resolved*, That the foregoing proposition covers, and is intended to embrace, the whole subject of Slavery agitation in Congress; and, therefore, the Democratic party of the Union, standing on this National platform, will abide by and adhere to a faithful execution of the acts known as the Compromise measures settled by the last Congress—the act for reclaiming fugitives from service or labor included; which act, being designed to carry out an express provision of the Constitution, cannot, with fidelity thereto, be repealed, nor so changed as to destroy or impair its efficiency.

"*Resolved*, That the Democratic party will resist all attempts at renewing, in Congress or out of it, the agitation of the Slavery question, under whatever shape or color the attempt may be made."

The Whig National Convention met in Baltimore two weeks later than its rival, and a caucus of the Southern delegates, held the night before its organization, unanimously resolved to insist on making the wisdom and finality of the Compromise of 1850 a plank in the Whig platform to be constructed by the Convention. They agreed upon a full draft of what they believed the Whig platform should be; which, on being presented to the friends of Mr. Webster, was accepted by them, and thus had a majority of the Convention pledged to it in advance of any general consultation on the subject.

On the first ballot for a Presidential candidate, Mr. Fillmore had 133 votes, Gen. Scott 131, Mr. Webster 29. On the next, Gen. Scott had 133, and Mr. Fillmore but 131. These proportions were nearly preserved through three or four days—Gen. Scott gaining slightly and unsteadily on Mr. Fillmore—till, on the fiftieth ballot, Gen. Winfield Scott received 142, and on the fifty-second 148. On the next, he was nominated; having 159 votes to 112 for Mr. Fillmore and 21 for Mr. Webster. William A. Graham, of North Carolina, was, on the second ballot, nominated for Vice-President.

The Southern platform had already been imposed on the Convention—the Slavery plank by a vote of 164 Yeas to 117 Nays. It is as follows:

"*Eighth*, That the series of acts of the XXXIst Congress known as the Compromise Measures of 1850—the act known as the Fugitive Slave law included—are received and acquiesced in by the Whig party of the United States as a settlement, in principle and substance, of the dangerous and exciting questions which they embrace; and, so far as they are concerned, we will maintain them, and insist on their strict enforcement, until time and experience shall demonstrate the necessity of further legislation to guard against the evasion of the laws on the one hand, and the abuse of their powers on the other—not impairing their present efficiency; and we deprecate all further agitation of the question thus settled, as dangerous to our peace, and will discountenance all efforts to continue or renew such agitation, whenever, wherever, or however, the attempt may be made; and we will maintain this system as essential to the nationality of the Whig party, and the integrity of the Union."

Gen. Scott made haste to plant himself unequivocally and thoroughly on the platform thus erected, which was in undoubted accordance with his own feelings and convictions. But his success in the canvass was by no means commensurate with the expectations of his friends. Many of the anti-Slavery Whigs, by whose efforts he had been nominated, supported him coldly because of the platform; while the intense *pro*-Slavery section of the party did not support him at all—distrusting, not him, but the influences which, they apprehended, might guide his councils.

The "Free Soil Democracy," who yet maintained a National organization on the basis of open and thorough hostility to Slavery Extension and all pro-Slavery compromises, held their nominating Convention at Pittsburg, Pennsylvania, on the 11th of August; presented John P. Hale, of New

Hampshire, for President, and GEORGE W. JULIAN, of Indiana, for Vice-President; and, though they carried no State, they polled a far stronger vote than they would or could have done but for the Whig platform aforesaid; and they made their gain wholly at the expense of Gen. Scott. When the polls were closed and the result made manifest, it appeared that he had carried only the States of Massachusetts, Vermont, Kentucky, and Tennessee—four in all, choosing 42 Electors; while Gen. Pierce had carried twenty-seven States, choosing 254 Electors. Never before was there such an overwhelming defeat of a party that had hoped for success. Even little Delaware had, for the first time—save only in the reëlection of Monroe—voted for a 'Democratic' President. But quite a number of States had been carried for Gen. Pierce by very close votes; so that the popular preponderance of his party was by no means so great as the electoral result would seem to indicate. In all the States except South Carolina (where the Electors are not chosen by the people, but where there was no serious opposition to Pierce and King) the popular vote summed up as follows: For Pierce, 1,601,274; for Scott, 1,386,580; for Hale, 155,825; Pierce over Scott, 214,694; over Scott and Hale together, 58,896. And, whatever else the Election might have meant, there was no doubt that the popular verdict was against 'Slavery agitation,' and in favor of maintaining the Compromise of 1850.[20]

XVII.

THE NEBRASKA-KANSAS STRUGGLE.

FRANKLIN PIERCE was inaugurated President on the 4th of March, 1853. Never were the visible omens more auspicious of coming years of political calm and National prosperity. Though a considerable Public Debt had been incurred for the prosecution and close of the Mexican War, yet the Finances were healthy and the Public Credit unimpaired. Industry and Trade were signally prosperous. The Tariff had ceased to be a theme of partisan or sectional strife. The immense yield of gold by California during the four preceding years had stimulated Enterprise and quickened the energies of Labor, and its volume showed as yet no signs of diminution. And, though the Fugitive Slave law was still denounced, and occasionally resisted, by Abolitionists in the Free States, while Disunionists still plot-

[20] On the day before that of the choice of Presidential Electors by the people, the writer met an old friend whom he had not before seen for years, but whom he had formerly known as an ardent and active Whig. Speaking to him of the morrow's contest, in the undoubting confidence of a political compatriot, he was met at first by blank reserve, and then a frank assertion: 'I shall not vote this year as I formerly did.' 'What does that mean?' 'Why, I have been down South since I last saw you, *and I don't think Slavery so bad as I once did.*' No question of Slavery had ever been broached between us; and there was now no Slavery issue between the great National parties; yet an instinct stronger than logic had taught him that, if he would uphold and maintain Slavery, he must vote the Democratic ticket.

ted in secret, and more openly prepared in Southern Commercial Conventions (having for their ostensible object the establishment of a general exchange of the great Southern staples directly from their own harbors with the principal European marts, instead of circuitously by way of New York and other Northern Atlantic ports), there was still a goodly majority at the South, with a still larger at the North and Northwest, in favor of maintaining the Union, and preserving the greatest practicable measure of cordiality and fraternity between the Free and the Slave States, substantially on the basis of the Compromise of 1850.

The region lying directly westward and northwestward of the State of Missouri, and stretching thence to the Rocky Mountains, was vaguely known as the "Platte Country" (from the chief river intersecting it), and its eastern frontier was mainly covered by Indian reservations, on which whites were forbidden to settle, down to a period so late as 1850. Two great lines of travel and trade stretched across it — one of them tending southwestward, and crossing the Arkansas on its way to Santa Fé and other villages and settlements in New Mexico; the other leading up the Platte, North Platte, and Sweetwater, to and through the South Pass of the Rocky Mountains, where it divides — one trail leading thence northwestward to the Columbia and to Oregon; the other southwestward to Salt Lake, the Humboldt, and California. The western boundary of Missouri was originally a line drawn due north as well as south from the point where the Kansas or Kaw river enters the Missouri; but in 1836 a considerable section lying west of this line, and between it and the Missouri, was quietly detached from the unorganized territory aforesaid and added to the State of Missouri, forming in due time the fertile and populous counties of Platte, Buchanan, Andrew, Holt, Nodaway, and Atchison, which contained in 1860 70,505 inhabitants, of whom 6,699 were slaves. This conversion of Free into Slave territory, in palpable violation of the Missouri Compromise, was effected so dexterously and quietly as to attract little or no public attention.

At the first session of the XXXIId Congress (1851-2) petitions were presented for a territorial organization of the region westward of Missouri and Iowa; but no action was had thereon until the next session, when Mr. Willard P. Hall, of Missouri, submitted[1] to the House a bill organizing the Territory of *Platte*, comprising this region. This bill being referred to the Committee on Territories, Mr. William A. Richardson, of Illinois, from said Committee, reported[2] a bill organizing the Territory of *Nebraska* (covering the same district); which bill, being sent to the Committee of the Whole and considered therein, encountered a formidable and unexpected Southern opposition, and was reported[3] from said Committee with a recommendation that it be rejected. An attempt by Mr. John Letcher, of Virginia, to lay it on the table, was defeated by a call of the Yeas and Nays; when it was engrossed, read a third time, and passed: Yeas 98; Nays 43.

[1] December 13, 1852. [2] February 2, 1853. [3] February 10th.

The bill now went to the Senate, with ample notice that a pro-Slavery cabal had been secretly formed to resist the organization of a new Territory on soil consecrated to Free Labor, as this had solemnly been, until a counterpoise could be found or devised, through the partition of Texas or otherwise. It reached the Senate on the 11th, and was sent to the Committee on Territories, from which Mr. Stephen A. Douglas reported it on the 17th without amendment. On the 2d of March (being the last day but one of the session), he moved that it be taken up; which was resisted and beaten: Yeas 20; Nays 25—the Nays nearly all from the South. He tried again next day, when Mr. Solon Borland, of Arkansas, moved that it *do lie on the table*, which prevailed: Yeas 23; Nays 17—as before. So the South defeated any organization at this time of a territory west of Missouri. No Senators from Slave States but those from Missouri sustained the bill; and Mr. Atchison, of that State, in supporting a motion to take up the bill, to which Mr. Rusk, of Texas, had objected, said:

"I must ask the indulgence of the Senate to say one word in relation to this matter. Perhaps there is not a State in the Union more deeply interested in this question than the State of Missouri. If not the largest, I will say the best portion of that Territory—perhaps the only portion of it that in half a century will become a State—lies immediately west of the State of Missouri. It is only a question of time, whether we will organize the Territory at this session of Congress, or whether we will do it at the next session; and, for my own part, I acknowledge now that, as the Senator from Illinois well knows, when I came to this city, at the beginning of the last session, I was perhaps as much opposed to the proposition as the Senator from Texas now is. The Senator from Iowa [Mr. A. C. Dodge] knows it; and *it was for reasons I will not not now mention or suggest*. But, Sir, I have, from reflection and investigation in my own mind, and from the opinions of others—my constituents, whose opinions I am bound to respect—come to the conclusion that now is the time for the organization of this Territory. It is the most propitious time. The treaties with the various Indian tribes, the titles to whose possessions must be extinguished, can better be made now than at any future time; for, as the question is agitated, and as it is understood, white men, speculators, will interpose and interfere, and the longer it is postponed the more we will have to fear from them, and the more difficult it will be to extinguish the Indian title in that country, and the harder the terms to be imposed. Therefore, Mr. President, for this reason, without going into detail, I am willing now that the question should be taken, whether we will proceed to the consideration of this bill or not."

Here was a distinct intimation,[4] from a leading propagandist of Slavery, that he was aware of a Southern conspiracy to prevent the organization, westward of the Missouri, of a new Territory which must necessarily be Free; but he had no faith in its success, and was anxious, for urgent local reasons, to have the organization proceed. But he was overborne, and the bill defeated.

The XXXIIId Congress met December 5, 1853. There was an overwhelming Democratic majority in either branch. Linn Boyd, of Kentucky, was chosen Speaker of the House. President Pierce, as he in his Inaugural had been most emphatic in his commendation of the Compromise of 1850, and in insisting that "the rights of the South" should be upheld, and "that the laws to enforce them be respected and obeyed, not with reluctance encouraged by abstract opinions as to their propriety in a different state of society, but cheerfully, and according to the de-

[4] December 15, 1852.

cisions of the tribunal to which their exposition belongs," so now, in his first Annual Message, he reiterated these recommendations, and added:

"Notwithstanding differences of opinion and sentiment which then existed in relation to details and specific provisions, the acquiescence of distinguished citizens, whose devotion to the Union can never be doubted, has given renewed vigor to our institutions, and restored a sense of repose and security to the public mind throughout the confederacy. *That this repose is to suffer no shock during my official term, if I have power to avert it, those who placed me here may be assured.*"

Mr. Augustus C. Dodge, of Iowa, submitted[5] to the Senate a bill "to organize the Territory of Nebraska," embracing (as before) the region lying westward of Missouri and Iowa, which was referred to the Committee on Territories; from which Mr. Douglas, of Illinois, reported[6] it with amendments. Still, no word in this bill proposed to repeal or meddle with the interdict on Slavery in this region laid by the Missouri Compromise of 1820. On the contrary, Mr. Douglas's Report accompanying the bill, while it raised the question of the original validity of the Missouri Restriction aforesaid, contained no hint that said Restriction had been removed by the legislation of 1850. The material portion of that Report is as follows:

"A question has arisen in regard to the right to hold slaves in the Territory of Nebraska, when the Indian laws shall be withdrawn, and the country thrown open to emigration and settlement. By the 8th section of 'an act to authorize the people of Missouri Territory to form a Constitution and State Government, and for the admission of such State into the Union on an equal footing with the original States, and to prohibit Slavery in certain territories,' approved March 6, 1820, it was provided; 'That in all that territory ceded by France to the United States under the name of Louisiana, which lies north of 36 degrees 30 minutes north latitude, not included within the limits of the State contemplated by this act, Slavery and involuntary servitude, otherwise than in punishment of crimes whereof the parties shall have been duly convicted, shall be, and are hereby, prohibited: *Provided always*, That any person escaping into the same, from whom labor or service is lawfully claimed in any State or Territory of the United States, such fugitive may be lawfully reclaimed, and conveyed to the persons claiming his or her labor or service as aforesaid.'

"Under this section, as in the case of the Mexican law in New Mexico and Utah, it is a disputed point whether Slavery is prohibited in the Nebraska country by *valid* enactment. The decision of this question involves the constitutional power of Congress to pass laws prescribing and regulating the domestic institutions of the various Territories of the Union. In the opinion of those eminent statesmen who hold that Congress is invested with no rightful authority to legislate upon the subject of Slavery in the territories, the 8th section of the act preparatory to the admission of Missouri is null and void; while the prevailing sentiment in large portions of the Union sustains the doctrine that the Constitution of the United States secures to every citizen an inalienable right to move into any of the Territories with his property, of whatever kind and description, and to hold and enjoy the same under the sanction of law. Your Committee do not feel themselves called upon to enter upon the discussion of these controverted questions. They involve the same grave issues which produced the agitation, the sectional strife, and the fearful struggle, of 1850. As Congress deemed it wise and prudent to refrain from deciding the matters in controversy then, either by affirming or repealing the Mexican laws, or by an act declaratory of the true intent of the Constitution, and the extent of the protection afforded by it to Slave property in the Territories, so your Committee are not prepared to recommend a departure from the course pursued on that memorable occasion, either by affirming or repealing the 8th section of the Missouri act, or by any act declaratory of the meaning of the Constitution in respect to the legal points in dispute."

This would seem conclusive; yet it is but fair to add the following, from near the close of the Report:

"From these provisions, it is apparent that the Compromise measures of 1850 affirm, and rest upon, the following propositions:

[5] Dec. 14, 1853.

[6] January 4, 1854.

"First,—That all questions pertaining to Slavery in the Territories, and the new States to be formed therefrom, are to be left to the decision of the people residing therein, by their appropriate representatives, to be chosen by them for that purpose."

The bill thus reported was soon after, on Mr. Douglas's motion, recommitted, and on the 23d reported again by him from his Committee on Territories, with material alterations. For, meantime,[6] Mr. Archibald Dixon,[7] of Kentucky, had given due notice that, whenever this bill should come up, he would offer the following amendment:

"SEC. 22. *And be it further enacted*, That so much of the 8th section of an act approved March 6, 1820, entitled 'An Act to authorize the people of the Missouri Territory 'to form a constitution and State government, and for the admission of such State 'into the Union on an equal footing with the 'original States, and to prohibit Slavery in 'certain territories,' as declares 'That, in all 'that territory ceded by France to the United States, under the name of Louisiana, 'which lies north of 36 degrees 30 minutes 'north latitude, Slavery and involuntary servitude, otherwise than in the punishment 'of crimes whereof the party shall have 'been duly convicted, shall be forever prohibited,' *shall not be so construed as to apply to the Territory contemplated by this act, or to any other Territory of the United States;* but that the citizens of the several States or Territories shall be at liberty to take and hold their slaves within any of the Territories or States to be formed therefrom, as if the said act, entitled as aforesaid, and approved as aforesaid, had never been passed."

This blunt proposition that the Missouri Compromise, in so far as its stipulations favored the consecration of the Territories to Free Labor, be utterly repudiated, now that so much of it as strengthened Slavery had taken full and vigorous effect, was received with more surprise than satisfaction by the engineers of the original measure. *The Union*, then the Democratic organ at Washington, promptly denounced it as a Whig device to divide and disorganize the Democratic party. It received no hearty welcome from any quarter—certainly none from Mr. Douglas, or any supporter of his Presidential aspirations. It had evidently been expected by them that his proposal to organize these territories, so expressly contemplated and covered by the inhibition of bondage contained in the Missouri act, in blank silence on the subject of Slavery, would be deemed a concession to Southern prejudices, if not to Southern interests. Yet, in the presence of this bolder, stronger, larger, and more practical concession, that of Mr. Douglas dwindled by contrast into insignificance.

Mr. Douglas, thus outbid, resolved to start afresh. On the 23d aforesaid, he reported from his Committee a bill so different from its predecessor as hardly to resemble it, save that it contemplated the same region. Instead of one Territory, to be called Nebraska, and stretching from the parallel of 36° 30′ north latitude on the south to that of 43° 30′ on the north, and from the western boundary of Missouri and Iowa on the east to the crests of the Rocky Mountains on the west, he now proposed to create *two* Territories, one to be composed of so much of said region as was directly west of the State of Missouri, to be known as KANSAS; the other to comprise the residue, and be known as NEBRASKA. (The south line of Kansas was moved northward from latitude 36° 30′ to latitude 37°, in order to make it conform to the boundary between the lands of the Cherokees and those of the Osages.) And, with reference to Slavery, the new bill contained these provisions:

[6] January 16th, 1854.

[7] Elected as a Whig—afterward a Democrat.

"SEC. 21. *And be it further enacted*, That, in order to avoid all misconstruction, it is hereby declared to be the true intent and meaning of this act, so far as the question of Slavery is concerned, to carry into practical operation the following propositions and principles, ***established by the Compromise measures of one thousand eight hundred and fifty***, to wit:

"First. That all questions pertaining to Slavery in the Territories, and in the new States to be formed therefrom, are to be left to the decision of the people residing therein, through their appropriate representatives.

"Second. That 'all cases involving title 'to slaves,' and 'questions of personal free-'dom,' are referred to the adjudication of the local tribunals, with the right of appeal to the Supreme Court of the United States.

"Third. That the provisions of the Constitution and laws of the United States, in respect to fugitives from service, are to be carried into faithful execution in all the 'organized Territories,' the same as in the States."

Proceeding to that section which provides for the election of a delegate to Congress from Kansas, instead of the original stipulation—

"That the Constitution, and all laws of the United States which are not locally inapplicable, shall have the same force and effect within the said Territory as elsewhere in the United States"—

The following important reservation was now added:

"Except the section of the act preparatory to the admission of Missouri into the Union, approved March 6, 1820, which was superseded by the principles of the Legislation of 1850, commonly called the Compromise measures, and is declared inoperative."

The section which authorized Nebraska to send a delegate was amended in precisely the same manner.

Mr. Douglas called up his new bill for consideration next morning; when not only Messrs. Chase and Sumner, but Mr. Norris, of New Hampshire, Gen. Cass, and other Democrats, desired that time be given to consider the grave changes which had just been made in the vital character of the measure. On the other hand, Messrs. Dawson, of Georgia, and Dixon, of Kentucky, were ready to sustain Mr. Douglas throughout. Mr. Dixon, expressing entire satisfaction with the new shape given to the bill, said:[8]

"I think it due to the Senate that they should have an opportunity of understanding precisely the bearings and the effect of the amendment which has been recently incorporated into the bill, as originally reported by the Committee—I mean that portion of the amendment which alludes to Slavery within the Territories to be organized—Nebraska and Kansas. So far as I am individually concerned, I am perfectly satisfied with the amendment reported by the Senator from Illinois, and which has been incorporated into the bill. If I understand it, it reaches a point which I am most anxious to attain—that is to say, it virtually repeals the act of 1820, commonly called the Missouri Compromise act, declaring that Slavery should not exist north of the line of 36° 30′ north latitude.

"I here take occasion to remark, merely with a view of placing myself right before the Senate, that I think my position in relation to this matter has been somewhat misunderstood.

"I have been charged, through one of the leading journals[9] of this city, with having proposed the amendment which I notified the Senate I intended to offer, with a view to embarrass the Democratic party. It was said that I was a Whig from Kentucky, and that the amendment proposed by me should be looked upon with suspicion by the opposite party. Sir, I merely wish to remark that, upon the question of Slavery, I know no Whiggery, and I know no Democracy. I am a pro-Slavery man. I am from a slaveholding State; I represent a slaveholding constituency; and I am here to maintain the rights of that people whenever they are presented before the Senate.

"The amendment which I notified the Senate that I should offer at the proper time, has been incorporated by the Senator from Illinois into the bill which he has reported to the Senate. The bill, as now amended, meets my views, and I have no objection to it. I shall, at the proper time, as far as I am able to do so, aid and assist the Senator from Illinois, and others who

[8] January 24, 1854.

[9] *The Union.*

are anxious to carry through this proposition, with the feeble abilities I may be able to bring to bear upon it. I think it due to myself to make this explanation, because I do not wish it to be understood that, upon a question like this, I have, or could have, any motive except that which should influence a man anxious to secure what he believes to be a great principle—that is, Congressional non-interference in all the Territories, so far as this great question of Slavery is concerned.

"I never did believe in the propriety of passing the Missouri Compromise. I thought it was the result of necessity. I never thought that the great Senator from Kentucky (Mr. Clay), when he advocated that measure, did so because his judgment approved it, but because it was the result of a combination of circumstances which drove him to the position he assumed; and I have never thought that that measure received the sanction either of his heart or of his head.

"The amendment, then, which I gave notice that I would propose—and which I intended to have proposed, if it had not been rendered wholly unnecessary by the amendment reported by the Senator from Illinois, from the Committee on Territories, of which he is the honored Chairman—I intended to offer, under the firm conviction that I was carrying out the principles settled in the Compromise acts of 1850; and which leave the whole question of Slavery with the people, and without any Congressional interference. For, over the subject of Slavery, either in the States or Territories of the United States, I have always believed, and have always contended, that Congress had no power whatever, and that, consequently, the act of 1820, commonly known as the Missouri Compromise act, is unconstitutional; and, at the proper time, I shall endeavor to satisfy the Senate and the country of the truth of these propositions."

To which Mr. Douglas responded as follows:

"As this discussion has begun, I feel it to be my duty to say a word in explanation. I am glad to hear the Senator from Kentucky say that the bill, as it now stands, accomplishes all that he desired to accomplish by his amendment, because his amendment seemed to myself, and to some with whom I have consulted, to mean more than what he now explains it to mean, and what I am glad he did not intend it should mean.

"We supposed that it not only wiped out the legislation which Congress has heretofore adopted, excluding Slavery, but that it affirmatively legislated Slavery into the Territories. The object of the Committee was neither to legislate Slavery in or out of the Territories; neither to introduce nor exclude it; but to remove whatever obstacle Congress had put there, and apply the doctrine of Congressional non-intervention, in accordance with the principles of the Compromise measures of 1850, and allow the people to do as they pleased upon this, as well as all other matters affecting their interests.

"The explanation of the honorable Senator from Kentucky shows that his meaning was not what many supposed it to be, who judged simply from the phraseology of the amendment. I deem this explanation due to the Senator and to myself."

Messrs. Webster, Clay, and Calhoun had all passed from the earth since the inception of Mr. Clay's Compromise in 1850. Not one of them lived to hear that that Compromise had lifted the interdict of Slavery from the whole region solemnly guaranteed to Free Labor forever by the Compromise of 1820. Mr. Webster, certainly, never dreamed of such a thing, when he vehemently denounced, as insane, malignant folly, the attempt to fasten a like prohibition on the bill organizing New Mexico—as an effort to debar slaveholding on snowy crags and arid deserts where no slave could be subsisted—as a superserviceable attempt to "reënact the laws of God," as if their Author were unequal to the task He had undertaken.

In the accord of Messrs. Douglas and Dixon, an undertone of discord may be detected. Mr. Dixon repudiates the restrictive provision of the Compromise of 1820 as void *ab initio*, for want of constitutional power to enact it. Congress *could not* lawfully exclude Slavery from the Federal domain—therefore, *did not*, to any purpose. Mr. Clay consented to that Restriction because he must, not because he would—(as if this were not always the case in compromises—each party conceding something he would gladly retain, in order to secure something else that is otherwise beyond his reach.) But that Mr. Clay deliberately bargained to secure what he greatly desired (the admission of Missouri), knowing that the stipulated consideration was utterly beyond the power of Congress, therefore a blank nullity—*that*, Mr. Dixon did not assert, nor would any true friend of the great Kentuckian's memory insinuate it. Whatever Mr. Dixon's belief on the subject, it is certain that Mr. Clay deemed the Missouri Compromise a valid contract, and that he never dreamed that it was either unauthorized by the Constitution or superseded by the Compromise of 1850. No champion, no adversary, of this latter arrangement ever suggested, whether as an argument for, or an objection to, this scheme, that one of its effects or incidents would be the repeal of the Missouri Restriction, and a consequent opening to Slavery of the region stretching westward and north-westward from Missouri.

Mr. Douglas, it will be seen, indorses none of Mr. Dixon's assumptions. He had misunderstood Mr. Dixon's original proposition, supposing that it intended to "legislate Slavery into the Territory." He could mean by this nothing more nor other than that he misunderstood Mr. Dixon's as a proposition to legislate Slave *law*—that is, law under which slaves could be legally held to service—into said Territory; the act of planting Slavery *in fact* there, being one which legislation might facilitate and invite; but which individual action must initiate and achieve. And he did not now contend that the legislation of 1850 had even removed the obstacle to such establishment, but only that the action he proposed was "in accordance with the *principles* of the Compromise measures of 1850"—that is to say, it applied to Kansas and Nebraska—Territories secured, upon due consideration, to Free Labor, by sacred agreement in 1820—a principle which Congress had, under very different circumstances, applied to New Mexico—a most unlike and peculiar region—in 1850.

Mr. Dixon, it will be remarked, had not yet attained to the ultimate orthodoxy of the South with respect to the rights of slaveholders in the Territories. He only held that Congress had no right to *exclude* them with their human chattels.[9] That it was bound to recognize and protect their property in slaves, and that the people of the Territories could have no right, prior to their organization as a State, to exclude or inhibit Slavery, were dogmas as yet confined to the more ardent devotees of Calhounism, and so far from being accepted, that they were scarcely comprehended by the great body of the supporters of the Compromise.

The amended bill, thus reported by Mr. Douglas, was debated at

[9] "Is it not hard," asked Mr. Badger, of North Carolina, during the debate on the Kansas-Nebraska bill, "if I should choose to emigrate to Kansas, that I should be forbidden to take my old mammy [slave-nurse] along with me?"—"The Senator entirely mistakes our position," responded Mr. Wade, of Ohio. "We have not the least objection, and would oppose no obstacle, to the Senator's migrating to Kansas, and taking his 'old mammy' along with him. We only insist that he shall not be empowered to *sell* her after taking her there."

length, and ably, by Messrs. Douglas and several others in favor, and by Messrs. Chase, Seward, Sumner, Wade, and others, in opposition. But the disparity in numbers between its supporters and its opponents was too great—nearly three for to one against it—to allow much interest to attach to the successive discussions and divisions, save as they serve to cast light on the real character of the measure, especially with respect to Slavery. A few of these will here be noted.

Mr. Chase, having attempted[10] to strike out so much of the clause last quoted as declares the Restriction of 1820 "superseded" by the Compromise of 1850, and been beaten by 30 Nays to 13 Yeas, Mr. Douglas[11] himself moved that said clause be stricken out, and replaced by the following:

"Which being inconsistent with the principle of Non-Intervention by Congress with Slavery in the States and Territories, as recognized by the legislation of 1850 (commonly called the Compromise measures), is hereby declared inoperative and void; it being the true intent and meaning of this act not to legislate Slavery into any Territory or State, nor to exclude it therefrom, but to leave the people thereof perfectly free to form and regulate their domestic institutions in their own way, subject only to the Constitution of the United States."

This, of course, prevailed: Yeas 35; Nays 10: whereupon Mr. Chase moved[12] to add thereto as follows:

"*Under which, the people of the Territory, through their appropriate representatives, may, if they see fit, prohibit the existence of Slavery therein.*"

This touchstone of the true nature and intent of the measure was most decisively voted down; the Yeas and Nays being as follows:

Yeas—Fessenden and Hamlin, of Maine; Sumner, of Massachusetts; Foot, of Vermont; Smith, of Connecticut; Fish and Seward, of New York; Chase and Wade, of Ohio; Dodge (Henry), of Wisconsin—10.

Nays—Norris and Williams, of New Hampshire; Toucey, of Connecticut; Brodhead, of Pennsylvania; Clayton, of Delaware; Stuart,[13] of Michigan; Pettit, of Indiana; Douglas and Shields, of Illinois; Dodge (A. C.) and Jones, of Iowa; Walker, of Wisconsin; Hunter and Mason, of Virginia; Pratt, of Maryland; Badger, of North Carolina; Butler and Evans, of South Carolina; Dawson, of Georgia; Fitzpatrick and C. C. Clay, of Alabama; Adams and Brown, of Mississippi; Benjamin and Slidell, of Louisiana; Morton, of Florida; Houston and Rusk, of Texas; Dixon, of Kentucky; Bell and Jones, of Tennessee; Atchison, of Missouri; Sebastian and Johnson, of Arkansas; Gwin and Weller, of California—36.

So the Senate decisively voted that the people of the new Territories, formed by this act from the region shielded from Slavery by the Compromise of 1820, should *not* have the right, under this organization, to prohibit Slavery, should they see fit.

On motion of Mr. Badger, of North Carolina, it was further (Yeas 35, Nays 6)

"*Provided*, That nothing herein shall be construed to revive or put in force any law or regulation which may have existed prior to the act of 6th of March, 1820, either protecting, establishing, prohibiting, or abolishing Slavery."

On motion of Mr. Clayton, of Delaware, it was further provided that immigrants from foreign countries who had merely declared their intention to become naturalized citizens should not be voters in these Territories. On this proposition, the Yeas were 23 (all from Slave States); the Nays 21 (all from Free States).

Mr. Chase now moved an amendment fixing a day of election, appointing commissioners to lay off Counties, etc., etc., and enabling the

[10] February 6th. [11] February 15th.

[12] March 2d.

[13] Gen. Cass, the inventor of "Popular Sovereignty," who was in his seat and voted just before, did not respond to the call of his name on this occasion.

people of these Territories to choose their own Governor as well as Legislature,—which was rejected; Yeas 10;[14] Nays 30.

So far, the bill had been acted on as in Committee of the Whole. On coming out of Committee, Mr. Clayton's amendment, above mentioned, was disagreed to—22 to 20—and the bill engrossed for its third reading by 29 to 12—and, at a late hour of the night[15]—or rather, morning—passed: Yeas 37; Nays[16] 14: whereupon the Senate, exhausted by struggle and excitement, adjourned over from Friday to the following Tuesday.

In the House, this bill was not taken up for more than two months after it had passed the Senate. There were scruples to vanquish, objections to remove or to soften, and machinery to adjust, in order to give the measure a chance of success. Meantime, the hum of public dissatisfaction rose louder and louder, and members who were soon to face Northern constituencies were reasonably reluctant to vote for it, unless the Democratic majorities in their districts were well-nigh impregnable.

A House bill (nearly a copy of that of Mr. Douglas) having been reported[17] by Mr. Richardson, of Illinois, from the Committee on Territories, Mr. English, of Indiana—a most unflinching Democrat—from the minority of said Committee, proposed to strike out the clause which we have seen reported by Mr. Douglas to the Senate, and adopted by that body, repealing the 8th section of the Missouri act, and insert instead the following:

"*Provided*, That nothing in this act shall be so construed as to prevent the people of said Territory, through the properly constituted legislative authority, from passing such laws, in relation to the institution of Slavery, as they may deem best adapted to their locality, and most conducive to their happiness and welfare; and so much of any existing act of Congress as may conflict with the above right of the people to regulate their domestic institutions in their own way, be, and the same is hereby, repealed."

It is highly probable that this proposition could not have been defeated on a call of the Yeas and Nays in the House—which was doubtless the reason why it was never acted on. The House bill was never taken up, save at a late day,[18] so as to enable the Senate bill to be moved as an amendment.

There was a violent struggle in the House for and against closing the debate on this measure, and it was finally agreed that said debate should terminate on Saturday the 20th. And now, Mr. Alex. H. Stephens, of Georgia, originated, and was enabled to execute, a parliamentary maneuver which, if recognized as legitimate, must prove an important aid to party despotism and a screen to vicious legislation through all future time. The right of a majority to prescribe a reasonable limit to discussion—to afford

[14] Messrs. Chase, Fessenden, Foot, Hamlin, Norris, Seward, Shields, Smith, Sumner, Wade—10.

[15] March 3d.

[16] Messrs. Bell, of Tennessee, Houston, of Texas, and Walker, of Wisconsin, who had voted against Mr. Chase's amendment above cited, and Mr. James, of Rhode Island, who had not voted on it at all, now voted Nay. Messrs. Bayard, of Delaware, Cass, of Michigan, Thompson, of Kentucky, Geyer, of Missouri, Thomson, of New Jersey, who did not vote for or against Gov. Chase's amendment, whereon we have given the Yeas and Nays, were now present and voted *for* the bill.

[17] January 31st.

[18] May 8th.

fair opportunity for debate, but insist that it shall close at a definite and not too distant day and hour—has become a part of our parliamentary law. But the right of a minority to seek to improve what it deems a vicious and mistaken measure—to soften, if it may, objectionable features which it is unable wholly to remove—is still sacred; and it has accordingly been established, after much experience of the evils of the opposite rule, that even a vote of the House, enforcing the Previous Question on a reluctant, struggling minority, does not cut off amendments which may have already been proposed, but only arrests debate and brings the House to vote successively on all the propositions legitimately before it, including, it may be, the engrossment of the bill. But Mr. Stephens, when the hour for closing the debate in Committee had arrived, moved *that the enacting clause of the bill be stricken out*, which was carried by a preconcerted and uncounteracted rally of the unflinching friends of the measure. Of course, all pending amendments were thus disposed of—the bill being reported as dead. Having thus got the bill out of Committee and before the House, Messrs. Stephens & Co. voted *not to agree to the report of the Committee of the Whole*,[19] thus bringing the House to an immediate vote on the engrossment of the bill. Mr. Richardson now moved an amendment in the nature of a substitute (being, in effect, the Senate's bill), and thereupon called the Previous Question, which was seconded: Yeas 116; Nays 90; when his amendment was adopted—Yeas 115; Nays 95; the bill ordered to be engrossed—Yeas 112; Nays 99; the Previous Question again ordered and sustained; and the bill finally passed: Yeas 113; Nays 100. Thus the opponents of the measure in the House were precluded from proposing any amendments or modifications whatever, when it is morally certain that, had they been permitted to do so, some such amendment as Gov. Chase's or Mr. English's would have been carried.

The Free States contributed 44 votes—all cast by Democrats—to the support of this measure. From the Slave States, 12 Whigs and 57 Democrats sustained it. Against it were 91 members from Free States, of whom 44 were chosen as Whigs, three as "Free Soil" proper, and 44 as Democrats. So that precisely as many Democrats from Free States voted for as against the final passage of the Nebraska bill. Only nine[20] members from Slave States opposed it, of whom but two[21] had been regarded as Democrats; and of these Col. Benton was not so regarded thereafter. Of the Whigs who so voted, but two[22] were returned to the next House.

The bill had thus passed the House in form as an original measure of that body, although it was in essence the amended Senate bill. Being sent[23] to the Senate as such, an at-

[19] Yeas (for agreeing) 97; Nays 117.

[20] VIRGINIA.—John S. Millson—1. NORTH CAROLINA.—Richard C. Puryear, Sion H. Rogers—2. TENNESSEE.—Robert M. Bugg, William Cullom, Emerson Etheridge, Nathaniel G. Taylor—4. LOUISIANA.—Theodore G. Hunt—1. MISSOURI.—Thomas H. Benton—1. OTHER SOUTHERN STATES.—None. Total—9.

[21] Messrs. Millson, of Virginia, and Benton, of Missouri.

[22] Messrs. Puryear, of North Carolina, and Etheridge, of Tennessee.

[23] May 24th.

tempt to amend it was voted down, and the bill ordered to be engrossed, by 35 Yeas to 13 Nays. It was immediately passed, and, being approved by President Pierce, became a law of the land.

The struggle which ensued for the practical possession of Kansas was one which Congress had thus clearly provoked and invited.

When the bill organizing Kansas and Nebraska was first submitted to Congress in 1853, all that portion of Kansas which adjoins the State of Missouri, and, in fact, nearly all the accessible portion of both Territories, was covered by Indian reservations, on which settlement by whites was strictly forbidden. The only exception was that in favor of Government agents and religious missionaries; and these, especially the former, were nearly all Democrats and violent partisans of Slavery. Among the missionaries located directly on the border was the Rev. Thomas Johnson, of the Methodist Church South, who was among the few who had already introduced and then held slaves in the territory which is now Kansas, in defiance of the Missouri Restriction. He was a violent politician of the Missouri border pattern, and in due time became President of the Council in the first Territorial Legislature of Kansas—elected almost wholly by non-resident and fraudulent votes. Within the three months immediately preceding the passage of the Kansas bill aforesaid, treaties were quietly made at Washington with the Delawares, Otoes, Kickapoos, Kaskaskias, Shawnees, Sacs, Foxes, and other tribes, whereby the greater part of the soil of Kansas lying within one or two hundred miles of the Missouri border was suddenly opened to White appropriation and settlement. These simultaneous purchases of Indian lands by the Government, though little was known of them elsewhere, were thoroughly understood and appreciated by the Missourians of the Western border, who had for some time been organizing "Blue Lodges," "Social Bands," "Sons of the South," and other societies, with intent to take possession of Kansas in behalf of Slavery. They were well assured, and they fully believed, that the object contemplated and desired, in lifting, by the terms of the Kansas-Nebraska bill, the interdict of Slavery from Kansas, was to authorize and facilitate the legal extension of Slavery into that region. Within a very few days after the passage of the Kansas-Nebraska act, hundreds of leading Missourians crossed into the adjacent Territory, selected each his quarter-section or larger area of land, put some sort of mark on it, and then united with his fellow-adventurers in a meeting or meetings intended to establish a sort of Missouri preëmption upon all this region. Among the resolves passed at one of these meetings, were the following:

> "That we will afford protection to no abolitionist as a settler of this Territory.
>
> "That we recognize the institution of Slavery as already existing in this Territory, and advise slaveholders to introduce their property as early as possible."

Information being received, soon after this, that associations were being formed in the Eastern States, designed to facilitate and promote the migration of citizens of those

States to Kansas, with intent to make her a Free State, a violent and general indignation of the borderers was thereby excited. Among others, a meeting was held at Westport, Mo., early in July, 1854, which adopted the following:

"*Resolved*, That this association will, whenever called upon by any of the citizens of Kansas Territory, hold itself in readiness together to assist and remove any and all emigrants who go there under the auspices of the Northern Emigrant Aid Societies.

"*Resolved*, That we recommend to the citizens of other Counties, particularly those bordering on Kansas Territory, to adopt regulations similar to those of this association, and to indicate their readiness to cöoperate in the objects of this first resolution."

Before the passage of these resolves, at least one person, who had strayed into the Territory with intent to settle there, and who was unable to convince the "Border Ruffians," already in possession, that he was one with them in faith and spirit, was seized by them, placed in a canoe without oars, and sent floating down the Missouri.

The first company, about thirty in number, of Eastern emigrants, under the auspices of the New England Emigrant Aid Society, reached Kansas before the end of July, and located on the site now known as Lawrence.[24] Two weeks later, they were joined by a second and larger company, numbering sixty or seventy. While these were still living in tents, but busily employed in erecting temporary houses, they were visited by a party of Missourians, one hundred strong, who were reinforced next day by one hundred and fifty more, who pitched their camp just across a ravine from the young canvas city, and sent over formal notification that "the Abolitionists must leave the Territory, never more to return to it." The settlers must have all their effects gathered together preparatory to leave by ten o'clock. The time was afterward extended to one o'clock, with abundant professions of a desire to prevent the effusion of blood. The Yankees, meantime, had organized and armed as a militia company, and were quietly drilling amid their tents, sending civil but decided answers to the repeated messages sent to them. Finally, having satisfied themselves that they could only prevent bloodshed by letting the Yankees alone, and going about their own business, the ruffians broke up their camp by piecemeal and stole away, at evening and during the night, back to their dens in Missouri.

President Pierce appointed Andrew H. Reeder, of Pennsylvania, Governor, and Daniel Woodson, of Arkansas, Secretary of Kansas, with judicial officers of whom a majority were from Slave States—one of them taking a number of slaves with him into the Territory. These officers reached Kansas, and established a Territorial Government there, in the autumn of 1854. All of them were, of course, Democrats; but Gov. Reeder's soundness on the vital question was early suspected at the South. *The Union* (Washington), President Pierce's immediate organ, promptly rebuked these suspicions, as follows:

"A gentleman in Virginia calls our attention to the fact that the enemies of President

[24] So named after Amos A. Lawrence, Treasurer of the Society.

Pierce in the South lay particular stress upon his appointment of Gov. Reeder as proof of his willingness to favor Free-Soilers, and asks us whether, at the time of his appointment, Gov. Reeder was regarded as a sound *national* Democrat. It is in our power to answer this question with entire confidence, and to say that, down to the time that Gov. Reeder went to Kansas to assume the duties of Governor of the Territory, there had not been, so far as we have ever heard, or so far as the President ever heard, a breath of suspicion as to his entertaining Free-Soil sentiments. He was appointed under the strongest assurances that he was strictly and honestly a *national* man. We are able to state, further, on very reliable authority, that, *whilst* Gov. Reeder was in Washington, at the time of his appointment, *he conversed with Southern gentlemen on the subject of Slavery, and assured them that he had no more scruples in buying a slave than a horse, and he regretted that he had not money to purchase a number to carry with him to Kansas.* We have understood that he repeated the same sentiments on his way to Kansas. We will repeat what we have had occasion to say more than once before—that no man has ever been appointed by President Pierce to office who was not at the time understood by him to be a faithful adherent to the Baltimore platform of 1852, on the subject of Slavery. If any appointment was made contrary to this rule, it was done under a misapprehension as to the appointment. We may add that the evidences of Gov. Reeder's soundness were so strong that President Pierce was slower than many others to believe him a Free-Soiler after he had gone to Kansas. It is, therefore, the grossest injustice to refer to Gov. Reeder's appointment as proof of the President's willingness to favor Free-Soilers."

An election for Delegate from Kansas was held near the close of November. There were probably less than two thousand adult white males then resident in the Territory; yet 2,871 votes were cast, whereof 1,114 were afterward ascertained to have been legal, while 1,729 were cast by residents of Missouri. At one poll, known as "110," 604 votes were cast, of which 20 were legal and 584 were illegal. John W. Whitfield,[25] an Indian agent, the Missouri candidate, had 597 of them. He received 2,268 in all, to 570 for all others. David R. Atchison, then a U. S. Senator from Missouri, in a speech in Platte County, Mo., a few weeks before the election, said:

"When you reside within one day's journey of the Territory, and when your *peace*, your *quiet*, and your *property*, depend upon your action, you can, without any exertion, *send* five hundred of your young men who will vote in favor of your institutions. Should each county in the State of Missouri only do its duty, the question will be decided quietly and peaceably at the ballot-box. If we are defeated, then Missouri and the other Southern States will have shown themselves recreant to their interests, and will deserve their fate."

The city of Atchison, named after this distinguished Senator, was founded[26] about this time by gentlemen of his faith, who established *The Squatter Sovereign* as their organ. One of its early issues contained the following significant paragraph:

"We can tell the impertinent scoundrels of *The Tribune* that they may exhaust an ocean of ink, their Emigrant Aid Societies spend their millions and billions, their representatives in Congress spout their heretical theories till doomsday, and his Excellency appoint abolitionist after free-soiler as our Governor, yet we will continue to lynch and hang, tar and feather and drown, every white-livered abolitionist who dares to pollute our soil."

Gov. Reeder, in the early months of 1855, had a census of the Territory taken, which showed a total population of 8,501, whereof 2,905 were voters and 242 slaves. He thereupon ordered an election for a first Territorial Legislature and for certain county officers, to be held on the 30th of March, which took place accordingly. All of border Missouri was on hand; and the invaders had

[25] A Tennesseean; last heard from in the Confederate army.

[26] On the Kansas bank of the Missouri; some thirty miles above Leavenworth.

been so nicely apportioned and directed to the several districts and polls that they elected all the members, with a single exception, in either House—the two Free-Soilers being chosen from a remote inland district which the Missourians had overlooked or did not care to reach. Although but 831 legal electors voted, there were no less than 6,320 votes polled. Even at Lawrence, where there were but 369 voters in all, and not half a dozen of them pro-Slavery, the vote returned was—pro-Slavery, 781; Free State, 253. At Marysville, where there were 24 legal voters, 328 votes were returned, all pro-Slavery. There was no disguise, no pretense of legality, no regard for decency. On the evening before and the morning of the day of election, nearly a thousand Missourians arrived at Lawrence, in wagons and on horseback, well armed with rifles, pistols, and bowie-knives, and two pieces of cannon loaded with musket balls. They had tents, music, and flags, and encamped in a ravine near the town. They held a meeting the night before the election at the tent of Claiborne F. Jackson.[27] Finding that they had more men than were needed to carry the Lawrence district, they dispatched companies of one to two hundred each to two other districts. Meeting one of the judges of election before the poll opened, they questioned him as to his intended course, and, learning that he should insist on the oath of residence, they first attempted to bribe and then threatened to hang him. In consequence of this threat, he failed to appear at the poll, and a Missourian was appointed in his stead. One of the remaining judges, refusing to receive Missouri votes, resigned under duress, and was replaced by another who made no objection. One Missourian voted for himself and then for his son, ten or eleven years old. Three of those they thus elected to the Legislature were residents of Missouri at the time. These details might be continued indefinitely, but it is needless. The Missourians voted at other polls with less circumspection, easily driving off all who objected to their proceedings, and then doing as they chose. *The Weston Reporter* (Missouri), of the day before, had said:

> "Our minds are already made up as to the result of the election in Kansas to-morrow. The pro-Slavery party will be triumphant, we presume, in nearly every precinct. Should the pro-Slavery party fail in this contest, it will not be because Missouri has failed to do her duty to assist her friends. It is a safe calculation that two thousand squatters have passed over into the promised land from this part of the State within four days."

The Platte Argus (Missouri), in its next issue, said:

> "It is to be admitted that they—the Missourians—have conquered Kansas. Our advice is, let them hold it, or die in the attempt."

A week or two thereafter, rumors were in circulation that the Governor did not indorse, in all respects, the legality of this election; whereupon *The Brunswicker* (Missouri) said:

> "We learn, just as we go to press, that Reeder has refused to give certificates to four of the Councilmen and thirteen members of the House! He has ordered an election to fill their places on the 22d of May.
>
> "This infernal scoundrel will have to be hemped yet."

The Parkville Luminary, issued in Platte County, Missouri, was the only journal on that side of the bor-

[27] Democratic Governor of Missouri, elected in 1860; died a Rebel refugee in Arkansas, 1862.

der that dared and chose to speak a word for the Free-State settlers of Kansas, maintaining their rights under the organic law. Though guarded and careful in its language, it could not escape the discipline meted out in that region to all who favored "Abolition." On the 14th of April, 1855, its office and materials were destroyed by a mob, and its editor constrained to flee for his life.

William Phillips, a Free-State lawyer of Leavenworth, saw fit to sign the protest against the wholesale frauds whereby the election at that place was carried. A few days thereafter, he was seized by a crowd of Missouri ruffians, taken by force to Weston, Mo., eight miles distant, and there tarred and feathered, ridden on a rail, and finally sold at auction to a negro, who was compelled to purchase him.

Gov. Reeder *did* set aside the election in the only six districts from which protests were seasonably forwarded to him, with distinct proof of frauds; whereupon, new elections were held in those districts, and all of them but Leavenworth were carried Free-Soil. Leavenworth, being directly on the Missouri border, was carried pro-Slavery by fraud and violence, as usual. The Free-State men elected at this second election were refused seats by the pro-Slavery majority, and the pro-Slavery men chosen on the regular day of election duly installed in their places.

The Legislature was called to meet at Pawnee City on the Kansas river, nearly a hundred miles west from the border. It was immediately adjourned, over the Governor's veto, to Shawnee Mission, directly on the line of Missouri. It proceeded to pass one act whereby the laws of Missouri generally were adopted and declared laws of Kansas, and other acts specially upholding and fortifying Slavery, whereof the following are but specimens:

"SEC. 1. *Be it enacted by the Governor and Legislative Assembly of Kansas*, That every person, bond or free, who shall be convicted of raising a rebellion or insurrection of slaves, free negroes, or mulattoes, in this Territory, shall suffer death.

"SEC. 2. Every free person, who shall aid or assist in any rebellion or insurrection of slaves, free negroes, or mulattoes, or shall furnish arms, or do any other act in furtherance of such rebellion or insurrection, shall suffer death.

"SEC. 3. If any free person shall, by speaking, writing, or printing, advise, persuade, or induce, any slaves to rebel, conspire against, or murder, any citizen of the Territory, or shall bring into, print, write, publish, or circulate, or cause to be brought into, written, printed, published, or circulated, or shall, knowingly, aid or assist in the bringing into, printing, writing, publishing, or circulating, in the Territory, any book, paper, magazine, pamphlet, or circular, for the purpose of inciting insurrection, rebellion, revolt, or conspiracy, on the part of the slaves, free negroes, or mulattoes, against the citizens of the Territory, or any part of them, such person shall suffer death.

"SEC. 4. If any person shall entice, decoy, or carry away, out of this Territory, any slave belonging to another, with the intent to deprive the owner thereof of the services of such slave, he shall be adjudged guilty of grand larceny, and, on conviction thereof, shall suffer death, or be imprisoned at hard labor for not less than ten years.

"SEC. 5. If any person shall aid or assist in enticing, decoying, or persuading, or carrying away, or sending out of this Territory, any slave belonging to another, with the intent to procure or effect the freedom of such slave, or deprive the owners thereof of the services of such slave, he shall be adjudged guilty of grand larceny, and, on conviction thereof, shall suffer death, or be imprisoned at hard labor for not less than ten years.

"SEC. 12. If any free person, by speaking or writing, shall assert or maintain that persons have not the right to hold slaves in this Territory, or shall introduce into this Territory, print, publish, write, circulate, or cause to be introduced into the Territory, or written, printed, published, and circulated in this Territory, any book, paper, magazine, pamphlet, or circular, containing any denial of the right of persons to hold slaves in this Territory, such person shall be deemed guilty of *felony*, and punished by imprisonment at hard labor for a term of not less than two years.

"SEC. 13. No person who is conscientiously opposed to holding slaves, or who does not admit the right to hold slaves in this Territory, shall sit as a juror on the trial of any prosecution for any violation of any of the sections of this act."

Another act of this remarkable Legislature, entitled "An act to punish persons decoying slaves from their masters," has this unique provision:

"SEC. 3. If any person shall entice, decoy, or carry away, out of any State or other Territory of the United States, any slave belonging to another, with intent to procure or effect the freedom of such slave, or to deprive the owner thereof of the services of such slave, and shall bring such slave into this Territory, he shall be adjudged guilty of grand larceny, in the same manner as if such slave had been enticed, decoyed, or carried away, out of this Territory; and in such case the larceny may be charged to have been committed in any county of this Territory, into or through which such slave shall have been brought by such person, and, on conviction thereof, the person offending shall suffer death."

This Legislature, whose acts were systematically vetoed by Gov. Reeder, but passed over his head, memorialized the President for his removal, which was, in due time, effected. Wilson Shannon,[28] of Ohio, was appointed in his stead. On his way to Kansas, he stopped at Westport, Mo., the headquarters of border ruffianism, and made a speech to those who crowded about him. In that speech, he declared that he considered the Legislature which had recently adjourned to Shawnee Mission a legal assembly, and regarded its laws as binding on the authorities and on every citizen of the Territory. He added:

"To one subject, however, he would allude—Slavery. His official life and character were not unknown to a portion, at least, of the citizens of Kansas. He had no intention of changing his political faith. He thought, with reference to Slavery, that, as Missouri and Kansas were adjoining States, —as much of that immense trade up the Missouri, which was already rivaling the commerce between the United States and some foreign countries, must necessarily lead to a great trade and perpetual intercourse between them,—it would be well if their institutions should harmonize; otherwise, there would be continual quarrels and border feuds. *He was for Slavery in Kansas* (loud cheers)."

The actual settlers of Kansas were little disposed to submit to the impudent and hostile usurpation which had seized their ballot-boxes and imposed on them a fraudulent Legislature. They held a mass convention at Big Springs on the 5th of September, wherein they repudiated the laws and officers imposed on Kansas by the Border-Ruffian election and Legislature, and refused to submit to them. They further resolved not to vote at the election for a Delegate to Congress, which the bogus Legislature had appointed to be held on the 1st of October. They called a Delegate Convention to be held at Topeka on the 19th of that month, whereat an Executive Committee for Kansas Territory was appointed, and an election for Delegate to Congress appointed for the second Tuesday in October. Gov. Reeder was nominated for Delegate. So, two rival elections for Delegate were held on different days, at one of which Whitfield (pro-Slavery), and at the other Reeder (Free-Soil), was chosen Delegate to Congress. And, on the 23d of October, a Constitutional Convention, chosen by the settlers under the Free-State organization aforesaid, assembled at Topeka,

[28] Elected Democratic Governor of Ohio over Thomas Corwin, in 1842,

and formed a Free-State Constitution, under which they asked admission into the Union as a State.

The XXXIVth Congress assembled at Washington, December 3d, 1855, no party having a majority in the House. Several weeks were consumed in fruitless ballotings for Speaker, until, finally, a majority voted—Yeas 113, Nays 104—that a plurality should suffice to elect after three more ballots. Under this rule, Nathaniel P. Banks, Jr., of Massachusetts, received 103 votes to 100 for William Aiken, of South Carolina, and 11 scattering. It was thereupon resolved—Yeas 155, Nays 40—that Mr. Banks had been duly elected Speaker. The House, on the 19th of March, resolved—Yeas 101, Nays 93—to send a Special Committee to Kansas, to inquire into the anarchy by this time prevailing there. That Committee was composed of Messrs. William A. Howard, of Michigan, John Sherman, of Ohio, and Mordecai Oliver, of Missouri, who immediately proceeded to Kansas, and there spent several weeks in taking testimony; which the majority, on their return to Washington, summed up in an able and searching Report. Their conclusions were as follows:

"*First:* That each election in the Territory, held under the organic or alleged Territorial law, has been carried by organized invasions from the State of Missouri, by which the people of the Territory have been prevented from exercising the rights secured to them by the organic law.

"*Second:* That the alleged Territorial Legislature was an illegally constituted body, and had no power to pass valid laws; and their enactments are, therefore, null and void.

"*Third:* That these alleged laws have not, as a general thing, been used to protect persons and property and to punish wrong, but for unlawful purposes.

"*Fourth:* That the election under which the sitting delegate, John W. Whitfield, holds his seat, was not held in pursuance of any valid law, and that it should be regarded only as the expression of the choice of those resident citizens who voted for him.

"*Fifth:* That the election under which the contesting delegate, Andrew H. Reeder, claims his seat, was not held in pursuance of law, and that it should be regarded only as the expression of the choice of the resident citizens who voted for him.

"*Sixth:* That Andrew H. Reeder received a greater number of votes of resident citizens than John W. Whitfield, for Delegate.

"*Seventh:* That, in the present condition of the Territory, a fair election cannot be held without a new census, a stringent and well-guarded election law, the selection of impartial judges, and the presence of United States troops at every place of election.

"*Eighth:* That the various elections held by the people of the Territory preliminary to the formation of the State Government, have been as regular as the disturbed condition of the Territory would allow; and that the Constitution framed by the Convention, held in pursuance of said elections, embodies the will of a majority of the people."

Whitfield held his seat, notwithstanding, to the end of the Congress, despite strenuous efforts by the Republican members to oust him; and a bill admitting Kansas as a State under her Free Constitution was first defeated in the House by 106 Yeas to 107 Nays, but afterward reconsidered and passed by 99 Yeas to 97 Nays. In the Senate, which was strongly pro-Slavery, it was promptly defeated.

Meantime, the settled antagonism in Kansas between the Federal authorities and the Territorial functionaries and enactments recognized and upheld by them on the one side, and the great mass of her people on the other, had resulted in great practical disorders. On the 21st of November, 1855, William Dow, a Free-State settler on the Santa Fé road, near Hickory Point, was shot dead in open day by one Coleman, a pro-Slavery neighbor, in plain sight of several persons. Dow was unarmed, and was set upon by three armed pro-Slavery men, who had no cause of quarrel with him but their difference in politics, although they made a pretense of claiming the land on which he had settled. The murderer fled to Missouri, but immediately returned to Shawnee Mission, and surrendered himself to Gov. Shannon, but was allowed to go at large. The body of the murdered man lay in the road from noon till evening, when Jacob Branson, the Free-State settler with whom he boarded, hearing of his death, went after and recovered it. Five days thereafter, a meeting of Free-State men was held at Hickory Point, at which the murder and its authors were forcibly denounced, and a Committee appointed to bring the murderers to justice. This meeting was made the pretext for bringing on a collision between the people and the authorities. Branson was soon after arrested on an affidavit of one of the three armed men who had compassed the death of Dow, who swore that he was in fear of his life. The arrest was made by a party headed by Samuel J. Jones, postmaster at Westport, Mo., and one of the foremost in the conspiracy by which Kansas had been so far subjugated to "Border-Ruffian" rule through the wholesale corruption of her ballot-boxes. For his zeal and efficiency in this work, the fraudulent Legislature at Shawnee Mission had made him sheriff of Douglas County, wherein are Lawrence and Hickory Point. Of course, the "Free-State" settlers, constituting a large majority of the people of that important county, scouted his assumption of official authority, regarding him as a deadly and dangerous foe. His *posse* was made up of pro-Slavery men, including two of those who had witnessed and abetted the murder of Dow, though Coleman —however active in raising, fitting out, and arming the party—had been persuaded not to accompany it. Branson was found by them asleep in his bed, and taken out by Jones, who professed his intent to take him to Lawrence for examination. Whether he did or did not entertain that purpose, he lingered and drank by the way, so that a party of the neighboring Free-State settlers, fifteen in number, was hastily collected, by which Jones and his party were intercepted near Blanton's Bridge over the Wakarusa, and Branson rescued from Jones's custody. There was no actual collision—not even a gun snapped—but the Free-State men formed across the road in a bright moonlight evening, and called Branson to come over to them, which he did, notwithstanding free threats of shooting on the part of Jones and his followers, answered by a cocking of Sharpe's rifles and revolvers on the other side. Jones, who had been speaking daggers up to this time, wisely concluded to use none, though his party was well armed, and decidedly the more numerous. Branson and his rescuers moved off toward Lawrence, the citadel of Free-State principles, which the discomfited sheriff protested he would soon visit at the head of five thousand men, and "wipe out." He accordingly called on Gov. Shannon to order out three thousand militia, to enable him to "execute the laws," and sent to President Pierce an affidavit that he had been resisted by "forty abolitionists." The call was promptly made by proclamation from the governor, and the whole Missouri border came over to execute vengeance on Lawrence and the Free-State men. This army encamped at Franklin, a pro-Slavery settlement, a few miles from Lawrence, and there remained several days, during which Thomas W. Barber, a Free-State man, returning from Lawrence to his home, seven miles off, was shot dead by some of them, but no other serious damage done. Finally, articles of negotiation and adjustment were agreed upon between Gov. Shannon and the Free-State leaders, in Lawrence, which suspended the feud for the present. The Missourians dispersed, and the troubled land once more had peace.

In the Spring of 1856, the pro-Slavery party on the Kansas border were reënforced by Col. Buford, from Alabama, at the head of a regiment of wild young men, mainly recruited in South Carolina and Georgia. They came in military array, armed, and with the avowed purpose of making Kansas a Slave State at all hazards. On one of their raids into Kansas, a party of Buford's men, who were South Carolinians, took a Mr. Miller prisoner, and, finding that he was a Free-State man, and a native of South Carolina, they gravely tried him for treason to his native State! He was found guilty, and escaped with his life only, losing his horse and money.

Kansas now swarmed with the minions of the Slave Power, intent on her subjugation; their pretext being the enforcement of the laws passed by the fraudulent Legislature.

On the morning of the 21st of May, 1856, Lawrence was surrounded and surprised by various parties of enemies, part of them under Gen. Atchison, who, with the "Platte County Rifles," and two pieces of artillery, approached from Lecompton on the west, while another force, composed in good part of the volunteers from the Atlantic Southern States, under Col. Buford, beleaguered it on the east. They bristled with weapons from the United States Armory, then in charge of the Federal officers in Kansas. Nearly all the pro-Slavery leaders then in Kansas, or hovering along the Missouri border, were on hand; among them, Col. Titus, from Florida, Col. Wilkes, from South Carolina, Gen. Stringfellow, a Virginian, Col. Boone, hailing from Westport, and many others of local and temporary fame. The entire force was about 800 strong, having possession of Mount Oread, a hill which commanded the town. The pretext for this raid was a desire to serve legal processes in Kansas, although deputy marshal Fain, who held a part of those processes, had been in Lawrence the evening before, and served two writs without a sign of resistance, as on several previous occasions. He now rode into the town with ten men, and arrested two leading Free-State citizens, no one making objection. Meantime, the *posse*, so called, were busy in the suburbs, breaking open houses and robbing their inmates. Fain remained in town until afternoon, eating dinner with his party at the principal hotel, but neglecting to pay for it; then returned to the camp on the hill, and was succeeded by "Sheriff Jones" of that county, whose authority, being derived from the sham Legislature, the people did not recognize. Jones rode into town at the head of twenty men, at three P. M., and demanded that all the arms should be given up to him, on pain of a bombardment. The people, unprepared to resist, consented to surrender their artillery, consisting of a twelve-pound howitzer, and four smooth-bore pieces, carrying each a pound ball. All these had been buried some days before, but were now dug up and made over to Jones. A few muskets were likewise surrendered by their owners. The pro-Slavery army now marched down the hill, and entered the south end of the town, where Atchison made a speech to them, declaring that the Free-State Hotel and the two Free-State printing-offices must be destroyed. "Sheriff Jones" declared that he had an order to that effect from Judge Lecompte, of the Federal Court. The whole force accordingly marched into the heart of the town, destroyed the printing-offices, and fired some fifty rounds from their cannon at the Free-State Hotel, which, being solidly built of stone, was not much damaged thereby. Four kegs of gun-powder were then placed in it and fired, but only two of them exploded, making little impression. Fire was now applied to the building, and it was burnt to the bare and blackened walls. The dwelling of Gov. Robinson[29] was next set on fire, and, though the flames were twice extinguished, it was finally consumed. The total loss to the citizens of Lawrence by that day's robbery and arson was estimated at $150,000. None of them were killed or wounded; but one of the ruffians shot himself badly, and another was killed by a brick or stone, knocked by one of their cannon from the upper story of the Free-State Hotel.

Such were the beginnings of the so-called "Kansas War," a desultory, wasteful, but not very bloody conflict, which continued, with alternations of activity and quiet, throughout the next year. One of its most noted incidents is known as the "battle of Black Jack," wherein 28 Free-State men, led by old John Brown, of Osawatomie, fought and defeated, on the open prairie, 56 "border ruffians," headed by Capt. H. Clay Pate, from Virginia, who professed to be an officer under Marshal Donaldson. It terminated in the surrender of Pate and all that remained of his band, twenty-one men, beside the wounded, with twenty-three horses and mules, wagons, provisions, camp-equipage, and a considerable quantity of plunder, obtained just before by sacking a little Free-State settlement, known as Palmyra.

The Legislature chosen under the Free-State Constitution was summoned to meet at Topeka on the 4th of July, 1856, and its members assembled accordingly, but were not allowed to organize, Col. Sumner,[30] with a force of regulars, dispersing them by order of President Pierce.

The village of Osawatomie, in the southern part of the Territory, was sacked and burned on the 5th of June by a pro-Slavery force, headed

[29] Elected Governor under the embryo organization, by the great body of her settlers, of Kansas as a Free State.

[30] Since known as Maj.-Gen. Edwin V. Sumner: fought bravely in several battles of the War: died at Syracuse, N. Y., early in 1863.

by Gen. Whitfield. But few of the male citizens were at home, and there was no resistance.

Leavenworth, being directly on the border, and easily accessible from a populous portion of Missouri, was especially exposed to outrages. It was long under the control of the pro-Slavery party, being a military post, and a point whence overland trains and mails were dispatched, and at which a vast Federal patronage was concentrated. The office of *The Territorial Register* (Free-State) was destroyed by a Missouri band, December 20, 1855. Many collisions and murders occurred here, and in the vicinity; and at length, on the recurrence of the municipal election (September 1, 1856), a large force, mainly of Missourians, took possession of the town; and, under the pretense of searching for arms, plundered and ravaged as they chose. William Phillips, a lawyer, refused to submit to their search, and stood on his defense. He killed two of his assailants, but was finally killed himself; while his brother, who aided him in his defense, had his arm shattered by a bullet. Phillips's house was burned, with several others, and every known Free-State man put on board a steamboat and sent down the river. It was boasted by the Missouri journals that not a single "abolition vote" was cast at that election!

Meantime, the emigrants flocking to Kansas from the Free States were arrested on their passage through Missouri and turned back: cannon being planted along the Missouri river to stop the ascending steamboats for this purpose. Not many of these emigrants were actually plundered, save of their passage-money, which was in no case returned. A large party was finally made up of those whose progress to their intended homes had been thus obstructed, who proceeded thither slowly and toilsomely, by a circuitous route through Iowa and Nebraska; but who, on entering Kansas, were met by a Federal military force, and all their arms taken from them.

Yet the immigration continued; so that, while the office-holders, the military, and all the recognized power and authority, were on the side of Slavery, the Free-State preponderance among the settlers constantly increased. The pro-Slavery forces made strong incursions or raids into the Territory from time to time, but subsided into Missouri after a few days; and, while a good share of the fighting, with most of the burning and plundering, was done by them, nearly all the building, the clearing, the plowing, and the planting, were the work of Free-State men. Meantime, dissipation, exposure, and all manner of irregularities, were constantly thinning the ranks of the pro-Slavery volunteers from the South, while many of the better class among them, disgusted and remorseful, abandoned their evil work, and shrank away to some region wherein they were less generally detested. Under all its persecutions and desolations, Kansas was steadily maturing and hardening into the bone and sinew of a Free State not only, but of one fitted by education and experience to be an apostle of the gospel of Universal Freedom.

The Democratic National Convention for 1856 met at Cincinnati on the 2d of June. John E. Ward, of Georgia, presided over its deliberations. On the first ballot, its votes for Presidential candidate were cast, for JAMES BUCHANAN, 135; Pierce, 122; Douglas, 33; Cass, 5. Buchanan gained pretty steadily, and Pierce lost; so that, on the ninth ballot, the vote stood: Buchanan, 147; Pierce, 87; Douglas, 56; Cass, 7. On the sixteenth, Mr. Buchanan had 168; Mr. Douglas, 121. And, on the seventeenth, Mr. Buchanan received the whole number, 296 votes, and was nominated. On the first ballot for Vice-President, John A. Quitman, of Mississippi, received the highest vote—59; but, on the second, his name was withdrawn, and JOHN C. BRECKINRIDGE, of Kentucky, was unanimously nominated.

The Convention, in its platform, after adopting nearly all the material resolves of its two immediate predecessors, unanimously

"1. *Resolved*, That, claiming fellowship with and desiring the coöperation of all who regard the preservation of the Union under the Constitution as the paramount issue, and repudiating all sectional parties and platforms concerning domestic Slavery, which seek to embroil the States and incite to treason and armed resistance to law in the Territories, and whose avowed purpose, if consummated, must end in civil war and disunion, the American Democracy recognize and adopt the principles contained in the organic laws establishing the Territories of Kansas and Nebraska, as embodying the only sound and safe solution of the Slavery question, upon which the great National idea of the people of this whole country can repose in its determined conservation of the Union, and non-interference of Congress with Slavery in the Territories or in the District of Columbia.

"2. That this was the basis of the Compromises of 1850, confirmed by both the Democratic and Whig parties in National Conventions; ratified by the people in the election of 1852, and rightly applied to the organization of the Territories in 1854.

"3. That, by the uniform application of the Democratic principle to the organization of Territories, and the admission of new States with or without domestic Slavery, as they may elect, the equal rights of all the States will be preserved intact, the original compacts of the Constitution maintained inviolate, and the perpetuity and expansion of the Union insured to its utmost capacity of embracing, in peace and harmony, every future American State that may be constituted or annexed with a republican form of government."

The dissolution of the Whig party, commenced by the imposition of the Southern platform on its National Convention of 1852, was consummated by the eager participation of most of its Southern members of Congress in the repudiation of the Missouri Compromise by the passage of the Kansas-Nebraska bill. Those, of whatever party in the past, who emphatically condemned that repudiation, and who united on that basis to ignore past political denominations, with a view to united action in the future, were first known simply as "anti-Nebraska," but gradually, and almost spontaneously, assumed the designation of "Republicans." As such, they carried most of the Free State elections of 1854, but were less decidedly successful in those of 1855. Their first National Convention was held at Pittsburgh, Pa., on the 22d of February, 1856; but no nominations were there made. Their nominating Convention met at Philadelphia on the 17th of June, Col. Henry S. Lane, of Indiana, presiding. JOHN C. FREMONT, of California, was nominated for President on the first ballot, receiving 359 votes to 196 for John McLean, of Ohio. WILLIAM L. DAYTON, of New Jersey, received 259 votes on the informal ballot, to 110 for Abraham Lincoln and 180 scattering, for Vice-President. Mr. Dayton was thereupon unanimously nominated. The more material resolves of this Convention are as follows:

"*Resolved*, That, with our republican fathers, we hold it to be a self-evident truth, that all men are endowed with the inalienable rights to life, liberty, and the pursuit of happiness; and that the primary object and ulterior design of our Federal Government were, to secure these rights to all persons within its exclusive jurisdiction; that, as our republican fathers, when they had abolished Slavery in all our National territory, ordained that no person should be deprived of life, liberty, or property, without due process of law, it becomes our duty to maintain this provision of the Constitution against all attempts to violate it, for the purpose of establishing Slavery in any territory of the United States, by positive legislation, prohibiting its existence and extension therein. That we deny the authority of Congress, of a Territorial Legislature, of any individual or association of individuals, to give legal existence to Slavery in any Territory of the United States, while the present Constitution shall be maintained.

"*Resolved*, That the Constitution confers upon Congress sovereign power over the Territories of the United States for their government; and that, in the exercise of this power, it is both the right and the duty of Congress to prohibit in the Territories those twin relics of barbarism—Polygamy and Slavery."

An "American" National Convention was held at Philadelphia on the 22d of February; all the States represented but Maine, Vermont, Georgia, and South Carolina. An "American" National Council (secret) had met three days before in the same place, and adopted a platform. The following plank is the most essential:

"The recognition of the right of native-born and naturalized citizens of the United States, permanently residing in any Territory thereof, to frame their Constitution and laws, and to regulate their domestic and social affairs in their own mode, subject only to the provisions of the Federal Constitution, with the privilege of admission into the Union whenever they have the requisite population for one Representative in Congress: *Provided, always*, that none but those who are citizens of the United States, under the Constitution and laws thereof, and who have a fixed residence in any such Territory, ought to participate in the formation of the Constitution, or in the enactment of laws, for said Territory or State."

This Council proceeded to condemn the National Administration, among other things, for "rëopening sectional agitation by the repeal of the Missouri compromise." This was not satisfactory to the "anti-Nebraska" members of the nominating Convention; on whose behalf, Mr. Killinger, of Pennsylvania, proposed the following:

"*Resolved*, That the National Council has no authority to prescribe a Platform of principles for this Nominating Convention; and that we will nominate for President and Vice-President no men who are not in favor of interdicting the introduction of Slavery into territory north of 36° 30′ by Congressional action."

This resolve was laid on the table, by 141 votes to 59. The "anti-Nebraska" delegates, to the number of about fifty, thereupon withdrew from the Convention. On the first ballot for President, MILLARD FILLMORE, of New York, received 71 votes; George Law, of N. Y., 27; and there were 45 scattering. On the next ballot, Mr. Fillmore received 179 to 64 for all others, and was nominated. On the first ballot for Vice-President, ANDREW JACKSON DONELSON, of Tennessee, received 181 votes to 24 scattering, and was unanimously nominated.

The nomination of Mr. Fillmore was ratified by a Whig Convention, which met at Baltimore on the 17th of September—Edward Bates, of Missouri, presiding.

Mr. Fillmore was absent in Europe when the American nomination was made; but, returning early in July, took ground emphatically against the Republican organization and effort. In his speech at Albany, he said:

"We see a political party presenting candidates for the Presidency and Vice-Presidency, selected, for the first time, from the Free States alone, with the avowed purpose of electing these candidates by the suffrages of one part of the Union only, to rule over the whole United States. Can it be possible that those who are engaged in such a measure can have seriously reflected upon the consequences which must inevitably follow, in case of success? Can they have the madness or the folly to believe that our Southern brethren would submit to be governed by such a Chief Magistrate? Would he be required to follow the same rule prescribed by those who elected him in making his appointments? If a man living south of Mason and Dixon's line be not worthy to be President or Vice-President, would it be proper to select one from the same quarter as one of his Cabinet Council, or to represent the nation in a foreign country? Or, indeed, to collect the revenue, or administer the laws of the United States? If not, what new rule is the President to adopt in selecting men for office that the people themselves discard in selecting *him?* These are serious but practical questions; and, in order to appreciate them fully, it is only necessary to turn the tables upon ourselves. Suppose that the South, having the majority of the electoral votes, should declare that they would only have slaveholders for President and Vice-President, and should elect such by their exclusive suffrages to rule over us at the North. Do you think we would submit to it? No, not for a moment. And do you believe that your Southern brethren are less sensitive on this subject than you are, or less jealous of their rights? If you do, let me tell you that you are mistaken. And, therefore, you must see that, if this sectional party succeeds, it leads inevitably to the destruction of this beautiful fabric, reared by our forefathers, cemented by their blood, and bequeathed to us as a priceless inheritance."

This speech is memorable not merely for its gross misapprehension of the grounds and motives of the Republican movement—representing its purposes as violent, aggressive, and sectional, when they date back to 1784, and trace their paternity to Jefferson, a Southron and a slaveholder—but because this was the first declaration by a Northern statesman of mark that the success of the Republicans would not only incite, but justify, a Southern rebellion. The facts that the "National Republicans," in 1828, supported John Q. Adams and Richard Rush—both from Free States—while their antagonists supported Andrew Jackson and John C. Calhoun, both slaveholders, and thus secured nearly every elector from the Slave States, are conveniently ignored by Mr. Fillmore.

The Presidential contest of 1856 was ardent and animated up to the October elections, wherein the States of Pennsylvania and Indiana were carried by the Democrats, rendering the election of Buchanan and Breckinridge a moral certainty. In despite, however, of that certainty, the Republicans carried New York by a plurality of 80,000, with the six New England States, and Ohio, Michigan, Wisconsin, and Iowa—giving Gen. Fremont 114 electoral votes. Mr. Buchanan carried Pennsylvania, New Jersey, Indiana, Illinois, California, with all the Slave States but Maryland, which voted alone for Mr. Fillmore. New Jersey, Illinois, and California, gave each a plurality only, not a majority, of her popular vote for the successful candidate. In the aggregate, Mr. Buchanan received 1,838,169 votes; Col. Fremont 1,341,264; and Mr. Fillmore 874,534: so that Mr. Buchanan, though he had a very decided plurality, lacked 377,629 votes of a majority over both his competitors. Of the electors, however, he had 174—a clear majority of 60. Major Breckinridge was, of course, chosen Vice-President by the same vote.

The disturbed and distracted condition of Kansas, resulting from the efforts of her Missouri neighbors to force Slavery upon her against her will, necessarily attracted the early attention of Mr. Buchanan's Administration. John W. Geary—the third or fourth of her Territorial Governors—had recently resigned and left in disgust, and the selection of a successor was an obvious and urgent duty. The President's choice fell on Hon. Robert J. Walker, formerly Senator from Mississippi, and Secretary of the Treasury under President Polk, who accepted the post with considerable reluctance. Frederick P. Stanton, for ten years a representative in Congress from Tennessee, was associated with him as Secretary.

Meantime, the double-headed action in Kansas proceeding, an immense majority of the settlers, though prevented by Federal force from effecting such an organization as they desired, utterly refused to recognize the Legislature chosen by the Missouri invaders, or the officers thereby appointed: consequently, each party held its own conventions and elections independent of the other. The pro-Slavery Legislature called a Constitutional Convention in 1857, which met at Lecompton on the first Monday of September. That Convention proceeded, of course, to form a pro-Slavery Constitution, which they pretended to submit to the people at an election held on the 21st of December following. But at this remarkable election, held expressly to ratify or reject a State Constitution, no one was allowed to vote against that Constitution. The vote was to be taken "For the Constitution *with* Slavery" or "For the Constitution *without* Slavery"—no others to be allowed or counted. It was accordingly so taken, and the following was the return:

For the Constitution *with* Slavery.........6,266.
For the Constitution *without* Slavery...... 567.

So the Constitution *with* Slavery was adopted. But, meantime, an election had been held, on the first Monday in October, for a Territorial Legislature under the bogus laws; and at this election most of the Free-State men, trusting to the assurances of Gov. Walker, had voted. Over 11,000 votes were polled, of which 1,600 were taken at a little precinct known as Oxford, on the Missouri border, where there were but 43 voters; and 1,200 were returned from McGee County, where no poll was opened. But, notwithstanding these enormous frauds, the Free-State preponderance was so decided that it carried the Legislature and elected a delegate to Congress. This Legislature, whose legality was now unquestioned, passed an act submitting the Lecompton Constitution to a vote of the people for or against it, on the 4th of January, 1858. This Constitution provided that "the rights of property in slaves now in the Territory shall in no manner be interfered with," and precluded any amendment prior to the year 1864; after which, amendments could be made with the concurrence of both houses of the legislature, and a majority of all the citizens of the State. Thus, while the people had not been allowed to vote *against* the Constitution, their seeming privilege of voting *for* it without Slavery was a delusion. In any case, Slavery was to have been protected and perpetuated. But, at the election authorized by the new Legislature, which the Missourians did not choose to recognize as valid, and therefore did not come over to vote at, the full poll was returned as follows:

For the Lecompton Constitution *with* Slavery,	138;
" " " " *without* "	24;
Against the Lecompton Constitution,	10,226;

giving a majority of over 10,000 against the said Constitution in any shape.

The XXXVth Congress organized at Washington, December 7, 1857. There being a large Democratic majority, Col. James L. Orr, of S. C., was elected Speaker. Mr. Buchanan, in his Annual, as also in a Special Message,[31] urged Congress to accept and ratify the Lecompton Constitution. Senator Douglas took strong ground against it. The Senate[32] passed—Yeas 32, Nays 25—a bill accepting this Constitution. But the House[33] adopted a substitute, prepared by Senator Crittenden, of Kentucky, and proposed in the House by Mr. Montgomery, a Douglas Democrat from Pennsylvania. This substitute required a re-submission of that Constitution to the people of Kansas, under such provisions and precautions as should insure a fair vote thereon. It was adopted by the House as a substitute for the Senate bill—Yeas, 92 Republicans, 22 Douglas Democrats, 6 Americans—total 120; Nays, 104 Democrats, 8 Americans—total 112. This amendment was rejected by the Senate, who asked a Committee of Conference; which, on motion of Mr. English, of Indiana, who had thus far acted with the Douglas men, was granted by 109 Yeas to 108 Nays. The bill reported from the Conference Committee proposed a submission to the people of Kansas of a proposition on the part of Congress to limit and curtail the grants of public lands and other advantages stipulated in behalf of said State in the Lecompton Constitution; and, in case of their voting to reject said proposition, then a new Convention was to be held and a new Constitution framed. This bill passed both Houses;[34] and under it the people of Kansas, on the 3d of August, voted, by an overwhelming majority, to reject the proposition: which was, in effect, to reject the Lecompton Constitution.

The Territorial Legislature had now passed completely into the hands of the Free-State party, and, under its guidance, a new Constitutional Convention assembled at Wyandot on the first Tuesday in March, 1859; the people having voted, by a majority of 3,881, to hold such Convention. The attempt to make Kansas a Slave State was now formally abandoned in favor of an effort to organize it as a Democratic Free State. This, however, failed—the Convention consisting of thirty-five Republicans to seventeen Democrats. A Free-State Constitution was duly framed, whereby the western boundary of the State was fixed at the twenty-third parallel of longitude west from Washington. This Constitution was adopted at an election held on the first Tuesday in October, whereat the majority for ratification was about 4,000. The first undisputed State election was held under it on the 6th of December following, when Republican officers and member of Congress were elected on a light vote, by majorities ranging from 2,000 to 2,500.

The Constitution framed by the

[31] February 2, 1858. [32] March 23, 1858. [33] April 1, 1858. [34] April 30, 1858.

Convention at Wyandot was laid before the House, February 10th, 1860. On the 15th, Mr. Grow, of Pennsylvania, introduced a bill for the admission of Kansas into the Union; which was read a first and a second time, and referred to the Committee on Territories. This bill was reported to the House from that Committee, and, on the 11th of April, it passed, under the Previous Question: Yeas 134; Nays 73. But the Senate, which was very strongly Democratic, stubbornly refused (32 to 27) to take it up, and adjourned, leaving Kansas still a Territory: so that, though every way qualified for and entitled to admission, she was remanded into territorial vassalage by the very men who had been so eager to admit her, two years before, when her population and every other element of strength and stability were considerably less. She was thus denied a voice in the election for President in 1860. At the next session of Congress, however, her application was renewed; and on the same day[35] that Messrs. Jefferson Davis, Clement C. Clay, Fitzpatrick, Mallory, and others, abandoned their seats and the Capitol to take part in the Southern Rebellion, a bill admitting her as a Free State under the Wyandot Constitution was called up by Gov. Seward, and passed the Senate: Yeas 36; Nays 16. One week later, on motion of Mr. Grow, of Pennsylvania, it was taken up in the House, out of regular order, by 119 to 42, and passed.

And thus, on the very threshold of our great struggle—no serious effort having been made by the slaveholders to colonize or conquer Nebraska—the arduous contest opened by Mr. Dixon's proposition to repeal the Missouri Restriction, was closed by the admission of Free Kansas as the thirty-fourth State of our Federal Union.

XVIII.

THE DRED SCOTT CASE.

Dred Scott, a negro, was, previously to 1834, held as a slave in Missouri by Dr. Emerson, a surgeon in the U. S. Army. In that year, the doctor was transferred to the military post at Rock Island, in the State of Illinois, and took his slave with him. Here, Major Taliaferro (also of the army) had, in 1835, in his service a black known as Harriet, whom he likewise held as his slave. The major was transferred that year to Fort Snelling, on the other side of the Missisippi, in what is now known as Minnesota, but was then an unorganized territory of the United States, expressly covered by the Slavery Prohibition included in the Missouri Compromise of 1820. Dr. Emerson was likewise transferred to Fort Snelling in 1836, and here bought Harriet of Major Taliaferro, and held her and Dred as his slaves; they being married to each other with his con-

[35] January 21, 1861.

sent soon after his arrival at the Fort. Two children were born to them; Eliza, in 1838, on board the steamboat Gipsy, on their way down the Mississippi, but still north of the Missouri line; Lizzie, seven years later, at Jefferson Barracks, in the State of Missouri. The doctor, with Dred, Harriet, and Eliza, returned thence to St. Louis, and he there continued to hold them as his slaves, until he sold them, several years later, to John F. A. Sanford, of the State and City of New York. Finally, Dred brought suit for his freedom, on the above state of facts, in the State Circuit Court of St. Louis County, Missouri, and obtained a verdict and judgment in his favor. But this was reversed by a judgment on a writ of error to the Supreme Court of that State, from which an appeal was taken to the courts of the United States, and the case came to trial in May, 1854. Having been fully heard by the Supreme Court at Washington, that court was about to decide it at its term of 1855–6; but the controlling majority of its Judges concluded, in view of the pending Presidential election, and the strong excitement which the Nebraska bill and the Kansas outrages had aroused throughout the Free States, to defer rendering judgment until its next session. It is quite probable that its action in the premises, if made public at the time originally intended, would have reversed the issue of that Presidential election. The eminent Chief Justice John Marshall, who had so long presided over that tribunal, and whose opinions had won for it a weight and influence rarely accorded to any court, died in 1835 at the ripe age of eighty. None of the Judges appointed by any predecessor of Gen. Jackson survived. Of the nine who now composed that august tribunal, eight had been selected from the ranks of the Democratic party, and most of them for other considerations than those of eminent legal ability or acquirements. John McLean, of Ohio, was placed on the bench, in 1829, by Gen. Jackson, in order to make room for a Postmaster-General who would remove from office the postmasters who had supported Mr. Adams and appoint Jacksonians to their places; which McLean—having been continued in office by Mr. Adams, though himself for Jackson—could not decently do. Roger B. Taney, of Maryland, was likewise appointed by Jackson in 1836, as a reward for his services in accepting the post of Secretary of the Treasury and removing the Federal deposits from the United States Bank, upon the dismissal of William J. Duane, of Pennsylvania, for refusing to make such removal. Mr. Taney, born in 1777, was an ultra Federalist previously to his becoming a Jacksonian, but always a devotee of prerogative and power. Of his associates, beside Judge McLean, only Samuel Nelson, of New York, and Benjamin R. Curtis, of Massachusetts, were ever presumed qualified, either by nature or attainments, for judicial eminence.

The decision and opinions of this Court, in the case of Dred Scott, had not been made public when Mr. Buchanan was inaugurated;[1] but that gentleman had undoubtedly been favored with a private intimation of their scope and bearing:

[1] March 4th, 1857.

hence the following prelusive suggestions of his Inaugural Address:

"We have recently passed through a Presidential contest, in which the passions of our fellow-citizens were excited to the highest degree by questions of deep and vital importance; but, when the people proclaimed their will, the tempest at once subsided, and all was calm.

"The voice of the majority, speaking in the manner prescribed by the Constitution, was heard; and instant submission followed. Our own country could alone have exhibited so grand and striking a spectacle of the capacity of man for self-government.

"What a happy conception, then, was it for Congress to apply this simple rule—that the will of the majority shall govern—to the settlement of the question of domestic Slavery in the territories! Congress is neither 'to legislate Slavery into any territory or State, nor to exclude it therefrom, but to leave the people thereof perfectly free to form and regulate their domestic institutions in their own way, subject only to the Constitution of the United States.' As a natural consequence, Congress has already prescribed that, when the Territory of Kansas shall be admitted as a State, it 'shall be received into the Union with or without Slavery, as their Constitution may prescribe at the time of their admission.'

"A difference of opinion has arisen in regard to the point of time when the people of a territory shall decide this question for themselves.

"This is, happily, a matter of but little practical importance. Besides, it is a judicial question, which legitimately belongs to the Supreme Court of the United States, before whom it is now pending, *and will, it is understood, be speedily and finally settled.* To their decision, in common with all good citizens, I shall cheerfully submit."

Not many days thereafter, the decision and opinions thus heralded, and commended as a new and admirable exemplification of "Popular Sovereignty," and the "happy conception" embodied in the Kansas-Nebraska bill, were revealed, with due trumpeting and laudation, to an expectant world. Chief Justice Taney, in pronouncing the decision of the Court, which nullified the Missouri Restriction, or *any* restriction by Congress on the boundless diffusion of Slavery throughout the territories of the Union, commenced by denying to Dred Scott, or to any person "whose ancestors were imported to this country and sold as slaves," any right to sue in a court of the United States. He said:

"The question before us is, whether the class of persons described in the plea in abatement compose a portion of this people, and are constituent members of this sovereignty? We think they are not, and that they are not included, and were not intended to be included, under the word 'citizens' in the Constitution, and can therefore claim none of the rights and privileges which that instrument provides for and secures to citizens of the United States. On the contrary, they were at that time considered as a subordinate and inferior class of beings, who had been subjugated by the dominant race, and, whether emancipated or not, yet remained subject to their authority, and had no rights or privileges but such as those who held the power and the Government might choose to grant them."

The Chief Justice proceeds to affirm, not only that no persons who had been, or whose ancestors had been, slaves, were regarded as citizens previously to, or at the time of, adopting the Federal Constitution, but that no State has, or can have, any right to confer citizenship on such persons. Bearing in mind the citations from our revolutionary and *post*-revolutionary history, embodied in the earlier chapters of this work,[2] the reader will be puzzled to decide whether Law, Humanity, or History, is most flagrantly defied in that portion of Chief Justice Taney's opinion which follows:

"In the opinion of the Court, the legislation and history of the times, and the language used in the Declaration of Independence, show, that neither the class of persons who had been imported as slaves, nor their descendants, whether they had become

[2] See pages 51–2, 107–8, etc., etc.

free or not, were then acknowledged as a part of the people, nor intended to be included in the general words used in that memorable instrument.

"It is difficult at this day to realize the state of public opinion in relation to that unfortunate race, which prevailed in the civilized and enlightened portions of the world at the time of the Declaration of Independence, and when the Constitution of the United States was framed and adopted. But the public history of every European nation displays it, in a manner too plain to be mistaken.

"They had, for more than a century before, been regarded as beings of an inferior order, and altogether unfit to associate with the white race, either in social or political relations; and so far inferior that *they had no rights which the white man was bound to respect;* and that the negro might justly and lawfully be reduced to Slavery for his benefit. He was bought and sold, and treated as an ordinary article of merchandise and traffic, whenever a profit could be made by it. This opinion was at that time fixed and universal in the civilized portion of the white race. It was regarded as an axiom in morals, as well as in politics, which no one thought of disputing, or supposed to be open to dispute; and men of every grade and position in society daily and habitually acted upon it in their private pursuits, as well as in matters of public concern, without doubting for a moment the correctness of this opinion.

"And in no nation was this opinion more firmly fixed or more uniformly acted upon than by the English Government and English people. They not only seized them on the coast of Africa, and sold them or held them in Slavery for their own use, but they took them as ordinary articles of merchandise to every country where they could make a profit on them, and were far more engaged in this commerce than any other nation in the world.

"The opinion thus entertained and acted upon in England was naturally impressed upon the colonies they founded on this side of the Atlantic. And, accordingly, a negro of the African race was regarded by them as an article of property, and held, and bought and sold as such, in every one of the thirteen colonies which united in the Declaration of Independence, and afterward formed the Constitution of the United States. The slaves were more or less numerous in the different colonies, as slave labor was found more or less profitable. But no one seems to have doubted the correctness of the prevailing opinion of the time."

The immortal language of the preämble to the Declaration of Independence, wherein "life, liberty, and the pursuit of happiness," are proclaimed the self-evident, inalienable rights of *all* men, might well stagger the most brazen and subtle attorney, but not a case-hardened Chief Justice. He tosses them aside in this fashion:

"The general words above quoted would seem to embrace the whole human family; and, if they were used in a similar instrument at this day, would be so understood. But it is too clear to dispute, that the enslaved African race were not intended to be included, and formed no part of the people who framed and adopted this Declaration; for, if the language, as understood in that day, would embrace them, the conduct of the distinguished men who framed the Declaration of Independence would have been utterly and flagrantly inconsistent with the principles they asserted; and, instead of the sympathy of mankind, to which they so confidently appealed, they would have deserved and received universal rebuke and reprobation.

"Yet the men who framed this declaration were great men—high in literary acquirements—high in their sense of honor—and incapable of asserting principles inconsistent with those on which they were acting. They perfectly understood the meaning of the language they used, and how it would be understood by others; and they knew that it would not, in any part of the civilized world, be supposed to embrace the negro race; which, by common consent, had been excluded from civilized Governments and the family of nations, and doomed to Slavery. They spoke and acted according to the then established doctrines and principles, and in the ordinary language of the day, and no one misunderstood them. The unhappy black race were separated from the white by indelible marks, and laws long before established, and were *never thought of or spoken of except as property*,[3] and when the claims of the owner or the profit of the trader were supposed to need protection.

"This state of public opinion had undergone no change when the Constitution was adopted, as is equally evident from its provisions and language."

Mr. Taney here deliberately asserts that "the unhappy black race"

[3] See, in refutation of this, the views of Henry Laurens, Dr. Hopkins, La Fayette, Washington, Jefferson, etc., as quoted in the earlier chapters of this work.

were "never thought of or spoken of except as property," before and when the Constitution was adopted, "as is equally evident from its provisions and language." Had he been asked to say, then, what the Constitution *can* mean by declaring (Art. I. § 2) that "representatives and direct taxes shall be apportioned among the several States which may be included in this Union, according to their respective numbers; which shall be determined by adding to the whole number of *free* persons, including those bound to service for a term of years, and excluding Indians not taxed, three-fifths of *all other persons*," he might have hesitated for an answer, but never blushed; since, very soon after this, he proceeds to argue that, when this same article of the Constitution (§ 9) declares that Congress shall not, prior to the year 1808, prohibit "the migration or importation of such *persons* as any of the States now existing shall think proper to admit," but a tax or duty may be imposed "on such importation, not exceeding ten dollars for each *person*," he coolly says, the importation which it thus sanctions, "was unquestionably of all *persons* of the race of which we are now speaking."

The Chief Justice proceeds to defy history and common sense by asserting that, in the days of the fathers, even emancipated blacks "were identified in the public mind with the race to which they belonged, and *regarded as a part of the slave population rather than the free*." He is so kind as to tell the people of the Free States that the efforts of Wesley, and Edwards, and Hopkins, and Franklin, and Jay, and all the other eminent divines, patriots, and statesmen, who appealed to their consciences and their hearts against Slavery as unjust and cruel, had no existence, or, at least, no effect—that Slavery was abolished by our fathers, not at all because it was felt to be wrong, but because it was found to be unprofitable in this particular locality. On this point, he says:

"It is very true that, in that portion of the Union where the labor of the negro race was found to be unsuited to the climate and unprofitable to the master, but few slaves were held at the time of the Declaration of Independence; and, when the Constitution was adopted, it had entirely worn out in one of them, and measures had been taken for its gradual abolition in several others. But this change had not been produced by any change of opinion in relation to this race; but because it was discovered, from experience, that slave labor was unsuited to the climate and productions of these States: for some of these States where it had ceased, or nearly ceased, to exist, were actively engaged in the Slave-Trade; procuring cargoes on the coast of Africa, and transporting them for sale to those parts of the Union where their labor was found to be profitable, and suited to the climate and productions. And this traffic was openly carried on, and fortunes accumulated by it, without reproach from the people of the States where they resided. And it can hardly be supposed that, in the States where it was then countenanced in its worst form—that is, in the seizure and transportation—the people could have regarded those who were emancipated as entitled to equal rights with themselves."

How utterly mistaken this is, the recollection of thousands will establish. The very few persons at the North who were openly engaged in this slave-trading, fifty or eighty years ago, though shrewd, wealthy, and powerful, were never held in good repute; and the stain of their nefarious traffic still sullies their innocent descendants. Bad as our great marts may be, and blinded by the lust of gain as our trading classes may seem, there never was an hour when it was desirable to be known on the exchange of New York or Boston as a slave-trader; and no man to-day blazons the fact that the wealth he inherits was obtained by successful ventures on the Slave-Coast.

Mr. Taney proceeds to show, after his fashion, that no State can make its black people citizens, because that would be very inconvenient and unsafe for the slaveholders of other States. "For," he says:

> "If they were so received, and entitled to the privileges and immunities of citizens, it would exempt them from the operation of the special laws and from the police regulations which they considered to be necessary for their own safety. It would give to persons of the negro race, who were recognized as citizens in any one State of the Union, the right to enter every other State whenever they pleased, singly or in companies, without pass or passport; and, without obstruction, to sojourn there as long as they pleased; to go where they pleased at every hour of the day or night without molestation, unless they committed some violation of law for which a white man would be punished; and it would give them the full liberty of speech in public and private upon all subjects upon which its own citizens might speak; to hold public meetings upon political affairs, and to keep and carry arms wherever they went. And all of this would be done in the face of the subject race of the same color, both free and slaves, and inevitably producing discontent and insubordination among them, and endangering the peace and safety of the State."

Having thus determined, to his own satisfaction, that Dred Scott, being a negro and descended from slaves, had no right to bring this suit, and no standing in the Federal Courts, and that the Court has no authority in the premises, the Chief Justice proceeds to *take* jurisdiction, in order to obtain a footing from which to nullify the Missouri Restriction and deny the right of Congress to exclude Slavery from any territory. To this end, he affirms that that clause of the Constitution (Art. IV. § 3) which says "Congress shall have power to dispose of and make all needful rules and regulations respecting the territory or other property belonging to the United States," applies only to such territory as belonged to the United States at the time the Constitution was framed! The territory covered by the Missouri Restriction, having all been acquired *since* that time, is not, in his view, subject to this provision.

He proceeds to affirm that, by the mere fact of our acquiring territory, "the Government and the citizen both enter it under the authority of the Constitution;" in other words, that the Constitution takes effect upon any territory that our Government may acquire, at the instant of such acquisition, in such manner as to create and uphold the right of every slaveholder to take his slaves thither and hold them there as property. But this particular and only clause of the Constitution relating to territory has no application or subsisting validity; because, if it had, it might enable Congress to prohibit Slavery therein. The Chief Justice, therefore, nullifies the Missouri Restriction, and all kindred restrictions, in the following terms:

> "Upon these considerations, it is the opinion of the Court that the act of Congress which prohibited a citizen from holding property of this kind in the territory of the United States north of the line therein mentioned, is not warranted by the Constitution, and it is therefore void; and that neither Dred Scott himself, nor any of his family, were made free by being carried into this territory, even if they had been carried there by the owner, with the intention of becoming a permanent resident."

But Dred's freedom was claimed on still another ground; viz.: that he had been taken by his master to the Free State of Illinois, and there retained some two or three years. But this the Chief Justice disposes of by declaring that his claim was not properly before the court; that the question raised by it was to be adjudged by the tribunals of Missouri alone; and he concludes as follows:

"Upon the whole, therefore, it is the judgment of this Court, that it appears by the record before us that the plaintiff in error is not a citizen of Missouri, in the sense in which that word is used in the Constitution; and that the Circuit Court of the United States, for that reason, had no jurisdiction in the case, and could give no judgment in it. Its judgment for the defendant must, consequently, be reversed, and a mandate issued, directing the suit to be dismissed for want of jurisdiction."

Justice Wayne, of Georgia, concurred "entirely in the opinion of the Court, as written and read by the Chief Justice, without any qualification of its reasoning or its conclusions."

Justice Nelson, of New York, concurred also in the conclusion of the Court, and favored an astonished world with the following sample of judicial logic:

"If Congress possesses power, under the Constitution, to abolish Slavery in a territory, it must necessarily possess the like power to *establish* it. It cannot be a one-sided power, as may suit the convenience or particular views of the advocates. It is a power, if it exist at all, over the whole subject."

But the power against which Mr. Nelson is contending is a power to *prohibit* by legislation certain forms of injustice and immorality. If, then, according to his reasoning, Congress should, by law, prohibit adultery, theft, burglary, and murder, in the territories of the Union, it would thereby affirm and establish its right to reward and encourage those crimes.

Mr. Justice Grier, of Pennsylvania, emitted all the additional light he had power to shed on the subject in the following commendably brief, but not otherwise commendable, opinion:

"I concur in the opinion delivered by Mr. Justice Nelson on the question discussed by him.

"I also concur with the opinion of the Court, as delivered by the Chief Justice, that the act of Congress of 6th of March, 1820, is unconstitutional and void; and that, assuming the facts as stated in the opinion, the plaintiff cannot sue as a citizen of Missouri in the courts of the United States. But, that the record shows a *prima facie* case of jurisdiction, requiring the Court to decide all the questions properly arising in it; and as the decision of the pleas in bar shows that the plaintiff is a slave, and therefore not entitled to sue in a court of the United States, the form of the judgment is of little importance; for, whether the judgment be affirmed or dismissed for want of jurisdiction, it is justified by the decision of the Court, and is the same in effect between the parties to the suit."

Mr. Justice Daniel, of Virginia, in announcing his opinion, seemed appalled by the magnitude of the issues involved in the question before the Court. The tremor and awe with which he had approached the subject may have blunted his judicial acumen, since his exhibitions of it were mainly confined to such assertions as these:

"Now, the following are truths which a knowledge of the history of the world, and particularly of that of our own country, compels us to know—that the African negro race have never been acknowledged as belonging to the family of nations; that as amongst them there never has been known or recognized by the inhabitants of other countries anything partaking of the character of nationality, or civil or political polity; that this race has been, by all the nations of Europe, regarded as subjects of capture or purchase, as subjects of commerce or traffic; and that the introduction of that race into every section of this country was not as members of civil or political society, but as slaves—as *property*, in the strictest sense of the term."

He proceeded in this vein to deny

the right or power of any State to elevate persons (or, as he would say, *property*) of African descent to citizenship of the United States, "by any direct or indirect proceeding," so as to entitle them to sue, or be sued, in the Federal tribunals. And, having thus put Dred Scott out of court, and finished the case, he proceeds to deal with the political questions introduced and discussed by Chief Justice Taney, in order "to put them finally to rest." He is horror-struck at the "inequalities," the disfranchisement, and the degradation, involved in the prohibition of Slavery in the Federal territories, which he reprehends and stigmatizes as follows:

"Nothing can be more conclusive to show the equality of this with every other right in all the citizens of the United States, and the iniquity and absurdity of the pretension to exclude or to disfranchise a portion of them, because they are the owners of slaves, than the fact that the same instrument, which imparts to Congress its very existence, and its every function, guarantees to the slaveholder the title to his property, and gives him the right to its reclamation throughout the entire extent of the nation; and, further, that the only private property which the Constitution has *specifically recognized*, and has imposed it as a direct obligation, both on the States and the Federal Government, to protect and *enforce*, is the property of the master in his slave; no other right of property is placed by the Constitution upon the same high ground, nor shielded by a similar guarantee."

There is much more of this, but the above must suffice. Mr. Daniel, pushing his doctrines to their legitimate result, pronounces the Ordinance of '87 only equal in constitutionality and validity with the Missouri Restriction—that is to say, essentially null and void.

Mr. Justice Campbell, of Alabama, followed with a general assent to the views of Chief Justice Taney.

Mr. Justice Catron, of Tennessee, concurs with Justice Nelson, that Dred Scott has no right to freedom, at the hands of this court, on the ground of his two years' residence in Illinois; but he dissents from the Chief Justice's notion that the power over the territories, expressly given to Congress by the Constitution, has no force or application *beyond* the territory possessed by us when that Constitution was framed. In fact, as he had been hanging men for the last twenty years under this very power, he could not well do otherwise. He says:

"It is due to myself to say, that it is asking much of a judge, who has for nearly twenty years been exercising jurisdiction from the Western Missouri line to the Rocky Mountains, and, on this understanding of the Constitution, inflicting the extreme penalty of death for crimes committed where the direct legislation of Congress was the only rule, to agree that he had all the while been acting in mistake, and as an usurper.

"More than sixty years have passed away since Congress has exercised power to govern the territories, by its legislation directly, or by territorial charters, subject to repeal at all times; and it is now too late to call that power in question, if this Court could disregard its own decisions, which it cannot do, as I think."

Several points in his opinion evince a sturdy independence; yet he concludes that that clause of the Constitution which provides that "the citizens of each State shall be entitled to all privileges and immunities of citizens in the several States," gives slaveholders an indefeasible right to carry their slaves into, and hold them in, the territories.

Col. Benton[4] observes that the

[4] In his "Historical and Legal Examination of that part of the Decision of the Supreme Court, in the Dred Scott case, which declares the unconstitutionality of the Missouri Compromise."

opinion of the Court, as pronounced by Chief Justice Taney in this celebrated case, is, in essence, but an amplification of certain resolves submitted by Mr. Calhoun to the United States Senate, in February, 1847, in the following language:

"*Resolved*, That the Territories of the United States belong to the several States composing this Union, and are held by them as their joint and common property.

"*Resolved*, That Congress, as the joint agent and representative of the States of the Union, has no right to make any law, or do any act whatever, that shall directly, or by its effects, make any discrimination between the States of this Union, by which any one of them shall be deprived of its full and equal rights in the territory of the United States, acquired or to be acquired.

"*Resolved*, That the enactment of any law which would directly, or by its effects, deprive the citizens of any of the States of this Union from emigrating, with their property, into any of the Territories of the United States, *would* make such a discrimination; and would, therefore, be a violation of the Constitution, and the rights of the States from which such citizens emigrated, and in derogation of that perfect equality which belongs to them as members of this Union, and would tend directly to subvert the Union itself."

The resolve submitted to the Democratic National Convention of 1848, by Mr. William L. Yancey, and unceremoniously rejected by it, 216 to 36, as will have been seen[5]—sets forth the same doctrine more concisely and abruptly.

Col. Benton, himself a life-long slaveholder and upholder of Slavery, thus forcibly refutes,[6] from a conservative and legal standpoint, the Calhoun-Yancey dogma:

"The prohibition of Slavery in a territory is assumed to work an inequality in the States, allowing one part to carry its property with it—the other, not. This is a mistake—a great error of fact—the source of great errors of deduction. The citizens of all the States, free and slave, are precisely equal in their capacity to carry their property with them into territories. Each may carry whatever is property by the laws of nature: neither can carry that which is only property by statute law; and the reason is, *because he cannot carry with him* THE LAW *which* MAKES *it property.* Either may carry the thing which is the subject of this local property; but neither can carry the law which makes it so. The Virginian may carry his man-slave; but he cannot carry the Virginian law which *makes* him a slave. The citizen of Massachusetts may carry the pile of money which, under a State law, constitutes a bank; but he cannot carry the law or charter which makes it a bank: and his treasure is only a pile of money; and, besides being impossible, it would be absurd, and confusion confounded, to be otherwise. For, if the citizen of one State may carry his Slave State law with him into a territory, the citizens of every other Slave State might do the same; and then what Babylonish confusion, not merely of tongues, but of laws, would be found there! Fifteen different codes, as the Slave States now number, and more to come. For every Slave State has a servile code of its own, differing from others in some respects—and in some, radically: as much so as land, in the eye of the law, differs from cattle. Thus, in some States, as in Virginia and others, slaves are only chattels: in others, as in Kentucky and Louisiana, they are real estate. How would all these codes work together in a territory under the wing of the Constitution, protecting all equally; no law of Congress there, or of the territory, to reconcile and harmonize them by forming them into one; no law to put the protecting power of the Constitution into action; but of itself, by its own proper vigor, it is to give general and equal protection to all slaveholders in the enjoyment of their property—each, according to the law of the State from which he came! For, there being no power in Congress, or the Territorial Legislature, to legislate upon Slavery, the whole subject is left to the Constitution and the State law! that law which cannot cross the State line! and that Constitution which gives protection to slave property but in one instance, and that only in States, not in Territories—the single instance of recovering runaways. The Constitution protect slave property in a territory! when, by that instrument, a runaway from the territory or into the territory cannot be reclaimed! Beautiful constitutional protection that! only one clause under it to protect slave property; and that limited, in express words, to fugitives between State and State! and but one clause in it to protect the master against his slaves, and that limited to States! and but one clause in it

[5] See page 192.

[6] In his "Examination," aforesaid.

to tax slaves as property, and that limited to States! and but one clause in it to give a qualified representation to Congress, and that limited to States. No; the thing is impossible. The owner cannot carry his Slave State law with him into the Territory; nor can he carry it into another Slave State, but must take the law which he finds there, and have his property governed by it; and, in some instances, wholly changed by it, and rights lost, or acquired, by the change."

To the same effect, Mr. Webster, when resisting, in 1848, the attempt, on a bill organizing the Territory of Oregon, to fasten a "rider" extending the Slave line of 36° 30′ to the Pacific, refuted this doctrine as follows:

"The Southern Senators say we deprive them of the right to go into these newly acquired territories with their property. We certainly do not prevent them from going into those territories with what is, in general law, called property. But these States have, by their local laws, created a property in persons; and they cannot carry these local laws with them. Slavery is created and exists by a local law, which is limited to a certain section; and it is asked that Congress shall establish a local law in other territories to enable Southern Senators to carry their particular law with them. No man can be held as a slave unless the local law accompany him."

Justice McLean, of Ohio, in his opinion dissenting from that of the Court in this case of Dred Scott, says:

"Will it be said that the slave is taken as property, the same as other property which the master may own? To this I answer, that colored persons are made property by the law of the State, and no such power has been given to Congress. Does the master carry with him the law of the State from which he removes into the territory? and does that enable him to coerce his slave in the territory? Let us test this theory: If this may be done by a master from one Slave State, it may be done by a master from every other Slave State. This right is supposed to be connected with the person of the master, by virtue of the local law. Is it transferable? May it be negotiated as a promissory note or bill of exchange? If it be assigned to a man from a Free State, may he coërce the slave by virtue of it? What shall this thing be denominated? Is it personal or real property? Or is it an indefinable fragment of sovereignty, which every person carries with him from his late domicile? One thing is certain, that its origin has been very recent, and it is unknown to the laws of any civilized country. It is said that the territories are the common property of the States, and that every man has a right to go there with his property. This is not controverted. But the Court say, a slave is not property beyond the operation of the local law which makes him such. Never was a truth more authoritatively and justly uttered by man. Suppose a master of a slave in a British island owned a million of property in England; would that authorize him to take his slaves with him to England? The Constitution, in express terms, recognizes the *status* of Slavery as founded on the municipal law: 'No person held to service or labor in one State, *under the laws thereof*, escaping to another, shall,' etc. Now, unless the fugitive escape from a place where, by the municipal law, he is held to labor, this provision affords no remedy to the master. What can be more conclusive than this? Suppose a slave escape from a territory where Slavery is not authorized by law, can he be reclaimed? In this case, a majority of the Court have said that a slave may be taken by his master into a territory of the United States, the same as a horse, or any other kind of property. It is true, this was said by the Court, as also many other things, which are of no authority. Nothing that has been said by them, which has not a direct bearing on the jurisdiction of the Court, against which they decided, can be considered as authority. I shall certainly not regard it as such. The question of jurisdiction, being before the Court, was decided by them authoritatively, but nothing beyond that question. A slave is not a mere chattel. He bears the impress of his Maker, and is amenable to the laws of God and man; and he is destined to an endless existence."

To the same effect, Justice Curtis, of Massachusetts, in *his* dissenting opinion, thus traverses the judgment of the Court:

"Is it conceivable that the Constitution has conferred the right on every citizen to become a resident on the territory of the United States with his slaves, and there to hold them as such, but has neither made nor provided for any municipal regulations which were essential to the existence of Slavery? Is it not more rational to conclude that they who framed and adopted the Constitution were aware that persons held to service under the laws of a State are property only to the extent and under the conditions fixed by those laws; and that they must cease to be available as property when their owners voluntarily place them permanently within another jurisdiction, where no municipal laws on the subject of Slavery exist?

"Moreover, if the right exists, what are its limits, and what are its conditions? If citizens of the United States have a right to take their slaves to a Territory, and hold them there as slaves, without regard to the laws of the Territory, I suppose this right is not to be restricted to the citizens of slave-holding States. A citizen of a State which does not tolerate Slavery can hardly be denied the power of doing the same thing. And what law of Slavery does either take with him to the Territory? If it be said to be those laws respecting Slavery which existed in the particular State from which each slave last came, what an anomaly is this! Where else can we find, under the laws of any civilized country, the power to introduce and permanently continue diverse systems of foreign municipal law, for holding persons in Slavery?"

Justice Curtis is an ultra conservative of the State-street (Boston) school—a life-long follower of Mr. Webster, especially in his later and more lamentable days—and yet his opinion delivered in this case evinces considerably more freedom and boldness than that of Judge McLean. Though couched in judicial and respectful language, it constantly, and pretty clearly, intimates not merely that the judgment of the Court is contrary both to law and to fact, but that its authors well *know* such to be the case. In reply to Chief Justice Taney's disquisition as to the opinions and views of our Revolutionary statesmen, Mr. Curtis bluntly says:

"To determine whether any free persons, descended from Africans held in Slavery, were citizens of the United States under the Confederation, and consequently at the time of the adoption of the Constitution of the United States, it is only necessary to know whether such persons were citizens of either of the States under the Confederation, at the time of the adoption of the Constitution.

"Of this, there can be no doubt. At the time of the ratification of the Articles of Confederation, all free, native-born inhabitants of the States of New Hampshire, Massachusetts, New York, New Jersey, and North Carolina, though descended from African slaves, were not only citizens of those States, but such of them as had the other necessary qualifications possessed the franchise of electors, on equal terms with other citizens."

He proceeds to cite, in support of this averment, the judgment of the Supreme Court of North Carolina in the case of the State against Manuel, wherein William Gaston—by far the most eminent jurist of whom that State could ever boast—pronounced the opinion of the Court in the following terms.

"According to the laws of this State, all human beings within it, who are not slaves, fall within one of two classes. Whatever distinctions may have existed in the Roman laws between citizens and free inhabitants, they are unknown to our institutions. Before our Revolution, all free persons born within the dominions of the King of Great Britain, whatever their color or complexion, were native-born British subjects—those born out of his allegiance were aliens. Slavery did not exist in England, but it did in the British Colonies. Slaves were not, in legal parlance, persons, but property. The moment the incapacity, the disqualification of Slavery was removed, they became persons, and were then either British subjects, or not British subjects, according as they were or were not born within the allegiance of the British king. Upon the Revolution, no other change took place in the laws of North Carolina than was consequent on the transition from a colony dependent on a European king to a free and sovereign State. Slaves remained slaves. British subjects in North Carolina became North Carolina freemen. Foreigners, until made members of the State, remained aliens. Slaves, manumitted here, became freemen; and therefore, if born within North Carolina, are citizens of North Carolina; and all free persons born within the State are born citizens of the State. The Constitution extended the elective franchise to every freeman who had arrived at the age of twenty-one, and paid a public tax; and it is a matter of universal notoriety, that, under it, free persons, without regard to color, claimed and exercised the franchise, until it was taken from free men of color a few years since, by our amended Constitution."

Continuing his review of the Chief Justice's assumptions, Judge Curtis says:

"It has been often asserted that the Constitution was made exclusively by and for the white race. It has already been shown that, in five of the thirteen original States, colored persons then possessed the elective franchise, and were among those by whom the Constitution was ordained and established. If so, it is not true, in point of fact, that the Constitution was made exclusively *by* the white race. And that it was made exclusively *for* the white race is, in my opinion, not only an assumption not warranted by anything in the Constitution, but contradicted by its open declaration, that it was ordained and established by the people of the United States, for themselves and their posterity. And, as free colored persons were then citizens of at least five States, and so, in every sense, part of the people of the United States, they were among those for whom and whose posterity the Constitution was ordained and established."

Judge Curtis is not content with refuting the logic of the Chief Justice. He seizes the weapons of his antagonist and turns them against him with decided effect. Witness the following:

"I do not deem it necessary to review at length the legislation of Congress having more or less bearing upon the citizenship of colored persons. It does not seem to me to have any considerable tendency to prove that it has been considered by the legislative department of the Government that no such persons are citizens of the United States. Undoubtedly, they have been debarred from the exercise of particular rights or privileges extended to white persons, but, I believe, always in terms which, by implication, admit that they *may* be citizens. Thus, the act of May 17, 1792, for the organization of the militia, directs the enrollment of every 'free, able-bodied, white male citizen.' An assumption that none but white persons are citizens, would be as inconsistent with the just import of this language, as that all citizens are able-bodied, or males.

"So the act of February 28, 1803 (2 *Stat. at Large*, 205), to prevent the importation of certain persons into States, when, by the laws thereof, their admission is prohibited, in its first section forbids all masters of vessels to import or bring 'any negro, mulatto, or other person of color, not being a native, *a citizen*, or registered seaman of the United States,' etc., etc.

"The acts of March 3, 1813, § 1 (2 *Stat. at Large*, 809), and March 1, 1817, § 3 (3 *Stat. at Large*, 351), concerning seamen, certainly imply that there may be persons of color, natives of the United States, who are not citizens of the United States. This implication is undoubtedly in accordance with the fact. For not only slaves, but free persons of color, born in some of the States, are not citizens. But there is nothing in these laws inconsistent with the citizenship of persons of color in others of the States, nor with their being citizens of the United States.

"Whether much or little weight should be attached to the particular phraseology of these and other laws, which were not passed with any direct reference to the subject, I consider their tendency to be, as already indicated, to show that, in the apprehension of their framers, color was not a necessary qualification for citizenship. It would be strange, if laws were found on our statute-book to that effect, when, by solemn treaties, large bodies of Mexican and North American Indians, as well as free colored persons of Louisiana, have been admitted to citizenship of the United States."

Mr. Curtis cites with effect the action of Congress in 1821 on the admission of Missouri, whereby that State was constrained to abandon and repudiate her attempt to prohibit the settlement of free negroes and mulattoes within her borders;[7] whereof he says:

"It is true, that neither this legislative declaration, nor anything in the Constitution or laws of Missouri, could confer or take away any privilege or immunity granted by the Constitution. But it is also true that it expresses the then conviction of the legislative power of the United States, that free negroes, as citizens of *some* of the States, might be entitled to the privileges and immunities of citizens in *all* the States."

He sums up his conclusions as to

[7] See page 80 of this work.

the right of Dred Scott to bring this action, as follows:

"*First.* That the free, native-born citizens of each State are citizens of the United States.

"*Second.* That, as free colored persons, born within some of the States, are citizens of those States, such persons are also citizens of the United States.

"*Third.* That every such citizen, residing in any State, has a right to sue, and is liable to be sued, in the Federal Courts, as a citizen of that State in which he resides.

"*Fourth.* That, as the plea to the jurisdiction in this case shows no facts except that the plaintiff was of African descent, and that his ancestors were sold as slaves, and as these facts are not inconsistent with his citizenship of the United States and his residence in the State of Missouri, the plea to the jurisdiction was bad, and the judgment of the Circuit Court overruling it was correct.

"I dissent, therefore, from that part of the opinion of the majority of the court in which it is held that a person of African descent cannot be a citizen of the United States; and I regret I must go further, and dissent both from what I deem their assumption of authority to examine the constitutionality of the act of Congress commonly called the Missouri Compromise act, and the grounds and conclusions announced in their opinion.

"Having first decided that they were bound to consider the sufficiency of the plea to the jurisdiction of the Circuit Court, and having decided that this plea showed that the Circuit Court had *not* jurisdiction, and consequently that this is a case to which the judicial power of the United States does not extend, they have gone on to examine the merits of the case as they appeared on the trial before the court and jury, on the issues joined on the pleas in bar, and so have reached the question of the power of Congress to pass the act of 1820. On so grave a subject as this, I feel obliged to say that, in my opinion, such an exertion of judicial power transcends the limits of the authority of the Court, as described by its repeated decisions, and, as I understand, acknowledged in this opinion of the majority of the Court."

Mr. Curtis proceeds to confute at length, and with decided ability, the doctrines of the majority, affirming the invalidity of the Missouri Restriction, and asserting the paramount right of each slaveholder to remove with his slaves into any territory of the United States, and there retain and control them under the ægis of the Federal Constitution. He shows, further, that the majority erred in upholding a majority of the Supreme Court of Missouri in overruling their own Chief Justice and their own former decisions, whereby it had been established, in accordance with kindred decisions in Louisiana, as in other Slave States, that a slave taken by his master, or removed with his assent, to a Free State, or to any country wherein Slavery is prohibited, becomes thereby a freeman, and cannot be returned or reduced again to Slavery. It cannot, however, be necessary to quote further on this head. He concludes:

"For these reasons, I am of the opinion that so much of the several acts of Congress as prohibited Slavery and involuntary servitude within that part of the Territory of Missouri lying north of thirty-six degrees thirty minutes north latitude, and west of the river Mississippi, were constitutional and valid laws.

"In my opinion, the judgment of the Circuit Court should be reversed, and the cause remanded for a new trial."

The majority of the Justices composing the Supreme Court, after deciding that Dred Scott had no standing in that Court, and that the case was, therefore, entirely beyond, or outside of, its jurisdiction, had proceeded to take and make jurisdiction, for the purpose of ousting Congress and the people from all right or power to exclude Slavery from the Federal Territories, organized or unorganized. Congress had repeatedly, and from the very origin of the Government, legislated on this subject, and to this end. The Supreme Court now interposes, in a case wherein it proclaims itself devoid of jurisdiction, and denies the validity of such legislation. The people are treated as inclining to usurp the power of excluding human bondage from their territorial possessions; so the Court decides that they have no rights in the premises, no power to act on the question. If twenty millions of freemen were unanimously and earnestly to insist that Freedom should be the law of their common territories, while but one slaveholder should claim the privilege of taking his slaves to and holding them in said territories, the claim of this one slaveholder, according to the Court, would override and defeat, conclusively, the earnest demands of those twenty millions of freemen. The war upon the Missouri Restriction, and against Slavery Inhibition in the Territories generally, had been commenced and prosecuted under the banner of "Popular Sovereignty;" and it was to this complexion it had come at last; and it was of this judgment, just about to be proclaimed to an astounded people, that Mr. Buchanan, in his Inaugural aforesaid, says:

> "The whole territorial question being thus settled upon the principle of Popular Sovereignty—a principle as ancient as free government itself—everything of a practical nature has been decided. No other question remains for adjustment; because all agree that, under the Constitution, Slavery in the States is beyond the reach of any human power, except that of the respective States themselves wherein it exists. May we not, then, hope that the long agitation on this subject is approaching its end, and that the geographical parties to which it has given birth, so much dreaded by the father of his country, will speedily become extinct?"

!

XIX.

OUR FOREIGN POLICY—CUBA.

THE foundations of our foreign policy were firmly and strongly laid during the Presidency, and under the councils, of Washington. To mind our own business, and leave other nations to manage their affairs, and to preserve, recast, or modify their respective governments, as to them shall seem fit and advantageous—to regard the rule actually established and operative in any nation as the rightful government of that nation, however widely divergent it may be from our own notions of what is wisest and most beneficent: such are its great cardinal principles. To Washington and his eminent compatriots in our Revolutionary struggle, and in the framing of our Federal Union, is the credit justly due of having originated and firmly upheld this policy, in defiance of popular passion, and under circumstances of great difficulty and embarrassment. But Jefferson, Madison, George Clinton, Gerry, and their associate founders of the Republican party, very generally yielded to this policy a tacit, if not positive and emphatic, approval. The mob of the seaboard cities, who shouted beneath the windows of Citizen Genet, burned Jay's treaty in the streets, and clamored violently for alliance with revolutionary France and war upon Tory England, were, of course, anti-Federal; and their voices and votes helped to strengthen the Republican opposition in Congress, and to swell the steadily-growing host that, in due time, ousted the Federalists from power, by electing Mr. Jefferson to the Presidency.

But Mr. Jefferson himself never shared in the blind passions by which he so largely profited. An earnest and unchanging devotee of cheap, simple, and frugal government, he profoundly realized that wars were costly, and alliances perilous; and, while he hated the British Government as embodying whatever was, at the same time, most pernicious to our country, and most seductive to her wealthy and commercial classes, he never, after our independence was achieved, was eager to tempt again the desperate chances, the certain devastations and enduring burdens, of war with Great Britain. Before the close of his Presidency,[1] the popular feeling would have fully justified and sustained him in declaring war, but he wisely forbore; and it was only after the strong infusion of young blood into the councils of the Republican party, through the election of Messrs. Clay, Grundy, Calhoun, John Holmes, etc., to Congress, that the hesitation of the cautious and philosophic Madison was overborne by their impetuosity, and war actually proclaimed.

When Washington and his advisers definitively resolved on preserving a strict neutrality between revolutionary France and the banded despots who assailed her, they did not entirely escape the imputation of ingratitude, if not positive bad faith. Our country was deeply indebted to France for the generous and vitally important assistance received from her in our Revolutionary struggle; and, although France was not—as nations, like individuals, seldom are—entirely disinterested in rendering that assistance, the advantage accruing to and the obligation incurred by us were scarcely lessened by that consideration. When barely two of our seven years' arduous struggle had passed, Louis XVI. decided to acknowledge our independence; and his minister soon after[2] united with our envoys in a treaty of alliance, whereof the preponderance of benefits was very greatly on our side. And among the stipulations of that treaty—a treaty whereby we profited too much in the general to be fastidious as to the particulars—was the following:

"Art. XI. The two parties guarantee mutually, from the present time and forever, against all other powers, to wit: The United States, to his Most Christian Majesty, the present possessions of the crown of France in America, as well as those which it may acquire by the future treaty of peace: And his Most Christian Majesty guarantees on his part to the United States their liberty, sovereignty, and independence, absolute and unlimited, as well in matters of government as commerce, and also their possessions, and the additions or conquests that their confederation may obtain during the war, from any of the dominions now or heretofore possessed by Great Britain in North America, conformably to the 5th and 6th articles above written, the whole as their possessions shall be fixed and assured to the said States, at the moment of the

[1] On the occasion of the outrageous attack on the frigate Chesapeake by the Leopard.

[2] February 6, 1778. This treaty was kept secret for several months.

cessation of their present war with England."

Such a guarantee could not, in the nature of things, endure and be fulfilled, unless the contracting parties were to become, in effect, one nation; or, at least, to be partners or confederates in all their future wars. In the case actually presented, the monarch with whom we made this treaty had been the enemy and the victim of the Jacobins, who claimed of us the fulfillment of this grave compact.

President Washington, in his Farewell Address[3] to his countrymen on taking leave of public life, thus summed up his convictions on the subject under contemplation:

"The great rule of conduct for us in regard to foreign nations is, in extending our commercial relations, to have with them as little political connection as possible. So far as we have already formed engagements, let them be fulfilled with perfect good faith. Here let us stop.

"Europe has a set of primary interests, which to us have none, or a very remote, relation. Hence, she must be engaged in frequent controversies, the causes of which are essentially foreign to our concerns. Hence, therefore, it must be unwise in us to implicate ourselves by artificial ties in the ordinary vicissitudes of her politics, or the ordinary combinations and collisions of her friendships or enmities.

"Our detached and distant situation invites and enables us to pursue a different course. If we remain one people, under an efficient government, the period is not far off when we may defy material injury from external annoyance; when we may take such an attitude as will cause the neutrality we may at any time resolve upon to be scrupulously respected; when belligerent nations, under the impossibility of making acquisitions from us, will not lightly hazard the giving us provocation; when we may choose peace or war, as our interests, guided by justice, shall counsel.

"Why forego the advantages of so peculiar a situation? Why quit our own to stand on foreign ground? Why, by interweaving our destiny with that of any part of Europe, entangle our peace and prosperity in the toils of European ambition, rivalships, interests, humor, or caprice?

"It is our true policy to steer clear of permanent alliances with any portion of the foreign world, so far, I mean, as we are now at liberty to do it; for let me not be understood as capable of patronizing infidelity to existing engagements. I hold the maxim no less applicable to public than to private affairs, that honesty is the best policy. I repeat, therefore, let those engagements be observed in their genuine sense. But, in my opinion, it is unnecessary and would be unwise to extend them."

No decided—at least no avowed—departure from this policy had occurred down to 1823, when President Monroe was required to address a new Congress under peculiar circumstances. The Spanish people had revolted against the despotism of their imbecile, treacherous monarch, Ferdinand VII., and had established a Constitution which left him still in possession of the trappings, but with little of the substance, of royalty. He was, of course, profoundly hostile to this change, though affecting to acquiesce in it. A congress[4] of the great powers of continental Europe, then united in a league, known as the "Holy Alliance," for the maintenance of their despotic authority and the repression of popular aspirations, had decreed the overthrow of this dangerous example; and, under its auspices, a French army of 100,000 men, led by the Duke d'Angoulême, a prince of the blood royal, had invaded Spain, and, meeting with little serious resistance, overthrown the Constitution and the Cortes, and restored to Ferdinand his beloved and grossly abused autocracy. Apprehensions were entertained that the discipline thus bestowed on Spain was about to

[3] September 17, 1796.

[4] Held at Verona, Italy, in 1822.

be extended to her revolted and nearly independent American colonies, whereby they should be reduced to abject servitude to their mother country, and to the despotism that now enthralled her. To such a consummation, Great Britain, as well as this country, was intensely opposed —quite as much, probably, for commercial as for political reasons. Mr. Canning, then the master-spirit of the British Cabinet, at least with respect to foreign affairs, hinted to our Government the expediency of a moral demonstration against the apprehended design of the Holy Alliance with regard to this Continent—a demonstration which could be made with less offense, yet with no less efficiency, from this side of the Atlantic than from the other. Thus prompted, Mr. Monroe spoke as follows:[5]

"Of events in that quarter of the globe with which we have so much intercourse, and from which we derive our origin, we have always been anxious and interested spectators. The citizens of the United States cherish sentiments the most friendly in favor of the liberty and happiness of their fellow-men on that side of the Atlantic. In the wars of the European powers, in matters relating to themselves, we have never taken any part, nor does it comport with our policy so to do. It is only when our rights are invaded or seriously menaced, that we resent injuries, or make preparation for our defense. With the movements in this hemisphere, we are of necessity more immediately connected, and by causes which must be obvious to all enlightened and impartial observers. The political system of the Allied Powers is essentially different in this respect from that of America. This difference proceeds from that which exists in their respective governments. And to the defense of our own, which has been achieved by the loss of so much blood and treasure, and matured by the wisdom of their most enlightened citizens, and under which we have enjoyed unexampled felicity, this whole nation is devoted. We owe it, therefore, to candor, and to the amicable relations existing between the United States and those powers, to declare, that we should consider any attempt on their part to extend their system to any portion of this hemisphere as dangerous to our peace and safety.

"With the existing colonies or dependencies of any European power, we have not interfered, and shall not interfere. But with the governments which have declared their independence and maintained it, and whose independence we have, on great consideration and on just principles, acknowledged, we could not view any interposition for the purpose of oppressing them, or controlling in any other manner their destiny, by any European power, in any other light than as the manifestation of an unfriendly disposition toward the United States. * * * * Our policy in regard to Europe, which was adopted at an early stage of the wars which have so long agitated that quarter of the globe, nevertheless, remains the same: which is, not to interfere in the internal concerns of any of its powers; to consider the government *de facto* as the legitimate government for us; to cultivate friendly relations with it; and to preserve those relations by a frank, firm, and manly policy; meeting, in all instances, the just claims of every power, submitting to injuries from none.

"But, in regard to these continents, circumstances are eminently and conspicuously different. It is impossible that the Allied Powers should extend their political system to any portion of either continent without endangering our peace and happiness; nor can any one believe that our southern brethren, if left to themselves, would adopt it of their own accord. It is equally impossible, therefore, that we should behold such interposition, in any form, with indifference. If we look to the comparative strength and resources of Spain and those new governments, and their distance from each other, it must be obvious that she can never subdue them. It is still the true policy of the United States to leave the parties to themselves, in the hope that other powers will pursue the same course."

In this remarkable passage, may probably be found the impulse to the invitation from several of the South American Republics to that Congress at Panama of representatives of American Republics, which Messrs. Adams and Clay so promptly and heartily accepted, and which the Opposition or Jackson party of 1825-6

[5] Seventh Annual Message, December 2, 1823.

so generally and resolutely opposed. That Congress proved, practically, a failure, whether through European intrigue, or Spanish-American jealousy and indolence, is not apparent. Our envoys[6] were duly appointed; but the strenuous opposition in our Senate[7] had so protracted the discussion that it was found too late for Mr. Sergeant to reach Panama at the time appointed for the meeting of the Congress;[8] and Mr. Anderson, then Minister to Colombia, when at Carthagena on his way to Panama, was attacked by a malignant fever, whereof he died.

But, long ere this, the jealousy of the slaveholders had been aroused, and their malign influence upon the course of our Government made manifest. Among the means employed to render the Panama Congress odious at the South, was the fact that John Sergeant, the more conspicuous of our envoys, had sternly opposed the admission of Missouri as a Slave State.[9]

The Spanish-American Republics had already decreed general emancipation; and fears were naturally expressed that they would extend this policy to Cuba, should they, as was then contemplated, combine to invade and conquer that island. Mr. Clay had already[10] written as Secretary of State to Mr. Alexander H. Everett, our Minister at Madrid, instructing him to urge upon Spain the expediency of acknowledging the independence of her lost colonies. He said:

"It is not for the new Republics that the President wishes to urge upon Spain the expediency of concluding the war. If the war should continue between Spain and the new Republics, and those islands [Cuba and Porto Rico] should become the object and theater of it, their fortunes have such a connection with the people of the United States, that they could not be indifferent spectators; and the possible contingencies of a protracted war might bring upon the Government

---

[6] John Sergeant, of Pennsylvania, and Richard C. Anderson, of Kentucky.

[7] In the course of the debate, Mr. John Randolph, of Virginia, said:

"Cuba possesses an immense negro population. In case those States [Mexico and Colombia] should invade Cuba at all, it is unquestionable that this invasion will be made with this principle,—the genius of universal emancipation,—this sweeping anathema against the white population in front,—and then, Sir, *what is the situation of the Southern States?*"

Mr. John M. Berrien, of Georgia, said:

"The question to be determined is this: with a due regard to the safety of the Southern States, can you suffer these islands (Cuba and Porto Rico) to pass into the hands of *buccaneers drunk with their new-born liberty?* If our interest and our safety shall require us to say to these new republics, 'Cuba and Porto Rico *must* remain as they are,' we are free to say it, and, by the blessing of God, *and the strength of our arms*, to enforce the declaration; and let me say to gentlemen, these high considerations *do* require it. The *vital* interests of *the South* demand it."

Mr. John Floyd, of Virginia, said [in the House]

"So far as I can see, in all its bearings, it [the Panama Congress] looks to the conquest of Cuba and Porto Rico; or, at all events, of tearing them from the crown of Spain. The interests, if not safety, of our own country, would rather require us to interpose to prevent such an event; and I would rather take up arms to prevent than to accelerate such an occurrence."

Mr. Josiah S. Johnston, of Louisiana, a friend of the Administration, parried these attacks as follows:

"We know that Colombia and Mexico have long contemplated the independence of the island [Cuba]. The final decision is now to be made, and the combination of forces and the plan of attack to be formed. What, then, at such a crisis, becomes the duty of the Government? Send your ministers instantly to the diplomatic assembly, where the measure is maturing. Advise with them—remonstrate—*menace*, if necessary—against a step so dangerous to us, and perhaps fatal to them."

[8] June 22, 1826.

[9] "And then, to cap the climax,
John Sergeant, too, must go—
A chief *who wants the darkies free*—
John Adams' son, my Jo!"
—'Federal Song' in *The Richmond Enquirer*.

[10] April 27, 1825.

of the United States duties and obligations, the performance of which, however painful it should be, they *might not be at liberty to decline.*"

In the same spirit, his instructions to Messrs. Anderson and Sergeant[11] contained the following passage:

"It is required by the frank and friendly relations which we most earnestly desire ever to cherish with the new Republics, that you should, without reserve, explicitly state that the United States have too much at stake in the fortunes of Cuba, to allow them to see with indifference a war of invasion prosecuted in a desolating manner, or to see employed, in the purposes of such a war, *one race of the inhabitants combating against another*, upon principles and with motives that must inevitably lead, if not to the extermination of one party or the other, to the most shocking excesses. The humanity of the United States in respect to the weaker, and which, in such a terrible struggle, would probably be the suffering, portion, and the duty to defend themselves against the *contagion* of such near and dangerous examples, would constrain them, even at the hazard of losing the friendship of Mexico and Colombia, to employ all the means necessary to their security."

Several years later, Mr. Van Buren, writing as Gen. Jackson's premier to Mr. C. P. Van Ness, our then Minister at Madrid, urges upon Spain, through him, the acknowledgment of South American independence, on this among other grounds:

"Considerations connected with *a certain class of our population* make it the interest of the Southern section of the Union that no attempt should be made in that island [Cuba] to throw off the yoke of Spanish dependence; the first effect of which would be the sudden emancipation of a numerous slave population, whose result could not but be very sensibly felt upon the adjacent shores of the United States."

Thus, so long as any revolution in Cuba, or displacement of the Spanish authority there, seemed likely to affect the stability or perpetuity of Slavery, our Government steadily, officiously opposed such revolution; and, while refusing, so early as 1825, to guarantee the possession of that island to Spain, and informally giving notice that we would never consent to its transfer to any more formidable power, seemed entirely satisfied with, and anxious for, its retention by Spain as her most precious and valued dependency—'The Queen of the Antilles.'

But, at length, having *re*ännexed Texas, the Slave Power fixed covetous eyes on this fertile, prolific island. In 1848, our Minister, under instructions from President Polk, made an offer of $100,000,000 for it, which was peremptorily, conclusively rejected. Directly thereafter, the South became agitated by 'fillibustering' plots for the invasion and conquest of that island, wherein real or pretended Cubans by nativity were prominent as leaders. President Taylor was hardly warm in the White House before he was made aware that these schemes were on the point of realization, and compelled to issue his proclamation[12] against them in these words:

"There is reason to believe that an armed expedition is about to be fitted out in the United States with an intention to invade the island of Cuba, or some of the provinces of Mexico. The best information which the Executive has been able to obtain points to the island of Cuba as the object of this expedition. It is the duty of this Government to observe the faith of treaties, and to prevent any aggression by our citizens upon the territories of friendly nations. I have, therefore, thought it necessary and proper to issue this Proclamation, to warn all citizens of the United States, who shall connect themselves with any enterprise so grossly in violation of our laws and our treaty obligations, that they will thereby subject themselves to the heavy penalties denounced against them by our acts of Congress, and will forfeit their claim to the protection of their country. No such persons must ex-

[11] May 8, 1826.

[12] August 11, 1849.

pect the interference of this Government, in any form, on their behalf, no matter to what extremities they may be reduced in consequence of their conduct. An enterprise to invade the territories of a friendly nation, set on foot and prosecuted within the limits of the United States, is, in the highest degree, criminal, as tending to endanger the peace, and compromit the honor, of this nation; and, therefore, I exhort all good citizens, as they regard our national reputation, as they respect their own laws and the Law of Nations, as they value the blessings of peace and the welfare of their country, to discountenance and prevent, by all lawful means, any such enterprise; and I call upon every officer of this Government, civil or military, to use all efforts in his power to arrest, for trial and punishment, every such offender against the laws providing for the performance of our sacred obligations to foreign powers."

This emphatic warning probably embarrassed and delayed the execution of the plot, but did not defeat it. Early in August, 1851—or soon after Gen. Taylor's death—an expedition under Lopez, a Cuban adventurer, sailed in a steamer from New Orleans—always the hotbed of the projects of the Slavery propagandists. About five hundred men embarked in this desperate enterprise, by which a landing was effected on the island of Cuba. All its expectations, however, of a rising in its behalf, or of any manifestation of sympathy on the part of the Cubans, were utterly disappointed. The invaders were easily defeated and made prisoners, when their leader was promptly *garroted* at Havana,[13] and a few of his comrades shot; but the greater number were sentenced to penal servitude in a distant Spanish possession, whence they were ultimately liberated by pardon.

The discipline proved effective. There was much talk of further expeditions against Cuba from one or another Southern city. A secret cabal, known as the "Order of the Lone Star," recruited adventurers and tried to raise funds through all the seaboard cities of the Union, and it was understood that Gen. John A. Quitman, of Mississippi, one of the ablest and strongest of Mr. Calhoun's disciples, had consented to lead the next expedition against Cuba; but none ever sailed. The "Order of the Lone Star" proved useful to Gen. Pierce in swelling his vote for President in 1852, and soon after subsided into nothingness.

As our Government had long expressed satisfaction with the possession of Cuba by Spain, while proclaiming hostility to its transfer to any other power, Great Britain and France determined to put our sincerity to the test; and, accordingly, in 1852, proposed to unite with us in a treaty mutually guaranteeing that island to Spain.[14] But Mr. Edward Everett, as Secretary of State to Mr. Fillmore, rejected the overture in an exceedingly smart dispatch.

The formal proposition for a joint agreement of perpetual renunciation, on the part of Great Britain, France, and the United States, respectively, of any covetous designs on Cuba,

[13] August 16th.

[14] The body of the Convention proposed to us, on the part of Great Britain and France, was in the following words:

"The high contracting parties hereby severally and collectively disclaim, both now and for hereafter, all intention to obtain possession of the island of Cuba; and they respectively bind themselves to discountenance all attempts to that effect on the part of any power or individuals whatever.

"The high contracting parties declare, severally and collectively, that they will not obtain or maintain, for themselves, or for any one of themselves, any exclusive control over the said island, nor assume nor exercise any dominion over the same."

was presented, on the 23d of April, to Mr. Webster, then our Secretary of State, and by him courteously acknowledged, six days later, in a note which, though not without demur, expressed the acquiescence of our Government in the general views expressed by France and England with reference to Cuba, and gave assurances that, "The President will take M. de Sartiges' communication into consideration, and give it his best reflections."

Mr. Webster being dead[15] and Mr. Everett duly installed as his successor, the latter answered[16] a note of M. de Sartiges, recalling Mr. Webster's attention to this subject, under date of July 8th. In this answer, our Government peremptorily declines, for various and elaborately stated reasons, any such convention or compact as that proposed to it by France and England. While still disclaiming, *pro forma*, any desire or intention on our part of acquiring Cuba, this document affords the strongest evidence of a contrary disposition. It assumes that the Senate would inevitably refuse its assent to the treaty proposed, and adds: "its certain rejection by that body would leave the question of Cuba in a more unsettled position than it is now." It doubts the constitutional power "to impose a permanent disability on the American Government for all coming time." It parades, with significant emphasis, the repeated and important acquisitions of territory by our Government, through the purchase of Louisiana in 1803, and of Florida in 1819, as also through the annexation of Texas; as to which, Mr. Everett—overdoing his part, as is natural in a Federalist turned fillibuster—volunteers the wholly gratuitous assertion that "there never was an extension of territory more naturally or justifiably made." Ignoring the fact that Great Britain has still possessions in this hemisphere nearly, if not quite, equal in extent to those of our own country, and that her important island of Jamaica is quite as near to Cuba as is any portion of our Southern coast, Mr. Everett says:

> "The President does not covet the acquisition of Cuba for the United States; at the same time, he considers the acquisition of Cuba as mainly an American question. The proposed convention proceeds on a different principle. It assumes that the United States have no other or greater interest in the question than France or England; whereas, it is necessary only to cast one's eye on the map to see how remote are the relations of Europe, and how intimate those of the United States, with this island."

If three strong men were traversing a desert in company with a fourth rich, but weak, companion, and two of them should propose to the other a mutual stipulation not to rob or otherwise abuse their weak brother, it could hardly fail to astonish them to hear their proposition declined, as contemplating an "entangling alliance"—a perplexing and troublesome undertaking, whereof no one could fully calculate the scope and ultimate consequences. Yet Mr. Everett sees fit to say that

> "There is another strong objection to the proposed agreement. Among the oldest traditions of the Federal Government is an aversion to political alliances with European powers. In his memorable Farewell Address, President Washington says: 'The great rule of conduct for us in regard to foreign nations is, in extending our com-

[15] Oct. 24th, 1852.

[16] December 1, 1852.

mercial relations, to have with them as little political connection as possible. So far as we have already formed engagements, let them be fulfilled with perfect good faith. Here let us stop.' President Jefferson, in his Inaugural Address in 1801, warned the country against 'entangling alliances.' This expression, now become proverbial, was unquestionably used by Mr. Jefferson in reference to the alliance with France of 1778—an alliance, at the time, of incalculable benefit to the United States; but which, in less than twenty years, came near involving us in the wars of the French Revolution, and laid the foundation of heavy claims upon Congress, not extinguished to the present day. It is a significant cöincidence, that the particular provision of the alliance which occasioned these evils was that under which France called upon us to aid her in defending her West Indian possessions against England. Nothing less than the unbounded influence of Washington rescued the Union from the perils of that crisis, and preserved our neutrality."

Mr. Everett proceeds:

"But the President has a graver objection to entering into the proposed convention. He has no wish to disguise the feeling that the compact, although equal in its terms, would be very unequal in substance. France and England, by entering into it, would disable themselves from obtaining possession of an island remote from their seats of government, belonging to another European power, whose natural right to possess it must always be as good as their own—a distant island in another hemisphere, and one which, by no ordinary or peaceful course of things, could ever belong to either of them. * * * The United States, on the other hand, would, by the proposed convention, disable themselves from making an acquisition which might take place without any disturbance of existing foreign relations, and in the natural order of things. The island of Cuba lies at our doors. It commands the approach to the Gulf of Mexico, which washes the shores of five of our States. It bars the entrance of that great river which drains half the North American continent, and with its tributaries forms the largest system of internal water communication in the world. It keeps watch at the doorway of our intercourse with California by the Isthmus route. If an island like Cuba, belonging to the Spanish crown, guarded the entrance of the Thames and the Seine, and the United States should propose a convention like this to France and England, those powers would assuredly feel that the disability assumed by ourselves was far less serious than that which we asked them to assume."

Mr. Everett, having thus, in effect, apprised the civilized world that the acquisition of Cuba *is* essential to our independence, and that we shall proceed in our own time to appropriate it, turns to give our slaveholders a meaning hint that they must not be too eager in the pursuit, or they will overreach themselves. He says:

"The opinions of American statesmen, at different times, and under varying circumstances, have differed as to the desirableness of the acquisition of Cuba by the United States. Territorially and commercially, it would, in our hands, be an extremely valuable possession. Under certain contingencies, it might be almost essential to our safety. Still, for *domestic* reasons, on which, in a communication of this kind, it might not be proper to dwell, the President thinks that the incorporation of the island into the Union at the present time, although effected with the consent of Spain, would be a hazardous measure; and he would consider its acquisition by force, except in a just war with Spain (should an event so greatly to be deprecated take place), as a disgrace to the civilization of the age."

In another place, he gives them another intimation of the solicitude with which our Government watches and wards against any subversion of Slavery in Cuba; saying:

"Even now, the President cannot doubt that both France and England would prefer any change in the condition of Cuba to that which is most to be apprehended, viz.: an *internal convulsion* which should renew the horrors and the fate of San Domingo"

But Cuba, it seems, is not merely a slaveholding, but a slave-trading dependency, which affords still another reason why Spain should lose and we gain it. Says Mr. Everett:

"I will intimate a final objection to the proposed convention. M. de Turgot and Lord Malmesbury put forward, as the reason for entering into such a compact, 'the attacks which have lately been made on the island of Cuba by lawless bands of adventurers from the United States, with the avowed design of taking possession of that island.' The President is convinced that the conclusion of such a treaty, instead of putting a stop to these lawless proceedings, would give a new and powerful impetus to them. It would strike a death-blow to the conservative policy hitherto pursued in this country toward Cuba. No administration of this Government, however strong in the public confidence in other respects, could stand a day under the odium of having stipulated with the Great Powers of Europe, that, in no future time, under no change of circumstances, by no amicable arrangement with Spain, by no act of lawful war (should that calamity unfortunately occur), by no consent of the inhabitants, should they, like the possessions of Spain on the American continent, succeed in rendering themselves independent; in fine, by no overruling necessity of self-preservation, should the United States ever make the acquisition of Cuba."

After all this, and much more of the same purport, a smile must have irradiated the countenance of even the most impassive European diplomatist on reading the concluding paragraph of Mr. Everett's dispatch, viz.:

"For these reasons, which the President has thought advisable, considering the importance of the subject, to direct me to unfold at some length, he feels constrained to decline respectfully the invitation of France and England to become parties to the proposed convention. He is persuaded that these friendly powers will not attribute this refusal to any insensibility on his part to the advantages of the utmost harmony between the great maritime States on a subject of such importance. As little will Spain draw any unfavorable inference from this refusal; the rather, as the emphatic disclaimer of any designs against Cuba on the part of this Government, *contained in the present note*, affords all the assurance which the President can constitutionally, or to any useful purpose, give, of a practical concurrence with France and England in the wish not to disturb the possession of that island by Spain."

Soon after the passage of the Nebraska bill, President Pierce, through a dispatch from Gov. Marcy as Secretary of State,[17] directed Messrs. James Buchanan, John Y. Mason, and Pierre Soulé, our Embassadors at London, Paris, and Madrid respectively, to convene in some European city, there to confer with regard to the best means of getting possession of Cuba. They met accordingly at Ostend,[18] and sat three days; adjourning thence to Aix-la-Chapelle, where they held sweet council together for several days more, and the result of their deliberations was transmitted to our Government in a dispatch known as the 'Ostend Manifesto.' In that dispatch, they say:

"We firmly believe that, in the course of human events, the time has arrived when the vital interests of Spain are as seriously involved in the sale, as those of the United States in the purchase, of the island, and that the transaction will prove equally honorable to both nations.

"Under these circumstances, we cannot anticipate a failure, unless, possibly, through the malign influence of foreign powers, who possess no right whatever to interfere in the matter.

"We proceed to state some of the reasons which have brought us to this conclusion; and, for the sake of clearness, we shall specify them under two distinct heads:

"1. The United States ought, if practicable, to purchase Cuba with as little delay as possible.

"2. The probability is great that the Government and Cortes of Spain will prove willing to sell it; because this would essentially promote the highest and best interests of the Spanish people.

"Then, 1. It must be clear to every reflecting mind that, from the peculiarity of its geographical position, and the considerations attendant on it, Cuba is as necessary to the North American republic as any of its present members, and that it belongs naturally to that great family of States of which the Union is the providential nursery.

"From its locality, it commands the mouth of the Mississippi, and the immense and annually increasing trade which must seek this avenue to the ocean.

"On the numerous navigable streams, measuring an aggregate course of some thirty thousand miles, which disembogue themselves through this magnificent river

[17] Dated Washington, August 16, 1854.

[18] October 9, 1854.

into the Gulf of Mexico, the increase of the population within the last ten years amounts to more than that of the entire Union at the time Louisiana was annexed to it.

"The natural and main outlet to the products of this entire population, the highway of their direct water-course with the Atlantic and the Pacific States, can never be secure, but must ever be endangered, whilst Cuba is a dependency of a distant power, in whose possession it has proved to be a source of constant annoyance and embarrassment to their interests.

"Indeed, the Union can never enjoy repose, nor possess reliable security, as long as Cuba is not embraced within its boundaries."

These arguments for the necessity of acquiring Cuba on our part, though not so strong intrinsically as might be adduced to justify the acquisition of Great Britain by France, are still further amplified; intermingled with demonstrations that Spain would be, pecuniarily, the gainer by the sale, and insults which would seem offered on purpose to render her compliance impossible. Witness these specimens:

"Such is her present wretched financial condition, that her best bonds are sold upon her own Bourse at about one-third of their par value; whilst another class, on which she pays no interest, have but a nominal value, and are quoted at about one-sixth the amount for which they were issued. Besides, these latter are held principally by British creditors, who may, from day to day, obtain the effective interposition of their own Government for the purpose of coercing payment. Intimations to that effect have been already thrown out from high quarters; and, unless some new source of revenue shall enable Spain to provide for such exigencies, it is not improbable that they may be realized.

"Extreme oppression, it is now universally admitted, justifies any people in endeavoring to relieve themselves from the yoke of their oppressors. The sufferings which the corrupt, arbitrary, and unrelenting local administration necessarily entails upon the inhabitants of Cuba, cannot fail to stimulate and keep alive that spirit of resistance and revolution against Spain, which has of late years been so often manifested. In this condition of affairs, it is vain to expect that the sympathies of the people of the United States will not be warmly enlisted in favor of their oppressed neighbors.

"We know that the President is justly inflexible in his determination to execute the neutrality laws; but, should the Cubans themselves rise in revolt against the oppression which they suffer, no human power could prevent citizens of the United States, and liberal-minded men of other countries, from rushing to their assistance. Besides, the present is an age of adventure, in which restless and daring spirits abound in every portion of the world.

"It is not improbable, therefore, that Cuba may be wrested from Spain by a successful revolution: and, in that event, she will lose both the island and the price which we are now willing to pay for it—a price far beyond what was ever paid by one people to another for any province."

Finally, Spain is frankly told by our model diplomatists that we will have Cuba at any rate; that resistance on her part will only serve to deprive her of the liberal bonus we are prepared to pay for its peaceful cession. Here is the language:

"But if Spain, dead to the voice of her own interest, and actuated by stubborn pride and a false sense of honor, should refuse to sell Cuba to the United States, then the question will arise, What ought to be the course of the American Government under such circumstances?

"Self-preservation is the first law of nature, with States as well as with individuals. All nations have, at different periods, acted upon this maxim. Although it has been made the pretext for committing flagrant injustice, as in the partition of Poland and other similar cases which history records, yet the principle itself, though often abused, has always been recognized. * * * * After we shall have offered Spain a price for Cuba far beyond its present value, and this shall have been refused, then it will be time to consider the question, Does Cuba, in the possession of Spain, seriously endanger *our internal peace* and the existence of our cherished Union?

"Should this question be answered in the affirmative, then, by every law, human and divine, we shall be justified in wresting it from Spain, if we possess the power: and this upon the very same principle that would justify an individual in tearing down the burning house of his neighbor if there was no other means of preventing the flames from destroying his own home.

"Under such circumstances, we ought

neither to count the cost nor regard the odds which Spain might enlist against us. We forbear to enter into the question whether the present condition of the island would justify such a measure. We should, however, be recreant to our duty, be unworthy of our gallant forefathers, and commit base treason against our posterity, should we permit Cuba to be Africanized and become a second St. Domingo, with all its attendant horrors to the white race, and suffer the flames to extend to our own neighboring shores, seriously to endanger, or actually to consume, the fair fabric of our Union.

"We fear that the course and current of events are rapidly tending toward such a catastrophe. We, however, hope for the best, though we ought certainly to be prepared for the worst."

When this dispatch was made public in Europe through the newspapers, the first sensation created by it was one of stubborn incredulity. The journal which contained it having a far higher reputation for enterprise than for accuracy, our minister at one of the minor courts did not hesitate at once to assure the diplomatic circle that it was a transparent and unquestionable hoax; and such it was quite commonly adjudged until later advices had left no room for doubt.

The civilized world, unhappily, was not now for the first time to make the acquaintance of the rule of the strongest. The partition of Poland, Napoleon's perfidious clutch of Spain and her royal Bourbons, with a portion of the doings of the triumphant despots who resettled Europe by dividing it among themselves at the Congress of Vienna in 1815, and several less conspicuous examples, had already guarded the intelligent classes against the delusion that, in Christendom any more than out of it, temptations to gigantic robbery will be uniformly resisted even by nations and their rulers—that rapacity ever needs any other excuse than the proximity and defenselessness of its prey. But, though the exactions of morality are often disregarded by monarchs and cabinets in our day, the requirements of decorum are very rarely defied and derided by any power north of the Mediterranean; and the blackest political crimes of the present age have usually been perpetrated in the abused names of Order, of Legitimacy, and of Religion. That the United States should covet Cuba, and seek by any means to acquire it, did not severely shock Europe's sense of decency; that we should openly, boldly, set forth such justifications of our lust, clearly did. The coarseness, the effrontery, and the shamelessness of the Ostend Manifesto seemed to carry the world back to the days of Attila or Genghis Khan, and to threaten the centers of civilization and refinement, the trophies of art and the accumulations of wealth, with a new irruption of barbarians from the remote, forbidding West. No other document that ever emanated from our Government was so well calculated to deepen and diffuse the distrust and apprehension wherewith the growth and power of our country had already come to be regarded by the more polite, intelligent, and influential classes of the Old World.

The doctrines of this Manifesto were in no respect disavowed, modified, or explained, by our Government. None of our citizens who had openly, notoriously contributed to fit out and man the Lopez expedition were brought to justice, or exposed to any punishment whatever. While strenuous efforts were made to procure the pardon and release of such Americans as had been captured while participating in that ill-fated adventure, evidence was soon afforded that the spirit which impelled to that crime would find aliment, but not satiety, in the conquest of Cuba. Very soon after the appearance of the Ostend Circular, one William Walker, a Tennessean, recently resident in California, left that State, at the head of a band as reckless and desperate as himself, for Nicaragua, which he entered in the character of ally to one of the factions habitually disputing the mastery of that, as well as of most other Spanish American countries. Though he never evinced much military or other capacity, Walker, so long as he acted under color of authority from the chiefs of the faction he patronized, was generally successful against the pitiful rabble styled soldiers by whom his progress was resisted, capturing[19] at last by surprise the important city of Granada, which was deemed the stronghold of the adverse faction, and assuming thereon the rank of General. But his very successes proved the ruin of the faction to which he had attached himself, by exciting the natural jealousy and alarm of the natives who mainly composed it; and his assumption, soon afterward, of the title of President of Nicaragua, speedily followed by a decree reëstablishing Slavery in that country, exposed his purpose and insured his downfall. As if madly bent on ruin, he proceeded to confiscate the steamboats and other property of the Nicaragua Transit Company, thereby arresting all American travel to and from California through that country, and cutting himself off from all hope of further recruiting his forces from the throngs of sanguine or of baffled gold-seekers, who might otherwise have been attracted to his standard. Yet he maintained the unequal contest for about two years, succumbing at last to a coalition of the Central American States, and surrendering his remnant of some two hundred men at Rivas.[20] By the interposition of Commander C. H. Davis, of our sloop of war St. Mary's, on the Pacific coast, he and sixteen of his party were brought away unharmed, and landed at Panama, whence he returned to this country, and immediately commenced at New Orleans the fitting out of a new Nicaraguan military expedition. Here he was arrested, and compelled to give bonds in the sum of two thousand dollars to desist from unlawful enterprises; notwithstanding which, he very soon left that city on a steamboat freighted with armed men and military stores, ostensibly for Mobile, but which, once at sea, headed for Nicaragua, landing him and his followers at Punta Arenas, Nov. 25th. Here Commodore Paulding of our Navy compelled him to surrender,[21] with one hundred and thirty-two of his followers, bringing him to New-York as a prisoner. President Buchanan, by Special Message to Congress,[22] condemned the Commodore for thus violating the sovereignty of a foreign country! and declined to hold Walker as a prisoner. Being thus set at liberty, the 'gray-eyed Man of Destiny' traversed the South, exciting the more fanatical Slavery propagandists to aid him in fitting out a third expedition, with which he got off from Mobile;[23] but was arrested near the

[19] October 13, 1855. [20] May 1, 1857. [21] December 8th. [22] January 7, 1858. [23] October 7th.

mouths of the Mississippi for having left port without a clearance. Being taken to New Orleans, he and his associates were tried before the Federal Court and all acquitted; when he immediately recommenced his operations, so that in June, 1860, he was again afloat, with an expedition bound to Central America. He, this time, landed on the island of Ruatan,[24] and finally at Truxillo,[25] which he took with little loss, thence issuing a proclamation to the people, assuring them, in the usual fashion, that he did not come to make war on them, but on their Government. Very soon, the President of Honduras appeared,[26] at the head of seven hundred men, while the commander of an English man-of-war in the harbor ordered Walker to decamp. He obeyed, marching with eighty men southward along the coast, and was soon captured,[27] brought back to Truxillo, tried by court-martial, condemned, and shot. He was small in size, cold in demeanor, of light complexion, slow of speech, and unimpressive in manner, and was often accused by his followers of utter recklessness as to their sufferings or perils. His death put a decided damper on the spirit whereof his later life was so striking a manifestation.

In the heyday of Walker's career, and while it was exciting much admiration among the more reckless youth of our great cities, especially at the South, the Democratic National Convention, which nominated Mr. Buchanan at Cincinnati, unanimously adopted the following:[28]

"1. *Resolved*, That there are questions connected with the foreign policy of this country, which are inferior to no domestic question whatever. The time has come for the people of the United States to declare themselves in favor of free seas, and progressive free-trade throughout the world, and, by solemn manifestations, to place their moral influence at the side of their successful example.

"2. *Resolved*, That our geographical and political position with reference to the other States of this continent, no less than the interest of our commerce, and the development of our growing power, requires that we should hold sacred the principles of the Monroe doctrine.

"3. *Resolved*, That the great highway which nature, as well as the States most immediately interested in its maintenance, has marked out for free communication between the Atlantic and the Pacific Oceans, constitutes one of the most important achievements realized by the spirit of modern times, in the unconquerable energy of our people; and that result would be secured by a timely and efficient exertion of the control which we have the right to claim over it; and no power on earth should be suffered to impede or clog its progress by any interference with relations that it may suit our policy to establish between our Government and the Government of the States within whose dominions it lies; we can under no circumstances surrender our *preponderance* in the adjustment of all questions arising out of it.

"4. *Resolved*, That, in view of so commanding an interest, the people of the United States cannot but sympathize with the efforts which are being made *by the people of Central America* to *regenerate*[29] that portion of the continent which covers the passage across the inter-oceanic isthmus.

"5. *Resolved*, That the Democratic party will expect of the next Administration that every proper effort be made to insure our *ascendency* in the Gulf of Mexico, and to maintain permanent protection to the great outlets through which are emptied into its waters the products raised out of the soil and the commodities created by the industry of the people of our western valleys and of the Union at large."

Hon. Albert G. Brown, Senator from Mississippi, visited Mr. Buchanan at Lancaster soon after his nomination for President in 1856, as one of the Committee appointed by the Convention to apprise him officially

[24] June 25th. [25] June 27th. [26] August 23d. [27] September 3d.

[28] May 22, 1856. [29] Alluding to Walker, then militant in Central America.

of the fact, and was, of course, very cordially received. After his return to Washington, he wrote[30] to his friend and constituent, Hon. S. R. Adams, an account of his interview, mainly devoted to a report of Mr. Buchanan's sayings on that occasion. Of these, the material portion is as follows:

"After thus speaking of Kansas and the Slavery issue, Mr. Buchanan passed to our foreign policy. He approved, in general terms, of the Cincinnati resolutions on this subject, but said that, while enforcing our own policy, we must at all times scrupulously regard the just rights and proper policy of other nations. He was not opposed to territorial extension. All our acquisitions had been fairly and honorably made. Our necessities might require us to make *other* acquisitions. He regarded the acquisition of *Cuba* as very desirable now, and it was likely to become a National necessity. Whenever we could obtain the island on fair, honorable terms, he was for taking it. But, he added, it must be a terrible necessity that would induce me to sanction any movement that would bring reproach upon us, or tarnish the honor and glory of our beloved country.

"After the formal interview was over, Mr. Buchanan said playfully, but in the presence of the whole audience, 'If I can be instrumental in settling the Slavery question upon the terms I have mentioned, and then add *Cuba* to the Union, I shall, if President, be willing to give up the ghost, and let Breckinridge take the Government.' Could there be a more noble ambition? * * * In my judgment, he is as worthy of Southern confidence and Southern votes as ever Mr. Calhoun was."[31]

The Republican National Convention of 1856, in the platform of principles framed and adopted by it, alluded to this subject as follows:

"*Resolved*, That the highwayman's plea that 'might makes right,' embodied in the Ostend Circular, was in every respect unworthy of American diplomacy, and would bring shame and dishonor on any government or people that gave it their sanction."

At the last Democratic National Convention, which met at Charleston, April 23, 1860, while discord reigned with regard to candidates and the domestic planks of their platform, there was one topic whereon a perfect unanimity was demonstrated. In the brief platform of the majority was embodied the following:

"*Resolved*, That the Democratic party are in favor of the acquisition of the island of Cuba, on such terms as shall be honorable to ourselves and just to Spain."

This resolve was first reported to the Convention by Mr. Avery, of N. C., from the majority of the grand Committee, was accepted on all hands, and was unanimously adopted by the bolting, or Breckinridge, as well as by the Douglas, or majority, Convention. It thus forms about the only surviving and authentic article of the Democratic creed, and may serve as the nucleus of a grand "reconstruction."

---

[30] June 18, 1856.

[31] Among the letters found by the Union soldiers at the residence of Jefferson Davis, in Mississippi, when in 1863 they advanced, under Gen. Grant, into the heart of that State, was the following from a prominent Democratic politician of Pennsylvania:

"PHILADELPHIA, *March* 7, 1850.

"MR. JEFFERSON DAVIS,—*My Dear Sir:* Can you tell me if Gen. Larmon is likely to remain much longer in Nicaragua? I should like to go to that country, and help *open it to civilization and niggers*. I could get strong recommendations from the President's special friends in Pennsylvania for the place were the mission vacant, and, I think, I would prove a live Minister.

"I am tired of being a white slave at the North, and long for a home in the sunny South.

"Please let me hear from you when you have leisure.

"Mrs. Brodhead joins me in sending kind remembrances to Mrs. Davis and yourself.

"Sincerely and gratefully your friend,

"JOHN BRODHEAD."

XX.

JOHN BROWN.

On the 17th of October, 1859, this country was bewildered and astounded, while the fifteen Slave States were convulsed with fear, rage, and hate, by telegraphic dispatches from Baltimore and Washington, announcing the outbreak, at Harper's Ferry, of a conspiracy of Abolitionists and negroes, having for its object the devastation and ruin of the South, and the massacre of her white inhabitants. A report that President Buchanan had been proclaimed Emperor and Autocrat of the North American continent, and had quietly arrested and imprisoned all the members of Congress and Judges of the Supreme Court, by way of strengthening his usurpation, would not have seemed more essentially incredible, nor have aroused a more intense excitement. Here follow the dispatches which gave the first tidings of this audacious and amazing demonstration:

"INSURRECTION AT HARPER'S FERRY!

"To the Associated Press:

"BALTIMORE, *Monday, Oct.* 17, 1859.

"A dispatch just received here from Frederick, and dated this morning, states that an insurrection has broken out at Harper's Ferry, where an armed band of Abolitionists have full possession of the Government Arsenal. The express train going east was twice fired into, and one of the railroad hands and a negro killed, while they were endeavoring to get the train through the town. The insurrectionists stopped and arrested two men, who had come to town with a load of wheat, and, seizing their wagon, loaded it with rifles, and sent them into Maryland. The insurrectionists number about 250 whites, and are aided by a gang of negroes. At last accounts, fighting was going on.

"The above is given just as it was received here. It seems very improbable, and should be received with great caution, until affirmed by further advices. A later dispatch, received at the railroad office, says the affair has been greatly exaggerated. The reports had their foundation in a difficulty at the Armory, with which negroes had nothing to do.

"BALTIMORE, 10 o'clock.

"It is apprehended that the affair at Harper's Ferry is more serious than our citizens seem willing to believe. The wires from Harper's Ferry are cut, and consequently we have no telegraphic communication with Monocacy Station. The southern train, which was due here at an early hour this morning, has not yet arrived. It is rumored that there is a stampede of negroes from this State. There are many other wild rumors, but nothing authentic as yet.

"BALTIMORE, *Monday, Oct.* 17—2 P. M.

"Another account, received by train, says the bridge across the Potomac was filled with insurgents, all armed. Every light in the town was extinguished, and the hotels closed. All the streets were in the possession of the mob, and every road and lane leading thereto barricaded and guarded. Men were seen in every quarter with muskets and bayonets, who arrested the citizens, and impressed them into the service, including many negroes. This done, the United States Arsenal and Government Pay-house, in which was said to be a large amount of money, and all other public works, were seized by the mob. Some were of the opinion that the object was entirely plunder, and to rob the Government of the funds deposited on Saturday at the Pay-house. During the night, the mob made a demand on the Wager Hotel for provisions, and enforced the claim by a body of armed men. The citizens were in a terrible state of alarm, and the insurgents have threatened to burn the town.

"The following has just been received from Monocacy, this side of Harper's Ferry:

"'The Mail Agent on the western-bound train has returned, and reports that the train was unable to get through. The town is in possession of the negroes, who arrest every one they can catch and imprison. The train due here at 3 p. m., could not get through, and the Agent came down on an empty engine.'"

Probably the more prevalent sensation at first excited by this intelligence was that of blank incredulity. Harper's Ferry being the seat of a National Armory, at which a large number of mechanics and artisans were usually employed by the Government, it was supposed by many that some collision respecting wages or hours of labor had occurred between the officers and the workmen, which had provoked a popular tumult, and perhaps a stoppage of the trains passing through that village on the Baltimore and Ohio Railroad; and that this, magnified by rumor and alarm, had afforded a basis for these monstrous exaggerations. Yet, as time wore on, further advices, with particulars and circumstances, left no room to doubt the substantial truth of the original report. An attempt had actually been made to excite a slave insurrection in Northern Virginia, and the one man in America to whom such an enterprise would not seem utter insanity and suicide, was at the head of it.

John Brown was sixth in descent from Peter Brown, a carpenter by trade, and a Puritan by intense conviction, who was one of the glorious company who came over in the Mayflower, and landed at Plymouth Rock, on that memorable 22d of December, 1620. The fourth in descent from Peter the pilgrim, was John Brown, born in 1728, who was captain of the West Simsbury (Connecticut) train-band, and in that capacity joined the Continental Army at New York in the Spring of 1776, and, after two months' service, fell a victim to camp-fever, dying in a barn a few miles north of the city. His grandson, John Brown, of Osawatomie, son of Owen and Ruth Brown, was born in Torrington, Conn., May 9, 1800. On his mother's side, he was descended from Peter Miles, an emigrant from Holland, who settled at Bloomfield, Conn., about 1700; and his grandfather on this side, Gideon Mills, also served in the Revolutionary war, and attained the rank of lieutenant.

When John was but five years old, his father migrated to Hudson, Ohio, where he died a few years since, aged eighty-seven. He was engaged, during the last war, in furnishing beef cattle to our forces on the northern frontier; and his son, John, then twelve to fourteen years of age, accompanied him as a cattle-driver, and, in that capacity, witnessed Hull's surrender at Detroit, in 1812. He was so disgusted with what he saw of military life that he utterly refused, when of suitable age, to train or drill in the militia, but paid fines or evaded service during his entire liability to military duty. In an autobiographical fragment, written by him in 1857, for a child who had evinced a deep interest in his Kansas efforts, speaking of himself in the third person, he says:

"During the war with England, a circumstance occurred that in the end made him a most determined Abolitionist, and led him to declare, or swear, eternal war with Slavery. He was staying, for a short time, with a very gentlemanly landlord, once a United States Marshal, who held a slave-boy near his own age, active, intelligent, and good-feeling, and to whom John was under considerable obligation for numerous little acts of kindness. The master made a great pet of John, brought him to table with his first company and friends—called their attention to every little smart thing he said or did, and to the fact of his being more than a hundred miles from home with a drove of cattle alone; while the negro boy (who was fully, if not more than, his equal,) was badly clothed, poorly fed and lodged in cold weather, and beaten before his eyes with iron shovels or any other thing that came first to hand. This brought John to reflect on the wretched, hopeless condition of fatherless and motherless slave children; for such children have neither fathers nor mothers to protect and provide for them. He sometimes would raise the question, Is God their Father?"

Young John had very little of what is called education; poverty and hard work being his principal teachers. At sixteen years of age, he joined the Congregational Church in Hudson; and from fifteen to twenty he learned the trade of tanner and currier. He returned to New England while still a minor, and commenced, at Plainfield, Mass., a course of study with a view to the Christian ministry; but, being attacked with inflammation of the eyes, which ultimately became chronic, he relinquished this pursuit and returned to Ohio, where he married his first wife, Dianthe Lusk, when a little more than twenty years of age. By her, he had seven children; the last of whom, born in 1832, was buried with her three days after its birth. He next year married Mary A. Day (who survives him), by whom he had thirteen children, of whom three sons were with him at Harper's Ferry, two of whom lost their lives there, and the third escaped. Eight of his children were living at the time of his death.

Brown worked for himself as a tanner and farmer five or six years in northern Ohio, and, for nine or ten years thereafter, in Crawford County, Pennsylvania, enjoying general respect as a sincere, earnest, upright, pious man. One who knew him in those days remembers that the wrong of Slavery was a favorite topic with him, and that, though stern in manner, he was often affected to tears when depicting the unmerited sufferings of slaves. So early as 1839, the idea of becoming himself a liberator of the unhappy race was cherished by him. From 1835 to 1846, he lived once more in northern Ohio, removing thence to Springfield, Mass., where he engaged in wool-dealing under the firm of Perkins & Brown, selling wool extensively on commission for growers along the southern shore of Lake Erie, and undertaking to dictate prices and a system of grading wools to the manufacturers of New England, with whom he came to an open rupture, which induced him at length to ship two hundred thousand pounds of wool to London, and go thither to sell it. This bold experiment proved a failure, wool bringing far higher prices in this country than in any other. He finally sold at a fearful loss and came home a bankrupt. But, meantime, he had traveled considerably over Europe, and learned something of the ways of the world.

In 1849, he removed with his family to North Elba, Essex County, New York, to some land given him by Gerrit Smith. He went thither expressly to counsel and benefit the negroes settled in that vicinity, on lands likewise bestowed upon them by our noblest philanthropist. The location was a hard one, high up among the glens of the Adirondack Mountains, rugged, cold, and bleak. The negroes generally became discouraged, in view of the incessant toil, privation, and hardships, involved in hewing a farm and a habitation out of the primitive wilderness, in a secluded, sterile region, and gave over in despair after a brief trial; but John Brown and his sons persevered, ultimately making homes for themselves, which, though not luxurious nor inviting, their families retain. In 1851, the father returned with his family to Akron, Ohio, where he once more carried on the wool business and managed the farm of a friend; but, in 1855, on starting for Kansas, he moved his family back to their own home at North Elba, where they remain, with his grave in the midst of them.

In 1854, his four elder sons—all by his first wife, and all living in Ohio—determined to migrate to Kansas. They went thither, primarily, to make that a Free State; secondly, to make homes for themselves and their families. They went unarmed, having a very inadequate idea of the nature and spirit of the fiend they were defying. They settled in Lykins County, southern Kansas, about eight miles distant from the present village of Osawatomie, and not far from the Missouri border. Here they were soon so harassed, threatened, insulted, and plundered, by gangs of marauding ruffians from Missouri, that they found it impossible to remain without arms, and they wrote to their father to procure such as they needed. He obtained them; and, to make sure work of it, went with them. Nearly all others went to Kansas in the hope of thereby improving their worldly condition, or, at least, of making homes there. John Brown went there for the sole purpose of fighting, if need were, for Liberty. He left his family behind him, for he had no intention of making Kansas his home. He was no politician, in the current acceptation of the term, having taken little or no interest in party contests for many years. His intimate follower and admiring biographer, Redpath, says of him:

"It has been asserted that he was a member of the Republican party. It is false. He despised the Republican party. It is true that, like every Abolitionist, he was opposed to the extension of Slavery: and, like the majority of anti-Slavery men, in favor, also, of organized political action against it. But he was too earnest a *man*, and too devout a Christian, to rest satisfied with the only action against Slavery consistent with one's duty as a *citizen*, according to the usual Republican interpretation of the Federal Constitution. It teaches that we must content ourselves with resisting the extension of Slavery. Where the Republicans said, 'Halt!' John Brown shouted, 'Forward! to the rescue!' He was an Abolitionist of the Bunker Hill school. He followed neither Garrison nor Seward, Gerrit Smith nor Wendell Phillips; but the Golden Rule and the Declaration of Independence, in the spirit of the Hebrew warriors, and in the God-applauded mode that they adopted. 'The Bible story of Gideon,' records a man who betrayed him, 'had manifestly a great influence on his actions.' He believed in human brotherhood and in the God of Battles; he admired Nat Turner, the negro patriot, equally with George Washington, the white American deliverer. He could not see that it was heroic to fight against a petty tax on tea, and war seven long years for a political principle, yet wrong to restore, by force of arms, to an outraged race, the rights with which their Maker had endowed them, but of which the South, for two centuries, had robbed them. The old man distrusted the Republican leaders. He thought that their success in 1860 would be a serious check to the cause he loved.[1] His reason was that the people had confidence in these leaders, and would believe that, by their action in Congress, they would peacefully and speedily abolish Slavery. That the people would be deceived—that the Republicans would become as conservative of Slavery as the Democrats themselves—he sincerely and prophetically believed. Apathy to the welfare of the slave would follow; and hence, to avert this moral and national calamity, he hurried on to Harper's Ferry.

"He was no politician. He despised that class with all the energy of his earnest and determined nature. He was too large a man to stand on any party platform. He planted his feet on the Rock of Ages—the Eternal Truth—and was therefore never shaken in his policy or principles."

[1] "'The Republicans of 1858 will be the Democrats of 1860'—a pithy prophecy, found among the manuscripts at Harper's Ferry—is a brief and clear statement of John Brown's ideas."

Of course, he was not pleased with what he found and saw in Kansas. There were too much policy, too much politics, and too general a regard for personal safety and comfort. He would have preferred a good deal less riding about, especially at night, with more solid fighting. Redpath, who visited him in his camp near Prairie City, not long before the battle of Black Jack, says:

"I shall not soon forget the scene that there opened to my view. Near the edge of the creek, a dozen horses were tied, all ready saddled for a ride for life, or a hunt after Southern invaders. A dozen rifles and sabres were stacked around the trees. In an open space, amid the shady and lofty woods, there was a great blazing fire with a pot on it; a woman, bare-headed, with an honest, sun-burnt face, was picking blackberries from the bushes; three or four armed men were lying on red and blue blankets on the grass; and two fine-looking youths were standing, leaning on their arms, on guard, near by. One of them was the youngest son of Old Brown, and the other was 'Charley,' the brave Hungarian, who was subsequently murdered at Osawatomie. Old Brown himself stood near the fire, with his shirt-sleeves rolled up, and a large piece of pork in his hand. He was cooking a pig. He was poorly clad, and his toes protruded from his boots. The old man received me with great cordiality, and the little band gathered about me. But it was for a moment only; for the Captain ordered them to renew their work. He respectfully but firmly forbade conversation on the Pottawatomie; and said that, if I desired any information from the company in relation to their conduct or intentions, he, as their Captain, would answer for them whatever it was proper to communicate.

"In this camp, no manner of profane language was permitted; no man of immoral character was allowed to stay, except as a prisoner of war. He made prayers, in which all the company united, every morning and evening; and no food was ever tasted by his men until the Divine blessing had been asked on it. After every meal, thanks were returned to the Bountiful Giver. Often, I was told, the old man would retire to the densest solitudes to wrestle with his God in secret prayer. One of his company subsequently informed me that, after these retirings, he would say that the Lord had directed him in visions what to do; that, for himself, he did not love warfare, but peace—only acting in obedience to the will of the Lord, and fighting God's battles for His children's sake.

"It was at this time that the old man said to me: 'I would rather have the small-pox, yellow fever, and cholera, all together in my camp, than a man without principles. It's a mistake, Sir,' he continued, 'that our people make, when they think that bullies are the best fighters, or that they are the men fit to oppose these Southerners. Give me men of good principles—God-fearing men, men who respect themselves—and, with a dozen of them, I will oppose any hundred such men as these Buford ruffians.'

"I remained in the camp about an hour. Never before had I met such a band of men. They were not earnest, but earnestness incarnate. Six of them were John Brown's sons."

In the August following, a new invasion, on an extensive scale, of Kansas, from the Missouri border, was planned and executed. Inflammatory proclamations were issued, which affirmed that the pro-Slavery settlers either had been or were about to be all killed or driven out of the Territory by the Abolitionists, and the Missourians were exhorted to rally all their forces for the conflict. Lexington, Mo., was assigned as the place, and August 20th as the time, of assemblage for La Fayette County, and New Santa Fe, Jackson County, as the general rendezvous. "Bring your guns, your horses, and your clothing, all ready to go on to Kansas: our motto will be this time, 'No Quarter!' Let no one stay away!" A similar appeal was issued from Westport, signed by Atchison, Stringfellow, and others. A force of two thousand men was, by virtue of these appeals, collected at the petty village of Santa Fe, directly on the border; but soon divided into two expeditions, one of which, led by Senator Atchison, was confronted at Bull's Creek by not more than half its number under Gen. J. H. Lane, and turned back without a fight—first halting, and refusing to advance against the determined front of the Free-State men, and finally disappearing in the course of the ensuing night. The other and smaller party, led by Gen. Reid, consisted of four to five hundred men, well armed with United States cannon, muskets, bayonets, and revolvers, and liberally supplied with ammunition. They pursued a more southerly course, and, at daylight on the morning of August 30th, approached the little village of Osawatomie, which was defended by barely thirty Free-State men; but their leader was old John Brown. His son Frederick was shot dead, about a mile and a half from the village, by the Rev. Martin White, who led the pro-Slavery advance or scouting party, before young Brown was aware of their hostile character. Two other Free-State men were likewise surprised and killed early in the morning.

John Brown, with his thirty compatriots, took position in great haste in the timber on the southern bank of the little river Osage, here known as the Marais-des-Cygnes, a little to the northwest of the village, and here fought the advance of the foe as they approached, until thirty-one or two of them were killed and from forty to fifty wounded. The Free-State men, fighting generally under cover against an undisciplined and badly managed force, lost but five or six in all; but the disproportion was too great, and, their ammunition becoming exhausted, they were forced to retreat, leaving Osawatomie to be sacked and burned again. Brown himself continued steadily firing, as well as directing his men, throughout the conflict, amid an incessant shower of grapeshot and bullets. Not until he saw the whites of the enemy's eyes did he give the order to his little band to retreat. The Ruffians killed the only wounded prisoner whom they took, as also a Mr. Williams, whom they found in Osawatomie, and who had taken no part in the conflict. The Missourians returned to their homes in triumph, boasting that they had killed old Brown and dispersed his band; but their wagon-loads of dead and wounded created a salutary awe, which was very efficient in preventing future invasions, or rendering them comparatively infrequent.

The Rev. Martin White, for his services in this expedition, was chosen a member of the next Lecompton (pro-Slavery) Legislature, which he attended; and, in the course of its deliberations, he entertained his fellow-members with a graphic and humorous account of his killing of Frederick Brown. When the session was finished, he started for home, but never reached it. His body was found cold and stiff on the prairie, with a rifle-ball through his vitals.

Six weeks after the Osawatomie fight, Capt. Brown was in Lawrence, stopping over Sunday on his way home from Topeka, when the startling announcement was made that 2,800 Missourians, under Atchison and Reid, were advancing upon that town. Not more than two hundred men in all could be rallied for its defense. Brown was unanimously chosen their leader. He made a speech from a dry-goods box in Main-street, opposite the post-office, substantially as follows:

"Gentlemen, it is said there are twenty-five hundred Missourians down at Franklin, and that they will be here in two hours. You can see for yourselves the smoke they are making by setting fire to the houses in that town. Now is probably the last opportunity you will have of seeing a fight; so that you had better do your best. If they should come up and attack us, don't yell and make a great noise, but remain perfectly silent and still. Wait till they get within twenty-five yards of you; get a good object; be sure you see the hind-sight of your gun: then fire. A great deal of powder and lead, and very precious time, are wasted by shooting too high. You had better aim at their legs than at their heads. In either case, be sure of the hind-sights of your guns. It is from this reason that I myself have so many times escaped; for, if all the bullets which have been aimed at me had hit me, I should have been as full of holes as a riddle."

He proceeded to post his men so admirably as to conceal entirely their paucity of numbers, taking advantage of a gentle ridge running east and west, at some distance south of the town. The hostile forces remained through the night about half a mile from each other, with a corn-field between, each man covered by the grass and the inequalities of the ground, their positions only revealed by the flashes and reports of their guns. When the sun rose next morning, the Missourians had decamped.

Capt. Brown left soon after for the East by the circuitous land route through Nebraska and Iowa; that through Missouri being closed against Free-State men. He took a fugitive slave in his wagon, and saw him safely on his way to freedom. He made two or three visits to the East in quest of aid and of funds, returning for the last time to Southern Kansas in the Autumn of 1858. Peace had finally been secured in all that part of the Territory lying north of the Kansas river, by the greatly increased numbers and immense preponderance of the Free-State settlers, rendering raids from Missouri, whether to carry elections or devastate settlements, too perilous to be lightly undertaken. When the Missourians still rallied, in obedience to habit, at Kansas elections, they did so at Oxford, Santa Fe, and other polls held just along the border, where they could suddenly concentrate force enough to make the operation a tolerably safe one. But Southern Kansas was still very thinly settled, in part by Missourians; while Fort Scott, a military post and land-office in the heart of that section, afforded a nucleus and a rallying-point for pro-Slavery terrorism. The Missourians, recognizing and acting under the Territorial Legislature and local officers created by the Border Ruffian irruptions and fraudulent elections, claimed to be the party of Law and Order, and often, if not usually, committed their outrages under the lead of a marshal or a sheriff. The Free-State men, repudiating and scouting those elections and their fruits, were regarded and treated, not only by the pro-Slavery party on either side of the border, but by the Federal Administration and its instruments in Kansas, as outlaws and criminals. At length, Fort Scott itself was captured[2] by Montgomery,[3] one of the boldest of the Free-State leaders, who, with 150 men, entered it by night, made temporary prisoners of its dignitaries, and liberated a Free-State man imprisoned there. Montgomery soon after surrendered himself to the Federal Governor of the Territory, when a treaty or understanding was had between them,

[2] Dec. 15, 1858.

[3] Since, Colonel of the First South Carolina (Colored) Volunteers.

under which the region gradually settled into comparative peace.

But, while the ferment was at its hight, and forces were gathering on both sides for the conflict, a slave named Jim came secretly across the border to Capt. Brown's cabin, and told him that himself and his family had been sold, and were to be sent off to Texas next day. Brown, with twenty men, divided into two parties, crossed the border in the night, liberated Jim and his family, and, proceeding to the house of another slaveholder, gave deliverance to five more slaves. The other party, under Kagi, called at several houses in search of slaves, but found none until they reached the residence of David Cruse, who, learning their object, seized his rifle and raised it to fire, but was instantly shot dead. He had but one slave, who accompanied his liberators on their retreat. One of the captured slaveholders was carried several miles into the Territory to prevent his raising a hue-and-cry for rescue.

A furious excitement throughout Western Missouri inevitably followed. The Governor offered a reward of three thousand dollars for the arrest of Brown, on his part; to which President Buchanan added two hundred and fifty dollars. It was reported that the slave population of the two adjacent Missouri counties was diminished from five hundred to fifty within a few weeks, mainly by removal for sale. The more moderate Free-State men earnestly disavowed all sympathy with Brown's doings over the border, or any acts of violence by Free-State men on their adversaries, not committed in necessary self-defense. Brown soon learned that he must leave Kansas, or remain there denounced and condemned by those who had hitherto been his friends. He resolved to leave, and started early in January, 1859, passing through Lawrence on his northward route. He had four white companions, three of whom afterward fought under him at Harper's Ferry, and three negroes, beside women and children. He was pursued by thirty pro-Slavery men from Lecompton so sharply that he was compelled to halt and prepare for a defense. He took possession of two deserted log-cabins in the wilderness, which his pursuers surrounded, at a respectful distance, and sent to Atchison and Lecompton for reënforcements. From Atchison, twelve men arrived, making their force forty-two to his eight. As they were preparing to attack, Brown and his seven companions suddenly issued from the wood, in order of battle, when the valorous *posse* turned and fled.[4] Not a shot was fired, as they, putting spurs to their horses, galloped headlong across the prairie, and were soon lost to the view. Only four men stood their ground, and these were made prisoners forthwith. Brown ordered them to dismount, and give their horses to his negroes. This command occasioned—not to say provoked—profane language on their part; whereupon he commanded silence, saying he would permit no blasphemy in his presence. At this, they only swore the louder and the harder. "Kneel!" exclaimed the stern Puri-

[4] They probably were already aware, though Brown was not, that a party of mounted men from Topeka were hastening to his rescue, and were then within a short distance

tan, suddenly presenting his pistol. There was no alternative but a deadly one, and they all knelt. "Now, pray!" It was probably their first attempt in that line for many years, and their success could hardly have been brilliant; but he kept them at it until they had at least manifested an obedient and docile spirit. They never swore again in his presence, though he held them prisoners for five days, compelling them, each and all, to pray night and morning. These four were from Atchison; and, being finally liberated, returned to that still pro-Slavery city, where one of them was green enough to tell the story of their capture, and their discipline under old John Brown. The laugh was so general and so hearty that they soon left, never to return.

Brown was joined, soon after this "Battle of the Spurs," by Kagi, with forty mounted men from Topeka, of whom seventeen escorted him safely to Nebraska City. He there crossed the Mississippi into Iowa, and traveled slowly through that State, Illinois, and Michigan, to Detroit, where he arrived on the 12th of March, crossing immediately into Canada, where his twelve blacks—one of them born since he left Missouri—were legally, as well as practically, free. All of them were industrious, prosperous, and happy, when last heard from, many months thereafter.

A secret convention, called by Brown, and attended only by such whites and blacks as he believed in thorough sympathy with his views, had assembled in a negro church at Chatham, Canada West, May 8, 1858; at which Convention a "Provisional Constitution and Ordinances for the People of the United States" had been adopted. It was, of course, drafted by Brown, and was essentially an embodiment of his political views. The nature of this Constitution is sufficiently exhibited in the following extracts:

"PREAMBLE.—*Whereas*, Slavery, throughout its entire existence in the United States, is none other than the most barbarous, unprovoked, and unjustifiable war of one portion of its citizens against another portion, the only conditions of which are perpetual imprisonment and hopeless servitude, or absolute extermination, in utter disregard and violation of those eternal and self-evident truths set forth in our Declaration of Independence:

"Therefore, We, the citizens of the United States, and the oppressed people, who, by a recent decision of the Supreme Court, are declared to have no rights which the white man is bound to respect, together with all the other people degraded by the laws thereof, do, for the time being, ordain and establish for ourselves the following Provisional Constitution and ordinances, the better to protect our people, property, lives, and liberties, and to govern our actions.

"ARTICLE I. *Qualifications of Membership.*—All persons of mature age, whether proscribed, oppressed, and enslaved citizens, or of proscribed and oppressed races of the United States, who shall agree to sustain and enforce the Provisional Constitution and ordinances of organization, together with all minor children of such persons, shall be held to be fully entitled to protection under the same."

"ART. XXVIII. *Property.*—All captured or confiscated property, and all property the product of the labor of those belonging to this organization, and of their families, shall be held as the property of the whole equally, without distinction, and may be used for the common benefit, or disposed of for the same object. And any person, officer or otherwise, who shall improperly retain, secrete, use, or needlessly destroy, such property, or any property found, captured, or confiscated, belonging to the enemy, or shall willfully neglect to render a full and fair statement of such property by him so taken or held, shall be guilty of a misdemeanor, and, on conviction, shall be punished accordingly.

"ART. XXIX. *Safety or Intelligence Fund.*—All money, plate, watches, or jewelry, captured by honorable warfare, found, taken, or confiscated, belonging to the enemy, shall be held sacred, to constitute a liberal safety or intelligence fund; and any person who shall improperly retain, dispose of, hide, use, or destroy, such money or other articles above named, contrary to the provisions and spirit of this article, shall be deemed guilty of theft, and, on conviction thereof, shall be punished accordingly. The Treasurer shall furnish the Commander-in-Chief at all times with a full statement of the condition of such fund, and its nature."

"ART. XXXIII. *Volunteers.*—All persons who may come forward, and shall voluntarily deliver up slaves, and have their names registered on the books of this organization, shall, so long as they continue at peace, be entitled to the fullest protection in person and property, though not connected with this organization, and shall be treated as friends, and not merely as persons neutral.

"ART. XXXIV. *Neutrals.*—The persons and property of all non-slaveholders who shall remain absolutely neutral shall be respected so far as circumstances can allow of it, but they shall not be entitled to any active protection.

"ART. XXXV. *No Needless Waste.*—The needless waste or destruction of any useful property or article by fire, throwing open of fences, fields, buildings, or needless killing of animals, or injury of either, shall not be tolerated at any time or place, but shall be promptly and peremptorily punished.

"ART. XXXVI. *Property Confiscated.*—The entire personal and real property of all persons known to be acting, either directly or indirectly, with or for the enemy, or found in arms with them, or found willfully holding slaves, shall be confiscated and taken whenever and wherever it may be found, in either Free or Slave States."

"ART. XLVI. *These Articles not for the Overthrow of Government.*—The foregoing articles shall not be construed so as in any way to encourage the overthrow of any State Government, or of the General Government of the United States, and look to no dissolution of the Union, but simply to amendment and repeal; and our flag shall be the same that our fathers fought under in the Revolution."

Under this Constitution, the offices of President and Commander-in-Chief were to be separate, and in all cases to be held by different persons. John Brown was chosen Commander-in-Chief; J. H. Kagi, Secretary of War; Owen Brown (son of John), Treasurer; Richard Realf, Secretary of State.

Brown returned to the States soon after his triumphal entry into Canada as a liberator, and was at Cleveland from the 20th to the 30th of March. He entered his name on the hotel-book, as "John Brown, of Kansas," advertised two horses for sale at auction; and, at the time of the sale, stood in front of the auctioneer's stand, notifying all bidders that the title might be considered defective, since he had taken the horses with the slaves whom he liberated in Western Missouri, finding it necessary to his success that the slaves should have horses, and that the masters should not. "But," he added, when telling the story afterward, "they brought a very excellent price."

Early in April following, he was in Ashtabula County, Ohio, sick of the ague. He visited his family in Essex County, New York, toward the end of that month. In May, he was in New York City, Rochester, and Boston, where he learned to manufacture crackers. On the 3d of June, he was at Collinsville, Conn., where he closed a contract for a thousand pikes, that he had ordered some time before.

He was soon afterward again in Northern Ohio, and in Western Pennsylvania, proceeding by Pittsburg and Bedford to Chambersburg, where he remained several days. He was in Hagerstown, Md., on the 30th, where he registered his name as "Smith, and two sons, from Western New York." He told his landlord that they had been farming in Western New York, but had been discouraged by losing two or three years' crops by frost, and they were now looking for a milder climate, in a lo-

VIEW OF HARPER'S FERRY.

cation adapted to wool-growing, etc. After looking about Harper's Ferry for several days, they found, five or six miles from that village, a large farm, with three unoccupied houses, the owner, Dr. Booth Kennedy, having died the last Spring. These houses they rented for a trifle until the next March, paying the rent in advance, purchasing for cash a lot of hogs from the family, and agreeing to take care of the stock on the farm until it could be sold, which they faithfully did. After they had lived there a few weeks, attracting no observation, others joined them from time to time, including two of Brown's young daughters; and one would go and another come, without exciting any particular remark. They paid cash for everything, were sociable and friendly with their neighbors, and seemed to pass their time mainly hunting in the mountains; though it was afterward remembered that they never brought home any game. On one occasion, a neighbor remarked to the elder Mr. Smith (as old Brown was called), that he had observed twigs and branches bent down in a peculiar manner; which Smith explained by stating that it was the habit of Indians, in traveling through a strange country, to mark their path thus, so as to be able to find their way back. He had no doubt, he said, that Indians passed over these mountains, unknown to the inhabitants.

Meantime, the greater number of the men kept out of sight during the day, so as not to attract attention, while their arms, munitions, etc., were being gradually brought from Chambersburg, in well-secured boxes. No meal was eaten on the farm, while old Brown was there, until a blessing had been asked upon it; and his Bible was in daily requisition.

The night of the 24th of October was originally fixed upon by Brown for the first blow against Slavery in Virginia, by the capture of the Federal Arsenal at Harper's Ferry; and his biographer, Redpath, alleges that many were on their way to be with him on that occasion, when they were paralyzed by the intelligence that the blow had already been struck, and had failed. The reason given for this, by one[5] who was in his confidence, is, that Brown, who had been absent on a secret journey to the North, suspected that one of his party was a traitor, and that he must strike prematurely, or not at all. But the women who had been with them at the Kennedy farm—the wives or daughters of one or another of the party—had already been quietly sent away; and the singular complexion of their household had undoubtedly begun to excite curiosity, if not alarm, among their neighbors. On Saturday, the 15th, a council was held, and a plan of operations discussed. On Sunday evening, another council was held, and the programme of the chief unanimously approved. He closed it with these words:

"And now, gentlemen, let me press this one thing on your minds. You all know how dear life is to you, and how dear your lives are to your friends; and, in remembering that, consider that the lives of others are as dear to them as yours are to you. Do not, therefore, take the life of any one if you can possibly avoid it; but, if it is neces-

[5] A certain "Col." Hugh Forbes, an English adventurer, and general dabbler in civil discord, who had been with Brown in Iowa, if not in Kansas, afterward figured as a revealer of his secrets, or what were alleged to be such. He had been disappointed in his pecuniary expectations.

sary to take life in order to save your own, then make sure work of it."

Harper's Ferry was then a village of some five thousand inhabitants, lying on the Virginia side of the Potomac, and on either side of its principal tributary, the Shenandoah, which here enters it from the South. Its site is a mere nest or cup among high, steep mountains; the passage of the united rivers through the Blue Ridge at this point having been pronounced by Jefferson a spectacle which one might well cross the Atlantic to witness and enjoy. Here the Baltimore and Ohio Railroad crosses the Potomac; and the rich valley of the Shenandoah is traversed, for a considerable distance hence, by the Winchester and Harper's Ferry Railroad. Washington is fifty-seven miles distant by turnpike; Baltimore eighty miles by railroad. Modest as the village then was, space had been with difficulty found for its habitations, some of which were perched upon ground four hundred feet above the surface of the streams. One of its very few streets was entirely occupied by the work-shops and offices of the National Armory, and had an iron railing across its entrance. In the old Arsenal building, there were usually stored from 100,000 to 200,000 stand of arms. The knowledge of this had doubtless determined the point at which the first blow of the liberators was to be struck.

The forces with which Brown made his attack consisted of seventeen white and five colored men, though it is said that others who escaped assisted outside, by cutting the telegraph wires and tearing up the railroad track. The entrance of this petty army into Harper's Ferry on Sunday evening, October 17th, seems to have been effected without creating alarm. They first rapidly extinguished the lights of the town; then took possession of the Armory buildings, which were only guarded by three watchmen, whom, without meeting resistance or exciting alarm, they seized and locked up in the guard-house. It is probable that they were aided, or, at least, guided, by friendly negroes belonging in the village. At half-past ten, the watchman at the Potomac bridge was seized and secured. At midnight, his successor, arriving, was hailed by Brown's sentinels, but ran, one shot being fired at him from the bridge. He gave the alarm, but still nothing stirred. At a quarter-past one, the western train arrived, and its conductor found the bridge guarded by armed men. He and others attempted to walk across, but were turned back by presented rifles. One man, a negro, was shot in the back, and died next morning. The passengers took refuge in the hotel, and remained there several hours; the conductor properly refusing to pass the train over, though permitted, at three o'clock, to do so.

A little after midnight, the house of Col. Washington was visited by six of Brown's men under Capt. Stevens, who captured the Colonel, seized his arms, horses, etc., and liberated his slaves. On their return, Stevens and party visited the house of Mr. Alstadtt and his son, whom they captured, and freed their slaves. These, with each male citizen as he appeared in the street, were confined in the Armory until they numbered between forty and fifty. Brown informed his prisoners that they could be liberated on condition of writing to their friends to send a negro apiece as ransom. At daylight, the train proceeded, Brown walking over the bridge with the conductor. Whenever any one asked the object of their captors, the uniform answer was, "To free the slaves;" and when one of the workmen, seeing an armed guard at the Arsenal gate, asked by what authority they had taken possession of the public property, he was answered, "By the authority of God Almighty!"

The passenger train that sped eastward from Harper's Ferry, by Brown's permission, in the early morning of Monday, October 17th, left that place completely in the military possession of the insurrectionists. They held, without dispute, the Arsenal, with its offices, workshops, and grounds. Their sentinels stood on guard at the bridges and principal corners, and were seen walking up and down the streets. Every workman, who ignorantly approached the Armory, as day dawned, was seized and imprisoned, with all other white males who seemed capable of making any trouble. By eight o'clock, the number of prisoners had been swelled to sixty-odd, and the work was still proceeding.

But it was no longer entirely one-sided. The white Virginians, who had arms, and who remained unmolested in their houses, prepared to use them. Soon after daybreak, as Brown's guards were bringing two citizens to a halt, they were fired on by a man named Turner, and, directly afterward, by a grocer named Boerly, who was instantly killed by the return fire. Several Virginians soon obtained possession of a room overlooking the Armory gates, and fired thence at the sentinels who guarded them, one of whom fell dead, and another — Brown's son Watson—was mortally wounded. Still, throughout the forenoon, the liberators remained masters of the town. There were shots fired from one side or the other at intervals, but no more casualties reported. The prisoners were by turns permitted to visit their families under guard, to give assurance that they still lived and were kindly treated. Had Brown chosen to fly to the mountains with his few followers, he might still have done so, though with a much slenderer chance of impunity than if he had, according to his original plan, decamped at midnight, with such arms and ammunition as he could bear away. Why he lingered, to brave inevitable destruction, is not certain; but it may fairly be presumed that he had private assurances that the negroes of the surrounding country would rise at the first tidings of his movement, and come flocking to his standard; and he chose to court the desperate chances of remaining where arms and ammunition for all could abundantly be had. True, he afterward said that he had arms enough already, either on or about his premises; but, if so, why seize Harper's Ferry at all?

At all events, if his doom was already sealed, his delay at least hastened it. Half an hour after noon, a militia force, one hundred strong, arrived from Charlestown, the county seat, and were rapidly disposed so as to command every available exit from the place. In taking the Shenandoah bridge, they killed one of the insurgents, and captured William Thompson, a neighbor of Brown at Elba, unwounded. The rifle-works were next attacked, and speedily carried, being defended by five insurgents only. These attempted to cross the river, and four of them succeeded in reaching a rock in the middle of it, whence they fought with two hundred Virginians, who lined either bank, until two of them were dead, and a third mortally wounded, when the fourth surrendered. Kagi, Brown's Secretary of War, was one of the killed. William H. Leeman, one of Brown's captains, being pursued by scores, plunged into the river, a Virginian wading after him. Leeman turned round, threw up his empty hands, and cried, "Don't shoot!" The Virginian fired his pistol directly in the youth's face—he was but twenty-two—and shattered his head into fragments.

By this time, all the houses around the Armory buildings were held by the Virginians. Capt. Turner, who had fired the first shot in the morning, was killed by the sentinel at the Arsenal gate, as he was raising his rifle to fire. Here Dangerfield Newby, a Virginia slave, and Jim, one of Col. Washington's negroes, with a free negro, who had lived on Washington's estate, were shot dead; and Oliver Brown, another of the old man's sons, being hit by a ball, came inside of the gate, as his brother Watson had done, lay quietly down without a word, and in a few moments was dead. Mr. Beckham, mayor of the town, who came within range of the insurgents' rifles as they were exchanging volleys with the Virginians, was likewise killed.

At the suggestion of Mr. Kitzmiller, one of Brown's prisoners, Aaron D. Stevens, one of his most trusted followers from Kansas, was sent out with a flag of truce to call a parley, but was instantly shot down by the Virginians, receiving six balls in his person. Thompson, their prisoner, was attacked by scores of them in the parlor where he was confined, but saved for the moment by a young lady throwing herself between him and their presented rifles, because, as she afterward explained, she "did not want the carpet spoiled." He was dragged out to the bridge, there shot in cold blood, and his body riddled with balls at the base of the pier, whither he had fallen forty feet from the bridge.

By this time, more militia had arrived from every quarter, and a party from Martinsburgh, led by a railroad conductor, attacked the Armory buildings in the rear, while a detachment of the same force assailed them in front. Brown, seeing that his assailants were in overwhelming force, retreated to the engine-house, where he repulsed his assailants, who lost two killed and six wounded.

Still, militia continued to pour in; the telegraph and railroad having been completely repaired, so that the Government at Washington, Gov. Wise at Richmond, and the authorities at Baltimore, were in immediate communication with Harper's Ferry, and hurrying forward troops from all quarters to overwhelm the remaining handful of insurgents, whom terror and rumor had multiplied to twenty times their actual number. At five, P. M., Capt. Simms arrived, with militia from Maryland, and completed the investment of the Armory buildings, whence eighteen prisoners had already been liberated upon the retreat of Brown to the engine-house.

Col. Baylor commanded in chief. The firing ceased at nightfall. Brown offered to liberate his prisoners, upon condition that his men should be permitted to cross the bridge in safety, which was refused. Night found Brown's forces reduced to three unwounded whites beside himself, with perhaps half a dozen negroes from the vicinity. Eight of the insurgents were already dead; another lay dying beside the survivors; two were captives mortally wounded, and one other unhurt. Around the few survivors were fifteen hundred armed, infuriated foes. Half a dozen of the party, who had been sent out at early morning by Brown to capture slaveholders, and liberate slaves, were absent, and unable, even if willing, to rejoin their chief. They fled during the night to Maryland and Pennsylvania; but most of them were ultimately captured. During that night, Col. Lee, with ninety United States marines and two pieces of artillery, arrived, and took possession of the Armory guard, very close to the engine-house.

Brown, of course, remained awake and alert through the night, discomfited and beyond earthly hope, but perfectly cool and calm. Said Gov. Wise, in a speech at Richmond soon after:

> "Col. Washington said that Brown was the coolest man he ever saw in defying death and danger. With one son dead by his side, and another shot through, he felt the pulse of his dying son with one hand, held his rifle with the other, and commanded his men with the utmost composure, encouraging them to be firm, and to sell their lives as dearly as possible."

Conversing with Col. Washington during that solemn night, he said he had not pressed his sons to join him in this expedition, but did not regret their loss—they had died in a good cause.

At seven in the morning, after a parley which resulted in nothing, the marines advanced to the assault, broke in the door of the engine-house by using a ladder as a battering-ram, and rushed into the building. One of the defenders was shot and two marines wounded; but the odds were too great; in an instant, all resistance was over. Brown was struck in the face with a saber and knocked down, after which the blow was several times repeated, while a soldier ran a bayonet twice into the old man's body. All the insurgents, it was said, would have been killed on the spot, had the Virginians been able to distinguish them with certainty from their prisoners.

Of course, all Virginia, including her Governor, rushed to Harper's Ferry upon learning that all was over, and the insurrection completely suppressed. The bleeding survivors were subjected to an alternation of queries and execrations, which they met bravely, as they had confronted the bullets of their numerous and ever-increasing foes. They answered frankly, save where their replies might possibly compromise persons still at liberty; and none of them sought to conceal the fact that they had struck for Universal Freedom at all hazards. The bearing of Brown was especially praised by his enemies (many of whom have since won notoriety in the ranks of the Rebellion), as remarkably simple and noble. Among others, Mr. C. L. Vallandigham, of Ohio, hastened to visit and catechise Brown, in the hope of making political capital out of his confessions, and was answered frankly and fully. On his return to Ohio, he said:

"It is in vain to underrate either the man or the conspiracy. Capt. John Brown is as brave and resolute a man as ever headed an insurrection; and, in a good cause, and with a sufficient force, would have been a consummate partisan commander. He has coolness, daring, persistency, the stoic faith and patience, and a firmness of will and purpose unconquerable. He is the farthest possible remove from the ordinary ruffian, fanatic, or madman. Certainly, it was one of the best planned and best executed conspiracies that ever failed."

On Wednesday evening, October 19th, after thirty hours of this discipline, the four surviving prisoners were conveyed to the jail at Charlestown under an escort of marines. Brown and Stevens, badly wounded, were taken in a wagon; Green and Coppoc, unhurt, walked between files of soldiers, followed by hundreds, who at first cried, "Lynch them!" but were very properly shamed into silence by Gov. Wise.

It is not necessary to linger here over the legal proceedings in this case; nor do the complaints, so freely made at the time, of indecent haste and unfair dealing, on the part of the Virginia authorities, seem fully justified. That the conviction and death of Brown and his associates were predetermined, is quite probable; but the facts and the nature of the case were notorious, beyond dispute; and Virginia had but this alternative—to hang John Brown, or to abolish Slavery. She did not choose to abolish Slavery; and she had no remaining choice but to hang John Brown. And as to trying him and Stevens while still weak and suffering severely from their wounds—neither able at times to stand up—it must be considered that the whole State had been terror-stricken by the first news of their attempt, and that fears of insurrection and of an armed rescue were still widely prevalent. That the lawyers of the vicinage who were assigned to the defense of the prisoners did their duty timidly and feebly, is certain; but they shared, of course, not only the prejudices but the terrors of their neighbors, and knew that the case, at any rate, was hopeless.

Brown's conduct throughout commanded the admiration of his bitterest enemies. When his papers were brought into court to be identified, he said: "I will identify any of my handwriting, and save all trouble. I am ready to face the music." When a defense of insanity was suggested rather than interposed, he repelled it with indignation. When, after his conviction, he was suddenly brought into court, on the 1st of November, to listen to the judgment, and directed to stand up, and say why sentence should not be passed upon him, though taken by surprise and somewhat confused, he spoke gently and tenderly as follows:

"In the first place, I deny every thing but what I have all along admitted—the design on my part to free the slaves. I intended certainly to have made a clear thing of that matter, as I did last winter, when I went into Missouri, and there took slaves without the snapping of a gun on either side, moved them through the country, and finally left them in Canada. I designed to have done the same thing again, on a larger scale. That was all I intended. I never did intend murder, or treason, or the destruction of property, or to excite or incite slaves to rebellion, or to make insurrection.

"I have another objection: and that is, it is unjust that I should suffer such a penalty. Had I interfered in the manner which I admit has been fairly proved—(for I admire the truthfulness and candor of the greater portion of the witnesses who have testified in this case)—had I so interfered in behalf of the rich, the powerful, the intelligent, the so-called great, or in behalf of any

VIEW IN THE SHENANDOAH VALLEY.

of their friends, either father, mother, brother, sister, wife, or children, or any of that class, and suffered and sacrificed what I have in this interference, it would have been all right, and every man in this Court would have deemed it an act worthy of reward rather than punishment.

"This Court acknowledges, as I suppose, the validity of the Law of God. I see a book kissed here which I suppose to be the Bible, or, at least, the New Testament. That teaches me that all things 'whatsoever I would that men should do unto me, I should do even so to them.' It teaches me, further, to 'remember those that are in bonds as bound with them.' I endeavored to act upon that instruction. I say, I am yet too young to understand that God is any respecter of persons. I believe that to have interfered as I have done, as I have always freely admitted I have done, in behalf of His despised poor, was not wrong, but right. Now, if it is deemed necessary that I should forfeit my life for the furtherance of the ends of justice, and mingle my blood further with the blood of my children, and with the blood of millions in this slave country whose rights are disregarded by wicked, cruel, and unjust enactments—I submit: so let it be done.

"Let me say one word further:

"I feel entirely satisfied with the treatment I have received on my trial. Considering all the circumstances, it has been more generous than I expected. But I feel no consciousness of guilt. I have stated from the first what was my intention and what was not. I never had any design against the life of any person, nor any disposition to commit treason, or excite slaves to rebel, or make any general insurrection. I never encouraged any man to do so, but always discouraged any idea of that kind.

"Let me say, also, a word in regard to the statements made by some of those connected with me. I hear it has been stated by some of them that I have induced them to join me. But the contrary is true. I do not say this to injure them, but as regretting their weakness. There is not one of them but joined me of his own accord, and the greater part at their own expense. A number of them I never saw, and never had a word of conversation with, till the day they came to me, and that was for the purpose I have stated.

"Now I have done."

Among the many letters addressed to him while in prison was one from Lydia Maria Child, who sought, but did not obtain, from the Virginia authorities, permission to visit him in his prison. Her letter to Brown was answered as follows:

"MRS. L. MARIA CHILD:

"My dear Friend (such you prove to be, though a stranger):—Your most kind letter has reached me, with the kind offer to come here and take care of me. Allow me to express my gratitude for your great sympathy, and at the same to propose to you a different course, together with my reasons for wishing it. I should certainly be greatly pleased to become personally acquainted with one so gifted and so kind; but I cannot avoid seeing some objections to it, under present circumstances. First, I am in charge of a most humane gentleman, who, with his family, have rendered me every possible attention I have desired, or that could be of the least advantage; and I am so far recovered from my wounds as no longer to require nursing. Then, again, it would subject you to great personal inconvenience and heavy expense, without doing me any good.

"Allow me to name to you another channel through which you may reach me with your sympathies much more effectually. I have at home a wife and three young daughters—the youngest but little over five years old, the oldest nearly sixteen. I have also two daughters-in-law, whose husbands have both fallen near me here. There is also another widow, Mrs. Thompson, whose husband fell here. Whether she is a mother or not, I cannot say. All these, my wife included, live at North Elba, Essex County, New York. I have a middle-aged son, who has been, in some degree, a cripple from his childhood, who would have as much as he could well do to earn a living. He was a most dreadful sufferer in Kansas, and lost all he had laid up. He has not enough to clothe himself for the winter comfortably. I have no living son, or son-in-law, who did not suffer terribly in Kansas.

"Now, dear friend, would you not as soon contribute fifty cents now, and a like sum yearly, for the relief of those very poor and deeply afflicted persons, to enable them to supply themselves and their children with bread and very plain clothing, and to enable the children to receive a common English education? Will you also devote your energies to induce others to join in giving a like amount, or any other amount, to constitute a little fund for the purpose named?

"I cannot see how your coming here can do me the least good, and I am quite certain you can do me immense good where you are. I am quite cheerful under all my afflicting circumstances and prospects; having, as I humbly trust, 'the peace of God, which passeth all understanding,' to rule in my heart. You may make such use of this as you see fit. God Almighty bless and reward you a thousand fold!

"Yours, in sincerity and truth,

"JOHN BROWN."

His letter to his family, written a week after his sentence to death, is as follows:

"CHARLESTOWN, JEFFERSON CO., VA.,
"8th Nov., 1859.

"Dear Wife and Children—Every one: I will begin by saying that I have in some degree recovered from my wounds, but that I am quite weak in my back, and sore about my left kidney. My appetite has been quite good for most of the time since I was hurt. I am supplied with almost every thing I could desire to make me comfortable, and the little I do lack (some articles of clothing, which I lost), I may perhaps soon get again. I am, besides, quite cheerful, having (as I trust) the peace of God, which 'passeth all understanding,' to 'rule in my heart,' and the testimony (in some degree) of a good conscience that I have not lived altogether in vain. I can trust God with both the time and the manner of my death, believing, as I now do, that for me at this time to seal my testimony (for God and humanity) with my blood, will do vastly more toward advancing the cause I have earnestly endeavored to promote, than all I have done in my life before. I beg of you all meekly and quietly to submit to this; not feeling yourselves in the least *degraded* on that account. Remember, dear wife and children all, that Jesus of Nazareth suffered a most excruciating death on the cross as a felon, under the most aggravating circumstances. Think, also, of the prophets, and apostles, and Christians of former days, who went through greater tribulations than you or I; and (try to) be reconciled. May God Almighty comfort all your hearts, and soon wipe away all tears from your eyes. To Him be endless praise. Think, too, of the crushed millions who 'have no comforter.' I charge you all never (in your trials) to forget the griefs of 'the poor that cry, and of those that have none to help them.' I wrote most earnestly to my dear and afflicted wife not to come on, for the present at any rate. I will now give her my reasons for doing so. First, it would use up all the scanty means she has, or is at all likely to have, to make herself and children comfortable hereafter. For let me tell you that the sympathy that is now aroused in your behalf may not always follow you. There is but little more of the romantic about helping poor widows and their children than there is about trying to relieve poor 'niggers.' Again, the little comfort it might afford us to meet again would be dearly bought by the pains of a final separation. We must part; and, I feel assured, for us to meet under such dreadful circumstances would only add to our distress. If she come on here, she must be only a gazing-stock throughout the whole journey, to be remarked upon in every look, word, and action, and by all sorts of creatures, and by all sorts of papers throughout the whole country. Again, it is my most decided judgment that in quietly and submissively staying at home, vastly more of generous sympathy will reach her, without such dreadful sacrifice of feeling as she must put up with if she comes on. The visits of one or two female friends that have come on here have produced great excitement, which is very annoying, and they cannot possibly do me any good. O Mary, do not come; but patiently wait for the meeting (of those who love God and their fellow-men) where no separation must follow. 'They shall go no more out forever.' I greatly long to hear from some one of you, and to learn any thing that in any way affects your welfare. I sent you ten dollars the other day. Did you get it? I have also endeavored to stir up Christian friends to visit and write to you in your deep affliction. I have no doubt that some of them, at least, will heed the call. Write to me, care of Capt. John Avis, Charlestown, Jefferson County, Va.

"'Finally, my beloved, be of good comfort.' May all your names be 'written in the Lamb's book of life'—may you all have the purifying and sustaining influence of the Christian religion—is the earnest prayer of your affectionate husband and father,

"JOHN BROWN.

"P. S. I cannot remember a night so dark as to have hindered the coming day, nor a storm so furious or dreadful as to prevent the return of warm sunshine and a cloudless sky. But, beloved ones, do remember that this is not your rest, that in this world you have no abiding-place or continuing city. To God and His infinite mercy I always commend you. J. B."

"Nov. 9."

During the forty-two days of his confinement at Charlestown, Brown received several visits from sympathizing Northern friends, many of whom had never before seen him. His wife, overcoming many obstacles, was finally permitted to spend a few hours in his cell, and to take supper with him a short time before his death. No Virginians, so far as is known, proffered him any words of kindness, unless it were the reverend clergy of the neighborhood, who tendered him the solace of religion after their fashion, which he civilly, but firmly, declined. He could not recognize any one who justified or palliated Slavery as a minister of the God he worshiped, or the Saviour in whom he trusted. He held arguments on several occasions with pro-Slavery clergymen, but recognized them as men only, and not as invested with any peculiar sanctity. To one of them, who sought to reconcile Slavery with Christianity, he said: "My dear Sir, you know nothing about Christianity; you will have to learn the A B Cs in the lesson of Christianity, as I find you entirely ignorant of the meaning of the word. I, of course, respect you as a gentleman; but it is as a *heathen* gentleman." The argument here closed.

The following characteristic letter was written by him, while under sentence of death, to a relative then residing in Windham, Ohio:

"CHARLESTOWN, JEFFERSON CO., VA.,
19th Nov., 1859.

"REV. LUTHER HUMPHREY—*My Dear Friend:* Your kind letter of the 12th instant is now before me. So far as my knowledge goes as to our mutual kindred, I suppose I am the first since the landing of Peter Brown from the Mayflower that has either been sentenced to imprisonment or to the gallows. But, my dear old friend, let not that fact alone grieve you. You cannot have forgotten how and where our grandfather (Captain John Brown) fell in 1776, and that he, too, might have perished on the scaffold had circumstances been but very little different. The fact that a man dies under the hand of an executioner (or otherwise) has but little to do with his true character, as I suppose. John Rogers perished at the stake, a great and good man, as I suppose: but his doing so does not prove that any other man who has died in the same way was good or otherwise. Whether I have any reason to 'be of good cheer' (or not) in view of my end, I can assure you that I feel so; and that I am totally blinded if I do not really experience that strengthening and consolation you so faithfully implore in my behalf. The God of our Fathers reward your fidelity! I neither feel mortified, degraded, nor in the least ashamed of my imprisonment, my chain, or my near prospect of *death by hanging.* I feel assured 'that not one hair shall fall from my head without the will of my heavenly Father.' I also feel that I have long been endeavoring to hold exactly 'such a *fast* as God has chosen.' See the passage in Isaiah which you have quoted. No part of my life has been more happily spent than that I have spent here, and I humbly trust that no part has been spent to better purpose. I would not say this boastingly; but 'thanks be unto God who giveth us the victory,' through infinite grace.

"I should be 60 years old were I to live till May 9, 1860. I have enjoyed much of life as it is, and have been remarkably prosperous, having early learned to regard the welfare and prosperity of others as my own. I have never, since I can remember, required a great amount of sleep, so that I conclude that I have already enjoyed full an average number of waking hours with those who reach their 'three-score years and ten.' I have not as yet been driven to the use of glasses, but can see to read and write quite comfortably. But, more than that, I have generally enjoyed remarkably good health. I might go on to recount unnumbered and unmerited blessings, among which would be some very severe afflictions; and those the most needed blessings of all. And now, when I think how easily I might be left to spoil all I have done or suffered in the cause of Freedom, I hardly dare wish another voyage, even if I had the opportunity. It is a long time since we met; but we shall now soon come together in our 'Father's house,' I trust. 'Let us hold fast that we already have,' remembering 'we shall reap in due time if we faint not.' 'Thanks be ever unto God, who giveth us the victory through Jesus Christ our Lord.' And now, my old warm-hearted friend, 'Good-bye.'

"Your affectionate cousin,
"JOHN BROWN."

The 2d of December was the day appointed for his execution. Nearly three thousand militia were early on the ground. Fears of a forcible rescue or of a servile insurrection prevented a large attendance of citizens. Cannon were so planted as to sweep every approach to the jail, and to blow the prisoner into shreds upon the first intimation of tumult. Virginia held her breath until she heard that the old man was dead.

Brown rose at daybreak, and continued writing with energy until half-past ten, when he was told to prepare to die. He shook hands with the sheriff, visited the cell of Copeland and Green, to whom he handed a quarter of a dollar each, saying he had no more use for money, and bade them adieu. He next visited Cook and Coppoc, the former of whom had made a confession, which he pronounced false; saying he had never sent Cook to Harper's Ferry, as he had stated. He handed a quarter to Coppoc also, shook hands with him, and parted. He then visited and bade a kindly good-bye to his more especial comrade, Stevens, gave him a quarter, and charged him not to betray his friends. A sixth, named Hazlett, was confined in the same prison, but he did not visit him, denying all knowledge of him.

He walked out of the jail at 11 o'clock; an eye-witness said—"with a radiant countenance, and the step of a conqueror." His face was even joyous, and it has been remarked that probably his was the lightest heart in Charlestown that day. A black woman, with a little child in her arms, stood by the door. He stopped a moment, and, stooping, kissed the child affectionately. Another black woman, with a child, as he passed along, exclaimed: "God bless you, old man! I wish I could help you; but I can't." He looked at her with a tear in his eye. He mounted the wagon beside his jailor, Capt. Avis, who had been one of the bravest of his captors, who had treated him very kindly, and to whom he was profoundly grateful. The wagon was instantly surrounded by six companies of militia. Being asked, on the way, if he felt any fear, he replied: "It has been a characteristic of me from infancy not to suffer from physical fear. I have suffered a thousand times more from bashfulness than from fear." The day was clear and bright, and he remarked, as he rode, that the country seemed very beautiful. Arrived at the gallows, he said: "I see no citizens here; where are they?" "None but the troops are allowed to be present," was the reply. "That ought not to be," said he; "citizens should be allowed to be present as well as others." He bade adieu to some acquaintances at the foot of the gallows, and was first to mount the scaffold. His step was still firm, and his bearing calm, yet hopeful. The hour having come, he said to Capt. Avis: "I have no words to thank you for all your kindness to me." His elbows and ankles being pinioned, the white cap drawn over his eyes, the hangman's rope adjusted around his neck, he stood waiting for death. "Capt. Brown," said the sheriff, "you are not standing on the drop. Will you come forward?" "I can't see," was his firm answer; "you must lead me." The sheriff led him forward to the center of the drop. "Shall I give you a handkerchief, and let you drop it as a signal?" "No; I am ready at any time; but do not keep me needlessly waiting." In defiance of this reasonable request, he was kept standing thus several minutes, while a military parade and display of readiness to repel an imaginary foe were enacted. The time seemed an hour to the impatient spectators; even the soldiers began to murmur—"Shame!" At last, the order was given, the rope cut with a hatchet, and the trap fell; but so short a distance that the victim continued to struggle and to suffer for a considerable time. Being at length duly pronounced dead, he was cut down after thirty-eight minutes' suspension. His body was conveyed to Harper's Ferry, and delivered to his widow, by whom it was borne to her far northern home, among the mountains he so loved, and where he was so beloved.[6]

There let it rest forever, while the path to it is worn deeper and deeper by the pilgrim feet of the race he so bravely though rashly endeavored to rescue from a hideous and debasing thraldom!

XXI.

THE PRESIDENTIAL CANVASS OF 1860.

The vote polled for Fremont and Dayton in 1856 considerably exceeded the solid strength, at that time, of the Republican party. It was swelled in part by the personal popularity of Col. Fremont, whose previous career of adventure and of daring—his explorations, discoveries, privations, and perils—appealed, in view of his comparative youth for a Presidential candidate, with resistless fascination, to the noble young men of our country; while his silence and patience throughout the canvass, under a perfect tempest of preposterous yet annoying calumnies, had contributed to widen the circle of his admirers and friends. A most wanton and brutal personal assault[1] on Senator Sumner, of Massachusetts, by Representative Brooks of South Carolina, abetted by Representatives Keitt, of South Carolina, and Edmundson, of Virginia, doubtless contributed also to swell the Republican vote of the following Autumn. Mr. Sumner had made an elaborate speech in the Senate on the Kansas question—a speech not without grave faults of conception and of style, but nowise obnoxious to the charge of violating the decencies of debate by unjustifiable personalities. Yet, on the assumption that its author had therein unwarrantably assailed and ridiculed Judge Butler—one of South Carolina's Senators, and a relative of Mr. Brooks—he was assaulted by surprise while sitting in his place (though a few minutes after the Senate had adjourned for the day), knocked to the floor senseless, and beaten, while helpless

[6] Cook, Coppoc, Copeland, and Green (a black), were hanged at Charlestown a fortnight after Brown—December 16th; Stevens and Hazlitt were likewise hanged on the 16th of March following. The confederates of Brown, who succeeded in making their escape, were Owen Brown, Barclay Coppoc, Charles P. Tidd, Francis Jackson Merriam, and Osborne P. Anderson, a colored man.

[1] May 22, 1856.

and unconscious, till the rage of his immediate assailant was thoroughly satiated. Mr. Sumner was so much injured as to be compelled to abandon his seat and take a voyage to Europe, where, under the best medical treatment, his health was slowly restored. The infliction on Brooks, by a Washington court, of a paltry fine[2] for this outrage, tended to deepen and diffuse popular indignation at the North, which the unopposed reëlection of Brooks—he having resigned, because of a vote of censure from a majority of the House—did not tend to allay. Of Fremont's aggregate vote—1,341,812—it is probable that all above 1,200,000 was given him on grounds personal to himself, or from impulses growing out of the Sumner outrage.

Accordingly, the elections of 1857 exhibited a diminution of Republican strength—the eleven States which had voted for Fremont, giving him an aggregate popular majority of over 250,000, now giving but little over 50,000 for the Republican tickets. All the New England States were still carried by the Republicans, but by majorities diminished, in the average, more than half, while that of Connecticut was reduced from 7,715 to 546. So, in Ohio, Gov. Chase was this year reëlected by 1,481, though Fremont had 16,623; while Gov. Lowe, in Iowa, had but 2,151, where Fremont had received 7,784; and Gov. Randall was chosen in Wisconsin by barely 118, where Fremont had received 13,247. No Republican State was actually revolutionized, however, but New York; where—owing, in part, to local questions and influences—Fremont's magnificent plurality of 80,000 was changed to a Democratic plurality of 18,000. It appeared in this, as in most other Free States, that the decline or dissolution of the "American" or Fillmore party inured mainly to the benefit of the triumphant Democracy; though Pennsylvania, and possibly Rhode Island, were exceptions. To swell the resistless tide, Minnesota and Oregon—both in the extreme North—each framed a State Constitution this year, and took position in line with the dominant party—Minnesota by a small, Oregon by an overwhelming majority—the two swelling by four Senators and four[3] Representatives the already invincible strength of the Democracy.

The Opposition was utterly powerless against this surge; but what they dare hardly undertake, Mr. Buchanan was able to effect. By his utterly indefensible attempt to enforce the Lecompton Constitution upon Kansas, in glaring contradiction to his smooth and voluble professions regarding "Popular Sovereignty," "the will of the majority," etc., etc., he enabled the Republicans, in 1858, to hold, by majorities almost uniformly increased, all the States they had carried the preceding year, and reverse the last year's majority against them in New York; carry Pennsylvania for the first time by over 26,000 majority; triumph even in New Jersey under an equiv-

[2] Of $300.

[3] Minnesota chose *three* Members to the House, on the assumption that her population was sufficient to warrant her in claiming that number—or, at least, soon would be. She has since chosen but two, being entitled to no more—in fact, hardly to so many—under the Census of 1860.

ocal organization; bring over Minnesota by a close vote; and swell their majority in Ohio to fully 20,000. They were beaten in Indiana on the State ticket by a very slender majority, but carried seven of the eleven Representatives in Congress, beside helping elect an anti-Lecompton Democrat in another district; while Michigan, Iowa, and Wisconsin, chose Republican tickets—as of late had been usual with them—by respectable majorities, and the last named by one increased to nearly 6,000. California and Oregon still adhered to Democracy of the most pro-Slavery type, by decisive majorities.

Illinois was this year the arena of a peculiar contest. Senator Douglas had taken so prominent and so efficient a part in the defeat of the Lecompton abomination, that a number of the leading Republicans of other States were desirous that their Illinois brethren should unite in choosing a Legislature pledged to return him, by a vote substantially unanimous, to the seat he had so ably filled. But it was hardly in human nature that those thus appealed to should, because of one good act, recognize and treat as a friend one whom they had known for nearly twenty years as the ablest, most indefatigable, and by no means the most scrupulous, of their adversaries. They held a sort of State Convention, therefore, and presented ABRAHAM LINCOLN as a Republican competitor for Mr. Douglas's seat; and he opened the canvass at once,[4] in a terse, forcible, and thoroughly "radical" speech, wherein he enunciated the then startling, if not absolutely novel, doctrine that *the Union cannot permanently endure half Slave and half Free.* Said Mr. Lincoln:

"If we could first know where we are, and whither we are tending, we could better judge what to do, and how to do it. We are now far into the fifth year since a policy was initiated with the avowed object and confident promise of putting an end to Slavery agitation. Under the operation of that policy, that agitation has not only not ceased, but has constantly augmented. In my opinion, it will not cease until a crisis shall have been reached and passed. 'A house divided against itself cannot stand.' I believe this Government cannot permanently endure half slave and half free. I do not expect the Union to be dissolved—I do not expect the house to fall—but I *do* expect that it will cease to be divided. It will become all one thing or all the other. Either the opponents of Slavery will arrest the further spread of it, and place it where the public mind shall rest in the belief that it is in the course of ultimate extinction; or its advocates will push it forward till it shall become alike lawful in all the States, old as well as new—North as well as South."

This almost prophetic statement, from one born in Kentucky, and who had been known, prior to the appearance of the Dred Scott decision, as a rather conservative Whig, was put forth, more than four months before Gov. Seward,[5] as if under a like premonition of coming events, said:

"These antagonistic systems are continually coming into closer contact, and collision results.

"Shall I tell you what this collision means? They who think that it is accidental, unnecessary, the work of interested or fanatical agitators, and therefore ephemeral, mistake the case altogether. *It is an irrepressible conflict* between opposing and enduring forces; and it means that the United States must and will, sooner or later, become either entirely a slave-holding nation, or entirely a free-labor nation. Either the cotton and rice-fields of South Carolina and the sugar plantations of Louisiana will ultimately be tilled by free labor, and Charleston and New Orleans become marts for legitimate merchandise alone, or else the rye-fields and wheat-fields of Massachusetts

[4] At Springfield, Ill., June 17, 1858.

[5] At Rochester, N. Y., Oct. 25, 1858.

and New York must again be surrendered by their farmers to slave culture and to the production of slaves, and Boston and New York become once more markets for trade in the bodies and souls of men. It is the failure to apprehend this great truth that induces so many unsuccessful attempts at final compromise between the Slave and Free States; and it is the existence of this great fact that renders all such pretended compromises, when made, vain and ephemeral."

Mr. Lincoln, in his brief Springfield speech, furnished the shortest and sharpest exposition ever yet given of the doctrine vaunted as 'Popular Sovereignty,' viz.:

"This necessity [for a popular indorsement of the policy embodied in the Nebraska-Kansas bill] had not been overlooked; but had been provided for, as well as might be, in the notable argument of 'Squatter Sovereignty,' otherwise called 'sacred right of self-government;' which latter phrase, though expressive of the only rightful basis of any government, was so perverted, in this attempted use of it, as to amount to just this: That, *if any one man choose to enslave another, no third man shall be allowed to object.*"

Mr. Douglas promptly joined issue; and an oral canvass of unequaled interest, considering the smallness of the stake, was prosecuted by these capable and practiced popular debaters, before immense audiences of their fellow-citizens, up to the eve of the State Election. In the event, Mr. Douglas was successful, securing 54 to 46 of the members of the Legislature, and being promptly reëlected by them; but the candidates favorable to Mr. Lincoln had a plurality of the popular vote.[6]

The Elections of 1859 were not especially significant, save that, in New York, what remained of the "American" party, instead of nominating a State ticket of their own men, adopted the expedient of selecting their candidates alternately from the tickets of the two great parties—of course, powerfully aiding that which must otherwise have been beaten throughout. The 25,000 votes thus cast elected three of the Democratic candidates by majorities of 328 to 1,450; while the Republicans placed on the "American ticket" had majorities ranging from 45,104 to 49,447; and one Republican candidate was chosen over the joint vote of both the adverse parties. In this "balance-of-power" movement of the Americans was foreshadowed the "Fusion" electoral tickets of 1860.

The indignant, scornful rhetoric wherewith Mr. Webster had scouted the suggestion, that Slavery might possibly be established in New Mexico, and spurned the idea of "reënacting the laws of God" by prohibiting it there, had scarcely died out of the public ear, when the Legislature of that vast Territory proceeded, at its session in 1859, to do the very thing which he had deemed so inconceivable. Assuming the legal existence of Slavery in that Territory, in accordance with the Dred Scott decision, the Legislature proceeded to pass "An act to provide for the protection of property in slaves," whereby severe penalties were provided for "stealing," or "enticing away" said property, or "inciting" said property to "discontent" or "insubordination." The spirit of this notable act is fairly exhibited in the following provisions:

[6] For Lincoln, 124,698; for Douglas, 121,130; Lincoln's plurality, 3,568. But over 4,000 Democratic votes were scattered and lost, in obedience to directions from Washington—Mr. Douglas's apprehended return being exceedingly distasteful to President Buchanan.

"SEC. 10. Any person may lawfully take up or apprehend any slave who shall have run away, or be absenting himself from the custody or service of his master or owner, and may lawfully use or employ such force as may be necessary to take up or apprehend such slave; and such person, upon the delivery of such slave to his master or owner, or at such place as his master or owner may designate, shall be entitled to demand or recover by suit any reward which may have been offered for the apprehension or delivery of such slave. And, if no reward have been offered, then such person so apprehending such slave shall, upon the delivery of such slave to his master or owner, or to the sheriff of the county in which such slave was apprehended, be entitled to demand and recover from such owner or master the sum of twenty dollars, besides ten cents for each mile of travel to and from the place where such apprehension was made.

"SEC. 11. If any sheriff of any county within this Territory shall fail or refuse to receive with proper care any runaway slave so offered to him for safe-keeping, by such person apprehending the same, or his agent, such sheriff shall, upon conviction thereof, be fined in a sum not less than five hundred dollars to the use of the Territory, shall further be liable to the owner of such slave for his value, recoverable by civil suit, and shall be ineligible for reëlection to the said office.

"SEC. 20. Any slave who shall conduct himself disorderly in a public place, or shall give insolent language or signs to any free white person, may be arrested and taken by such person before a justice of the peace, who, upon trial and conviction, in a summary manner, shall cause his constable to give such slave any number of stripes upon his or her bare back, not exceeding thirty-nine.

"SEC. 21. When any slave shall be convicted of any crime or misdemeanor, for which the penalty assigned by law is, in whole or in part, the fine of a sum of money, the court passing sentence on him may, in its discretion, substitute for such fine corporal punishment, or *branding*, or stripes.

"SEC. 26. No slave shall be permitted to go from the premises of his owner or master after sunset and before sunrise, without a written pass, specifying the particular place or places to which such slave is permitted to go; and any white person is authorized to take any slave who, upon demand, shall not exhibit such pass, before any justice of the peace, who, upon summary investigation, shall cause such slave to be whipped with not more than thirty-nine stripes upon his or her bare back, and to be committed to the jail, or custody of a proper officer, to be released the next day, on demand and payment of costs by the owner or master."

Another act passed by the same Legislature, "Amendatory of the law relative to contracts between masters and servants" (*peons*), has this unique provision, which might have afforded a hint to South Carolina in her worst estate:

"SEC. 4.—No Court of this Territory shall have jurisdiction, nor shall take cognizance, of any cause for the correction that masters may give their servants for neglect of their duties as servants; for they are considered as domestic servants to their masters, and they should correct their neglect and faults; for, as soldiers are punished by their chiefs, without the intervention of the civil authority, by reason of the salary they enjoy, an equal right should be granted those persons who pay their money to be served in the protection of their property; *Provided*, That such correction shall not be inflicted in a cruel manner, with clubs or stripes."

These acts were directly inspired from Washington, and were enacted under the supervision and tutelage of the Federal officers stationed in the Territory. Some of these were personally slaveholders; others were only anxious to commend themselves to the notice and favor of their superiors; and it was easy for them to persuade the ignorant Mexicans, who mainly composed the Legislature, that such acts would cause the heavenly dews of Federal patronage to fall in boundless profusion on the arid, thirsty hills of their Territory. And, while the number of slaves held in New Mexico might never be great, its salubrity, and the ease wherewith a mere subsistence is maintained there, might well have commended it to favor as a breeding-ground of black chattels for the unhealthy swamps and lowlands of Arkansas and Louisiana. In any case its subservience to the Slave Power was assured by the mere legalization of life-long bondage and unrequited labor on its narrow but fertile intervales, and in its mines of precious ore.

The XXXVIth Congress assembled at Washington Monday, December 5, 1859. The Senate was still strongly Democratic, though the Republican minority therein had grown gradually, until it numbered twenty-four. Indiana, Minnesota, California, and Oregon, were still represented by Democrats, as were in part Pennsylvania, Ohio, and Illinois; but the strong anti-Lecompton wave of 1858 had swept into the House delegations from New York, New Jersey, Pennsylvania, Ohio, Wisconsin, Iowa, and Minnesota, decidedly hostile to the Administration; and these, with unanimous Republican delegations from all the New England States, left no clear majority for any party. On the first ballot for Speaker, Thomas S. Bocock, Dem., of Virginia, received eighty-six votes; John Sherman, Rep., of Ohio, sixty-six; Galusha A. Grow, Rep., of Pennsylvania, forty-three: twenty-two were divided between three "Americans" or Southern Whigs, and thirteen were scattered mainly upon anti-Lecompton Democrats: whole number cast, 230; necessary for a choice, 116.

Mr. Burnett, of Kentucky, now moved that the House adjourn till to-morrow, which was negatived—Yeas 100; Nays 130: whereupon Mr. John B. Clark,[7] of Missouri, rose, and, amid a shower of objections and interruptions, proposed the following preämble and resolution:

"*Whereas*, certain members of this House, now in nomination for Speaker, did indorse and recommend the book hereinafter mentioned,

"*Resolved*, That the doctrines and sentiments of a certain book called 'The Impending Crisis of the South—How to meet it,' purporting to have been written by one Hinton R. Helper, are insurrectionary and hostile to the domestic peace and tranquillity of the country; and that no member of this House who has indorsed and recommended it, or the compend from it, is fit to be Speaker of this House."

The book thus advertised was written by a young North Carolinian of the poorer middle class, who, having migrated to California, and spent some time in the Northern States, had imbibed ideas respecting Slavery which it was not safe to express in his native State. Those ideas he had embodied in his "Impending Crisis," which was, in substance, a vehement appeal to the poor whites of the South against persistence in servility to the slaveholders, backed by ample statistics, proving Slavery specially injurious and degrading to them, as well as baleful and blighting to the entire South. This book, being deemed effective as an anti-Slavery argument, whether in the North or in the South, had been recommended to general attention, in a circular signed by two thirds, at least, of the Republican members of the last Congress, including, of course, many of those returned to the present. Messrs. Sherman and Grow, between whom the Republican vote for Speaker was divided, were both among the signers of this circular. Hereupon, Mr. Clark proceeded to make, amid interruptions and questions of order, such a speech as a slaveholder might be expected to make on such a theme; urging

---

7 Since known as an active and bitter Rebel.

that no man who had recommended such a book as Helper's ought to be chosen Speaker, and insisting on discussing the contents and bearings of that book at leisure; whilst several Republican members, instead of reprehending this discreditable interruption of the proper business of the House, and demanding that the Clerk should proceed to call the roll for another attempt to elect a Speaker, rose to deprecate, and explain, and apologize, and insist that, if they *had* signed a recommendation of any such book, it was in total ignorance of its contents, which they utterly condemned and repudiated. Thus, amid great confusion, Mr. Clark carried the point he was aiming at; and the House, after one more refusal—Yeas 113; Nays 115—consented to adjourn at a little past two o'clock, without taking a second ballot for Speaker.

In the Senate, also, Slavery agitation was commenced from the Democratic side, even before that body had been fairly organized, by a resolve, introduced by Mr. Mason, of Virginia, calling for the most elaborate inquiry into the recent tragedy at Harper's Ferry, and requiring the Select Committee thereon to report "what legislation may, in their opinion, be necessary for the future preservation of the peace of the country," etc.; and hereupon the Senate plunged into a discussion, which lasted several days.

Mr. Clark, in like manner, resumed his dissertation on Helper immediately on the assembling of the House next morning, having all manner of documents read from the Clerk's desk; and spinning out his remarks to the utmost length. When he had closed, Mr. John A. Gilmer,[8] of N. C., moved a substitute, condemning all attempts at renewing Slavery agitation; whereupon Mr. Washburne, of Ill., moved that the whole subject be laid on the table, which was defeated by a tie vote: Yeas 116; Nays 116: and the debate went on, simultaneously with that on John Brown and his doings in the Senate. A second ballot for Speaker was not obtained until the close of the third day's proceedings, when Mr. Sherman received 107 votes; Mr. Bocock 88; Mr. Gilmer 22; and there were 14 scattering. And still the two Houses continued to debate John Brown and Helper, by way of discouraging Slavery agitation, interspersed with readings of the choicest and spiciest extracts from Helper, and occasional ballots for Speaker—Mr. Sherman's vote rising to 112, while 116 were necessary for a choice. The total vote was diminished, after a few days, as members paired off and left Washington; but Mr. Sherman continued to lack from three to five of an election; until finally, after eight weeks had been thus spent, he peremptorily declined; and Mr. William Pennington—ex-Governor of New Jersey, and now, for the first time, a member of the House—was presented in his stead. Mr. Bocock was also withdrawn, and the entire pro-Slavery strength concentrated, so far as possible, on Mr. Wm. N. H. Smith, "American," of N. C. The next (fortieth) ballot gave Pennington 115; Smith 113; John G. Davis, anti-Lecompton Dem., of Ind., 2; and there were 4 scattering: necessary to a choice 118. Finally, on the forty-fourth ballot,[9] Mr. Smith's name

[8] "American."

[9] February 1, 1860.

having been withdrawn, the vote was declared: for Pennington 117; John A. McClernand, Dem., 85; John A. Gilmer, Amer., 16; and there were 15 scattering. Mr. Henry Winter Davis, of Md., who had hitherto voted with the Americans, now cast his vote for Pennington, and elected him—he having the exact number necessary to a choice. John W. Forney, anti-Lecompton Dem., was soon after elected Clerk by a close vote.

The majority in the Senate was not merely Democratic of the Lecompton or extreme pro-Slavery caste; it was especially hostile to Senator Douglas, and determined to punish him for his powerful opposition to the Lecompton bill, by reading him out of the party. To this end, Mr. Jefferson Davis submitted[10] an elaborate series of resolves, whereof the following is the most material:

"4. *Resolved*, That neither Congress nor a Territorial Legislature, whether by direct legislation or legislation of an indirect and unfriendly nature, possess the power to annul or impair the constitutional right of any citizen of the United States to take his slave property into the common Territories; but it is the duty of the Federal Government there to afford for that, as for other species of property, the needful protection; and, if experience should at any time prove that the Judiciary does not possess power to insure adequate protection, it will then become the duty of Congress to supply such deficiency."

These resolutions he modified, "after a conference with friends," and submitted afresh,[11] presenting the material proposition in this shape:

"4. *Resolved*, That neither Congress nor a Territorial Legislature, whether by direct legislation or legislation of an indirect and unfriendly character, possesses power to annul or impair the constitutional right of any citizen of the United States to take his slave property into the common Territories, and there hold and enjoy the same while the territorial condition remains."

The discussion of the series consumed a large share of the time and attention of the Senate during the entire session. It ultimately transpired that they were the work of a 'Lecompton' or regular Democratic caucus, and that their ulterior object was the reading of Mr. Douglas, and other tenacious champions of 'Popular Sovereignty,' out of the Democratic party. At length,[12] the Senate came to a vote on the first of the series, which was as follows:

"1. *Resolved*, That, in the adoption of the Federal Constitution, the States adopting the same acted severally as free and independent sovereignties, delegating a portion of their powers to be exercised by the Federal Government for the increased security of each against dangers, *domestic* as well as foreign; and that any intermeddling by any one or more States, or by a combination of their citizens, with the domestic institutions of the others, on any pretext whatever, political, moral, or religious, with a view to their disturbance or subversion, is in violation of the Constitution, insulting to the States so interfered with, endangers their domestic peace and tranquillity—objects for which the Constitution was formed—and, by necessary consequence, tends to weaken and destroy the Union itself."

This resolve was aimed directly at the Republicans, and was passed by a strict party vote—that is, by the votes of all others in the affirmative, against the Republicans in the negative: Yeas 36; Nays 19.[13]

---

[10] Feb. 2, 1860. [11] Feb. 29, 1860.

[12] May 24, 1860.

[13] Yeas—Messrs. Benjamin, Bigler, Bragg, Bright, Brown, Chesnut, C. C. Clay, Clingman, Crittenden, Davis, Fitzpatrick, Green, Gwin, Hammond, Hemphill, Hunter, Iverson, Johnson, of Ark., Johnson, of Tenn., Kennedy, Lane (Oregon), Latham, Mallory, Mason, Nicholson, Pearce, Polk, Powell, Pugh, Rice, Sebastian, Slidell, Thomson, of N. J., Toombs, Wigfall, and Yulee—36.

Nays—Messrs. Bingham, Chandler, Clark, Collamer, Dixon, Doolittle, Fessenden, Foot, Foster, Grimes, Hale, Hamlin, Harlan, King, Simmons, Sumner, Ten Eyck, Wade, and Wilson—19.

"2. *Resolved*, That negro Slavery, as it exists in fifteen States of this Union, composes an important portion of their domestic institutions, inherited from their ancestors, and existing at the adoption of the Constitution, by which it is recognized as constituting an important element in the apportionment of powers among the States, and that no change of opinion or feeling on the part of the non-slaveholding States of the Union, in relation to this institution, can justify them or their citizens in open or covert attacks thereon, with a view to its overthrow; and that all such attacks are in manifest violation of the mutual and solemn pledge to protect and defend each other, given by the States respectively on entering into the constitutional compact which formed the Union, and are a manifest breach of faith, and a violation of the most solemn obligations."

This was adopted: Yeas 36; Nays 20; the division being identical with the foregoing, save that Mr. Trumbull, of Illinois, was now present, adding one to the Republican vote.

While the above resolve was under consideration, Mr. Harlan, of Iowa, moved to add to it as follows:

"But the free discussion of the morality and expediency of Slavery should never be interfered with by the laws of any State, or of the United States; and the freedom of speech and of the press, on this and every other subject of domestic and national policy, should be maintained inviolate in all the States."

This was rejected: Yeas 20; Nays 36 (as upon the adoption of the second resolve, with the order reversed).

"3. *Resolved*, That the Union of these States rests on the equality of rights and privileges among its members; and that it is especially the duty of the Senate, which represents the States in their sovereign capacity, to resist all attempts to discriminate either in relation to persons or property in the Territories, which are the common possessions of the United States, so as to give advantages to the citizens of one State which are not equally assured to those of every other State."

This was also adopted—Yeas 36; Nays 18: the Yeas, as upon the first vote; as also the Nays, except that Messrs. Grimes and King did not vote.

The next was the touchstone—its passage by a party vote the object of the movement. It reads:

"4. *Resolved*, That neither Congress nor a Territorial Legislature, whether by direct legislation or legislation of an indirect and unfriendly character, possesses power to annul or impair the constitutional right of any citizen of the United States to take his slave property into the common Territories, and there hold and enjoy the same while the territorial condition remains."

This important resolve—the sentence and death-knell of "Popular Sovereignty"—was passed by the decisive majority of thirty-five Yeas to twenty-one Nays[14]—every Democratic Senator present but Mr. Pugh, of Ohio, voting for it; though Messrs. Latham, of California, Fitch, of Indiana, Rice, of Minnesota, and perhaps one or two others, had been known in other days as friends of Mr. Douglas, and champions of his doctrine. Mr. Douglas himself was absent through-

[14] YEAS—Messrs. Thomson (John R.,) of New Jersey, Bigler, of Pennsylvania, Rice, of Minnesota, Bright, of Indiana, Gwin and Latham, of California, Lane, of Oregon—in all, *seven* from Free States; with Messrs. Kennedy and Pearce, of Maryland, Hunter and Mason, of Virginia, Bragg and Clingman, of North Carolina, Chesnut and Hammond, of South Carolina, Iverson and Toombs, of Georgia, C. C. Clay and Fitzpatrick, of Alabama, Brown and Davis, of Mississippi, Benjamin and Slidell, of Louisiana, Mallory and Yulee, of Florida, Hemphill and Wigfall, of Texas, Crittenden and Powell, of Kentucky, A. Johnson and Nicholson, of Tennessee, Green and Polk, of Missouri, R. W. Johnson and Sebastian, of Arkansas—28 from Slave States alone—every Slave State but Delaware being fully represented, and casting its full vote for this proposition. Total 35.

The NAYS were—Messrs. Fessenden and Hamlin, of Maine, Clark and Hale, of New Hampshire, Sumner and Wilson, of Massachusetts, Simmons, of Rhode Island, Dixon and Foster, of Connecticut, Collamer and Foot, of Vermont, King, of New York, Ten Eyck, of New Jersey, *Pugh* and Wade, of Ohio, Trumbull, of Illinois, Brigham and Chandler, of Michigan, Doolittle, of Wisconsin, Grimes and Harlan, of Iowa—21.

out, by reason of sickness. The negative vote on this grave proposition was made up of the twenty Republicans aforesaid, and Mr. Pugh. Neither Mr. Crittenden, nor either of the Maryland Senators, had the courage to oppose a proposition whereby Mr. Jefferson Davis and his confederates were permitted to brand, by an imposing vote of the Senate, not only the Republicans, but the Douglas or anti-Lecompton Democrats also—composing an immense majority of the people of the Free States—in effect, as unfaithful to their Constitutional obligations, and making war on the guaranteed rights of the South.

Mr. Clingman, of North Carolina, proposed the following:

"*Resolved*, That the existing condition of the Territories of the United States *does not* require the intervention of Congress for the protection of property in slaves."

To this, Mr. Collamer, of Vermont, moved to alter the amendment, so as to make it read:

"*Resolved*, That the existing condition of the Territories of the United States does not, and, in our opinion, *never will*, require," etc.

This was rejected—Yeas 16; Nays 33. Then Mr. Clingman's amendment was adopted: Yeas 26; Nays 23.[15]

"5. *Resolved*, That, if experience should at any time prove that the Judicial and Executive authority do not possess means to insure adequate protection to constitutional rights in a Territory, and if the territorial government should fail or refuse to provide the necessary remedies for that purpose, it will be the duty of Congress to supply such deficiency."

Mr. Clingman proposed to amend this, as follows:

"*Provided*, That it is not hereby intended to assert the duty of Congress to provide a system of laws for the maintenance of Slavery."

This was rejected—Yeas 12; Nays 31—only Messrs. Clark, Clingman, Dixon, Foot, Foster, Hale, Hamlin, Latham, Pugh, Ten Eyck, Trumbull, and Wilson, voting in the affirmative.

The original resolution was then adopted; as follows: Yeas 35; Nays 2—Messrs. Hamlin and Trumbull: the Yeas being as upon the adoption of the first resolve, with the subtraction of Messrs. Brown and Thomson, and the addition of Mr. Ten Eyck.

"6. *Resolved*, That the inhabitants of a Territory of the United States, when they rightfully form a Constitution to be admitted as a State into the Union, may then, for the first time, like the people of a State when forming a new Constitution, decide for themselves whether Slavery, as a domestic institution, shall be maintained or prohibited within their jurisdiction; and 'they shall be admitted into the Union, with or without Slavery, as their constitution may prescribe at the time of their admission.'"

This was also adopted, as follows: Yeas 33—same as on the first resolve, less Brown, Mallory, and Pugh; Nays 12—Bingham, Chandler, Dixon, Foot, Foster, Hale, Pugh, Simmons, Ten Eyck, Trumbull, Wade, and Wilson.

"7. *Resolved*, That the provision of the Constitution for the rendition of fugitives from service or labor, without the adoption of which the Union could not have been formed, and the laws of 1793 and 1850, which were enacted to secure its execution, and the main features of which, being similar, bear the impress of nearly seventy years of sanction by the highest judicial authority, should be honestly and faithfully observed and maintained by all who enjoy the bene-

[15] YEAS—Messrs. Bigler, Bingham, Bragg, Chandler, Clark, Clingman, Collamer, Crittenden, Dixon, Doolittle, Foot, Grimes, Hale, Hamlin, Harlan, Johnson, of Tennessee, Kennedy, Latham, Polk, Pugh, Simmons, Ten Eyck, Toombs, Trumbull, Wade, and Wilson—26.

NAYS—Messrs. Benjamin, Bright, Brown, Chesnut, Clay, Davis, Fitzpatrick, Green, Hammond, Hunter, Iverson, Lane, Mallory, Mason, Nicholson, Pearce, Powell, Rice, Saulsbury, Sebastian, Slidell, Wigfall, and Yulee—23. [All from Slave States but Bright, Lane, and Rice.]

fits of our compact of union, and that all acts of individuals or of State Legislatures to defeat the purpose or nullify the requirements of that provision, and the laws made in pursuance of it, are hostile in character, subversive of the Constitution, and revolutionary in their effect."

This, the last of the series, was likewise adopted, as follows: Yeas 36; Nays 6: Yeas as in the first instance, except that Messrs. Pearce and Thompson did not vote, their places being filled by Messrs. Ten Eyck and Thomson; while the Nays were Messrs. Chandler, Clark, Foot, Hale, Wade, and Wilson.

The Senate then proceeded, on motion of Mr. Wilson, of Massachusetts, to reconsider Mr. Clingman's resolution hitherto given—Mr. Wilson stating that, for himself and his friends, they wished to have nothing to do with any part of the series, and therefore moved the reconsideration; which prevailed: Yeas 26; Nays 8. And the resolution of Mr. Clingman, being reconsidered, was rejected.

And so, Mr. Jefferson Davis's entire series, without the change of a comma, affirming and emphasizing the worst points of the Dred Scott decision, and asserting as vital truths propositions which even the *Southern* Democracy voted down when first presented to a Democratic National Convention by Mr. Yancey in 1848, were now adopted by the United States Senate as necessary deductions from the fundamental law of the land.

The Democratic National Convention of 1856 had decided that its successor should meet at Charleston, S. C., which it accordingly did, on the 23d of April, 1860.

Abundant premonitions of a storm had already been afforded. One delegation from the State of New York had been chosen by the Convention which nominated State officers at Syracuse the preceding Autumn; while another had been elected by districts, under the auspices of Mr. Fernando Wood, then Mayor of the Commercial Emporium. The former was understood to favor the nomination of Senator Douglas for President; the latter to oppose it, and incline to entire acquiescence in whatever the South might propose or desire. Two delegations had, in like manner, been chosen from Illinois, under similar auspices. The National Committee had issued tickets to what it esteemed the regular, or anti-Wood, delegation from New York, admitting them to seats in the Convention, and excluding their competitors. Francis B. Flournoy, of Arkansas, was chosen temporary Chairman; Gen. Caleb Cushing, of Massachusetts, was, on the second day, made permanent President, and a Committee on Platform, consisting of one member from each State, appointed. On the third day, the contests were decided in favor of the anti-Wood delegation from New York and the Douglas men from Illinois. On the fourth, no progress was made. On the fifth, Mr. Avery, of North Carolina, from a majority of the Committee on Platform (17 to 14), but representing a minority of the People and of the Electors of President, reported a series, whereof the material proposition was as follows:

"*Resolved*, That the platform adopted at Cincinnati be affirmed, with the following resolutions:

"That the National Democracy of the United States hold these cardinal principles on the subject of Slavery in the Territories: First, That Congress has no power to abolish Slavery in the Territories; second, that the Territorial Legislature has no power to abolish Slavery in the Territories, nor to prohibit the introduction of slaves therein, nor any power to destroy or impair the right of property in slaves by any legislation whatever."

Mr. Henry B. Payne, of Ohio, on behalf of the members of said Committee from all the Free States but California, Oregon, and Massachusetts—States entitled to choose 172 Electors, while those represented in the majority report were entitled to but 127 Electors—reported a platform, which, as finally modified, was presented by Mr. Samuels, of Iowa, in the following shape:

"1. *Resolved*, That we, the Democracy of the Union, in Convention assembled, hereby declare our affirmance of the resolutions unanimously adopted and declared as a platform of principles by the Democratic Convention at Cincinnati, in the year 1856, believing that Democratic principles are unchangeable in their nature, when applied to the same subject-matters; and we recommend, as the only further resolutions, the following:

"Inasmuch as differences of opinion exist in the Democratic party as to the nature and extent of the powers of a Territorial Legislature, and as to the powers and duties of Congress, under the Constitution of the United States, over the institution of Slavery within the Territories:

"2. *Resolved*, That the Democratic Party will abide by the decisions of the Supreme Court of the United States on the questions of Constitutional law.

"3. *Resolved*, That it is the duty of the United States to afford ample and complete protection to all its citizens, whether at home or abroad, and whether native or foreign.

"4. *Resolved*, That one of the necessities of the age, in a military, commercial, and postal point of view, is speedy communication between the Atlantic and Pacific States; and the Democratic Party pledge such constitutional government aid as will insure the construction of a railroad to the Pacific coast, at the earliest practicable period.

"5. *Resolved*, That the Democratic party are in favor of the acquisition of the Island of Cuba, on such terms as shall be honorable to ourselves and just to Spain.

"6. *Resolved*, That the enactments of State Legislatures to defeat the faithful execution of the Fugitive Slave Law, are hostile in character, subversive of the Constitution, and revolutionary in their effect."

Mr. Avery's report from the majority was ultimately modified by him so as to read as follows:

"*Resolved*, That the platform adopted by the Democratic party at Cincinnati be affirmed, with the following explanatory resolutions:

"*First*. That the government of a Territory organized by an act of Congress, is provisional and temporary; and, during its existence, all citizens of the United States have an equal right to settle with their property in the Territory without their rights, either of person or property, being destroyed or impaired by congressional or territorial legislation.

"*Second*. That it is the duty of the Federal Government, in all its departments, to protect, when necessary, the rights of persons and property in the Territories, and wherever else its constitutional authority extends.

"*Third*. That when the settlers in a Territory having an adequate population form a State Constitution, the right of sovereignty commences, and, being consummated by admission into the Union, they stand on an equal footing with the people of other States; and the State thus organized ought to be admitted into the Federal Union, whether its constitution prohibits or recognizes the institution of Slavery.

"*Fourth*. That the Democratic party are in favor of the acquisition of the Island of Cuba, on such terms as shall be honorable to ourselves and just to Spain, at the earliest practicable moment.

"*Fifth*. That the enactments of State legislatures to defeat the faithful execution of the Fugitive Slave Law, are hostile in character, subversive of the Constitution, and revolutionary in their effect.

"*Sixth*. That the Democracy of the United States recognize it as the imperative duty of this Government to protect the naturalized citizen in all his rights, whether at home or in foreign lands, to the same extent as its native-born citizens.

"*Whereas*, one of the greatest necessities of the age, in a political, commercial, postal and military point of view, is a speedy communication between the Pacific and Atlantic coasts: Therefore, be it

"*Resolved*, That the Democratic party do hereby pledge themselves to use every means in their power to secure the passage of some bill, to the extent of the constitutional authority of Congress, for the construction of a Pacific Railroad, from the Mississippi River to the Pacific Ocean, at the earliest practicable period."

[The report concludes with resolves 5 and 6 of the Douglas platform, for which see preceding column.]

Gen. Benj. F. Butler, of Massachusetts, disagreeing with both these reports, proposed simply to reäffirm the Cincinnati platform, and there stop.

The majority report, it will be noted, was concurred in by the representatives, in Committee, of each of the fifteen Slave States, with those of California and Oregon. Mr. Avery, in introducing it, very frankly and fairly set forth its object, and the grounds of difference with the minority, as follows:

"I have stated that we demand at the hands of our Northern brethren upon this floor that the great principle which we cherish should be recognized, and in that view I speak the common sentiments of our constituents at home; and I intend no reflection upon those who entertain a different opinion, when I say that the results and ultimate consequences to the Southern States of this confederacy, if the Popular Sovereignty doctrine be adopted as the doctrine of the Democratic party, would be as dangerous and subversive of their rights as the adoption of the principle of Congressional intervention or prohibition. We say that, in a contest for the occupation of the Territories of the United States, the Southern men encumbered with slaves cannot compete with the Emigrant Aid Society at the North. We say that the Emigrant Aid Society can send a voter to one of the Territories of the United States, to determine a question relating to Slavery, for the sum of $200; while it would cost the Southern man the sum of $1500. We say, then, that, wherever there is competition between the South and the North, that the North can and will, at less expense and difficulty, secure power, control, and dominion over the Territories of the Federal Government; and if, then, you establish the doctrine that a Territorial Legislature which may be established by Congress in any Territory has the right, directly or indirectly, to affect the institution of Slavery, then you can see that the Legislature by its action, either directly or indirectly, may finally exclude every man from the slaveholding States as effectually as if you had adopted the Wilmot Proviso out and out. * * *

"But we are told that, in advocating the doctrine we now do, we are violating the principles of the Cincinnati platform. They say that the Cincinnati platform is a Popular Sovereignty platform; that it was intended to present and practically enforce that great principle. Now, we who made this report deny that this is the true construction of the Cincinnati platform. We of the South say that, when we voted for the Cincinnati platform, we understood, from the fact that the Territories stand in the same position as the District of Columbia, that non-interference and non-intervention in the Territories was that same sort of non-interference and non-intervention practiced in the District of Columbia. Now, we maintain that Congress has no right to prohibit or abolish Slavery in the District of Columbia. Why? Because it is an existing institution. It becomes the duty of Congress under the Constitution to protect and cherish the right of property in slaves in that District, because the Constitution does not give them the power to prohibit or establish Slavery. Every session of Congress, Northern men, Southern men, men of all parties, are legislating to protect, cherish and uphold, the institution of Slavery in the District of Columbia. * * *

"It is said that the Cincinnati platform is ambiguous, and that we must explain it. At the South, we have maintained that it had no ambiguity; that it did not mean Popular Sovereignty; but our Northern friends say that it *does* mean Popular Sovereignty. Now, if we are going to explain it and to declare its principles, I say, let us either declare them openly, boldly, squarely, or let us leave it as it is in the Cincinnati Platform. I want, and we of the South want, no more doubtful platforms upon this or any other question. We desire that this Convention should take a bold, square stand. What do the minority of the committee propose? Their solution is to leave the question to the decision of the Supreme Court, and agree to abide by any decision that may be made by that tribunal between the citizens of a Territory upon the subject. Why, gentlemen of the minority, you cannot help yourselves! That is no concession to us. There is no necessity for putting that in the platform, because I take it for granted that you are all law-abiding citizens. Every gentleman here from a non-slaveholding State is a law-abiding citizen; and, if he be so, why we know that, when there is a decision of the Supreme Court, even adverse to his views, he will submit to it. * * *

"You say that this is a judicial question. We say that it is not. But, if it be a judicial question, it is immaterial to you how the platform is made, because all you will have to say is, 'This is a judicial question; the majority of the Convention were of one opinion; I may entertain my own opinion upon the question; let the Supreme Court settle it.' * * *

"Let us make a platform about which there can be no doubt, so that every man, North and South, may stand side by side on all issues connected with Slavery, and advocate the same principles. That is all we ask. All we demand at your hands is, that there shall be no equivocation and no doubt in the popular mind as to what our principles are."

Mr. Payne, on the other side, quoted at length from the Cincinnati platform, from Mr. Buchanan's letter of acceptance, and from speeches of Howell Cobb, John C. Breckinridge, James L. Orr, A. H. Stephens, Judah P. Benjamin, James A. Bayard, James M. Mason, Robert Toombs, etc., to show that 'Non-Intervention' with 'Popular Sovereignty' was the original and established Democratic doctrine with regard to Slavery in the Territories.

The debate was continued, amid great excitement and some disorder, until Monday, April 30th, when the question was first taken on Gen. Butler's proposition; which was defeated—Yeas 105; Nays 198—as follows:

YEAS—Maine, 3; Massachusetts, 8; Connecticut, 2½; New Jersey, 5; Pennsylvania, 16½; Delaware, 3; Maryland, 5½; Virginia, 12½; North Carolina, 10; Georgia, 10; Missouri, 4½; Tennessee, 11; Kentucky, 9; Minnesota, 1½; Oregon, 3—105.

NAYS—Maine, 5; New Hampshire, 5; Vermont, 5; Massachusetts, 5; Rhode Island, 4; Connecticut, 3½; New York, 35; New Jersey, 2; Pennsylvania, 10½; Maryland, 2½; Virginia, 2½; South Carolina, 8; Florida, 3; Alabama, 9; Louisiana, 6; Mississippi, 7; Texas, 4; Arkansas, 4; Missouri, 4½; Tennessee, 1; Kentucky, 3; Ohio, 23; Indiana, 13; Illinois, 11; Michigan, 6; Wisconsin, 5; Iowa, 4; Minnesota, 2½; California, 4—198.

The question was next taken on the regular minority report, as presented in a modified form by Mr. Samuels; which was adopted, by the following vote:

YEAS—Maine, 8; New Hampshire, 5; Vermont, 5; Massachusetts, 7; Rhode Island, 4; Connecticut, 6; New York, 35; New Jersey, 5; Pennsylvania, 12; Maryland, 3½; Virginia, 1; Missouri, 4; Tennessee, 1; Kentucky, 2½; Ohio, 23; Indiana, 13; Illinois, 11; Michigan, 6; Wisconsin, 5; Iowa, 4; Minnesota, 4—165.

NAYS—Massachusetts, 6; New Jersey, 2; Pennsylvania, 15; Delaware, 3; Maryland, 4½; Virginia, 14; North Carolina, 10; South Carolina, 8; Georgia, 10; Florida, 3; Alabama, 9; Louisiana, 6; Mississippi, 7; Texas, 4; Arkansas, 4; Missouri, 5; Tennessee, 11; Kentucky, 9½; California, 4; Oregon, 3—138.

Hereupon, Mr. L. P. Walker, of Alabama, presented the written protest of the delegates from that State, 28 in number, showing that they were expressly instructed by the State Convention which elected them not to acquiesce in or submit to any 'Squatter Sovereignty' platform, but to withdraw from the Convention in case such a one should be adopted. Among the resolves so adopted and made binding on their delegates by the Alabama State Convention, were the following:

"1. *Resolved, by the Democracy of the State of Alabama in Convention assembled*, That, holding all issues and principles upon which they have heretofore affiliated and acted with the National Democratic Party to be inferior in dignity and importance to the great question of Slavery, they content themselves with a general reäffirmance of the Cincinnati platform as to such issues, and also indorse said platform as to Slavery, together with the following resolutions:

"2. *Resolved further*, That we reäffirm so much of the first resolution of the platform adopted in the Convention by the Democracy of this State, on the 8th of January, 1856, as relates to the subject of Slavery, to wit: 'The unqualified right of the people of the Slaveholding States to the protection of their property in the States, in the Territories, and in the wilderness in which Territorial Governments are as yet unorganized.'

"3. *Resolved further*, That, in order to meet and clear away all obstacles to a full enjoyment of this right in the Territories, we reaffirm the principle of the 9th resolution of the Platform adopted in Convention by the Democracy of this State, on the 14th of February, 1848, to wit: 'That it is the duty of the General Government, by all proper legislation. to secure an entry into those

Territories to all the citizens of the United States, together with their property of every description; and that the same should be protected by the United States while the Territories are under its authority.'

"4. *Resolved further*, That the Constitution of the United States is a compact between sovereign and co-equal States, united upon the basis of perfect equality of rights and privileges.

"5. *Resolved further*, That the Territories of the United States are common property, in which the States have equal rights, and to which the citizens of every State may rightfully emigrate, with their slaves or other property recognized as such in any of the States of the Union, or by the Constitution of the United States.

"6. *Resolved further*, That the Congress of the United States has no power to abolish Slavery in the Territories, or to prohibit its introduction into any of them.

"7. *Resolved further*, That the Territorial Legislatures, created by the legislation of Congress, have no power to abolish Slavery, or to prohibit the introduction of the same, or to impair by unfriendly legislation the security and full enjoyment of the same within the Territories; and such constitutional power certainly does not belong to the people of the Territories in any capacity, before, in the exercise of a lawful authority, they form a Constitution preparatory to admission as a State into the Union; and their action, in the exercise of such lawful authority, certainly cannot operate or take effect before their actual admission as a State into the Union.

"8. *Resolved further*, That the principles enunciated by Chief Justice Taney, in his opinion in the *Dred Scott* case, deny to the Territorial Legislature the power to destroy or impair, by any legislation whatever, the right of property in slaves, and maintain it to be the duty of the Federal Government, in *all* of its departments, to protect the rights of the owner of such property in the Territories; and the principles so declared are hereby asserted to be the rights of the South, and the South should maintain them.

"9. *Resolved further*, That we hold all of the foregoing propositions to contain *cardinal principles*—true in themselves—and just and proper and necessary for the safety of all that is dear to us; and we do hereby instruct our delegates to the Charleston Convention to present them for the calm consideration and approval of that body—from whose justice and patriotism we anticipate their adoption.

"10. *Resolved further*, That our delegates to the Charleston Convention are hereby expressly instructed to insist that said Convention shall adopt a platform of principles, recognizing distinctly the rights of the South, as asserted in the foregoing resolutions; and if the said National Convention shall refuse to adopt, in substance, the propositions embraced in the preceding resolutions, prior to nominating candidates, our delegates to said Convention are hereby positively instructed to withdraw therefrom.

"11. *Resolved further*, That our delegates to the Charleston Convention shall cast the vote of Alabama as a unit, and a majority of our delegates shall determine how the vote of this State shall be given.

"12. *Resolved further*, That an Executive Committee, to consist of one from each Congressional District, be appointed, whose duty it shall be, in the event that our delegates withdraw from the Charleston Convention, in obedience to the 10th resolution, to call a Convention of the Democracy of Alabama, to meet at an early day to consider what is best to be done."

The Alabama delegation concluded with the following statement:

"The points of difference between the Northern and the Southern Democracy are:

"1. As regards the *status* of Slavery as a political institution in the Territories whilst they remain Territories, and the power of the people of a Territory to exclude it by unfriendly legislation; and

"2. As regards the duty of the Federal Government to protect the owner of slaves in the enjoyment of his property in the Territories so long as they remain such.

"This Convention has refused, by the Platform adopted, to settle either of these propositions in favor of the South. We deny to the people of a Territory any power to legislate against the institution of Slavery; and we assert that it is the duty of the Federal Government, in all its departments, to protect the owner of slaves in the enjoyment of his property in the Territories. These principles, as we state them, are embodied in the Alabama Platform.

"Here, then, is a plain, explicit and direct issue between this Convention and the constituency which we have the honor to represent in this body.

"Instructed, as we are, not to waive this issue, the contingency, therefore, has arisen, when, in our opinion, it becomes our duty to withdraw from this Convention. We beg, Sir, to communicate this fact through you, and to assure the Convention that we do so in no spirit of anger, but under a sense of imperative obligation, properly appreciating its responsibilities and cheerfully submitting to its consequences."

The Alabama delegation, which

included ex-Gov. John A. Winston, Wm. L. Yancey, Reuben Chapman, ex-M. C., and other prominent citizens, thereupon withdrew from the Convention.

Mr. Barry, of Mississippi, next announced the withdrawal of the entire Mississippi delegation. Mr. Glenn, of Mississippi, stated the grounds of such withdrawal, as follows:

"Sir, at Cincinnati we adopted a Platform on which we all agreed. Now answer me, ye men of the North, of the East, of the South, and of the West, what was the construction placed upon that Platform in different sections of the Union? You at the West said it meant one thing; we of the South said it meant another. Either we were right or you were right; we were wrong or you were wrong. We came here to ask you which was right and which was wrong. You have maintained your position. You say that you cannot give us an acknowledgment of that right, which I tell you here now, in coming time will be your only safety in your contests with the Black Republicans of Ohio and of the North. (Cheers.)

"Why, sir, turn back to the history of your own leading men. There sits a distinguished gentleman, Hon. Charles E. Stuart, of Michigan, once a representative of one of the sovereign States of the Union in the Senate, who then voted that Congress had the constitutional power to pass the Wilmot Proviso, and to exclude Slavery from the Territories; and now, when the Supreme Court has said that it has not that power, he comes forward and tells Mississippians that that same Congress is impotent to protect that same species of property! There sits my distinguished friend, the Senator from Ohio (Mr. Pugh), who, but a few nights since, told us from that stand that, if a Territorial Government totally misused their powers or abused them, Congress could wipe out that Territorial Government altogether. And yet, when we come here and ask him to give us protection in case that Territorial Government robs us of our property and strikes the star which answers to the name of Mississippi from the flag of the Union, so far as the Constitution gives her protection, he tells us, with his hand upon his heart—as Gov. Payne, of Ohio, had before done—that they will part with their lives before they will acknowledge the principle which we contend for.

"Gentlemen, in such a situation of things in the Convention of our great party, it is right that we should part. Go your way, and we will go ours. The South leaves you —not like Hagar, driven into the wilderness, friendless and alone—but I tell Southern men here, and, for them, I tell the North, that, in less than sixty days, you will find a united South standing side by side with us. (Prolonged and enthusiastic cheering.)"

Mr. Mouton, of Louisiana, briefly announced that all the delegates from his State but two would withdraw from the Convention, and protested against the right of the two to act or cast any vote in behalf of the State.

Hon. James Simons, of South Carolina, announced the withdrawal of the delegation from that State, in a communication signed by all the thirteen members thereof, in the words following:

"We, the undersigned delegates appointed by the Democratic State Convention of South Carolina, beg leave respectfully to state that, according to the principles enunciated in their Platform at Columbia, the power, either of the Federal Government or of its agent, the Territorial Government, to abolish or legislate against property in slaves, by either direct or indirect legislation, is especially denied; and, as the Platform adopted by the Convention palpably and intentionally prevents any expression affirming the incapacity of the Territorial Government so to legislate, that they would not be acting in good faith to their principles, or in accordance with the wishes of their constituents, to longer remain in this Convention, and they hereby respectfully announce their withdrawal therefrom."

Mr. John Milton, of Florida, next announced the unanimous withdrawal of the delegation from that State, in a protest signed by five delegates, which was read by Mr. Eppes, whereof the essential portion is as follows:

"Florida, with her Southern sisters, is entitled to a clear and unambiguous recognition of her rights in the Territories; and this being refused, by the rejection of the majority report, we protest against receiving the Cincinnati Platform with the interpretation that it favors the doctrine of Squatter Sovereignty in the Territories—which doctrine, in the name of the people represented by us, we repudiate."

Mr. Guy M. Bryan, of Texas, next announced the withdrawal of the entire delegation from that State. In their protest against the platform adopted by the Convention, they declared

"That it is the right of every citizen to take his property, of any kind, including slaves, into the common territory belonging equally to all the States of the Confederacy, and to have it protected there under the Federal Constitution. Neither Congress nor a Territorial Legislature, nor any human power, has any authority, either directly or indirectly, to impair these sacred rights; and, they having been affirmed by the decision of the Supreme Court in the *Dred Scott* case, we declare that it is the duty of the Federal Government, the common agent of all the States, to establish such government, and enact such laws for the Territories, and so change the same, from time to time, as may be necessary to insure the protection and preservation of these rights, and prevent every infringement of the same. The affirmation of this principle of the duty of Congress to simply protect the rights of property, is nowise in conflict with the heretofore established and well-recognized principle of the Democratic party, that Congress does not possess the power to legislate Slavery into the Territories, or to exclude it therefrom.

"It is sufficient to say that, if the principles of the Northern Democracy are properly represented by the opinion and action of the majority of the delegates from that section on this floor, we do not hesitate to declare that their principles are not only not ours, but, if adhered to and enforced by them, will destroy this Union."

Mr. B. Burrow, of Arkansas, announced the withdrawal of three delegates from that State, for these reasons:

"1st. Because the numerical majority have usurped the prerogatives of the States in setting aside the Platform made by the States, and have thus unsettled the basis of this Convention, and thereby permanently disorganized its constitution. Its decrees, therefore, become null and void.

"2d. Because we were positively instructed by the Democracy of Arkansas to insist on the recognition of the equal rights of the South in the common Territories, and protection to those rights by the Federal Government, prior to any nomination of a candidate; and, as this Convention has refused to recognize the principles required by the State of Arkansas, in her popular Convention first, and twice subsequently reässerted by Arkansas, together with all her Southern sisters, in the report of a Platform in this Convention; and, as we cannot serve two masters, we are determined first to serve the Lord our God. We cannot ballot for any candidate whatsoever."

Mr. J. P. Johnson, on behalf of that portion of the Arkansas delegation who had concluded *not* to leave the Convention until after time had been afforded for consultation, said he hesitated, "because he conceived that the stability of the Union itself was involved in the action taken here by the Southern representatives."

The Georgia delegation here asked leave to retire for consultation, which was granted. Messrs. Bayard and Whiteley—Senator and Representative in Congress from Delaware—now retired from the Convention and joined the seceders. Mr. Saulsbury, the other Senator, gave his reasons for *not* retiring at this time, and the Convention adjourned for the night.

Next morning, May 1st, Mr. Henry L. Benning presented a notification from twenty-six of the thirty-four delegates from Georgia, that they had decided to withdraw from the Convention—four of them in obedience to a vote of the majority, which they had opposed.

Mr. Johnson, of Arkansas, now announced the withdrawal, after due consideration and consultation, of the remainder of the delegation from his State; but Mr. F. B. Flournoy gave notice that he did not concur in this action.

The formal protest and withdrawal of ten delegates from Louisiana was now presented. It states that these delegates act in obedience to a resolution passed by the Democracy of Louisiana in State Convention at Baton Rouge, March 5, 1860, in the following words:

"*Resolved*, That the Territories of the United States belong to the several States as their common property, and not to individual citizens thereof; that the Federal Constitution recognizes property in slaves; and, as such, the owner thereof is entitled to carry his slaves into any Territory in the United States; to hold them there as property; and, in case the people of the Territories, by inaction, unfriendly legislation or otherwise, should endanger the tenure of such property, or discriminate against it by withholding that protection given to other species of property in the Territories, it is the duty of the General Government to interpose, by the active exertion of its constitutional power, to secure the rights of the slaveholder."

The two remaining delegates from Louisiana gave notice that, though they did not personally desire to withdraw from the Convention, they should be governed by the action of the majority of their delegation.

Mr. W. B. Gaulden, of Georgia, made a speech against the course taken by his colleagues, on the following grounds:

"I am not in favor of breaking up this Government upon an impracticable issue,—upon a mere theory. I believe that this doctrine of protection to Slavery in the Territories is a mere theory, a mere abstraction. (Applause.) Practically, it can be of no consequence to the South, for the reason that the infant has been strangled before it was born. (Laughter.) You have cut off the supply of slaves; you have crippled the institution of Slavery in the States by your unjust laws; and it is mere folly and madness now to ask for protection for a nonentity—for a thing which is not there. We *have* no slaves to carry to these Territories. We can never make another Slave State with our present supply of slaves. But, if we could, it would not be wise; for the reason that, if you make another Slave State from your new Territories with the present supply of slaves, you will be obliged to give up another State—either Maryland, Delaware, or Virginia—to Free Soil upon the North. Now, I would deal with this question, fellow-Democrats, as a practical one. When I can see no possible practical good to result to the country from demanding legislation upon this theory, I am not prepared to disintegrate and dismember the great Democratic party of this Union. * * * *

"I would ask my friends of the South to come up in a proper spirit, ask our Northern friends to give us *all* our rights, and take off the ruthless restrictions which cut off the supply of slaves from foreign lands. As a matter of right and justice to the South, I would ask the Democracy of the North to grant us this thing; and I believe they have the patriotism and honesty to do it, because it is right in itself. I tell you, fellow-Democrats, that the African Slave-trader is the true Union man. (Cheers and laughter.) I tell you that the slave-trading of Virginia is more immoral, more unchristian in every possible point of view, than that African Slave-trade which goes to Africa and brings a heathen and worthless man here, makes him a useful man, Christianizes him, and sends him and his posterity down the stream of time to enjoy the blessings of civilization. (Cheers and laughter.) Now, fellow-Democrats, so far as any public expression of the State of Virginia—the great Slave-trading State of Virginia—has been given, they are all opposed to the African Slave-trade.

"Dr. Reed, of Indiana—I am from Indiana, and I am in favor of it.

"Mr. Gaulden—Now, gentlemen, we are told, upon high authority, that there is a certain class of men who strain at a gnat and swallow a camel. Now, Virginia, which authorizes the buying of Christian men, separating them from their wives and children, from all the relations and associations amid whom they have lived for years, rolls up her eyes in holy horror when I would go to Africa, buy a savage, and introduce him to the blessings of civilization and Christianity. (Cheers and laughter.)

"Capt. Rynders, of N. Y.—You can get one or two recruits from New York to join with you.

"The President.—The time of the gentleman has expired. (Cries of "Go on! Go on!")

"The President stated that, if it was the unanimous wish of the Convention, the gentleman could proceed.

"Mr. Gaulden.—Now, fellow-Democrats, the slave-trade in Virginia forms a mighty and powerful reason for its opposition to the African slave-trade, and in this remark I do not intend any disrespect to my friends from Virginia. Virginia, the Mother of States and of statesmen, the Mother of Presidents, I apprehend may err as well as other mortals. I am afraid that her error in this regard lies in the promptings of the almighty dollar. It has been my fortune to go into that noble old State to buy a few darkies; and I have had to pay from $1,000 to $2,000 a head, when I could go to Africa and buy better negroes for $50 apiece. (Great laughter.) Now, unquestionably, it is to the interest of Virginia to break down the African slave-trade, when she can sell her negroes at $2,000. She knows that the African slave-trade would break up her monopoly, and hence her objection to it. If any of you Northern Democrats—for I have more faith in you than I have in the carpet-knight Democracy of the South—will go home with me to my plantation in Georgia, but a little way from here, I will show you some darkies that I bought in Maryland, some that I bought in Virginia, some in Delaware, some in Florida, some in North Carolina; and I will also show you the pure African, the noblest Roman of them all. (Great laughter.) Now, fellow-Democrats, my feeble health and failing voice admonish me to bring the few remarks I have to make to a close. (Cries of "Go on, go on.") I am only sorry that I am not in a better condition than I am to vindicate before you to-day the words of truth, of honesty, and of right, and to show you the gross inconsistencies of the South in this regard. I come from the First Congressional District of the State of Georgia. I represent the African slave-trade interest of that section. (Applause.) I am proud of the position I occupy in that respect. I believe that the African slave-trader is a true missionary, and a true Christian (applause); and I have pleaded with my delegation from Georgia to put this issue squarely to the Northern Democracy, and say to them, Are you prepared to go back to first principles, and take off your unconstitutional restrictions, and leave this question to be settled by each State? Now, do this, fellow-citizens, and you will have peace in the country. But, so long as your Federal Legislature takes jurisdiction of this question, so long will there be war, so long will there be ill-blood, so long will there be strife, until this glorious Union of ours shall be disrupted and go out in blood and night forever. I advocate the repeal of the laws prohibiting the African Slave-trade, because I believe it to be the true Union movement. I do not believe that sections whose interests are so different as the Southern and Northern States can ever stand the shocks of fanaticism, unless they be equally balanced. I believe that, by reöpening this trade, and giving us negroes to populate the Territories, the equilibrium of the two sections will be maintained."

The Convention now proceeded to ballot for President, having first adopted, by a vote of 141 to 112, the rule requiring two-thirds of a full Convention to nominate. Candidates were put in nomination, and, on the first ballot, STEPHEN A. DOUGLAS, of Illinois, received 145½ votes; Robert M. T. Hunter, of Virginia, 42 votes; James Guthrie, of Kentucky, 35 votes; Andrew Johnson, of Tennessee, 12; Daniel S. Dickinson, of New York, 7; Joseph Lane, of Oregon, 6; Isaac Toucey, of Connecticut, 2½; Jefferson Davis, of Mississippi, 1½; Franklin Pierce, of New Hampshire, 1. On the next ballot, Mr. Douglas had 147; and he continued to gain slowly to the thirty-second, when he received 152½ votes. He fell off on the thirty-sixth to 151½, which vote he continued to receive up to the fifty-seventh ballot, on which Guthrie received 65½, Hunter 16, Lane 14, Dickinson 4, and Jefferson Davis 1. The Convention (May 3d), on motion of Mr. Russell, of Virginia, by a vote of 195 to 55, adjourned, to reässemble at Baltimore on Monday, the 18th of June; recommending to the Democratic party of the several States whose delegations had withdrawn, to fill their places prior to that day.

The seceding delegates assembled at St. Andrew's Hall—Senator Bayard, of Delaware, in the chair—and adopted the platform reported to the Convention by Mr. Avery, as aforesaid; and, after four days' deliberations, adjourned to meet at Richmond, Va., on the second Monday in June. The Wood delegates from New York attended this meeting, but were not admitted as members.

The regular Convention reässembled at the Front-street Theater in

Baltimore, pursuant to adjournment. Some days were spent in considering the credentials of contesting delegates from certain Southern States. The decisions of the Convention were such as to increase the strength of Senator Douglas. When it was concluded, Mr. Russell, of Virginia, Mr. Lander, of North Carolina, Mr. Ewing, of Tennessee, Mr. Johnson, of Maryland, Mr. Smith, of California, Mr. Saulsbury, of Delaware, Mr. Caldwell, of Kentucky, and Mr. Clark of Missouri, announced the withdrawal of the whole, or of a part, of the delegations from their respective States. Gen. Cushing resigned the chair of the Convention, which was immediately taken by Gov. David Tod, of Ohio (a Vice-President at Charleston), amid enthusiastic cheers. Gen. B. F. Butler, of Massachusetts, announced the determination of a majority of the delegates from his State not to participate further in its deliberations. He said:

"We have not discussed the question, Mr. President, whether the action of the Convention, in excluding certain delegates, could be any reason for withdrawal. We now put our withdrawal before you, upon the simple ground, among others, that there has been a withdrawal in part of a majority of the States, and further (and that, perhaps, more personal to myself), upon the ground that I will not sit in a Convention where the African slave-trade—which is piracy by the laws of my country—is approvingly advocated. (Great sensation.)"

The Convention now proceeded to vote for President; and, on the first ballot, Mr. Douglas had 173½; Guthrie 10, Breckinridge 5, and there were 3 scattering. On the next ballot, Mr. Douglas had 181½, Breckinridge 7½, Guthrie 5½; whereupon, on motion of Mr. Sanford E. Church, of New York, the following resolution was adopted:

"*Resolved unanimously*, That Stephen A. Douglas, of the State of Illinois, having now received two-thirds of all the votes given in this Convention, is hereby declared, in accordance with the rules governing this body, and in accordance with the uniform customs and rules of former Democratic National Conventions, the regular nominee of the Democratic party of the United States, for the office of President of the United States."

Hon. BENJAMIN FITZPATRICK, of Alabama, was now nominated for Vice-President, receiving 198½ votes to 1 scattering. [He declined, two days thereafter, and the National Committee substituted Hon. HERSCHEL V. JOHNSON, of Georgia.]

Gov. Wickliffe, of Louisiana, now offered the following resolve, as an addition to the platform adopted at Charleston:

"*Resolved*, That it is in accordance with the true interpretation of the Cincinnati Platform, that, during the existence of the Territorial Governments, the measure of restriction, whatever it may be, imposed by the Federal Constitution on the power of the Territorial Legislatures over the subject of the domestic relations, as the same has been, or shall hereafter be, finally determined by the Supreme Court of the United States, should be respected by all good citizens, and enforced with promptness and fidelity by every branch of the General Government."

Mr. Payne, of Ohio, moved the previous question, and this was also adopted, with but two dissenting votes.

The Seceders' Convention, which met, first at Richmond on the 11th of June, adjourned thence to Baltimore, and finally met at the Maryland Institute on the 28th of June. Twenty-one States were fully or partially represented. Hon. Caleb Cushing was chosen its President. Mr. Avery, of North Carolina, submitted his Charleston platform, which was unanimously adopted. It was resolved that the next Democratic National Convention should be held at Philadelphia.

The Convention now proceeded to ballot for a candidate for President, when JOHN C. BRECKINRIDGE, of Kentucky, received the unanimous vote —105—of the delegates present; and Gen. JOSEPH LANE, of Oregon, was nominated for Vice-President by a similar vote. And then, after a speech from Mr. Yancey, the Convention finally adjourned.

The "Constitutional Union" (late "American") party held a Convention at Baltimore on the 19th of May; and, on the second ballot, nominated JOHN BELL, of Tennessee, for President; he receiving 138 votes to 114 for all others. Sam Houston, of Texas, had 57 votes on the first, and 69 on the second ballot. EDWARD EVERETT, of Massachusetts, was then unanimously nominated for Vice-President. The Convention, without a dissenting voice, united on the following

PLATFORM:

"*Whereas*, Experience has demonstrated that Platforms adopted by the partisan Conventions of the country have had the effect to mislead and deceive the people, and at the same time to widen the political divisions of the country, by the creation and encouragement of geographical and sectional parties; therefore,

"*Resolved*, That it is both the part of patriotism and of duty to *recognize* no political principle other than THE CONSTITUTION OF THE COUNTRY, THE UNION OF THE STATES, AND THE ENFORCEMENT OF THE LAWS, and that, as representatives of the Constitutional Union men of the country in National Convention assembled, we hereby pledge ourselves to maintain, protect, and defend, separately and unitedly, these great principles of public liberty and national safety, against all enemies, at home and abroad; believing that thereby peace may once more be restored to the country, the rights of the People and of the States reëstablished, and the Government again placed in that condition of justice, fraternity, and equality, which, under the example and Constitution of our fathers, has solemnly bound every citizen of the United States to maintain a more perfect union, establish justice, insure domestic tranquillity, provide for the common defense, promote the general welfare, and secure the blessings of liberty to ourselves and our posterity."

The "Republican" National Convention met at Chicago, Ill., on Wednesday, May 16th. All the Free States were strongly represented, with Delaware, Maryland, Virginia, Kentucky, Missouri, the District of Columbia, and the Territories of Kansas and Nebraska. There was a delegation present claiming to represent Texas, but it was afterward found to be fraudulent. David Wilmot, of Pennsylvania, was chosen temporary Chairman, and George Ashmun, of Massachusetts, President. A Platform Committee of one from each State and Territory was appointed on the first day, from which Committee a report was submitted on the evening of the second, when it was immediately and unanimously adopted. That report or Platform is as follows:

"*Resolved*, That we, the delegated representatives of the Republican electors of the United States, in Convention assembled, in discharge of the duty we owe to our constituents and our country, unite in the following declarations:

"1. That the history of the nation, during the last four years, has fully established the propriety and necessity of the organization and perpetuation of the Republican party; and that the causes which called it into existence are permanent in their nature, and now, more than ever before, demand its peaceful and constitutional triumph.

"2. That the maintenance of the principle promulgated in the Declaration of Independence and embodied in the Federal Constitution, 'That all men are created equal; that they are endowed by their Creator with certain inalienable rights; that among these are life, liberty, and the pursuit of happiness; that, to secure these rights, governments are instituted among men, deriving their just powers from the consent of the governed,' is essential to the preservation of our Republican institutions; and that the Federal Constitution, the Rights of the States, and the Union of the States, must and shall be preserved.

"3. That to the Union of the States this nation owes its unprecedented increase in population, its surprising development of material resources, its rapid augmentation of wealth, its happiness at home and its honor abroad; and we hold in abhorrence all schemes for Disunion, come from whatever source they may: And we congratulate the country that no Republican member of Congress has uttered or countenanced the threats of Disunion so often made by Democratic members, without rebuke and with applause from their political associates; and we denounce those threats of Disunion, in case of a popular overthrow of their ascendency, as denying the vital principles of a free government, and as an avowal of contemplated treason, which it is the imperative duty of an indignant People sternly to rebuke and forever silence.

"4. That the maintenance inviolate of the rights of the States, and especially the right of each State to order and control its own domestic institutions according to its own judgment exclusively, is essential to that balance of powers on which the perfection and endurance of our political fabric depend; and we denounce the lawless invasion by armed force of the soil of any State or Territory, no matter under what pretext, as among the gravest of crimes.

"5. That the present Democratic Administration has far exceeded our worst apprehensions, in its measureless subserviency to the exactions of a sectional interest, as especially evinced in its desperate exertions to force the infamous Lecompton Constitution upon the protesting people of Kansas; in construing the personal relation between master and servant to involve an unqualified property in persons; in its attempted enforcement, everywhere, on land and sea, through the intervention of Congress and of the Federal Courts, of the extreme pretensions of a purely local interest; and in its general and unvarying abuse of the power intrusted to it by a confiding people.

"6. That the people justly view with alarm the reckless extravagance which pervades every department of the Federal Government; that a return to rigid economy and accountability is indispensable to arrest the systematic plunder of the public treasury by favored partisans; while the recent startling developments of frauds and corruptions at the Federal metropolis, show that an entire change of administration is imperatively demanded.

"7. That the new dogma that the Constitution, of its own force, carries Slavery into any or all of the Territories of the United States, is a dangerous political heresy, at variance with the explicit provisions of that instrument itself, with contemporaneous exposition, and with legislative and judicial precedent; is revolutionary in its tendency, and subversive of the peace and harmony of the country.

"8. That the normal condition of all the territory of the United States is that of Freedom: That, as our Republican fathers, when they had abolished Slavery in all our national territory, ordained that 'no person should be deprived of life, liberty, or property, without due process of law,' it becomes our duty, by legislation, whenever such legislation is necessary, to maintain this provision of the Constitution against all attempts to violate it; and we deny the authority of Congress, of a territorial legislature, or of any individuals, to give legal existence to Slavery in any Territory of the United States.

"9. That we brand the recent reöpening of the African slave-trade, under the cover of our national flag, aided by perversions of judicial power, as a crime against humanity and a burning shame to our country and age; and we call upon Congress to take prompt and efficient measures for the total and final suppression of that execrable traffic.

"10. That in the recent vetoes, by their Federal Governors, of the acts of the Legislatures of Kansas and Nebraska, prohibiting Slavery in those Territories, we find a practical illustration of the boasted Democratic principle of Non-Intervention and Popular Sovereignty embodied in the Kansas-Nebraska bill, and a demonstration of the deception and fraud involved therein.

"11. That Kansas should, of right, be immediately admitted as a State, under the Constitution recently formed and adopted by the House of Representatives.

"12. That, while providing revenue for the support of the General Government by duties upon imports, sound policy requires such an adjustment of these imposts as to encourage the development of the industrial interests of the whole country: and we commend that policy of national exchanges which secures to the working men liberal wages, to agriculture remunerating prices, to mechanics and manufacturers an adequate reward for their skill, labor, and enterprise, and to the nation commercial prosperity and independence.

"13. That we protest against any sale or alienation to others of the Public Lands held by actual settlers, and against any view of the Homestead policy which regards the settlers as paupers or suppliants for public bounty; and we demand the passage by Congress of the complete and satisfactory

Homestead measure which has already passed the House.

"14. That the Republican Party is opposed to any change in our Naturalization Laws, or any State legislation by which the rights of citizenship hitherto accorded to immigrants from foreign lands shall be abridged or impaired; and in favor of giving a full and efficient protection to the rights of all classes of citizens, whether native or naturalized, both at home and abroad.

"15. That appropriations by Congress for River and Harbor improvements of a National character, required for the accommodation and security of an existing commerce, are authorized by the Constitution, and justified by the obligations of Government to protect the lives and property of its citizens.

"16. That a Railroad to the Pacific Ocean is imperatively demanded by the interests of the whole country; that the Federal Government ought to render immediate and efficient aid in its construction; and that, as preliminary thereto, a daily Overland Mail should be promptly established.

"17. Finally, having thus set forth our distinctive principles and views, we invite the coöperation of all citizens, however differing on other questions, who substantially agree with us in their affirmance and support."

The Convention, having already decided, by a vote of 331 to 130, that a majority vote only of the delegates should be required to nominate, proceeded, on the morning of the third day of its session, to ballot for a candidate for President of the United States, with the following result:

	1st Ballot.	*2d.*	*3d.*
William H. Seward, of New York	173½	184½	180
Abraham Lincoln, of Illinois	102	181	231½
Simon Cameron, of Pennsylvania	50½	Withdrawn	
Salmon P Chase, of Ohio	49	42½	24½
Edward Bates, of Missouri	48	35	22
William L. Dayton, of New Jersey	14	10	Withdr'n
John McLean, of Ohio	12	8	5
Jacob Collamer, of Vermont	10	Withdrawn	
Scattering	6	4	2

ABRAHAM LINCOLN having, on the third ballot, within two and a half votes of the number necessary to nominate him, Mr. David K. Cartter, of Ohio, before the result was announced, rose to change four votes from Chase to Lincoln, giving the latter a clear majority. Mr. McCrillis, of Maine, followed, changing ten votes from Seward to Lincoln; Mr. Andrew, of Massachusetts, also changed a part of the vote of that State from Seward to Lincoln; and Mr. B. Gratz Brown, of Missouri, changed the eighteen votes of that State from Bates to Lincoln. Others followed, until Mr. Lincoln had 354 out of 466 votes, and was declared duly nominated. On motion of Mr. Wm. M. Evarts, of New York, seconded by Mr. John A. Andrew, of Massachusetts, the nomination was made unanimous.

In the evening, the Convention proceeded to ballot for Vice-President, when HANNIBAL HAMLIN, of Maine, received, on the first ballot, 194 votes; Cassius M. Clay, of Kentucky, 101½; and there were 165½ cast for other candidates. On the second ballot, Mr. Hamlin received 367 votes to 99 for all others, and was declared duly nominated. On motion of Mr. George D. Blakey, of Kentucky, the nomination was made unanimous.

On motion of Mr. Joshua R. Giddings, of Ohio, it was

"*Resolved*, That we deeply sympathize with those men who have been driven, some from their native States and others from the States of their adoption, and are now exiled from their homes on account of their opinions; and we hold the Democratic party responsible for the gross violations of that clause of the Constitution which declares that citizens of each State shall be entitled to all the privileges and immunities of citizens of the several States."

And then, after a brief speech by the President, the Convention adjourned, with nine hearty cheers for the ticket.

The canvass for the Presidency, thus opened, was distinguished from all that had preceded it, not more by the number of formidable contestants, than by the sharpness with which the issues were defined by three of the contending parties. It was, in effect, proclaimed by three of the leading Southern delegates in the Charleston Convention: "The last Presidential election was won by ambiguity, double-dealing, deception—by devising a platform that meant one thing at the North, and another at the South. But, we are resolved to have no more of this. We shall now succeed on a clear exhibition of our principles, or not at all." And the champions of Popular Sovereignty, who controlled most of the delegations from Free States, were nearly as frank, and quite as firm. Said a leading supporter of Senator Douglas—Mr. George E. Pugh, of Ohio[16]—in the Charleston Convention:

"Thank God that a bold and honest man [Mr. Yancey] has at last spoken, and told the whole truth with regard to the demands of the South. It is now plainly before the Convention and the country that the South *does* demand an advanced step from the Democratic party." [Mr. Pugh here read the resolves of the Alabama Democratic State Convention of 1856, to prove that the South was *then* satisfied with what it now rejects. He proceeded to show that the Northern Democrats had sacrificed themselves in battling for the rights of the South, and instanced one and another of the delegates there present, who had been defeated and thrown out of public life thereby. He concluded:] "And now, the very weakness thus produced is urged as a reason why the North should have no weight in forming the platform! The Democracy of the North are willing to stand by the old landmarks—to reäffirm the old faith. They will deeply regret to part with their Southern brethren. But, if the gentlemen from the South can only abide with us on the terms they now propound, *they must go*. The North-West must and will be heard and felt. The Northern Democrats are not children, to be told to stand here—to stand there—to be moved at the beck and bidding of the South. Because we are in a minority on account of our fidelity to our constitutional obligations, we are told, in effect, that we must put our hands on our mouths, and our mouths in the dust. Gentlemen," said Mr. Pugh, "you mistake us—*we will not do it.*"

The Southern leaders gave repeated and earnest warnings to this effect: "Gentlemen from the North! look well to your doings! If you insist on your 'Squatter Sovereignty' platform, in full view of its condemnation by the Supreme Court in the Dred Scott case, you break up the Democratic party—nay, more: you break up the Union! The unity of the Democratic party is the last bond that holds the Union together: that snapped, there is no other that can be trusted for a year." Discarding that of the "Constitutional Union" party as meaning anything in general and nothing in particular, the Lincoln, Douglas, and Breckinridge parties had deliberately planted themselves, respectively, on the following positions:

1. *Lincoln.*—Slavery can only exist by virtue of municipal law; and there is no law for it in the Territories, and no power to enact one. Congress can establish or legalize Slavery nowhere, but is bound to prohibit it in or exclude it from any and every Federal Territory, whenever and wherever there shall be necessity for such exclusion or prohibition.

2. *Douglas.*—Slavery or No Slavery in any Territory is entirely the affair of the white inhabitants of such Territory. If they choose to have it, it is their right; if they choose *not* to have it, they have a right to exclude or prohibit it. Neither Congress nor the people of the Union, or of any part of it, outside of said Territory, have any right to meddle with or trouble themselves about the matter.

3. *Breckinridge.*—The citizen of any State has a right to migrate to any Territory, taking with him anything which is property by the law of his own State, and hold, enjoy,

[16] Recently, U. S. Senator from that State; elected over Gov. Chase in 1853–4; succeeded by him in turn in 1859–60; since, a candidate for Lieut. Governor, under Vallandigham, in 1863.

and be protected in, the use of such property in said Territory. And Congress is bound to render such protection wherever necessary, whether with or without the coöperation of the Territorial Legislature.

We have seen how thoroughly this last doctrine is refuted by Col. Benton in his strictures on the Dred Scott decision. If it were sound, any blackleg might, with impunity, defy the laws of any Territory forbidding the sale of lottery tickets or other implements of gambling. Or the Indian trader might say to the United States Agent: "Sir, I know you have a law authorizing and directing you to destroy every drop of liquor you find offered or kept for sale on an Indian reservation; but my liquor is *property*, according to the laws of my State, and you cannot touch it. I have a Constitutional *right* to take my property into any Territory, and there do with it as I please—so, Hands off!" He who does not know that this is not law, nor compatible with the most vital functions of government, can hardly have considered the matter patiently or thoughtfully.

The Douglas platform was practically eviscerated by the ready acceptance at Baltimore of Gov. Wickliffe's resolve making the dicta of the Supreme Court absolute and unquestionable with regard to Slavery in the Territories. The Dred Scott decision was aimed directly at 'Squatter Sovereignty:' the case, after being once disposed of on an entirely different point, was restored to life expressly to cover this ground. Ambiguous as was the Cincinnati platform, the upholder of 'Popular Sovereignty' in the Territories, who, at the same time, regards the Dred Scott decision as binding law, and its authors as entitled to make further and kindred decrees controlling his vote and action with regard to the extension of Slavery, maintains positions so inconsistent and contradictory as to divest him of all moral power in the premises—all freedom of effective action.

The canvass was opened with great spirit and vigor by Mr. Douglas in person; he speaking in nearly every Free, and in many if not most of the Slave States, in the course of the Summer and Autumn. A ready and able debater, he necessarily attracted large crowds to his meetings, and infused something of his own fiery impetuosity and tireless energy into the breasts of his supporters.

But the odds were soon seen to be too great; since the partisans of Breckinridge, not content with their manifest preponderance in all the Slave States, insisted on organizing in and dividing the Democratic strength of the Free States as well. Nay, more: in several of those States—Pennsylvania, New Jersey, Connecticut, California, and Oregon—the leaders of the Democracy in previous contests were mainly found ranged on the side of Breckinridge; while, in nearly or quite every Free State, enough adherents of the Southern platform were found to organize a party and nominate a Breckinridge ticket, rendering the choice of the Douglas Electors in most Free States hardly possible.

The Democrats, as we have seen, had divided on a question of principle—one deemed, on either side, of overwhelming consequence. Pathetic entreaties and fervid appeals had been lavished at Charleston on futile attempts to bring them to an agreement, that the party first and the Union next might be saved from imminent dissolution. Personal aspirations, doubtless, had their weight; but the South could have taken any candidate—perhaps even Douglas himself—if he were standing squarely, openly, on the Avery or Breckinridge platform; and so, probably, could the Northern delegates have consented to support Breckinridge or Howell Cobb on the Payne-Samuels or Douglas platform. Never was an issue more broadly made or clearly defined as one of conflicting, incompatible assumptions. And nowhere in the Slave States did the Breckinridge men consent to any compromise, partnership, coälition, or arrangement, with the partisans of Douglas, though aware that their antagonism would probably give several important States to the Bell-Everett ticket. But the Douglasites of the Free States, on their part, evinced a general readiness to waive their prestige of regularity, and support Electoral tickets made up from the ranks of each anti-Republican party. Thus, in New York, the "Fusion" anti-Lincoln ticket was made up of ten supporters of Bell and Everett, seven of Breckinridge and Lane, and the residue friends of Douglas. No doubt, there was an understanding among the managers that, if all these could elect Mr. Douglas, their votes should be cast solid for him; but the contingency thus contemplated was at best a remote one, while the fact that those who had the prestige of Democratic regularity consented to bargain and combine with bolters and "Know-Nothings," tended to confuse and bewilder those who "always vote the regular ticket," and were accustomed to regard a Democratic bolter with more repugnance than a life-long adversary. The portents, from the outset, were decidedly unfavorable to Mr. Douglas's election.

And, from the shape thus given to the canvass, his chances could not fail to suffer. The basis of each anti-Lincoln coälition could, of course, be nothing else than hostility to the Republican idea of excluding Slavery from the territories. Now, the position directly and thoroughly antagonistic to this was that of the Breckinridge party, which denied the right to exclude, and proclaimed the *right* of each slaveholder to carry Slavery into any territory. The position of Mr. Douglas was a mean between these extremes; and, in an earnest, arduous struggle, the prevailing tendency steadily is away from the mean, and toward a positive and decided position on one side or the other. The great mercantile influence in the seaboard cities had one controlling aim in its political efforts—to conciliate and satisfy the South, so as to keep her loyal to the Union. But Douglasism, or "Squatter Sovereignty," *did not* satisfy the South—in fact, since the failure to establish Slavery in Kansas, was regarded with special loathing by many Southrons, as an indirect and meaner sort of Wilmot Proviso. Wherever a coälition was effected, the canvass was thenceforth prosecuted on a basis which was a mumbling compromise between the Bell and the Breckinridge platforms, but which was usually reticent with regard to "Popular Sovereignty."

But the salient feature of the canvass was the hearty accord of the coälesced parties North of the Potomac, in attributing to the Republican platform and to Mr. Lincoln apprehended consequences that were, by the South, attributed to Douglas and "Squatter Sovereignty." The Democratic National Convention and party had been broken up, not because of any suspicion of Republicanism affecting either faction, but because the South would not abide the doctrine of Mr. Douglas, with regard to Slavery in the Territories. Yet here were his supporters appealing to the people from every stump to vote the coälition ticket, in order to conciliate the South, and save the country from the pangs of dissolution! It was not easy to realize that the Pughs, Paynes, Richardsons, Churches, etc., who had so determinedly bearded the South at Charleston and at Baltimore, defying threats of disruption and disunion, were the very men who now exhorted the People to vote the coälition Electoral tickets, in order to dispel the very dangers which they had persistently invoked, by supporting the Payne-Samuels platform, and nominating Douglas for President.

It is more difficult to treat calmly the conduct of the "American," "Conservative," "Union," or Bell-Everett party of the South; or, more accurately, to reconcile its chosen attitude and professions in the canvass with the course taken by thousands of its members immediately on the announcement of the result, with the ultimate concurrence of many more, including even the eminent and hitherto moderate and loyal Tennessean whom it had deliberately presented as an embodiment of its principles by nominating him for the Presidency. That party was mainly composed of admiring disciples of Clay and Webster, who had sternly resisted Nullification on grounds of principle, and had united in the enthusiastic acclaim which had hailed Webster as the triumphant champion of our Nationality, the "great expounder of the Constitution," in his forensic struggle with Hayne. It had proudly pointed to such men as William Gaston, of North Carolina, Sergeant S. Prentiss, of Mississippi, Edward Bates, of Missouri, George W. Summers, of Virginia, John J. Crittenden, of Kentucky, and James L. Petigru, of South Carolina, as the exponents of its principles, the jewels of its crown. It had nominated and supported Bell and Everett on a platform which meaningly proclaimed fidelity to "The Union, the Constitution, and the Enforcement of the Laws," as its distinctive ground. To say that it meant by this to stand by the Union until some other party should, in its judgment, violate the Constitution, is to set the human understanding at defiance. It either meant to cling to the Constitution and Union at all hazards and under all circumstances, and to insist that the laws should be enforced throughout the country, or it was guilty of seeking votes under false pretenses. Unlike the Douglas Democracy, it was a distinct, well-established party, which had a definitive existence, and at least a semblance of organization in every Slave State but South Carolina. It had polled a majority of the Southern vote for Harrison in 1840, for Taylor in 1848, had just polled nearly forty per cent.. of that vote for Bell, and might boast its full share of the property, and more than its share of the intelligence and respectability, of the South. This party had but to be courageously faithful to its cardinal principle and to its abiding convictions to avert the storm of civil war. Had its leaders, its orators, its presses, spoken out promptly, decidedly, unconditionally, for the Union at all hazards, and for settling our differences in Congress, in the Courts, and at the ballot-box, it would have prevented the effusion of rivers of precious blood. It was perfectly aware that the Republicans and their President elect were powerless, even if disposed, to do the South any wrong; that the result of the elections already held had secured[17] an anti-Republican majority in either branch of the ensuing Congress; that the Supreme Court was decidedly and, for a considerable period, unchangeably on the same side. In the worst conceivable event of the elections yet to come, no bill could pass respecting the Territories, or anything else, which the "Conservatives" should see fit unitedly to oppose. And yet, South Carolina had scarcely indicated unmistakably her purpose, when many Bell-Unionists of Georgia, Alabama, and other Southern States, began to clamor and shout for Secession. They seemed so absorbingly intent on getting, for once, on the stronger side, that they forgot the controlling fact that the side on which God is has always at last the majority.

The early State Elections of 1860 had not been favorable to the Republicans. They had begun by carrying New Hampshire by 4,443—a satisfactory majority; but were next beaten in Rhode Island—an independent ticket, headed by William Sprague for Governor, carrying the State over theirs, by 1,460 majority. In Connecticut, Gov. Buckingham had been reëlected by barely 541 majority, in nearly 80,000 votes—the heaviest poll ever had there at a State Election. It was evident that harmony at Charleston would have rendered the election of a Democratic President morally certain. But, after the disruption there, things were bravely altered. Maine, early in September, elected a Republican Governor by 18,091 majority; Vermont directly followed, with a Republican majority of 22,370; but when Pennsylvania and Indiana, early in October, declared unmistakably for Lincoln—the former choosing Andrew G. Curtin her Governor by 32,164 majority over Henry D. Foster, who had the hearty support of all three opposing parties; while Indiana chose Gen. Henry S. Lane by 9,757 over T. A. Hendricks, his only competitor, with seven out of eleven Representatives in Congress, and a Republican Legislature—it was manifest that only a miracle could prevent the success of Lincoln and Hamlin the next month.

Yet the mercantile fears of convulsion and civil war, as results of Mr. Lincoln's election, were so vivid and earnest that the contest at the North was still prosecuted by his combined adversaries with the energy of desperation. New York, especially, was the arena of a struggle as intense, as

[17] New York had chosen 10; Pennsylvania 7; New Jersey 3; Ohio 8; Indiana 4; Illinois 5; and Missouri 6 anti-Republicans to the House; rendering it morally certain that, but for Secession, Mr Lincoln would have had to face an Opposition Congress from the start.

vehement, and energetic, as had ever been known. Her drawn battle of the year before, and the perfect accord in this contest of the anti-Republican parties, gave grounds for hope, if not confidence, that she might now be carried against Lincoln, especially as the City was expected to give a far larger majority for "Fusion" than she had ever yet given for any man or party. Abundance of money for every purpose doubtless contributed to the animation of the struggle on this side, while painful apprehensions of Southern revolt, in case Lincoln should be elected, rendered the "merchant princes," whose wealth was largely, if not wholly, locked up in the shape of Southern indebtedness, ready to bleed freely for even a hope of preventing a result they so dreaded as fatal to their business, their prosperity, and their affluence.

Gov. Seward—who had made a political tour through the North-West during the Autumn, wherein his speeches in behalf of the Republican cause and candidates were of a remarkably high order, alike in originality, dignity, and perspicuity—closed the canvass, the night before Election, in an address to his townsmen at Auburn, which concluded with these truthful and memorable words:

"Now here is the trinity in unity and unity in trinity of the political church, just now come to us by the light of a new revelation, and christened 'Fusion.' And this 'Fusion' party, what is the motive to which it appeals? You may go with me into the streets to-night, and follow the 'Little Giants,' who go with their torchlights, and their flaunting banners of 'Popular Sovereignty;' or you may go with the smaller and more select and modest band, who go for Breckinridge and Slavery; or you may follow the music of the clanging bells; and, strange to say, they will all bring you into one common chamber. When you get there, you will hear only this emotion of the human heart appealed to, Fear,—fear that, if you elect a President of the United States according to the Constitution and the laws to-morrow, you will wake up next day, and find that you have no country for him to preside over! Is not that a strange motive for an American patriot to appeal to? And, in that same hall, amid the jargon of three discordant members of the 'Fusion' party, you will hear one argument; and that argument is, that, so sure as you are so perverse as to cast your vote singly, lawfully, honestly, as you ought to do, for one candidate for the Presidency, instead of scattering it among three candidates, so that no President may be elected, this Union shall come down over your heads, involving you and us in a common ruin!

"Fellow-citizens, it is time, high time, that we know whether this is a Constitutional government under which we live. It is high time that we know, since the Union is threatened, who are its friends, and who are its enemies. The Republican party, who propose, in the old, appointed, constitutional way, to choose a President, are every man of them loyal to the Union. The disloyalists, wherever they may be, are those who are opposed to the Republican party, and attempt to prevent the election of a President. I know that our good and esteemed neighbors—(Heaven knows I have cause to respect, and esteem, and honor, and love them, as I do; for such neighbors as even my Democratic neighbors, no other man ever had)—I know that they do not avow, nor do they mean to support, or think they are supporting, disunionists. But I tell them, that he who proposes to lay hold of the pillars of the Union, and bring it down into ruin, *is* a disunionist; and that every man who quotes him, and uses his threats and his menaces as an argument against our exercise of our duty, is an abettor, unconscious though he may be, of disunion; and that, when to-morrow's sun shall have set, and the next morning's sun shall have risen on the American people, rejoicing in the election of Abraham Lincoln to the Presidency, those men who to-day sympathize with, uphold, support, and excuse the disunionists, will have to make a sudden choice, and choose whether, in the language of the Senator from Georgia, they will go for treason, and so make it respectable, or whether they will go with us for Freedom, for the Constitution, and for eternal Union."

XXII.

SECESSION.

THE choice of Presidential Electors, which formerly took place at the discretion of the several States within a limited range, is now required, by act of Congress, to be made on the same day throughout—namely, on the Tuesday next succeeding the first Monday in November. This fell, in 1860, on the 6th of the month; and it was known, before that day had fully expired, that ABRAHAM LINCOLN had been clearly designated by the People for their next President, through the choice by his supporters of a majority of the whole number of Electors. Every Free State but New Jersey had chosen the entire Lincoln Electoral ticket; and in New Jersey the refusal of part of the Douglas men to support the "Fusion" ticket (composed of three Douglas, two Bell, and two Breckinridge men), had allowed four of the Lincoln Electors to slip in over the two Bell and the two Breckinridge Electors on the regular Democratic ticket. The three Lincoln Electors who had to confront the full vote of the coalesced anti-Republican parties were defeated by about 4,500 majority. And, although this was not ascertained that night, nor yet the fact that California and Oregon had gone with the other free States, yet there were 169 Lincoln Electors chosen (out of 303) outside of these three States; *with* these, Mr. Lincoln had 180, to 123 for all others. Of these, Breckinridge had 72; Bell 39 (from Virginia, Kentucky, and Tennessee); and Douglas barely 12—those of Missouri (9) and 3, as aforesaid, from New Jersey. But, though nowhere in the Electoral, Mr. Douglas was second in the Popular, vote, as will be seen by the following table, wherein the "Fusion" vote is divided between the parties which contributed to it, according to the best estimate that can now be made of their strength respectively:

FREE STATES.

STATES.	LINCOLN.	*Douglas.*	*Breckinridge.*	*Bell.*
Maine	62,811	26,693	6,368	2,046
New Hampshire	37,519	25,881	2,112	441
Massachusetts	106,353	34,372	5,939	22,331
Rhode Island	12,244	*4,000	*1,000	2,707
Connecticut	43,972	15,522	14,641	3,291
Vermont	33,808	6,849	218	1,969
New York	353,804	*203,329	*50,000	*50,000
New Jersey	58,324	*30,000	*30,000	*2,801
Pennsylvania	268,030	*78,871	*100,000	12,776
Ohio	231,610	187,232	11,405	12,194
Indiana	139,033	115,509	12,295	5,306
Illinois	172,161	160,215	2,404	4,913
Michigan	88,480	65,057	805	405
Wisconsin	86,110	65,021	888	161
Minnesota	22,069	11,920	748	62
Iowa	70,409	55,111	1,048	1,748
California	39,173	38,516	34,334	6,817
Oregon	5,270	3,951	5,006	183
Total Free States	1,831,180	1,128,049	279,211	130,151

* "Fusion" vote apportioned according to the estimated strength of the several contributing parties.

SLAVE STATES.

STATES.	LINCOLN.	*Douglas.*	*Breckinridge.*	*Bell.*
Delaware	3,815	1,023	7,337	3,864
Maryland	2,294	5,966	42,482	41,760
Virginia	1,929	16,290	74,323	74,681
North Carolina	(no ticket)	2,701	48,539	44,990
South Carolina	[Chosen by the Legislature.]			
Georgia	(no ticket)	11,590	51,889	42,886
Alabama	(no ticket)	13,651	48,831	27,875
Mississippi	(no ticket)	3,283	40,797	25,040
Kentucky	1,364	25,651	53,143	66,058
Tennessee	(no ticket)	11,350	64,209	69,274
Missouri	17,028	58,801	31,317	58,372
Arkansas	(no ticket)	5,227	28,732	20,094
Louisiana	(no ticket)	7,625	22,681	20,204
Florida	(no ticket)	367	8,543	5,437
Texas	(no ticket)	(no ticket)	47,548	†15,438
Total Slave States	26,430	163,525	570,871	515,973
Grand Total	1,857,610	1,291,574	850,082	646,124

† This anti-Breckinridge vote was cast for a "Fusion" Electoral ticket, but almost entirely by old 'Whigs' or Bell men.

Lincoln over Douglas, 566,036; Do. over Bell, 1,211,486; do. over Breckinridge, 1,007,528.

Lincoln has less than all his opponents combined, by 930,170.

Breckinridge had in the Slave States over Bell, 54,898; do. over Douglas, 407,346; do. over Douglas and Lincoln, 380,916.

Breckinridge lacks of a majority in the Slave States, 135,057.

From an early stage of the canvass, the Republicans could not help seeing that they had the potent aid, in their efforts, of the *good wishes* for their success of at least a large proportion of the advocates of Breckinridge and Lane. The toasts drunk with most enthusiasm at the Fourth-of-July celebrations throughout South Carolina pointed to the probable election of Mr. Lincoln as the necessary prelude to movements whereon the hearts of all Carolinians were intent. Southern "Fire-Eaters" canvassed the Northern States in behalf of Breckinridge and Lane, but very much to the satisfaction of the friends of Lincoln and Hamlin. The "Fusion" arrangements, whereby it was hoped, at all events, to defeat Lincoln, were not generally favored by the "Fire-Eaters" who visited the North, whether intent on politics, business, or pleasure; and, in some instances, those who sought to commend themselves to the favor of their Southern patrons or customers, by an exhibition of zeal in the "Fusion" cause, were quietly told: "What you are doing looks not to the end *we* desire: *we* want *Lincoln* elected." In no Slave State did the supporters of Breckinridge unite in any "Fusion" movement whatever; and it was a very open secret that the friends of Breckinridge generally—at all events, throughout the Slave States—next to the all but impossible success of their own candidate—preferred that of the Republicans.[1] In the Senate throughout the preceding Session, at Charleston, at Baltimore, and ever since, they had acted precisely as they would have done, had they preëminently desired Mr. Lincoln's success, and determined to do their best to secure it.

And now, a large majority of Lincoln Electors had been carried, rendering morally certain his choice by the Electoral Colleges next month, and his inauguration on the 4th of March ensuing. So the result contemplated and labored for by at least *two* of the four contending parties in the canvass had been secured.

What next?

In October, 1856, a Convention of Southern Governors was held at Raleigh, N. C., at the invitation of Gov. Wise, of Virginia. This gathering was kept secret at the time; but it was afterward proclaimed by Gov. Wise that, had Fremont been elected, he would have marched at the head of twenty thousand men to Washington, and taken possession of the Capitol, preventing by force Fremont's inauguration at that place.

In the same spirit, a meeting of the prominent politicians of South

[1] *The Washington Star*, then a Breckinridge organ, noticing, in September, 1860, the conversion of Senator Clingman, of North Carolina, from the support of Douglas to that of Breckinridge, said:

"While we congratulate him on the fact that his eyes are at length open to the (to the South) dangerous tendency of the labors of Douglas, we hail his conversion as an evidence of the truth of our oft-repeated declaration, that, ere the first Monday in November, every honest and unselfish Democrat throughout the South will be found arrayed against Douglas-Freesoilism, as being far more dangerous to the South than the election of Lincoln; because it seeks to create a Free-Soil party there; while, if Lincoln triumphs, the result cannot fail to be a South united in her own defense—the only key to a full and—we sincerely believe—a peaceful and happy solution of the political problem of the Slavery question."

Columns like the above might be quoted from the Breckinridge journals of the South, showing that they regarded the success of Douglas as the great peril, to be defeated at all hazards.

Carolina was held at the residence of Senator Hammond, near Augusta, on the 25th of October, 1860. Gov. Gist, ex-Gov. Adams, ex-Speaker Orr, and the entire delegation to Congress, except Mr. Miles, who was kept away by sickness, were present, with many other men of mark. By this cabal, it was unanimously resolved that South Carolina should secede from the Union in the event of Lincoln's then almost certain election. Similar meetings of kindred spirits were held simultaneously, or soon afterward, in Georgia, Alabama, Mississippi, Florida, and probably other Slave States. By these meetings, and by the incessant interchange of messages, letters, and visits, the entire slaveholding region had been prepared, so far as possible, for disunion in the event of a Republican, if not also of a Douglas, triumph.

The Legislature of South Carolina does not regularly meet until the fourth Monday in November; but, the recent act of Congress requiring a choice of Presidential Electors prior to that time, Gov. Gist had good reason for calling the Legislature of 1860 to meet in advance of the regular day. It met, according to his summons, at Columbia, on Monday, Nov. 5 (the day before the choice of Presidential Electors throughout the Union), when Mr. W. D. Porter, of Charleston, was chosen President of the Senate. On taking the Chair, he said:

"I do not seek now to lift the veil that hides the future from our sight; but we have all an instinctive feeling that we are on the eve of great events. His Excellency, the Governor, in the terms of his call, has summoned us to take action, if advisable, for the safety and protection of the State. Heretofore, we have consulted for its convenience and well-being; now, its destiny, its very existence, depends upon our action. It was the old injunction, in times of great peril, to the Roman consuls, to take care that the Republic sustained no detriment; this charge and injunction is now addressed to us. All that is dear and precious to this people—life, fortune, name, and history—all is committed to our keeping for weal or for woe, for honor or for shame. Let us do our part, so that those who come after us shall acknowledge that we were not unworthy of the great trusts devolved upon us, and not unequal to the great exigencies by which we were tried. Above all things, let us be of one mind. We are all agreed as to our wrongs. Let us sacrifice all differences of opinion, as to the time and mode of remedy, upon the altar of patriotism, and for the sake of the great cause. In our unanimity will be our strength, physical and moral. No human power can withstand or break down a united people, standing upon their own soil and defending their homes and firesides. May we be so united, and may the great Governor of men and of nations inspire our hearts with courage, and inform our understandings with wisdom, and lead us in the way of honor and of safety."

Gov. Gist (whose term expired with the current year) communicated to both Houses his Annual Message, immediately on their organization. It is as follows:

"EXECUTIVE DEPARTMENT,
"COLUMBIA, S. C., Nov. 5, 1860.

"*Gentlemen of the Senate and House of Representatives:*

"The act of Congress, passed in the year 1846, enacts that the electors of President and Vice-President shall be appointed on the Tuesday next after the first Monday of the month of November, of the year in which they are to be appointed. The annual meeting of the Legislature of South Carolina, by a constitutional provision, will not take place until the fourth Monday in November instant. I have considered it my duty, under the authority conferred upon me to convene the Legislature on extraordinary occasions, to convene you, that you may, on to-morrow, appoint the number of Electors of President and Vice-President to which this State is entitled.

"Under ordinary circumstances, your duty could be soon discharged by the election of Electors representing the choice of the people of the State; but, in view of the threatening aspect of affairs, and the strong probability of the election to the Presidency of a sectional candidate, by a party committed to the support of measures, which, if carried out, will inevitably destroy our equality in the Union, and ultimately reduce the Southern States to mere provinces of a consolidated despotism, to be governed by a fixed majority in Congress hostile to our institutions, and fatally bent upon our ruin, I would respectfully suggest that the Legislature remain in session, and take such action as will prepare the State for any emergency that may arise.

"That an exposition of the will of the people may be obtained on a question involving such momentous consequences, I would earnestly recommend that, in the event of Abraham Lincoln's election to the Presidency, a Convention of the people of this State be immediately called, to consider and determine for themselves the mode and measure of redress. My own opinions of what the Convention should do are of little moment; but, believing that the time has arrived when every one, however humble he may be, should express his opinions in unmistakable language, I am constrained to say that the only alternative left, in my judgment, is the secession of South Carolina from the Federal Union. The indications from many of the Southern States justify the conclusion that the secession of South Carolina will be immediately followed, if not adopted simultaneously, by them, and ultimately by the entire South. The long-desired coöperation of the other States having similar institutions, for which so many of our citizens have been waiting, seems to be near at hand; and, if we are true to ourselves, will soon be realized. The State has, with great unanimity declared that she has the right peaceably to secede, and no power on earth can rightfully prevent it.

"If, in the exercise of arbitrary power, and forgetful of the lessons of history, the Government of the United States should attempt coërcion, it will become our solemn duty to meet force by force; and, whatever may be the decision of the Convention, representing the Sovereignty of the State, and amenable to no earthly tribunal, it shall, during the remainder of my administration, be carried out to the letter, regardless of any hazard that may surround its execution.

"I would also respectfully recommend a thorough reörganization of the Militia, so as to place the whole military force of the State in a position to be used at the shortest notice, and with the greatest efficiency. Every man in the State, between the ages of eighteen and forty-five, should be well armed with the most efficient weapons of modern warfare, and all the available means of the State used for that purpose.

"In addition to this general preparation, I would recommend that the services of ten thousand volunteers be immediately accepted; that they be organized and drilled by officers chosen by themselves, and hold themselves in readiness to be called on upon the shortest notice. With this preparation for defense, and with all the hallowed memories of past achievements, with our love of liberty, and hatred of tyranny, and with the knowledge that we are contending for the safety of our homes and firesides, we can confidently appeal to the Disposer of all human events, and safely trust our cause in His keeping. WM. H. GIST."

Mr. James Chesnut, Jr., one of the United States Senators from South Carolina, was among the large number of leading politicians in attendance at the opening of the legislative session. He was known as a zealous advocate of Secession, and as such was serenaded on the evening of November 5th, aforesaid. Being called out to speak, Mr. Chesnut (as reported by telegraph to *The Charleston Courier*) said:

"Before the setting of to-morrow's sun, in all human probability, the destiny of this confederated Republic would be decided. He solemnly thought, in all human probability, that the Republican party would triumph in the election of LINCOLN as President. In that event, the lines of our enemies seem to be closing around us; but they must be broken. They might see in the hurried paths of these starched men of livery the funeral cortege of the Constitution of the country. Peace, hope, independence, liberty, power, and the prosperity of Sovereign States, may be draped as chief mourners; still, in the rear of this procession, there is the light of the glorious past, from which they might rekindle the dying blaze of their own altars. We see it all—know it all—feel it all; and, with heaven's help, we will meet it all.

"It was evident that we had arrived at the initial point of a new departure. We have two ways before us, in one of which, whether we will or not, we must tread; for, in the event of this issue, there would be no repose. In both lie dangers, difficulties, and troubles, which no human foresight can foreshadow or perceive; but they are not equal in magnitude. One is beset with humiliation, dishonor, *émeutes*, rebellions—with submission, in the beginning, to all, and at all times, and confiscation and slavery in the end. The other, it is true, has its difficulties and trials, but no disgrace. Hope, duty, and honor, shine along the path. Hope beacons you at the end. Before deciding, consider well the ancient and sacred maxim —'Stand upon the ancient way—see which is the right, good way, and walk in it.'

"But the question now was, Would the South submit to a Black Republican President and a Black Republican Congress, which will claim the right to construe the Constitution of the country and administer the Government in their own hands, not by the law of the instrument itself, nor by that of the fathers of the country, nor by the practices of those who administered seventy years ago, but by rules drawn from their own blind consciences and crazy brains. They call us inferiors, semi-civilized barbarians, and claim the right to possess our lands, and give them to the destitute of the Old World and the profligates of this. They claim the dogmas of the Declaration of Independence as part of the Constitution, and that it is their right and duty to so administer the Government as to give full effect to them. The people now must choose whether they would be governed by enemies, or govern themselves.

"For himself, he would unfurl the Palmetto flag, fling it to the breeze, and, with the spirit of a brave man, determine to live and die as became our glorious ancestors, and ring the clarion notes of defiance in the ears of an insolent foe. He then spoke of the undoubted right to withdraw their delegated powers, and it was their duty, in the event contemplated, to withdraw them. It was their only safety.

"Mr. C. favored separate State action; saying the rest would flock to our standard."

Hon. Wm. W. Boyce—then, and for some years previously, a leading Representative in Congress from South Carolina—was, in like manner, serenaded and called out by the enthusiastic crowd of Secessionists, at Columbia, on the following evening. He concluded a speech denunciatory of the Republicans, as follows:[2]

"The question then is, What are we to do? In my opinion, the South ought not to submit. If you intend to resist, the way to resist in earnest is to act; the way to enact revolution is to stare it in the face. I think the only policy for us is to arm as soon as we receive authentic intelligence of the election of Lincoln. It is for South Carolina, in the quickest manner, and by the most direct means, to withdraw from the Union. Then we will not submit, whether the other Southern States will act with us or with our enemies.

"They cannot take sides with our enemies; they must take sides with us. When an ancient philosopher wished to inaugurate a great revolution, his motto was to dare! to dare!"

"Mr. Boyce was followed by Gen. M. E. Martin, Cols. Cunningham, Simpson, Richardson, and others, who contended that to submit to the election of Lincoln is to consent to a lingering death."

There was great joy in Charleston, and wherever "Fire-Eaters" most did congregate, on the morning of November 7th. Men rushed to shake hands and congratulate each other on the glad tidings of Lincoln's election. *Now*, it was felt, and exultingly proclaimed, the last obstacle to "Southern independence" has been removed, and the great experiment need no longer be postponed to await the pleasure of the weak, the faithless, the cowardly. It was clear that the election had resulted precisely as the master-spirits had wished and hoped. *Now*, the apathy, at least of the other Cotton States, must be overcome; *now*, South Carolina—that is, her slaveholding oligarchy—will be able to achieve her long-cherished purpose of breaking up the Union, and founding a new confederacy on her own ideas, and on the 'peculiar institution' of the South. Men thronged the streets, talking, laughing, cheering,[3] like mariners long becalmed

[2] This, and nearly all the proceedings at Columbia at this crisis, are here copied directly from the columns of *The Charleston Courier*.

[3] Dispatch to *The New York Herald*, dated Washington, Nov. 8, 1860:

"A dispatch, received here to-day from a leading and wealthy gentleman in Charleston, states that the news of Lincoln's election was received there with cheers and many manifestations of approbation."

The Charleston Mercury of the 7th or 8th exultingly announced the same fact.

on a hateful, treacherous sea, whom a sudden breeze had swiftly wafted within sight of their longed-for haven, or like a seedy prodigal, just raised to affluence by the death of some far-off, unknown relative, and whose sense of decency is not strong enough to repress his exultation.

Thus stimulated, the Legislature did not hesitate nor falter in the course marked out for it by the magnates of the State oligarchy. Joint resolves, providing for the call of a Convention at some early day, with a view to unconditional secession from the Union, were piled upon each other with great energy, as if nearly every member were anxious to distinguish himself by zeal in the work. Among others, Mr. Robert Barnwell Rhett, on the second day of the session, offered such resolves, calling for the choice of a Convention on the 22d of November; the delegates to meet at Columbia on the 17th of December.

Mr. Moses and others offered similar resolves in the Senate; where Mr. Lesesne, of Charleston, attempted to stem, or, rather, to moderate, the roaring tide, by inserting the thinnest end of the wedge of "Coöperation." His resolves are, in terms, as follows:

"1st. *Resolved*, That the ascendency of the hostile, sectional, anti-Slavery party, styling themselves the Republican party, would be sufficient and proper cause for the dissolution of the Union and formation of a Southern Confederacy.

"2d. *Resolved*, That, in case of the election of the candidates of that party to the office of President and Vice-President of the United States, instead of providing unconditionally for a Convention, the better course will be to empower the Governor to take measures for assembling a Convention *so soon as any one of the other Southern States shall, in his judgment, give satisfactory assurance or evidence of her determination to withdraw from the Union.*"

In support of this proposition, Mr. Lesesne spoke ably and earnestly, but without effect. "Coöperation" had been tried in 1850–1, and had signally failed to achieve the darling purpose of a dissolution of the Union; so the rulers of Carolina opinion would have none of it in 1860.

Still another effort was made in the House (November 7th), by Mr. Trenholm, of Charleston—long conspicuous in the councils of the State—who labored hard to make "Coöperation" look so much like Secession that one could with difficulty be distinguished from the other. His proposition was couched in the following terms:

"*Resolved*, That the Committee on the Military of the Senate and House of Representatives, be instructed to meet during the recess, and to prepare a plan for arming the State, and for organizing a permanent Military Bureau; and that the said Committee be instructed to report by bill to their respective Houses on the first day of the reässembling of the General Assembly.

"*Resolved*, That the Committee of Ways and Means of the House of Representatives be instructed to sit during the recess, and prepare a bill for raising supplies necessary to carry into effect the measure recommended by the Military Committee, and to report by bill on the first day of the reässembling of the General Assembly.

"*Resolved*, That the Governor be requested immediately to apply the one hundred thousand dollars, appropriated by the last General Assembly, to the purchase of arms.

"*Resolved*, That immediately after the election of the Commissioner to the State of Georgia, this General Assembly do take a recess until the third Monday, being the nineteenth day, of November, instant, at 7 o'clock.

"*Resolved*, As the sense of this General Assembly, that the election of a Black Republican to the Presidency of the United States, will be the triumph and practical application of principles incompatible with the peace and safety of the Southern States.

"*Resolved*, That a Commissioner be elected, by joint ballot of the Senate and House of Representatives, whose duty it shall be, in the event of Mr. Lincoln's election, to proceed immediately to Milledgeville, the seat of government of the State of Georgia, whose legislature will then be in session, to announce to the government of that State that South Carolina, in view of the impending danger, will immediately put herself in a state of efficient military defense, and will cordially coöperate with the State of Georgia in measures for the protection of Southern interests; and to express the readiness of this State to coöperate with the State of Georgia, in the event of Mr. Lincoln's election, in withdrawing at once from the confederacy; and to recommend the calling of a Convention simultaneously in both States, to carry this measure into effect; and to invite the coöperation of all the Southern States in withdrawing from the present Union, and forming a separate Southern Confederacy."

These resolves coming up for consideration on the 9th, Mr. McGowan, of Abbeville, made a zealous effort to stem the furious current; pleading earnestly and plausibly for Coöperation—that is, for consultation with other Slave States, and for action in obedience to their mutual determination. He said:

"Coöperation with our Southern sisters has been the settled policy of South Carolina for at least ten years past. We have long been satisfied with the causes for a dissolution of this Union. We thought we saw long ago what was coming, and only awaited the action of our Southern sisters. This being the case, it would seem strange, now that the issue is upon us—when our need is the sorest—that we should ignore our past policy, and, in the very crisis of the conflict, cease to ask for Coöperation.

"Lincoln's election is taken as *an occasion* for action, but with us it is not the only *cause* for action. We have delayed for the last ten years for nothing but Coöperation. He thought it the best and wisest policy to remain in the Union, with our Southern sisters, in order to arrange the time when, and the manner how, of going out, and nothing else.

"It is perfectly manifest that the recorded policy of this State for the last ten years has been the policy of Secession in coöperation with other Southern States.

"But is that not fortified by both history and philosophy?—by the nature of the thing itself, and the fate of other nations? The Southern States of this Union have more motives, more inducements, and *more necessities*, for concert and Union, than any people that has lived in the tide of time. They are one in soil and climate; one in productions, having a monopoly of the Cotton region; one in institutions; and, more than all, one in their wrongs under the Constitution. Add to all this that they alone, of all the earth, have a peculiar institution—African Slavery—which is absolutely necessary for them; without which they would cease to exist, and against which, under the influence of a fanatical sentiment, the world is banded. Upon the subject of this institution, we are *isolated* from the whole world, who are not only indifferent, but inimical to it; and it would seem that the very weight of this outside pressure would compel us to unite.

"Besides, the history of the world is pregnant with admonition as to the necessity of union. The history of classic Greece, and especially that awful chapter upon the Peloponnesian war, appeals to us. The history of poor, dismembered Poland cries to us. The history of the Dutch Republic claims to be heard. Modern Italy and the States of Central America are now, at this moment, crying to us to unite. All history teaches us that 'United we stand, divided we fall.' All the Southern States would not be too many for our confederacy, whose flag would float, honored upon every sea, and under whose folds every citizen would be sure of protection and security. My God! what is the reason we cannot unite? It seems to me that we might with propriety address to the whole South the pregnant words of Milton:

'Awake! arise! or be forever fallen!'

"South Carolina has sometimes been accused of a paramount desire to lead or to disturb the councils of the South. Let us make one last effort for Coöperation, and, in doing so, repel the false and unfounded imputation.

"Mr. Speaker, I think all of us desire to consolidate the sentiment of the South. All of us prefer Coöperation. It is, therefore, immensely important that we should take no false step, and omit nothing that might tend to that end. I am utterly opposed, now and forever, to taking any step backward in this matter, and therefore it is that I am anxious that we should take no false step. It is better to consider in advance of action than after action. When we act, we must stand upon that action against the world in arms. It will strengthen our arms and nerve our hearts in doing that, if we shall be able to say that this course was not taken hastily or from impulse, but after mature deliberation, and a last effort for that which we all desire so much—Coöperation.

Then, if we fail, and a Convention is called under these circumstances, I and all of us will stand by the action of that Convention. Whatever may be our individual opinions, we will obey the mandate of the State thus pronounced.

"Whenever she, after exhausting all proper and becoming efforts for union, resolves upon her course, we will have no option, as we will have no desire, to do otherwise than rally under her banner. If the State, in her sovereign capacity, determines that her secession will produce the coöperation which we have so earnestly sought, then it shall have my hearty approbation. And if, in the alternative, she determines to let us forego the honor of being first, for the sake of promoting the common cause, let us declare to Georgia, the Empire State of the South—the Keystone of the Southern Arch, which is our nearest neighbor westward, and lying for a great distance alongside of our own territory—that we are willing to follow in her lead, and together take our place among the nations of the earth.

"If South Carolina, in Convention assembled, deliberately secedes—separate and alone, and, without any hope of coöperation, decides to cut loose from her moorings, surrounded as she is by Southern sisters in like circumstances—I will be one of her crew, and, in common with every true son of hers, will endeavor, with all the power that God has given me, to

'Spread all her canvas to the breeze,
Set every threadbare sail,
And give her to the God of storms,
The lightning and the gale.'"

Mr. Mullins, of Marion, followed; and his reply to McGowan's speech is worthy of record here, since it clearly betrays the consciousness of the disunionists that they were a lean minority of the Southern people, who might be precipitated, bullied, or dragged into treason, but whom there was no rational hope of reasoning or even seducing into it. He said:

"South Carolina had tried Coöperation, but had exhausted that policy. The State of Virginia had discredited the cause which our Commissioner went there to advocate, although she treated him, personally, with respect; but she had as much as said there were *no* indignities which could drive her to take the leadership for Southern rights. *If we wait for Coöperation, Slavery and State Rights would be abandoned*, State Sovereignty and the cause of the South lost forever, and we would be subjected to a dominion the parallel to which was that of the poor Indian under the British East India Company. When they had pledged themselves to take the State out of the Union, and placed it on record, then he was willing to send a Commissioner to Georgia, or any other Southern State, to announce our determination, and to submit the question whether they would join us or not. *We have it from high authority, that the representative of one of the Imperial Powers of Europe, in view of the prospective separation of one or more of the Southern States from the present confederacy, has made propositions in advance for the establishment of such relations between it and the Government about to be established in this State, as will insure to that power such a supply of Cotton for the future* as their increasing demand for that article will require: this information is perfectly authentic."

Thus, it will be seen that foreign intrigue was already hand-and-glove with domestic treason in sapping the foundations of our Union and seeking peculiar advantages from its overthrow.

Mr. Edmund Ruffin, of Virginia, had for many years been the editor of a leading Agricultural monthly, and had thus acquired a very decided influence over the planters of the South. A devotee of Slavery, he had hastened to Columbia, on the call of the Legislature, to do his utmost for Secession. He was, of course, serenaded in his turn by the congregated Union-breakers, on the evening of the 7th, and addressed them from the balcony of the Congaree House. The following is a synopsis of his response:

"He said the question now before the country he had studied for years. It had been the one great idea of his life. The defense of the South, he verily believed, was only to be secured through the lead of South Carolina. As old as he was, he had come here to join them in that lead. *He wished Virginia was as ready as South Carolina, but, unfortunately, she was not;* but, circumstances being different, it was perhaps better that Virginia and all other border States remain quiescent for a time, to serve as guard against the North. The first drop of blood spilled on the soil of South Carolina, would bring Virginia and every Southern State with them. By remaining in the Union for a time, she would not only prevent coërcive legislation in Congress, but any attempt for our subjugation. No argument in favor of resistance was wanted now. As soon as he had performed his duty in Virginia as a citizen, he came as fast as steam could bring him to South Carolina. He was satisfied if anything was to be done, it was to be done *here*. He had no doubt it *would* be done, and the sooner the better. Every day delayed was a day lost to the cause. They should encourage and sustain their friends, and they would frighten their enemies.

"There was no fear of Carolina remaining alone. She would soon be followed by other States. Virginia and half a dozen more were just as good and strong, and able to repel the enemy, as if they had the whole of the slaveholding States to act with them. Even if Carolina remained alone—not that he thought it probable, but supposing so—it was his conviction that she would be able to defend herself against any power brought against her. Multitudes spoke and said the issue was one of courage and honor, or of cowardice, desertion, and degradation."

A number of second and third-rate traitors followed this Ruffin in a similar vein, but their remarks were not deemed worth reporting.

But, that evening, the busy telegraph reported from Charleston the more important resignation of the leading Federal officers for South Carolina, in anticipation of her seceding. The U. S. District Court had met there in the morning, District Judge Magrath presiding. The Grand Jury—of course, by preconcert—formally declined to make any presentments, because of

"The verdict of the Northern section of the confederacy, solemnly announced to the country, through the ballot-box, on yesterday, having swept away the last hope for the permanence, for the stability of the Federal Government of these sovereign States; and the public mind is constrained to lift itself above the consideration of details in the administration of Law and Justice, up to the vast and solemn issues which have been forced upon us. These issues involve the existence of the Government of which this Court is the organ and minister. In these extraordinary circumstances, the Grand Jury respectfully decline to proceed with their presentments. They deem this explanation due to the Court and to themselves."

Judge Magrath received this communication with complaisance, and thereupon resigned his office; saying:

"The business of the term has been disposed of, and, under ordinary circumstances, it would be my duty to dismiss you to your several avocations, with my thanks for your presence and aid. But now I have something more to do, the omission of which would not be consistent with propriety. In the political history of the United States, an event has happened of ominous import to fifteen slaveholding States. The State of which we are citizens has been always understood to have deliberately fixed its purpose whenever that event should happen. Feeling an assurance of what will be the action of the State, I consider it my duty, without delay, to prepare to obey its wishes. That preparation is made by the resignation of the office I have held. For the last time, I have, as a Judge of the United States, administered the laws of the United States within the limits of the State of South Carolina.

"While thus acting in obedience to a sense of duty, I cannot be indifferent to the emotions it must produce. That department which, I believe, has best maintained its integrity and preserved its purity, has been suspended. So far as I am concerned, the Temple of Justice, raised under the Constitution of the United States, is now closed. If it shall never be again opened, I thank God that its doors have been closed before its altar has been desecrated with sacrifices to tyranny."

C. J. Colcock, Collector at Charleston, and James Conner, U. S. District Attorney, likewise resigned; and it was announced that B. C. Pressley, Sub-Treasurer, would follow, "so soon as was consistent with due respect and regard for our present excellent Chief Magistrate [Buchanan], by whose appointment he holds the office."

In the face of such multiform and high-seasoned incitements to go ahead, the efforts of those members of the

ALEXANDER H. STEPHENS
HENRY A. WISE
R. BARNWELL RHETT
JEFFERSON DAVIS
JAMES M. MASON
JOHN B. FLOYD
JOHN SLIDELL
WILLIAM L. YANCEY
ROBERT TOOMBS
ISHAM G. HARRIS
Entered according to act of Congress in the year 1864 by O. D. Case & Co. in the Clerk's office of the District Court of the United States for the District of Connecticut
CONFEDERATE CHIEFTAINS.

Legislature who would gladly have held back were paralyzed and their remonstrances silenced. They dared neither to speak nor to vote as their convictions impelled.

All pleadings and efforts for delay, for reflection, for calm consideration, were stifled or fruitless. A bill calling a Convention, with the distinct purpose of secession, passed the Senate on the 9th and the House on the 12th. December 6th was the day appointed for the election of delegates; the Convention to meet on the 17th of that month. Whereupon, Gov. Hammond resigned his seat in the U. S. Senate, as his colleague, Mr. Chesnut, had already done.

On the same day (Nov. 12), a Military Convention of Georgians was held at Milledgeville, which was attended and addressed by Gov. Joseph E. Brown of that State. He affirmed the right of secession, and the duty of other Southern States to sustain South Carolina in the step she was then taking. 'He would like to see Federal troops dare attempt the coërcion of a seceding Southern State! For every Georgian who fell in a conflict thus incited, the lives of two Federal soldiers should expiate the outrage on State Sovereignty.' The Convention, thus harangued, voted, about two to one, for secession; and though it had, of course, no legal or official authority, its action was doubtless potent in precipitating the 'Empire State of the South' into the abyss of Disunion.

The foregoing detailed, methodical statement of the process whereby Secession was inaugurated in South Carolina, and of the conceptions and purposes developed by that process, seems to render needless a like particularity with regard to the subsequent proceedings in that and other States. The germ of the entire movement, with the ideas whereon it was based, is clearly exhibited in the doings at Columbia and Charleston, during those memorable early days of November, 1860. And, though South Carolina ostentatiously precipitated the catastrophe by her single, sovereign fiat, it is not doubted that she did so upon full understanding with the "Chivalry" of nearly, or quite every Slave State. These had, of course, apprised her own master-spirits, in their conferences at watering-places and other fashionable resorts during the preceding Summer and Autumn, that, though they could not bring their several States to march abreast with her in the enterprise of National disruption and dissolution, they should have little difficulty in inducing them to fly to her rescue in case she went boldly forward in the predetermined course, and thus exposed herself to imminent peril on behalf of their common and most cherished interest, Slavery.[4] Theirs was the strategy of the leader of a forlorn hope, who, seeing his storming party hesitate and waver in the breach, or under the wall of the hostile fortress, throws his flag for-

[4] On the first day of the South Carolina Secession Convention, at Columbia, December 17, 1860, Hon. William Porcher Miles, M. C. from the Charleston District, one of the delegates, made a short speech against adjournment to Charleston, on account of the epidemic (small-pox) at Columbia; saying that he was just from Washington, where he had been in consultation with Southern friends representing every other Southern State, who had unanimously urged the utmost haste in the consummation of South Carolina's secession. He would adjourn to no other place until the Ordinance of Secession had passed.—See *Charleston Courier*, December 18, 1860.

ward among the enemy, and rushes, sword in hand, to its recovery, calculating that his soldiers will thereupon instinctively spring to his and its rescue at all hazards. The event proved the efficiency of the method, if not the perfect accuracy of the calculation.

But the long-standing conspiracy for Disunion was favored, at this crisis, by very powerful incidental influences, whereof the principal were as follows:

1. No public opposition to Slavery having, for many years, been permitted in the slave-holding region, save at a very few points like St. Louis, where the Free-Labor interest had, from the force of circumstances, silently and suddenly achieved a practical preponderance, the journals, the religious organizations, and the political parties, were all immeasurably subservient to the Slave Power. In fact, the chief topic of political contention, whether in the press or on the stump, had for twenty years been the relative soundness and thoroughness of the rival parties in their devotion to Slavery. On this ground, Gen. Jackson had immensely the advantage of J. Q. Adams, so far as the South was concerned, when they were rival candidates for the Presidency; as Gen. Harrison had some advantage of Mr. Van Buren; Mr. Polk of Mr. Clay; Gen. Taylor of Gen. Cass; Gen. Pierce of Gen. Scott; and, lastly, Major Breckinridge of John Bell. In Kentucky, in the State canvass of 1859, Mr. Joshua F. Bell, "American" candidate for Governor, had tried hard to "cut under" his Democratic antagonist, Beriah Magoffin, but had failed, and been signally defeated. His more spotless record as a Slavery propagandist had enabled the supporters of Breckinridge to carry even Maryland for him against Bell, in 1860. And now, the readiness to back South Carolina, or, at least, to shield her from harm, was presented as a touchstone of earnestness, to those of all parties, who had for years so loudly vaunted their own and their party's matchless devotion to "Southern rights."

2. The patronage of the Federal Government throughout the fifteen Slave States, being wielded and bestowed by the Southern members[5] of Mr. Buchanan's Cabinet, was almost entirely monopolized by their fellow-conspirators. The Collectors of Customs, Postmasters, Marshals, etc., who had good reason to apprehend the loss of their comfortable places on Mr. Lincoln's accession to power, were generally "ripe for treasons, stratagems, and spoils." Many, if not most of them, were early and active promoters of the Slaveholders' Rebellion, even while easily deriving large emoluments from the Government they were plotting to destroy.

3. The Legislatures and party Conventions of all the Slave States had long been in the habit[6] of unanimously resolving that they would never submit to exclusion from the Territories, "Black-Republican domination," etc., etc. Those who were really Unionists were apt to let these resolves pass as a matter of course,

[5] Howell Cobb, of Georgia, Secretary of the Treasury; John B. Floyd, of Virginia, Secretary of War; Jacob Thompson, of Mississippi, Secretary of the Interior. Aaron V. Brown, of Tennessee, Mr. Buchanan's first Postmaster-General, died, and was succeeded, in 1859, by Joseph Holt, of Kentucky, who stood by the Union.

[6] See, as a specimen, the Alabama resolves—on pages 312–13.

regarding them as a sort of theatrical, sheet-iron thunder, which might scare the North into greater subserviency to the Slave Power, and, at the worst, could do no harm. And now, these resolves were triumphantly quoted by the conspirators, and the people asked whether they *meant* any thing by passing them, or were only uttering threats which they never intended to make good.

4. The Governors of nearly all the Slave States, including even Delaware, had actively and zealously supported Breckinridge, and had thus justified the withdrawal of a majority of the Southern delegates from the Charleston Convention, on grounds not essentially differing from those whereon Disunion was now urged. The action now taken by South Carolina was very fairly claimed to be a direct and necessary sequence of that bolt. The Governors and other leading politicians who had supported Breckinridge and Lane in the recent canvass, were held to have thereby pledged themselves to prosecute that policy to its legitimate results. And most of them were fully aware of and ready to meet this expectation. Hence, South Carolina had scarcely thrown up her signal rocket, announcing the outbreak of the long meditated revolution, when it was responded to by proclamations and calls of Legislatures in most of the Slave States.

Texas was not originally of the number. Her leading politicians had shown the cloven foot a year too soon, by nominating, early in 1859, a State ticket pledged to favor the re-öpening of the African Slave-Trade, which was a well-understood Shibboleth of the South-Western plotters of Disunion. Hardin R. Runnells, a Mississippian, who was the incumbent, was placed at its head as a candidate for Governor. The people were alarmed by this bold step; Gen. Sam Houston took the field in opposition to it as an independent Union candidate for Governor; and, though there was no political organization in the State but that which he confronted, while Texas had gone overwhelmingly for Pierce against Scott, and for Buchanan against Fillmore, Gen. Houston carried it with all ease, beating Runnells by 8,670 majority,[7] in by far the largest vote ever yet polled in the State. Andrew J. Hamilton, running as a Unionist for Congress, in the Western District, in like manner beat T. N. Waul, the regular Democratic candidate, by 448[8] majority. In the Eastern District, John H. Reagan,[9] Democrat, had no serious opposition.

Gen. Houston was thus in a position to thwart the Texan conspirators, had he evinced either principle or courage, when they commenced operating to take their State out of the Union at the close of 1860. He did refuse to call the Legislature, or a Convention; whereupon the conspirators called the Legislature themselves, by a document signed by sixty of their number, having just as much legal validity and force as a harangue at a negro camp-meeting. But the Disunionists were thoroughly united, determined, and ready; while their adversaries, owing to Houston's pu-

[7] Houston, 36,170; Runnells, 27,500.

[8] Hamilton, 16,409; Waul, 15,961.

[9] Since, Confederate Postmaster-General. Reagan was elected to Congress from Eastern Texas in 1859, by 20,565 votes to 3,541 for Judge W. B. Ochiltree; but Houston for Governor had 4,183 majority in the District at that election; showing that Reagan had no serious opposition.

sillanimity, were as sheep without a shepherd, in a fair way to be transformed into mutton. Had there been a loyal soldier in command of that large portion of our small regular army stationed in Texas, ostensibly for the defense of her exposed Northern and Western frontier, he might have formed a nucleus for an effective rally for the Union. But Mr. John B. Floyd was at the head of the War Department, and had taken care that this force should be wielded by a thorough-going traitor, who would paralyze, and, in due time, betray it into the hands of his fellows. Houston was allowed to remain in office, despised by the implacable enemies to whom he truckled, and despising himself, until they were ready to dispense with him; when he obsequiously resigned, enduring an ignominious existence in their midst until he found relief from it in death, some two years thereafter.

Virginia had recently chosen for her Governor Mr. John Letcher, whose position was nearly as peculiar as Houston's. The genuine Southrons had long professed to be Democrats for Slavery's sake; Letcher, at heart, and formerly by open avowal, regarding human bondage as a blunder if not a crime, was pro-Slavery for the sake of the Democratic party, whereof he had ever been a bigoted devotee, and which had promoted and honored him beyond any other estimate of his merits but his own. Transferred from the House of Representatives to the Governorship[10] by the election of 1859, he, as a life-long champion of regular nominations and strict party discipline, had supported Douglas for President in 1860, and thereby thrown himself into a very lean minority[11] of his party. He had, of course, much leeway to make up to reïnstate himself in that party's good graces, and hence early and zealously lent himself to the work of the conspirators.

The course of Gov. Beriah Magoffin, of Kentucky, was in striking contrast with that of his Southern peers. He, too, had supported Breckinridge; while his party owed its recently acquired ascendency in his State, and he his election, to the deepening conviction of the slaveholding interest that no other party than the Democratic possessed at once the power and the will to rule the country in conformity to its wishes and presumed interests. But Kentucky had already repeatedly declared for the Union—conspicuously in her August State Election of 1860, and again in choosing Bell Electors, and giving the rival candidates for President some Forty Thousand more votes than she gave her own Breckinridge, who, but for her apprehensions and dread of disunion, would probably have received her vote. Gov. Magoffin now issued an address to the people of Kentucky, wherein he wisely and forcibly said:

"To South Carolina, and such other States as may wish to secede from the Union, I would say: The geography of this country will not admit of a division; the mouth and sources of the Mississippi river cannot be separated without the horrors of civil war. We cannot sustain you in this movement merely on account of the election of Lincoln. Do not precipitate us, by premature action, into a revolution or civil war, the consequences of which will be most frightful to all of us. It may yet be avoided. There is still hope, faint though it be. Kentucky is a border State, and has suffered more than

[10] Vote for Governor: Letcher, Dem., 77,112; Goggin, Am., 71,543.

[11] Democratic vote of Virginia: Breckinridge, 74,323; Douglas, 16,290.

all of you. She claims that, standing upon the same sound platform, you will sympathize with her, and stand by her, and not desert her in her exposed, perilous border position. She has a right to claim that her voice, and the voice of reason, and moderation, and patriotism, shall be heard and heeded by you. If you secede, your representatives will go out of Congress, and leave us at the mercy of a Black Republican Government. Mr. Lincoln will have no check. He can appoint his Cabinet, and have it confirmed. The Congress will then be Republican, and he will be able to pass such laws as he may suggest. The Supreme Court will be powerless to protect us. We implore you to stand by us, and by our friends in the Free States; and let us all, the bold, the true and just men in the Free and the Slave States, with a united front, stand by each other, by our principles, by our rights, our equality, our honor, and by the Union under the Constitution. I believe this is the only way to save it; and we can do it."

Gov. Elias N. Conway, of Arkansas, transmitted his Annual Message to the new Legislature of that State on the 19th of November, 1860, when nearly all the Slave States were alive with drumming and drilling,[12] and frantic with telegraphing and haranguing in behalf of Secession; yet he said nothing on the subject. It is a fair presumption that he disapproved of the entire business. But his successor, Henry M. Rector, had been chosen[13] the preceding August, and he made haste to do the bidding of the conspirators.

In all the other Slave States south of Maryland, the Governors were heart and soul in the Disunion conspiracy, and called Legislatures to meet in extra session, issued vehement Proclamations, concocted and put forth incendiary Messages, or did whatever else the master-spirits of the conspiracy required. Their associates and subordinates in office were of like faith and purpose; and it may fairly be assumed that at least four-fifths of all those in office in the Slave States, whether under the National or any State Government, on the 6th of November, 1860, were ardent advocates of Secession.

In Missouri, Mr. Claiborne F. Jackson had been chosen Governor[14] as a Douglas Democrat; but that designation was entirely delusive. Having achieved what he considered the regular Democratic nomination for Governor, he thought he could not

[12] Extract from a letter in *The New York Herald* of Nov. 9, dated

CHARLESTON, Nov. 5, 1860.

"As a mark of the popular inclination toward resistance, it is a fact of some significance that the echoes of the word 'coërcion' had hardly reached our borders before the whole State was bristling with spontaneous organizations of Minute-Men—irregular forces, it is true, but, nevertheless, formidable, because armed to the teeth with weapons to which they have been accustomed from early youth, and animated with the idea that they are defending all that is near and dear to them. The elaborate disclaimers, on the part of some of the Lincoln papers, of any design to molest the State, even if she secedes, have no weight whatever here. People very justly argue that, if coërcion should be attempted, the Minute-Men will be wanted; and, if the State should not be molested in her independence, it will be a great advantage to have such a body of men always at command.

"At this time, it is impossible to describe the extent of the Minute-Men movement. There is not a hamlet in the State that has not its squad, either of mounted men or infantry. They are drilling every night, and have generally adopted Hardee's Tactics, which, because less monotonous, are preferred by our impetuous young men to the old, heavy infantry drill. Not a night passes that we do not hear in the streets of Charleston the tramp of large bodies of armed men, moving with the quick Zouave step, and with admirable discipline and precision."

This, it will be seen, was *before* Lincoln's election; and, of course, before any public steps had been taken toward Secession. As the movement extended to other States, its military manifestations were nearly everywhere such as are portrayed above.

[13] As a stump candidate; by 30,577 votes to 28,618 for R. H. Johnson, regular Democrat.

[14] Election of August, 1860: C. F. Jackson (Douglas) 74,446; Sam. Orr (Bell) 66,583; Hancock Jackson (Breck.) 11,416; Gardenhire (Lincoln) 6,135.

afford to bolt the regular Democratic nomination for President, and so gave at least a nominal support to Douglas, who thus obtained the vote of Missouri in November, when Gov. J. and a large proportion of his supporters were in feeling and purpose with the backers of Breckinridge. He was fully in the hands of the conspirators from the start, and in due time united openly in the Rebellion. Outside of Missouri, the Douglas Democracy had been so thoroughly, overwhelmingly beaten in the vote of the Slave States for President—as thoroughly in Delaware or Maryland as in Georgia or Arkansas—that they seemed to be crushed out of life, or anxious to merge their distinctive character by a plunge into the common abyss of Rebellion. Mr. Douglas himself, being catechised on the subject,[15] frankly declared that, should Lincoln be chosen President, he would *not* consider that a cause for resistance, but should adhere to and uphold the Union. Yet the result of the election had hardly transpired when his friend Gov. Letcher of Virginia, Mr. George N. Sanders, of Kentucky, who had been one of his busiest and noisiest champions, and many more such, made haste to swell the gathering cohorts of Secession. The ablest and most respectable of their number was Mr. Alex. H. Stephens, of Georgia, whose courage and loyalty endured at least a week after those of his late compatriots had bidden them a final adieu. The Legislature of Georgia having assembled,[16] Mr. Stephens presented himself and spoke [17] boldly as well as ably against the meditated treason; saying:

"The first question that presents itself is, Shall the people of the South secede from the Union in consequence of the election of Mr. Lincoln to the Presidency of the United States? My countrymen, I tell you frankly, candidly, and earnestly, that I do not think that they ought. In my judgment, the election of no man, constitutionally chosen to that high office, is sufficient cause for any State to separate from the Union. It ought to stand by and aid still in maintaining the Constitution of the country. To make a point of resistance to the Government—to withdraw from it, because a man has been constitutionally elected—puts us in the wrong. We are pledged to maintain the Constitution. Many of us have sworn to support it. Can we, therefore, for the mere election of a man to the Presidency—and that, too, in accordance with the prescribed forms of the Constitution—make a point of resistance to the Government, and, without becoming the breakers of that sacred instrument ourselves, withdraw ourselves from it? Would we not be in the wrong? Whatever fate is to befall this country, let it never be laid to the charge of the people of the South, and especially of the people of Georgia, that we were untrue to our National engagements. Let the fault and the wrong rest upon others. If all our hopes are to be blasted, if the Republic is to go down, let us be found to the last moment standing on the deck, with the Constitution of the United States waving over our heads. (Applause.) Let the fanatics of the North break the Constitution, if such is their fell purpose. Let the responsibility be upon them. I shall speak presently more of their acts; but let not the South, let us not be the ones to commit the aggression. We went into the election with this people; the result was different from what we wished; but the election has been constitutionally held. Were we to make a point of resistance to the Government, and go out of the Union on that account, the record would be made up hereafter against us.

"But, it is said, Mr. Lincoln's policy and principles are against the Constitution, and that, if he carries them out, it will be destructive of our rights. Let us not anticipate a threatened evil. If he violates the Constitution, then will come our time to act. Do not let us break it, because, forsooth, *he* may. If he does, that is the time for us to strike. (Applause.) I think it would be injudicious and unwise to do this sooner. I do not anticipate that Mr. Lincoln will do anything to jeopardize our safety or security, whatever may be his spirit to do it; for

[15] While speaking at Norfolk, Va., during the canvass of 1860.

[16] At Milledgeville, Nov. 8, 1860.

[17] At the State House, Nov. 14, 1860.

he is bound by the constitutional checks which are thrown around him, which, at this time, render him powerless to do any great mischief. This shows the wisdom of our system. The President of the United States is no Emperor, no Dictator—he is clothed with no absolute power. He can do nothing unless he is backed by power in Congress. The House of Representatives is largely in the majority against him. In the Senate, he will also be powerless. There will be a majority of four against him: This, after the loss of Bigler, Fitch, and others, by the unfortunate dissensions of the Democratic party in their States. Mr. Lincoln cannot appoint an officer without the consent of the Senate—he cannot form a Cabinet without the same consent. He will be in the condition of George III. (the embodiment of Toryism), who had to ask the Whigs to appoint his Ministers, and was compelled to receive a Cabinet utterly opposed to his views; and so Mr. Lincoln will be compelled to ask of the Senate to choose for him a Cabinet, if the Democracy of that body choose to put him on such terms. He will be compelled to do this, or let the Government stop, if the National Democratic men—for that is their name at the North—the conservative men in the Senate—should so determine. Then, how can Mr. Lincoln obtain a Cabinet which would aid him, or allow him, to violate the Constitution?

"Why, then, I say, should we disrupt the bonds of this Union, when his hands are tied—when he can do nothing against us?"

Warming with his argument, Mr. Stephens did not hesitate, before concluding his speech, to say:

"I believe in the power of the people to govern themselves when wisdom prevails, and passion is silent. Look at what has already been done by them for their advancement in all that ennobles man. There is nothing like it in the history of the world. Look abroad, from one extent of the country to the other; contemplate our greatness: we are now among the first nations of the earth. Shall it, then, be said that our institutions, founded upon principles of self-government, are a failure?

"Thus far it is a noble example, worthy of imitation. The gentleman (Mr. Cobb), the other night, said it had proven a failure. A failure in what? In growth? Look at our expanse in National power! Look at our population and increase in all that makes a people great! A failure? Why, we are the admiration of the civilized world, and present the brightest hopes of mankind.

"*Some of our public men have failed in their aspirations; that is true; and from that comes a great part of our troubles.* (Prolonged applause.)

"No! there is no failure of this Government yet. We have made great advancement under the Constitution; and I cannot but hope that we shall advance still higher. Let us be true to our cause."

This was frank and noble; yet there was a dead fly in the ointment, which sadly marred its perfume. That was a distinct avowal of the right of the State to overrule his personal convictions, and plunge him into treason to the Nation. Years before, Henry Clay, when catechised by Jefferson Davis in the Senate, set forth the true American doctrine on this point, as follows:

"Mr. President, I have heard with pain and regret a confirmation of the remark I made, that the sentiment of Disunion has become familiar. I hope it is confined to South Carolina. I do not regard as my duty what the honorable Senator seems to regard as his. If Kentucky to-morrow unfurls the banner of resistance, I never will fight under that banner. I owe a *paramount* allegiance to the whole Union—a *subordinate* one to my own State." [18]

[18] Mr. Clay, at another time, at a caucus of Southern members of Congress, was asked whether, in a certain contingency, Kentuckians would go for Disunion. He promptly replied: "No, Sir: Kentuckians view Disunion as itself the greatest of evils, and as a remedy for nothing."

The following letter likewise embodies the ruling conviction of his life, which under no circumstances could he be induced to depart from:

"WASHINGTON, *Dec.* 22, 1849.

"MY DEAR SIR:—My object in writing to you now is one of great importance, and I wish you to lead off in it.

"The feeling for Disunion among some of the intemperate Southern politicians is stronger than I supposed it could be. The masses generally, even at the South, are, I believe, yet sound; but they may become inflamed and perverted. The best counteraction of that feeling is to be derived from popular expressions at public meetings of the people. Now, what I would be glad to see, is such meetings held throughout Kentucky. For, you must know, that the Disunionists count upon the coöperation of our patriotic State. Cannot you get up a large, powerful meeting of both

Mr. Stephens was, in his earlier years, an admirer and follower of Mr. Clay; but, since 1850, he had gone a roving after strange gods. He now said:

"Should Georgia determine to go out of the Union, I speak for one, though my views may not agree with them, whatever the result may be, I shall bow to the will of her people. Their cause is my cause, and their destiny is my destiny; and I trust this will be the ultimate course of all. The greatest curse that can befall a free people is civil war. But, as I said, let us call a Convention of the people; let all these matters be submitted to it; and, when the will of a majority of the people has thus been expressed, the whole State will present one unanimous voice in favor of whatever may be demanded."

Of course, Mr. Stephens was taken at his word. A Convention *was* called; a majority of delegates secured for Disunion; an Ordinance of Secession passed; and Mr. Stephens sank from the proud position of a citizen of the American Republic into that of Vice-President of the Confederacy of slaveholding traitors and their benighted, misguided satellites and dupes.

The South Carolina Convention met at Columbia on the appointed day—December 17th. Gen. D. F. Jamison, its temporary Chairman, on being called to preside, paraded the wrongs of the South in the admission of California, organization and settlement of Kansas, etc., etc., and trusted that "the door is now closed *forever* against any further connection[19] with the Northern confederacy," etc., etc., etc. He further trusted that "we shall not be diverted from our purpose by any dictates *from without;*" and that the Convention, in inaugurating such a movement, would heed the counsels of a master-spirit of the French Revolution, whose maxim was, to "*dare, and again to dare, and without end to dare.*"

Mr. Chas. G. Memminger[20] having suggested that the members, on the roll being called, advance and be sworn, a delegate responded: "Oh no! that is not required; we came not to *make*, but to *unmake*, a government."

Gen. Jamison was, on the fifth ballot, chosen President. At the evening session of the first day, Hon. John A. Elmore, a Commissioner from Alabama, and Hon. Charles Hooker, a Commissioner from Mississippi, were introduced by the President, and successively addressed the Convention—of course, in favor of prompt and unconditional Secession. Mr. Elmore said:

"I am instructed by the Governor of Alabama to say that he desires, and, he be-

---

parties, if possible, at Lexington, at Louisville, etc., etc., to express in strong language their determination to stand by the Union? Now is the time for salutary action, and you are the man to act. I inclose some resolutions, which, or some similar to them, I should be happy to see adopted. H. CLAY."

"To Gen. LESLIE COMBS."

[19] Early in 1860, an eminent New York lawyer visited Charleston professionally, and was detained in that city several weeks, mingling freely with her citizens and the guests at her principal hotel. Though never a candidate for office, he took a warm interest in public affairs, and had always acted with the 'Whig,' 'American,' or 'Conservative' party. Soon after his return to New York, some old associates called to consult him on political affairs, and were astounded to hear that his views had undergone a complete change. "What can that mean?" "It means this," was his well-considered reply; "that I have spent the past month in the South; that I find the Union a sham; that we are, in effect, two peoples, between whom an early war is inevitable; and that, in that war, I mean to stand by my own hearth and kindred. Good morning, gentlemen!"

[20] Since, Confederate Secretary of the Treasury.

lieves, our State desires (and I unite my voice with him in that opinion), that the action of the Convention be immediate and prompt. [Applause.] It will give the cause strength, not only in Alabama, as we believe, and of which I have a right to speak, but I believe it will give the cause strength in the *other* States, which are united with you in sentiment."

On motion of Mr. Inglis, it was unanimously, and amid tremendous cheering,

"*Resolved*, That it is the opinion of the Convention that the State of South Carolina should forthwith secede from the Federal Union, known as the United States of America."

The small-pox then raging in Columbia, the Convention adjourned to 'Secession Hall' in Charleston, where it met next day. Mr. Buchanan's last Annual Message having been received, Judge Magrath, of Charleston, offered the following, which was debated next day, but does not seem to have passed:

"*Resolved*, That so much of the Message of the President of the United States as relates to what he designates the property of the United States in South Carolina, be referred to a Committee to report of what such property consists, how the same was acquired, or, whether the purposes for which it was so acquired can be enjoyed by the United States after the State of South Carolina shall have seceded, consistently with the dignity and safety of the State; and that said Committee further report the value of the property of the United States not in South Carolina, and the value of the share thereof to which South Carolina may be entitled upon an equal division thereof among the States. [Great applause in the galleries."]

The President announced an address from a portion of the Legislature of Georgia, which he thought should not be made public; so it was not. It was afterward understood to be an appeal from fifty-two members of said Legislature for delay and consultation among the Slave States.

The next day, Hon. J. A. Elmore communicated a dispatch from the Governor of Alabama, in these words:

"MONTGOMERY, ALA., Dec. 17, 1860.
"Tell the Convention to listen to no proposition of compromise or delay.
"A. B. MOORE."

Among the utterances of this Convention, the following seem especially significant and memorable:

Mr. Parker said:

"Mr. President, it appears to me, with great deference to the opinions that have been expressed, that the public mind is fully made up to the great occasion that now awaits us. *It is no spasmodic effort that has come suddenly upon us; it has been gradually culminating for a long period of thirty years, At last, it has come to that point where we may say, the matter is entirely right.*"

Mr. Inglis said:

"Mr. President, if there is any gentleman present who wishes to debate this matter, of course this body will hear him. But, as to delay for the purpose of discussion, I, for one, am opposed to it. As my friend (Mr. Parker) has said, *most of us* have had this matter under consideration for the last twenty years; and I presume that we have, by this time, arrived at a decision upon the subject."

And Hon. Lawrence M. Keitt—

"*I have been engaged in this movement ever since I entered political life.* I am content with what has been done to-day, and with what will take place to-morrow. We have carried the body of this Union to its last resting-place, and now we will drop the flag over its grave. After that is done, I am ready to adjourn, and leave the remaining ceremonies for to-morrow."

And Mr. Robert Barnwell Rhett—

"The Secession of South Carolina is not an event of a day. *It is not anything produced by Mr. Lincoln's election*, or by the non-execution of the Fugitive Slave Law. It has been a matter which has been gathering head for thirty years. * * * The point in which I differ from my friend is this: He says he thought it expedient to put this great question before the world upon this simple matter of wrongs—on the question of Slavery; and that question turned upon the Fugitive Slave Law. Now, in regard to the Fugitive Slave Law, I myself doubted its constitutionality, and doubted it on the floor of the Senate, when I was a member of that body. The States, acting in their sovereign capacity, should be responsible for the rendition of fugitive slaves. That was our best security."

It was, on motion of Mr. Hayne, resolved that a Commissioner be sent to each Slave State, with a copy of the Secession Ordinance, with a view to hasten coöperation on the part of those States; also, that three Commissioners be sent to Washington, with a copy of the same, to be laid before the President, to treat for the delivery of the United States property in South Carolina over to the State, on the subject of the Public Debt, etc.

The Ordinance of Secession was reported from a Committee of seven on the fourth day (Dec. 20th), and immediately passed, without dissent. (Yeas 169.) It is in the following words:

"*An Ordinance to dissolve the Union between the State of South Carolina, and other States united with her under the compact entitled the Constitution of the United States of America:*

"We, the people of the State of South Carolina, in Convention assembled, do declare and ordain, and it is hereby declared and ordained, that the Ordinance adopted by us in Convention, on the 23d day of May, in the year of our Lord 1788, whereby the Constitution of the United States of America was ratified, and also all Acts and parts of Acts of the General Assembly of this State ratifying the amendments of the said Constitution, are hereby repealed; and that the Union now subsisting between South Carolina and other States, under the name of the United States of America, is hereby dissolved."

A formal "Declaration of Causes, which induced the Secession of South Carolina," was in like manner reported and adopted. Its substance and force are entirely derived from and grounded on the alleged infidelity of the Free States to their constitutional obligations with respect to Slavery, but more especially in the non-rendition of fugitive slaves. New York, among other States, is herein charged (of course by mistake) with having passed acts to obstruct the return of such fugitives. Indiana and Illinois are likewise among the States thus erroneously accused. The Constitution is pronounced a compact between sovereign States, and the Convention proceeds:

"We maintain that, in every compact between two or more parties, the obligation is mutual; that the failure of one of the contracting parties to perform a material part of the agreement, entirely releases the obligation of the other; and that, where no arbiter is provided, each party is remitted to his own judgment to determine the fact of failure, with all its consequences."

No grievance of any name or nature is alleged or insinuated, but such as flow from anti-Slavery feeling and action in the Free States, culminating in the election of Lincoln. The Declaration concludes as follows:

"We, therefore, the people of South Carolina, by our delegates in Convention assembled, appealing to the Supreme Judge of the world for the rectitude of our intentions, have solemnly declared that the Union heretofore existing between this State and the other States of North America is dissolved, and that the State of South Carolina has resumed her position among the nations of the world, as a separate and independent State, with full power to levy war, conclude peace, contract alliances, establish commerce, and to do all other acts and things which independent States may of right do."

On motion of Mr. W. F. De Saussure, it was further

"*Resolved*, That the passage of the Ordinance be proclaimed by the firing of artillery and the ringing of the bells of the city, and such other demonstrations as the people may deem appropriate on the passage of the great act of deliverance and liberty."

The President, at a quarter past 1, announced that the Ordinance had unanimously passed; whereupon there burst forth a pent-up flood of congratulatory and jubilant speeches, and then the Convention adjourned, to meet again in the evening for a more formal ratification, at which the Governor [21] and Legislature were invited to attend. Then and there, the Ordinance, having been duly engrossed, was read by the President, then signed by all the delegates in alphabetical order, and thereupon displayed by the President to the enthusiastic crowd, with a declaration that "the State of South Carolina is now and henceforth a free and independent commonwealth." And then, with wild, prolonged, exulting huzzas, the assemblage dispersed; and the Charleston papers began to print thenceforth their daily quantum of intelligence from the non-seceding States as "Foreign News."

Georgia, as was arranged and expected, was the first State to follow South Carolina in her fatal plunge. Her new Legislature, moved by an impassioned Message from her Governor, Joseph E. Brown, passed [22] a bill appropriating $1,000,000 to arm and equip the State; and, on the 18th, a bill calling a Convention of delegates, to be chosen in the several counties on the 2d of January ensuing, and to meet one week thereafter. The Convention bill passed by a unanimous vote; the Convention thus chosen and convened finally passed [23] an Ordinance of Secession: Yeas 208; Nays 89. The names of A. H. Stephens and Herschel V. Johnson, late Douglas leaders in the South, were recorded among the Nays.[24]

Alabama was held back by a scruple on the part of her Governor, Andrew B. Moore, who declined to act decisively until the Presidential Electors in the several States had met, and a majority cast their votes for Lincoln. He issued his call on the 6th, and the election of delegates was held on the 24th of December. The Secessionists claimed a popular majority of 50,000 in the votes of the several counties; but when the Convention [25] passed an Ordinance of Secession,[26] by a vote of 61 to 39, it was claimed that the minority, being mainly from the Northern counties, where the free population is proportionally far more numerous than among the great plantations of the South, represented more freemen than did the majority.

Florida, through her Legislature, voted [27] to call a Convention. That Convention met at Tallahassee,[28] and passed [29] an Ordinance of Secession: Yeas 62; Nays 7. Several delegates elected expressly as Unionists voted for Secession.

Mississippi assembled her Legislature, on the call of Gov. John J. Pettus, at Jackson; and a Convention was thereby called to meet at the same place, January 7th; and a Se-

[21] Francis W. Pickens, newly chosen by the Legislature; an original Nullifier and life-long Disunionist, "born insensible to fear." He was in Congress (House) from 1835 to 1843; sent as Minister to Russia by Buchanan in 1858.

[22] November 13, 1860. [23] January 18, 1861.

[24] "A sad thing to observe is, that those who are determined on immediate secession have not the coolness, the capacity, or the nerve, to propose something *after* that. We must secede, it is said; but, what then we are to do, nobody knows, or, at least, nobody says. This is extremely foolish, and more wicked than foolish. All sorts of business are going to wreck and ruin, because of the uncertainty of the future. No statesmanship has ever been exhibited yet, so far as we know, by those who will dissolve the Union. South Carolina considers it her policy to create a collision with the Federal authorities *for the purpose of arousing the South from her slumber*. Never was there a greater mistake." —*Augusta* (*Ga.*) *Chronicle and Sentinel*, January 1, 1861.

[25] Assembled at Montgomery, January 7th.

[26] January 11, 1861. [27] December 1, 1860.

[28] January 3, 1861. [29] January 10th.

cession Ordinance was passed by it two days thereafter: Yeas 84; Nays 15. Mississippi having, next to South Carolina, the largest proportional Slave population of any State in the Union, it is probable that this action more nearly conformed to the real sentiment of her reading, governing class, than that of any other State which is claimed as having seceded.

In Louisiana, Gov. Thomas O. Moore, an extensive planter and slaveholder, cherishing the prejudices of his class, called[30] her new Legislature to meet at Baton Rouge, December 10th. This lost no time in calling[31] a Convention, by which an Ordinance of Secession was passed:[32] Yeas 103; Nays 17. But a New Orleans journal, which had not yet fallen into treason, confidently asserted that a majority of the people who voted for delegates to that Convention had voted for Union delegates, and challenged the Secessionists to publish and scrutinize the popular vote. This they were finally impelled to do, figuring out a small majority for their own side. It was plain that, while every Secessionist voted and many Unionists abstained, the vote for Union and that for Secession delegates were just about equal. As made up by the Secessionists, they stood: For Secession, 20,448; Against it, 17,296. The vote for Secession is only two-fifths of the vote cast for President just before. The Convention *refused*—84 to 45—to submit their act to a vote of the people.

In Texas, a Convention—called, as we have seen—assembled at Austin, January 28th, passed[33] an Ordinance of Secession: Yeas 166; Nays 7. *This* ordinance was submitted to a popular vote, and ratified by a considerable majority; it being very much safer, in most districts, to vote Secession than not at all, and not to vote at all than to vote Union.

Arkansas, in spite of her Governor's reticence, was blest with a Convention;[34] her Legislature voting a call for one; but her popular vote showed a Union majority, and the conspirators were baffled for the time.

North Carolina was under the rule, but not at first under the control, of the conspirators. Among the dispatches flying, thick as hail, over the South the day after Lincoln's election, was the following:

> "RALEIGH, N. C., Nov. 7, 1860.
> "The Governor and Council are in session. The people are very much excited. *North Carolina is ready to secede.*"

The Governor (John W. Ellis) and Legislature being of the Breckinridge school of Democracy, it was easy to call a Convention, but difficult to assemble one without giving the People some voice in the premises. And they, upon the appointed day of election, not only chose a strong majority of Union delegates, but voted further (for fear of what *might* happen) that the Convention should not meet at all. Yet that same Convention was, directly after the reduction of Sumter, called together, and voted the State out of the Union!

So, in Virginia, where Gov. Letcher had early and heartily entered into the counsels of the Disunionists, the Legislature was called by him to meet in extra session at Richmond on the 7th of January, which it did, and[35] passed a bill calling a Convention;

[30] November 26, 1860. [31] December 17, 1860.
[32] January 26, 1860.
[33] February 1, 1861. [34] November 16, 1860.
[35] January 13, 1861.

but the people returned an overwhelming Union majority; which, so late as April 4th, by 89 to 45, decided *not* to pass an Ordinance of Secession.

Missouri, under Gov. C. F. Jackson's rule, had a Democratic Legislature, which voted[36] to call a Convention; but that body, when convened, was found to be decidedly and inflexibly Union. The pretended Secession of the State, some time afterward, was the work of unauthorized persons, and had not a shadow of legal validity.

So, Tennessee, whose Legislature met January 7th, though her Governor, Isham G. Harris, was thoroughly with the Disunionists, could not be induced to take the first step in their company.[37]

In Kentucky, the open Secessionists were but a handful, and were unable to make any show of strength in the Legislature. The few slave-traders, some scions of the planting aristocracy, with quite a number of politicians of bygone eminence and power (many, if not most, of them 'Whigs' of other days), were early enlisted in the movement, and sought to counterbalance, if not conceal, their paucity of numbers by intense bitterness and preternatural activity. They were enabled, through the timidity and twaddling of the leading politicians who had supplanted them in place and power, to exert a baleful influence over the course of their State throughout the ensuing year, but never to drive or lure her to the brink of Secession.

So, in Maryland, which was early visited by emissaries from the seceded States, who exerted every art to drag her after them into the abyss. They were patiently, respectfully treated; feasted and toasted by the aristocratic few, but nowise encouraged or sympathized with by the great body of the industrious classes. Gov. Thomas H. Hicks, though a slaveholder, and not very determined nor consistent in his course at the outset of the Rebellion, met the original appeal for Secession with a decided rebuff. Being strongly memorialized to convene the Legislature in extra session, he responded[38] as follows:

"Identified, as I am, by birth, and every other tie, with the South—a slaveholder, and feeling as warmly for my native State as any man can do—I am yet compelled by my sense of fair dealing, and my respect for the Constitution of our country, to declare that I see nothing in the bare election of Mr. Lincoln which would justify the South in taking any steps tending toward a separation of these States. Mr. Lincoln being elected, I am willing to await further results. If he will administer the Government in a proper and patriotic manner, we are all bound to submit to his Administration, much as we may have opposed his election.

"As an individual, I will very cheerfully sustain him in well doing, because my suffering country will be benefited by a constitutional administration of the Government. If, on the contrary, he shall abuse the trust

---

[36] January 16, 1861.

[37] *The Nashville Banner*, a leading journal of the old Whig school, contained late in January, 1860, the following warning of the treacherous schemes that were then culminating in Tennessee:

"Let every true, honest citizen of the South beware. The vilest, most damnable, deep-laid and treacherous conspiracy that was ever concocted in the busy brain of the most designing knave, is being hatched to destroy his liberties by breaking up this Government. If the people do not rise in their strength and put back these meddling politicians, the latter will chloroform them with sectional prejudice, and then ride over them rough-shod before they can recover from the narcotic. The political tricksters, who see their power slipping from their grasp, are playing a desperate game, and will not 'lose a trick' if they can help it. Let honest men see that the double-dealers do not 'stock the cards.'"

[38] November 27, 1861.

confided to him, I shall be found as ready and determined as any other man to arrest him in his wrong courses, and to seek redress of our grievances by any and all proper means."

Delaware had, in 1858, chosen William Burton (Democrat) for Governor by 7,758 votes to 7,544 for his Opposition rival; Democracy in Delaware being almost exclusively based on Slavery, and having at length carried the State by its aid. The great body of the party, under the lead of Senator James A. Bayard, had supported Breckinridge, and were still in sympathy with his friends' view of 'Southern Rights,' but not to the extent of approving South Carolina remedies. Their Legislature met at Dover, January 2, 1861. Gov. Burton, in his Message, said:

"The cause of all the trouble is the persistent war of the Abolitionists upon more than two billions of property; a war waged from pulpits, rostrums, and schools, by press and people—all teaching that Slavery is a crime and a sin, until it has become the opinion of a portion of one section of the country. The only remedy for the evils now threatening is *a radical change of public sentiment* in regard to the whole question. The North should retire from its untenable position immediately."

Mr. Dickenson, Commissioner from Mississippi, having addressed the two Houses jointly in advocacy of Secession, they passed, directly thereafter, separately and unanimously, the following:

"*Resolved*, That, having extended to the Hon. H. Dickenson, Commissioner from Mississippi, the courtesy due him as the representative of a sovereign State of the confederacy, as well as to the State he represents, we deem it proper, and due to ourselves and the people of Delaware, to express our unqualified disapproval of the *remedy* for the existing difficulties suggested by the resolutions of the Legislature of Mississippi."

Before the opening of 1861, a perfect reign of terror had been established throughout the Gulf States. A secret order, known as "Knights of the Golden Circle," or as "Knights of the Columbian Star," succeeding that known, six or seven years earlier, as the 'Order of the Lone Star,' having for its ostensible object the acquisition of Cuba, Mexico, and Central America, and the establishment of Slavery in the two latter, but really operating in the interest of Disunion, had spread its network of lodges, grips, passwords, and alluring mystery, all over the South, and had ramifications even in some of the cities of the adjoining Free States. Other clubs, more or less secret, were known as 'The Precipitators,' 'Vigilance Committee,' 'Minute Men,' and by kindred designations; but all of them were sworn to fidelity to 'Southern Rights;' while their members were gradually prepared and ripened, wherever any ripening was needed, for the task of treason. Whoever ventured to condemn and repudiate Secession as the true and sovereign remedy for Southern wrongs, in any neighborhood where Slavery was dominant, was thenceforth a marked man, to be stigmatized and hunted down as a 'Lincolnite,' 'Submissionist,' or 'Abolitionist.' One refugee planter from Southern Alabama, himself a slaveholder, but of northern birth, who barely escaped a violent death, because of an intercepted letter from a relative in Connecticut, urging him to free his slaves and return to the North, as he had promised, stated[39] that he had himself been

[39] To Mr. O. J. Victor, author of '*The History of the Southern Rebellion*,' who knew him well, and vouches for his integrity. (See his vol. i., p. 134.) See to the same effect the testimony of Hon. A. J. Hamilton, of Texas, Rev. Mr. Aughey, of Mississippi, and hundreds of others. South-

obliged to join the 'Minute Men' of his neighborhood for safety, and had thus been compelled to assist in hanging six men of Northern birth because of their Union sentiments; and he personally knew that not less than *one hundred* men had been hung in his section of the State and in the adjoining section of Georgia, during the six weeks which preceded his escape in December, 1860.

When, therefore, the time at length arrived,[40] in pursuance of a formal invitation from South Carolina, for the assembling at Montgomery of a Convention of delegates from all the States which should, by that time, have seceded from the Union, with a view to the formation of a new Confederacy, the States which had united in the movement were as follows:

States.	*Free Population in 1860.*	*Slaves.*	*Total.*
South Carolina	301,271	402,541	703,812
Georgia	595,097	462,232	1,057,329
Alabama	529,164	435,132	964,296
Mississippi	354,700	436,696	791,396
Louisiana	376,280	333,010	709,290
Florida	78,686	61,753	140,439
Texas*	421,750	180,682	602,432
Total Seceded	2,656,948	2,312,046	4,968,994
Non-Seceded Slave States	5,633,005	1,638,297	7,271,302
Total Slave States	8,289,953	3,950,343	12,240,296

* Texas had seceded; but her delegates had not reached Montgomery when the time arrived for organizing the Convention.

The Slave States and District which had *not* united in the movement, were as follows:

States.	*Free Population in 1860.*	*Slaves.*	*Total.*
Arkansas	324,323	111,104	435,427
Delaware	110,420	1,798	112,218
Kentucky	930,223	225,490	1,155,713
Maryland	599,846	87,188	687,034
Missouri	1,067,352	114,965	1,182,317
North Carolina	661,586	331,081	992,667
Tennessee	834,063	275,784	1,109,847
Virginia	1,105,192	490,887	1,596,079
Dist. Columbia	71,895	3,181	75,076
Total	5,704,900	1,641,478	7,346,378

So that, after the conspiracy had had complete possession of the Southern mind for three months, with the Southern members of the Cabinet, nearly all the Federal officers, most of the Governors and other State functionaries, and seven-eighths of the prominent and active politicians, pushing it on, and no force exerted against nor in any manner threatening to resist it, a majority of the Slave States, with two-thirds of the free population of the entire slaveholding region, was openly and positively adverse to it; either because they regarded the alleged grievances of the South as exaggerated if not unreal, or because they believed that those wrongs would rather be aggravated than cured by Disunion.

XXIII.

"PEACE" EFFORTS AT THE NORTH.

In one of Beaumarchais's comedies, a green reveler in every advantage and luxury that noble birth and boundless wealth can secure, asks an attendant the odd question, "What have I *done* that I should enjoy all these blessings?"—and is answered, with courtly deference and suavity,

ern *unanimity* (in certain localities) for Secession, was such as violence and terror have often produced in favor of the most universally detested men and measures all over the world. Such an apparent unanimity was doubtless secured, but at the expense of not less than ten thousand precious lives, taken because the victims would not conceal and deny their invincible affection for their whole country.

[40] February 4, 1861.

"Your Highness condescended to be born."

The people of the United States had, in an unexceptionably legal and constitutional manner, chosen for their President an eminently conservative, cautious, moderate citizen, of blameless life and unambitious spirit, born in slaveholding Kentucky, but now resident in free Illinois, who held, with Jefferson and nearly all our Revolutionary sages and patriots, that Human Slavery is an evil which ought not to be diffused and strengthened in this Nineteenth Century of Christian light and love. Hereupon, the ruling oligarchy in certain States, who had done nothing to prevent, but much, indirectly yet purposely, to secure this result, resolved to rend the Republic into fragments, tearing their own fragment away from the residue. What should be done about it?

The natural, obvious answer springs at once to every unquivering lip—"Convince the disturbers that their only safe course is to desist and behave themselves. They might have had a President who is not a Republican, had they chosen: having done their best to elect one who *is*, they must now accept the result they have contributed to insure, until the evolutions of four years shall bring around the opportunity for another, and, if they will, a more acceptable choice."

Far otherwise was the actual response of the Republic to her spoiled children, and their most unreasonably factious demonstration. Instead of treating their outbreak as culpable and flagrant disloyalty, to be rebuked, abandoned, repented, and desisted from, the first impulse from almost every side was to inquire on what terms and by what means they could be mollified, bribed, beseeched, into remaining peaceably in the Union.

This was but following in the beaten track. Vehement threats of secession and dissolution were among the established means whereby an aristocracy of less than one-tenth of the American people had for sixty years swayed, almost uninterruptedly, the destinies of the Nation. Why should they not again resort to the expedient which had so often proved effectual? Why should not the response be substantially the same now as it had hitherto been? And why should not those whose success furnished the pretext for this treason be charged with the evil, and inculpated as themselves the traitors?

Had not, for a generation, the upholding of a rule based on caste, and a denial to the humblest class of all political rights in half the Union, and of all social and civil, as well as political, rights in another third of it, been commended and glorified as *Democracy?*

Had not every assertion, however broad and general, of the right of each rational being to "life, liberty, and the pursuit of happiness," been stigmatized as *Sectionalism?*

Had not a simple adhesion to the policy of Jefferson and the fathers, as to Slavery in the Territories, been denounced as *Radicalism*, and as "making war on fifteen States?"

Had not ravaging and subjugating foreign lands, with intent to curse them with human bondage, been glorified as "extending the area of Freedom?"

Had not the maintenance of the rights of constitutional majorities, and of the duty of universal submission to the popular will, constitutionally ascertained and declared, been stigmatized as inciting to disunion and anarchy?

And who could expect that half a century of such utter perversion of the plainest, least equivocal, most obvious terms, should not bear bitter fruit? The inebriate, who fancies the square in which he lives revolving about him, and gravely holds his latch-key in hand, waiting till his door shall in due order present itself, labors under substantially the same hallucination, and is usually certain to cherish it until he awakes to prosaic realities—to bruises, self-reproach, headache, and remorse.[1]

Nearly forty years ago, the great and good Channing, after listening to Benjamin Lundy, wrote to Mr. Webster in apprehension that the South would regard and resent any attempt at the North to promote or hasten the removal of her giant curse as impelled by hostility or ill-will, though nothing was further from our intention.[2] The good Doctor can scarcely have read with adequate attention, or at least not with the utmost profit, the urgent, impassioned adjurations of the demoniacs to the Saviour of mankind, for forbearance and 'non-intervention.' "Let us alone," was their habitual entreaty: "What have we to do with thee?" "Art thou come to torment us before the time?" No delicacy of handling, no gentleness of treatment, could have pacified them: they must be left undisturbed and unobserved, or irritation and excitement were unavoidable.

Twenty or thirty years ago, there existed in Charleston, S. C., an association for social and intellectual enjoyment, known as 'The Wistar

[1] Von Muller, one of the present King of Prussia's grave and reverend councilors of state, in his younger and wittier days, celebrated this inversion of the perceptive faculties, in verses still popular in Germany, and which have been rendered into English, as follows:

"OUT OF THE TAVERN.

"Out of the tavern I've just stepped to-night:
Street! you are caught in a very bad plight;
Right hand and left are both out of place—
Street! you are drunk!—'t is a very clear case!

"Moon! 't is a very queer figure you cut—
One eye is staring, whilst t' other is shut;
Tipsy, I see; and you're greatly to blame:
Old as you are, 't is a terrible shame.

"Then the street lamps—what a scandalous sight!
None of them soberly standing upright;
Rocking and swaggering—why, on my word,
Each of the lamps is as drunk as a lord!

"All is confusion—now isn't it odd,
I am the only thing sober abroad?
Sure it were rash with this crew to remain;
Better go into the tavern again."

[2] The following is a portion of Dr. Channing's letter:

"BOSTON, *May* 14, 1848.

"MY DEAR SIR:—I wish to call your attention to a subject of general interest.

"A little while ago, Mr. Lundy, of Baltimore, the editor of a paper called 'The Genius of Universal Emancipation,' visited this part of the country to stir us up to the work of abolishing Slavery at the South; and the intention is to organize societies for this purpose. I know of few objects into which I should enter with more zeal; but I am aware how cautiously exertions are to be made for it in this part of the country. I know that our Southern brethren interpret every word from this region on the subject of Slavery as an expression of hostility. I would ask if they cannot be brought to understand us better, and if we can do any good till we remove their misapprehensions. It seems to me that, before moving in this matter, we ought to say to them distinctly: 'We consider Slavery as your calamity, not your crime; and we will share with you the burden of putting an end to it. We will consent that the public lands shall be appropriated to this object; or that the General Government shall be clothed with power to apply a portion of revenue to it.'

"I throw out these suggestions merely to illustrate my views. We must first let the Southern States see that we are their *friends* in this affair; that we sympathize with them, and, from principles of patriotism and philanthropy, are willing to share the toil and expense of abolishing Slavery; or I fear our interference will avail nothing. I am the more sensitive on this subject, from my increased solicitude for the preservation of the Union. I know no public interest so important as this."—*Webster's Works*, vol. v., p. 366.

Club.' Many, if not most, of the more intelligent and cultivated class belonged to it, and strangers of like breeding were freely invited to its weekly or bi-weekly meetings. It was its rule to select, at each gathering, some subject for conversational discussion at the next. At one of these meetings, the economic results of Slavery were incidentally brought into view; when the few remarks dropped from one and another developed a decided difference of opinion —the native Carolinians expressing a conviction that 'the institution' was profitable; while two or three members or guests of Northern birth indicated a contrary impression. Hereupon, some one asked, 'Why not select this as the topic for our next meeting?' 'Agreed!' was the unbroken response; and the point was settled. It was distinctly stipulated that no ethical, ethnological, religious, or other aspect of the main problem, should be considered—nothing but the simple, naked question—'Is it economically advantageous to a community to hold slaves?' Hereupon, the assemblage quietly dissolved.

At the evening designated for the next regular meeting, the 'Yankee' members of the club were duly on hand, prepared and eager for the expected discussion; but not a Carolinian was present! Some old head had determined that no such discussion should take place—at least, in Charleston—and had given a hint which had operated as a command. Though the interest in the subject had seemed general at the last meeting, and the disposition to discuss it mutual and cordial, not a man now appeared to speak for Slavery. The 'Yankees' enjoyed or endured each other's society throughout the evening, sipped their coffee with due decorum, and dispersed at the proper hour, without an opportunity for discussion, leaving the proposed debate to stand adjourned over to the opening of the bombardment of Fort Sumter, in the year of grace 1861.

"Why can't you let Slavery alone?" was imperiously or querulously demanded at the North, throughout the long struggle preceding that bombardment, by men who should have seen, but would not, that Slavery never let the North alone, nor thought of so doing. "Buy Louisiana for us!" said the slaveholders. "With pleasure." "Now Florida!" "Certainly." Next: "Violate your treaties with the Creeks and Cherokees; expel those tribes from the lands they have held from time immemorial, so as to let us expand our plantations." "So said, so done." "Now for Texas!" "You have it." "Next, a third more of Mexico!" "Yours it is." "Now, break the Missouri Compact, and let Slavery wrestle with Free Labor for the vast region consecrated by that Compact to Freedom!" "Very good. What next?" "Buy us Cuba, for One Hundred to One Hundred and Fifty Millions." "We have tried; but Spain refuses to sell it." "Then wrest it from her at all hazards!" And all this time, while Slavery was using the Union as her catspaw—dragging the Republic into iniquitous wars and enormous expenditures, and grasping empire after empire thereby—Northern men (or, more accurately, men at the North) were constantly asking why people living in the Free States could not let Slavery alone, mind their own business, and expend their surplus philanthropy on the poor at their own doors, rather than on the happy and contented slaves!

The Slave Power, having resolved to destroy the Union—having taken decided steps to that end—several States having definitively seceded, or prepared to secede, from the Union, without giving the least intimation that they could be swerved from this purpose by any pledge or act whatever, on the part of the Free States—what was the North to do?

"Let us try the virtue of new protestations, new prostrations, more groveling abasements," was the instinctive, urgent, unanimous response of that large portion of the politicians and traders of the Free States who had already reduced servility to a science. Without the least warrant, in defiance of the most explicit declarations, it was assumed that Secession was but a "strike" of the Slave Power for more complete, unresisted sway over the Union, rather than for utter and final escape from it.

Whoever has carefully considered the platforms and the action of the respective parties which confronted each other during the canvass and in the election of 1860, must realize that Secession could be met in but one of four ways:

1. By substantial acquiescence in the movement, and in its proposed result.

2. By proffering such new concessions and guarantees to Slavery as should induce the conspirators to desist from their purpose, and return to loyalty and the Union.

3. By treating it as Rebellion and Treason, and putting it down, if need be, by the strong arm.

4. By so acting and speaking as to induce a pause in the movement, and permit an appeal "to Philip sober"—from the South inflamed by passionate appeals and frenzied accusations,[3] to the South, enlightened, calmed, and undeceived, by a few months of friendly, familiar discussion, and earnest expostulation.

The first of these alternatives had few open advocates in the Free States; but there were some who even went the length of declaring Secession a constitutional right,[4] to be exercised by any State whenever her own con-

[3] At a great public meeting held at Mobile, Alabama, November 15, 1860, a "Declaration of Causes," twenty-two in number, was put forth; from which we select the following:

"The following brief, but truthful history of the Republican party, its acts and purposes, affords an answer to these questions:

"It claims to abolish Slavery in the districts, forts, arsenals, dockyards, and other places ceded to the United States. To abolish the inter-State Slave-Trade, and thus cut off the Northern Slave States from their profits of production, and deprive the Southern of their sources of supply of labor. * * *

"It has denied the extradition of murderers, marauders, and other felons.

"It has concealed and shielded the murderer of masters or owners, in pursuit of fugitive slaves. * * *

"It has advocated negro equality, and made it the ground of positive legislation, hostile to the Southern States.

"It opposes protection to Slave property on the high seas, and has justified piracy itself in the case of the Creole. * * *

"It has invaded Virginia, and shed the blood of her citizens on her own soil. * * *

"It has announced its purpose of total abolition in the States and everywhere, as well as in the territories, and districts, and other places ceded."

[4] *The New York Herald*, of November 11, 1860, closes a glowing picture of the growth, condition, and prospects of the city of New York, as follows:

"If, however, Northern fanaticism should triumph over us, and *the Southern States should exercise their* UNDENIABLE RIGHT *to secede from the Union*, then the city of New York, the river counties, the State of New Jersey, and, very

victions of safety and interest should prompt her to that resort—or, if not exactly a right, then a heroic remedy for grievous wrongs, which could not be practically resisted.[5]

The second was urgently advocated by the entire "Democratic" and "Conservative" strength of the Free States, and by nearly all that still openly clung to the Union in the Slave States.

The third was the natural, spontaneous impulse of the great mass of Republicans, who could not see why their adversaries should not submit unqualifiedly to the result of a fair and honest election, as *they* had uniformly done, constitutionally resisting any unwarranted act or attempt of the President elect or his supporters, whenever the occasion should arise. But they found it difficult to realize that those who still retained predominance in both branches of Congress, and in the Supreme Court—who might have had, moreover, a Democratic President, had they chosen to support the candidate of a majority of that party—and who had still the active and earnest sympathy of a large majority of the American People—could cherish any real fears of usurpation and aggression from the numerical minority, or the President they had been permitted to choose. It was with little patience that the great body of the Republicans heard suggestions from any of their leaders or oracles of overtures looking to "conciliation" and "peace" through new concessions, in the face of the now chronic menace of Disunion.

The asserted right of Secession is one which no government or nation ever did or can concede without signing its own death-warrant. When the Federal Constitution was before the States for ratification, vehemently and formidably opposed, and its adoption, in several States, for a time successfully resisted, there was manifest danger of its failure in New York, as well as in two other great leading States, Virginia and Massachusetts. To the New York Convention, sitting at Poughkeepsie, the people had returned a majority of delegates hostile to ratification. The friends of the Constitution were constrained to resort to delay, to policy, and to propositions of amendment, to overcome or wear out the resistance they had

likely, Connecticut, would separate from those New England and Western States, where the black man is put upon a pinnacle above the white. New York City is for the Union first, and the gallant and chivalrous South afterward."

[5] A correspondent of the *Boston Courier*, of November, 1860, after contending that the South has ample cause for seceding, says:

"It is perfectly competent for South Carolina to notify the President officially, that she no longer belongs to the confederacy. This she can do at any moment. The Federal officers, from the district judge, collector, and marshal, to the humblest postmaster, can resign their places. Everybody agrees that this can readily be done at once, and without difficulty or any quarrel. Suppose so much to be done, and that President Buchanan should appoint a new Judge and a new Collector, who should repair to Charleston and demand the payment of duties upon any imported goods. Suppose, upon a refusal to pay the duties exacted, the Collector should do what all the Collectors are bound to do—seize the goods. The owner would have to furnish a bond to the government for their value. The owner would protest against giving one, and only give it, as the lawyers say, when in *duress*. In any suit upon such a bond, when the question of coërcion in making it was tried, who would compose the jury? They must belong to South Carolina. We have made these suggestions simply to satisfy any reader how very easily the mere matter of peaceable secession can be accomplished, and how futile would be all attempts to enforce Federal laws in any State by the aid of officers appointed from abroad.

"Practically, therefore, a peaceable secession will be very apt to work a final separation of the State which desires it, and, ultimately, a general dissolution of the confederacy."

encountered. In this dilemma, Alexander Hamilton wrote to James Madison to ask if the Constitution might not be accepted provisionally, with liberty to recede from the Union formed by it, if experience should justify the apprehensions of its adversaries. Mr. Madison promptly and wisely responded[6] in the negative, stating that such conditional acceptance had been agitated at Richmond, and rejected as, in fact, no ratification at all. In the same spirit, Mr. Clay likened our Constitutional Union to a marriage, which is either indissoluble at the pleasure of one or both parties, or else no marriage at all.

The Virginia Convention which ratified the Federal Constitution, in the preämble to its Ordinance of Ratification, declared that it was the "impression" of the People of their State that the powers granted by said Constitution, being derived from the People of *the United States*, may rightfully be resumed *by them*, whenever those powers shall be perverted to their injury or oppression. But this is nothing else than the fundamental doctrine of the republican system—that governments are made for the People, not the People for governments; and that the People, consequently, may, from time to time, modify their forms of government in accordance with their riper experience and their enlightened convictions—respecting, of course, the limitations and safeguards they may have seen fit to establish. This right had been set forth, with remarkable clearness and force, in the preämble to the Declaration of Independence, and by many of our patriot sages in later days. John Quincy Adams—never remarkably inclined to popularize forms of government—had distinctly affirmed it in a speech in Congress; so had Abraham Lincoln, in one of his debates with Senator Douglas. But the right of a people to modify their institutions is one thing, and the right of a small fraction or segment of a people to break up and destroy a Nation, is quite another. The former is Reform; the latter is Revolution.[7]

[6] Col. Hamilton, having first set before Mr. Madison the formidable obstacles to ratification, proceeded as follows:

"You will understand that the only qualification will be the *reservation* of the right to recede, in case our amendments have not been decided upon in one of the modes pointed out by the Constitution within a certain number of years—perhaps five or seven. If this can, in the first instance, be admitted as a ratification, I do not fear any further consequences."

But Madison knew no *ifs* in the ratification of our federal pact. His reply, in full, is as follows:

"New York, *Sunday Evening.*

"My Dear Sir:—Yours of yesterday is this instant come to hand, and I have but a few minutes to answer it.

"I am sorry that your situation obliges you to listen to propositions of the nature you describe. My opinion is, that a reservation of a right to withdraw, if amendments be not decided on under the form of the Constitution within a certain time, is a *conditional* ratification; that it does not make New York a member of the new Union; and, consequently, that she could not be received on that plan. Compacts must be reciprocal—this principle would not, in such a case, be preserved. The Constitution requires an adoption, *in toto* and *forever*. It has been so adopted by the other States. An adoption for a limited time would be as defective as an adoption of some of the Articles only. In short, any *condition* whatever must vitiate the ratification. What the new Congress, by virtue of the power to admit new States, may be *able* and disposed to do in such case, I do not inquire, as I suppose that is not the material point at present. I have not a moment to add more than my fervent wishes for your success and happiness. The idea of reserving a right to withdraw was started at Richmond, and considered as a conditional ratification, which was itself abandoned as worse than a rejection. Yours, James Madison, Jr."

[7] Hon. Reverdy Johnson, who lived in the same house with John C. Calhoun from 1845 to 1849, and enjoyed a very close intimacy with

But, while it was impossible to concede the asserted right of Secession—that is, of State withdrawal at pleasure from the Union—(for, even if the Constitution is to be regarded as nothing more than a compact, it is evident—as Mr. Jefferson observed,[8] in speaking of our old Articles of Confederation: "When two parties make a compact, there results to each the power of compelling the other to execute it")—it is not impossible so to expound and apply the original, organic, fundamental right of a people to form and modify their political institutions, as to justify the Free States in consenting to the withdrawal from the Union of the Slave, provided it could be made to appear that such was the deliberate, intelligent, unconstrained desire of the great body of their people. And the South had been so systematically, so outrageously, deluded by demagogues on both sides of the Slave line, with regard to the nature and special importance of the Union *to the North*—it being habitually represented as an immense boon conferred on the Free States by the Slave, whose withdrawal would whelm us all in bankruptcy and ruin—that it might do something toward allaying the Southern inflammation to have it distinctly and plainly set forth that the North had no desire to enforce upon the South the maintenance of an abhorred, detested Union. Accordingly—the second day after Mr. Lincoln's election had been assured at the polls—the following leading article appeared[9] in *The New York Tribune:*

"GOING TO GO.—The people of the United States have indicated, according to the forms prescribed by the Constitution, their desire that Abraham Lincoln, of Illinois, shall be their next President, and Hannibal Hamlin, of Maine, their Vice-President. A very large plurality of the popular vote has been cast for them, and a decided majority of Electors chosen, who will undoubtedly vote for and elect them on the first Wednesday in December next. The electoral votes will be formally sealed up and forwarded to Washington, there to be opened and counted, on a given day in February next, in the presence of both Houses of Congress; and it will then be the duty of Mr. John C. Breckinridge, as President of the Senate, to declare Lincoln and Hamlin duly elected President and Vice-President of these United States.

"Some people do not like this, as is very natural. Dogberry discovered, a good while ago, that 'When two ride a horse, one must ride behind.' That is not generally deemed the preferable seat; but the rule remains unaffected by that circumstance. We know how to sympathize with the defeated; for

---

him, in a letter to Edward Everett, dated Baltimore, June 24, 1861, says:

"He [Calhoun] did me the honor to give me much of his confidence, and frequently his Nullification doctrine was the subject of conversation. Time and time again have I heard him, and with ever-increased surprise at his wonderful acuteness, defend it on constitutional grounds, and distinguish it, *in that respect*, from the doctrine of Secession. This last he never, with me, placed on any other ground than that of revolution. This, he said, was to destroy the Government; and no Constitution, the work of sane men, ever provided *for its own destruction*. The other was to preserve it—was, practically, but to amend it, and in a constitutional mode."

To the same effect, Hon. Howell Cobb—since, a most notable Secessionist—in a letter to the citizens of Macon, Ga., in 1851, said:

"When asked to concede the right of a State to secede at pleasure from the Union, with or without just cause, we are called upon to admit that the framers of the Constitution did that which was never done by any other people possessed of their good sense and intelligence—that is, *to provide, in the very organization of the Government, for its own dissolution*. It seems to me that such a course would not only have been an anomalous proceeding, but wholly inconsistent with the wisdom and sound judgment which marked the deliberations of those wise and good men who framed our Federal Government. While I freely admit that such an opinion is entertained by many for whose judgment I entertain the highest respect, I have no hesitation in declaring that the convictions of my own judgment are well settled, that no such principle was contemplated in the adoption of our Constitution."

[8] Letter to Col. Carrington, April 4, 1787.

[9] November 9, 1860.

we remember how *we* felt, when Adams was defeated; and Clay, and Scott, and Fremont. It is decidedly pleasanter to be on the winning side, especially when—as now—it happens also to be the *right* side.

"We sympathize with the afflicted; but we cannot recommend them to do any thing desperate. What is the use? They are beaten now; they may triumph next time: in fact, they have generally had their own way: had they been subjected to the discipline of adversity so often as we have, they would probably bear it with more philosophy, and deport themselves more befittingly. We live to learn: and one of the most difficult acquirements is that of meeting reverses with graceful fortitude.

"The telegraph informs us that most of the Cotton States are meditating a withdrawal from the Union, because of Lincoln's election. Very well: they have a right to meditate, and meditation is a profitable employment of leisure. We have a chronic, invincible disbelief in Disunion as a remedy for either Northern or Southern grievances. We cannot see any necessary connection between the alleged disease and this ultra-heroic remedy; still, we say, if any one sees fit to meditate Disunion, let him do so unmolested. That was a base and hypocritic row that was once raised, at Southern dictation, about the ears of John Quincy Adams, because he presented a petition for the dissolution of the Union. The petitioner had a right to make the request; it was the Member's duty to present it. And now, if the Cotton States consider the value of the Union debatable, we maintain their perfect right to discuss it. Nay: we hold, with Jefferson, to the inalienable right of communities to alter or abolish forms of government that have become oppressive or injurious; and, if the Cotton States shall decide that they can do better out of the Union than in it, we insist on letting them go in peace. The right to secede may be a revolutionary one, but it exists nevertheless; and we do not see how one party can have a right to do what another party has a right to prevent. We must ever resist the asserted right of any State to remain in the Union, and nullify or defy the laws thereof: to withdraw from the Union is quite another matter. And, whenever a considerable section of our Union shall deliberately resolve to go out, we shall resist all coërcive measures designed to keep it in. We hope never to live in a republic, whereof one section is pinned to the residue by bayonets.

"But, while we thus uphold the practical liberty, if not the abstract right, of secession, we must insist that the step be taken, if it ever shall be, with the deliberation and gravity befitting so momentous an issue. Let ample time be given for reflection; let the subject be fully canvassed before the people; and let a popular vote be taken in every case, before Secession is decreed. Let the people be told just why they are asked to break up the confederation; let them have both sides of the question fully presented; let them reflect, deliberate, then vote; and let the act of Secession be the echo of an unmistakable popular fiat. A judgment thus rendered, a demand for separation so backed, would either be acquiesced in without the effusion of blood, or those who rushed upon carnage to defy and defeat it, would place themselves clearly in the wrong.

"The measures now being inaugurated in the Cotton States, with a view (apparently) to Secession, seem to us destitute of gravity and legitimate force. They bear the unmistakable impress of haste—of passion—of distrust of the popular judgment. They seem clearly intended to precipitate the South into rebellion before the baselessness of the clamors which have misled and excited her, can be ascertained by the great body of her people. We trust that they will be confronted with calmness, with dignity, and with unwavering trust in the inherent strength of the Union, and the loyalty of the American people."

Several other Republican journals, including some of the most influential, held similar language, and maintained a position not unlike that of *The Tribune*. None of them countenanced the right of a State to secede from the Union, or regarded it as more defensible than the right of a stave to secede from the cask which it helps to form; nor did they regard the effervescence now exhibited at the South as demonstrating a real desire on the part of her people to break up the Union. But they said impressively to that people: "Be calm; let us be heard; allow time for deliberation and the removal of prejudice; unite with us in calling a Convention of the States and People; and, if that Convention shall be unable to agree on such amendments to the Constitution as shall remove existing discontent, and your people shall still, with any approach to unanimity, insist on disunion, you shall go in peace. Neither Congress nor the President has any power to sanction a dissolution of the Union; but wait for and unite in a Convention, and our differences shall somehow be adjusted without fraternal bloodshed."

With the same general object, but contemplating a different method of attaining it, the veteran Editor of *The Albany Evening Journal*—whose utterances were widely regarded as deriving additional consequence from his intimate and almost life-long association with Gov. Seward—took ground, at an early day, in favor of concessions calculated—at all events, intended—to calm the ebullition of Southern blood. Being sharply criticised therefor, by several of his contemporaries, he replied[10] to them generally as follows:

"The suggestions, in a recent number of *The Journal*, of a basis of settlement of differences between the North and the South, have, in awakening attention and discussion, accomplished their purpose. We knew that in no quarter would these suggestions be more distasteful than with our own most valued friends. We knew that the occasion would be regarded as inopportune. We knew also the provocations in the controversy were with our opponents. Nothing is easier, certainly, than to demonstrate the rightfulness of the position of the Republican party—a party that was created by the repeal of the Missouri Compromise, and owes its recent triumph to the determination of Slavery to extend and perpetuate its political dominion, aided by two successive and besotted Federal Administrations.

"But, unfortunately, the pending issue is to be decided irrespective of its merits. The election of Mr. Lincoln is the pretext for, and not the cause of, Disunion. The design originated with Mr. Calhoun; who, when he failed to be chosen President of the whole Union, formed the scheme of dividing it, and devoted the remainder of his life in training the South up to the treason now impending. Mr. Calhoun had, in McDuffie, Hayne, and other statesmen, eloquent auxiliaries. The contagion extended to other Southern States; and, by diligence, activity, discipline, and organization, the whole people of the Gulf States have come to sympathize with their leaders. The masses are, in their readiness for civil war, in advance of their leaders. They have been educated to believe us their enemies. This has been effected by systematic misrepresentations of the sentiments and feelings of the North. The result of all this is, that, while the Southern people, with a unanimity not generally understood, are impatient for Disunion, more than one half of them are acting in utter ignorance of the intentions, views, and feelings, of the North. Nor will the leaders permit them to be disabused. Those leaders know that Mr. Lincoln will administer the Government in strict and impartial obedience to the Constitution and laws, seeking only the safety and welfare of the whole people, through the prosperity and glory of the Union. For this reason, they precipitate the conflict; fearing that, if they wait for a provocation, none will be furnished, and that, without fuel, their fires must be extinguished.

"This question, involving the integrity of the Union and the experiment of self-government, we repeat, will be decided irrespective of its merits. Three miserable months of a miserable Administration must 'drag its slow length along' before the Republican Administration can act or be heard. During these three months, its baleful influences will be seen and felt in the demoralization of popular sentiment. Its functionaries and its journals will continue to malign the North and inflame the South; leaving, on the 4th of March, to their successors an estate as wretchedly encumbered and dilapidated as imbecile or spendthrift ever bequeathed. Mismanaged as that estate has been, and wretched as its present condition is, we regard it as an inestimable, priceless, and precious inheritance—an inheritance which we are unwilling to see wholly squandered before we come into possession.

"To our dissenting friends, who will not question our devotion to freedom, however much they may mistrust our judgment, we submit a few earnest admonitions:

"1. There is imminent danger of a dissolution of the Union.

"2. This danger originated in the ambition and cupidity of men who desire a Southern despotism; and in the fanatic zeal of Northern Abolitionists, who seek the emancipation of slaves regardless of consequences.

"3. The danger can only be averted by such moderation and forbearance as will

[10] November 30, 1860.

draw out, strengthen, and combine the Union sentiment of the whole country.

"The Disunion sentiment is paramount in at least seven States; while it divides and distracts as many more. Nor is it wise to deceive ourselves with the impression that the South is not in earnest. It *is* in earnest; and the sentiment has taken hold of all classes with such blind vehemence as to 'crush out' the Union sentiment.

"Now, while, as has been said, it is easy to prove all this unjust and wrong, we have to deal with things as they are—with facts as they exist—with people blinded by passion. Peaceable Secession is not intended; nor is it practicable, even if such were its object. Mad, however, as the South is, there is a Union sentiment there worth cherishing. It will develop and expand as fast as the darkness and delusion, in relation to the feelings of the North, can be dispelled. This calls for moderation and forbearance. We do not, when our dwelling is in flames, stop to ascertain whether it was the work of an incendiary before we extinguish the fire. Hence our suggestions of a basis of adjustment, without the expectation that they would be accepted, in terms, by either section, but that they might possibly inaugurate a movement in that direction. The Union is worth preserving. And, if worth preserving, suggestions in its behalf, however crude, will not be contemned. A victorious party can afford to be tolerant—not, as our friends assume, in the abandonment or abasement of its principles or character—but in efforts to correct and disabuse the minds of those who misunderstand both.

"Before a final appeal—before a resort to the 'rough frown of war'—we should like to see a Convention of the People, consisting of delegates appointed by the States. After more than seventy years of 'wear and tear,' of collision and abrasion, it should be no cause of wonder that the machinery of government is found weakened, or out of repair, or even defective. Nor would it be found unprofitable for the North and South, bringing their respective griefs, claims, and proposed reforms, to a common arbitrament, to meet, discuss, and determine upon a future.

"It will be said that we have done nothing wrong, and have nothing to offer. This, supposing it true, is precisely the reason why we should both propose and offer whatever may, by possibility, avert the evils of civil war, and prevent the destruction of our, hitherto, unexampled blessings of Union.

"Many suppose that the North has nothing to lose by a division of the Union. Some even say that we must be gainers by it. We do not, for obvious reasons, intend to discuss this aspect of the question. But it is a mistake—a serious and expensive mistake. The North and South were wisely and by a good Providence united. Their interests, their welfare, their happiness, their glory, their destiny, is one. Separated, while the North languishes, the South becomes, first, a despotism, running riot, for a season, with unrestrained African Slavery, to share in time the fate of every tropical nation, whether despotism, monarchy, or republic. That fate, induced by the indolence, luxury, and laxity of the privileged few over the oppressed, degraded, and enslaved many, is anarchy and destruction. That fate is written in the history of all enslaved nations—its ancient, seared, and crumbling, but instructive, monuments are seen in Egypt, in Italy, in Central America, and in Mexico.

"These are the evils—and they are not imaginary—that we desire to avert. But, conscious of the feebleness of a single voice in such a tempest, there is little to expect but to abide its peltings. The Republican party now represents one side of a controversy fraught with the safety and welfare of this Government and nation. As an individual, we shall endeavor to do our duty; and, as we understand it, that duty does not consist in folded arms, or sealed ears, or closed eyes. Even if, as say our Rochester and Syracuse friends—and they are such, in the truest meaning of the word—the North stands, in all respects, blameless in this controversy, much is needed to correct the impression of the Southern people; many of whom, truly informed, would join us in defending the Union. We do not mistake the mission of the Republican party in assuming that, while defending free territory from aggression, it maintains and upholds the supremacy of the Constitution and laws. The people have intrusted the Government to our keeping; and we must not abuse their confidence or disappoint their expectations.

"We intend to answer in detail the questions raised by *The Democrat* and *Journal*. It is proper, though perhaps scarcely necessary, to say that, in this solicitude for the Union, we think and speak only for ourself. We are either better, or not so well, informed of the condition of the country and the bearings of this controversy as others—either in advance of or behind the intelligence of the times. But, as we speak only for ourself, nobody else can be compromised or harmed."

However well intended and (under certain aspects) salutary, it may well be questioned whether either of these overtures was not calculated to do more harm than good. Each was, of course, intended to strengthen the Unionists of the South—the former by showing that the North did not regard the Slave States as a conquest, of which it was about to take possession, nor yet as a heritage whence were derived its subsistence and wealth; but rather that it looked on their people as misguided, excited brethren, with whom we were anxious to discuss all differences freely, settle them (if possible) amicably, or part—if part we must—in kindness and mutual good-will. The latter, in a like spirit, was plainly designed to induce the Southrons to bring their grievances to the bar of amicable investigation and discussion, by assuring them that the North stood ready to redress every wrong to the extent of its power. But the chronic misapprehension at the South of any other language from the North than that of abject servility, was then, as ever, deserving of thoughtful consideration. The palpable fact that the North recoiled with shuddering aversion from a conflict of arms with the South, was hailed by the Secessionists as a betrayal of conscious weakness and unmanly fear; while the proffer of fresh concessions and a new compromise was regarded by Southern Unionists as an assurance that they had only to ask, and they would receive—that the North would gladly do anything, assent to anything, retract anything, to avert the impending shock of war.

For the great mails, during the last few weeks of 1860, sped southward, burdened with letters of sympathy and encouragement to the engineers of Secession, stimulating if not counseling them to go forward in their predetermined course. A very few of the writers indorsed Secession as a right, and favored it as an end; but the great majority wished it carried no further than would be necessary to frighten, or bully the 'Black Republicans' out of what they termed their 'principles,' and sink them, with their 'conservative' fellow-citizens, into measureless abasement at the footstool of the Slave Power. And nearly every current indication of public sentiment pointed to this as the probable result, provided 'the South' should only evince a willingness to accept the prostration, and graciously forgive the suppliant. As trade fell off, and work in the cities and manufacturing villages was withered at the breath of the Southern sirocco, the heart of the North seemed to sink within her; and the Charter Elections at Boston, Lowell, Roxbury, Charlestown, Worcester, etc., in Massachusetts, and at Hudson, etc., in New York, which took place early in December, 1860, showed a striking and general reduction of Republican strength. What must and could be done to placate the deeply offended and almost hopelessly alienated South, was the current theme of conversation, and of newspaper discussion.

Of the meetings held to this end, the most imposing may fairly be cited as a sample of the whole. The city of Philadelphia had given a small majority for Lincoln over all his competitors. Her Mayor, Alexander Henry, though of 'American' antecedents, had been among his supporters. On the 10th of December, he issued an official Proclamation, "by advice of the Councils" of the city, summoning the whole people thereof to assemble on the 13th in Independence Square, there to "counsel together," in view of the fact that

Disunion appeared to be imminent, unless the "loyal people, casting off the spirit of party, should, in a special manner, avow their unfailing fidelity to the Union, and their abiding faith in the Constitution and laws."

The meeting was held accordingly; called to order by the President of the Common Council, prayed for by Bishop Potter, and the speaking initiated by Mayor Henry, who, after cautioning his hearers to discard "all *sordid* and *self-interested* views," and to avow their "unbroken attachment to the Union," and their determination to "leave no honest effort untried to preserve its integrity," proceeded to set forth the provocations to Secession, and the proper means of counteracting it, after this fashion:

"My fellow-citizens, I should be false to the position in which you have placed me—I should be recreant to my sense of duty—if I withheld an avowal of the truth which this occasion demands. I speak to you frankly, my fellow-citizens; I tell you that, if, in any portion of our confederacy, sentiments have been entertained and cherished which are inimical to the civil rights and social institutions of any other portion, those sentiments should be relinquished and discountenanced. (Cheers.) The family discipline which you choose to adopt for your own fireside, whilst it does not violate the law under which you dwell, is your rightful prerogative; and you are prompt to resist the officious intermeddling of others, however well intended. (Applause.) The social institutions of each State in this Union are equally the rightful prerogatives of its citizens; and, so long as those institutions do not contravene the principles of your Federal compact, none may justly interfere with, or righteously denounce them. (Applause.) The efficient cause of the distracted condition of our country is to be found in the prevalent belief of the citizens of the South that their brethren of the North are, as a community, arrayed against a social institution which they regard as essential to their prosperity. You are ready to aver truthfully that such belief is mistaken and unfounded; but it becomes all who are actuated by an earnest brotherhood to see to it that, where public sentiment has been misled, it shall be restored to its standpoint of twenty-five years since. The misplaced teachings of the pulpit, the unwise rhapsodies of the lecture-room, the exciting appeals of the press, on the subject of Slavery, must be frowned down by a just and law-abiding people. (Great applause.) Thus, and thus only, may you hope to avoid the sectional discord, agitation, and animosity, which, at frequently recurring periods, have shaken your political fabric to its center, and, at last, have undermined its very foundation."

Hon. Joseph R. Ingersoll (old-line Whig, but anti-Lincoln) followed in a far less humiliating strain, but urging the immediate, unconditional repeal of the State act antagonistic to the Fugitive Slave Law; which proposition was hailed with enthusiastic cheers. He closed as follows:

"We are all one country. It is a farce to suppose that this country will be divided. (Applause.) It will be united in peace or in war. (Applause.) You may see, perhaps, legions brought against legions, in a domestic fury that shall be worse than the fury of a foreign enemy, and they will be united in doing harm. While we, in the center of the country, will endeavor to interpose kindness and peace, in order to restore the country to the situation in which it was left at the death of Washington, let us be determined to maintain the rights of the whole country, and extend the feeling of fellowship over all the land. (Great cheering.)"

Judge George W. Woodward[11] spoke next, commencing by an assault on Mr. Lincoln's premonition that 'the Union must become all Slave or all Free,' and proceeding to indicate the exclusion of Slavery from the territories as a dogma which must be given up, or the Union was lost. Here is his statement and condemnation of the policy inaugurated by Thomas Jefferson:

"The inexorable exclusion of slave property from the common territories, which the Government holds in trust for the people of all the States, is a natural and direct step

[11] Of the State Supreme Court; since, beaten as the Democratic candidate for Governor, in 1863, by 15,238 majority. A consistent antagonist of 'coërcion.'

toward the grand result of extinguishing slave property, and was one of the record issues of the late election. This policy must be considered as approved also. Not that every man who voted for the successful nominee meant to affirm that a trustee for several coëqual parties has a right, in law or reason, to exclude the property of some and admit that of others of the parties for whom he holds; but so is the record. The South seems inclined to accept the judgment. She holds the property that is to be shut out of the territories—that is to be restricted, cribbed, and confined more and more until it is finally extinguished. Everywhere in the South, the people are beginning to look out for the means of self-defense. Could it be expected that she would be indifferent to such events as have occurred?—that she would stand idle, and see measures concerted and carried forward for the annihilation of her property in slaves? Several States propose to retire from the confederacy; and that justly alarms us. We come together to consider what may be done to prevent it; and we are bound, in fidelity to ourselves and others, to take the measure of the whole magnitude of the danger."

The Judge proceeded to set forth that the questions raised among our fathers by the introduction of Slavery had been wisely settled:

"If the Anglo-Saxon loves liberty above all other men, he is not indifferent to gain and thrift, and is remarkable for his capacity of adaptation, whereby he takes advantage of any circumstances in which he finds himself placed. And, accordingly, by the time the colonists were prepared to throw off the British yoke, and to assume among the Powers of the earth the separate and equal station to which the laws of nature and of nature's God entitled them, it had been discovered that the unwelcome workers, against whose introduction such earnest protests had been made, could be turned to profitable account in the Southern States—that the African constitution was well adapted to labor in latitudes which alone could produce some of the great staples of life—and that the North, which could not employ them profitably, would be benefited by such employment as the South could afford. Considerations of humanity also, as well as the rights of private property, entered into the discussions of that day. What was best for an inferior race, thrust unwillingly upon a superior? That both should be free? or that the inferior should serve the superior, and the superior be bound by the law of the relation to protect the inferior? That was a great question; and, like all the questions of that day, it was wisely settled. The Northern States abolished their Slavery; and so gratified their innate love of freedom—but they did it gradually, and so did not wound their love of gain. They *sold out Slavery to the South;* and they received a full equivalent, not only in the price paid down, but in the manufacturing and commercial prosperity which grew up from the productions of slave labor. When the Constitution came to be formed, some of the Northern States still held slaves; but several had abolished the institution, and it must have been apparent that natural causes would force it ultimately altogether upon the South. The love of liberty was as intense as ever, and as strong at the South as at the North; and the love of gain was common also to both sections. Here were two master passions to be adjusted, under circumstances of the gravest delicacy. They *were* adjusted, in the only manner possible. Concessions and compromises—consideration for each others' feelings and interests—sacrifices of prejudices, forbearance, and moderation—these were the means by which the 'more perfect Union' was formed. And what a work it was! If the Union had never brought us a single blessing, the Constitution of the United States would still have been a magnificent monument to the unselfish patriotism of its founders. Not an alliance merely, but a close and perfect Union, between people equally ambitious, equally devoted to freedom, equally bent on bettering their condition, but separated by State lines and jealous of State rights—one section seeks its prosperity under institutions which were to make every man a freeman—the other under institutions which tolerated negro Slavery. Had the Constitution failed to work out the beneficent results intended, here was an instance of human efforts to do good, which would forever have challenged the admiration of mankind. But it did *not* fail, thank God! it has made us a great and prosperous nation, and the admiration of the world for the motives of the founders, is swallowed up in wonder at the success of their work. But all this the 'irrepressible conflict' ignores. The passion for liberty has burned out all memories of the compromise and the compact in these Northern communities, which, under the false name of Liberty bills, obstruct the execution of the bargain. What part of the purposes of the founders are the 'underground railroads' intended to promote? Whence came these excessive sensibilities, that cannot bear a few slaves in a remote territory until the white people establish a Constitution? What does that editor or preacher know of the Union, and of the men who made it, who habitually reviles and misrepresents the Southern people, and excites the ignorant and the thoughtless in our midst to hate and persecute them? Be not deceived. Let me not prophesy smooth things, and cry Peace, when there is no peace. Let the truth be spoken, be heard, be pondered, if we mean to save the Union."

Judge Woodward concluded his address to this non-partisan Union meeting after this fashion:

"Have I not a right to say that a Government which was all-sufficient for the country fifty years ago, when soil and climate and State sovereignty were trusted to regulate the spread of Slavery, is insufficient today, when every upstart politician can stir the people to mutiny against the domestic institutions of our Southern neighbors—when the ribald jests of seditious editors like Greeley and Beecher can sway legislatures and popular votes against the handiwork of Washington or Madison—when the scurrilous libels of such a book as Helper's become a favorite campaign document, and are accepted by thousands as law and gospel both —when jealousy and hate have extinguished all our fraternal feelings for those who were born our brethren, and who have done us no harm?"

Mr. Charles E. Lex (who had voted for Lincoln) made an apologetic and deprecatory speech, wherein he said:

"However they may suppose the contrary, our affections are *not* alienated from our Southern friends; and, even now, the rumor of any damage to them from a domestic source would bring to their aid a legion of young men from this State—ay, and of those more advanced in life—ready to assist them in the emergency, and willing to shed their blood in their defense. I appeal to you, citizens of Philadelphia, whether I am not speaking the truth. What, then, can we say to them? What more than we have expressed in the resolutions we have offered? If they are really aggrieved by any laws upon our statute-books opposed to their rights—if, upon examination, any such are found to be in conflict with the Constitution of these United States—nay, further: if they but serve to irritate our brethren of the South, whether constitutional or not, I, for one, have no objection that they should instantly be repealed. They are not necessary to our existence as a State. We have lived without them in years that are past, and we can live without them again. I am not here, however, to concede that, in this respect, our noble commonwealth has done any intentional wrong; but if, in our calm judgment, it shall appear that our feelings, in the slightest degree warped, have apparently inflicted any injury, she is noble and generous enough manfully to repair it. Let the Fugitive Slave Law be executed in its full intent and spirit. It is the law of the land; let it be implicitly obeyed. We might, perhaps, have desired to have a few of its provisions modified; but let it remain as it is, however liable these portions may be to Northern criticism, if the South deem it necessary for the protection of her rights. Let us, too, submit, as we have hitherto cheerfully done, to the decisions of the Supreme Court of the United States. It is the great bulwark of the Constitution. Its judgments should be final and conclusive, and not be questioned in any quarter. Whilst the free discussion of every question is the privilege of every citizen of the Republic, let us discountenance any denunciation of Slavery, or of those who maintain that institution, as intemperate and wrong, whether they are promulgated in the lecture-room, at the political gathering, or from the sacred desk."

Mr. Theodore Cuyler followed in a kindred strain, illustrating his notion of what was required to bring back the seceders and restore fraternal concord to the Union, as follows:

"Let us of the North get back to our true position. Let us first set the example of perfect obedience to the Constitution and the laws; and then, when we shall have pulled the beam from our own eye, we may talk to our brother of the mote in his. Let us return the fugitive from labor, as we are bound to do; or, if we permit his rescue by unlawful violence, compensate his owner for the loss. Let us repeal our obnoxious Personal Liberty bills—those mean evasions of the plainest duty; let us receive our brother of the South, if he will come among us for a little time, attended by his servant, and permit him thus to come. We are bound by a sacred compact not to interfere or meddle with the institution of Slavery as it exists in many of our sister States; and yet the pulpit and the press, and many of our public halls, are eloquent with violent and inflammatory appeals touching this subject, whose mischief, extending far beyond the boundary of our own Commonwealth, extends into the very heart of neighboring States. Who shall say, fellow-citizens, how much of our present peril springs from this very cause? Can we wonder that our Southern brother feels that the heart of his Northern fellow-citizen is shut against him? Can we forget that these appeals have reached the Slaves themselves, and filled with dread and apprehension the once quiet and happy homes of many, very many, Southern masters? Fellow-citizens, although the law may be powerless, yet there is a moral force which can and would arrest this evil. I appeal to you earnestly—to each one of you individually—by every lawful means in your power, to put an end to the violent and inflammatory discussion of this unhappy subject. The past, the present, and the future, appeal to you eloquently to be true to your country and to yourselves. Never before has constitutional liberty assumed so fair a form among men as here with us. Never before, under its influence and protection, has any people been so speedily and happily borne to great prosperity; until now the imagination sinks in the effort to contemplate that glorious future on whose very threshold our feet have stood. Can it be that madness and fanaticism—can it be that selfishness and sectionalism—are about to destroy this noblest form of government, freighted as it is with the highest hopes of humanity? (Loud cheers.)"

Mr. Isaac Hazlehurst closed the discussion in a far manlier spirit. Himself a 'Conservative,' the 'American' candidate for Governor in 1857, he had no palinode to offer for Northern 'fanaticism,' and no thought of crouching to Southern treason. On the contrary, he spoke, with singular and manly directness, as follows:

"Fellow-citizens, it is no time for party, because there are no party questions to be discussed. We are here for the purpose of endeavoring to preserve the Union of these States. The American Union was made perfect by the people of these States, and by the people of these States it is to be maintained and preserved. It is not a question of '*must* be preserved,' but, in the language of Gen. Jackson, 'it *shall* be preserved.' (Applause.) * * * I say, fellow-citizens, that Pennsylvania has been true to the Constitution and the Union. She has always been loyal to it. There is no doubt upon that subject. She has nothing whatever to repent of; and we will maintain these principles as presented by your resolutions. I care not where the traitors are—I care not where they hide themselves—the first arm that is raised against the Constitution and the Union, I will bring all that I have to their defense—all that I have to secure the enforcement of the laws. ('Good!' Cheers.)"

Of the resolutions in which the spirit of this meeting was embodied, these are the most significant:

"*Resolved*, 4. That the people of Philadelphia hereby pledge themselves to the citizens of the other States that the statute-books of Pennsylvania shall be carefully searched at the approaching session of the Legislature, and that every statute, if any such there be, which, in the slightest degree, invades the constitutional rights of citizens of a sister State, will be at once repealed; and that Pennsylvania, ever loyal to the Union, and liberal in construing her obligations to it, will be faithful always in her obedience to its requirements.

"*Resolved*, 5. That we recognize the obligations of the act of Congress of 1850, commonly known as the Fugitive Slave Law, and submit cheerfully to its faithful enforcement; and that we point with pride and satisfaction to the recent conviction and punishment, in this city of Philadelphia, of those who had broken its provisions by aiding in the attempted rescue of a slave, as proof that Philadelphia is faithful in her obedience to the law; and furthermore, that we recommend to the Legislature of our own State the passage of a law which shall give compensation, in case of the rescue of a captured slave, by the county in which such rescue occurs, precisely as is now done by existing laws in case of destruction of property by violence of mobs.

"*Resolved*, 6. That, as to the question of the recognition of slaves as property, and as to the question of the rights of slaveholders in the territories of the United States, the people of Philadelphia submit themselves obediently and cheerfully to the decisions of the Supreme Court of the United States, whether now made or hereafter *to be* made; and they pledge themselves faithfully to observe the Constitution in these respects, as the same has been or may be expounded by that august tribunal. And, further: they recommend that whatever points of doubt exist touching these subjects be, in some amicable and lawful way, forthwith submitted to the consideration of said Court; and that its opinion be accepted as the final and authoritative solution of all doubts as to the meaning of the Constitution on controverted points.

"*Resolved*, 7. That all denunciations of Slavery, as existing in the United States, and of our fellow-citizens who maintain that institution, and who hold slaves under it, are inconsistent with the spirit of brotherhood and kindness which ought to animate all who live under and profess to support the Constitution of the American Union."

That the meaning of all this was—"In the hope of winning back the seceded States, and of retaining the trade, custom, and profits, which we have hitherto derived from the slave-holders, we hereby solemnly pledge ourselves never more to say or do, nor let our neighbors say or do, aught calculated to displease said slaveholders or offend the Slave Power," was promptly demonstrated. Mr. George W. Curtis, one of our most attractive and popular public speakers, had been engaged by 'the People's Literary Institute' of Philadelphia to lecture on the evening after the great meeting, and had announced as his subject, "The Policy of Honesty." What reflections were suggested by that topic or title to the engineers of the meeting, can only be inferred from the following notification:

"Office of the Mayor of the City of Philadelphia, Dec. 10, 1860.

"Dear Sir:—The appearance of George W. Curtis, Esq., as a lecturer before the People's Literary Institute, on Thursday evening next, will be extremely unwise. If I possessed the lawful power, I would not permit his presence on that occasion.

"Very respectfully, etc.

"Alexander Henry, Mayor.

"James W. White, Esq., Chairman."

The following letter from the owner of the Hall betrays a common impulse, if not a common origin, with the foregoing:

"Concert Hall, December 11, 1860.

"Dear Sir:—I have been *officially* informed that, in the event of G. W. Curtis lecturing in this Hall on Thursday evening next, a riot is anticipated. Under these circumstances, I cannot permit the Hall to be used on that occasion. Respectfully,

"Thomas A. Andrews.

"J. W. White, Esq."

So the *Lincoln* city of Philadelphia, like a good many other Northern cities, made *her* bid for slave-holding forbearance and patronage—no one observing, nor even hinting, that the North had rights and grievances, as well as the South—that "sectional" aspirations, aggressions, encroachments, were not confined to Free States; and that, in the conciliation so generally and earnestly commended, the Slave Power might fairly be asked to accord *some* consideration, some respect, if not to make some concession, to that generous, loving spirit, which recognizes a brother in the most repulsive form of Humanity, which keenly feels that wrong and degradation to any necessarily involve reproach and peril to all, and will rest content with nothing short of Universal Justice and Impartial Freedom.

XXIV.

'CONCILIATION' IN CONGRESS.

The XXXVIth Congress reconvened for its second and last session on Monday, December 3, 1860, and President Buchanan transmitted his fourth and last Annual Message next day. After briefly stating therein that the year then closing had been one of general health, ample harvests, and commercial prosperity, he plunged into the great political controversy of the day after this fashion:

"Why is it, then, that discontent now so

extensively prevails, and the Union of the States, which is the source of all these blessings, is threatened with destruction? The long-continued and intemperate interference of the Northern people with the question of Slavery in the Southern States has at length produced its natural effects. The different sections of the Union are now arrayed against each other; and the time has arrived, so much dreaded by the Father of his Country, when hostile geographical parties have been formed. I have long foreseen, and often forewarned my countrymen of the now impending danger. This does not proceed solely from the claims on the part of Congress or the Territorial Legislatures to exclude Slavery from the territories, nor from the efforts of different States to defeat the execution of the Fugitive Slave law.

"All or any of these evils might have been endured by the South without danger to the Union (as others have been), in the hope that time and reflection might apply the remedy. The immediate peril arises, not so much from these causes, as from the fact that the incessant and violent agitation of the Slavery question throughout the North for the last quarter of a century has at length produced its malign influence on the slaves, and inspired them with vague notions of freedom. Hence, a sense of security no longer exists around the family altar. This feeling of peace at home has given place to apprehensions of servile insurrection. Many a matron throughout the South retires at night in dread of what may befall herself and her children before the morning. Should this apprehension of domestic danger, whether real or imaginary, extend and intensify itself until it shall pervade the masses of the Southern people, then disunion will become inevitable. Self-preservation is the first law of nature, and has been implanted in the heart of man by his Creator for the wisest purpose; and no political union, however fraught with blessings and benefits in all other respects, can long continue, if the necessary consequence be to render the homes and the firesides of nearly half the parties to it habitually and hopelessly insecure. Sooner or later, the bonds of such a Union must be severed. It is my conviction that this fatal period has not yet arrived; and my prayer to God is, that He would preserve the Constitution and the Union throughout all generations.

"But let us take warning in time, and remove the cause of danger. It cannot be denied that, for five-and-twenty years, the agitation at the North against Slavery in the South has been incessant. In 1835, pictorial handbills and inflammatory appeals were circulated extensively throughout the South, of a character to excite the passions of the slaves; and, in the language of Gen. Jackson, 'to stimulate them to insurrection, and produce all the horrors of a servile war.' This agitation has ever since been continued by the public press, by the proceedings of State and County Conventions, and by Abolition sermons and lectures. The time of Congress has been occupied in violent speeches on this never-ending subject; and appeals, in pamphlet and other forms, indorsed by distinguished names, have been sent forth from this central point, and spread broadcast over the Union.

"How easy would it be for the American people to settle the Slavery question forever, and to restore peace and harmony to this distracted country!

"They, and they alone, can do it. All that is necessary to accomplish the object, and all for which the Slave States have ever contended, is, to be let alone, and permitted to manage their domestic institutions in their own way. As sovereign States, they, and they alone, are responsible before God and the world for the Slavery existing among them. For this, the people of the North are not more responsible, and have no more right to interfere, than with similar institutions in Russia or in Brazil. Upon their good sense and patriotic forbearance, I confess I greatly rely."

How a sane man *could* talk in this way, in full view of the Texas, Nebraska, and Kansas struggles of the last few years, and of the persistent efforts to acquire Cuba, and "regenerate" Central America in the interest of the Slave Power, is one of the problems reserved for solution in some future and higher existence. To expose its inconsistency with notorious facts were a waste of time and effort; to lose temper over it were even a graver mistake: the proper, fittest frame of mind wherein to contemplate it is one of silent wonder.

Mr. Buchanan proceeded to argue that the election of Mr. Lincoln "does not of itself afford just cause for dissolving the Union;" that "from the very nature of his office, and its high responsibilities, he must necessarily be conservative;" that no single act has ever passed Congress, unless we may possibly except *the Missouri Compromise*,[1] impairing, in the slightest degree, the rights of the South in their property in slaves; that no such act *could* be passed, in the present or in the next Congress; that the Dred Scott decision had covered all the ground contended for by the Slave States, rendering null and void a recent act of the Legislature of Kansas, abolishing Slavery in that Territory; that all acts of State Legislatures intended to defeat the execution of the Fugitive Slave law were nullities, the Supreme Court having so decided and sustained that law at every point; nevertheless, the States that have passed such acts ought, and should be urged, to repeal them; that, should they not be repealed, "the injured States" "would be justified in revolutionary resistance to the Government of the Union" (for unfaithfulness to constitutional obligations by those whom that Government could not control); that there is *no* reserved or constitutional right of State Secession from the Union, which was clearly intended to be perpetual; that the Federal Government is required, and the States expressly forbidden, to do many things essential to the idea of sovereignty; that the Federal Government "has precisely the same right to exercise its power for the people of all these States, in the enumerated cases, that each one of them possesses over subjects not delegated to the United States;" that the Federal Constitution is a part of the Constitution of each State, and is binding upon the people thereof; that the people of States aggrieved or oppressed by Federal power have the right of revolutionary resistance, but no other—and yet, if any State *should* see fit to secede from and defy the Union, there is no help for it! Let us hear Mr. Buchanan more fully on this point:

"What, in the mean time, is the responsibility and true position of the Executive? He is bound by solemn oath, before God and the country, 'to take care that the laws be faithfully executed;' and from this obligation he cannot be absolved by any human power. But what, if the performance of this duty, in whole or in part, has been rendered impracticable by events over which he could have exercised no control? Such, at the present moment, is the case throughout the State of South Carolina, so far as the laws of the United States to secure the administration of justice by means of the Federal Judiciary are concerned. All the Federal officers within its limits, through whose agency alone these laws can be carried into execution, have already resigned. We no longer have a District Judge, a District Attorney, or a Marshal, in South Carolina. In fact, the whole machinery of the Federal Government necessary for the distribution of remedial justice among the people has been demolished, and it would be difficult, if not impossible, to replace it.

"The only acts of Congress on the statute-book, bearing upon this subject, are those of 28th February, 1795, and 3d March, 1807. These authorize the President, after he shall have ascertained that the Marshal, with his *posse comitatus*, is unable to execute civil or criminal process in any particular case, to call out the militia and employ the Army and Navy to aid him in performing this service, having first, by Proclamation, commanded the insurgents to 'disperse, and retire peaceably to their respective abodes, within a limited time.' This duty cannot, by possibility, be performed in a State where no judicial authority exists to issue process, and where there is no Marshal to execute it; and where, even if there were such an officer, the entire population would constitute one solid combination to resist him."

But why cannot the President ap-

[1] The Ordinance of 1787, reäffirmed under the Constitution in 1789, is thus clearly affirmed by Mr. Buchanan to be *not* in derogation of 'Southern Rights.' This, be it remembered, as well as the Missouri Compromise itself, had the hearty support of the entire South.

point a new District Judge, a new Marshal, to replace those who have resigned? If no one of the vicinage will or dare accept these trusts, why not fill them from loyal States? If these shall be resisted, will it not be at the proper peril of the insurgents? If the Federal Government can be driven out of a State, and compelled to *stay* out, by the cheap process of bullying two or three Federal officers into resigning, and bullying others out of daring to take their places, is ours a real government at all?

The President, proceeding, set forth the main issue as follows:

"The question, fairly stated, is: Has the Constitution delegated to Congress the power to coërce into submission a State which is attempting to withdraw, or has actually withdrawn, from the confederacy? If answered in the affirmative, it must be on the principle that the power has been conferred upon Congress to declare and to make war against a State. After much serious reflection, I have arrived at the conclusion that no such power has been delegated to Congress, or to any other department of the Federal Government. It is manifest, upon an inspection of the Constitution, that this is not among the specific and enumerated powers granted to Congress: and it is equally apparent that its exercise is not 'necessary and proper for carrying into execution' any one of these powers."

The contrast between this logic and that of Gen. Jackson in like circumstances[2] has already been noted. But it is difficult to realize that such transparent sophistry can have deceived even its author. The President had already truly stated that

"The Executive has no authority to decide what shall be the relations between the Federal Government and South Carolina. He has been invested with no such discretion. He possesses no power to change the relations heretofore existing between them; much less to acknowledge the independence of that State."

The act of Secession, so called, was therefore—at least, so far as the President was concerned—a simple nullity. He could know South Carolina only as one of the States composing our Union, whose citizens were consequently citizens of the United States, and bound to uphold their Constitution and obey their laws. If any or many of those citizens chose to break and defy those laws, it was his simple and imperative duty to cause them to be faithfully executed, at whatever inconvenience or peril to the law-breakers. No President had ever suggested or imagined that the opposition of any State to the Fugitive Slave law, for example, could absolve him from the duty of enforcing that law. This is the President's duty in the premises, and the whole of it,—to "take care that the laws be faithfully executed."[3] The Constitution and laws being, by express provision, "the supreme law of the land; * * * anything in the Constitution or laws of any State to the contrary notwithstanding,"[4] the real question was not—'Has the Constitution delegated to Congress the power to coërce a State?' but 'Has any State a reserved, inherent power to coërce the Union into acquiescence in the overthrow of the Federal Constitution, the subversion of the laws, and the destruction of our Nationality?' The President is bound to know no legitimate power within the Union acting in hostility to the Constitution and laws he has solemnly sworn to uphold and enforce. Whoever and whatever stands in the way of such enforcement, he can regard only as law-breakers, insurgents, and traitors.

[2] See pages 94–100.

[3] Federal Constitution, Art. II., § 3.

[4] *Ibid.* Art. VI., § 2. See also Webster's Reply to Hayne, pages 86–8.

Of course, having decided not to perform his sworn duty, the President proceeded to lecture the people whom he thus betrayed on the duty of buying off the banded traitors by new concessions and guarantees; saying:

"The fact is, that our Union rests upon public opinion, and can never be cemented by the blood of its citizens shed in civil war. If it cannot live in the affections of the people, it must one day perish. Congress possess many means of preserving it by conciliation; but the sword was not placed in their hand to preserve it by force."

But, if it cannot be 'cemented,' can it be *un*cemented, dissolved, and destroyed, 'by the blood of its citizens, shed in civil war?' If it can, then is it the most stupendous mockery and sham which ever duped and deluded mankind.

His panacea for the ills experienced or imminently impending was an "explanatory amendment" of the Constitution, which should operate as a "final settlement" of the true construction of the Federal pact on three special points:

"1. An express recognition of the right of property in slaves in the States where it now exists or may hereafter exist.

"2. The duty of protecting this right in all the common territories throughout their territorial existence, and until they shall be admitted as States into the Union, with or without Slavery, as their Constitution may prescribe.

"3. A like recognition of the right of the master to have his slave, who has escaped from one State to another, restored and 'delivered up' to him, and of the validity of the Fugitive Slave law enacted for this purpose, together with a declaration that all State laws impairing or defeating this right are violations of the Constitution, and are consequently null and void."

Behind this pitiable exhibition was an elaborate opinion[5] from Hon. Jeremiah S. Black, of Pennsylvania, Mr. Buchanan's Attorney-General, sustaining and elaborating the President's most fatal errors. After setting forth, in a most grudging and technical fashion, the occasions in which the President is authorized to use force in support of the violated laws of the land, Mr. Black proceeds as follows:

"But what if the feeling in any State against the United States should become so universal that the Federal officers themselves (including Judges, District Attorneys, and Marshals) would be reached by the same influence, and resign their places? Of course, the first step would be to appoint others in their stead, if others could be got to serve. But, in such event, it is more than probable that great difficulty would be found in filling the offices. We can easily conceive how it might become altogether impossible. We are, therefore, obliged to consider what can be done in case we have no Courts to issue judicial process, and no ministerial officers to execute it. In that event, troops would certainly be out of place, and their use wholly illegal. If they are sent to aid the Courts and Marshals, there must *be* Courts and Marshals to be aided. Without the exercise of these functions, which belong exclusively to the civil service, the laws cannot be executed in any event, no matter what may be the physical strength which the Government has at its command. Under such circumstances, to send a military force into any State, with orders to act against the people, would be simply making war upon them."

That is to say: A little rebellion may be legally and constitutionally repressed; but a great one cannot be.

'If we have no Courts' where they are needed, we should constitute them; and, 'if we have no ministerial officers,' we should appoint them. The President is expressly clothed with the requisite power, and has no right to refrain from exercising it. If no man now living in South Carolina dare serve as District Judge or Marshal, then one should be sent thither who has no repugnance and

[5] Dated November 20, 1860.

no fear, and be backed by a competent force. The President could have found a thousand qualified persons to take either position, had he chosen. The fact that the insurgents were locally formidable—even omnipotent—only hightened the imperative necessity of dealing with them promptly and sternly. And, if jurors could not there be found to render verdicts according to law, then the culprits should be removed to some region where treason, at the worst, was not universal. But 'The slothful man says, There is a lion in the way;' and he who has determined not to do his duty, will never lack excuses for repudiating it.

Mr. Black closed his disorganizing opinion as follows:

"If it be true that war cannot be declared, nor a system of general hostilities carried on, by the Central Government against a State, then it seems to follow that an attempt to do so would be *ipso facto* an expulsion of such State from the Union. Being treated as an alien and an enemy, she would be compelled to act accordingly. And, if Congress shall break up the present Union by unconstitutionally putting strife, and enmity, and armed hostility, between different sections of the country, instead of the 'domestic tranquillity' which the Constitution was meant to insure, will not all the States be absolved from their Federal obligations? Is any portion of the people bound to contribute their money or their blood to carry on a contest like that?

"The right of the General Government to preserve itself in its whole constitutional vigor, by repelling a direct and positive aggression upon its property or its officers, cannot be denied. But this is a totally different thing from an offensive war to punish the people for the political misdeeds of State Governments, or to prevent a threatened violation of the Constitution, or to enforce an acknowledgment that the Government of the United States is supreme. The States are colleagues of one another; and, if some of them should conquer the rest and hold them as subjugated provinces, it would totally destroy the whole theory upon which they are now connected.

"If this view of the subject be as correct as I think it is, then the Union must utterly perish at the moment when Congress shall arm one part of the people against another, for any purpose beyond that of merely protecting the General Government in the exercise of its proper constitutional functions."

Strange as it must now seem, this assertion of the radical impotence of the Government, this avowal of a fixed purpose to 'let the Union slide,' on the part of the President and his legal adviser, were received in Congress with general and concerted taciturnity on the part of the upholders, and with a bounteous display of indignation on that of the banded assailants, of the National life. Mr. A. R. Boteler,[6] of Virginia, moved a reference of so much of the Message as related to our National perils to a Select Committee of one from each State; which in due time prevailed, and a very fair Committee was appointed—Thomas Corwin, of Ohio, Chairman; with a large preponderance of the more moderate 'Republicans' and pro-Slavery men in its composition. Mr. Speaker Pennington, who framed the Committee, was strongly inclined to 'conciliation,' if that could be effected on terms not disgraceful to the North; and at least six of the sixteen Republicans placed on the Committee desired and hoped that an adjustment might yet be achieved. No member of extreme anti-Slavery views was associated with them.

But it was soon evident that no 'concession' or 'conciliation' was desired by a large portion of the pro-

[6] From the Potomac district next above Washington; originally a 'Whig'; then 'American'; elected to this Congress and supported for Speaker as 'Union'; now, zealous for 'concession' and 'peace'; an open traitor from the day of Virginia's secession.

Slavery members. Mr. Clingman of N. C.—who came into Congress as a 'Whig' of very moderate views regarding Slavery, but had finally turned Democrat under the impulse of zeal for 'Southern Rights,' and been thereupon promoted from the House to the Senate, and who had changed from Douglas to Breckinridge toward the end of the Presidential canvass just closed—assailed the Message, so soon as it had been read, and broadly intimated that no concession would satisfy the South. The repeal of all 'Personal Liberty bills,' etc., he observed, "would not be satisfactory to the State from which I come." He protested against "waiting for an overt act" before seceding, and against further parley or negotiation between the Free and the Slave States. Said he:

"They want to get up a free debate, as the Senator from New York [Mr. Seward] expressed it, in one of his speeches. But a Senator from Texas told me the other day *that a great many of these free debaters were hanging from the trees of that country* [Texas]. I have no doubt they would run off a great many slaves from the Border States, so as to make them Free States; and then, Sir, when the overt act was struck, we should have a hard struggle. I say, therefore, that our policy is not to let this thing continue. That, I think, is the opinion of North Carolina. I think the party for immediate secession is gaining ground rapidly. It is idle for men to shut their eyes to consequences like this, if anything can be done to avert the evil, while we have power to do it."

Messrs. Albert G. Brown, of Mississippi, Louis T. Wigfall, of Texas, and Alfred Iverson, of Georgia, spoke in a similar strain, but even more plainly. Said Mr. Iverson:

"Gentlemen speak of concession—of the repeal of the Personal Liberty bills. Repeal them all to-morrow, and you cannot stop this revolution. It is not the Liberty laws but the mob law which the South fears. They do not dread these overt acts; for, without the power of the Federal Government, by force, under Republican rule, their institution would not last ten years; and they know it. They intend to go out of this Union, and he believed this. Before the 4th of March, five States will have declared their independence, and he was satisfied that three other States would follow as soon as the action of their people can be had. Arkansas will call her Convention, and Louisiana will follow. And, though there is a clog in the way in the 'lone star' of Texas, in the person of her Governor, who will not consent to call the Legislature, yet the public sentiment is so strong that even her Governor may be overridden; and, if he will not yield to that public sentiment, *some Texan Brutus may arise to rid his country of this old, hoary-headed traitor.* [Great sensation.] There has been a good deal of vaporing and threatening; but they came from the last men who would carry out their threats. Men talk about their eighteen millions; but we hear a few days afterward of these same men being switched in the face, and they tremble like a sheep-stealing dog. There will be no war. The North, governed by such far-seeing statesmen as the Senator from New York [Mr. Seward], will see the futility of this. In less than twelve months, a Southern Confederacy will be formed; and it will be the most successful Government on earth. The Southern States, thus banded together, will be able to resist any force in the world. We do not expect war; but we will be prepared for it; and we are not a feeble race of Mexicans either."

Messrs. Crittenden, of Kentucky, and Saulsbury, of Delaware, both spoke pleadingly for 'conciliation' and the Union, but to deaf ears.

A caucus of Southern members was held on Saturday evening, December 8th; but it only served to develop more clearly the broad line of demarkation between the Unionists and the Disunionists. Messrs. Albert G. Brown, of Mississippi, and John Slidell, of Louisiana, were among the most fierce for Secession. Messrs. Jefferson Davis, of Mississippi, and James M. Mason, of Virginia, favored further efforts, or, at least, further waiting, for conciliation. Messrs. Crittenden, Bayard, and several other 'Border-State' Senators, more earnestly urged this course.

Monday, December 9th, being 'resolution day' in the House, was signalized by the broaching of several new devices for saving the Union. Mr. John Sherman, of Ohio, suggested a faithful observance, on all hands, of the requirements and compromises of the Constitution, with an immediate division of the territories into embryo States, with a view to their prompt admission into the Union. Mr. John Cochrane, of New York, revived the old scheme of dividing the territories between Free and Slave Labor on the line of 36° 30′. Mr. English, of Indiana, proposed substantially the same thing. Mr. Noell, of Missouri, proposed an abolition of the office of President of the United States, and a division of the Union into three districts, each to elect one member of an 'Executive Council,' to which the functions of President should be intrusted. He suggested, moreover, a 'restoration of the equilibrium between the Free and Slave States,' by a division of several of the latter into two or more States each. Mr. Thomas C. Hindman,[7] of Arkansas, proposed to so amend the Constitution as to protect slave property in the territories, etc., etc., and that any State which should pass an act impairing or defeating the operation of the Fugitive Slave law should thereupon be deprived of her right of representation in Congress. Mr. Charles H. Larrabee, of Wisconsin, proposed a Convention of the States. All these projects were referred to the Grand Select Committee aforesaid.

That Committee, December 13th, after four days' earnest deliberation, united in a resolve, moved by Mr. Justin S. Morrill, of Vermont, as a substitute for one moved by Mr. William McKee Dunn, of Indiana, affirming the necessity of proffering to the Slave States "additional and more special guarantees of their peculiar rights and interests." Mr. Morrill's affirmation was as follows:

"*Resolved*, That, in the opinion of the Committee, the existing discontents among the Southern people, and the growing hostility among them to the Federal Government, are greatly to be regretted; and that any reasonable, proper, and constitutional remedies, necessary to preserve the peace of the country and the perpetuation of the Union, should be promptly and cheerfully granted."

Twenty-two votes were cast for this proposition, including those of all the members from Slave States who voted. Two (Messrs. Boyce, of South Carolina, and Hawkins, of Florida) were absent. Mr. Reuben Davis was present, but did not vote. The Nays (eight) were all Republicans.

On motion of Mr. Garnett B. Adrain (Douglas Democrat) of New Jersey, the House,[8] by 151 Yeas to 14 Nays:

"*Resolved*, That we deprecate the spirit of disobedience to the Constitution, wherever manifested; and that we earnestly recommend the repeal of all statutes by the State Legislatures in conflict with, and in violation of, that sacred instrument, and the laws of Congress passed in pursuance thereof."

Mr. Owen Lovejoy (Republican) of Illinois, hereupon proposed this counterpart to the foregoing:

"*Whereas*, The Constitution of the United States is the supreme law of the land, and ready and faithful obedience to it a duty of all good and law-abiding citizens: Therefore,

"*Resolved*, That we deprecate the spirit

[7] Since, a Rebel Brigadier.

[8] December 17th.

of disobedience to the Constitution, wherever manifested; and that we earnestly recommend the repeal of all nullification laws; and that it is the duty of the President of the United States to protect and defend the property of the United States."

The Yeas were 124; the Nays *none*—most of the Southern members refusing to vote.

Mr. Isaac N. Morris (Democrat) of Illinois, next moved

"That we have seen nothing in the past, nor do we see anything in the present, either in the election of Abraham Lincoln to the Presidency, or otherwise, to justify a dissolution of the Union," etc., etc.

On this, the Yeas were 115; Nays 44. Two of the Nays were Northern Democrats.[9]

On the same day, a resolve, by Mr. Lazarus W. Powell, of Kentucky, proposing a Committee of Thirteen on the absorbing topic, came up in the Senate, and Mr. Benjamin F. Wade, of Ohio, uttered some weighty words on the general subject. Having shown that the Government had hitherto been under the control of the Slave Power—that the personal rights and safety of Northern men of anti-Slavery views were habitually violated in the South—that the present pointed antagonism between the Free and the Slave States had been caused by a great change of opinion, not at the North, but at the South, he continued:

"The Republican party holds the same opinion, so far as I know, with regard to your 'peculiar institution' that is held by every civilized nation on the globe. We do not differ in public sentiment from England, France, Germany, and Italy, on the subject of Slavery.

"I tell you frankly that we *did* lay down the principle in our platform, that we would prohibit, if we had the power, Slavery from invading another inch of the free soil of this Government. I stand to that principle today. I have argued it to half a million of people, and *they* stand by it—they have commissioned *me* to stand by it; and, so help me God, I will! I say to you, while we hold this doctrine to the end, there is no Republican, or Convention of Republicans, or Republican paper, that pretends to have any right in your States to interfere with your peculiar and local institutions. On the other hand, our platform repudiates the idea that we have any right, or harbor any ultimate intention, to invade or interfere with your institution in your own States. * * *

"I have disowned any intention, on the part of the Republican party, to harm a hair of your heads. We hold to no doctrine that can possibly work you any inconvenience—any wrong—any disaster. We have been, and shall remain, faithful to all the laws—studiously so. It is not, by your own confessions, that Mr. Lincoln is expected to commit any overt act by which you may be injured. You will not even wait for any, you say; but, by anticipating that the Government *may* do you an injury, you will put an end to it—which means, simply and squarely, that you intend to rule or ruin this Government. * * *

"As to compromises, I supposed that we had agreed that the day of compromises was at an end. The most solemn we have made have been violated, and are no more. Since I have had a seat in the Senate, one of considerable antiquity was swept from our statute-book; and when, in the minority, I stood up here, and asked you to withhold your hands—that it was a solemn, sacred compact between nations—what was the reply? That it was nothing but an act of Congress, and could be swept away by the same majority which enacted it. That *was* true in fact, and true in law; and it showed the weakness of compromises. * * *

"We beat you on the plainest and most palpable issue ever presented to the American people, and one which every man understood; and now, when we come to the capital, we tell you that our candidates must and shall be inaugurated—must and shall administer this Government precisely as the Constitution prescribes. It would not only be humiliating, but highly dishonorable to us, if we listened to any compromise by which we should set aside the honest verdict of the people. When it comes to that, you have no government, but anarchy intervenes, and civil war may follow; and all the evils that human imagination can raise may be consequent on such a course as that. The American people would lose the sheet-anchor of their liberties whenever it is denied on this floor that a majority, fairly given, shall rule. I know not what others may do; but

[9] Daniel E. Sickles of New York; Thomas B. Florence, of Pennsylvania.

I tell you that, with that verdict of the people in my pocket, and standing on the platform on which these candidates were elected, I would suffer anything before I would compromise in any way. I deem it no case where we have a right to extend courtesy and generosity. The absolute right, the most sacred that a free people can bestow upon any man, is their verdict that gives him a full title to the office he holds. If we cannot stand there, we cannot stand anywhere; and, my friends, any other verdict would be as fatal to you as to us."

The venerable and Union-loving JOHN J. CRITTENDEN, of Kentucky—the Nestor of the Bell-Everett party—who had first entered Congress as a Senator forty-four years before—who had served, at different times, no less than twenty years, in the upper House of Congress; and who, after filling, for a season, the post of Attorney-General under Gen. Harrison, and again under Mr. Fillmore, was now, in his fullness of years, about to give place to a Democrat,[10] elected because of the greater confidence of the slaveholding interest in the Democratic than in the adverse party—came forward to tender *his* peace-offering; and no anti-Republican in Congress or in the country could have risen whose personal character and history could have more disposed the Republicans to listen to him with an anxious desire to find the acceptance of his scheme compatible with their principles and their sense of public duty. His olive-branch was as follows:

"*A Joint Resolution proposing certain amendments to the Constitution of the United States:*

"*Whereas*, serious and alarming dissensions have arisen between the Northern and the Southern States, concerning the rights and security of the rights of the slaveholding States, and especially their rights in the common territory of the United States; *and whereas*, it is eminently desirable and proper that these dissensions, which now threaten the very existence of this Union, should be permanently quieted and settled by constitutional provisions, which shall do equal justice to all sections, and thereby restore to the people that peace and good-will which ought to prevail between all the citizens of the United States: Therefore,

"*Resolved, by the Senate and House of Representatives of the United States of America, in Congress assembled* (two-thirds of both Houses concurring), That the following articles be, and are hereby, proposed and submitted as amendments to the Constitution of the United States, which shall be valid, to all intents and purposes, as part of said Constitution, when ratified by Conventions of three-fourths of the several States:

"ARTICLE 1. In all the territory of the United States now held, or hereafter acquired, situate north of latitude 36° 30′, Slavery or involuntary servitude, except as a punishment for crime, is prohibited, while such territory shall remain under territorial government. In all the territory south of said line of latitude, Slavery of the African race is hereby recognized as existing, and shall not be interfered with by Congress, but shall be protected as property by all the departments of the territorial government during its continuance. And when any territory, north or south of said line, within such boundaries as Congress may prescribe, shall contain the population requisite for a member of Congress, according to the then Federal ratio of representation of the people of the United States, it shall, if its form of government be republican, be admitted into the Union, on an equal footing with the original States; with or without Slavery, as the Constitution of such new State may provide.

"ART. 2. Congress shall have no power to abolish Slavery in places under its exclusive jurisdiction, and situate within the limits of States that permit the holding of slaves.

"ART. 3. Congress shall have no power to abolish Slavery within the District of Columbia, so long as it exists in the adjoining States of Virginia and Maryland, or either, nor without the consent of the inhabitants, nor without just compensation first made to such owners of slaves as do not consent to such abolishment. Nor shall Congress, at any time, prohibit officers of the Federal Government, or members of Congress whose duties require them to be in said District, from bringing with them their slaves, and holding them as such during the time their duties may require them to remain there, and afterward taking them from the District.

[10] John C. Breckinridge; chosen to take Mr. Crittenden's seat on the 4th of March, 1861.

"ART. 4. Congress shall have no power to prohibit or hinder the transportation of slaves from one State to another, or to a territory in which slaves are, by law, permitted to be held, whether that transportation be by land, navigable rivers, or by the sea.

"ART. 5. That, in addition to the provisions of the third paragraph of the second section of the fourth article of the Constitution of the United States, Congress shall have power to provide by law, and it shall be its duty to provide, that the United States shall pay to the owner who shall apply for it, the full value of his fugitive slaves in all cases where the marshal, or other officer whose duty it was to arrest said fugitive, was prevented from so doing by violence or intimidation, or where, after arrest, said fugitive was rescued by force, and the owner thereby prevented and obstructed in the pursuit of his remedy for the recovery of his fugitive slave under the said clause of the Constitution and the laws made in pursuance thereof. And in all such cases, when the United States shall pay for such fugitive, they shall have the right, in their own name, to sue the county in which said violence, intimidation, or rescue, was committed, and recover from it, with interest and damages, the amount paid by them for said fugitive slave. And the said county, after it has paid said amount to the United States, may, for its indemnity, sue and recover from the wrong-doers or rescuers by whom the owner was prevented from the recovery of his fugitive slave, in like manner as the owner himself might have sued and recovered.

"ART. 6. No future amendment of the Constitution shall affect the five preceding articles; nor the third paragraph of the second section of the first article of the Constitution; nor the third paragraph of the second section of the fourth article of said Constitution; and no amendment shall be made to the Constitution which shall authorize or give to Congress any power to abolish or interfere with Slavery in any of the States by whose laws it is, or may be, allowed or permitted.

"*And whereas, also*, besides those causes of dissension embraced in the foregoing amendments proposed to the Constitution of the United States, there are others which come within the jurisdiction of Congress, and may be remedied by its legislative power; *And whereas*, it is the desire of Congress, as far as its power will extend, to remove all just cause for the popular discontent and agitation which now disturb the peace of the country and threaten the stability of its institutions: Therefore,

"*Resolved, by the Senate and House of Representatives in Congress assembled*, That the laws now in force for the recovery of fugitive slaves are in strict pursuance of the plain and mandatory provisions of the Constitution, and have been sanctioned as valid and constitutional by the judgment of the Supreme Court of the United States; that the slaveholding States are entitled to the faithful observance and execution of those laws; and that they ought not to be repealed, or so modified or changed as to impair their efficiency; and that laws ought to be made for the punishment of those who attempt, by rescue of the slave, or other illegal means, to hinder or defeat the due execution of said laws.

"2. That all State laws which conflict with the fugitive slave acts of Congress, or any other Constitutional acts of Congress, or which, in their operation, impede, hinder, or delay, the free course and due execution of any of said acts, are null and void by the plain provisions of the Constitution of the United States; yet those State laws, void as they are, have given color to practices, and led to consequences, which have obstructed the due administration and execution of acts of Congress, and especially the acts for the delivery of fugitive slaves; and have thereby contributed much to the discord and commotion now prevailing. Congress, therefore, in the present perilous juncture, does not deem it improper, respectfully and earnestly, to recommend the repeal of those laws to the several States which have enacted them, or such legislative corrections or explanations of them as may prevent their being used or perverted to such mischievous purposes.

"3. That the act of the 18th of September, 1850, commonly called the Fugitive Slave law, ought to be so amended as to make the fee of the Commissioner, mentioned in the eighth section of the act, equal in amount in the cases decided by him, whether his decision be in favor of or against the claimant. And, to avoid misconstruction, the last clause of the fifth section of said act, which authorizes the person holding a warrant for the arrest or detention of a fugitive slave to summon to his aid the *posse comitatus*, and which declares it to be the duty of all good citizens to assist him in its execution, ought to be so amended as to expressly limit the authority and duty to cases in which there shall be resistance, or danger of resistance or rescue.

"4. That the laws for the suppression of the African Slave-Trade, and especially those prohibiting the importation of slaves into the United States, ought to be more effectual, and ought to be thoroughly executed; and all further enactments necessary to those ends ought to be promptly made."

A white man and an Indian, says the legend, once went hunting in partnership; and the net product of their joint efforts was a turkey and an owl, which were to be divided between them. "I will take the turkey," said the white man, "and you may have the owl; or *you* may have the owl, and *I'll* take the turkey." "Ah, but," demurred the Indian, "you don't say 'turkey' *once* to *me*."

I. For a generation, the Free North had been struggling against a series of important measures, forming a system of public policy, whereof the purpose and necessary effect were the diffusion and aggrandizement of Slavery. Mr. Crittenden, by coöperating therein, to a certain extent, had clearly affirmed, to that extent, the right and justice of this resistance. He had earnestly opposed the violation of our public faith solemnly plighted to the Creek and Cherokee Indians; he had struggled manfully against the annexation of Texas. True, he had not openly condemned and resisted the repudiation of the Missouri Compact; but his studied silence on that topic, in view of the Southern *furor* in favor of the Nebraska Bill, proves clearly his tacit concurrence in the Northern repugnance to that measure. So also with regard to the projected purchase or seizure of Cuba. Yet this struggle of the North, its importance and its justice, are utterly ignored in this plan of 'adjustment' and 'conciliation;' while the South is proffered guarantees of the perpetuity of Slavery in the District of Columbia as well as in the Slave States, with the utmost facilities and aids to slave-hunting ever known in any country. The show of concession, in the foregoing project, to Northern convictions, relates to the 'mint, anise and cummin' of the great controversy; it proffers to the Free States no guarantee on a single point ever deemed by them essential. Then as to the territories: Mr. Crittenden's proposition, in substance, is, that the North shall not merely permit, but establish and guarantee, Slavery in all present and *future* territories of the Union south of 36° 30′. The direct incitement herein proffered, the strong temptation held out, to fillibustering raids upon Mexico, Central America, Cuba, Hayti, etc., could never be ignored. The Slave Power would have claimed this as a vital element of the new compromise—that she had surrendered her just claim to all territory north of 36° 30′ for the conceded right to acquire and enjoy new territory south of that line, and would have insisted on her 'pound of flesh' —a rigorous fulfillment of the compact. Her Sam Houstons, William Walkers and Bickleys would have plotted at home and plundered abroad, in the character of apostles, laboring to reädjust the disturbed equilibrium of the Union by acquiring for the South that to which she was entitled by the Crittenden Compromise.

II. The essence and substance of Mr. Crittenden's 'adjustment' inhere in his proposition that, of the vast territories acquired by us from Mexico, with all that may be acquired hereafter, so much as lies south of the parallel 36° 30′, shall be absolutely surrendered and guaranteed to Slavery. But this very proposition was made, on behalf of the South, by Gen. Burt, of S. C., in 1847, and was then defeated by the decisive vote of

114 to 82—*not one* Whig, and but *four* Democrats, from the Free States, sustaining it.[11] It was defeated again in the next Congress, when proposed by Mr. Douglas, in 1848: Yeas 82; Nays 121; only *three* Democrats and *no* Whig from Free States sustaining it.[12] The Republican party was now required, in the year 1861, to assent to a partition of the territories, and an establishment of Slavery therein, which both the Whig and the Democratic parties of the Free States had repeatedly, and all but unanimously, rejected before there *was* any Republican party. Thus the North, under the lead of the Republicans, was required to make, on pain of civil war, concessions to Slavery which it had utterly refused when divided only between the 'conservative' parties of fifteen or twenty years ago.

III. The vital principle of this, as of all compromises or projects of conciliation proposed from the South to the North, was this: '*You* shall regard Slavery as *we* do, and agree with us that it is beneficent and right. We will concede that it is not desirable nor profitable in *your* harsh climate, on your rugged soil; and you must concur with us in affirming that it is the very thing for *our* fervid suns and fertile vales. Then we will go forward, conquering, annexing, settling, planting, and filling the markets of the world with our great staples, while you shall be amply enriched by our commerce and by our constantly expanding markets for your food and manufactures.' In other words, Slavery was henceforth to be regarded, on all hands, as the basis at once of our National industry and our National policy.

IV. As a part of this compact, the North was to silence her lecturers, muzzle her press, chloroform her pulpits, and bully her people into a silence respecting Slavery, which should be broken only by the utterance of vindications and panegyrics. Already the great publishing houses of our Northern cities had been very generally induced to mutilate the works they from time to time issued, by expunging from them every passage or sentiment obnoxious to the fastidious, exacting taste of the slaveholders. Some of our authors—Mr. James K. Paulding conspicuous among them—had revised their own works, and issued new editions, wherein their old-time utterances adverse to Slavery had been supplanted by fulsome adulations of the system or vehement abuse of its opponents. Our Missionary, Tract, and other religious organizations, had very generally been induced to expurgate their publications and their efforts of all anti-Slavery ideas. Our great popular churches had either bent to the storm or been broken by it. And now, the work was to be completed by a new and comprehensive 'adjustment,' taking the place and, in part, the name of that 'Compromise' which the Slave Power had first forced upon the North and then coolly repudiated; an adjustment which was to bind the Free States over to perpetual complicity in slaveholding, and perpetual stifling of all exposure of, or remonstrance against, the existence, the domination, and the diffusion of Slavery.

These strictures are neither impelled nor colored by any unkindly feeling toward Mr. Crittenden, whose

[11] See pages 196–7.

[12] See pages 197–8.

patriotism and fairness they are not designed to impeach. He doubtless considered carefully and well what the South could be induced to accept; and he undoubtingly believed this to be embodied and presented in his plan of compromise. A slaveholder himself; born, educated, and living amid the influences of the institution; he could not or did not realize that his conditions would seem inadmissible to any but the narrowest and most miserable fanatics. Assuming his premises, regarding the matter exclusively from his standpoint, and putting conscience and consistency entirely out of the question, his proposal was fair enough; and its cordial adoption would doubtless have exhilarated the stock market, and caused general rejoicing on exchanges and around the dinner-tables of merchant princes. Its advocates, with good reason, claimed a large majority of the people in its favor, and clamored for its submission to a direct popular vote. Had such a submission been accorded, it is very likely that the greater number of those who voted at all would have voted to ratify it.

But, on the other hand, these facts deserve consideration:

I. The Democratic and 'Conservative' politicians who united on the Crittenden Compromise, and clamored for its adoption, had had control of Congress and the Federal Executive through seven-eighths of our past national history. If this were the true panacea for our troubles respecting Slavery, why had they not applied it long ago? Why not adopt it under Polk or Fillmore, Pierce or Buchanan, without waiting to the last sands of their departing power? Why not unite upon it as their platform in the Presidential contest of 1860? Why call upon the Republicans to help them do, after forty years of controversy, what they might themselves have done, without help, almost any time during those forty years? Why repudiate, against the most urgent remonstrances, in 1854, a compromise which, so far as it went, was substantially identical with this, and now ask those whom they then overbore to unite with them in ratifying another and a worse, in 1861?

II. The 'Conservatives,' so called, were still able to establish this Crittenden Compromise by their own proper strength, had they been disposed so to do. The President was theirs; the Senate strongly theirs; in the House, they had a small majority, as was evinced in their defeat of John Sherman for Speaker. Had they now come forward and said, with authority: 'Enable us to pass the Crittenden Compromise, and all shall be peace and harmony,' they would have succeeded without difficulty. It was only through the withdrawal of pro-Slavery members that the Republicans had achieved an unexpected majority in either House. Had those members chosen to return to the seats still awaiting them, and to support Mr. Crittenden's proposition, they could have carried it without difficulty.

III. But it was abundantly evident that the passage of this measure would *not* restore the Union. Several States had already plunged into Secession, their oracles avowing that they wanted *no* concession, and would be satisfied with none. Every suggestion that they should wait for some overt act, at least for some official declaration, from Mr. Lincoln, had been spurned by them. They made haste to secede, from fear that concessions *would* be offered—that their pretexts for disruption would somehow be obviated. To send concessions after them, in their scornful, imperious, insulting stampede, would be inviting them to heap new and more dishonoring indignities on the nation they were defying. It was, in fact, to justify their past treason, and incite them to perseverance and greater daring in the evil way they had chosen.

IV. Our 'conservative' Supreme Court, by its Dred Scott decision, had denied to Congress all power to exclude Slavery from a single acre of the common territories of the Union; it had held the Missouri Compromise invalid on this very ground; and now, the North was called to reënact and extend that very line of demarkation between Free and Slave territory which the Court had pronounced a nullity. True, Mr. Crittenden proposed that the new compromise should be ingrafted upon the Constitution; but that only increased the difficulty of effecting the adjustment, without assuring its validity. For, if the new Southern doctrines respecting property, and the rights of property, and the duty of protecting those rights, and the radical inability of the Government to limit or impair them, be sound, then the guarantee to Free Labor of the territory north of 36° 30′, must prove delusive. Indeed, Mr. Jefferson Davis, at a meeting of the Select Committee framed to consider these very resolutions, proposed, on the 26th of December, the following:

"*Resolved*, That it shall be declared, by amendment of the Constitution, that property in slaves, recognized as such by the local law of any of the States of the Union, shall stand on the same footing, in all constitutional and Federal relations, as any other species of property so recognized; and, like other property, shall not be subject to be divested or impaired by the local law of any other State, either in escape thereto, or by the transit or sojourn of the owner therein. And in no case whatever shall such property be subject to be divested or impaired by any legislative act of the United States, or any of the territories thereof."

When the Senate came to act[13] upon Mr. Crittenden's proposition, Mr. Anthony, of Rhode Island—a very moderate, conservative Republican—made a new overture which ought to have closed the controversy. Announcing his intention to vote for the substitute proposed by Mr. Daniel Clark, of New Hampshire, as "abstractly true," and more in accordance with his idea of the mode in which our troubles should be composed, Mr. Anthony proceeded:

"I believe, Mr. President, that, if the danger which menaces us is to be avoided at all, it must be by legislation; which is more ready, more certain, and more likely to be satisfactory, than constitutional amendment. The main difficulty is the territorial question. The demand of the Senators on the other side of the chamber, and of those whom they represent, is, that the territory South of the line of the Missouri Compromise shall be open to their peculiar property. All this territory, except the Indian reservation, is within the limits of New Mexico, which, for a part of its northern boundary, runs up two degrees beyond that line. This is now a slave territory; made so by territorial legislation; and Slavery exists there, recognized and protected. Now, I am willing, so soon as Kansas can be admitted, to vote for the admission of New Mexico as a State, with such Constitution as the people may adopt.

"This disposes of all the territory that is adapted to slave labor, or that is claimed by the South. It ought to settle the whole question. Surely, if we can dispose of all the territory that we have, we ought not to

[13] January 16, 1861

quarrel over that which we have not, and which we have no very honest way of acquiring. Let us settle the difficulties that threaten us now, and not anticipate those which may never come. Let the public mind have time to cool; let us forget, in the general prosperity, the mutual dependence and the common glory of our country, that we have ever quarreled over the question that we have put at rest; and perhaps when, in the march of events, the northern provinces of Mexico are brought under our sway, they may come in without a ripple on the political sea, whose tumultuous waves now threaten to ingulf us all in one common ruin.

"In offering to settle this question by the admission of New Mexico, we of the North who assent to it propose a great sacrifice, and offer a large concession. We propose to take in a State that is deficient in population, and that possesses but imperfectly many of the elements of a member of the Union, and that will require, in one form or another, even after its admission, the aid of the General Government. But we make the offer in a spirit of compromise and good feeling, which we hope will be reciprocated.

"And now, Mr. President, I appeal to Senators on the other side, when we thus offer to bridge over seven-eighths of the frightful chasm that separates us, will you not build the other eighth? When, with outstretched arms, we approach you so near, that by reaching out your hands you can clasp ours in the fraternal grasp from which they should never be separated, will you, with folded arms and closed eyes, stand upon extreme demands which you know we cannot accept, and for which, if we did, we could not carry our constituents?"

There was no response to this; and the Senate, after having refused—30 to 25—to postpone the subject to take up the Kansas Admission bill, proceeded to vote on Mr. Clark's substitute, which was in these words:

"*Resolved*, That the provisions of the Constitution are ample for the preservation of the Union, and the protection of all the material interests of the country; that it needs to be obeyed rather than amended; and that an extrication from our present dangers is to be looked for in strenuous efforts to preserve the peace, protect the public property, and enforce the laws, rather than in new guarantees for peculiar interests, compromises for particular difficulties, or concessions to unreasonable demands.

"*Resolved*, That all attempts to dissolve the present Union, or overthrow or abandon the present Constitution, with the hope or expectation of constructing a new one, are dangerous, illusory, and destructive; that, in the opinion of the Senate of the United States, no such reconstruction is practicable; and, therefore, to the maintenance of the existing Union and Constitution should be directed all the energies of all the departments of the Government, and the efforts of all good citizens."

The vote was now taken on this substitute, which was adopted, as follows:

YEAS.—Messrs. Anthony, Baker, Bingham, Cameron, Chandler, Clark, Collamer, Dixon, Doolittle, Durkee, Fessenden, Foot, Foster, Grimes, Hale, Harlan, King, Seward, Simmons, Sumner, Ten Eyck, Trumbull, Wade, Wilkinson, and Wilson—25 [all Republicans].

NAYS.—Messrs. Bayard, Bigler, Bragg, Bright, Clingman, *Crittenden*, Fitch, Green, Gwin, Hunter, Johnson, of Tennessee, *Kennedy*, Lane, of Oregon, Mason, Nicholson, Pearce, Polk, Powell, Pugh, Rice, Saulsbury, and Sebastian—23 [all Democrats, but two Bell-Conservatives, in *italics*].

Messrs. Iverson, of Georgia, Benjamin and Slidell, of Louisiana, Hemphill and Wigfall, of Texas, and R. W. Johnson, of Arkansas—who had voted just before against taking up the Kansas bill—had now absented themselves or sat silent, and allowed Mr. Clark's resolves to supplant Mr. Crittenden's, which were thus defeated. They doubtless did this in obedience to a resolve, preconcerted with Messrs. Davis, Toombs, etc., to accept no adjustment or concession which did not receive the vote of a majority of the Republicans.

In the last hours of the session,[14] the subject was called up by Mr. J. M. Mason, of Virginia, when Mr. Clark's substitute aforesaid was reconsidered and rejected—22 to 14—in order to have a direct vote on the

[14] March 2, 1861.

Crittenden proposition; which was then defeated: Yeas 19 ['Conservatives']; Nays 20 [Republicans]; as before. Several more Southern Senators had meantime seceded and left.

Mr. Lazarus W. Powell, of Kentucky, having moved[15] the appointment of a Select Committee of Thirteen on the crisis at which the country had now arrived, the Senate assented, and Vice-President John C. Breckinridge[16] appointed Messrs. Powell, Hunter, Crittenden, *Seward*, Toombs, Douglas, *Collamer*, Davis, *Wade*, Bigler, Rice, *Doolittle*, and *Grimes* on said Committee—five of the thirteen Republicans (in *italics*). Mr. Davis [Jefferson] asked to be excused from serving, but finally consented. The Committee met two or three days thereafter, and held several animated sessions, but to little purpose. Mr. Crittenden's main proposition—the line of 36° 30′—was voted down after full discussion: Yeas Messrs. Bigler, Crittenden, Douglas, Rice, and Powell—5; Nays, Messrs. *Davis*, Doolittle, Collamer, Wade, *Toombs*, Grimes, and *Hunter*—7: absent, Mr. Seward. Messrs. Hunter, Toombs, and Davis, it is said, would have supported it, had it been proposed and sustained by the Republicans. The remaining propositions of Mr. Crittenden received generally a majority of the whole number of votes, but were not considered adopted; the Committee having agreed upon a rule that nothing should be so considered that did not receive a majority both of the Republican and the anti-Republican votes. When the Committee met again,[17] Mr. Seward submitted the following proposition:

"*First.* No amendment shall be made to the Constitution which will authorize or give to Congress any power to abolish or interfere, in any State, with the domestic institutions thereof, including that of persons held to service or labor by the laws of such State."

This was adopted by the following vote:

YEAS—Messrs. Powell, Hunter, Crittenden, Seward, Douglas, Collamer, Wade, Bigler, Rice, Doolittle, and Grimes—11.

NAYS—Messrs. Davis and Toombs—2.

"*Second,* The Fugitive Slave law of 1850 shall be so amended as to secure to the alleged fugitive a trial by jury."

This, having been amended, on motion of Mr. Douglas, so as to have the alleged fugitive sent for trial to the State from which he was charged with escaping, was voted down—all the Republicans and Mr. Crittenden sustaining it; all the rest opposing it.

Mr. Seward[18] further proposed, and the Republicans sustained, the following:

"*Resolved,* That, under the fourth section of the fourth article of the Constitution, Congress should pass an efficient law for the punishment of all persons engaged in the armed invasion of any State from another by combinations of individuals, and punishing all persons in complicity therewith, on trial and conviction, in the State or District where their acts of complicity were committed, in the Federal Courts."

This was negatived by the solid vote of the anti-Republican members.

It can hardly be necessary to trace further the abortive proceedings of this Committee. They came to nothing, through no want of good-will on the part of a majority of its members, but because most or all of those from the South could or would accept nothing as sufficient short of an utter and shameful repudiation by the Republicans of the vital principle of their party—the consecration of

[15] December 5, 1860. [16] December, 20, 1860. [17] December 24th. [18] December 26th.

the Territories to Free Labor. Thus: Mr. Robert Toombs, of Georgia, having submitted a series of propositions, which were, in substance, the Breckinridge platform, without waiting a vote or any decisive action thereon, made haste to telegraph to Georgia, for effect upon her approaching election, as follows:

"WASHINGTON, Dec. 23, 1860.

"I came here to secure your constitutional rights, *and* to demonstrate to you that you can get no guarantee for those rights from your Northern confederates.

"The whole subject was referred to a Committee of thirteen in the Senate. I was appointed on the Committee, and accepted the trust. I submitted propositions, which, so far from receiving a decided support from a single member of the Republican party of the Committee, were all treated with derision and contempt.

"A vote was then taken in the Committee on amendments to the Constitution, proposed by Hon. J. J. Crittenden; and each and all of them were voted against, unanimously, by the Black Republican members of the Committee.

"In addition to these facts, a majority of the Black Republican members of the Committee declared distinctly that they had no guarantees to offer; which was silently acquiesced in by the other members.

"The Black Republican members of the Committee are representative men of the party and section, and, to the extent of my information, truly represent them.

"The Committee of thirty-three on Friday adjourned for a week, without coming to any vote, after solemnly pledging themselves to vote on all the propositions then before them, that day. It is controlled by the Black Republicans, your enemies, who only seek to amuse you with delusive hopes until your election, that you may defeat the friends of Secession.

"If you are deceived by them, it shall not be my fault. I have put the test fairly and frankly. It is decisive against you now. I tell you, upon the faith of a true man, that all further looking to the North for security for your constitutional rights, ought to be instantly abandoned.

"It is fraught with nothing but ruin to yourselves and to your posterity. Secession, by the 4th day of March next, should be thundered from the ballot-box by the unanimous voice of Georgia, on the 2d day of January next. Such a voice will be your best guarantee for liberty, tranquillity, and glory. R. TOOMBS."

Though it is neither essential nor practicable here to record all the abortive projects of 'conciliation' submitted to Congress at this fruitlessly fruitful session, that presented by Mr. C. L. Vallandigham, of Ohio, deserves notice, as the fullest and most logical embodiment yet made of Mr. Calhoun's subtile device for enabling a minority to obstruct and baffle the majority under a political system preserving the forms of a republic.

Mr. V., after a preämble, setting forth "the tendency of stronger governments to enlarge their powers and jurisdiction at the expense of weaker," "and of majorities to usurp and abuse power, and oppress minorities;" also affirming that "sectional divisions can no longer be suppressed," etc., etc., proposed[19] that Congress should recommend to the States a radical change of the Federal Constitution, by adding thereto as follows:

"ARTICLE XIII. Sec. 1. The United States are divided into four sections, as follows:

"The States of Maine, New Hampshire, Vermont, Massachusetts, Rhode Island, Connecticut, New York, New Jersey, and Pennsylvania; and all new States annexed and admitted into the Union or formed or erected within the jurisdiction of said States, or by the junction of two or more of the same or of parts thereof, or out of territory acquired north of said States, shall constitute one section, to be known as THE NORTH.

"The States of Ohio, Indiana, Illinois, Michigan, Wisconsin, Minnesota, Iowa, and Kansas, and all new States annexed or admitted into the Union, or erected within the jurisdiction of any of said States, or by the junction of two or more of the same, or of parts thereof, or out of territory now held or hereafter acquired north of latitude 36° 30′ and east of the crest of the Rocky Mountains, shall constitute another section, to be known as THE WEST.

"The States of Oregon and California, and

[19] February 7, 1861.

all new States annexed or admitted into the Union, or formed or erected within the jurisdiction of any of said States, or by the junction of two or more of the same, or of parts thereof, or out of territory now held or hereafter acquired west of the crest of the Rocky Mountains and of the Rio Grande, shall constitute another section, to be known as THE PACIFIC.

"The States of Delaware, Maryland, Virginia, North Carolina, South Carolina, Georgia, Florida, Alabama, Mississippi, Louisiana, Texas, Arkansas, Tennessee, Kentucky, and Missouri, and all new States annexed or admitted into the Union, or formed or erected within the jurisdiction of any of said States, or by the junction of two or more of the same, or of parts thereof, or out of territory acquired east of the Rio Grande and south of latitude 36° 30′, shall constitute another section, to be known as THE SOUTH.

"SEC. 2. On demand of one-third of the Senators of any one of the sections on any bill, order, resolution, or vote, to which the concurrence of the House of Representatives may be necessary, except on a question of adjournment, a vote shall be had by sections; and a majority of the Senators from *each section* shall be necessary to the passage of each bill, order, or resolution, and to the validity of every such vote.

"SEC. 3. Two of the Electors of President and Vice-President shall be appointed by each State, in such manner as the Legislature thereof may direct, for the State at large. The other Electors to which each State may be entitled shall be chosen in the respective Congressional Districts into which the State may, at the regular decennial period, have been divided, by the electors of each District having the qualifications requisite for electors of the most numerous branch of the State Legislature. A majority of all the Electors in *each of the four sections* in this article established, shall be necessary to the choice of President and Vice-President; and the concurrence of a majority of the States of each section shall be necessary to the choice of President by the House of Representatives, and of the Senators from each section to the choice of Vice-President by the Senate, whenever the right of choice shall devolve upon them respectively.

"SEC. 4. The President and Vice-President shall hold their offices each during the term of six years; and neither shall be eligible to more than one term except by the votes of two-thirds of all the Electors of each section, or of the States of each section, whenever the right of choice of President shall devolve upon the House of Representatives; or of the Senators from each section, whenever the right of choice of Vice-President shall devolve upon the Senate.

"SEC. 5. The Congress shall provide by law for the case of a failure by the House of Representatives to choose a President, and of the Senate to choose a Vice-President, whenever the right of choice shall devolve upon them respectively, declaring what officer shall then act as President; and such officer shall then act accordingly until a President shall be elected. The Congress shall also provide by law for a special election for President and Vice-President in such case, to be held and completed within six months of the expiration of the term of office of the last preceding President, and to be conducted in all respects as provided for in the Constitution for regular elections of the same officers; except that, if the House of Representatives shall not choose a President, should the right of choice devolve upon them, within twenty days of the opening of the certificates and counting of the Electoral votes, then the Vice-President shall act as President, as in the case of the death or other constitutional disability of the President. The term of office of the President chosen under such special election shall continue six years from the 4th day of March preceding such election.

"ART. XIV. No State shall secede, without the consent of the Legislatures of all the States of *the section* to which the State proposing to secede belongs. The President shall have power to adjust with seceding States all questions arising by reason of their secession; but the terms of adjustment shall be submitted to the Congress for their approval before the same shall be valid.

"ART. XV. Neither the Congress nor a Territorial Legislature shall have power to interfere with the right of the citizens of any of the States within either of the sections to migrate, upon equal terms with the citizens of the States within either of the other sections, to the territories of the United States; nor shall either have power to destroy or impair any rights of either person or property in the territories. New States annexed for admission into the Union, or formed or erected within the jurisdiction of the other States, or by the junction of two or more States, or parts of States, and States formed with the consent of Congress, out of any territory of the United States, shall be entitled to admission upon an equal footing with the original States, under any Constitution establishing a government republican in form, which the people thereof may ordain, whenever such States shall contain, within an area of not less than thirty thousand square miles, a population equal to the then existing ratio of representation for one member of the House of Representatives."

Dr. Franklin—who failed to perceive the wisdom of dividing a legislature into two 'houses'—once compared said device to that of a Dutchman, who, having a loaded wagon stuck fast in a bog, hitched a span of horses to either end and 'whipped up both ways.' It is not certain that he might not have thus extricated his load—or, at least, overturned it; for even our old Confederation, though a feeble and vicious, was not an impossible frame-work of government. We could not have so rapidly increased in wealth or power under it; yet we need not have permanently held in the scale of nations a lower rank than that of Switzerland or Sweden. But this project of Mr. Vallandigham, if adopted, would have given us a government which no civilized people could have endured through a quarter of a century—a government embodying in an aggravated form all the vices of the old Confederation, with few or none of its virtues—a government requiring a President, yet rendering his election a rare and happy accident—a Congress wherein the passage of a single act of any decided importance would be the event of a decade—a rule hardly to be endured, yet not to be escaped without a revolution. For the chief end of this, as of nearly every kindred contrivance of the session, was the construction of a balance whereby three hundred thousand slaveholders would weigh down twenty millions of freemen, and a section which systematically repels immigration, degrades industry, and discourages improvement, be rendered enduringly equal in power and consideration with one cherishing a policy radically antagonistic to this. Yet this inevitable disparity in growth and strength between the Free and the Slave States was the basis of all Southern discontent with the Union, and to counteract or overbear it the object of every device for the removal of Southern grievances and the redress of Southern wrongs.

The House Committee of Thirty-three encountered the same obstacles, and achieved a like failure, with its counterpart in the Senate. Mr. Albert Rust, of Arkansas, submitted to it[20] a proposition which was substantially identical with Mr. Crittenden's, and which he presented as the ultimatum of the South. It was voted down some days afterward: Yeas 12; Nays 15: no Republican sustaining it. On the 18th, Mr. Henry Winter Davis, of Md., offered the following, which was adopted unanimously:

"*Resolved, by the Senate and House of Representatives*, That the several States be respectfully requested to cause their statutes to be revised, with a view to ascertain if any of them are in conflict with, or tend to embarrass or hinder, the execution of the laws of the United States, made in pursuance of the second section of the IVth Article of the Constitution of the United States, for the delivering up of persons held to labor by the laws of any State and escaping therefrom; and the Senate and House of Representatives earnestly request that all enactments having such tendency be forthwith repealed, as required by a just sense of constitutional obligations, and by a due regard for the peace of the Republic. And the President of the United States is requested to communicate these resolutions to the Governors of the several States, with the request that they will lay the same before the Legislatures thereof respectively."

Mr. Thomas Corwin, of Ohio, from a majority of this Committee, made an elaborate report, on the 14th of January, 1861, favoring concession

[20] December 17th.

and compromise, but *not* the line of 36° 30.' Messrs. C. C. Washburne, of Wisconsin, and Mason W. Tappan, of N. H., tendered a minority report, setting forth that, in view of the Rebellion, now in progress, no concessions should be made. They closed by submitting the resolve which had been offered in the Senate by Mr. Clark, of N. H., and which has already been given.

Messrs. Birch, of California, and Stout, of Oregon, submitted a separate minority report, proposing a Convention of the States to amend the Federal Constitution. This proposal had been voted down by 15 to 14 in the Committee, and it was likewise voted down in the House: Yeas 64; Nays 108.

The Crittenden proposition was moved in the House, as a substitute for Mr. Corwin's, and rejected: Yeas 80; Nays 113.

The conclusions of the Grand Committee, as reported by Mr. Corwin and sustained by the House, were as follows:

"1. *Resolved, by the Senate and House of Representatives of the United States of America in Congress assembled*, That all attempts, on the part of the Legislatures of any of the States, to obstruct or hinder the recovery and surrender of fugitives from labor, are in derogation of the Constitution of the United States, inconsistent with the comity and good neighborhood which should prevail among the several States, and dangerous to the peace of the Union.

2. [Mr. H. Winter Davis's proposition, already given on page 386.]

"3. *Resolved*, That we recognize Slavery as now existing in fifteen of the United States, by the usages or the laws of those States; and we recognize no authority, legally or otherwise, outside of a State where it so exists, to interfere with slaves or Slavery in such States, in disregard of the rights of their owners or the peace of Society.

"4. *Resolved*, That we recognize the justness and propriety of a faithful execution of the Constitution, and laws made in pursuance thereof, on the subject of fugitive slaves, or fugitives from service or labor, and discountenance all mobs, or hindrances to the execution of such laws; and that citizens of each State shall be entitled to all the privileges and immunities of citizens in the several States.

"5. *Resolved*, That we recognize no such conflicting element in its composition, or sufficient cause from any source for a dissolution of this Government; that we are not sent here to destroy, but to sustain and harmonize, the institutions, and to see that equal justice is done to all parts of the same; and, finally, to perpetuate its existence on terms of equality and justice to all the States.

"6. *Resolved*, That the faithful observance, on the part of all the States, of all their constitutional obligations to each other, and to the Federal Government, is essential to the peace of the country.

"7. *Resolved*, That it is the duty of the Federal Government to enforce the Federal laws, protect the Federal property, and preserve the Union of these States.

"8. *Resolved*, That each State is requested to revise its statutes, and, if necessary, so to amend the same as to secure, without legislation by Congress, to citizens of other States traveling therein, the same protection as citizens of such State enjoy; and that she also protect the citizens of other States traveling or sojourning therein against popular violence or illegal summary punishment, without trial, in due form of law, for imputed crimes.

"9. *Resolved*, That each State be also respectfully requested to enact such laws as will prevent and punish any attempt whatever in such State to recognize or set on foot the lawless invasion of any other State or territory.

"10. *Resolved*, That the President be requested to transmit copies of the foregoing resolutions to the Governors of the several States, with a request that they be communicated to their respective Legislatures."

The Speaker decided Mr. Corwin's report an indivisible proposition, and the House, after refusing to lay it on the table, finally passed it by the decisive majority of 83: Yeas 136; Nays 53: the proportion of Republicans to anti-Republicans being about the same in the Yeas as in the Nays.

Mr. Corwin further reported a joint resolution proposing an amendment to the Constitution, whereby any future amendment giving Congress power over Slavery in the States is forbidden; which was defeated, not receiving the requisite two-thirds—Yeas 123; Nays 71. It was reconsidered, however, on motion of Mr. Daniel Kilgore, of Indiana, seconded by[21] Mr. Benjamin Stanton, of Ohio; adopted: Yeas 133; Nays 65: and the Senate concurred: Yeas 24; Nays 12.

This closed the efforts in Congress to disarm the sternly purposed Rebellion, by yielding without bloodshed a substantial triumph to the Rebels.

At this session, after the withdrawal of Southern members in such numbers as to give the Republicans a large majority in the House and a practical control of the Senate, three separate acts were passed, organizing the Territories of Colorado, Nevada, and Dakotah respectively—the three together covering a very large proportion of all the remaining territory of the United States. All these acts were silent with regard to Slavery; leaving whatever rights had accrued to 'the South' under the Constitution, as interpreted and affirmed by the Supreme Court in the Dred Scott decision, not merely unimpaired, but unassailed and unquestioned, by any Federal legislation or action. The passage of these acts in this form was certainly intended to soothe the prevalent madness, and to strengthen the Unionists of the South, especially of the Border States; though it does not seem to have had any such effect. And, indeed, it is not probable that *any* concession could have been made, after the withdrawal of Toombs, Davis, etc., from Washington, that would not have evoked the stern answer—'Too late!'

XXV.

PEACE DEMOCRACY—PEACE CONFERENCE.

On the 31st of January, 1861, a Democratic State Convention, called to consider the impending peril of Disunion, assembled at Tweddle Hall, Albany. It was probably the strongest and most imposing assemblage of delegates ever convened within the State. Not less than thirty of them had been chosen to seats in Congress, while three[1] of them had been Democratic candidates for Governor; one of them once elected, and since chosen again. Though called as 'Democratic,' there was a large and most respectable representation of the old Whig party, with a number who had figured as 'Americans.' No Convention which had nominations to make, or patronage to dispose of, was ever so influentially constituted. All sympathizing State officers and members of the Legislature were formally invited to participate in its deliberations. Sanford E. Church, of Albion, was temporary Chairman, and Judge Amasa J. Parker, of Albany, Presi-

[21] February 28, 1861.

[1] Horatio Seymour, Amasa J. Parker, and William Kelly.

dent. On taking the Chair, Judge Parker said:

"This Convention has been called with no view to mere party objects. It looks only to the great interests of State. We meet here as conservative and representative men who have differed among themselves as to measures of governmental policy, ready, all of them, I trust, to sacrifice such differences upon the altar of our common country. He can be no true patriot who is not ready to yield his own prejudices, to surrender a favorite theory, and to clip even from his own party platform, where such omission may save his country from ruin otherwise inevitable. [Loud cheers.]

"The people of this State demand the peaceful settlement of the questions that have led to disunion. They have a right to insist that there shall be conciliation, concession, compromise. While yet the pillars of our political temple lie scattered on the ground, let them be used to reconstruct the edifice. The popular sentiment is daily gathering strength, and will overwhelm in its progress alike those who seek to stem it on the frail plank of party platforms and those who labor to pervert it to mere party advantage. [Cheers.]"

The venerable Alex. B. Johnson, of Utica, followed, in an address which lauded the good understanding which had always existed between the Democratic party and the South; which he attributed to a mutual dread of the undue extension and aggrandizement of Federal power. He said:

"To a superficial observer, our difficulties consist of revolutionary movements in the Southern States; but these movements are only symptoms of a disorder, not the disorder itself; and, before we can treat the disorder understandingly, with a view to its remedy, we must understand its cause; and we shall find it in the avowed principles on which the late presidential election was conducted to its final triumph—principles inculcating sectional hate in place of federal kindness; in direct contravention with the dying injunctions of the Father of his Country, and of the most eminent of his successors in the presidency, General Jackson."

He proceeded to blame the Republicans, "whose principles and conduct have produced the mischief," for refusing to give 'the South' such guarantees of her rights as are required; adding:

"What the guarantees should be is in vain for us to prescribe, having no power to either inaugurate them or to conduct them to a successful consummation; but, speaking for the Democratic party of this State, and of, we believe, the whole Union, and, indeed, for a vast body of citizens not identified with any party, we feel safe in saying that no guarantee will be unwelcome that shall give the South, and all its property, the same rights that are or shall be possessed by the North and its property: the same rights which the South possessed at the commencement of the confederacy: Slavery being at that time no object of antagonism, but the common institution of all the States but one; and we will accord this equality the more readily, by reason that any settlement which shall continue any inequality between the North and the South will be prejudicial to the permanency of the settlement, and hence should not be offered by the North, even if the South, from a love of the Union, should be willing to remain therein with less than an equality of its advantages."

He considered the prescribed modes of amending the Constitution, and then continued:

"Possibly, all remedies may be withheld till the seceded States shall have become confederated together and refuse to return. In the possibility of this unhappy determination, and which the present aspect of parties compels us to consider, we are certain that the will of a large portion of the citizens of this State is against any armed coërcion, on the part of the General or State governments, to restore the Union by civil war; and, in this connection, we have seen with disapprobation the haste evinced by our Legislature to imbrue their hands in fraternal blood, and the pernicious zeal which, without even the apology of any legislative direction, induced the transmission of this aggressive intention to the governors of not only the seceded States, but of the Border States, who, at the time, were struggling to restrain their citizens from secession, and thus revealing to us, that, unless our Northern people interfere, the mistaken sectionalism, which has produced our present misfortunes, is not to be corrected by any evidence of its destructiveness, but is to be continued by partisans, till the South is either subjugated or destroyed. The advocates of this horrid violence against the doctrines of our Declaration of Independence, and which, if successful in its object, would constitute a more radical revolution in our form of government than even secession, certainly mistake not only the age in which we live, but the people whom they represent, and who sympathize in no desire to take a bloody revenge on those who think they can live more peacefully and prosperously alone, than in a Union with those who have, for years, irritated them almost to madness, by denouncing them as a reproach and a disgrace."

Mr. Johnson concluded in these words:

"But we are asked, rather triumphantly, 'Have we a government?' The question is intended to imply, that the government must be strong enough for self-preservation, whatever may become a necessary means. The answer is, that the government is as strong as its founders could agree to make it. Its weakness in emergencies like the present was foreseen by the men that framed the Constitution; but they soon perceived that they must take the Constitution as it now stands, or no confederation could be formed. If, therefore, we now attempt to strengthen the government by coërcive action, which all men know its founders would have rejected with scorn, *we* are the revolutionists, and not the South; so jealous, indeed, were the States of Federal interference, that its protection of them against domestic violence was prohibited, till the disturbed State applied for protection by its legislature, or by its chief executive when the legislature could not be convened. If, then, the States would not accept protection from the general government till it was demanded, how much less would they have accepted coërcion against their own actions! The government was strong enough while cemented by mutual good fellowship; but no government, and ours the least of all, is sufficiently strong to resist incessant aggravations. Finally, if Congress and our States cannot, or will not, win back our Southern brethren, let us, at least, part as friends; and then possibly, if experience shall, as we suppose it will, show the departed States that, in leaving the Union, they have only deserted a happy home, they may be willing to sue us to readmit them; or, if they shall find a permanent separation more desirable than Union, we may still exist together as useful and profitable neighbors, assisting each other when either is threatened by injustice from the nations of Europe; and the two sections, instead of wasting their time and energies in quarreling with each other about Slavery, will at least have more time to severally employ all their energies in seeking their own prosperity in their own way."

Gov. Horatio Seymour followed, berating the Republicans generally, but especially those in Congress, as the responsible authors of the perils now darkening the National sky. Referring to the refusal of the Republicans in Congress to coöperate in the legalization of Slavery in the territories, he asked:

"What spectacle do we present to-day? Already six States have withdrawn from this confederacy. Revolution has actually begun. The term 'secession' divests it of none of its terrors, nor do arguments to prove secession inconsistent with our Constitution stay its progress, or mitigate its evils. All virtue, patriotism, and intelligence, seem to have fled from our National Capitol; it has been well likened to the conflagration of an asylum for madmen—some look on with idiotic imbecility; some in sullen silence; and some scatter the firebrands which consume the fabric above them, and bring upon all a common destruction. Is there one revolting aspect in this scene which has not its parallel at the Capitol of your country? Do you not see there the senseless imbecility, the garrulous idiocy, the maddened rage, displayed with regard to petty personal passions and party purposes, while the glory, the honor, and the safety of the country are all forgotten? The same pervading fanaticism has brought evil upon all the institutions of our land. Our churches are torn asunder and desecrated to partisan purposes. The wrongs of our local legislation, the growing burdens of debt and taxation, the gradual destruction of the African in the Free States, which is marked by each recurring census, are all due to the neglect of our own duties, caused by the complete absorption of the public mind by a senseless, unreasoning fanaticism. The agitation of the question of Slavery has thus far brought greater social, moral, and legislative evils upon the people of the free States than it has upon the institutions of those against whom it has been excited. The wisdom of Franklin stamped upon the first coin issued by our government, the wise motto, 'Mind your business!' The violation of this homely proverb, which lies at the foundation of the doctrines of local rights, has, thus far, proved more hurtful to the meddlers in the affairs of others than to those against whom this pragmatic action is directed."

Gov. Seymour proceeded to argue that the North had, thus far, had greatly the advantage in the division or disposition of the Federal territories—that the claims put forth on behalf of the South were just and reasonable—that the difference ought to be settled by compromise—that we have no alternative but compromise or civil war—adding:

"We are advised by the conservative States of Virginia and Kentucky that, if force is to be used, it must be exerted against the united South. It would be an act of folly and madness, in entering upon this contest, to underrate our opponents, and thus subject ourselves to the disgrace of defeat in an inglorious warfare. Let us also see if successful coërcion by the North is less revolutionary than successful secession by the South. Shall we prevent revolution by being foremost in overthrowing the principles of our government, and all that makes it valuable to our people, and distinguishes it among the nations of the earth?"

Gov. Seymour proceeded to dilate on the valor and sagacity of the men of the South—the extent of their coast-line, rendering its effectual blockade nearly impossible—the ruin of our own industry which must result from civil war—and to urge afresh the necessity of compromise; saying:

"The question is simply this—'Shall we have compromise *after* war, or compromise *without* war?'"

He urged that a compromise was required, not to pacify the States which have seceded from the Union, but to save the Border States from following, by strengthening the hands of their Unionists.

There is no point whereon men are apt to evince more generosity than in the sacrifice of other men's convictions. What *they* may consider vital principles, but which *we* regard as besotted prejudices or hypocritical pretenses, we are always willing to subordinate to any end which we consider beneficent. In fact, a frank, ingenuous confession of the errors and sins of his adversaries is one of the politician's commonest exhibitions of sincerity and patriotism. Thus Gov. Seymour continues:

"Let us take care that *we* do not mistake passion and prejudice and partisan purposes for principle. The cry of 'no compromise' is false in morals; it is treason to the spirit of the Constitution; it is infidelity in religion: the cross itself is a compromise, and is pleaded by many who refuse all charity to their fellow-citizens. It is the vital principle of social existence; it unites the family circle; it sustains the church, and upholds nationalities.

"But the Republicans complain that, having won a victory, we ask them to surrender its fruits. We do not wish them to give up any political advantage. We urge measures which are demanded by the honor and the safety of our Union. Can it be that they are less concerned than we are? Will they admit that they have interests antagonistic to those of the whole commonwealth? Are they making sacrifices, when they do that which is required by the common welfare?"

Had New England and some other of the Fremont States revolted, or threatened to revolt, after the election of 1856, proclaiming that they would never recognize nor obey Mr. Buchanan as President, unless ample guarantees were accorded them that Kansas should thenceforth be regarded and treated as a Free Territory or State, would any prominent Democrat have thus insisted that this demand should be complied with? Would he have urged that the question of Freedom or Slavery in Kansas should be submitted to a direct popular vote, as the only means of averting civil war? Yet Gov. Seymour demanded the submission of the Crittenden Compromise to such a vote, under circumstances wherein (as Gov. Seward had so forcibly stated) "the argument of fear" was the only one relied on, and Republicans were to be coërced into voting for that Compromise, or staying away from the polls; not that their convictions had changed one iota, but because they could only thus avert the unutterable woes and horrors of a gigantic and desperate civil war.

Mr. James S. Thayer (a Whig of other days) followed in a speech which urged the call, by the Legislature, of a constitutional State Convention, to march abreast with similar Conventions in the Border Slave States, in quest of "some plan of adjustment on this great question of difference between the North and the South." He continued:

"If we cannot, we can at least, in an authoritative way and a practical manner, arrive at the basis of a peaceable separation [renewed cheers]; we can at least by discussion enlighten, settle, and concentrate the public sentiment in the State of New York upon this question, and save it from that fearful current, that circuitously, but certainly, sweeps madly on, through the narrow gorge of 'the enforcement of the laws,' to the shoreless ocean of civil war. [Cheers.] Against this, under all circumstances, in every place and form, we must now and at all times oppose a resolute and unfaltering resistance. The public mind will bear the avowal, and let us make it—that if a revolution of force is to begin, *it shall be inaugurated at home.* [Cheers.] And if the incoming Administration shall attempt to carry out the line of policy that has been foreshadowed, we announce that, when the hand of Black Republicanism turns to blood-red, and seeks from the fragment of the Constitution to construct a scaffolding for coërcion—another name for execution—we will reverse the order of the French Revolution, and save the blood of the people by making those who would inaugurate a reign of terror the first victims of a national guillotine.[2] [Enthusiastic applause.]"

Mr. Thayer proceeded to argue that Southern Secession, under the circumstances, was justified by urgent considerations of necessity and safety. He said:

"The Democratic and Union party at the North made the issue at the last election with the Republican party that, in the event of their success, and the establishment of their policy, the Southern States not only would go out of the Union, but would have adequate cause for doing so. [Applause.] Who of us believed that, with the government in the hands of a party whose avowed policy was no more slave States, no further extension of Slavery, and asserting the power and duty of Congress to prohibit it in all the territories, that the Southern States *would* remain in the Union? It seems to me, thus encompassed and menaced, they could not, with safety to their largest interest, and any prudent consideration for their future condition and welfare, continue in the confederacy. What would become, in twenty-five years, of 8,000,000 of white people and 4,000,000 of slaves, with their natural increase, walled in by Congressional prohibition, besieged and threatened by a party holding the seats of Federal power and patronage, that, according to the doctrine of the President elect, must 'arrest the further spread of Slavery,' and place the institution itself 'where the public mind will rest satis-

[2] *The Bangor* (Maine) *Union* of about this date (copied approvingly into *The Cincinnati Enquirer* of February 8th), said:

"The difficulties between the North and the South must be compromised, or the separation of the States SHALL BE PEACEABLE. If the Republican party refuse to go the full length of the Crittenden Amendment—which is the very least the South can or ought to take—then, here in Maine, not a Democrat will be found who will raise an arm against his brethren of the South. From one end of the State to the other, let the cry of the Democracy be, COMPROMISE OR PEACEABLE SEPARATION."

The Detroit Free Press of February 3d or 4th (copied into *The Cincinnati Enquirer* of February 6th), more boldly and frankly said:

"We can tell the Republican Legislature, and the Republican Administration of Michigan, and the Republican party everywhere, one thing: that, if the refusal to repeal the Personal Liberty laws shall be persisted in, and if there shall not be a change in the present seeming purpose to yield to no accommodation of the National difficulties, and if troops shall be raised in the North to march against the people of the South, *a fire in the rear will be opened upon such troops, which will either stop their march altogether, or wonderfully accelerate it.*

"In other words, if, in the present posture of the Republican party toward the National difficulties, war shall be waged, *that war will be fought in the North.* We warn it that the conflict, which it is precipitating, will not be with the South, *but with tens of thousands of people in the North.* When civil war shall come, it will be here in Michigan, and here in Detroit, and in every Northern State."

fied in the belief that it is in the course of ultimate extinction?'

"This is the position I took, with 313,000 voters in the State of New York, on the 6th of November last. I shall not recede from it; having admitted that, in a certain contingency, the Slave States would have just and adequate causes for a separation. Now that the contingency has happened, I shall not withdraw that admission, because they have been unwise or unreasonable in the 'time, mode, and measure of redress.' [Applause.]

"Aside from particular acts that do not admit of any justification, those who imagine that the Southern States do not well know what they are about, forget that they have been for fifteen years looking at this thing with all its importance to their largest interest, as well as to their safety, and mistake the deep and deliberate movement of a revolution for the mere accidents and incidents which always accompany it. [Applause.] There are some Democrats and Union men who, when the fever for a fight has subsided, will wake up and wonder that they mistook the madness of passion for the glow of patriotism. Again: we should consider that, whatever may be our construction of the Constitution under which we live, as to any right under it for one or more States to go out of the Union, when six States, by the deliberate, formal, authoritative action of their people, dissolve their connection with the government, and nine others say that that dissolution shall be final if the seceding members so choose, announcing to the North, 'No interference; we stand between you and them.' Can you bring them back? No! Enforcement of the laws in six States is a war with fifteen. And, after all, to speak plainly on this subject, and reveal the true secret of the utter repugnance of the people to resort to any coërcive measures, it is within their plain judgment and practical common sense, that the very moment you go outside the narrow circle of the written letter and provisions of the Constitution of the United States, you are confronted with the great world of facts, and find this is not a consolidated government; not a government of the whole people in the sense and meaning now attached to it. [Applause.]"

Mr. Thayer proceeded to speak of "coërcion" in terms which go far to elucidate the outcry since made against alleged usurpations and disregard of personal rights in dealing with partisans of the Rebellion. Said he:

"It is announced that the Republican Administration will enforce the laws against and in all the seceding States. A nice discrimination must be exercised in the performance of this duty: not a hair's breadth outside the mark. You remember the story of William Tell, who, when the condition was imposed upon him to shoot an apple from the head of his own child, after he had performed the task, he let fall an arrow. 'For what is that?' said Gesler. 'To kill thee, tyrant, had I slain my boy!' [Cheers.] Let one arrow winged by the Federal bow strike the heart of an American citizen, and who can number the avenging darts that will cloud the heavens in the conflict that will ensue? [Prolonged applause.] What, then, is the duty of the State of New York? What shall we say to our people when we come to meet this state of facts? That the Union must be preserved. But if that cannot be, what then? *Peaceable separation.* [Applause.] Painful and humiliating as it is, let us temper it with all we can of love and kindness, so that we may yet be left in a comparatively prosperous condition, in friendly relations with another Confederacy. [Cheers.]"

The Committee on Resolutions having reported, the venerable ex-Chancellor, Reuben H. Walworth, appeared on the platform in support of the second, which earnestly deprecated civil war; saying:

"Civil War will not restore the Union, but will defeat, forever, its reconstruction."

Said the ex-Chancellor:

"It would be as brutal, in my opinion, to send men to butcher our own brothers of the Southern States, as it would be to massacre them in the Northern States. We are told, however, that it is our duty to, and we must, enforce the laws. But why—and what laws are to be enforced? There were laws that were to be enforced in the time of the American Revolution, and the British Parliament and Lord North sent armies here to enforce them.

"But what did Washington say in regard to the enforcement of those laws? That man—honored at home and abroad more than any other man on earth ever was honored—did he go for enforcing the laws? No, he went to resist laws that were oppressive against a free people, and against the injustice of which they rebelled. [Loud cheers.]

"Did Lord Chatham go for enforcing the laws? No, he gloried in defence of the liberties of America. He made that memorable declaration in the British Parliament, 'If I was an American citizen instead of being as I am, an Englishman, I never would submit to such laws—never, never, never!' [Prolonged applause.]"

A single voice was raised in dissent from these inculcations. A Mr. Elseffer having proposed to amend one of the reported resolutions by an assertion that, if the Federal Government should undertake to "use force," "under the specious and untenable pretense of enforcing the laws," it would "plunge the nation into civil war," and been warmly supported therein by Mr. Thayer and others, Hon. Geo. W. Clinton,[3] of Buffalo, rose in opposition, and said:

"We all agree in detesting the very thought of war. [Applause.] But is our country gone? Is the Union dissolved? Is there no government binding these States in peace and harmony! Why, the proposition was before you, ten minutes ago, that this Union was dissolved, and you voted it down. God grant it may for ever continue! [Applause.] Oh! let us conciliate our erring brethren who, under a strange delusion, have, as they say, seceded from us; but, for God's sake, do not let us humble the glorious government under which we have been so happy!—which has done, and, if we will by judicious means sustain it, will yet do, so much for the happiness of mankind. [Applause.]

"Gentlemen: I hate to use a word that would offend my Southern brother, erring as he does; but we have reached a time when, as a man—if you please, as a Democrat—I must use plain terms. There is no such thing as legal secession. There is no such thing, I say, unless it is a secession which is authorized by the original compact,—and the Constitution of these United States was intended to form a firm and perpetual Union. [Cheers.] There is no warrant for it in the Constitution. Where, then, do you find the warrant for it? It is in the unhappy delusion of our Southern brethren, who doubt our love for them and our attachment to the Constitution. Let us remove that illusion. We will try to do it. But if secession be not lawful, oh! what is it! I use the term reluctantly but truly—it is rebellion! [Cries of 'No! No! revolution.'] It is rebellion! rebellion against the noblest government that man ever framed for his own benefit and for the benefit of the world."

"[A Voice: We are all rebels, then.]"

"Judge Clinton: May be so, sir. Gentlemen, this secession doctrine is not a new thing. The people have passed upon it. They passed upon it in the last war. You may do what you please, my friend; but I never, never can be prevailed upon to see, by any process of reasoning, by any impulse of feeling, that the Hartford Convention was not what the people of the Union pronounced it—a damnable treason. [Applause.] What is it—this secession? I am not speaking of the men. I love the men, but I hate treason. What is it, but the nullification of all the rights of the United States, and the execution of the laws! A threat to reject them, in arms! It is nullification by the wholesale. I, for one, have venerated Andrew Jackson, and my blood boiled, in old time, when that brave patriot and soldier of Democracy said—'The Union—it must and shall be preserved!' [Loud applause.] Preserve it! Preserve it! Why should we preserve it, if it would be the thing that these gentlemen would make it—that this amendment would make it! Why should we love a government that has no dignity and no power? [Applause.] Admit the doctrine, and what have you? A government that no man who is a freeman ought to be content for one day to live under. Admit it, and any State, of its own sovereign will, may retire from the Union! Look at it for a moment. Congress, for just cause,—for free trade or sailor's rights—declares war. Oh! where is your government! Why should it! What right has it to declare war! The Constitution invested that power in it, but one State says, 'War is not for me—I secede.' And so another and another, and the government is rendered powerless. * * *

"I understand this amendment to have this point, and no other. It is perfectly nugatory and useless, unless it has this point, because all the other points for which it can provide are already provided for in the resolution. It is this: You shall use no force to protect the property of the United States, to retain it in your possession, or to collect your revenue for the common benefit, and the payment of the common debt. Now, I am willing to say, that the government is false to itself, false to us, and false to all, if it should use more than necessary force for these purposes; but I am not prepared to humble the general government at the feet of the seceding States. [Applause.] I am unwilling to say to the government, 'You must abandon your property—you must

[3] Son of the illustrious De Witt Clinton.

cease to collect the revenues, because you are threatened!'

"In other words, gentlemen, it seems to me—and I know I speak the wishes of my constituents,—that, while I abhor coërcion, in one sense, as war, I wish to preserve the dignity of the government of these United States as well. [Applause.]"

Mr. Elseffer's amendment was thereupon withdrawn, and the original resolutions unanimously adopted.

They are eight in number; whereof the first affirms that "the crisis into which the country has been thrown" has been produced by "the conflict of sectional passions;" and that the calamities now imminent of civil war can only be averted by concessions. The second condemns a resort to civil war, on the part of the Federal Government, asserting that "civil war will not restore the Union, but will defeat, for ever, its reconstruction." The third calls for conciliation, concession, and compromise, declaring that "it would be monstrous to refuse them." The fourth declares that it is eminently fit that we should listen to the appeals of loyal men in the Border States. The fifth approves of the Crittenden proposition, and urges that it be submitted by the Legislature to a vote of the electors of this State. The sixth urges upon Congress "adequate measures of conciliation," and requests the Legislature to take steps toward the summoning of a Convention of the States. The seventh urges a compliance with the request of the Legislature of Virginia for a meeting of Commissioners at Washington, and asks the Legislature of New York to appoint Commissioners thereto; and, in case of its failure, names seven eminent citizens—not one of them a Republican—as such Commissioners. The eighth implores "the States in the attitude of secession to stay the sword and save the nation from civil war," so as to give time for perfecting a compromise; appealing also to the non-seceded Southern States to act in a similar spirit. Committees were appointed to present these resolutions to Congress and to the State Legislature, as also to correspond with other States; and then the Convention adjourned, after empowering its President to reconvene it in his discretion.

The action of this Convention was of great moment under two distinct aspects; first, as indicating truly and clearly the light in which the Secession movement was regarded by the 'conservative' politicians of the North;[4] secondly, as revealing to the

[4] *The Albany Argus*, for example, of November 10, 1860—four days after the election of Mr. Lincoln—thus clearly and temperately expressed the view generally taken of the Secession movement by the Democratic journals of the Free States:

"We are not at all surprised at the manifestations of feeling at the South. We expected and predicted it; and for so doing were charged by the Republican press with favoring disunion; while, in fact, we simply correctly appreciated the feeling of that section of the Union. We sympathize with and justify the South, as far as this—their rights have been invaded to the extreme limit possible within the forms of the Constitution, and, beyond this limit, their feelings have been insulted and their interests and honor assailed by almost every possible form of denunciation and invective; and, if we deemed it certain that the real *animus* of the Republican party could be carried into the administration of the Federal Government, and become the permanent policy of the nation, we should think that all the instincts of self-preservation and of manhood rightfully impelled them to a resort to revolution and a separation from the Union, and we would applaud them and wish them God speed in the adoption of such a remedy."

In the same spirit, *The Rochester Union*, two or three days later, argued that the threatened secession of the Slave States was but a counterpoise of the Personal Liberty bills and other

South the probable action of those 'conservatives,' should the Union be constrained to defend itself by force against a slaveholding effort for its disintegration and overthrow. And, whatever may have been the intent of those assembled, it is certain that the sentiments expressed by Messrs. Parker, A. B. Johnson, Seymour, Thayer, etc., and the approving response which they elicited, were hailed by the engineers of Secession as proof positive that they would either not be forcibly opposed at all, or would have no difficulty in overcoming, by the help of their sympathizing friends and allies in the Free States, any resistance to their purpose that might be offered.[5] Mr. Roscoe Conkling attests that, when the proceedings of this Convention reached Washington, they were hailed with undisguised exultation by the Secessionists still lingering in the halls of Congress; one of whom said to him triumphantly, "If your President should attempt coërcion, he will have more opposition *at the North* than he can overcome."[6]

The "Peace Conference," or Congress, so called, was assembled on the unanimous invitation of the Legisla-

measures of antagonism to slaveholding at the North. Said *The Union:*

"Restricting our remarks to actual violations of the Constitution, the North have led the way, and for a long period have been *the sole offenders* or aggressors. For many years, laws have been on the statute-books of Northern States, which were passed with the avowed object of preventing the 'delivering up' of fugitive slaves, which the Constitution says, '*shall be* delivered up.' Owing to their different circumstances, *Northern* States have been enabled to secure their cherished object by violating the Constitution in a way that does not necessitate secession from, or a dissolution of, the Union. Owing to *their* peculiar circumstances, the *Southern* States cannot retaliate upon the North without taking ground for secession from or a dissolution of the Union. But, in resorting to this mode and measure of redress, they simply followed the example set by Northern States in *violating the Constitution to such an extent as they deem necessary to secure their objects.* The Northern States stopped at one given point in their career of nullification, because they had no object to gain by going further. The Southern States propose to stop at another given point, which, in their judgment, is indicated by the necessities of their position."

[5] *The Albany Argus* of Nov. 12, 1860, said:

"Should secession from the Union be actually attempted by South Carolina alone, or in connection with other States, it will be a most important question for the present and next Administration, how it shall be treated. Shall it be met by force? Shall the military power of the Government be employed to retain seceding States within the Union, and compel them to yield obedience to the requirements of the Constitution? Waiving, in what we now have to say, all question about the *right* of secession, we believe that, as a matter of practical administration, neither Mr. Buchanan nor Mr. Lincoln will employ force against the seceding States. If South Carolina, or any other State, through a convention of her people, shall formally separate herself from the Union, probably both the present and the next Executive will simply let her alone, and quietly allow all the functions of the Federal Government within her limits to be suspended. *Any other course would be madness;* as it would at once enlist all the Southern States in the controversy, and plunge the whole country into a civil war. The first gun fired in the way of forcing a seceding State back to her allegiance to the Union, would probably prove the knell of its final dismemberment. As a matter of policy and wisdom, therefore, independent of the question of right, we should deem resort to force most disastrous."

[6] *The New York Herald* of November 9th—the third day after that of the Presidential election—in its leading editorial, had said:

"For far less than this [the election of Lincoln], our fathers seceded from Great Britain; and *they left revolution organized in every State, to act whenever it is demanded by public opinion.* The confederation is held together only by public opinion. Each State is organized as a complete government, holding the purse and wielding the sword, *possessing the right to break the tie of the confederation as a nation might break a treaty, and to repel coërcion as a nation might repel invasion.* * * * Coërcion, if it were possible, is out of the question."

The Charleston Courier of November, 1860, announced the formation of Military organizations in various parts of the North in defense of 'Southern rights.' Allentown, Pa., was specified as one of the points at which such forces were mustering and drilling.

ture of Virginia,[7] and convened[8] in Washington one month prior to Mr. Lincoln's inauguration. Thirteen Free States were represented, viz.: Maine, New Hampshire, Vermont, Massachusetts, Rhode Island, Connecticut, New York, New Jersey, Pennsylvania, Ohio, Indiana, Illinois, and Iowa; and seven Slave States, viz.: Delaware, Maryland, Virginia, North Carolina, Kentucky, Tennessee, and Missouri. Ex-President John Tyler, of Virginia, was called to the Chair. On motion of Mr. James Guthrie, of Kentucky, it was[9]

"*Resolved*, That a Committee of one from each State be appointed by the Commissioners thereof, to be nominated to the President, and to be appointed by him, to whom shall be referred the resolutions of the State of Virginia, and the other States represented, and all propositions for the adjustment of existing difficulties between States; with authority to report what they may deem right, necessary, and proper, to restore harmony and preserve the Union; and that they report on or before Friday."

This Committee was composed as follows:

Maine, Lot M. Morrill; *New Hampshire*, Asa Fowler; *Vermont*, Hiland Hall; *Massachusetts*, Francis B. Crowninshield; *Rhode Island*, Samuel Ames; *Connecticut*, Roger S. Baldwin; *New York*, David Dudley Field; *New Jersey*, Peter D. Vroom; *Pennsylvania*, Thomas White; *Ohio*, Thomas Ewing; *Indiana*, Charles B. Smith; *Illinois*, Stephen F. Logan; *Iowa*, James Harlan; *Delaware*, Daniel M. Bates; *North Carolina*, Thomas Ruffin; *Virginia*, James A. Seddon; *Kentucky*, James Guthrie; *Maryland*, Reverdy Johnson; *Tennessee*, F. K. Zollicoffer; *Missouri*, A. W. Doniphan.

Mr. Guthrie, from the majority of said Committee, on the 15th, made a report, recommending several amendments to be ingrafted on the Federal Constitution; which amendments, as perfected and voted on by the Conference, will hereafter be given.

Gov. Roger S. Baldwin [Republican], of Connecticut, made a dissenting report; recommending that, instead of the aforesaid amendments, this body adopt and recommend the suggestion of the Legislature of Kentucky—that of a General Convention of the States. [His proposition will be given in full, in connection with its disposal by the Conference.]

Mr. James A. Seddon, of Virginia, made another minority report, wherein he affirms that the majority report would not be acceptable to Virginia,

[7] Adopted January 19, 1861.

So early as Nov. 30, 1860, Gov. John Letcher, of Virginia, who, as a Douglas Democrat and former anti-Slavery man, was regarded as among the most moderate of Southern politicians, in answer to a Union letter from Rev. Lewis P. Clover, a Democrat of Springfield, Ill., had said:

"I now consider the overthrow of the Union absolutely certain. South Carolina will secede; and the chain, once broken, is not very likely to be reünited. * * * Unless something shall be *speedily* done to quiet the apprehensions of the South, the Union is gone beyond all hope."

Mr. Clover replied, stating that he had shown Gov. L.'s letter to Mr. Lincoln (who asked Mr. C., whether it was just to hold *him* responsible for the Personal Liberty bills, etc., which he had never favored), and trusting that the President elect would "be found a friend to the South." Gov. Letcher responded (Dec. 25, 1860), saying:

"I regard the government as now doomed, beyond a contingency, to destruction. * * * I have lost all hope, as I see no disposition in the free States to adjust the controversy. We have just heard from Washington that the Republicans have presented their ultimatum; and I say to you, in sincerity and sorrow, that it will never be assented to. I believe ninety-nine men out of every hundred in Virginia will repudiate it with scorn. Conservative as I am, and laboring as I have been for months to secure an adjustment, before I will assent to that proposition, I will welcome civil war with all its horrors. It would be dishonorable in the South to accept it; and my motto is, 'Death before dishonor.'"

Such were the *Southern Unionists* whom the Republicans were expected to conciliate, and stigmatized as repelling.

[8] February 4th. [9] On the 6th.

because it gave less to the South than even the Crittenden Compromise; whereas, Virginia required the whole of that, and something *more*. He proposed sundry amendments to the Federal Constitution, in addition to the guarantee to Slavery, forever, of all territory south of 36° 30′; one of which secures to every slaveholder the right to take his slave through any non-slaveholding State or territory, in passing from one slaveholding State or territory to another; and also secures to him protection for his slaves as property, while at sea on such a journey. Another is in these words:

"ARTICLE 7. Sec. 1. The elective franchise and the right to hold office, whether Federal, State, territorial, or municipal, shall not be exercised by persons who are, in whole or in part, of the African race."

Another of these amendments presumes, and recognizes, the right of peaceable State secession, undertaking to guard against its abuses.

Mr. Charles A. Wickliffe, of Kentucky, proposed that this Convention request the several States which have passed Personal Liberty bills, to abrogate them; also, that they allow slaves to be carried across their soil respectively.

Mr. Amos Tuck [Republican], of New Hampshire, submitted an Address to the People of the United States, "deploring the divisions and distractions that now afflict our country," but deprecating secession or violence, and insisting that "the Constitution of the United States, properly understood and fairly enforced, is equal to every exigency." Mr. Tuck's address closed with three resolutions; which will be given hereafter.

Gov. S. P. Chase, of Ohio, proposed that this Convention adjourn to the 4th of April, to enable other States to be represented therein: but this was not agreed to.

After several days' discussion and consideration, with votes upon various amendments, Mr. David Dudley Field, of New York, moved to amend the Committee's report, by striking out § 7, and inserting as follows:

"ARTICLE 1. No State shall withdraw from the Union without the consent of all the States, given in a Convention of the States, convened in pursuance of an act passed by two-thirds of each House of Congress."

This proposition was rejected,[10] as follows:

AYS—Connecticut, Illinois, Indiana, Iowa, Maine, Massachusetts, New York, New Hampshire, Vermont, Kansas—10.

NOES—Delaware, Kentucky, Maryland, Missouri, New Jersey, North Carolina, Ohio, Pennsylvania, Rhode Island, Tennessee, Virginia—11.

Mr. Guthrie's report at length coming up for action thereon, Gov. Baldwin moved a substitution for said report of his proposition aforesaid; which was in the following words:

"*Whereas*, unhappy differences exist which have alienated from each other portions of the people of the United States to such an extent as seriously to disturb the peace of the nation, and impair the regular and efficient action of the Government within the sphere of its constitutional powers and duties:

"*And whereas*, the Legislature of the State of Kentucky has made application to Congress to call a Convention for proposing amendments to the Constitution of the United States:

"*And whereas*, it is believed to be the opinion of the people of other States that amendments to the Constitution are or may become necessary to secure to the people of the United States, of every section, the full and equal enjoyment of their rights and liberties, so far as the same may depend for their security and protection on the powers granted to or withheld from the General Government, in pursuance of the national purposes for which it was ordained and established:

"*And whereas*, it may be expedient that such amendments as any of the States may

[10] February 26, 1861.

desire to have proposed, should be presented to the Convention in such form as the respective States desiring the same may deem proper:

"This convention does, therefore, recommend to the several States to unite with Kentucky in her application to Congress to call a Convention for proposing amendments to the Constitution of the United States, to be submitted to the Legislatures of the several States, or to conventions therein, for ratification, as the one or the other mode of ratification may be proposed by Congress, in accordance with the provision in the fifth article of the Constitution:"

which was defeated by the following vote:

AYS—Connecticut, Illinois, Iowa, Maine, Massachusetts, New York, New Hampshire, Vermont—8.

NOES—Delaware, Indiana, Kentucky, Maryland, Missouri, New Jersey, North Carolina, Ohio, Pennsylvania, Rhode Island, Tennessee, Virginia, Kansas—13.

Mr. Seddon's project, excluding that part which provides for State secession, was likewise moved as a substitute, and defeated by the following vote:

AYS—Kentucky, Missouri, North Carolina, Virginia—4.

NOES—Connecticut, Delaware, Illinois, Indiana, Maine, Massachusetts, Maryland, New Jersey, New York, New Hampshire, Ohio, Pennsylvania, Rhode Island, Tennessee, Vermont, Kansas—16.

Mr. James B. Clay,[11] of Kentucky, now moved a very long substitute, which was substantially Mr. Seddon's over again; which was rejected by the following vote:

AYS—Kentucky, Missouri, North Carolina, Tennessee, Virginia—5.

NOES—Connecticut, Delaware, Illinois, Indiana, Maine, Massachusetts, Maryland, New Jersey, New York, New Hampshire, Ohio, Pennsylvania, Rhode Island, Vermont—14.

Mr. Tuck's proposition, consisting of an address and three resolves, was now moved as a substitute. His resolves were as follows:

"1st. *Resolved*, That this Convention recognize the well understood proposition that the Constitution of the United States gives no power to Congress, or any branch of the Federal Government, to interfere in any manner with Slavery in any of the States; and we are assured, by abundant testimony, that neither of the great political organizations existing in the country contemplates a violation of the spirit of the Constitution in this regard, or the procuring of any amendment thereof, by which Congress, or any department of the General Government, shall ever have jurisdiction over Slavery in any of the States.

"2d. *Resolved*, That the Constitution was ordained and established, as set forth in the preamble, by the people of the United States, in order to form a more perfect Union, establish justice, insure domestic tranquillity, provide for the common defense, promote the general welfare, and secure the blessings of liberty to themselves and their posterity; and when the people of any State are not in full enjoyment of all the benefits intended to be secured to them by the Constitution, or their rights under it are disregarded, their tranquillity disturbed, their prosperity retarded, or their liberty imperiled, by the people of any other State, full and adequate redress can and ought to be provided for such grievances.

"3d. *Resolved*, That this Convention recommend to the Legislatures of the several States of the Union to follow the example of the Legislatures of the States of Kentucky and Illinois, in applying to Congress to call a Convention for the proposing of amendments to the Constitution of the United States, pursuant to the fifth article thereof."

The Conference refused thus to substitute, by the following vote:

AYS—Connecticut, Illinois, Indiana, Iowa, Maine, Massachusetts, New York, New Hampshire, Vermont—9.

NOES—Delaware, Kentucky, Maryland, Missouri, New Jersey, North Carolina, Ohio, Pennsylvania, Rhode Island, Tennessee, Virginia—11.

The question was next taken on the *first* section of Mr. Guthrie's plan of constitutional amendment, as follows:

"SECTION 1. In all the present territory of the United States, north of the parallel of thirty-six degrees and thirty minutes of north latitude, involuntary servitude, except in punishment of crime, is prohibited. In all the present territory south of that line, the status of persons held to involuntary

[11] Son of Henry Clay; since a prominent Rebel; died in Canada in January, 1864.

service or labor, as it now exists, shall not be changed; nor shall any law be passed by Congress or the Territorial Legislature to hinder or prevent the taking of such persons from any of the States of this Union to said territory, nor to impair the rights arising from said relation; but the same shall be subject to judicial cognizance in the federal courts, according to the course of the common law. When any territory north or south of said line, within such boundary as Congress may prescribe, shall contain a population equal to that required for a member of Congress, it shall, if its form of government be republican, be admitted into the Union on an equal footing with the original States, with or without involuntary servitude, as the constitution of such State may provide."

This proposition was affirmed[11] and recommended by the following vote:

Ays—Delaware, Illinois, Kentucky, Maryland, New Jersey, Ohio, Pennsylvania, Rhode Island, Tennessee—9.

Noes—Connecticut, Iowa, Maine, Massachusetts, North Carolina, New Hampshire, Vermont, Virginia—8.

New York,[12] Indiana, and Kansas were equally divided, and so cast no vote. The section was declared adopted.

The *second* section had been so amended during the debates as to read as follows:

"Section 2. No territory shall be acquired by the United States, except by discovery, and for naval and commercial stations, depots, and transit-routes, without the concurrence of a majority of all the Senators from States which allow involuntary servitude, and a majority of all the Senators from States which prohibit that relation; nor shall territory be acquired by treaty, unless the votes of a majority of the Senators from each class of States hereinbefore mentioned be cast as a part of the two-thirds majority necessary to the ratification of such treaty."

This was likewise adopted—New York and Kansas being still divided—by the following vote:

Ays—Delaware, Indiana, Kentucky, Maryland, Missouri, New Jersey, Ohio, Pennsylvania, Rhode Island, Tennessee, Virginia—11.

Noes—Connecticut, Illinois, Iowa, Maine, Massachusetts, North Carolina, New Hampshire, Vermont—8.

Mr. Guthrie next moved the adoption of the *third* section of his Committee's report; amended by the Convention so as to read as follows:

"Section 3. Neither the Constitution nor any amendment thereof shall be construed to give Congress power to regulate, abolish, or control, within any State, the relation established or recognized by the laws thereof touching persons held to labor or involuntary service therein, nor to interfere with or abolish involuntary service in the District of Columbia without the consent of Maryland and without the consent of the owners, or making the owners who do not consent just compensation; nor the power to interfere with or prohibit representatives and others from bringing with them to the District of Columbia, retaining, and taking away, persons so held to labor or service; nor the power to interfere with or abolish involuntary service in places under the exclusive jurisdiction of the United States within those States and Territories where the same is established or recognized; nor the power to prohibit the removal or transportation of persons held to labor or involuntary service in any State or Territory of the United States to any other State or Territory thereof where it is established or recognized by law or usage; and the right during transportation, by sea or river, of touching at ports, shores, and landings, and of landing in case of distress, shall exist; but not the right of transit in or through any State or Territory, or of sale or traffic, against the laws thereof. Nor shall Congress have power to authorize any higher rate of taxation on persons held to labor or service than on land.

"The bringing into the District of Columbia of persons held to labor or service for sale, or placing them in depots to be afterwards transferred to other places for sale as merchandise, is prohibited."

This section was adopted by the following vote—New York and Kansas not voting, because equally divided:

Ays—Delaware, Illinois, Kentucky, Maryland, Missouri, New Jersey, North Carolina, Ohio, Pennsylvania, Rhode Island, Tennessee, Virginia—12.

Noes—Connecticut, Indiana, Iowa, Maine, Massachusetts, New Hampshire, Vermont—7.

[11] February 27th.

[12] Through the necessary absence from the Conference of a Republican Commissioner, [Mr. David Dudley Field] leaving his colleagues five to five.

Mr. Guthrie next moved the adoption of the *fourth* section of the report, which had been so amended as to read thus:

"SECTION 4. The third paragraph of the second section of the fourth article of the Constitution shall not be construed to prevent any of the States, by appropriate legislation, and through the action of their judicial and ministerial officers, from enforcing the delivery of fugitives from labor to the person to whom such service or labor is due."

This also was carried, by the following vote—New York and Kansas still equally divided:

AYS—Connecticut, Delaware, Illinois, Indiana, Kentucky, Maryland, Missouri, New-Jersey, North Carolina, Ohio, Pennsylvania, Rhode Island, Tennessee, Vermont, Virginia—15.

NOES—Iowa, Maine, Massachusetts, New-Hampshire—4.

Mr. Guthrie next moved the adoption of the *fifth* section of the report, so amended as to read as follows:

"SECTION 5. The foreign slave trade is hereby forever prohibited; and it shall be the duty of Congress to pass laws to prevent the importation of slaves, coolies, or persons held to service or labor, into the United States and the Territories from places beyond the limits thereof."

This section was adopted, as follows:

AYS—Connecticut, Delaware, Illinois, Indiana, Kentucky, Maryland, Missouri, New-Jersey, New York, New Hampshire, Ohio, Pennsylvania, Rhode Island, Tennessee, Vermont, Kansas—16.

NOES—Iowa, Maine, Massachusetts, North Carolina, Virginia—5.

Mr. Guthrie next moved the adoption of the *sixth* section of the report; amended thus:

"SECTION 6. The first, third, and fifth sections, together with this section of these amendments, and the third paragraph of the second section of the first article of the Constitution, and the third paragraph of the second section of the fourth article thereof, shall not be amended or abolished without the consent of all the States."

This was adopted by the following vote—New York again divided, and not voting:

AYS—Delaware, Illinois, Kentucky, Maryland, Missouri, New Jersey, Ohio, Pennsylvania, Rhode Island, Tennessee, Kansas—11.

NOES—Connecticut, Indiana, Iowa, Maine, Massachusetts, North Carolina, New Hampshire, Vermont, Virginia—9.

Mr. Guthrie next moved the adoption of the *seventh* section of the report; amended to read as follows:

"SECTION 7. Congress shall provide by law that the United States shall pay to the owner the full value of his fugitive from labor, in all cases where the marshal, or other officer, whose duty it was to arrest such fugitive, was prevented from so doing by violence or intimidation from mobs or riotous assemblages, or when, after arrest, such fugitive was rescued by like violence or intimidation, and the owner thereby deprived of the same; and the acceptance of such payment shall preclude the owner from further claim to such fugitive. Congress shall provide by law for securing to the citizens of each State the privileges and immunities of citizens in the several States."

This section was adopted by the following vote—New York still divided:

AYS—Delaware, Illinois, Indiana, Kentucky, Maryland, New Jersey, New Hampshire, Ohio, Pennsylvania, Rhode Island, Tennessee, Kansas—12.

NOES—Connecticut, Iowa, Maine, Missouri, North Carolina, Vermont, Virginia—7.

The report having been thus adopted by sections, Gov. Chase, of Ohio, demanded a vote upon the entire plan of conciliation together; which President Tyler decided unnecessary, as the whole plan had been adopted by sections.

Mr. T. E. Franklin, of Pennsylvania, moved the following independent proposition:

"*Resolved*, As the sense of this Convention, that the highest political duty of every citizen of the United States is his allegiance to the Federal Government created by the Constitution of the United States, and that no State of this Union has any constitutional right to secede therefrom, or to absolve the citizens of such State from their allegiance to the Government of the United States."

Mr. Barringer, of North Carolina,

moved that this proposition do lie on the table; which was defeated by 12 States to 9: but, on motion of Mr. Ruffin, of North Carolina, the consideration of Mr. Franklin's proposition was indefinitely postponed, as follows:

AYS—Delaware, Kentucky, Maryland, Missouri, New Jersey, North Carolina, Ohio, Rhode Island, Tennessee, Virginia—10.

NOES—Connecticut, Illinois, Indiana, Iowa, Maine, Massachusetts, Pennsylvania—7.

Mr. J. A. Seddon, of Virginia, moved once more his proposition, requiring an amendment of the Constitution, whereby the assent of a majority of the Senators from the slaveholding States and a like majority of the Senators from the non-slaveholding States is required to give validity to any act of the Senate, as also recognizing and legalizing State-secession from the Union; which was laid on the table.

Mr. Guthrie then offered the following preämble to the propositions which had been agreed to:

"*To the Congress of the United States:*

"The Convention assembled upon the invitation of the State of Virginia, to adjust the unhappy differences which now disturb the peace of the Union and threaten its continuance, make known to the Congress of the United States that their body convened in the city of Washington on the 4th instant, and continued in session until the 27th.

"There were in the body, when action was taken upon that which is here submitted, one hundred and thirty-three Commissioners, representing the following States: Maine, New Hampshire, Vermont, Massachusetts, Rhode Island, Connecticut, New York, New Jersey, Pennsylvania, Delaware, Maryland, Virginia, North Carolina, Tennessee, Kentucky, Missouri, Ohio, Indiana, Illinois, Iowa, Kansas.

"They have approved what is herewith submitted, and respectfully request that your honorable body will submit it to conventions in the States as an article of amendment to the Constitution of the United States."

This was adopted; and President Tyler requested to present the 'plan of adjustment' to Congress forthwith.

And then the Convention adjourned without day.

The above plan of conciliation was immediately communicated by President Tyler to Vice-President Breckinridge, who laid it before the Senate without delay: and, on motion of Mr. Crittenden, it was referred to a Select Committee of five, to be reported to the Senate next day.

Mr. Crittenden reported it accordingly.[13] Gov. Seward, from the Republican minority of said Committee, presented a substitute for that project, as follows:

"*A joint resolution concerning a National Convention to propose amendments to the Constitution of the United States.*

"*Whereas*, the Legislatures of the States of Kentucky, New Jersey, and Illinois, have applied to Congress to call a Convention for proposing amendments to the Constitution of the United States: Therefore,

"*Be it resolved*, etc., That the Legislatures of the other States be invited to take the subject into consideration, and to express their will on that subject to Congress, in pursuance of the fifth article of the Constitution."

Mr. Hale, of New Hampshire, and others, strenuously objected to a consideration of the majority report at this time; so that its second reading was postponed until next day: when, on motion of Mr. Douglas, it was made the special order for noon of the day following; when Gen. Joseph Lane, of Oregon, made a long speech against 'coërcion,' and in favor of the Southern view of State Rights. Mr. Andrew Johnson, of Tennessee, followed, speaking very strongly and earnestly in favor of maintaining the Union.

[13] February 28th.

At length, the Senate, on motion of Mr. Douglas, voted—Yeas 25; Nays 11—to postpone the consideration of this, in favor of the House proposition of amendment, already referred to, and which had passed that body; providing

"that no amendment shall be made to the Constitution which will authorize or give to Congress the power to interfere, within any State, with the domestic institutions thereof," etc.

This proposed amendment was finally concurred in by the Senate: Yeas 24; Nays 12: as follows:

YEAS—Messrs. Anthony, Baker, Bigler, Bright, Crittenden, Dixon, Douglas, Foster, Grimes, Gwin, Harlan, Hunter, Johnson, of Tennessee, Kennedy, Latham, Mason, Morrill, Nicholson, Polk, Pugh, Rice, Sebastian, Ten Eyck, and Thomson—24.

NAYS—Messrs. Bingham, Chandler, Clark, Doolittle, Durkee, Foot, King, Sumner, Trumbull, Wade, Wilkinson, and Wilson—12.

And then the Senate returned to the consideration of the Crittenden proposition, for which Mr. Clark's proposition, already given,[14] was again offered as a substitute, and voted down: Yeas 14; Nays 22.

Finally, Mr. Crittenden moved that the Peace Conference proposition be substituted for his own original project of conciliation; which the Senate refused, by the following vote:

YEAS—Messrs. Crittenden, Douglas, Harlan, Johnson, of Tennessee, Kennedy, Morrill, and Thomson—7.

NAYS—Messrs. Bayard, Bigler, Bingham, Bright, Chandler, Clark, Dixon, Fessenden, Foot, Foster, Grimes, Gwin, Hunter, Lane, Latham, Mason, Nicholson, Polk, Pugh, Rice, Sebastian, Sumner, Ten Eyck, Trumbull, Wade, Wigfall, Wilkinson, and Wilson—28.

So the Senate, by four to one, disposed of the scheme of the Peace Commissioners, and proceeded to vote, directly thereafter, on Mr. Crittenden's original proposition, which was defeated—Yeas 19, Nays 20—as has been stated.

The proceedings of the Peace Conference were likewise presented to the House,[15] but not acted upon in that body—the report of the Committee of Thirty-three being held entitled to preference.

Thus ended in failure the more or less earnest efforts to avert the gathering storm of war by some project of 'Compromise' or 'Conciliation,' to be enacted by Congress preliminary to its being ingrafted on the Constitution. And, as it has been very widely asserted and believed that the Republicans evinced an unbending disposition, stubbornly refusing to make any concession, any sacrifice, for the preservation of peace and National integrity, it may be well to consider what they actually did and proffered. The foregoing pages show that

I. They were at all times willing, and more than willing, to unite in the call of a Convention of the States, which would have inherent power to deal thoroughly with all the questions whereon the differences termed 'sectional' had arisen, and wherein their opponents were morally certain to have a large majority of votes. President Lincoln at an early day, Gov. Morgan, the Republicans in the Peace Conference, etc., etc., had indicated their concurrence in the call of a Convention. But this resort, though originally suggested by the Legislature of Kentucky, was voted down in the Peace Conference by the aid of all the Slave States represented—Kentucky among them.

II. The Republicans likewise

---

[14] See page 382.

[15] March 1, 1861.

evinced a willingness to pay for slaves who should be lost to their owners through popular interposition to defeat their return to bondage from the Free States to which they had escaped. Mr. Tuck's proposition in the 'Peace Conference,' Gov. Baldwin's, and nearly every authentic or influential utterance from the same side, admitted the duty of the North, if it could no longer return such fugitives, to pay their value to those injured or aggrieved by this failure to make good the constitutional stipulation. Had the South presented as her ultimatum—"Pay us cash[16] for every slave whom we shall hereafter lose through your repugnance to slave-hunting"—the exaction would have been acceded to as reasonable and just.

III. The North could not, without shame and conscious guilt, consent to diffuse and uphold Slavery on territory that came to us free.[17] But Gov. Anthony, of Rhode Island, formally offered,[18] in the Senate, to unite in the immediate admission of New Mexico (which then included Arizona) as a State, under such Constitu-

[16] During the preceding discussion in the Conference, Gov. S. P. Chase, of Ohio (February 6th), after stating frankly to the Southern Commissioners that those from the Free States could not surrender the principle of Slavery Restriction as to the territories, and that, if they did, it would do no good, as their constituents would disavow and repudiate them, proceeded as follows:

"Aside from the Territorial question—the question of Slavery outside of Slave States—I know of but one serious difficulty. I refer to the question concerning fugitives from service. The clause in the Constitution concerning this class of persons is regarded by almost all men, North and South, as a stipulation for the surrender to their masters of slaves escaping into Free States. The people of the Free States, however, who believe that slaveholding is wrong, cannot and will not aid in the reclamation, and the stipulation becomes therefore a dead letter. You complain of bad faith; and the complaint is retorted by denunciations of the cruelty which would drag back to bondage the poor slave who has escaped from it. You, thinking Slavery right, claim the fulfillment of the stipulation; we, thinking Slavery wrong, cannot fulfill the stipulation without consciousness of participation in wrong. Here is a real difficulty; but it seems to me not insuperable. It will not do for us to say to you, in justification of non-performance, 'The stipulation is immoral, and therefore we cannot execute it;' for you deny the immorality, and we cannot assume to judge for you. On the other hand, you ought not to exact from us the literal performance of the stipulation when you know that we cannot perform it without conscious culpability. A true solution of the difficulty seems to be attainable by regarding it as a simple case where a contract, from changed circumstances, cannot be fulfilled exactly as made. A court of equity in such a case decrees execution as near as may be. It requires the party who cannot perform to make a compensation for non-performance. Why cannot the same principle be applied to the rendition of fugitives from service? We cannot surrender—but we can compensate. Why not, then, avoid all difficulties on all sides, and show respectively good faith and good will, by providing and accepting compensation where masters reclaim escaping servants and prove their right of reclamation under the Constitution? Instead of a judgment for rendition, let there be a judgment for compensation, determined by the true value of the services, and let the same judgment assure freedom to the fugitive. The cost to the National Treasury would be as nothing in comparison with the evils of discord and strife. All parties would be gainers."

[17] Mr. Webster, in one of his latest speeches—at Buffalo, May 22, 1851—said:

"If the South wish any concession from me, they won't get it—not a hair's breadth of it. If they come to my house for it, they will not find it. I concede nothing. * * * No matter what may be said at the Syracuse Convention, or any other assemblage of insane persons. I never would consent that there should be one foot of Slave Territory beyond what the old Thirteen States had at the time of the formation of the Union. Never, never! The man can't show his face to me, and prove that I ever departed from that doctrine. He would sneak away, or slink away, or hire a mercenary Heep, that he might say what a mercenary apostate from liberty Daniel Webster has become. He knows himself to be a hypocrite and a falsifier. * * * All that I now say is, that, *with the blessing of God*, I will *not now nor hereafter, before the country or the world, consent to be numbered among those who introduced new Slave Power into the Union. I will do all in my power to prevent it.*"

Mr. Clay's deliberate and emphatic declaration that *he* would never consent nor be constrained "to vote for the positive introduction of Slavery either south or north of that line" (36° 30′), will be found on page 205.

[18] See page 381.

tion as her people should see fit to frame and adopt—New Mexico being at that moment a Slave Territory by act of her Legislature—to say nothing of the Dred Scott decision. That would have given the South a firm hold on nearly every acre of our present territory whereon she could rationally hope ever to plant Slavery—*provided* the people of New Mexico should see fit to ingraft Slavery on their State, as they seemed, under Democratic training, to have done on their Territory.

IV. The House—which had become strongly Republican through the withdrawal of most of the representatives from Cotton States—passed the conciliatory and practical resolves reported by Mr. Corwin from the Committee of Thirty-three—passed them by an overwhelming majority. The Senate would have promptly concurred, had it been intimated or probable that such concurrence would have arrested and rolled back the surge of Secession.

V. Both Houses united in passing the Joint Resolve from said Committee which, being ratified by the required proportion of the States, would have precluded forever any action of Congress adverse to the perpetuation of Slavery in such States as should desire such perpetuation. This, too, would have been readily perfected, had 'the South' evinced any inclination to be satisfied and pacified thereby. But it was very generally treated by them as of no value. Senator Mason, of Virginia, spoke of it derisively as, in substance, one of the planks of the Chicago [Republican] Platform. And the artillery of Secession soon dispelled all desire of, or motive for, ratifying it.

VI. There were very many Republicans—and those by no means without consideration or influence—who would have cheerfully consented to a peaceful withdrawal from the Union of the Cotton States, with such others as might have chosen to accompany them, had these accorded *time* for decently effecting and assenting to such a separation, after first allowing the Free States a fair opportunity to submit to and urge upon the people of the South their reasons for deprecating it. To this end, the calling of a National Convention and the election of delegates thereto were deemed indispensable prerequisites. Such a Convention could have acted decisively on the main question and all subordinate points—such as the rightful disposal, by apportionment or otherwise, of the public lands and other property belonging to the Union, with the public debt owed by it.

VII. The North did, as we have seen, organize three new Territories at this Session, in utter silence respecting Slavery, and in such manner as left 'the South' in full possession of all the rights accruing to her from the Federal Constitution, as expounded in the Dred Scott decision. This was done, not in accordance with the views and feelings of the Republicans, who reported and passed the bills, but as a peace-offering and a concession to those Southern Unionists who were constantly protesting that *they* cared nothing for the extension of Slavery—in fact, were rather opposed to it—but would not tamely submit to see a stigma placed on their section and her 'institution' by Northern votes.

Yet all this was fruitless, because the North, in the full flush of a long-awaited and fairly achieved triumph, did not see fit to repudiate the cherished and time-honored principle for which it had patiently, ardently struggled. No other successful party was ever before required, at such a moment, to surrender its principle, its consistency, its manhood, on peril of National disruption and overthrow. There was no concession from the other side—no real compromise—but a simple, naked exaction that the Republicans should stultify and disgrace themselves, by admitting that they were fundamentally wrong, and that, instead of electing their President, they should have been defeated.[19]

What 'the South' and its friends really required of the North was partnership, coöperation, complicity, in the work of extending, diffusing, and fortifying Slavery, such as it had secured in the annexation of Texas. That Slavery was a great National interest—the broad and solid base of our industrial economy and commercial prosperity—the slaves confined, indeed, to one section of the Union, because there most profitably employed, but laboring for the benefit of Northern[20] manufacturers and merchants as much as for that of Southern planters and factors—that we must all watch and work to give that interest wider scope by the conquest of more territory, and by the maintenance at all hazards of Slavery in Cuba, etc.—and that all anti-Slavery discussion or expostulation must be systematically suppressed, as sedition, if not treason—such was the gist of the Southern requirement. A long-haired, raving Abolitionist in the furthest North, according to 'conservative' ideas, not merely disturbed the equilibrium of Southern society, but undermined the fabric of our National prosperity. He must be squelched,[21] or there could be no further Union. Haman, surrounded by the power and pomp of his dazzling exaltation, bitterly says, "All this availeth me nothing, so long as I see Mordecai, the Jew, sitting at the king's gate."[22]

Hence 'the South' would accord no time, allow no canvass by Northern men of the Slave States in the hope of disabusing their people of the prejudice that we were their natural, implacable enemies.[23] They gave us but this alternative—"Consent to Disunion—let us wrest from the Republic such portion of it as we choose to have—or meet us in the shock of battle! Your country or your life!"

—And so we were plunged into the horrors of Civil War.

---

[19] *The Cincinnati Enquirer* of January 15, 1861, has a letter from 'A Citizen of Highland County,' which puts the case squarely thus:

"There is only one possible remedy which can save the country, and restore harmony and peace; and that is a total abandonment of the dogmas of Lincoln, and the adoption of another and opposite object—'the recognition of the equality of all the States in the territories of the United States, and the strict enforcement of all the laws protecting and securing slave property under the Constitution.' This principle is recognized in the proposition of Senator Crittenden; and when the madness and violence of such men as John Sherman, Ben. Wade, and Horace Greeley shall be humbled, and when wise and patriotic statesmen shall be looked for and found as guides and counselors for the peace of the nation, then may we rejoice in the prospect of restoring our country to that prosperity and happiness which we had before the spirit of Abolitionism and of hate blasted this fair heritage of our fathers. Let the entire South to the border, including Kentucky, Maryland, Virginia, and Missouri, take a bold, dignified, and patriotic position, and demand as a right that which the North—redeemed from the curse of Abolitionism—will have the magnanimity and patriotism to yield."

[20] See Judge Woodward's speech, page 364.

[21] See Mayor Henry's speech; also his letter forbidding G. W. Curtis's lecture, pages 363–7.

[22] Esther v., 13.

[23] See Senator Clingman, page 373.

XXVI.

THE UNION—THE CONFEDERACY.

If Hudibras was right in his assumption, that there is and can be no fighting where one party gives all the blows—the other being content with meekly and patiently receiving them—then it might be plausibly contended that our great Civil War was initiated by the bombardment of Fort Sumter, or by the attempt to supply its famishing garrison, some weeks after Mr. Lincoln's inauguration. But Wit stands opposed to Reason in this case, as in many others. The first attempt in the interest of Secession to dispossess the Union, by force, of any property or position held by it, even though not seriously opposed, was as truly an act of war as though it had been desperately resisted, at the cost of hundreds of lives.

The Secession of South Carolina[1] was hailed with instant and general exultation by the plotters of Disunion in nearly every Slave State. There were celebrations, with parades, music, cannon-firing, speeches, etc., on that evening or the following day, at New Orleans, Mobile, Memphis, etc. Even at Wilmington, Del., where the Secessionists were few indeed, the event was honored by a salute of a hundred guns. Senator Andrew Johnson was still more honored, on the 22d, by being burned in effigy by the Secessionists of Memphis. While the Northern cities were anxious, apprehensive, and paralyzed, it was noted that at Baltimore, though no formal celebration was had, people seemed relieved and cheerful; the streets were gayly crowded, and business was better. At Washington, Mr. Garnett, of Virginia, exultingly announced the fact of South Carolina's secession in the House; whereupon, three or four Southrons clapped their hands. There was no further public manifestation in Congress; and none north of the Virginia line, save in Wilmington, as aforesaid.

A mere handful of Federal troops, under Maj. Robert Anderson, watched rather than garrisoned the forts in Charleston harbor. Of these, Fort Moultrie, though the older and weaker, was mainly tenanted by the soldiers, being the more convenient to the city; but it could not have been held a day against a serious assault. Its garrison found themselves suddenly surrounded by scowling, deadly foes,[2] too numerous to be resisted. During the night of the 26th, Maj. Anderson properly and prudently transferred his entire command to Fort Sumter, taking with them, or after them, all provisions, munitions, etc., that could conveniently be transported. The removal was effected by means of two schooners, which made several trips during the night, passing directly by the harbor guard-boat

[1] December 20, 1860.

[2] *The Charleston Mercury* of the 22d said:

"The garrison in our harbor will not be strengthened. The reënforcement of the forts, at this time and under present circumstances, means coërcion—war. When the forts are demanded and refused to be delivered up to those in whom is invested the title of eminent domain, and for whose defense and protection alone they

Nina, and affecting no concealment. A full moon was shining in a clear sky. When all that could be had been removed, the remaining gun-carriages, etc., were burnt, so as to prevent their use in any future attack upon Sumter. No resistance was offered; perhaps none of a serious nature could have been; for Maj. Anderson's act was evidently unanticipated in Charleston; but it was gravely complained of as a breach of faith—President Buchanan, it was implied, rather than distinctly alleged,[3] having promised that the military *status* should not be changed, without due notice. The news of Anderson's movement sent a thrill through the hearts of many, who felt that we were silently drifting toward a sea of fraternal blood.

Almost simultaneously with this transfer, a popular excitement was aroused in Pittsburgh, Pa., by information that an order had been received from the War Department for an extensive transfer of arms, especially of heavy ordnance, from the Alleghany Arsenal near that place to the South and South-West.[4] That such transfers had been quietly going on for months, did not reconcile the stanch Republicans of our American Birmingham to further operations of the kind, now palpably in the interest of Southern treason. A public meeting was called; dispatches sent to Washington; and an order obtained suspending the meditated transfer. The citizens' meeting was held on the evening of the 27th; and its resolves, while they deprecated any lawless resistance to official orders, called urgently on the President to purge his Cabinet of every one known to be in complicity with treason or rebellion against the Federal Government and Union.

John B. Floyd, Secretary of War, resigned his post on the 29th, alleging the course of the President, in refusing to order Major Anderson back to

were ceded and built up; and when, the Federal Government showing a hostile purpose, it shall become necessary and proper for us to obtain possession, then it will be right for the world and Black Republicanism to expect that the State, by her authorities, will move in the premises. *The people will obey the call for war, and take the forts.*"

The Charleston Courier of December 4, 1860, has a speech by Mr. Edward M'Crady at a Secession meeting in that city a few days previously, which concludes as follows:

"I do not counsel any precipitate action; nor do I fear anything from the forts—they are ours, not merely in part. They were placed there on *our* soil for *our* protection; and, whenever the separation comes, they must fall into our possession. They will be ours as surely as we secede; and we will secede as surely as the sun will rise to-morrow."

[3] *The Charleston Courier* of the 29th said:

"Major Robert Anderson, United States Army, *has achieved the unenviable distinction of opening civil war between American citizens by an act of gross breach of faith.* He has, under counsels of a panic, deserted his post at Fort Moultrie, and, under false pretexts, has transferred his garrison and military stores and supplies to Fort Sumter."

And *The Charleston Mercury* said:

"Major Anderson alleges that the movement was made without orders, and upon his own responsibility, and that he was not aware of such an understanding. He is a gentleman, and we will not impugn his word or his motives. But it is due to South Carolina and to good faith that the act of this officer should be repudiated by the Government, and that the troops be removed forthwith from Fort Sumter."

[4] The order was as follows:

"Send *immediately* to Ship Island, near Balize, (mouth of Mississippi), 46 cannon, and to Galveston 78 cannon," naming the kinds.

The schedule was as follows:

21 ten-inch Columbiads,	15,200 lbs.	=	319,200 lbs.
21 eight-inch ditto	9,240 "	=	194,040 "
4 32-pounders (iron),	7,250 "	=	29,000 "
46 to Ship Island.			
Total weight of metal,			542,240 lbs.
23 ten-inch Columbiads,	15,200 lbs.	=	349,600 lbs.
48 eight-inch ditto	9,240 "	=	443.520 "
7 32-pounders (iron),	7,250 "	=	50,750 "
78 to Galveston.			
Total weight of metal,			843,870 lbs.

Fort Moultrie, as his reason. He asserted that *he* had promised South Carolina that no change should be made in the disposition of our forces in Charleston harbor—which is exceedingly probable. He asked permission to "vindicate *our* honor, and prevent civil war" by "withdrawing the Federal garrison altogether from the harbor of Charleston." This not being accorded, he declared that he could no longer hold his office, "under my convictions of patriotism, nor with honor." The President mildly accepted his resignation, and appointed Joseph Holt, of Kentucky, to succeed him.

By the middle of December, Hon. Caleb Cushing, of Mass., was dispatched to Charleston by President Buchanan as a Commissioner or confidential agent of the Executive. His errand was a secret one. But, so far as its object was allowed to transpire, he was understood to be the bearer of a proffer from Mr. Buchanan that he would not reënforce Major Anderson, nor initiate any hostilities against the Secessionists, provided they would evince a like pacific spirit, by respecting the Federal authority down to the close of his Administration—now but a few weeks distant. Gen. Cushing had been in Charleston a few months earlier as an anti-Douglas delegate to, and President of, the Democratic National Convention, and then stood in high favor with her aristocracy: on this occasion, however, he was soon given to understand that he had fallen from grace; that his appearance in the character of an advocate or representative of Federal authority had cast a sudden mildew on his popularity in that stronghold of Secession. He remained but five hours in Charleston; having learned within that time that the rulers of South Carolina would make no promises and enter into no arrangements which did not recognize or imply the independence of their State. He returned directly to Washington, where his report was understood to have been the theme of a stormy and protracted Cabinet meeting.

Directly after Major Anderson's removal to Fort Sumter, the Federal arsenal in Charleston, containing many thousand stand of arms and a considerable quantity of military stores, was seized by the volunteers, now flocking to that city by direction of the State authorities; Castle Pinckney, Fort Moultrie, and Sullivan's Island, were likewise occupied by them, and their defenses vigorously enlarged and improved. The Custom-House, Post-Office, etc., were likewise appropriated, without resistance or commotion; the Federal officers having them in charge being original, active, and ardent Secessionists. The lights in the light-houses were extinguished, and the buoys in the intricate channel of the harbor were removed, so that no ocean craft could enter or depart without the guidance of a special pilot. Additional fortifications, defending the city and commanding the harbor approaches, were commenced and pushed rapidly forward; some of them having direct reference, offensive and defensive, to Fort Sumter. And still the volunteers came pouring in; nearly all from the interior of South Carolina; though abundant proffers of military aid were received from all parts of the South. The first company from another State, consisting of eighty men, was organized in Savannah, and reached Charleston December 23d. Capt. N. L. Coste, of the U. S. revenue service, in command of the cutter William Aiken, in Charleston harbor, turned her over to the State authorities, and enlisted, with his crew, in the service of South Carolina. This day, the Palmetto, or South Carolina, flag was formally raised over the Custom-House and the Post-Office at Charleston; and it was announced next morning that Gov. Pickens had been tendered the services of volunteers from Georgia and Alabama, as well as from all parts of South Carolina.

Mr. Jacob Thompson, Secretary of the Interior, having left his post to visit North Carolina in the character of a Secession Commissioner from Mississippi, a heavy defalcation was discovered[5] in his Department. A South Carolina clerk named Godard Bailey, who was custodian of a large amount of State bonds belonging to the Indian Trust Fund, had abstracted therefrom bonds and coupons amounting in the aggregate to $870,-000, and had disappeared. Mr. Thompson was notified by letter of the fraud, and, returning,[6] called at once upon the President to announce it. An investigation was forthwith ordered; but neither the key of the safe nor the clerk who had charge of it could be found. Mr. Bailey was at length discovered, but could not or would not produce the key. The Department was then surrounded by a police force, which no clerk was allowed to pass, the safe broken open, and the extent of the robbery discovered. An examination of Mr. Bailey elicited the following facts:

The firm of Russell, Majors & Waddell held a very large contract for the transportation of army supplies from Leavenworth and other points on the Missouri river to the army stationed at Camp Floyd, in Utah; under which they were to receive from the Treasury about one million dollars per annum. The contractors being pressed for funds, Mr. Floyd had been induced to accept their drafts on his department, in anticipation of future service, to the amount of nearly or quite a million of dollars. These acceptances, being manifestly irregular, could with difficulty, and but to a moderate extent, be negotiated; so that the embarrassment of the contractors was thereby scarcely mitigated. Under these circumstances, it appears, Mr. Russell had been made acquainted with Mr. Bailey, and had, by some means, induced the latter to supply him with a large amount of bonds from the safe under his control, substituting therefor Mr. Floyd's acceptances aforesaid. The bonds he had hypothecated in Wall-street and raised money thereon. As our national sky darkened, the bonds depreciated, and the lenders called on Mr. Russell for additional security, which he furnished in the shape of more bonds, supplied by Bailey; who, finding himself inextricably involved, addressed, on the 18th, a letter to Secretary Thompson, disclosing the more material facts, and pleading that he had taken the bonds only to save the honor of Secretary Floyd, which, he was assured, had been compromised by his advances to Russell & Co. He did this on the faith of promises that all should be made right in due

[5] December 24th.

[6] December 25th.

season: but, being called upon by the Indian Bureau for the coupons, payable January 1st, on the abstracted securities, he found himself unable to respond, and was driven to a confession. The Government being at that moment penniless, the revenue shrunk to less than half its ordinary dimensions by the stoppage of importations, and the necessity for borrowing urgent, this development, casting doubt on the integrity of men high in authority, gave a staggering blow to the public credit. The Grand Jury at Washington indicted[7] Floyd on two counts: first, for malfeasance; second, for conspiracy with Bailey and Russell to defraud the Government; but he was by this time far from that city, absorbed in the work of luring Virginia into the toils of treason.

The disintegration of the Cabinet had commenced so early as December 10th, when Mr. Howell Cobb, thoroughly in the counsels of the secessionists, resigned the control of the Treasury, whereof the bankrupt and hopeless condition supplied him with an excuse, though not the reason, for his retirement. Mr. Philip Francis Thomas, of Md., previously Commissioner of Patents, was appointed in his stead. Gen. Lewis Cass resigned the post of Secretary of State on the 14th, directly after a long and exciting Cabinet session. He did so because he could not consent to render himself responsible for, or be implicated in, the President's refusal to reënforce, provision, and sustain Maj. Anderson and his little force, holding the forts in Charleston harbor. He did not rush into the newspapers; yet he made no secret of his conviction that the course on which the President had decided was a fatally mistaken one, and led directly to National subversion and ruin. Attorney-General Black—a lifelong and intimate personal friend of the President—took charge, by his direction, of the State Department.

Messrs. R. W. Barnwell, James L. Orr, and ex-Gov. Adams, Commissioners from the State of South Carolina, reached Washington on the 26th, under instructions to negotiate with the Federal Executive a partition of all the properties and interests of the sovereign and independent State of South Carolina in the Union from which she had seceded. Every one of them knew perfectly that the President had no more constitutional power or right to enter upon such a negotiation than he had to cede the country bodily to Russia, France, or Great Britain. They were, of course, received civilly, and treated respectfully, but informed that the President could only regard and meet them as citizens of the United States. They left, on their return, nine days afterward; sending farewell letters to the President, which are scarcely average samples of diplomatic suavity.

Georgia having given[8] a large popular majority for Secession, her authorities immediately took military possession of the Federal arsenal at Augusta, as also of Forts Pulaski and Jackson, commanding the approaches by sea to Savannah.

North Carolina had not voted to secede, yet Gov. Ellis simultaneously seized the U. S. Arsenal at Fayetteville, with Fort Macon, and other fortifications commanding the approaches to Beaufort and Wilming-

[7] On the 30th.

[8] January 2, 1861.

ton. Having done so, Gov. E. coolly wrote to the War Department that he had taken the step to preserve the forts from seizure by mobs!

In Alabama, the Federal arsenal at Mobile was seized on the 4th, by order of Gov. Moore. It contained large quantities of arms and munitions. Fort Morgan, commanding the approaches to Mobile, was likewise seized, and garrisoned by State troops.

The steamer Star of the West left New York unannounced, during the night of January 5th, laden with reënforcements and supplies for Fort Sumter. A dispatch from that city reached the South Carolina authorities next day, advising them of her destination and objects. Secretary Thompson likewise sent a dispatch from Washington to the same effect, directly after leaving the Cabinet council in which he had ascertained the facts. He resigned his office on the 8th, asserting that the attempt to reënforce Fort Sumter was a violation of the promises of the Executive. The Star of the West, having 250 soldiers and ample provisions on board, appeared off the bar at Charleston on the 9th. Attempting to steam up the harbor to Fort Sumter, she was fired upon from Fort Moultrie and a battery on Morris Island, and, being struck by a shot, put about, and left for New York, without even communicating with Major Anderson.

In Louisiana, the Federal arsenal at Baton Rouge was seized by order of Gov. Moore on the 11th. Forts Jackson and St. Philip, commanding the passage up the Mississippi to New Orleans, and Fort Pike, at the entrance of Lake Pontchartrain, were likewise seized and garrisoned by State troops. The Federal Mint and Custom-House at New Orleans were left untouched until February 1st, when they, too, were taken possession of by the State authorities.

In St. Louis, the Custom-House, Sub-Treasury, and Post Office were garrisoned by a handful of Federal soldiers as a protection against a similar movement.

Mr. Thomas, after a very few days' service, resigned control of the Treasury, and was succeeded by Gen. John A. Dix, of New York.

In Florida, Fort Barrancas and the Navy Yard at Pensacola were seized by Florida and Alabama forces on the 13th; Commander Armstrong surrendering them without a struggle. He ordered Lieut. Slemmer, likewise, to surrender Forts Pickens and McRae; but the intrepid subordinate defied the order, and, withdrawing his small force from Fort McRae to the stronger and less accessible Fort Pickens, announced his determination to hold out to the last. He was soon after besieged therein by a formidable volunteer force; and a dispatch from Pensacola announced that "Fort McRae is being occupied and the guns manned by the allied forces of Florida, Alabama, and Mississippi."

Col. Hayne, as agent of Gov. Pickens, reached Washington on the 12th; and on the 16th demanded the surrender of Fort Sumter, as essential to a good understanding between the two nations of South Carolina and the United States. The Legislature of the former had, on the 14th, formally resolved, that "any attempt by the Federal Government to reënforce Fort Sumter will be regarded as an act of open hostility, and a declaration of war."

The revenue cutter Cass, stationed at Mobile, was turned over by Capt. J. J. Morrison to the authorities of Alabama at the end of January. The McClellan, Capt. Breshwood, stationed on the Mississippi below New Orleans, was, in like manner, handed over to those of Louisiana. Gen. Dix had sent down a special agent to secure them, but he was too late. The telegraph dispatch whereby Gen. Dix directed him, "If any person attempts to haul down the American flag, shoot him on the spot," sent an electric thrill through the loyal heart of the country.

Finally, tidings reached Washington, about the end of February, that Brig.-Gen. Twiggs, commanding the department of Texas, had disgracefully betrayed his trust, and turned over his entire army, with all[9] the posts and fortifications, arms, munitions, horses, equipments, etc., to Gen. Ben. M'Culloch, representing the authorities of Texas, now fully launched upon the rushing tide of treason. The Union lost by that single act at least half its military force, with the State of Texas, and the control of our Mexican frontier; while two millions of dollars could hardly have replaced, in that crisis, the property thus filched from the Republic. And, to add to the extent of the disaster, the ship Star of the West, which, after its return from its abortive mission to Fort Sumter, was dispatched, laden with munitions and supplies, for the army of the frontier, went into the harbor of Indianola utterly unsuspicious of the transformation which had been there effected, and became[10] an easy prey to the exultant Rebels.

The defensive fortifications located within the seceding States were some thirty in number, mounting over three thousand guns, and having cost at least Twenty Millions of dollars. Nearly all these had been seized and appropriated by the Confederates before Mr. Lincoln's inauguration, with the exception of Fortress Monroe (Virginia), Fort Sumter (South Carolina), Fort Pickens (Florida), and the fortresses on Key West and the Tortugas, off the Florida coast. To offset these, they had full possession of Fort Macon, North Carolina, though that State had utterly refused to unite in the conspiracy, with the extensive and costly Navy Yard at Pensacola, and the Southern Arsenals, which their Floyd had crammed[11] with arms

[9] The following is a list of the property given up to the State of Texas by Gen. Twiggs:

1,800 mules, valued at $50 each	$90,000
500 wagons, " " 140 "	70,000
950 horses, " " 150 "	142,500
500 harness, " " 50 "	25,000
Tools, wagon materials, iron, nails, horse and mule-shoes	250,000
Corn (at this port)	7,000
Clothing	150,000
Commissary stores	75,000
Ordnance stores	400,000
Total	$1,209,500

exclusive of public buildings to which the Federal Government has a title. Much of the property is estimated at the original cost, its value in Texas being much greater, and worth to the State at least a million and a half of dollars.—*San Antonio Herald*, Feb. 23d.

[10] April 20, 1861.

[11] Mr. Edward A. Pollard, in his "Southern [Rebel] History of the War," page 40, thus sums up the cheap initial conquests of the Confederacy:

"On the incoming of the Administration of Abraham Lincoln, on the 4th of March, the rival government of the South had perfected its organization; the separation had been widened and envenomed by the ambidexterity and perfidy of President Buchanan; the Southern people, however, still hoped for a peaceful accomplishment of their independence, and deplored war between the two sections, as 'a policy detrimental to the civilized world.' The revolution, in the mean time, had rapidly gathered, not only in moral power, but in

and munitions with direct reference to this contingency.[12] Add to these the Army of the Frontier, with all its arms, munitions, trains, animals, and provisions, with the Southern revenue-cutters, Mints, Custom-Houses, Sub-Treasuries, etc. (over half a million of dollars in gold having been seized in that at New Orleans alone); and it may be safely estimated that the Rebellion had possessed itself of Thirty Millions' worth of Federal property before Mr. Buchanan left the White House; which was increased to Forty Millions by the seizure of Harper's Ferry Arsenal, and the Norfolk Navy Yard, with its ships of war, munitions, and two thousand cannon, before a single blow was struck on the side of the Union.

The Convention of South Carolina called,[13] on motion of Mr. R. Barnwell Rhett, a Convention of such slaveholding States as should, meantime, have seceded from the Union, to meet at Montgomery, Alabama, February 4th, which was acceded to.

The Convention took place accordingly, and a provisional framework of government was adopted for "the Confederate States of America" on the 9th; which was superseded by a permanent Constitution,[14] substantially a copy of the Federal Constitution, except in these particulars: The President and Vice-President are chosen for six years; and the President may not be reëlected while in office. He may not remove from office any functionaries, but members of his Cabinet, without referring the same, with his reasons therefor, to the Senate. The heads of departments may each, by law, be accorded a seat on the floor of either House, with the privilege of discussing any measures pertaining to his department. This Constitution further provides that

"No bounties shall be granted from the Treasury, nor shall any duties or taxes on importations be levied to promote or foster any branch of industry."

"The citizens of each State * * * * shall have the right of transit and sojourn in any

the means of war and muniments of defense. Fort Moultrie and Castle Pinckney had been *captured* by the South Carolina troops; Fort Pulaski, the defense of the Savannah, had been *taken;* the Arsenal at Mount Vernon, Alabama, with 20,000 stand of arms, had been *seized* by the Alabama troops; Fort Morgan, in Mobile Bay, had been *taken;* Forts Jackson, St. Philip, and Pike, near New Orleans, had been *captured* by the Louisiana troops; the New Orleans Mint and Custom-House had been *taken;* the Little Rock Arsenal had been *seized* by the Arkansas troops [though Arkansas had refused to secede]; and, on the 16th of February, Gen. Twiggs had *transferred* the public property in Texas to the State authorities. All of these events had been accomplished without bloodshed. Abolitionism and Fanaticism had not yet lapped blood. But reflecting men saw that the peace was deceitful and temporizing; that the temper of the North was impatient and dark; and that, if all history was not a lie, the first incident of bloodshed would be the prelude to a war of monstrous proportions."

[12] Mr. E. Pollard, aforesaid, writing his 'Southern' History of the struggle at Richmond, after having been in public employment at Washington throughout Buchanan's Administration, himself one of the original traitors, and always in their counsels, says:

"It had been supposed that the Southern people, poor in manufactures as they were, and in the haste for the mighty contest that was to ensue, would find themselves but illy provided with arms to contend with an enemy rich in the means and munitions of war. This disadvantage had been provided against by the timely act of one man. Mr. Floyd, of Virginia, when Secretary of War under Mr. Buchanan's Administration, had, by a single order, effected the transfer of 115,000 improved muskets and rifles from the Springfield Armory and Watervliet Arsenal to different Arsenals at the South. Adding to these the number of arms distributed by the Federal Government to the States in preceding years of our history, and those purchased by the States and citizens, it was safely estimated that the South entered upon the war with one hundred and fifty thousand small arms of the most approved modern pattern and the best in the world."

[13] December 27th. [14] Adopted March 11th.

State of this Confederacy with their slaves and other property; and the right of property in said slaves shall not thereby be impaired."

"No slave or other person held to service or labor in any State or territory of the Confederate States, under the laws thereof, escaping or lawfully carried into another, shall, in consequence of any law or regulation therein, be discharged from such service or labor, but shall be delivered up on claim of the party to whom such slave belongs, or to whom such service or labor may be due."

"The Confederate States may acquire new territory * * * * in all such territory the institution of negro Slavery, as it now exists in the Confederate States, shall be recognized and protected by Congress and by the territorial government; and the inhabitants of the several Confederate States and territories shall have the right to take to such territory any slaves lawfully held by them in any of the States or territories of the Confederate States."

Jefferson Davis, of Mississippi, was, by the Congress, unanimously elected President, and Alexander H. Stephens, of Georgia, Vice-President, of the Confederacy for the current year; and they, too, were reëlected, without dissent, for a full term of six years, by a popular vote in the ensuing Autumn.

Mr. Davis reached Montgomery on the 17th by a special train from Jackson, his progress being one continual ovation. He made twenty-five speeches [15] on the route to enthusiastic crowds, and was welcomed on his arrival at Montgomery by a vast concourse. He was inaugurated next day with most imposing ceremonies.

Mr. Davis's Inaugural was a temperate and carefully studied document. Assuming the right of Secession as inherent in "the sovereign States now composing this Confederacy," to be exercised whenever, in their judgment, the compact by which they acceded to the Union "has been perverted from the purposes for which it was ordained, and ceased to answer the ends for which it was established," and that its exercise "merely asserted the right which the Declaration of Independence of 1776 defined to be inalienable," he avers of their recent action that "it is, by the abuse of language, that their act has been denominated revolution." "They formed a new *alliance*," he continues, [ignoring their solemn compact in the Federal Constitution by which they had covenanted with each other that "No State shall enter into any treaty, *al-*

[15] *The True Delta* (New Orleans) of February 16, contains the following telegraphic synopsis of Mr. Davis's speech on leaving Jackson for Montgomery:

"He alluded to the difficulties of constructing a new government, and how these difficulties are enhanced by the threatening elements in the North. It may be that we will be confronted by war, that the attempt will be made to blockade our ports, to starve us out; but they know little of the Southern heart, of Southern endurance. No amount of privation could force us to remain in a Union on unequal terms. England and France would not allow our great staple to be dammed up within our present limits; the starving thousands in their midst would not allow it. We have nothing to apprehend from blockade. But, if they attempt invasion by land, *we must take the war out of our territory*. If war must come, *it must be upon Northern, and not upon Southern, soil*. In the mean time, if they were prepared to grant us peace, to recognize our equality, all is well."

And the following extract from one of those speeches, made at Stevenson, Alabama, faithfully embodies the joyous anticipations with which the struggle, then imminent, was commenced by the Confederates:

"Your Border States will gladly come into the Southern Confederacy within sixty days, as we will be their only friends. England will recognize us, and a glorious future is before us. The grass will grow in the Northern cities, where the pavements have been worn off by the tread of commerce. We will carry war where it is easy to advance—where food for the sword and torch await our armies in the densely populated cities; and though they [the enemy] may come and spoil our crops, we can raise them as before; while they cannot rear the cities which took years of industry and millions of money to build."

liance, or *confederation*."] The Federal Government is termed by him "the *agent* through whom they communicated with foreign nations," which they have now "changed"—that is all. In short, the chief of the Confederacy talks as though his people had acted in a very natural and common-place manner in voting for President of the United States, and then, being beaten in the contest, seceding from the Union, framing a new Confederacy, and electing him President for the ensuing term, for which they had failed to elect Major Breckinridge. And, as they had cotton to sell, which the North, with nearly all other civilized countries, wished to buy, their policy was necessarily one of peace; and he argued that the old Union would inevitably and gladly, for cotton's sake, if for no other, cultivate peace with them.

There was an undertone in this Inaugural, however, which plainly evinced that the author expected nothing of the sort. "If we may not hope to avoid war," says Mr. Davis, "we may at least expect that posterity will acquit us of having needlessly engaged in it." "We have entered upon a career of independence, and it *must* be inflexibly pursued through *many years* of controversy with our late associates of the Northern States." Hence, he very properly called upon his Congress, in addition to the services of the Militia, to provide for a Navy, and "a well-instructed, disciplined Army, more numerous than would usually be required as a *peace* establishment"—which was putting quite as fine a point on it as the truth would warrant.

Mr. Davis carefully refrained from any other allusion to Slavery, or the causes of estrangement between the North and the South, than the following:

"With a Constitution differing only from that of our fathers in so far as it is explanatory of their well-known intent, freed from sectional conflicts, which have interfered with the pursuit of the general welfare, it is not unreasonable to expect that the States from which we have parted may seek to unite their fortunes to ours, under the Government which we have instituted. For this, your Constitution makes adequate provision; but beyond this, if I mistake not, the judgment and will of the people are, that union with the States from which they have separated is neither practicable nor desirable. To increase the power, develop the resources, and promote the happiness of the Confederacy, it is requisite there should be so much homogeneity that the welfare of every portion should be the aim of the whole. Where this does not exist, antagonisms are engendered, which must and should result in separation."

Mr. Stephens, the Vice-President of the 'Confederacy,' proved far less reticent and more candid. On his return from the Convention or Congress whereby the 'Confederacy' had been cemented, and he chosen its Vice-President, he was required to address a vast assemblage at Savannah,[16] and did so in elaborate exposition and defense of the new Confederate Constitution. After claiming that it preserved all that was dear and desirable of the Federal Constitution, while it embodied very essential improvements on that document, in its prohibition of Protective Duties and Internal Improvements by Confederate authority; in its proffer to Cabinet Ministers of seats in either House of Congress, with the right of debate; and in forbidding the reëlection of a President while in office, Mr. Stephens proceeded:

"But, not to be tedious in enumerating the numerous changes for the better, allow

[16] March 21. 1860.

me to allude to one other—though last, not least: the new Constitution has put at rest *forever* all the agitating questions relating to our peculiar institution—African Slavery as it exists among us—the proper *status* of the negro in our form of civilization. *This was the immediate cause of the late rupture and the present revolution.* Jefferson, in his forecast, had anticipated this, as the 'rock upon which the old Union would split.' He was right. What was conjecture with him is now a realized fact. But whether he comprehended the great truth upon which that rock *stood* and *stands*, may be doubted. *The prevailing ideas entertained by him and most of the leading statesmen at the time of the formation of the old Constitution were, that the enslavement of the African was in violation of the laws of nature; that it was wrong in principle, socially, morally, and politically.* It was an evil they knew not well how to deal with; but the general opinion of the men of that day was, that, somehow or other, in the order of Providence, the institution would be evanescent and pass away. This idea, though not incorporated in the Constitution, was the prevailing idea at the time. The Constitution, it is true, secured every essential guarantee to the institution while it should last; and hence no argument can be justly used against the constitutional guarantees thus secured, because of the common sentiment of the day. *Those ideas, however, were fundamentally wrong. They rested upon the assumption of the equality of races. This was an error.* It was a sandy foundation; and the idea of a Government built upon it—when the storm came and the wind blew, it *fell.*

"*Our new government is founded upon exactly the opposite ideas; its foundations are laid, its corner-stone rests upon, the great truth that the negro is not equal to the white man; that Slavery, subordination to the superior race, is his natural and normal condition.* [Applause.] *This, our new Government, is the first in the history of the world, based upon this great physical, philosophical, and moral truth.* This truth has been slow in the process of its development, like all other truths in the various departments of science. It is so, even amongst us. Many who hear me, perhaps, can recollect well that this truth was not generally admitted, even within their day. The errors of the past generation still clung to many, so late as twenty years ago. Those at the North who still cling to these errors with a zeal above knowledge, we justly denominate fanatics. All fanaticism springs from an aberration of the mind; from a defect in reasoning. It is a species of insanity. One of the most striking characteristics of insanity, in many instances, is, forming correct conclusions from fancied or erroneous premises; so with the anti-Slavery fanatics: their conclusions are right if their premises are. They assume that the negro is equal, and hence conclude that he is entitled to equal privileges and rights, with the white man. If their premises were correct, their conclusions would be logical and just; but, their premises being wrong, their whole argument fails. I recollect once of having heard a gentleman from one of the Northern States, of great power and ability, announce in the House of Representatives, with imposing effect, that we of the South would be compelled, ultimately, to yield upon this subject of Slavery; that it was impossible to war successfully against a principle in politics, as it was in physics or mechanics—that the principle would ultimately prevail—that we, in maintaining Slavery, as it now exists with us, were warring against a principle—a principle founded in nature—the principle of the equality of man. The reply I made to him was, that, upon his own grounds, we should succeed; that he and his associates in their crusade against our institutions would ultimately fail. The truth announced, that it was as impossible to war successfully against a principle in politics as in physics and mechanics, I admitted; but told him it was he, and those acting with him, who were warring against a principle. They were attempting to make things equal which the Creator had made unequal.

"In the conflict thus far, success has been on our side complete, throughout the length and breadth of the Confederate States. It is upon this, as I have stated, our social fabric is firmly planted; and I cannot permit myself to doubt the ultimate success of a full recognition of this principle throughout the civilized and enlightened world.

"As I have stated, the truth of this principle may be slow in development, as all truths are, and ever have been, in the various branches of science. It was so with the principles announced by Galileo—it was so with Adam Smith, and his principles of political economy. It was so with Harvey, and his theory of the circulation of the blood. It is stated that not a single one of the medical profession, living at the time of the announcement of the truths made by him, admitted them. Now, they are universally acknowledged. May we not, therefore, look with confidence to the ultimate universal acknowledgment of the truths upon which our system rests? It is the first government ever instituted upon principles in strict conformity with nature, and the ordination of Providence, in furnishing the materials of human society. Many governments have been founded upon the principle of enslaving certain classes; but the classes thus enslaved were of the same race, and their enslavement in violation of the laws of nature. *Our* system commits no such violation of nature's laws. The negro, by nature, or by the curse against Canaan, is fitted for that condition which he occupies in our system. The architect, in the construction of buildings, lays the foundation with the proper material—the granite—then comes the brick or the marble. The substratum of *our* society is made of the material fitted by nature for it; and by experience we know that it is the best, not only for the superior, but for the inferior race, that it should be so. It is, indeed, in conformity with the Creator. *It is not for us to inquire into the wisdom of His ordinances, or to question them.* For His own purposes, He has made one race to differ from another, as He has made 'one star to differ from another in glory.'

"The great objects of humanity are best attained when conformed to His laws and decrees, in the formation of governments as well as in all things else. Our Confederacy is founded upon principles in strict conformity with these laws. This stone, which was rejected by the first builders, '*is become the chief stone of the corner*' in our new edifice. [Applause.]

"I have been asked, What of the future? It has been apprehended by some that we would have arrayed against us the civilized world. I care not who or how many they may be; when we stand upon the eternal principles of truth, we are obliged to and must triumph. [Immense applause.]"

With regard to future accessions to the Confederacy, Mr. Stephens said:

"Our growth by accessions from other States will depend greatly upon whether we present to the world, as I trust we shall, a better government than that to which they belong. If we do this, North Carolina, Tennessee, and Arkansas, cannot hesitate long; neither can Virginia, Kentucky, and Missouri. They will necessarily gravitate to us by an imperious law. We made ample provision in our Constitution for the admission of other States. It is more guarded—and wisely so, I think—than the old Constitution on the same subject; but not too guarded to receive them so fast as it may be proper. Looking to the distant future—and perhaps not *very* distant either—it is not beyond the range of possibility, and even probability, that all the great States of the North-West shall gravitate this way, as well as Tennessee, Kentucky, Missouri, Arkansas, etc. Should they do so, our doors are wide enough to receive them; *but not until they are ready to assimilate with us in principle.*

"The process of disintegration in the old Union may be expected to go on with almost absolute certainty. We are now the nucleus of a growing power; which, if we are true to ourselves, our destiny, and our high mission, will become the controlling power on this continent. To what extent accessions will go on, in the process of time, or where it will end, the future will determine. So far as it concerns States of the old Union, they will be upon no such principle of *reconstruction* as is now spoken of, but upon *reörganization* and new assimilation. [Loud applause.] Such are some of the glimpses of the future as I catch them."

Mr. Abraham Lincoln, on the 11th of February, left his home at Springfield, Illinois, for Washington, receiving on the way advices that he had been, upon a careful canvass and comparison of the Electoral votes by Congress, proclaimed[17] by Vice-President Breckinridge the duly elected President of the United States, for four years from the 4th of March ensuing. Immense crowds surrounded the stations at which the special train halted wherein he, with his family and a few friends, was borne eastward through Indianapolis, Cincinnati, Columbus, Pittsburgh, Cleveland, Erie, Buffalo, Albany, New York City, Trenton, Newark, Philadelphia, Lancaster, and Harrisburg, on his way to the White House. He was everywhere received and honored as the chief of a free people; and his unstudied remarks in reply to the complimentary addresses which he day by day received indicated his decided disbelief in any bloody issue of our domestic complications.

Thus, at Indianapolis, where he spent the first night of his journey, he replied to an address of welcome from Gov. Morton, as follows:

[17] February 13th.

"FELLOW-CITIZENS OF THE STATE OF INDIANA: I am here to thank you much for this magnificent welcome, and still more for the very generous support given by your State to that political cause which, I think, is the true and just cause of the whole country and the whole world. Solomon says, 'There is a time to keep silence;' and, when men wrangle by the month with no certainty that they mean the same thing while using the same word, it perhaps were as well if they *would* keep silence. The words 'coërcion' and 'invasion' are much used in these days, and often with some temper and hot blood. Let us make sure, if we can, that we do not misunderstand the meaning of those who use them. Let us get the exact definitions of these words, not from dictionaries, but from the men themselves, who certainly deprecate the things they would represent by the use of the words. What, then, is 'coërcion'? What is 'invasion'? Would the marching of an army into South Carolina without the consent of her people, and with hostile intent toward them, be invasion? I certainly think it would be 'invasion,' and 'coërcion' also, if the South Carolinians were forced to submit. *But, if the United States should merely hold and retake her own forts and other property, and collect the duties on foreign importations, or even withhold the mails from places where they were habitually violated, would any or all these things be 'invasion' or 'coërcion'?* Do our professed lovers of the Union, but who spitefully resolve that they will resist coërcion and invasion, understand that such things as these on the part of the United States would be 'coërcion' or 'invasion' of a State? If so, their idea of means to preserve the object of their great affection would seem to be exceedingly thin and airy. If sick, the little pills of the homœopathist would be much too large for it to swallow. In their view, the Union, as a family relation, would seem to be no regular marriage, but rather a sort of free-love arrangement, to be maintained on 'passional attraction.' By the way, in what consists the special sacredness of a State? I speak not of the position assigned to a State in the Union by the Constitution; for that is the bond we all recognize. That position, however, a State cannot carry out of the Union with it. I speak of that assumed primary right of a State to rule all which is less than itself, and to ruin all which is larger than itself. If a State and a County, in a given case, should be equal in extent of territory and equal in number of inhabitants, in what, as a matter of principle, is the State better than the County? Would an exchange of names be an exchange of rights? Upon principle, on what rightful ground may a State, being no more than one-fiftieth part of the nation in soil and population, break up the nation, and then coërce a proportionally larger subdivision of itself in the most arbitrary way? What mysterious right to play tyrant is conferred on a district of country, with its people, by merely calling it a State?

"Fellow-citizens, I am not asserting anything. I am merely asking questions for you to consider. And now, allow me to bid you farewell."

At Columbus, Ohio, he said:

"I have not maintained silence from any want of real anxiety. It is a good thing that there is no more than anxiety; for there is nothing going wrong. It is a consoling circumstance that, when we look out, there is nothing that really hurts anybody. We entertain different views upon political questions: but nobody is suffering anything. This is a most consoling circumstance; and from it we may conclude that all we want is time, patience, and a reliance on that God who has never forsaken this people."

At Pittsburgh, Pennsylvania, on the 15th, he said:

"Notwithstanding the troubles across the river [the speaker pointing southwardly across the Monongahela, and smiling], there is no crisis but an artificial one. What is there now to warrant the condition of affairs presented by our friends over the river? Take even their own views of the questions involved, and there is nothing to justify the course they are pursuing. I repeat, then, there is no crisis, except such a one as may be gotten up at any time by turbulent men, aided by designing politicians. My advice to them, under the circumstances, is to keep cool. If the great American people only keep their temper both sides of the line, the trouble will come to an end, and the question which now distracts the country be settled, just as surely as all other difficulties, of a like character, which have originated in this Government, have been adjusted. Let the people on both sides keep their self-possession, and, just as other clouds have cleared away in due time, so will this great nation continue to prosper as heretofore."

At Philadelphia, being required to assist at the solemn raising of the United States flag over Independence Hall, Mr. Lincoln, in reply to an address of welcome by Mr. Theodore Cuyler, said:

"I have often pondered over the dangers incurred by the men who assembled here, and framed and adopted that Declaration of

Independence. I have pondered over the toils that were endured by the officers and soldiers of the army who achieved that Independence. I have often inquired of myself, what great principle or idea it was that kept this confederacy so long together. It was not the mere matter of the separation of the Colonies from the mother-land; but *that sentiment in the Declaration of Independence which gave Liberty, not alone to the people of this country, but, I hope, to the world, for all future time.* It was that which gave promise that, in due time, the weight would be lifted from the shoulders of all men. This is a sentiment embodied in the Declaration of Independence. Now, my friends, can this country be saved on that basis? If it can, I will consider myself one of the happiest men in the world, if I can help to save it. If it cannot be saved on that basis, it will be truly awful. But, if this country cannot be saved without giving up that principle, I was about to say that I would rather be assassinated on this spot than surrender it. Now, in my view of the present aspect of affairs, there need be no bloodshed or war. There is no necessity for it. I am not in favor of such a course; and I may say, in advance, that there *will* be no bloodshed, unless it be forced upon the Government, and then it will be compelled to act in self defense."

Arrived at Harrisburg, however, on the 22d, Mr. Lincoln, looking across the slave line, experienced suddenly a decided change in the political barometer. It had been arranged that he should next day pass through Baltimore, the center of a grand procession—a cynosure of admiring eyes—the object of enthusiastic acclamations—as he had, thus far, passed through nearly all the great cities of the Free States. But Baltimore was a slaveholding city, and the spirit of Slavery was nowhere else more rampant and ferocious. The mercantile and social aristocracy of that city had been sedulously, persistently, plied by the conspirators for disunion with artful suggestions that, in a confederacy composed exclusively of the fifteen Slave States, Baltimore would hold the position that New York enjoys in the Union, being the great ship-building, shipping, importing and commercial emporium, whitening the ocean with her sails, and gemming Maryland with the palaces reared from her ample and ever-expanding profits. That aristocracy had been, for the most part, thoroughly corrupted by these insidious whispers, and so were ready to rush into treason. At the other end of the social scale was the mob—reckless and godless, as mobs are apt to be, especially in slaveholding communities—and ready at all times to do the bidding of the Slave Power. Between these was the great middle class, loyal and peacefully inclined, as this class usually is—outnumbering both the others, but hitherto divided between the old pro-Slavery parties, and having arrived, as yet, at no common understanding with regard to the novel circumstances of the country and the events visibly impending.

The city government was in the hands of the Breckinridge Democracy, who had seized it under a cry of reform; and the leaders of that Democracy were deep in the counsels of treason. It had been proclaimed, in many quarters, and through various channels, that Mr. Lincoln should never live to be inaugurated; and *The Baltimore Republican* of the 22d had a leading article directly calculated to incite tumult and violence on the occasion of Mr. Lincoln's passage through the city.[18] The police

[18] *The Baltimore Exchange* of February 23d, significantly said:

"Mr. Lincoln, the President elect of the United States, will arrive in this city with his suite this afternoon by special train from Harrisburgh, and will proceed, we learn, directly to Washington. It is to be hoped that no opportunity will be afforded him—or that, if it be afforded, he will not embrace it—to repeat in our

was directed by Marshal George P. Kane, who, after a sojourn in Fort McHenry, fled in 1863 to the congenial associations of Richmond and the Confederate Army. It being considered certain that an attempt to assassinate the President would be made, under cover of mob violence, should he pass through the city as was originally intended, Mr. Lincoln was persuaded to take the cars secretly, during the evening of the 22d, and so passed through Baltimore, unknown and unsuspected, early on the morning of the 23d—reaching Washington about the hour that he was expected to leave Harrisburg. The prudence of this step has since been abundantly demonstrated; but it wounded, at the time, the sensibilities of many friends, who would have much preferred to form an escort of one hundred thousand armed men to see him safely through Baltimore, than to have him pass through it clandestinely and like a hunted fugitive.

The 4th of March, 1861, though its early morning had been cloudy and chilly, was a remarkably bright and genial day at Washington. To the children of harsh New England, it seemed more like May than March. Expectations and threats of convulsion had rather increased than lessened the throng, wherein all sections of the unseceded States were liberally represented, though the Federal District and the adjacent counties of Maryland and Virginia doubtless supplied by far the larger share of it. Menaces that the President elect would never be permitted to take the oath of office—that he would be assassinated in the act, if no other mode of preventing it should promise success—had been so freely and loudly made,[19] that apprehensions of some concerted attempt at violence or tumult were widely entertained and fully justified. Lieut.-Gen. Scott had taken the fullest military precautions that his limited force of regulars—perhaps one thousand in all—would permit; and there was a considerable muster of uniformed Militia. The procession, partly civic, which escorted the retiring and incoming Presidents, who rode in the same carriage, to the Capitol, was quite respectable—unusually so for that non-enthusiastic, and, as yet, strongly pro-Slavery, metropolis.

The Senate had been sitting through most of the preceding forty-eight hours, though this was Monday, and barely concluded the labors of the session in time to allow Vice-President Breckinridge to resign the Chair in a few courteous words, and take his seat on the floor as a member, while Vice-President Hamlin left the floor to take the Chair with as little parade—the two thus exchanging places. This done, and several other new Senators beside Mr. Breckinridge having been sworn in, the space in the Chamber allotted for this occasion to the Embassadors of Foreign Powers ('Dixie' not included) was promptly filled by the diplomatic body in full dress; the magnates blazing with stars and orders. Soon, the Justices of the Supreme Court entered in a body, and the assemblage rose in silent homage, and

midst the sentiments which he is reported to have expressed yesterday in Philadelphia."

[The "sentiments" thus deprecated are those uttered in reply to Mr. Cuyler, and quoted on the preceding page.]

[19] In Richmond and other journals.

stood till they were seated. The remaining space on the floor was now filled to its utmost capacity by members of the House, just adjourned; and it was soon afterward announced that the Presidential party had entered the edifice. On its appearance, the whole assemblage proceeded to the magnificent and spacious Eastern portico of the Capitol, on which a platform had been erected, and in front of which a considerable space had been cleared, and was held, by the Military. The President elect was barely introduced to the vast concourse by Col. Edward D. Baker, Senator from Oregon, and received with cheers from perhaps a fourth of the thirty thousand persons confronting him. Silence having succeeded, Mr. Lincoln unrolled a manuscript, and, in a firm, clear, penetrating voice, read the following

INAUGURAL ADDRESS.

Fellow-Citizens of the United States:

In compliance with a custom as old as the Government itself, I appear before you to address you briefly, and to take, in your presence, the oath prescribed by the Constitution of the United States to be taken by the President, before he enters on the execution of his office.

I do not consider it necessary, at present, for me to discuss those matters of administration about which there is no special anxiety or excitement. Apprehension seems to exist among the people of the Southern States, that, by the accession of a Republican Administration, their property and their peace and personal security are to be endangered. There has never been any reasonable cause for such apprehension. Indeed, the most ample evidence to the contrary has all the while existed, and been open to their inspection. It is found in nearly all the published speeches of him who now addresses you. I do but quote from one of those speeches, when I declare that "I have no purpose, directly or indirectly, to interfere with the institution of Slavery in the States where it exists." I believe I have no lawful right to do so; and I have no inclination to do so. Those who nominated and elected me, did so with the full knowledge that I had made this, and many similar declarations, and had never recanted them. And, more than this, they placed in the platform, for my acceptance, and as a law to themselves and to me, the clear and emphatic resolution which I now read:

"*Resolved*, That the maintenance inviolate of the rights of the States, and especially the right of each State to order and control its own domestic institutions according to its own judgment exclusively, is essential to that balance of power on which the perfection and endurance of our political fabric depend; and we denounce the lawless invasion by armed force of the soil of any State or Territory, no matter under what pretext, as among the gravest of crimes."

I now rëiterate these sentiments; and, in doing so, I only press upon the public attention the most conclusive evidence of which the case is susceptible, that the property, peace, and security, of no section are to be in anywise endangered by the now incoming Administration.

I add, too, that all the protection which, consistently with the Constitution and the laws, can be given, will be cheerfully given to all the States, when lawfully demanded, for whatever cause, as cheerfully to one section as to another.

There is much controversy about the delivering up of fugitives from service or labor. The clause I now read is as plainly written in the Constitution as any other of its provisions:

"No person held to service or labor in one State under the laws thereof, escaping into another, shall, in consequence of any law or regulation therein, be discharged from such service or labor, but shall be delivered up on claim of the party to whom such service or labor may be due."

It is scarcely questioned that this provision was intended by those who made it for the reclaiming of what we call fugitive slaves; and the intention of the lawgiver is the law.

All members of Congress swear their support to the whole Constitution—to this provision as well as any other. To the proposition, then, that slaves whose cases come within the terms of this clause "shall be delivered up," their oaths are unanimous. Now, if they would make the effort in good temper, could they not, with nearly equal unanimity, frame and pass a law by means of which to keep good that unanimous oath?

There is some difference of opinion whether this clause should be enforced by National or by State authority; but surely that difference is not a very material one. If the slave is to be surrendered, it can be of but little consequence to him or to others by which authority it is done; and should any one, in any case, be content that this oath shall go unkept on a merely unsubstantial controversy as to how it shall be kept?

Again, in any law upon this subject, ought not all the safeguards of liberty known in civilized and humane jurisprudence to be introduced, so that a free man be not, in any case, surrendered as a slave? And might it not be well at the same time to provide by law for the enforcement of that clause in the Constitution which guarantees that "the citizens of each State shall be entitled to all the privileges and immunities of citizens in the several States?"

I take the official oath to-day with no mental reservations, and with no purpose to construe the Constitution or laws by any hypercritical rules; and, while I do not choose now to specify particular acts of Congress as proper to be enforced, I do suggest that it will be much safer for all, both in official and private stations, to conform to and abide by all those acts which stand unrepealed, than to violate any of them, trusting to find impunity in having them held to be unconstitutional.

It is seventy-two years since the first inauguration of a President under our National Constitution. During that period, fifteen different and very distinguished citizens have in succession administered the executive branch of the government. They have conducted it through many perils, and generally with great success. Yet, with all this scope for precedent, I now enter upon the same task, for the brief constitutional term of four years, under great and peculiar difficulties.

A disruption of the Federal Union, heretofore only menaced, is now formidably attempted. I hold that, in the contemplation of universal law and of the Constitution, the Union of these States is perpetual. Perpetuity is implied, if not expressed, in the fundamental law of all national governments. It is safe to assert that no government proper ever had a provision in its organic law for its own termination. Continue to execute all the express provisions of our national Constitution, and the Union will endure forever, it being impossible to destroy it except by some action not provided for in the instrument itself.

Again, if the United States be not a government proper, but an association of States in the nature of a contract merely, can it, as a contract, be peaceably unmade by less than all the parties who made it? One party to a contract may violate it—break it, so to speak; but does it not require all to lawfully rescind it? Descending from these general principles, we find the proposition that in legal contemplation the Union is perpetual, confirmed by the history of the Union itself.

The Union is much older than the Constitution. It was formed, in fact, by the Articles of Association in 1774. It was matured and continued in the Declaration of Independence in 1776. It was further matured, and the faith of all the then thirteen States expressly plighted and engaged that it should be perpetual, by the Articles of Confederation, in 1778; and, finally, in 1787, one of the declared objects for ordaining and establishing the Constitution was to form a more perfect union. But, if the destruction of the Union by one or by a part only of the States be lawfully possible, the Union is less than before, the Constitution having lost the vital element of perpetuity.

It follows from these views that no State, upon its own mere motion, can lawfully get out of the Union; that resolves and ordinances to that effect, are legally void; and that acts of violence within any State or States against the authority of the United States, are insurrectionary or revolutionary, according to circumstances.

I therefore consider that, in view of the Constitution and the laws, the Union is unbroken, and, to the extent of my ability, I shall take care, as the Constitution itself expressly enjoins upon me, that the laws of the Union shall be faithfully executed in all the States. Doing this, which I deem to be only a simple duty on my part, I shall perfectly perform it, so far as is practicable, unless my rightful masters, the American people, shall withhold the requisite power, or in some authoritative manner direct the contrary.

I trust this will not be regarded as a menace, but only as the declared purpose of the Union that it will constitutionally defend and maintain itself.

In doing this, there need be no bloodshed or violence, and there shall be none unless it is forced upon the national authority.

The power confided to me *will be used to hold, occupy, and possess the property and places belonging to the Government*, and collect the duties and imposts; but, beyond what may be necessary for these objects, there will be no invasion, no using of force against or among the people anywhere.

Where hostility to the United States shall be so great and so universal as to prevent competent resident citizens from holding the Federal offices, there will be no attempt to force obnoxious strangers among the people for that object. While the strict legal right may exist of the Government to enforce the exercise of these offices, the attempt to do so would be so irritating, and so nearly impracticable withal, that I deem it better to forego for the time the uses of such offices.

The mails, unless repelled, will continue to be furnished in all parts of the Union.

So far as possible, the people everywhere shall have that sense of perfect security which is most favorable to calm thought and reflection.

The course here indicated will be followed, unless current events and experience shall show a modification or change to be proper; and in every case and exigency my best discretion will be exercised according to the circumstances actually existing, and with a view and hope of a peaceful solution of the national troubles, and the restoration of fraternal sympathies and affections.

That there are persons, in one section or another, who seek to destroy the Union at all events, and are glad of any pretext to do it, I will neither affirm nor deny. But, if there be such, I need address no word to them.

To those, however, who really love the Union, may I not speak? Before entering upon so grave a matter as the destruction of our national fabric, with all its benefits, its memories, and its hopes, would it not be well to ascertain why we do it? Will you hazard so desperate a step, while any portion of the ills you fly from, have no real existence? Will you, while the certain ills you fly to are greater than all the real ones you fly from? Will you risk the commission of so fearful a mistake? All profess to be content in the Union if all constitutional rights can be maintained. Is it true, then, that any right, plainly written in the Constitution, has been denied? I think not. Happily, the human mind is so constituted, that no party can reach to the audacity of doing this.

Think, if you can, of a single instance in which a plainly-written provision of the Constitution has ever been denied. If, by the mere force of numbers, a majority should deprive a minority of any clearly-written constitutional right, it might, in a moral point of view, justify revolution; it certainly would, if such right were a vital one. But such is not our case.

All the vital rights of minorities and of individuals are so plainly assured to them by affirmations and negations, guaranties and prohibitions, in the Constitution, that controversies never arise concerning them. But no organic law can ever be framed with a provision specifically applicable to every question which may occur in practical administration. No foresight can anticipate, nor any document of reasonable length contain, express provisions for all possible questions. Shall fugitives from labor be surrendered by National or by State authority? The Constitution does not expressly say. Must Congress protect Slavery in the Territories? The Constitution does not expressly say. From questions of this class spring all our constitutional controversies, and we divide upon them into majorities and minorities.

If the minority will not acquiesce, the majority must, or the government must cease. There is no alternative for continuing the government but acquiescence on the one side or the other. If a minority in such a case will secede rather than acquiesce, they make a precedent which in turn will ruin and divide them; for a minority of their own will secede from them whenever a majority refuses to be controlled by such a minority. For instance, why not any portion of a new confederacy, a year or two hence, arbitrarily secede again, precisely as portions of the present Union now claim to secede from it? All who cherish disunion sentiments are now being educated to the exact temper of doing this. Is there such perfect identity of interests among the States to compose a new Union as to produce harmony only, and prevent renewed secession? Plainly, the central idea of secession is the essence of anarchy.

A majority held in restraint by constitutional check and limitation, and always changing easily with deliberate changes of popular opinions and sentiments, is the only true sovereign of a free people. Whoever rejects it, does, of necessity, fly to anarchy or to despotism. Unanimity is impossible; the rule of a minority, as a permanent arrangement, is wholly inadmissible. So that, rejecting the majority principle, anarchy or despotism in some form is all that is left.

I do not forget the position assumed by some that constitutional questions are to be decided by the Supreme Court, nor do I deny that such decisions must be binding in any case upon the parties to a suit, as to the object of that suit, while they are also entitled to very high respect and consideration in all parallel cases by all other departments of the government; and, while it is obviously possible that such decision may be erroneous in any given case, still, the evil effect following it, being limited to that particular case, with the chance that it may be overruled and never become a precedent for other cases, can better be borne than could the evils of a different practice.

At the same time, the candid citizen must confess that, if the policy of the government upon the vital questions affecting the whole people is to be irrevocably fixed by the decisions of the Supreme Court, the instant they are made, as in ordinary litigation between parties in personal actions, the people will have ceased to be their own masters, having to that extent practically resigned their government into the hands of that eminent tribunal.

Nor is there in this view any assault upon the court or the judges. It is a duty from which they may not shrink, to decide cases properly brought before them; and it is no fault of theirs if others seek to turn their decisions to political purposes. One section of our country believes Slavery is right and ought to be extended, while the other believes it is wrong and ought not to be extended; and this is the only substantial dispute; and the fugitive slave clause of the constitution, and the law for the suppression of the foreign slave-trade, are each as well enforced, perhaps, as any law can ever be in a community where the moral sense of the people imperfectly supports the law itself. The great body of the people abide by the dry legal obligation in both cases, and a few break over in each. This, I think, cannot be perfectly cured, and it would be worse in both cases after the separation of the sections than before. The foreign slave-trade, now imperfectly suppressed, would be ultimately revived, without restriction, in one section; while fugitive slaves, now only partially surrendered, would not be surrendered at all, by the other.

Physically speaking, we cannot separate—we cannot remove our respective sections from each other, nor build an impassable wall between them. A husband and wife may be divorced, and go out of the presence and beyond the reach of each other; but the different parts of our country cannot do this. They cannot but remain face to face; and intercourse, either amicable or hostile, must continue between them. Is it possible, then, to make that intercourse more advantageous or more satisfactory after separation than before? Can aliens make treaties easier than friends can make laws? Can treaties be more faithfully enforced between aliens than laws can among friends? Suppose you go to war, you cannot fight always; and when, after much loss on both sides and no gain on either, you cease fighting, the identical questions as to terms of intercourse are again upon you.

This country, with its institutions, belongs to the people who inhabit it. Whenever they shall grow weary of the existing government, they can exercise their constitutional right of amending, or their revolutionary right to dismember or overthrow it. I cannot be ignorant of the fact that many worthy and patriotic citizens are desirous of having the national Constitution amended. While I make no recommendation of amendment, I fully recognize the full authority of the people over the whole subject, to be exercised in either of the modes prescribed in the instrument itself; and I should, under existing circumstances, favor, rather than oppose, a fair opportunity being afforded the people to act upon it.

I will venture to add, that to me the Convention mode seems preferable, in that it allows amendments to originate with the people themselves, instead of only permitting them to take or reject propositions originated by others not especially chosen for the purpose, and which might not be precisely such as they would wish either to accept or refuse. I understand that a proposed amendment to the Constitution (which amendment, however, I have not seen) has passed Congress, to the effect that the Federal Government shall never interfere with the domestic institutions of States, including that of persons held to service. To avoid misconstruction of what I have said, I depart from my purpose not to speak of particular amendments, so far as to say that, holding such a provision to now be implied constitutional law, I have no objection to its being made express and irrevocable.

The chief magistrate derives all his authority from the people, and they have conferred none upon him to fix the terms for the separation of the States. The people themselves, also, can do this if they choose; but the Executive, as such, has nothing to do with it. His duty is to administer the present government as it came to his hands, and to transmit it unimpaired by him to his successor. Why should there not be a patient confidence in the ultimate justice of the people? Is there any better or equal hope in the world? In our present differences, is either party without faith of being in the right? If the Almighty Ruler of nations, with His eternal truth and justice, be on your side of the North, or on yours of the South, that truth and that justice will surely prevail by the judgment of this great tribunal, the American people. By the frame of the Government under which we live, this same people have wisely given their public servants but little power for mischief, and have with equal wisdom provided for the return of that little to their own hands at very short intervals. While the people retain their virtue and vigilance, no administration, by any extreme wickedness or folly, can very seriously injure the Government in the short space of four years.

My countrymen, one and all, think calmly and well upon this whole subject. Nothing valuable can be lost by taking time.

If there be an object to hurry any of you, in hot haste, to a step which you would never take deliberately, that object will be frustrated by taking time; but no good object can be frustrated by it.

Such of you as are now dissatisfied still have the old Constitution unimpaired, and, on the sensitive point, the laws of your own framing under it; while the new administration will have no immediate power, if it would, to change either.

If it were admitted that you who are dissatisfied hold the right side in the dispute, there is still no single reason for precipitate action. Intelligence, patriotism, Christianity, and a firm reliance on Him who has never yet forsaken this favored land, are still competent to adjust, in the best way, all our present difficulties.

In your hands, my dissatisfied fellow-countrymen, and not in mine, is the momentous issue of civil war. The Government will not assail you.

You can have no conflict without being yourselves the aggressors. You can have no oath registered in Heaven to destroy the Government; while I shall have the most solemn one to "preserve, protect, and defend" it.

I am loath to close. We are not enemies, but friends. We must not be enemies. Though passion may have strained, it must not break, our bonds of affection.

The mystic chords of memory, stretching from every battle-field and patriot grave to every living heart and hearthstone all over this broad land, will yet swell the chorus of the Union, when again touched, as surely they will be, by the better angels of our nature.

The habitual tone of this remarkable paper is deprecatory, not to say apologetic. Mr. Lincoln evidently composed it under the fixed impression that 'the South' needed but to be disabused of her impressions and apprehensions of Northern hostility to restore her to loyalty and the whole land to peace. If she can be made to feel that the new rule does not desire to meddle with Slavery in the States which cherish it, but will hunt and return fugitive slaves to the extent of its ability, then Secession will be given up, and the country restored to peace and harmony! That, certainly, is an amiable view of the situation; but it was not justified by a close study and thorough comprehension of our recent political history.

Mr. Lincoln's suggestion that the dictum of the Supreme Court, though law to the suitor whom it bore hard upon, does not bind the people not to entertain and vote in conformity to an adverse conviction, though in full accordance with the action of 'the South' in regard to the Alien and Sedition laws, the Creek and Cherokee treaties,[19] etc., and, in fact, to the action of all parties when overruled by that Court, was not calculated to please and conciliate 'the South.' Yet no adversary of a United States Bank ever felt himself restrained from opposing and voting against such a Bank as unconstitutional by the fact that the Court had adjudged it otherwise. No one imagines that a decision by that Court that Slavery had *no* right to enter the territories would have been regarded and treated by 'the South' as the end of controversy on that point.[20] But, having obtained, in the Dred Scott case, an opinion that slaveholders *might* take their human chattels to any territory, and there hold them, claiming ample protection from the Government in so doing, they were fully resolved to make the most of it, and not at all disposed to acquiesce in the suggestion that, on questions essentially political, the American People are a higher authority than even their Supreme Court.

The weakest portion of this document is its inconsiderate talk about an "invasion" of the States by the Federal Government, and its *quasi* pledge not to appoint Federal offi-

[19] See pages 105–6.

[20] See Mr. John Van Buren on this point, page 213. For Mr. Jefferson's views, see pages 83–4; for Gen. Jackson's, see pages 104–6.

cers for communities unanimously hostile to the authority of the Union. A surgeon who should volunteer a pledge not to disturb or meddle with any proud flesh he might find in his patient's wounds, would hardly expect to augment thereby that patient's confidence in his skill; nor could a priest who should stipulate never to assail any other than unpopular and repudiated sins, expect to win a high regard either for his authority or his sanctity. The fact that the sovereignty of the Union is coëxtensive, and, *at least*, coördinate with that of the States, is here clearly lost sight of. To say, in effect, to rebels against the National authority, "You may expel that authority wholly from your vicinage by killing a few of its leading upholders, and thus terrifying the residue into mute servility to your will," is not the way to suppress a rebellion.

The strong point of this Inaugural is its frank and plump denial of the fundamental Secession dogma that our Union is a league,[21] formed in 1787. "The Union is much older than the Constitution," says Mr. Lincoln, truly and pertinently. Had the Constitution been rejected by the States, the Union would nevertheless have subsisted. Ours is '*one* country'—made so by God and His Providence, revealed through the whole of its recorded history; its '*more perfect* Union' is but a step in its development—not the cause of its existence. Hence, Secession is not "the dissolution of a league," as Mr. Jefferson Davis asserts, but a treasonable, though futile, effort to disorganize and destroy a nation.

Mr. Lincoln's rejection of Disunion as physically impossible—as forbidden by the geography and topography of our country—is a statesmanlike conception that had not before been so clearly apprehended or so forcibly set forth. And, in truth, not one-tenth of the then active Secessionists ever meditated or intended Disunion as permanent. They proposed to destroy the Union in order to reconstitute it according to their own ideas, with Slavery as its corner-stone. To kick out the New England States, rural New York, and that 'fanatical' section of the West that is drained by the Great Lakes and the St. Lawrence—such was the constant inculcation of pro-Slavery journalists and politicians throughout that eventful Winter and Spring. Free States were to be admitted into the Confederacy, on condition of their fully

[21] *The New York Herald* of November 9th, contained an instructive letter dated Charleston, November 5th, 1860, from which the following is an extract:

"It must be understood that there is a radical difference in the patriotism of a Northerner and a Southerner. The Northerner invariably considers himself as a citizen of the Union; he regards the Federal army and navy as his country's army and navy, and looks upon the Government at Washington as a great consolidated organization, of which he forms an integral part, and to which whatever love of country he may possess is directed. Beyond paying the State taxes, voting for State officers, and seeking redress primarily in the State courts, he has very little idea of any special fealty being due to his own particular State.

"The Southerner, on the other hand, generally (and the South Carolinian always) repudiates this theory of consolidation. He feels that he owes allegiance to his own State, and to her alone; he is jealous of her rights and honor, and will never admit that any step taken in obedience to her mandate can involve the idea of treason. The Federal Government is, in his eyes, but the embodiment of certain powers delegated by the States from motives of policy. Let those motives be once removed or counterbalanced, and he holds that the State has no longer any reason for maintaining a connection which it was her right, at any time, to have dissolved. These being the views of the people of South Carolina, the threats of Douglas and the Black Republicans have only served to confirm the wavering and knit together the citizens of the various sections of the State."

abjuring all manner of anti-Slavery sentiment and inculcation evermore, and becoming Slave States. A few Southern fanatics, who deemed nothing needed but the reöpening of the African Slave-Trade to render 'the South' the mistress of the world, wished to be rid of all 'Yankee' association and contamination evermore; but the great mass, even in the Cotton States, regarded Secession but as a device for bringing the North to its knees, and binding it over to future docility to every exaction of the Slave Power.

Mr. Lincoln fondly regarded his Inaugural as a resistless proffering of the olive-branch to 'the South'; the conspirators everywhere interpreted it as a challenge to war.[22] And when the former had taken the oath, solemnly administered to him by Chief Justice Taney, the two Presidents wended their way back, duly escorted, to the White House, at whose door Mr. Buchanan bade Mr. Lincoln a cordial good-by, retiring to the residence of his friend and beneficiary, Robert Ould, whom he had made U. S. District Attorney, and who, though from Maryland, soon after fled to Richmond, and entered at once the military service of the Confederacy.

XXVII.

OMINOUS PAUSE.

President Lincoln, on the day after his inauguration, submitted to the new Senate the names of those whom he had chosen to preside over the several Departments, and who thus became, by a usage which has no express warrant in the Constitution, his official counselors. They were

William H. Seward, of New York, *Secr'y of State;*
Salmon P. Chase, of Ohio, *Secretary of the Treasury;*
Simon Cameron, of Pennsylvania, *Secretary of War;*
Gideon Welles, of Connecticut, *Secr'y of the Navy;*
Caleb B. Smith, of Indiana, *Secretary of the Interior;*
Edward Bates, of Missouri, *Attorney-General;*
Montgomery Blair, of Maryland, *Postmaster-General.*

---

[22] It were idle to quote the Disunion press, even of the yet unseceded States, to prove this; since *their* strictures may well be imagined. The following, from professedly loyal journals, are worth recording:

"The Inaugural, as a whole, breathes the spirit of mischief. It has only a conditional conservatism—that is, the lack of ability or some inexpediency to do what it would. It assumes despotic authority, and intimates the design to exercise that authority to any extent of war and bloodshed, qualified only by the *withholding* of the requisite means to the end by the American people. The argumentation of the address is puerile. Indeed, it has no quality entitled to the dignity of an argument. It is a shaky specimen of special pleading, by way of justifying the unrighteous character and deeds of the fanaticism which, lifted into power, may be guilty, as it is capable, of any atrocities. There is no Union spirit in the address, it is sectional and mischievous, and studiously withholds any sign of recognition of that equality of the States upon which the Union can alone be maintained. If it means what it says, it is the knell and requiem of the Union, and the death of hope."—*Baltimore Sun.*

"Mr. Lincoln stands to-day where he stood on the 6th of November last, *on the Chicago Platform.* He has not receded a single hair's breadth. *He has appointed a Cabinet in which there is no slaveholder—a thing that has never before happened since the formation of the Government;* and in which there are but two nominally Southern men, and both bitter Black Republicans of the radical dye. Let the Border States ignominiously *submit* to the Abolition rule of this Lincoln Administration, if they like; but *don't let the miserable submissionists pretend to be deceived.* Make any base or cowardly excuse but this."—*Philadelphia Pennsylvanian.*

Mr. Jefferson Davis, ruling at Montgomery, had already constituted *his* Cabinet, which consisted of

ROBERT TOOMBS, of Georgia, *Secretary of State;*
CHARLES G. MEMMINGER, of South Carolina, *Secretary of the Treasury;*
LEROY POPE WALKER, of Alabama, *Secretary of War;*

to which were afterward added

STEPHEN R. MALLORY, of Florida, *Sec'ry of the Navy;*
JOHN H. REAGAN, of Texas, *Postmaster-General.*

Thus the two Governments stood face to face, holding positions and maintaining assumptions so palpably, utterly incompatible as to necessitate an early collision; and that collision must, in the nature of things, produce a crash that would shake the continent. Still, there was great and wise reluctance, at least on this side, to precipitate or to initiate hostilities. In spite of appearances, President Lincoln,[1] and the advisers in whom he most trusted, seemed still incredulous as to the inevitability and imminence of a clash of arms. Gov. Seward, the new Secretary of State, had for months been apparently the most resolute of optimists with regard to a happy issue from our internal complications. At the New England Dinner[2] in New York, he had confidently predicted a settlement of all our troubles within the ensuing sixty days. That term had sped; yet his faith in a peaceful solution of our differences appeared as buoyant as ever, and seemed to be shared by the President, whose "Nobody hurt as yet" had become a watchword among the obstinate believers in 'Manifest Destiny' and the unparalleled rationality, wisdom, intelligence, and self-control, of the peerless American People.

Does this look like infatuation? If the wisdom that comes to-morrow were the genuine article, every man would be a Solomon. Remember that, for more than seventy years, no man had seen an American hand lifted against the symbol of our Nationality. Neither Shays's Rebellion,[3] in Massachusetts, nor the Whisky Rebellion,[4] so called, in western Pennsylvania, had really purposed aught beyond the removal or redress of temporary grievances which were deemed intolerable. Even old John Brown—fanatic as he was; madman as many held him—never dreamed of dividing the country which he sought to purge of its most flagrant wrong; his Canada Constitution expressly stipulated[5] that the Union should be preserved, and its flag retained and cherished by his adherents. Since the close of our Revolutionary struggle, no man had seen, in the Free States, any other banner floating over a regiment of our people than the Stars and Stripes; though the waves of party spirit had often run mountain high,[6] and we had seemed just on the brink of disruption and civil war, yet the dreaded collision had always been somehow averted, and the moment of fiercest excitement, of widest alienation, had

---

[1] The writer revisited Washington for a day or two, some two weeks or more after Mr. Lincoln's inauguration, and was surprised to see and hear on every hand what were, to him, convincing proofs that an early collision with the 'Confederates' was not seriously apprehended in the highest quarters.

[2] Anniversary of the Landing of the Pilgrims, December 22, 1860.

[3] In 1786–7.

[4] In 1795.

[5] See pages 287–8.

[6] During the War of 1812, it was common in New England for the antagonist parties to take opposite sides of the 'broad aisle' of the 'meeting-house' wherein their respective 'town meetings' were held, and so remain during the day, conferring and counseling among themselves, but rarely mingling with or speaking civilly to members of the adverse party.

often been the immediate precursor of a halcyon era of reconciliation, peace, and fraternal harmony. It was not easy for Northern men, especially those who had never visited and sojourned at the South, to comprehend and reälize the wide prevalence and intensity of anti-National sentiment and feeling in those localities whose social order, industry, and business, were entirely based on Slavery. Neither envying nor hating the Southerners, while lamenting their delusions and resisting their exactions, it was hard indeed for many, if not most, of the citizens of the Free States to realize that we stood on the brink of a volcano whose rumblings preluded an eruption of blood as well as ashes.

Scarcely a week after Mr. Lincoln's inauguration, his Secretary of State was served with the following:

"WASHINGTON, *March* 12, 1861.
"Hon. WILLIAM H. SEWARD,
Secretary of State of the United States:

"SIR:—The undersigned have been duly accredited by the Government of the Confederate States of America as Commissioners to the Government of the United States, and, in pursuance of their instructions, have now the honor to acquaint you with that fact, and to make known, through you, to the President of the United States, the objects of their presence in this Capital.

"Seven States of the late Federal Union having, in the exercise of the inherent right of every free people to change or reform their political institutions, and through Conventions of their people, withdrawn from the United States, and reässumed the attributes of sovereign power, delegated to it, have formed a Government of their own. The Confederate States constitute an independent nation, *de facto* and *de jure*, and possess a Government perfect in all its parts and endowed with all the means of self-support.

"With a view to a speedy adjustment of all questions growing out of this political separation, upon such terms of amity and good-will as the respective interests, geographical contiguity, and future welfare, of the two nations may render necessary, the undersigned are instructed to make to the Government of the United States overtures for the opening of negotiations, assuring the Government of the United States that the President, Congress, and people of the Confederate States earnestly desire a peaceable solution of these great questions; that it is neither their interest nor their wish to make any demand which is not founded in strict justice, nor do any act to injure their late confederates.

"The undersigned have now the honor, in obedience to the instructions of their Government, to request you to appoint as early a day as possible, in order that they may present to the President of the United States the credentials which they bear and the objects of the mission with which they are charged.

"We are, very respectfully,
"Your obedient servants,
"JOHN FORSYTH,
"MARTIN J. CRAWFORD."

To this virtual Declaration of War, under the guise of an overture looking to negotiation, settlement, and amity, Gov. Seward responded as follows:[7]

"*Memorandum.*

"DEPARTMENT OF STATE,
"WASHINGTON, *March* 15, 1861.

"Mr. John Forsyth, of the State of Alabama, and Mr. Martin J. Crawford, of the State of Georgia, on the 11th inst., through the kind offices of a distinguished Senator, submitted to the Secretary of State their desire for an unofficial interview. This request was, on the 12th inst., upon exclusively public considerations, respectfully declined.

"On the 13th inst., while the Secretary was preöccupied, Mr. A. D. Banks, of Virginia, called at this Department, and was received by the Assistant Secretary, to whom he delivered a sealed communication, which he had been charged by Messrs. Forsyth and Crawford to present to the Secretary in person.

"In that communication, Messrs. Forsyth and Crawford inform the Secretary of State that they have been duly accredited by the Government of the Confederate States of America as Commissioners to the Govern-

[7] This reply was withheld, upon consultation with John A. Campbell, of Alabama, (then and till May 2d thereafter a Justice of the U. S. Supreme Court,) until twenty-three days subsequent to its date. Judge C. would seem to have been, even then, acting as a Confederate, despite his oath of office, though misunderstood by Gov. S. as laboring to preserve the Union.

ment of the United States, and they set forth the objects of their attendance at Washington. They observe that seven States of the American Union, in exercise of a right inherent in every free people, have withdrawn, through conventions of their people, from the United States, reässumed the attributes of sovereign power, and formed a government of their own, and that those Confederate States now constitute an independent nation *de facto* and *de jure*, and possess a government perfect in all its parts and fully endowed with all the means of self-support.

"Messrs. Forsyth and Crawford, in their aforesaid communication, thereupon proceeded to inform that, with a view to a speedy adjustment of all questions growing out of the political separation thus assumed, upon such terms of amity and good-will as the respective interests, geographical contiguity, and the future welfare of the supposed two nations might render necessary, they are instructed to make to the Government of the United States overtures for the opening of negotiations, assuring this Government that the President, Congress, and people of the Confederate States earnestly desire a peaceful solution of these great questions, and that it is neither their interest nor their wish to make any demand which is not founded in strictest justice, nor do any act to injure their late confederates.

"After making these statements, Messrs. Forsyth and Crawford close their communication, as they say, in obedience to the instructions of their Government, by requesting the Secretary of State to appoint as early a day as possible, in order that they may present to the President of the United States the credentials which they bear and the objects of the mission with which they are charged.

"The Secretary of State frankly confesses that he understands the events which have recently occurred, and the condition of political affairs which actually exists in the part of the Union to which his attention has thus been directed, very differently from the aspect in which they are presented by Messrs. Forsyth and Crawford. He sees in them, not a rightful and accomplished revolution and an independent nation, with an established government, but rather a perversion of a temporary and partisan excitement to the inconsiderate purposes of an unjustifiable and unconstitutional aggression upon the rights and the authority vested in the Federal Government, and hitherto benignly exercised, as from their very nature they always must be exercised, for the maintenance of the Union and the preservation of liberty, and the security, peace, welfare, happiness, and aggrandizement of the American People. The Secretary of State therefore avows to Messrs. Forsyth and Crawford that he looks patiently but confidently for the cure of evils which have resulted from proceedings so unnecessary, so unwise, so unusual, and so unnatural, not to irregular negotiations, having in view new and untried relations with agencies unknown to and acting in derogation of the Constitution and laws, but to regular and considerate action of the people of those States, in coöperation with their brethren in the other States, through the Congress of the United States, and such extraordinary Conventions, if there be any need thereof, as the Federal Constitution contemplates and authorizes to be assembled.

"It is, however, the purpose of the Secretary of State not to engage in any discussion of these subjects, but simply to set forth his reasons for declining to comply with the request of Messrs. Forsyth and Crawford.

"On the 4th of March inst., the newly elected President of the United States, in view of all the facts bearing upon the present question, assumed the executive Administration of the Government, first delivering, in accordance with an early, honored custom, an Inaugural Address to the people of the United States. The Secretary of State respectfully submits a copy of this address to Messrs. Forsyth and Crawford.

"A simple reference will be sufficient to satisfy those gentlemen that the Secretary of State, guided by the principles therein announced, is prevented altogether from admitting or assuming that the States referred to by them have, in law or in fact, withdrawn from the Federal Union, or that they could do so in the manner described by Messrs. Forsyth and Crawford, or in any other manner than with the consent and concert of the people of the United States, to be given through a National Convention, to be assembled in conformity with the provisions of the Constitution of the United States. Of course, the Secretary of State cannot act upon the assumption, or in any way admit, that the so called Confederate States constitute a foreign Power, with whom diplomatic relations ought to be established.

"Under these circumstances, the Secretary of State, whose official duties are confined, subject to the direction of the President, to the conducting of the foreign relations of the country, and do not at all embrace domestic questions, or questions arising between the several States and the Federal Government, is unable to comply with the request of Messrs. Forsyth and Crawford, to appoint a day on which they may present the evidences of their authority and the objects of their visit to the President of the United States. On the contrary, he is obliged to state to Messrs. Forsyth and Crawford that he has no authority, nor is he at liberty, to recognize them as diplomatic agents, or hold correspondence or other communication with them.

"Finally, the Secretary of State would observe that, although he has supposed that he might safely and with propriety have adopted these conclusions without making any reference of the subject to the Executive, yet, so strong has been his desire to practice entire directness, and to act in a spirit of perfect respect and candor toward Messrs. Forsyth and Crawford, and that portion of the Union in whose name they present themselves before him, that he has cheerfully submitted this paper to the President, who cöincides generally in the views it expresses, and sanctions the Secretary's decision declining official intercourse with Messrs. Forsyth and Crawford."

These memorable papers are too lucid to require or justify extended comment. The Commissioners, it will be seen, place the alleged Secession of the Cotton States expressly and exclusively on the true and proper ground—"the inherent right of every *free* people to change or reform their political institutions"—in other words, the Right of Revolution—thus precluding all discussion as to the pretended *constitutional* right, or reservation of right, to secede at will from the Union. But this position, however wisely and honorably taken, does not at all preclude the question which *Mr. Lincoln* was bound to ask, and, in some way, to answer—"What right have *I*, the fairly chosen Chief Magistrate of the Union—chosen, too, at an election wherein the seven States now alleged to have seceded fully participated—to recognize those States as a foreign nation, as independent of the remaining States as Russia or Peru? How will such recognition, and the action necessarily consequent thereon, accord with my solemn oath of office, and the weighty obligations it imposes? How with my duty to those loyal citizens of the United States who are also citizens or residents of the States which acknowledge Mr. Jefferson Davis as their political Chief?" To these questions, inevitably presenting themselves to every intelligent mind, Messrs. Forsyth and Crawford indicate no reply whatever. They represented a power which had declined coöperation with even a majority of the Slave States—which had not even considered the propriety of calling a National Convention—and which now proffered to the Union no compromise, no middle ground, but the naked alternative of 'Surrender or fight!'

Gov. Seward's reply, though pacific in temper, and evidently animated by a hope that hostilities may yet be avoided, is eminently frank and explicit. That the Executive could recognize Messrs. Forsyth and Crawford only as citizens of the United States, not as plenipotentiaries of an independent and foreign power—that the alleged secession and confederation of the seven States in question was not, and could not be, recognized by the Government as valid; their secession being impliedly, and their confederation expressly, forbidden by the Federal Constitution—that there could be *no* secession save through the agency of a National Convention, which those States had declined to invoke, and were now unwilling to submit to—that their alleged grievances could be redressed only through such Convention, or by the Congress of the United States, wherein the right of those States to an equal representation had been, and still was, unquestioned—and that the President had been consulted respecting, and fully concurred in, these views of his Secretary of State—so much seems plainly set forth in this 'memorandum,' with all the perspicuity which can be attained through the employment of our mother tongue. How is it possible, then, that complaint should nevertheless be made that the Confederates were deluded by Gov. Seward into anticipations of an early and easy concession of their independence?

Yet that charge *is* made; and, since it rests wholly on the testimony of a Confederate who once held, and had not then resigned, the exalted position of a Justice of the United States Supreme Court, it may be well to consider it fully. The testimony is that of Judge Campbell aforesaid, (a prominent disciple of Mr. Calhoun), who, about the time of his taking final leave of Washington to enter more openly into the service of the Confederacy, wrote to Gov. Seward as follows:

"WASHINGTON CITY,
"SATURDAY, *April* 13, 1861.

"SIR:—On the 15th March ult., I left with Judge Crawford, one of the Commissioners of the Confederate States, a note in writing to the following effect:

'I feel entire confidence that Fort Sumter will be evacuated in the next ten days. And this measure is felt as imposing great responsibility on the Administration.

'I feel an entire confidence that no measure changing the existing status, prejudicious to the Southern Confederate States, is at present contemplated.

'I feel an entire confidence that an immediate demand for an answer to the communication of the Commissioners will be productive of evil, and not of good. I do not believe that it ought, at this time, to be pressed.'

"The substance of this statement I communicated to you the same evening by letter. Five days elapsed, and I called with a telegram from Gen. Beauregard, to the effect that Sumter was not evacuated, but that Maj. Anderson was at work making repairs.

"The next day, after conversing with you, I communicated to Judge Crawford, in writing, that the failure to evacuate Sumter was not the result of bad faith, but was attributable to causes consistent with the intention to fulfill the engagement; and that, as regarded Pickens, I should have notice of any design to alter the existing status there.

Mr. Justice Nelson was present at these conversations, three in number, and I submitted to him each of my communications to Judge Crawford, and informed Judge C. that they had his (Judge Nelson's) sanction. I gave you, on the 22d March, a substantial copy of the statement I had made on the 15th.

"The 30th of March arrived, and at that time a telegram came from Gov. Pickens, inquiring concerning Col. Lamon, whose visit to Charleston, he supposed, had a connection with the proposed evacuation of Fort Sumter.

"I left that with you, and was to have an answer the following Monday (1st April). On the first of April, I received from you a statement, in writing, 'I am satisfied the Government will not undertake to supply Fort Sumter without giving notice to Gov. Pickens.' The words 'I am satisfied' were for me to use as expressive of confidence in the remainder of the declaration.

"The proposition, as originally prepared, was, 'The President *may desire* to supply Sumter, but will not do so,' etc., and your verbal explanation was that you did not believe any such attempt would be made, and that there was no design to reënforce Sumter.

"There was a departure here from the pledges of the previous month; but, with the verbal explanation, I did not consider it a matter then to complain of—I simply stated to you that I had that assurance previously.

"On the 7th April, I addressed you a letter on the subject of the alarm that the preparations by the Government had created, and asked you if the assurances I had given were well or ill founded. In respect to Sumter, your reply was, 'Faith as to Sumter fully kept—wait and see.' In the morning's paper, I read, 'An authorized messenger from President Lincoln informed Gov. Pickens and Gen. Beauregard that provisions would be sent to Fort Sumter peaceably, *or otherwise by force.*'

"This was the 8th of April, at Charleston, the day following your last assurance, and is the evidence of the full faith I was invited to *wait for* and *see*. In the same paper, I read that intercepted dispatches disclose the fact that Mr. Fox, who had been allowed to visit Maj. Anderson, on the pledge that his purpose was pacific, employed his opportunity to devise a plan for supplying the fort by force, and that this plan had been adopted by the Washington Government, and was in process of execution.

"My recollection of the date of Mr. Fox's visit carries it to a day in March. I learn he is a near connection of a member of the Cabinet.

"My connection with the commissioners and yourself was superinduced by a conversation with Justice Nelson. He informed me of your strong disposition in favor of peace, and that you were oppressed with a demand of the Commissioners of the Confederate States for a reply to their first letter, and that you desired to avoid, if possible, at that time. I told him I might, perhaps, be of some service in arranging the difficulty. I came to your office entirely at his request, and without the knowledge of the Commissioners. Your depression was obvious to both Judge Nelson and myself. I was gratified at the character of the counsels you were desirous of pursuing, and much impressed with your observation that a civil war might be prevented by the success of my mediation. You read a letter of Mr. Weed, to show how irksome and responsible the withdrawal of troops from Sumter was. A portion of my communication to Judge Crawford on the 15th of March was founded upon these remarks, and the pledge to evacuate Sumter is less forcible than the words you employed. Those words were, 'Before this letter reaches you [a proposed letter by me to President Davis], Sumter will have been evacuated.'

"The Commissioners who received those communications conclude they have been abused and overreached. The Montgomery Government hold the same opinion. The Commissioners have supposed that my communications were with you, and, upon that hypothesis, prepared to arraign you before the country in connection with the President. I placed a peremptory prohibition upon this, as being contrary to the terms of my communications with them. I pledged myself to them to communicate information upon what I considered as the best authority, and they were to confide in the ability of myself, aided by Judge Nelson, to determine upon the credibility of my informant.

"I think no candid man who will read over what I have written, and consider for a moment what is going on at Sumter, will agree that the equivocating conduct of the Administration, as measured and interpreted in connection with these promises, is the proximate cause of the great calamity.

"I have a profound conviction that the telegrams of the 8th of April, of Gen. Beauregard, and of the 10th of April, of Gen. Walker, the Secretary of War, can be referred to nothing else than their belief that there has been systematic duplicity practiced upon them throughout. It is under an oppressive sense of the weight of this responsibility that I submit to you these things for your explanation.

"Very respectfully,

"John A. Campbell,

"*Associate Justice of the Supreme Court.*

"Hon. Wm. H. Seward,

"*Secretary of State.*"

Judge Campbell, it will be noted, takes up the thread of the furtive negotiations exactly where the Commissioners had dropped it. They had made their demand on the 12th; had been answered by Gov. Seward on the 15th; but the answer withheld; for on this day Judge C. makes his first appearance on the scene, with an assurance to the Commissioners that *he* felt "entire confidence that Fort Sumter would be evacuated within the next ten days," if the Commissioners would not push matters too hurriedly to a crisis. Still later, he gave these Commissioners assurances that no attempt would be made to supply the closely invested and scantily provisioned garrison of Fort Sumter, until due notice of the intent had been given to Gov. Pickens; which promise was fulfilled to the letter.

Judge Campbell quotes Justice Nelson as testifying to Gov. Seward's "strong disposition in favor of peace." Who ever denied or doubted it? But did he ever avow an inclination to *Peace on the basis of Disunion?* That is the vital point; and it is not covered, even by assertions, on the part of the Confederates. That he clung tenaciously to the hope of some 'adjustment' or 'conciliation,' whereby civil war might be averted, and the just authority of the Federal Government acknowledged and respected by the Confederate States, is manifest; and that is the whole truth, and affords a simple and obvious explanation of what seems to Confederates so mysterious, so crafty, or so atrocious. The manifest, controlling fact is, that the parties to this unique correspondence occupied positions so contrasted, so incompatible, that it was scarcely possible that they should seriously engage in a negotiation, much less bring it to a happy issue. It was much as if a plenipotentiary should address the government to which he was accredited in Greek, knowing no other tongue, and his dispatch be received and answered by one who was equally ignorant of any language but Choctaw. The only possible result of such diplomacy is a postponement of hostilities; and that seems, in this case, to have been achieved: for the Confederate envoys, in shaking from their feet the dust of Washington and returning to their own 'nation,' addressed, on the 9th of April, a vituperative letter to Gov. Seward, whereof all that is not mere rhetoric, of a peculiarly Southern stamp, or has not already been herein stated, is as follows:

"The undersigned clearly understand that you have declined to appoint a day to enable them to lay the objects of the mission with which they are charged before the President of the United States, because so to do would be to recognize the independence and separate nationality of the Confederate States. This is the vein of thought that pervades the memorandum before us. The truth of history requires that it should distinctly appear upon the record that the undersigned *did not ask the Government of the United States to recognize the independence* of the Confederate States. They only asked an audience to adjust, in a spirit of amity and peace, *the new relations springing from a manifest and accomplished revolution* in the government of the late Federal Union. Your refusal to entertain these overtures for a peaceful solution, the active naval and military preparations of this Government, and a formal notice to the commanding general of the Confederate forces in the harbor of Charleston that the President intends to provision Fort Sumter, by forcible means, if necessary, are viewed by the undersigned, and can only be received by the world, as a declaration of war against the Confederate States; for the President of the United States knows that Fort Sumter cannot be provisioned without the effusion of blood. The undersigned, in behalf of their Government and people, accept the gage of battle thus thrown down to them; and, appealing to God and the judgment of mankind for the righteousness of their cause, the people of the Confederate States will defend their liberties to the last against this flagrant and open attempt at their subjugation to sectional power."

As the world has not been gratified with a sight of the credentials and instructions of these gentlemen, it may be discourteous to assume that their eagerness to "accept the gage of battle" carried them beyond the strict limits of their powers and duties; but the subtile casuistry which enabled them to discriminate between a recognition of Confederate independence and an "audience to adjust the new relations springing from a manifest and accomplished revolution," might have secured to them fame and fortune in some more poetic and imaginative vocation.

As the Commissioners seem to apprehend that they would be charged with a lack of energy if it should be understood that they had allowed the Government of the United States nearly four weeks wherein to decide between recognizing — or, if they choose, admitting and acting upon — the independence of the Confederate States, and an acceptance of the "gage of battle," it may be requisite to give one more extract from their valedictory, as follows:

"This delay was assented to for the express purpose of attaining the great end of the mission of the undersigned, to wit: a pacific solution of existing complications. The inference, deducible from the date of your memorandum, that the undersigned had, of their own volition and without cause, consented to this long hiatus in the grave duties with which they were charged, is therefore not consistent with a just exposition of the facts of the case. The intervening twenty-three days were employed in active unofficial efforts, the object of which was to smooth the path to a pacific solution, the distinguished personage alluded to [Judge Campbell] coöperating with the undersigned; and every step of that effort is recorded in writing, and now in possession of the undersigned and of their Government. It was only when all these anxious efforts for peace had been exhausted, and it became clear that Mr. Lincoln had determined to appeal to the sword to reduce the people of the Confederate States to the will of the section or party whose President he is, that the undersigned resumed the official negotiation temporarily suspended, and sent their secretary for a reply to their note of March 12th."

But that the Confederacy was allowed, in no respect, to suffer by this brief breathing-spell mistakenly accorded by her plenipotentiaries to the Union—that the 'peace' which we enjoyed was of an equivocal and one-sided character—will appear, not only from the close investment of menaced Fort Sumter—with which no one was allowed to communicate, save by Gov. Pickens's gracious permission—but by the active, aggressive hostility to Federal authority manifested throughout the South, as evinced in the following order:

"HEAD-QUARTERS TROOPS CONFEDERATE STATES,
NEAR PENSACOLA, FLA., *March* 18, 1861.

"The Commanding General learns with surprise and regret that some of our citizens are engaged in the business of furnishing supplies of fuel, water, and provisions, to the armed vessels of the United States now occupying a threatening appearance off this harbor.

"That no misunderstanding may exist upon this subject, it is announced to all concerned that this traffic is strictly forbidden; and all such supplies which may be captured in transit to said vessels, or to Fort Pickens, will be confiscated.

"The more effectually to enforce this prohibition, no boat or vessel will be allowed to visit Fort Pickens, or any of the United States naval vessels, without special sanction.

"Col. John H. Forney, Acting Inspector-General, will organize an efficient Harbor Police for the enforcement of this order.

"By command of Brigadier General
"BRAXTON BRAGG.
"ROBERT C. WOOD, Jr., *Ass't. Adj't.-Gen.*"

And, all through the seceded States, those Unionists who dared to indicate their devotion to the flag of their fathers were being treated with a still more active and positive illustration of Confederate amity than was accorded to the garrison of Sumter and the fleet off Pensacola.

Whether President Lincoln did or did not, for some days after his inauguration, incline to the withdrawal of Major Anderson and his brave handful from closely beleaguered Sumter, is not certain. It *is* certain that great doubt and anxiety on this point pervaded the country. Some of the newspaper correspondents at Washington, who were very properly and keenly on the watch for the least indication of the Presidential purpose, telegraphed, quite confidently, on the 14th, that Sumter was to be peaceably evacuated; that Gen. Scott had given his opinion that this was a military necessity; that the fortress was so surrounded and enveloped by Confederate forts and batteries that it could not now be reënforced, nor even provisioned, save at an enormous and unjustifiable cost of human blood; so that there was no practical alternative to its abandonment.

The new Senate, which had been convened for the 4th by President Buchanan to act upon the nominations of his successor, remained sitting in Extra Session until the 28th; and its Democratic members—now reduced by Secession and by changes to a decided minority—urgently and pertinaciously demanded from the majority some declaration of the President's purpose. "Are we to have coërcion and civil war, or concession and peace?" was the burden of their inquiries. Messrs. T. L. Clingman,[7] of North Carolina, Bayard, of Delaware, and Breckinridge,[8] of Kentucky, who were all three close allies in the past of the Confederate chiefs, and two of them, since, open participants in the Rebellion, were prominent and pertinacious in pushing these inquiries; but Mr. Douglas, of Illinois, united in them, talking as if the President were at perfect liberty to enforce the laws or not, at his discretion, and as if his attempting to do it would render him responsible for lighting the flames of civil war. He distinctly advocated the surrender of the Southern fortresses; saying:

"We certainly cannot justify the holding of forts there, much less the recapturing of those which have been taken, unless we intend to reduce those States themselves into subjection. * * * We cannot deny that there is a Southern Confederacy, *de facto*, in existence, with its capital at Montgomery. We may regret it. *I* regret it most profoundly; but I cannot deny the truth of the fact, painful and mortifying as it is."

No Democrat in the Senate, and no organ of Democratic opinion out of the Senate, proffered an assurance or an exhortation to the President, tending to encourage and support him in upholding the integrity and enforcing the laws of the Union; and not Democrats only, but those who, in the late Presidential contest, had made "the Union, the Constitution, and the enforcement of the laws," their platform and their battle-cry, now spoke and acted precisely as would a community who, seeing their sheriff set forth to serve a precept upon a band of desperate law-breakers, were to ask him why he did not desist from his aggressive project, and join them in preserving the peace. The Republicans of the Senate were either unable or unwilling to shed any additional light on the purposes of the Executive—the resolution in regard to them, offered by Mr. Douglas, being laid on the table by a party vote: Yeas 23; Nays 11. But, before the Senate adjourned, it was very generally understood—certainly among Republicans—that the Southern forts were *not* to be surrendered, and that the Union was to be maintained.

The month of March had nearly worn away prior to any outward manifestations, by the 'new lords' at Washington, of a firm resolve to discard the policy of indecision and inaction whereby their predecessors had permitted the Republic's strongholds, arms, munitions, and treasure, to be seized and turned against her by the plotters of Disunion.[9] So late as the 21st of that month, the astute and

[7] Mr. Clingman offered the following resolution:

"*Resolved*, That, in the opinion of the Senate, it is expedient that the President withdraw all Federal troops from the States of South Carolina, Georgia, Florida, Alabama, Mississippi, Texas, and Louisiana, and abstain from all attempts to collect revenue in these States."

[8] Mr. Breckinridge finally offered the following resolution; action on which—together with that of Mr. Clingman—was precluded by the adjournment of the Senate:

"*Resolved*, That the Senate recommend and advise the removal of the United States troops from the limits of the Confederate States."

[9] *The New Orleans Bee*, one of the most respectable of Southern journals, in its issue of March 10th, thus expressed the universal conviction of the Southrons that no fight could be educed from the North:

"The Black Republicans are a cowardly set, after all. They have not the courage of their own convictions. They tamper with their principles. Loathing Slavery, they are willing to incur almost any sacrifice rather than surrender the Border States. Appearances indicate their disposition even to forego the exquisite delight of sending armies and fleets to make war on the Confederate States, rather than run the risk of forfeiting the allegiance of the frontier Slave States. We see by this how hollow and perfidi-

rarely over-sanguine Vice-President Stephens[10] congratulated his hearers that their revolution had thus far been accomplished without shedding a drop of blood—that the fear of deadly collision with the Union they had renounced was nearly dispelled—that the Southern Confederacy had now a population considerably larger than that of the thirteen United Colonies that won their independence through a seven years' struggle with Great Britain—that its area was not only considerably larger than that of the United Colonies, but larger than that of both France and the Austrian Empire—larger than that of France, Spain, Portugal, and the British Isles altogether. He estimated the property of the Confederate States as worth *Twenty-two Thousand Millions of Dollars;* while the last Census makes that of the entire Union but Sixteen Thousand Millions—an understatement, doubtless. That the remaining Slave States would break away from the Union and join the Confederacy was regarded by him as a matter of course. "They will necessarily *gravitate* to us by an imperious law." As to such others as might be deemed desirable acquisitions, Mr. Stephens spoke more guardedly, yet no less complacently, as was previously seen.[11]

This was by no means idle gasconade or vain-glorious presumption. Throughout the Free States, eminent and eager advocates of adhesion to the new Confederacy by those States—or so many of them as might hope to find acceptance—were widely heard and heeded. The New England[12] States (except, possibly, Connecticut), it was agreed, need indulge no such hope—*their* sins were past forgiveness, and their reprobation eternal. So with the more 'fanatical' States of the North-West; so, perhaps, with Western New York and Northern Ohio. The remaining States and parts of States, it was assumed, might easily and wisely fit themselves for adhesion to, and acceptance by, the Southern Confederacy by expelling or suppressing all 'fanatics,' and adopting the Montgomery Constitution, thus legalizing slaveholding as well as slavehunting on their soil. Among those who were understood to urge such adhesion were Gov. Seymour, of New York, Judge Woodward and

ous is their policy, and how inconsistent are their acts with their professions. The truth is, they abhor Slavery; but they are fully alive to the danger of losing their power and influence, should they drive Virginia and the other Border States out of the Union. They chafe, doubtless, at the hard necessity of permitting South Carolina and her sisters to escape from their thraldom; but it *is* a necessity, and they must, perforce, submit to it."

[10] In his speech at Savannah, already quoted.

[11] See pages 416–18.

[12] *The New York Herald* of December 9, 1860, has a Washington dispatch of the 8th relative to a caucus of Southern Senators then being held at the Capitol, which said:

"The current of opinion seems to set strongly in favor of a reconstruction of the Union, without the New England States. The latter States are supposed to be so fanatical in their views as to render it impossible that there should be any peace under a government to which they were parties."

And Gov. Letcher, of Virginia, in his Message of January 7, 1861, after suggesting "that a commission, to consist of two of our most intelligent, discreet, and experienced statesmen," should be appointed to visit the Legislatures of the Free States, to urge the repeal of the Personal Liberty bills which had been passed, said:

"In renewing the recommendation at this time, I annex a modification, and that is, that commissioners shall not be sent to either of the *New England* States. The occurrences of the last two months have satisfied me that New England Puritanism has no respect for human constitutions, and so little regard for the Union that they would not sacrifice their prejudices, or smother their resentments, to perpetuate it."

Francis W. Hughes,[13] of Pennsylvania, Rodman M. Price,[14] of New Jersey, etc., etc.

Kindred in idea, though diverse in its mode of operations, was an association organized at New York during this month, naming itself the "American Society for promoting National Unity," whereof Prof. Samuel F. B. Morse (of telegraphic fame and fortune) was made President, while *The Journal of Commerce* became its accredited organ. The cardinal idea of this fraternity was the restoration and conservation of National Unity through the conversion of all dissidents to the faith that African Slavery is ordained by God, for the improvement and blessing of both the Whites and the Blacks. The programme of this society thus illustrates the bland, benignant piety wherein the movement was grounded:—

"We believe that the time has come when such evil teachings [Abolitionism] should be firmly and boldly confronted, not by the antagonisms of doubtful and perishable weapons, but by 'the Word of God, which liveth and abideth for ever,' as expounded by a broad and faithful recognition of His moral and providential government over the world. It is with this view that we propose an organized effort," etc., etc.

"Our attention will not be confined to Slavery; but this will be, at present, our main topic. Four millions of immortal beings, incapable of self-care, and indisposed to industry and foresight, are providentially committed to the hands of our Southern

Arguments nearly identical with the foregoing were used to like purpose by Gov. Seymour, of New York, but in private conversations only.

[13] For many years, Chairman of the Democratic State Committee.

[14] Formerly Representative in Congress from California; since, Democratic Governor of New Jersey. Gov. Price's letter to L. W. Burnett, Esq., of Newark, N. J., appeared in *The Newark Mercury* of April 4, 1861. He says:

"If we find that to remain with the North, separated from those who have, heretofore, consumed our manufactures, and given employment to a large portion of our labor, deprived of that reciprocity of trade which we have hitherto enjoyed, our Commerce will cease, European competition will be invited to Southern markets, our people be compelled to seek employment elsewhere, our State becoming depopulated and impoverished, thereby affecting our agricultural interest, which has not yet felt the crisis—commerce and manufactures being always first to feel political and financial embarrassments. But at last the blow will be felt by all; even now, the farmers' products are at ruinous prices at the West. These are the prospective results of remaining with the present Northern confederacy. Whereas, to join our destiny with the South will be to continue our trade and intercourse, our prosperity, progress, and happiness, uninterrupted, and perhaps in an augmented degree. Who is he that would advise New Jersey to pursue the path of desolation when one of prosperity is open before her, *without any sacrifice of principle or honor*, and without difficulty or danger; besides being the course and policy, in my judgment, most likely to reünite all the States under the glorious 'Stars and Stripes?'

"The action of our State will prove influential and, perhaps, potential, from our geographical position, upon the adjoining great States of Pennsylvania and New York; and I am confident that the people of those States, whose interests are identical with our own to a considerable degree, will, when they elect, choose also to cast their lot with the South. And, after them, the Western and North-Western States will be found in the same balance, which would be, essentially, a reconstruction of the old Government. What is the difference whether we go to the South, or they come to us? I would rather be the magnanimous brother or friend, to hold out the hand of reconciliation, than he who, as magnanimously, receives the proffer.

"It takes little discernment to see that one policy will enrich us, and the other impoverish us. Knowing our rights and interests, we dare maintain them. The Delaware River only separates us from the State of Delaware for more than one hundred miles. A portion of our State extends south of Mason and Dixon's line, and south of Washington city. The Constitution made at Montgomery has many modifications and amendments desired by the people of this State, and none they would not prefer to disunion. We believe that Slavery is no sin; 'that the negro is not equal to the white man; that Slavery—subordination to the superior race —is his natural and normal condition;' still, we might desire some change in the Constitution, which time may effect; but, as a whole, it is, in my opinion, the only basis upon which the country can be saved; and, as the issue between the North and the South has been a practical one (the question of territorial rights was immaterial, and, practically, nothing to us), let us, then, save the country—let us do that which is most likely to reünite the States, speedily and peacefully."

friends. This stupendous trust they cannot put from them, if they would. Emancipation, were it possible, would be *rebellion* against Providence, and destruction to the colored race in our land. We at the North rid ourselves of no responsibility by assuming an attitude of hostility to Slavery, and thus sundering the bonds of State fellowship; we only put it out of our power to do the good which both humanity and religion demand. Should we not rather recognize the Providence of God, in His placing such a vast multitude of the degraded and dependent sons of Africa in this favored land, and cheerfully coöperate, by all needful labors and sacrifices, with His benevolent design to save and not to destroy them? Under a Providential dispensation, lifting them up from the degradation and miseries of indolence and vice, and exacting of them due and needful labor, they can certainly be trained and nurtured, as many have been, for the services and joys of heaven; and, if the climate and institutions of the South are such that our fellow-citizens there can afford to take the onerous care of them, in return for their services, should we not gladly consent? They freely concede to us our conscientious convictions, our rights, and all our privileges: should we not as freely concede to them theirs? Why should we contend? Why paralyze business, turn thousands of the industrious and laborious poor out of employment, sunder the last ties of affection that can bind these States together, destroy our once prosperous and happy nation, and perhaps send multitudes to premature graves—and all for what? Is not such a course a struggle of arrogant assumption against the Providence of the Most High? and, if persisted in, will it not surely bring down His heavy and prolonged judgments upon us?"

Such were the means whereby many conservative and Christian men were intent on preserving our National unity, and reviving the sentiment of fraternity among our people, in March and the beginning of April, 1861.

XXVIII.

FORT SUMTER.

WHETHER the hesitation of the Executive to reënforce Fort Sumter was real or only apparent, the reserve evinced with regard to his intentions was abundantly justified. The President, in his Inaugural Address, had kindly and explicitly set forth his conception of the duties and responsibilities assumed in taking his oath of office. No man of decent understanding who can read our language had any reason or right to doubt, after hearing or perusing that document, that he fully purposed, to the extent of his ability, to maintain the authority and enforce the laws of the Union on every acre of the geographical area of our country. Hence, secessionists in Washington, as well as South of that city, uniformly denounced that manifesto as a declaration of war, or as rendering war inevitable. The naked dishonesty of professed Unionists inquiring—as even Senator Douglas,[1] for two weeks, persisted in doing—whether

[1] Mr. Douglas—though one of the most zealous advocates of the Crittenden Compromise, and though he, as such, strangely employed all his great ability throughout the winter of '60–'61 to demonstrate that the Republicans ought to act, in accordance not with their own principles and convictions, but with his—and who talked and acted in this vein through most of the Sen-

SUNSET VIEW OF FORT SUMTER BEFORE THE BOMBARDMENT.

Mr. Lincoln *intended peace or war*, was a sore trial to human patience. A government which cannot uphold and vindicate its authority in the country which it professes to rule is to be pitied; but one which does not even *attempt* to enforce respect and obedience is a confessed imposture and sham, and deserves to be hooted off the face of the earth. Nay, more: it was impossible for ours to exist on the conditions prescribed by its domestic foes. No government can endure without revenue; and the Federal Constitution (Art. I. § 9) expressly prescribes that

"No preference shall be given, by any regulation of commerce or revenue, to the ports of one State over those of another; nor shall vessels bound to or from one State be obliged to enter, clear, or pay duties, in another."

But here were the ports of nearly half our Atlantic and Gulf coasts sealed against the commerce and navigation of the other half, save on payment of duties utterly unknown to our laws; while goods could be entered at those ports at quite other (and generally lower) rates of impost than those established by Congress. Hence, importers, with good reason, refused to pay the established duties at Northern ports until the same should be exacted at Southern as well; so that three months' acquiescence by the President in what was untruly commended as the "Peace policy," would have sunk the country into anarchy and whelmed the Government in hopeless ruin.

Still, no one is required to achieve the impossible, though to attempt what to others will seem such may sometimes be accepted by the unselfish and intrepid as a duty; and this practical question confronted the

ate's called Session, which followed—yet, when war actually grew out of the conflicting pretensions of the Union and the Confederacy, took nobly and heartily the side of his whole country. But, even before the close of the called Session, a decided change in his attitude, if not in his conceptions, was manifest. On the 25th of March, replying to a plea for 'Peace,' on the basis of 'No Coërcion,' by Senator J. C. Breckinridge, of Kentucky, he thus thoroughly exposed the futility of the main pretext for Disunion:

"From the beginning of this Government down to 1859, Slavery was prohibited *by Congress* in some portion of the territories of the United States. But now, for the first time in the history of this Government, *there is no foot of ground in America where Slavery is prohibited by act of Congress.* You, of the other side of this chamber, by the unanimous vote of every Republican in this body, and of every Republican in the House of Representatives, have organized all the territories of the United States on the principle of non-intervention, by Congress, with the question of Slavery—leaving the people to do as they please, subject only to the limitations of the Constitution. Hence, I think the Senator from Kentucky fell into a gross error of fact as well as of law when he said, the other day, that you had not abated one jot of your creed—that you had not abandoned your aggressive policy in the territories, and that you were now pursuing the policy of *excluding* the Southern people from all the territories of the United States. * * * There never has been a time since the Government was founded when the right of the slaveholders to emigrate to the territories, to carry with them their slaves, and to *hold* them on an equal footing with all other property, *was as fully and distinctly recognized in all the territories as at this time, and that, too, by the unanimous vote of the Republican party in both Houses of Congress.*

"The Senator from Kentucky [Mr. Breckinridge] has told you that the Southern States, still in the Union, will never be satisfied to remain in it unless they get terms that will give them either a right, in common with all the other States, to emigrate into the territories, or that will secure to them their rights in the territories on the principle of an equitable division. These are the *only* terms on which, as he says, those Southern States now in the Union will consent to remain. I wish to call the attention of that distinguished Senator to the fact that, under the law *as it now stands*, the South has all the rights which he claims. First, Southern men *have* the *right* to emigrate into all the territories, and to carry their Slave property with them, on an equality with the citizens of the other States. Secondly, they *have* an equitable partition of the territories assigned by law, viz.: *all is Slave Territory up to the thirty-seventh degree, instead of up to the parallel of thirty-six degrees thirty minutes—a half degree more than they claim.*"

President on the threshold: 'What *means* have I at command wherewith to compel obedience to the laws?' Now, the War Department had, for nearly eight years prior to the last few weeks, been directed successively by Jefferson Davis and John B. Floyd. The better portion of our little army had been ordered by Floyd to Texas, and there put under the command of Gen. Twiggs, by whom it had already been betrayed into the hands of his fellow-traitors. The arms of the Union had been sedulously transferred by Floyd from the Northern to the Southern arsenals. The most effective portion of the Navy had, in like manner, been dispersed over distant seas. But, so early as the 21st of March, at the close of a long and exciting Cabinet session, it appears to have been definitively settled that Fort Sumter was *not* to be surrendered without a struggle; and, though Col. G. W. Lay, an Aid of Gen. Scott, had visited Charleston on the 20th, and had a long interview with Gov. Pickens and Gen. Beauregard, with reference, it was said, to the terms[2] on which Fort Sumter should be evacuated, if evacuated at all, the 25th brought to Charleston Col. Ward H. Lamon, a confidential agent of the President, who, after an interview with the Confederate authorities, was permitted to visit the fort, and hold unrestricted intercourse with Major Anderson, who apprised the Government through him that their scanty stock of provisions would suffice his little garrison only till the middle of April. Col. Lamon returned immediately to Washington, and was said to have reported there, that, in Major Anderson's opinion as well as in his own, the relief of the fortress was impracticable.

By this time, however, very decided activity began to be manifest in the Navy Yards still held by the Union. Such ships of war as were

[2] *The New York Herald* of April 9th has a dispatch from its Washington correspondent, confirming one sent twenty-four hours earlier to announce the determination of the Executive to provision Fort Sumter, which thus explains the negotiations, and the seeming hesitation, if not vacillation, of March:

"The peace policy of the Administration has been taken advantage of by the South, while, at the same time, their representatives have been here begging the President to keep hands off. While he was holding back, in the hope that a forbearing disposition, on the part of the authorities of the seceded States, would be manifested, to his great surprise, he found that, instead of peace, they were investing every fort and navy yard with Rebel troops and fortifications, and actually preparing to make war upon the Federal Government. Not only this, but, while the Administration was yielding to the cry against coërcion, for the purpose, if possible, of averting the calamity of civil war, the very men who were loudest against coërcion were preparing for it; the Government was losing strength with the people; and the President and his Cabinet were charged with being imbecile and false to the high trust conferred upon them.

"At last, they have determined to enforce the laws, and to do it vigorously; but not in an aggressive spirit. When the Administration determined to order Major Anderson out of Fort Sumter, some days since, they also determined to do so on one condition: namely, *that the fort and the property in it should not be molested, but allowed to remain as it is.* The authorities of the Confederacy would not agree to this, but manifested a disposition to get possession of the fort and United States property therein. The Government would not submit to any such humiliation.

"It was immediately determined to keep Major Anderson in Fort Sumter, and to supply him with provisions forthwith. * * * There is no desire to put additional men into the fort, unless resistance is offered to the attempt to furnish Major Anderson with supplies. The fleet will not approach Charleston with hostile intent; but, in view of the great military preparations about Fort Sumter, the supply vessels will go prepared to reply promptly to any resistance of a warlike character that may be offered to a peaceful approach to the fort. The responsibility of opening the war will be thrown upon the parties who set themselves in defiance to the Government. It is sincerely hoped, by the Federal authorities here, that the leaders of the secessionists will not open their batteries."

at hand were rapidly fitted for service and put into commission; while several swift ocean steamers of the largest size were hurriedly loaded with provisions, munitions, and forage. By the 6th or 7th of April, nearly a dozen of these vessels had left New York and other Northern ports, under sealed orders. Lieut. Talbot, who had arrived at Washington on the 6th, from Fort Sumter, bearing a message from Major Anderson that his rigidly restricted supplies of fresh food from Charleston market had been cut off by the Confederate authorities, and that he must soon be starved into surrender, if not relieved, returned to Charleston on the 8th, and gave formal notice to Gov. Pickens that the fort would be provisioned at all hazards. Gen. Beauregard immediately telegraphed the fact to Montgomery; and, on the 10th, received orders from the Confederate Secretary of War to demand the prompt surrender of the fort, and, in case of refusal, to *reduce* it. The demand was accordingly made in due form at 2 P. M., on the 11th, and courteously declined. But, in consequence of additional instructions from Montgomery—based on a suggestion of Major Anderson to his summoners that he would very soon be starved out, if not relieved—Gen. Beauregard, at 11 P. M., again addressed Major Anderson, asking him to state at what time he would evacuate Fort Sumter, if unmolested; and was answered that he would do so at noon on the 15th, "should I not receive, prior to that time, controlling instructions from my Government, or additional supplies." This answer was judged unsatisfactory; and, at 3:20 A. M., of the 12th, Major Anderson was duly notified that fire would be opened on Fort Sumter in one hour.

Punctual to the appointed moment, the roar of a mortar from Sullivan's Island, quickly followed by the rushing shriek of a shell, gave notice to the world that the era of compromise and diplomacy was ended—that the Slaveholders' Confederacy had appealed from sterile negotiations to the 'last argument' of aristocracies as well as kings. Another gun from that island quickly repeated the warning, waking a response from battery after battery, until Sumter appeared the focus of a circle of volcanic fire. Soon, the thunder of fifty heavy breaching cannon, in one grand volley, followed by the crashing and crumbling of brick, stone, and mortar around and above them, apprised the little garrison that their stay in those quarters must necessarily be short. Unless speedily relieved by a large and powerful fleet, such as the Union did not then possess, the defense was, from the outset, utterly hopeless.

It is said that the Confederate leaders expected to reduce the fort within a very few hours; it is more certain that the country was disappointed by the inefficiency of its fire and the celerity of its reduction. But it was not then duly considered that Sumter was never intended to withstand a protracted cannonade from batteries solidly constructed on every side of it, but to resist and repel the ingress of fleets from the Ocean—a service for which it has since proved itself admirably adapted. Nor was it sufficiently considered that the defensive strength of a fortress inheres largely in its ability to compel its assailants to commence operations for its reduction at a respectful distance, and to make their approaches slowly, under conditions that secure to its fire a great superiority over that of the besiegers. But here were the assailants, in numbers a hundred to one, firing at short range from batteries which had been constructed and mounted in perfect security, one of them covered with iron rails so adjusted as to glance the balls of the fortress harmlessly from its mailed front. Had Major Anderson been ordered, in December, to defend his post against all aggressive and threatening demonstrations, he could not have been shelled out of it by a thirty hours' bombardment. But why officers' quarters and barracks of wood should ever have been constructed in the center of such a fort—or rather, why they should have been permitted to stand there after the hostile intentions of the Confederates had been clearly proclaimed—is not obvious. That shells and red-hot balls would be rained into this area—that the frail structures which nearly filled it would inevitably take fire, and not only imperil magazines, cartridges, and everything else combustible, but prevent the working of the guns, was palpable from the outset. To have committed to the surrounding waves every remaining particle of wood that was not essential to the defense, would seem the manifest work of the night which preceded the opening of the bombardment, after the formal demand that the fort be surrendered. To do this while yet unassailed and unimperiled, instead of rolling barrel after barrel of precious powder into the sea under the fire of a dozen batteries, with the whole center of the fortress a glowing furnace, and even the casemates so hot that their tenants could only escape roasting by lying flat on the floor and drawing their breath through wet blankets, would seem the dictate of the simplest forecast.

So, when we read that "the guns, without tangents or scales, and even destitute of bearing-screws, were to be ranged by the eye, and fired 'by guess,'" we have an ample explanation of the inefficiency of their fire, but none of the causes of this strange and fatal lack of preparation for a contest that had so long been imminent. It might seem as if Sumter had been held only that it should be assailed with impunity and easily taken.

It was at 7 o'clock—nearly three hours after the first shot came crashing against her walls—that Sumter's garrison, having deliberately eaten their breakfast—whereof salt pork constituted the staple—fired their first gun. They had been divided into three squads or reliefs, each in succession to man the guns for four hours, and then be relieved by another. Capt. Arthur Doubleday commanded the first on duty, and fired the first gun. Only the casemate guns were commonly fired—those on the parapet being too much exposed to the shot and shell pouring in from every quarter to render their use other than a reckless, bootless waste of life. The fire of the fort was so weak, when compared to that of its assailants, as to excite derision rather than apprehension on their part. It was directed at Fort Moultrie, the Cummings' Point battery, and Sullivan's Island, from which a masked battery of heavy columbiads, hitherto unsuspected by the garrison, had opened on their walls with fearful effect. The floating battery, faced with railroad bars, though planted very near to Sumter, and seemingly impervious to her balls, was far less effective. A new *English* gun, employed by the Confederates, was remarked by the garrison as wonderfully accurate and efficient; several of its shots entering their embrasures, and one of them slightly wounding four men. But the casemates were shell-proof; the officers constantly warned their men against needless exposure; so that, though the peril from fire and from their own ammunition was even greater than that from the enemy's guns, not one was seriously hurt. And, though Fort Moultrie was considerably damaged, and the little village of Moultrieville—composed of the Summer residences of certain wealthy citizens of Charleston — was badly riddled, it was claimed, and seems undisputed, that no one was mortally wounded on the side of the assailants. So bloodless was the initiation of the bloodiest struggle that America ever witnessed.

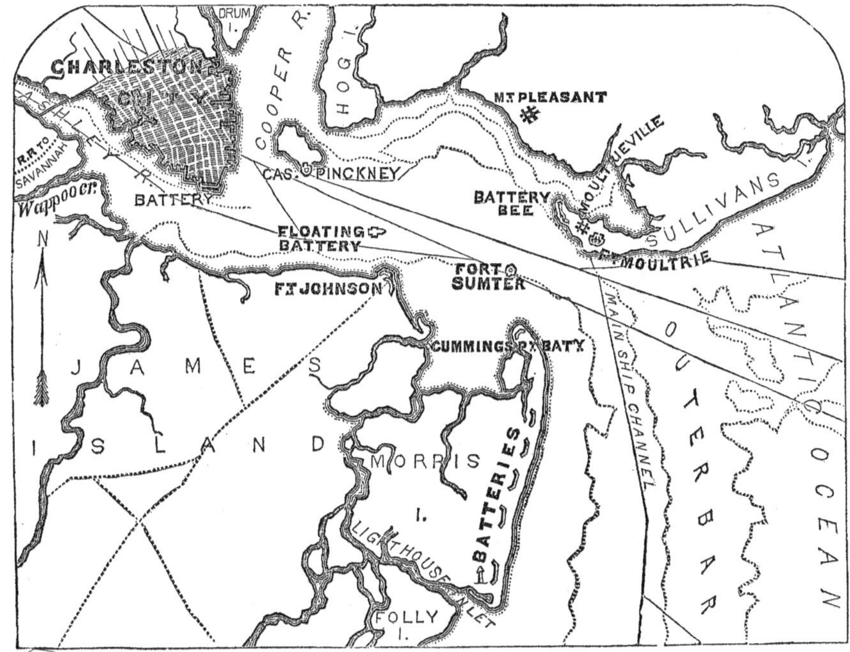

CHARLESTON HARBOR AND FORT SUMTER.

But, though almost without casualty, the contest was not, on the side of the Union, a mere mockery of war: it even served to develop traits of heroism. Says one of those who participated in the perils of the defense:

"The workmen [Irish laborers, hired in New York for other than military service] were at first rather reluctant to assist the soldiers in handling the guns; but they gradually took hold and rendered valuable assistance. Few shots were fired before every one of them was desperately engaged in the conflict. We had to abandon one gun on account of the heavy fire made upon it. Hearing the fire renewed, I went to the spot. I there found a party of workmen engaged in serving it. I saw one of them stooping over, with his hands on his knees, convulsed with joy, while the tears rolled down his powder-begrimed cheeks. 'What are you doing here with that gun?' I asked. 'Hit it right in the center,' was the reply; the man meaning, that his shot had taken effect in the center of the floating battery."

Says another eye-witness:

"Shells burst with the greatest rapidity

in every portion of the work, hurling the loose brick and stone in all directions, breaking the windows, and setting fire to whatever wood-work they burst against. The solid-shot firing of the enemy's batteries, and particularly of Fort Moultrie, was directed at the barbette [unsheltered] guns of Fort Sumter, disabling one ten-inch columbiad [they had but two], one eight-inch columbiad, one forty-two pounder, and two eight-inch seacoast howitzers, and also tearing a large portion of the parapet away. The firing from the batteries on Cummings' Point was scattered over the whole of the gorge or rear of the fort, till it looked like a sieve. The explosion of shells, and the quantity of deadly missiles that were hurled in every direction and at every instant of time, made it almost certain death to go out of the lower tier of casemates, and also made the working of the barbette or upper [uncovered] guns, which contained all our heaviest metal, and by which alone we could throw shells, quite impossible. During the first day, there was hardly an instant of time that there was a cessation of the whizzing of balls, which were sometimes coming half a dozen at once. There was not a portion of the work which was not taken in reverse from mortars.

"On Friday, before dinner, several of the vessels of the fleet, beyond the bar, were seen through the port-holes. They dipped their flag. The commander ordered Sumter's flag to be dipped in return, which was done, while the shells were bursting in every direction. [The flag-staff was located in the parade, which was about the center of the open space within the fort.] Sergeant Hart saw the flag of Fort Sumter half-way down, and, supposing it had been cut by the enemy's shot, rushed out through the fire to assist in getting it up. Shortly after it had been re-raised, a shell burst and cut the halliards, but the rope was so intertwined around the halliards, that the flag would not fall. The cartridges were exhausted by about noon, and a party was sent to the magazines to make more of the blankets and shirts; the sleeves of the latter being readily converted to the use desired. Another great misfortune was, that there was not an instrument in the fort by which they could weigh the powder; which, of course, destroyed all approach to accuracy of firing. Nor had they tangent-screws, breech-slides, or other instruments with which to point a gun.

"When it became so dark as to render it impossible to see the effect of their shot, the port-holes were closed for the night, while the batteries of the Secessionists continued their fire unceasingly.

"During Friday, the officers' barracks were three times set on fire by the shells, and three times put out under the most galling and destructive cannonade. This was the only occasion on which Maj. Anderson allowed the men to expose themselves without an absolute necessity. The guns on the parapet—which had been pointed the day before—were fired clandestinely by some of the men slipping up on top.

"The firing of the rifled guns from the iron battery on Cummings' Point became extremely accurate in the afternoon of Friday, cutting out large quantities of the masonry about the embrasures at every shot, throwing concrete among the cannoneers, and slightly wounding and stunning others. One piece struck Sergeant Kernan, an old Mexican war veteran, hitting him on the head and knocking him down. On being revived, he was asked if he was hurt badly. He replied: 'No; I was only knocked down *temporarily;*' and he went to work again. * * *

"For the fourth time, the barracks were set on fire early on Saturday morning, and attempts were made to extinguish the flames; but it was soon discovered that red-hot shot were being thrown into the fort with fearful rapidity, and it became evident that it would be impossible to put out the conflagration. The whole garrison was then set to work, or as many as could be spared, to remove the powder from the magazines, which was desperate work, rolling barrels of powder through the fire.

"Ninety-odd barrels had been rolled out through the flames, when the heat became so intense as to make it impossible to get out any more. The doors were then closed and locked, and the fire spread and became general. The wind so directed the smoke as to fill the fort so full that the men could not see each other; and, with the hot, stifling air, it was as much as a man could do to breathe. Soon, they were obliged to cover their faces with wet cloths in order to get along at all, so dense was the smoke and so scorching the heat.

"But few cartridges were left, and the guns were fired slowly; nor could more cartridges be made, on account of the sparks falling in every part of the works. A gun was fired every now and then, only to let the fleet and the people in the town know that the fort had not been silenced. The cannoneers could not see to aim, much less where they hit.

"After the barracks were well on fire, the batteries directed upon Fort Sumter increased their cannonading to a rapidity greater than had been attained before. About this time, the shells and ammunition in the upper service-magazines exploded, scattering the tower and upper portions of the building in every direction. The crash of the beams, the roar of the flames, and the shower of fragments of the fort, with the blackness of the smoke, made the scene indescribably terrific and grand. This continued for several hours. Meanwhile, the main gates were burned down, the chassis of the barbette guns were burned away on the gorge, and the upper portions of the towers had been demolished by shells.

"There was not a portion of the fort where a breath of air could be got for hours, except through a wet cloth. The fire spread to the men's quarters on the right hand and on the left, and endangered the powder which had been taken out of the magazines. The men went through the fire and covered the barrels with wet cloths; but the danger of the fort's blowing up became so imminent that they were obliged to heave the barrels out of the embrasures. While the powder was being thrown overboard, all the guns of Moultrie, of the iron floating battery, of the enfilade battery, and of the Dahlgren battery, worked with increasing vigor.

"All but four barrels were thus disposed of, and those remaining were wrapped in many thicknesses of wet woolen blankets. But three cartridges were left, and these were in the guns. About this time, the flag-staff of Fort Sumter was shot down, some fifty feet from the truck; this being the ninth time that it had been struck by a shot. The man cried out, 'The flag is down! it has been shot away!' In an instant, Lieut. Hall rushed forward, and brought the flag away. But the halliards were so inextricably tangled that it could not be righted; it was therefore nailed to the staff, and planted upon the ramparts, while batteries in every direction were playing upon them."

The fleet from New York, laden with provisions for the garrison, had appeared off the bar by noon of the day on which fire was opened, but made no effort to fulfill its errand. To have attempted to supply the fort would have, at best, involved a heavy cost of life, probably to no purpose. Its commander communicated by signals with Major Anderson, but remained out of the range of the enemy's fire till after the surrender; when he returned as he came.

Meantime, the boom of heavy ordnance and the telegraph had borne far and wide the eagerly awaited tidings that the war for which South Carolina had so long been impatient had actually begun; and from every side thousands flocked to the spectacle as to a long expected holiday. Charleston herself was drunk with excitement and joyous exultation. Her entire white population, and her gay crowds of well-dressed[3] visitors, thronged her streets and quays, noting the volume and resonant thunder of the Confederate cannonade, and the contrasted feebleness of that by which it was replied to.[4] That seven thousand men, after five months of careful preparation, could overcome seventy, was regarded as an achievement ranking with the most memorable deeds of Alexander or Hannibal, Cæsar or Napoleon. Champagne flowed on every hand like water; thousands quaffed, and feasted on the richest viands, who were ere long to regard rancid pork as a dainty, and tea and coffee as faintly remembered luxuries. Beauregard shot up like Jonah's gourd to the altitude of the world's greatest captains; and "Damnation to the Yankees!" was drunk with rapture by enthusiastic crowds whose heads were sure to ache to-morrow with what they had drunk before. Already, in the ardent imagination of her Chivalry, the Confederacy had established its independ-

[3] The New York merchants who sold the costly fabrics are still waiting for their pay.

[4] A Charleston dispatch, dated April 13th, says:

"Had the surrender not taken place, Fort Sumter would have been stormed to-night. The men are crazy for a fight.

"The bells have been chiming all day, guns firing, ladies waving handkerchiefs, people cheering, and citizens making themselves generally demonstrative. *It is regarded as the greatest day in the history of South Carolina.*"

—Such it undoubtedly was.

ence beyond dispute, and was about to conquer and lay waste the degenerate, cowardly North.

The credit of putting an end to this most unequal contest is due to Louis T. Wigfall, late a Senator from the State of Texas, now styling himself a Confederate Brigadier. Wigfall—a Carolinian by birth, a Nullifier by training, and a duelist by vocation—had the faults and virtues of his caste; and one of the latter is a repugnance to witnessing a conflict between parties too palpably ill-matched. Seeing that the fire of Sumter was only maintained as a matter of pride—for the fainting garrison had quite enough to do at fighting the flames that had burned their quarters, and in rolling out their powder to prevent its explosion—Wigfall seized a skiff on the afternoon of Saturday (the second day of the bombardment), and made direct toward the almost silenced and thoroughly harmless fortress. He was soon at the side of the fort, and, showing his face at an embrasure, waving a white handkerchief on the point of his sword, he asked to be presented to Maj. Anderson. No objection being made, he crawled through the embrasure into the casemate, and was there met by several officers, to whom he urged the futility of further resistance. "Let us stop this firing," said he; "you are on fire, and your flag is down. Let us quit." "No," replied Lieut. Davis, "our flag is *not* down. Step out here, and you will see it waving over the ramparts." Wigfall persisted that the resistance had no longer any justification, and urged one of the officers to wave his white flag toward Moultrie; and, this being declined, proceeded to wave it himself. Finally, a corporal was induced to relieve him in this, but to no purpose. About this time, Maj. Anderson approached, to whom Wigfall announced himself (incorrectly) as a messenger from Gen. Beauregard, sent to inquire on what terms he would evacuate the fortress. Maj. Anderson calmly replied: "Gen. Beauregard is already acquainted with my *only* terms." After a few more civil interchanges of words, to no purpose, Wigfall retired, and was soon succeeded by ex-Senator Chesnut, and ex-Representatives Roger A. Pryor and W. Porcher Miles, who assured Maj. A. that Wigfall had acted entirely without authority. Maj. A. thereupon ordered his flag, which had been lowered, to be raised again; but his visitors requested that this be delayed for further conference; and, having reported to Beauregard, returned, two or three hours afterward, with a substantial assent to Maj. Anderson's conditions. The latter was to evacuate the fort, his garrison to retain their arms, with personal and company property, and march out with the honors of war, being conveyed to whatever port in the loyal States they might indicate. Considering his hopeless condition, these terms were highly honorable to Maj. Anderson, and hardly less so to Gen. Beauregard; though it was the manifest interest of the Confederates not only to stop their prodigal expenditure of ammunition at the earliest moment, but to obtain possession of the coveted fortress in as effective a state as possible—each day's additional bombardment subtracting seriously from its strength and efficiency, as a defense of Charleston after it should have fallen into their hands.

MAJ. GEN. JOHN C. FREMONT.
MAJ. GEN. BENJ. F. BUTLER.
LIEUT. GEN. WINFIELD SCOTT.
MAJ. GEN. IRWIN McDOWELL.
MAJ. GEN. JOHN E. WOOL.
MAJ. GEN. HENRY W. HALLECK.
MAJ. GEN. A. E. BURNSIDE.
MAJ. GEN. DAVID HUNTER.
MAJ. GEN. GEO. B. McCLELLAN.
MAJ. GEN. JOSEPH HOOKER.
MAJ. GEN. DON CARLOS BUELL.
BRIG. GEN. ROBERT ANDERSON.
Entered according to act of Congress A.D. 1864 by O. D. Case & Co in the Clerk's Office of the District Court of the United States for the District of Connecticut
Eng. by J. C. Buttre, New York
UNION GENERALS

While Charleston resumed and intensified her exulting revels,[5] and the telegraph invited all 'Dixie' to share the rapture of her triumph, the weary garrison extinguished the fire still raging, and lay down to rest for the night. The steamboat Isabel came down next morning to take them off; but delay occurred in their removal by tug to her deck, until it was too late to go out by that day's tide. When the baggage had all been removed, a part of the garrison was told off as gunners to salute their flag with fifty guns; the Stars and Stripes being lowered with cheers at the firing of the last gun. Unhappily, there was at that fire a premature explosion, whereby one of the gunners was killed, and three more or less seriously wounded. The men were then formed and marched out, preceded by their band, playing inspiring airs, and taken on board the Isabel, whereby they were transferred to the Federal steamship Baltic, awaiting them off the bar, which brought them directly to New York, whence Maj. Anderson dispatched to his Government this brief and manly report:

"STEAMSHIP BALTIC, OFF SANDY HOOK, *April* 18, 1861.

"The Honorable S. CAMERON,
Secretary of War, Washington, D. C.:

"SIR: Having defended Fort Sumter for thirty-four hours, until the quarters were entirely burned, the main gates destroyed, the gorge-wall seriously injured, the magazine surrounded by flames, and its door closed from the effects of the heat, four barrels and three cartridges of powder only being available, and no provisions but pork remaining, I accepted terms of evacuation offered by Gen. Beauregard (being the same offered by him on the 11th instant, prior to the commencement of hostilities), and marched out of the fort on Sunday afternoon, the 14th instant, with colors flying and drums beating, bringing away company and private property, and saluting my flag with fifty guns.

"ROBERT ANDERSON,
"Major First Artillery."

XXIX.

THE CALL TO ARMS.

WHETHER the bombardment and reduction of Fort Sumter shall or shall not be justified by posterity, it is clear that the Confederacy had no alternative but its own dissolution. Five months had elapsed since the Secession movement was formally inaugurated—five months of turmoil, uncertainty, and business stagnation, throughout the seceded States. That section was deeply in debt to the merchants and manufacturers of the Northern cities, as well as to the slave-breeders and slave-traders of the Border States; and, while many creditors were naturally urgent for their pay, few desired or consented to extend their credits in that quarter. Secession had been almost everywhere followed, if not preceded, by

[5] "Bishop Lynch (Roman Catholic), of Charleston, S. C., celebrated on Sunday the bloodless victory of Fort Sumter with a Te Deum and congratulatory address. In all the churches, allusions were made to the subject. The Episcopal Bishop, wholly blind and feeble, said it was his strong persuasion, confirmed by travel through every section of South Carolina, that the movement in which the people were engaged was begun by them in the deepest conviction of duty to God; and God had signally blessed their dependence on Him. If there is a war, it will be purely a war of self-defense."—*New York Tribune, April* 16.

a suspension of specie payments by the Banks; and, though the lawyers in most places patriotically refused to receive Northern claims for collection, a load of debt weighed heavily on the planting[1] and trading classes of the entire South, of whom thousands had rushed into political convulsion for relief from the intolerable pressure. Industry, save on the plantations, was nearly at a stand; never before were there so many whites vainly seeking employment. The North, of course, sympathized with these embarrassments through the falling off in its trade, especially with the South, and through the paucity of remittances; but our currency was still sound, while Southern debts had always been slow, and paid substantially at the convenience of the debtors, when paid at all. Still, the feeling that the existing suspense and apprehension were intolerable, and that almost any change would be an improvement, was by no means confined to the South.

Secession, as we have seen, had been initiated by the aid of the most positive assurances that, once fairly in progress, every Slave State would speedily and surely unite in it; yet, up to this time, but seven of the fifteen Slave States, having a decided minority of the population, and a still more decided minority of the *white* inhabitants, of that 'section,' had justified the sanguine promise. On the contrary, the so-called 'Border States,' with Tennessee and Arkansas, had voted *not* to secede, and most of them by overwhelming majorities; save that Kentucky, Maryland, and Delaware, had scarcely deigned to take the matter into consideration. And, despite Vice-President Stephens's glowing rhetoric, it was plain that the seceded States did not and could not suffice to form a nation. Already, the talk in their aristocratic circles of Protectorates and imported Princes[2] betrayed their own consciousness of this. Either to attack the Union, and thus provoke

[1] The following private letter from a South Carolina planter to an old friend settled in Texas, gives a fair idea of the situation:

"ABBEVILLE C. H., S. C., *Jan.* 24, 1861.

"DEAR SIR:—I desire you to procure for me, and send by mail, a Texas Almanac. Six months since, I felt perfectly willing to remain in South Carolina; but I can remain here no longer. At the election of Lincoln, we all felt that we must resist. In this move, I placed myself among the foremost, and am yet determined to resist him to the bitter end. I had my misgivings, at first, of the idea of separate Secession; but thought it would be but for a short time, and at small cost. In this manner, together with thousands of other Carolinians, we have been mistaken. Everything is in the wildest commotion. My bottom land on Long Cone, for which I could have gotten thirty dollars per acre, I now cannot sell at any price. All our young men, nearly, are in and around Charleston. Thither we have sent many hundreds of our negroes (*I* have sent twenty) to work. Crops were very short last year; and it does now seem that nothing will be planted this coming season. All are excited to the highest pitch, and not a thought of the future is taken. Messengers are running here and there, with and without the Governor's orders. We have no money. A forced tax is levied upon every man. I have furnished the last surplus dollar I have. I had about $27,000 in the bank. At first, I gave a check for $10,000; then $5,000; then the remainder. It is now estimated that we are spending $25,000 per day, and no prospect of getting over these times. It was our full understanding, when we went out of the Union, that we would have a new Government of *all* the Southern States. Our object was to bring about a collision with the authorities at Washington, which all thought would make all join us. Although we have sought such collision in every way, we have not yet got a fight, and the prospect is very distant. I want the Almanac to see what part of Texas may suit me. I want to raise cotton principally, but must raise corn enough to do me. I cannot live here, and must get away. Many are leaving now; at least 10,000 negroes have left already; and, before long, one-third of the wealth of South Carolina will be in the West. I desire you to look around and help me to get a home. As ever yours,

"ROBERT LYON."

[2] Wm. H. Russell, of *The London Times*, in his

a war, or to sink gradually but surely out of existence beneath a general appreciation of weakness, insecurity, and intolerable burdens, was the only choice left to the plotters and upholders of Secession.

And, though signally beaten in the recent elections of the non-seceded Slave States, they had yet a very strong party in most of those States —stronger in wealth, in social standing, and in political activity and influence, than in numbers. A majority of these had been able to bring the Conventions or the Legislatures of their respective States to say, with tolerable unanimity, "If the Black Republicans attempt to *coërce* the seceded States, we will join them in armed resistance." It was indispensable, therefore, to their mutual purposes, that there *should* be 'coërcion.'

So late as April 4th—a month after the return of her 'Commissioners' from the abortive Peace Conference —Virginia, through her Convention, by the decisive vote of 89 to 45, refused to pass an Ordinance of Secession. Still, her conspirators worked on, like those of the other 'Border States,' and claimed, not without plausible grounds, that they were making headway. Richmond was the focus of their intrigues, as it was of her Slave-trade; but it was boasted that, whereas two of her three delegates to the Convention were chosen as Unionists, she would now give a decided majority for Secession. *The Richmond Whig*,[3] the time-honored organ of her Whig 'Conservatives,'

"Diary, North and South," writing at Charleston, April 18, 1861, says:

"These tall, thin, fine-faced Carolinians are great materialists. Slavery, perhaps, has aggravated the tendency to look at all the world through parapets of cotton-bales and rice-bags; and, though more stately and less vulgar, the worshipers here are not less prostrate before the 'almighty dollar' than the Northerners. Again, cropping out of the dead level of hate to the Yankee, grows its climax in the profession, from nearly every one of the guests, that he would prefer a *return to British rule* to any reunion with New England. * * * They affect the agricultural faith and the belief of a landed gentry. It is not only over the wine-glass—why call it cup?—that they ask for a Prince to reign over them. I have heard the wish repeatedly expressed within the last two days that *we could spare them one of our young Princes*, but never in jest or in any frivolous manner."

Mr. Russell's letters from Charleston to *The Times* are to the same effect, but more explicit and circumstantial.

[3] *The Richmond Whig* of November 9, 1860, had the following:

"Because the Union was creäted by the voluntary consent of the original States, it does not follow that such consent can be withdrawn at will by any single party to the compact, and its obligations and duties, its burdens and demands, be avoided. A government resting on such a basis would be as unstable as the ever-shifting sands. The sport of every popular excitement, the victim of every conflicting interest, of plotting ambition or momentary impulse, it would afford no guarantee of perpetuity, while the hours bring round the circuit of a single year. To suppose that a single State could withdraw at will, is to brand the statesmen of the Revolution, convinced of the weakness and certain destruction of the old Confederation of States, of laboring to perpetuate the evil they attempted to remedy. The work, which has been the marvel of the world, would be no government at all; the oaths taken to support and maintain it would be bitter mockery of serious obligations; and nothing would exist to invite the confidence of citizens or strangers in its protection.

"Less strong would it be than a business partnership of limited time. From this, neither party who has entered into it can escape, except by due course of law. Withdrawal of one member carries no rights of possession of property or control of the affairs of the partnership, unless the injunctions of legal tribunals are invoked to restrain all action until the matter in dispute is settled. A State seceding knows no law to maintain its interest nor vindicate its rights. The right to secede, on the other hand, places the Government more at the mercy of popular whim than the business interest of the least mercantile establishment in the country is placed, by the law of the land."

Such were the just and forcibly stated convictions of a leading journal, which soon after became, and has since remained, a noisy oracle of Secession.

who had secured her vote for Bell and Everett, had been changed—by purchase, it was said—and was now as zealous for Secession as hitherto against it. Finally, her Convention resolved, on the 4th aforesaid, to send new Commissioners to wait on President Lincoln, and appointed Messrs. William Ballard Preston, Alex. H. H. Stuart, and George W. Randolph (of whom the last only was formerly a Democrat, and was chosen as a Secessionist), to proceed to Washington on this errand. They did not obtain their formal audience until the 13th—the day of Fort Sumter's surrender—when its bombardment, if not its capture also, was already known in that city—and there was a grim jocosity in their appearance at such an hour to set before the harassed President such a missive as this:

"*Whereas*, in the opinion of the Convention, the uncertainty which prevails in the public mind as to the policy which the Federal Executive intends to pursue toward the seceded States is extremely injurious to the industrial and commercial interests of the country, tends to keep up an excitement which is unfavorable to the adjustment of the pending difficulties, and threatens a disturbance of the public peace: therefore,

"*Resolved*, That a Committee of three delegates be appointed to wait on the President of the United States, present to him this preämble, and respectfully ask him to communicate to this Convention the policy which the Federal Executive intends to pursue in regard to the Confederate States."

To this overture, after duly acknowledging its reception, Mr. Lincoln replied as follows:

"In answer, I have to say that, having, at the beginning of my official term, expressed my intended policy as plainly as I was able, it is with deep regret and mortification I now learn that there is a great and injurious uncertainty in the public mind as to what that policy is, and what course I intend to pursue. Not having, as yet, seen occasion to change, it is now my purpose to pursue the course marked out in that Inaugural Address. I commend a careful consideration of the document as the best expression I can give to my purposes. As I then and therein said, I now repeat, 'The power confided in me will be used to hold, occupy, and possess, property and places belonging to the Government, and to collect the duties on imports; but, beyond what is necessary for these objects, there will be no invasion, no using of force against or among the people anywhere.' By the words 'property and places belonging to the Government,' I chiefly allude to the military posts and property which were in possession of the Government when it came into my hands. But if, as now appears to be true, in pursuit of a purpose to drive the United States authority from these places, an unprovoked assault has been made upon Fort Sumter, I shall hold myself at liberty to repossess it, if I can, like places which had been seized before the Government was devolved upon me; and, in any event, I shall, to the best of my ability, repel force by force. In case it proves true that Fort Sumter has been assaulted, as is reported, I shall, perhaps, cause the United States mails to be withdrawn from all the States which claim to have seceded, believing that the commencement of actual war against the Government justifies and, possibly, demands it. I scarcely need to say that I consider the military posts and property, situated within the States which claim to have seceded, as yet belonging to the United States as much as they did before the supposed secession. Whatever else I may do for the purpose, I shall not attempt to collect the duties and imposts by any armed invasion of any part of the country; not meaning by this, however, that I may not land a force deemed necessary to relieve a fort on the border of the country. From the fact that I have quoted a portion of the Inaugural Address, it must not be inferred that I repudiate any other part, the whole of which I reäffirm, except so far as what I now say of the mails may be regarded as a modification."

With this answer, the Commissioners retired; and the next important news from Virginia reached Washington *via* Montgomery and New Orleans, which cities had been exhilarated to the point of cheering and cannon-firing, by dispatches from Richmond, announcing the fact that the Convention had, in secret, taken their State out of the Union, and united her fortunes with those of the

Confederacy.[4] The vote by which this result was achieved stood 88 to 55—the majority greatly strengthened, doubtless, if not secured, by an act of the Confederate Congress forbidding the importation of slaves from States out of the Confederacy—an act which, so long as Virginia adhered to the Union, struck a staggering blow at the most important and productive branch of her industry. And, while the fact of her secession was still unproclaimed, her authorities at once set whatever military forces they could muster in motion to seize the Federal Navy Yard at Norfolk (Portsmouth) and the Arsenal at Harper's Ferry.

As the news of the attack on Sumter flashed over the country, an intense and universal excitement was aroused in the Free as well as the Slave States. Indignation was paramount in the former; exultation ruled throughout the latter.[5] Many at the North obstinately refused to credit the tidings; and, when news of the surrender of the fort so speedily followed, the number of the incredulous was even increased. All doubt, however, was dispelled when the journals of Monday morning, April 15th, displayed conspicuously the following

"PROCLAMATION.

"WHEREAS, the laws of the United States have been for some time past, and now are, opposed, and the execution thereof obstructed, in the States of South Carolina, Georgia, Alabama, Florida, Mississippi, Louisiana, and Texas, by combinations too powerful to be suppressed by the ordinary course of judicial proceedings, or by the powers vested in the marshals by law: now, therefore, I, Abraham Lincoln, President of the United States, in virtue of the power in me vested by the Constitution and the laws, have thought fit to call forth the Militia of the several States of the Union to the aggregate number of 75,000, in order to suppress said combinations, and to cause the laws to be duly executed.

"The details for this object will be immediately communicated to the State authorities through the War Department.[6] I appeal to all loyal citizens to favor, facilitate, and aid, this effort to maintain the honor, the integrity, and existence, of our national Union, and the perpetuity of popular Government, and to redress wrongs already long enough endured. I deem it proper to say that the first service assigned to the forces hereby called forth will probably be to repossess the forts, places, and property which have been seized from the Union; and in every event the

[4] *The New York Herald* of April 13th had a Charleston dispatch of the 12th, which thus correctly expresses the Confederate idea:

"The first shot [at Fort Sumter] from Stevens's battery was fired by the venerable Edmund Ruffin, of Virginia. That ball will do more for the cause of Secession in Virginia than volumes of stump speeches."

[5] *The New York Herald* of the 14th had the following:

"RICHMOND, VA., *April* 13, 1861.

"There is great rejoicing here over the news from Charleston.

"One hundred guns have been fired to celebrate the surrender of Fort Sumter.

"Confederate flags are everywhere displayed; while music and illuminations are the order of the evening.

"Gov. Letcher has just been serenaded. He made a non-committal speech.

"The streets are crowded with people, and the utmost enthusiasm and excitement prevails."

[6] The Circular from the War Department, which was sent to the Governors along with this Proclamation, explained that the call was for regiments of infantry or riflemen only—each regiment to be composed of 780 men—the apportionment of regiments to the several States called on being as follows:

State		State	
Maine	1	Virginia	3
New Hampshire	1	North Carolina	2
Vermont	1	Kentucky	4
Massachusetts	2	Arkansas	1
Rhode Island	1	Missouri	4
Connecticut	1	Ohio	13
New York	17	Indiana	6
New Jersey	4	Illinois	6
Pennsylvania	16	Michigan	1
Delaware	1	Iowa	1
Tennessee	2	Minnesota	1
Maryland	4	Wisconsin	1

The 94 regiments thus called for would form a total of 73,391 men—the residue of the 75,000 being expected from the Federal District.

utmost care will be observed, consistently with the objects aforesaid, to avoid any devastation, any destruction of, or interference with, property, or any disturbance of peaceful citizens of any part of the country; and I hereby command the persons composing the combinations aforesaid, to disperse and retire peaceably to their respective abodes, within twenty days from this date.

"Deeming that the present condition of public affairs presents an extraordinary occasion, I do hereby, in virtue of the power in me vested by the Constitution, convene both Houses of Congress. The Senators and Representatives are, therefore, summoned to assemble at their respective chambers at 12 o'clock, noon, on Thursday, the 4th day of July next, then and there to consider and determine such measures as, in their wisdom, the public safety and interest may seem to demand.

"In witness whereof, I have hereunto set my hand, and caused the seal of the United States to be affixed.

"Done at the City of Washington, this 15th day of April, in the year of our Lord one thousand eight hundred and sixty-one, and of the independence of the United States the eighty-fifth.

"ABRAHAM LINCOLN.

"By the President:

"WM. H. SEWARD, *Secretary of State*."

This Proclamation was received throughout the Free States with very general and enthusiastic approval. Nearly all of them on this side of the Rocky Mountains had Republican Governors and Legislatures, who vied with each other in proffers of men, money, munitions, and everything that could be needed to vindicate the authority and maintain the integrity of the Union. The only[7] Governor not elected as a Republican was William Sprague, of Rhode Island—an independent 'conservative'—who not merely raised promptly the quota required of him, but volunteered to lead it to Washington, or wherever its services might be required. No State was more prompt and thorough in her response, and none sent her troops into the field more completely armed and serviceably equipped, than did Rhode Island. Among the privates in her first regiment was one worth a million dollars, who destroyed the passage-ticket he had bought for a voyage to Europe, on a tour of observation and pleasure, to shoulder his musket in defense of his country and her laws.

Hitherto, the Democrats and other 'conservatives' of the Free States had seemed[8] to sympathize rather with 'the South' than with the new Administration, in so far as they were at variance, though not usually to the extent of justifying Secession. Now, public meetings, addresses, enlistments, the mustering of companies and of regiments on all sides, seemed for a time to indicate an almost unbroken unanimity in support of the Government. The spirit of the hour is very fairly exhibited in the leading article of *The New York Tribune* of April 15th, as follows:

"Fort Sumter is lost, but freedom is saved. There is no more thought of bribing or coaxing the traitors who have dared to aim their cannon-balls at the flag of the Union, and those who gave their lives to defend it. It seems but yesterday that at least two-thirds of the journals of this city were the virtual allies of the Secessionists, their apologists, their champions. The roar of the great circle of batteries pouring their iron hail upon devoted Sumter has struck them all dumb. It is as if one had made a brilliant and effective speech, setting forth the innocence of murder, and, having just bidden adieu to the cheers and the gas-lights, were to be confronted by the gory form and staring eyes of a victim of assassination, the first fruit of his oratorical success.

"For months before the late Presidential election, a majority of our journals predicted forcible resistance to the Government as the natural and necessary result of a Republican triumph; for months since, they have been cherishing and encouraging the Slaveholders' Rebellion, as if it were a very natural

[7] Those of California and Oregon were exceptions; but, being far away, and not called on for Militia, their views were then undeveloped.

[8] See especially pages 355-6, and thenceforward.

and proper proceeding. Their object was purely partisan—they wished to bully the Republican Administration into shameful recreancy to Republican principle, and then call upon the people to expel from power a party so profligate and so cowardly. They did not succeed in this; they *have* succeeded in enticing their Southern *protégés* and sometime allies into flagrant treason. * * *

"Most of our journals lately parading the pranks of the Secessionists with scarcely disguised exultation, have been suddenly sobered by the culmination of the slaveholding conspiracy. They would evidently like to justify and encourage the traitors further, but they dare not; so the Amen sticks in their throat. The aspect of the people appalls them. Democrat as well as Republican, Conservative and Radical, instinctively feel that the guns fired at Sumter were aimed at the heart of the American Republic. Not even in the lowest groggery of our city would it be safe to propose cheers for Beauregard and Gov. Pickens. The Tories of the Revolution were relatively ten times as numerous here as are the open sympathizers with the Palmetto Rebels. It is hard to lose Sumter; it is a consolation to know that in losing it we have gained a united people. Henceforth, the loyal States are a unit in uncompromising hostility to treason, wherever plotted, however justified. Fort Sumter is temporarily lost, but the country is saved. Live the Republic!"

Dissent from this view did, indeed, seem for the moment almost, but not entirely, silenced. The opposite conception was temperately set forth, on the evening of that day, by *The New York Express*, as follows:

"The 'irrepressible conflict' started by Mr. Seward and indorsed by the Republican party, has at length attained to its logical, foreseen result. That conflict, undertaken 'for the sake of humanity,' culminates now in inhumanity itself, and exhibits the afflicting spectacle of brother shedding brother's blood.

"Refusing the ballot before the bullet, these men, flushed with the power and patronage of the Federal Government, have madly rushed into a civil war, which will probably drive the remaining Slave States into the arms of the Southern Confederacy, and dash to pieces the last hope for a reconstruction of the Union.

"To the gallant men who are so nobly defending their flag within the walls of Fort Sumter, the nation owes a debt of eternal gratitude—not less than to the equally gallant and patriotic spirits, who, in like obedience to the demands of duty, are periling their lives and shedding their blood in the heroic, but, as yet, unsuccessful endeavor to afford them succor. But, to the cold-blooded, heartless demagogues who started this civil war—themselves magnanimously keeping out of the reach of bodily harm—we can only say, You must find your account, if not at the hands of an indignant people, then in the tears of widows and orphans. The people of the United States, it must be borne in mind, petitioned, begged, and implored these men, who are become their accidental masters, to give them an opportunity to be heard before this unnatural strife was pushed to a bloody extreme; but their petitions were all spurned with contempt; and now the bullet comes in to decide the issue!"

In another editorial, *The Express* said:

"The great fact is upon us. Civil war has commenced. Where it will end, is known only to that Higher Power 'that shapes our ends, rough-hew them as we will.' Of one thing, however, we are thoroughly convinced—the South can never be subjugated by the North, nor can any marked successes be achieved against them. They have us at every advantage. They fight upon their own soil, *in behalf of their dearest rights*—for their public institutions, their homes, and their property. They are abundantly supplied with all the means and appliances for the contest; are commanded by officers who have fought and won battles by the side of those against whom they are now arrayed, with ranks filled by men as intelligent, patriotic, and brave, as e'er faced a foe, and a determination never to be defeated. * * *

"*The South, in self-preservation, has been driven to the wall, and forced to proclaim its independence. A servile insurrection and wholesale slaughter of the whites will alone satisfy the murderous designs of the Abolitionists.* The Administration, egged on by the halloo of the Black Republican journals of this city, has sent its mercenary forces to *pick a quarrel and initiate the work of desolation and ruin.* A call is made for an army of volunteers, under the pretense that an invasion is apprehended of the Federal capital; and the next step will be to summon the slave population to revolt and massacre."

The Utica [N. Y.] *Observer* more pointedly said:

"Of all the wars which have disgraced the human race, it has been reserved for our own enlightened nation to be involved in the most useless and foolish one. What advantage can possibly accrue to any one from this war, however prolonged it might be? Does any suppose that millions of free white Americans in the Southern States, who will soon be arrayed against us, can be conquered by any efforts which can be brought against them? Brave men, fighting on their own soil, and, as they believe, for their freedom and dearest rights, can never be subjugated. The war may be prolonged until we are ourselves exhausted, and become an easy prey to military despotism or equally fatal anarchy; but we can never conquer the South. Admit, if you please, that they are rebels and traitors: they are beyond our reach. Why should we destroy ourselves in injuring them?

"Who are to fight the battles of sectional hatred in this sad strife? The Seceders will fight; but will the Abolitionists, who have combined with them to overthrow the Union, make themselves food for powder? If this could be so—if ten thousand picked fire-eaters of either side could be arrayed against each other, and would fight until, like the Kilkenny cats, all were destroyed—the country would be the better for it. But, while the Secessionist defends himself, the Abolitionist will sneak in the back-ground, leaving those to do the fighting who have no interest in the bloody strife, no hatred against their brethren. The best we can hope is, that, at the end of a fearful struggle, when the country becomes tired of gratifying a spirit of fanaticism, we shall have peace through a treaty in which both sides must make sacrifices, but each must agree to respect the rights of the other. How much better to make such a treaty now, before further bloodshed, before worse hatreds are engendered!"

The Bangor Union (Maine) still more boldly said:

"Democrats of Maine! the loyal sons of the South have gathered around Charleston, as your fathers of old gathered about Boston, in defense of the same sacred principles of liberty—principles which *you* have ever upheld and defended with your vote, your voice, and your strong right arm. Your sympathies are with the defenders of the truth and the right. Those who have inaugurated this unholy and unjustifiable war are no friends of yours—no friends of Democratic Liberty. Will you aid them in their work of subjugation and tyranny?

"When the Government at Washington calls for volunteers or recruits to carry on the work of subjugation and tyranny under the specious phrase of 'enforcing the laws,' 'retaking and protecting the public property,' and 'collecting the revenue,' let every Democrat fold his arms, and bid the minions of Tory despotism do a Tory despot's work. Say to them fearlessly and boldly, in the language of England's great Lord, the Earl of Chatham, whose bold words in behalf of the struggling colonies of America, in the dark hours of the Revolution, have enshrined his name in the heart of every friend of freedom and immortalized his fame wherever the name of liberty is known—say, in his thrilling language: 'If I were a Southerner, as I am a Northerner, while a foreign troop was landed in my country, I would never lay down my arms—*never*, *never*, NEVER!'"

The Albany Argus more cautiously and guardedly said:

"The first gun of civil war is heard, whose reverberations are yet to echo through the civilized world—the signal of events of which no man can tell the end. A fearful responsibility is due to those who have brought this crisis upon the country. War is not the least of calamities. If the Federal Government were about to sacrifice its treasures and fleets and armies to rebuke the Spanish usurpation in Saint Domingo—if this armament were intended to repel Mexican aggression, or to assert our right to San Juan against English pretension—every citizen would gladly rally to the support of the Government. But it is between the States of the Union that the war is to be declared; and its provocations are to be found in the aggressions of section against section, and the defiance of constitutional guarantees. It is a civil war that opens—a war whose successes are without glory, whose noblest deeds are without honor, for they are won in fratricidal conflict, and their cost is fratricidal blood. If this were even a natural, intelligent assertion of Government authority, it would appeal to the moral sentiment of the country. If its object and result were to restore the Union and reëstablish the Constitution over these States, it might be worth all the sacrifices it imposed. For ourselves, we should place no impediments in its way, but bid it God speed to its end. Every Democrat in the North would take the same position. But it cannot, in any event, have this effect. It cannot restore; it can only destroy. There are those who believe that it is the deliberate purpose of the Administration to terminate, in a war in which sectional passions shall be aroused to the utmost hight, the connection between the North and the South, and to cut off all possible hope of reconstruction. If this *is* the purpose of the Administration, they have lost no time in its execution. The deed of separation is sealed in the first blood shed in this conflict."

The Journal of Commerce (New York) said:

"We will not undertake, at this moment, to apportion the measure of folly and crime, on either side, which has led to the present catastrophe. No doubt it has been precipitated by the sending of a fleet with troops, by the United States Government, for the relief (as was understood) of Sumter. And, on the other hand, it may be said that this action of the United States Government was occasioned by the cutting off of supplies from Fort Sumter by the Confederate authorities, which rendered it necessary to send them from New York or some other point. To this, again, it may be replied, that the cutting off of supplies by the Confederate authorities was caused by the long continued delay of the United States authorities to take or consent to any measures of adjustment of the pending differences, thus leaving the Confederate authorities subject to the necessity of maintaining a large military force at Charleston for an indefinite period, or abandoning their claims altogether. The Confederate authorities must, however, bear the responsibility (and it is a heavy one) of commencing the actual firing."

The Boston Post still more mildly said:

"The people must speak in their primary capacity, if they would save their country from a miserable destiny—if they would secure to their families and themselves peace and safety. This should be done in a legal manner. An Extra Session of Congress should be called at once. And, if that body prove incompetent to the duty required, then a National Convention should be convened; and, if all measures for a satisfactory adjustment fail, after full hearing and answers to statements of discontent, and a portion of our country declare its determination, at all events, to dissolve its association with another portion, let it depart in peace, if possible; but, if it be not possible, then we shall feel that we have done all that Christianity, reason, and patriotism could demand, and be prepared to meet the last dreadful issue with a sustaining conscience."[8]

The New York Herald of the 15th put forth a 'leader,' whereof the drift is exhibited in the following extracts:

"Earnestly laboring in behalf of peace, from the beginning of these sectional troubles down to this day, and for the maintenance of the Union through mutual concessions, we do not, even yet, utterly despair of arresting this civil war before it shall have passed beyond the reach of reason. In any event, the people of this metropolis owe it to themselves, to their material and political interests, to their social security and to the country at large, to make a solemn and imposing effort in behalf of peace. To this end, we again call upon our fellow-citizens of this island, irrespective of creed or party, to meet together in an earnest consultation upon the ways and means of peace. The Government at Washington and that at Montgomery, confronted with the horrors of civil war, may yet recoil from them.

"The conservative city of New York, guiltless of any agency in precipitating upon the two sections of this great country this causeless and senseless appeal to arms, has the right, and has some power, to speak to the North and the South in behalf of peace."

The Herald of the next day contained a leading article in substantial accordance with the new drift of public sentiment, even among 'conservatives:' saying:

"The measures that have been adopted, within the last few days, by the Government of Mr. Lincoln, entirely change the aspect of public affairs. Had a similar course been pursued five months ago, the last would have been heard of Secession before now. Not the firing of a gun would have been

[8] *The True American* (Trenton, N. J.), and, so far as can now be traced, every other prominent Democratic journal issued in New Jersey, blamed the Administration and the 'Black Republicans' for inciting and provoking 'the South' to rebellion and civil war, in substantial accordance with the foregoing views of *The New York Express* and *The Albany Argus*. *The Pennsylvanian* (Philadelphia), and *The Patriot and Union* (Harrisburg), with nearly every other leading Democratic journal in Pennsylvania, also treated the war now opening as provoked, if not wantonly commenced, by the 'Black Republicans.' So with the ablest and most widely circulated Democratic journals of Connecticut. *The Chicago Times*, *The Detroit Free Press*, and *Ohio Statesman* (Columbus), likewise regarded and treated the conflict as one which the Republicans had unwarrantably commenced, or, at least, incited. Few or none of these, however, counseled acquiescence in Disunion—much less, a surrender of Washington and Maryland.

needed; the fortifications upon the coast would have been rendered impregnable against local attacks; and, with the exception of South Carolina, no State would have withdrawn from the Union. Such a policy was strongly recommended to Mr. Buchanan's Administration, at the time, by *The New York Herald;* but treason in his Cabinet, and the atrocious perfidy of many others who surrounded him, prevented his acts from corresponding with the exigencies of the period. It is better, however, late than never.

* * * "The time has passed for such public peace meetings, in the North, as were advocated, and might have effected some beneficial result, a few weeks since. War will make the Northern people a unit. Republicans look upon it as inevitable, and Democrats have been gradually becoming disgusted at the neglect and ingratitude with which they have been treated by a section for which they have faithfully borne the heat and burden of conflict for so many years. Fire-eaters have accustomed themselves to adopt an indiscriminate tone of hostility toward citizens of the non-slaveholding States, which would have, long ago, alienated their friends, but that the party attachment of the latter has been founded upon principles, not recklessly to be abandoned.

"The policy adopted by Mr. Lincoln, as set forth in his Proclamation and his speech to the Virginia Commissioners, is, on the whole, approved by the masses of the community. It cannot harm the North eventually; and, if the damage it may inflict upon the South is to be regretted, it will be none the less well, if it secures final peace to the country."

That those who for years had zealously maintained that a simple adherence to the policy of Jefferson with regard to the exclusion of Slavery from the territories was an unwarranted and unjustifiable war upon 'the South,' impelled by 'fanaticism' and 'sectional' hate, should, by the mere crashing of a few balls against the walls of a Federal fortress, be converted to an entirely different view of the past and present attitude of the combatants, was not to be expected. That the hated 'Abolitionists' were the real, responsible, culpable authors of the long foreseen and deeply deplored collision, was doubtless still the belief of thousands who saw no adequate reason for insisting on it at this juncture, and in whose minds indignation at the Secessionists, not only as factious and unpatriotic, but as untrue and ungrateful to their 'conservative' friends in the Free States, for the moment overbore all countervailing considerations. But, despite this undertone of demur and dissatisfaction, it is certain that the North had never before seemed so nearly and enthusiastically unanimous and determined as in devotion to the maintenance of the Union for the month or two succeeding the reduction of Fort Sumter.

Very different was the impression made on the public mind of the South by the same occurrences—strikingly diverse was the reception there accorded to the President's Proclamation.

On the evening of April 12th, the Confederates congregated at their capital, Montgomery, held high carnival over the tidings that Beauregard had, by order, opened fire that morning on Fort Sumter. As was natural, their Secretary of War, Mr. Leroy Pope Walker, was called out for a speech, and, in his response, predicted that the Confederate flag would float, before the 1st of May, over Washington City,[9] as it might, ultimately, over Faneuil Hall itself.

[9] *The New York Herald* of April 10th, after proclaiming in its 'leader' that 'civil war is close at hand,' and announcing that Lieut. Talbot had been stopped in Charleston on his return from Washington to Major Anderson in Fort Sumter says:

"Anticipating, then, the speedy inauguration of civil war at Charleston, at Pensacola, or in

This declaration was, very naturally, at once flashed over the whole country; and it was well known that a portion of the Confederate forces were dispatched northward from Charleston directly after the fall of Sumter.[10] Yet, in the face of these notorious facts, Gov. Letcher responded to the President's call on Virginia for Militia to defend the capital in the following terms:

"I have only to say that the militia of Virginia will not be furnished to the powers at Washington for any such use or purpose as they have in view. Your object is to subjugate the Southern States; and a requisition made upon me for such an object—an object, in my judgment, not within the purview of the Constitution or the Act of 1795—will not be complied with. You have chosen to inaugurate civil war; and, having done so, we will meet you in a spirit as determined as the Administration has exhibited toward the South."

To the same effect, Gov. Ellis, of North Carolina—who had long been thoroughly in the interest and counsels of the plotters of Disunion—responded to the call as follows:

"RALEIGH, *April* 15, 1861.

"Honorable SIMON CAMERON,

"*Secretary of War:*

"Your dispatch is received, and, if genuine—which its extraordinary character leads me to doubt—I have to say in reply, that I regard the levy of troops made by the Administration for the purpose of subjugating the States of the South, as in violation of the Constitution, and a usurpation of power. I can be no party to this wicked violation of the laws of the country, and to this war upon the liberties of a free people. You can get no troops from North Carolina. I will reply more in detail when your call is received by mail. JOHN W. ELLIS,

"Governor of North Carolina."

Gov. Isham G. Harris, of Tennessee—likewise a thorough sympathizer with South Carolina—responded as follows:

"Tennessee will not furnish a single man for coërcion, but fifty thousand, if necessary, for the defense of our rights and *those of our brethren.*"

Texas, or, perhaps, at all these places, the inquiry is forced upon us, What will be the probable consequences? We apprehend that they will be: first, the secession of Virginia and the other border Slave States, and their union with the Confederate States; secondly, the organization of an army for the removal of the United States ensign and authorities from every fortress or public building within the Confederate States, *including the White House, the Capitol, and other public buildings at Washington.* After the secession of Virginia from the United States, *it is not likely that Maryland can be restrained from the same decisive act.* She will follow the fortunes of Virginia, and will undoubtedly claim that, in withdrawing from the United States, *the District of Columbia reverts into her possession* under the supreme right of revolution. Here we have verge and scope enough for a civil war of five, ten, or twenty years' duration.

"What for? To 'show that we have a Government'—to show that the seceded States are still in our Union, and are still subject to its laws and authorities. This is the fatal mistake of Mr. Lincoln, and his Cabinet, and his party. The simple truth—patent to all the world—is, that the seceded States *are* out of the Union, and are organized under an independent Government of their own. The authority of the United States, within the borders of this independent Confederacy, has been completely superseded, except in a detached fort here and there. We desire to restore this displaced authority in its full integrity. How is this to be done? By entering into a war with the seceded States for the continued occupation of those detached forts? No. A war will only widen the breach, and enlarge and consolidate this Southern Confederacy, on the one hand; while, on the other hand, it will bring ruin upon the commerce, the manufactures, the financial and industrial interests, of our Northern cities and States, and may end in an oppressive military despotism.

"How then are we to restore these seceded States to the Union? We can do it only by conciliation and compromise."

[10] *The Mobile Advertiser* about this time, had the following:

"We are prepared to fight, and the enemy is not. Now is the time for action, while he is yet unprepared. Let the fife sound 'Gray Jackets over the Border,' and let a hundred thousand men, with such arms as they can snatch, get over the border as quickly as they can. Let a division enter every Northern border State, destroy railroad connection to prevent concentration of the enemy, and the desperate strait of these States, the body of Lincoln's country, will compel him to a peace—or compel his successor, should Virginia not suffer him to *escape from his doomed capital.* Kentucky and Tennessee are offering to send legions south to our aid. Their route is *north.* They place themselves at the orders of our Government—and we have not yet heard that our Government has ordered them *south.*"

From Union-loving Kentucky, this reply was rendered:

"FRANKFORT, April 16, 1861.

"Hon. SIMON CAMERON, *Secretary of War:*

"Your dispatch is received. In answer, I say emphatically that Kentucky will furnish no troops for the wicked purpose of subduing her sister Southern States.

"B. MAGOFFIN,
"Governor of Kentucky."

Four days prior to the date of this exhibition of Kentucky loyalty, the following telegram had flown all over the country:

"LOUISVILLE, Ky., April 12, 1861.

"Dispatches have come here to hold the Kentucky volunteer regiment in readiness to move at a moment's notice from the War Department *at Montgomery*."

This formal order from the *Confederate* Government to the Kentuckians enlisted for its service does not seem to have evoked a remonstrance from her Governor. It was only the call for Kentuckians to maintain the integrity of the Republic and enforce the authority of its Government that aroused his abhorrence of its "wicked purpose."

The Louisville Journal—chief oracle of Bell-Everett 'conservatism' in Kentucky—then, as before and since, professedly devoted to the Union—thus responded to the President's call:

"The President's Proclamation has reached us. We are struck with mingled amazement and indignation. The policy announced in the Proclamation deserves the unqualified condemnation of every American citizen. It is unworthy not merely of a statesman but of a man. It is a policy utterly harebrained and ruinous. If Mr. Lincoln contemplated this policy in his Inaugural Address, he is a guilty dissembler; if he has conceived it under the excitement aroused by the seizure of Fort Sumter, he is a guilty Hotspur. In either case, he is miserably unfit for the exalted position in which the enemies of the country have placed him. Let the people instantly take him and his Administration into their own hands, if they would rescue the land from bloodshed, and the Union from sudden and irretrievable destruction."[11]

Few or no journals issued in the Slave States—save a portion of those of St. Louis and Knoxville—gave the call a more cordial greeting than this.

Gov. Claiborne F. Jackson,[12] of Missouri, gave these among his reasons for disregarding and defying the President's call:

"It is illegal, unconstitutional, revolutionary, inhuman, diabolical, and cannot be complied with."

He added:

"Not one man will the State of Missouri furnish to carry on so unholy a crusade."

Gov. Burton, of Delaware, deferred his response to the 26th, and then stated that "the laws of this State do not confer upon the Executive any authority allowing him to comply with such requisition." He proceeded, however, formally and officially, to "recommend the formation of volunteer companies for the protection of the lives and property of the citizens of *this State* against violence of any sort to which they may be exposed. For these purposes, such companies, when formed, will be under the control of the *State* authorities, though not subject to be ordered by the Executive into the United States service—the law not vesting in him such authority. They will, however, have the option of offering their services to the General Government for the defense of its Capital and the support of the Constitution and laws of the country."

[11] *The National Intelligencer*—perhaps the only journal of note issued south of Mason and Dixon's line that did not utterly execrate the President's call—thus mildly indicated [April 16th] its dissent from the policy thereby initiated:

"For ourselves, we have to express the hope and belief that, until the meeting of Congress, the President will employ the forces of the Government in purely defensive purposes, guarding all points threatened with attack, and awaiting, in the mean time, the counsel and coöperation of the people's representatives, before proceeding to ulterior measures; and upon those representatives, when they are assembled, we shall, without questioning the *legal rights* of the Government, urge the impolicy of advising and consenting to the recapture of forts and public property, which we do not want in States out of the Union, and which, certainly, cannot be permanently regained to the Union by military force."

[12] April 16th.

In other words: Gov. Burton called for an organization of the Militia of Delaware, not in obedience to the requisition of the President, nor in support of the integrity and authority of the Union, but to be wielded by himself, as circumstances should eventually dictate. And, in consistency with this, neither the Governor nor the great body of his political adherents rendered any aid or encouragement whatever to the Government down to the close of his official life, which happily terminated with the year 1862.

Gov. Hicks, of Maryland, made at first no direct, but several indirect, responses to the President's call. He issued, on the 18th, a Proclamation, assuring the people of Maryland of his desire to preserve "the honor and integrity of *the State*," and to maintain "within her limits, that *peace* so earnestly desired by all good citizens." He exhorted them to "abstain from all heated controversy upon the subject," and pledged them that "all powers vested in the Governor will be strenuously exerted to preserve the peace and maintain inviolable the honor and integrity *of Maryland*;" adding his assurance that "no troops will be sent from Maryland, *unless* it may be for the defense of the National capital"—that being the express purpose for which the President had required them. Finally, this model Southern Unionist apprised them that

"The people of this State will, in a short time, have the opportunity afforded them, in a special election for Members of the Congress of the United States, to express their devotion to the Union, *or their desire to see it broken up*."

In other words: Maryland might, at any time, relieve herself of all her engagements and obligations to her sister States in the Union by giving a Disunion majority on her vote for Members of Congress! Surely, no Secessionist could go further or ask more than that! Yet this was the response of the *only* Governor of a Slave State who had claimed votes for his party in the late Presidential canvass on the ground of its especial and unflinching devotion to "the Union, the Constitution, and the enforcement of the laws."

Mayor Brown, of Baltimore—being thoroughly in the confidence as well as the interest of the Disunionists—was but too happy to indorse and reïterate these sentiments. In a Proclamation of even date with the foregoing, he "heartily concurs" in the Governor's views aforesaid, "and will earnestly coöperate with his efforts to maintain peace and order in the city of Baltimore;" but he more especially approves and takes delight in the Governor's assurance that "no troops shall be sent from Maryland to the soil of any other State." Of course, he responds to the Governor's suggestion that, at the approaching election, the people of Maryland may vote themselves out of the Union, if a majority shall see fit to do so. He is sure that, if the Governor's counsels shall be heeded, "the storm of war which now threatens the country will, at least, pass over *our* beloved State and leave it unharmed; but, if they shall be disregarded, *a fearful and fratricidal strife may at once burst forth in our midst*."

These hints and covert menaces were destined to receive a prompt and tragical explication.

The President's call was issued on the morning of the 15th; and, on the evening of the 16th, several companies from Pennsylvania had reached Washington and reported for duty. In the afternoon of the 17th, the Sixth Massachusetts—the first full regiment that responded to the call—started from Boston by rail, leaving the Fourth all but ready to follow. On the 18th, more Pennsylvania Volunteers, including an artillery company, reported at Washington, having that day passed through Baltimore—mauger the Governor's and Mayor's Proclamations aforesaid—without objection or impediment. The Sixth Massachusetts—one thousand strong—enjoyed that day a magnificent ovation in New York, and passed on southward at night, reaching Baltimore by train about noon on the 19th, utterly unsuspecting and unprepared for the reception that awaited them.

But the Secessionists of Baltimore had been intensely excited, on the 18th, by the arrival of emissaries from Charlestown, Va., instructed to exact not only pledges but guarantees from the managers of the Baltimore and Ohio Railroad that no Federal troops should be permitted to pass over their main line, and that no munitions should be removed thereon from the Federal Arsenal at Harper's Ferry! In case of their refusal, their great bridge over the Potomac at that point should be blown up. Hereupon, an immense meeting of "The National Volunteer Association" was held at evening in Monument Square—T. Parkin Scott presiding; he, with Wilson C. N. Carr and William Burns (President of said Association) being the speakers. All these were rank Disunionists, and the Association was organized in the interest of Secession. None of the speakers directly advocated attacks on the Northern troops about to pass through the city; but each was open in his hostility to 'coërcion,' and ardently exhorted his hearers to organize, arm, and drill, for the conflict now inevitable. Carr said:

> "I do not care how many Federal troops are sent to Washington; they will soon find themselves surrounded by such an army from Virginia and Maryland that escape to their homes will be impossible; and when the 75,000 who are intended to invade the South shall have polluted that soil with their touch, the South will exterminate and sweep them from the earth." [Frantic cheering and yelling.]

The meeting broke up with stentorian cheers for 'the South' and for 'President Davis.'

To add fuel to the raging flames, news arrived next morning that Lieut. Jones, who was in charge of the Federal Arsenal and other property at Harper's Ferry, with barely forty-five regulars, learning that a force of 2,500 Virginia Militia was advancing to seize that post, had evacuated it during the night, after endeavoring, in the face of a suddenly gathered force of Virginians, to destroy by fire the National property, including fifteen thousand Springfield muskets there deposited. These were somewhat injured; but the Confederates are understood to have ultimately repaired and used most of them. Lieut. Jones fled across the thin western strip of Maryland to Chambersburg, Pa., losing three of his men. He left the Ferry at 10 o'clock, P. M., and reached Hagerstown, Md., thirty miles distant, next morning; having blown up and destroyed the public property so far as possible, but saving none of it to the Government.

At the hight of the frenzied excitement created by these tidings, the Massachusetts Sixth, with ten companies of the Philadelphia Washington brigade, under Gen. Small, having left Philadelphia at 3 A. M., of the 19th, reached Baltimore, in a train of seventeen passenger cars, containing over two thousand persons, mainly soldiers. The train stopped at the Camden station, on the east side of the city, a little before noon. The five foremost cars, containing a portion of the Massachusetts men, were here detached, and drawn singly through the city by four horses each. There being no horses for the remainder, the residue of the regiment, of whom but a small portion were armed, left the cars and formed in the street, waiting the arrival of horses. None came; for the Secession mob who filled the streets had covered the track, immediately behind the five cars aforesaid, with heavy anchors, timber, stones, and other obstructions—piled, in one instance, to a hight of fifteen feet—and, by the help of these, were prepared to prevent the passage of any more cars. Meantime, the residue of the regiment, as they formed, were assailed by showers of stones and other missiles, hurled from the streets and the house-tops, whereby several of them were knocked down and otherwise badly injured. In the confusion thus created among the raw, unarmed soldiers, a rioter came behind the last platoon, seized the musket of one of the volunteers, and shot him dead. Hereupon, the soldiers were ordered to fire; and those who had guns and ammunition did so, with some effect. This caused the mob to recoil; and the soldiers, learning that the track had been obstructed, closed their ranks, and commenced their march of two miles and a half through the streets of the city to the Washington dépôt, surrounded and followed by the howling, pelting mob. Mayor Brown and a strong detachment of police marched at the head of the troops, opening a way before them through the vast and angry crowd. Missiles still poured upon them from every quarter; and, in some cases, heavy pieces of iron were cast out of second and third-story windows upon their heads. One man was crushed down by one of these iron billets. The front of the column received little injury; but the rioters closed in upon and attempted to cut off a portion of the rear, which, being hardly pressed, was at length ordered to fire; and the order was obeyed. Several volleys were fired by a small portion of the regiment, whereby eleven of the mob were killed, and four severely wounded. Of the soldiers, three were slain, and eight seriously injured. Most of the remaining volunteers reached the Washington dépôt and crowded into the cars, which were dispatched, so soon as possible, for Washington. Fifteen of the soldiers who went on with their comrades were so injured by the missiles that, on reaching the capital, they were sent to the hospital. The train was repeatedly fired at from the hills and woods along the route, but at too great distance to do harm. At the Jackson bridge, it was stopped by the removal of several rails, which were promptly relaid, under the protection of the troops.

The Pennsylvanians were left behind; and, being entirely unarmed, Gen. Small decided that they should not proceed. He attempted to have the cars in which they remained drawn back out of the city, but without immediate success. Soon, a portion of the mob, desisting from the pursuit of the Massachusetts men, turned upon these, and commenced a violent stoning of the cars, whereby the windows were broken and several men severely injured. The Pennsylvanians sprang from the cars, and engaged in a hand-to-hand fight with their assailants, being aided to some extent by Baltimore Unionists. An irregular fight was here kept up for nearly two hours, during which ten or twelve soldiers were badly hurt, and one or two killed. Finally, Police Marshal Kane appeared on the ground, and, being very influential with the Secessionists, soon stopped the fight; when the Pennsylvanians, returning to the cars, were started on the back track to Philadelphia, where they arrived late that night.

At 4 P. M. of that day—the soldiers from the Free States having all departed—a great meeting of the triumphant rioters, under a Maryland flag, was held in Monument Square. After a rebel speech by Dr. A. C. Robinson, Mayor Brown harangued the multitude in favor of peace and order, which was received with evident disrelish; but, when he added that he disapproved of the President's call, and would not have responded to it, had *he* been Governor, the rioters recognized their friend. He told them that he had conferred with Gov. Hicks, who had united with him in telegraphing to Washington and to Philadelphia that no more Northern troops must be sent through Maryland, and had received assurances from the President of the Philadelphia and Baltimore railroad that *he* would send none without further consultation and concert with the authorities of Baltimore and Maryland. Gov. Hicks further concurred with him in the opinion that it is folly and madness for one portion of this great nation to attempt the subjugation of another portion. It can never be done. [Cheers.] A deputation was sent for the Governor, who duly appeared, and, standing under the Maryland flag, addressed the assemblage. He said:

> "I coïncide in the sentiment of your worthy Mayor. After three conferences, we have agreed; and I bow in submission to the people. I am a Marylander; I love my State, and I love the Union; but I will suffer my right arm to be torn from my body before I will raise it to strike a sister State."

Hereupon, the meeting adjourned.

That night, Baltimore, and, in fact, nearly all Maryland, were completely in the hands of the Secessionists. The Unionists were terrified, paralyzed, silenced, and they generally shrank from observation. The rebel mob—partially armed from the gunstores—paraded the streets of Baltimore unopposed, broke in the doors and windows of the President-street railroad dépôt, and demanded the muskets which they insisted were in the building, and were allowed to appoint a Committee to search it, and report. The Committee examined it, was satisfied, and reported that there were no arms; so they left. Ex-Gov. Louis E. Lowe harangued the mob, under the Maryland flag, from the portico of Barnum's Hotel; pledging them ample assistance from his [Frederick] county. With the full assent, if not by express direction, of Mayor Brown and Police Marshal Kane, the telegraph wires connecting Baltimore with the Free States were cut, and the railroad bridges northward and north-eastward from Baltimore, on the railroads to Philadelphia and Harrisburg, burned; thus shutting off Washington and the Government from all communication with the Northern, as Gov. Letcher and his backers had just excluded them from all intercourse with the Southern, States. The telegraphic communication westward was preserved, to enable the master-spirits to dispatch to their confederates in Western Maryland such messages as this to one at Frederick, who soon after joined the Confederate army:

"To BRADLEY T. JOHNSON, Esq.:

"Thank you for your offer. Bring your men by the first train, and we will arrange with the railroad afterward. *Streets red with Maryland blood.*

"Send expresses over the mountains and valleys of Maryland and Virginia for the riflemen to come without delay. Further hordes [of Union volunteers] will be down upon us to-morrow [the 20th]. We will fight them, and whip them, or die.

"GEO. P. KANE."

Mayor Brown sent three envoys to the President, bearing a dispatch indorsed by Gov. Hicks, wherein he says:

"The people are exasperated to the highest degree by the passage of troops, and the citizens are unusually decided in the opinion that no more troops should be ordered to come.

"The authorities of the city did their best to-day to protect both strangers and citizens, and to prevent a collision, but in vain; and, but for their great efforts, a fearful slaughter would have occurred.

"Under these circumstances, it is my solemn duty to inform you that it is not possible for more soldiers to pass through Baltimore, unless they fight their way at every step. I, therefore, hope and trust, and most earnestly request, that no more troops be permitted or ordered by the Government to pass through the city. If they should attempt it, the responsibility for the bloodshed will not rest upon me."

The Committee telegraphed back the following message:

"WASHINGTON, April 20, 1861.

"To MAYOR BROWN, Baltimore: We have seen the President and Gen. Scott. We bear from the former a letter to the Mayor and Governor, declaring that no troops shall be brought through Baltimore, if, in a military point of view, without opposition, they can be marched around Baltimore.

H. L. BOND,
J. C. BRUNE, GEO. W. DOBBIN."

The President of the Baltimore and Ohio railroad had already responded to a similar message as follows:

"GENTLEMEN: I have the honor to acknowledge the receipt of your communication of this date, in which you advise that the troops now here be sent back to the 'borders of Maryland.' Most cordially approving this advice, I have just telegraphed the same to the Philadelphia, Wilmington, and Baltimore railroad company, and this company will act in accordance therewith.

"J. W. GARRETT, President."

Gov. Andrew, of Massachusetts, having telegraphed to Mayor Brown as follows:

"I pray you to cause the bodies of our Massachusetts soldiers, dead in Baltimore, to be laid out, preserved in ice, and tenderly sent forward by express to me. All expenses will be paid by the Commonwealth:"

Mayor Brown responded as follows:

"SIR: No one deplores the sad events of yesterday in this city more deeply than myself, but they were inevitable. Our people viewed the passage of armed troops of another State, through the streets, as an invasion of our soil, and could not be restrained. The authorities exerted themselves to the best of their ability, but with only partial success. Gov. Hicks was present, and concurs in all my views as to the proceedings now necessary for our protection. When are these scenes to cease? Are we to have a war of sections? God forbid! The bodies of the Massachusetts soldiers could not be sent on to Boston, as you requested, all communication between this city and Philadelphia by railroad, and with Boston by steamers, having ceased; but they have been placed in cemented coffins, and will be placed with proper funeral ceremonies in the mausoleum of Green Mount Cemetery, where they shall be retained until further directions are received from you. The wounded are tenderly cared for. I appreciate your offer; but Baltimore will claim it as her right to pay all expenses incurred."

Gov. Andrew promptly rejoined:

"Dear Sir: I appreciate your kind attention to our wounded and our dead, and trust that, at the earliest moment, the remains of our fallen will return to us. I am overwhelmed with surprise that a peaceful march of American citizens over the highway to the defense of our common capital should be deemed aggressive to Baltimoreans. Through New York, the march was triumphal."

At 3 A. M., on Sunday, April 21st, Mayor Brown received a message from the President, requesting Gov. Hicks and himself to proceed immediately to Washington for consultation. Gov. Hicks being no longer in the city, Mayor Brown, on further conference, went without him, taking three friends—whereof, at least two were ardent Secessionists—to bear him company. They reached Washington at 10 A. M., and were admitted to an immediate interview with the President, attended by the Cabinet and Gen. Scott. Mr. Lincoln urged, with abundant reason, that he had no choice between bringing troops through Maryland and surrendering the capital to armed treason. He finally appealed to Gen. Scott, who gave his military opinion that troops might be brought through Maryland by way of Annapolis or the Relay House, without passing through Baltimore. The Mayor dilated on the fearful excitement of the Baltimoreans, and the impossibility of his answering for the consequences, if more Northern troops should appear in that city. He adroitly added that his jurisdiction was confined to the city, and that he could make no promises as to the behavior of the Marylanders on either side of it. In his official report of the interview, Mr. Brown says:

"The Mayor and his companions availed themselves of the President's full discussion of the questions of the day to urge upon him respectfully, but in the most earnest manner, a course of policy which would give peace to the country, and especially the withdrawal of all orders contemplating the passage of troops through any part of Maryland."

On returning to the cars, the Mayor received a dispatch from railroad President Garrett, announcing the approach of troops (Pennsylvanians) by railroad from Harrisburg to Cockeysville, a few miles north of Baltimore, and that the city was greatly excited thereby; whereupon, Messrs. Brown & Co. returned to the President, and demanded a further audience, which was granted. The dispatch was submitted; and the President and Gen. Scott agreed that the Pennsylvania soldiers, who had thus unwittingly profaned the soil of Maryland by daring to advance over it to the defense of the National Metropolis, should be turned back to Harrisburg.

There is not much more of this nature to be recorded; but, among the Baltimoreans who, next day, visited Washington to second the demands of Messrs. Brown & Co., and confirm the impression which it was hoped they had made, was a Committee from the Young Men's Christian Association, who modestly petitioned that the President should put an end to the unnatural conflict now imminent by yielding to the demands of the South. To this end, they advised that the Federal forces already in Washington should be disbanded; but, at all events, that no more should be marched across the territory of

Maryland. The President, in reply, called their attention to the fact that the capital was imminently threatened; that he was informed that Rebel batteries were being erected on the Virginia bank of the Potomac to command the passage of that river; that the Rebel Government had determined to establish forthwith its headquarters in the house where this interview was held; and that the only effect of yielding to their prayers would be the destruction of the Government as well as his own death or captivity. The Young Christians, of course, disclaimed any purpose to produce such a catastrophe; to which the President replied that their *intent* mattered little, since the *effect* of the course demanded by Baltimore could be no other than this. To a similar but more formal representation from Gov. Hicks, objecting to the passage of Northern troops across any portion of Maryland, Gov. Seward returned the following most moderate and conciliatory answer:

"Department of State, *April* 22, 1861.

"His Excellency Thos. H. Hicks,

"*Governor of Maryland:*

"Sir: I have had the honor to receive your communication of this morning, in which you inform me that you have felt it to be your duty to advise the President of the United States to order elsewhere the troops then off Annapolis, and also that no more may be sent through Maryland; and that you have further suggested that Lord Lyons be requested to act as mediator between the contending parties in our country, to prevent the effusion of blood.

"The President directs me to acknowledge the receipt of that communication, and to assure you that he has weighed the counsels which it contains with the respect which he habitually cherishes for the Chief Magistrates of the several States, and especially for yourself. He regrets, as deeply as any magistrate or citizen of the country can, that demonstrations against the safety of the United States, with very extensive preparations for the effusion of blood, have made it his duty to call out the force to which you allude.

"The force now sought to be brought through Maryland is intended for nothing but the defense of this capital. The President has necessarily confided the choice of the national highway which that force shall take in coming to this city to the Lieutenant-General commanding the Army of the United States, who, like his only predecessor, is not less distinguished for his humanity than for his loyalty, patriotism, and distinguished public services. The President instructs me to add that the national highway thus selected by the Lieutenant-General has been chosen by him, upon consultation with prominent magistrates and citizens of Maryland, as the one which, while a route is absolutely necessary, is furthest removed from the populous cities of the State, and with the expectation that it would, therefore, be the least objectionable one.

"The President cannot but remember that there has been a time in the history of our country, when a General of the American Union, with forces designed for the defense of its Capital, was not unwelcome anywhere in the State of Maryland, and certainly not at Annapolis, then, as now, the capital of that patriotic State, and then, also, one of the capitals of the Union.

"If eighty years could have obliterated all the other noble sentiments of that age in Maryland, the President would be hopeful, nevertheless, that there is one that would forever remain there and everywhere. That sentiment is that no domestic contention whatever, that may arise among the parties of this Republic, ought in any case to be referred to any foreign arbitrament—least of all to the arbitrament of an European monarchy.

"I have the honor to be, with distinguished consideration, your Excellency's most obedient servant,

"William H. Seward."

The spirit in which these negotiations were regarded throughout the loyal States is very fairly exhibited in the following letter:

"New York, *April* 25, 1861.

"*To the President of the United States:*

"Sir: The people of the Free States have now been for some time cut off from communication with the capital of their country by a mob in the city of Baltimore. The troops of the General Government have been attacked and shot down by the mob in their passage through that city, in pursuance to the orders of the Government. The lines of communication have been destroyed, and the authority of the General Government has been set at defiance. This state of things has been permitted to continue for nearly a week; and our troops going to the capital have been delayed, and have had to find their way by irregular and circuitous routes, very much to their inconvenience. Citizens of the Free States have either been prevented altogether from visiting the capital or from returning thence to their homes, or have been compelled to run the gauntlet, been subjected to all sorts of insult and danger, and have had to resort to the most circuitous routes by private conveyance and at exorbitant expense. All facilities by mail and telegraph have been cut off by the same unlawful assemblage in Baltimore and other parts of Maryland, at a time when free communication is so much required between the Free States and Washington.

"The public mind is already excited to the highest point that this state of things has been so long tolerated; and the people are determined that free and uninterrupted communication with the seat of Government shall be immediately established, not by circuitous routes, but by the direct lines of communication that they have heretofore traveled over. *And it is demanded* of the Government that they at once take measures to open and establish those lines of communication, and that they protect and preserve them from any further interruption. Unless this is done, the people will be compelled to take it into their own hands, let the consequences be what they may, and let them fall where they will. It is certainly desirable that this be done through the regularly constituted authorities at Washington; and the Government is earnestly desired to act without delay.

"There is entire unanimity on the part of the people of the Free States to sustain the Government and maintain the Union.

"I trust, Mr. President, that this letter will not be received unkindly; as, in writing it, I simply do what I feel it to be my duty as a citizen to do in this extraordinary state of things.

"I have the honor to be, Sir, your most obedient servant, GEORGE LAW."

Maryland, as we have seen, was practically, on the morning of the 20th of April, a member of the Southern Confederacy. Her Governor spoke and acted the bidding of a cabal of the ablest and most envenomed traitors. At their instance, he summoned the Legislature to meet in extra session at Annapolis on the 26th; while it was notorious that a majority of that body would probably vote her immediately out of the Union, and would, at best, proclaim her neutral in the struggle now opening—would forbid the passage of Federal troops across her soil; and not only forbid, but resist it. Baltimore was a Secession volcano in full eruption; while the counties south of that city were overwhelmingly in sympathy with the Slaveholders' Rebellion, and their few determined Unionists completely overawed and silenced. The counties near Baltimore, between that city and the Susquehanna, were actively coöperating with the Rebellion, or terrified into dumb submission to its behests. The great populous counties of Frederick, Washington, and Alleghany, composing Western Maryland—having few slaves—were preponderantly loyal; but they were overawed and paralyzed by the attitude of the rest of the State, and still more by the large force of rebel Virginians—said to be 5,000 strong—who had been suddenly pushed forward to Harper's Ferry, and who, though not in season to secure the arms and munitions there deposited, threatened Western Maryland from that commanding position. Thus, only the county of Cecil, in the extreme north-east, remained fully and openly loyal to the Union; that county lying this side of the Susquehanna, and being connected with the Free States by railroad and telegraph.

The Eighth Massachusetts, under Gen. Benjamin F. Butler, reached Perryville, on the east bank of the Susquehanna, on the 20th, and found its progress here arrested by burned bridges, and the want of cars on the other side. But Gen. Butler was not a man to be stopped by such impediments. Seizing the spacious and commodious railroad ferry steamer Maryland, he embarked his men thereon, and appeared with them early next morning before Annapolis, the political capital of Maryland, thirty miles south of Baltimore, and about equi-distant with that city from Washington, wherewith it is connected by a branch or feeder of the Baltimore road. He found this city virtually in rebellion, with its branch railroad aforesaid dismantled, and partially taken up, in the interest of Secession. Here, too, were the Naval Academy and the noble old frigate Constitution; the latter without a crew, and in danger of falling, at any moment, into the hands of the enemy. He at once secured the frigate, landed next day unopposed, took possession of the city, and was soon reënforced by the famous Seventh regiment, composed of the flower of the young chivalry of New York City, which had been transported from Philadelphia direct by the steamboat Boston. The Maryland returned forthwith to Perryville for still further reënforcements, munitions, and supplies—no one in Annapolis choosing, or daring, for some time, to sell anything to the Union soldiers. Gen. Butler was met at Annapolis by a formal protest from Gov. Hicks against his landing at that place, or at any other point in Maryland; the specific objection to his occupying Annapolis being that the Legislature had been called to meet there that week. Gen. Butler, in reply, suggested that, if he could obtain means of transportation to Washington, he would gladly "vacate the capital prior to the sitting of the Legislature, and not be under the painful necessity of incommoding your beautiful city while the Legislature is in session."

On the morning of the 24th—several other regiments having meantime arrived—Gen. Butler put his column in motion, the Massachusetts Eighth in advance, closely followed by the New York Seventh. They kept the line of the railroad, repairing it as they advanced. A dismantled engine, which they found on the way, was refitted and put to use. The day proved intensely hot. Many of the men had had little or nothing to eat for a day or two, and had scarcely slept since they left Philadelphia. Some fell asleep as they marched; others fell out of the ranks, utterly exhausted; one was sunstruck, and had to be sent back, permanently disabled. The people whose houses they passed generally fled in terror at the first sight of the Northern Goths, who, they had been told, had come to ravage and desolate the South. Nothing to eat could be bought; and, as they did not choose to take without buying, they hungrily marched, building bridges and laying rails by turns, throughout the day and the following night. The Seventy-first New York followed the next day, and passed, four miles out, the camp of Gov. Sprague's Rhode Island regiment, by whom they were generously supplied with provisions. Arrived at the Annapolis Junction, the soldiers were met by cars from Washington, in which they proceeded on the 25th—the New York Seventh in the advance—to that city, and were hailed with rapture by its loyal denizens, who composed, perhaps, one-half of its entire population. Washington had, for a week, been isolated from the North, while surrounded and threatened by malignant foes. A spirited body of volunteers—temporary sojourners at or casual visitors to the capital—under Cassius M. Clay as Colonel, had stood on guard during those dark days[13] and darker nights; and these, in addition to the small force of regulars commanded by Gen. Scott, had constituted, up to this time, the entire defensive force of the Federal metropolis.

The Legislature of Maryland convened in extra session, in accordance with Gov. Hicks's call, not at Annapolis, but at Frederick—far from any Union force, but within easy striking distance of the Confederates at Harper's Ferry. Gov. Hicks, in his Message (April 27th), recapitulated most of the facts just related, adding that Gen. Butler, before landing at Annapolis, asked permission to do so, but was refused. He said: "The people of Annapolis, though greatly exasperated, acting under counsel of the most prudent citizens, refrained from molesting or obstructing the passage of the troops through the city." Again:

"Notwithstanding the fact that our most learned and intelligent citizens admit the right of the Government to transport its troops across our soil, it is evident that a portion of the people of Maryland are opposed to the exercise of that right. I have done all in my power to protect the citizens of Maryland, and to preserve peace within our borders."

Gov. Hicks admits that he has been somewhat swerved from his true course by "the excitement prevailing among our people during the last few days;" but he restates his deliberate and well-considered position, as follows:

"It is of no consequence now to discuss the causes which have induced our troubles. Let us look to our distressing present and to our portentous future. The fate of Maryland, and, perhaps, of her sister border Slave States, will undoubtedly be seriously affected by the action of your honorable body. Therefore should every good citizen bend his energies to the task before us; and therefore should the animosities and bickerings of the past be forgotten, and all strike hands in the bold cause of restoring peace to our State and to our country. I honestly and most earnestly entertain the conviction that the only safety of Maryland lies in maintaining a *neutral* position between our brethren of the North

---

[13] *The Richmond Examiner*, of April 23d, contained this article:

"The capture of Washington City is perfectly within the power of Virginia and Maryland, if Virginia will only make the effort by her constituted authorities; nor is there a single moment to lose. The entire population pant for the onset; there never was half the unanimity among the people before, nor a tithe of the zeal, upon any subject, that is now manifested to take Washington, and drive from it every Black Republican who is a dweller there.

"From the mountain-tops and valleys to the shores of the sea, there is one wild shout of fierce resolve to capture Washington City, at all and every human hazard. That filthy cage of unclean birds must and will assuredly be purified by fire. The people are determined upon it, and are clamorous for a leader to conduct them to the onslaught. The leader will assuredly arise; ay, and that right speedily.

"It is not to be endured that this flight of Abolition harpies shall come down from the black North for their roosts in the heart of the South, to defile and brutalize the land. They come as our enemies; they act as our most deadly foes; they promise us bloodshed and fire; and this is the only promise they have ever redeemed. The fanatical yell for the immediate subjugation of the whole South is going up hourly from the united voices of all the North; and, for the purpose of making their work sure, they have determined to hold Washington City as the point whence to carry on their brutal warfare.

"Our people can take it—they *will* take it—and Scott, the arch-traitor, and Lincoln, the Beast, combined, cannot prevent it. The just indignation of an outraged and deeply injured people will teach the Illinois Ape to repeat his race and retrace his journey across the borders of the Free negro States still more rapidly than he came; and Scott, the traitor, will be given the opportunity, at the same time, to try the difference between 'Scott's Tactics' and the Shanghae Drill for quick movements.

"Great cleansing and purification are needed and will be given to that festering sink of iniquity, that wallow of Lincoln and Scott—the desecrated city of Washington; and many indeed will be the carcasses of dogs and caitiffs that will blacken the air upon the gallows before the great work is accomplished. So let it be!"

and of the South. We have violated no right of either section. We have been loyal to the Union. The unhappy contest between the two sections has not been commenced or encouraged by us, although we have suffered from it in the past. The impending war has not come by any act or wish of ours. We have done all we could to avert it. We have hoped that Maryland and other Border Slave States, by their conservative position and love for the Union, might have acted as mediators between the extremes of both sections, and thus have prevented the terrible evils of a prolonged civil war. Entertaining these views, I cannot counsel Maryland to take sides against the General Government, until it shall commit outrages upon us which would justify us in resisting its authority. As a consequence, I can give no other counsel than that we shall array ourselves for Union and peace, and thus preserve our soil from being polluted with the blood of brethren. Thus, if war must be between the North and South, we may force the contending parties to transfer the field of battle from our soil, so that *our* lives and property may be secure."

The Legislature, thus instructed, decided *not* to secede from the Union—unanimously in the Senate—53 to 13 in the House; but proceeded to pass an act to provide for the public safety, constituting a 'State Board' of seven, whereof all were rank Secessionists but Gov. Hicks; which Board was to have full control over the organization and direction of the military forces of Maryland; appointing all officers above the rank of captain. This Board was to have full power to adopt measures for the safety, peace and defense of the State; and was directed to proscribe no officer for "his political opinions." Its oath of office included no promise of allegiance to the Federal Constitution or Government. The purpose of this measure was more fully developed by a report from the Committee on Federal Relations, in which the President was charged with acts of tyranny and schemes of subjugation; and the attempt to bring the State, step by step, into collision with the Federal Government clearly revealed. But by this time the strength and resolution of the Free States had been demonstrated, and the sober second thought of Maryland began to assert its ascendency. The violence and preternatural activity of the Secessionists had, for a time, concealed the paucity of their numbers; but it was now evident that they were scarcely a third of the entire white population, and less than a fourth in all that major portion of the State lying north and west of Baltimore.

A Home Guard of Unionists was organized in Frederick, comprising her most substantial citizens. A great Union meeting was held in Baltimore on the evening of May 4th; whereat the creation of the Board of Public Safety, and all kindred measures, were unsparingly denounced. Next day, Gen. Butler pushed forward two regiments from the Annapolis Junction to the Relay House, nine miles from Baltimore, and controlling the communications between that city and Frederick. On the 9th, a force of 1,300 men from Perryville debarked at Locust Point, Baltimore, under cover of the guns of the Harriet Lane, and quietly opened the railroad route through that city to the Relay House and Washington, encountering no opposition. Gen. Butler took permanent military possession of the city on the 13th, while a force of Pennsylvanians from Harrisburg advanced to Cockeysville, reöpening the Northern Central railroad. The Legislature adopted, on the 10th, the following:

"*Whereas*, The war against the Confederate States is unconstitutional and repugnant to civilization, and will result in a bloody and shameful overthrow of our institutions; and, while recognizing the obligations of Maryland to the Union, we sympathize with the South in the struggle for their rights—for the sake of humanity, we are for peace and reconciliation, and solemnly protest against this war, and will take no part in it.

"*Resolved*, That Maryland implores the President, in the name of God, to cease this unholy war, at least until Congress assembles; that Maryland desires and consents to the recognition of the independence of the Confederate States. The military occupation of Maryland is unconstitutional, and she protests against it, though the violent interference with the transit of Federal troops is discountenanced; that the vindication of her rights be left to time and reason, and that a Convention, under existing circumstances, is inexpedient."

The Federal authority having been fully reëstablished in Baltimore, and the Union troops within or upon her borders decidedly outnumbering the Confederate, the Secession fever in the veins of her people subsided as rapidly as it had risen. Having been accustomed from time immemorial to acquiesce in whatever the slaveholding interest proposed, and seeing that interest thoroughly affiliated with the plotters of Disunion, the great majority had consulted what seemed the dictates of prudence and personal safety by flocking to what appeared, in view of the temporary weakness and paralysis of the Federal Government, the strong side—the side whereon were evinced confidence, energy, and decision. Under like influences, Maryland would have been voted out of the Union as promptly, and by as decisive a majority, as Virginia or Tennessee was. Another week's exhibition of the spirit in which Mayor Brown and the Young Christians were allowed to press their impudent demands at the White House, and to return thence to Baltimore not even arrested, would have thrown her headlong into the arms of treason.

Her Legislature finally adjourned on the 14th, after having sent an embassy to Montgomery in quest of 'peace;' which was so received and answered by Davis as to convey to the South the impression that Maryland was in sympathy with the Rebellion. On the 14th, also, Gov. Hicks issued an official Proclamation, calling for four regiments of volunteers, in answer to the President's requisition. The route through Baltimore being fully reöpened, and communication restored between the Free States and Washington, the safety of the capital was secured; regiment after regiment pouring into it by almost every train, until, by the end of May, not less than fifty thousand men—raw and undisciplined, indeed, but mainly of the best material for soldiers—held the line of the Potomac, or guarded the approaches to the capital. And still, from every side, the people of the loyal States were urging more regiments upon the Government, and begging permission to swell the ranks of the Union armies, so as to overmatch any conceivable strength of the rebels.

Baltimore was still, and was destined, for years, to remain, the focus and hiding-place of much active though covert treason; her Confederates maintaining constant communication with Richmond, and continually sending men, as well as medicines, percussion caps, and other pressingly needed supplies, to the Rebel armies, mainly across the lower Potomac, through the southern counties of the State; which, being thoroughly 'patriarchal' in their social and industrial polity, preponderantly and ardently sympathized with the Rebel cause.

XXX.

PROGRESS OF SECESSION.

The Convention of Virginia, whereof a great majority had been elected as Unionists, was, nevertheless, bullied, as we have seen, at the hight of the Southern frenzy which followed the reduction of Fort Sumter, into voting their State out of the Union.[1] In order to achieve this end, it was found necessary to consent to a submission of the ordinance to a popular vote; and the 23d of May was appointed for the election. But, in utter mockery of this concession, the conspirators proceeded forthwith to act upon the assumption that the vote of the Convention was conclusive, and the State already definitively and absolutely out of the Union. Within twenty-four hours after the vote of the Convention to secede, and while that vote was still covered by an injunction of secrecy, they had set on foot expeditions for the capture of the Federal Arsenal, arms and munitions, at Harper's Ferry, as also for that of the Norfolk Navy Yard. So early as the night of the 16th, the channel of Elizabeth River, leading up from Hampton Roads to Norfolk, was partially obstructed in their interest by sinking two small vessels therein, with intent to preclude the passage, either way, of Federal ships of war. The number appears to have been increased during the following nights; while a hastily collected military force, under Gen. Taliaferro—a Virginia brigadier who reached Norfolk from Richmond on the 18th—was reported to be preparing to seize the Navy Yard and Federal vessels during the night of Saturday, the 20th. The Southern officers of the Yard, having done the cause of the Union all the harm they could do under the mask of loyalty, resigned and disappeared in the course of that day. The Navy Yard was in charge of Capt. McCauley, a loyal[2] officer, but a good deal past the prime of life. A young Decatur or Paul Jones would have easily held it a week against all the Virginian Militia that could have been brought within range of its guns, and would never have dreamed of abandoning it while his cartridges held out. No man fit to command a sloop of war would have thought of skulking away from a possession so precious and important, until he had, at least, seen the whites of an enemy's eyes. For here were the powerful forty-gun steam frigate Merrimac, richly worth a million dollars even in time of peace, with the Cumberland, the Germantown, the Plymouth, the Raritan, the Columbia, and the Dolphin, beside the huge old three-decker Pennsylvania, the dismantled seventy-fours Delaware and Columbus, with nearly two thousand[3] cannon, some thou-

[1] April 17th, 1861.

[2] That is to say: Capt. McCauley has never renounced the service, but still draws the pay of an officer of the U. S. Navy.

[3] The Report to the Senate of its Select Committee, appointed to investigate this shameful transaction, made by Hon. John P. Hale, April 18th, 1862, says:

"According to the returns received at the Ordnance bureau of the Navy Department, it appears that there were seven hundred and

sand stand of arms, and immense quantities of munitions, naval stores, timber, etc.; the whole having cost, in peace, more than ten millions of dollars, while its value at this time was absolutely incalculable. The

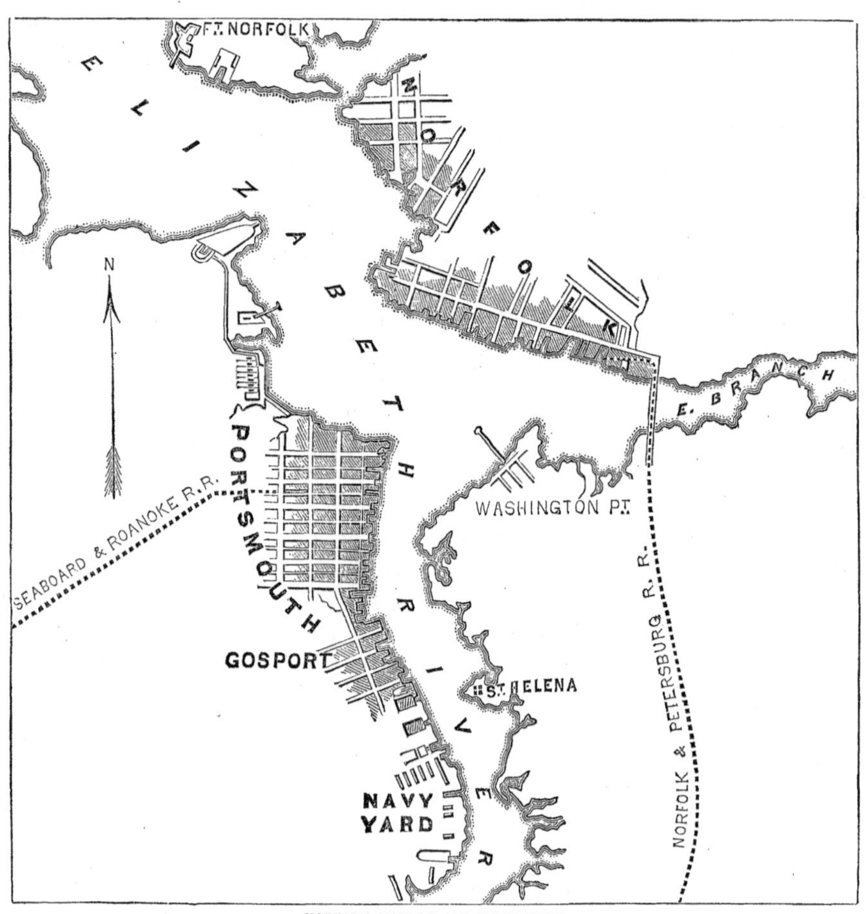

NORFOLK, HARBOR AND NAVY-YARD.

Federal magazine, just below Norfolk, apparently left without a guard, had been broken open the night before by the Rebels, and robbed of

sixty-eight guns in the Yard. Other evidence, however, taken by the Committee, goes to show quite conclusively that there were in the Yard at the time of the evacuation at least two thousand pieces of heavy ordnance, of which about three hundred were new Dahlgren guns, and the remainder were of old patterns. Captain Paulding walked about among them on the 18th of April, and estimated that there were between two and three thousand. Captain McCauley, who must be supposed to have had ample means of knowledge on the subject, thinks there were nearly three thousand pieces of cannon. Mr. James H. Clements, a reliable and intelligent man, testifies that he was familiar with the guns at the Yard, and thinks he speaks within bounds when he puts the number of them at eighteen hundred; and he explains very satisfactorily the discrepancy between the account in the Ordnance bureau and the estimates of the witnesses already mentioned, and of others who appeared before the Committee, stating the number of guns variously at from fifteen hundred to three thousand. Upon the whole evidence, the Committee are forced to the conclusion that there were as many as two thousand pieces of artillery of all calibers in and about the Yard at the time of its abandonment, comprising the armaments of three line-of-battle ships and several frigates."

over four thousand kegs of powder. Capt. McCauley, with all these formidable ships of war, cannon, and munitions, had several hundred good and true men under his command. He had received, some days before, express orders to send the Merrimac forthwith to Philadelphia, and had had her fitted out for the voyage, under the direction of Chief Engineer Isherwood, who was sent thither from Washington on purpose; but, when she was reported all ready but her guns, he declined to order them on board—or, rather, gave the order, but very soon countermanded it—excusing his vacillation or perplexity by his dread of exasperating the Rebels, and referring to the reported obstructions sunk in the channel, which the Merrimac, properly handled, would have crushed like an egg-shell, and thus passed over without a check to her progress. Finally, on the evening of the 20th, he gave orders to scuttle all the ships but the Cumberland, preparatory to flight—as if this were not the very course to preserve them for the future use of the Rebels.

The steam frigate Pawnee, Capt. Hiram Paulding, left Washington on the evening of the 19th, and arrived, at 4 P. M. of the 20th, abreast of Fortress Monroe. Here she took on board Col. Wardrop's regiment of Massachusetts volunteers, 450 strong, raising her fighting force to some six hundred men. She now steamed cautiously and slowly up the river to the Navy Yard, which she reached soon after 8 o'clock. Capt. Paulding had instructions from the Secretary of the Navy, directing him to take command at Norfolk, on his arrival there, and to act as circumstances should dictate; but, at all events, to save the public property from falling into the hands of traitors. He found the guns in the Navy Yard rendered useless by Capt. McCauley's orders, and nearly all the ships of war disabled—several of them already sinking. Among the scuttled was the Merrimac—alone worth all the rest—barely the Cumberland having been reserved to bear away the expectant fugitives. Still, Capt. Paulding might have held his position a week against all the traitors yet developed in Virginia; and that week would have brought at least 30,000 men to his aid. But, without awaiting the firing of a shot, or even the appearance of a foe, he proceeded at once to transfer, with the utmost haste, books, papers, money, and some other of the most portable portions of the public property, to the Pawnee and the Cumberland; not even saving the small arms, of which his Government stood in urgent need. The cannon he abandoned were (or had been) partially spiked; but so inefficiently, with nails, etc., that they were promptly and easily restored by the Rebels to a serviceable condition. The muskets, revolvers, etc., were broken, and, with great quantities of shot and shell, thrown into the water. Several hours were spent in this work—the marine barracks, in the center of the Yard, being set on fire, about midnight, to give light for its continuance.

Lieut. H. A. Wise[4] had accompanied Capt. Paulding from Washington, and was detailed by him, on or before their arrival, to board the Merrimac and bring her out, if possible; and he was accordingly on her

[4] Since, of the Naval Ordnance Bureau.

deck at the earliest moment. He found her partially filled with water, and rapidly filling—a block, which he threw from her lower deck into her hold, indicating by the splash that the water was already over her orlop deck. He returned immediately, and reported the fact to Capt. Paulding, who thereupon decided to desist from further attempts to save her, but to mutilate the guns in the Yard, fire the vessels, ship-houses, and other structures, and blow up the (stone) dry dock. Some of the old and relatively worthless guns were dismantled by knocking off their trunnions; but the new Dahlgren guns proved so tough that not one of them was or could thus be rendered useless. Capt. Paulding now recalled the order he had given Lieut. Wise to blow up the dry dock, and ordered trains to be laid instead, so that, at a signal, the ships might be fired. This was accordingly done; but the previous partial submersion of the ships, under Capt. McCauley's unaccountable order to scuttle them, of course prevented their destruction. Thus, when the Plymouth was reached in its turn by Lieut. Wise, she had sunk below her upper deck, so flooding the train that it could not be fired. Lieut. Wise, who narrowly escaped with a scorching from the inconceivably rapid combustion of the upper portion of the Merrimac, when he fired his train while on board of her, pulled down the channel in his small boat after the escaping vessels, and got on board the Pawnee below Craney Island, when seven or eight miles on her way. The Pawnee, towing the Cumberland, moved slowly down the river at 4 A. M. (high tide), brilliantly lighted on their course by the remaining vessels and all the combustible property left behind. The Cumberland, drawing seventeen feet of water, grounded in passing one of the vessels sunk in the channel, but was got off, an hour or two afterward, uninjured. No molestation was offered them by the Rebels, who, very naturally, thought themselves fortunate in so easily obtaining possession of what was left behind. Most of the vessels were destroyed; but the Merrimac, the best of them all, though badly burned above the water-line, was saved by the Rebels, and, in due time, metamorphosed into the iron-clad Virginia, with which such memorable havoc was wrought in Hampton Roads. A crowd from Norfolk and Portsmouth burst into the Yard, so soon as our ships had fairly departed, and saved for the uses of treason whatever they could, including the dry dock, which had been mined, but not fired, and was readily filled with water. At 6 o'clock, a volunteer company had taken formal possession in the name of Virginia, and raised her flag over the ruins. By 7, the work of unspiking cannon had commenced; and, by 9, several guns had been planted along the dock, where they might serve in resisting the return of the Yankees under some more intrepid leader than he who had just slunk away. It was said that Gen. Taliaferro was drunk throughout the night, and was with difficulty aroused at 6 in the morning to hear that all was over. Two officers of the Pawnee, who were left to fire the Navy Yard, were cut off or bewildered by the rapid spread of the conflagration, and compelled to cross, by skiff, to Norfolk, where they were instantly taken prisoners. No lives were lost.

Thus ended the most shameful, cowardly, disastrous performance that stains the annals of the American Navy.[5]

Many, perhaps most, of the Union delegates to the Virginia Convention left it directly after the passage of the Ordinance of Secession, feeling that they had no longer any business in such company. The residue proceeded, in utter contempt of their own vote directing the submission of the act to the people, to adopt and ratify the Confederate Constitution; and to enter[6] into a convention with the Confederacy, through A. H. Stephens, whereby all the public property, naval stores, munitions of war, etc., acquired by their State at Norfolk and elsewhere, from the United States, were turned over to said Confederacy; and it was agreed that

"the whole military force and military operations, offensive and defensive, of said Commonwealth, in the impending conflict with the United States, shall be under the chief control and direction of the President of said Confederate States, upon the same principles, basis, and footing, as if said Commonwealth were now, and during the interval, a member of said Confederacy."

This agreement was approved and ratified by the Convention on the 25th; although, so early as April 20th, the movement of Confederate troops, from Alabama, Georgia, and South Carolina, to Richmond, had commenced. The treaty of offensive and defensive alliance negotiated by Vice-President Stephens did not, therefore, inaugurate that movement: it could but regulate and perhaps augment it.

[5] It is impossible to interpret the course of many officers of the Army and Navy in this and similar emergencies, save on the presumption that they were in doubt as to whether they ought, as loyal men, to stand by the 'Black Republican' rulers who had just been invested with power at Washington or side with the militant champions of that Slave Power which had somehow become confounded, in their not very lucid or intelligent conceptions, with the Constitution and the Union. At all events, it is certain that their indecision or pusillanimity potently aided to crush out the Unionism of the South, and came very near wrecking the Union itself. Mr. Hale's Report, already cited, says:

"The aid which might have been derived from the workmen in the Yard, and other loyal citizens of Norfolk and Portsmouth, is, in some degree, a matter of conjecture, and it is not proposed to introduce it as an element in the decision of this question. During the closing days of the United States authority at Norfolk, the revolt had acquired such strength, momentum, and confidence, that perhaps no material assistance of this kind was to be depended upon. It is proper to remark, however, that there was abundant evidence before the Committee that at least a majority of the citizens of both Norfolk and Portsmouth were on the side of the Union, and would have been warmly and openly so had the Government shown a strong hand and a timely determination to defend itself. *An election for mayor was held in Portsmouth a few days previous to the surrender, at which the Union candidate was elected by an overwhelming majority.* A voluntary military association, considerable in numbers and influence, was formed in Norfolk for the exclusive purpose of assisting in the defense of the Yard against the insurgents, proffered their services, and offered such tests of their fidelity as should have at once secured their acceptance by the authorities of the Yard. How suicidal a policy was pursued, all know and remember. The Government exhibited such utter feebleness and irresolution, and the enemy so much vigor and fierce purpose, unencumbered by scruples of any kind, that it is not strange that the friends of the Union, finding themselves unsupported by the Government they were anxious to serve and protect, should finally yield to the tempest of treason and passion surging around them, and find, in a compulsory submission and in silence, at least a refuge from the insults and outrages of a ferocious revolutionary mob. But, so irrepressible was the loyal feeling of many of the citizens of Norfolk, that, on the evening of the 20th of April, they *greeted the arrival of the "Pawnee" at the dock with cheer on cheer*, under the supposition that she had come to reënforce and hold the Yard, and bring them deliverance from the perils and dishonor of a war against that Union which they loved. That hope was cruelly disappointed by the hasty attempt to destroy the Yard; and the Government afforded the loyal men at Norfolk—as, indeed, everywhere else at that time—every possible reason for *the conviction that the Rebellion was the winning side, and that devotion to the Government could end only in defeat, loss, and death.*"

[6] April 24th.

A complete reign of terror had, by this time, been established throughout Eastern or Old Virginia. Immigrants from Free States were hunted out on suspicion of Unionism, unless they chose to enlist at once in the Rebel army; and only the most violent and obstreperous sympathy with Secession could save them from personal outrage. Appeals from those who had formerly figured as inflexible Unionists were circulated through the journals, calling upon all true Virginians to stand by the action of their State, and thereby preserve her from the horrors of an intestine war. Thus, Mr. A. H. H. Stuart—a leading Whig of other days, an eminent member of Congress, afterward Secretary of the Interior under President Fillmore—who had been elected to the Convention as a Unionist from the strong Whig county of Augusta, and had opposed Secession to the last, now wrote a letter to *The Staunton Spectator*, maintaining this position:

"In my judgment, it is the duty of all good citizens to *stand by the action of the State*. It is no time for crimination or recrimination. We cannot stop now to inquire who brought the troubles upon us, or why. It is enough to know that they *are* upon us; and we must meet them like men. We must stand shoulder to shoulder. Our State is threatened with invasion, and we must repel it as best we can. The only way to preserve peace is to present a united front. If we show divisions among ourselves, the enemy will be encouraged by them, and may make them the pretext for sending armies into our borders for the purpose of sustaining the hands of the disaffected. Our true policy, then, is to stand together as one man in the hour of danger, and leave our family feuds to be adjusted after the contest is over."

To the same effect, but a little more boldly, Mr. James M. Mason, late a Senator of the United States, wrote as follows:

"*To the Editor of the Winchester Virginian:*

"The question has been frequently put to me—'What position will Virginia occupy, should the Ordinance of Secession be rejected by the people at the approaching election?' And the frequency of the question may be an excuse for giving publicity to the answer.

"The Ordinance of Secession withdrew the State of Virginia from the Union, with all the consequences resulting from the separation. It annulled the Constitution and laws of the United States within the limits of this State, and absolved the citizens of Virginia from all obligations and obedience to them.

"Hence, it follows, if this Ordinance be rejected by the people, the State of Virginia will remain in the Union, and the people of the State will remain bound by the Constitution of the United States; and obedience to the government and laws of the United States will be fully and rightfully enforced against them.

"It follows, of course, that, in this war now carried on by the Government of the United States against the seceding States, Virginia must immediately *change sides*, and, under the orders of that Government, *turn her arms against her Southern sisters.*

"From this, there can be no escape. As a member of the Union, all her resources of men and money will be at once at the command of the Government of the Union.

"Again: for mutual defense, immediately after the Ordinance of Secession passed, a treaty or 'military league' was formed by the Convention in the name of the people of Virginia, with the Confederate States of the South, by which the latter were bound to march to the aid of our State against the invasion of the Federal Government. And we have now in Virginia, at Harper's Ferry and at Norfolk, in face of the common foe, several thousands of the gallant sons of South Carolina, of Alabama, of Louisiana, Georgia and Mississippi, who hastened to fulfill the covenant they made, and are ready and eager to lay down their lives, side by side with our sons, in defense of the soil of Virginia.

"If the Ordinance of Secession is rejected, not only will this 'military league' be annulled, but it will have been made a trap to inveigle our generous defenders into the hands of their enemies.

"Virginia remaining in the Union, duty and loyalty to her obligations to the Union will require that those Southern forces shall not be permitted to leave the State, but shall be delivered up to the Government of the Union; and those who refuse to do so will be guilty of treason, and be justly dealt with as traitors.

"Treason against the United States consists as well 'in adhering to its enemies and giving them aid' as in levying war.

"If it be asked—'What are those to do, who, in their consciences, cannot vote to separate Virginia from the United States?'—the answer is simple and plain: Honor and duty alike require that they should *not vote* on the question; *if they retain such opinions, they must* LEAVE THE STATE.

"None can doubt or question the truth of what I have written; and none can vote against the Ordinance of Secession, who do not thereby (whether ignorantly or otherwise) vote to place himself and his State in the position I have indicated. J. M. MASON.

"*Winchester, Va., May* 16, 1861."

Under the influence of such inculcations, backed by corresponding action, the more conspicuous Unionists being hunted out, and the greater number silenced and paralyzed, the election was a perfect farce,[7] throughout both Eastern and South-Western Virginia. Even Alexandria—always, hitherto, strongly Union—gave but 106 Union votes to over 900 Secession; while in lower Virginia scarcely a Union vote was polled. Thus, when the conspirators came to announce the result, they reported that, including the votes taken in camp, 125,950 had been cast for Secession to 20,373 for the Union; but they significantly added that this did not include the vote of several Western counties, which were in such a state of confusion that no returns therefrom had been received!

North-Western Virginia, including more than a third of the geographical area of the State, with from one-fifth to one-fourth of its white population, had, for many years, chafed under the sway of the slaveholding oligarchy in the East. Repeated struggles respecting bases of legislative apportionment, of taxation, etc., and on questions of internal improvement, had clearly indicated that the antagonism between the East and the West was founded in natural causes, and could not be compromised nor overcome. When opportunity presented, the West had repeatedly protested against the perpetuation of Slavery, but still more earnestly against the subordination of all her interests and rights to the incessant exactions of the Slave Power; though her ruling politicians and presses were usually held in subjection to the dominant interest by the preponderating power of the East. Her people had but to look across the Ohio, whereto their streams tended and their surplus produce was sent, to convince them that their connection with the Old Dominion was unfortunate and injurious.

Ten years prior to this, Muscoe R. H. Garnett,[8] a leading politician of Old Virginia, writing privately to his friend and compatriot, William H. Trescott,[9] of South Carolina, who had sounded him with regard to the aid to be expected from Virginia, in case South Carolina should then secede from the Union, had responded[10] as follows:

"I believe thoroughly in our own theories, and that, if Charleston did not grow quite so fast in her trade with other States, yet the relief from Federal taxation would vastly

[7] *The Louisville Journal* of June 1st, said:

"The vote of Virginia last week on the question of Secession was a perfect mockery. The State was full of troops from other States of the Confederacy; while all the Virginia Secessionists, banded in military companies, were scattered in various places to overawe the friends of Union or drive them from the polls. The Richmond Convention, in addition to other acts of usurpation, provided that polls should be opened in all the military encampments, besides the ordinary voting places. * * * No man voted against Secession on Thursday last but at the peril of being lynched or arrested as an incendiary dangerous to the State."

[8] Democratic representative in Congress from 1857 to 1861; since then, in the Rebel Congress.

[9] Assistant Sec'ry of State under Buchanan.

[10] Richmond, May 3, 1851.

stimulate your prosperity. If so, the *prestige* of the Union would be destroyed, and you would be the nucleus for a Southern confederation at no distant day. But I do not doubt, from all I have been able to learn, that the Federal Government would use force, beginning with the form most embarrassing to you, and least calculated to excite sympathy: I mean a naval blockade. In that event, could you withstand the reaction of feeling which the suffering commerce of Charleston would probably manifest? Would you not lose that in which your strength consists, the union of your people? I do not mean to imply an opinion; I only ask the question. If you force this blockade, and bring the Government to direct force, the feeling in Virginia would be very great. I trust in God it would bring her to your aid. But it would be wrong in me to deceive you by speaking certainly. I cannot express the deep mortification I have felt at her course this winter. But I do not believe that the course of the Legislature is a fair expression of the popular feeling. In the East, at least, the great majority believe in the right of Secession, and feel the deepest sympathy with Carolina in opposition to measures which they regard as she does. But the west—Western Virginia—there is the rub! Only 60,000 slaves to 494,000 whites.[11] When I consider this fact, and the kind of argument which we have heard in this body,[12] I cannot but regard with the greatest fear, the question whether Virginia would assist Carolina in such an issue."

Mr. Garnett had clearly and truly foreseen that Western Virginia must necessarily constitute a formidable obstacle to the triumph of Secession. The forty-two counties which now compose the State of West Virginia, had, in 1860, a free population of 349,642, with only 12,771 slaves, or but one slave to nearly thirty white persons; and even this small number of slaves were, in good part, held in the counties of Greenbrier, Monroe and Hampshire, lying on the southern verge of the new State, and, for the most part, adhering to old Virginia in the struggle for Disunion. In the nature of things, this people were not, and could not be, disposed to divide the Republic, and place themselves on the most exposed and defenseless frontier of a far smaller and weaker nation, in the interest, and for the supposed benefit, of human Slavery. And yet this enormous sacrifice was required of them by the slaveholding conspiracy, which, since it could not hope to win them by persuasion, was preparing to subject them to its sway by force of arms: and it was a secret condition of the adhesion of Virginia to the Confederacy that her territorial area was, in no case, to be curtailed by any treaty of peace that might ultimately be made with the Union.

On the other hand, the accession of Virginia to the Confederacy had rendered a peaceful concession of Southern independence a moral, and well nigh a geographical, impossibility. West Virginia—but more especially that long, narrow strip, strangely interposed between Pennsylvania and Ohio, (locally designated "The Panhandle,") could not be surrendered by the Union without involving the necessity of still further national disintegration. For this "Panhandle" stretches northerly to within a hundred miles of Lake Erie, nearly severing the old from the new Free States, and becoming, in the event of its possession by a foreign and hostile power, a means of easily interposing a military force so as to cut off all communication between them. If the people of the Free States could have consented to surrender their brethren of West Virginia to their common foes, they could not have relinquished their territory without

[11] Mr. Garnett counts the Valley (Shenandoah,) as a portion of Western Virginia.

[12] Mr. G. was then a member of a Virginia State Convention.

consenting to their own ultimate disruption and ruin. West Virginia was thus the true key-stone of the Union arch.

The Legislature of TENNESSEE, which assembled at Nashville January 7th, 1861, and elected Breckinridge Democrats for officers in both Houses, had, on the 19th, decided to call a State Convention, subject to a vote of the people. That vote was taken early in March; and, on the 10th, the result was officially proclaimed as follows: for the Union 91,803; for Disunion 24,749; Union majority 67,054. Several counties did not render their returns; and it was said that their vote would reduce the Union majority to something over 50,000; but the defeat of the Secessionists was admitted to be complete and overwhelming.

Still, the conspirators for Disunion kept actively plotting and mining; and, by means of secret societies, and all the machinery of aristocratic sedition, believed themselves steadily gaining. They had no hope, however, of hurling their State into the vortex of treason, save on the back of an excitement raised by actual collision and bloodshed. Up to the hour of the bombardment of Sumter, though the Governor and a majority of the Legislature were fully in their interest, they remained a powerless minority of the people.

When the news of that bombardment was received, and the excitement created by it was at its hight, the leaders of the 'conservative' or Union party were beguiled into a fatal error. On the 18th, they issued from Nashville an address to the people of Tennessee, wherein, after glancing at the leading events which had just occurred on the seaboard, they proceeded to say:

"Tennessee is called upon by the President to furnish two regiments; and the State has, through her Executive, refused to comply with the call. This refusal of our State *we fully approve*. We commend the wisdom, the justice, and the humanity, of the refusal. We unqualifiedly disapprove of secession, both as a constitutional right, and as a remedy for existing evils; we equally condemn the policy of the Administration in reference to the seceded States. But, while we, without qualification, condemn the policy of coërcion, as calculated to dissolve the Union forever, and to dissolve it in the blood of our fellow-citizens, and regard it as sufficient to justify the State in refusing her aid to the Government, in its attempt to suppress the revolution in the seceded States, we do not think it our duty, considering her position in the Union, and in view of the great question of the peace of our distracted country, to take sides against the Government. Tennessee has wronged no State nor citizen of this Union. She has violated the rights of no State, north or south. She has been loyal to all where loyalty was due. She has not brought on this war by any act of hers. She has tried every means in her power to prevent it. She now stands ready to do any thing within her reach to stop it. And she ought, as we think, to *decline joining either party*. For, in so doing, she would at once terminate her grand mission as peace-maker between the States of the South and the General Government. Nay, more: the almost inevitable result would be the transfer of the war within her own borders; the defeat of all hopes of reconciliation; and the deluging of the State with the blood of her own people.

"The present duty of Tennessee is to maintain a position of independence—taking sides with the Union and the peace of the country against *all* assailants, whether from the North or the South. Her position should be to maintain the sanctity of her soil from the hostile tread of any party.

"We do not pretend to foretell the future of Tennessee, in connection with the other States, or in reference to the Federal Government. We do not pretend to be able to tell the future purposes of the President and Cabinet in reference to the impending war. But, should a purpose be developed by the Government of overrunning and subjugating our brethren of the seceded States, we say, unequivocally, that it will be the duty of the State to resist at all hazards, at any cost, *and by arms*, any such purpose or attempt.

And, to meet any and all emergencies, she ought to be *fully armed;* and we would respectfully call upon the authorities of the State to proceed at once to the accomplishment of this object.

"Let Tennessee, then, prepare thoroughly and efficiently for coming events. In the mean time, let her, as speedily as she can, hold a conference with her sister slaveholding States yet in the Union, for the purpose of devising plans for the preservation of the peace of the land. Fellow-citizens of Tennessee! we entreat you to bring yourselves up to the magnitude of the crisis. Look in the face impending calamities! Civil war—what is it? The bloodiest and darkest pages of history answer this question. To avert this, who would not give his time, his talents, his untiring energy—his all? There may be yet time to accomplish every thing. Let us not despair. The Border Slave States may prevent this civil war: and why shall they not do it?"

Of course, these gentlemen were, though unconsciously, on the high road to open treason, whither they all arrived ere the lapse of many weeks. How they saved their State from the woes of civil war, and preserved her soil from the tread of hostile armies, is already well known. Of the many who weakly, culpably allowed themselves to be beguiled or hurled into complicity in the crime of dividing and destroying their country, there is no name whereon will rest a deeper, darker stigma than that of John Bell.

Conservatism having thus bound itself hand and foot, and cast its fettered and helpless form at the feet of rampant, aggressive treason, the result was inevitable. An emissary from the Confederate traitors, in the person of Henry W. Hilliard,[13] of Alabama, forthwith appeared upon the scene. The Legislature secretly adopted[14] a resolve that the Governor might or should appoint "three Commissioners on the part of Tennessee to enter into a military league with the authorities of the Confederate States, and with the authorities of such other slaveholding States as may wish to enter into it; having in view the protection and defense of the entire South against the war which is now being carried on against it." The Governor appointed as such Commissioners Messrs. Gustavus A. Henry, Archibald O. W. Totten, and Washington Barrow; who lost no time in framing a Convention "between the State of Tennessee and the Confederate States of America," whereof the vital provisions are as follows:

"*First:* Until the said State shall become a member of said Confederacy, according to the Constitutions of both powers, *the whole military force and military operations, offensive and defensive, of said State, in the impending conflict with the United States, shall be under the chief control and direction of the Confederate States*, upon the same basis, principles and footing, as if said State were now and during the interval a member of said Confederacy. Said force, together with those of the Confederate States, is to be employed for the common defense.

"*Second:* The State of Tennessee will, upon becoming a member of said Confederacy, under the permanent Constitution of said Confederate States, if the same shall occur, *turn over to said Confederate States all the public property, naval stores and munitions of war*, of which she may then be in possession, acquired from the United States, on the same terms and in the same manner as the other States of said Confederacy have done in like cases."

This convention—concluded on the 7th—was submitted to the Legislature, still in secret session, and ratified: in Senate, Yeas 14; Nays 6; absent or not voting, 5. In the House, Yeas 43; Nays 15; absent or not voting, 18. This Legislature had, on the preceding day, passed an ordinance of Secession, whereof the first two, and most essential, articles are as follows:

"*First:* We, the people of the State of

[13] Formerly a Whig member of Congress.

[14] May 1, 1861.

Tennessee, waiving an expression of opinion as to the abstract doctrine of secession, but asserting the right, as a free and independent people, to alter, reform or abolish our form of government in such manner as we think proper, do ordain and declare that all the laws and ordinances by which the State of Tennessee became a member of the Federal Union of the United States of America are hereby abrogated and annulled, and that all obligations on our part be withdrawn therefrom; and we do hereby resume all the rights, functions and powers, which, by any of said laws and ordinances, were conveyed to the Government of the United States, and absolve ourselves from all the obligations, restraints and duties, incurred thereto; and do hereby henceforth become a free, sovereign and independent State.

"*Second:* We, furthermore, declare and ordain that Article 10, sections 1 and 2 of the Constitution of the State of Tennessee, which requires members of the General Assembly, and all officers, civil and military, to take an oath to support the Constitution of the United States, be, and the same are hereby, abrogated and annulled, and all parts of the Constitution of the State of Tennessee making citizenship of the United States a qualification for office, and recognizing the Constitution of the United States as the supreme law of this State, are, in like manner, abrogated and annulled."

This Ordinance, with a pendant providing for the adoption of the Confederate Constitution, was nominally submitted to a popular vote of the State, to be taken on the 8th of June ensuing; but such a submission, after "all the public property, naval stores and munitions of war" and the whole "military operations, offensive and defensive, of the said State," were placed "under the chief control and direction of the President of the Confederate States," was, of course, a farce.[15]

The network of railroads checkering the State, and especially the great line connecting Virginia, through Knoxville and Chattanooga, with the Cotton States, was instantly covered with Rebel soldiers, and all freedom of opinion and expression, on the side of the Union, completely crushed out. Gov. Harris, on the 24th of June, issued his proclamation, declaring that the vote of the 8th had resulted as follows:

	Separation.	*No Separation.*
East Tennessee....	14,780	32,923
Middle "	58,265	8,198
West "	29,127	6,117
Military Camps....	2,741	(none)
Total........	104,913	47,238

But a Convention of the people of East Tennessee—a region wherein the immense preponderance of Union sentiment still commanded some degree of freedom for Unionists—held at Greenville on the 17th, and wherein thirty-one counties were represented by delegates, adopted a declaration of grievances, wherein they say:

"We, the people of East Tennessee, again assembled in a Convention of our delegates, make the following declaration in addition to that heretofore promulgated by us at Knoxville, on the 30th and 31st days of May last:

"So far as we can learn, the election held in this State on the 8th day of the present month was free, with but few exceptions, in no part of the State, other than East Tennessee. In the larger portion of Middle and West Tennessee, no speeches or discussions in favor of the Union were permitted.[16] Union papers were not allowed to circulate. Measures were taken, in some parts of West Tennessee, in defiance of the Constitution and laws, which allow folded tickets, to have

[15] *The Louisville Journal* of May 13th, said:

"The spirit of Secession appears to have reached its culminating point in Tennessee. Certainly, the fell spirit has, as yet, reached no higher point of outrageous tyranny The whole of the late proceeding in Tennessee has been as gross an outrage as ever was perpetrated by the worst tyrant of all the earth. The whole Secession movement, on the part of the Legislature of that State, has been lawless, violent and tumultuous. The pretense of submitting the Ordinance of Secession to the vote of the people of the State, after placing her military power and resources at the disposal and under the command of the Confederate States without any authority from the people, is as bitter and insolent a mockery of popular rights as the human mind could invent."

[16] An attempt, a short time before the election,

the ballots numbered in such manner as to mark and expose the Union voters. A Disunion paper, *The Nashville Gazette*, in urging the people to vote an open ticket, declared that 'a thief takes a pocket-book or effects an entrance into forbidden places by stealthy means—a tory, in voting, usually adopts pretty much the same mode of procedure.' Disunionists, in many places, had charge of the polls; and Union men, when voting, were denounced as Lincolnites and Abolitionists. The unanimity of the votes in many large counties, where, but a few weeks ago, the Union sentiment was so strong, proves beyond doubt that Union men were overawed by the tyranny of the military law, and the still greater tyranny of a corrupt and subsidized press. * * * Volunteers were allowed to vote in and out of the State, in flagrant violation of the Constitution. From the moment the election was over, and before any detailed statement of the vote in the different counties had been published, and before it was possible to ascertain the result, it was exultingly proclaimed that Separation had been carried by from fifty to seventy thousand votes. This was to prepare the public mind, to enable the Secessionists to hold possession of the State, though they should be in a minority. The final result is to be announced by a Disunion Governor, whose existence depends upon the success of Secession; and no provision is made by law for an examination of the vote by disinterested persons, or even for contesting the election. For these and other causes, we do not regard the result of the election as expressive of the will of a majority of the freemen of Tennessee."[17]

The people of East Tennessee—a mountainous, pastoral region, like New Hampshire or the Tyrol, wherein Slavery never had and never could have any substantial foothold—she having about one slave to twenty freemen—earnestly petitioned and entreated permission to remain in the Union; and, if the residue of the State were resolved to go out, then they asked of it to be set off and quit-claimed, so that they might enjoy "the right, as a free and independent people, to alter, reform, or abolish our form of government in such manner as we see proper," which the legislators of their State, in their Ordinance of Secession, had solemnly asserted. But they were at once given to understand that this could not be granted. The right aforesaid was recognized by the Confederates as inhering in all who sought to destroy the Union, not in those who essayed to preserve or adhere to it. So East Tennessee—isolated from her natural allies by the shameful neutrality of Kentucky—was ruthlessly trampled under the iron heel of the Rebellion. Her bolder Unionists were shot down like wolves, or hung by scores like sheep-stealing dogs; while those more cautious or reticent were outlawed and hunted from their State. For weary months and years, she lay helpless and bleeding in the grasp of her blood-thirsty foes, while thousands of her sons were torn from their homes by a merciless conscription, and compelled to fight and die for the traitorous cause they abhorred.

to hold a Union meeting at Paris, Tenn., resulted in the death of two Union men—shot by the Disunionists; and a notice that Hon. Emerson Etheridge would speak at Trenton, Tenn., elicited the following correspondence:

"TRENTON, TENN., April 16, 1861.

"To J. D. C. ATKINS and R. G. PAYNE:

"Etheridge speaks here on Friday. Be here to answer him Friday or next day."

The following is the answer to the above:

"MEMPHIS, April 16, 1861.

"*To Messrs.* ———: I can't find Atkins. Can't come at that time. If Etheridge speaks for the South, we have no reply. If against it, *our only answer to him and his backers must be cold steel and bullets.* R. G. PAYNE."

[17] Parson Brownlow, in his "Experiences among the Rebels," says:

"For Separation and Representation at Richmond, East Tennessee gave 14,700 votes. *One-half of that number were Rebel troops, having no authority under the Constitution to vote at any election.* For No Separation and No Representation, East Tennessee gave 33,000 straight-out *Union* votes, with at least 5,000 quiet citizens deterred from coming out by threats of violence and by the presence of drunken troops at the polls to insult them."

The State of NORTH CAROLINA, though never deliberately and intelligently hostile to the Union, became a much easier prey to the conspirators. Her Democratic Legislature—reconvened at Raleigh, November 19th, 1860—had refused, a month later, to pass a bill to arm the State, though visited and entreated to that end by Hon. Jacob Thompson, then a member of Mr. Buchanan's Cabinet; and had adjourned[18] without even calling a Convention. This, as we have seen, did not prevent Gov. Ellis taking military possession of the Federal forts near Beaufort and Wilmington (January 2d), on the pretext that, if *he* did not do it, a mob would! He proceeded to reconvene the Legislature in extra session, and to worry it into calling a Convention; for which, an election was duly held.[19] But the act making this call provided that the people, when electing delegates, might vote that the Convention should or should not meet. They profited by the gracious permission, and, while electing a Union Convention by an immense majority, voted—to guard against accidents—that the Convention should *not* meet: their vote—quite a heavy one—standing: *For* holding, 46,672; *Against* holding, 47,323: majority for No Convention, 651. This vote temporarily checked all open, aggressive movements in the interest of Disunion, but did not arrest nor diminish the efforts of its champions. On the contrary, a great State Rights Convention was assembled at Raleigh on the 22d of March, and largely attended by leading Disunionists from South Carolina, Virginia, and other States. Its spirit and its demonstrations left no doubt of the fixed resolve of the master-spirits to take their State out of the Union, even in defiance of a majority of her voters. But they concluded to await the opportunity which South Carolina was preparing. This opportunity was the taking of Fort Sumter; when Gov. Ellis proceeded to seize the U. S. Branch Mint at Charlotte[20] and the Federal Arsenal at Fayetteville;[21] and thereupon[22] to call an extra session of the Legislature. This session commenced May 1st, and in a few days thereafter resulted in the passage of the following:

"*Whereas*, By an unwarranted and unprecedented usurpation of power by the Administration at Washington City, the Government of the United States of America has been subverted; *and whereas*, the honor, dignity, and welfare, of the people of North Carolina imperatively demand that they should resist, at all hazards, such usurpation; *and whereas*, there is an actual state of revolution existing in North Carolina, and our sister State of Virginia, making common cause with us, is threatened with invasion by the said Administration; now, therefore,

"*Resolved*, That his Excellency, the Governor, be authorized to tender to Virginia, or to the Government of the Confederate States, such portion of our volunteer forces now, or that may be hereafter, under his command, as may not be necessary for the immediate defense of North Carolina."

The Legislature proceeded at once to call a Convention; delegates to be elected on the 13th, and the Convention to assemble on the 20th. On that day, the Convention assembled—having been elected under the influence of the Fort Sumter effervescence and of such assertions as are contained in the preamble just quoted. Mr. Thomas L. Clingman, late of the U. S. Senate, having been delegated by the Legislature to the Confederate Congress at Montgomery, on the 14th, submitted to that body the following:

[18] December 22d. [19] January 30, 1861. [20] April 20th. [21] April 22d. [22] April 26th.

"*Resolution, authorizing the Governor to use all the powers of the State, civil and military, consistent with the Constitution, to protect the persons and property of our citizens, and to maintain and defend the honor of North Carolina.*

"*Whereas*, The Constitution of the United States has been entirely subverted, and its Government has been converted into a military despotism, by the usurpations of the Administration of Abraham Lincoln; *And whereas*, the said Abraham Lincoln has promulgated a proclamation declaring the ports of North Carolina in a state of blockade, and directing our ships engaged in lawful commerce to be seized; *And whereas*, such measures are, by the laws of civilized nations, only to be resorted to against a foreign State, and one against which war has been declared; *And whereas*, North Carolina has no alternative, consistent with her safety and honor, but to accept the position thus assigned to her, as being that of an independent and foreign State:

"*Therefore, be it resolved*, That the Governor is hereby authorized to use all the powers of the State, civil and military, consistent with the Constitution, to protect the persons and property of our citizens, and to maintain and defend the honor of North Carolina.

"A true copy, from the minutes of the House of Commons of North Carolina.

"EDWARD CANTWELL, C. H. C."

By such statements, wholly uncontradicted, the loyalty and patriotism of North Carolina were, for the moment, utterly paralyzed. The people, assured by those they had learned to trust that the Federal Government had been utterly subverted by usurpation, and that a military despotism, headed by Abraham Lincoln, was making unprovoked war upon them, which their honor and their interests alike required them to resist, were passive, bewildered and helpless instruments in the hands of the conspirators. The Convention, on the very day of its assembling, passed an Ordinance of Secession by a unanimous vote, and forthwith linked the efforts and fortunes of North Carolina with those of the traitors, by adopting and ratifying the Confederate Constitution.

It has been widely represented, and, to some extent, believed, that the failure of the Peace Conference or Congress, so called, with the refusal of the Republicans to pass the Crittenden Compromise, backed by President Lincoln's Inaugural, was generally received throughout the Slave States as a declaration of war on the South, and, as such, resented by large and controlling acquisitions to the ranks of the Disunionists in the hitherto unseceded States. The true view is widely different from this. We have seen that the Virginia Convention refused, so late as April 4th, by a vote of nearly two to one, to pass an Ordinance of Secession.

The ARKANSAS Convention assembled about the 1st of March; and, on the 16th, was waited on by William S. Oldham, a member of the Confederate Congress and a Commissioner from Jefferson Davis, bearing a message from that potentate, dated March 9th—four days after the adjournment of Congress, and when the contents of Mr. Lincoln's Inaugural were familiar to the entire South. The Convention listened to Mr. Davis's letter, wherein he dilated on the identity of institutions and of interests between his Confederacy and the State of Arkansas, urging the adhesion of the latter to the former; and, after taking two days to deliberate, a majority—39 to 35—voted *not* to secede from the Union. The Convention proceeded, however, to resolve that a vote of the people of their State should be taken on the 1st of August ensuing—the ballots reading "Secession" or "Coöperation"—the Convention to stand adjourned to August 17th; when, if it should appear that Secession had received a majority, this should be regarded as an instruction from their constituents to pass the Ordinance, which they had now rejected; and so, having elected five delegates to a proposed Conference of the Border States, at Frankfort, Ky., May 27th, the Convention stood adjourned.[23] Yet this identical Convention was reconvened upon the reception of the news from Fort Sumter, and proceeded, with little hesitation, to pass an Ordinance of Secession,[24] by a vote of 69 to 1. That Ordinance asserts that this Convention, by resolves adopted March 11th, had pledged "the State of Arkansas to resist to the last extremity any attempt on the part of such power to coërce any State that seceded from the old Union." The Ordinance proceeds to set forth that the Legislature of Arkansas had, on the 18th of October, 1836, by virtue of authority vested therein by the Convention which framed the State Constitution, adopted certain propositions made to that State by Congress, which propositions "were freely accepted, ratified, and irrevocably confirmed, as articles of compact and union between the State of Arkansas and the United States;" which *irrevocable* compact this Convention proceeded formally to *revoke* and annul, and to declare "repealed, abrogated, and fully set aside," by the identical act which withdraws Arkansas from the Union and absolves its citizens from all allegiance to its Government!

The meaning of this may not be understood without explanation. The soil or public lands of Arkansas, before there was any such State or Territory, had belonged fully and absolutely to the Union, having been acquired by it in the purchase of Louisiana. To that soil, thus purchased and paid for, and the Indian title thereto at a still further cost extinguished, Congress had not chosen either to alienate or imperil its title by the creation and admission of the State of Arkansas. As a prerequisite, therefore, of such admission, said State was required to enter into an irrevocable compact never to claim nor exercise ownership of said public lands, until that title should be ceded and conveyed, upon due consideration, by the Union, to individual or other purchasers. Having thus become a State and been admitted into the Union by virtue of this irrevocable compact, Arkansas proceeds to revoke the compact and seize the lands!

The 'conservatives' in the Convention—that is, those who were opposed to Secession at its earlier meeting—now issued an address, justifying their change of position by the fact that the Federal Government had determined to use force against the seceded States, and adding:

> "*The South is 'our country;'* and, while we are satisfied that, up to the moment when the Government committed the folly and wickedness of making war upon the seceded States, the conservative party in Arkansas was largely in the ascendant, we cannot believe that her soil is polluted by a being base and cowardly enough to stop to consider, in casting his lot in the unequal struggle in which she is engaged, whether she is 'right or wrong.'"

The 'conservatism' of these gentlemen, it seems, had not been shocked by the military seizure by Secession-

[23] March 22d.

[24] May 6, 1861.

ists, two weeks previous, of the Federal arsenal at Napoleon,[25] containing 12,000 Springfield muskets and a large amount of munitions and stores; nor by that of Fort Smith,[26] also containing valuable deposits of arms, munitions, and Indian goods. These, and many kindred acts of violence and outrage on the side of disunion, had been committed without a shadow of disguise, and with no other excuse than the treason of the perpetrators—Solon Borland, late U. S. Senator, having led the party that captured Fort Smith. 'Coërcion' was abhorred and execrated only when exercised in defense of the Union.

Missouri was found in a most anomalous condition on the breaking out of the great struggle, destined so severely to try her integrity, as well as that of the nation. Though her slaves were less than a tenth of her total population, and her real interests were bound up in the triumph of Free Labor and the maintenance of the Union, yet her managing politicians, of the Calhoun or extreme pro-slavery school, had contrived for years to wield and enjoy her power and patronage, by keeping a firm and skillful hold on the machinery of the Democratic party. They had thus succeeded, through a long and bitter canvass, in hunting Col. Thomas H. Benton—once the autocrat of the State—out of the Senate, and, ultimately, out of public life. In accordance with their settled policy, the most of them had professed to support Senator Douglas for President in 1860; and, on the strength of their regularity as Democrats, had elected Claiborne F. Jackson as Governor, Thomas C. Reynolds as Lieut. Governor, and a Legislature either thoroughly committed or easily molded to their ultimate schemes.

Of this Legislature, the Senate had instructed[27] its Committee on Federal Relations to report a bill calling a State Convention, which, in due time, became a law.[28] The Convention was accordingly chosen and held; but, when it came to assemble, not one avowed Disunionist was found among its members. Even Sterling Price, a Democratic ex-Governor, who in due time became one of the ablest and most successful of Rebel Generals, had secured his election only by a profession of Unionism. Its Committee on Federal Relations, through its Chairman, Judge H. R. Gamble,[29] reported at length, on the 9th of March—four days after Mr. Lincoln's Inaugural had been read all over the country—in pointed opposition to the views of the Disunionists. After discussing the questions which agitated the country from a Southern point of view, with the usual complaints of Northern fanaticism, intermeddling, and aggression, condemning coërcion, whether employed by or against the seceded States, and warmly indorsing the Crittenden Compromise, the Convention, on the report of this Committee,

"*Resolved*, That at present, there is no adequate cause to impel Missouri to dissolve her connection with the Federal Union; but, on the contrary, she will labor for such an adjustment of the existing troubles as will secure peace, rights, and equality, to all the States.

"*Resolved*, That the people of this State are devotedly attached to the institutions of our country, and earnestly desire that, by a fair and amicable adjustment, the present causes of disagreement may be removed,

[25] April 23d. [26] April 24th. [27] Jan. 5th, 1861. [28] Jan. 16th. [29] Afterward made Governor.

the Union perpetuated, and peace and harmony restored between the North and the South."

And hereupon the Convention adjourned[30] to the third Monday in December, after appointing seven delegates to the proposed Border-State Convention, and a Committee with power to call an earlier meeting of this body, if deemed necessary.

The Legislature, however, remained in session, completely under the control of Gov. Jackson and his Disunion allies; and one of its most notable acts provided a metropolitan police for the city of St. Louis, under the control of five Commissioners, to be appointed by the Governor; who, of course, took care that a decided majority of them should be Secessionists. Thus, the practical control of the chief city of the State, and of the entire Missouri valley, was seized by the enemies of the Union.

Fort Sumter having been captured, and a most insulting, defiant refusal returned to the President's requisition for troops by Gov. Jackson, he proceeded[31] to call an extra session of his Legislature, to begin May 2d, "for the purpose of enacting such laws and adopting such measures as may be necessary for the more perfect organization and equipment of the Militia of this State, and to raise money and such other means as may be required to place the State in a proper attitude of defense." Orders were issued by his Adjutant-General, Hough, to the Militia officers of the State, to assemble their respective commands May 3d, to go into encampment for a week. The Legislature having been on that day reconvened by him, the Governor transmitted to it a Message, denouncing the President's call for troops as "unconstitutional and illegal, tending toward a consolidated despotism." Though he did not venture, directly, to advocate secession, he did all he could and dared to promote it; urging the Legislature to appropriate a large sum to arm the State and place it in a posture of defense. He said:

"Our interests and sympathies are identical with those of the slaveholding States, and necessarily unite our destiny with theirs. The similarity of our social and political institutions, our industrial interests, our sympathies, habits, and tastes, our common origin, territorial congruity, all concur in pointing out our duty in regard to the separation now taking place between the States of the old Federal Union."

The Legislature obsequiously obeyed his behests; giving him, so far as it could, the entire control of the military and pecuniary resources of the State.

Had not these machinations been countervailed, Missouri would have soon fallen as helplessly and passively into the hands of the Confederates as did North Carolina or Arkansas. Her slaveholders, though not numerous, constituted her political and social aristocracy. They were large landholders, mainly settled in the fertile counties[32] stretched along both banks of the Missouri river, through the heart of the State, and exerting a potent control over the poorer, less intelligent, and less influential pioneers, who thinly overspread the rural counties north and south of them.

[30] March 22d. [31] April 22d.

[32] Of the 114,965 slaves held in 1860 in the entire State, no less than 50,280 were held in twelve Counties stretching along the Missouri river: viz: Boone, 5,034; Callaway, 4,527; Chariton, 2,837; Clay, 3,456; Cooper, 3,800; Howard, 5,889; Jackson, 3,944; Lafayette, 6,367; Pike, 4,056; Platte, 3,313; St. Charles, 2,181; Saline, 4,876. Probably two-thirds of all the slaves in the State were held within 20 miles of that river.

The mercantile aristocracy of St. Louis was predominantly devoted to their supposed interests and docile to their commands. But for St. Louis on one side and Kansas on the other, Missouri could scarcely have been saved. But Kansas had a population whom the rough experiences of previous years had educated into deadly hostility to the Slave Power; while St. Louis possessed, in her liberty-loving Germans, in her intelligent and uncompromising citizens of eastern lineage, and in *The St. Louis Democrat*—a journal of high character and extensive influence, which could neither be bought nor frightened into recreancy to the interests of Free Labor—the elements of powerful resistance to the meditated treason. Although the Governor had so promptly and abusively repelled President Lincoln's requisition, a full regiment had been raised by Col. Frank P. Blair, while four others were in process of formation in St. Louis, within ten days from the issue of the President's call.

The Federal Arsenal in Western Missouri was located at Liberty, Clay County, in the midst of a strongly pro-Slavery population. As it had been often robbed with impunity to arm the 'Border Ruffians' for their repeated raids into Kansas, it was naturally supposed that it might now be drawn upon for its entire contents in behalf of what was essentially the same cause. Accordingly, on the 20th, it was seized by a strong force, and the guns and munitions therein deposited carried off to arm and equip the gathering hosts of treason.

But the Federal Arsenal at St. Louis had a garrison of several hundred regulars, under the command of Capt. Nathaniel Lyon, who promptly made arrangements, not to destroy, but to protect and defend, its stores of arms and munitions. During the night of the 25th of April, the great bulk of these were quietly but rapidly transferred to a steamboat, and removed to Alton, Ill., whence they were mainly conveyed to Springfield, the capital of that State, foiling the Secessionists, who were organizing a 'State Guard' in the vicinity with a view to their capture, and who had, for several days, been eagerly and hopefully awaiting the right moment to secure these arms. Having thus sent away all that were not needed, Capt. Lyon and Col. Blair, on the morning of May 10th, suddenly surrounded the State Guard at Camp Jackson, at the head of 6,000 armed Unionists and an effective battery, and demanded their surrender—allowing half an hour for compliance with this peremptory request. Gen. D. M. Frost, in command of the camp, being completely surprised, had no alternative but compliance. Twenty cannon, twelve hundred new rifles, several chests of muskets, large quantities of ammunition, etc., most of which had recently been received from the Baton Rouge Arsenal, now in Confederate hands, were among the 'spoils of victory.'

The news of this exploit preceded the return of the Unionists from the camp to the city; and the chagrin of the embryo Rebels impelled them to proceed from insults to violence. At length, one of the Unionist regiments (German) were impelled to fire upon its assailants, when twenty-two persons fell dead—one of them a woman. A furious excitement was aroused by this tragedy, but inquiries established the endurance and forbearance of the volunteers, so long as patience was a virtue.

The rage and hate of the Secessionists were intensified by this serious blow; but they took care not to provoke further collision. The unquestioned fact that the streets and alleys of the discomfited State Guard's 'Camp Jackson' were named after Davis, Beauregard, etc., was not needed to prove the traitorous character of the organization. Capt. Lyon was made Brigadier-General of the First Brigade of Missouri Volunteers.

Gen. William S. Harney returned from the East to St. Louis on the 12th, and took command of the Union forces. Nine days thereafter, he entered into a truce or compact with Gen. Sterling Price, whereof the object was the pacification of Missouri. But this did not prevent the traitors from hunting and shooting Unionists in every part of the State where Slavery and treason were locally in the ascendant—thousands having been driven in terror from their homes before the end of May. Some of them were served with notices from one or another of the secret societies of Rebels overspreading the State. In at least one instance, a citizen was arrested and sent to Jefferson City, to be tried by Court Martial on a charge of raising a Union company; and, on the 22d, the American flag was taken down from its staff in front of the Post Office in St. Joseph, and the authorities of that city (in the Northwest corner of the State) formally resolved that no American flag should be planted within its limits. Gen. Harney's compact with Price, proving a protection to treason only, was repudiated at Washington, and Gen. Harney himself superseded in the command of the department by Gen. Lyon.

Gov. Jackson thereupon[33] issued a circular, professing to regard the Harney compact as still in force, and insisting that "the people of Missouri should be permitted, in peace and security, to decide upon their future course; that they could not be subjugated," etc., etc. Very soon,[34] an interview was had, at St. Louis, between Gen. Price, on behalf of the Governor, and Gen. Lyon and Col. Blair, on the side of the Union; whereat Gen. Price demanded, as a vital condition of peace, that no Federal troops should be stationed in, or allowed to pass through, the State. Gen. Lyon peremptorily refused compliance. Jackson and Price returned that night to Jefferson City; and the next morning brought tidings to St. Louis that the Gasconade railroad bridge had been burnt, as also a portion of the bridge over the Osage river, and the telegraph wires cut, under the direction of a son of the Governor. On the back of this came a proclamation from Jackson, calling out 50,000 State Militia to repel Federal invasion, and closing as follows:

"In issuing this proclamation, I hold it to be my most solemn duty to remind you that Missouri is still one of the United States; that the Executive department of the State Government does not arrogate to itself the power to disturb that relation; that power has been wisely vested in the Convention, which will, at the proper time, express your sovereign will; and that, meanwhile, it is your duty to obey all constitutional requirements of the Federal Government. But it is equally *my* duty to advise you that *your first allegiance is due to your own State*, and that you are under no obligation whatever

[33] June 4th.

[34] June 11th.

to obey the unconstitutional edicts of the military despotism which has introduced itself at Washington, nor submit to the infamous and degrading sway of its wicked minions in this State. No brave-hearted Missourian will obey the one or submit to the other. *Rise, then, and drive out ignominiously the invaders*, who have dared to desecrate the soil which your labors have made fruitful, and which is consecrated by your homes."

Thus, though Missouri had authoritatively and overwhelmingly refused to leave the Union, her Governor made war upon it, and, mustering all the forces of Slavery and treason, proceeded openly to cast in his and their lot with the fortunes of the Great Rebellion.

KENTUCKY, despite the secret affiliation of her leading politicians with the traitors, whom many of them ultimately joined, refused from the outset, through the authentic action of her people, to unite her fortunes with those of the Rebellion. Though she had, for some years, been a 'Democratic' State—casting her Presidential vote for Buchanan and Breckinridge, in 1856, by some seven thousand majority[35]—the cloven foot of treason had no sooner been exhibited, by the disruption of the Democratic party at Charleston, than her people gave unmistakable notice that they would acquiesce in no such purpose. Her State Election occurred not long afterward,[36] when Leslie Combs, 'Union' candidate for Clerk of her highest Court (the only office filled at this election by the general vote of the State), was chosen by the magnificent majority of 23,223 over his leading competitor, and 11,423 over the combined votes of all[37] others. If Maj. Breckinridge had been made their candidate for President by the bolters with any idea of thereby seducing 'the home of Henry Clay' from her loyalty, that hope was ill-grounded, as the Presidential election more conclusively demonstrated—Bell and Everett carrying the State by a large plurality.[38] Yet her Democratic Governor, Magoffin,[39] though he forcibly protested[40] against the headlong impetuosity wherewith South Carolina persisted in dragging the South into Disunion—summoned her[41] Legislature to meet in extra session, and, on its assembling,[42] addressed to it a Message, urging the call of a State Convention, wherein he premises that

"We, the people of the United States, are no longer one people, united and friendly. The ties of fraternal love and concord, which once bound us together, are sundered. Though the Union of the States may, by the abstract reasoning of a class, be construed still to exist, it is really and practically—to an extent, at least—fatally impaired. The confederacy is rapidly resolving itself into its original integral parts, and its loyal members are intent upon contracting wholly new relations. Reluctant as we may be to realize the dread calamity, the great fact of revolution stares us in the face, demands recognition, and will not be theorized away. Nor is the worst yet told. We are not yet encouraged to hope that this revolution will be bloodless. A collision of arms has even occurred between the Federal Government and the authorities of a *late* member of the Union, and the issue threatens to involve the whole country in fratricidal war. It is under these circumstances of peculiar gloom that you have been summoned. * * * In view of the partial disruption of the Union, the secession of eight or ten States, the establishment of a Southern Confederated Republic, and the adminis-

[35] Buchanan 74,642; Fillmore 67,416; Fremont 314. [36] August 6, 1860.

[37] Combs 68,165; M'Clarty (Breckinridge) 44,942; Bolling (Douglas) 10,971; Hopkins (Lincoln) 829.

[38] Bell 66,058; Breckinridge 53,143; Douglas 25,651; Lincoln 1,364.

[39] Elected in 1859. [40] See page 340.

[41] December 27, 1860. [42] January 17, 1861.

tration of this Government upon the principles of the Chicago Platform—a condition of our country, most likely, near at hand—what attitude will Kentucky hold, and by virtue of what authority shall her external relations be determined? Herein are involved issues of momentous consequence to the people. It is of vital importance to our own safety and domestic peace that these questions be solved in accordance with the will of a majority of our people. * * * The ordinary departments of the Government are vested with no power to conduct the State through such a revolution. Any attempt, by either of these departments, to change our present external relations, would involve a usurpation of power, and might not command that confidence and secure the unanimity so essential to our internal safety."

The Legislature heard him patiently, but refused to follow him. It declined to call a State Convention, but proposed instead a National Convention to revise the Federal pact, and a 'Peace Conference' at Washington; which latter was duly held, as we have already seen. No action looking to Disunion could be extracted from that Legislature, which adjourned soon afterward. And, though the Secessionists sought to atone for their paucity of numbers by preternatural activity, especially through their secret organizations, as 'Knights of the Golden Circle,' etc., and called a 'State Rights' Convention, to meet at Frankfort on the 22d of March, by a secret circular, wherein they assumed that Disunion was an accomplished fact, nothing of importance had been effected by them when the roar of the batteries encircling Fort Sumter called the nation to arms.

Gov. Magoffin, having refused, with insult, to respond to the President's call for Militia to maintain the Union, summoned the Legislature to meet once more, in extra session, assigning, as one reason therefor, the necessity of promptly putting the State in a complete position for defense. His call was issued April 18th; and, on the evening of that day, an immense Union meeting was held at Louisville, whereof James Guthrie, Archibald Dixon, and other 'conservatives,' were the master-spirits. This meeting resolved against Secession, and against any forcible resistance thereto—in favor of arming the State, and against using her arms to put down the rampant treason at that moment ruling in Baltimore as well as in Richmond, and ostentatiously preparing for a speedy rush upon Washington. Two of its resolves will sufficiently exhibit the inconsequence and unreason of this species of conservatism: viz:

"*Resolved, First:* That, as the Confederate States have, by overt acts, commenced war against the United States, without consultation with Kentucky and their sister Southern States, Kentucky reserves to herself the right to choose her own position; and that, while her natural sympathies are with those who have a common interest in the protection of Slavery, she still acknowledges her loyalty and fealty to the Government of the United States, which she will cheerfully render until that Government becomes aggressive, tyrannical, and regardless of our rights in slave property.

"*Second:* That the National Government should be tried by its acts; and that the several States, as its peers in their appropriate spheres, will hold it to a rigid accountability, and require that its acts should be fraternal in their efforts to bring back the seceded States, and not sanguinary or coërcive."

The red-hot balls fired into Sumter by the traitors had hardly cooled, when Kentucky Unionism insulted the common-sense and nauseated the loyal stomach of the Nation by this astounding drivel. The consequences may well be imagined. Not a single Rebel in all the State was induced by it to relax his efforts in behalf of slaveholding treason; and men, munitions, and supplies were openly, and almost daily, dispatched to the mustering Rebel hosts in the South and Southeast; while, for months, nothing was done by that State for the cause of the Union. The first regiment of Kentuckians raised for the Union armies was encamped on the free side of the river, in deference to urgent representations from professed Unionists and to Kentucky's proclaimed neutrality.

The meeting further resolved:

"*Eighth:* That we look to the young men of the Kentucky State Guard as the bulwarks of the safety of our Commonwealth; and we conjure them to remember that they are pledged equally to fidelity to the United States and to Kentucky."

That 'State Guard,' organized by Gen. Simon B. Buckner, under the auspices of Gov. Magoffin, became a mere recruiting and drilling convenience of the Rebel chiefs—its members being dispatched southward so fast as ripened for their intended service. Ultimately, having corrupted all he could, Buckner followed them into the camp of open treason,[43] and was captured at the head of a portion of them at the taking of Fort Donelson.

The Legislature having reässembled,[44] Magoffin read them another lecture in the interest of the Rebellion. The Union was gone—the Confederacy was a fixed fact—it would soon be composed of ten, and perhaps of thirteen, States; President Lincoln was a usurper, "mad with sectional hate," and bent on subjugating or exterminating the South. The Federal Government was rolling up a frightful debt, which Kentucky would not choose to help pay, etc., etc. Whereupon, he again urged the call of a Convention, with a view to State independence and self-protection.

The Legislature had been chosen in 1859, and had a Democratic majority in either House, but not a Disunion majority. It could not be induced to call a Convention, nor even to favor such neutrality as Magoffin proposed. Yet he presumed to issue[45] a Proclamation of Neutrality, denouncing the war as a "horrid, unnatural, lamentable strife," forbidding either the Union or the Confederate Government to invade the soil of Kentucky, and interdicting all "hostile demonstrations against *either* of the aforesaid *sovereignties*" by citizens of that State, "whether incorporated in the State Guard or otherwise." Had he been an autocrat, this might have proved effectual. But the Legislature refused to indorse his Proclamation; refused to vote him Three Millions wherewith to "arm the State;" and so amended the Militia Law as to require the 'State Guard' to swear allegiance to the *Union* as well as to Kentucky. Senator Louis H. Rousseau,[46] among others, spoke[47] decidedly, boldly, in opposition to all projects of Disunion or semi-Disunion; saying:

"When Kentucky goes down, it will be in blood. Let that be understood. She will not go as other States have gone. Let the responsibility rest on you, where it be-

[43] *The Louisville Journal* of Sept. 27th denounced the treachery of Buckner in the following terms:

"Away with your pledges and assurances—with your protestations, apologies, and proclamations, at once and altogether! Away, parricide! Away, and do penance forever!—be shriven or be slain—away! You have less palliation than Attila—less boldness, magnanimity, and nobleness than Coriolanus. You are the Benedict Arnold of the day! You are the Catiline of Kentucky; Go, then, miscreant!"

[44] April 28th. [45] May 20th.

[46] Since, a gallant Union General. [47] May 22d.

longs. It is all your work, and whatever happens will be your work. We have more right to defend our Government than you have to overturn it. Many of us are sworn to support it. Let our good Union brethren at the South stand their ground. I know that many patriotic hearts in the seceded States still beat warmly for the old Union—the old flag. The time will come when we shall all be together again. The politicians are having their day. The *people* will yet have theirs. I have an abiding confidence in the *right*, and I know this Secession movement is all wrong. There is, in fact, not a single substantial reason for it. If there is, I should be glad to hear of it; our Government has never oppressed us with a feather's weight. The direst oppression alone could justify what has brought all our present suffering upon us. May God, in His mercy, save our glorious Republic!"

The Legislature adjourned on the 24th—the Senate having just resolved that

"Kentucky will not sever connection with the National Government, nor take up arms for either belligerent party; but arm herself for the preservation of peace within her borders;" and tendering their services as mediators to effect a just and honorable peace.

Rev. Robert J. Breckinridge—always a devoted Unionist, because never a devotee of Slavery—in an address at Cincinnati, one year later, declared that Kentucky was saved from the black abyss by her proximity to loyal Ohio, Indiana, and Illinois, whose Governors, it was known, stood pledged to send ten thousand men each to the aid of her Unionists whenever the necessity for their presence should be indicated. Had she been surrounded as Tennessee and North Carolina were, she must have fallen as they did. She would have so fallen, not because a majority of her people were disloyal, but because the traitors were better organized, more determined, more belligerent, and bent on success at any cost.

They would have succeeded, because the behests of the slaveholding caste are habitually accepted and obeyed as law in every slaveholding community.

An election for delegates to the proposed "Peace Convention" was held May 4th, and resulted in an immense Union majority—7,000 in Louisville, and over 50,000 in the State. The Secessionists, ascertaining their numerical weakness, and unwilling to expose it, withdrew their tickets a few days previously, and took no part in the election.

The "Peace Convention" assembled May 27th; but Virginia, at whose instance it was called, sent no delegates, and none were present but from Kentucky, save four from Missouri and one from Tennessee. John J. Crittenden presided. Among the delegates were some who have since proved traitors; but the great majority were earnestly devoted to the Union. And yet, this Convention failed to assert the imperative duty of obedience to its constituted authority, without which the Union is but a name for anarchy. It deprecated civil war as abhorrent and ruinous, and exhorted the people to "hold fast to that sheet-anchor of republican liberty, the principle that the will of the majority, constitutionally and legally expressed, must govern;" yet failed to charge those who, defying this principle, were plunging the whole land into confusion and carnage, with the full responsibility of their acts, or to call on the people to put them down. It still harped on the wrongs of the South, though condemning her rebellion; exhorted the North to "discard that sectional and unfriendly spirit, which has contributed so much to inflame the feelings of the Southern people;" proposed a voluntary Convention of all the States, to devise "measures of peaceable adjustment;" and indicated what those measures should be, by gravely recommending

"*First:* That Congress shall at once propose such constitutional amendments as will secure to slaveholders their legal rights, and allay their apprehensions in regard to possible encroachments in the future.

"*Second:* If this should fail to bring about the results so desirable to us, and so essential to the best hopes of our country, then let a voluntary Convention be called, composed of delegates from the people of all the States, in which measures of peaceable adjustment may be devised and adopted, and the nation rescued from the continued horrors and calamities of civil war."

While 'conservatives' were thus discoursing, the bolder traitors went on arming and drilling, until the southwestern half of the State was virtually subject to their sway; while, from every quarter, troops were forwarded to their armies in the field; and the triumphant Secessionists of Tennessee, from their grand camp at Nashville, were threatening to open the road to Louisville, whence supplies were not sent them so freely as they deemed required by their needs or their dignity.

The climax was reached when[48] Gen. Buckner proclaimed that he had entered into a compact with Gen. McClellan, commanding the Federal department of the Ohio, whereby the latter stipulated that no Union troops should press the soil of Kentucky, which State should be sustained in her chosen attitude of neutrality; and, in case 'the South' should plant an army on her soil, Kentucky should be required to show them out—if they did not go, or, if she failed to expel them, *then* the United States might interpose; but our forces must be withdrawn so soon as the Rebels had been expelled! Gen. McClellan promptly denied that he had made any such treaty—or, in fact, any treaty at all. He had had an interview with Buckner, at the request of the latter, who had promised to drive out any Confederate force that should invade Kentucky—that was all. No doubt remained that Buckner had drawn largely on his imagination; proclaiming, as agreed on, much that he had scarcely ventured to propose.

Gov. Magoffin having appointed June 20th as the day for electing Representatives in Congress, in deference to the President's call of an Extra Session, the election was held accordingly, and resulted in the choice of *nine* Unionists to *one* Secessionist (H. C. Burnett, who fled to the Rebels, after serving through the called session.) The vote of the State showed an aggregate of 92,365 for the 'Union' to 36,995 for the Secession candidates, giving a majority of 55,370 for the former. And this election was held when no Federal soldier trod the soil of Kentucky; under a Governor at heart with the Rebels; and after every effort had been exhausted to win her to the side of treason. The Southern frenzy had affected but a small minority of her people; while the terrorism which had coërced so many States into submission to the will of the conspirators was rendered powerless by the proximity of loyal and gallant communities. Kentucky voted as nearly every Slave State would have done, but for the amazing falsehoods

[48] June 10th, 1861.

which were diffused among their people, while none dared to contradict them—while thousands dared not be loyal to their country, because the more reckless minions of the Slave Power stood ready to execute its condign vengeance on all who dared oppose its darling project, or who should in any manner dispute its sway.

XXXI.

THE FORCES IN CONFLICT.

Mr. Jefferson Davis, in his Special Message to his Congress,[1] wherein he asserts that war has been declared against the Confederacy by President Lincoln's Proclamation of April 15th, heretofore given, with more plausibility asserts that the Democratic party of the Free States stands publicly committed to the principles which justify the secession and confederation of the States owning his sway, by its reïterated affirmation and adoption of "the Resolutions of '98 and '99,"[2] and that the whole country had ratified this committal by large majorities, in the reëlection as President of Mr. Jefferson, in the first election of Mr. Madison, and in the election of Gen. Pierce. Assuming this as a basis, Mr. Davis had no difficulty in convincing those whom he more immediately addressed, that, for his confederates to surprise, capture, or otherwise obtain, through the treachery of their custodians, the forts, arsenals, armories, custom-houses, mints, sub-treasuries, etc., etc., of the Union, in their respective States—even (as in the case of North Carolina and Arkansas) those which had not seceded—was a peaceful, regular, legitimate, legal procedure; while to resist such spoliation and maintain the right of the Union to possess and control the property it had created and hitherto enjoyed, was unjustifiable aggression and unprovoked war. Mr. Lincoln (said Mr. Davis) had no constitutional right to issue "the declaration of war against this Confederacy which has prompted me to convoke you." It was his duty to have quietly let the Confederates help themselves, by virtue of shot and shell, to such portions of the property of the Union as they should see fit to touch and take. In fact, this whole Message, like several which succeeded it, evinces the consciousness of its author that he had no longer to square his assertions by what was regarded, out of the Confederacy, as historic truth, or his deductions by what the civilized world had estab-

[1] Montgomery, April 29, 1861.

[2] He says:

"From a period as early as 1798, there had existed in all the States a party, almost uninterruptedly in the majority, based upon the creed that *each State* was, in the last resort, the *sole judge*, as well of its wrongs as of the mode and measure of redress. * * * The Democratic party of the United States repeated, in its successful canvass of 1836, the declaration, made in numerous previous political contests, that it would faithfully abide by and uphold the principles laid down in the Kentucky and Virginia Legislatures of [1798 and] 1799, and that it adopts those principles as constituting one of the main foundations of its political creed."

lished as the dictates of human reason. Thus, he does not hesitate to assert that

"In the Inaugural Address delivered by President Lincoln, in March last, he asserts a maxim, which he plainly deems to be undeniable, that the theory of the Constitution requires, in *all* cases, that the majority shall govern." * * * *

"The climate and soil of the Northern States soon proved unpropitious to the continuance of Slave Labor; while, the reverse being the case at the South, * * * the Northern States consulted their own interests by *selling their Slaves to the South and prohibiting Slavery within their limits.*"

Now, not one-fifth of the slaves held in the Northern States, just before or at the time they respectively abolished Slavery, were sold to the South—as hundreds of them, still living, can bear witness; nor is it true that Slavery was ever proved unsuited to or unprofitable in the North, *in the judgment of her slaveholders.* Had the slaveholding caste been as omnipotent here as in the South, controlling parties, politics, and the press, Slavery would have continued to this day. It was by the *non*-slaveholding possessors of influence and power, here as everywhere else, that Slavery was assailed, exposed, reprobated, and ultimately overthrown. No class ever yet discovered that aught which ministered so directly and powerfully to its own luxury, sensuality, indolence, and pride, as Slavery does to those of the slaveholders, was either unjust, pernicious, or unprofitable.

With greater truth and plausibility, Mr. Davis assured his Congress that

"There is every reason to believe that, at no distant day, other States, identical in political principles and community of interest with those which you represent, will join this Confederacy."

This expectation was, in good part, fulfilled. When Mr. Davis was next[3] called to address his Congress—which had meantime adjourned from Montgomery to Richmond—in announcing the transfer of the Executive departments likewise to the new capital, he said:

"*Gentlemen of the Congress of the Confederate States of America:*

"My Message addressed to you at the commencement of the last session contained such full information of the state of the Confederacy as to render it unnecessary that I should now do more than call your attention to such important facts as have occurred during the recess, and the matters connected with the public defense.

"I have again to congratulate you on the accession of new members to our Confederation of free and equally sovereign States. Our beloved and honored brethren of North Carolina and Tennessee have consummated the action foreseen and provided for at your last session; and I have had the gratification of announcing by Proclamation, in conformity with the law, that these States were admitted into the Confederacy. The people of Virginia also, by a majority previously unknown in our history, have ratified the action of her Convention uniting her fortunes with ours. The States of Arkansas, North Carolina, and Virginia, have likewise adopted the permanent Constitution of the Confederate States; and no doubt is entertained of its adoption by Tennessee, at the election to be held early in next month."

The Confederacy having thus attained its full proportions prior to any serious collision between its armies and those of the Union, we may now properly consider and compare the relative strength of the opposing parties about to grapple in mortal combat.

I. The total population of the United States, as returned by the Census of 1860, somewhat exceeded Thirty-one Millions,[4] whereof the Free States, with all the territories, contained Nineteen,[5] and the Slave States, including the District of Columbia, over Twelve[6] Millions. As the Free States all ad-

[3] July 20, 1861.

[4] 31,443,790

[5] 19,128,143.

[6] 12,315,372.

hered to the Union, while, of the Slave States, Delaware, Maryland, Kentucky, and Missouri[7] did *not* unite with the Confederacy, the preponderance of population in the adhering over that of the seceded States was somewhat more than two to one. The disparity in wealth between the contending parties was at least equal to this; so that there was plausibility in the claim of the Confederates to that sympathy which the generous usually extend to the weaker party in a life-and-death struggle. In Manufactures, Commerce, Shipping, etc., the preponderance was immensely on the side of the Union.

II. The prestige of regularity, of legitimacy, and of whatever the Old World implies by the comprehensive term 'Order,' was likewise on the side of the Union. The Confederacy appeared as a disturber of preëxisting arrangements, and thus of the general peace. Its fundamental theories of State Sovereignty, Right of Secession, etc., were utter novelties to the mass of mankind, and were at war with the instincts and prepossessions of nearly all who could understand them. The greatness and security, wealth and power, of England were based on the supersedure of the Heptarchy by the Realm, and on the conversion of Scotland and Ireland, respectively, from jealous and hostile neighbors into integral portions of the British commonwealth. France, feeble and distracted while divided into great feudatories, became strong and commanding from the hour that these were absorbed into the power and influence of the monarchy, and Burgundy, Picardy, Anjou, etc., became mere geographical designations of portions of the nation 'one and indivisible.' Italy, through her at length half-realized aspirations of so many weary centuries — Germany, still in fragments, in defiance of her ardent hopes and wishes, the imposing and venerable anarchy that Voltaire pronounced her, four generations back—Poland, through her lamentable partition—and nearly every great calamity which modern history had taught mankind to deplore—protested against such disintegrations as the Confederacy had initiated, and not less against the principles on which they were justified. And especially did the Democracy of Europe — the party of Progress and Reform of whatever country — instinctively revolt against doctrines and practices which tended unmistakably backward to the ages alike of national and of individual impotence, wherein peoples were weak, though castes were strong; to the ages of barbarism and of feudalism, wherein nobles and chieftains were mighty, but laws and magistrates of small account. The Democracy of Europe were never for one moment misled or confused by the Confederates' pretensions as to reserved rights and constitutional liberty. Their instinct at once recognized their deadly foe through all his specious disguises. Men who had, as conspirators and revolutionists, been tenanting by turns the dungeons and dodging the gibbets of 'Divine Right' from boyhood, repudiated with loathing any affiliation with *this* rebellion; and no word of cheer ever reached the ears of its master-spirits from Kossuth, Mazzini,

[7] Kentucky and Missouri are *claimed* as having done so; and, hence, were both represented, from an early day, in the Confederate Congress. But the claim is baseless and impudent.

Victor Hugo, Ledru Rollin, Louis Blanc, Garibaldi, or any other of those who, defying the vengeance of despots, have consecrated their lives and sacrificed personal enjoyment to the championship of the Rights of Man.

III. The Confederates had vastly the advantage in the familiarity of their people with the use of arms,[8] and in their addiction to and genius for the art of war. The Northern youth of 1860 were not nearly so familiar with the use of the hunter's rifle or fowling-piece as were their ancestors of 1770. The density of our population had expelled desirable game almost entirely from all the New-England States but Maine; in the prairie States, it rapidly disappears before the advancing wave of civilized settlement and cultivation. Our Indian wars of the present century have nearly all been fought on our western and south-western borders; our last war with Great Britain was condemned as unwise and unnecessary by a large proportion of the Northern people; so was the war upon Mexico: so that it may be fairly said that, while the South and South-West had been repeatedly accustomed to hostilities during the present century, the North and East had known very little[9] of war but by hearsay since the peace which secured our independence, eighty years ago.

IV. The Rebels had a decided advantage in the fact that, on the main question underlying the great issue they had made up—the question of upholding, strengthening, extending, and perpetuating Slavery, or (on the other hand) restricting, confining, weakening it, with a view to its ultimate extinction—they had the active sympathy of a decided majority of the American people. The vote for President in 1860[10] had shown that scarcely more than two-fifths of the American People were even so far hostile to Slavery to wish its farther diffusion arrested. Had political action been free in the Slave States, they would probably have swelled Mr. Lincoln's poll to fully Two Millions; but, on the other hand, the hopeless distraction and discouragement of the pro-Slavery forces so paralyzed effort on that side, by demonstrating its futility, as seriously to diminish the anti-Lincoln vote. Had there been but one instead of three pro-Slavery tickets in the field, its vote in Maine, New Hampshire,

[8] A Southern gentleman, writing from Augusta, Ga., in February, 1861, said:

"Nine-tenths of our youth go constantly armed; and the common use of deadly weapons is quite disregarded. No control can be exercised over a lad after he is fourteen or fifteen years of age. He then becomes 'Mr.' so-and-so, and acknowledges no master."

The street-fights, duels, etc., so prominent among the 'peculiar institutions' of the South, doubtless conduced to the ready adaptation of her whites to a state of war.

[9] Pollard, in his "Southern History" of our struggle, smartly, if not quite accurately, says:

"In the war of 1812, the North furnished 58,552 soldiers; the South 96,812—making a majority of 37,030 in favor of the South. Of the number furnished by the North—

Massachusetts furnished	3,110
New Hampshire "	897
Connecticut "	387
Rhode Island "	637
Vermont "	181
In all	5,162

While the State of South Carolina furnished 5,696.

In the Mexican War,

Massachusetts furnished	1,047
New Hampshire "	1
The other New England States	0,000
In all	1,048

The whole number of troops contributed by the North to the Mexican War was 23,054; while the South contributed 43,630—very nearly double—and, in proportion to her population, four times as many soldiers as the North."

[10] Lincoln 1,857,610; all others 2,787,780.

Connecticut, Pennsylvania, Ohio, Illinois, and (in fact) nearly every Free State, would have been far heavier than that actually returned; so it will be but fair to estimate the pro-Slavery voters of the entire Union as preponderating in just about the proportion of Three Millions to Two. In other words, three-fifths of the entire American People (the Blacks being then of little more account, politically, than so many cattle) sympathized with the Rebellion in so far as its animating purpose was the fortification, diffusion, and aggrandizement of Slavery.

And this explains that exaggeration of the importance as well as of the beneficence of human chattelhood which is seen to pervade all the earlier harangues, manifestoes, and State papers, circulated or uttered in the interest of Disunion. He would underrate the sagacity of the conspirators, and impute to them a blind fanaticism which they never felt, who should fail to take into account the state of antecedent opinion whereon these were designed to operate. Let him but consider that, throughout thirteen of the fifteen Slave States, no journal of any note or influence had for many years been issued which was not an ardent champion and eulogist of Slavery—that no man could be chosen to Congress from any district in those thirteen States, and none from more than two districts of the entire fifteen, who was not a facile and eager instrument of the Slave Power, even though (as in West Virginia) their inhabitants well understood that Slavery was to them a blight and a curse—that every prominent and powerful religious organization throughout the South was sternly pro-Slavery, its preachers making more account in their prelections of Ham and Onesimus than of Isaiah and John the Baptist—and he will be certain to render a judgment less hasty and more just. There were probably not a hundred white churches south of the Potomac and Ohio which would have received an avowed Abolitionist into their communion, though he had been a Jonathan Edwards in Orthodoxy, a Wesley in piety, or a Bunyan in religious zeal. The Industry, Commerce, and Politics of the South were not more squarely based on Slavery than was its Religion. Every great national religious organization had either been rendered pliant and subservient to the behests of Slavery or had been shivered by its resistance thereto. And no sooner had Secession been inaugurated in the South than the great Protestant denominations which had not already broken their connection with the North proceeded unanimously and with emphasis to do so—the Protestant Episcopalians, who had never received a word of reproof for slaveholding from their Northern brethren, unanimously taking the lead, followed by the still more numerous Baptists. And even the Southern Press, incendiary and violent as it was, was outstripped by the Southern pulpit in the unanimity and vehemence of its fulminations in behalf of Secession.[11]

[11] Of the sermons with which the South was carpeted—'thick as Autumnal leaves that strew the brooks in Vallombrosa'—between November, 1860, and May, 1861, that entitled "Slavery a Divine Trust," by Rev. B. M. Palmer, of New-Orleans, was perhaps the most forcible and noteworthy. In it, Mr. Palmer says:

"In determining our duty in this emergency,

And not in the South only, but in the North also, had the temples and organizations of religion been gradually molded and manipulated into a more guarded but not less effective subserviency to the Slave Power. Of the many periodicals edited and issued in the interest of the Roman Catholic faith and polity, hardly one had ever indicated even a wish that Slavery should fall; while a large majority were among its most vehement, unshrinking champions. The case was scarcely better with those sustained by the Protestant Episcopalians; while, among the organs of the other great denominations, Slavery had about as many apologists as assailants. The godless ruffianism and rowdy lawlessness of the North were, of course, as thoroughly pro-Slavery as those of the South—conscious baseness and ill-deserving always requiring somewhat to look down upon and to trample underfoot; and he who has nothing else to boast of always seeking to make the most of the [constructive] whiteness of his skin. It thus chanced that, in this, as in some other controversies, the sleek sanctity and the rough rascality at the respective extremities of the social scale were found acting in concert, as when the Jewish hierarchy were aided in compassing the death of Jesus by the rabble cry of 'Crucify him!' alternated with clamors for the release of Barabbas the robber.

V. The Rebellion had, at the outset of the struggle, the immense advantage always enjoyed by the belligerent who alone has a positive creed, a definite purpose, and is moving directly, consistently, toward his proclaimed goal. It said, 'I stand for Slavery—strike for Slavery—put all at risk for Slavery—and I demand the sympathy and succor of all who concur with me in regarding Slavery as just and beneficent.' And what it thus boldly and reasonably demanded it naturally and generally secured. There were slaveholders of the Revolutionary school—relics of the era or inheritors of the faith of Washington and Jefferson—who re-

it is necessary that we should first ascertain the nature of the trust providentially committed to us. * * The particular trust assigned to such a people becomes the pledge of Divine protection; and their fidelity to it determines the fate by which it is overtaken. * * *

"If, then, the South is such a people, what, at this juncture, is their providential trust? I answer, that it is *to conserve and perpetuate the institution of domestic Slavery as now existing.* * * For us, as now situated, the duty is plain, of conserving and transmitting the system of Slavery, with the freest scope for its natural development and *extension.* * * *

"*This duty is bounden upon us again, as the constituted guardians of the slaves themselves.* Our lot is not more implicated in theirs than is their lot in ours; in our mutual relations, we survive or we perish together. The worst foes of the black race are those who have intermeddled in their behalf. We know, better than others, that every attribute of their character fits them for dependence and servitude.

"By nature, the most affectionate and loyal of all races beneath the sun, they are also the most helpless; and no calamity can befall them greater than the loss of that protection they enjoy under this patriarchal system. * * *

"Last of all, in this great struggle, *we defend the cause of God and of religion.* The Abolition spirit is undeniably atheistic. * * It is nowhere denied that the first article in the creed of the dominant party is the restriction of Slavery within its present limits. * * *

"This argument, then, which sweeps over the entire circle of our relations, touches the four cardinal points of duty *to ourselves, to our slaves, to the world, and to Almighty God.* It establishes the nature and solemnity of our present trusts *to preserve and transmit our existing system of domestic servitude, with the right, unchanged by man, to go and root itself wherever Providence and nature may carry it.* This trust we will discharge, in the face of the worst possible peril. Though war be the aggregation of all evils, yet, should the madness of the hour appeal to the arbitration of the sword, we will not shrink, even from the baptism of fire. If modern crusaders stand in serried ranks upon some plain of Esdraelon, there shall we be in defense of our trust. Not till the last man has fallen behind the last rampart, shall it drop from our hands."

pudiated Secession and clung to the Union; but there was not an earnest devotee of human chattelhood—whether in the South or in the North—whether in America or in Europe—whether a Tory aristocrat, scorning and fearing the unwashed multitude, or an Irish hod-carrier, of the latest importation, hating 'naygurs,' and wishing them all 'sint back to Africa, where they belong'—whose heart did not throb in open or secret sympathy with the Slaveholders' Rebellion. Many did this whose judgments told them that Secession was a mistake—a rash, headlong staking of momentous interests on the doubtful chances of a mortal strife that might easily and safely have been avoided; but, after all, the truth remained, that whoever really loved Slavery did not and could not regard the Rebellion otherwise than with tenderness, with forbearance, with that 'fellow feeling' that 'makes wondrous kind,' and insists that the mistakes it sees and admits shall be regarded and treated with generous allowance. There were thousands in the Free States, never really for bondage, whom party ties and party necessities had held in silent, passive complicity with the Slave Power through years, whose bonds were snapped like glass by the concussion of the first cannon-shot of the war; but whoever was really pro-Slavery was at heart an apologist for if not an active partisan of the Slaveholders' Rebellion—not merely at first, but so long as his affections were unweaned from the grim and gory idol of their early love.

On the other hand, the Unionists were fettered, their unity threatened, their enthusiasm chilled, their efficiency impaired, by the complication of the struggle with the problem of Slavery. They stood for Law, Order, and Established Right; all which were confidently, plausibly claimed as guarantors of Slavery. They were struggling to preserve the Union; yet their efforts, even in their own despite, tended to unsettle and endanger that which, in the conception of many, was the Union's chief end and function. Even the loyal Millions were not ripe, at the outset—though they might, by a heroic leader, have been surely and rapidly ripened—for stern dealing with the source of all our woes. Hence, the proffer of new concessions, new guarantees to Slavery, backed by vehement protestations of devotion to its chartered rights, which marked the initial stages of the struggle. The reflecting few remembered how kindred professions—doubtless sincere—of unshaken, invincible loyalty to the British Crown, were constantly reïterated by our fathers in all the earlier stages of their Revolutionary struggle; and how like protestations of loyalty to the throne and person of Louis XVI. were persisted in by the leaders of the French in their great convulsion, down to within a short period of the abolition of the monarchy, closely followed by the execution of the monarch. So History repeats its great lessons, and must, so long as the nature of Man remains essentially unchanged. The Republicans of 1860 purposed no more than the Secessionists a speedy and violent overthrow of Slavery. Each were but instruments in the hands of that benign, inscrutable Power which 'shapes our ends, rough-hew them as we will;' but, in their common blindness, the advantage was with those who seemed to be struggling more directly, logically, fearlessly toward their avowed end.

VI. The strong reliance of the Rebels on their Cotton, as so vitally necessary to the maritime Powers of Europe that it would compel them speedily to recognize the independence of the Confederacy, and even to aid in its achievement, by forcibly raising the foreseen blockade of their ports, was not justified by the event. Communities, like individuals, are apt to magnify their own consequence, and to fancy the rest of mankind subsisting by their favor, if not on their bounty. ("Soldiers!" said a General, going into battle, "remember that you are Portuguese!") The Southrons, in their impetuosity and conceit, seem not to have duly considered that *their* dependence on others was in the direct ratio of the dependence of others on them, and that Europe could dispense with their Cotton with (at least) as little inconvenience as they could forego the receipt of whatsoever its proceeds might purchase. Yet it is manifest that a region which produced for sale only a few great staples, which western Europe could not produce and must largely buy, and which bought freely of whatever Europe most desired to sell, would be regarded with partiality by her manufacturing and trading classes, when contrasted with an adversary who largely bought Cotton and Tobacco, and made Wares and Fabrics to sell. It is but stating the most obvious truth to assert that—regarding the Southrons as generous, lavish customers, and the Yankees as sharp, close-fisted, tricky, dangerous rivals, the responsible authors of the American tariffs, whereby their exports to the New World were restricted and their profits seriously curtailed—the fabricating, trading, banking classes across the Atlantic were, for the most part, early and ardent partisans of Disunion.

VII. That the ingrain Tories, Aristocrats, and Reäctionists of the Old World should be our instinctive, implacable foes, was inevitable. For eighty years, this Republic had been not only a standing but a growing refutation of their most cherished theories, their vital dogmas. A New England town meeting, wherein the shoemaker moves that $6,000 be this year raised by it for the support of common schools, and is seconded by the blacksmith—neither of them worth, perhaps, the shop wherein by daily labor he earns his daily bread—the wagon-maker moving to amend by raising the sum to $8,000, and the doctor making a five-minutes' speech to show why this should or should not prevail—when the question is taken, first on the amendment, then on the main proposition—either of them standing or falling as a majority of those present shall decide—such is a spectacle calculated to strike more terror to the soul of Kingcraft than would the apparition of a score of speculating Rousseaus or fighting Garibaldis; and its testimony to the safety and beneficence of intelligent democracy increases in weight with every year of its peaceful and prosperous endurance. When it has quietly braved unharmed the shocks and mutations of three-quarters of a century, assertions of its utter insecurity and baselessness—solemn assurances that it cannot possibly stand, and must inevitably topple at the first serious trial—sound very much like fresh predictions of a repeatedly postponed, but still confidently expected, 'end of the world.' Carlyle once remarked that the British people, having considered and condemned all the arguments for retaining the Corn-Laws that could be expressed in language, were still waiting to see whether there might not be some reasons therefor quite *un*utterable. So the people of Europe, having endured the burdens and fetters of Aristocracy and Privilege throughout three generations, on the strength of assurances that all democracies were necessarily violent, unstable, regardless of the rights of Property, inimical to Social Order, and incompatible with tranquillity and thrift, had begun very generally to direct the attention of their self-appointed guides and rulers to the actual condition of the Model Republic, and to ask them how they reconciled their theories with *that*. The question was an ugly one, to which not even a plausible answer could be given, until Jefferson Davis supplied one. Hope and gratitude on the one hand, apprehension and dread on the other, made the hereditary masters and chief priests of the Old World the natural, instinctive allies of the Slaveholders' Rebellion. Hence, of all the British military or naval officers, the high-born functionaries, who visited our country during the struggle, few even affected neutrality or reserve, while the great majority were the open, ardent partisans of the Rebel cause.

VIII. The vastness of the territory occupied by the belligerents, the rugged topography of much of the country over which the contest was fought, the general badness of American roads, with the extraordinary facilities newly afforded to military operations by the Railroad and the Electric Telegraph, secured enormous advantages to the party standing generally on the defensive. The Confederate President, sitting in his cabinet at Montgomery or Richmond, could thence dispatch a message to his lieutenant in Florida or on the Rio Grande, and receive a response the next day—perhaps the next hour—while *our* President or General-in-Chief could not hear of operations at Pensacola or New Orleans for a week or more, and so could not give seasonably the orders required to repair a disaster or improve a victory. The recovery of New Orleans was first learned in Washington through Richmond journals; and so of many other signal Union triumphs. A corps could be sent from Virginia to Tennessee or Mississippi, by the Confederates, in half the time that was required to countervail the movement on our side. If they chose to menace Newbern, N. C., or our forces on the Sea Islands of South Carolina, they could do so with troops drawn from Richmond or Chattanooga before we could learn that any had started. True, as the war wore on, and their railroads wore out—more especially after their territory was cut in two by the opening of the Mississippi—this advantage was materially lessened; but the ruggedness of the country remained; while the badness of American, especially of Southern, roads, afforded undiminished, and, to a European, inconceivably, great advantages to the party acting on the defensive.

IX. The Confederates had a superiority from the first in this, that their leaders and officers were thoroughly *in earnest*. Their chief had been educated at West Point, had fought through the Mexican War, had been four years at the head of the War Department, and been succeeded therein by Floyd, a man after his own heart, who left the service, at the close of 1860, in precisely that state which was deemed most favorable to their great design. One, if not both, of them knew personally almost every officer in our service; knew the military value of each; knew that he was pliant or otherwise to the behests of slaveholding treason. They knew whom to call away to help organize and lead their own forces, and who, even if loyal, would serve them better in our armies than he could do in their own. The immense advantages they thus secured can never be overestimated. Their Generals exposed their lives in leading or repelling charges with a reckless courage which made promotions rapid in their ranks; and, where the troops on both sides are raw and undisciplined, the bravest and most determined officers, if capable, are seldom beaten. In the course of the war, eminent courage and conspicuous cowardice were often displayed on either side; but the Rebels were seldom beaten through the pusillanimity, never through the treachery, of their leaders.

On the other hand, President Lincoln, without military education or experience, found himself suddenly plunged into a gigantic and, to him, most unexpected war, with no single member of his Cabinet even pretending to military genius or experience, and with the offices of his army filled to his hand by those who were now the chiefs of the Rebellion. His officers were all strangers to him; many of them superannuated and utterly inefficient, yet bearing names associated with remembered heroism, and not to be shelved without invoking popular as well as personal reprobation. How should an Illinois lawyer, fresh from comparative obscurity, and who never witnessed the firing of a platoon or read a page of Vauban, presume to say, even had he dared to think, that the illustrious Lieutenant-General at the head of our armies, covered all over with the deep scars of wounds received in glorious conflicts nearly half a century ago, no longer possessed the mental vigor requisite to the planning of campaigns or the direction of military movements? The bare suggestion, on Mr. Lincoln's part, would have been generally scouted as the acme of ignorant conceit and fool-hardy presumption.

But not merely was it true that, while Jefferson Davis was not only able to place every man in his service exactly in the position he deemed him fitted for, while Abraham Lincoln had neither the requisite knowledge[12] nor the legal authority to do likewise with *our* officers, the fact that every one who went over to the Confederates thereby proved that his *heart* was in their cause, gave that side a just confidence in their mili-

[12] "Mr. Lincoln," said an officer who called at the White House during the dark days, when Washington was isolated and threatened from every side, "every one else may desert you, but *I* never will." Mr. Lincoln thanked and dismissed him to his duties. Two days afterward, he learned that this modern Peter had absconded to take service with the Rebels. His name was J. Bankhead Magruder, then a Lieut. Col. of Artillery; since, a Confederate Major-General.

tary leaders which was wanting in ours. The bitter distich—

> "Heaven takes the good, too good on earth to stay,
> And leaves the bad, too bad to take away,"

has a qualified application to this case. Of the army officers—some two hundred in number—who went over to the Rebellion, not one fancied that he was consulting his own ease or physical comfort in so doing. Say they were ambitious, 'sectional,' traitorous, forsworn, or whatever you will: it is barely possible that some of them shared the prevalent Southern delusion that the North would not fight; but it is not probable that their error on this point at all approached that of their stay-at-home compatriots, who supposed the North[13] a small patch of country mainly devoted to the production of schoolmasters, counter-jumpers, peddlers, and keepers of watering-place hotels, all keen at a bargain, but never to be driven into a fight. Perhaps no other class of the Southern people were so free from the prevalent delusion on this head as were their relatively educated, widely-traveled, observant army officers, who, abandoning the service of their whole country, proffered their swords and their lives to the cause of Human Slavery. On the other hand, the indolent, the stolid, the consciously inefficient, who aspired to light work and easy living, naturally clung to a service wherein they had found what they most desired. The Confederacy *might* fail; the Union, even though defeated and curtailed, could not well absolutely go down. Many thus remained whose hearts inclined to the other side, but who did not believe the overthrow or disruption of the Union would prove a light undertaking.

X. The more flagrant instances of official cowardice or imbecility which these pages must often record, will sometimes prompt the question—"Were these men downright traitors?" And the general answer must be: Consciously, purposely, according to their own conceptions, they were not. They did not desire, nor seek to compass, the division of the republic. Many of them were not even bewildered by the fatal delusion of State omnipotence. They hoped for and sought such an issue from our perilous complications as would leave our country undivided, and stronger, more powerful, greater than before. But they had undoubtingly imbibed that one-sided, narrow, false conception of the genius and history of our political fabric which identifies Slavery with the Constitution, making the protection and conservation of the former the chief end of our National existence—not a local and sectional excrescence, alien and hostile to the true nature and paramount ends of our system, to be borne with patience and restrained from diffusing its virus until opportunity should be presented for its safe eradication. To this large and influential class of our officers, the Rebellion seemed a sad mistake, impelled and excused by the factious, malignant, unjustifiable refusal of the Republicans to give 'the South' her 'rights' in the territories; and they controllingly desired that there should be the least possible

[13] "Do you know John Williams?" asked a Southern young lady of average education, addressing her Yankee school-mistress.—"No, I do not happen to recollect any person of that name." "Why, I supposed you *must* know him—he came from the North."

fighting until cool reflection and the enormous cost of the struggle should calm or overbear the rage of extremists on both sides, and induce rëunion on the basis, substantially, of the Crittenden Compromise. Whoever keeps this explanation in mind will be enabled by it to comprehend movements, delays, vacillations, obstinate torpors, and even whole abortive campaigns, which must otherwise seem utterly unaccountable.

XI. The Rebellion had, moreover, a decided advantage in the respect that *all* its partisans, civil as well as military, were thoroughly in earnest, and ready to prove their faith by their works. "You are a Unionist," said a Baltimorean to a New York friend —"I don't doubt it. But are you ready to *fight* for the Union? *I* am a Secessionist, and am going to *fight* for Secession." There were few real Secessionists who shrank from this test of their sincerity. On the side of the Union were the calm calculations of interest, the clear suggestions of duty, the inspirations of a broad, benignant patriotism; but these were tame and feeble impulses when contrasted with the vengeful hate, the quivering, absorbing rage, the stormy wrath, which possessed the great body of the Secessionists, transforming even women into fiends. These impulses were sedulously cultivated and stimulated by the engineers of Disunion, through the uncontradicted diffusion by their journals of the most atrocious forgeries [14] and the most shameless inventions.[15] The North was habitually represented to the ignorant masses of the South as thirsting for their blood and bent on their extermination—as sending forth her armies instructed to ravish, kill, lay waste, and destroy; and the pulpit was not far behind the press in disseminating these atrocious falsehoods. Hence, the Southern militia, and even conscripts, were impelled by a hate or horror of their adversaries which rendered them valiant in their own despite, making them sometimes victors where the memories of their grandfathers at Charleston and at Guilford, and of their fathers at Bladensburg, had led their foes to greatly undervalue their prowess and their efficiency.

XII. Whether Slavery should prove an element of strength or of weakness to the Rebellion necessarily depended on the manner in which it should be

---

[14] *The Louisville (Ky.) Courier* of June, 1861, published the following infamous fabrication as from *The New York Tribune*, and it immediately ran the rounds of the journals of the Confederacy:

"*From the New York Tribune.* 'DO YOU HEAR? THE BEAUTY AND THE BOOTY SHALL BE YOURS, ONLY CONQUER THESE REBELS OF THE SOUTH BEFORE THE NEXT CROP COMES IN. The next crop will be death to us! Let it be hewn down in the field, burned, trampled, lost; or, if you have the opportunity, ship it to New York, and we will build up Gotham by the prices it must bring next season. We shall have the monopoly of the markets, having duly subjected our vassals in the South. Go ahead, brave fellows, Zouaves of New York, whom we were apt to spit upon, though you do the work at fires. Go ahead! Don't mind yellow fever; don't mind black vomit; don't mind bilious fever, or cholera, or measles, or small pox, or hot weather, or hard living, or cold steel, or hot shot! Go!'"

[15] *The Norfolk (Va.) Herald* of April 22d, said: "It is rumored that Lincoln has been *drunk for three days*, and that Capt. Lee has command at the Capitol; and also that Col. Lee, of Virginia, who lately resigned, is *bombarding Washington* from Arlington Hights. If so, it will account for his not having arrived here to take command, as was expected."

The New Orleans Picayune of about May 15th, 1861, said:

"All the Massachusetts troops now in Washington are negroes, with the exception of two or three drummer boys. Gen. Butler, in command, is a native of Liberia. Our readers may recollect old Ben, the barber, who kept a shop in Poydras-street, and emigrated to Liberia with a small competence. Gen. Butler is his son."

treated by the defenders of the Union. It was a nettle, which, handled timidly, tenderly, was certain to sting the hand that thus toyed with it; the only safety lay in clutching it resolutely and firmly. Slavery had made the Rebellion; Slavery coërced the South into a silence that counterfeited unanimity by howling 'Abolitionist!' on the track of every one who refused to seem a traitor to his country, and sending its bloodhounds and Thugs to throttle or knife him. An aristocracy of three hundred thousand families, haughty, high-spirited, trained to arms, and accustomed to rule all who approached them, wielding all the resources and governing the conduct not only of Four Millions of Slaves, but of nearly twice that number of free persons, who served the woolly man-owners as merchants, factors, lawyers, doctors, priests, overseers, navigators, mechanics, slave-hunters, etc., etc., never dreaming that they could cherish any opinions but such as the planting aristocracy prescribed, was no contemptible foe. So long as their slaves should remain obedient to their orders and docile to their will, knowing nothing but what they were told, and hoping for nothing beyond their daily rations of corn and pork, a community of Twelve Millions, holding an area of nearly One Million square miles—the governing caste conscripting the Poor Whites to fill its armies, and using the labor of the slaves to feed and clothe them—presented to its foes on every side a front of steel and flame. Only by penetrating and disintegrating their phalanx, so that its parts should no longer support each other, but their enforced cohesion give place to their natural antagonism, could its power be broken and its persistence overborne.

And here it may be instructive to note that the paramount loyalty to his *State*, vaunted by the Southron as the keystone of his political arch, always resolved itself, on a searching analysis, into devotion to Slavery. Thus, when Virginia seceded, we have seen Alex. H. H. Stuart, with other eminent 'conservatives,' who had, up to this point, resisted Disunion, now take ground in its favor; while Magoffin, C. F. Jackson, etc., always insisted that it was to *his State* that each citizen owed his first and highest duty. A favored officer in our regular army transmitted his resignation, to be tendered in case *his State* seceded, and was not cashiered therefor, as he should have been promptly and finally. All over the South, men said, 'This Secession is madness—it will ruin all concerned—I have resisted it to the best of my ability—but *my State* has seceded nevertheless, and I must *go with my State*.' But, on the other hand, Sterling Price, Humphrey Marshall, James B. Clay, Richard Hawes, Simon B. Buckner, William Preston, Charles S. Morehead, and scores like them—in good part old Whigs, who could not help knowing better—never seemed to imagine that the *refusal* of their respective States to secede laid them under the smallest obligation to restrain their traitorous propensities. 'State Sovereignty' was potent only to authorize and excuse treason to the Union—never to restrain or prevent it.

XIII. The Southern leaders entered upon their great struggle with the Union under the impression—which, with the more sanguine, amounted to undoubting confidence—that they were to be largely aided by coöperation and diversion on the part of their Northern friends and allies. They did not, for a moment, suppose that the Free States were to be, even in appearance, a unit against their efforts.[16] Doubtless, there was disappointment on both sides—the North believing that there could never fail to be an open and active Union party at the South; while the South counted on like aid from the North; but there was this material difference between the two cases: The Southern leaders had received innumerable assurances, through a series of years, of Northern sympathy and aid in the anticipated struggle for their 'rights;' while probably no single Republican had received a letter or message from any Southron of note, urging that no concession be made, but that the Disunionists be crowded to the wall, and compelled to back square out or fight. On the contrary, almost every Southern plea for the Union had assumed as its basis that the North could, would, and should, be induced to recede from its position of resistance to Slavery Extension, or else ———. The alternative was not always plainly expressed; but the inference was irresistible, that Southern Unionism differed from Secessionism in that it proposed allowing the North a month or two longer wherein to back out of its chosen position before visiting its perverseness with the retribution of fire and sword. 'Wait a little longer,' was the burden of Southern appeals for persistence in Unionism: 'the North is preparing to recede: she will presently agree, rather than fight, to give us, at least, the Crittenden Compromise.' But suppose she should *not*—what then? This question was sometimes answered, sometimes not; but the logical inference was inevitable: 'Then we will unite with you in a struggle for Disunion.' Here were the toils in which Virginia Unionism had immeshed itself before the bombardment of Sumter, and which foredoomed it to suicide directly thereafter.

The more earnest and resolute Southerners had been talking of their 'rights' and their 'wrongs,' for a number of years, in such a definite, decisive way that they felt that no one could justifiably fail to comprehend them. Some of them were Disunionists outright—regarded separation as at all events desirable for the South, and certain to enhance her prosperity, wealth, and power. Others preferred to remain in the Union, if they could shape its policy and mold it to their will; but the

[16] *The New Orleans Picayune* of February 21st, 1861, had a letter from its New York correspondent 'Antelope,' dated the 13th, which, with reference to Mr. Lincoln's speech, two days earlier, at Indianapolis, said:

"Lincoln even goes so far as to intimate that hostile armies will march across the seceded States to carry out the darling project of recapture, and the 'enforcement of the laws,' but he surely could not have counted the dreadful and sickening result when such a course wandered through his hot and frenzied brain. March hostile armies through the Southern States! Why, where are the armies to come from that are to take up the march? Where are the loans of money to come from to carry on this diabolical and fiendish crime? An *American* army sufficiently powerful cannot be raised to do it; while, as regards the raising of moneys to prosecute the fratricidal strife, New York, the banking emporium of the Union, will refuse, point blank, to advance a dollar for so unholy a purpose. * * *

"No! no! The South is too terribly in earnest for our bankers to furnish the sinews wherewith to whip it back to its 'allegiance;' and, if the atrocious game should still be persisted in, instead of having the funds to work with, the new Government of Mr. Lincoln will find itself flat upon its back."

former class, though few at first, had been steadily gaining from the latter. Each of these were constantly, openly saying, "Give us our rights *in* the Union, or we will secure them by going *out* of the Union." When, therefore, they received messages of sympathy and cheer from their Northern compatriots in many arduous struggles, they could not but understand their assurances of continued and thorough accord as meaning what was implied by like assurances from Southern sources.

Among the captures by Gen. Grant's army, during his glorious Mississippi campaign of 1863, were several boxes of the letters and private papers of Jefferson Davis, found in an out-house on a plantation between Jackson and Vicksburg. Several of these letters were given to the public by their captors, many of them bearing the signatures of Northern men of note, who have never denied their authenticity. These letters throw a clear light on the state of Southern opinion which induced the Secession movement of 1860–61, and are therefore essential contributions to the history of that period. As such, a portion of them will here be given.

So early as 1850, James Buchanan (not yet President) wrote to Mr. Davis, complaining that 'the South' was disposed to be too easily satisfied, with regard to her 'rights' in the territories. In this 'private and confidential' letter, dated Wheatland, March 16th, he says:

"So far from having in any degree recoiled from the Missouri Compromise, I have prepared a letter to sustain it, written with all the little ability of which I am master. You may ask, why has it not been published? The answer is very easy. From a careful examination of the proceedings in Congress, it is clear *that Non-Intervention is all that will be required by the South.* Webster's speech is to be the base of the compromise—it is lauded to the echo by distinguished Southern men—and what is it? Non-intervention; *and Non-Intervention simply because the Wilmot Proviso is not required to prevent the curse of Slavery from being inflicted on the Territories.* Under these circumstances, it would be madness in me to publish my letter, and take higher ground for the South than they have taken for themselves. This would be to out-Herod Herod, and to be more Southern than the South. It could do no good, but might do much mischief.

"The truth is, the South have got themselves into a condition on this question from which it appears to me now they cannot extricate themselves. My proposition of the Missouri Compromise was at once abandoned by them, and the cry was Non-Intervention. They fought the battle at the last Presidential election with this device upon their banners. The Democracy of Pennsylvania are now everywhere rallying to Non-Intervention. They suppose in doing this they are standing by the South in the manner most acceptable to their Southern brethren. Our Democratic journals are praising the speech of Webster,[17] because all the appearances are that it is satisfactory to the South. It is now too late to change front with any hope of success. You may retreat with honor upon the principle that you can carry your slaves to California, and hold them there under the Constitution, and refer the question to the Supreme Court of the United States. I am sorry, both for your sakes and my own, that such is the condition in which you are placed.

"*I say for my own sake*, because I can never yield the position which I have deliberately taken in favor of the Missouri Compromise; and I shall be assailed by fanatics and free-soilers as long as I live, for having gone further in support of the rights of the South than Southern Senators and Representatives. I am committed for the Missouri Compromise, *and that committal shall stand.*

"Should there be any unexpected change in the aspect of affairs at Washington which would hold out the hope that the publication of my Missouri Compromise letter would do any good, it shall yet be published."

In this spirit, Northern aspirants and office-seekers had for years been

[17] Mr. Webster's deplorably famous speech of March 7th, 1850.

egging on the leaders of Southern opinion to take higher ground in opposition to Northern 'fanaticism' and in assertion of 'Southern rights.' Gen. John A. Quitman, of Mississippi—an able and worthy disciple of Mr. Calhoun—in a letter written shortly before his death, stated that Senator Douglas, just prior to the Cincinnati Convention of 1856, made complaints to him of the disposition of Southern men to be too easily satisfied, substantially like those of Mr. Buchanan, just quoted. He suggested that they should boldly demand *all* their rights, and accept nothing less. In this spirit, the following letter from a leading Democrat of Illinois, formerly Governor of that State, was written after the secession of South Carolina:

"BELLVILLE, Ill., Dec. 28, 1860.

"DEAR FRIENDS: I write to you because I cannot well avoid it. I am, in heart and soul, for the South, as they are right in the principles and possess the Constitution.

"If the public mind will bear it, the seat of Government, the Government itself, and the Army and Navy, ought to remain with the South and the Constitution. I have been promulgating the above sentiment, although it is rather revolutionary. A Provisional Government should be established at Washington to receive the power of the out-going President, and for the President elect to take the oath of office out of slave territory.

"Now I come to the point. All the Slave States must separate from the North and come together. The Free States will not concede an atom, but are bent on the destruction of Slavery. Why, in God's name, cannot the Northern Slave States see this fact, as clear as noonday before their eyes?

"The general secession ought to be accomplished before the 4th of March. Mr. Buchanan deserves immortal honor for keeping down bloodshed. In one hour, by telegraph, he could order Fort Moultrie to fire on Charleston, and the war would rage over the Union. I am, in heart and soul, against war; but the best way to keep peace is to be able to defend yourselves.

"If the Slave States would unite and form a Convention, they might have the power to coërce the North into terms to amend the Constitution so as to protect Slavery more efficiently.

"You will pardon this letter, as it proceeds from friendly motives, from

"Your friend, JOHN REYNOLDS.

"To the Hon. Jeff. Davis and Ex-Governor Wm. Smith."

Prof. Charles W. Hackley, of Columbia College, New York, writing two days earlier to Mr. Davis, to suggest a moderate and reasonable mean between the Northern and the Southern positions respecting the territories, commences: "My sympathies are entirely with 'the South'"—an averment which doubtless meant much more to the receiver than was intended by the writer. Yet it is probable that nine out of every ten letters written from the North to the South during that boding Winter, if they touched on public affairs at all, were more exceptionable and misleading than was this one.

Ex-President Pierce wrote, almost a year previously, and in prospect of the Presidential nomination for 1860, as follows:

CLARENDON HOTEL, Jan. 6, 1860.

MY DEAR FRIEND: I wrote you an unsatisfactory note a day or two since. I have just had a pleasant interview with Mr. Shepley, whose courage and fidelity are equal to his learning and talents. He says he would rather fight the battle with you as the standard-bearer, in 1860, than under the auspices of any other leader. The feeling and judgment of Mr. S. in this relation is, I am confident, rapidly gaining ground in New England. Our people are looking for "the Coming Man." One who is raised by all the elements of his character above the atmosphere ordinarily breathed by politicians. A man really fitted for this emergency by his ability, courage, broad statesmanship and patriotism. Col. Seymour (Tho's. H.) arrived here this morning, and expressed his views in this relation in almost the identical language used by Mr. Shepley. It is true that, in the present state of things at Washington, and throughout the country, no man can predict what changes two or three months may bring forth. Let me suggest that, in the morning debates of Congress, full justice seems to me not to have been done to the Democracy of the North. I do not believe that our friends at the South have any just idea of the state of feeling, hurrying at this moment to the pitch of intense exasperation, between those who respect their political obligations, and those who have apparently no impelling power but that which a fanatical position on the subject of domestic Slavery imparts. Without discussing the question of right—of abstract power to secede—I have never believed that actual disruption of the Union can occur without blood; *and if through the madness of Northern Abolitionists that dire calamity must come, the fighting will not be along Mason and Dixon's line merely. It will be within our own borders, in our own streets, between the two classes of citizens to whom I have referred. Those who defy law and scout constitutional obligations, will, if we ever reach the arbitrament of arms, find occupation enough at home.* Nothing but the state of Mrs. Pierce's health would induce me to leave the country now, although it is quite likely that my presence at home would be of little service. I have tried to impress upon our people, especially in N. H. and Connecticut, where the only elections are to take place during the coming Spring, that, while our Union meetings are all in the right direction and well enough for the present, they will not be worth the paper upon which their resolutions are written unless we can overthrow political Abolitionism at the polls, and repeal the unconstitutional and obnoxious laws which in the cause of "Personal Liberty" have been placed upon our statute-books. I shall look with deep interest, and not without hope, for a decided change in this relation. Ever and truly your friend, FRANKLIN PIERCE.

Hon. JEFF. DAVIS, Washington, D. C.

Such are specimens of the *Northern* letters wherewith Southern statesmen were misled into the belief that the North would be divided into hostile camps whenever the South should strike boldly for her 'rights.' It proved a grievous mistake; but it was countenanced by the habitual tone of 'conservative' speakers and journals throughout the canvass of 1860, and thence down to the collision at Sumter. Even then, the *spirit* which impelled these assurances of Northern sympathy with, and readiness to do and dare for, 'the South,' was not extinguished, though its more obvious manifestations were in good part suppressed for a season. A very few persons—hardly a score in all—of the most uncontrollable Southern sympathies, left the North to enter the Confederate armies; but many thousands remained behind, awaiting the opportunity, which disappointment and disaster were soon to present, wherein they might take ground against the prosecution of the 'Abolition War,' and in favor of a 'compromise' that was not to be had—at all events and on any terms, of 'Peace.' There is, or has been, a quite general impression, backed by constant and confident assertions, that the people of the Free States were united in support of the War until an anti-Slavery aspect was given to it by the Administration. Yet that is very far from the truth. There was no moment wherein a large portion of the Northern Democracy were not at least passively hostile to any form or shade of 'coërcion;' while many openly condemned and stigmatized it as atrocious, unjustifiable aggression. And this opposition, even when least vociferous, sensibly subtracted from the power and diminished the efficiency of the North.

XIV. Whether there was greater unanimity at the South or at the North in sustaining the Union or the Confederacy in the prosecution of their struggle, will, perhaps, never be conclusively determined. There were moments during its progress when the South appeared almost a unit for Secession, while the disheartened North seemed ready to give up the contest for the Union; as there were crises wherein the Rebellion seemed to reel on the brink of speedy dissolution: but neither of these can justly be taken as an accurate test of the average popular sentiment of the respective sections. Yet we have seen that a majority of the Southern people could never, until frenzied by the capture of Fort Sumter, and by official assurances (undenied in *their* hearing) that Lincoln had declared unprovoked and utterly unjustifiable war upon them, be induced to lift hostile hands against their country; and that Secession was only forced down the throats of those who accepted it by violence, outrage, and terror. A few additional facts on this head, out of thousands that might be cited, will here be given:

Rev. John H. Aughey, a Presbyterian clergyman of Northern birth, but settled in Northern Mississippi for some years prior to the outbreak of the Rebellion, in his "Iron Furnace,"[18] gives a synopsis of a Secession speech to which he listened in Atala county, Miss., just after President Lincoln's election, running thus:

> "The halter is the only argument that should be used against the submissionists; and I predict that it will soon, very soon, be in force.
>
> "We have glorious news from Tallahatchie. Seven tory submissionists were hanged there in one day; and the so-called Union candidates, having the wholesome dread of hemp before their eyes, are not canvassing the county," etc., etc.

When the election was held for delegates to the Convention which assumed the power to take Mississippi out of the Union, Mr. Aughey attended it, and says:

> "Approaching the polls, I asked for a Union ticket, and was informed that none had been printed, and that it would be advisable to vote the Secession ticket. I thought otherwise; and, going to a desk, made out a Union ticket, and voted it, amidst the frowns and suppressed murmurs of the judges and bystanders; and, as the result proved, I had the honor of depositing the *only* vote in favor of the Union which was polled in that precinct. I knew of many who were in favor of the Union, but who were intimidated by threats, and by the odium attending it, from voting at all."

Such was the case at thousands of polls throughout the South, or wherever the Confederates were strong enough to act as their hearts prompted. Mr. Clingman's boast, in the Senate, that 'free debaters' were 'hanging on trees' down his way, was uttered, it should be noted, in December, 1860. And thus it was that several Counties in Tennessee[19] gave not a single vote against Secession, while Shelby (including Memphis) gave 7,132 for Secession to *five* against it, and a dozen others gave respectively 3, 7, 9, 11, 12, 13, 14, 16, 17, 20, 23, and 28 votes for the Union to many thousands for Secession. There was only the semblance of an election. "If you vote the Union ticket, you must prepare to leave the State," said Senator Mason; and the more reckless and less responsible Secessionists readily translated such words into deeds. Where Slavery had undivided sway, a voter had just the same liberty to be a Unionist as he had to be an Abolitionist—that is, none at all.

But there were many communities, and even entire counties, throughout the South, wherein Slavery had but a nominal or limited existence; as in Texas, thirty-four counties—some of them having each a considerable free population—were returned, in 1860, as containing each less than a hundred slaves. Some of these could be,

[18] Philadelphia, W. S. and Alfred Martin, 1863.

[19] Franklin, Humphreys, Lincoln.

and were, controlled by their managing politicians, holding offices and earning perquisites by the grace of the Slave Power enthroned at the State capital; others were incorrigible, and were managed in this way: In Grayson county (having 8,187 inhabitants, of whom 1,291 were slaves), when Secession was proposed, a county meeting was held, to consider the project; by which, after discussion, it was decided to negative the movement, and hold no election for delegates to the proposed State Convention. This gave the Secessionists the opportunity they wanted. *They* proceeded to hold an election, and to choose delegates, who helped vote the State out of the Union. And this was one case like many others.

Gen. Edward W. Gantt, who had, in August, 1860, been chosen to Congress as an independent Democrat, from the Southern district of Arkansas, and who was an early and ardent Secessionist, testifies, since his reclamation to Unionism, that the poor farmers and other industrious non-slaveholders of his region were never Secessionists—that, where he had always been able to induce three-fourths of them to vote with him as a Democrat, he could not persuade half of them to sustain him as a Secessionist—that their hearts were never in the cause; and that those who could be persuaded to vote for it did so reluctantly, and as though it went against the grain. No rational doubt can exist that, had time been afforded for consideration, and both sides been generally heard, a free and fair vote would have shown an immense majority, even in the Slave States, against Secession.

For the Union was strong—immensely strong—in the traditions, the affections, the instincts, and the aspirations, of the great majority of the American People. Its preservation was inseparably entwined with their glories, their interests, and their hopes. In the North, no one had, for forty years, desired its dissolution, unless on account of Slavery; at the South, the case was essentially the same. No calculations, however imposing and elaborate, had ever convinced any hundred persons, on whichever side of the slave line, that Disunion could be really advantageous to either section. No line could be drawn betwixt 'the South' and 'the North' which would not leave one or the other exposed to attack—none which six plain citizens, fairly chosen from either section, could be induced to adopt as final. Multitudes who supported Secession did so only as the most efficacious means of inducing the North to repudiate the 'Black Republicans' and agree to the Crittenden or some kindred Compromise—in short, to bully the North into giving the South her 'rights'—never imagining, at the outset, that this could be refused, or that Disunion would or could be really, conclusively effected. Thousands died fighting under the flag of treason whose hearts yearned toward the old banner, and whose aspiration for an 'ocean-bound republic'—one which should be felt and respected as first among nations—could not be quenched even in their own life-blood. And, on the other hand, the flag rendered illustrious by the triumphs of Gates and Greene and Washington—of Harrison, Brown, Scott, Macomb, and Jackson—of Truxtun, Decatur, Hull, Perry, Porter, and McDonough—was throughout 'a tower of strength' to the Unionists. In the hours darkened by shameful defeat and needless disaster, when the Republic seemed rocking and reeling on the very brink of destruction—when Europe almost unanimously pronounced the Union irretrievably lost, and condemned the infatuation that demanded persistence in an utterly hopeless contest—the heart of the loyal Millions never faltered, nor was their faith shaken that, in spite of present reverses, the flag of their fathers would float once more over Richmond and Charleston and Montgomery, over Raleigh, Atlanta, and Houston, the symbol of National authority and power, accepted, beloved, and rejoiced in, by a great, free, happy people.

XXXII.

WEST VIRGINIA.

The Virginia Convention of 1861, of which a majority assumed to vote their State out of the Union, as we have seen, had been elected not only as Unionists, but under an express stipulation that their action should be valid only in case of its submission to and indorsement by a vote of the People. How shamefully that condition was evaded and circumvented, we have seen. The vote to secede, taken on the 17th of April, and already anticipated by acts of hostility to the Union under the authority of the State, was, so far as possible, kept secret until the 25th, when it was proclaimed by Gov. Letcher that the Convention had, on the preceding day, adopted the provisional Constitution of the Confederate States, and placed the entire military power of the State under the control of Jefferson Davis, by a 'convention,' whereof the material provision is as follows:

"1st. Until the union of said Commonwealth with said Confederacy shall be perfected, and said Commonwealth shall become a member of said Confederacy, according to the Constitutions of both Powers, the whole military force and military operations, offensive and defensive, of said Commonwealth, in the impending conflict with the United States, shall be under the chief control and direction of the President of said Confederate States, upon the same principle, basis, and footing, as if said Commonwealth were now, and during the interval, a member of said Confederacy."

Thus it will be seen that the Unionists of Virginia were liable, that day and every day thereafter, to be called out as militia, and ordered to assault Washington, seize Pittsburg, or invade any portion of the loyal States, as Davis and his subordinates might direct; and, having thus involved themselves in the guilt and peril of flagrant treason against the Union, they were to be allowed, a month later, to vote themselves out of the Confederacy and back into the Union again! The stupendous impudence of this mockery of submission was so palpable as almost to shield it from the reproach of imposture; and, as if to brush aside the last fig-leaf of disguise, Letcher, nine days thereafter,[1] issued a fresh proclamation, calling out the militia of the State to repel

[1] May 3d, 1861.

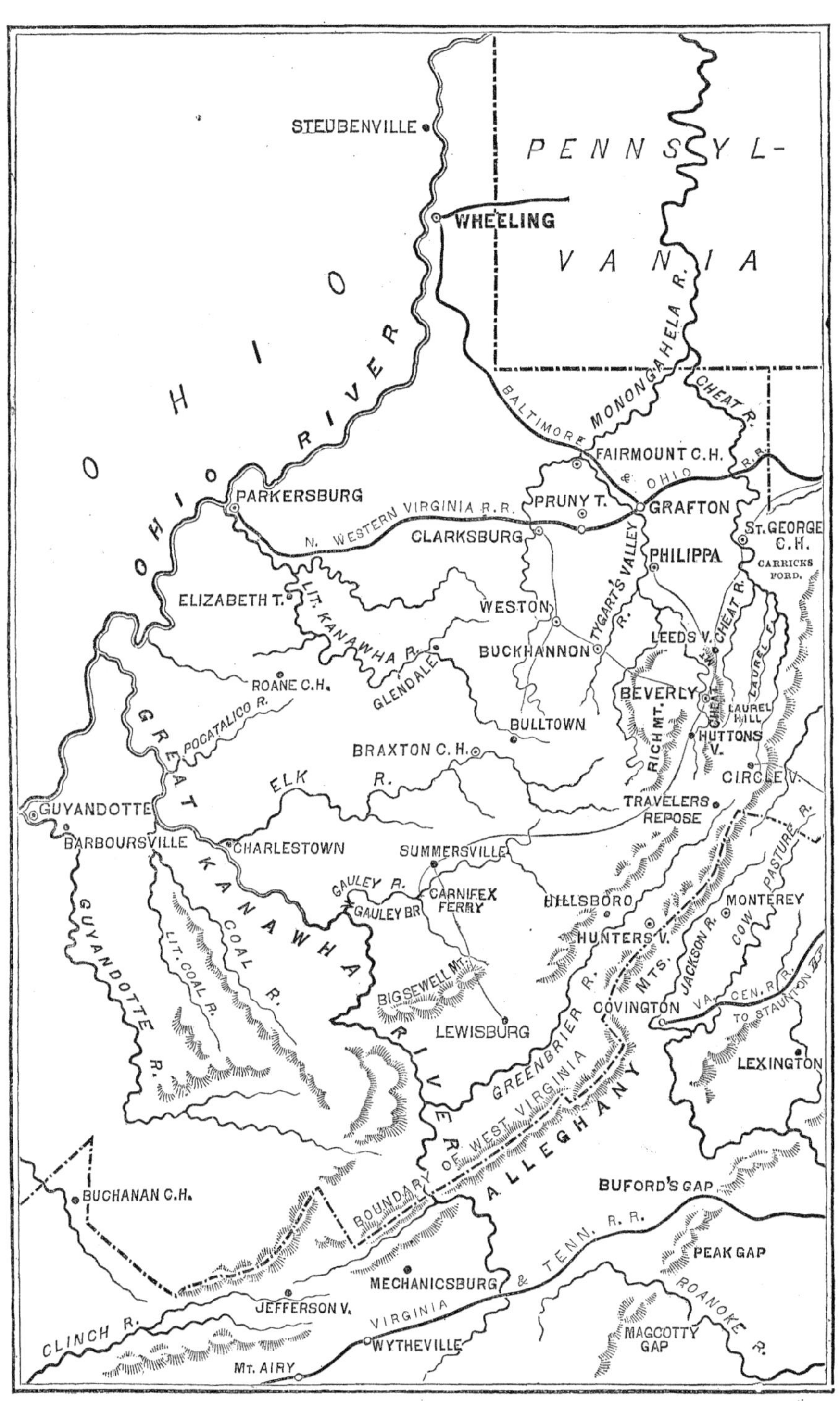

WEST VIRGINIA.

apprehended invasion from "the Government at Washington," and designating twenty points throughout the State—five or six of them westward of the mountains—at which the militia from the adjacent counties respectively were required to assemble forthwith, for organization and service; and, only three days later[2]—still seventeen days prior to that on which the people were to vote for or against Secession—the State was formally admitted into and incorporated with the Confederacy, and Gen. Robert E. Lee[3] put in chief command of the Confederate forces in Virginia—by this time, largely swelled by arrivals from South Carolina, Georgia, Alabama, and other Rebel States.

The people of West Virginia, thus summoned, in the name of their State, to fight against the country they loved for a Rebellion they abhorred, saw the toils closing fast around them, and realized that they must awake and resist, or they would soon be helpless under the feet of their betrayers. Rebel officers, appointed from Richmond, were busily at work, enlisting and mustering their young men for the uses of treason, under the guise of obedience to lawful and constitutional authority. On the 4th, a strong and spirited Union mass meeting was held at Kingwood, Preston county, near the north line of the State, at which the most determined hostility to Secession was avowed, and the separation of Western from Old Virginia demanded. The meeting further resolved to vote, on the appointed day, for a member of Congress—not that of the Confederacy, but that of the Union. A like meeting, impelled by a similar spirit, was held at Wheeling on the following day, whereby adherence to the Union was affirmed, separation from Eastern Virginia demanded, and a determination evinced to render no further tribute, whether military or pecuniary, to the Rebel rule at Richmond. Hon. John S. Carlile was especially decided and zealous in advocacy of separation. Another great Union meeting was held at Wheeling on the 11th, which was addressed in the same spirit by Mr. Carlile, as also by Francis H. Pierpont. The response of the masses was unanimous and enthusiastic. On the 13th, a Convention of delegates, representing thirty-five counties of West Virginia, assembled at Wheeling, to reiterate more formally the general demand that Secession be repudiated, and West Virginia severed from the Old Dominion. This Convention adjourned on the 15th, after calling a provisional Convention, to assemble on the 11th of June. The delegates were to be chosen on the 26th of May; on which day, about forty Counties held regular elections, and chose delegates in accordance with the call—usually, by a heavy vote.

The provisional Convention met on the designated day. Arthur J. Boreman was chosen permanent Chairman; and John S. Carlile, on the 13th, reported, from the Committee on Business, a Declaration, denouncing the usurpation by which the Convention at Richmond had pretended to sever Virginia from the Union, repudiating the idea of allegiance to the Southern Confederacy, and vacating the offices of all who adhered to the Rebellion. In the debate which followed, Mr. Car-

[2] May 6th.

[3] Late a Colonel of Cavalry in the U. S. regular Army.

lile opposed an immediate division of the State; but Mr. Dorsey, of Monongahela, who urged it, being supported by Pierpont and others, obtained, on the 20th, a unanimous vote in favor of ultimate separation—Yeas 56. The Convention had voted, two days earlier, by 57 to 17, that the separation of Western from Eastern Virginia was one of its paramount objects. In the afternoon of that day, Francis H. Pierpont, of Marion county, was chosen Governor, Daniel Palsley, of Mason county, Lieutenant-Governor, with five members to form an Executive Council. These elections were all unanimous. The Convention, it will be noted, was a Convention of Virginia, wherein the loyal counties and loyal people were represented, so far as the Rebellion did not prevent; and all this action was taken, not in behalf of *West* Virginia as such, but of *loyal* Virginia. The Legislature, which met soon after at Wheeling, was a Legislature of Virginia, elected on the regularly appointed day of election — eastern as well as western counties being represented therein; and this Legislature, as well as the Convention, heartily assented to the formation of the new State of West Virginia. This action was taken, throughout, on the assumption that the loyal people of a State constitute the State; that traitors and rebels, who repudiate all respect for or loyalty to the Constitution and Government of the country, have no right to control that Government; and that those people of any State who heartily recognize and faithfully discharge their obligations as loyal citizens, have a right to full and perfect protection from the Republic they thus cling to and uphold. Congress, after due deliberation, assented to and ratified this claim, admitting the new State of West Virginia[4] into the Union as the equal of her elder sisters; her people being henceforth under no other obligation to the authorities of Old Virginia than are the people of that State to the authorities of her young sister across the Alleghanies.

Of course, neither the Rebels in arms, nor their sympathizers anywhere, were delighted with this application of the principle of secession. Gov. Letcher, in a Special Message,[5] treated it as one of the chief sources of his general unhappiness. He says:

> "President Lincoln and his Cabinet have willfully and deliberately proposed to violate every provision of the third section of the fourth article of the Constitution, which each one of them solemnly swore or affirmed, in the presence of Almighty God, to 'preserve, protect, and defend.' That section is in these words:
>
> "'New States may be admitted by the Congress into this Union; but no new State shall be formed or erected within the jurisdiction of any other State, nor any State formed by the junction of two or more States or parts of States, without the consent of the Legislatures of the States concerned, as well as of the Congress.'"

The answer to this is ready and simple: President Lincoln and his Cabinet do not regard John Letcher as Governor of that State of Virginia which is a member of our Federal Union. The Governor of *that* Virginia is Francis H. Pierpont; and its Legislature is that which, elected by loyal Virginians, assembled at Wheeling, and gave its free, hearty, and almost unanimous assent to the division of the old and the formation of the new State. All this must be as plain to Letcher as to Lincoln. Those who

[4] First named *Kanawha*, after its principal river.

[5] January 6th, 1862.

hold that Letcher and his fellow-conspirators had a legal right to precipitate their State into treason, so as to bind her loyal, Union-loving citizens to follow and sustain them therein, will echo his lamentations; but those who stand by their country and her Government take a different view of the matter.[6]

All direct communication between Western Virginia and Washington was, and remained, interrupted for some weeks after the primary[7] Rebel foray on Harper's Ferry. The Rebels remained in force at that point, completely controlling travel and transportation on the Baltimore and Ohio road. They finally obstructed that road altogether by destroying[8] several bridges farther west; continuing to hold and to strengthen their position at Harper's Ferry. Two companies of Confederate or State militia entered the village of Clarksburg, the capital of Harrison county, on the 20th, but found themselves speedily outnumbered by the Union militia of that place, on whose demand they surrendered their arms and dispersed without a contest.

Although some thousands of West Virginians had volunteered to fight for the Union, none of them were encamped on the soil of their State until after the election held[9] to ratify or reject the Ordinance of Secession. The Government, assured that Western Virginia was overwhelmingly for the Union, doubtless chose not to have that unanimity attributed, even falsely, to the presence of a Union force. The Virginians who volunteered were mustered in and organized at Camp Carlile, in Ohio, opposite Wheeling, under the command of Col. Kelly, himself a Virginian. George B. McClellan, who had been appointed a Major-General and assigned to the command of the Department of the Ohio, remained at Cincinnati, his home. Three days after the election aforesaid, he issued from that city a spirited address "To the Union men of Western Virginia," wherein he says:

"The General Government has long enough endured the machinations of a few factious Rebels in your midst. Armed traitors have in vain endeavored to deter you from expressing your loyalty at the polls. Having failed in this infamous attempt to deprive you of the exercise of your dearest rights, they now seek to inaugurate a reign of terror, and thus force you to yield to their schemes, and submit to the yoke of the traitorous conspiracy, dignified by the name of the Southern Confederacy. They are destroying the property of citizens of your State, and ruining your magnificent railways. The General Government has heretofore carefully abstained from sending troops across the Ohio, or even from posting them along its banks, although frequently urged by many of your prominent citizens to do so.

"It determined to await the result of the State election, desirous that no one might be able to say that the slightest effort had been made from this side to influence the free expression of your opinions, although the many agencies brought to bear upon you by the Rebels were well known. You have now shown, under the most adverse circumstances, that the great mass of the people of Western Virginia are true and loyal to that beneficent Government under which we and our fathers have lived so long."

A brief and stirring address to his soldiers was issued simultaneously with the above; and, both being read

[6] A Union soldier who, having been taken prisoner by the Rebels and paroled, was, in the Summer of 1862, in camp on Governor's Island, New-York, was asked by a regular army officer—"What is your regiment?" He answered: "The 6th Virginia." "*Virginia?*" rejoined the Westpointer; "*then you ought to be fighting on the other side.*" Of course, this patriot will naturally be found among those who consider the division of Virginia a usurpation and an outrage.

[7] Night of April 18th.

[8] May 16th.

[9] May 23d.

to those in Camp Carlile that evening, the 1st Virginia, 1,100 strong, Col. Kelly, crossed to Wheeling early next morning, closely followed by the 16th Ohio, Col. Irvine. The 14th Ohio, Col. Steedman, crossed simultaneously, and quietly occupied Parkersburg, the terminus of the Northwestern branch of the Baltimore and Ohio road. A rebel force, then holding Grafton, which connected the branch aforesaid with the main or Wheeling division of the railroad, had meditated a descent on Wheeling; but, finding themselves anticipated and outnumbered, they obstructed and destroyed the railroad west of them, so that the Unionists did not reach Grafton till the morning of the 30th. On the 31st, both tracks having been repaired, a force of seven or eight thousand men was collected at this point, under the immediate command of Gen. Morris; the Rebels having been pushed back, without resistance, to Philippi, the capital of Barbour county, some fifteen miles southward, and entirely off the line of the railroad. From this place, Col. G. A. Porterfield, as commander of the Virginia Rebel forces, issued the following proclamation:

"FELLOW-CITIZENS: I am in your section of Virginia, in obedience to the legally constituted authorities thereof, with the view of protecting this section of the State from invasion by foreign forces, and to protect the people in the full enjoyment of their rights—civil, religious, and political. In the performance of my duties, I shall endeavor to exercise every charitable forbearance, as I have hitherto done. I shall not inquire whether any citizens of Virginia voted for or against the Ordinance of Secession. My only inquiry shall and will be as to who are the enemies of our mother—the Commonwealth of Virginia. My duty now compels me to say to all, that the citizens of the Commonwealth will at all times be protected by me and those under my command. Those who array themselves against the State will be treated as her enemies, according to the laws thereof.

"Virginians! allow me to appeal to you, in the name of our common mother, to stand by the voice of your State, and especially to repel invasion from any and every quarter. Those who reside within the State, who invite invasion, or who in any manner assist, aid, or abet invaders, will be treated as enemies to Virginia. I trust that no Virginian, whether native-born or adopted, will refuse to defend his State and his brothers against invasion and injury. Virginians! be true; and, in due time, your common mother will come to your relief.

"Already, many of you have rallied to the support of the honor of your State, and the maintenance of your liberties. Will you continue to be freemen, or will you submit to be slaves? Will you allow the people of other States to govern you? Have you forgotten the precepts of Madison and Jefferson?[10] Remember that 'the price of liberty is eternal vigilance.' Virginia has not made war. War has been made upon her and her time-honored principles. Shall she be vindicated in her efforts to maintain the liberties of her people? or shall she bow her head in submission to tyranny and oppression? It seems to me that the true friend of rational liberty cannot hesitate. Strike for your State! Strike for your liberties! Rally! rally at once in defense of your mother!"

Gen. McClellan having ordered that Philippi be captured by surprise, the attempt was made on the night of June 2d. Two brigades of two regiments each approached the Rebel camp by different roads. They were to have enveloped the town by 4 A. M. of the 3d; but the roads were bad, the night intensely dark and stormy, and the division under Col. Kelly, which had to make the longer march—twenty-two miles—did not, because it could not, arrive in season. The Rebels, only six or eight hundred in number, could make no successful stand against the forces already in their front, and were evidently pre-

[10] The omission of *Washington's* name here is most appropriate and significant.

paring for a hurried retreat. The Unionists, under Cols. Dumont and Lander, opened with artillery and promptly charged with infantry, when the dismayed Rebels, after a momentary resistance, fled. Col. Kelly's division came in at this instant, and fell upon the Rebels, who were utterly demoralized and dispersed. Col. Kelly received a severe wound from a pistol-shot through the lungs, and two Unionists were killed. The Rebels lost sixteen killed and ten prisoners, with all their provisions, munitions, and tents, and nearly all their arms. Porterfield, gathering up such portion of his forces as he could find, retreated hastily to Beverly, and thence to Huttonsville; where the Rebel array was rapidly increased by conscription, and Gov. Wise placed in command.

Gen. McClellan arrived at Grafton on the 23d, and at once issued a proclamation severely condemning the guerrilla warfare to which the Rebels were addicted. On the 25th, he issued a second address to his soldiers, exhorting them to forbear pillage and outrage of every kind, remembering always that the people were their friends. His forces were rapidly augmented, till they amounted, by the 4th of July, to over 30,000 men; while the Rebels in his front could hardly muster 10,000 in all. He therefore resolved to advance. The Rebel main force, several thousand strong, under Gen. Robert S. Garnett, was strongly intrenched on Laurel Hill, a few miles north of Beverly, the capital of Randolph county, holding the road to Philippi; while a smaller detachment, under Col. John Pegram, was intrenched upon the summit and at either base of Rich Mountain,[11] where passes the turnpike from Beverly westward to Buckhannon—his position being a strong one, three or four miles distant from the Rebel main body. McClellan, after reconnoitering, and determining by scouts the position of the enemy, decided, first, to attack and crush Pegram; and, to this end, sent Col. Rosecrans to make a détour of eight miles through the mountains, and gain the turnpike two or three miles in the rear of Pegram. This was successfully accomplished; but a dragoon, dispatched by McClellan with orders to Rosecrans, was captured during the day, and the plan of attack discovered. The Rebels were found intrenched on the top of the mountain, with three cannon. Rosecrans, who had marched since daylight through forests and thickets of laurel, under a cold, pelting rain, by mountain bridle-paths, and, in part, through trackless woods, had, of course, no artillery. He approached the Rebel position about noon, and was immediately opened upon by their guns, which made much noise to little purpose. The vigorous musketry fire, soon opened on either side, was little more effective, because of the rain, the inequalities of the ground, and the density of the low, bushy forest. But the Unionists were largely superior in numbers, and, after half an hour of this random firing, were ordered to fix and charge

[11] "Rich Mountain is a gap in the Laurel Hill Range, where the Staunton and Western turnpike crosses it between Buckhannon and Beverly, and about four or five miles out of the latter place. It is about as far from Laurel Hill proper (that is, where the Beverly and Fairmount turnpike crosses it, and where the enemy is intrenched) as Beverly is. It is also about twenty-five miles from Buckhannon."—*Wheeling Intelligencer.*

bayonets, which orders were promptly and vigorously obeyed. The Rebels at once took to flight, leaving their cannon, wagons, tents, provisions, and stores, with 135 dead.

Gen. McClellan remained throughout the day inactive in front of Col. Pegram's position, awaiting advices from Rosecrans, that failed to reach him. Pegram, better advised of Rosecrans' operations, and justly alarmed for his own safety, attempted to escape during the following night, but found it impossible, and was compelled, after a day's hiding in the forest, to surrender[12] his remaining force—about 600 men—at discretion.

Gen. McClellan pushed on to Beverly, which he entered early next morning, flanking Gen. Garnett's position at Laurel Hill, and compelling him to a precipitate flight northward. Six cannon, two hundred tents, sixty wagons, and over one hundred prisoners, were the trophies of this success. The Rebel loss in killed and wounded was about 150; the Union about 50. Gen. Garnett, completely flanked, thoroughly worsted, and fearfully outnumbered, abandoned his camp at Laurel Hill without a struggle, crossing the Laurel Mountains eastward, by a by-road, into the narrow valley of Cheat river, traversed by one wretched road, which he took care to make worse for his pursuers by felling trees across it at every opportunity. It rained incessantly. This valley is seldom more than a wooded glen; whence he hoped to escape across the main ridge of the Alleghanies eastward into Hardy county. Provisions and supplies of every kind were scarce enough with the fugitives, and, for the most part, with their pursuers also. Rain fell incessantly, swelling the unbridged rivulets to torrents. Skirmishes were frequent; and four companies of a Georgia regiment, being cut off from the main body, were taken prisoners. At length, having crossed the Cheat at a point known as Carrick's Ford, which proffered an admirable position for defense, Garnett turned to fight; and, though the Union forces rapidly came up in overpowering numbers, and opened a heavy fire both of musketry and artillery, yet the strong and sheltered position of the Confederates enabled them for some time to hold the ford, twice repulsing efforts to cross it. Col. Taliaferro, commanding the Rebel rearguard, finally withdrew by order, having exhausted his cartridges and lost about thirty men. The position had by this time been flanked by Col. Dumont, with his 7th Indiana, who had fairly gained the crest on the right, when he was ordered to turn it on the left; and, marching down the bluff and through the middle of the stream, between the two armies firing over their heads, the regiment, forcing its way through the tangled thicket of laurel, appeared on the right flank of the Rebels, who thereupon fled. The road crosses the stream again a quarter of a mile below; and here a desperate attempt was made by Garnett to rally his forces for another struggle; but in vain. They received and returned one volley, when they started to run—they being, at least, 3,000, and the Indianians, directly upon them, barely 600; but there were enough more not far behind. Gen. Garnett exerted himself desperately to hold his men, without success; and,

[12] July 12th.

while so doing, was shot through the body by Sergt. Burlingame, and fell dead without a groan. A slight, boyish Georgian—probably an Aid—alone stood by him to the last, and shared his fate.[13] Gen. McClellan, with a large portion of his force, had not united in this chase, but had moved southerly from Beverly, several miles, to Huttonsville; whence, on the next day,[14] he telegraphed to Washington that

> "Gen. Garnett and his forces have been routed, and his baggage and one gun taken. His army are completely demoralized. Gen. Garnett was killed while attempting to rally his forces at Carricksford, near St. George.
>
> "We have completely annihilated the enemy in Western Virginia.
>
> "Our loss is about thirteen killed, and not more than forty wounded; while the enemy's loss is not far from two hundred killed; and the number of prisoners we have taken will amount to at least one thousand. We have captured seven of the enemy's guns in all.
>
> "A portion of Garnett's forces retreated; but I look for their capture by Gen. Hill, who is in hot pursuit."

This expectation was not realized. The pursuit was only continued two miles beyond the ford; when our weary soldiers halted, and the residue of the Rebels, under Col. Ramsey, turning sharply to the right, made their way across the mountains, and joined Gen. Jackson at Monterey.

A strong Union force, under Gen. Cox, made an advance from Guyandotte simultaneously with Gen. McClellan's on Beverly, capturing Barboursville after a slight skirmish, and moving eastward to the Kanawha, and up that river. At Scarytown, some miles below Charleston, a detachment of 1,500 Ohio troops, under Col. Lowe, was resisted[15] by a smaller Rebel force, well posted, under Capt. Patton, and repulsed, with a loss of 57 men. Five officers, including two Colonels, who went heedlessly forward, without their commands, to observe the fight, rode into the Rebel lines, and were captured. The Rebels abandoned the place that night, leaving their leader dangerously wounded to become a prisoner.

Gen. Cox pushed steadily forward, reaching Charleston, the capital of Kanawha county, on the 25th. Gov. Wise, who commanded the Rebels in this quarter, had expected here to make a stand; but, discouraged by the tidings which had reached him, some days before, of Garnett's disasters, continued his flight up the river. Gen. Cox pursued, reaching, on the 29th, Gauley bridge, which Wise had burned to impede pursuit. The people of that valley, and, indeed, of nearly all Western Virginia—being Unionists—complained that the Rebels mercilessly plundered them of every thing eatable; which was doubtless true to a great extent, and, for the most part, unavoidable. In the race up the Kanawha valley, Wise succeeded, to the last, in keeping ahead, which was the only military success he ever achieved. He

[13] *The Cincinnati Gazette's* correspondent, 'Agate,' in describing the battle, says:

"Among the enemy's wounded was a young *Massachusetts boy*, who had received a shot in the leg. He had been visiting the South, and had been impressed into the Rebel service. As soon as the battle began, he broke from the Rebel ranks, and attempted to run down the hill and cross over to our side. His own lieutenant saw him in the act, and shot him with a revolver. Listen to such a tale as that I did, by the side of the sad young sufferer, and tell me if your blood does not boil hotter than ever before, as you think, not of the poor deluded followers, but of the leaders, who, for personal ambition and personal spite, began this infernal rebellion."

[14] July 14th. [15] July 17th

retreated to Lewisburg, the capital of Greenbrier, one of the few counties west of the main ridge of the Alleghanies which, having a considerable number of slaves, and having been settled entirely from Old Virginia, has evinced a preponderating devotion to the Rebel Cause.

Here he was reënforced, and outranked, about August 1st, by Gen. John B. Floyd, who, under the influence of the inspiring news from Bull Run, and the depletion of the Federal forces by the mustering out of service of the three months' men, was soon able to assume the offensive. Keeping well to the right of New River—the main affluent which unites near Gauley bridge with the Gauley to form the Kanawha—he surprised the 7th Ohio, Col. Tyler, while at breakfast at Cross Lanes, near Summersville,[16] and routed it with a loss of some 200 men. Moving thence southerly to Carnifex Ferry, he was endeavoring to gain the rear of Gen. Cox, who was still south of him, when he was himself attacked by Gen. Rosecrans, who, at the head of nearly 10,000 men, came rapidly down upon him from Clarksburg, nearly a hundred miles northward. Most of the Union troops had marched seventeen miles that day, when, at 3 o'clock P. M. of the 10th, they drew up in front of Floyd's strong and well-fortified position on the north bank of the Gauley, just below the mouth of Meadow river. Rosecrans ordered a reconnoissance in force by Benham, which was somewhat too gallantly executed, resulting in a short, but severe action, wherein the advantage of position was so much on the side of the Confederates that their loss must have been considerably less than ours, which was about two hundred, including Col. Lowe, of the 12th Ohio, killed, and Col. Lytle, of the 10th, severely wounded, as was Lieut.-Col. White, of the 12th. Col. McCook's Ohio brigade (Germans) at one time received an order to storm the Rebel intrenchments, and welcomed it with a wild delight, which showed how gladly and thoroughly it would have been obeyed; but it was an order which Rosecrans had not given, and which, after a careful observation of the works, he countermanded. Instead of assaulting, he directed a more thorough reconnoissance to be made, and the troops to be so posted as to be ready for decisive work early in the morning. But, when daylight dawned, the enemy were missing. Floyd, disappointed in the expected support of Wise, and largely outnumbered, had wisely withdrawn his forces under cover of the night, abandoning a portion of his equipage, much baggage, and a few small arms, but no cannon.[17] He rapidly retreated some thirty miles to Big Sewell Mountain, and thence to Meadow Bluff, whither he was not closely followed.

Wise strengthened the position on Big Sewell, named it Camp Defiance, and there remained.

Gen. Lee, arriving from the North with a considerable Rebel force, took

[16] The capital of Nicholas county.

[17] Pollard says of this conflict:

"The successful resistance of this attack of the enemy, in the neighborhood of Carnifex Ferry, was one of the most remarkable incidents of the campaign in Western Virginia. The force of Gen. Floyd's command was 1,740 men; and from 3 o'clock P. M. until night-fall it sustained, with unwavering determination and the most brilliant success, an assault from an enemy between eight and nine thousand strong, made with small-arms, grape, and round-shot, from howitzers and rifled cannon."

command of both Floyd's and Wise's troops, swelling his army to 20,000 men. Rosecrans, after remaining several days in his front at Big Sewell, retreated thirty miles to the Gauley, and was not pursued; Gen. Lee being soon after recalled to take a command on the coast, and Gov. Wise ordered to report at Richmond.

Gen. Lee, before leaving the North, had made a strong reconnoissance in force rather than a serious attack, on the position held by Gen. Reynolds on Cheat Mountain, in Randolph county, not far from the arena of Garnett's and of Pegram's disasters. There was skirmishing on the 12th, 13th, and 14th of September, during which Col. John A. Washington, one of Gen. Lee's aids, was killed, with nearly one hundred other Rebels. The Union loss was nearly equal to this, mainly in prisoners. Reynolds's force was about half that of his assailants, but so strongly posted that Lee found it impossible to dislodge him, and retired to his camp at Greenbrier. Here Reynolds, whose forces were equal, if not superior, to those in his front, after Lee's departure for the South, paid a return visit to the Rebels, now commanded by Gen. H. R. Jackson, of Georgia, on the 3d of October. Reynolds, in turn, found his adversary's position too strong to be carried by assault, and retreated unpursued, after a desultory contest of several hours.

On the 10th of November, at 8 P. M., Col. Jenkins, with his regiment of Rebel cavalry, which had been engaged for some time in guerrilla warfare, dashed into the village of Guyandotte, on the Ohio river, near the Kentucky line, surprising the Union forces stationed there and taking over a hundred prisoners. All who resisted were killed by the guerrillas, who left hastily next morning, with all the plunder they could carry. Col. Zeigler, of the 5th [loyal] Virginia, who arrived early next morning, ordered the houses of the Secessionists to be burned, on the assumption that they had instigated the Rebel raid, and furnished the information which rendered it safe and successful; and, the leading citizens being mostly rebels, the village was mainly consumed. This destruction was generally condemned as barbarous, though the charge was probably true, and would have justified any penalty that might have been inflicted on those only who supplied the information.

Rosecrans having posted himself at Gauley Mount, on New River, three miles above its junction with the Gauley, Floyd and Wise, after Lee's departure, took position on the opposite (south) side of New River, and amused themselves by shelling the Union teamsters engaged in supplying our army. Here Rosecrans attempted to flank and surprise them, but was first defeated by a great flood in the river, rendering it impassable; and next by the failure of Gen. Benham to gain Floyd's rear and obstruct his retreat, as he had been ordered to do. The attack in front was duly made,[18] but Floyd retreated unmolested by Benham, and but faintly pursued. On the 14th, his rear-guard of cavalry was attacked and driven by Benham; its Colonel, St. George Croghan, being killed. No further pursuit was attempted. Floyd retreated to Peterstown, more than

[18] November 12th.

fifty miles southward. And thus died out the campaign in the southern part of West Virginia.

In the north-east, Gen. Kelly, who held and guarded the Alleghany section of the Baltimore and Ohio Railroad, starting from New Creek on the night of October 25th, advanced rapidly to Romney, the capital of Hampshire county, driving out a Rebel battalion and capturing two cannon, sixty prisoners, several hundred stand of arms, with all the camp equipage, provisions, and munitions. By this spirited dash, West Virginia was nearly cleared of armed Rebels.

Gen. R. H. Milroy, who had succeeded Gen. Reynolds in command at Cheat Mountain, attempted, soon afterward,[19] a similar dash on the Rebels in his front, strongly posted at Alleghany Summit, twenty-two miles distant, on the turnpike to Staunton. To this end, he moved forward with 3,200 men, nearly half of which were directed to make a détour by the old Greenbrier road, to assault the enemy's left. The combination failed. The flank movement, under Col. Moody, of the 9th Indiana, was not effected in time. The Rebel forces, consisting of four regiments, under Col. Edward Johnson, were neither surprised nor dismayed; and the attack in front, led by Col. James A. Jones, of the 25th Ohio, though gallantly made, did not succeed. The Rebels, finding themselves superior in numbers as well as position, attacked in turn, and were likewise repulsed, as also in an attempted flank movement. Still, Milroy, having lost 150 men, with his ranks still further depleted by the skulking of his raw troops, had begun to retreat before Col. Moody, at 8 A. M., commenced his flank attack, which was of course a failure. Milroy retreated unpursued to his old camp. But, not discouraged, he dispatched Major Webster, of the 25th Ohio, with 800 men, on the last day of the year, to break up a Rebel post at Huntersville, fifty miles south, on the Greenbrier. The weather was cold; the ground covered with snow; yet the march was made in three days, the Rebel force driven out, and six buildings, filled with provisions and forage, destroyed by fire; the expedition returning without loss or accident. Here closed the campaign of 1861 in Western Virginia, with scarcely a Rebel uniform or picket to be seen, on that side of the Alleghany Mountains.[20]

---

[19] December 12th.

[20] Though the crest of the main ridge of the Alleghanies is the natural and proper line of demarcation between 'the Old Dominion' and new, or West Virginia, and pretty accurately discriminates the Counties wherein Slavery and Secession did, from those wherein they did not, at any time, predominate, yet three or four Counties—Monroe, Greenbrier, &c.—which geographically pertain to West Virginia, have, either voluntarily or under duress, adhered to Old Virginia and the Rebellion.

NOTE.—The originally proposed State of *Kanawha* included within her boundaries only the Counties of Virginia lying north and west of, but not including, McDowell, Mercer, Monroe, Greenbrier, and Pocahontas—thirty-nine in all, with a total population in 1860 of 280,691, whereof 6,894 were slaves. The Constitution of WEST VIRGINIA expressly included the five counties above named, making the total population 315,969, of whom 10,147 were slaves. It further provided that the counties of Pendleton, Hardy, Hampshire, Frederick, Berkeley, Jefferson, and Morgan, might also be embraced within the new State, provided their people should, by vote, express their desire to be—which they, excepting those of Frederick, in due time, did—raising the population, in 1860, of the new State to 376,742, and entitling it to three representatives in Congress.

XXXIII.

EAST VIRGINIA—BULL RUN.

If the North had been, or at least had seemed, obstinately apathetic, because skeptical as to the probability or the imminence of Civil War, it was fully and suddenly undeceived by the developments that swiftly followed the bombardment of Fort Sumter, but especially by the occurrences in Baltimore and the attitude of Maryland. For a few weeks, all petty differences seemed effaced, all partisan jealousies and hatreds forgotten. A few 'conservative' presses sought to stem the rushing tide; a few old Democratic leaders struggled to keep the party lines distinct and rigid; but to little purpose. Twelve States, whose Legislatures happened to be sitting in some part of April or May, 1861, tendered pecuniary aid to the Government, amounting, in the aggregate, to nearly Nineteen Millions of Dollars; while some Five Millions were as promptly contributed, in the cities and chief towns of the North, to clothe and equip volunteers. Railroads and steamboats were mainly employed in transporting men and munitions to the line of the Potomac or that of the Ohio. Never before had any Twenty Millions of people evinced such absorbing and general enthusiasm. But for the deplorable lack of arms, Half a Million volunteers might have been sent into camp before the ensuing Fourth of July.

President Lincoln issued, on the 27th of April, a proclamation announcing the blockade of the coast of Virginia and North Carolina; due evidence having been afforded that Virginia had formally and North Carolina practically adhered to the Rebellion. Some weeks were required to collect and fit out the vessels necessary for the blockade of even the chief ports of the Rebel States; but the month of May[1] saw this undertaking so far completed as to make an entrance into either of those ports dangerous to the blockade-runner. On the 3d, the President made a further call for troops—this time requiring 42,000 additional volunteers for three years; beside adding ten regiments to the regular army — about doubling its nominal strength. A large force of volunteers, mainly Pennsylvanians, was organized at Chambersburg, Pa., under the command of Major-Gen. Robert Patterson, of the Pennsylvania militia; while Gen. Butler, having completed the taming of Baltimore, by planting batteries on the highest points and sending a few of her more audacious traitors to Fort McHenry, was made[2] a Major-General, and placed in command of a Department composed of tide-water Virginia with North Carolina. George B. McClellan, John C. Fremont (then in Europe), and John A. Dix had already[3] been appointed Major-Generals in the regular army

[1] Richmond and Norfolk, the 8th; Charleston, the 11th; New Orleans and Mobile, the 27th; Savannah, the 28th.

[2] May 16th.

[3] May 1st and speedily thereafter.

LIEUT. GEN. THOMAS J. JACKSON
MAJ. GEN. JOHN C. BRECKINRIDGE
MAJ. GEN. STERLING PRICE
GEN. ROBERT E. LEE
GEN. JOSEPH E. JOHNSTON
LIEUT. GEN. G. P. T. BEAUREGARD
GEN. BRAXTON BRAGG
MAJ. GEN. SIMON B. BUCKNER
LIEUT. GEN. LEONIDAS POLK
MAJ. GEN. A. SIDNEY JOHNSTON
LIEUT. GEN. JOHN C. PEMBERTON
LIEUT. GEN. JAMES LONGSTREET
Entered according to act of Congress AD 1864 by O.D. Case & Co. in the Clerks Office of the District Court for the District of Connecticut.
Engraved by J.C. Buttre, New York
CONFEDERATE GENERALS

—Gen. Dix commanding in New-York. Lieut. Gen. Winfield Scott, at Washington, was commander-in-chief, as well as in immediate charge of the large force rapidly pouring into the capital and its environs—in part, by steamboat up the Potomac; in part, by way of the Railroad through Baltimore. There were cities that hailed the Union soldiers with greater enthusiasm, but none that treated them with more civility and deference, than Baltimore, from and after Butler's arrival in that city; though he somewhat embarrassed the trade of that hitherto thriving mart by searching for and seizing large quantities of arms, secreted in her cellars or snugly stowed away in the holds of her vessels, awaiting transportation to lower Virginia. One of his last and most important seizures was that of the person of George P. Kane, Marshal of Police; who, making all possible opposition to captures of arms designed for the Rebels, was taken also to the Fort, that he might see that they were in safe hands. Unluckily, he, like other traitors, was not retained there so long as he should have been; but this was by no fault of Gen. Butler, who was ordered to take command at Fortress Monroe, whither he repaired on the 22d, and where he soon found himself at the head of some 15,000 raw but gallant soldiers.

It had been decided that no offensive movement should be made prior to the 24th (the day after the farce of voting to ratify the Ordinance of Secession)—the Government having apparently resolved that no Union soldier should, on that day, tread the soil of Virginia, save within the narrow limits, or immediately under the frowning walls, of Fortress Monroe. So Gen. Butler soon found some ten or twelve thousand Confederates in his front, under command of Gens. Huger and Magruder, (both recently of the regular army,) with earthworks and batteries facing him at every commanding point, well mounted with powerful guns from the spoils of the Norfolk Navy Yard. The white population in that slaveholding neighborhood was so generally disloyal that, of a thousand inhabitants of the little village of Hampton, lying just under the guns of the fort, but a hundred remained on the 1st of June.[4]

Gen. Butler found his position so cramped by the proximity and audacity of the Rebels, whose cavalry and scouts almost looked into the mouths of his guns, that he resolved on enlarging the circle of his Virginia acquaintance; to which end he seized and fortified the point known as Newport News, at the mouth of James river; and, on the 9th of June, ordered a reconnoissance in force for some eight or ten miles northward, with intent to surround, surprise, and capture, the Rebel position nearest him, known as Little Bethel. To this end, Col. Abram Duryea's Zouaves were dispatched from Hampton at 1 o'clock next morning, followed by Col. F. Townsend's 3d New-York, an hour later, with directions to gain the rear of Little Bethel, so as to cut off the retreat of the Rebels; while Col. Phelps, with a Vermont battalion, supported by Bendix's New-York

[4] This village was burnt, August 9th, by Magruder's order, that it might no longer afford shelter to our troops. An attempt was at first made to attribute this devastation to the Unionists.

regiment, was to approach that post in front, ready to attack at daybreak. The whole expedition was under the command of Gen. E. W. Pierce, a militia Brigadier from Massachusetts.

Gen. Butler had given precise orders and directed the use of ample precautions to avoid collision in the darkness between the several portions of our own forces. Yet, just before daybreak, at a junction of roads, some two miles from Little Bethel, the regiments of Col. Bendix and Col. Townsend neared each other;

TEN MILES AROUND FORTRESS MONROE.

and the former, mistaking the latter for enemies, opened fire with both artillery and musketry, whereby two of Col. Townsend's men were killed, and eight or ten seriously, besides a large number slightly wounded. The mistake was soon discovered; but not until the whole expedition had been thrown into confusion—those in advance, with reason, presuming that the Rebels were assaulting their rear, and preparing for defense on this presumption. The Rebels at Little Bethel were, of course, alarmed, and made good their retreat. Gen. Pierce sent back to Gen. Butler for reënforcements; and another regiment was ordered up to his support. Col. Duryea had already surprised and captured a picket-guard of the enemy, consisting of thirty persons, who were sent prisoners to the fort.

Gen. Pierce, finding only a hastily deserted camp at Little Bethel, pushed on to Big Bethel, several miles further. Here he found a substantial, though hastily constructed, breastwork, protected from assault by a deep creek, with 1,800 Confederates, under Col. J. B. Magruder, behind it. Gen. Pierce, who, probably, had never before seen a shot fired in actual war, ordered an attack; planting his few small guns in the open field, half a mile from the well-sheltered Rebel batteries in his front. Our balls, of course, buried themselves harmlessly in the Rebel earthworks;[5] while our men, though partially screened by woods and houses, were exposed to a deadly fire from the Rebels. For four hours, the action thus continued—necessarily with considerable loss on our side and very little on the other. Finally, a more determined assault was made by a part of our infantry, led by Major Theodore Winthrop, Aid to Gen. Butler, who was shot dead while standing on a log, cheering his men to the charge. His courage and conduct throughout the fight rendered him conspicuous to, and excited the admiration of, his enemies. Lieut. John T. Greble, of the 2d regular artillery, was likewise killed instantly by a ball through the head, while serving his gun in the face of the foe. Our total loss, in the advance and the attack, was hardly less than 100 men; while the Rebels reported theirs at 1 killed and 7 wounded. Gen. Pierce, whose inexperience and incapacity had largely contributed to our misfortune, finally ordered a retreat, which was made, and in good order; the Rebels following for some miles with cavalry, but at a respectful distance. And, so conscious were their leaders that they owed their advantage to accident, that they abandoned the position that night, and retreated so far as Yorktown, ten miles up the Peninsula.[6] No further collisions of moment occurred in this department that season. Gen. Butler was succeeded by Gen. Wool on the 16th of August.

Reports of a contemplated Rebel invasion of the North, through Maryland, were current throughout the month of May, countenanced by the fact that Maryland Hights, opposite Harper's Ferry, were held by Johnston through most of that month, while a considerable force appeared opposite Williamsport on the 19th, and seemed to meditate a crossing. A rising in Baltimore, and even a dash on Philadelphia, were among their rumored purposes. Surveys and reconnoissances had been made by them of Arlington Hights and other eminences on the Virginia side of the Potomac, as if with intent to plant batteries for the shelling of Washington. But the Union forces, in that State and Maryland, increased so rapidly, that any offensive movement

[5] Pollard says: "The only injury received from their artillery was the loss of a mule."

[6] Col. (since, Major-Gen.) D. H. Hill, who commanded the 1st North Carolina in this affair, in his official report, after claiming a victory, says:

"Fearing that heavy reënforcements would be sent up from Fortress Monroe, we fell back at nightfall upon our works at Yorktown."

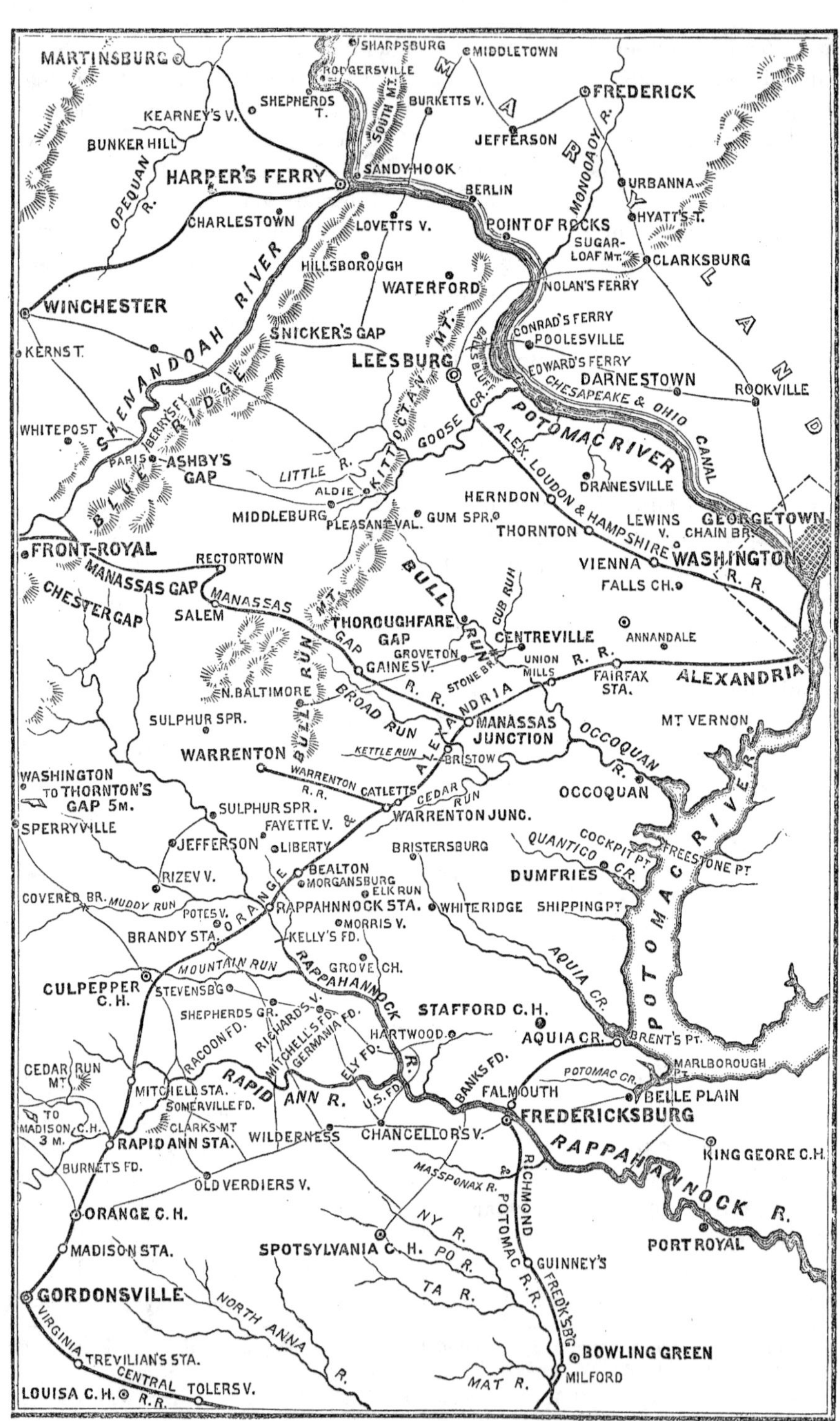

WASHINGTON AND VICINITY.

in that quarter on the part of the Rebels would have been foolhardy in the extreme. Finally, on the night of the 23d—the day of her election aforesaid—Gen. Scott gave the order for an advance; and, before morning, 10,000 Unionists were planted on the 'sacred soil.' Gen. Mansfield superintended the crossing of the Long Bridge; while Gen. McDowell conducted that over the Chain Bridge at Georgetown; whence the 69th New York, Col. Corcoran, was pushed forward to seize the crossing of the Orange and Manassas Gap Railway, some miles westward. The New-York Fire Zouaves, Col. Ellsworth, moved by steamers directly on Alexandria; but the Rebels in that city had either been warned by treachery, or were alarmed by the menacing appearance of the gunboat Pawnee, and had very generally escaped when the Zouaves landed. Some 300 of them, mainly civilians, were captured by the New York 69th, in their flight on the railroad aforesaid. No resistance was met at any point. But Col. Ellsworth, seeing a Secession flag flying from the 'Marshall House' at Alexandria, stepped in, with four followers, and took it down. Passing down the stairs, he was met by one Jackson, the hotel-keeper, who, raising a double-barreled gun, shot Ellsworth dead on the spot. He was himself instantly shot in turn by Francis E. Brownell, one of Col. Ellsworth's followers; and the two who, at one moment, confronted each other as strangers but as mortal foes, the next lay side by side in death. Jackson's deed, which, at the North, was shudderingly regarded as assassination, at the South, was exulted over as an exhibition of patriotic heroism; and a subscription was at once set on foot for the benefit of his family. This incident was rightly regarded by many as indicative of the terrible earnestness of the contest upon which the American people were now entering.

Gen. McDowell, having firmly established himself on the right bank of the Potomac for several miles opposite to and below Washington, proceeded to fortify his position, but made no further offensive demonstrations for several weeks; whose quiet was broken only by a brisk dash into and through the village of Fairfax Court-House by Lieut. C. H. Tompkins, of the 2d regular cavalry—resulting in a loss of six on either side—and by an ambuscade at Vienna.

Late on Monday, June 17th, Gen. Robert C. Schenck, under orders from Gen. McDowell, left camp near Alexandria, with 700 of Col. McCook's 1st Ohio, on a railroad train, and proceeded slowly up the track toward Leesburg, detaching and stationing two companies each at Fall's Church and at two road-crossings as he proceeded. He was nearing Vienna, thirteen miles from Alexandria, with four remaining companies, numbering 275 men, utterly unsuspicious of danger, when, on emerging from a cut and turning a curve, eighty rods from the village, his train was raked by a masked battery of two guns, hastily planted by Col. Gregg,[7] who had been for two or three days scouting along our front, with about 800 Rebels, mainly South Carolinians, and who, starting that morning from Dranesville, had been tearing up the track at Vienna, and had started to return

[7] Afterward, Gen. Maxcy Gregg; Governor elect of South Carolina; killed at Fredericksburg.

to Dranesville when they heard the whistle of Gen. Schenck's locomotive. Several rounds of grape were fired point-blank into the midst of the Ohio boys, who speedily sprang from the cars, and formed under the protection of a clump of trees on the side of the track. The engineer, who was backing the train, and, of course, in the rear of it, instantly detached his locomotive, and started at his best speed for Alexandria, leaving the cars to be burnt by the Rebels, and the dead and wounded to be brought off in blankets by their surviving comrades. The Rebels, deceived by the cool, undaunted bearing of our force, did not venture to advance, for fear of falling into a trap in their turn; so that our loss in men was but 20, including one captain. The Rebels, of course, lost none. Each party retreated immediately—the Rebels to Fairfax Court House.

As very much has since been said, on both sides, with partial justice, of outrages and barbarities, devastation and rapine, whereof 'the enemy' is always assumed to be guilty, the following manifesto, issued by a Confederate chief at the very outset of the contest, and before it could have had any foundation in fact, casts light on many similar and later inculpations:

"HEAD-QUARTERS, DEP'T OF ALEXANDRIA,
CAMP PICKENS, June 5th, 1861.

"A PROCLAMATION.

"*To the people of the Counties of Loudoun, Fairfax, and Prince William:*

"A reckless and unprincipled tyrant has invaded your soil. Abraham Lincoln, regardless of all moral, legal, and constitutional restraints, has thrown his Abolition hosts among you, who are murdering and imprisoning your citizens, confiscating and destroying your property, and committing other acts of violence and outrage, too shocking and revolting to humanity to be enumerated.

"All rules of civilized warfare are abandoned, and they proclaim by their acts, if not on their banners, that their war-cry is 'Beauty and Booty.' All that is dear to man—your honor, and that of your wives and daughters—your fortunes and your lives, are involved in this momentous contest.

"In the name, therefore, of the constituted authorities of the Confederate States—in the sacred cause of constitutional liberty and self-government, for which we are contending—in behalf of civilization itself—I, G. T. Beauregard, Brigadier-General of the Confederate States, commanding at Camp Pickens, Manassas Junction, do make this my Proclamation, and invite and enjoin you, by every consideration dear to the hearts of freemen and patriots, by the name and memory of your Revolutionary fathers, and by the purity and sanctity of your domestic firesides, to rally to the standard of your State and country; and, by every means in your power, compatible with honorable warfare, to drive back and expel the invaders from your land.

I conjure you to be true and loyal to your country and her legal and constitutional authorities, and especially to be vigilant observers of the movements and acts of the enemy, so as to enable you to give the earliest authentic information at these headquarters, or to the officers under my command.

"I desire to assure you that the utmost protection in my power will be given to you all. G. T. BEAUREGARD,
"Brigadier-General Commanding."

Three days before, and in utter unconsciousness of the fulmination which Beauregard was preparing, Gen. McDowell, in command of our forces in his front, had issued the following:

"HEAD-QUARTERS DEP'T OF N. E. VIRGINIA,
ARLINGTON, June 2d, 1861.

"GENERAL ORDER No. 4.—Statements of the amount, kind, and value, of all private property taken and used for Government purposes, and of the damage done in any way to private property, by reason of the occupation of this section of the country by the United States troops, will, as soon as practicable, be made out and transmitted to department head-quarters of brigades by the commanders of brigades, and officers in charge of the several fortifications. These statements will exhibit:

"*First.* The quantity of land taken possession of for the several field-works, and the kind and value of the crops growing thereon, if any.

"*Second.* The quantity of land used for the several encampments, and the kind and value of the growing crops, if any.

"*Third.* The number, size, and character of the buildings appropriated to public purposes.

"*Fourth.* The quantity and value of trees cut down.

"*Fifth.* The kind and extent of fencing, etc., destroyed.

"These statements will, as far as possible, give the value of the property taken, or of the damage sustained, and the name or names of the owners thereof. Citizens who have sustained any damage or loss as above will make their claims upon the commanding officers of the troops by whom it was done, or, in cases where these troops have moved away, upon the commander nearest them.

"These claims will accompany the statement above called for. The commanders of brigades will require the assistance of the commanders of regiments or detached companies, and will make this order known to the inhabitants in their vicinity, to the end that all loss or damage may, as nearly as possible, be ascertained while the troops are now here, and by whom, or on whose account, it has been occasioned, that justice may be done alike to the citizen and to the Government. The name of the officer or officers, in case the brigade commanders shall institute a board to fix the amount of loss or damage, shall be given in each case.

"By order of Brig. Gen. McDowell.

"James B. Fry, Ass't Adj't-General."

Of course, this order does not prove that no outrage was committed, no wanton injury inflicted, by our soldiers, in this or other portions of the Confederacy. War cannot afford to be nice in the selection of its instruments; and probably no campaign was ever prosecuted through a friendly, much more a hostile, region, wherein acts of violence and spoliation were not perpetrated by soldiers on the defenseless inhabitants of the country. But that the commanders on our side, and, in fact, on both sides, were generally earnest and vigilant in repressing and punishing these excesses, is the simple truth, which should be asserted and insisted on for the honor of our country and her people.

Gen. Robert Patterson, with about 20,000 men, broke camp at Chambersburg, June 7th, and advanced to Hagerstown, while Col. Lew. Wallace, on his right, took quiet possession of Cumberland, and made a dash upon Romney, which he easily captured. Gen. Joseph E. Johnston, commanding the Rebels, burned the bridge at Point of Rocks on the 7th, and evacuated Harper's Ferry on the 14th, destroying the superb railway bridge over the Potomac. He retreated upon Winchester and Leesburg, after having destroyed the armory and shops at the Ferry—the machinery having been already sent off to Richmond. The Chesapeake Canal and the several railroads in this region were thoroughly dismantled. The Potomac was crossed at Williamsport, by Gen. Thomas, on the 16th. But, for some reason, this advance was countermanded, and our troops all recrossed on the 18th—Gen. Patterson remaining at Hagerstown. The Rebels at once returned to the river, completing the work of destruction at Harper's Ferry, and conscripting Unionists as well as Confederates to fill their ranks. Patterson recrossed the Potomac at Williamsport on the morning of July 2d, at a place known as 'Falling Waters,' encountering a small Rebel force under Gen. Jackson (afterward known as 'Stonewall'), who, being outnumbered, made little resistance, but fell back to Martinsburg, and ultimately to Bunker Hill. On the 7th, an order to advance on Winchester was given, but not executed. Finally, on the 15th, Patterson moved forward to

Bunker Hill, on the direct road to and nine miles from Winchester, which he occupied without resistance.

On the 17th, he turned abruptly to the left, moving away from the enemy in his front, and marching to Charlestown, twelve miles eastward, near the Potomac, leaving Johnston at full liberty to lead his entire force to Manassas. The consequences of this extraordinary movement by Patterson were so important and so disastrous as to demand for it the fullest elucidation.

Maj.-Gen. Charles W. Sanford, of New York, who was second in command to Gen. Patterson during this campaign, testifies[8] positively that he was dispatched from Washington by Gen. Scott and the Cabinet, on the 6th of July, to report to Patterson and serve under him, because of the latter's tardiness and manifest indisposition to fight—that he reported to Patterson at Williamsport, with two fresh regiments, on the 10th; was there placed in command of a division composed of 8,000 New York troops, and delivered orders from Gen. Scott, urging "a forward movement as rapidly as possible"—that Patterson then had 22,000 men and two batteries; that delay ensued at Martinsburg; but that the army advanced from that place—on the 15th—to Bunker Hill, nine miles from Johnston's fortified camp at Winchester—Sanford's division moving on the left or east of the other two; that Patterson visited him (Sanford)—whose pickets were three miles further ahead—that afternoon, after the army had halted, and complimented him on his comfortable location; to which he (S.) responded—"Very comfortable, General; but when shall we move on?" to which Patterson replied—but this is so important that we must give the precise language of Gen. Sanford's sworn testimony:

"He hesitated a moment or two, and then said: 'I don't know yet when we shall move. And, if I did, I would not tell my own father.' I thought that was rather a queer sort of speech to make to me, under the circumstances. But I smiled and said: 'General, I am only anxious that we shall get forward, that the enemy shall not escape us.' He replied: 'There is no danger of that. I will have a reconnoissance to-morrow, and we will arrange about moving at a very early period.' He then took his leave.

"The next day, there was a reconnoissance on the Winchester turnpike, about four or five miles below the General's camp. He sent forward a section of artillery and some cavalry, and they found a post and log fence across the Winchester turnpike, and some of the enemy's cavalry on the other side of it. They gave them a round of grape. The cavalry scattered off, and the reconnoissance returned. That was the only reconnoissance I heard of while we were there. My own pickets went further than that. But it was understood, the next afternoon, that we were to march forward at daylight. I sent down Col. Morell, with 40 men, to open a road down to Opequan creek, within five miles of the camp at Winchester, on the side-roads I was upon, which would enable me, in the course of three hours, to get between Johnston and the Shenandoah river, and effectually bar his way to Manassas. I had my ammunition all distributed, and ordered my men to have 24 hours' rations in their haversacks, independent of their breakfast. We were to march at 4 o'clock the next morning. I had this road to the Opequan completed that night. I had then with me, in addition to my eight regiments, amounting to about 8,000 men and a few cavalry, Doubleday's heavy United States battery of 20 and 30-pounders, and a very good Rhode Island battery. And I was willing to take the risk, whether Gen. Patterson followed me up or not, of placing myself between Johnston and the Shenandoah river, rather than let Johnston escape. And, at 4 o'clock, I should have moved over that road for that purpose, if I had had no further orders. But, a little after 12 o'clock at night [July 16th–17th], I received a long order of three pages from Gen. Patterson, instructing me to move on *to Charlestown*, which is nearly at right angles to the road I was going to move on, and

[8] Before the Joint Committee of Congress on the Conduct of the War.

twenty-two miles from Winchester. This was after I had given my orders for the other movement.

"*Question by the Chairman:* [Senator Wade] And that left Johnston free?

"*Answer:* Yes, sir; left him free to make his escape, which he did. * * *

"*Question:* In what direction would Johnston have had to move to get by you?

"*Answer:* Right out to the Shenandoah river, which he forded. He found out from his cavalry, who were watching us, that we were actually leaving, and he started at 1 o'clock that same day, with 8,000 men, forded the Shenandoah where it was so deep that he ordered his men to put their cartridge-boxes on their bayonets, got out on the Leesburg road, and went down to Manassas. * * *

"*Question by the Chairman:* Did Patterson assign any reason for that movement?

"*Answer:* I was, of course, very indignant about it, and so were all my officers and men; so much so that when, subsequently, at Harper's Ferry, Patterson came by my camp, there was a universal groan—against all discipline, of course, and we suppressed it as soon as possible. The excuse given by Gen. Patterson was this: that he had received intelligence that he could rely upon that Gen. Johnston had been reënforced by 20,000 men from Manassas, and was going to make an attack upon him; and, in the order which I received that night—a long order of three pages—I was ordered to occupy all the communicating roads, turning off a regiment here, and two or three regiments there, and a battery at another place, to occupy all the roads from Winchester to the neighborhood of Charlestown, and all the cross-roads, and hold them all that day, until Gen. Patterson's whole army went by me to Charlestown; and I sat seven hours in the saddle near a place called Smithfield, while Patterson, with his whole army, went by me on their way to Charlestown, he being apprehensive, as he said, of an attack from Johnston's forces.

"*Question by Mr. Odell:* You covered this movement?

"*Answer:* Yes, sir. Now the statement that he made, which came to me through Col. Abercrombie, who was Patterson's brother-in-law, and commanded one division in that army, was that Johnston had been reënforced; and Gen. Fitz-John Porter reported the same thing to my officers. Gen. Porter was then the chief of Patterson's staff, and was a very excellent officer, and an accomplished soldier. They all had got this story, which was without the slightest shadow of foundation; *for there had not a single man arrived at the camp since we had got full information that their force consisted of* 20,000 *men*, of whom 1,800 were sick with the measles. The story was, however, that they had ascertained, by reliable information, of this reënforcement. Where they got their information, I do not know. None such reached *me;* and I picked up deserters and other persons to get all the information I could; and we since have learned, as a matter of certainty, that Johnston's force never did exceed 20,000 men there. But the excuse Patterson gave was, that Johnston had been reënforced by 20,000 men from Manassas, and was going to attack him. That was the reason he gave then for this movement. But, in this paper he has lately published, he hints at another reason—another excuse—which was that it was by order of Gen. Scott. Now, I know that the peremptory order of Gen. Scott to Gen. Patterson, repeated over and over again, was this—I was present on several occasions when telegraphic communications went from Gen. Scott to Gen. Patterson: Gen. Scott's orders to Gen. Patterson were that, if he were strong enough, he was to attack and beat Johnston. But, if not, then he was to place himself in such a position as to keep Johnston employed, and prevent him from making a junction with Beauregard at Manassas. That was the repeated direction of Gen. Scott to Gen. Patterson; and it was because of Patterson's hesitancy, and his hanging back, and keeping so far beyond the reach of Johnston's camp, that I was ordered to go up there and reënforce him, and assist him in any operations necessary to effect that object. The excuse of Gen. Patterson now is, that he had orders from Gen. Scott to move to Charlestown. Now, that is not so. But this state of things existed: Before the movement was made from Martinsburg, Gen. Patterson suggested to Gen. Scott that Charlestown would be a better base of operations than Martinsburg, and suggested that he had better move on Charlestown, and thence make his approaches to Winchester; that it would be better to do that than to move directly to Winchester from Martinsburg; and Gen. Scott wrote back to say that, if he found that movement a better one, he was at liberty to make it. But Gen. Patterson had already commenced his movement on Winchester direct from Martinsburg, and had got as far as Bunker Hill; so that the movement which he had formerly suggested, to Charlestown, was suppressed by his own act. But that is the pretense now given in his published speech for making the movement from Bunker Hill to Charlestown, which was a retreat, instead of the advance which the movement to Charlestown he first proposed to Gen. Scott was intended to be. * *

"*Question by the Chairman:* I have heard it suggested that he undertook to excuse this movement on the ground that the time of many of his troops had expired, and they refused to accompany him.

"*Answer:* That, to my knowledge, is untrue. The time of none of them had expired when this movement was made. All the troops that were there were in the highest condition for the service. These three-months' men, it may be well to state to you who are not military men, were superior to any other volunteer troops that we had, in point of discipline. They were the disciplined troops of the country. The three-months' men were generally the organized troops of the different States—New-York, Pennsylvania, etc. We had, for instance, from Patterson's own city, Philadelphia, one of the finest regiments in the service, which was turned over to me, at their own request; and the most of my regiments were disciplined and organized troops. They were all in fine condition, anxious, zealous, and earnest for a fight. They thought they were going to attack Johnston's camp at Winchester. Although I had suggested to Gen. Patterson that there was no necessity for that, the camp being admirably fortified with many of their heavy guns from Norfolk, I proposed to him to place ourselves between Johnston and the Shenandoah, which would have compelled him to fight us there, or to remain in his camp, either of which would have effected Gen. Scott's object. If I had got into a fight, it was very easy, over this road I had just been opening, for Patterson to have reënforced me and to have come up to the fight in time. The proposition was to place ourselves between Johnston's fortified camp and the Shenandoah, where his fortified camp would have been of no use to him.

"*Question:* Even if you had received a check there, it would have prevented his junction with the forces at Manassas?

"*Answer:* Yes, sir; I would have risked a battle with my own division rather than Johnston should have escaped. If he had attacked me, I could have taken a position where I could have held it, while Patterson could have fallen upon him and repulsed him.

"*Question by Mr. Odell:* Had you any such understanding with Patterson?

"*Answer:* I told him I would move down on this side-road in advance, leaving Gen. Patterson to sustain me if I got into a fight. So, on the other hand, if he should attack Patterson, I was near enough to fall upon Johnston's flank and to support Patterson. By using this communication of mine to pass Opequan creek—where, I had informed Patterson, I had already pushed forward my pickets, [200 men in the day and 400 more at night,] to prevent the enemy from burning the bridge—it would have enabled me to get between Johnston and the Shenandoah river. On the morning of our march to Charlestown, Stuart's Cavalry, which figured so vigorously at Bull Run, was upon my flank all day. They were apparently about 800 strong. I saw them constantly on my flank for a number of miles. I could distinguish them, with my glass, with great ease. Finally, they came within about a mile of the line of march I was pursuing, and I sent a battery around to head them off, and the 12th regiment across the fields in double-quick time to take them in the rear. I thought I had got them hemmed in. But they broke down the fences, and went across the country to Winchester, and I saw nothing more of them. They were then about eight miles from Winchester, and must have got there in the course of a couple of hours. That day, at 1 o'clock—as was ascertained from those who saw him crossing the Shenandoah—Johnston started from Winchester with 8,000 men, forded the Shenandoah, and got to Manassas on Friday night; and his second in command started the next day with all the rest of the available troops—something like 9,000 men; leaving only the sick, and a few to guard them, in the camp at Winchester—and they arrived at the battle-field in the midst of the fight, got out of the cars, rushed on the battle-field, and turned the scale. I have no doubt that, if we had intercepted Johnston, as we ought to have done, the battle of Bull Run would have been a victory for us instead of a defeat. Johnston was, undoubtedly, the ablest general they had in their army."[9]

Patterson remained at Charlestown, idle and useless, until the 22d; when, learning of the disaster at Bull Run,

[9] If any Unionist is curious to see, and has the patience to read, all the excuses which can be trumped up for Patterson's conduct throughout this wretched business, he will find them embodied and skillfully marshaled in Mr. Fitz John Porter's testimony before the Joint Committee [of the XXXVIIth Congress] on the Conduct of the War, vol. ii. pp. 152–59. I see nothing therein that essentially contradicts Gen. Sanford's testimony, or is calculated to relieve Gen. Patterson from the grave imputations which that testimony must fix in the breast of every loyal American. All that it seems to establish is a perfect identity of principles, sympathies, and purposes, between Porter and Patterson, with a rare skill in framing excuses on the part of the former.

he fell back hastily to Harper's Ferry;[10] where, on the 25th, he was superseded by Gen. N. P. Banks.

The movement of the Union Grand Army, commanded in the field by Gen. Irwin McDowell, but directed from Washington by Lieut. Gen. Scott, commenced on Tuesday, July 16th. Gen. Tyler's column, in the advance, bivouacked that night at Vienna, four and a half miles from Fairfax Court House. It rested next night at Germantown, two miles beyond Fairfax; and, on Thursday, at 9 o'clock A. M., pushed on to and through Centerville, the Rebels retiring quietly before it. Three miles beyond that village, however, the Rebels were found strongly posted at Blackburn's ford, on BULL RUN, and, on being pressed, showed fight. This was at 1½ o'clock P. M. A spirited conflict, mainly with artillery, resulted—the Rebels being in heavy force, under the immediate command of Gen. James Longstreet. The Unionists, more exposed, as well as outnumbered, finally drew back, leaving the Rebel position intact. The losses were nearly equal: 83 on our side; 68 on the other. Sherman's battery, Capt. Ayres, did most of the actual fighting, supported by Col. Richardson's brigade, consisting of the 1st Massachusetts, 12th New-York, and 2d and 3d Michigan. Regarded as a reconnoissance in force, the attack might be termed a success; since the result demonstrated that the main Rebel army was in position along the wooded valley of Bull Run, half-way between Centerville and Manassas Junction, and purposed to remain.

Gen. McDowell's army was moved up to and concentrated around the ridge on which Centerville is situated during the 18th and 19th, with intent to advance and attack the Rebels, posted along Bull Run and between that stream and Manassas Junction, on Saturday, the 20th. But delay was encountered in the reception of adequate subsistence, which did not arrive till Friday night. During Saturday, three days' rations were distributed and issued, and every preparation made for moving punctually at 2 o'clock next morning. Meantime, Beauregard, maintaining an absolute quiet and inoffensiveness on his front, and fully informed by spies and traitors of every movement between him and Washington, had hastily gathered from every side all the available forces of the Confederacy, including 15,000, or nearly the

[10] On the day of McDowell's advance to Centerville, and of the collision at Blackburn's Ford, Gen. Scott telegraphed complainingly to Patterson as follows:

"WASHINGTON, July 18th, 1861.

"MAJOR-GEN. PATTERSON, etc.: I have certainly been expecting you to beat the enemy. If not, to hear that you have felt him strongly, or, at least, had occupied him by threats and demonstrations. You have been at least his equal, and, I suppose, superior, in numbers. Has he not stolen a march and sent reënforcements toward Manassas Junction? A week is enough to win a victory. * *

"WINFIELD SCOTT."

To this, Patterson responded as follows:

"CHARLESTOWN, July 18th, 1861.

"COL. E. D. TOWNSEND, A. A. G., etc.: Telegram of to-day received. The enemy has stolen *no* march upon me. I have kept him actively employed, and, by threats and reconnoissances in force, caused him to be reënforced. I have accomplished more in this respect than the General-in-Chief asked, or could well be expected, in the face of an enemy far superior in numbers, with no line of communication to protect. * * * * R. PATTERSON."

At this very moment, Patterson *knew* that he had, by his flank march to Charlestown, completely relieved Johnston from all apprehension of attack or disturbance, and left him perfectly free to reënforce Beauregard with his entire army.

full strength, of Gen. Johnston's Army of the Shenandoah, and had decided to assume the offensive and attack our forces before Gen. Patterson could come up to join them. Had our advance been made on Saturday, as we originally intended, it would have encountered but two-thirds of the force it actually combated; had it been delayed a few hours longer, we should have stood on the defensive, with the immense advantage of knowing the ground, and of choosing the positions whereon to fight. Such are the overruling casualties and fatalities of war.

Bull Run is a decent mill-stream, fordable, in summer, at intervals of

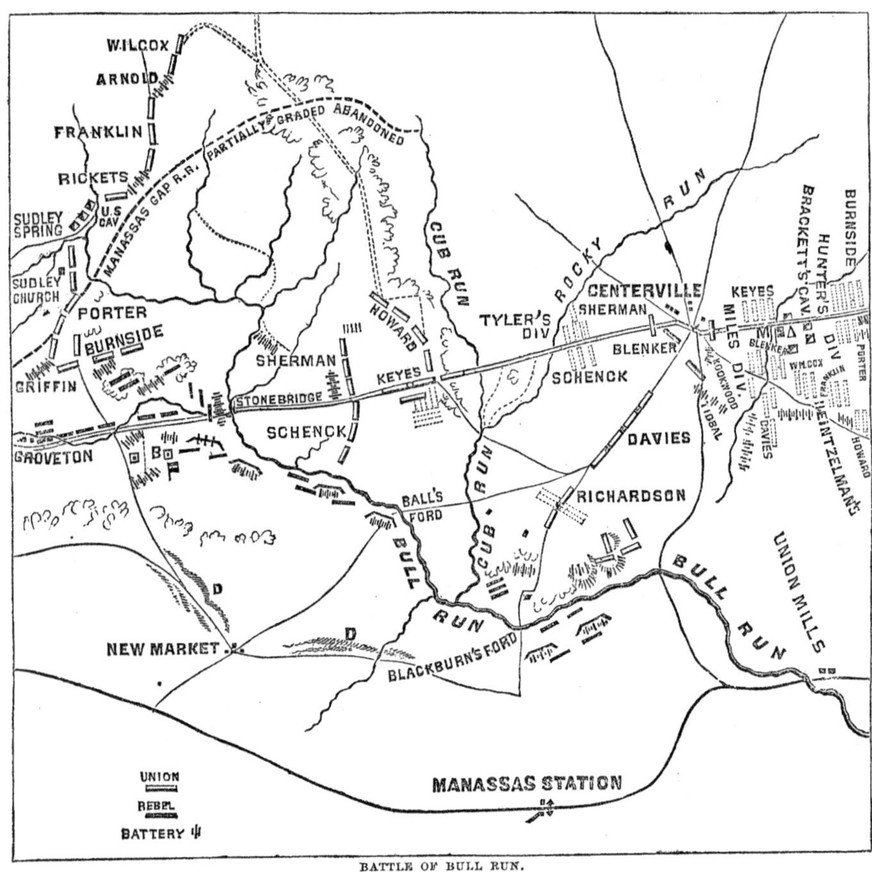

BATTLE OF BULL RUN.

half a mile to a mile. Its immediate valley is generally narrow and wooded, inclosed by bluffs, neither high nor very steep, but affording good positions for planting batteries to command the roads on the opposite side, so screened by woods and brush as to be neither seen nor suspected until the advancing or attacking party is close upon them. This fact explains and justifies Gen. McDowell's (or Scott's) order of battle. This was, briefly: to menace the Rebel right by the advance of our 1st division on the direct road from Centreville to Manassas Junction, while making a more serious demonstration on the road running due west from Centerville to Groveton and Warrenton, and crossing Bull Run by the Stone Bridge; while the real or main attack was to be made by a column 15,000 strong, composed of the 2d (Hunter's) and 3d (Heintzelman's) divisions, which, starting from their camps a mile or two east and southeast of Centerville, were to make a considerable détour to the right, crossing Cub Run, and then Bull Run at a ford known as Sudley Spring, three miles above the Stone Bridge, thus turning the Rebel left, and rolling it up on the center, where it was to be taken in flank by our 1st division (Tyler's) crossing the Stone Bridge at the right moment, and completing the rout of the enemy. The 5th division (Miles's) was held in reserve at Centerville, not only to support the attacking columns, but to guard against the obvious peril of a formidable Rebel advance on our left across Blackburn's Ford to Centerville, flanking our flank movement, capturing our munitions and supplies, and cutting off our line of retreat. The 4th division (Runyon's) guarded our communications with Alexandria and Arlington; its foremost regiment being about seven miles back from Centerville.

The movement of our army was to have commenced at 2½ o'clock A. M., and the battle should have been opened at all points at 6 A. M.; but our raw troops had never been brigaded prior to this advance, and most of their officers were utterly without experience; so that there was a delay of two or three hours in the flanking divisions reaching the point at which the battle was to begin. Gen. Tyler, in front of Stone Bridge, opened with his artillery at 6½ A. M., eliciting no reply; and it was three hours later when Hunter's advance, under Col. Burnside, crossed at Sudley Spring; his men, thirsty with their early march that hot July morning, stopping as they crossed to drink and fill their canteens. Meantime, every movement of our forces was made manifest to Beauregard, watching them from the slope two or three miles west, by the clouds of dust that rose over their line of march; and regiment after regiment was hurried northward by him to meet the imminent shock. No strength was wasted by him upon, and scarcely any notice taken of, our feint on his right; but, when Burnside's brigade, after crossing at Sudley, had marched a mile or so through woods down the road on the right of Bull Run, and come out into a clear and cultivated country, stretching thence over a mile of rolling fields down to Warrenton turnpike, he was vigorously opened upon by artillery from the woods in his front, and, as he pressed on, by infantry also. Continuing to advance, fighting, followed and supported by Hunter's entire division, which was soon joined on its left by Heintzelman's, which had crossed the stream a little later and further down, our attacking column reached and crossed the Warrenton road from Centerville by the Stone Bridge, giving a hand to Sherman's brigade of Tyler's division, and all but clearing this road of the Rebel batteries and regiments, which here resisted our efforts,[11] under the immediate com-

[11] Beauregard's official report of the battle, which was dated Manassas, August 26th, (after he had received and read all our official reports,) says of the state of the battle at this time:

"Heavy losses had now been sustained on our side, both in numbers and in the personal worth

mand of Gen. Joseph E. Johnston. Here Griffin's battery, which, with Rickett's, had done the most effective fighting throughout, was charged with effect by a Rebel regiment, which was enabled to approach it with impunity by a mistake of our officers, who supposed it one of our own. Three different attacks were repulsed with slaughter, and the battery remained in our hands, though all its horses were killed. At 3 P. M., the Rebels had been driven a mile and a half, and were nearly out of sight, abandoning the Warrenton road entirely to our victorious troops. Gen. Tyler, on hearing the guns of Hunter on our right, had pushed Sherman's, and soon after Keyes's, brigade, over the Run to assail the enemy in his front, driving them back after a severe struggle, and steadily advancing until checked by a heavy fire of artillery from batteries on the hights above the road, supported by a brigade of Rebel infantry strongly posted behind breastworks. A gallant charge by the 2d Maine and 3d Connecticut temporarily carried the buildings behind which the Rebel guns were sheltered; but the breastworks were too strong, and our men, recoiling from their fire, deflected to the left, moving down the Run under the shelter of the bluff, covering the efforts of Captain's Alexander's pioneers to remove the heavy abatis, whereby the Rebels had obstructed the road up from the Stone Bridge. This had at length been effected; and Schenck's brigade and Ayres' battery, of Tyler's division, were on the point of crossing the Run to aid in completing our triumph.

But the Rebels, at first out-numbered at the point of actual collision, had been receiving reënforcements nearly all day; and, at this critical moment, Gen. Kirby Smith,[12] who had that morning left Piedmont, fifteen miles distant, with the remaining brigade of Gen. Johnston's army, appeared on the field. Cheer after cheer burst from the Rebel hosts, but now so downcast, as this timely reënforcement rushed to the front of the battle.[13] Smith almost instantly

of the slain. The 8th Georgia regiment had suffered heavily, being exposed, as it took and maintained its position, to a fire from the enemy, already posted within a hundred yards of their front and right, sheltered by fences and other cover. It was at this time that Lieut. Col. Gardner was severely wounded, as also several other valuable officers; the Adjutant of the regiment, Lieut. Branch, was killed, and the horse of the regretted Bartow was shot under him. The 4th Alabama also suffered severely from the deadly fire of the thousands of muskets which they so dauntlessly fronted, under the immediate leadership of Bee himself. Its brave Colonel, E. J. Jones, was dangerously wounded, and many gallant officers fell, slain or *hors de combat.*

"Now, however, with the surging mass of over 14,000 Federal infantry pressing on their front, and under the incessant fire of at least twenty pieces of artillery, with the fresh brigades of Sherman and Keyes approaching—the latter already in musket-range—our lines gave back, but under orders from Gen. Bee.

"The enemy, maintaining their fire, pressed their swelling masses onward as our shattered battalions retired: the slaughter for the moment was deplorable, and has filled many a Southern home with life-long sorrow.

"Under this inexorable stress, the retreat continued until arrested by the energy and resolution of Gen. Bee, supported by Bartow and Evans, just in the rear of the Robinson House, and Hampton's Legion, which had been already advanced, and was in position near it.

"Imboden's battery, which had been handled with marked skill, but whose men were almost exhausted, and the two pieces of Walton's battery, under Lieut. Richardson, being threatened by the enemy's infantry on the left and front, were also obliged to fall back. Imboden, leaving a disabled piece on the ground, retired until he met Jackson's brigade, while Richardson joined the main body of his battery near the Lewis House."

[12] A Connecticut traitor.

[13] *The Richmond Dispatch* of August 1st has a spirited account of the battle, by an eye-witness, writing at Manassas Junction, July 22d; from which we extract the following:

fell from his horse, wounded; but the command of his brigade was promptly assumed by Col. Arnold Elzey,[14] who pressed forward, backed by the whole reässured and exultant Rebel host, who felt that the day was won. Our soldiers, who had been thirteen hours marching and fighting, weary, hungry, thirsty, continually encountering fresh Rebel regiments, and never seeing even a company hurrying to their own support, became suddenly dismayed and panic-stricken. Elzey's and Early's[15] fresh battalions filled the woods on their right, extending rapidly toward its rear, firing on them from under cover, and seeming, by their shots and cries, to be innumerable. Two or three of our regiments recoiled, and then broke, rushing down to the Run. Jefferson Davis, who had left Richmond at 6 A. M., reached the Junction at 4, and galloped to the battle-field just in time, it was said, to witness the advance of his cavalry, 1,500

"Between 2 and 3 o'clock, large numbers of men were leaving the field, some of them wounded, others exhausted by the long struggle, who gave us gloomy reports; but, as the firing on both sides continued steadily, we felt sure that our brave Southerners had not been conquered by the overwhelming hordes of the North. It is, however, due to truth to say that the result at this hour hung trembling in the balance. We had lost numbers of our most distinguished officers. Gens. Bartow and Bee had been stricken down; Lieut. Col. Johnson, of the Hampton Legion, had been killed; Col. Hampton had been wounded. But there was at hand the fearless General whose reputation as a commander was staked on this battle: Gen. Beauregard promptly offered to lead the Hampton Legion into action, which he executed in a style unsurpassed and unsurpassable. Gen. Beauregard rode up and down our lines, between the enemy and his own men, regardless of the heavy fire, cheering and encouraging our troops. About this time, a shell struck his horse, taking his head off, and killing the horses of his Aids, Messrs. Ferguson and Hayward. Gen. Beauregard's Aids deserve honorable mention, particularly those just named, and Cols. W. Porcher Miles, James Chestnut, John L. Manning, and A. R. Chisholm. Gen. Johnston also threw himself into the thickest of the fight, seizing the colors of a Georgia regiment, and rallying them to the charge. His staff signalized themselves by their intrepidity, Col. Thomas being killed and Major Mason wounded.

"Your correspondent heard Gen. Johnston exclaim to Gen. Cocke, just at the critical moment, 'Oh, for four regiments!' His wish was answered; for in the distance our reënforcements appeared. The tide of battle was turned in our favor by the arrival of Gen. Kirby Smith, from Winchester, with 4,000 men of Gen. Johnston's division. Gen. Smith heard, while on the Manassas railroad cars, the roar of battle. He stopped the train, and hurried his troops across the fields to the point just where he was most needed. They were at first supposed to be the enemy, their arrival at that point of the field being entirely unexpected. The enemy fell back, and a panic seized them. Cheer after cheer from our men went up, and we knew the battle had been won."

The Louisville Courier, a thoroughly Secession sheet, had an account from its correspondent, "Se De Kay," who was an officer in the Kentucky battalion attached to Gen. Johnston's army, which reached the battle-field among the last, and who, writing from Manassas, Monday, July 22d, after stating that Beauregard had been driven two miles, says:

"The fortunes of the day were evidently against us. Some of our best officers had been slain, and the flower of our army lay strewn upon the field, ghastly in death or gaping with wounds. At noon, the cannonading is described as terrific. It was an incessant roar for more than two hours, the havoc and devastation at this time being fearful. *McDowell, with the aid of Patterson's division of* 20,000 *men, had nearly outflanked us, and they were just in the act of possessing themselves of the railway to Richmond. Then all would have been lost. But, most opportunely—I may say providentially—at this juncture, Gen. Johnston, with the remnant of his division*—our *army, as we fondly call it, for we have been friends and brothers in camp and field for three months—reäppeared and made one other desperate struggle to obtain the vantage-ground.* Elzey's brigade of Marylanders and Virginians led the charge; and right manfully did they execute the work."

[14] A Marylander who did *not* 'go with his State.'

[15] Beauregard's report of the battle says:

"Col. Early, who, by some mischance, did not receive orders until 2 o'clock, which had been sent him at noon, came on the ground immediately after Elzey, with Kemper's 7th Virginia, Hay's 7th Louisiana, and Barksdale's 13th Mississippi regiments. This brigade, by the personal direction of Gen. Johnston, was marched by the Holkham house, across the fields to the left, entirely around the woods through which Elzey had passed, and under a severe fire, into a position in line of battle near Chinn's house, outflanking the enemy's right."

strong, under Lieut. Col. Stuart, on the heels of our flying troops. He telegraphed that night to his Congress as follows:

"MANASSAS JUNCTION, Sunday night.

"Night has closed upon a hard-fought field. Our forces were victorious. The enemy was routed, and fled precipitately, abandoning a large amount of arms, ammunition, knapsacks, and baggage. The ground was strewed for miles with those killed, and the farm-houses and the ground around were filled with wounded.

"Pursuit was continued along several routes, toward Leesburg and Centerville, until darkness covered the fugitives. We have captured several field-batteries, stands of arms, and Union and State flags. Many prisoners have been taken. Too high praise cannot be bestowed, whether for the skill of the principal officers, or for the gallantry of all our troops. The battle was mainly fought on our left. *Our force was* 15,000; that of the enemy estimated at 35,000.

"JEFFERSON DAVIS."

Had Davis been aware of the utter demoralization of our soldiers by panic, he would doubtless have had them pursued, not only *toward* Centerville, but, if possible, *into* and beyond it; and he would not have needed so grossly to understate the strength of his army in order to magnify his victory.

Before 3 P. M., there had been fitful cannonading and skirmishing, but no serious engagement, on our left.[16] But, when our defeat on the right became manifest, Gen. Johnston[17] again ordered Ewell to advance and attack; which he did, but was received by the 2d brigade, Col. T. A. Davis, with so rapid and spirited a fire of grape and canister that he precipitately retreated. There were still more than three hours of good daylight when the Rebels saw our routed right rushing madly from the field,[18] like frightened sheep, yet their pursuit amounted to nothing. They came across Bull Run, preceded by their cavalry, and seem to have taken a deliberate, though rather distant, survey of the 5th division, drawn up in good order along the slope west of Centerville, and eagerly expecting their advance. But they appear to have been aware that their victory was a lucky accident, and they did not choose to submit its prestige to the chances of another fray. Having gratified their thirst for knowledge, considerably out of musket-shot, they returned to their previous hiding-places in the woods skirting Bull

[16] Beauregard says, in his official report, that he sent orders to Gen. Ewell, holding his extreme right at the Union Mills ford, next south of Blackburn's (on Bull Run), to advance and attack; and that they did advance a mile toward Centerville on the Union Mills road, but retreated again "under a sharp fire of artillery, in consequence of the miscarriage of orders."

[17] Gen. Johnston, who had joined Beauregard, at Winchester on the 20th, was the ranking officer, and entitled to command: but, after listening to Beauregard's plans, promptly acceded to them, and directed him to carry them into execution. As Davis himself finally arrived on the field, the Rebel army may be said to have had three commanders-in-chief during the course of the battle.

[18] A correspondent of *The New York Tribune*, who witnessed and described the battle and the flight, says:

"Notwithstanding all that I had seen, it seemed incredible that our whole army should melt away in a night; and so I remained at Centerville, trusting that, by the morning, a sort of reorganization would have taken place, and that our front would still oppose the enemy. At 7 A. M., I started toward the battle-field; and, on reaching a considerable acclivity, was amazed to find that no vestige of our troops remained, excepting a score or two of straggling fugitives, who followed the tracks of those who had gone before. While returning to Centerville, a group of Rebel cavalry passed, who looked inquiringly, but did not question. Their conversation turned upon the chances of cutting off the retreat at Fairfax Court House. After seeking Mr. Waud, an artist from New York, who also lingered, I went straight to Fairfax. As we passed the church used as a hospital, the doctors came out, and, finding what was the condition of affairs, walked rapidly away. I do not wish to say that they deserted the wounded. They may have returned, for aught I know."

Run.[19] During the fore part of the night, some of our men, who had not been stampeded, went down toward the battle-field and brought away one or two guns, which had been abandoned in the flight, but not captured by the enemy. Our 5th division, constituting the reserve, now become the rear-guard, of our army, remained in position until after midnight; when, under peremptory orders from Gen. McDowell, it commenced its deliberate retreat to the environs of Washington.[20]

Gen. McDowell reports our losses in this engagement at 481 killed and 1,011 wounded, but says nothing of how many wounded or others were taken prisoners.[21] Gen. Beauregard reports the Rebel loss at 269 killed and 1,533 wounded;[22] in all, 1,852; saying nothing of any loss in prisoners, of whom two or three hundred were taken by our soldiers in the early part of the battle, and duly forwarded to Washington. He says he had sent 1,460 wounded and other prisoners to Richmond, and estimates

[19] Beauregard, in his official report, thus lamely explains this modesty:

"Early's brigade, meanwhile, joined by the 19th Virginia regiment, Lieut. Col. Strange, of Cocke's brigade, pursued the now panic-stricken, fugitive enemy. Stuart, with his cavalry, and Beckham, had also taken up the pursuit along the road by which the enemy had come upon the field that morning; but, soon encumbered by prisoners, who thronged his way, the former was unable to attack the mass of the fast-fleeing, frantic Federalists. Withers's, R. J. Preston's, Cash's, and Kershaw's regiments, Hampton's Legion and Kemper's battery, also pursued along the Warrenton road by the Stone Bridge, the enemy having opportunely opened a way for them through the heavy abatis which my troops had made on the west side of the bridge, several days before. *But this pursuit was soon recalled, in consequence of a false report, which unfortunately reached us, that the enemy's reserves, known to be fresh and of considerable strength, were threatening the position of Union Mills Ford.*"

[20] The impression that the Rebels, had they pursued, might have captured or dispersed our flying forces, is unsustained by facts. For between the panic-stricken fugitives and the victors were not merely the reserve (5th) division, which remained in position, and had not fired a shot, but the 1st (Tyler's) division forming our left, which had suffered little loss, but had signally repulsed the demonstration made upon it at the close of the fight; while the better portion of our beaten right and center, including the regular infantry and cavalry, still stood its ground and sternly faced the foe. Maj. Barry, our Chief of Artillery in the battle, in his official report, after noticing the loss of ten of his guns at the close, through the flight of their supporting infantry, says:

"The army having retired upon Centerville, I was ordered by Gen. McDowell in person, to post the artillery in position to cover the retreat.

"The batteries of Hunt, Ayres, Tidball, Edwards, Green, and the New-York 8th regiment, (the latter served by volunteers from Wilcox's brigade,) 20 pieces in all, were at once placed in position; and thus remained until 12 o'clock P. M., when, orders having been received to retire upon the Potomac, the batteries were put in march, and, covered by Richardson's brigade, retired in good order and without haste, and, early next morning, reöccupied their former camps on the Potomac."

Col. J. B. Richardson, commanding the 4th brigade of Tyler's division, remained unmolested in position one mile in advance of Centerville, on the Blackburn's Ford road, until 2 A. M. of Monday; then retreated, per order, through Centerville to Fairfax and Arlington, entirely unassailed.

[21] Among our killed were Col. James Cameron, brother of the Secretary of War—of the 79th New York (Highlanders); Col. Slocum, and Major Ballou, of the 2d Rhode Island; and Lieut. Col. Haggerty, of the 69th New York. Among our wounded were Gen. David Hunter and Gen. S. P. Heintzelman—commanding divisions; Col. Oliver B. Wilcox, of Michigan; Col. Gilman Marston, of the 1st New Hampshire; Col. A. M. Wood, of the 14th New York; Col. H. W. Slocum, of the 27th New York; and Col. N. L. Farnham, of the 11th New York (Fire Zouaves). Col. Wilcox was also taken prisoner, as well as Col. Michael Corcoran, of the 69th New York (Irish), and Maj. James D. Potter, of the 38th New York—both slightly wounded.

[22] "Se De Kay," a Rebel officer, writing to *The Louisville Courier* from Manassas Junction, on the 22d, says:

"*Our loss is fully two thousand killed and wounded.* Among the killed are Gen. Bee, of South Carolina; Gen. E. K. Smith, [a mistake], Gen. Bartow, of Georgia; Col. Moore and all the Alabama field officers; Col. Fisher and the North Carolina field officers; Adjt. Branch, of Georgia, and a host of other leading men."

[five weeks after the fight] that the number may be increased to 1,600. That is certainly a very lean exhibit of prisoners as the fruit of so decisive a victory; but the fleetness of our soldiers is to be taken into the account. He guesses that our losses will amount to 4,500 in killed, wounded, and prisoners, and adds:

"The ordnance and supplies captured include *some* 28 [23] field-pieces of the best character of arms,[24] with over 100 rounds of ammunition for each gun, 37 caissons, 6 forges, 4 battery-wagons, 64 artillery horses, completely equipped, 500,000 rounds of small-arms ammunition, 4,500 sets of accouterments, over 500 muskets, some 9 regimental and garrison flags, with a large number of pistols, knapsacks, swords, canteens, blankets, a large store of axes and intrenching tools, wagons, ambulances, horses, camp and garrison equipage, hospital stores, and some subsistence."

At 7 A. M., of Monday, the 22d, the last of our stragglers and wounded left Centerville, which a Rebel cavalry force was about to enter. But there was no pursuit, and no loss on our part after the battle, but of what our men threw away. Beauregard explains his failure to pursue, after our discomfiture, as follows:

"An army which had fought like ours on that day, against uncommon odds, under a July sun, most of the time without water and without food, except a hastily snatched meal at dawn, was not in condition for the toil of an eager, effective pursuit of an enemy immediately after the battle.

"On the following day, an unusually heavy and unintermitting fall of rain intervened to obstruct our advance, with reasonable prospect of fruitful results. Added to this, the want of a cavalry force of sufficient numbers made an efficient pursuit a military impossibility."

The forces actually engaged in this celebrated battle, so decisive in its results and so important in its consequences, were probably not far from 25,000 on either side;[25] while the combatants actually on the battle-field, or so near it as to be practically at the disposal of the respective command-

[23] Our reports admit a loss of 17 guns; other accounts make it 22. Beauregard, writing on the 26th of August, should have been able to state the exact number. His statement of the number of muskets taken at "over 500," including all those dropped by our dead and wounded, proves that the stories told by excited correspondents and other fugitives, of our men throwing away everything that could impede their flight, were gross exaggerations.

[24] Gen. Heintzelman, in his official report of the battle, giving an account of his retreat by the circuitous road on which he had advanced, says:

"Having every reason to fear a vigorous pursuit from the enemy's fresh troops, I was desirous of forming a strong rear-guard; but neither the efforts of the officers of the regular army, nor the coolness of the regular troops with me, could induce them to form a single company. We relied entirely for our protection on one section of artillery and a few companies of cavalry. Most of the road was favorable for infantry, but unfavorable for cavalry and artillery. About dusk, as we approached the Warrenton turnpike, we heard a firing of rifled cannon on our right, and learned that the enemy had established a battery enfilading the road. Capt. Arnold, with his section of artillery, attempted to run the gauntlet and reach the bridge over Cub Run, about two miles from Centerville, but found it obstructed with broken vehicles, and was compelled to abandon his pieces, as they were under the fire of these rifled cannon. The cavalry turned to the left, and, after passing through a strip of woods and some fields, struck a road which led them to some camps occupied by our troops in the morning, through which we gained the turnpike. At about 8 P. M., we reached the camps we had occupied in the morning. Had a brigade from the reserve advanced a short distance beyond Centerville, nearly one-third of the artillery lost might have been saved, as it was abandoned at or near this crossing."

These were the only guns lost by us, save those abandoned for want of horses, on the immediate field of conflict.

[25] Pollard, in his "Southern History," says:

"Our effective force of all arms ready for action on the field, on the eventful morning, was less than 30,000 men."

This was before the arrival of that portion of Johnston's army led to the field by Kirby Smith, and afterward commanded by Elzey, or the brigade of Early—to say nothing of the reënforcements that were received during the day from the direction of Richmond.

ers, were, on either side, not far from 35,000. But the Rebels, who were somewhat the fewer at day-break, fought under the encouraging stimulus of a knowledge that every hour, as it passed, added to their strength; that each railroad train arriving at the Junction, brought fresh brigade after brigade to their support;[26] and these, as they arrived, were hastened to that part of the field whereon their services could be most effective: while our men, who had been called to arms at 2 o'clock in the morning, and had generally thrown aside their knapsacks and haversacks to facilitate their movements, had been fourteen hours marching—some of them on the double-quick for miles—or fighting, and were utterly exhausted and faint with hunger and thirst; while not a single company had been added to their numbers. Some regiments fought badly, and had been demoralized and dispersed prior to the general catastrophe; but the great majority evinced a courage and devotion which, under favoring auspices, would have commanded victory. They gave way only when hope seemed dead—when the ever-increasing hosts of their foes not only outnumbered them in their front, but filled the woods on their right flank, exposing them to an enfilading fire, which they could not return with effect; and, their defeat once confessed, the confusion and panic of their flight are explained, not excused, by the fact that, owing to the long détour they had necessarily made in advancing to the attack, pursuant to the plan of battle, their line of retreat lay in part along the front of the foe, much of whose strength was actually nearer to Centerville than they were when the fortunes of the day turned against them.

The causes of this disaster, so shamefully misstated and perverted at the time, are now generally understood. No one could, at this day, repeat the misrepresentations that for the moment prevailed, without conscious, palpable guilt and ignominy. The true, controlling reasons of our defeat are, briefly, these:

I. The fundamental, fatal error on our side was that spirit of hesitation, of indecision, of calculated delay, of stolid obstruction, which guided[27] our Military councils, scattering our

[26] Mr. Julius Bing, on his return from captivity at Richmond, having been taken prisoner on the battle-field, after seeing and hearing all that he could on both sides, reports as follows:

"Beauregard's force at Bull Run was 27,000; which was increased by 8,000 of Johnston's the day before, and by 5,000 more during the engagement. This statement is confirmed from an independent and trustworthy source."

[27] *The New York Times* of July 26th contained a carefully prepared statement, by its Editor, of a conversation with Gen. Scott at his own dinner-table on the Tuesday before the battle; wherein Gen. Scott developed his conception of the strategy required for the overthrow of the Rebellion, as follows:

"If the matter had been left to him, he said, he would have commenced by a perfect blockade of every Southern port on the Atlantic and on the Gulf Then he would have collected a large force at the capital for defensive purposes, and another large one on the Mississippi for offensive operations. The Summer months, during which it is madness to take troops south of St. Louis, should have been devoted to tactical instruction—and, with the first frosts of Autumn, he would have taken a column of 80,000 well-disciplined troops down the Mississippi—and taken every important point on that river, New Orleans included. *It could have been done, he said, with greater ease, with less loss of life, and with far more important results, than would attend the marching of an army to Richmond.* At eight points, the river would probably have been defended, and eight battles would have been necessary; but, in every one of them, success would have been made certain for us. The Mississippi and the Atlantic once ours, the Southern States would have been compelled, by the natural and inevitable pressure of events, to seek, by a return to the Union, escape from the

forces and paralyzing our efforts. Had any real purpose of suppressing the Rebellion been cherished by Gen. Scott, he would never have scattered our eastern forces along the line of the Potomac and Chesapeake, from Cumberland to Fortress Monroe, divided into three or four distinct armies, under the command of militia officers who had never smelt burning powder, unless in a squirrel-hunt. His advance across the Potomac, after having been put off so long as possible, was made, as we have seen, on the 24th of May. Within one week thereafter, a column of 50,000 men should have taken the road to Richmond, with their commander in their

ruin that would speedily overwhelm them, out of it. 'This,' said he, 'was *my* plan. But I am only a subordinate. It is my business to give advice when it is asked, and to obey orders when they are given. *I shall do it.* There are men in the Cabinet who know much more about war than I do, and who have far greater influence than I have in determining the plan of the campaign. There never was a more just and upright man than the President—never one who desired more sincerely to promote the best interest of the country. But there are men among his advisers who consult their own resentments far more than the dictates of wisdom and experience, and *these men will probably decide the plan of the campaign.* I shall do, or attempt, whatever I am ordered to do. *But they must not hold me responsible.* If I am ordered to go to Richmond, I shall endeavor to do it. But I know perfectly well that they have no conception of the difficulties we shall encounter. I know the country—how admirably adapted it is for defense, and how resolutely and obstinately it will be defended. I would like nothing better than to take Richmond; now that it has been disgraced by becoming the capital of the Rebel Confederacy, I feel a resentment toward it, and should like nothing better than to scatter its Congress to the winds. But I have lived long enough to know that human resentment is a very bad foundation for public policy; and these gentlemen will live long enough to learn it also. I shall do what I am ordered. I shall fight when and where I am commanded. *But, if I am compelled to fight before I am ready, they shall not hold me responsible.* These gentlemen must take the responsibility of their acts, as I am willing to take that of mine. But they must not throw *their* responsibility upon my shoulders.'

"This is the substance and very nearly the language of a portion of Gen. Scott's conversation on the occasion referred to. It proves conclusively that he was opposed to the advance upon Richmond by way of Manassas, at that time."

Hon. Francis P. Blair, in a speech in the House (Aug. 1st, 1861), after repelling the false imputation that Gen. Scott had been constrained by the President (his only superior) to fight this battle prematurely, in opposition to the dictates of his own judgment, stated that

"The President, after he had information that Gen. Johnston had escaped through the hands of Gen. Patterson and had joined Gen. Beauregard on Friday evening, went to Gen. Scott, and suggested the propriety of waiting until Patterson's corps could come up and reënforce the army that was then before Manassas; but, so firmly fixed was Gen. Scott's determination to attack the enemy then and there, that the President's suggestion was disregarded. The Secretary of War also returned from the field before the battle, and endeavored to induce Gen. Scott to send forward reënforcements; he urged it again and again; and finally succeeded in having five regiments sent, two of which reached Centerville before the retreat commenced."

Mr. Blair then took up the above statement of *The Times*, and thus dealt with it:

"I do not believe that it was Gen. Scott's plan. I do not think he would promulgate his plan. I think, even, that, if such was his plan, gentlemen, without arrogating to themselves any superior military knowledge, might well dissent from it. I do not profess to have any knowledge of military matters at all; and yet I can say that any such plan as that would lead to a fatal disaster to our country, in the relations which it would bring about between the people of the Northern and Southern States; in the relations it would bring about between our Government and foreign governments, and between the Union men in the Border States and their enemies. I think it would be a fatal mistake. I am well satisfied that it is not the plan of the Government, and will not be acted upon, whether Gen. Scott favors it or not. That is the plan which the Confederate troops and authorities are in favor of, and they have proceeded upon it. Their desire is to make the whole of this war within the Border States, and escape themselves scot free—not only free from Scott, but from all our other Generals. They wish to enjoy entire quietude, in order to raise their cotton, that they may hold it out to foreign nations as a bribe to break our blockade. That is their object and their heart's desire.

"They wish, also, to intrench themselves within those Border States, where they can get plenty of subsistence, and wring a reluctant support from the Union men of those States. The counties of Alexandria and Fairfax gave an immense Union vote when the question was submitted to them; and, at the last vote upon the Ordinance of Secession, they would have given the same vote for the Union if they had not been restrained by the bayonets of the Confederate troops; for, in whatever part of Virginia they

midst, even though he had to travel in an ambulance. Moving slowly, steadily, cautiously forward, our army should have been reënforced by two or three fresh regiments each day, being exercised in field maneuvers at every opportunity. On or before the 1st day of July, this array, one hundred thousand strong, should have been before Richmond, not then fortified to any serious extent, and should have replaced the Stars and Stripes on the steeples of that city by the Fourth, at latest. That we had ample force to do this, is now beyond doubt; for the Rebels, gathering all their strength from the Shenandoah on the one side to the James on the other, were barely able, on the 21st—three weeks after we should have been before Richmond—to beat a third of our regiments that might and should have confronted them.[28]

II. The flagrant disobedience and defection of Gen. Patterson,[29] unaccountable on any hypothesis consist-

were free from the Confederate bayonets, they gave a majority of votes against Secession. The same was the case in Tennessee. Any such plan as that which *The Times* says is Gen. Scott's plan of carrying on the war would leave the unarmed Union men of the Border States and of the Southern States at the mercy of the armies of the Confederate States. It would leave the 25,000 majority in East Tennessee, the vast majority in Missouri, and everywhere else, at the mercy of the Rebels.

"I say, further, that, if we remain idle for such a period of time, doing nothing upon the borders of these revolted States, however great an army we might possess, we should, by so doing, proclaim to the world that we were unable to enter those States and put down Rebellion; and the governments of Europe would make it a pretext for acknowledging the independence of those States.

"It is manifest, therefore, that such important political considerations must enter largely into any plan of campaign; and no plan is admissible which, by its delays, destroys the business of the country, leaves the Union men of the Border States and their property a prey to the Rebels, and gives a pretext to foreign Powers to interfere for the purpose of forcing our blockade."

That the policy of 'wait and get ready,' involved, in fact, a virtual admission of the independence of the Confederacy, while enabling the Rebels to crush out the last vestiges of Unionism in the South, as also to cover all the important points with impregnable fortifications, erected in good part by slave labor, is too obvious to need enforcement. It was the policy of all who wished to save the Union by surrendering at discretion to the Rebels, bidding them do what they pleased with the Constitution, the Government, the territories, so that they would but consent to endure us as fellow-countrymen.

[28] That Gen. Scott, though loyal and Union-loving, was always in favor of buying off the Rebellion by compromises and concessions, and averse to what was most unjustly termed 'coërcion' and 'invasion,' is no secret. How eagerly he jumped upon the 'finality' platform when nominated for President, in 1852, and ordered a grand salute of one hundred guns in honor of the passage of Mr. Guthrie's Compromise propositions in the "Peace Conference" of 1861, are matters of record. That he sought to have Fort Sumter evacuated, a month later, as a "military necessity," is well known. Two or three weeks thereafter, on the very morning that the Rebels opened fire on Sumter, *The National Intelligencer*, of April 12th, contained the following, which was widely understood to have been inspired, if not directly written, by him:

"There is a general and almost universal desire that no coërcive measures should be resorted to, so as to induce actual collision of arms between the States that say they have seceded and the Government of the United States, until all peaceful remedies have been exhausted, yet:

"Great confidence is inspired by an exhibition of the actual strength and power of the Government. It gratifies national pride to have the consciousness that the Government is in possession of power, and that, when it is not exercised, it may receive the credit of forbearance. There would be an objection that this attribute of power should be directed, at the present moment, to any specific end; even though that end should be the execution of the laws. But nothing can be more evident than that universal satisfaction is felt and security inspired by the knowledge that the power of the Government is ready, at a moment's notice, to be applied and used."

[29] Pollard, in his "Southern History," blandly says:

"The best service which the army of the Shenandoah could render was to prevent the defeat of that of the Potomac. To be able to do this, it was necessary for Gen. Johnston to defeat Gen. Patterson, or to elude him. The latter course was the more speedy and certain, and was, therefore, adopted. Evading the enemy by the disposition of the advance guard under Col.

ent with the possession, on his part, of courage, common sense, and loyalty.[30]

III. The failure of Gen. Scott to send forward with Gen. McDowell a force adequate to provide against all contingencies. The fact that 20,000 volunteers remained idle and useless, throughout that eventful Sunday, in and immediately around Washington—Scott having obstinately resisted entreaties that they should be dispatched to the front—insisting that McDowell had "men enough"—that he needed no cavalry, etc.—of itself attests strongly the imbecility and lack of purpose that then presided over our military councils.[31]

IV. The Rebels were kept thoroughly acquainted by their confederates, left by Davis, Floyd, etc., in our service, with everything that took place or was meditated[32] on our side; and so were able to anticipate and baffle every movement of our armies.[33] Thus, a military map or plan of the region directly west of Washington had been completed for use at the War Department barely two days before our advance reached Centerville; but, the movement being rapid, the Rebels left here many articles in their hasty flight, and, among them, a copy of this map, which was supposed to be unknown to all but a few of our highest officers. It was so throughout. Washington swarmed

Stuart, our army moved through Ashley's Gap to Piedmont, a station of the Manassas Gap railroad. Hence, the infantry were to be transported by the railway, while the cavalry and artillery were ordered to continue their march. Gen. Johnston reached Manassas about noon on the 20th, preceded by the 7th and 8th Georgia regiments and by Jackson's brigade, consisting of the 2d, 4th, 5th, 27th, and 33d Virginia regiments. He was accompanied by Gen. Bee, with the 4th Alabama, the 2d, and two companies of the 11th Mississippi. The president of the railroad had assured him that the remaining troops should arrive during the day."

[30] Patterson was a Breckinridge Democrat of the extreme pro-Slavery type—of that type whose views were expressed by *The Pennsylvanian*—(see page 428). When, on the reception of the tidings of Fort Sumter's surrender, a great popular uprising took place in Philadelphia, as in other cities, and immense crowds paraded the streets, demanding that the flag of the Union should be everywhere displayed, Gen. Patterson's was one of the mansions at which this public exaction of an avowal of sympathy with the outraged symbol of our Union was longest and most sturdily resisted.

[31] W. H. Russell, writing from Washington to *The London Times* on the 19th, two days before the battle—doubtless obtaining his information from authentic sources—thus states the disposition of our forces at that moment:

Under McDowell, at Fairfax and Centerville . .	30,000
Under Patterson, on the Shenandoah	22,000
Under Mansfield, in and about Washington . . .	16,000
Under Butler, at and near Fortress Monroe . .	11,000
Under Banks, in and near Baltimore	7,400
Total	86,400

Thus, while the Rebels concentrated, from Richmond on the south to Winchester on the north, all their available strength upon Manassas, and had it in hand before the close of the battle, McDowell had but little more than a third of our corresponding forces wherewith to oppose it—he acting on the offensive. In other words, we fought with 35,000 men, a battle in which we might and should have had 75,000.

[32] Mr. Julius Bing, a German by birth but British by naturalization, who was on the battlefield as a spectator, and was there taken prisoner, and conducted next morning to Beauregard's head-quarters, whence he was sent to Richmond, and who seems to have had the faculty of making himself agreeable to either side, stated, after his return, that among the men he met at Beauregard's head-quarters, at the Junction, was Col. Jordan, formerly of our War Department, who boasted that he had received,

"Before the attack at Bull Run, a cipher dispatch from some well-informed person within our lines, giving full details of our movements, including the particulars of the plan of battle, the time at which operations would commence, and the number of our troops."

[33] A correspondent of *The New York Tribune*, in his account of the battle, says:

"A remarkable fact to be considered is, that the enemy seemed perfectly acquainted with our plans. The feint of Col. Richardson availed nothing, since the Rebel force had nearly all been withdrawn from that position. Our combined attack was thoroughly met, and at the very points where partial surprises had been anticipated."

with traitors, many of them holding official positions of the gravest responsibility; and whatever it was important to Beauregard to know he speedily ascertained. To cross the Potomac, a little below or above our camps, was never difficult; and, once across, trusty messengers knew where to find fleet horses and sure guides to take them to the Rebel lines. The Confederate chiefs knew which among our officers meant them any harm, and which might be confidently trusted never to take them at disadvantage. They evidently had no more apprehension that Patterson would obstruct or countervail the march of Johnston to Manassas than that Breckinridge or Burnett would do them mortal harm in Congress.

V. The fall, very early in the action, of Gen. David Hunter,[34] commanding the 2d or leading division, was most untimely and unfortunate. He was so seriously wounded that he was necessarily borne from the field. Gen. Heintzelman,[35] commanding the 3d division, was also wounded; not as severely, but so as to disable him. Gen. McDowell either had control of Runyon's division, guarding his line of communication, or he had not. If he had, he should have ordered the bulk of it to advance that morning on Centerville, so as to have had it well in hand to precipitate on the foe at the decisive moment; or, if he was so hampered by Scott that he was not at liberty to do this, he should have refused to attack, and resigned the command of the army, rather than fight a battle so fettered. After the mischief was done, Runyon's division was ordered forward from Fairfax—of course, to no purpose. But it should, at least, have been promptly employed to block completely with its bayonets the roads leading to Washington, sternly arresting the flight of the panic-stricken fugitives, and gathering them up into something which should bear once more the semblance of an army.

VI. The original call of President Lincoln on the States, for 75,000 militia to serve three months, was a deplorable error. It resulted naturally from that obstinate infatuation which *would* believe, in defiance of all history and probability, that an aristocratic conspiracy of thirty years' standing, culminating in a rebellion based on an artificial property valued at Four Thousand Millions of Dollars, and wielding the resources of ten or twelve States, having nearly ten millions of people, was to be put down in sixty or ninety days by some process equivalent to reading the Riot Act to an excited mob, and sending a squad of police to disperse it. Hence, the many prisoners of war taken with arms in their hands, in West Virginia and Missouri, had, up to this time, been quite commonly permitted to go at large on taking an oath [36] of fidelity to the Constitution —a process which, in their view, was about as significant and imposing as taking a glass of cider. The Government had only to call for any number of men it required, to serve during the pleasure of Congress, or till the overthrow of the Rebellion, and

[34] Colonel of the 3d cavalry in the regular service.

[35] Colonel in the regular service.

[36] For the first year of the war, no regular list of prisoners taken by us—not even of those paroled—was kept at the War Department; hence, we fell deplorably behind in our account current with the Rebels.

they could have been had at once. Regiments were pressed upon it from all sides; and the hotels of Washington were crowded by keen competitors for the coveted privilege of raising more batteries and fresh battalions. None asked for shorter terms to serve, or would have then hesitated to enlist for the war. It was entirely proper to call out the organized and uniformed militia as minutemen to defend Washington and protect the public property until volunteers could be raised; but no single regiment should have been organized or enlisted, during that springtide of National enthusiasm, for any term short of the duration of the war.

VII. It is impossible not to perceive that the Rebel troops were better handled, during the conflict, than ours. Gen. McDowell, who does not appear to have actively participated in any former battle but that of Buena Vista, where he served as Aid to Gen. Wool, seems to have had very little control over the movements of his forces after the beginning of the conflict. Gov. Sprague, who fought through the day as brigadier with the 2d Rhode Island, whose Colonel, Slocum, and Major, Ballou, were both left dead on the battle-field, observed to one who asked him, near the close of the fight, what were his orders, that he had been fighting all day without any. In short, our army was projected like a bolt, not wielded like a sword.

VIII. Although our army, before fighting on that disastrous day, was largely composed of the bravest and truest patriots in the Union, it contained, also, much indifferent material. Many, in the general stagnation and dearth of employment, had volunteered under a firm conviction that there would be no serious fighting; that the Rebels were not in earnest; that there would be a promenade, a frolic, and, ultimately, a compromise, which would send every one home, unharmed and exultant, to receive from admiring, cheering thousands the guerdon of his valor. Hence, some regiments were very badly officered, and others gave way and scattered, or fled, just when they were most needed.

IX. Col. D. J. Miles, a Marylander, commanding the 5th (reserve) division, was drunk throughout the action, and playing the buffoon; riding about to attract observation, with two hats on his head, one within the other. As, however, he was pretty certainly a traitor, and was not ordered to advance, it is hardly probable that his drunkenness did any serious damage, save as it disgusted and disheartened those whose lives were in his hands.

No one who did not share in the sad experience will be able to realize the consternation which the news of this discomfiture—grossly exaggerated—diffused over the loyal portion of our country. Only the tidings which had reached Washington up to 4 o'clock—all presaging certain and decisive victory—were permitted to go north by telegraph that day and evening; so that, on Monday morning, when the crowd of fugitives from our grand army was pouring into Washington, a heedless, harmless, worthless mob, the loyal States were exulting over accounts of a decisive triumph. But a few hours brought different advices; and these were as much worse than the truth as the former had been better: our army had been utterly destroyed—cut to pieces, with a loss of twenty-five to thirty thousand men, beside all its artillery and munitions, and Washington lay at the mercy of the enemy, who were soon to advance to the capture and sack of our great commercial cities. Never before had so black a day as that black Monday lowered upon the loyal hearts of the North; and the leaden, weeping skies reflected and hightened, while they seemed to sympathize with, the general gloom. It would have been easy, with ordinary effort and care, to have gathered and remanded to their camps or forts around Alexandria or Arlington, all the wretched stragglers to whom fear had lent wings, and who, throwing away their arms and equipments, and abandoning all semblance of military order or discipline, had rushed to the capital to hide therein their shame behind a cloud of exaggerations and falsehoods. The still effective batteries, the solid battalions, that were then wending their way slowly back to their old encampments along the south bank of the Potomac, depressed but unshaken, dauntless and utterly unassailed, were unseen and unheard from; while the panic-stricken racers filled and distended the general ear with their tales of impregnable intrenchments and masked batteries, of regiments slaughtered, brigades utterly cut to pieces, etc., making out their miserable selves to be about all that was left of the army. That these men were allowed thus to straggle into Washington, instead of being peremptorily stopped at the bridges, and sent back to the encampments of their several regiments, is only to be accounted for on the hypothesis that the reason of our military magnates had been temporarily dethroned, so as to divest them of all moral responsibility.

The consequences of this defeat were sufficiently serious. Our 75,000 three months' men, whose term of enlistment, for the most part, expired within the three weeks following the battle, generally made haste to quit the service and seek their several firesides at the earliest possible moment.[37] Our armies were thus depleted with a rapidity rarely equaled; and the Government, which, throughout the preceding month, had been defending itself as best it could against importunities and entreaties to be allowed to furnish a regiment here or a bat-

[37] Gen. McDowell, in his official report, in giving his reasons for fighting as and when he did, says:

"I could not, as I have said more early, push on faster, nor could I delay. A large and the best part of my forces were three months' volunteers, whose term of service was about to expire, but who were sent forward as having long enough to serve for the purpose of the expedition. On the eve of the battle, the 4th Pennsylvania regiment of volunteers, and the battery of volunteer artillery of the New York 8th militia, whose term of service expired, insisted on their discharge. I wrote to the regiment, expressing a request for them to remain a short time; and the Hon. Secretary of War, who was at the time on the ground, tried to induce the battery to remain at least five days. But in vain. They insisted on their discharge that night. It was granted: and, the next morning, when the army moved forward into battle, *these troops moved to the rear to the sound of the enemy's cannon.*

"In the next few days, day by day, I should have lost ten thousand of the best armed, drilled, officered, and disciplined troops in the army. In other words, every day, which added to the strength of the enemy, made us weaker."

It should here be added, that a member of the New York battery aforesaid, who was most earnest and active in opposing Gen. McDowell's request, and insisting on an immediate discharge, was, at the ensuing election, in full view of all the facts, chosen Sheriff of the city of New-York—probably the most lucrative office filled by popular election in the country.

tery there, was glad thenceforth to take all that offered, and to solicit where it had been so earnestly solicited. The nation awoke from a dream of invincibility and easy triumph to find itself inextricably involved in a desperate and dubious struggle for life. And the thinly disguised or utterly undisguised exultation wherewith the news of this disaster was received by thousands whose sympathy with the Rebels had hitherto been suppressed, or only indulged in secret, proved that, in the struggle now upon us, the Republic could not count on the support even of all those who still claimed to be loyal to the Constitution and Union.

On the other hand, the Rebellion was immensely strengthened and consolidated by its victory. Tens of thousands throughout the South, who had hitherto submitted in silence to proceedings which they condemned and deplored, but lacked the power or the courage to resist, yet whose hearts were still with their whole country and the old flag, now abandoned the Union as hopelessly lost, and sought, by zeal in the cause of the Rebellion, to efface the recollection of their past coldness and infidelity; while no one who had previously been a Rebel any longer cherished a shadow of doubt that the independence of the Confederacy was secured. The vote of Tennessee for Secession, the sudden uprising of a great Rebel army in Missouri, and the strengthening of the cause and its defenders everywhere, owe much of their impulse to the dispatches which flashed over the rejoicing South assurances that the grand army of the North, 35,000 to 50,000 strong, had been utterly routed and dispersed by Beauregard's 15,000 to 20,000 Confederates.

Yet it is to be added that, whatever the exultation of one party, the depression of the other was not without its compensations. The North, at first stunned, was ultimately rather chastened and sobered than disheartened or unnerved by its great disaster; while the South, intoxicated by its astounding success, expended in fruitless exultation energies that might better have been devoted to preparation for future and more determined struggles. If, as the Confederates were told, 15,000 of their raw recruits, badly armed and provided, had sufficed to rout and scatter double or treble their number of Yankees, superbly equipped for the contest, what need could there be for self-denial, and sacrifice, and a general volunteering to recruit their victorious armies? They hastily concluded that the struggle was virtually over—that nothing remained but to prescribe the terms on which peace should be accorded to the vanquished; and this delusion continued for months undispelled and effective.

And thus, while the instant effect of the tidings was the doubling of the Rebel numbers in the field and a reduction of ours by half, yet a few weeks sufficed to efface this disparity, and the expiration of three months saw our forces swelled once more till they exceeded those of the enemy. The Nation, flung headlong to the earth, and temporarily paralyzed by her fall, rose at length with a truer appreciation of the power, the purpose, and the venom of her foes, and a firmer resolve that they should be grappled with and overcome.

XXXIV.

THE EXTRA SESSION.

The XXXVIIth Congress convened, pursuant to the President's summons, in Extra Session, at noon on the 4th of July; when, on a call of the roll, an ample quorum of either House was found in attendance, including full delegations from Kentucky,[1] Missouri,[2] Maryland,[3] and Delaware.[4] Tennessee had not yet chosen Representatives; and, when she did choose, at her regular State election, five weeks later, only the three districts east of the mountains elected members to the Union Congress; and, of these, one—Thomas A. R. Nelson—being arrested by the Rebels while on his way to Washington, regained his liberty by renouncing the Union and professing adherence to the Rebellion. Of the seceded States, only Arkansas chose Representatives to Congress in 1860; and these renounced their seats by open and active adhesion to the Southern Confederacy. In the Senate, the four States first named were fully represented; while Andrew Johnson was present from Tennessee, making 44 in all. Western Virginia had chosen three members at the regular State election in April, while another had been elected by a light vote, either then or subsequently, from the district lying along the Potomac, above and below Harper's Ferry. Of Representatives, 157 in all answered to their names at the first call. Galusha A. Grow [Republican], of Pennsylvania, was chosen Speaker, and Emerson Etheridge [Bell-Everett], of Tennessee, Clerk of the House. John W. Forney [Douglas], of Pennsylvania, was soon afterward elected Clerk of the Senate.

President Lincoln's Message was transmitted to both Houses on the following day. It was largely devoted to a recital of occurrences already narrated. It did not distinctly avow that the Government had ever

[1] The Representatives from Kentucky had been chosen a few weeks before at a special election, wherein nine districts elected 'conservative' or pro-Slavery Unionists, while the 1st reëlected, by a considerable majority, Henry C. Burnett, a Secessionist, who only served through the Extra Session, and then fled to participate openly in the Rebellion. The only remaining district seriously contested was the 8th (Fayette, Bourbon, etc.), which elected John J. Crittenden (Union) over William E. Simms (late Democrat, now Secessionist), by 8,272 to 5,706. The aggregate vote of the State showed a preponderance of more than two to one for the Union.

[2] The members from this State had been chosen in August, 1860: five of them as Democrats; one (Francis P. Blair,) as a Republican; another (James S. Rollins) as a Bell-Everett Unionist. One of the Democrats had already gone over to the Rebellion, as two more of them did afterward.

[3] Maryland had very recently chosen her Representatives at a special election, wherein each district elected a professed Unionist—the 6th (south-western) by barely 162 majority. But Henry May, elected as a Democrat over Winter Davis in the Baltimore city district, by 8,424 votes to 6,214, received the unanimous and ardent support of the Secessionists, and, as afterward appeared, for very good reasons.

[4] Delaware had elected George P. Fisher (Unionist), in 1860, by the combined vote of the Lincoln and Bell parties—giving him 257 majority over Biggs (Breckinridge); while Reed (Douglas) drew away 761 votes.

purposed the evacuation of Fort Sumter, but set forth the material facts as follows:

"On the 5th of March (the present incumbent's first full day in office), a letter of Major Anderson, commanding at Fort Sumter, written on the 28th of February, and received at the War Department on the 4th of March, was, by that Department, placed in his hands. This letter expressed the professional opinion of the writer, that reënforcements could not be thrown into that fort within the time for his relief rendered necessary by the limited supply of provisions, and with a view of holding possession of the same, with a force of less than twenty thousand good and well-disciplined men. This opinion was concurred in by all the officers of his command, and their *memoranda* on the subject were made inclosures of Major Anderson's letter. The whole was immediately laid before Lieut.-Gen. Scott, who at once concurred with Major Anderson in opinion. On reflection, however, he took full time, consulting with other officers, both of the Army and of the Navy, and, at the end of four days, came reluctantly but decidedly to the same conclusion as before. He also stated, at the same time, that no such sufficient force was then at the control of the Government, or could be raised and brought to the ground within the time when the provisions in the fort would be exhausted. In a purely military point of view, this reduced the duty of the Administration in the case to the mere matter of *getting the garrison safely out of the fort.*"

Thus baffled with regard to Fort Sumter, the Administration had resolved to reënforce and provision Fort Pickens, Fla., simply as an indication of its purpose to maintain, in the South, the constitutional rights of the Government; and had dispatched the steamship Brooklyn to Pensacola for that purpose; but had been defeated in its effort, because

"the officer commanding the Sabine, to which vessel the troops had been transferred from the Brooklyn, acting upon some *quasi* armistice of the late Administration (and of the existence of which the present Administration, up to the time the order was dispatched, had only too vague and uncertain rumors to fix attention), had refused to land the troops."

The news of this failure reached Washington "just one week before the fall of Sumter;" and thereupon the President proceeded at once to notify Gov. Pickens, of South Carolina, that he should provision Fort Sumter. "Whereupon, the fort was attacked and bombarded to its fall, without even awaiting the arrival of the provisioning expedition."

The President sets forth the course with regard to the seceded States which he had endeavored to pursue, until forced to abandon it by violence and bloodshed on their part, as follows:

"The policy chosen looked to the exhaustion of all peaceful measures before a resort to any stronger ones. It sought only to hold the public places and property not already wrested from the Government, and to collect the revenue; relying for the rest on time, discussion, and the ballot-box. It promised a continuance of the mails, at Government expense, to the very people who were resisting the Government; and it gave repeated pledges against any disturbance to any of the people, or any of their rights. Of all that which a President might constitutionally and justifiably do in such a case, everything was forborne, without which it was believed possible to keep the Government on foot."

But this policy it was neither the interest nor the disposition of the Confederates, as such, to acquiesce in. The naked fact that it was deemed advisable on the part of the Union, raises the presumption that it would not answer the ends of the Secessionists. Says the President:

"They have forced upon the country the distinct issue: 'immediate dissolution or blood.'

"And this issue embraces more than the fate of these United States. It presents to the whole family of man the question, whether a constitutional republic or democracy—a government of the people by the same people—can or cannot maintain its territorial integrity against its own domestic foes. It presents the question, whether discontented individuals, too few in numbers to control administration, according to organic law, in any case, can always, upon the pretenses made in this case, or on any other pretenses, or arbitrarily, without any pretense, break up their government, and thus practically put an end to free government upon the earth. It forces us to ask: 'Is there in all republics this inherent and fatal weakness?' 'Must a government, of necessity, be too *strong* for the liberties of its own people, or too *weak* to maintain its own existence?'

"So viewing the issue, no choice was left but to call out the war power of the Government; and so, to resist force employed for its destruction by force employed for its preservation."

After a brief exposure of the deceit and violence which governed the issue of the pretended submission, in Virginia and other States, of the question of Secession to a vote of the people, after they had been bound hand and foot to the car of the Confederacy, Mr. Lincoln says:

"The people of Virginia have thus allowed this giant insurrection to make its nest within her borders; and this Government has no choice left but to deal with it where it finds it. And it has the less regret, as the loyal citizens have, in due form, claimed its protection. Those loyal citizens this Government is bound to recognize and protect, *as being Virginia.*"

With regard to the self-styled neutrality of Kentucky, as of other States which had, by this time, passed out of that chrysalis condition into open rebellion, the President forcibly says:

"In the Border States, so called—in fact, the Middle States—there are those who favor a policy which they call 'armed neutrality;' that is, an arming of these States to prevent the Union forces passing one way, or the Disunion the other, over their soil. This would be disunion completed. Figuratively speaking, it would be building an impassable wall along the line of separation—and yet, not quite an impassable one; for, under the guise of neutrality, it would tie the hands of the Union men, and freely pass supplies from among them to the insurrectionists, which it could not do as an open enemy. At a stroke, it would take all the trouble off the hands of Secession, except only what proceeds from the external blockade. It would do for the Disunionists that which, of all things, they most desire—feed them well, and give them disunion without a struggle of their own. It recognizes no fidelity to the Constitution, no obligation to maintain the Union; and, while very many who favored it are, doubtless, loyal citizens, it is, nevertheless, very injurious in effect."

As to the work directly in hand, the President thus briefly proclaims:

"It is now recommended that you give the legal means for making this contest a short and decisive one; that you place at the control of the Government, for the work, at least four hundred thousand men and $400,000,000. That number of men is about one-tenth of those of proper ages within the regions where, apparently, *all* are willing to engage; and the sum is less than a twenty-third part of the money value owned by the men who seem ready to devote the whole. A debt of $600,000,000 *now* is a less sum per head than was the debt of our Revolution when we came out of that struggle; and the money value in the country now bears even a greater proportion to what it was *then* than does the population. Surely, each man has as strong a motive *now* to *preserve* our liberties as each had then to *establish* them.

"A right result, at this time, will be worth more to the world than ten times the men and ten times the money."

The cool assumptions and fluent sophistries of the Confederates, with regard to State Rights, are very frankly and thoroughly handled by the President; but those who are familiar with the teachings of Webster and Jackson on this subject can need no further argument. Mr. Lincoln thus deals with the fiction of 'State Sovereignty:'

"The States have their *status* IN the Union; and they have *no other* legal *status.* If they break from this, they can only do so against law and by revolution. The Union, and not themselves separately, procured their independence and their liberty. By conquest or purchase, the Union gave each of them whatever of independence and liberty it has. The Union is older than any of the States, and, in fact, it created them *as* States. Originally, some independent colonies made the Union; and, in turn, the Union threw off their old dependence for them and made them States, such as they are. Not one of them ever had a State constitution independent of the Union."

As to the proper division, or partition, of powers between the Federal and the State governments, he says:

"Whatever concerns the whole should be confided to the whole—to the General Government; while whatever concerns *only* the State should be left exclusively *to* the State. This is all there is of original principle about it. Whether the National Constitution, in defining boundaries between the two, has applied the principle with exact accuracy, is not to be questioned. We are all bound by that defining, without question."

As to the abstract justice and rightfulness of Secession, he says:

"What is now combated is the principle that Secession is *consistent* with the Constitution—is *lawful* and *peaceful*. It is not contended that there is any express law for it; and nothing should ever be implied as law which leads to unjust or absurd consequences. The nation purchased, with money, the countries out of which several of these States were formed. Is it just that they shall go off without leave, and without refunding? The nation paid very large sums (in the aggregate, I believe, nearly a hundred millions) to relieve Florida of the aboriginal tribes. Is it just that she shall now be off without consent, or without making any return? The nation is now in debt for money applied to the benefit of these so-called seceding States, in common with the rest. Is it just, either that creditors shall go unpaid, or the remaining States pay the whole? A part of the present National debt was contracted to pay the old debts of Texas. Is it just that she shall leave, and pay no part of this herself?

"Again: If one State may secede, so may another; and when all shall have seceded, none is left to pay the debts. Is this quite just to creditors? Did we notify them of this sage view of ours when we borrowed their money? If we now recognize this doctrine, by allowing the seceders to go in peace, it is difficult to see what we can do if others choose to go, or to extort terms upon which they will promise to remain."

The following illustration of the essential unreasonableness of Secession is ingenious and striking:

"If all the States, save one, should assert the power to *drive* that one out of the Union, it is presumed the whole class of seceder politicians would at once deny the power, and denounce the act as the greatest outrage upon State Rights. But suppose that precisely the same act, instead of being called 'driving the one out,' should be called 'the seceding of the others from that one:' it would be exactly what the seceders claim to do; unless, indeed, they make the point, that the one, because it is a minority, may rightfully do what the others, because they are a majority, may *not* rightfully do."

No mention of Slavery as the grand, inciting cause of the Rebellion occurs in this Message; yet there is significance in the fact, stated by the President, that, while all the Free States had been, beyond exception, firm, hearty, and zealous in responding to his calls for troops:

"None of the States commonly called Slave States, except Delaware, gave a regiment through regular State organization. A few regiments have been organized within some others of those States, by individual enterprise, and received into the Government service."

But that this is essentially a contest between aristocratic assumption and popular liberty the President perceives, and does not hesitate to declare. He says:

"Our adversaries have adopted some declarations of independence, in which, unlike the good old one penned by Jefferson, they omit the words 'all men are created equal.' Why? They have adopted a temporary National Constitution, in the preamble of which, unlike our good old one signed by Washington, they omit, 'We, the people,' and substitute 'We, the deputies of the sovereign and independent States.' *Why?* Why this deliberate pressing out of view the rights of men and the authority of the people?

"This is essentially a people's contest. On the side of the Union, it is a struggle for maintaining in the world that form and substance of government whose leading object is to elevate the condition of men—to lift artificial weights from all shoulders—to clear the paths of laudable pursuit for all—to afford all an unfettered start and a fair chance in the race of life. Yielding to partial and temporary departures, from necessity, this is the leading object of the Government for whose existence we contend.

"I am most happy to believe that the plain people understand and appreciate this. It is worthy of note that while, in this the Government's hour of trial, large numbers of those in the Army and Navy who have been favored with the offices have resigned, and proved false to the hand that pampered them, not one common soldier or common sailor is known to have deserted his flag.

"Great honor is due to those officers who remained true, despite the example of their treacherous associates; but the greatest honor, and most important fact of all, is the unanimous firmness of the common soldiers and common sailors. To the last man, so far as known, they have successfully resisted the traitorous efforts of those whose commands, but an hour before, they obeyed as absolute law. This is the patriotic instinct of plain people. They understand, without an argument, that the destroying the Government which was made by Washington means no good to *them*.

"Our popular government has often been called an experiment. Two points in it our people have already settled: the successful *establishing* and the successful *administering* of it. One still remains: its successful *maintenance* against a formidable internal attempt to overthrow it. It is now for them to demonstrate to the world that those who can fairly carry an election can also suppress a rebellion; that ballots are the rightful and peaceful successors of bullets; and that, when ballots have fairly and constitutionally decided, there can be no successful appeal back to bullets; that there can be no successful appeal except to ballots themselves, at succeeding elections. Such will be a great lesson of peace; teaching men that what they cannot take by an election, neither can they take by a war—teaching all the folly of being the beginners of a war."

He concludes his Message with these impressive and memorable words:

"It was with the deepest regret that the Executive found the duty of employing the war power, in defense of the Government, forced upon him. He could but perform this duty, or surrender the existence of the Government. No compromise by public servants could, in this case, be a cure; not that compromises are not often proper, but that no popular government can long survive a marked precedent, that those who carry an election can only save the Government from immediate destruction by giving up the main point upon which the people gave the election. The people themselves, and not their servants, can safely reverse their own deliberate decisions.

"As a private citizen, the Executive could not have consented that these institutions shall perish; much less could he, in betrayal of so vast and so sacred a trust as these free people had confided to him. He felt that he had no moral right to shrink, not even to count the chances of his own life, in what might follow. In full view of his great responsibility, he has, so far, done what he has deemed his duty. You will now, according to your own judgment, perform yours. He sincerely hopes that your views and your action may so accord with his as to assure all faithful citizens who have been disturbed in their rights, of a certain and speedy restoration to them, under the Constitution and the laws.

"And, having thus chosen our course, without guile and with pure purpose, let us renew our trust in God, and go forward without fear and with manly hearts."

Several of the opening days of the Session were mainly devoted by the House to the consideration of disputed claims to seats—there being rival claimants from Oregon, from Nebraska, and from the Ist district of Pennsylvania, beside three members in all from Virginia, whereof two (Messrs. Carlile and Whaley) were chosen from Western districts, by heavy votes, on the regular day of election; while the other (Mr. Upton) was chosen under different auspices. The Convention which passed the Ordinance of Secession had assumed power to annul or suspend the law which provides that a regular election shall be held, and Members of Congress semi-annually chosen thereat, on the fourth Thursday of May; but the people of West Virginia had treated this action of the Convention as a nullity, not having been ratified by a popular vote, as the law calling the Convention required; and had elected in its despite. Congress approved and sustained this action, and Messrs. Carlile and Whaley held their seats with very little dissent. There was more demur as to Mr. Upton's case—his poll being light, the time and manner of his election irregular, and he having voted in Ohio the preceding November; but he was not unseated. The remaining contests involved no question connected with Slavery or secession. On the 8th, the House, on motion of Mr. Holman (Dem.), of Ind., modified at the suggestion of Mr. Hickman (Republican), of Pa.,

"*Resolved*, That the House, during the present extraordinary session, will only consider bills and resolutions concerning the military and naval operations of the Government, and the financial affairs therewith connected, and the general questions of a judicial character; and all bills and resolutions of a private character, and all other bills and resolutions not directly connected with the raising of revenue, or affecting the military or naval affairs of the Government, shall be referred to the appropriate Committees without debate, to be considered at the next regular session of Congress."

On the 9th, Mr. Lovejoy, of Ill., moved the following:

"*Resolved*, That, in the judgment of this House, it is no part of the duty of the soldiers of the United States to capture and return fugitive slaves."

After a strenuous effort to rule this out of order, as precluded by the resolve before quoted, a vote was taken on a motion of Mr. Mallory, of Ky., that it do lie on the table; which was negatived: Yeas 66; Nays 81. Mr. Lovejoy's resolve was then adopted: Yeas 92; Nays 55; [the Yeas all Republicans; Nays, all the Democrat and Border-State conservatives, with Messrs. Sheffield, of R. I., Fenton, of N. Y., Horton, of Ohio, Wm. Kellogg, of Ill., Nixon, of N. J., and Woodruff, of Conn.]

On the 10th, Mr. Clark, of N. H., proposed, and on the 11th the Senate adopted, the following:

"*Whereas*, a conspiracy has been formed against the peace, union, and liberties of the People and Government of the United States; and, in furtherance of such conspiracy, a portion of the people of the States of Virginia, North Carolina, South Carolina, Tennessee, Arkansas, and Texas, have attempted to withdraw those States from the Union, and are now in arms against the Government; *And whereas*, James M. Mason and Robert M. T. Hunter, Senators from Virginia; Thomas L. Clingman and Thomas Bragg, Senators from North Carolina; James Chesnut, Jr., a Senator from South Carolina; A. O. P. Nicholson, a Senator from Tennessee; William K. Sebastian and Charles B. Mitchell, Senators from Arkansas; and John Hemphill and Louis T. Wigfall, Senators from Texas, have failed to appear in their seats in the Senate, and to aid the Government in this important crisis; and it is apparent to the Senate that said Senators are engaged in said conspiracy for the destruction of the Union and Government, or, with full knowledge of such conspiracy, have failed to advise the Government of its progress, or aid in its suppression: Therefore,

"*Resolved*, That the said Mason, Hunter, Clingman, Bragg, Chesnut, Nicholson, Sebastian, Mitchell, Hemphill, and Wigfall, be, and they hereby are, each and all of them, expelled from the Senate of the United States."

Messrs. Bayard, of Del., and Latham, of Cal., sought to have this so modified as merely to declare the seats of the indicated Senators vacant and strike their names from the roll; but the Senate rejected the amendment (Yeas 11; Nays 32) and passed the original resolve: Yeas 31 Republicans and McDougall, of Cal.,—in all, 32;

NAYS — Messrs. Bayard, Breckinridge, Bright, Johnson, of Mo., Johnson, of Tenn., Latham, Nesmith, Polk, Powell, and Rice—10.

The Vice-President thereupon declared the resolve adopted by a two-thirds vote.

On the 10th, a bill reported from the Committee of Commerce, by Mr. Washburne, of Ill., providing for the collection of revenue from imports—adapting our revenue laws to the state of facts created by a formidable rebellion—authorizing the President to designate other places as ports of delivery instead of those held by Rebels—also, to close, by proclamation, ports so held—to prohibit all intercourse between loyal and insurgent districts, etc. etc.—was passed, under the Previous Question—Yeas 136;

NAYS—Messrs. Burnett, (Ky.,) Harding, (Ky.,) Norton, (Mo.,) George H. Pendleton, (Ohio,) Reid, (Mo.,) Robinson, (Ill.,) Vallandigham, (Ohio,) Voorhees, (Ind.,) Wadsworth, (Ky.,) and Wood, (N. Y.)—10.

This bill came up in the Senate, on the 12th; and, after a brief debate, was passed: Yeas 36;

NAYS—Messrs. Breckinridge, (Ky.,) Bright, (Ind.,) Johnson, (Mo.,) Kennedy, (Md.,) Polk, (Mo.,) and Powell, (Ky.)—6.

The House, on the 10th, likewise passed its first Loan bill—authorizing the Secretary of the Treasury to borrow Two Hundred and Fifty Millions of Dollars, for the support of the Government and the prosecution of the War. Mr. Vallandigham, of Ohio, made an elaborate speech, in thorough-going opposition to the bill and to the entire policy of 'coërcion;' submitting, in reply to a question from Mr. Holman (Dem.), of Ind., the following proposition, as embodying his views touching the general subject, but asking no present action thereon:

"*Resolved*, That the Federal Government is the agent of the people of the several States composing the Union; that it consists of three distinct departments—the legislative, the executive, and the judicial—each equally a part of the Government, and equally entitled to the confidence and support of the States and the people; and that it is the duty of every patriot to sustain the several departments of the Government in the exercise of all the constitutional powers of each which may be necessary and proper for the preservation of the Government in its principles and in its vigor and integrity, and to stand by and to defend to the utmost the flag which represents the Government, the Union, and the country."

MR. HOLMAN. "While the gentleman censures the Administration, let me ask him whether, with his own constituents, he is resolved that the Union shall be maintained.

MR. VALLANDIGHAM. "My votes shall speak for me on that subject. My position is defined in the resolution just read. I am answerable only to my conscience and to my constituents, and not to the gentleman from Indiana."

The bill passed under the previous question: Yeas 150;

NAYS—Messrs. Burnett, of Ky., Norton and Reid, of Mo., Vallandigham, of Ohio, and B. Wood, of N. Y. [The three first-named went over to the Rebels soon after the close of the session.]

On the 11th, the Army Appropriation bill being under consideration in Committee of the Whole, Mr. Vallandigham moved to add this proviso:

"*Provided, however*, That no part of the money hereby appropriated shall be employed in subjugating, or holding as a conquered province, any sovereign State now or lately one of the United States; nor in abolishing or interfering with African Slavery in any of the States."

The proviso was voted down, and the bill (appropriating $161,000,000) reported and passed.

On the 13th, the bill calling out Half a Million Volunteers being under consideration, Mr. Vallandigham moved to add to it (as he had already done in Committee of the Whole) the following:

"*Provided further*, That, before the President shall have the right to call out any more volunteers than are now in the service, he shall appoint seven Commissioners, whose mission it shall be to accompany the army on its march, to receive and consider such propositions, if any, as may at any time be submitted by the Executive of the so-called Confederate States, or of any one of them, looking to a suspension of hostilities, and the return of said States, or any of them, to the Union, or to obedience to the Federal Constitution and authorities."

The amendment was voted down without a division, and the bill passed.

This day, Messrs. John S. Carlile and Waitman T. Willey presented themselves as Senators from the State of Virginia (not the new State of *West* Virginia, since organized), vice Hunter and Mason, expelled as traitors. They presented credentials, setting forth their appointment by Gov.

Pierpont to fill the existing vacancies. Messrs. Bayard and Saulsbury, of Del., strenuously resisted their admission—the former wishing their credentials referred to the Committee on the Judiciary. Mr. Powell, of Ky., also opposed their acceptance as Senators; which was advocated by Messrs. Andrew Johnson, of Tenn., Latham, of Cal., Trumbull, of Ill., Collamer, of Vt., and Ten Eyck, of N. J. Mr. Bayard's motion to refer was voted down: Yeas—Messrs. Bayard, Bright, Polk, Powell, and Saulsbury; Nays 35: And Messrs. Carlile and Willey were then sworn in and took their seats.

On motion of Mr. F. P. Blair, the House this day expelled John B. Clark, a member-elect from Missouri (but who had not taken his seat), because he had

"taken up arms against the Government of the United States, and now holds a commission in what is called the State Guard of Missouri, under the Rebel Government of that State, and took part in the engagement at Booneville against the United States forces."

This was adopted (after an attempt to send it to the Committee of Elections), by Yeas 94 to Nays 45, (nearly, but not entirely, a party vote).

On the 15th, Mr. B. Wood, of N. Y., moved that it be

"*Resolved*, That this Congress recommend the Governors of the several States to convene their Legislatures, for the purpose of calling an election to select two delegates from each congressional district, to meet in general Convention at Louisville, in Kentucky, on the first Monday in September next: the purpose of the said Convention to be to devise measures for the restoration of peace to the country."

On motion of Mr. Washburne, of Ill., this was laid on the table: Yeas 92; Nays 51.

Mr. Wm. Allen (Dem.), of Ohio, moved that it be

"*Resolved*, That, whenever the States now in rebellion against the General Government shall cease their rebellion and become loyal to the Union, it is the duty of the Government to suspend the further prosecution of the present war.

"*Resolved*, That it is no part of the object of the present war against the rebellious States to interfere with the institution of Slavery therein."

This was ruled out of order without dissent.

Mr. Vallandigham here moved a long series of resolves, condemning as unconstitutional the increase of the Army, the blockade of the ports of the insurgent States, the seizure of dispatches in the telegraph offices, the arbitrary arrest of persons suspected of complicity with treason, and nearly every important act of the President in resistance to the Rebellion. On motion of Mr. Lovejoy, of Ill., these resolves were unceremoniously laid on the table.

A bill, introduced by Mr. Hickman, of Pa., defining and punishing conspiracies against the United States—providing that persons who conspire to overthrow, put down, or destroy by force, the government of the United States, or to levy war against the same, may be arraigned for trial before any U. S. district or circuit court, and, on due conviction, may be punished by fine not exceeding $5,000, or by imprisonment for not more than six years, was now called up and passed: Yeas 123; Nays 7. Most of the Nays were opposed not to the bill, but to the precipitancy of its passage. The Senate concurred, a few days thereafter, and the bill became a law.

Mr. McClernand (Dem.), of Ill., moved, and the House, by 121 to 5, voted, that

"*Whereas*, a portion of the people of the

United States, in violation of their Constitutional obligations, have taken up arms against the National Government, and are now striving, by aggressive and iniquitous war, to overthrow it, and break up the Union of these States: Therefore,

"*Resolved*, That this House hereby pledges itself to vote for any amount of money and any number of men which may be necessary to insure a speedy and effectual suppression of such Rebellion, and the permanent restoration of the Federal authority everywhere within the limits and jurisdiction of the United States."

NAYS—Messrs. Burnett, Grider, (Ky.,) Norton, Reid, and Wood—5.

Mr. Potter, of Wisc., offered the following, which was adopted:

"*Resolved*, That the Committee on the Judiciary be directed to inquire whether Hon. Henry May, a Representative in Congress from the fourth district of the State of Maryland, has not been found holding criminal intercourse and correspondence with persons in armed rebellion against the Government of the United States, and to make report to the House as to what action should be taken in the premises; and that said Committee have power to send for persons and papers, and to examine witnesses on oath or affirmation; and that said Hon. Henry May be notified of the passage of this resolution, if practicable, before action thereon by the Committee."

Mr. May, being ill, was not then in his seat; but, the Committee having reported, on the 18th, that no evidence had been presented to them tending to inculpate Mr. May, he took the floor, and made what he termed a personal explanation, avowing that he had been to Richmond on an errand of conciliation and peace, evincing intense hostility to the Administration and the War on its part, and very thorough sympathy, at least, with the Baltimore friends of the Rebels. He said:

"At the time I received notice of this accusation, it was under my consideration whether I could, with honor, come here, and enter upon the duties of a Representative upon this floor. The humiliation that I felt at the condition of my constituents, bound in chains; absolutely without the rights of a free people in this land; every precious right belonging to them, under the Constitution, prostrated and trampled in the dust; military arrests in the dead hour of the night; dragging the most honorable and virtuous citizens from their beds, and confining them in forts; searches and seizures the most rigorous and unwarrantable, without pretext of justification; that precious and priceless writ of *habeas corpus*, for which, from the beginning of free government, the greatest and best of men have lived and died—all these prostrated in the dust; and hopeless imprisonment inflicted without accusation, without inquiry or investigation, or the prospect of a trial—Sir, is there a representative of the people of the United States here in this body, acknowledging the sympathy due to popular rights and constitutional liberty, who does not feel indignant at the perpetration of these outrages?"

With regard to his permission to visit Richmond, he said:

"I did not feel at liberty to go across the Potomac without permission of the authorities of this Government. And so, I felt it my duty to wait on the Chief Magistrate, and tell him, as I did, most frankly and fully, the objects of my visit. I did not ask for his sanction; I did not desire it. I did not wish to embarrass the Chief Magistrate in such a way. I had no claim upon his confidence; I had no right to ask him for any commission or authority; but I felt it was my duty to state to him distinctly the objects which governed me, and obtain his permission to cross the Potomac. It was most distinctly understood, between the President and me, that I took *no* authority from him—none whatever; that I asked for none, and disclaimed asking for any; that I went on the most private mission on which a humble citizen could go. I asked his consent, also, to obtain from the military authorities a pass. Having jurisdiction on the other side of the Potamac, they were to be consulted, and the necessary formalities observed. The President authorized me to say to Gen. Scott that I had conversed with him, and that, while he gave no sanction whatever to my visit to Richmond, he did not object to my going there on my own responsibility."

Mr. May carefully avoided all disclosure of the purport of his conferences with the Rebel chiefs at Richmond; but it was manifest that he visited and was received by them as a sympathizing friend, and that his communications were not intended to discourage them in their efforts. The conclusion is irresistible, that he went to Richmond hoping to elicit from the Confederate chiefs some proffer, overture, or assent, looking to reünion on their own terms, but had been utterly disappointed and rebuffed. He closed as follows:

"Mr. Speaker, all the crime, all the treason of this act, rests on me, and me alone; and I am content, in the sight of high Heaven, to take it and press it to my heart."

Mr. Francis Thomas, of Maryland, replied ably and thoroughly to Mr. May's assaults on the Administration and its policy of 'coërcion;' pointing to the recent vote of the People of Maryland (44,000 "Union" to 24,000 "Peace") as their verdict on the issues whereon the President was arraigned by his colleague. He said:

"The apportionment of representatives in the Legislature was made in old colonial times. It has been modified; but, up to this day and hour, the majority of the people of Maryland have no voice in the choice of their Legislature. Under our new Constitution, however, the majority, by a general ticket, elect a Governor; and, at the last election, they elected one responsive to the sentiment that beats warmly in the hearts of the people of Maryland. But the Legislature of Maryland, elected two years ago, not with a view to this issue, have been engaged in embarrassing the Governor in all his measures of policy. One of those measures, which Gov. Hicks thought a very prudent measure under the existing state of things in Maryland, was to collect the arms held by private citizens, without distinction of party. This the Legislature prevented from being carried into execution, and passed a law which goes very far to secure arms in the hands of individuals. Why? If the citizens of Maryland are for warring against the Government, they should not be permitted to have arms. If they are for peace, they do not need them; for the arm of the United States protects them, and the banner of the confederacy floats over them. Why, then, have the Legislature interposed obstructions, by law, to the collection of arms? Do they think it prudent to leave them in the hands of private holders, to be concealed where they cannot be found? It could not be for the purpose of upholding the laws of the Union. It could not be to uphold the statutes of Maryland. The President of the United States is faithful to his duty; and the people of Maryland are faithful to theirs."

The bill providing for the reörganization of the Army being this day before the Senate, Mr. Powell, of Kentucky, proposed to add to it the following:

"*And be it further enacted*, That no part of the Army or Navy of the United States shall be employed or used in subjecting or holding as a conquered province any sovereign State now or lately one of the United States."

Mr. J. H. Lane, of Kansas, moved to amend this, by adding,

"Unless a military necessity shall exist in enforcing the laws and maintaining the Constitution of the Union."

A very able and earnest debate arose hereon, wherein Messrs. Powell, Polk, and Bright, on the one hand, and Messrs. Sherman, of Ohio, Browning, of Illinois, Lane, of Kansas, Fessenden, of Maine, etc., on the other, took part. Mr. Lane's amendment was rejected by Yeas 11 (all Republicans) to

NAYS—Messrs. Breckinridge, Bright, Browning, Carlile, Doolittle, Fessenden, Foster, Grimes, Hale, Harris, Howe, Johnson, of Tenn., Johnson, of Mo., Kennedy, Latham, McDougall, Morrill, Nesmith, Polk, Powell, Saulsbury, Sherman, Ten Eyck, and Willey—24.

Mr. Sherman, of Ohio, now moved the following as a substitute for Mr. Powell's proposition:

"*And be it further enacted*, That the purposes of the military establishment provided for in this act are to preserve the Union, to defend the property, and to maintain the constitutional authority, of the Government."

This was adopted, after debate; Yeas 33; Nays 4. [Breckinridge and Powell, of Ky., Johnson and Polk, of Missouri.]

As Mr. Powell's amendment was thus superseded, Mr. Breckinridge now moved the following, as an addition to the amendment just adopted:

"But the Army and Navy shall not be employed for the purpose of subjugating any State, or reducing it to the condition of a Territory or province, or to abolish Slavery therein."

This was rejected by the following vote:

YEAS—Messrs. Breckinridge, Bright, W. P. Johnson, of Mo., Kennedy, Latham, Nesmith, Polk, Powell, and Saulsbury—9.

NAYS—Messrs. Anthony, Bingham, Browning, Carlile, Chandler, Clark, Collamer, Cowan, Doolittle, Fessenden, Foot, Foster, Grimes, Hale, Harlan, Harris, Howe, Johnson, of Tenn., King, Lane, of Ind., Lane, of Kansas, McDougall, Morrill, Pomeroy, Sherman, Sumner, Ten Eyck, Wade, Willey, and Wilson—30.

The original amendment was then rejected, so as to strike out all these declaratory propositions, and leave the bill as it came from the Committee of the Whole; when it was engrossed, read a third time, and passed.

Bearing in mind that this debate occurred three days before the battle of Bull Run, that it was initiated by a pro-Slavery Democrat from Kentucky, and that it occurred when loyal men still generally and confidently expected that the Rebellion would soon be suppressed, leaving Slavery intact, it may be well to note some of the significant intimations which it elicited from the more conservative Republicans; as follows:

MR. DIXON (of Conn.) "Mr. President, the Senator from Kentucky [Mr. Powell] has alluded to remarks of mine, and has said that I have declared on this floor, that, if it were necessary to abolish Slavery in order to save the Union, Slavery should be abolished. Mr. President, I have said no such thing. What I said was this: that, if the war should be persisted in, and be long protracted, on the part of the South, and, in the course of its progress, it should turn out that either this Government or Slavery must be destroyed, then the people of the North—the *conservative* people of the North—would say, 'Rather than let the Government perish, let Slavery perish.' That is what I said; and I say it now, and shall continue at all times to say the same; not, by any means, as a threat, but as a warning and an admonition."

MR. BROWNING (of Ill.) "Mr. President, I cannot say, in common with the Senator from Virginia [Mr. Carlile], that I regret that this amendment has been proposed to the Senate. I shall certainly vote against it; it does not meet my views, nor receive my approbation; but it may still be well that it has been offered; as it affords us an opportunity of comparing notes, understanding the opinions of each other, and giving the country at large a distinct understanding of what the purpose and intentions of the Congress of the United States are. I speak only for one; I intend to speak very briefly, but very plainly, my sentiments on this subject.

"I differ, furthermore, from the Senator from Virginia, in the supposition that the institution of Slavery has had nothing to do in involving the country in the calamities which now press upon it. Had it not been for the sentiments and opinions which are engendered, fostered, and cherished by the institution of Slavery, I cannot persuade myself to believe that there ever would have been found a disloyal heart to the American Constitution upon the American continent. I believe that the whole trouble has grown out of the institution of Slavery, and its presence among us; and (as I remarked) the sentiments and opinions which it necessarily engenders, fosters, and cherishes. The war, it is true, is not a war for the extermination of Slavery. With the institution of Slavery where it exists, the General Government has nothing, as a Government, to do; nor has the General Government ever assumed the power of, in any shape or manner, controlling the institution of Slavery, or its management, in the States where it exists. The General Government has never been aggressive either upon the Slave States or upon the institution of Slavery. These troubles have all grown out of precisely the opposite—not the aggressions of the General Government, or of the Free States—but out of the aggressions of Slavery itself, and its continual struggles for expansion and extension to countries where it had no right to go, and where our fathers never intended it should go. If Slavery had been content to remain where the Constitution placed it—if it had been content with the privileges and immunities which the Constitution guaranteed to it—the Free States and the Slave States of this Union could have lived together in a perpetual bond of fraternity.

"Mr. President, History gives no instance, in my judgment, of such long-suffering and forbearance as there has been, not by the people of the Slave States, but as there has been exhibited by the people of the Free

States of this Union, in the endurance of outrages, wrongs, and oppressions, that they have suffered at the hands of that institution, and those who maintain the institution, and have suffered from their strong and enduring devotion to the General Government—to the institutions that our fathers achieved for us, and transmitted to us. I think I should not be at all mistaken in asserting that, for every slave that has ever been seduced from the service of his owner, by the interference of citizens of the Free States with the institution where it exists, more than ten free white men of the Free States of this Union have been outraged—every privilege of freedom trodden upon—every right of person violated—by lawless mobs in the Slave States. We have borne all this uncomplainingly; we have borne it without a murmur, because we were willing to bear it—willing to make the sacrifice, for the sake of the glorious institutions that were the common property and common blessing of us all.

"Mr. President, we have not invited this war: the people of the loyal States of the Union are in no degree responsible for the calamities that are now upon the country: we gave no occasion for them. There is, in the history of man, no instance of so stupendous a conspiracy, so atrocious a treason, so causeless a rebellion, as that which now exists in this country; and for what purpose? What wrong had we ever done to the Slave States, or to the institution of Slavery? I have heard, in all the assaults that have been made on this Administration, no single specification of one injustice that they had ever suffered at the hands of the General Government, or at the hands of the Free States, or of the people of the Free States.

"Mr. President, I am not prepared to admit, either—as some gentlemen take pains to explain—that this is not a war of subjugation. If it is not a war of subjugation, what is it? What was it set on foot for, if it is not for the sole, identical purpose of subjugating the atrocious Rebellion that exists in the country?"

Mr. SHERMAN. "My friend will allow me?"

Mr. BROWNING. "Certainly."

Mr. SHERMAN. "My friend misunderstood my language. I said distinctly that it was not the purpose of this war to subjugate a State, a political community; but I will go as far as he or any other living man to uphold the Government against all rebellious citizens, whether there be one or many of them in a State. If nine-tenths of the people of any State rebel against the authority of this Government, the physical power of this Government should be brought to reduce those citizens to subjection. The State survives; and, I have no doubt, the State of South Carolina, and the State of Florida, and the State of Virginia, will be represented on this floor long after the honorable Senator and I have filled the mission allotted to us."

Mr. BROWNING. "I trust so. I will not stop to deal with technicalities; I care not whether you call it the subjugation of the people or the subjugation of the State, where all the authorities of a State, where all the officers, who are the embodiment of the power of the State, who speak for the State, who represent the government of the State, where they are all disloyal and banded in treasonable confederation against this Government, I, for one, am for subjugating *them;* and you may call it the subjugation of the State, or of the people, just as you please. I want this Rebellion put down, this wicked and causeless treason punished, and an example given to the world that will teach them that there is a power in the freemen of this continent to maintain a constitutional government.

"Why, Mr. President, it is just a struggle to-day—the whole of this fight is about that, and nothing else—whether there shall be any longer any such thing as government on this continent or not; and the very moment that the doctrine of Secession, the very moment that the astounding heresy of Secession, is admitted, in any sense or in any degree, government is overthrown; because, if there be any such thing as a right existing in a State to secede at any time at her will—causelessly to dismember this Union and overthrow this Government—there is an end to all constitutions and all laws; and it is a struggle to-day for the life of the nation. *They* have assailed that life: *we* have not done it; and all that the Government has done, and all that the Administration proposes to do, is in necessary self-defense against assaults that are made upon the very life of the nation. * * * Now, Mr. President, one thing more. It is better that people everywhere should understand precisely what is going on, what has happened, and what is to happen. For one, I should rejoice to see all the States in rebellion return to their allegiance; and, if they return, if they lay down the arms of their rebellion, and come back to their duty and their obligations, they will be as fully protected now, and at all times hereafter, as they have ever been before, in all their rights, including the ownership, use, and management of slaves. Let them return to their allegiance; and I, for one, am now for giving to the Slave States as fully and completely all the protection of the Constitution and laws as they have ever enjoyed in any past hour of our existence.

"But, sir, let us understand another thing. As I have already said, the power to terminate this war now is not with us. The power is with us, but not to terminate it instantly. We will terminate it, if it is not terminated, as it should be, by those who began it. But, sir, I say, for one—I speak for myself, and myself only, but I believe, in so speaking, I utter the sentiments which will burst from every free heart in all the Northern States of the confederacy—that, if our brethren of the South *do* force upon us the distinct issue—'Shall this Government be overthrown, and it and all the hopes for civil liberty, all the hopes for the oppressed and down-trodden of all the despotisms of the earth, go down in one dark, dreary night of hopelessness and despair?'—if they force upon us the issue whether the Government shall go down, to maintain the institution of Slavery, or whether Slavery shall be obliterated, to sustain the Constitution and the Government for which our fathers fought and bled, and the principles that were cemented in their blood—I say, sir, when the issue comes, when they force it upon us, that one or the other is to be overthrown, then I am for the Government and against Slavery; and my voice and my vote shall be for sweeping the last vestige of barbarism from the face of the continent. I trust that necessity may not be forced on us; but, when *it is* forced upon us, let us meet it like men, and not shrink from the high and holy and sacred duties that are laid upon us, as the conservators not only of government, but as the conservators of the eternal principles of justice and freedom for the whole human family.

"It is better, Mr. President, that we should understand each other; and I repeat, in conclusion, that, when the issue comes—and *if* it comes—it comes because it is forced upon us; it comes upon us as a hard, unwelcome necessity—I trust we shall be found adequate to the emergency; I trust that our hearts will not fail us in the day of that terrible conflict—for it is *to be* a terrible one, if this war goes on. If rebellion does not recover of its madness—if American citizens will continue so infatuated as to prosecute still further this unnatural war against the best and most blessed Government that the world has ever known—this issue may be forced upon us. I say it is not true, as gentlemen have ventured to assert, that, if it were known by the people of the great Northwest that, in any possible contingency, this war might result in the overthrow and extermination of Slavery, they would no longer give their support to this Government. If it were known or believed by the people of the great Northwest that this Government should become so recreant to its duties as to shrink from meeting that great question, when forced upon us, in my opinion, they would descend in an avalanche upon this Capitol, and hurl us from the places we should be unworthy to fill.

"We do not desire this issue; we do not want this necessity; but we have no power to prevent it; and it is better that the people everywhere should understand that, if the necessity is forced upon us, our choice is promptly, instantly, manfully made, and made for all time—that we make the decision, and we will abide by the decision, to stand by the Government; and, if it does go down—if not only this nation, but the great brotherhood of mankind everywhere, is to witness that unspeakable and unheard of calamity of the overthrow of constitutional government here—let us go down in a manly effort to sustain and uphold it, and *to sweep away the causes that brought upon us all this trouble.*" * * * * * *

Mr. Carlile, of Va., having demurred to these views, Mr. Browning rejoined, as follows:

"If he understood me as announcing any wish or any intention that this war should be a war waged against Slavery, he totally misapprehended my meaning."

Mr. Carlile. "I did *not* so understand the Senator."

Mr. Browning. "For I took especial pains to say that I would rejoice to see this war terminated; and, if the institution still existed when it is terminated, I should be for giving it then, as we had always done heretofore, in the best faith in the world, every possible protection that the Constitution and laws intended it should have; but that, if the issue was forced upon us—as it might be—to make a choice between the Government, on the one side, and Slavery on the other, then I was for the Government."

Mr. Sherman, of Ohio. "I do not understand either the Senator from Kansas on my right, or the Senator from Connecticut, or the Senator from Kansas behind me, to say that it is the purpose of this war to abolish Slavery. It is not waged for any such purpose, or with any such view. They have all disclaimed it. Why, then, does the Senator [Mr. Powell] insist upon it? I will now say, and the Senator may make the most of it, that, rather than see one single foot of this country of ours torn from the national domain by traitors, I will myself see the slaves set free; but, at the same time, I utterly disclaim any purpose of that kind. If the men who are now waging war against the Government, fitting out pirates against our commerce, going back to the old mode of warfare of the middle ages, should prosecute this Rebellion to such an extent that there is no way of conquering South Carolina, for instance, except by emancipating her slaves, I say, Emancipate her slaves and conquer her rebellious citizens; and, if they have not people there enough to elect members of Congress and Senators, we will *send* people there. Let there be no misunderstanding my position; I wish it distinctly understood; but, at the same time, I utterly disclaim that it was any purpose, or idea, or object of this war to free the slaves. On the contrary, I am in favor of the Constitution as it is; I am in favor of giving the people—the loyal people—of the Southern States, every constitutional right that they now possess. I voted last Winter to change the Constitution for their benefit—to give them new guarantees, new conditions. I would not do that now; but I did last Winter. I will give them all the Constitution gives them, and no more."

Mr. John J. Crittenden, of Ky., on the 19th, submitted to the House the following:

"*Resolved by the House of Representatives of the Congress of the United States*, That the present deplorable civil war has been forced upon the country by the Disunionists of the Southern States now in revolt against the constitutional Government, and in arms around the capital; that, in this national emergency, Congress, banishing all feeling of mere passion or resentment, will recollect only its duty to the whole country; that this war is not waged, on our part, in any spirit of oppression, nor for any purpose of conquest or subjugation, nor purpose of overthrowing or interfering with the rights or established institutions of those States; but to defend and maintain the supremacy of the Constitution, and to preserve the Union, with all the dignity, equality, and rights, of the several States unimpaired; and, as soon as these objects are accomplished, the war ought to cease."

Mr. Stevens, of Pa., objecting,

The resolution could not be considered forthwith; but it was taken up on Monday, and, on motion of Mr. Burnett, of Ky., divided—the vote being first taken on so much of the resolution as precedes and includes the word "capital," which was adopted by Yeas 121; Nays—Messrs. Burnett and Reid—(Rebels:) when the remainder was likewise adopted: Yeas 117; Nays—Messrs. Potter, of Wis., and Riddle, of Ohio—(Republicans.) Mr. Burnett declined to vote.

It is worthy of record that on this sad day, while Washington, crowded with fugitives from the routed Union Grand Army, seemed to lie at the mercy of the Rebels, Congress legislated calmly and patiently throughout; and the House, on motion of Mr. Vandever, of Iowa, unanimously

"*Resolved*, That the maintenance of the Constitution, the preservation of the Union, and the enforcement of the laws, are sacred trusts which must be executed; that no disaster shall discourage us from the most ample performance of this high duty; and that we pledge to the country and the world the employment of every resource, national and individual, for the suppression, overthrow, and punishment of Rebels in arms."

Mr. Andrew Johnson, of Tenn., on the 24th, moved in the Senate a resolution identical with that of Mr. Crittenden, so recently adopted by the House; which was zealously opposed by Messrs. Polk and Breckinridge, and, on special grounds, by Mr. Trumbull, who said:

"As that resolution contains a statement which, in my opinion, is untrue, that this capital is surrounded by armed men, who started this revolt, I cannot vote for it. I shall say 'Nay.'

"I wish to add one word. The revolt was occasioned, in my opinion, by people who are not here nor in this vicinity. It was started in South Carolina. I think the resolution limits it to a class of persons who were not the originators of this Rebellion."

But the resolution was nevertheless adopted, by the following vote:

Yeas—Messrs. Anthony, Browning, Chandler, Clark, Cowan, Dixon, Doolittle, Fessenden, Foot, Foster, Grimes, Harlan, Harris, Howe, Johnson, of Tenn., Kennedy, King, Lane, of Ind., Lane, of Kansas, Latham, Morrill, Nesmith, Pomeroy, Saulsbury, Sherman, Ten Eyck, Wade, Wilkinson, Willey, and Wilson—30.

Nays—Messrs. Breckinridge, Johnson, of Mo., Polk, Powell, Trumbull—5.

This day, the Senate considered a bill to confiscate property used for insurrectionary purposes by persons engaged in rebellion or forcible resistance to the Government; and Mr. Trumbull, of Ill., moved the following amendment:

"*And be it further enacted*, That whenever any person, claiming to be entitled to the service or labor of any other person, under the laws of any State, shall employ such person in aiding or promoting any insurrection, or in resisting the laws of the United States, or shall permit him to be so employed, he shall forfeit all right to such service or labor, and the person whose labor or service is thus claimed shall be thenceforth discharged therefrom—any law to the contrary notwithstanding."

This proposition was advocated by Mr. Ten Eyck, of N. J., who had opposed it two days before, in Committee, but who now urged its passage on the assumption that slaves had been engaged on the Rebel side in the battle of Bull Run. Mr. Pearce, of Md., earnestly opposed it, saying:

"It will inflame suspicions which have had much to do with producing our present evils; will disturb those who are now calm and quiet; inflame those who are restless; irritate numbers who would not be exasperated by any thing else; and will, in all probability, produce no other real effect than these. Being, then, useless, unnecessary, and irritating, it is, in my opinion, unwise."

The vote was then taken, and the amendment adopted: Yeas 33; Nays—Breckinridge and Powell, of Ky., Johnson and Polk, of Mo., Kennedy and Pearce, of Md.—6. The bill was then engrossed, read a third time, and passed.

When this bill reached the House, it encountered a most strenuous and able opposition from Messrs. Crittenden and Burnett, of Ky., Vallandigham and Pendleton, of Ohio, and Diven, of N. Y.

Mr. Cox, of Ohio, moved (August 2d) that the bill do lie on the table; which was negatived: Yeas 57; Nays 71.

Mr. Thaddeus Stevens closed a vigorous speech in its favor with this impressive admonition:

"If this war is continued long, and is bloody, I do not believe that the free people of the North will stand by and see their sons and brothers and neighbors slaughtered by thousands and tens of thousands by rebels, with arms in their hands, and forbear to call upon their enemies to be our friends, and to help us in subduing them. I, for one, if it continues long, and has the consequences mentioned, shall be ready to go for it, let it horrify the gentleman from New York [Mr. Diven] or anybody else. That is *my* doctrine: and that will be the doctrine of the whole free people of the North before two years roll around, if this war continues.

"As to the end of the war, until the Rebels are subdued, no man in the North thinks of it. If the Government are equal to the people—and I believe they are—there will be no bargaining, there will be no negotiation, there will be no truces with the Rebels, except to bury the dead, until every man shall have laid down his arms, disbanded his organization, submitted himself to the Government, and sued for mercy. And, sir, if those who have the control of the Government are not fit for this task, and have not the nerve and mind for it, the people will take care that there are others who are—although, sir, I have not a bit of fear of the present Administration or of the present Executive.

"I have spoken more freely, perhaps, than gentlemen within my hearing might think politic; but I have spoken just what I felt. I have spoken what I believe will be the result; and I warn Southern gentlemen that, if this war is to continue, there will be a time when my friend from New York [Mr. Diven] will see it declared by this free nation that every bondman in the South—belonging to a Rebel, recollect; I confine it to them—shall be called upon to aid us in war against their masters, and to restore this Union."

The bill was now recommitted, on motion of Mr. Pendleton, of Ohio; and an attempt by Mr. Stevens to reconsider this decision was defeated by laying on the table—Yeas 71; Nays 61. It was reported back next day from the Judiciary Committee by Mr. Bingham, of Ohio, so amended as to strike out the section relating to slaves—adopted on motion of Mr.

Trumbull as aforesaid—and insert instead the following:

"SEC. 4. *And be it further enacted*, That, whenever hereafter, during the present insurrection against the Government of the United States, any person claimed to be held to labor or service, under the laws of any State, shall be required or permitted by the person to whom such labor or service is claimed to be due, or by the lawful agent of such person, to take up arms against the United States, or shall be required or permitted by the person to whom such service or labor is claimed to be due, or his lawful agent, to work or be employed in or upon any fort, navy-yard, dock, armory, ship, or intrenchment, or in any military or naval service whatever, against the Government and lawful authority of the United States, then, and in every such case, the person to whom such service is claimed to be due shall forfeit his claim to such labor, any law of the State or of the United States to the contrary notwithstanding; and whenever thereafter the person claiming such service or labor shall seek to enforce his claim, it shall be a full and sufficient answer to such claim, that the person whose service or labor is claimed had been employed in hostile service against the Government of the United States, contrary to the provisions of this act."

Mr. Bingham called for the previous question on the reading of the bill, as thus amended, which was seconded. Mr. Holman, of Indiana, moved that the bill be laid on the table; which was beaten: Yeas 47; Nays 66. The amendment of the Judiciary Committee was then agreed to; the bill, as amended, ordered to be read a third time, and passed, as follows:

YEAS—Messrs. Aldrich, Alley, Arnold, Ashley, Babbitt, Baxter, Beaman, Bingham, Francis P. Blair, Samuel S. Blair, Blake, Buffinton, Chamberlain, Clark, Colfax, Frederick A. Conkling, Covode, Duell, Edwards, Eliot, Fenton, Fessenden, Franchot, Frank, Granger, Gurley, Hanchett, Harrison, Hutchins, Julian, Kelley, Francis W. Kellogg, William Kellogg, Lansing, Loomis, Lovejoy, McKean, Mitchell, Justin S. Morrill, Olin, Potter, Alex. H. Rice, Edward H. Rollins, Sedgwick, Sheffield, Shellabarger, Sherman, Sloan, Spaulding, Stevens, Benj. F. Thomas, Train, Van Horne, Verree, Wallace, Charles W. Walton, E. P. Walton, Wheeler, Albert S. White, and Windom—60.

NAYS—Messrs. Allen, Ancona, Joseph Baily, George H. Browne, Burnett, Calvert, Cox, Cravens, Crisfield, Crittenden, Diven, Dunlap, Dunn, English, Fouke, Grider, Haight, Hale, Harding, Holman, Horton, Jackson, Johnson, Law, May, McClernand, McPherson, Mallory, Menzies, Morris, Noble, Norton, Odell, Pendleton, Porter, Reid, Robinson, James S. Rollins, Sheil, Smith, John B. Steele, Stratton, Francis Thomas, Vallandigham, Voorhees, Wadsworth, Webster, and Wickliffe—48.

The bill, thus amended, being returned to the Senate, Mr. Trumbull moved a concurrence in the House amendment, which prevailed by the following vote:

YEAS—Messrs. Anthony, Bingham, Browning, Clark, Collamer, Dixon, Doolittle, Fessenden, Foot, Foster, Grimes, Hale, Harris, King, Lane, of Ind., Lane, of Kansas, McDougall, Sherman, Simmons, Sumner, Ten Eyck, Trumbull, Wade, and Wilson—24.

NAYS—Messrs. Breckinridge, Bright, Carlile, Cowan, Johnson, of Mo., Latham, Pearce, Polk, Powell, Rice, and Saulsbury—11.

Mr. Clark, of New Hampshire, submitted[5] the following:

"*Be it resolved by the Senate and House of Representatives of the United States of America, in Congress assembled*, That we, as representatives of the people and States, respectively, do hereby declare our fixed determination to maintain the supremacy of the Government and the integrity of the Union of all these United States; and to this end, as far as we may do so, we pledge the entire resources of the Government and people, until all rebels shall submit to the one and cease their efforts to destroy the other."

Which was adopted: Yeas 34; Nays 1—Mr. Breckinridge.

Mr. S. S. Cox, of Ohio,[6] asked the House to suspend its rules to enable him to offer the following:

"*Whereas*, it is the part of rational beings to terminate their difficulties by rational methods, and, inasmuch as the differences between the United States authorities and the seceding States have resulted in a civil war, characterized by bitter hostility and extreme atrocity; and, although the party in the seceded States are guilty of

[5] July 25, 1861.

[6] July 29th.

breaking the national unity and resisting the national authority: Yet,

"*Be it resolved*, First: That, while we make undiminished and increased exertions by our Navy and Army to maintain the integrity and stability of this Government, the common laws of war, consisting of those maxims of humanity, moderation, and honor, which are a part of the international code, ought to be observed by both parties, and for a stronger reason than exists between two alien nations, inasmuch as the two parties have a common ancestry, history, prosperity, glory, Government, and Union, and are now unhappily engaged in lacerating their common country. Second: That, resulting from these premises, while there ought to be left open, as between two alien nations, the same means for preventing the war being carried to outrageous extremities, there ought, also, to be left open some means for the restoration of peace and Union. Third: That, to this end—the restoration of peace and union on the basis of the Constitution—there be appointed a Committee of one member from each State, who shall report to this House, at its next session, such amendments to the Constitution of the United States as shall assuage all grievances, and bring about a reconstruction of the national unity; and that, for the preparation of such adjustment, and the conference requisite for that purpose, there be appointed a commission of seven citizens of the United States, consisting of Edward Everett, of Massachusetts, Franklin Pierce, of New Hampshire, Millard Fillmore, of New York, Reverdy Johnson, of Maryland, Martin Van Buren, of New York, Thomas Ewing, of Ohio, and James Guthrie, of Kentucky, who shall request from the so-called Confederate States the appointment of a similar commission, and who shall meet and confer on the subject in the city of Louisville, on the first Monday of September next. And that the Committee appointed from this House notify said Commissioners of their appointment and function, and report their action to the next session, as an amendment of the Constitution of the United States, to be proposed by Congress to the States for their ratification, according to the fifth article of the Constitution."

The House refused to suspend: Yeas 41; Nays 85.

Mr. Waldo P. Johnson,[7] of Mo., proposed (Aug. 5th) to add to the bill providing for an increase of the Engineer Corps the following:

"*And be it further enacted*, That this Congress recommend the Governors of the several States to conveue their Legislatures for the purpose of calling an election to select two delegates from each Congressional district, to meet in general Convention at Louisville, in Kentucky, on the first Monday in September next; the purpose of the said Convention to be to devise measures for the restoration of peace to our country."

Mr. CARLILE, of Va. "Mr. President, there is no one, perhaps, within the limits of the Union, who is more anxious that peace should be restored to our country than I am; but, sir, in the presence of a large, organized army, engaged in an effort to overthrow the institutions of the country, and permanently to divide these States that have so long existed as one people, I do not think any such proposition as this ought to be made until that army shall be disbanded, and until an offer to meet those who desire peace shall be made to them by those who are engaged in this Rebellion. I cannot, therefore, entertaining these views, vote for the amendment offered by the Senator from Missouri—not that I would not go as far as he will go, or any other Senator on this floor, to allay the strife in our land; but I think that propositions of this kind, coming from the Senate of the United States at this hour, are inopportune; and, instead of aiding the effort that may be made for peace, they will prolong the civil war that is now raging in the country."

Mr. McDOUGALL, of Cal. "I wish merely to amend the remark made by the Senator from Virginia. He says this proposition would be inopportune. I say it would be intensely cowardly."

Mr. Johnson's proposition was rejected by the following vote:

YEAS — Messrs. Bayard, Breckinridge, Bright, Johnson, of Mo., Latham, Pearce, Polk, Powell, and Saulsbury—9.

NAYS—Messrs. Baker, Browning, Carlile, Chandler, Clark, Collamer, Cowan, Dixon, Doolittle, Fessenden, Foot, Foster, Grimes, Harris, Howe, King, Lane, of Ind., Lane, of Kansas, McDougall, Morrill, Rice, Sherman, Sumner, Ten Eyck, Trumbull, Wade, Wilkinson, Wilmot, and Wilson—29.

The bill increasing the pay of soldiers being that day under consideration, Mr. Wilson, of Mass., moved to add the following:

"*And be it further enacted*, That all the acts, proclamations, and orders of the Presi-

[7] Who, with his colleague, Trusten Polk, openly joined the Rebels soon afterward.

dent of the United States, after the 4th of March, 1861, respecting the Army and Navy of the United States, and calling out or relating to the militia or volunteers from the States, are hereby approved, and in all respects legalized and made valid, to the same intent, and with the same effect, as if they had been issued and done under the previous express authority and direction of the Congress of the United States."

The amendment was agreed to, and the bill thereupon passed, as follows: Yeas 33;

NAYS—Messrs. Breckinridge, Kennedy, Polk, Powell, and Saulsbury—5.

This bill was, the same day, reconsidered, and the above amendment, being moved afresh, was again adopted: Yeas 37;

NAYS—Messrs. Breckinridge, Bright, Kennedy, Pearce, and Powell—5.

So the amendment was once more agreed to, and the bill passed.

The bill being thus returned to the House, Mr. Vallandigham moved to strike out the above section, which was defeated by the following vote:

YEAS—Messrs. Allen, Ancona, George H. Browne, Calvert, Cox, Crisfield, Jackson, Johnson, May, Noble, Pendleton, James S. Rollins, Sheil, Smith, Vallandigham, Voorhees, Wadsworth, Ward, and Webster—19.

NAYS—74.

The bill was thereupon passed.

Mr. Calvert, of Md., offered the following:

"That, whilst it is the duty of Congress, by appropriate legislation, to strengthen the hands of Government in its efforts to maintain the Union and enforce the supremacy of the laws, it is no less our duty to examine into the original causes of our dissensions, and to apply such remedies as are best calculated to restore peace and union to the country: Therefore, it is

"*Resolved* (The Senate concurring herein), that a Joint Committee, to consist of nine members of this House and four members of the Senate, be appointed to consider and report to Congress such amendments to the Constitution and laws as may be necessary to restore mutual confidence and insure a more perfect and endurable Union amongst these States."

This proposition was laid on the table: Yeas 72; Nays 39—nearly a party division. And Mr. Diven, of N. Y., thereupon asked the unanimous consent of the House to enable him to offer the following:

"*Resolved*, That, at a time when an armed rebellion is threatening the integrity of the Union, and the overthrow of the Government, any and all resolutions or recommendations designed to make terms with armed rebels are either cowardly or treasonable."

Mr. Vallandigham objected; and the House refused to suspend the rules: Noes 36; Ays 56—not two-thirds.

The session terminated by adjournment at noon, August 6th, having lasted but thirty-three days.

XXXV.

MISSOURI.

WE have seen Conventions of the people of several States coolly assume the power, asserted or reserved in no one of their respective Constitutions, to take those States out of the Union, and absolve their people from all obligation to uphold or obey its Government, in flagrant defiance of that Federal charter, framed for and adopted by the people of the United States, and by them recognized and accepted as the supreme law of the land, anything in the Constitution and laws of any State to the contrary notwithstanding. We have seen one of these Conventions assume and exercise the right of revoking a fundamental compact between the State and the Union, which is, by its express terms, irrevocable. We have seen State Legislatures, in default of Conventions, usurp, practically, this tremendous power of secession; and have heard a now loyal Governor proclaim that a popular majority for Secessionists, in an election of mem-

MAP OF MISSOURI.

bers of Congress, might serve to nullify the obligation of the citizens of that State to the Federal Constitution and Union. We are now to contemplate more directly the spectacle of a State plunged into secession and civil war, not in obedience to, but in defiance of, the action of her Convention and the express will of her people—not, even, by any direct act of her Legislature, but by the will of her Executive alone.[1] Gov. Jackson,

[1] Pollard, in his "Southern History," says: "Upon the election of Abraham Lincoln, the Border States were unwilling to rush into dissolution until every hope of a peaceful settlement

as we have seen, having found the Convention, which his Legislature had called, utterly and emphatically intractable to the uses of treason, had reconvened his docile Legislature.[2] But even this body could not be induced to vote the State out of the Union. Below that point, however, it stood ready enough to aid the bolder conspirators; and its pliancy was taxed to the utmost. The State School Fund, the money provided to pay the July interest on the heavy State Debt, and all other available means, amounting in the aggregate to over three millions of dollars, were appropriated to military uses, and placed at the disposal of Jackson, under the pretense of arming the State against any emergency. By another act, the Governor was invested with despotic power—even verbal opposition to his assumptions of authority being constituted treason; while every citizen liable to military duty was declared subject to draft into active service at Jackson's will, and an oath of obedience to the State Executive exacted. Under these acts, Jackson appointed ex-Gov. Sterling Price Major-General of the State forces, with nine Brigadiers—Parsons, M. L. Clark, John B. Clark, Slack, Harris, Rains, McBride, Stein, and Jeff. Thompson, commanding in so many districts into which the State was divided. These Brigadiers were ordered by Maj. Gen. Price to muster and organize the militia of their several districts so fast as possible, and send it with all dispatch to Booneville and Lexington, two thriving young cities on the Missouri, respectively some forty and one hundred miles west of Jefferson, and in the heart of the slaveholding region. This call having been made, Jackson and Price, fearing an attack from the Federal forces gathering at St. Louis, started westward with their followers, reaching Booneville on the 18th of June. Price, being sick, kept on by steamboat to Lexington.

They had not moved too soon. Gen. Lyon and his army left St. Louis by steamboats on the 13th, and reached Jefferson City on the morning of the 15th, only to find that the Confederate chiefs had started when he did, with a good hundred miles advantage in the race. Reëmbarking on the 16th, he reached Rockport, nearly opposite Booneville, next morning, and espied the Rebel encampment just across the river. In it were collected some two or three thousand men, only half armed, and not at all drilled, under the immediate command of Col. Marmaduke. Jackson, utterly disconcerted by Lyon's unexpected rapidity of movement, had ordered his 'State Guard' to be disbanded, and no resistance to be offered. But Marmaduke determined to fight, and started for the landing, where he hoped to surprise and cut up the Unionists while debarking. He met Lyon advancing in good order, and was easily routed by him, losing two guns, with much camp-equipage, clothing, etc. His raw infantry were dispersed, but his strength in cavalry saved him from utter destruction.

Jackson fled to Warsaw, on the Osage, some eighty miles south-west.

---

of the question had vanished. This was the position of Missouri, to whose Convention *not a single Secessionist was elected.* Gov. Price was elected from his district as a Union man, without opposition; and, on the assembling of the Convention, was chosen its President." [2] May 3d.

Fifteen miles north of that place, at Camp Cole, a half-organized regiment of Unionists, under Capt. Cook, was asleep in two barns, with no pickets out save northward, when, during the night of the 18th, they were surprised by a Rebel force from the southward, under Col. O'Kane, and utterly routed—being unable to offer any serious resistance. Capt. Cook and a portion of his followers barely escaped with their lives.[3] Jackson, reënforced by O'Kane, halted two days at Warsaw, then continued his retreat some fifty miles to Montevallo, in Vernon County, near the west line of the State, and was here joined on the 3d of July by Price, with such aid as he had been able to gather at Lexington and on his way. Their united force is stated by Pollard at 3,600. Being pursued by Lyon, they continued their retreat next day, halting at 9 P. M., in Jasper County, twenty-three miles distant. Ten miles hence, at 10 A. M., next morning, they were confronted by a Union force 1,500 strong, under Col. Franz Sigel, who had been dispatched from St. Louis by the South-western Pacific road, to Rolla, had marched thence to Springfield, and had pushed on to Mount Vernon, Lawrence County, hoping to prevent a junction between Jackson and some forces which his Brigadiers were hurrying to his support. Each army appears to have started that morning with intent to find and fight the other; and such mutual intentions are seldom frustrated. Sigel found the Rebels, halted after their morning march, well posted, vastly superior in numbers and in cavalry, but inferior in artillery, which he accordingly resolved should play a principal part in the battle. In the cannonade which ensued, he inflicted great damage on the Rebels and received very little, until, after a desultory combat of three or four hours, the enemy resolved to profit by their vast superiority in cavalry by outflanking him, both right and left. This compelled Sigel to fall back on his baggage-train, three miles distant, which was otherwise at the mercy of the enemy. The retreat was made in perfect order, with two cannon on either flank, two in front, and four in the rear, keeping the Rebel cavalry at a respectful distance; save when, at the crossing of Dry Fork creek, where the road passes between bluffs, an effort was made to stop him by massing a strong cavalry force in his front. This was easily routed by bringing all his guns to bear upon it; when he continued his retreat to Carthage, and through that town to Sarcoxie, some fifteen miles eastward. It was well, indeed, that he did so; for Jackson's force was augmented, during that night and next morning, by the arrival of Price from the southward, bringing to his aid several thousand Arkansas and Texas troops, under Gens. Ben. McCulloch and Pearce. Our loss in the affair of Carthage was 13 killed and 31 wounded—not one of

[3] It seems to be pretty well agreed that Cook's men were about 400 in number: but he reported that he was attacked by 1,200, while Pollard makes O'Kane's force only 350. Cook's account makes his loss 23 killed, 20 wounded, and 30 prisoners; while Pollard says we lost 206 killed, a large number wounded, and over 100 taken prisoners; while the Rebels lost but 4 killed, 15 or 20 wounded, and captured 362 muskets. Such are the materials out of which History is necessarily distilled. Pollard is probably the nearer right in this case.

them abandoned to the enemy; while the Rebels reported their loss at 40 to 50 killed and 125 to 150 wounded. Sigel, now outnumbered three or four to one, was constrained to continue his retreat, by Mount Vernon, to Springfield; where Gen. Lyon, who had been delayed by lack of transportation, joined and outranked him on the 10th.

Meantime, Gen. Harris, Jackson's Brigadier for north-eastern Missouri, had rallied a considerable force at Paris, near the Mississippi, and hence commenced the work of destroying the Hannibal and St. Joseph Railroad. Col. Smith's Union force attacked him on the 10th at Palmyra, whence Harris fell back to Monroe, fifiteen miles west, where he destroyed much of the railroad property. Here he was again attacked by Smith, and worsted, losing one gun and 75 prisoners. He thereupon disappeared; but continued actively organizing guerrilla parties, and sending them out to harass and plunder Unionists, destroying their property through all this section, until he finally joined Price, with 2,700 men, at the siege of Lexington. In fact, all over Missouri, partisan fights and guerrilla outrages were now the order of the day.

The State Convention reässembled at Jefferson City July 20th, and proceeded—52 to 28—to declare[4] the offices of Governor, Lieut. Governor, Secretary of State, with those of members of the Legislature, vacant by the treason of their occupants, and all the acts of said Executive and Legislature, in contravention of the Federal Constitution, and in hostility to the Union, null and void. They designated the first Monday of the November ensuing as a day of election, whereat the people should ratify or disapprove this decisive action; and, meantime, elected Hamilton R. Gamble Governor, Willard P. Hall Lieut. Governor, and Mordecai Oliver Secretary of State. These officers were that day inaugurated, and the Convention, immediately thereupon, adjourned to the third Monday in December. Their action was ratified, of course, and the functionaries above named continued in their respective offices. These proceedings were met by a proclamation from the Rebel Lieut. Governor, Reynolds, styling himself acting Governor, dated New Madrid, July 31st; wherein he declares that he has been absent for two months, as a Commissioner of Missouri to the Confederate States, and that now

"I return to the State, to accompany, in my official capacity, one of the armies which the warrior statesman,[5] whose genius now presides over the affairs of *our half of the Union*, has prepared to advance against the common foe. * * *

"I particularly address myself to those who, though Southerners in feeling, have permitted a love of peace to lead them astray from the State cause. You now see the State authorities about to assert, with powerful forces, their constitutional rights; you behold the most warlike population on the globe, the people of the lower Mississippi valley, about to rush, with their gleaming bowie-knives and unerring rifles, to aid us in driving out the Abolitionists and their Hessian allies. If you cordially join our Southern friends, the war must soon depart Missouri's borders; if you still continue, either in apathy, or in indirect support of the Lincoln Government, you only bring ruin upon yourselves by fruitlessly prolonging the contest. The road to peace and internal security is only through union with the South. We will receive you as brothers, and let bygones be bygones. Rally to the Stars and Bars, in union with our glorious ensign of the Grizzly Bear!"

Jackson followed this (August 6th)

[4] July 30th.

[5] Jefferson Davis, to wit.

by a Declaration of Independence, mainly made up of abuse of the Federal Government, and its efforts to maintain its authority in Missouri. He thus established his right to take that State out of the Union:

"By the recognized universal public law of all the earth, war dissolves all political compacts. Our forefathers gave as one of their grounds for asserting their independence that the King of Great Britain had 'abdicated government here, by declaring us out of his protection, and waging war upon us.' The people and Government of the Northern States of the late Union have acted in the same manner toward Missouri, and have dissolved, by war, the connection heretofore existing between her and them.

"The General Assembly of Missouri, the recognized political department of her Government, by an act approved May 10th, 1861, entitled, 'An act to authorize the Governor of the State of Missouri to suppress rebellion and repel invasion,' has vested in the Governor, in respect to the rebellion and invasion now carried on in Missouri by the Government and people of the Northern States and their allies, power and authority 'to take such measures, as in his judgment he may deem necessary or proper, to repel such invasion or put down such rebellion.'

"Now, therefore, by virtue of the authority in me vested by said act, I, Claiborne F. Jackson, Governor of the State of Missouri, appealing to the Supreme Judge of the world for the rectitude of my intentions, and firmly believing that I am herein carrying into effect the will of the people of Missouri, do hereby, in their name, by their authority, and on their behalf, and subject at all times to their free and unbiased control, make and publish this provisional declaration, that, by the acts of the people and Government of the United States of America, the political connection heretofore existing between said States and the people and Government of Missouri is and ought to be totally dissolved; and that the State of Missouri, as a sovereign, free, and independent republic, has full power to levy war, conclude peace, contract alliances, establish commerce, and to do all other acts and things which independent States may of right do."

On the strength of the preceding, there was negotiated at Richmond, on the 31st of October ensuing, by E. C. Cabell and Thomas L. Snead, on the part of Jackson, and R. M. T. Hunter acting for Davis, an offensive and defensive alliance between Missouri and the Confederacy; whereby all the military force, matériel of war, and military operations of the former were transferred to the said Davis, as though she were already in the Confederacy; to which was added a stipulation that she should, so soon as possible, be admitted into the Confederacy; and she has since been represented in its Congress, although no election for members thereof was ever held by her people.

The Rebels, largely reënforced from the South, and immensely strong in cavalry, soon overran all southern Missouri, confining Gen. Lyon to Springfield and its immediate vicinity. Aware of their great superiority in numbers, Lyon waited long for reënforcements; but the disaster at Bull Run, and the general mustering out of service of our three-months' men, prevented his receiving any. At length, hearing that the enemy were advancing in two strong columns, from Cassville on the south and Sarcoxie on the west, to overwhelm him, he resolved to strike the former before it could unite with the latter. He accordingly left Springfield, August 1st, with 5,500 foot, 400 horse, and 18 guns; and, early next morning, encountered at Dug Springs a detachment of the enemy, whom he lured into a fight by pretending to fly, and speedily routed and dispersed. The Rebels, under McCulloch, thereupon recoiled, and, moving westward, formed a junction with their weaker column, advancing from Sarcoxie to strike Springfield from the west. Lyon thereupon retraced his steps to Springfield. The Rebels, now commanded by Price, their best General, advanced slowly and warily, reaching Wilson's Creek, ten miles south of Springfield, on the 7th. Lyon purposed here to surprise them by a night attack; but it was so late when all was ready that he deferred the attempt until the 9th, when he again advanced from Springfield in two columns; his main body, led by himself, seeking the enemy in front; while Sigel, with 1,200 men, was to gain their rear by their right.

Price had planned an attack on our camps that night; but, jealousies arising, had resigned the chief command to McCulloch, who had recalled the order to advance, because of the intense darkness of the night. At 5 A. M., of August 10th, Lyon opened

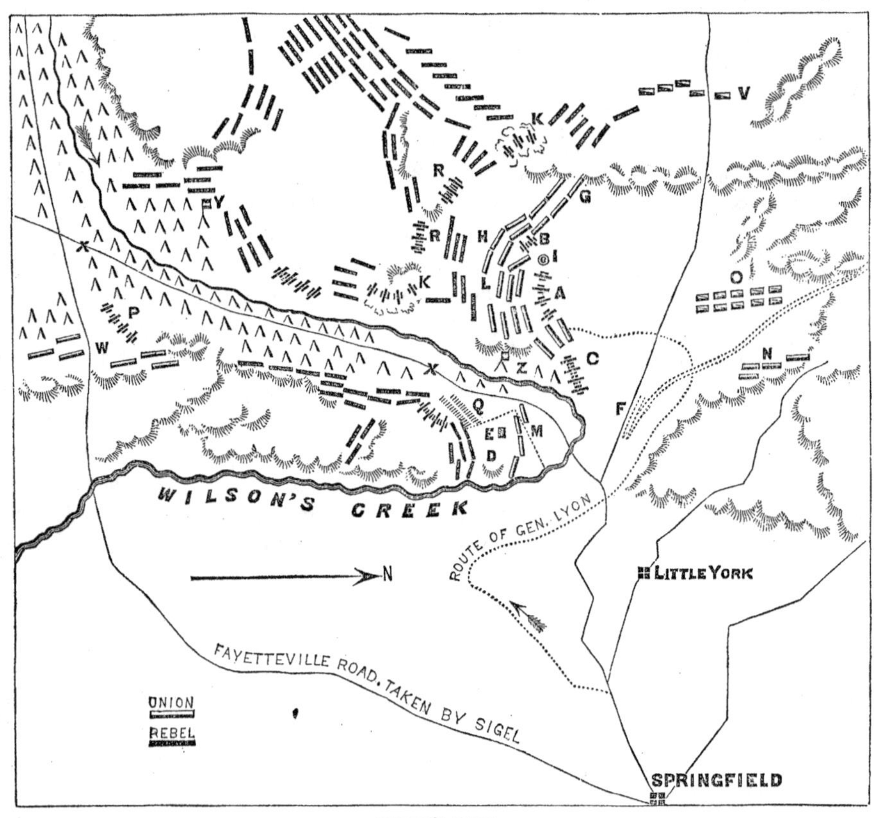

WILSON'S CREEK.

Explanations to the Plan of the Battle of Wilson's Creek.

A Capt. Totten's Battery.
B Section of Totten's Battery.
C Dubois's Battery.
D Cornfield, } hotly contested.
E Log House, }
F Road to Cassville.
G 2d Missouri Volunteers.
H 2d Kansas Volunteers.
I Spot where Gen. Lyon fell.
K Rebel batteries masked.
L 1st Kansas, 1st Missouri, 1st Iowa, and Capt. Shaler's Battalion.
M Capt. Plummer's Battalion.
N Home Guards.
O Kansas Rangers (Cavalry).
P Col. Sigel's Position.
Q Part of Rebel train.
R Concealed Rebel Batteries.
V Rebel Cavalry.
W Sigel's Brigade, 3d and 5th Missouri.
X Road through Rebel camp.
Y McCulloch's Head-Quarters.
Z Rains's Head-Quarters.

upon the Rebels in front, while Sigel, with his 1,200 men and 6 guns, almost simultaneously, assailed the rear of the enemy's right. The battle was obstinate and bloody; but the disparity of numbers was too great, and the division of forces proved, therefore, a mistake. The Rebels, at first surprised by Sigel's unexpected attack, and most gallantly charged by him, gave way before him; and he soon secured a commanding position for his artillery. But the weakness of his force was now manifest; and he was deceived by the advance of a Rebel regiment, which was mistaken by his men for Lyon's victorious vanguard, and thus came close to them unopposed. At a signal, Sigel was assailed by two batteries and a strong column of infantry, and instantly thrown into confusion. The enemy's fire was so hot that our cannoneers were driven by it from their pieces, the horses killed, and five guns captured. Our infantry fell back in confusion, followed and assailed by large bodies of Rebel cavalry. Of Sigel's 1,200, less than 400 were present at the next roll-call. One of his regiments, 400 strong, under Col. Salomon, was composed of three-months' men, who had already overstaid their term of enlistment, and who had reluctantly consented to take part in this battle; but who, when charged by an overwhelming Rebel force, were suddenly seized with a fit of home-sickness, and fled in all directions.

Meantime, our front or main advance, under Gen. Lyon, had waked up the great body of the Rebels; Capt. Totten's and Lieut. Dubois's batteries opening upon their immense masses with great vigor and decided effect. Very soon, the infantry on both sides were brought into action; and the 1st Missouri, 1st and 2d Kansas, and 1st Iowa regiments, with Steele's battalion of regulars, won immortal honor by the persistent and heroic gallantry with which they for hours maintained their ground against immense odds. The Rebels were repeatedly driven back in confusion, and the firing would be nearly or quite suspended for ten to twenty minutes; when, perceiving their decided superiority in numbers, since the rout and flight of Sigel's command, the Confederate officers would rally their men and bring them once more to the charge. Meantime, Gen. Lyon, who had led out his little army to fight against his own judgment, upon the representation of Gen. Sweeny, that to abandon all south-west Missouri without a battle would be worse than a defeat, and who had evinced the most reckless bravery throughout, had been twice wounded, and had had his horse killed under him. The second ball struck him in the head, and seemed for the moment to confuse him. He walked a few paces to the rear, saying to Maj. Schofield, his Adjutant, "I fear the day is lost;" to which Schofield responded, "No, General; let us try them once more." Maj. Sturgis offered him his own horse, which Lyon at first declined, but soon after mounted, and, bleeding from his two wounds, swung his hat in the air, and called upon the troops nearest him to prepare for a bayonet-charge on the lines of the enemy. The 2d Kansas rallied around him, but in a moment its brave Col. Mitchell fell severely wounded, and his soldiers cried out: "We are ready to follow—who will lead us?" "*I* will lead you!" replied

Lyon; "come on, brave men!" and at that moment a third bullet struck him in his breast, and he fell mortally wounded.

Still, the battle was not lost. For the enthusiastic, death-defying valor of the Unionists had repelled the assaults of their enemies along their entire front, and scarcely a shot was fired for the twenty minutes following Gen. Lyon's death. Maj. Sturgis, in his official report of the battle, says:

"After the death of Gen. Lyon, when the enemy fled and left the field clear, so far as we could see, an almost total silence reigned for a space of twenty minutes. Maj. Schofield now informed me of the death of Gen. Lyon, and reported for orders. The responsibility which now rested upon me was duly felt and appreciated. Our brave little army was scattered and broken; over 20,000 foes were still in our front; and our men had had no water since 5 o'clock the evening before, and could hope for none short of Springfield, twelve miles distant; if we should go forward, our own success would prove our certain defeat in the end; if we retreated, disaster stared us in the face; our ammunition was well-nigh exhausted; and, should the enemy make this discovery, through a slackening of our fire, total annihilation was all we could expect. The great question in my mind was, 'Where is Sigel?' If I could still hope for a vigorous attack by him on the enemy's right flank or rear, then we could go forward with some hope of success. If he had retreated, there was nothing left for us but to retreat also. In this perplexing condition of affairs, I summoned the principal officers for consultation. The great question with most was, 'Is retreat possible?' The consultation was brought to a close by the advance of a heavy column of infantry from the hill, where Sigel's guns had been heard before. Thinking they were Sigel's men, a line was formed for an advance, with the hope of forming a junction with him. These troops wore a dress much resembling that of Sigel's brigade, and carried the American flag. They were, therefore, permitted to move down the hill within easy range of Dubois's battery, until they had reached the covered position at the foot of the ridge on which we were posted, and from which we had been fiercely assailed before; when, suddenly, a battery was planted on the hill in our front, and began to pour upon us shrapnell and canister—a species of shot not before fired by the enemy. At this moment, the enemy showed his true colors, and at once commenced along our entire lines the fiercest and most bloody engagement of the day. Lieut. Dubois's battery on our left, gallantly supported by Maj. Osterhaus's battalion and the rallied fragments of the Missouri 1st, soon silenced the enemy's battery on the hill, and repulsed the right wing of his infantry. Capt. Totten's battery, in the center, supported by the Iowas and regulars, was the main point of attack. The enemy could frequently be seen within twenty feet of Totten's guns, and the smoke of the opposing lines was often so confounded as to seem but one. Now, for the first time during the day, our entire line maintained its position with perfect firmness. Not the slightest disposition to give way was manifested at any point; and, while Capt. Steele's battery, which was some yards in front of the line, together with the troops on the right and left, were in imminent danger of being overwhelmed by superior numbers, the contending lines being almost muzzle to muzzle, Capt. Granger rushed to the rear and brought up the supports of Dubois's battery, consisting of two or three companies of the 1st Missouri, three companies of the 1st Kansas, and two companies of the 1st Iowa, in quick time, and fell upon the enemy's right flank, and poured into it a murderous fire, killing or wounding nearly every man within sixty or seventy yards. From this moment, a perfect rout took place throughout the Rebel front, while ours, on the right flank, continued to pour a galling fire into their disorganized masses.

"It was then evident that Totten's battery and Steele's little battalion were safe. Among the officers conspicuous in leading this assault were Adj. Hezcock, Capts. Burke, Miller, Maunter, Maurice, and Richardson, and Lieut. Howard, all of the 1st Missouri. There were others of the 1st Kansas and 1st Iowa who participated, and whose names I do not remember. The enemy then fled from the field.

"A few moments before the close of the engagement, the 2d Kansas, which had firmly maintained its position, on the extreme right, from the time it was first sent there, found its ammunition exhausted, and I directed it to withdraw slowly, and in good order, from the field, which it did, bringing off its wounded, which left our right flank exposed, and the enemy renewed the attack at that point, after it had ceased along the whole line; but it was gallantly met by Capt. Steele's battalion of regulars, which had just driven the enemy from the right of the center, and, after a sharp engagement, drove him precipitately from the field.

"Thus closed—at about half-past 11

o'clock—an almost uninterrupted conflict of six hours. The order to retreat was given soon after the enemy gave way from our front and center, Lieut. Dubois's battery having been previously sent to occupy, with its supports, the hill in our rear. Capt. Totten's battery, as soon as his disabled horses could be replaced, retired slowly with the main body of the infantry, while Capt. Steele was meeting the demonstrations upon our right flank. This having been repulsed, and no enemy being in sight, the whole column moved slowly to the high, open prairie, about two miles from the battle-ground; our ambulances, meanwhile, passing to and fro, carrying off our wounded. After making a short halt on the prairie, we continued our march to Springfield.

"It should be here remembered that, just after the order to retire was given, and while it was undecided whether the retreat should be continued, or whether we should occupy the more favorable position of our rear, and await tidings of Col. Sigel, one of his non-commissioned officers arrived, and reported that the Colonel's brigade had been totally routed, and all his artillery captured, Col. Sigel himself having been either killed or made prisoner. Most of our men had fired away all their ammunition, and all that could be obtained from the boxes of the killed and wounded. Nothing, therefore, was left to do but to return to Springfield; where 250 Home Guards, with two pieces of artillery, had been left to take care of the train. On reaching the Little York road, we met Lieut. Farrand, with his company of dragoons, and a considerable portion of Col. Sigel's command, with one piece of artillery. At 5 o'clock, P. M., we reached Springfield."

Of course, the Confederates claimed the result as a success; and with good reason, since they stood on the defensive and held the field, and could show as trophies five of Sigel's six guns; but there is no pretense, on their part, of having pursued those whom they claimed to have beaten; and McCulloch's first official report only says of our army, "They have met with a signal *repulse*"—which was the truth. He admits a loss of 265 killed, 800 wounded, and 30 missing. Our official reports make our loss 223 killed, 721 wounded, and 292 missing.[6] McCulloch says: "My effective force was 5,300 infantry, 15 pieces of artillery, and 6,000 horsemen, armed with flint-lock muskets, rifles, and shot-guns. There were other horsemen with the army, who were entirely unarmed, and, instead of being a help, were continually in the way." Lieut. Col. Merritt, of the 1st Iowa, in his report, says:

"The enemy brought to the field 14,000 well-armed and well-disciplined troops, and 10,000 irregular troops; and our own force amounted to about 5,000 troops in the early part of the engagement, and considerably less than 4,000 troops for the concluding four hours of it."

Maj. Sturgis, in his official report of the battle, says:

"That 3,700 men, after a fatiguing night-march, attacked the enemy, numbering 23,000, on their own ground, and, after a bloody conflict of six hours, withdrew at their pleasure, is the best eulogium I can pass on their conduct that day."[7]

[6] It was very hard for our soldiers engaged in the main or front attack to admit that the day went against us, when they never saw the faces of the Rebels throughout the fight without seeing their backs directly afterward. Thus Col. John B. Plummer, 11th Missouri (who was badly wounded), testifies before the Committee on the Conduct of the War:

"I have but little more to say in regard to the battle except that we whipped them. * * * I was severely wounded, and, in the course of an hour and a half, was myself in an ambulance. I did not see the latter part of the action, but Major Schofield stated to me that, after the last repulse, it was a perfect rout—that the enemy fled in the wildest confusion. Everybody says that. * * * Schofield also stated that, in attempting to ride forward to reconnoiter and see where the enemy were, their dead were piled up so thick that he could not ride over them, but had to make a considerable détour.

"There was a flag of truce sent out after our return to Springfield, as I heard. A young doctor of the army went out with it, with a few men and some wagons, to obtain the body of Gen. Lyon, and to look for our wounded left on the field. He told me that Gen. McCulloch remarked to a non-commissioned officer—a sergeant—who attended the party, 'Your loss was very great; but ours was four times yours;' and I think it but a fair estimate to put their loss at least as high as 4,000 men, killed and wounded."

[7] Gen. Lyon's entire force, as returned by his

He further says:

"Our total loss, in killed, wounded, and missing, amounts to 1,235—that of the enemy will probably reach 3,000."

Beyond doubt, the Rebel army was considerably larger than ours—probably about two to one. It embodied not only the mass of the Missouri Rebels under Gen. Price, as well as those of Arkansas under McCulloch, but a considerable force, also, from Texas, with one regiment from Louisiana. Among its losses were Col. Weightman, commanding a brigade of Missourians, while Gens. Slack and Clark were severely, and Gen. Price slightly wounded. Yet the preponderance of losses was undoubtedly on our side; that of Lyon alone being a national disaster.[8] McCulloch, from his camp *near* Springfield, on the 12th, after learning that the Union army, under Sturgis and Sigel, had retreated from that city, issued an exulting proclamation, in which he said:

"We have gained over them a great and signal victory. Their general-in-chief is slain, and many of their other general officers wounded; their army is in full flight; and now, if the true men of Missouri will rise up and rally around our standard, the State will be redeemed. * * *

"Missouri must be allowed to choose her own destiny—no oaths binding your consciences. I have driven the enemy from among you. The time has now arrived for the people of the State to act. You can no longer procrastinate. Missouri must now take her position, be it North or South."

In an order to his army, issued that day, he says:

"The flag of the Confederacy now floats *near* Springfield, the stronghold of the enemy,"—

proving that he did not, even yet, feel strong enough to attack that city. But Springfield was neither fortified nor provisioned for a siege; while the immense preponderance of the Rebels in cavalry would have enabled them to cut off our supplies from every quarter: a retreat was, therefore, wisely determined on, and commenced during the night of the 14th. On the 19th, our little army, with a baggage train five miles long, reached Rolla utterly unmolested. Indeed, it does not seem to have been even pursued.[9]

John C. Fremont had, on the 9th of July, been appointed to the command of the Western District, including the States of Illinois, Kentucky, Missouri, and Kansas, with the Territories stretching westward of these; but was still in New-York, endeavoring to obtain necessary arms, equipments, and munitions, when

---

Adjutant, J. C. Kelton, on the 8th of August (the day before the battle), was 5,368; which included his sick and wounded in hospital, all who were absent on special duty, and his guard left in Springfield. It is, therefore, certain that he fought the battle of Wilson's Creek with less than 5,500, and, after the rout of Sigel, with less than 4,500. We have seen that the Rebels, by their own account, had at least twice this number in the field, beside those left in camp for want of arms.

[8] Pollard, in his "Southern History," says:

"The death of Gen. Lyon was a serious loss to the Federals in Missouri. He was an able and dangerous man—a man of the times, who appreciated the force of audacity and quick decision in a revolutionary war. To military education and talents, he united a rare energy and promptitude. No doubts or scruples unsettled his mind. A Connecticut Yankee, without a trace of chivalric feeling or personal sensibility—one of those who submit to insult with indifference, yet are brave on the field—he was this exception to the politics of the late regular army of the United States, that he was an unmitigated, undisguised, and fanatical Abolitionist."

[9] Pollard, in his "Southern History," says:

"Shortly after the battle, the Confederate army returned to the frontier of Arkansas; Gens. McCulloch and Price having failed to agree upon the plan of a campaign in Missouri."

tidings were received of the Union disaster at Bull Run. He left that city on the evening of that day (July 22d), and reached St. Louis on the 25th.

The bad news had, of course, preceded him; and he found most of the Union soldiers in his department just ready to be mustered out of service at the close of their three months' enlistment—disaffected, because unpaid; while arms, money, and nearly everything else required by the public exigency, were wanting. The Unionists were temporarily stunned and almost paralyzed by their great and unexpected disaster near Washington. The energies of the Government were absorbed in hurrying to the Potomac every available regiment and battery from whatever quarter; while the Secessionists, exultant and sanguine, were preparing on all sides to push their advantage promptly and to the utmost.

Lieut. Gov. Reynolds, in a proclamation to the people of Missouri, dated New Madrid, July 31st, with good reason assured them, that "the sun which shone in its full, midday splendor at Manassas, is about to rise upon Missouri." Every young slaveholder instinctively snatched his rifle, mounted his horse, and started for the nearest Rebel camp. Each old one stayed at home, professed neutrality, if the Union sentiment of his neighborhood were decidedly predominant, but sent his older sons to reënforce Jackson and Price. Wherever, as in north-eastern Missouri, and along the great lines of railroad, Rebel armies could not be maintained, there guerrilla bands were organized, to operate with vigor by night, hiding in the forests, or dispersing to their homes and pretending to be peaceful citizens, by day. The bolder traitors were ready and eager for open hostilities; the more cowardly would follow their leaders in a midnight raid on a peaceful Union settlement, or aid them in burning railroad bridges. Kentucky, though hitherto closed against Union soldiers, received without objection large bodies of Rebels from Tennessee and below, and, from her thoroughly disloyal Western district, formidably threatened Cairo. Gen. Fremont's position and its difficulties are very forcibly depicted in the private letter which he addressed, five days after his arrival, to the President, as follows:

"HEAD-QUARTERS WESTERN DEPARTMENT,
"ST. LOUIS, July 30th, 1861.

"MY DEAR SIR: You were kind enough to say that, as occasions of sufficient gravity arose, I might send you a private note.

"I have found this command in disorder; nearly every county in an insurrectionary condition, and the enemy advancing in force by different points of the Southern frontier. Within a circle of fifty miles around Gen. Prentiss, there are about 12,000 of the Confederate forces;[10] and 5,000 Tennessee and Arkansas men, under Hardee, well armed with rifles, are advancing upon Ironton. Of these, 2,000 are cavalry, which, yesterday morning, were within twenty-four hours' march of Ironton. Col. Bland, who had been seduced from this post, is falling back upon it. I have already reënforced it with one regiment; sent another this morning, and fortified it. I am holding the railroad to Ironton and that to Rolla, so securing our connections with the South. Other measures, which I am taking, I will not trust to a letter; and I write this only to inform you as to our true condition, and to say that, if I can obtain the material aid I am expecting, you may feel secure that the enemy will be driven out, and the State reduced to order. I have ordered Gen. Pope back to North Missouri, of which he is now in command. I am sorely pressed for want of arms. I have arranged with Adams's Express Company to bring me everything

[10] That is, in Kentucky and south-eastern Missouri, threatening Cairo, where Prentiss commanded.

with speed, and will buy arms to-day in New-York. Our troops have not been paid, and some regiments are in a state of mutiny; and the men whose term of service is expired generally refuse to reënlist. I lost a fine regiment last night, from inability to pay them a portion of the money due. This regiment had been intended to move on a critical post last night. The Treasurer of the United States has here $300,000 entirely unappropriated. I applied to him yesterday for $100,000 for my Paymaster, Gen. Andrews, but was refused. We have not an hour for delay. There are three courses open to me: One, to let the enemy possess himself of some of the strongest points in the State, and threaten St. Louis, which is insurrectionary. Second: to force a loan from Secession banks here. Third: to use the money belonging to the Government, which is in the Treasury here. Of course, I will neither lose the State, nor permit the enemy a foot of advantage. I have infused energy and activity into the department, and there is a thoroughly good spirit in officers and men. This morning, I will order the Treasurer to deliver the money in his possession to Gen. Andrews, and will send a force to the Treasury to take the money, and will direct such payments as the exigency requires. I will hazard everything for the defense of the department you have confided to me, and I trust to you for support.

"With respect and regard, I am yours truly,
"J. C. Fremont,
"Major General Commanding.
"To the President of the United States."

Gen. Fremont, in his testimony before the Committee on the Conduct of the War, thus explains his action in the premises:

"A glance at the map will make it apparent that Cairo was the point which first demanded immediate attention. The force under Gen. Lyon could retreat, but the position at Cairo could not be abandoned; the question of holding Cairo was one which involved the safety of the whole Northwest. Had the taking of St. Louis followed the defeat of Manassas, the disaster might have been irretrievable; while the loss of Springfield, should our army be compelled to fall back upon Rolla, would only carry with it the loss of a part of Missouri—a loss greatly to be regretted, but not irretrievable.

"Having reënforced Cape Girardeau and Ironton, by the utmost exertions I succeeded in getting together and embarking with a force of 3,800 men, five days after my arrival in St. Louis.

"From St. Louis to Cairo was an easy day's journey by water, and transportation abundant. To Springfield, was a week's march; and, before I could have reached it, Cairo would have been taken, and with it, I believe, St. Louis.

"On my arrival at Cairo, I found the force under Gen. Prentiss reduced to 1,200 men; consisting mainly of a regiment which had agreed to await my arrival. A few miles below, at New Madrid, Gen. Pillow had landed a force estimated at 20,000, which subsequent events showed was not exaggerated. Our force, greatly increased to the enemy by rumor, drove him to a hasty retreat, and permanently secured the position. * * *

"I returned to St. Louis on the 4th, having, in the mean time, ordered Col. Stephenson's regiment from Booneville, and Col. Montgomery from Kansas, to march to the relief of Gen. Lyon.

"Immediately upon my arrival from Cairo, I set myself at work, amid incessant demands upon my time from every quarter, principally to provide reënforcements for Gen. Lyon.

"I do not accept Springfield as a disaster belonging to my administration. Causes, wholly out of my jurisdiction, had already prepared the defeat of Gen. Lyon before my arrival at St. Louis."

Adj. Gen. Harding, whom Gen. Fremont found, by appointment of Gen. Lyon, in practical command at St. Louis, says:

"Gen. Fremont was not inattentive to the situation of Gen. Lyon's column, and went so far as to remove the garrison of Booneville in order to send him aid. During the first days of August, troops arrived in the city in large numbers. Nearly all of them were unarmed; all were without transportation. Regiment after regiment lay for days in the city without any equipments, for the reason that the Arsenal was exhausted, and arms and accouterments had to be brought from the East. From these men, Gen. Lyon would have had reënforcements, although they were wholly unpracticed in the use of the musket and knew nothing of movements in the field; but, in the mean time, the battle of the 10th of August was fought."

News of Gen. Lyon's repulse and death reached St. Louis on the 13th. Gen. Fremont thereupon decided to fortify that city with all possible dispatch, as a permanent and central base of operations; to fortify and garrison, likewise, Cape Girardeau, Ironton, Rolla, and Jefferson City; using for this purpose hired labor so far as possible, so that his raw recruits, even though unarmed, might be drilled and fitted for service so rapidly as might be; when, on the receipt of sufficient arms, he would take the field at the head of a numerous and effective army, and speedily regain all that should have, meantime, been lost. He now issued the following stringent and stirring general order:

"HEAD-QUARTERS OF THE WESTERN DEP'T,
"ST. LOUIS, August 31st.

"Circumstances, in my judgment, of sufficient urgency, render it necessary that the Commanding General of this department should assume the administrative power of the State. Its disorganized condition, the helplessness of the civil authority, the total insecurity of life, and the devastation of property by bands of murderers and marauders, who infest nearly every county in the State, and avail themselves of the public misfortunes and the vicinity of a hostile force to gratify private and neighborhood vengeance, and who find an enemy wherever they find plunder, finally demand the severest measures to repress the daily increasing crimes and outrages which are driving off the inhabitants and ruining the State. In this condition, the public safety and the success of our arms require unity of purpose, without let or hindrance to the prompt administration of affairs.

"In order, therefore, to suppress disorders, to maintain, as far as now practicable, the public peace, and to give security and protection to the persons and property of loyal citizens, I do hereby extend and declare established martial law throughout the State of Missouri. The lines of the army of occupation in this State are, for the present, declared to extend from Leavenworth, by way of the posts of Jefferson City, Rolla, and Ironton, to Cape Girardeau, on the Mississippi river. All persons who shall be taken with arms in their hands, within these lines, shall be tried by Court-Martial, and, if found guilty, will be shot. The property, real and personal, of all persons in the State of Missouri who shall take up arms against the United States, or shall be directly proven to have taken active part with their enemies in the field, is declared to be confiscated to the public use; and their slaves, if any they have, are hereby declared free men.

"All persons who shall be proven to have destroyed, after the publication of this order, railroad tracks, bridges, or telegraphs, shall suffer the extreme penalty of the law.

"All persons engaged in treasonable correspondence, in giving or procuring aid to the enemies of the United States, in disturbing the public tranquillity by creating and circulating false reports or incendiary documents, are in their own interest warned that they are exposing themselves.

"All persons who have been led away from their allegiance are required to return to their homes forthwith; any such absence, without sufficient cause, will be held to be presumptive evidence against them.

"The object of this declaration is to place in the hands of the military authorities the power to give instantaneous effect to existing laws, and to supply such deficiencies as the conditions of war demand. But it is not intended to suspend the ordinary tribunals of the country, where the law will be administered by the civil officers in the usual manner and with their customary authority, while the same can be peaceably exercised.

"The Commanding General will labor vigilantly for the public welfare, and, in his efforts for their safety, hopes to obtain not only the acquiescence, but the active support, of the people of the country."

"J. C. FREMONT, Maj.-Gen. Com."

This order, so far as it declared the slaves of Rebels to be free, was subsequently overruled and annulled by President Lincoln, as will hereafter be seen.

Gen. Price, very naturally, did not see fit to await the fulfillment of Gen. Fremont's programme. Though abandoned by McCulloch, with the bulk of the Confederate army, he moved northward from Springfield about the middle of August, receiving reënforcements continually, and, deflecting to the west as he advanced, pushed back a far inferior force of Unionists under Gen. Lane, after a little brush, at the crossing of a stream known as Dry Wood, and sent a detachment to and occupied Fort Scott, on the edge of Kansas, which was found evacuated. Thence, advancing north by east unopposed, he reached Warrensburg on the 10th of September, and, on the 11th, drew up before Lexington.[11] Here Col. Mulligan, of the Irish (Chicago) Brigade, at the head of 2,780 Union soldiers, with barely forty rounds of ammunition, and eight small guns, had taken post on a hill northeast of the city, and, in confident expectation of being soon relieved, awaited and defied the overwhelming numbers of the Rebels, who were rapidly swelled by the arrival of Gen. Harris from the north side of the river, and by reënforcements and volunteers from all quarters, until they numbered not less than 25,000, with 13 guns.

Col. Mulligan's position, naturally

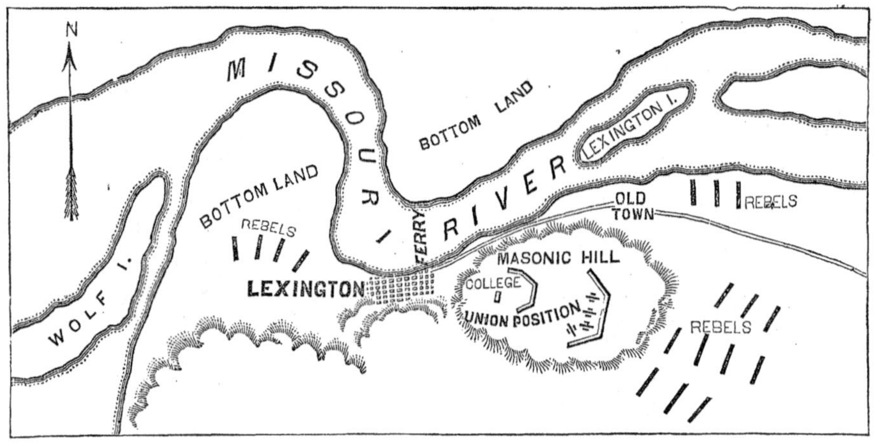

LEXINGTON.

strong, included a large college and its grounds, comprising an area of at least fifteen acres, and had been hastily but effectively fortified by earthworks, which were somewhat strengthened after the commencement of the siege. An industrious cannonade was opened from four different points on the beleaguered Unionists, but with little effect. Some outer works were taken, and some Rebel sharpshooters took possession of a dwelling which overlooked our intrenchments, but were readily driven out by an intrepid charge. No general, determined assault was made—Gen. Price not caring to rush his raw levies upon substantial breastworks, and evidently perceiving that the garrison must soon be forced to surrender.

Gen. Fremont, at St. Louis, was apprised, on the 13th, of Mulligan's arrival at Lexington; and another dispatch on the same day informed him that Price was reported near Warrensburg with 5,000 to 15,000 men; also that Gen. Jeff. C. Davis, commanding, at Jefferson City, a district which included Lexington, was

[11] A young city of five or six thousand inhabitants, the capital of Lafayette County, situated on the south bank of the Missouri, 240 miles west of St. Louis, and 50 or 60 from the nearest point on the North Missouri Railroad, or on that portion of the Pacific Road yet completed. The river was then at so low a stage as to be navigable only by boats of an inferior class.

giving vigilant attention to Price's movements. That same day brought, by telegraph, pressing demands for more troops from Gen. Grant, commanding at Cairo; and the next—the 14th—brought peremptory orders from Gen. Scott to "send 5,000 well-armed infantry to Washington without a moment's delay." Gen. Robert Anderson, commanding in Kentucky, was also calling urgently on Gen. Fremont, his immediate superior, for reënforcements to save Louisville, then threatened by the Rebels, who were rapidly 'annexing' Kentucky. Gen. Fremont had at that time scattered over his entire department, and confronted at nearly every point by formidable and often superior numbers of Rebels, a total of 55,693 men; whereof over 11,000 occupied Fort Holt and Paducah, Ky., warding off the menaced advance of the Rebels in force on Cairo and St. Louis; some 10,000 more held Cairo and important points in its vicinity; while Gen. Pope, in North Missouri, had 5,500; Gen. Davis, at Jefferson City, 9,600, and there were 4,700 at Rolla, and 3,000 at Ironton; leaving less than 7,000 at St. Louis. Gen. Lane, on the frontier of Kansas, had 2,200; and these, with a good part of Pope's command under Gen. Sturgis, and a large proportion of Davis's at Jefferson City, were disposable for the relief of Lexington, toward which point they were directed and expected to move so rapidly as possible. On the 13th, two regiments were ordered from St. Louis to Jefferson City, and two others from that point to Lexington. Fremont, pressed on every side, thus responded by telegraph, on the 15th, to the requisition upon him for five regiments for Washington City:

"Reliable information from the vicinity of Price's column shows his present force to be 11,000 at Warrensburg and 4,000 at Georgetown, with pickets extending toward Syracuse. Green is making for Booneville, with a probable force of 3,000. Withdrawal of force from this part of Missouri risks the State; from Paducah, loses Western Kentucky. As the best, I have ordered two regiments from this city, two from Kentucky, and will make up the remainder from the new force being raised by the Governor of Illinois."

The Rebels of north-eastern Missouri—reported at 4,500—led by Cols. Boyd and Patton, marched from St. Joseph, on the 12th, toward Lexington, where they doubtless had been advised that they would find Price on their arrival. Two parties of Unionists started in pursuit from different points on the North Missouri Railroad, directed to form a junction at Liberty, Clay county. Lieut. Col. Scott, of the Iowa 3d, reached that point at 7 A. M., on the 17th, and, not meeting there the expected coöperating force from Cameron, under Col. Smith, pushed on to Blue Mills Landing, on the Missouri, where he attacked the Rebels—now commanded by Gen. David R. Atchison—and was promptly and thoroughly routed. Col. Smith, who had been delayed by rains and bad roads, reached Liberty by dark, and there met Scott's beaten and demoralized regiment. They now moved together to the Landing (on the 18th); but found that the Rebels had all crossed the river and pushed on to Lexington, thirty miles distant. Smith thereupon returned to St. Joseph; and Gen. Sturgis, who was advancing by another route to the relief of Lexington, being confronted by a superior Rebel force under Gen. Parsons, likewise retreated northward, with the loss (Pollard says) of all his tents and camp equipage. Gen. Pope had telegraphed Gen. Fremont, on the 16th, from Palmyra, as follows:

"The troops I sent to Lexington will be there the day after to-morrow [18th], and consist of two full regiments of infantry, four pieces of artillery, and 150 irregular horse. These, with the two Ohio regiments, which will reach there on Thursday [19th], will make a reënforcement of 4,000 men and four pieces of artillery."

Unhappily, all these calculations proved futile. No part of Gen. Pope's 4,000 men and four pieces of artillery reached the beleaguered and sorely pressed Mulligan; nor did any of the reënforcements ordered to his support from all quarters. On the 17th, he was cut off from the river by the enemy, and thus deprived of water—save such as was poured upon him from the skies, which his unsheltered soldiers caught in their blankets, and then wrung out into camp-dishes, to assuage their thirst. The ferry-boats were likewise seized by the Rebels, to prevent his escaping, as well as to preclude the receipt of reënforcements. Rations became short; and the Missouri Home Guard, who constituted a good part of our forces, were early dispirited, refused to fight, and clamored for a surrender. Our artillery had very little and very bad ammunition; while the Illinois cavalry, composing a sixth of our forces, had only their pistols to fight with. Great numbers of the horses that had been brought within our intrenchments had been killed by the Rebel cannon, creating a stench which was scarcely tolerable. The Rebels made four charges without success; but finally, at 2 P. M., Friday, the 20th, they pushed up a movable breastwork of hemp-bales, two deep, along a line of forty yards in length, to within ten rods of our works. Maj. Beckwith, of the Home Guards—8th Missouri, whose Colonel (White) had been killed during that day's fighting—raised a white flag, and the defense was over.[12] The Rebels ceased firing;

[12] Col. Mulligan, in his official account of the siege, says:

"At 9 A. M., of the 18th, the drums beat to arms, and the terrible struggle commenced. The enemy's force had been increased te 28,000 men and 13 pieces of artillery. They came on as one dark, moving mass; men armed to the teeth, as far as the eye could reach—men, men, men were visible. They planted two batteries in front, one on the left, one on the right, and one in the rear, and opened with a terrible fire, which was answered with the utmost bravery and determination. Our spies had informed us that the Rebels intended to make one grand rout, and bury us in the trenches of Lexington. The batteries opened at 9 o'clock; and for three days they never ceased to pour deadly shot upon us. About noon, the hospital was taken. It was situated on the left, outside of the intrenchments. I had taken for granted, never thought it necessary to build fortifications around the sick man's couch. I had thought that, among civilized nations, the soldier sickened and wounded in the service of his country would, at least, be sacred. But I was inexperienced, and had yet to learn that such was not the case with Rebels. They besieged the hospital, took it, and from the balcony and roof their sharpshooters poured a deadly fire within our intrenchments. It contained our chaplain and surgeon and 120 wounded men. It could not be allowed to remain in the possession of the enemy. A company of the Missouri 13th [Dutch] was ordered forward to retake the hospital. They started on their errand, but stopped at the breastworks, 'going not out, because it was bad to go out.' A company of the Missouri 14th was sent forward; but it also shrank from the task, and refused to move outside the intrenchments. The Montgomery Guard, Capt. Gleason, of the Irish brigade, were then brought out. The Captain admonished them that the others had failed; and, with a brief exhortation to uphold the name they bore, gave the word to 'charge.' The distance was eight hundred yards. They started out from the intrenchments, first quick, then double-quick, then on a run, then faster. The enemy poured a deadly shower of bullets upon them; but on they went, a wild line of steel, and, what is better than steel, human will. They stormed up the slope to the hospital door, and, with irresistible bravery, drove the enemy before them, hurling them far down the hill beyond. At the head of those brave fellows, pale as marble, but not pale from fear, stood that gallant officer, Capt. Gleason. He said, 'Come on, my brave boys!' and in they rushed. But, when their brave captain returned, it was with a shot

the Home Guards left the outer defenses and retired within the line of inner intrenchments, saying they would fight no longer, and raising the white flag over the center of our works. Col. Mulligan, who had been twice wounded this day, called his officers around him, and they decided that nothing remained but to surrender. Of course, no terms could now be made. Price agreed that the privates on our side should be paroled—he having none too much food for his own; but the officers must be retained as prisoners of war, with all arms and equipments.

The losses during this fight were probably much the greater on the side of the Rebels; Price, indeed, makes them barely 25 killed and 75 wounded; but this probably includes only returns from such portion of his forces as were regularly organized and mustered; while nearly half his men were irregulars, of whom no account was taken. Our loss was 40 killed and 120 wounded.

Gen. Fremont, who had good reason to believe that Sturgis had already reënforced Mulligan, and that Lane and Pope had done or would do so that day, enabling him to hold his position, directed Davis by telegraph, on the 18th, to push forward 5,000 men to the crossing of Lamine Creek by the Pacific Railroad, with a view to intercept Price's retreat at the Osage. Late on the 22d, he received from Pope the sad tidings of Mulligan's surrender; and, on the 27th, he left St. Louis for Jefferson City, expecting that Price would try to maintain himself at some point on or near the Missouri, where lay his chief strength.

But Price was too crafty for this. By good luck, as well as good generalship, he had struck us a damaging blow, and was determined to evade its return. On the very day that Fremont left St. Louis, he put his force in motion southward and southwestward. He, of course, made feints of resuming the offensive, threatening the forces closing upon him from three sides, as if about to precipitate his full strength upon this or that particular foe, which, with his immense superiority in cavalry, was not a difficult feat. Our troops, of course, fell back or advanced cautiously; and, meantime, his infantry and artillery were making the best possible time southward. Pollard says he in two days crossed the Osage with 15,000 men in two common flatboats, and that Fremont was fifteen days in building pontoon bridges, and crossing after him. This is untrue; but a General who lived from hand to mouth on the country he traversed, moving but few and light guns, with very little ammunition, and who was careful to destroy whatever means of transit he no longer wished to use, breaking down bridges and burning boats, could easily outstrip his more heavily laden pursuer.

Price continued his flight to Neosho, in the south-west corner of the State, where he found McCulloch, with 5,000 Arkansas Confederates; and where Jackson assembled the fag-end of his old Legislature, and had an Ordinance of Secession formally passed by it—a most super-

through the cheek and another through the arm, and with but fifty of the eighty he had led forth. The hospital was in their possession. This charge was one of the most brilliant and reckless in all history, and to Capt. Gleason belongs the glory."

fluous ceremony, since Missouri had already been admitted into the Confederacy, on his own application, and he had exactly as good a right to take her out of the Union as his Legislative remnant[13] had—that is, none at all. Price, though powder was none too abundant with him, wasted one hundred good cannon-charges in honor of this ridiculous performance. After stopping ten days at Neosho, Price, finding that Fremont was in pursuit, retreated to Pineville, in the extreme south-west corner of the State; and, dreading to be pressed further, because many of his Missourians had enlisted expressly for the defense of their own State, and would naturally object to following him into another, had decided (says Pollard) not to abandon Missouri without a battle.

Gen. Fremont pushed westward from Jefferson City, some thirty miles, to Tipton, then the western terminus of the Pacific Railroad, nearly due south of Booneville, where he spent some time in organizing and equipping his green army, preparatory to a pursuit of Jackson and Price, who, it was reasonably supposed, would not surrender their State without a battle; and we had, by this time, had quite enough of fighting without due concentration and preparation on our side. Here he was visited, Oct. 13th, by Gen. Cameron, Secretary of War, accompanied by Adjt. Gen. Thomas and suite, who came away discouraged and dissatisfied. The heavy Autumn rains had set in some days before, and turned the rich soil of the prairies into a deep, adhesive mire, wherein the wheels of artillery and other heavily laden carriages sunk to the hubs, rendering the movement of cannon, munitions, and provisions, exceedingly slow and difficult. Fremont's army—by this time swelled to 30,000 men, including 5,000 cavalry and 86 guns—was still very inadequately provided with transportation for half its numbers. Meantime, his order emancipating the slaves of Rebels had excited a furious and powerful opposition, resulting in a deafening clamor for his removal, which was urgently pressed on the President, it was understood, by the two members of his Cabinet best entitled to be heard with regard to affairs in Missouri. Gen. Cameron carried an order relieving him from command, which he was instructed to present or withhold, at his discretion. He did not present it, but brought away an unfavorable impression, which was embodied and emphasized in Adjt. Gen. Thomas's report. Those who accompanied Gens. Cameron and Thomas on this visit, and who were on terms of intimacy with them throughout, reported, on their return, that Fremont's campaign was a failure—that he could never

[13] Mr. Isaac N. Shambaugh, a representative of De Kalb county in this Legislature, and a follower hitherto of Jackson, in an address to his constituents dated January 21, 1862, says:

"It is doubtless known to most of you that the House of Representatives of our State consists of 133 members, and the Senate of 33 members, and that, in order to constitute a quorum constitutionally competent to the transaction of any business, there must be present at least 67 members of the House and 17 members of the Senate. Instead of this, there were present at the October session referred to [at Neosho] but 35 members of the House of Representatives and 10 members of the Senate. A few days afterward, when we had adjourned to Cassville, one additional Senator and five additional Representatives made their appearance; and, these being all that were at any time present, it need scarcely be added that all the pretended legislation at either place was a fraud, not only upon the people of the *State*, but upon the Government of the *Confederate* States, as well as the *United* States."

get his army across the Osage—certainly not to Springfield; and that southern Missouri was virtually given over to Rebel possession.

These gloomy apprehensions were destined to be signally dispelled. Gen. Fremont moved southward immediately thereafter, reaching Warsaw on the 17th. Thither Sigel had preceded him. Five days thereafter, the bridging of the Osage had been completed, and the army, as it crossed, pressed rapidly forward.

Meantime, on the 21st, a spirited fight had occurred at Fredericktown, in the south-east, which section had hitherto been overrun almost at will by Rebel bands directed by Jeff. Thompson, one of Jackson's brigadiers, termed the "Swamp Fox" by his admirers. Capt. Hawkins, of the Missouri (Union) cavalry, having been ordered thither on a reconnoissance from Pilot Knob, on the north-east, engaged and occupied Thompson while Gen. Grant, commanding at Cape Girardeau, on the Mississippi, sent a superior force, under Col. Plummer, to strike him from the east. Meantime, Col. Carlile, with a considerable body of infantry, moved up from Pilot Knob to support Hawkins. When all these advanced, the disparity in numbers was so great as to preclude a serious contest; so that Thompson, though strongly posted, was overpowered, and, after two hours' fighting, constrained to fly, leaving 60 dead behind him, including Col. Lowe, his second in command. Thompson was hotly pursued for twenty miles, and his banditti thoroughly demoralized and broken up.

The advance of Gen. Fremont's army was preceded by a squadron of 'Prairie Scouts,' led by Maj. Frank J. White, who had recently distinguished himself by a forced march of sixty miles on Lexington, which he captured without loss on the morning of the 16th, taking 60 or 70 prisoners, considerable property, and releasing a number of Unionists captured with Mulligan, including two colonels. Lexington and its vicinity being strongly Rebel, Maj. White abandoned it on the 17th, and moved southerly by Warrensburg and Warsaw to the front, which they struck at Pomme de Terre river, fifty-one miles north of Springfield. Still pushing ahead, Maj. White was joined, on the 24th, by Maj. Zagonyi, of the 'Fremont Body-Guard,' who assumed command, and, marching all night, resolved to surprise and capture Springfield next day. Maj. White, being very ill, was left at a farm-house to recover; but in a few hours started in a wagon, with a guard of six men, to overtake his command, and soon found himself in a Rebel camp a prisoner, and in imminent danger of assassination. He had moved on the direct road to Springfield, while Zagonyi had made a détour of twelve miles to the right, hoping thus to surprise the enemy in Springfield, who, he was advised, were fully 2,000 strong.

The two commands combined numbered hardly 300 sabers, when, on reaching the outskirts of Springfield, they found 1,200 infantry and 400 cavalry well posted on the crown of a hill, prepared for and awaiting them. Zagonyi did not quail. To his officers he said: "Follow me, and do like me!" to his soldiers—

"Comrades, the hour of danger has come: your first battle is before you. The enemy is 2,000 strong, and you are 300. If any of you would turn back, you can do so now."

Not a man stepped from the ranks. He then added:

"I will lead you. Let the watchword be, '*The Union and Fremont!*' Draw sabers! By the right flank—quick trot—*march!*"

With a ringing shout, the thin battalion dashed eagerly forward.

A miry brook, a stout rail-fence, a narrow lane, with sharpshooters judiciously posted behind fences and trees—such were the obstacles to be overcome before getting at the enemy. A fence must be taken down, the lane traversed, the sharpshooters defied, before a blow could be struck. All was the work of a moment; but when that moment had passed, seventy of their number were stretched dead or writhing on the ground. Maj. Dorsheimer, an Aid to Fremont, who came up soon after, thus describes the close of the fight:

"The remnant of the Guard are now in the field under the hill; and, from the shape of the ground, the Rebel fire sweeps with the roar of a whirlwind over their heads. A line of fire upon the summit marks the position of the Rebel infantry; while nearer, and on the top of a lower eminence to the right, stand their horse. Up to this time, no guardsman has struck a blow, but blue coats and bay horses lie thick along the bloody lane. Their time has come. Lieut. Maythenyi, with 30 men, is ordered to attack the cavalry. With sabers flashing over their heads, the little band of heroes spring toward their tremendous foe. Right upon the center they charge. The dense mass opens, the blue-coats force their way in, and the whole Rebel squadron scatter in disgraceful flight through the cornfields in the rear. The boys follow them, sabering the fugitives. Days afterward, the enemy's horse lay thick among the uncut corn.

"Zagonyi holds his main body until Maythenyi disappears in the cloud of Rebel cavalry; then his voice rises through the air. 'In open order—charge!' The line opens out to give play to their sword-arm. Steeds respond to the ardor of their riders; and, quick as thought, with thrilling cheers, the noble hearts rush into the leaden torrent which pours down the incline. With unabated fire, the gallant fellows press through. The fierce onset is not even checked. The foe do not wait for them—they waver, break, and fly. The guardsmen spur into the midst of the rout, and their fast-falling swords work a terrible revenge. Some of the boldest of the Southrons retreat into the woods, and continue a murderous fire from behind trees and thickets. Seven guard horses fall upon a space not more than twenty feet square. As his steed sinks under him, one of the officers is caught around the shoulders by a grape-vine, and hangs dangling in the air until he is cut down by his friends. The Rebel foot are flying in furious haste from the field. Some take refuge in the fair-ground; some hurry into the cornfields; but the greater part run along the edge of the wood, swarm over the fence into the road, and hasten to the village. The guardsmen follow. Zagonyi leads them. Over the loudest roar of battle rings his clarion voice—'Come on, Old Kentuck![14] I'm with you!' and the flash of his sword-blade tells his men where to go. As he approaches a barn, a man steps from behind the door and lowers his rifle; but, before it has reached a level, Zagonyi's saber-point descends upon his head, and his life-blood leaps to the very top of the huge barn-door.

"The conflict now rages through the village—in the public square, and along the streets. Up and down, the Guards ride in squads of three or four, and, wherever they see a group of the enemy, charge upon and scatter them. It is hand to hand. No one but has a share in the fray."

Zagonyi wisely evacuated the town at night-fall, knowing that by night he was at the mercy of the Rebels, if they should muster courage to return and attack him. Of his 300 men, 84 were dead or wounded.

Maj. White, who had escaped from his captors, taking captive in turn their leader, arrived next morning, at the head of a score of improvised Home Guards, to find himself 'monarch of all he surveyed.' He had 24 men, of whom he stationed 22 as pickets on the outskirts, and held the balance in reserve. At noon, he re-

[14] Of the Guard, 100 were Kentuckians.

ceived a Rebel flag of truce, asking permission to bury their dead; which, he said, must be referred to Gen. Sigel, from whom he, the next hour, forwarded the permission required.[15] White drew in a part of his pickets, stationed them between the village and the bloody field of yesterday's conflict, and the Rebels quietly buried their dead. He did not venture to remain through the night, but fell back upon Sigel, who reached Springfield by a forced march of thirty miles, on the evening of the 27th. Asboth came up with another division on the 30th; and Lane, with the Kansas brigade, was not long behind him. But Hunter, McKinstry, and Pope, with their respective divisions, were still struggling with the badness of the roads from thirty to forty miles back. Pope arrived November 1st, having marched seventy miles in two days; and McKinstry came in just behind him.

On the morning of Nov. 2d, a messenger brought to Springfield an order from Gen. Scott[16] removing Fremont from his command, and directing him to turn it over to Gen. Hunter, who had not yet arrived. This was sad news to the great bulk of the army, which had been collected and equipped with such effort; which had driven the Rebels almost out of Missouri without loss; and which confidently expected to meet and beat them within the State, and to chase the fragments of their army through Little Rock, and, ultimately, to New Orleans. Hunter not having yet arrived, and the enemy being reported in force at Wilson's Creek, it was determined in council to march out and give him battle next morning; but Hunter came up that night, and the command was turned over to him by Fremont.

It does not seem that their advices of the Rebels' proximity were well-founded. Pollard asserts that they were then at Pineville, some fifty miles from Springfield; but adds that Gen. Price had made preparations to receive Fremont, determined not to abandon Missouri without a battle. It must therefore be regarded as a national misfortune that the order superseding Gen. Fremont arrived at this time; for it is not possible that his army—superior in numbers and in equipment to the Rebels, and inspired by enthusiastic devotion to its chief—could have been beaten.

Gen. Fremont departed for St. Louis early next morning, accompanied by his Body-Guard as a special escort. That Guard, it is sad to say, though enlisted for three years, and composed of the very best material, were mustered out of service, by order of Gen. McClellan, soon afterward.

That Gen. Fremont—placed in so important a command, and frantically entreated for reënforcements from so many sides at once—committed some errors of judgment, is very probable. It may be he should have divined earlier than he did that Price would not strike at Jefferson City or Booneville, which he seemed to threaten, but would take the safer course of swooping down on Lexington, so much further west. It may be that he should have foreseen that the ferry-boats at Lexington, instead of being kept out of the reach of the Rebels, would be allowed to fall into their hands; and that neither Davis,

[15] Sigel was then forty miles distant.

[16] Scott was himself retired the day before.

nor Pope, nor Sigel, nor Smith, nor Lane, would be enabled to reach that point in season to save Mulligan; though the series of blunders and fatalities by which all succor was precluded, could not happen twice in a century. Had he known that the Rebels would not attack Louisville, nor Cairo, nor make a demonstration, by way of Cape Girardeau, on St. Louis, backed by an insurrection in that city, he might have stripped that vital point of troops, and rushed everything to the relief of Mulligan. He certainly had reason to believe that Pope's promise to push 4,000 men to Lexington by the 18th or 19th would be fulfilled; and that these, with the forces of Sturgis and Smith, and those that Davis might have sent at any time after he had learned that the Rebels were concentrating on Lexington, would be sufficient. Had even the imperative call for five regiments to be dispatched to Washington been forborne,[17] it is probable that Mulligan would have been saved.

But none of his errors, if errors they were, can compare in magnitude with that which dictated a second abandonment of Springfield and retreat to Rolla by our army, five days after Hunter had assumed command. No doubt, this was ordered from Washington; but that order was most mistaken and disastrous. We had already once abandoned southwestern Missouri; and, even then, Lyon had wisely and nobly decided that it were better to risk a probable defeat than to give up a Union-loving people to the mercy of their enemies, without making a determined effort to save them. But now there was no such exigency. We were too strong to be beaten; and might have routed Price near Pineville, chasing the wreck of his army into Arkansas, thus insuring a dispersion of large numbers of the defeated Missourians to their homes; and then 5,000 men, well intrenched, could have held Springfield against all gainsayers, until the next Spring. But our second retreat, so clearly wanton and unnecessary, disheartened the Unionists and elated the Secessionists of all southern Missouri. It made our predominance in any part of that State appear exotic and casual, not natural and permanent. It revived all the elements of turbulence, anarchy, and rapine, which the uncontested ascendency of our cause, under Fremont, had temporarily stilled. The Secession strongholds along and even above the Missouri river were galvanized into fresh activity in guerrilla outrages and murders, by the unexpected tidings that we had abandoned southern Missouri without a blow, and were sneaking back to our fastnesses along the lines of completed railroads, and within striking distance of St. Louis.

Gen. Henry W. Halleck succeeded to the command of the Missouri department, November 12th. But meantime, Gen. Ulysses S. Grant, in command at Cairo, had made a spirited demonstration on the little steamboat landing known as Belmont, on the Missouri side of the Mississippi, opposite Columbus, Ky. Columbus was then the head-quarters of the Secession force observing and threatening Cairo, while the Rebellion, protected by similar demonstrations of Con-

[17] This order, when partially executed, was withdrawn, but too late for the emergency.

federate strength at different points throughout the State, was greedily absorbing and annexing Kentucky, without encountering any forcible opposition from her 'loyal' authorities. Requesting Gen. Smith, commanding the Union garrison at Paducah, to make a feint of attacking Columbus from the north-east, Gen. Grant, sending a small force of his own down the Kentucky side of the great river to Ellicott's Mills, twelve miles from Columbus, embarked (Nov. 6th) 2,850 men, mainly Illinoisans, upon four steamboats, convoyed by the gunboats Tyler and Lexington, and dropped down the river to Island No. 1, eleven miles above Columbus, where they remained until 7 A. M. of the 7th, when they proceeded to Hunter's Point, some two to three miles above the ferry connecting Columbus with Belmont, where the whole array was debarked on the Missouri shore, formed in line of battle, and pushed forward as rapidly as possible, to overwhelm the somewhat inferior force of Rebels encamped at Belmont. This movement was rather annoyed than checked by a small Rebel detachment promptly thrown forward to impede its progress; but by 11 o'clock our little army was formed westward of and facing the Rebel camp, which was found well protected by a strong abatis nearly surrounding it on every side but that of the river. Fighting their way through this with great gallantry, though stoutly resisted by the Rebels, the Unionists reached and carried the camp, capturing several guns, and driving the enemy completely over the bluff down to the bank of the river. The tents of the Rebels were promptly fired, and their blankets and camp equipage destroyed with them. But, by this time, Maj. Gen. Polk, commanding in Columbus, had been thoroughly waked up, and, perceiving his camp across the river in possession of our forces, had trained some of his heaviest guns to bear from the hights on that side of

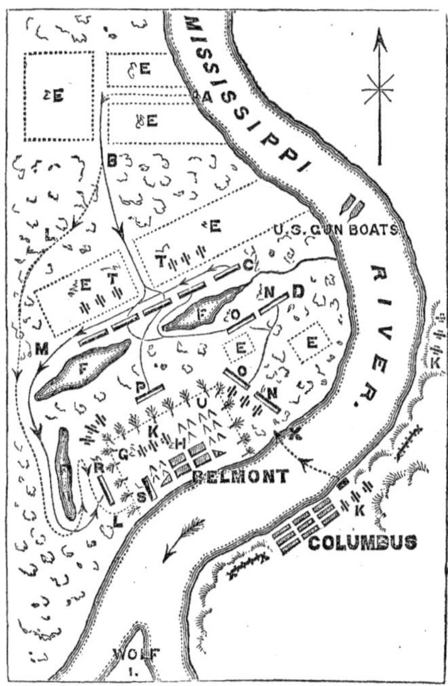

BATTLE OF BELMONT.

the river upon the position of our victorious regiments, which was much lower, and thoroughly exposed to their fire, which our men had no means of effectively returning.[18] Meantime, he had sent over three re-

18 *The Chicago Journal* has a letter from its Cairo correspondent, from which we extract the following spirited account of the battle:

"The design was to reach Belmont just before daylight; but, owing to unavoidable delays in embarking, it was 8 o'clock before the fleet reached Lucas Bend, the point fixed upon for debarkation. This is about three miles north of Columbus, Ky., on the Missouri side.

"The enemy were encamped on the high ground back from the river, and about two and a half miles from the landing. From their position, they could easily see our landing, and had

giments, under Gen. Pillow, to the immediate relief of his routed and sorely pressed fugitives; while three others, under Gen. Cheatham, had been landed between our soldiers and their boats, with intent to cut off their retreat; and, finally, as his fears of a direct attack on Columbus were dispelled, Polk himself crossed over with two additional regiments, making eight in all, or not less than 5,000 men, who were sent as reënforcements to the three regiments, under Col. Tappan, who originally held the place. Of course, our exhausted and largely outnumbered soldiers could do nothing better than to cut their way through the fresh troops obstructing their return to their boats, which they did with great gallantry and success, bringing off all their own guns, with the two best of those they had captured from the Rebels, and gaining their boats about 5 P. M., with a loss of two caissons, some ammunition and baggage, and of about 400

ample time to dispose of their forces to receive us, which they did with all dispatch. They also sent a detachment of light artillery and infantry out to retard our march, and annoy us as much as possible.

"A line of battle was formed at once on the levee, Col. Fouke taking command of the center, Col. Buford of the right, and Col. Logan of the left.

"The advance from the river bank to the Rebel encampment was a running fight the entire distance, the Rebels firing and falling back all the way; while our troops gallantly received their fire without flinching, and bravely held on their course, regardless of the missiles of death that were flying thick and fast about them. The way was of the most indifferent character, lying through woods with thick underbrush, and only here and there a path or a rough country road.

"The three divisions kept within close distance of each other, pressing over all obstacles and overcoming all opposition; each striving for the honor of being first in the enemy's camp. This honor fell to the right division, led by Col. Buford. It was the gallant 27th Illinois, who, with deafening cheers, first waved the Stars and Stripes in the midst of the Rebels' camping-ground.

"The scene was a terribly exciting one—musketry and cannon dealing death and destruction on all sides; men grappling with men in a fearful death-struggle; column after column rushing eagerly up, ambitious to obtain a post of danger; officers riding hither and thither in the thickest of the fight, urging their men on, and encouraging them to greater exertions; regiments charging into the very jaws of death with frightful yells and shouts, more effective, as they fell upon the ears of the enemy, than a thousand rifle-balls—and, in the midst of all, is heard one long, loud, continuous round of cheering as the Star-Spangled Banner is unfurled in the face of the foe, and defiantly supplants the mongrel colors that had, but a moment before, designated the spot as Rebel ground.

"The 22d boys have the honor of having silenced and captured a battery of twelve pieces, which had been dealing destruction with marked success. The 30th had been badly cut up by this battery, and were straining every nerve to capture it. They express considerable disappointment that the prize was snatched from them. They turned away in search of new laurels; and, in charging into the very midst of the camp, were drawn into an ambuscade, where they were again suffering terribly, though maintaining their ground unflinchingly, when the 31st came to their assistance.

"An impetuous and irresistible charge was then made, that drove the Rebels in all directions, and left the field in possession of the Federal forces. The Rebel camps were fired, and, with all their supplies, ammunition, baggage, etc., were totally destroyed.

"The discovery, on the Kentucky side, that we were in possession of their camp, led to an opening of the Rebel batteries from that direction upon us. Their fire was very annoying; the more so as we were not in a position to return it.

"Just at this juncture, the report was brought to Gen. Grant, by Lieut. Pittman, of the 30th Illinois, who had, with his company (F), been on scouting duty, that heavy reënforcements were coming up to the Rebels from the opposite side of the river. Indeed, the report was also made that the enemy were pouring over the river in immense numbers, and the danger was imminent that our retreat would be cut off. The order to fall back to the boats was therefore given, but not a moment too soon.

"The way was already filled with Rebel troops; and, as we had fought our way up to the encampment, so we were obliged to fight back to our boats, and against desperate odds. But the men were not lacking in courage, and fought like veterans, giving ample evidence of their determination. Every regiment of Federal troops suffered more or less severely in their return march; but the general opinion prevails that the Rebels suffered far greater losses than we.

"Wherever they made a stand, we put them to flight; and, although we lost many brave men, either killed, wounded, or taken prisoners, we made at least two of their men bite the dust for every one that fell from our ranks. Our regiments all reached their boats, though with considerably thinned ranks."

killed, wounded, and taken prisoners.[19] Col. Dougherty, of the 22d Illinois, was severely wounded and taken prisoner. Col. Lauman, of the 7th Iowa, and Maj. McClurken, of the 30th Illinois, were also badly wounded; while among the killed were Lieut. Col. Wentz, of the 7th Iowa, Capts. Brolaski, Markle, and Lieut. Dougherty. Gens. Grant and McClernand, who evinced the most reckless bravery throughout, each had his horse shot under him. The 22d Illinois lost 23 killed and 74 wounded, including Capts. Challenor and Abbott, who were taken prisoners. The 7th Iowa lost 26 killed and 80 wounded, including nearly all its field officers.[20] The entire Rebel loss[21] was from 600 to 1,000; among them, Col. John V. Wright,[22] of the 13th Tennessee, and Maj. Butler, of the 11th Louisiana, killed.

It is morally certain that the Rebel loss in this action was the greater; yet, for lack of proper combinations, and because of the fact that, of the 10,000 men we might and should have had in the action, less than 4,000 were actually present, the prestige of victory inured to the Rebels, who chased our weary men to their boats, and fired at them, as they, having cut their cables in their haste, steamed up the river. When our gunboats, gaining a proper distance from the shore, obtained the range of the exulting Rebels on the bank, the latter promptly desisted and retired.

[19] Gen. Grant, in his official report, dated Cairo, Nov. 12th, says:

"Our loss was about 84 killed, 150 wounded—many of them slightly—and about an equal number missing."

A letter preserved in *The Rebellion Record*, dated Camp McClernand, Cairo, Nov. 8th, says:

"The Memphis returned at midnight. The expedition that went down upon her with flags of truce report the whole number of our dead, found and buried by them upon the battle-field, at 85. This includes all. The Rebels acknowledge their loss to be 350 killed."

A private in Taylor's battery writes:

"After we got out into the river, and in range, we opened with three of our guns, together with the gunboats: and the way we dropped the shell among them was a caution. The firing did not cease till sundown."

This private sums up the battle as follows:

"To recapitulate: We had about 4,000 men; attacked about 3,000 at Belmont, and drove them from the field; when they were reënforced by 4,000 from above and 3,000 below, together with cavalry and four batteries from Columbus, and their heavy guns from the bluffs opposite playing down upon our men all the time; they could look right down on the battle from the shore, where Pillow was said to be in command."

The Memphis Avalanche's (Rebel) account of the battle says:

"We have 91 prisoners and over 100 of their wounded in our hands."

[20] Capt. Foote's official report of the participation of his gunboats in this affair, states the loss of those gunboats at 1 killed and 2 wounded; and, with regard to the general result, says:

"My opinion is, after careful inquiry, as stragglers are still coming in, that our loss of killed, wounded, and missing, will amount to 500 persons, together with 25 baggage wagons, 100 horses, 1,000 overcoats, and 1,000 blankets."

[21] Pollard, with unusual candor, says:

"The list of our [Rebel] killed, wounded, and missing, numbers 632."

A Rebel account of the battle by an eye-witness, printed in *The Memphis Appeal*, gives the official loss in four regiments at 364, and says the loss in the others has not been announced; but if in the same ratio, it must have been over a thousand. And yet *The Memphis Avalanche* bulletin says:

"Capt. John Morgan estimates the loss of our entire army at about 100 killed, and less than 200 wounded."

[22] Col. Wright had for some years been a Democratic member of Congress, and an intimate friend, as well as compatriot, of Hon. Philip B. Fouke, a Democratic member from Tennessee. When they parted, at the close of the session of 1860–61, Wright said to his friend: "Phil., I expect the next time we meet, it will be on the battle-field." Sure enough, their next meeting was in this bloody struggle, where Wright fell mortally wounded, and 60 of his men were taken prisoners by Col. Fouke's regiment.

XXXVI.

ON THE SEABOARD AND OCEAN.

On Sunday, June 2d, 1861, while the Minnesota, then blockading the harbor of Charleston, was looking after a suspicious vessel that was observed to the southward, a little schooner of some fifty tuns, carrying an ugly-looking 18-pounder mounted on a swivel amidships, and manned by twenty-two men, of whom not more than half could find room at once under the shelter of her deck, slipped out from under the lee of Fort Sumter, by the north channel, taking first a northward course, so as to allay suspicion on board the blockader, but intending to stretch boldly across the Gulf Stream to Great Abaco, and lie in wait near the Hole-in-the-Wall for unarmed Yankee merchantmen trafficking between Northern ports and Cuba.

She was lucky at the outset, almost beyond her hopes; falling in, when scarcely a day at sea, with the brig Joseph, of Rockland, Me., laden with sugar from Cardenas, Cuba, for Philadelphia. Setting an American flag in her main rigging, to indicate her wish to speak the stranger, the privateer easily decoyed the Joseph within speaking distance, when he ordered her captain to lower his boat and come on board. This command having been readily obeyed, the merchantman was astounded by the information, fully authenticated by the 18-pounder aforesaid, that he was a prize to the nameless wasp on whose deck he stood, which had unquestionable authority from Mr. Jefferson Davis to capture all vessels belonging to loyal citizens of the United States. There was plainly nothing to be said; so the Yankee skipper said nothing; but was held a prisoner on board his captor, while a prize-crew of eight well-armed men was sent on board the Joseph, directed to take her with her men into Georgetown, S. C.

At 5 P. M., of that day, a brig hove in sight; and the Confederate schooner at once made all sail directly toward her, expecting, by the easy capture of a second richly laden merchantman, to complete a good day's work, even for June. On nearing her, however, he was astonished in turn by a show of teeth—quite too many of them for his one heavy grinder. Putting his craft instantly about, he attempted, by sharp sailing, to escape; but it was too late. He was under the guns of the U. S. brig Perry, Lieut. E. G. Parrott commanding, which at once set all sail for a chase, firing at intervals, as signals that her new acquaintance was expected to stop. The Savannah—for that word, displayed in raised letters on the front part of her trunk cabin, seemed to be, or at least to have been, her name—did not appear to comprehend; for she sent four shots at the Perry, one of which passed through her rigging. So the chase continued till 8 o'clock P. M., when the Perry had hauled so close to the puzzling little craft as to order her by trumpet to heave to, when the schooner lowered all her sails, and her officers ran below. In a few moments, the two quarter-boats of the Perry were alongside, and their crews leaped upon the flyaway's deck; when all remaining mystery as to her character was thoroughly dispelled. Her men at once stepped forward and surrendered their side-arms; and, perceiving there was no bloodshed, the leaders soon emerged from the cabin, and did likewise. All were promptly transferred to the Perry, and returned in her to Charleston bar; whence they were dispatched, on the 7th, as prisoners, in what had been their own vessel, to New York, where they arrived, in charge of Midshipman McCook and a prize crew, on the 15th. They were arraigned and some of them tried as pirates, but not convicted—Mr. Jefferson Davis, by a letter to President Lincoln, dated Richmond, July 6th, declaring that he would retaliate on our prisoners in his hands any treatment that might be inflicted on them. No answer was returned to this letter; but the privateer's crew were ultimately exchanged, like other prisoners of war.

The Savannah's rough experience was repeated, two months later, by the Petrel, formerly the U. S. revenue cutter Aiken, but turned over to South Carolina by her officers in the infancy of Secession. Running out of Charleston on a cruise, the Petrel soon encountered the St. Lawrence, gunboat, and, mistaking her for a merchantman, fired at her as a summons to surrender. The St. Lawrence at once returned the compliment with a broadside, sinking the Rebel craft off-hand, with five of her crew. The residue, thirty-six in number, were sent to Fort Mifflin, on the Delaware, as prisoners.

Gen. Benj. F. Butler sailed, August 26, 1861, from Fortress Monroe, as commander of a military and naval force whose destination was secret. It consisted of the fifty-gun frigates Minnesota, Wabash, and Cumberland, with four smaller national vessels and two steam transports, carrying 800 soldiers, with two tugs laden with supplies; the Naval force under the command of Com. Stringham. Arriving the second night off the entrance through Hatteras Inlet to Pamlico Sound, it was found defend-

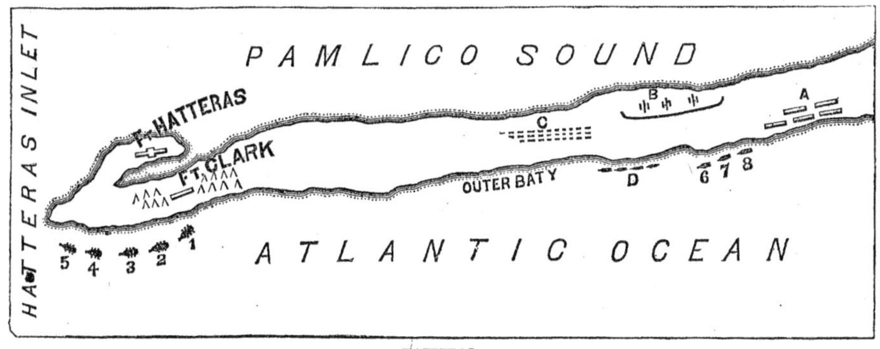

HATTERAS.

Explanations to the plan of the Bombardment of Forts Hatteras and Clark.

A. United States troops and marines.
B. Masked Batteries.
C. Scouting parties awaiting the bombardment.
D. Small Boats.
1. Cumberland.
2. Wabash.
3. Minnesota.
4 and 5. Susquehanna and Monticello, during the afternoon of the bombardment.
6, 7, and 8. Steamers Pawnee, Harriet Lane, and Monticello, protecting the landing of troops.

ed by the new Forts Hatteras and Clark, mounting five and ten guns respectively, with five more ready for mounting on the more important work; the whole defended by 700 Confederates, under Com. S. Barron, late of the Federal Navy; the infantry consisting of the 7th North Carolina, Col. Martin.

The forts were found far less formidable than they doubtless would have been a few weeks later. The bombardment was commenced at 10 A. M., of the 28th; Fort Hatteras replying, with signal industry, to little purpose; its gunners being evidently inexperienced and unskilled. Fort Clark had little or nothing to say; and was next morning found to have been already abandoned.

The Sound being still open, a heavily laden transport reënforced Fort Hatteras during the night; but this did no good. The bombardment having been reöpened by our ships on the morning of the 29th, and it being evident that to continue the contest was simply to condemn his men to useless slaughter, Com. Barron, at 11 A. M., raised the white flag, and, on consultation, offered to surrender the fort with its contents, on condition that the garrison should be allowed to retire. Gen. Butler declined the proffer; but proposed, in his turn, to guarantee to officers and men, on capitulation, the treatment of prisoners of war; and this was ultimately accepted. The spoils were 715 prisoners, 25 cannon, 1,000 stand of arms, and a considerable quantity of provisions and stores. Our loss was next to nothing. And the secret of the expedition had been so well kept that, for several days thereafter, blockade-runners from various quarters ran into the inlet as a Confederate shelter, and fell an easy prey to our arms.

No effort being made by the Confederates to retake this important position, Gen. Butler, with most of our vessels, had departed on other service; when Col. Hawkins, commanding at Hatteras, dispatched, late in September, the 20th Indiana, Col. Brown, to the petty hamlet on the Hatteras Bank, known as Chicamicomico, near Cape Hatteras, and some fifteen or twenty miles north-east of the Inlet. The excuse for this perilous division of his forces was the protection of the native residents, who claimed to be Unionists. A few days thereafter (Sept. 29th), the propeller Fanny, which had transported the regiment to Chicamicomico, and was now proceeding through the Sound, carrying thither a full cargo of stores and 40 men, was pounced upon by three armed steamers from the main land, and easily captured; and, six days thereafter, Col. Brown discovered five Rebel steamers emerging from Croatan Sound, with evident intent to attack him. To this end, they landed a superior force above his position, and then proceeded to land a detachment further down, intending to cut off his retreat and compel his surrender. Col. Brown, however, destroyed his tents and stores, and made a rapid march to the Hatteras Lighthouse, with a loss of about 50 stragglers taken prisoners. Col. Hawkins, by this time fully apprised of the Rebel movement, soon started, with six companies, to the rescue; while the Susquehanna and Monticello, our only two fighting vessels at the Inlet, moved up to the vicinity of the Lighthouse, to take a

THE U. S. FRIGATE ST. LAWRENCE SINKING THE PRIVATEER "PETREL," AUG. 1, 1861.

hand in the business. Doubling Cape Hatteras next morning, the Monticello, Lieut. Braine, came upon the main Rebel force at 1½ P. M., and opened upon them with shells, putting them instantly to flight, with great slaughter. The bank or beach between the ocean and the Sound, being less than a mile wide, afforded little protection to the fugitives, who sustained an incessant fire from the Monticello for two hours; and two of our shells are said to have penetrated two Rebel sloops laden with men, tearing them to pieces and destroying all on board. Had our land forces efficiently coöperated, most of the Rebels might have been taken; as it was, Col. Brown returned unmolested to the fort.

Fort Pickens, on the western extremity of Santa Rosa Island, commanding the main entrance to Pensacola harbor, was saved to the Union, as we have seen,[1] by the fidelity and prompt energy of Lieut. Slemmer. It was reënforced soon after the fall

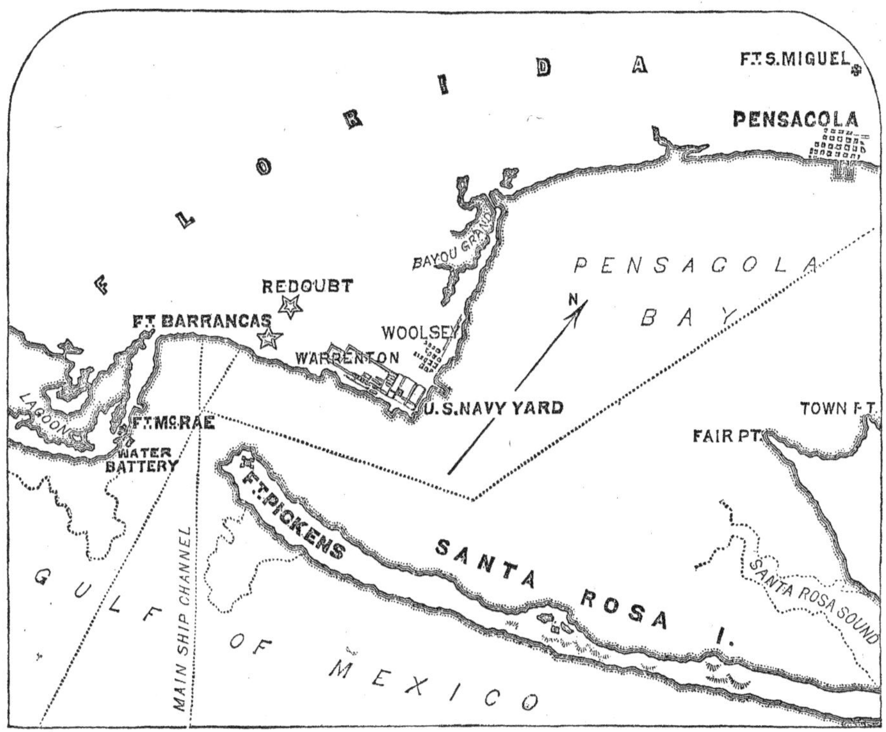

MAP OF FORT PICKENS, PENSACOLA, ETC.

of Sumter, and its defense confided to Col. Harvey Brown. A formidable Rebel force, ultimately commanded by Gen. Braxton Bragg, was assembled, early in the war, at Pensacola, and long threatened an attack or bombardment, which, on our side, was eagerly awaited.

Com. William Mervine, commanding the Gulf Blockading Squadron, having observed that a schooner named the Judah was being fitted

[1] Page 412.

out in the harbor of Pensacola as a privateer, with intent to slip out some dark night, prepared to cruise against our commerce, planned an expedition to destroy her. During the night of Sept. 13th, four boats, carrying 100 men, commanded by Lieut. Russell, put off from Com. Mervine's flag-ship Colorado, approaching the schooner at 3½ A. M., of the 14th. The privateer's crew, duly warned, opened a fire of musketry as the boats neared her; but were speedily driven from her deck by our boarders, and she set on fire and burned to the water's edge, when she sunk. Her gun, a 10-inch columbiad, was spiked, and sunk with her. All was the work of a quarter of an hour, during which our side had 3 killed and 12 wounded. As the Judah lay directly off the Navy Yard, where a thousand Rebels were quartered, this was one of the most daring and well-executed achievements of the year.

Finally, during the intensely dark night of Oct. 9th, a Confederate force crossed silently from Pensacola to Santa Rosa Island, with intent to surprise and destroy the camp of the 6th New York (Wilson's Zouaves), some two miles distant from Fort Pickens. The attack was well planned and well made. The surprise seems to have been complete. The Zouaves were instantly driven from their camp, which was thoroughly destroyed; but the darkness, which had favored the surprise, invested every step beyond the camp with unknown perils; and, when day broke, the Rebels had no choice but to retreat as swiftly as possible to their boats, eight miles distant. Of course, they were followed, and harassed, and fired upon after they had reëmbarked; and it was claimed, on our side, that their loss exceeded 300; but, as they left but 21 dead on the island, and 30 prisoners, the claim is simply absurd. Our loss was 60, and theirs probably a little more. But several thousand Rebels were kept at Pensacola throughout the campaign by less than 1,000 on our side; and, when they finally decamped, they had no choice but to surrender the Naval Floating Dock and Railway, with much other public property, to the flames, to prevent their easy recovery to the Union.

The blockade of the mouths of the Mississippi, naturally difficult, because of their number and distances, was successfully evaded on the 1st of July by the steam privateer Sumter, Capt. Raphael Semmes, who, darting swiftly from point to point throughout those portions of the West India waters known to be most thickly studded with our merchantmen, made some twelve or fifteen captures in hardly so many days, and then ran into the friendly British port of Nassau, where he was promptly supplied with everything necessary to a vigorous prosecution of his devastating career. Having continued it some time longer with great success, he finally ran into the British harbor of Gibraltar, where the Federal gunboat Tuscarora soon found him and his vessel, and, anchoring in the Spanish port of Algesiras, just opposite, where no law would compel her to remain twenty-four hours after the Sumter had departed, she held the privateer fast until relieved by the Kearsarge, by which the blockade was persistently maintained until the Confederate officers abandoned their vessel—professing to sell her—and betook themselves to Liverpool, where a faster and better steamer, the Alabama, had meantime been constructed, and fitted out for their service. So the Nashville, which ran out of Charleston during the Summer, and, in due time, appeared in British waters, after burning (Nov. 19th) the Harvey Birch merchantman within sight of the English coast, ran into Southampton, where lay the Tuscarora; which, if permitted to pursue, would have made short work of her soon after she left, but was compelled to remain twenty-four hours to insure her escape. This detention is authorized by the law of nations, though it has not always been respected by Great Britain: Witness her capture of the Essex and Essex Junior in the harbor of Valparaiso, and her destruction of the Gen. Armstrong privateer in the port of Fayal, during the war of 1812. But the concession of such belligerent rights and immunities to a power which has neither recognized national existence nor maritime strength will yet be regretted by Great Britain, as affording an unfortunate and damaging precedent.

In October—the communications between our blockading forces in the Gulf and the loyal States being fitful and tedious—the North was startled by the following bulletin, which appeared as a telegram from New Orleans to the Richmond papers:

"FORT JACKSON, Oct. 12, 1861.

"Last night, I attacked the blockaders with my little fleet. I succeeded, after a very short struggle, in driving them *all* aground on the Southwest Pass bar, except the Preble, *which I sunk.*

"I captured a prize from them; and, after they were fast in sand, I peppered them well.

"There were no casualties on our side. It was a complete success. HOLLINS."

Commander Hollins, formerly of our Navy, and more notorious than famous for his bombardment of Greytown, Nicaragua, had drawn rather liberally on his imagination in the above. His prize was a deserted coal-boat; he had not sunk the Preble; and his 'peppering' was done at a prudent distance, and with little or no effect. But he had burst upon our squadron blockading the mouths of the Mississippi, at 3.45 A. M. of that day, with a flotilla composed of his ram Manassas, three fire-rafts, and five armed steamers. The ram struck our flag steamship Richmond, Capt. Pope, staving in her side below the water-line, and, for the moment, threatening her destruction. Our squadron, consisting of the Richmond, Preble, Vincennes, and Water Witch, instantly slipped their cables, and ran down the South-west Pass, very much as they would have done had all on board been considerably frightened. Commander Robert Handy, of the Vincennes, ran his vessel aground in the flight, and deserted her, with all his men; setting a slow-match to destroy her, which happily failed. His vessel was recovered unharmed. The fire-rafts were entirely avoided; the Rebel steamboats not venturing within range of the Richmond's guns; while Hollins's haste to telegraph his victory seems to have cost him all its legitimate fruits. Beyond the destruction of the fire-ships, the losses on either side were of no account.

On the 29th of October, another and far stronger naval and military expedition set forth from Hampton Roads, and, clearing the capes of Virginia, moved majestically southward.

Gen. T. W. Sherman commanded the land forces, consisting of thirteen volunteer regiments, forming three brigades, and numbering not less than 10,000 men; while the fleet—commanded by Com. Samuel F. Du Pont—embraced the steam-frigate Wabash, 14 gunboats, 22 first-class and 12 smaller steamers, with 26 sailing vessels. After a stormy passage, in which several transports were disabled, and four absolutely lost, Com. Du Pont, in his flag-ship, came to off Port Royal, S. C., during the night of November 3d and 4th; and, after proper soundings and reconnoissances, which developed the existence of a new fort on either side of the entrance, the Commodore brought his most effective vessels into action at 9 A. M., on Thursday, November 7th, taking the lead in his flag-ship, the Wabash—the gunboats to follow at intervals in due order. Thus the fighting portion of the fleet steamed slowly up the bay by the forts, receiving and returning the fire of the batteries on Bay Point as they passed up, and

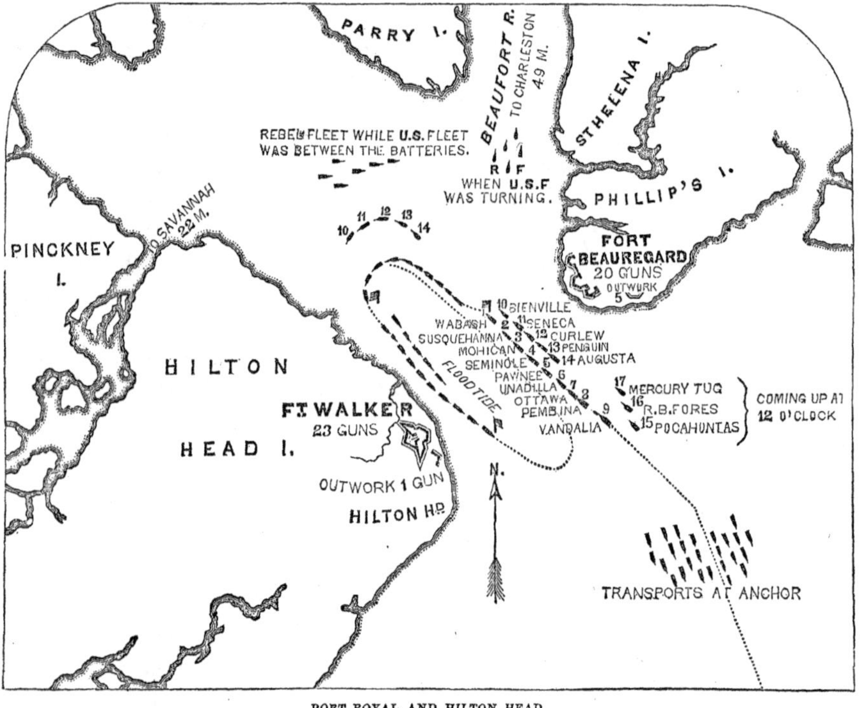

PORT ROYAL AND HILTON HEAD.

EXPLANATION.—Nos. 10, 11, 12, 13, and 14, in the back-ground, are the positions of the smaller Federal gunboats.

exchanging like compliments with the stronger fort on Hilton Head as they came down. Thus no vessel remained stationary under fire; so that the enemy were at no time enabled to gain, by experiment and observation, a perfect aim. The day was lovely; the spectacle magnificent; the fight spirited, but most unequal. Despite the general presumption that batteries, well manned and served, are superior to ships when not iron-clad, the terrible rain of shot and shell upon the gunners in the Rebel forts soon proved beyond human endurance. The smaller gunboats at length took positions whence their fire was most annoying, yet could not be effectively returned; while the Bienville, on her second promenade, steamed close in to the main Rebel fort, and fired her great guns with such effect as almost to silence the enemy. The Wabash, on her third round, came within six hundred yards of the fort, firing as calmly and heavily as at the outset. The battle had thus raged nearly five hours, with fearful carnage and devastation on the part of the Rebels and very little loss on ours, when the overmatched Confederates, finding themselves slaughtered to no purpose, suddenly and unanimously took to flight; their commander, Gen. T. F. Drayton,[2] making as good time as the best of them.[3] The Rebel forts were fully manned by 1,700 South Carolinians, with a field battery of 500 more stationed not far distant. The negroes, save those who had been driven off by their masters, or shot while attempting to evade them, had stubbornly remained on the isles; and there was genuine pathos in the prompt appearance of scores of them, rushing down to the water-side, with their scanty stock of valuables tied up in a handkerchief, and begging to be taken on board our ships. The idea that our occupation might be permanent seems not to have occurred to them; they only thought of escaping at all hazards from their life-long, bitter bondage.

Had this blow been followed up as it might have been, Charleston, or Savannah, or both, could have been easily and promptly captured. The Confederate defeat was so unexpected, so crushing, and the terror inspired by our gunboats so general and profound, that nothing could have withstood the progress of our arms. But Gen. Sherman had not been instructed to press his advantages, nor had he been provided with the light-draft steamers, row-boats, and other facilities, really needed for the improvement of his signal victory. He did not even occupy Beaufort until December 6th, nor Tybee Island, commanding the approach to Savannah, until December 20th; on which day, a number of old hulks of vessels were sunk in the main ship channel leading up to Charleston between Morris and Sullivan's islands—as others were, a few days afterward, in the passage known as Maffit's channel—with intent to impede the midnight flitting of blockade-runners. These obstructions were denounced in Europe as barbarous, but proved simply inefficient.

Meantime, the slaveholders of all the remaining Sea Islands stripped them of slaves and domestic animals, burned their cotton, and other crops which they were unable to remove, and fled to Charleston and the interior. Not a slaveholder on all that

[2] He was brother to Commander E. Drayton, of the U. S. gunboat Pocahontas, who was in the thickest of the fight on the side of his whole country. Capt. Steadman, of the Bienville, was likewise a South Carolinian.

[3] This flight, however hurried and reckless, was fully justifiable. They had to run six miles across the island to Seabrook, where they took boat for Savannah, and where any one of our idle armed vessels might easily have intercepted and captured them all. All their works on Hilton Head and the adjacent islands, with about 40 guns, most of them new and large, were utterly abandoned; and, when our forces took possession, soon after, of Beaufort, they found but one white person remaining, and he drunk.

coast remained himself, or left his family to live once more, under the flag of the Union. Gen. Sherman issued a pleading, beseeching proclamation to induce them to do so; but none who could read would receive a copy of it, and it fell a dead letter. Soon, the negroes who remained on the islands under our control were set to work at preparing the cotton for market; and, though assured by the master caste that, if they fell into the hands of the Yankees, they would certainly be sent to Cuba and sold, they could not be made to believe that any worse fortune than they had hitherto experienced was in store for them; and their number was steadily augmented by emigrants from the mainland; especially after schools began to be established among them.

The steamship Theodora ran out of Charleston harbor during the night of Oct. 12th, conveying James M. Mason, of Va., Confederate Envoy to Great Britain, and John Slidell, of La., likewise accredited to France. The Theodora duly reached Cardenas, Cuba; whence her official passengers repaired to Havana, and, on the 7th of November, left that port, in the British mail steamer Trent, for St. Thomas, on their way to England. The U. S. steamship San Jacinto, Capt. Wilkes, had left Havana on the 2d, and was watching for them in the Bahama Channel, 240 miles from Havana, when, at 11:40 A. M., of the 8th, he sighted the Trent; and, after a civil request to heave to had been declined by her, a shell was fired across her bow, which brought her to reason. Lieut. Fairfax, with a boat's crew, immediately boarded her in quest of the Embassadors; when Messrs. Mason and Slidell, with their Secretaries, Eustis and McFarland, were compelled to change their vessel and their destination. Their families were left undisturbed, and no effort made to obtain their papers. But the Embassadors and their Secretaries were brought to the United States, and confined, by order of the Government, in Fort Warren, near Boston.

Secretary Welles, in his Annual Report of naval proceedings for the year ending Dec. 2d, 1861, thus fully and frankly adopted and justified the capture:

> "The prompt and decisive action of Capt. Wilkes on this occasion merited and received the emphatic approval of the Department; and, if a too generous forbearance was exhibited by him in not capturing the vessels which had these Rebel enemies on board, it may, in view of the special circumstances, and of its patriotic motives, be excused; but it must by no means be permitted to constitute a precedent hereafter for the treatment of any case of similar infraction of neutral obligations by foreign vessels engaged in commerce or the carrying-trade."

By a decided majority of the publicists of the United States, as well as by the great mass of our people, this seizure was deemed abundantly justified by the doctrines and practices of Great Britain, but especially by her long continued and never disavowed habit of impressing seamen from our merchant vessels, on the assumption that they were natives of Great Britain, and therefore liable at all times and indefeasibly to be remanded into her service, wherever found. In the able and carefully prepared manifesto [7] whereby George IV., then Prince Regent, explained and justified the conduct of his Government touching the matters in con-

[7] Dated *Westminster* Jan. 9th, 1813.

troversy between it and our own, this doctrine is set forth as follows:

"The Order in Council of the 23d of June being officially communicated in America, the Government of the United States saw nothing in the repeal of the Orders which should, of itself, restore peace, unless Great Britain were prepared, in the first instance, substantially to relinquish the right of impressing her own seamen, when found on board American merchant ships. * * *

"If America, by demanding this preliminary concession, intends to deny the validity of that right, in that denial Great Britain cannot acquiesce; nor will she give countenance to such a pretension, by acceding to its suspension, much less to its abandonment, as a basis on which to treat. * * * The British Government has never asserted any exclusive right, as to the impressment of British seamen from American vessels, which it was not prepared to acknowledge as pertaining equally to the Government of the United States, with respect to American seamen when found on board British merchant ships. * * *

"His Royal Highness can never admit that, in the exercise of the undoubted, and, hitherto, undisputed, right of searching neutral vessels, in time of war, the impressment of British seamen, when found therein, can be deemed any violation of a neutral flag. Neither can he admit that the taking such seamen from on board such vessels can be considered, by any neutral State, as a hostile measure, or a justifiable cause of war.

"There is no right more clearly established than the right which a sovereign has to the allegiance of his subjects, more especially in time of war. Their allegiance is no optional duty, which they can decline at pleasure. It is a call which they are bound to obey. It began with their birth, and can only terminate with their existence."

In the Queen's Proclamation of Neutrality between the United States and the Confederates, dated May 13th, 1861, there occurs this express and proper inhibition:

"And we do hereby further warn all our loving subjects, and all persons whatsoever entitled to our protection, that, if any of them shall presume, in contempt of this Royal Proclamation, and of our high displeasure, to do any acts in derogation of their duty as subjects of a neutral sovereign, in the said contest, or in violation or contravention of the law of nations in that behalf—as, for example and more especially, by entering into the military service of either of the said contending parties as commissioned or non-commissioned officers or soldiers; or by serving as officers, sailors, or marines, on board any ship, or vessel of war, or transport of or in the service of either of the said contending parties; or by serving as officers, sailors, or marines, on board any privateer bearing letters of marque of or from either of the said contending parties; or by engaging to go, or going, to any place beyond the seas with intent to enlist or engage in any such service; or by procuring, or attempting to procure, within Her Majesty's dominions, at home or abroad, others to do so; or by fitting out, arming, or equipping, any ship or vessel, to be employed as a ship of war, or privateer, or transport, by either of the said contending parties; or by breaking, or endeavoring to break, any blockade lawfully and actually established by or on behalf of either of the said contending parties; or *by carrying officers*, soldiers, *dispatches*, arms, military stores or materials, or any article or articles considered and deemed to be contraband of war, according to the law or modern usage of nations, for the use or service of either of the said contending parties, all persons so offending will incur and be liable to the several penalties and penal consequences by the said statute, or by the law of nations, in that behalf imposed or denounced.

"And we do hereby declare that all our subjects and persons entitled to our protection, who may misconduct themselves in the premises, will do so at their peril and of their own wrong, and that they will in nowise obtain any protection from us against any liability or penal consequences; but will, on the contrary, incur our high displeasure by such misconduct."

Now, there was no shadow of doubt that the Trent was consciously, willingly, employed in carrying very important officers and dispatches for the Confederates; rendering them the greatest possible service, and one which could not safely be effected in vessels bearing their own flag. It was not at all the case of dispatches carried unconsciously, innocently, in the public mails of mail steamers; but just such an interference to the prejudice of the one and the advantage of the other belligerent as British Courts of Admiralty had been accustomed to condemn; forfeiting the vessel and cargo of the offender. Great Britain, however, would not see it in this light. Com. Wilkes's act was an outrage—an insult—which must be promptly atoned for at the peril of war. Such was the purport of the language held by a large majority of her publicists and journals; and a peremptory demand was promptly made, through her Embassador, Lord Lyons, for the unconditional surrender of Messrs. Mason and Slidell and their secretaries. France seconded and supported the requirement of Great Britain, in a considerate and courteous dispatch, wherein she justly claimed to have hitherto uniformly accorded with the United States in a liberal interpretation and generous assertion of the rights of neutrals in war. This demand of Great Britain—to the great disappointment and chagrin of the Confederates, who confidently expected that war between the United States and England must speedily and certainly ensue—was complied with by our Government—Gov. Seward, in an able dispatch, basing that compliance more immediately on the failure of Capt. Wilkes to bring the Trent into port for adjudication on the legality of his act, whereby her voyage had been temporarily arrested and two of her passengers forcibly abstracted.

And thus, at the close of the year 1861, the imminent peril of war with that European Power most able to injure us, because of her immense naval strength, as well as of the proximity of her American possessions, was wisely averted; though it was bitterly felt that her demand would at least have been more courteously and considerately made but for the gigantic war in which we were already inextricably involved by the Slaveholders' Rebellion.

XXXVII.

KENTUCKY.

We have seen[1] that Kentucky emphatically, persistently, repeatedly, by overwhelming popular majorities, refused—alike before and after the formal inauguration of war by the Confederate attack on Fort Sumter—to ally herself with the Rebellion, or to stand committed to any scheme looking to Disunion in whatever contingency. Her Democratic Governor and Legislature of 1860–61, with most of her leading Democratic, and many of her Whig, politicians, were, indeed, more or less cognizant of the Disunion conspiracy, and were more or less intimate and confidential with its master-spirits. But they looked to very different ends. The Southrons proper, of the school of Calhoun, Rhett, Yancey, and Ruffin, regarding Disunion as a chief good under any and all circumstances, made its achievement the great object of their life-long endeavor, and regarded Slavery in the territories, fugitive slaves and their recovery, compromises, John Brown raids, etc., only as conducive to or impeding its consummation; while

[1] P. 492–7.

REAR AD. DAVID G. FARRAGUT
REAR AD. L. M. GOLDSBOROUGH
REAR AD. SAMUEL F. DU PONT
REAR AD. ANDREW H. FOOTE
COM. CHARLES WILKES
REAR AD. JOHN A. DAHLGREN
REAR AD. DAVID D. PORTER
REAR AD. CHARLES H. DAVIS
COM. HENRY W. MORRIS
CAPT. JAMES H. WARD
CAPT. CHARLES S. BOGGS
CAPT. JOHN L. WORDEN
Entered according to act of Congress A.D. 1864 by O. D. Case & Co. in the clerks office of the District Court of the U.S. for the District of Connecticut.
Engraved by J. C. Buttre, New York.
UNION NAVAL OFFICERS

the 'State-Rights' apostles of the Border-State school contemplated Secession, and everything pertaining thereto, primarily, as means of perfecting and perpetuating the slaveholding ascendency in the Union as it was. Hence, we have seen Gov. Magoffin[2] protest against the secession of South Carolina and the Cotton States, not as a treasonable repudiation of their constitutional duties, but as a chimerical futility, and as a betrayal of the slaveholding Border States into the power of the 'Black Republicans.'

Kentucky, as we have shown,[3] nine weeks after the reduction of Fort Sumter, gave an aggregate of 92,365 votes for Union to 36,995 for Secession candidates, in choosing, at a special election, her representatives in the XXXVIIth Congress, while, as yet, no Federal soldier stood armed on her soil, and while her Legislature, Governor, and most of his associate State officers, were the Democratic compatriots of Breckinridge, Burnett, and Buckner. Only a single district elected a Secessionist, by four-sevenths of its total vote; and he its old member, who had hitherto received far larger majorities, running as a Democrat, in a district where the Democratic party had, since 1826, uniformly commanded overwhelming majorities. That district, at the western extremity of the State, hemmed in between West Tennessee, Southern Missouri, and that portion of Illinois widely known as 'Egypt,' and traversed by the great Southern rivers Tennessee and Cumberland, had, in fact, for more than a quarter of a century, been alien from Kentucky in character and sympathies, as it proved itself in this case. The residue of the State elected only Unionists to Congress, by a popular majority of almost three to one.

This majority was very nearly maintained at her regular State election (August 5th), when—Magoffin being still Governor, Buckner commander of the State Guard, and the local offices mainly held by 'State-Rights' Democrats, with the recent Union rout and disaster at Bull Run tending still further to unmask and develop all the latent treason in the State—a new Legislature was chosen, wherein Unionism of a very decided type predominated in the proportion of nearly three to one.[4]

[2] See pp. 340–41. [3] P. 496.

[4] Pollard, in his "Southern History," fully admits, while he denounces and deplores, the hostility of Kentucky to the Rebel cause—saying:

"It is not to be supposed for a moment that, while the position of Kentucky, like that of Maryland, was one of reproach, it is to mar the credit due to that portion of the people of each, who, in the face of instant difficulties, and at the expense of extraordinary sacrifices, repudiated the decision of their States to remain under the Federal Government, and expatriated themselves that they might espouse the cause of liberty in the South. The honor due such men is, in fact, increased by the consideration that their States remained in the Union, and compelled them to fly their homes, that they might certify their devotion to the South and her cause of independence. Still, the justice of history must be maintained. The demonstrations of sympathy with the South on the part of the States referred to—Maryland and Kentucky—considered either in proportion to what was offered the Lincoln Government by these States, or with respect to the numbers of their population, were sparing and exceptional; and although these demonstrations on the part of Kentucky, from the great and brilliant names associated with them, were perhaps even more honorable and more useful than the examples of Southern spirit offered by Maryland, it is unquestionably though painfully true, that the great body of the people of Kentucky were the active allies of Lincoln, and the unnatural enemies of those united to them by lineage, blood, and common institutions."

Those who love and honor the name of Henry Clay will thank the author of the "Southern History" for the following undesigned but richly merited homage to the character and influence of that great man:

"It is certainly defective logic, or, at best, an

A determined Union Legislature having thus been elected but not yet assembled, Gov. Magoffin, feeling that his time was short, and that any further mischief to the Union cause at his hands must be done quickly, addressed to the President of the United States, by the hands of two 'Commissioners,' the following cool epistle:

"COMMONWEALTH OF KENTUCKY,
"EXECUTIVE DEPARTMENT, FRANKFORT,
"August 19, 1861.
"To His Excellency, ABRAHAM LINCOLN,
"*President of the United States:*

"SIR: From the commencement of the unhappy hostilities now pending in this country, the people of Kentucky have indicated an earnest desire and purpose, as far as lay in their power, while maintaining their original political status, to do nothing by which to involve themselves in the war. Up to this time, they have succeeded in securing to themselves and to the State, peace and tranquillity as the fruits of the policy they adopted. My single object now is to promote the continuance of these blessings to the people of this State.

"Until within a brief period, the people of Kentucky were quiet and tranquil, free from domestic strife, and undisturbed by internal commotion. They have resisted no law, rebelled against no authority, engaged in no revolution; but constantly proclaimed their firm determination to pursue their peaceful avocations, earnestly hoping that their own soil would be spared the presence of armed troops, and that the scene of conflict would be kept removed beyond the border of their State. By thus avoiding all occasions for the introduction of bodies of armed soldiers, and offering no provocation for the presence of military force, the people of Kentucky have sincerely striven to preserve in their State domestic peace, and avert the calamities of sanguinary engagements.

"Recently, a large body of soldiers have been enlisted in the United States Army, and collected in military camps in the central portion of Kentucky. This movement was preceded by the active organization of companies, regiments, etc., consisting of men sworn into the United States service, under officers holding commissions from yourself. Ordnance, arms, munitions, and supplies of war, are being transported into the State, and placed in large quantities in these camps. In a word, an army is now being organized and quartered within the State, supplied with all the appliances of war, without the consent or advice of the authorities of the State, and without consultation with those most prominently known and recognized as loyal citizens. This movement now imperils that peace and tranquillity which, from the beginning of our present difficulties, have been the paramount desire of this people, and which, up to this time, they have secured to the State.

"Within Kentucky, there has been, and is likely to be, no occasion for the presence of military force. The people are quiet and tranquil, feeling no apprehension of any occasion arising to invoke protection from the Federal arm. They have asked that their territory be left free from military occupation, and the present tranquillity of their communications left uninvaded by soldiers. They do not desire that Kentucky shall be required to supply the battle-field for the contending armies, or become the theater of the war.

"Now, therefore, as Governor of the State of Kentucky, and in the name of the people I have the honor to represent, and with the single and earnest desire to avert from their peaceful homes the horrors of war, I urge the removal from the limits of Kentucky of the military force now organized and in camp within the State. If such action as is hereby urged be promptly taken, I firmly believe the peace of the people of Kentucky will be preserved, and the horrors of a bloody war will be averted from a people now peaceful and tranquil.

"B. MAGOFFIN."

The President, declining to receive Magoffin's Commissioners otherwise than as private citizens, returned this terse and pungent reply to their master's request:

inadequate explanation, which attributes the subserviency of a large portion of the people of Kentucky to the views of the Lincoln Government to the perfidy of a party or the adroitness of its management. However powerful may be the machinery of party, it certainly has not the power of belying public sentiment for any considerable length of time. The persistent adhesion of a large portion of the Kentucky people to the Northern cause must be attributed to permanent causes; and among these were, first, an essential unsoundness on the Slavery question, under the influences of the peculiar philosophy of Henry Clay, who, like every great man, left an impress upon his State, which it remained for future even more than contemporary generations to attest."

"WASHINGTON, D. C., Aug. 24, 1861.
"To his Excellency, B. MAGOFFIN,
"*Governor of the State of Kentucky:*

"SIR: Your letter of the 19th inst., in which you 'urge the removal from the limits of Kentucky of the military force now organized and in camp within that State,' is received.

"I may not possess full and precisely accurate knowledge upon this subject; but I believe it is true that there *is* a military force in camp within Kentucky, acting by authority of the United States; which force is not very large, and is not now being augmented.

"I also believe that some arms have been furnished to this force by the United States.

"I also believe that this force consists exclusively of Kentuckians, having their camp in the immediate vicinity of their own homes, and not assailing or menacing any of the good people of Kentucky.

"In all I have done in the premises, I have acted upon the urgent solicitation of many Kentuckians, and in accordance with what I believed, and still believe, to be the wish of a majority of all the Union-loving people of Kentucky.

"While I have conversed on the subject with many eminent men of Kentucky, including a large majority of her members of Congress, I do not remember that any one of them, or any other person, except your Excellency and the bearers of your Excellency's letter, has urged me to remove the military force from Kentucky or to disband it. One other very worthy citizen of Kentucky *did* solicit me to have the augmenting of the force suspended for a time.

"Taking all the means within my reach to form a judgment, I do not believe it is the popular wish of Kentucky that the force shall be removed beyond her limits; and, with this impression, I must respectfully decline to remove it.

"I most cordially sympathize with your Excellency in the wish to preserve the peace of my own native State, Kentucky; but it is with regret I search for and cannot find, in your not very short letter, any declaration or intimation that you entertain any desire for the preservation of the Federal Union.

"ABRAHAM LINCOLN."

The Legislature convened September 3d, but was not fully organized till the 5th, when Magoffin submitted a Message based on the assumption of Kentucky's proper and perfect neutrality between the belligerents North and South of her; complaining that she had suffered in her commerce and property from the acts of either; but more especially that a Federal force had recently been organized and encamped in the heart of that State without the permission of her lawful authorities—(Beriah Magoffin, to wit;) whereupon he proposed to so amend an act of the late Legislature as to enable the Military Board to borrow money for the purchase of arms and munitions for the defense of the State, etc., etc. He desired the Legislature authoritatively to request all Military organizations within the State, not under her authority, to be disbanded forthwith; and complained of the introduction of arms by the Federal Government and their distribution among private citizens, which—considering that the incipient Rebels obtained a large proportion thereof, and in due time carried them off to the camps of the Secession forces—was unreasonable. On the main question at issue, he said:

"Kentucky has meant to await the exhausting of all civil remedies before she will reconsider the question of assuming new external relations; but I have never understood that they will tamely submit unconditionally to the aggressions of the North; that they renounce their sympathy with the people of her aggrieved sister States; nor that they will approve of a war to subjugate the South. Still can I not construe any of their votes as meaning that they will prosecute a coërcive war against their Southern brethren. They meant only that they have still some hope of the restoration and perpetuation of the Union; and, until that hope is blasted, they will not alter their existing relations. Their final decision will be law to me; and I will execute every constitutional act of their representatives as vigilantly and faithfully as though it originated with myself."

These few words elicited no sympathetic response from the Legislature, fresh from the people, and imbued with their sentiments. On the contrary, the House, six days thereafter, resolved—71 to 26—that the Governor be directed to order by proclamation the Confederate troops encamped on the soil of that State to *de*camp immediately. An attempt so to amend the resolution as to require all *Union* as well as Disunion forces to quit the State, was decidedly voted down; and the two Houses united in passing, by overwhelming votes, the following:

"*Resolved*, That Kentucky's peace and neutrality have been wantonly violated, her soil has been invaded, and the rights of her citizens have been grossly infringed, by the so-called Southern Confederate forces. This has been done without cause: therefore,

"*Be it enacted by the General Assembly of the Commonwealth of Kentucky*, That the Governor be requested to call out the military force of the State to expel and drive out the invaders.

"*Resolved*, That the United States be invoked to give that aid and assistance, that protection against invasion, which is guaranteed to each one of the States by the 4th section of the 4th article of the Constitution of the United States.

"*Resolved*, That Gen. Robert Anderson be, and he is hereby, requested to enter immediately upon the active discharge of his duties in this military district.

"*Resolved*, That we appeal to the people of Kentucky, by the ties of patriotism and honor, by the ties of common interest and common defense, by the remembrances of the past, and by the hopes of future National existence, to assist in expelling and driving out the wanton invaders of our peace and neutrality, the lawless invaders of our soil."

These resolves were adopted—in the House by 68 to 26, and in the Senate by 26 to 8.

Magoffin promptly vetoed them. The Legislature as promptly passed them over his veto by overwhelming majorities. Gen. Grant, commanding at Cairo, had already telegraphed to the Legislature, Sept. 5th, that Western Kentucky had been invaded by a large Rebel force, who were then holding and fortifying strong positions on the east bank of the Mississippi at Hickman and Chalk Bluffs. The Legislature referred this dispatch to a Special Committee, which telegraphed thereupon to Gov. Harris, of Tennessee, who thus responded:

"The Confederate troops that landed at Hickman last night did so without my knowledge or consent; and, I am confident, also without the consent of the President. I have telegraphed President Davis, requesting their immediate withdrawal."[5]

Gen. Grant did not see fit to depend on the fair promises of Gov. Harris, nor the amenity of Gen. Bishop Leonidas Polk, nor yet of President Davis, for the safety of his department, but occupied, next morning, Paducah, on the south bank of the Ohio, near the mouth of the Tennessee, with two regiments and a battery, finding Rebel flags flying over many of the buildings in that little city, in anticipation of the speedy appearance of a Confederate force, re-

[5] Gov. Magoffin communicated to the Legislature, Sept. 9th, a message to him from the four Commissioners of the Governor of Tennessee, in explanation of the reason why the Confederates had not been withdrawn from Kentucky, from which the following is an extract:

"The undersigned yesterday received a verbal message, through a messenger, from Gov. Harris. The message was, that Gov. Harris had, by telegraphic dispatch, requested Gen. Polk to withdraw the Confederate troops from Kentucky, and that Gen. Polk had declined to do so; that Gov. Harris then telegraphed to Secretary Walker, at Richmond, requesting that Gen. Polk be ordered to withdraw his troops from Kentucky; and that such order was issued from the War Department of the Confederacy; that Gen. Polk replied to the War Department that the retention of the post was a military necessity, and that the retiring from it would be attended by the loss of many lives. This embraces the message received.

"The messenger, it is true, in conversation, said that he had heard in Nashville that Secretary Walker had sent a dispatch to Gen. Buckner, giving Gen. Polk a discretion to hold to or withraw from the occupation of the post in Kentucky."

ported 3,800 strong, and but sixteen miles distant. He found there large quantities of prepared rations and of leather for the expected Rebel army, and put them to a better use. In his proclamation, thereupon issued, he said:

"I have come among you not as an enemy, but as your fellow-citizen; not to maltreat or annoy you, but to respect and enforce the rights of all loyal citizens. An enemy, in rebellion against our common Government, has taken possession of and planted his guns on the soil of Kentucky, and fired upon you. Columbus and Hickman are in his hands. He is moving upon your city. I am here to defend you against this enemy; to assist the authority and sovereignty of your Government. I have nothing to do with opinions, and shall deal only with armed Rebellion and its aiders and abettors. You can pursue your usual avocations without fear. The strong arm of the Government is here, to protect its friends and punish its enemies. Whenever it is manifest that you are able to defend yourselves, maintain the authority of the Government, and protect the rights of loyal citizens, I shall withdraw the forces under my command. U. S. GRANT,
"Brig. General Commanding."

Bishop Polk had not then occupied Columbus, as Gen. Grant supposed; but he did so next day, with a force of ten regiments, six batteries, and three battalions of cavalry. Of course, the promise of Gov. Harris that he should be withdrawn was not fulfilled, and the fact that Grant had now crossed the Ohio was made an excuse for this invasion. In other words: the people of Kentucky, through their then freshly chosen Legislature, having decided to remain in and be loyal to the Union, the Confederates regarded this as justifying them in seizing any portion of that State of which they should deem the occupancy advantageous to their cause; and, in fact, Gen. Zollicoffer,[6] commanding their forces in East Tennessee, had already occupied Cumberland Gap, and advanced through that pass into Kentucky, at least so early as the 5th; though no pretense of Federal invasion, accomplished or meditated, was, in that quarter, justified. But East Tennessee was earnestly and unchangeably loyal to the Union—had so voted by more than two to one at the recent State Election; and it had become necessary to surround her with Confederate camps, and cut her off from all communication with the loyal States, to prevent a general uprising of her hardy mountaineers in defense of the cause they loved.

Gen. Robert Anderson assumed command, at Louisville, of the Department of Kentucky, Sept. 20th; and the organization of Union volun-

[6] Zollicoffer telegraphed, Sept. 14th, to Magoffin as follows:

"The safety of Tennessee requiring, I occupy the mountain passes at Cumberland, and the three long mountains in Kentucky. For weeks, I have known that the Federal commander at Hoskins's Cross-Roads was threatening the invasion of East Tennessee, and ruthlessly urging our people to destroy our own road and bridges. I postponed this precautionary movement until the despotic Government at Washington, refusing to recognize the neutrality of Kentucky, had established formidable camps in the center and other parts of the State, with the view, first, to subjugate your gallant State, and then ourselves. Tennessee feels, and has ever felt, toward Kentucky as a twin-sister; their people are as one people in kindred, sympathy, valor, and patriotism. We have felt, and still feel, a religious respect for Kentucky's neutrality. We will respect it as long as our safety will permit. If the Federal force will now withdraw from their menacing position, the force under my command shall immediately be withdrawn."

"The despotic Government at Washington" could hardly, with reason, be blamed for refusing to recognize the neutrality of Kentucky, when Kentucky herself did that very thing with a decision and emphasis quite equal to those evinced in President Lincoln's reply to Magoffin. Zollicoffer's "religious respect," therefore, was paid to something exceedingly convenient to his cause, but which, if it ever had been, no longer existed.

teers was thenceforth actively promoted. On the 25th, a bill calling out 40,000 volunteers for the defense of the State and Union passed the House by a vote of 67 to 13; the Senate concurring by a vote of 21 to 5. On that day, the Senate, by 16 to 10, passed a bill providing that any and every Kentuckian who shall have voluntarily joined the Rebel force invading the State, shall be incapable of inheriting any property in Kentucky, unless he shall return to his allegiance within sixty days; and, on the next day, the House Judiciary Committee, having reported that, in its judgment, Congress had not transcended its powers in imposing taxes for the preservation of the Union, was discharged from further consideration of the subject by a vote of 67 to 13; and the Senate concurred without a division.

On the 16th, Zollicoffer advanced to Barboursville, Ky., capturing the camp of a regiment of Kentucky Unionists, who fled at his approach.

The changed attitude and determined purpose of Kentucky encouraged the Federal Government to take some decided steps in defense of its own existence. Ex-Gov. Morehead,[7] a most inveterate traitor, was arrested at his residence near Louisville, and taken thence to Fort Lafayette, in New York harbor, wherein he was long confined, and whence he should not have been released. Warned by this blow, ex-Vice-President John C. Breckinridge, Hon. Wm. Preston, late Minister to Spain, Thomas B. Monroe, sr., U. S. District Judge, Thomas B. Monroe, jr., Secretary of State, Col. Humphrey Marshall, late 'American' member of Congress, Col. George W. Johnson, Capt. John Morgan, and several other prominent traitors, escaped about this time to the Rebel camps in Southern Kentucky, and passed thence into Tennessee or Virginia, where they openly gave in their adhesion to the Southern Confederacy. Judge Monroe formally renounced his office and his allegiance, and was adopted a citizen of the Confederacy in open court at Nashville, October 3d. Breckinridge and Humphrey Marshall were promptly made Confederate Brigadier-Generals.

Zollicoffer, on entering Kentucky, issued an order promising that no citizen of that State should be molested in person or property unless found in arms for the Union, or somehow giving aid and comfort to the National cause. Of course, this did not save active Unionists from seizure, abuse, and confinement, nor the pigs, fowls, cattle, etc., whether of Unionists or Confederates, from wholesale confiscation by his loosely organized and undisciplined banditti, who swept over the poor and thinly settled mountainous region wherein the Cumberland and Kentucky rivers have their sources, devouring and destroying all before them.

Mr. Breckinridge, on finding himself safely within the Confederate lines, issued an elaborate and bitter Address, announcing his resignation

[7] Charles S. Morehead, formerly a Whig representative in Congress from the Lexington district, afterward 'American' Governor of the State from 1855 to 1859, was originally a Unionist of the Henry Clay school; but, having become largely interested in slaves and cotton-growing in Mississippi, was now and evermore a devotee of the Slave Power—hence a Disunionist. He bore an active and baleful part in the Peace Conference of February, 1861; and was thenceforth, though professing moderation, fully in the counsels of the Secessionists.

of his seat in the Senate, and the dissolution of the Union; demonstrating, after his fashion, the unconstitutionality of struggling to uphold the Constitution; the atrocity of the despotism which had ventured to arrest a few of the many traitors actively at work to subvert the National Government; and charging the Legislature of his State with "woeful subserviency to every demand of Federal despotism and woeful neglect of every right of the Kentucky citizen," etc., etc. Here is a specimen of his rhetoric:

"I would speak of these things with the simple solemnity which their magnitude demands; yet it is difficult to restrain the expression of a just indignation while we smart under such enormities. Mr. Lincoln has thousands of soldiers on our soil, nearly all from the North, and most of them foreigners, whom he employs as his instruments to do these things. But few Kentuckians have enlisted under his standard; for we are not yet accustomed to his peculiar form of liberty.

"I will not pursue the disgraceful subject. Has Kentucky passed out of the control of her own people? Shall hirelings of the pen, recently imported from the North, sitting in grand security at the Capital, force public opinion to approve these usurpations and point out victims? Shall Mr. Lincoln, through his German mercenaries, imprison or exile the children of the men who laid the foundations of the Commonwealth, and compel our noble people to exhaust themselves in furnishing the money to destroy their own freedom? Never, while Kentucky remains the Kentucky of old!—never, while thousands of her gallant sons have the will and the nerve to make the State sing to the music of their rifles!"

It is clear that Mr. Breckinridge, in his exodus from Kentucky, had perpetrated a serious blunder. As a declaimer in the Senate, in chorus with Vallandigham, Voorhees, and May, he was worth far more to the Confederacy than as a Brigadier in its military service; and even the election of Garret Davis in his stead did not fully compensate the Rebellion for the loss of its boldest and most unscrupulous champion in the Federal Congress.

Gen. W. T. Sherman, early in October, succeeded Gen. Anderson in command of the district of Kentucky. The Rebels, with an art which they had already brought to perfection, imposed on him, with success, as on Gen. McClellan and other of our commanders, a most exaggerated notion of the amount of their forces; so that, when Kentucky might easily have been cleared of armed foes by a concerted and resolute advance, Sherman was telegraphing furiously to the War Department for large reënforcements; and, when visited at Louisville, on the 18th, by Secretary Cameron and Adjt.-Gen. Thomas, he gravely informed them that he should need 200,000 men to recover and hold Kentucky; when, in fact, there were not 40,000 Rebels in arms within the limits of that State.

Pollard, writing of the early part of November, says:

"Despite the victory of Belmont, our situation in Kentucky was one of extreme weakness, and entirely at the mercy of the enemy, if he had not been imposed upon by false representations of the number of our forces at Bowling Green.

* * * "About the middle of September, Gen. Buckner advanced, with a small force of about 4,000 men, which was increased, by the 15th of October, to 12,000; and, though other accessions of force were received, it continued at about the same strength until the end of November, measles and other diseases keeping down the effective force. The enemy's force then was reported to the War Department at 50,000; and an advance was impossible."

The Unionists of south-eastern Kentucky were mustering and organizing under Col. Garrard at a point known as Camp Wild-Cat, when Zollicoffer advanced (Oct. 20th) with seven regiments and a light battery, to attack and disperse them. Gen. Schoepf, who had just reached the camp, assumed command of the Union forces prior to the attack, which was made on the morning of the 21st. The Rebels were superior in numbers; but the Unionists had a strong position, and very easily beat off their assailants, who made two attacks to no purpose, and were repulsed and driven away without serious loss on either side.

A considerable Rebel force, under Col. John S. Williams, having been collected at Piketon, the capital of Pike, the easternmost county of Kentucky, at the head of the Big Sandy, Gen. Wm. Nelson, commanding the Union forces in Eastern Kentucky, started from Prestonburg, Nov. 8th, in quest of them. Having not less than 3,000 men, while Williams reports his full strength at 1,010, Nelson had, at 11 o'clock, A. M., of the 7th, dispatched Col. Apperson, of the 33d Ohio, with nearly half his force, to gain the rear of Piketon by a circuitous route through that rugged, almost roadless region, so as to inclose the Rebels between two fires, and compel their surrender. It was first telegraphed that this movement had proved a perfect success; but Williams, who seems to have been thoroughly posted throughout, retarded Nelson's direct advance by smart, judicious skirmishing in the positions assuring him the greatest advantage, while he hurried off the cattle and other spoils industriously collected from that poor, thinly-settled region, on the road to Pound Gap, whither he retreated on the 9th—his rear-guard of 400 leaving Piketon just as Nelson was entering it. The loss of either party in this affair was inconsiderable—not over 100—but the conduct of our soldiers was faultless, and their patient endurance of fatigue, exposure, and privation, most commendable. Williams—who appears to have admirably timed and managed his retreat—reported his force stronger at Pound Gap on the 13th than it was at Piketon on the 8th.

The heroic Unionists of East Tennessee, who had anxiously expected and awaited the arrival of a Union force since the opening of the struggle, were led to believe, after our successes at Camp Wild-Cat and other points, that its appearance would not much longer be delayed. Many of them stole through the woods and over the mountains to join it and hasten its march; while many of those who remained at home conspired to burn the more important railroad bridges throughout their section, in order to preclude the arrival of reënforcements to their Rebel oppressors during the struggle supposed to be just at hand. They succeeded in burning three or four, but failed with regard to others; and all of them who were captured by the Rebels while engaged in or escaping from these attempts were promptly consigned to an ignominious death.

The hopes of the loyal Tennesseeans were strangely and utterly blasted. Gen. Schoepf, in command of our army which, after the repulse of the Rebel attack on Camp Wild-Cat, confronted Zollicoffer, after advancing two or three days in the direction of Cumberland Gap, was induced, by a favorite stratagem of the Rebels, to believe that an overwhelming Confederate force was advancing on his right flank from Bowling Green, and about to pounce upon and annihilate him. There was not a shadow of foundation for this story: the Rebels at Bowling Green were glad enough to keep still, and not expose their weakness, knowing well that Sherman might and would have crushed them, had he been aware of it; yet, without waiting to verify this absurd report, Gen. Schoepf faced about and raced two days toward the Ohio, as if for dear life, strewing the road with wrecked wagons, dead horses, baggage, etc., and leaving East Tennessee to her fate. The bitter disappointment and agony of her gallant sons in his army, who but now confidently supposed themselves about to see the old flag floating in triumph from the spires of Knoxville and Jonesville, can but faintly be realized.

On the 18th of November, the Kentucky Secessionists held a Convention at Russellville, in the southernmost of her counties, behind their principal camp at Bowling Green, and organized what they termed a 'Provisional' Government—perhaps from their inability to make any provision for its support. Geo. W. Johnson, of Scott county, was here chosen Governor;[8] the party having had enough of popular elections, in which they never had any success or made a respectable figure. They chose, likewise, a "Legislative Council," which they clothed with ample powers; and this Council proceeded to appoint Commissioners to negotiate for the admission of Kentucky into the Southern Confederacy! No cavils as to the authority of these gentlemen to speak for Kentucky were raised at Richmond; and, on the 16th of December, *The Louisville Courier* (now issued at Nashville) gravely announced that said Council had this day chosen a full delegation to the Confederate Congress, composed as follows:

Henry C. Burnett,	George W. Ewing,
John Thomas,	Dr. D. V. White,
Thomas L. Burnett,	John M. Elliott,
S. H. Ford,	Thomas B. Monroe,
Thomas B. Johnson,	George B. Hodge.

How it happened that two of these persons—Messrs. Henry C. Burnett and Thomas B. Monroe—were, that same day, sworn in as *Senators*[9] from Kentucky at Richmond, it is not easy to understand; but it is of no consequence. They had probably been appointed, several days before, by 'Governor' Johnson. Suffice it that, since then, Kentucky has been regularly represented in the Confederate Congress, though no popular election thereto was ever held on her soil, and no shadow of consent ever given by her to such delegation of power. Of late, her representatives in that Congress have been chosen by the Kentuckians serving in the Rebel armies; which, though not very regular, seems straightforward and business-like. They represent bayonets; let them be chosen accordingly.[10]

[8] Johnson being killed in the battle at Shiloh next Spring, he was somehow succeeded in his shadowy Governorship by Richard Hawes—a weak old man who, some quarter of a century before, had twice represented, as a Whig, the Lexington district in Congress.

[9] So announced next morning in *The Norfolk Day-Book.*

[10] *The Louisville Journal* of Oct. 12th sharply said:

"Hundreds of those exceedingly sensitive Kentuckians, who so eloquently proclaimed that they could never take up arms against the Southern States, inasmuch as those States were Kentucky's sisters, have now taken up arms for the conquest of Kentucky herself! Is n't that enough to make the devil laugh?"

XXXVIII.

THE POTOMAC—BALL'S BLUFF—DRANESVILLE.

The disaster at Bull Run, and the amazing imbecility betrayed in allowing several of the regiments there routed to continue their panic-stricken, disorderly flight over the bridges into Washington, whence many soldiers, and even officers, dispersed to their respective homes, had dispelled all lingering illusions as to the capacity of Gen. Scott for the conduct of a great war. Though it was still deemed a military necessity to conceal the failure of his faculties, to excuse his blunders, and even, in some instances, to eulogize his abilities as well as magnify his services, the urgent, imperative need of replacing him by a younger and more vigorous commander was felt by every intelligent Unionist. It was he, Winfield Scott, and none other, who had precipitated a third of our forces, on or near the line of the Potomac, into a decisive conflict with seven-eighths of the Rebel strength in Virginia, in defiance of every dictate of prudence and of common sense. Neither the President, nor the Secretary of War, nor Gen. McDowell, nor the maligned and detested Radicals—who were naturally anxious that our 75,000 three-months' men should not be disbanded and sent home without having been of the least positive service—had ever desired or expected any such conflict as this. It was Gen. Scott who had given the orders under which Gen. McDowell advanced and fought on Sunday, the 21st of July. Gen. Cameron, the Secretary of War, who was at Centerville during the preceding day, saw plainly that our regiments at the front were not so many as they should be, and returned hastily that evening to Washington to procure a countermand of the order for battle; but arrived too late to see Gen. Scott and obtain it. Badly as Patterson had behaved, he had reported, on the 18th, by telegraph to Scott, his flank movement to Charlestown; which, any one could see, left Gen. Johnston at perfect liberty to hasten, with all his available force, to the aid of Beauregard at Manassas. And, on the 20th—the day before Bull Run—he had telegraphed to Scott that Johnston had actually departed on that errand.[1] Though Gen. Scott remained nominally in chief command until the last day of October, he was practically superseded

[1] Gen. Scott, in commenting on Gen. Patterson's testimony in a deliberately written statement, made to the Committee on the Conduct of the War, says:

"As connected with this subject, I hope I may be permitted to notice the charge made against me, on the floor of Congress, that I did not stop Brig. Gen. McDowell's movement upon Manassas Junction after I had been informed of the reënforcement sent thither from Winchester, though urged to do so by one or more members of the Cabinet. Now, it was, at the reception of that news, too late to call off the troops from the attack; and, beside, though opposed to the movement at first, we had all become animated and sanguine of success; and it is not true that I was urged by anybody in authority to stop the attack; which was commenced as early, I think, as the 18th of July."

forthwith by the formation of a new military department of Washington and of north-eastern Virginia, which Gen. George B. McClellan was summoned, by telegraph, from that of Western Virginia to preside over. This change was officially announced on the 25th of July; on which day Gen. McClellan arrived at Philadelphia, and there received a most enthusiastic ovation. He proceeded next morning to Washington.

Gen. McClellan found the army intrusted with the defense of the capital reduced, by defeat, desertions, and the mustering out of most of the three-months' men, to 50,000 infantry, 1,000 cavalry, and 650 artillery, with 30 field-guns. The city was protected, on the Virginia side of the Potomac, by hastily-constructed but substantial earthworks, on which some heavy guns were mounted. But, if the Rebels had chosen to ford the Potomac a few miles above, either Washington or Baltimore lay at their mercy, provided they could defeat this army in the open field. They did not, however, see fit to risk so bold a movement; though military critics believe that, for the two weeks succeeding their victory at Bull Run, it might have been attempted with reasonable prospect of success. They could probably have thrown across the river a force nearly or quite equal in numbers to that which defended Washington, whereof at least 5,000 would necessarily have been retained in the earthworks on the Virginia side; while the prestige of their recent victory, and the consequent demoralization of our troops, secured to the Rebels decided advantages, which each succeeding week was morally certain to diminish. They did not, however, attempt to cross the Potomac in force, nor even to provoke another battle on its south bank; but, having advanced their lines, soon after their victory, to Munson's Hill, a few miles from Alexandria, they only remained there until a night attack had been planned on our side; when, promptly forewarned by traitors, they hastily withdrew to Fairfax. It does not appear that the main body of their army ever deliberately took position this side of Centerville.

Gen. McClellan commenced[2] by ordering the officers and men of his army out of Washington, where too many, especially of the former, had hitherto been indulged in idling away their time, to the neglect of their duties and the damage of their morals. Col. Andrew Porter, of the 16th regulars, was appointed Provost Marshal to carry this order into effect. The organization of the Army into brigades was soon afterward[3] effected; and these brigades were ultimately[4] formed into divisions. But the formation of army corps was, for some reason, postponed and delayed, until finally[5] it was peremptorily directed by the President.

Meantime, the patient, loyal, earnest North, soon recovering from the shock of its astounding discomfiture, had been soberly but resolutely raising new regiments and new batteries for a more determined and more energetic prosecution of the struggle forced upon it by slaveholding treason. Every State, county, and township, addressed itself zealously to the work of recruiting and equipping; so that,

[2] July 30th, 1861. [3] Aug. 4th. [4] Oct. 15th. [5] March 8th, 1862.

by the middle[6] of October, Gen. McClellan found himself at the head of fully 150,000 men—an army superior in numbers, in intelligence, and in the essential quality of its material, to any ever led into battle by Napoleon, and by far the largest and most effective which had ever been seen on this continent. It was not only far better drilled and fitted for service than that with which Gen. McDowell had advanced to Centerville and Bull Run, but it was better constituted, in that its members—not one of them a conscript—had enlisted for a term of years, after all sixty-day hallucinations had been dispelled, and with a full knowledge that they were to encounter the hardships, the perils and the privations of protracted and inexorable war.

Gen. McClellan held his first grand parade at the close of September, when 70,000 men of all arms were assembled, maneuvered, and reviewed; a larger army than had ever before been concentrated on any field in America. Apprehensions were expressed that the Rebels would improve this opportunity to attack some portion of our lines; but they were not strong enough to warrant such a venture. Still, regiment after regiment, battery after battery, was poured from the North into Washington, and thence distributed to the several camps assigned them on either side of the Potomac, until the mere bulk of our quiescent forces, the necessity for ground whereon to station them, compelled an advance of our lines—the light troops covering the Rebel front retiring whenever pressed. Lewinsville was reöccupied by our army on the 9th, Vienna on the 16th, and Fairfax Court House on the 17th of October; the Confederates recoiling without firing a shot to Centerville and Manassas. On the 16th, Gen. Geary, under orders from Gen. Banks, in Maryland, advanced to and captured Bolivar Hights, overlooking Harper's Ferry. Leesburg, the capital of Loudoun county, Va., was mistakenly reported evacuated by the Confederates on the 17th; Gen. McCall, with a considerable Union force, moving up the right bank of the Potomac to Dranesville, whence his scouts were pushed forward to Goose Creek, four miles from Leesburg. On the 19th and 20th, McCall made two reconnoissances in the direction of Leesburg, encountering no enemy, and being assured by those he met that the Rebels had abandoned that town some days before. Thus advised, Gen. McClellan, on the 20th, directed the following dispatch to be sent to Gen. Stone, at Poolesville, Md., where he was watching and guarding the line of the Potomac from the Maryland side of the river:

"Received October 20, 1861, from Camp Griffin.

"Gen. McClellan desires me to inform you that Gen. McCall occupied Dranesville yesterday, and is still there; will send out heavy reconnoissances to-day in all directions from that point. The General desires that you keep a good lookout on Leesburg, to see if this movement has the effect to drive them away. Perhaps a slight demonstration on

---

[6] Gen. McClellan, in his carefully elaborated "Report," says:

"By the 15th of October, the number of troops in and about Washington, inclusive of the garrison of the city and Alexandria, the city guard, and the forces on the Maryland shore of the Potomac below Washington, and as far as Cumberland above, the troops under the command of Gen. Dix at Baltimore and its dependencies, were as follows:

Total present for duty	133,201
" sick	9,290
" in confinement	1,156
Aggregate present	143,647
" absent	8,404
Total	152,051"

your part would have the effect to move them. A. V. COLBURN,
"Ass't Adjt. General.
"BRIG.-GEN. STONE, *Poolesville*."

Gen. Stone at once ordered Col. Devens, of the 15th Massachusetts, to transfer two flat-boats from the Chesapeake and Ohio canal, opposite Harrison's Island, to the river at that point, and therewith to ferry over his regiment to the island; which was promptly done. About dark, in obedience to a verbal order, Devens sent Capt. Philbrick, with fifteen or twenty men, across to the Virginia shore, which he ascertained was not picketed by the enemy, and ascended the steep bank known as BALL'S BLUFF, which here rises about one hundred and fifty feet to the level of the adjacent country. Pushing out a small distance from the Bluff, Philbrick returned and reported that he had discovered a small camp of the enemy, which did not appear to be well guarded. This report was sent by Col. Devens to Gen. Stone, who thereupon issued the following order:

"HEAD-QUARTERS CORPS OF OBSERVATION,
"POOLESVILLE, Oct. 20, 1861—10½ P. M.

"SPECIAL ORDER NO. —.

"Col. Devens will land opposite Harrison's Island, with five companies of his regiment, and proceed to surprise the camp of the enemy discovered by Capt. Philbrick in the direction of Leesburg. The landing and march will be effected with silence and rapidity.

"Col. Lee, 20th Massachusetts volunteers, will, immediately after Col. Devens's departure, occupy Harrison's Island with four companies of his regiment, and will cause the four-oared boat to be taken across the island to the point of departure of Col. Devens. One company will be thrown across to occupy the hights on the Virginia shore, after Col. Devens's departure, to cover his return.

"Two mountain howitzers will be taken silently up the tow-path, and carried to the opposite side of the island, under the orders of Col. Lee.

"Col. Devens will attack the camp of the enemy at daybreak, and, having routed, will pursue them as far as he deems prudent, and will destroy the camp, if practicable, before returning. He will make all the observations possible on the country; will, under all circumstances, keep his command well in hand, and not sacrifice them to any supposed advantage of rapid pursuit.

"Having accomplished this duty, Col. Devens will return to his present position, unless he shall see one on the Virginia side, near the river, which he can undoubtedly hold until reënforced, and one which can be successfully held against largely superior numbers. In such case, he will hold on and report.

"CHAS. P. STONE, Brig.-General."

"Great care will be used by Col. Devens to prevent any unnecessary injury of private property; and any officer or soldier straggling from the command, for curiosity or plunder, will be instantly shot.

"CHAS. P. STONE, Brig.-General."

Col. Devens accordingly commenced crossing his force a little after midnight, and had his five companies formed on the top of the bluff so soon as it was light enough to find his way thither. Col. Lee likewise crossed about a hundred men, and took position this side of him. Scouts, dispatched right and left, returned and reported that they could find no enemy. Advancing, so soon as it was light, to the supposed Rebel camp reported to him the night before, Col. D. found it no camp at all, but an optical illusion, created by moonlight glimmering through a row of trees and presenting the appearance of a row of tents. Having advanced to within a mile of Leesburg without discovering a trace of an enemy, Col. D. halted in a wood, unperceived, as he supposed, by any foe, sent a messenger to Gen. Stone, and awaited further orders.

At 7 A. M., a body of riflemen appeared on his right, but fell back when approached; when Rebel cavalry became visible on the road to Leesburg. Col. Devens hereupon, about 8 A. M., fell back to the bluff, in perfect order and unmolested, and there soon received a message from Gen. Stone to remain, and he would be supported. He now counted his force, and ascertained that it numbered 28 officers and 625 men.

At noon, or a little after, he was attacked by musketry from the woods surrounding on three sides the field of barely six acres, in which his men were formed, and at once fell back some sixty yards to obtain a better position. An hour later, being still

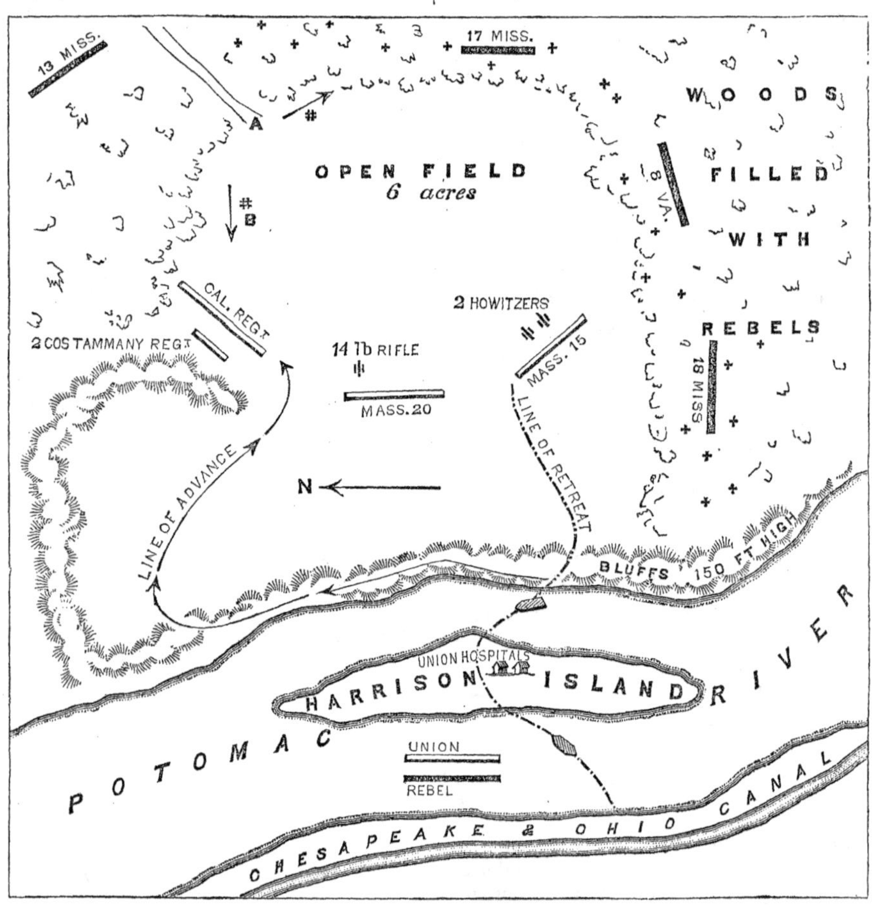

BATTLE OF BALL'S BLUFF.

A. Path by which the Rebels tried to enter the open field. B. Flank movement attempted by the Rebels; defeated by the California Regiment.

unsupported, he fell back again nearly to the edge of the bluff, where he was soon after reënforced, as he had been promised, by the California regiment, Col. E. D. Baker,[7] who, being the ranking officer, assumed command — having received from Gen. Stone an order to support Col. Devens, or withdraw his force to the Maryland shore, at his discretion. It seems that Col. Baker had doubts, on reaching the river, whether

[7] U. S. Senator from Oregon; formerly in Congress from Illinois, and a Colonel in the Mexican War.

to reënforce or withdraw Col. Devens's men; but, hearing that the enemy were already upon Col. D., he decided that he had no choice but to reënforce.

The main current of the Potomac passes Harrison's Island on the Maryland side, where three flat-boats or scows, with a joint capacity of 125 persons, were used by our men; while only a life-boat and two small skiffs, together carrying from 25 to 30 men, were employed on the Virginia side of the island. Finally, one of the scows or flat-boats was taken around to that side. But the crossing of the river, here quite rapid, was still difficult and tedious; while it does not seem that competent persons had been detailed to supervise and effect it. A narrow, winding path led up from the immediate brink of the river to the open field on which our troops were formed, with the enemy swarming in the woods belting that field on three sides, within musket-shot. Col. Baker reached it between 1 and 2 o'clock, P. M. His entire force consisted of the New York Tammany regiment, Col. Milton Cogswell, the California regiment, Lieut.-Col. Wistar, and portions of the 15th Massachusetts, Col. Devens, and 20th, Col. Lee —in all, 1,900 men.[8] The Rebels by whom they were assailed comprised the 8th Virginia, 13th, 17th, and 18th Mississippi, forming the brigade of Gen. Evans.[9] Col. Baker had barely completed the formation of his men, when his right was heavily assailed by the enemy; the attack gradually proceeding to the center and left, and the struggle thus continuing for two hours with desperate energy on both sides, but with far greater loss on ours, because of the uncovered position of our men. Col. Baker insisted on exposing himself with the most reckless bravery, and fell, shot through the head, a little before 5 o'clock. As our men, falling fast, began to waver, and some portions of the line to give way, in view of this calamity, Col. Cogswell, who succeeded to the command, resolved to charge the enemy on his left, and cut his way through to Edwards's Ferry, two or three miles, where Gen. Stone was known to be in force; but, upon attempting this movement, it was met by a fresh Mississippi regiment advancing from the direction of the Ferry, under whose destructive fire our decimated, discouraged troops gave way, and retreated in disorder down the bluff, just as darkness was drawing on. The triumphant Rebels now advanced from all sides to the bluff, and fired with impunity on the disorderly, straggling mass below. Meantime, the flat-boat on that side of the island, being overloaded, was soon riddled and sunk; the life-boat and skiffs were upset and lost; and the work of unresisted slaughter went on. Some were shot on the bank; others while attempting to swim to the island; while a number were carried down by the current and drowned. A few escaped in the darkness, by stealing along the bank of the river unobserved, and finally reached our lines in safety. But our actual loss by that bloody disaster

[8] California regiment, 570; Tammany, 360; 15th Massachusetts, 653; 20th Massachusetts, 318: total, 1,901.

[9] Gen. Evans's official report states his forces in the engagement at 1,709; which evidently does not include the 13th Mississippi, with six guns, held in reserve, and so posted as to repel aid to our side from Edwards's Ferry.

was not less than 1,000 men; of whom nearly 300 were killed outright, and more than 500, including the wounded, taken prisoners.[10]

Meantime, Gen. Stone had directed Gen. Gorman to throw across the river at Edwards's Ferry a small force, which made a cautious reconnoissance for about three miles on the road to Leesburg, when, coming suddenly upon a Mississippi regiment, it exchanged volleys and returned. Gen. Gorman's entire brigade was thrown over at this point during the day; but, as it did not advance, its mere presence on the Virginia side of the Potomac, so far from the scene of actual combat, subserved no purpose. After the disaster was complete, Gen. Stone, about 10 P. M., arrived on the ground from which our ill-starred advance was made; as did Gen. Banks at 3 next morning, and Gen. McClellan on the evening of that day. But it was now too late. No relief was sent while relief could have availed. Even McCall retired from Dranesville southward on the day of the fatal fight.

Col. Baker has been widely blamed for rashness in this conflict, and even for disregard of orders—it would seem most unjustly. The following orders, found in his hat after his death, deeply stained with his life-blood, are all the foundation for this charge:

"EDWARDS'S FERRY, Oct. 21st, 1861.
"COL. E. D. BAKER, Commander of brigade:
"COLONEL: In case of heavy firing in front of Harrison's Island, you will advance the California regiment of your brigade, or retire the regiments under Cols. Lee and Devens, now on the [almost rendered illegible with blood] Virginia side of the river, at your discretion—assuming command on arrival.
"Very respectfully, Colonel, your most obedient servant, CHARLES P. STONE,
"Brig.-General Commanding."

The second order was received on the battle-field, by the hand of Col. Cogswell, an hour before the death of Col. Baker, who had put it in his hat without reading it. It is as follows:

"HEAD-QUARTERS CORPS OF OBSERVATION,
"EDWARDS'S FERRY, Oct. 22d, 11.50.
"E. D. BAKER, Commanding brigade:
"COLONEL: I am informed that the force of the enemy is about 4,000, all told. If you can push them, you may do so as far as to have a strong position near Leesburg, if you can keep them before you, avoiding their batteries. If they pass Leesburg and take the Gum Spring road, you will not follow far, but seize the first good position to cover that road.
"Their desire is to draw us on, if they are obliged to retreat, as far as Goose Creek, where they can be reënforced from Manassas, and have a strong position.
"Report frequently, so that, when they are pushed, Gorman can come up on their flank. Yours, respectfully and truly,
"CHARLES P. STONE,
"Brig.-General Commanding."

How Stone expected Baker to 'push' 4,000 men with 1,900, in an advanced and unsupported position, where the 4,000 might at any moment be increased to 10,000 or to 20,000, is not obvious. And why was not Gorman sent forward to come up on their flank, at any rate; without waiting for 1,900 men to 'push' 4,000 beyond Leesburg to a good point for covering that place?

As to Col. Baker's reading or not reading this dispatch, it must be considered that he was at that moment engaged with a superior force, and

[10] Gen. Evans, in his report, claims 710 prisoners, including wounded, and guesses that we had "1,300 killed, wounded, and drowned." He thus makes our loss exceed by over 100 all our force engaged in the battle! He reports his own loss at 155 only, including Col. E. R. Burt, 18th Mississippi, killed. Gen. Evans says he had no cannon in the fight—which is true; for his artillery was where it could serve him best—by blocking the road from Edwards's Ferry.

that retreat on his part was simple ruin. He must repulse the enemy assailing him then and there, or be destroyed; for no force that Stone might now send to his relief could be brought up in time to save him.

The Ball's Bluff tragedy, grossly misrepresented as it was in Rebel bulletins and exulting narratives, tended to confirm and extend the vain-glorious delusion which was already sapping the foundations, if not of Rebel strength, at least of Rebel energy. Gen. Evans officially reported that he had fought and beaten 8,000 men, commanded by Gen. Stone—his troops using the musket alone; while the Unionists employed artillery, and fired on him with long-range guns from the Maryland shore! and that his brigade had driven "an enemy *four times their number* from the soil of Virginia, killing and taking prisoners a greater number than our whole force engaged." These fables were repeated in general orders, with the necessary effect of inflating the whole Confederate people with an inordinate conceit of their own prowess, and misleading them into an intense contempt for Yankee cowardice and inefficiency. The natural consequences of this delusive swagger were evinced in the encounters of the ensuing Spring.

On the other hand, Ball's Bluff dispelled, though at a terrible cost, some of the aspersions which had been sedulously propagated with regard to the spirit and *morale* of the Union rank and file. Whoever asked of any champion of the prevailing strategy why our armies stood idle, and as if paralyzed, in the presence of inferior forces of Rebels, were assured, in a confidential whisper, that our men had been so demoralized and spirit-broken by their rout at Bull Run, that there was no fight in them—that a whole brigade would take to their heels at the sight of a Rebel regiment advancing to the charge. Ball's Bluff repelled and dissipated this unworthy calumny—by showing that our soldiers, though most unskillfully handled, precipitated into needless perils, entrapped, surrounded, hopeless, had still the courage to fight and the manhood to die.

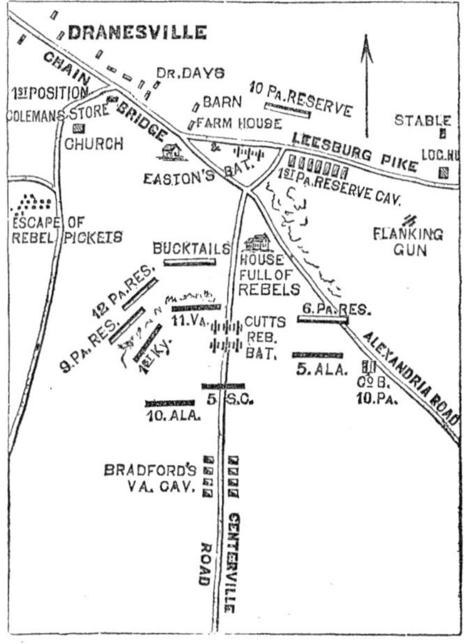

DRANESVILLE.

At 6 A. M., of Dec. 20th, Gen. E. O. C. Ord, commanding the 3d Pennsylvania brigade, in pursuance of orders from Gen. George A. McCall, commanding the division holding the right of Gen. McClellan's army, moved forward from Camp Pierpont toward Dranesville, Loudoun County, Va., instructed to drive back the enemy's pickets, procure a supply of forage, and capture, if possible, a small cavalry force scouting betwixt Dranesville and the Potomac. Gen. Ord's brigade consisted of the 9th, Col. C. F. Jackson, 10th, Col. J. S. McCalmont, 12th, Col. John H. Taggart, the Bucktail Rifles, Lt.-Col. T. L. Kane, a part of the 6th, with Easton's battery and two squadrons of cavalry; in all, about 4,000 men. While halting to load forage just east of Dranesville, he was attacked by a Rebel brigade, led by Gen. J. E. B. Stuart, composed of the 11th Virginia, the 6th South Carolina, 10th Alabama, 1st Kentucky, the Sumter Flying Artillery, and detachments from two cavalry regiments—the whole force numbering, according to Rebel accounts, only 2,500. Stuart appears to have been likewise on a foraging excursion; as he had with him about 200 wagons, which probably returned empty of aught but wounded men. They came up the road leading southwardly from Dranesville to Centerville, some fifteen miles distant, and were foolishly pushed on to attack, though the advantage in numbers, in position, and even in artillery, appears to have been decidedly on our side. They were, of course, easily and badly beaten; the Pennsylvanians fighting with cool intrepidity and entire confidence of success. Our aggregate loss was but 9 killed and 60 wounded—among the latter, Lieut.-Col. Kane, who led his men with signal gallantry. The Rebels lost, by their own account, 230; among them, Col. Forney, of the 10th Alabama, wounded, and Lieut. Col. Martin, killed. They left 25 horses dead on the field, with two caissons—one of them exploded,—running off their guns by hand; the 6th South Carolina, out of 315 present, losing 65—in part, by the fire of the 1st Kentucky (Rebel), which, mistaking them for Unionists, poured a murderous volley into them at forty yards' distance. It was a foolish affair on the part of Stuart, who was palpably misled by the gasconade of Evans, with regard to his meeting and beating more than four to one at Ball's Bluff. When he found himself overmatched, losing heavily, and in danger of being outflanked and destroyed, the Rebel General withdrew rapidly, but in tolerable order, from the field; and Gen. McCall, who came up at this moment, wisely decided not to pursue; since a Rebel force thrice his own might at any moment be interposed between him and his camp. Each party returned to its quarters that night.

The victory of Dranesville, unimportant as it may now seem, diffused an immense exhilaration throughout the Union ranks. It was a fitting and conclusive answer to every open assertion or whispered insinuation impeaching the courage or the steadiness of our raw Northern volunteers. The encounter was purely fortuitous, at least on our side; two strong foraging parties, believed by our men to be about equal in numbers, had met on fair, open ground; had fought a brief but spirited duel, which had ended in the confessed defeat and flight of the Rebels, whose loss was at least twice that they inflicted on us. Admit that they were but 2,500 to our 4,000; the Army of the Potomac, now nearly 200,000[11] strong, and able to advance on the enemy

[11] Gen. McClellan, in his deliberately prepared, loudly trumpeted, and widely circulated Report,

with not less than 150,000 sabers and bayonets, eagerly awaited the long-expected permission to prove itself but fairly represented in that casual detachment which had fought and won at Dranesville.

In every other quarter, our arms were in the ascendant. The blow well struck by Butler and Stringham at Hatteras, had never been retaliated. The Rebels' attempt to cut off Brown's regiment at Chicamicomico had resulted in more loss to them than to us. Du Pont's triumph at Port Royal had dealt a damaging blow to our foes, and inflicted signal injury on the original plotters of treason, without loss to our side. In West Virginia, the campaign was closing with the prestige of success and superiority gilding our standards, and with at least nine-tenths of the whole region securely in our hands. In Missouri, Gen. Fremont—though vehemently reproached for not advancing and fighting sooner, and though never enjoying facilities for obtaining arms, munitions, or any material of war, at all comparable to those at all times eagerly accorded to McClellan—had collected, organized, armed, and provided, a movable column of nearly 40,000 men, at whose head he had pushed Price—one of the very ablest of the Rebel chieftains—to the furthest corner of the State, and was on the point of hunting him thence into Arkansas or eternity, when the order which deprived him of his command was received at Springfield on the 2d of November. Yet then and throughout the Winter, Gen. McClellan, who had been called to command at Washington on the same day that Fremont left New York for St. Louis, stood cooped up and virtually besieged in the defenses of Washington, holding barely ground enough in Virginia to encamp and maneuver his army; while the Rebels impudently obstructed the navigation of the lower Potomac, on one hand, by batteries erected at commanding points on the Virginia shore, while the Baltimore and Ohio Railroad was dismantled and obstructed by them at Harper's Ferry and further west on the other; leaving the city of Washington, as well as his vast army, dependent on the single track of the Branch Railroad for all their subsistence and supplies, throughout the tedious Winter that followed.

The Confederates had not yet enforced a general Conscription; and, though volunteering was widely stimulated by Police discipline and Lynch law, while the more ignorant and ill-informed young women of many slaveholding localities were envenomed Secessionists, refusing to give any but the most furious countenance to young men who hesitated to enlist, yet the white population of the States actually controlled by the Rebels was so very far inferior in numbers to that of the loyal North and West, that the Rebel armies were necessarily and vastly the less numerous likewise.

Gen. McClellan, indeed, appears to have estimated their numbers in Eastern Virginia at 150,000; but the information on which he acted differed

states the force under his more immediate command on the 1st of December—that is, the force then in the Federal District, Maryland, Delaware, and the small patch of Eastern Virginia opposite Washington held by him—at 198,213; whereof 169,452 were "fit for duty." This does not include Gen. Wool's command at and near Fortress Monroe. On the 1st of January following, he makes his total 219,707; on the 1st of February, 222,196.

widely from that of his subordinates who spent the Winter in camp in Virginia, while he remained snugly housed in Washington. Gen. Wadsworth, who saw and (until forbidden) questioned the 'contrabands' and other deserters who came within our lines from Centerville and vicinity that Autumn and Winter, was confident that 60,000 was the highest number they ever had encamped in our front; and these we might have assailed at a day's notice with 120,000; and, by taking three days for preparation, with 150,000. Why not?

The weather was magnificent; the roads hard and dry, till far into Winter. An artillery officer wonderingly inquired: "What is such weather *for*, if not fighting?"

The loyal masses—awed by the obloquy heaped on those falsely accused of having caused the disaster at Bull Run by their ignorant impatience and precipitancy—stood in silent expectation. They still kept raising regiment after regiment, battery after battery, and hurrying them forward to the all-ingulfing Army of the Potomac, to be in time for the decided movement that must be just at hand—but the torrent was there drowned in a lake of Lethean stagnation. First, we were waiting for reënforcements—which was most reasonable; then, for the requisite drilling and fitting for service—which was just as helpful to the Rebels as to us; then, for the leaves to fall—so as to facilitate military movements in a country so wooded and broken as Virginia; then, for cannon—whereof we had already more than 200 first-rate field-guns in Virginia, ready for instant service: and so the long, bright Autumn, and the colder but still favorable December, wore heavily away, and saw nothing of moment attempted. Even the Rebel batteries obstructing the lower Potomac were not so much as menaced—the Navy laying the blame on the Army; the Army throwing it back on the Navy—probably both right, or, rather, both wrong: but the net result was nothing done; until the daily repetition of the stereotyped telegraphic bulletin, "All quiet on the Potomac"—which had at first been received with satisfaction; afterward with complacency; at length evoked a broad and general roar of disdainful merriment.

And so, Winter at last settled down upon that vast, gallant, most effective army, Two Hundred Thousand strong, able and ready, on any fair field, to bear down at a charge all the Rebels in their front without coming to a stand; yet lying thus beleaguered and paralyzed, shivering and dying in the tents to which they had been so suddenly transferred from their comfortable homes—not allowed to build themselves huts, such as the Rebels had, because that would reveal to the country the fact that nothing was to be attempted till Spring or later; expecting, hoping every day to receive the long-awaited order to advance; but seeing night after night close in without it; and sinking into homesickness and disease, which employment for body and mind would readily have repelled and dissipated.

Is this obstinate fixity, this rooted neglect and waste of the grandest opportunities, explicable? Not by the hypothesis of a constitutional aversion to the shedding of blood—that is, of other men's—on the part of our 'Young Napoleon;' for he was at that moment among the most eager to have our country involved in still another great war, by a refusal, on the part of our Government, to surrender Mason and Slidell. Not even Vallandigham was more belligerent in *that* direction. Constitutional timidity and irresolution—an overwhelming sense of responsibility and inadequacy to so stupendous a trust—were probably not without their influence in the premises. But, beyond and above all these, there was doubtless a slowly awakened consciousness that Slavery was the real assailant of our National existence, and that to put down the Rebellion by a positive, determined exertion of force, was to seal the doom of its inciting cause, which had so recently transformed into downright traitors so many high officers who once honored and loved our Union and its flag. It was hard for one who had long been arguing and voting that, in our current politics, Slavery was not the aggressor, but the innocent victim, to unlearn this gross error in a year; and Gen. McClellan is essentially slow. But, in the high position to which he had been so suddenly exalted, it was hard also *not* to see that, in order to save both Slavery and the Union, there must be little fighting and a speedy compromise—that fighting must be postponed, and put off, and avoided, in the hope that financial embarrassment, a foreign war, or some other complication, would compel the mutual adoption of some sort of Crittenden Compromise, or kindred 'adjustment,' whereby the Slave Power would graciously condescend to take the Union afresh into its keeping, and consent to a reünion, which would be, in effect, an extension of the empire of Jefferson Davis to the Canada frontier, and a perpetual interdict of all Anti-Slavery discussion and effort throughout the Republic. On this hypothesis, and on this alone, Gen. McClellan's course while in high command, but especially during that long Autumn and Winter, becomes coherent and comprehensible.

The Rebels, so vastly outnumbered and overmatched in every thing but leadership, were, of course, too glad to be allowed to maintain a virtual siege of Washington, with all but one of its lines of communication with the loyal States obstructed, to make any offensive movement; and the only assault made that Winter upon our General-in-Chief's main position, was repelled with prompt, decided energy. The circumstances were as follows:

A portion of the melodious Hutchinson family, having been attracted to Washington by the novelty of finding the public halls of that city no longer barricaded against the utterance of humane and generous sentiments, had there solicited of the Secretary of War permission to visit the camps across the Potomac, in order to break the monotony and cheer the ruggedness of Winter with the spontaneous, unbought carol of some of their simple, heartfelt songs. Gen. Cameron gave their project not merely his cordial assent, but his emphatic commendation; and, thus endorsed, they received Gen. McClellan's gracious permission. So they passed over to the camps, and were singing to delighted crowds of soldiers, when an officer's quick ear caught the drift of what sounded like *Abolition!* Forthwith, there were commotion, and effervescence, and indignation, rising from circle to circle of the military aristocracy, until they reached the very highest, drawing thence the following order:

"*By direction of Maj.-Gen. McClellan, the permit given to the Hutchinson Family to sing in the camps, and their pass to cross the Potomac, are revoked, and they will not be allowed to sing to the troops.*"

As the then freshly uttered stanzas of JOHN G. WHITTIER, which thus caused the peremptory, ignominious suppression and expulsion of the Hutchinsons, are of themselves a memorable and stirring portion of the history of our time, they may fitly—as they will most worthily—close this volume:

"EIN FESTE BURG IST UNSER GOTT."[12]
(Luther's Hymn.)

WE wait beneath the furnace-blast
  The pangs of transformation:
Not painlessly doth God recast
  And mold anew the nation.
    Hot burns the fire
    Where wrongs expire;
    Nor spares the hand
    That from the land
  Uproots the ancient evil.

The hand-breadth cloud the sages feared
  Its bloody rain is dropping;
The poison-plant the fathers spared
  All else is overtopping.
    East, West, South, North,
    It curses earth;
    All justice dies,
    And fraud and lies
  Live only in its shadow.

What gives the wheat-field blades of steel?
  What points the rebel cannon?
What sets the roaring rabble's heel
  On th' old star-spangled pennon?
    What breaks the oath
    Of th' men o' th' South?
    What whets the knife
    For the Union's life?—
  Hark to the answer: SLAVERY!

Then waste no blows on lesser foes,
  In strife unworthy freemen:
God lifts to-day the vail, and shows
  The features of the demon!
    O North and South,
    Its victims both,
    Can ye not cry,
    "Let Slavery die!"
  And Union find in Freedom?

What though the cast-out spirit tear
  The nation in his going?
We, who have shared the guilt, must share
  The pang of his o'erthrowing!
    Whate'er the loss,
    Whate'er the cross,
    Shall they complain
    Of present pain
  Who trust in God's hereafter?

For who that leans on His right arm
  Was ever yet forsaken?
What righteous cause can suffer harm
  If He its part has taken?
    Though wild and loud
    And dark the cloud,
    Behind its folds
    His hand upholds
  The calm sky of To-Morrow!

Above the madd'ning cry for blood,
  Above the wild war-drumming,
Let Freedom's voice be heard, with good
  The evil overcoming.
    Give prayer and purse
    To stay the Curse
    Whose wrong we share,
    Whose shame we bear,
  Whose end shall gladden Heaven!

In vain the bells of war shall ring
  Of triumphs and revenges,
While still is spared the evil thing
  That severs and estranges.
    But blest the ear
    That yet shall hear
    The jubilant bell
    That rings the knell
  Of Slavery forever!

Then let the selfish lip be dumb,
  And hushed the breath of sighing:
Before the joy of peace must come
  The pains of purifying.
    God give us grace,
    Each in his place,
    To bear his lot.
    And, murmuring not,
  Endure and wait and labor!

[12] 'Our God is a strong fortress,' (or castle.)

ADDITIONAL NOTES.

I.

It is stated on page 119 that "the Synod of Kentucky *adopted* a report on Slavery which condemned slaveholding broadly and thoroughly," etc. That statement is not literally accurate. The Synod met at Danville, in the Autumn of 1835, and appointed a Committee of ten—five ministers and five elders—who were instructed to "digest and prepare a plan for the moral and religious instruction of our slaves, and for their future emancipation," etc. The Committee did its duty faithfully, and the report in due time appeared—its character being such as is indicated in the text. The result was duly submitted to the Synod at its next meeting, at Bardstown, in 1836; but no action was taken thereon, beyond noting on the Synod's records the reception of the report, which had meantime been printed, and had excited some feeling among the slaveholders.

II.

The statement on page 120, respecting the attitude of the New School Presbyterian Church toward Slavery, is held by members of that Church to require qualification, in view of its more recent action on the subject. The material facts are as follows:

At the session of the General Assembly at Cleveland, Ohio, for 1857, a report on Slavery of the Committee on Bills and Overtures, after having been debated with great animation for the better part of a week, was finally adopted (June 3d), by the decisive majority of 169 yeas to 26 nays. This report is largely devoted to a recital of the former testimonies of the Presbyterian Church on the general subject, and is leveled at the new Southern doctrine that Slavery is essentially beneficent and just—a doctrine notoriously at variance with that originally maintained by this Church. The Report says:

"We are especially pained by the fact that the Presbytery of Lexington, South, have given official notice to us that a number of ministers and ruling elders, as well as many church-members, in their connection, hold slaves 'from principle' and 'of choice,' 'believing it to be, according to the Bible, right,' and have, without any qualifying explanation, assumed the responsibility of sustaining such ministers, elders, and church-members, in their position. We deem it our duty, in the exercise of our constitutional authority, 'to bear testimony against error in doctrine, or immorality in practice, in any church, Presbytery, or Synod,' to disapprove and earnestly condemn the position which has been thus assumed by the Presbytery of Lexington, South, as one which is opposed to the established convictions of the Presbyterian Church, and must operate to mar its peace and seriously hinder its prosperity, as well as bring reproach on our holy religion; and we do hereby call on the Presbytery to review and rectify their position. Such doctrine and practice cannot be permanently tolerated in the Presbyterian Church. May they speedily melt away under the illuminating and mellowing influence of the Gospel and grace of God our Saviour!

"We do not, indeed, pronounce a sentence of indiscriminate condemnation upon all our brethren who are, unfortunately, connected with the system of Slavery. We tenderly sympathize with all those who deplore the evil, and are honestly doing all in their power for the present well-being of their slaves, and for their complete emancipation. We would aid, and not embarrass, such brethren. And yet, in the language of the General Assembly of 1818, we would 'earnestly warn them against unduly extending the plea of necessity; against making it a cover for the love and practice of Slavery, or a pretense for not using efforts that are lawful and practicable to extinguish this evil.'"

Upon the announcement of this vote, Rev. James G. Hamner, of the Synod of Virginia, presented the protest of twenty-two Southern members of the Assembly against this doctrine of the Report, saying:

"We protest—Because, while past General Assemblies have asserted that the system of Slavery is wrong, they have heretofore affirmed that the slaveholder was so controlled by State laws, obligations of guardianship, and humanity, that he was, as thus situated, without censure or odium as the master. This averment in the testimony of past Assemblies has so far satisfied the South, as to make it unnecessary to do more than protest against the mere anti-Slavery part of such testimony.

"We protest, then, now, That the present act of the Assembly is such an assertion, without authority from the word of God, or the organic law of the Presbyterian body.

"We protest that such action is, under present conditions, the virtual exscinding of the South, whatever be the motives of those who vote the deed.

"We protest, that such indirect excision is unrighteous, oppressive, uncalled for—the exercise of usurped power—destructive of the unity of the Church—hurtful to the North and the South—and adding to the peril of the Union of these United States."

From the date of this action—which seems to have been but a more explicit reäffirmance of the older testimonies of the Church against Slavery, and to have stopped far short of declaring slaveholding inconsistent with the Christian character—the New School Presbyterian Church had hardly a foothold in the Slave States.

III.

The Albany Evening Journal of May 20th, 1861, commenting on a very abusive attack on Gov. Seward, in a then recent *Richmond Whig*, with regard to his assurances to or through Judge Campbell, respecting Fort Sumter, says:

"If the Secretary of State were at liberty to reply to ex-Judge Campbell, revealing all that passed between them on several occasions, not only no imputation of insincerity would rest upon the Secretary, but the facts would seriously affect Judge Campbell's well-established reputation for candor and frankness. These revelations would furnish no evidence of either the 'falsehood' or 'duplicity' of Governor Seward; for there was nothing of either in his conversations.

"We violate no confidence in saying that Judge Campbell balanced long between Loyalty and Secession; the preponderance, up to a late day, being in favor of the Union. If he at any time looked with favor or satisfaction upon Secession, he was much and generally misunderstood. If he did not seriously contemplate remaining in the Union and upon the Bench, he was misunderstood. If, during that period of mental trial, he was acting in harmony with the leading enemies of the Union, he was grossly misunderstood.

"That Gov. Seward conversed freely with Judge Campbell, we do not deny; nor do we doubt, that, in those conversations, at one period, he intimated that Fort Sumter would be evacuated. He certainly believed so; founding his opinion upon a knowledge of Gen. Scott's recommendation. Subsequently, the President deemed it his duty to authorize an effort to reënforce and provision that fortress. We do not know whether Gov. Seward met Judge Campbell after that change of purpose; but he was not at liberty, if they did meet, to reveal what was so well kept.

"But, whatever Gov. Seward said or intimated to Judge Campbell, was true at the time it was said.

"That Judge Campbell reported to the Confederate President half that he said or intimated, is more than doubtful."

IV.

The statement on pages 449–50, that the original attack on Fort Sumter was impelled by a stringent, imperative political necessity—that hostilities were inaugurated, to prevent the else inevitable crumbling away and utter collapse of the Confederacy—has received additional confirmation since that portion of this work was stereotyped, through an averment of Hon. Jere. Clemens, late U. S. Senator from Alabama, who, in a Union meeting held at the city of his residence, Huntsville, Ala., March 13, 1864, said:

"Before I declare this meeting adjourned, I wish to state a fact in relation to the commencement of the war: Some time after the ordinance of Secession was passed, I was in Montgomery, and called upon President Davis, who was in that city. Davis, Memminger, the Secretary of War, Gilchrist, the member from Lowndes County, and several others, were present. As I entered, the conversation ceased. They were evidently discussing the propriety of firing upon Fort Sumter. Two or three of them withdrew to a corner of the room; and I heard Gilchrist say to the Secretary of War, '*It must be done. Delay two months, and Alabama stays in the Union. You must sprinkle blood in the faces of the people.*'"

The Secretary of War in question was Mr. Leroy Pope Walker, also a citizen of Huntsville, who made, the evening after Fort Sumter's surrender, a public proclamation that the Rebels would have possession of Washington City within a month. He was an original Secessionist; while Senator Clemens, with most of the people of their county (Madison), clung to the Union, so long as they could with safety. That Mr. Clemens has fabricated such a statement with regard to two of his neighbors, by whom it might so easily be refuted, if untrue, will hardly be suggested.

V.

That the speedy capture and occupation of Washington by the Confederates were confidently anticipated by their chiefs, as among the earliest and most inevitable results of the War they were inaugurating, has, perhaps, been sufficiently established in due course; but, since the Governors of Virginia, North Carolina, Kentucky, Tennessee, and Missouri, with others, boldly and broadly charged President Lincoln with wantonly inaugurating civil war, by his Proclamation calling out 75,000 militia for the defense of the Federal metropolis, it may be proper to accumulate evidence on this head. Here is what Wm. H. Russell, *The Times's* correspondent, who was in the South when Sumter was reduced, records in his 'Diary,' under the date of April 20th, 1861, just after dining at Charleston with W. H. Trescott, W. Porcher Miles, Gov. Manning, and other pioneers of Disunion:

"The Secessionists are in great delight over Gov. Letcher's proclamation, calling out troops and volunteers; and it is hinted that *Washington will be attacked*, and *the nest of Black Republican vermin, which haunt the capital, be driven out.*"

VI.

It is stated on page 348, that the North Carolina Convention, which ultimately passed an Ordinance of Secession, was the same which the people of that State originally elected to keep her in the Union, and decided should not meet. The fact appears to have been otherwise—that the Convention which did the deed was a new one, elected just after the reduction of Fort Sumter, and under the popular conviction that Mr. Lincoln was waging an unprovoked war on 'the South.'

ANALYTICAL INDEX.

A.

B.

C.

D.

E.

F.

G.

H.

I.

J.

M.

N.

O.

Q.

R.

S.

T.

U.

V.

W.

Y.

Z.

END OF VOL. I.

www.ingramcontent.com/pod-product-compliance
Lightning Source LLC
LaVergne TN
LVHW021052110826
845150LV00001B/49

* 9 7 8 1 4 2 5 5 6 7 6 7 5 *